STUDENT'S *t* CRITICAL VALUES

This table shows the *t*-value that defines the area for the stated degrees of freedom (ν).

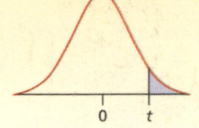

	Confidence Level						Confidence Level			
	.80	.90	.95	.98	.99		.80	.90	.95	.98	.99
	Significance Level for Two-Tailed Test						Significance Level for Two-Tailed Test				
	.20	.10	.05	.02	.01		.20	.10	.05	.02	.01
	Significance Level for One-Tailed Test						Significance Level for One-Tailed Test				
ν	.10	.05	.025	.01	.005	ν	.10	.05	.025	.01	.005
1	3.078	6.314	12.706	31.821	63.656	36	1.306	1.688	2.028	2.434	2.719
2	1.886	2.920	4.303	6.965	9.925	37	1.305	1.687	2.026	2.431	2.715
3	1.638	2.353	3.182	4.541	5.841	38	1.304	1.686	2.024	2.429	2.712
4	1.533	2.132	2.776	3.747	4.604	39	1.304	1.685	2.023	2.426	2.708
5	1.476	2.015	2.571	3.365	4.032	40	1.303	1.684	2.021	2.423	2.704
6	1.440	1.943	2.447	3.143	3.707	41	1.303	1.683	2.020	2.421	2.701
7	1.415	1.895	2.365	2.998	3.499	42	1.302	1.682	2.018	2.418	2.698
8	1.397	1.860	2.306	2.896	3.355	43	1.302	1.681	2.017	2.416	2.695
9	1.383	1.833	2.262	2.821	3.250	44	1.301	1.680	2.015	2.414	2.692
10	1.372	1.812	2.228	2.764	3.169	45	1.301	1.679	2.014	2.412	2.690
11	1.363	1.796	2.201	2.718	3.106	46	1.300	1.679	2.013	2.410	2.687
12	1.356	1.782	2.179	2.681	3.055	47	1.300	1.678	2.012	2.408	2.685
13	1.350	1.771	2.160	2.650	3.012	48	1.299	1.677	2.011	2.407	2.682
14	1.345	1.761	2.145	2.624	2.977	49	1.299	1.677	2.010	2.405	2.680
15	1.341	1.753	2.131	2.602	2.947	50	1.299	1.676	2.009	2.403	2.678
16	1.337	1.746	2.120	2.583	2.921	55	1.297	1.673	2.004	2.396	2.668
17	1.333	1.740	2.110	2.567	2.898	60	1.296	1.671	2.000	2.390	2.660
18	1.330	1.734	2.101	2.552	2.878	65	1.295	1.669	1.997	2.385	2.654
19	1.328	1.729	2.093	2.539	2.861	70	1.294	1.667	1.994	2.381	2.648
20	1.325	1.725	2.086	2.528	2.845	75	1.293	1.665	1.992	2.377	2.643
21	1.323	1.721	2.080	2.518	2.831	80	1.292	1.664	1.990	2.374	2.639
22	1.321	1.717	2.074	2.508	2.819	85	1.292	1.663	1.988	2.371	2.635
23	1.319	1.714	2.069	2.500	2.807	90	1.291	1.662	1.987	2.368	2.632
24	1.318	1.711	2.064	2.492	2.797	95	1.291	1.661	1.985	2.366	2.629
25	1.316	1.708	2.060	2.485	2.787	100	1.290	1.660	1.984	2.364	2.626
26	1.315	1.706	2.056	2.479	2.779	110	1.289	1.659	1.982	2.361	2.621
27	1.314	1.703	2.052	2.473	2.771	120	1.289	1.658	1.980	2.358	2.617
28	1.313	1.701	2.048	2.467	2.763	130	1.288	1.657	1.978	2.355	2.614
29	1.311	1.699	2.045	2.462	2.756	140	1.288	1.656	1.977	2.353	2.611
30	1.310	1.697	2.042	2.457	2.750	150	1.287	1.655	1.976	2.351	2.609
31	1.309	1.696	2.040	2.453	2.744	∞	1.282	1.645	1.960	2.326	2.576
32	1.309	1.694	2.037	2.449	2.738						
33	1.308	1.692	2.035	2.445	2.733						
34	1.307	1.691	2.032	2.441	2.728						
35	1.306	1.690	2.030	2.438	2.724						

Note: As *n* increases, critical values of Student's *t* approach the *z*-values in the last line of this table. A common rule of thumb is to use *z* when *n* > 30, but that is *not* conservative.

Applied Statistics

in Business and Economics

THE MCGRAW-HILL/IRWIN SERIES

Operations and Decision Sciences

BUSINESS STATISTICS

Aczel and Sounderpandian, **Complete Business Statistics,** *Sixth Edition*

ALEKS for Business Statistics

Bowerman and O'Connell, **Business Statistics in Practice,** *Fourth Edition*

Bowerman, O'Connell, and Orris, **Essentials of Business Statistics,** *First Edition*

Bryant and Smith, **Practical Data Analysis: Case Studies in Business Statistics, Volumes I, II, and III**

Cooper and Schindler, **Business Research Methods,** *Ninth Edition*

Delurgio, **Forecasting Principles and Applications,** *First Edition*

Doane and Seward, **Applied Statistics in Business and Economics,** *First Edition*

Doane, **LearningStats CD-Rom** *1.2,* *First Edition*

Doane, Mathieson, and Tracy, **Visual Statistics** *2.0,* *Second Edition*

Gitlow, Oppenheim, Oppenheim, and Levine, **Quality Management,** *Third Edition*

Lind, Marchal, and Wathen, **Basic Statistics for Business and Economics,** *Fifth Edition*

Lind, Marchal, and Wathen, **Statistical Techniques in Business and Economics,** *Twelfth Edition*

Merchant, Goffinet, and Koehler, **Basic Statistics Using Excel for Office XP,** *Third Edition*

Kutner, Nachtsheim, Neter, and Li, **Applied Linear Statistical Models,** *Fifth Edition*

Kutner, Nachtsheim, and Neter, **Applied Linear Regression Models,** *Fourth Edition*

Sahai and Khurshid, **Pocket Dictionary of Statistics,** *First Edition*

Siegel, **Practical Business Statistics,** *Fifth Edition*

Wilson, Keating, and John Galt Solutions, Inc., **Business Forecasting,** *Fifth Edition*

Zagorsky, **Business Information,** *First Edition*

QUANTITATIVE METHODS AND MANAGEMENT SCIENCE

Hillier and Hillier, **Introduction to Management Science,** *Second Edition*

Stevenson and Ozgur, **Introduction to Management Science with Spreadsheets,** *First Edition*

Applied Statistics

in Business and Economics

David P. Doane
Oakland University

Lori E. Seward
University of Colorado

McGraw-Hill Irwin

Boston   Burr Ridge, IL   Dubuque, IA   Madison, WI   New York   San Francisco   St. Louis
Bangkok   Bogotá   Caracas   Kuala Lumpur   Lisbon   London   Madrid   Mexico City
Milan   Montreal   New Delhi   Santiago   Seoul   Singapore   Sydney   Taipei   Toronto

APPLIED STATISTICS IN BUSINESS AND ECONOMICS

Published by McGraw-Hill/Irwin, a business unit of The McGraw-Hill Companies, Inc., 1221 Avenue of the Americas, New York, NY, 10020. Copyright © 2007 by The McGraw-Hill Companies, Inc. All rights reserved. No part of this publication may be reproduced or distributed in any form or by any means, or stored in a database or retrieval system, without the prior written consent of The McGraw-Hill Companies, Inc., including, but not limited to, in any network or other electronic storage or transmission, or broadcast for distance learning.

Some ancillaries, including electronic and print components, may not be available to customers outside the United States.

This book is printed on acid-free paper.

1 2 3 4 5 6 7 8 9 0 VNH/VNH 0 9 8 7 6

ISBN-13: 978-0-07-296693-0 (student edition)
ISBN-10: 0-07-296693-9 (student edition)
ISBN-13: 978-0-07-296696-1 (instructor's edition)
ISBN-10: 0-07-296696-3 (instructor's edition)

Editorial director: *Brent Gordon*
Executive editor: *Richard T. Hercher, Jr.*
Senior developmental editor: *Wanda J. Zeman*
Senior marketing manager: *Douglas Reiner*
Senior media producer: *Victor Chiu*
Lead project manager: *Pat Frederickson*
Production supervisor: *Debra R. Sylvester*
Coordinator freelance design: *Artemio Ortiz Jr.*
Senior photo research coordinator: *Jeremy Cheshareck*
Photo researcher: *Keri Johnson*
Senior media project manager: *Rose M. Range*
Cover design: *JoAnne Schopler*
Interior design: *Artemio Ortiz Jr.*
Cover image: *Corbis®*
Typeface: *10/12 Times New Roman*
Compositor: *Interactive Composition Corporation*
Printer: *Von Hoffmann Corporation*

Library of Congress Cataloging-in-Publication Data

Doane, David P.
    Applied statistics in business and economics / David P. Doane, Lori E. Seward.
        p. cm. — (McGraw-Hill/Irwin series operations and decision sciences)
    Includes index.
    ISBN-13: 978-0-07-296693-0 (alk. paper)
    ISBN-10: 0-07-296693-9 (student ed.)
    ISBN-13: 978-0-07-296696-1 (alk. paper)
    ISBN-10: 0-07-296696-3 (instructors ed.) 1. Commercial statistics. 2. Management—Statistical methods.
3. Economics—Statistical methods. 4. Statistics. I. Seward, Lori Welte, 1962– II. Title. III. Irwin/McGraw-Hill series in operations and decision sciences
    HF1017.D55 2007
    519.5—dc22   2005056294

www.mhhe.com

David P. Doane

David P. Doane is Professor of Quantitative Methods in Oakland University's Department of Decision and Information Sciences. He earned his Bachelor of Arts degree in mathematics and economics at the University of Kansas in 1966 and his PhD from Purdue University's Krannert Graduate School in 1969. His research and teaching interests include applied statistics, forecasting, and statistical education. He is co-recipient of three National Science Foundation grants to develop software to teach statistics and to create a computer classroom. He is a long-time member of the American Statistical Association and INFORMS, serving in 2002 as President of the Detroit ASA chapter, where he remains on the board. He has consulted with government, health care organizations, and local firms. He has published articles in many academic journals and is the author of *LearningStats* (McGraw-Hill, 2003, 2007) and co-author of *Visual Statistics* (McGraw-Hill, 1997, 2001).

Lori E. Seward

Lori E. Seward is a Senior Instructor of Systems in the Leeds School of Business at the University of Colorado—Boulder. She earned her Bachelor of Science and Master of Science degrees in Industrial Engineering at Virginia Tech in 1984 and 1985. After several years working as a reliability and quality engineer in the paper and automotive industries, she earned her PhD from Virginia Tech in 1998. She joined the Leeds faculty in 1998. Her teaching interests include applied statistics, quality management, and supply-chain management and she has taken the lead in using advanced technology tools for enhancing the classroom and learning experience in large lecture courses. She served as the Chair of the INFORMS Teachers' Workshop for the annual 2004 meeting. Her most recent article was published in *The International Journal of Flexible Manufacturing Systems* (Kluwer Academic Publishers, 2004).

To Robert Hamilton Doane-Solomon

David

To Eric Michael and William Samuel Seward

Lori

PREFACE

As recently as a decade ago our students used to ask us, "**How** do I use statistics?" Today we more often hear, "**Why** should I use statistics?," *Applied Statistics in Business and Economics* has attempted to provide real meaning to the use of statistics in our world by using real business situations and real data and appealing to your need to know *why* rather than just *how*.

With over 50 years of teaching statistics between the two of us, we feel we have something to offer you—the 21st-century student. Seeing how you've changed as the new century unfolds has required us to adapt and seek out better ways of instruction. So we wrote *Applied Statistics in Business and Economics* to meet four distinct objectives that we felt were not being met by the many textbooks currently available.

Objective 1: Communicate the Meaning of Variation in a Business Context   Variation exists everywhere in the world around us. Successful businesses know how to measure variation. They also know how to tell when variation should be responded to and when it should be left alone. We'll show you how businesses do this.

Objective 2: Use Real Data and Real Business Applications   Examples, case studies, and problems are taken from published research or real applications whenever possible. Hypothetical data are used when it seems the best way to illustrate a concept. You can usually tell the difference by examining the footnotes citing the source.

Objective 3: Incorporate Current Statistical Practices and Offer Practical Advice   With the increased reliance on computers, statistics practitioners have changed the way they use statistical tools. We'll show you the current practices and explain why they are used the way they are. We will also tell you when each technique should *not* be used.

Objective 4: Provide More In-Depth Explanation of the Why and Let the Software Take Care of the How   It is critical that you understand the importance of communicating with data. Today's computer capabilities make it much easier to summarize and display data than ever before. We demonstrate easily mastered software techniques using the common software available. We also spend a great deal of time on the idea that there are risks in decision making and those risks should be quantified and directly considered in every business decision.

Our experience tells us that you want to be given credit for the experience you bring to the college classroom. We have tried to honor this by choosing examples and exercises set in situations that will draw on your already vast knowledge of the world around you and knowledge you have gained from other classes you have taken. Emphasis is on thinking about data, choosing appropriate analytic tools, using computers effectively, and recognizing limitations of statistics. We bring your attention to newer methods of analysis that are changing the field of statistics. Business disciplines have adapted to the world around us and we have responded to this by emphasizing applications in health care administration, economics, and entrepreneurship.

Software

There are different types of software for statistical analysis, ranging from Excel's functions to stand-alone packages. Excel is used throughout this book because it is available everywhere. But calculations are illustrated using MegaStat, whose Excel-based menus and spreadsheet format offer more capability than Excel's Data Analysis Tools. MINITAB menus and examples are also included to point out similarities and differences of these tools. To assist those of you who need extra help or "catch up" work, the student CD contains tutorials or demonstrations on using Excel or MINITAB for the tasks of each chapter. At the end of each chapter is a list of *LearningStats* and *Visual Statistics* demonstrations, case studies, and applications that illustrate the concepts from the chapter. From the CD, you can install MegaStat, *LearningStats,* and *Visual Statistics* on your own computer.

Math Level

The assumed level of mathematics is pre-calculus, though there are rare references to calculus where it might help the better-trained reader. All but the simplest proofs and derivations are omitted, but key assumptions are stated clearly. You are advised what to do when these assumptions are not fulfilled. Worked examples are included for basic calculations, but the textbook does assume that computers will do all calculations after the statistics class is over. Thus, *interpretation* is paramount. End-of-chapter references and suggested Web sites are given so that interested readers can deepen their understanding. *LearningStats* includes a brief review and self-test on basic math concepts used in the textbook.

Exercises

Simple practice exercises are placed within each section. End-of-chapter exercises tend to be more integrative or to be embedded in more realistic contexts. The end-of-chapter exercises encourage you to try alternative approaches and discuss ambiguities or underlying issues when the statistical tools do not quite "fit" the situation. Many exercises invite mini-essays (at least a sentence or two) rather than just quoting a formula. Exercises marked * involve optional chapter material or more time-consuming answers (*not* tougher math). Answers to odd-numbered exercises are in the back of the book. The CD has Excel data sets for each chapter's examples and exercises, so there is no need to enter a lot of data.

LearningStats

LearningStats is a major supplement. It is intended to let you explore data and concepts at your own pace, ignoring material you already know and focusing on things that interest you. Students who have used *LearningStats* say that they continue to find it useful *after* the class is over, sometimes for projects in other classes they are taking or to finally understand a difficult concept (e.g., what does 95 percent confidence mean?). *LearningStats* is a menu-driven system that has two parts:

Demonstrations
Illustrations, examples, and case studies using Microsoft™ Excel, PowerPoint, and Word, with suggested exercises for individual inquiry. Many case studies use simulation (e.g., to illustrate sampling). Samples of student reports and presentations are included for chapters that require data analysis.

Data Sets
Thousands of variables, many of which were collected by students. Files are grouped by data type (cross-sectional or time-series) and topic (e.g., food, health, etc.). In some data sets, short file names are provided to facilitate import of data into MINITAB™ or other statistical packages (e.g., *Visual Statistics,* SPSS).

ACKNOWLEDGMENTS

The authors would like to acknowledge some of the many people who have helped with this book. Dorothy Duffy permitted use of the chemistry lab for the experiments on Hershey Kisses, Brach's jelly beans, and Sathers gum drops. Nainan Desai and Robert Edgerton explained the proper use of various kinds of engineering terminology. Case studies and examples were suggested by Kevin S. Nathan and Kenneth M. York. Thomas W. Lauer and Floyd G. Willoughby permitted quotation of a case study. Richard W. Hartl of Memorial Hospital and Kathryn H. Sheehy of Crittenton Hospital provided data for case studies. Kevin Murphy, John Sase, T.J. Wharton, and Kenneth M. York permitted questionnaires to be administered in their classes. Ian S. Bradbury, Winson Taam, and especially Ron Tracy and Robert Kushler gave generously of their time as expert statistical consultants. Don Smith and Dana Cobb contributed greatly to the *LearningStats* databases. Jonathan G. Koomey of E.O. Lawrence Berkeley National Laboratory offered valuable suggestions on visual data presentation.

Mark Isken has reliably provided Excel expertise and has suggested health care applications for examples and case studies. John Seeley and Jeff Whitbey provided regression databases. John Savio and the Michigan State Employees Credit Union provided ATM data. The Siena Research Institute has made its poll results available. The Public Interest Research Group of Michigan (PIRGIM) has generously shared data from its field survey of prescription drug prices.

We are grateful for the careful proofreading and suggestions offered by Frances J. Williams, William G. Knapp, John W. Karkowski, Nirmala Ranganathan, Thomas H. Miller, Clara M. Michetti, Fielder S. Lyons, Catherine L. Tatem, Anup D. Karnalkar, Richard G. Taylor, Ian R. Palme, Rebecca L. Curtiss, and Todd R. Keller. Dozens of other individuals have provided examples and cases which are cited in the text and *LearningStats* software.

For reviewing the material on quality, we wish to thank Kay Beauregard, Administrative Director at William Beaumont Hospital, and Ellen Barnes and Karry Roberts of Ford Motor Company. Reviewers of the *LearningStats* software have made numerous suggestions for improvement, which we have tried to incorporate. In particular, we wish to thank Lari H. Arjomand of Clayton College & State University, Richard P. Gebhart of the University of Tulsa, Kieran Mathieson of Oakland University, Vincent F. Melfi of Michigan State University, J. Burdeane Orris of Butler University, Joe Sullivan of Mississippi State University, and Donald L. Westerfield of Webster University.

A special debt of gratitude is due to Carol Rose for her careful copyediting and editorial suggestions, Wanda Zeman for coordinating the project, and especially Dick Hercher for guiding us at every step, solving problems, and encouraging us along the way. We are grateful to Ardith Baker of Oral Roberts University for her timely and detailed suggestions for improving the manuscript. Thanks to the many reviewers who provided such valuable feedback including criticism which made the book better, some of whom reviewed several drafts of the manuscript. Any remaining errors or omissions are the authors' responsibility.

Lari H. Arjomand	*Clayton College & State University*
Ardith Baker	*Oral Roberts University*
Bruce Barrett	*University of Alabama*
Mary Beth Camp	*Indiana University—Bloomington*
Alan R. Cannon	*University of Texas—Arlington*
Alan S. Chesen	*Wright State University*
Chia-Shin Chung	*Cleveland State University*
Bernard Dickman	*Hofstra University*
Lillian Fok	*University of New Orleans*
James C. Ford	*SAS Institute, North America*
Ellen Fuller	*Arizona State University*
Richard P. Gebhart	*University of Tulsa*
Betsy Greenberg	*University of Texas—Austin*
Don Gren	*Salt Lake Community College*
Kemal Gursoy	*Long Island University*
Mickey A. Hepner	*University of Central Oklahoma*
Johnny C. Ho	*University of Texas—El Paso*
Mark G. Kean	*Boston University*
Jerry LaCava	*Boise State University*
Carl Lee	*Central Michigan University*
Glenn Milligan	*The Ohio State University*
Robert M. Nauss	*University of Missouri—St. Louis*

Cornelius Nelan	*Quinnipiac University*
J. B. Orris	*Butler University*
Dane K. Peterson	*Southwest Missouri State University*
Don R. Robinson	*Illinois State University*
Sue Schou	*Idaho State University*
Bill Seaver	*University of Tennessee—Knoxville*
William E. Stein	*Texas A&M University*
Stanley Stephenson	*Southwest Texas State University*
Joe Sullivan	*Mississippi State University*
Patrick Thompson	*University of Florida*
Raja P. Velu	*Syracuse University*
Janet Wolcutt	*Wichita State University*
Jack Yurkiewicz	*Pace University*
Zhen Zhu	*University of Central Oklahoma*

Thanks to the participants in our focus groups and symposia on teaching business statistics in Chicago, Burr Ridge, Huntington Beach, and Las Vegas who provided so many teaching ideas and insights into their particular students and courses. We hope you will be able to see in the book and the teaching package consideration of those ideas and insights.

Nathan Adams	*Middle Tennessee State University*
David Ahlberg	*Santa Clara University*
Sung Ahn	*Washington State University*
M. Imam Alam	*University of Northern Iowa*
Mostafa Aminzadeh	*Towson University*
Ron Barnes	*University of Houston—Downtown*
Ali Behnezhad	*California State University—Northridge*
Lisa Betts	*Kent State University*
Pam Boger	*Ohio University*
Mary Beth Camp	*Indiana University—Bloomington*
Giorgio Canarella	*California State University—Los Angeles*
Alan R. Cannon	*University of Texas—Arlington*
Alan S. Chesen	*Wright State University*
Paul Choi	*DeVry University—Long Beach*
James Cochran	*Louisiana Tech University*
Robert Collins	*Marquette University*
Tom Davis	*University of Dayton*
Dovalee Dorsett	*Baylor University*
Mark Eakin	*University of Texas at Arlington*
Chris Ellis	*Florida International University*
Kathryn Ernstberger	*Indiana University—Southwest*
Grace Esimai	*University of Texas at Arlington*
Mark Ferris	*Saint Louis University*
Paula FitzGibbon	*Case Western Reserve University*
Jean Foss	*University of New Orleans*

Dan Ganster	*University of Arkansas*
Gail Gemberling	*University of Texas—Austin*
Wayne Gober	*Middle Tennessee State University*
Betsy Greenberg	*University of Texas—Austin*
Don Gren	*Salt Lake Community College*
A.M.M. Jamal	*Southeastern Louisiana University*
Arthur Jeffrey	*University of South Alabama*
Chun Jin	*Central Connecticut State University*
L. Van Jones	*Texas Christian University*
Ron Klimberg	*Saint Joseph's University*
Carl Lee	*Central Michigan University*
Seung-Dong Lee	*University of Alabama—Birmingham*
Dennis Lin	*Pennsylvania State University*
Rutilio Martinez	*University of Northern Colorado*
Ralph May	*Southwestern Oklahoma State University*
Bruce McCullough	*Drexel University*
Brad McDonald	*Northern Illinois University*
Elaine McGivern	*Dusquesne University*
Herb McGrath	*Bowling Green State University*
Altaf Memon	*University of Maryland*
Stuart Milne	*Georgia Institute of Technology*
Cornelius Nelan	*Quinnipiac University*
Lakshmi Nigam	*Quinnipiac University*
Richard Numrich	*Community College of Southern Nevada*
Ted Oleson	*University of Nevada—Reno*
Rene Ordonez	*Southern Oregon University*
J. B. Orris	*Butler University*
Barbara Osyk	*University of Akron*
Thomas Page	*Michigan State University*
Edward Pappanastos	*Troy State University*
Wes Payne	*Southwest Tennessee State CC*
Dennis Petruska	*Youngstown State University*
Joseph Petry	*University of Illinois—Champaign*
Stephen Pollard	*California State University—Los Angeles*
Harold Rahmlow	*Saint Joseph's University*
Darlene Riedemann	*Eastern Illinois University*
Mary Anne Rothermel	*University of Akron*
Amar Sahay	*Salt Lake Community College*
Hedayeh Samavati	*Purdue University—Ft. Wayne*
James Schmidt	*University of Nebraska*
Sue Schou	*Idaho State University*
William Stein	*Texas A&M University*
Stan Stephenson	*Texas State University*

Scott Stevens	*James Madison University*
Victoria Stodden	*San Jose State University*
Erich Studer-Ellis	*University of Maryland*
Cheikna Sylla	*New Jersey Institute of Technology*
Faye F. Teer	*James Madison University*
Joseph Van Matre	*University of Alabama*
Joseph Verref	*DeVry University—Pomona*
Mike Vineyard	*University of Memphis*
Bret Wagner	*Western Michigan University*
Don Wardell	*University of Utah*
Rachel Webb	*Portland State University*
Donald Westerfield	*Webster University*
Janet Wolcutt	*Wichita State University*
Bahman Zangenah	*Northeastern University*
Zhiwei Zhu	*University of Louisiana—Lafayette*

BRIEF CONTENTS

CONTENTS

Applied Statistics

in Business and Economics

Overview of Statistics

Chapter Learning Objectives

When you finish this chapter you should be able to

- Define statistics and explain some of its uses in business.

- List reasons for a business student to study statistics.

- State the common challenges facing data analysts.

- Explain why written communication is important.

- Know the basic rules for effective writing and oral presentations.

- Tell what an executive summary is and why it's important.

- List and explain common statistical pitfalls.

Statistics is the science of collecting, organizing, analyzing, interpreting, and presenting data. Some experts prefer to call statistics *data science,* a trilogy of tasks involving data modeling, analysis, and decision-making. Here are some alternative definitions.

Statistics

"I like to think of statistics as the science of learning from data . . ."
Jon Kettenring, ASA President, 1997

"The mathematics of the collection, organization, and interpretation of numerical data, especially the analysis of population characteristics by inference from sampling."
American Heritage Dictionary®*

"Statistical analysis involves collecting information, evaluating it, drawing conclusions, and providing guidance in what information is reliable and which predictions can be trusted."
American Statistical Association

In contrast, a **statistic** is a single measure, reported as a number, used to summarize a sample data set. Many different measures can be used to summarize data sets. You will learn throughout this textbook that there can be different measures for different sets of data and different measures for different types of questions about the same data set. Consider, for example, a sample data set that consists of heights of students in a university. There could be many different uses for this data set. Perhaps the manufacturer of graduation gowns wants to know how long to make the gowns; the best *statistic* for this would be the *average* height of the students. But an architect designing a classroom building would want to know how high the doorways should be, and would base measurements on the *maximum* height of the students. Both the average and the maximum are examples of a *statistic.*

Finally, a **statistician** is an expert with at least a master's degree in mathematics or statistics or a trained professional in a related application area of science or social science. Senior statisticians usually hold a doctorate. Yet any college graduate is expected to know something about statistics, and anyone who creates graphs or interprets data is "doing statistics" without an official title.

---

* *American Heritage Dictionary of the English Language,* 4th Ed. Copyright © 2000 by Houghton Mifflin Company. Used with permission.

1.2
WHY STUDY STATISTICS?

Knowing statistics will make you a better consumer of other people's data. Even if you don't plan to be a professional statistician, you should know enough to handle everyday data problems, to feel confident that others cannot deceive you with spurious arguments, and to know when you've reached the limits of your expertise. Statistical knowledge gives your company a competitive advantage against organizations that cannot understand their internal or external market data. And mastery of basic statistics gives you, the individual manager, a competitive advantage as you work your way through the promotion process, or when you move to a new employer. Here are some more reasons to study statistics.

Communication

The language of statistics is widely used in science, social science, education, health care, engineering, and even the humanities. In all areas of business (accounting, finance, human resources, marketing, information systems, operations management) workers use statistical jargon to facilitate communication. In fact, statistical terminology has reached the highest corporate strategic levels (e.g., "Six Sigma" at GE and Motorola). And in the multinational environment, the specialized vocabulary of statistics permeates language barriers to improve problem-solving across national boundaries.

Computer Skills

Whatever your computer skill level, it can be improved. Every time you create a spreadsheet for data analysis, write a report, or make an oral presentation, you bring together skills you already have, and learn new ones. Specialists with advanced training design the databases and decision support systems, but you must expect to handle daily data problems *without* experts. Besides, you can't always find an "expert," and, if you do, the "expert" may not understand your application very well. You need to be able to analyze data, use software with confidence, prepare your own charts, write your own reports, and make electronic presentations on technical topics.

Information Management

Statistics can help you handle either too little or too much information. When insufficient data are available, statistical surveys and samples can be used to obtain the necessary market information. But most large organizations are closer to drowning in data than starving for it. Statistics can help summarize large amounts of data and reveal underlying relationships. You've heard of data mining? Statistics is the pick and shovel that you take to the data mine.

Technical Literacy

Many of the best career opportunities are in growth industries propelled by advanced technology. Marketing staff may work with engineers, scientists, and manufacturing experts as new products and services are developed. Sales representatives must understand and explain technical products like pharmaceuticals, medical equipment, and industrial tools to potential customers. Purchasing managers must evaluate suppliers' claims about the quality of raw materials, components, software, or parts.

Career Advancement

Whenever there are customers to whom services are delivered, statistical literacy can enhance your career mobility. Multi-billion-dollar companies like Blue Cross, Citibank, Microsoft, and Wal-Mart use statistics to control cost, achieve efficiency, and improve quality. Without a solid understanding of data and statistical measures, you may be left behind.

Quality Improvement

Large manufacturing firms like Boeing or General Motors have formal systems for continuous quality improvement. The same is true of insurance companies and financial service firms like Vanguard or Fidelity, and the federal government. Statistics helps firms oversee their suppliers, monitor their internal operations, and identify problems. Quality improvement goes far beyond statistics, but every college graduate is expected to know enough statistics to understand its role in quality improvement.

There are two primary kinds of statistics:

- *Descriptive statistics* refers to the collection, organization, presentation, and summary of data (either using charts and graphs or using a numerical summary).
- *Inferential statistics* refers to generalizing from a sample to a population, estimating unknown parameters, drawing conclusions, and making decisions.

Figure 1.1 identifies the tasks within each.

FIGURE 1.1

Overview of statistics

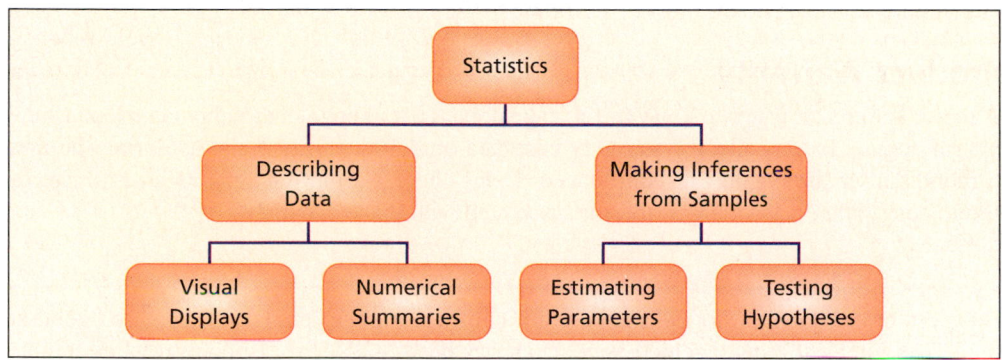

Now let's look at some of the ways statistics is used in business.

Auditing

A large firm pays over 12,000 invoices to suppliers every month. The firm has learned that some invoices are being paid incorrectly, but they don't know how widespread the problem is. The auditors lack the resources to check all the invoices, so they decide to take a sample to estimate the proportion of incorrectly paid invoices. How large should the sample be for the auditors to be confident that the estimate is close enough to the true proportion?

Marketing

A marketing consultant is asked to identify likely repeat customers for Amazon.com, and to suggest co-marketing opportunities based on a database containing records of 5 million Internet purchases of books, CDs, and DVDs. How can this large database be mined to reveal useful patterns that might guide the marketing strategy?

Health Care

An outpatient cognitive retraining clinic for victims of closed-head injuries or stroke evaluates 100 incoming patients using a 42-item physical and mental assessment questionnaire. Each patient is evaluated independently by two experienced therapists. From their evaluations, can we conclude that the therapists agree on the patient's functional status? Are some assessment questions redundant? Do the initial assessment scores accurately predict the patients' lengths of stay in the program?

Quality Control

A manufacturer of rolled copper tubing for radiators wishes to improve its product quality. It initiates a triple inspection program, sets penalties for workers who produce poor-quality output, and posts a slogan calling for "zero defects." The approach fails. Why?

Purchasing

A retailer's shipment of 200 DVD players reveals 4 with defects. The supplier's historical defect rate is .005. Has the defect rate really risen, or is this simply a "bad" batch?

Medicine

An experimental drug to treat asthma is given to 75 patients, of whom 24 get better. A placebo is given to a control group of 75 volunteers, of whom 12 get better. Is the new drug better than the placebo, or is the difference within the realm of chance?

Forecasting

The Home Depot carries 50,000 different products. To manage this vast inventory, it needs a weekly order forecasting system that can respond to developing patterns in consumer demand. Is there a way to predict weekly demand and place orders from suppliers for every item, without an unreasonable commitment of staff time?

Product Warranty

A major automaker wants to know the average dollar cost of engine warranty claims on a new hybrid engine. It has collected warranty cost data on 4,300 warranty claims during the first 6 months after the engines are introduced. Using these warranty claims as an estimate of future costs, what is the margin of error associated with this estimate?

1.4 STATISTICAL CHALLENGES

Business professionals who use statistics are not mere number crunchers who are "good at math." As Jon Kettenring succinctly said, "Industry needs holistic statisticians who are nimble problem solvers" (www.amstat.org). Consider the criteria listed below:

The ideal statistician

- Is technically current (e.g., software-wise).
- Communicates well.
- Is proactive.
- Has a broad outlook.
- Is flexible.
- Focuses on the main problem.
- Meets deadlines.
- Knows his/her limitations and is willing to ask for help.
- Can deal with imperfect information.
- Has professional integrity.

Clearly, many of these characteristics would apply to any *business* professional.

Working with Imperfect Data

In mathematics, exact answers are expected. But statistics lies at the messy interface between theory and reality. For instance, suppose a new air bag design is being tested. Is the new air bag design safer for children? Test data indicate the design may be safer in some crash situations, but the old design appears safer in others. The crash tests are expensive and time-consuming, so the sample size is limited. A few observations are missing due to sensor failures in the crash dummies. There may be random measurement errors. If you are the data analyst, what can you do? Well, you can know and use generally accepted statistical methods, clearly state any assumptions you are forced to make, and honestly point out the limitations of your analysis. You can use statistical tests to detect unusual data points or to deal with missing data. You can give a range of answers under varying assumptions. But occasionally, you need the courage to say, "No useful answer can emerge from this data."

Dealing with Practical Constraints

You will face constraints on the type and quantity of data you can collect. Automobile crash tests can't use human subjects (*too risky*). Telephone surveys can't ask a female respondent whether or not she has had an abortion (*sensitive question*). We can't test everyone for HIV (*the world is not a laboratory*). Survey respondents may not tell the truth or may not answer all the questions (*human behavior is unpredictable*).

Upholding Ethical Standards

Safeguards are in place not only to protect professional integrity but also to minimize ethical breaches. For example, all data analysts must know and follow accepted procedures, maintain data integrity, carry out accurate calculations, report procedures faithfully, protect confidential information, cite sources, and acknowledge sources of financial support. Further, because legal and ethical issues are intertwined, there are specific ethical guidelines for statisticians concerning treatment of human and animal subjects, privacy protection, obtaining informed consent, and guarding against inappropriate uses of data. For further information about ethics, see the American Statistical Association's ethical guidelines (www.amstat.org), which have been extensively reviewed by the statistics profession.

Ethical dilemmas for a nonstatistician are likely to involve conflicts of interest or competing interpretations of the validity of a study and/or its implications. For example, suppose a market research firm is hired to investigate a new corporate logo. The CEO lets you know that she strongly favors a new logo, and it's a big project that could earn you a promotion. Yet, the market data have a high error margin and could support either conclusion. As a manager, you will face such situations. Statistical practices and statistical data can clarify your choices.

Using Consultants

Someone once said the main thing you need to know about statisticians is when to call for one. An hour with an expert at the *beginning* of a project could be the smartest move a manager can make. When should a consultant be hired? When your team lacks certain critical skills, or when an unbiased or informed view cannot be found inside your organization. Expert consultants can handle domineering or indecisive team members, personality clashes, fears about adverse findings, and local politics. Large and medium-sized companies may have in-house statisticians, but smaller firms only hire them as needed. If you hire a statistical expert, you can make better use of the consultant's time by learning how consultants work. Read books about statistical consulting. If your company employs a statistician, take him or her to lunch!

SECTION EXERCISES

1.1   Select *two* of the following scenarios. Explain why you selected each, and give an example of how statistics might be useful to the person in the scenario.
   a. An auditor is looking for inflated broker commissions in stock transactions.
   b. An industrial marketer is representing her firm's compact, new low-power LCD screens to the military.
   c. A plant manager is studying absenteeism at assembly plants in three states.
   d. An automotive purchasing agent is comparing defect rates in steel shipments from three vendors of steel.
   e. A personnel executive is examining job turnover by gender in a fast-food chain.
   f. An intranet manager is studying e-mail usage rates by employee job classification.
   g. A retirement planner is studying mutual fund performance for six different types of asset portfolios.
   h. A hospital administrator is studying surgery scheduling to improve facility utilization rates.

1.2   (a) How much statistics does a student need in *your* chosen field of study? Why not more? Why not less? (b) How can you tell when the point has been reached where you should call for an expert statistician? List some costs and some benefits that would govern this decision.

1.3   (a) Should the average business school graduate expect to use computers to manipulate data, or is this a job better left to specialists? (b) What problems arise when an employee is weak in quantitative skills? Based on your experience, is that common?

1.4   "Many college graduates will not use very much statistics during their 40-year careers, so why study it?" (a) List several arguments for and against this statement. Which position do you find more convincing? (b) Replace the word "statistics" with "accounting" or "foreign language" and repeat this exercise. (c) On the Internet, look up the Latin phrase *reductio ad absurdum*. How is this phrase relevant here?

1.5   How can statistics help organizations deal with (a) information overload? (b) insufficient information? Give an example from a job you have held where statistics might have been useful.

Mini Case   1.1

Lessons from NASA

Former President Lyndon Baines Johnson observed, "A President's hardest task is not to *do* what is right, but to *know* what is right." What's missing is wisdom, not courage. Given incomplete or contradictory data, people have trouble making decisions (remember *Hamlet*?). Sometimes the correct choice is obvious in retrospect, as in NASA's space shuttle disasters. On January 28, 1986, *Challenger* exploded shortly after takeoff, due to erosion of O-rings that had become brittle in freezing overnight temperatures at Cape Canaveral. The crux of the matter was a statistical relationship between brittleness and temperature. Data on O-ring erosion were available for 22 prior shuttle flights. The backup O-rings (there were two layers of O-rings) had suffered no erosion in 9 prior flights at launch temperatures in the range 72°F–81°F, but significant erosion in 4 of 13 prior flights at temperatures in the range 53°F–70°F. However, the role of temperature was by no means clear. NASA and Morton-Thiokol engineers had debated the erratic data inconclusively, including the night before the launch.

After the *Challenger* accident, it was clear that the risk was underestimated. Two *statistical* issues were the degree to which backup layer O-rings provided redundant protection and the correct way to predict O-ring erosion at the *Challenger* launch temperature of 36°F when the lowest previous launch temperature had been 53°F. Two possible *ethical* issues were that NASA officials did not scrub the launch until they understood the problem better and that the astronauts, as participants in a dangerous experiment, had insufficient opportunity for informed consent. NASA's 100 percent previous success record was undoubtedly a factor in everyone's self-confidence, including the astronauts'.

On February 1, 2003, space shuttle *Columbia* burned on re-entry. The heat shield failure was apparently due to tiles damaged by falling foam insulation from the fuel tanks, loosened by vibration during launch. Prior to the *Columbia* disaster in 2003, foam-damaged tiles had been noted 70 times in 112 flights. In retrospect, review of the data showed that some previous flights may have come close to *Columbia*'s fate. This is a *statistical* issue because the heat shield had worked 70 times despite being damaged. Is it surprising that NASA officials believed that the tiles were resistant to foam damage? The statistical and ethical issues are similar to those in the *Challenger* disaster. Organizational inertia and pressure to launch have been blamed in both cases, favoring a risky interpretation of the data.

These disasters remind us that decisions involving data and statistics are always embedded in organizational culture. NASA's evaluation of risk differs from most businesses, due to the dangers inherent in its cutting-edge exploration of space. At the time of the *Challenger* launch, the risk of losing a vehicle was estimated at 1 in 30. At the time of the *Columbia* re-entry accident, the risk was estimated at 1 in 145. For nonhuman launches the risk is about 1 in 50 (2 percent) compared with 2 space shuttle losses in 113 flights (1.8 percent). By comparison, the risk of losing a commercial airline flight is about 1 in 2,000,000.

Sources: yahoo.com; www.nasa.gov; *The New York Times*, February 2, 2003.

Written and oral communication skills are critical for success in business. Table 1.1 lists the key business skills needed for *initial* and *long-range* success, as well as some common *weaknesses*.

1.5

WRITING AND PRESENTING REPORTS

For **Initial** *Job Success*	For **Long-Range** *Job Success*	***Most Common*** Weaknesses
Report writing	Managerial accounting	Communication skills
Accounting principles	Managerial economics	Writing skills
Mathematics	Managerial finance	Immaturity
Statistics	Report writing	Unrealistic expectations
	Oral communication	

TABLE 1.1
Skills Needed for Success in Business

Rules for "Power" Writing

Why is writing so important? Because someone may mention your report on warranty repairs during a meeting of department heads, and your boss may say "OK, make copies of that report so we can all see it." Next thing you know, the CEO is looking at it! Wish you'd taken more care in writing it? To avoid this awkward situation, set aside 25 percent of your allotted project time to *write* the report. You should always outline the report *before* you begin. Then complete the report in sections. Finally, ask trusted peers to review the report, and make revisions as necessary. Keep in mind that you may need to revise more than once. If you have trouble getting started, consult a good reference on technical report-writing.

Writing Style

While you may have creative latitude in how to organize the flow of ideas in the report, it is essential to answer the assigned question succinctly. Describe what you did and what conclusions you reached, listing the most important results first.

Use section headings to group related material and avoid lengthy paragraphs. Your report is your legacy to others who may rely on it. They will find it instructive to know about difficulties you encountered. Provide clear data so others will not need to waste time checking your data and sources. Consider placing technical details in an appendix to keep the main report simple.

If you are writing the report as part of a team, an "editor-in-chief" must be empowered to edit the material so that it is stylistically consistent, has a common voice, and flows together. Allow enough lead time so that all team members can read the final report and give their comments and corrections to the editor-in-chief.

Avoid Jargon   Experts use jargon to talk to one another, but outsiders may find it obscure or even annoying. Technical concepts must be presented so that others can understand them. If you can't communicate the importance of your work, your potential for advancement will be limited. Even if your ideas are good and hundreds of hours went into your analysis, readers up the food chain will toss your report aside if it contains too many cryptic references like SSE, MAPE, or 3-Sigma Limits.

Make It Attractive   Reports should have a title page, descriptive title, date, and author names. It's a good idea to use footers with page numbers and dates (e.g., Page 7 of 23—Draft of 10/8/06) to distinguish revised drafts.

Use wide margins so readers can take notes or write comments. Select an appropriate typeface and point size. Times Roman, Garamond, and Arial are widely accepted.

Call attention to your main points by using subheadings, bullets, **boldfaced type,** *italics,* large fonts, or **color,** but use special effects *sparingly.*

Spelling and Grammar

To an educated reader, incorrect grammar or spelling errors are conspicuous signs of sloppy work. You don't recognize your errors—that's why you make them. Get someone you trust to red-pencil your work. Study your errors until you're sure you won't repeat them.

Remember that Microsoft specializes in software, not English, so don't rely on spelling and grammar checkers. Here are some examples that passed the spell-checker, but each contains two errors. Can you spot them quickly?

Original	*Correction*
• "It's effects will transcend our nation's boarders."	(its, borders)
• "We cannot except this shipment on principal."	(accept, principle)
• "They seceded despite there faults."	(succeeded, their)
• "This plan won't fair well because it's to rigid."	(fare, too)
• "The amount of unhappy employees is raising."	(number, rising)

Your best bet? Keep a dictionary handy! You can refer to it for both proper spelling and grammatical usage.

Organizing a Technical Report

Report formats vary, but a business report usually begins with an *executive summary* limited to a *single page*. Attach the full report containing discussion, explanations, tables, graphs, interpretations, and (if needed) footnotes and appendices. Use appendices for backup material. There is no single acceptable style for a business report but the following would be typical:

- Executive Summary (1 page maximum)
- Introduction (1 to 3 paragraphs)
  - Statement of the problem
  - Data sources and definitions
  - Methods utilized
- Body of the Report (as long as necessary)
  - Discussion, explanations, interpretations
  - Tables and graphs, as needed
- Conclusions (1 to 3 paragraphs)
  - Statement of findings (in order of importance)
  - Limitations (if necessary)
  - Future research suggestions
- Bibliography and Sources
- Appendices (if needed for lengthy or technical material)

Writing an Executive Summary

The goal of an ***executive summary*** is to permit a busy decision-maker to understand what you did and what you found out *without reading the rest of the report*. In a statistical report, the executive summary *briefly* describes the task and goals, data and data sources, methods that were used, main findings of the analysis, and (if necessary) any limitations of the analysis. The main findings will occupy most of the space in the executive summary. Each other item may only rate a sentence or two. The executive summary is limited to a single page (maybe only two or three paragraphs) and should avoid technical language.

An excellent way to evaluate your executive summary is to hand it to a peer. Ask him/her to read it and then tell you what you did and what you found out. If the peer cannot answer precisely, then your summary is deficient. The executive summary must make it *impossible to miss your main findings*. Your boss may judge you and your team by the executive summary alone. S/he may merely leaf through the report to examine key tables or graphs, or may assign someone to review your full report.

Tables and Graphs

Tables should be embedded in the narrative (*not* on a separate page) near the paragraph in which they are cited. Each table should have a number and title, positioned above the table. Graphs should be embedded in the narrative (*not* on a separate page) near the paragraph in which they are discussed. Each graph should have a number and title, positioned below the graph. A graph may make things clearer. Compare Table 1.2 and Figure 1.2. Which do you prefer?

Nation	Top Five Stocks
United States	14.7
Japan	17.6
United Kingdom	31.1
Australia	32.4
France	32.6
Canada	40.5
Germany	43.2
Hong Kong	47.0
Netherlands	61.9
Switzerland	65.5
Ireland	78.6

TABLE 1.2

Stock Market Index Concentration ($n = 11$ nations)

Top5Share

Source: Rolf Banz and Sarah Clough, "Globalization Reshaping World's Financial Markets," *Journal of Financial Planning* 15, no. 4 (2002), p. 73. Copyright © 2002. Used with permission.

FIGURE 1.2

Stock market concentration ($n = 11$ nations)

Rules for Presenting Oral Reports

The goals of an oral report are *not the same* as those of a written report. Your oral presentation must only *highlight* the main points. If your presentation does not provide the answer to an audience question, you can say, "Good question. We don't have time to discuss that further here, but it's covered in the full report. I'll be happy to talk to you about it at the end of the presentation." Or, give a brief answer so they know you did consider the matter. Keep these tips in mind while preparing your oral presentation:

* Select just a few key points you most want to convey.
* Use simple charts and diagrams to get the point across. (See Figure 1.3 for an example.)
* Use **color** and *fonts* creatively to **emphasize a point.**
* Levity is nice on occasion, but avoid gratuitous jokes.
* Have backup slides or transparencies just in case.
* Rehearse to get the timing right (don't go too long).
* Refer the audience to the written report for details.
* Imagine yourself in the audience. Don't bore yourself!

FIGURE 1.3

Pictures help make the point

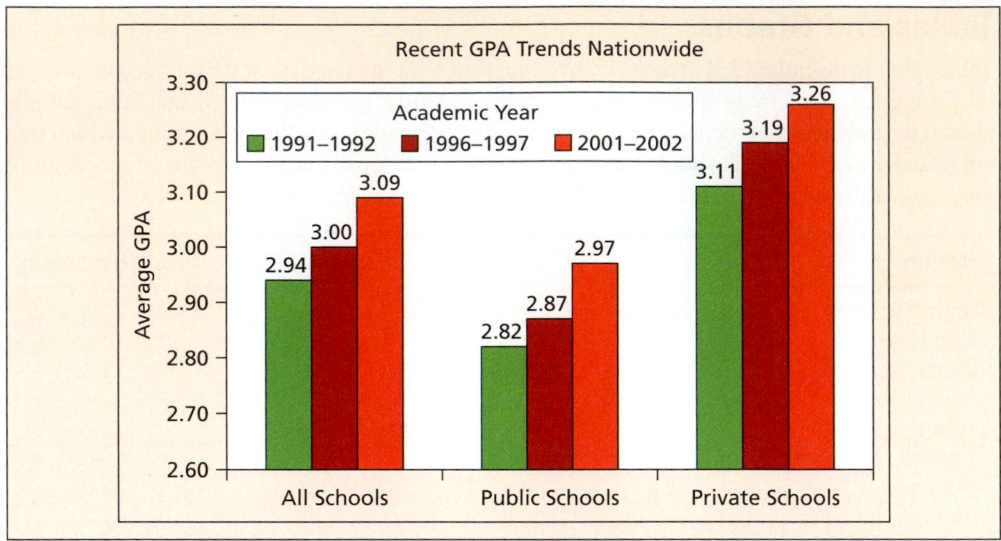

The Three Ps

Pace   Many presenters speak too rapidly—partly because they are nervous and partly because they think it makes them look smarter.

Slow down! Take a little time to introduce yourself, introduce your data, and explain what you are trying to do. If you skip the basic background and definitions, many members of the audience will not be able to follow the presentation and will have only a vague idea what you are talking about.

Planning   Create an outline to organize the ideas you want to discuss. Remember to keep it simple! You'll also need to prepare a verbal "executive summary" to tell your audience what your talk is about. Before you choose your planned opening words, *"Our team correlated robbery with income,"* you should ask yourself:

- Is the audience familiar with correlation analysis?
- Should I explain that our data came from the FBI and the 2000 U.S. Census?
- Will they know that our observations are averages for the 50 U.S. states?
- Will they know that we are talking about per capita robbery rates (not total robberies)?
- Will they know that we are using per capita personal income (not median family income)?
- Should I show them a few data values to help them visualize the data?

Don't bury them in detail, but make the first minute count. If you ran into problems or made errors in your analysis, it's OK to say so. The audience will sympathize.

Check the raw data carefully—you may be called on to answer questions. It's hard to defend yourself when you failed to catch serious errors or didn't understand a key definition.

Practice   Rehearse the oral presentation to get the timing right. Maybe your employer will send you to training classes to bolster your presentation skills. Otherwise consider videotaping yourself or practicing in front of a few peers for valuable feedback. Technical presentations may demand skills different from the ones you used in English class, so don't panic if you have a few problems.

SECTION EXERCISES

1.6   Discuss and criticize each of these two executive summaries from student reports, noting both good and bad points. Is the summary succinct? Was the purpose of the investigation clear? Were the methods explained? Are the main findings stated clearly? Were any limitations of the study noted? Is jargon a problem? How might each summary be improved?

a. "We weighed 10 Tootsie Rolls chosen randomly without replacement from a finite population of 290. The sample mean was calculated at 3.3048 grams and the sample standard deviation was 0.1320 grams. A 95 percent confidence interval using Student's *t* without FPCF was 3.2119 grams to 3.3977 grams."

b. "The November issue of *Money* magazine contained an estimated proportion of pages with advertisements of between 53 percent and 67 percent with an estimated mean advertisements per page between 0.5 and 1.3. The November issue consisted of 222 pages, and the sample consisted of the first 100 even-numbered pages."

1.7   (a) Which of these two displays (table or graph) is more helpful in describing the experience level of a sample of 49 financial planners? Why? (b) Write a one-sentence summary of the data. (Data are from T. Potts, J. E. Schoen, M. E. Loeb, and F. S. Hulme, "Effective Retirement for Family Business Owner-Managers," *Journal of Financial Planning* 14, no. 6 (June 2001), p. 110.)
FinancePlan

Financial Planners' Years of Experience	Frequency
Under 10	4
11 to 15	6
16 to 20	15
21 to 25	12
26 to 30	9
31 to 35	2
36 or more	1
Total	49

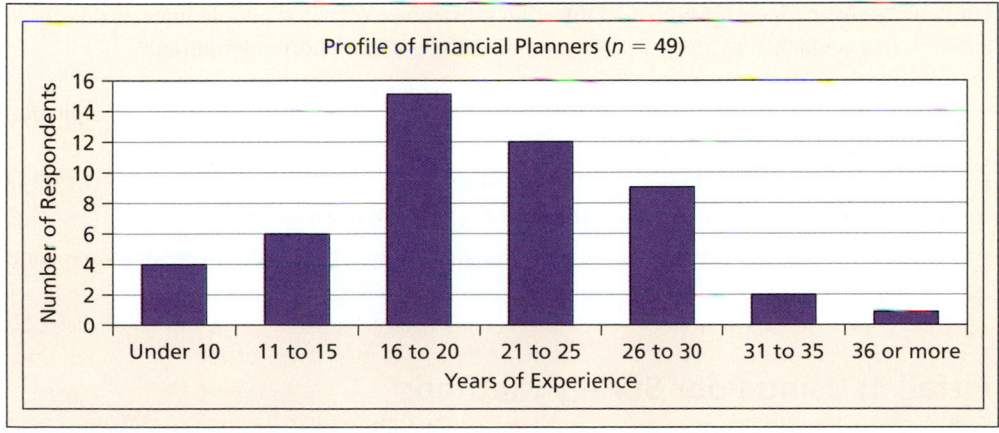

1.8   Go to the Web and use your favorite search engine to look up key words like "technical writing" or "scientific reports." Print one or two excerpts from Web sites that you found particularly interesting or useful, and write a few sentences explaining why you liked them.

1.9   Cite a situation from your work, daily life, or general reading where numerical facts could be presented in more than one way. What were the ethical implications for each alternative? How was it resolved? What was the result?

1.6
STATISTICAL PITFALLS

We use statistical tools to compare *empirical data* (data collected through observations and experiments) against theories. If the data doesn't support our theory, we reject or revise our theory. In *The Wall Street Journal,* in *Money* magazine, and on CNN you see stock market experts with theories to "explain" the current market (bull, bear, or pause). But each year brings new experts and new theories, and the old ones vanish. Logical pitfalls abound in both the data collection process and the reasoning process. Let's look at some.

Pitfall 1: Making Conclusions about a Large Population from a Small Sample

"My Aunt Harriet smoked all her life and lived to 90. Smoking doesn't hurt you." Good for her. But does one case prove anything? Five customers are asked if the new product design is an improvement. If three say yes, should the company implement the new design? If 10 patients try a new asthma medication and one gets a rash, can we conclude that the medication caused the rash? How large a sample is needed to make conclusions? Fortunately statisticians have developed clear rules about sample sizes. Until you learn them, it's OK to raise your pennant hopes when your favorite baseball team wins five games in a row.

Pitfall 2: Making Conclusions from Nonrandom Samples

"Rock stars die young. Look at Buddy Holly, Jimi Hendrix, Janis Joplin, Jim Morrison, John Lennon, and Kurt Cobain." But we are looking only at those who *did* die young. What about the thousands who are alive and well or who lived long lives? Similarly, we should be careful about generalizing from retrospective studies of people who have heart attacks, unless we also study those who do not have heart attacks. (From Arnold Barnett, "How Numbers Can Trick You," *Technology Review,* October 1994, p. 40.)

Pitfall 3: Attaching Importance to Rare Observations from Large Samples

Unlikely events happen if we take a large enough sample. Yet some people draw strong inferences from events that are not surprising when looking at the entire population.

- "Mary in my office won the lottery. Her system must have worked." Millions of people play the lottery. Someone will eventually win.
- "Bill's a sports genius. He predicted every Notre Dame football win last season." Millions of sports fans make predictions. A few of them will call every game correctly.
- "Tom's SUV rolled over. SUVs are dangerous." Millions of people drive SUVs, so some will roll over.

Pitfall 4: Using Poor Survey Methods

Did your instructor ever ask a question like "How many of you remember the simplex method from your math class?" One or two timid hands (or maybe none) are raised, even though the topic was covered. Did the math department not teach the simplex method? Or did students not "get it"? More likely, the instructor has used a poor sampling method and a vaguely worded question. It's difficult for students to respond to such a question in public, for they assume (often correctly) that if they raise a hand the instructor is going to ask them to explain it, or that their peers will think they are showing off. An anonymous survey or a quiz on the simplex method would provide better insight.

Pitfall 5: Assuming a Causal Link Based on Observation ———•

Association does not prove causation. You've probably heard that. But many people draw unwarranted conclusions when no cause-and-effect link exists. Consider anecdotes like these:

- "Murder rates were higher during the full moon in Miami last year. I guess the moon makes people crazy." But what about cities that saw a *decrease* in murders during the same full moon?

- "Most shark attacks occur between 12 P.M. and 2 P.M. Sharks must be hungrier then." Maybe it's just that more people go swimming near midday. If a causal link exists, it would have to be shown in a carefully controlled experiment.

On the other hand, association may warrant further study when common sense suggests a potential causal link. For example, many people believed that smoking was harmful decades before scientists showed *how* smoking leads to cancer, heart disease, and emphysema. A cell phone user who develops cancer might blame the phones. Yet almost everyone uses cell phones, and very few get cancer. A statistical analysis would consider factors like occupation, smoking, alcohol use, birth control pills, diet, and exercise, along with cell phone usage.

Pitfall 6: Making Generalizations about Individuals from Observations about Groups ———•

"Men are taller than women." Yes, but only in a statistical sense. Men are taller *on average,* but many women are taller than many men. We should avoid reading too much into **statistical generalizations.** Instead, ask how much *overlap* is in the populations that are being considered. Often, the similarities transcend the differences.

Pitfall 7: Unconscious Bias ———•

Without obvious fraud (tampering with data), researchers can unconsciously or subtly allow bias to color their handling of data. For example, for many years it was assumed that heart attacks were more likely to occur in men than women. The symptoms of heart disease are more obvious in men than women and therefore doctors tend to catch heart disease earlier in men than women. Recent studies now show that heart disease is the number one cause of death in women over the age of 25. (See Lori Mosca et al., "Evidence-based Guidelines for Cardiovascular Disease Prevention in Women," *American Heart Association* 109, no. 5 (February 2004), pp. 672–93.)

Pitfall 8: Attaching Practical Importance to Every Statistically Significant Study Result ———•

Statistically significant effects may lack practical importance. A study published in *The American Statistician* of over 500,000 Austrian military recruits showed that those born in the spring averaged 0.6 cm taller than those born in the fall (J. Utts, vol. 57, no. 2 (May 2003), pp. 74–79). But who would notice? Would prospective parents change their timing in hopes of having a child 0.6 cm taller? Similarly, cost-conscious businesses know that some significant product improvements cannot support a valid business case. Consumers cannot perceive small improvements in durability, speed, taste, and comfort if the products already are "good enough." For example, Seagate's Cheetah 147GB disk drive already has a mean time between failure (MTBF) rating of 1.4 million hours (about 160 years in continuous use). Would a 10 percent improvement in MTBF matter to anyone?

1.10 "Radar detector users have a lower accident rate than non-users. Moreover, detector users seem to be better citizens. The study found that detector users wear their seat belts more and even vote more than non-users." (a) Assuming that the study is accurate, do you think there is cause-and-effect? (b) If everyone used radar detectors, would voting rates and seat-belt usage rise?

1.11 A lottery winner told how he picked his six-digit winning number (5-6-8-10-22-39): number of people in his family, birth date of his wife, school grade of his 13-year-old daughter, sum of his birth date and his wife's, number of years of marriage, and year of his birth. He said, "I try to pick numbers that mean something to me." The State Lottery Commissioner called this method "the screwiest I ever heard of . . . but apparently it works." (a) From a statistical viewpoint, do you agree that this method "works"? (b) Based on your understanding of how a lottery works, would someone who picks 1-2-3-4-5-6 because "it is easy to remember" have a lower chance of winning?

1.12 "Smokers are much more likely to speed, run red lights, and get involved in car accidents than non-smokers." (a) Can you think of reasons why this statement might be misleading? *Hint:* Make a list of six factors that you think would cause car accidents. Is smoking on your list? (b) Can you suggest a causal link between smoking and car accidents?

1.7
STATISTICS: AN EVOLVING FIELD

Statistics is a relatively young field, having been developed mostly during the 20th century, although its roots hark back several centuries to early mathematicians in China and India. Its mathematical frontiers continue to expand, aided by the power of computers. Major developments of the late 20th century include exploratory data analysis (EDA), computer-intensive statistics, design of experiments, robust product design, advanced Bayesian methods, graphical methods, and data mining. In this book you will only get a glimpse of statistical methods and applications. But you can find many reference works that tell the story of statistics and famous statisticians (see Related Reading). The Web has many resources, including college statistics Web sites and biographies of famous statisticians.

Chapter Summary

Statistics is the science of collecting, organizing, analyzing, interpreting, and presenting data. A **statistician** is an expert with at least a master's degree in mathematics or statistics, while a **data analyst** is anyone who works with data. **Descriptive statistics** is the collection, organization, presentation, and summary of data with charts or numerical summaries. **Inferential statistics** refers to generalizing from a sample to a population, estimating unknown parameters, drawing conclusions, and making decisions. Statistics is used in all branches of business. **Statistical challenges** include imperfect data, practical constraints, and ethical dilemmas. Effective **technical report writing** requires attention to style, grammar, organization, and proper use of tables and graphs. Business data analysts must learn to write a good **executive summary** and learn the *3 Ps* for oral presentations: pace, planning, and practice. Statistical tools are used to test theories against empirical data. Pitfalls include nonrandom samples, incorrect sample size, and lack of causal links. The field of statistics is relatively new and continues to grow as mathematical frontiers expand.

Key Terms

descriptive statistics, *5*	inferential statistics, *5*	statistician, *3*
empirical data, *14*	statistic, *3*	statistical generalization, *15*
executive summary, *10*	statistics, *3*	

Chapter Review

1. Define (a) statistic; (b) statistics.
2. List three reasons to study statistics.
3. List three applications of statistics.
4. List four skills needed by statisticians. Why are these skills important?

5. List five rules for good writing. Why are good writing skills important?

6. (a) List some typical components of a technical report. (b) What does an executive summary include? What is its purpose?

7. (a) List three rules for using tables and graphs. (b) List three tips for making effective oral reports.

8. List three challenges faced by statisticians.

9. List five pitfalls or logical errors that may ensnare the unwary statistician.

CHAPTER EXERCISES

1.13 A survey of beginning students showed that a majority strongly agreed with the statement, "I am afraid of statistics." Why might this attitude exist among students who have not yet taken a statistics class? Would a similar attitude exist toward an ethics class? Explain your reasoning.

1.14 Under a recent U.S. Food and Drug Administration (FDA) standard for food contaminants, 3.5 ounces of tomato sauce can have up to 30 fly eggs, and 11 ounces of wheat flour can contain 450 insect fragments. How could statistical sampling be used to see that these standards of food hygiene are not violated by producers?

1.15 A statistical consultant was retained by a linen supplier to analyze a survey of hospital purchasing managers. After looking at the data, she realized that the survey had missed several key geographic areas and included some that were outside the target region. Some survey questions were ambiguous. Some respondents failed to answer all the questions or gave silly replies (one manager said he worked 40 hours a day). Of the 1,000 surveys mailed, only 80 were returned. (a) What alternatives are available to the statistician? (b) Might an imperfect analysis be better than none? (c) If you were the consultant, how might you respond to the supplier?

1.16 Ergonomics is the science of making sure that human surroundings are adapted to human needs. How could statistics play a role in the following:
   a. Choosing the height of an office chair so that 95 percent of the employees (male and female) will feel it is the "right height" for their legs to reach the floor comfortably.
   b. Designing a drill press so its controls can be reached and its forces operated by an "average employee."
   c. Defining a doorway width so that a "typical" wheelchair can pass through without coming closer than 6 inches from either side.
   d. Setting the width of a parking space to accommodate 95 percent of all vehicles at your local Wal-Mart.
   e. Choosing a font size so that a highway sign can be read in daylight at 100 meters by 95 percent of all drivers.

1.17 A research study showed that 7 percent of "A" students smoke, while nearly 50 percent of "D" students do. (a) List in rank order six factors that you think affect grades. Is smoking on your list? (b) If smoking is not a likely cause of poor grades, can you suggest reasons why these results were observed? (c) Assuming these statistics are correct, would "D" students who give up smoking improve their grades?

1.18 A research study by the Agency for Healthcare Research Quality showed that adolescents who watched more than 4 hours of TV per day were more than five times as likely to start smoking as those who watched less than 2 hours a day. The researchers speculate that TV actors' portrayals of smoking as personally and socially rewarding were an effective indirect method of tobacco promotion (*Note:* Paid television tobacco ads are illegal). List in rank order six factors that you think cause adolescents to start smoking. Did TV portrayals of attractive smokers appear on your list? (Data are from the *AHRQ Newsletter,* no. 269, January 2003, p. 12).

1.19 The Graduate Management Aptitude Test (GMAT) is used by many graduate schools of business as one of their admission criteria. GMAT scores for selected undergraduate majors are shown below. Using your own reasoning and concepts in this chapter, criticize each of the following statements.
   a. "Philosophy majors must not be interested in business since so few take the GMAT."
   b. "More students major in engineering than in English."
   c. "If marketing students majored in physics, they would score better on the GMAT."
   d. "Physics majors would make the best managers."

GMAT Scores and Undergraduate Major, 1984–1989   GMAT

Major	Average GMAT Score	Number Taking Test
Accounting	483	25,233
Computer Science	508	7,573
Economics	513	16,432
Engineering	544	29,688
English	507	3,589
Finance	489	20,001
Marketing	455	15,925
Philosophy	546	588
Physics	575	1,223

Source: Graduate Management Admission Council, *Admission Office Profile of Candidates,* October 1989, pp. 27–30.

1.20 (a) Which of these two displays (table or graph) is more helpful in visualizing the relationship between chest circumference and body fat for 100 randomly chosen men? Explain. (b) Do you see anything unusual in the data? Explain. (Data are from Roger W. Johnson, "Fitting Percentage of Body Fat to Simple Body Measurements," *Journal of Statistics Education* 4, no. 1 (1996).)   **BodyFat**

	Body Fat (%)				
Chest (cm)	0 < 10	10 < 20	20 < 30	30 < 40	Row Tot
80 < 90	5	7	2	0	14
90 < 100	12	15	11	0	38
100 < 110	7	7	18	4	36
110 < 120	0	2	3	5	10
120 < 130	0	0	0	1	1
130 < 140	0	0	0	1	1
Col Tot	24	31	34	11	100

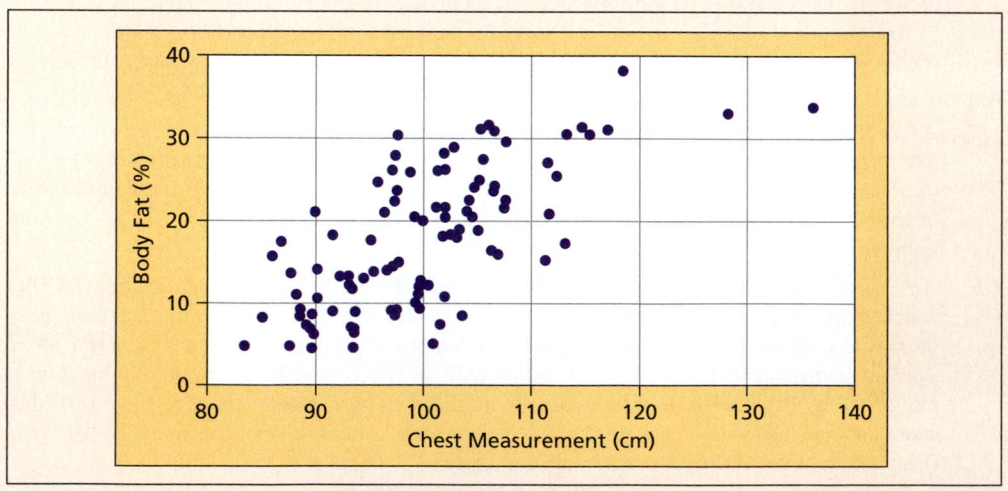

1.21 Each of the following is an actual writing sample, mostly from student projects. In each, find as many errors of spelling and/or grammar as you can, and correct them.

a. "Its' R^2 value is quite close to 1 indicating it is a good fit to the actual data. I feel that G.E., one of the most respected corporations in the world, because of its' strong management and name recognition, not to mention its' valuable assets, is poised for steady growth over the next decade."

b. "If a countries unemployment rate is to high it could cause a down swing in their economics structure."

c. "This forecast is very unlikely, because you cannot have a negative amount of people unemployed."

d. "It is not a well designed graph because it's title is too long and there isn't any axis labels."

e. "This graph has no clear concise boarder to give it a sense of containment. With this graph especially since it is dealing with actually three seperate pieces of information. In this graph, the same data is presented but in a deceptive manor. Its sources weren't as specific as they should of been."

1.22 Choose *three* of the following statisticians and use the Web to find out a few basic facts about them (e.g., list some of their contributions to statistics, when they did their work, whether they are still living, etc.).

Florence Nightingale	John Wilder Tukey	Genichi Taguchi
Gertrude Cox	William Cochran	Helen Walker
Sir Francis Galton	Siméon Poisson	George Box
W. Edwards Deming	S. S. Stevens	Sam Wilks
The Bernoulli family	R. A. Fisher	Carl F. Gauss
Frederick Mosteller	George Snedecor	William S. Gosset
William H. Kruskal	Karl Pearson	Thomas Bayes
Jerzy Neyman	C. R. Rao	Bradley Efron
Egon Pearson	Abraham De Moivre	
Harold Hotelling	Edward Tufte	

Related Reading

Practical Guides

Boen, James R. *The Human Side of Statistical Consulting.* Wadsworth, 1982.

Chatfield, Christopher. *Problem Solving: A Statistician's Guide.* Chapman and Hall, 1988.

Coleman, S.; T. Greenfield; R. Jones; C. Morris; and I. Puzey. *The Pocket Statistician.* Wiley, 1996.

Everitt, B. S. *The Cambridge Dictionary of Statistics.* 2nd ed. Cambridge University Press, 2002.

Kanji, Gopal K. *100 Statistical Tests.* Sage Publications, 1999.

Kruskal, William H.; and Judith M. Tanur. *International Encyclopedia of Statistics, Vol. I and II.* The Free Press, 1978.

Newton, Rae R.; and Kjell Erik Rudestam. *Your Statistical Consultant.* Sage Publications, 1999.

Sahei, Hardeo; and Anwer Khurshid. *Pocket Dictionary of Statistics.* McGraw-Hill, 2002.

Utts, Jessica. "What Educated Citizens Should Know About Statistics and Probability." *The American Statistician* 57, no. 2 (May 2003), pp. 74–79.

Effective Writing

Harris, Robert A. *Writing with Clarity and Style.* Pyrczak Publishing, 2003.

Michaelson, Herbert B. *How to Write and Publish Engineering Papers and Reports.* 3rd ed. Oryx, 1990.

Pyrczak, Fred; and Randall Bruce. *Writing Empirical Research Reports.* 4th ed. Pyrczak Publishing, 2003.

Radke-Sharpe, N. "Writing as a Component of Statistics Education." *The American Statistician* 45, November 1991, pp. 292–93.

Sabin, William A. *The Gregg Reference Manual.* 9th ed. Glencoe/McGraw-Hill, 2000.

Sides, Charles H. *How to Write and Present Technical Information.* Oryx, 1991.

Strunk, William J.; and E. B. White. *The Elements of Style.* Prentice-Hall, 1999.

Tichy, H. J. *Effective Writing for Engineers, Managers, and Scientists.* 2nd ed. Wiley, 1988.

Ethics

Nash, Laura L. *Good Intentions Aside: A Manager's Guide to Resolving Ethical Problems.* Harvard University Press, 1990.

Vardeman, Stephen B.; and Max D. Morris. "Statistics and Ethics: Some Advice for Young Statisticians." *The American Statistician* 57, February 2003, pp. 21–26.

History of Statistics

Gani, J. *The Making of Statisticians.* Springer-Verlag, 1982.

Heyde, C. C.; and E. Seneta. *Statisticians of the Centuries.* Springer-Verlag, 2001.

Johnson, Norman L.; and Samuel Kotz. *Leading Personalities in Statistical Science from the Seventeenth Century to the Present.* Wiley, 1997.

Statistics: Uses and Misuses

Almer, Ennis C. *Statistical Tricks and Traps.* Pyrczak Publishing, 2000.

Barnett, Arnold. "How Numbers Can Trick You." *Technology Review,* October 1994, pp. 38–45.

Gould, Stephen Jay. *The Mismeasure of Man.* W. W. Norton, 1996.

LearningStats Unit 00   Basic Skills

Even if you already know how to use Microsoft® Office tools (Excel, Word, PowerPoint), there may be features that you have never tried or skills you can improve. One objective of *LearningStats* is to show you how to use software applications (especially Excel) *in the context of statistics* for calculations, reports, and presentations. Excel is emphasized but there are also helpful tips on statistical reports using Word and PowerPoint. At your own pace, you should examine each demonstration. Some material will already be familiar to you, but you may pick up a few new tips. If you don't know anything about Excel, Word, or PowerPoint, you should consult additional sources, but you can still use *LearningStats*.

Topic	LearningStats Modules
Microsoft® Office	Excel Tips
	Word Tips
	PowerPoint Tips
	Checklist of Office Skills
Excel	Excel Basics
	Excel Embellishments
	Excel Functions
	Excel Advanced Features
Math Review	Math Review

Key: = PowerPoint   = Word   = Excel

LearningStats Unit 01   Overview of Statistics   [LS]

LearningStats Unit 01 introduces statistics, report-writing, and professional ethical guidelines. Modules are designed for self-study, so you can proceed at your own pace, concentrate on material that is new, and pass quickly over things that you already know. Your instructor may assign specific modules, or you may decide to check them out because the topic sounds interesting. In addition to helping you learn about statistics, they may be useful as references later on.

Topic	*LearningStats Modules*
Overview	What Is Statistics?
	Web Resources
	Statistics Software
Report writing	Effective Writing
	Technical Report Writing
	The Executive Summary
	The Oral Presentation
	Common Errors
	Writing Self-Test 1
	Writing Self-Test 2
	Writing Self-Test 3
Ethics	Ethical Guidelines

Key: = PowerPoint   = Word   = Excel

Data Collection

Chapter Learning Objectives

When you finish this chapter you should be able to

- Use basic terminology for describing data and samples.

- Explain the distinction between numerical and attribute data.

- Recognize levels of measurement in data and ways of coding data.

- Recognize a Likert scale and know how to use it.

- Explain the difference between time series and cross-sectional data.

- Use the correct terminology for samples and populations.

- Explain the common sampling methods and how to implement them.

- Find everyday print or electronic data sources.

- Describe basic elements of survey design, survey types, and sources of error.

In scientific research, data arise from experiments whose results are recorded systematically. In business, data usually arise from accounting transactions or management processes (e.g., inventory, sales, payroll). Much of the data that statisticians analyze were recorded without explicit consideration of their statistical uses, yet important decisions may depend on the data. How many pints of type A blood will be required at Mt. Sinai Hospital next Thursday? How many dollars must State Farm keep in its cash account to cover automotive accident claims next November? How many yellow three-quarter sleeve women's sweaters will Lands' End sell this month? To answer such questions, we usually look at historical data.

Data: Singular or Plural?

Data is the plural of the Latin *datum* (a "given" fact). This traditional usage is preferred in Britain, and especially in scientific journals, where over 90 percent of the references use data as a plural ("These data show a correlation . . ."). But in the popular press (newspapers, magazines) you will often see "data" used synonymously with "information" and hence as a singular ("The compressed data is stored on a CD . . ."). The singular usage is especially common in the United States and is becoming more common in the United Kingdom, rather to the chagrin of the educated populace.

Subjects, Variables, and Data Sets

In this book, we will use *data* as a plural and *data set* when we refer to a particular collection of data as a whole. Each data value is an *observation.* A *subject* or *individual* is an item for study. An example of a subject would be an employee in your company or an invoice statement generated last month. A *variable* is a characteristic of the subject or individual. An example of a variable might be the employee's income. An observation of that variable is the amount of the employee's income. Table 2.1 shows a small data set with eight subjects, five variables, and 40 observations (eight subjects times five variables).

TABLE 2.1

A Small Multivariate Data Set (5 variables, 8 subjects)

SmallData

Case	Name	Age	Income	Position	Gender
1	Frieda	45	$67,100	Personnel director	F
2	Stefan	32	56,500	Operations analyst	M
3	Barbara	55	88,200	Marketing VP	F
4	Donna	27	59,000	Statistician	F
5	Larry	46	36,000	Security guard	M
6	Alicia	52	68,500	Comptroller	F
7	Alec	65	95,200	Chief executive	M
8	Jaime	50	71,200	Public relations	M

TABLE 2.2

Number of Variables and Typical Tasks

Data Set	Variables	Typical Tasks
Univariate	One	Histograms, descriptive statistics, frequency tallies
Bivariate	Two	Scatter plots, correlations, simple regression
Multivariate	More than two	Multiple regression, data mining, modeling

A data set may consist of many variables. The questions that can be explored and the analytical techniques that can be used will depend upon the data type and the number of variables. This textbook starts with *univariate data sets* (one variable), then moves to *bivariate data sets* (two variables) and *multivariate data sets* (more than two variables), as illustrated in Table 2.2.

Data Types

A data set may contain a mixture of *data types*. Two broad categories are **attribute data** and **numerical data,** as shown in Figure 2.1.

FIGURE 2.1

Data types

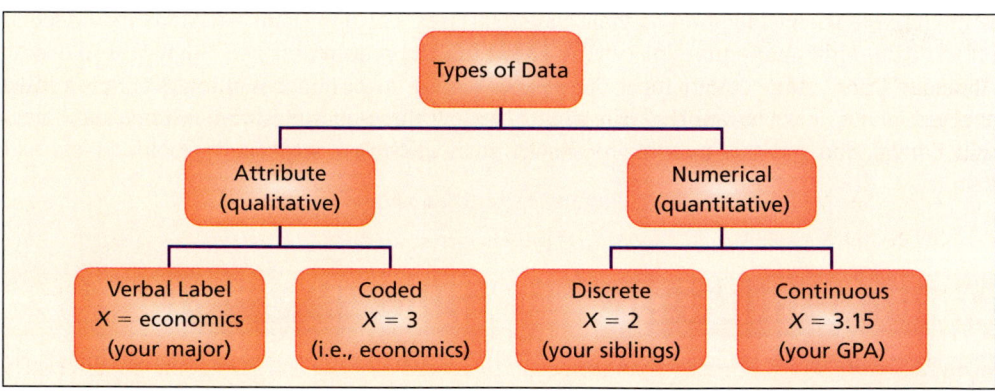

Attribute Data   *Attribute* data (also called *categorical, nominal,* or *qualitative*) have values that are described by words rather than numbers. For example:

Structural lumber type (e.g., $X =$ fir, hemlock, pine).

Automobile style (e.g., $X =$ full, midsize, compact, subcompact).

Mutual fund type (e.g., $X =$ load, no-load).

You might imagine that attribute data would be of limited statistical use, but in fact there are many statistical methods that can handle attribute data.

Data Coding   Using numbers to represent categories to facilitate statistical analysis is called *coding.* For example, a database might classify movies using numerical codes:

1 = Action, 2 = Classic, 3 = Comedy, 4 = Horror,

5 = Romance, 6 = Science Fiction, 7 = Western, 8 = Other

Coding an attribute as a number does *not* make the data numerical. The movie codes are assigned arbitrarily, and the codes do not imply a ranking. However, sometimes attribute codes do imply a ranking:

1 = Bachelor's, 2 = Master's, 3 = Doctorate

Rankings may exist if we are measuring an underlying continuum, such as political orientation:

1 = Liberal, 2 = Moderate, 3 = Conservative

Binary Data   A *binary variable* has only two values, indicating the presence (1) or absence (0) of a characteristic of interest. For example, for an individual:

Employment	*Education*	*Marital status*
1 = employed	1 = college graduate	1 = currently married
0 = not employed	0 = not college graduate	0 = not currently married

The codes are arbitrary. A variable like gender could be coded in many ways:

Like This	*Or Like This*	*Or Like This*
1 = female	0 = female	1 = female
0 = male	1 = male	2 = male

Here again the coding itself has no numerical meaning, so binary variables are *attribute* data.

Numerical Data   *Numerical* or *quantitative* data arise from counting, measuring something, or from some kind of mathematical operation. For example:

Number of auto insurance claims filed in March (e.g., $X = 114$ claims).

Sales for last quarter (e.g., $X = \$4,920,115$).

Percent of mortgage applicants who are retired (e.g., $X = 22.7$ percent).

Most accounting data, economic indicators, and financial ratios are quantitative, as are physical measurements (length, weight, time, speed).

Discrete Data   Numerical data can be further broken down into two types. A variable with a countable number of values that can be represented by an integer is *discrete*. You can recognize integer data because their description begins with "number of." For example:

Number of Medicaid patients in a hospital waiting room (e.g., $X = 2$).

Number of takeoffs at Chicago's O'Hare Airport in a given hour (e.g., $X = 37$).

We express such data as integer variables because we cannot observe a fractional number of patients or takeoffs.

Continuous Data   A numerical variable that can have any value within an interval is *continuous*. This would include things like physical measurements (e.g., length, weight, time, speed) and financial variables (e.g., sales, assets, price/earnings ratios, inventory turns). For example:

Weight of a package of Sun-Maid raisins (e.g., $X = 427.31$ grams).

Hourly fuel flow in a Cessna Citation V (e.g., $X = 1390.67$ pounds).

These are continuous variables because any interval (e.g., $422 < X < 428$) contains infinitely many possible values.

Rounding   Apparent ambiguity is introduced when we round continuous data to whole numbers (e.g., your weight this morning). However, the underlying measurement scale is continuous. That is, a package of Sun-Maid raisins is labeled 425 grams, but on an accurate scale its weight would be a noninteger (e.g., 427.31). Precision depends on the instrument we use to measure the continuous variable. We generally treat financial data (dollars, euros, pesos) as continuous even though retail prices go in discrete steps of .01 (i.e., we go from \$1.25 to \$1.26). The FM radio spectrum is continuous, but only certain discrete values are observed (e.g., 104.3) because of Federal Communications Commission rules. Conversely, we sometimes treat discrete data as continuous when the range is very large (e.g., SAT scores) and small differences (e.g., 604 or 605) aren't of much importance. This topic will be discussed in later chapters. If in doubt, just think about how X was measured and whether or not its values are countable.

SECTION EXERCISES

2.1   Explain the difference between an observation and a variable.

2.2   Give an example of (a) attribute data, (b) discrete numerical data, and (c) continuous numerical data.

2.3   What type of data (attribute, discrete numerical, or continuous numerical) is each of the following variables? If there is any ambiguity about the data type, explain why the answer is unclear.
a. The manufacturer of your car.
b. Your college major.
c. The number of college credits you are taking.
d. Your GPA.
e. The miles on your car's odometer.
f. The fat grams you ate for lunch yesterday.
g. Your dog's age.

2.4   What type of data (attribute, discrete numerical, or continuous numerical) is each of the following variables? If there is any ambiguity, explain why the answer is unclear.
a. Length of a TV commercial.
b. Number of peanuts in a can of Planter's Mixed Nuts.
c. Occupation of a mortgage applicant.
d. Flight time from London Heathrow to Chicago O'Hare.
e. Name of the airline with the cheapest fare from New York to London.
f. Blouse size purchased by a Marks and Spencer customer.

2.5   (a) Give three original examples of discrete data. (b) Give three original examples of continuous data. In each case, explain and identify any ambiguities that might exist. *Hint:* Do not restrict yourself to published data. Consider data describing your own life (e.g., your sports performance, financial data, or academic data). You need *not* list all the data, merely describe them and show a few typical data values.

2.6   Look at data sets in LearningStats under Cross-Sectional Data > Cars. Find an example of (a) a univariate data set, (b) a bivariate data set, and (c) a multivariate data set.

2.2 LEVEL OF MEASUREMENT

Statisticians sometimes refer to four levels of measurement for data: *nominal, ordinal, interval,* and *ratio* (see Table 2.3). This typology was proposed over 60 years ago by psychologist S. S. Stevens. The allowable statistical tests depend on the measurement level.

Nominal Measurement

Nominal measurement is the weakest level of measurement and the easiest to recognize. *Nominal data* (from Latin *nomen* meaning "name") merely identify a *category*. "Nominal" data are the same as "qualitative," "attribute," "categorical," or "classification" data. For example,

TABLE 2.3
Levels of Measurement

Level of Measurement	Characteristics	Example
Nominal	Categories only	Eye color (blue, brown, green, hazel)
Ordinal	Rank has meaning	Bond ratings (Aaa, Baa1, C1, etc.)
Interval	Distance has meaning	Temperature (17° Celsius)
Ratio	Meaningful zero exists	Accounts payable ($21.7 million)

the following survey questions yield nominal data:

Did you file an insurance claim last month?

1. Yes   2. No

Which kind of laptop do you own?

| 1. Acer | 2. Apple | 3. Compaq | 4. Dell | 5. Gateway | 6. HP |
| 7. IBM | 8. Micron | 9. Sony | 10. Toshiba | 11. Other | 12. None |

We usually code nominal data numerically. However, the codes are arbitrary placeholders with no numerical meaning, so it is improper to perform mathematical analysis on them. For example, we would not calculate an average using the laptop data (1 through 12). This may seem obvious, yet people have been known to do it. Once the data are in the computer, it's easy to forget that the "numbers" are only categories. With nominal data, the only permissible mathematical operations are counting (e.g., frequencies) and a few simple statistics such as the mode.

Ordinal Measurement

Ordinal data codes connote a *ranking* of data values. For example:

What size automobile do you usually drive?

1. Full-size   2. Compact   3. Subcompact

How often do you use Microsoft Access?

1. Frequently   2. Sometimes   3. Rarely   4. Never

Thus, a 2 (Compact) implies a larger car than a 3 (Subcompact). Like nominal data, these ordinal numerical codes lack the properties that are required to compute many statistics, such as the average. Specifically, there is no clear meaning to the *distance* between 1 and 2, or between 2 and 3, or between 3 and 4 (what would be the distance between "Rarely" and "Never"?). Other examples of ordinal scales can be found in a recruiter's rating of job candidates (outstanding, good, adequate, weak, unsatisfactory), S&P credit ratings (AAA, AA+, AA, AA−, A+, A, A−, B+, B, B−, etc.) or job titles (president, group vice-president, plant manager, department head, clerk). Ordinal data can be treated as nominal, but not vice versa. Ordinal data are especially common in social sciences, marketing, and human resources research. There are many useful statistical tests for ordinal data.

Interval Measurement

The next step up the measurement scale is **interval data,** which not only is a rank but also has meaningful intervals between scale points. Examples are the Celsius or Fahrenheit scales of temperature. The interval between 60°F and 70°F is the same as the interval between 20°F and 30°F. Since intervals between numbers represent *distances,* we can do mathematical operations such as taking an average. But because the zero point of these scales is arbitrary, we can't say that 60°F is twice as warm as 30°F, or that 30°F is 50 percent warmer than 20°F. That is, ratios are not meaningful for interval data. The absence of a meaningful zero is a key characteristic of interval data.

Likert Scales   A special case of interval data is the **Likert scale,** which is frequently used in survey research. You have undoubtedly seen such scales. Typically, a statement is made and the respondent is asked to indicate his or her agreement/disagreement on a five-point or seven-point scale using verbal anchors. The *coarseness* of a Likert scale refers to the number of scale points (typically 5 or 7). For example:

"College-bound high school students should be required to study a foreign language." (check one)

❏	❏	❏	❏	❏
Strongly Agree	Somewhat Agree	Neither Agree Nor Disagree	Somewhat Disagree	Strongly Disagree

A neutral midpoint ("Neither Agree Nor Disagree") is allowed if we use an *odd* number of scale points (usually 5 or 7). Occasionally, surveys may omit the neutral midpoint to force the

TABLE 2.4	*Likert Coding: 1 to 5 scale*	*Likert Coding: −2 to +2 scale*
Examples of Likert-Scale Coding: "How will a change in inflation affect the investment climate?"	5 = Will help a lot 4 = Will help a little 3 = No effect on investment climate 2 = Will hurt a little 1 = Will hurt a lot	+2 = Will help a lot +1 = Will help a little 0 = No effect on investment climate −1 = Will hurt a little −2 = Will hurt a lot

respondent to "lean" one way or the other. Likert data are coded numerically (e.g., 1 to 5) but any equally spaced values will work, as shown in Table 2.4.

By choosing the verbal anchors carefully, researchers believe that the *intervals* are the same (e.g., the distance from 1 to 2 is "the same" as the *interval,* say, from 3 to 4). However, ratios are not meaningful (i.e., here 4 is not twice 2). The assumption that Likert scales produce interval data justifies a wide range of statistical calculations, including averages, correlations, and so on. Researchers use many Likert-scale variants.

"How would you rate your marketing instructor?" (check one)

❑ Terrible   ❑ Poor   ❑ Adequate   ❑ Good   ❑ Excellent

Respondents may prefer having verbal labels for each category but researchers who are uncomfortable with the labels can put verbal anchors only on the end points, where 1 = "very poor" and 5 = "very good."

"How would you rate your marketing instructor?" (check one)

Very Bad   ❑   ❑   ❑   ❑   ❑   Very Good

This avoids intermediate scale labels and permits any number of scale points, but lacks a concrete interpretation (what does a "3" mean?).

Ambiguity   Grades are usually coded numerically (A = 4, B = 3, C = 2, D = 1, F = 0) and are used to calculate a mean GPA. But is the *interval* from 3.0 to 4.0 really the same as the *interval* from 1.0 to 2.0? Is there an underlying reality ranging from 0 to 4 that we are measuring? Most people seem to think so, although the conservative procedure would be to limit ourselves to statistical tests that assume only ordinal data.

Ratio Measurement

Ratio measurement is the strongest level of measurement. *Ratio data* have all the properties of the other three data types, but in addition possess a *meaningful zero* that represents the absence of the quantity being measured. Because of the zero point, ratios of data values are meaningful (e.g., $20 million in profit is twice as much as $10 million). Balance sheet data, income statement data, financial ratios, physical counts, scientific measurements, and most engineering measurements are ratio data because zero has meaning (e.g., a company with zero sales sold nothing). Having a zero point does *not* restrict us to positive data. For example, profit is a ratio variable (e.g., $4 million is twice $2 million) yet firms can have negative profit.

Zero does *not* have to be observable in the data. Newborn babies, for example, cannot have zero weight, yet baby weight clearly is ratio data (i.e., an 8-pound baby is 33 percent heavier than a 6-pound baby). What matters is that the zero is an absolute reference point. The Kelvin temperature scale is a ratio measurement because its absolute zero represents the absence of molecular vibration, while zero on the Celsius scale is merely a convenience (note that 30° C is not "twice as much temperature" as 15° C).

Lack of a true zero is often the quickest test to defrock variables masquerading as ratio data. For example, a Likert scale (+2, +1, 0, −1, −2) is *not* ratio data despite the presence of zero because the zero (neutral) point does not connote the absence of anything. As an acid test, ask yourself whether 2 (strongly agree) is twice as much "agreement" as 1 (slightly agree). Some classifications are debatable. For example, college GPA has a zero, but does it represent the absence of learning? Does 4.00 represent "twice as much" learning as 2.00?

Question	If "Yes"	
Q1. Is there a meaningful zero point?	Ratio data (all statistical operations are allowed)	**TABLE 2.5** **Recognizing** **Measurement Level**
Q2. Are intervals between scale points meaningful?	Interval data (common statistics allowed, e.g., means and standard deviations)	
Q3. Do scale points represent rankings?	Ordinal data (restricted to certain types of nonparametric statistical tests)	
Q4. Are there discrete categories?	Nominal data (only counting allowed, e.g., finding the mode)	

Table 2.5 offers a procedure to recognize data types. Start out assuming ratio data, and ask questions in the order shown. Each time the answer is "no," slide to the next lower level of measurement. If Q1–Q3 are all "no," you have nominal data. Although beginning statistics textbooks usually emphasize interval or ratio data, there are textbooks that emphasize other kinds of data, notably in behavioral research (e.g., psychology, sociology, marketing, human resources).

Changing Data by Recoding

We can recode ratio measurements *downward* into ordinal or nominal measurements (but not conversely). For example, doctors may classify systolic blood pressure as "normal" (under 130), "elevated" (130 to 140), or "high" (140 or over). The recoded data are ordinal, since the ranking is preserved. Intervals may be unequal. For example, U.S. air traffic controllers classify planes as "small" (under 41,000 pounds), "large" (41,001 to 254,999 pounds), and "heavy" (255,000 pounds or more). Such recoding is done to simplify the data when the exact data magnitude is of little interest; however, it discards information by mapping stronger measurements into weaker ones.

SECTION EXERCISES

2.7   Which type of data (nominal, ordinal, interval, ratio) is each of the following variables? Explain.
a. Number of hits in Game 1 of the next World Series.
b. Baltimore's standing in the American League East (among seven teams).
c. Field position of a baseball player (catcher, pitcher, etc.).
d. Temperature on opening day (Celsius).
e. Salary of a randomly chosen American League pitcher.
f. Freeway traffic on opening day (light, medium, heavy).

2.8   Which type of data (nominal, ordinal, interval, ratio) is each of the following variables? Explain.
a. Number of employees in the Wal-Mart store in Hutchinson, Kansas.
b. Number of merchandise returns on a randomly chosen Monday at a Wal-Mart store.
c. Temperature (in Fahrenheit) in the ice-cream freezer at a Wal-Mart store.
d. Name of the cashier at register 3 in a Wal-Mart store.
e. Birth month of the cashier at register 3 in a Wal-Mart store.
f. Social security number of the cashier at register 3 in a Wal-Mart store.

2.9   Give an original example of each type of data (nominal, ordinal, interval, ratio) from your own life (e.g., your finances, sporting activities, education).

2.10   Which type of data (nominal, ordinal, interval, ratio) is the response to each question? If you think that the level of measurement is ambiguous, explain why.
a. How would you describe your level of skill in using Excel? (check one)
  ❏ Low   ❏ Medium   ❏ High
b. How often do you use Excel? (check one)
  ❏ Rarely   ❏ Often   ❏ Very Often
c. Which version of Excel do you use? (check one)
  ❏ 2000   ❏ XP   ❏ 2003   ❏ Other
d. I spend _____ hours a day using Excel.

2.3

TIME SERIES VERSUS CROSS-SECTIONAL DATA

Time Series Data

If each observation in the sample represents a different equally spaced point in time (years, months, days) we have *time series data.* The *periodicity* is the time between observations. It may be annual, quarterly, monthly, weekly, daily, hourly, etc. Examples of *macroeconomic* time series data would include national income (GDP, consumption, investment), economic indicators (Consumer Price Index, unemployment rate, Standard & Poor's 500 Index), and monetary data (M1, M2, M3, prime rate, T-bill rate, consumer borrowing, federal debt). Examples of *microeconomic* time series data would include a firm's sales, market share, debt/equity ratio, employee absenteeism, inventory turnover, and product quality ratings. For time series, we are interested in *trends and patterns over time* (e.g., annual growth in consumer debit card use from 1999 to 2006).

Cross-Sectional Data

If each observation represents a different individual unit (e.g., a person, firm, geographic area) at the same point in time, we have *cross-sectional data.* Thus, traffic fatalities in the 50 U.S. states for a given year, debt/equity ratios for the Fortune 500 firms in the last quarter of a certain year, last month's Visa balances for a bank's new mortgage applicants, or GPAs of students in a statistics class would be cross-sectional data. For cross-sectional data, we are interested in *variation among observations* (e.g., collection period for accounts receivable in 10 Subway franchises) or in *relationships* (e.g., whether collection period correlates with sales volume in 10 Subway franchises).

Some variables (such as unemployment rates) could be either time series (monthly data over each of 60 months) or cross-sectional (January's unemployment rate in 50 different largest cities). We can combine the two (e.g., monthly unemployment rates for the 13 Canadian provinces or territories for the last 60 months) to obtain *pooled cross-sectional and time series data*.

SECTION EXERCISES

2.11 Which type of data (cross-sectional or time series) is each variable?
a. Scores of 50 students on a midterm accounting exam last semester.
b. Bob's scores on 10 weekly accounting quizzes last semester.
c. Average score by all takers of the state's CPA exam for each of the last 10 years.
d. Number of years of accounting work experience for each of the 15 partners in a CPA firm.

2.12 Which type of data (cross-sectional or time series) is each variable?
a. Value of Standard & Poor's 500 stock price index at the close of each trading day last year.
b. Closing price of each of the 500 stocks in the S&P 500 index on the last trading day this week.
c. Dividends per share paid by General Motors common stock for the last 20 quarters.
d. Latest price/earnings ratios of 10 stocks in Bob's retirement portfolio.

2.13 Which type of data (cross-sectional or time series) is each variable?
a. Mexico's GDP for each of the last 10 quarters.
b. Unemployment rates in each of the 31 states in Mexico at the end of last year.
c. Unemployment rate in Mexico at the end of each of the last 10 years.
d. Average home value in each of the 10 largest Mexican cities today.

2.14 Give an original example of a time series variable and a cross-sectional variable. Use your own experience (e.g., your sports activities, finances, education).

Sample or Census?

A *sample* involves looking only at some items selected from the population but a *census* is an examination of all items in a defined population. The accuracy of a census can be illusory. For example, the U.S. decennial census cannot locate every individual in the United States (the 1990 census is thought to have missed 8 million people while the 2000 census is believed to have overcounted 1.3 million people). Reasons include the extreme mobility of the U.S. population and the fact that some people do not want to be found (e.g., illegal immigrants) or do not reply to the mailed census form. Further, budget constraints make it difficult to train enough census field workers, install data safeguards, and track down incomplete responses or nonresponses. For these reasons, U.S. censuses have long used sampling in certain situations. Many statistical experts advised using sampling more extensively in the 2000 decennial census, but the U.S. Congress decided that an actual headcount must be attempted.

When the quantity being measured is volatile, there cannot be a census. For example, The Arbitron Company tracks American radio listening habits using over 2.6 million "Radio Diary Packages." For each "listening occasion," participants note start and stop times for each station. Panelists also report their age, sex, and other demographic information. Table 2.6 outlines some situations where a sample rather than a census would be preferred, and vice versa.

Situations Where a Sample May Be Preferred:	Situations Where a Census May Be Preferred
Infinite Population No census is possible if the population is infinite or of indefinite size (an assembly line can keep producing bolts, a doctor can keep seeing more patients).	**Small Population** If the population is small, there is little reason to sample, for the effort of data collection may be only a small part of the total cost.
Destructive Testing The act of measurement may destroy or devalue the item (measuring battery life, testing auto crashworthiness).	**Large Sample Size** If the required sample size approaches the population size, we might as well go ahead and take a census.
Timely Results Sampling may yield more timely results than a census (checking wheat samples for moisture and protein content, checking peanut butter for aflatoxin contamination).	**Database Exists** If the data are on disk, we can examine 100% of the cases. But auditing or validating data against physical records may raise the cost.
Accuracy Instead of spreading limited resources thinly to attempt a census, our budget might be better spent to hire experienced staff, improve training of field interviewers, and improve data safeguards.	**Legal Requirements** Banks must count *all* the cash in bank teller drawers at the end of each business day. The U.S. Congress forbade sampling in the 2000 decennial population census.
Cost Even if it is feasible to take a census, the cost, either in time or money, may exceed our budget.	
Sensitive Information A trained interviewer might learn more about sexual harassment in a large organization through in-depth interviews of a small sample of employees rather than trying to interview all employees, and confidentiality may also be improved.	

TABLE 2.6
Sample or Census?

FIGURE 2.2

Population versus sample

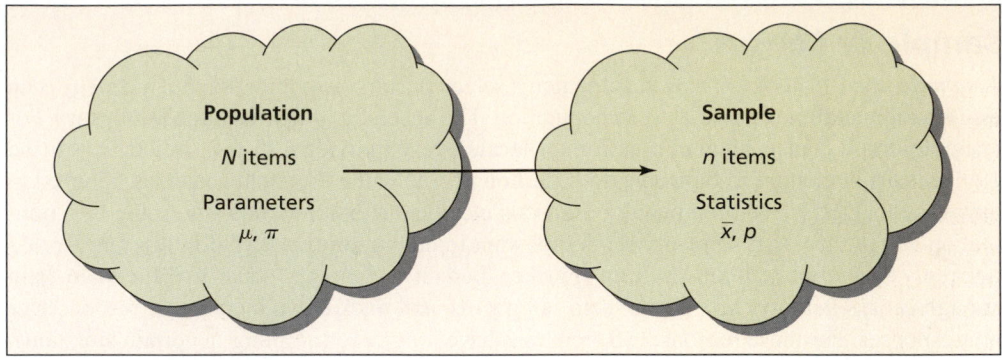

Parameters and Statistics

From a sample of n items, chosen from a population, we compute *statistics* that can be used as estimates of *parameters* found in the population. To avoid confusion, we use different symbols for each parameter and its corresponding statistic. Thus, the population mean is denoted μ (the Greek letter mu) while the sample mean is $\bar{x}$. The population proportion is denoted π (the Greek letter pi) while the sample proportion is p. Figure 2.2 illustrates this idea.

Parameter or Statistic?

A **parameter** is any measurement that describes an entire population. Usually, the parameter value is unknown since we rarely can observe the entire population. Parameters are often (but not always) represented by Greek letters.

A **statistic** is any measurement computed from a sample. Usually, the statistic is regarded as an estimate of a population parameter. Sample statistics are often (but not always) represented by Roman letters.

For example, suppose we want to know the mean (average) repair cost for auto air-conditioning warranty claims, or the proportion (percent) of 25-year-old concert-goers who have permanent hearing loss. Since a census is impossible, these parameters would be estimated using sampling. For the sample statistics to provide good estimates of the population parameters, the population must be carefully specified and the sample must be drawn scientifically so the sample items are representative of the population.

Target Population

The *target population* is the population in which we are interested. Suppose we wish to estimate the proportion of potential consumers who would purchase a $20 Harley-Davidson desk calendar. Is the target population all drivers? Only male drivers over age 16? Only drivers with incomes over $25,000? Only motorcycle owners? By answering questions such as these, we not only identify the target population but also are forced to define our business goals more clearly.

The *sampling frame* is the group from which we take the sample. If the frame differs from the target population, then our estimates will be of little use. Examples of frames are phone directories, voter registration lists, alumni association mailing lists, or marketing databases. Other examples might be:

- Names and addresses of all registered voters in Colorado Springs, Colorado.
- Names and addresses of all vehicle owners in Ventura County, California.
- E-mail addresses of all L. L. Bean customers who have placed online orders.

EXAMPLE

Gasoline Price Survey

The sample for the U.S. Energy Information Administration's survey of gasoline prices is drawn from a frame of approximately 115,000 retail gasoline outlets, constructed from purchased private commercial sources and EIA sources, combined with zip codes from private lists. Individual frames are mapped to the county level by using zip codes, and outlets are assigned to standard metropolitan statistical areas from Census Bureau definitions. (For details, see www.eia.doe.gov.)

Finite or Infinite?

A population is *finite* if it has a definite size, *N*, even if its size is unknown. For example, the number of cars in a McDonald's parking lot or the number of MBA students enrolled at the University of Kansas will be finite. A population is treated as *infinite* if it is of arbitrarily large size. For instance, assembly lines can produce indefinitely large numbers of M&Ms, aspirin tablets, or loaves of bread. Thus, quality process control samples of *n* items usually come from *effectively infinite* populations. But if a sample comes from a particular batch and we wish to make inferences about that specific batch, we could regard the batch as a finite population. When a population is known to be very large relative to the sample, a statistician may treat the population as infinite.

Rule of Thumb

A population may be treated as infinite when *N* is at least 20 times *n* (i.e., when $N/n > 20$).

SECTION EXERCISES

2.15 Would you use a sample or a census to measure each of the following? Why? If you are uncertain, explain the issues.
a. The model years of the cars driven by each of your five closest friends.
b. The model years of the cars driven by each student in your statistics class.
c. The model years of the cars driven by each student in your university.
d. The model years of the cars driven by each professor whose classes you are taking.

2.16 Is each of the following a parameter or a statistic? If you are uncertain, explain the issues.
a. The average price/earnings ratio for all 500 stocks in the S&P index.
b. The proportion of all stocks in the S&P 500 index that had negative earnings last year.
c. The proportion of energy-related stocks in portfolios owned by 50 investors.
d. The average rate of return for stock portfolios recommended by 50 brokers.

2.17 Would you use a sample or a census to measure each of the following? Why? If you are uncertain, explain the issues.
a. The mean time battery life of your laptop computer in continuous use.
b. The number of students in your statistics class who brought laptop computers to class today.
c. The average price paid for a laptop computer by students at your university.
d. The percentage of disk space available on laptop computers owned by your five closest friends.

2.18 The target population is all students in your university. You wish to estimate the average current Visa balance for each student. How large would the university student population have to be in order to be regarded as effectively infinite in each of the following samples?
a. A sample of 10 students.
b. A sample of 50 students.
c. A sample of 100 students.

2.5 SAMPLING METHODS

There are two main categories of sampling methods. In ***probability sampling,*** items are chosen by randomization or a chance procedure. ***Nonprobability sampling*** is less scientific but is sometimes used for expediency. Six common sampling methods are shown in Table 2.7.

Simple Random Sample

We denote the population size by *N* and the sample size by *n*. In a ***simple random sample,*** every item in the population of *N* items has the same chance of being chosen in the sample of *n* items. A physical experiment to accomplish this would be to write each of the *N* data values on a poker chip, and then to draw *n* chips from a bowl after stirring it thoroughly. But we can accomplish the same thing if the *N* population items appear on a numbered list, simply by choosing *n* integers at random between 1 and *N*. But we must take care not to allow any bias to creep into the selection process.

TABLE 2.7   **Six Sampling Methods**

Probability Samples		Nonprobability Samples	
Simple Random Sample	Use random numbers to select items from a list (e.g., Visa cardholders).	Judgment Sample	Use expert knowledge to choose "typical" items (e.g., which employees to interview).
Systematic Sample	Select every *k*th item from a list or sequence (e.g., restaurant customers).	Convenience Sample	Use a sample that happens to be available (e.g., ask co-worker opinions at lunch).
Stratified Sample	Select randomly within defined strata (e.g., by age, occupation, gender).		
Cluster Sample	Like stratified sampling except strata are geographical areas (e.g., zip codes).		

For example, suppose we want to select one student at random from a list of 48 students (see Figure 2.3). If you were asked to "use your judgment," you would probably pick a name in the middle, thereby biasing the draw against those individuals at either end of the list. Instead, we rely on *random numbers*. In this example, we used Excel's function =RANDBETWEEN(1,48) to pick a random integer between 1 and 48. The number was 44, so Stephanie was selected. There is no bias since all values from 1 to 48 are *equiprobable* (i.e., equally likely to occur).

FIGURE 2.3

Picking on Stephanie

Random person **44**

1	Adam	17	Haitham	33	Moira
2	Addie	18	Jackie	34	Nathan
3	Anne	19	Jennie	35	Oded
4	Aristo	20	Joel	36	Pablo
5	Balaji	21	Judy	37	Pat
6	Dean	22	Kay	38	Peter
7	Dennis	23	Kristina	39	Randy
8	Diana	24	LaDonna	40	Rick
9	Don	25	Latrice	41	Sarah
10	Ellen	26	Laura	42	Shamel
11	Erik	27	Leah	43	Sid
12	Floyd	28	Lindsay	**44**	**Stephanie**
13	Frances	29	Loretta	45	Stephen
14	Gadis	30	Lou	46	Sylvia
15	Ginnie	31	Majda	47	Tara
16	Giovanni	32	Mario	48	Tim

82134	14458	66716	54269	31928	46241	03052	00260	32367	25783
07139	16829	76768	11913	42434	91961	92934	18229	15595	02566
45056	*439*39	31188	43272	11332	99494	19348	97076	95605	28010
10244	19093	*516*78	63463	85568	70034	82811	23261	48794	63984
12940	84434	50087	*201*89	58009	66972	05764	10421	36875	64964
84438	45828	40353	28925	*119*11	53502	24640	96880	93166	68409
98681	67871	71735	64113	90139	*334*66	65312	90655	75444	30845
43290	96753	18799	49713	39227	15955	*461*67	63853	03633	19990
96893	85410	88233	22094	30605	79024	01791	*388*39	85531	94576
75403	41227	00192	16814	47054	16814	81349	92264	*010*28	29071
78064	92111	51541	76563	69027	67718	06499	71938	17354	*126*80
*262*46	71746	94019	93165	96713	03316	75912	86209	12081	57817
98766	67312	96358	21351	86448	31828	86113	78868	67243	06763
37895	51055	11929	44443	15995	72935	99631	18190	85877	31309
27988	81163	52212	25102	61798	28670	01358	60354	74015	18556
19216	53008	44498	19262	12196	93947	90162	76337	12646	26838
28078	86729	69438	24235	35208	48957	53529	76297	41741	54735
34455	61363	93711	68038	75960	16327	95716	66964	28634	65015
53510	90412	70438	45932	57815	75144	52472	61817	41562	42084
30658	18894	88208	97867	30737	94985	18235	02178	39728	66398

TABLE 2.8
1,000 Random Digits
🔹 **RandomDigits**

Random Number Tables

Another method (somewhat obsolete) to select random numbers between 1 and *N* is a table of random digits. A table of random digits has the property that, no matter how we pick our digits (up, down, diagonally, etc.) each digit 0 through 9 is equally likely. Table 2.8 shows 1,000 random digits arranged in 10 columns and 20 rows of five-digit blocks.

Setting Up a Rule

NilCo wants to award cash "customer loyalty" prizes to 10 of its customers from a list of 875 who made purchases last month. To get 10 three-digit random numbers between 001 and 875, we define *any consistent rule* for moving through the table. For example, we can point a finger at random to choose a starting point. In Table 2.8, we started in the second column in the third row. Our rule is to choose the first three digits of this five-digit block, move to the right one column, down one row, and repeat. When we reach the end of a line, we wrap around to the other side of the table and continue. We discard any number greater than 875 and move on. If we get a duplicate, we move on. The chosen 10 three-digit random numbers are highlighted in the table:

439, 516, 201, 119, 334, 461, 388, 010, 126, 262

By chance, no number greater than 516 was selected. Without random numbers, you might have an unconscious tendency to try to "cover" the range from 1 to 875 "evenly," but that would *not* be random.

With or Without Replacement?

The same number could have occurred more than once (it didn't happen in the NilCo illustration). If we allow duplicates, we are **sampling with replacement.** Using the bowl analogy, if we throw each chip back in the bowl and stir the contents before the next draw, an item can be chosen again. Duplicates are unlikely when the sample size *n* is much smaller than the population size *N*. People instinctively prefer **sampling without replacement** because drawing the same item more than once seems to add nothing to our knowledge. However, using the same sample item more than once does not introduce any *bias* (i.e., no systematic tendency to over- or underestimate whatever parameter we are trying to measure).

TABLE 2.9

Some Ways to Get 10 Random Integers Between 1 and 875

Excel—Option A	Enter the Excel function =RANDBETWEEN(1,875) into 10 spreadsheet cells. Press **F9** to get a new sample.
Excel—Option B	Enter the function =INT(1+875*RAND()) into 10 spreadsheet cells. Press **F9** to get a new sample.
Internet	The Web site www.random.org will give you many kinds of excellent random numbers (integers, decimals, etc).
MINITAB	Use MINITAB's Random Data menu with the Integer option, as shown in Figure 2.4.

FIGURE 2.4

MINITAB random integer generation

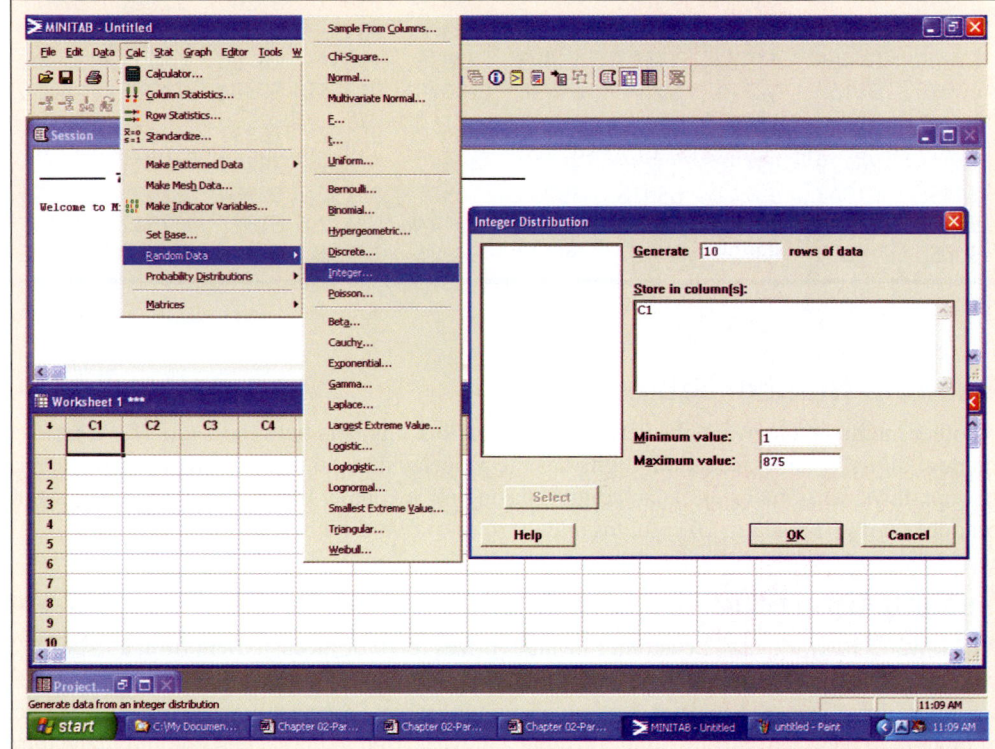

Computer Methods

Because computers are easier, we rarely use random number tables. Table 2.9 shows a few alternative ways to choose 10 integers between 1 and 875. All are based on a software algorithm that creates uniform decimal numbers between 0 and 1. Excel's function =RAND( ) does this, and many pocket calculators have a similar function. We call these *pseudo-random* generators because even the best algorithms eventually repeat themselves (after a cycle of millions of numbers). Thus, a software-based random data encryption scheme could conceivably be broken. To enhance data security, Intel and other firms are examining hardware-based methods (e.g., based on thermal noise or radioactive decay) to prevent patterns or repetition. Fortunately, most applications don't require that degree of randomness, so Excel's and MINITAB's random numbers are good enough for most purposes.

Row/Column Data Arrays

When the data are arranged in a rectangular array, we can choose an item at random by picking a row and column at random. For example, here is a 4 × 3 array containing the names of the 12 largest general merchandise companies in the United States. We select a random column between 1 and 3 and a random row between 1 and 4, so that every company has the same chance of being chosen. In this case, we used Excel's =RANDBETWEEN function to choose row 3 and column 3 (Target).

Dillard's	Kmart	Saks
Dollar General	Kohl's	Sears Roebuck
Federated Dept. Stores	May Dept. Stores	Target
J. C. Penney	Nordstrom	Wal-Mart Stores

Randomizing a List

To randomize a list (assuming it is in a spreadsheet) we can insert the Excel function =RAND( ) beside each row. This creates a column of random decimal numbers between 0 and 1. Copy the random numbers and paste them in the same column using Paste Special > Values to "fix" them (otherwise they will keep changing). Then sort all the columns by the random number column, and *voilà*—the list is now random! Figure 2.5 uses this method to randomize an alphabetized list of 12 students. The first n items on the randomized list can be used as a random sample.

This method is especially useful when the list is very long (perhaps millions of lines). The first n items are a random sample of the entire list, for they are as likely as any others. This method was used to create several of the *LearningStats* data sets (e.g., Cross-Sectional Data—Health ClaimsSample100.xls).

Systematic Sample

Another method of random sampling is to choose every kth item from the list, starting from a randomly chosen entry among the first k items on the list. This is called **systematic sampling.** Figure 2.6 shows how to sample every fourth item, starting from item 2, resulting in a sample of $n = 20$ items from a list of $N = 78$ items.

A systematic sample of n items from a population of N items requires that periodicity k be approximately N/n. For example, to choose 25 companies from a list of 501 companies in

FIGURE 2.5

Randomizing a list
RandomNames

Names in Alphabetical Order				Names in Random Order			
Rand	*Name*	*Major*	*Gender*	*Rand*	*Name*	*Major*	*Gender*
0.382091	Claudia	Accounting	F	0.143539	Dave	Human Res	M
0.730061	Dan	Economics	M	0.229854	Marcia	Accounting	F
0.143539	Dave	Human Res	M	0.334449	Ryan	MIS	M
0.906060	Kalisha	MIS	F	0.382091	Claudia	Accounting	F
0.624378	LaDonna	Finance	F	0.402726	Victor	Marketing	M
0.229854	Marcia	Accounting	F	0.431740	Rachel	Oper Mgt	F
0.604377	Matt	Undecided	M	0.604377	Matt	Undecided	M
0.798923	Moira	Accounting	F	0.624378	LaDonna	Finance	F
0.431740	Rachel	Oper Mgt	F	0.730061	Dan	Economics	M
0.334449	Ryan	MIS	M	0.798923	Moira	Accounting	F
0.836594	Tammy	Marketing	F	0.836594	Tammy	Marketing	F
0.402726	Victor	Marketing	M	0.906060	Kalisha	MIS	F

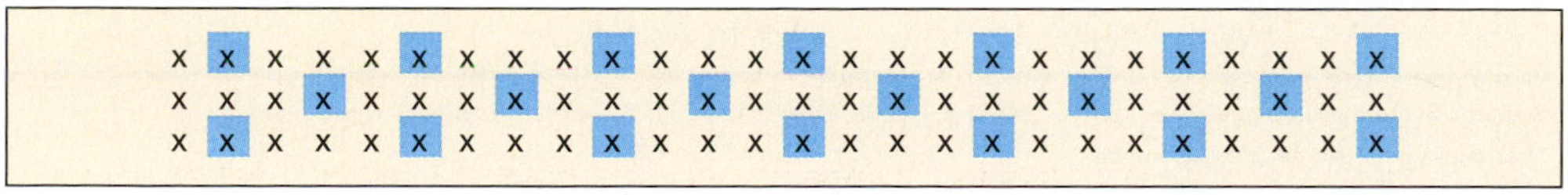

FIGURE 2.6

Systematic sampling

Mini Case 2.1 (Table 2.10), we chose every twentieth stock ($k = 501/25 \approx 20$). Systematic sampling should yield acceptable results unless patterns in the population happen to recur at periodicity k. For example, weekly pay cycles ($k = 7$) would make it illogical to sample bank check cashing volume every Friday. A less obvious example would be a machine that stamps a defective part every twelfth cycle due to a bad tooth in a 12-tooth gear, which would make it misleading to rely on a sample of every twelfth part ($k = 12$). But periodicity coincident with k is not typical or expected in most situations.

An attraction of systematic sampling is that it can be used with unlistable or infinite populations, such as production processes (e.g., testing every 5,000th light bulb) or political polling (e.g., surveying every tenth voter who emerges from the polling place). Systematic sampling is also well-suited to linearly organized physical populations (e.g., pulling every tenth patient folder from alphabetized filing drawers in a veterinary clinic).

Mini Case   2.1

CEO Compensation

To sample the compensation of the CEOs of the 501 largest companies in the United States listed in *Forbes'* annual survey, take every twentieth company in the alphabetized list, starting (randomly) with the thirteenth company. The starting point (the thirteenth company) is chosen at random. This yields the sample of 25 CEOs, shown in Table 2.10. While it would be very time-consuming to examine all 501 executives, this sample should provide a representative cross-section.

TABLE 2.10   CEO Compensation in 25 Large U.S. Firms*   🦅   **CEOComp**

Observation	Firm	CEO	One-Year Total ($000)
1	Allegheny Energy	Alan J. Noia	$ 1,530
2	Analog Devices	Jerald G. Fishman	16,550
3	AutoNation	Michael J. Jackson	1,898
4	BJ Services	J. W. Stewart	23,354
5	Cendant	Henry R. Silverman	40,472
6	Coca-Cola Enterprises	Lowry F. Kline	8,725
7	Costco Wholesale	James D. Sinegal	6,078
8	DST Systems	Thomas A. McDonnell	29,644
9	EOG Resources	Mark G. Papa	785
10	Fleming Cos.	Mark S. Hansen	4,476
11	Gillette	James M. Kilts	2,840
12	Hibernia	J. Herbert Boydstun	1,231
13	ITT Industries	Louis J. Giuliano	3,022
14	Laboratory Corp. Amer.	Thomas P. Mac Mahon	10,385
15	Marshall & Ilsley	Dennis J. Kuester	6,510
16	Micron Technology	Steven R. Appleton	949
17	Noble Drilling	James C. Day	5,066
18	Park Place Entertain.	Thomas E. Gallagher	975
19	Principal Financial	J. Barry Griswell	2,321
20	RJ Reynolds Tobacco	Andrew J. Schindler	5,552
21	Smurfit-Stone	Patrick J. Moore	1,549
22	Synovus Financial	James H. Blanchard	1,800
23	Union Pacific	Richard K. Davidson	1,681
24	Visteon	Peter J. Pestillo	1,366
25	Wm. Wrigley, Jr.	William Wrigley, Jr.	1,697

Source: CEO Compensation, *Forbes,* May 13, 2002, pp. 116–38. Copyright © 2005 Forbes Inc. Reprinted by permission.

*Compensation is for the latest fiscal year.

Stratified Sample

Sometimes we can improve our sample efficiency by utilizing prior information about the population. This method is applicable when the population can be divided into relatively homogeneous subgroups of known size (called *strata*). Within each *stratum,* a simple random sample of the desired size could be taken. Alternatively, a random sample of the whole population could be taken, and then individual strata estimates could be combined using appropriate weights. This procedure, called **stratified sampling,** can reduce cost per observation and narrow the error bounds. For a population with L strata, the population size N is the sum of the stratum sizes:

$$N = N_1 + N_2 + \cdots + N_L.$$

The weight assigned to stratum j is $w_j = N_j/N$ (i.e., each stratum is weighted by its known proportion of the population).

To illustrate, suppose we want to estimate smallpox vaccination rates among employees in state government, and we know that our target population (those individuals we are trying to study) is 55 percent male and 45 percent female. Suppose our budget only allows a sample of size 200. To ensure the correct gender balance, we could sample 110 males and 90 females. Alternatively, we could just take a random sample of 200 employees. Although our random sample probably will not contain *exactly* 110 males and 90 females, we can get an overall estimate of vaccination rates by *weighting* the male and female sample vaccination rates using $w_M = 0.55$ and $w_F = 0.45$ to reflect the known strata sizes.

Applications of Stratified Sampling

The Consumer Price Index is a stratified sample of 90,000 items from 364 categories, chosen from about 20,000 retail stores in 85 geographically distributed areas (strata) that are chosen to be as homogeneous as possible. Similarly, to estimate the unemployment rate each month, the Bureau of Labor Statistics conducts a survey of 50,000 households in about 2,000 counties and cities in all 50 states. Data are *stratified* using known weights for factors such as occupation, race, and gender. To ensure continuity yet to allow the panel to rotate, a household is kept in the panel for 4 consecutive months, is out of the survey for 8 months, is included for 4 more months, and finally is replaced by a new household.

Cluster Sample

Cluster samples are essentially strata consisting of geographical regions. We divide a region (say, a city) into subregions (say, blocks, subdivisions, or school districts). In one-stage cluster sampling, our sample consists of all elements in each of k randomly chosen subregions (or clusters). In two-stage cluster sampling, we first randomly select k subregions (clusters) and then choose a random sample of elements within each cluster. Figure 2.7 illustrates how four elements could be sampled from each of three randomly chosen clusters using two-stage cluster sampling.

Because elements within a cluster are proximate, travel time and interviewer expenses are kept to a minimum. Cluster sampling is useful when:

- Population frame and stratum characteristics are not readily available.
- It is too expensive to obtain a simple or stratified sample.
- The cost of obtaining data increases sharply with distance.
- Some loss of reliability is acceptable.

Although cluster sampling is cheap and quick, it is often reasonably accurate because people in the same neighborhood tend to be similar in income, ethnicity, educational background, and so on. Cluster sampling is useful in political polling, surveys of gasoline pump prices, studies of crime victimization, vaccination surveys, or lead contamination in soil. A hospital may contain clusters (floors) of similar patients. A warehouse may have clusters (pallets) of

FIGURE 2.7

Two-stage cluster sampling

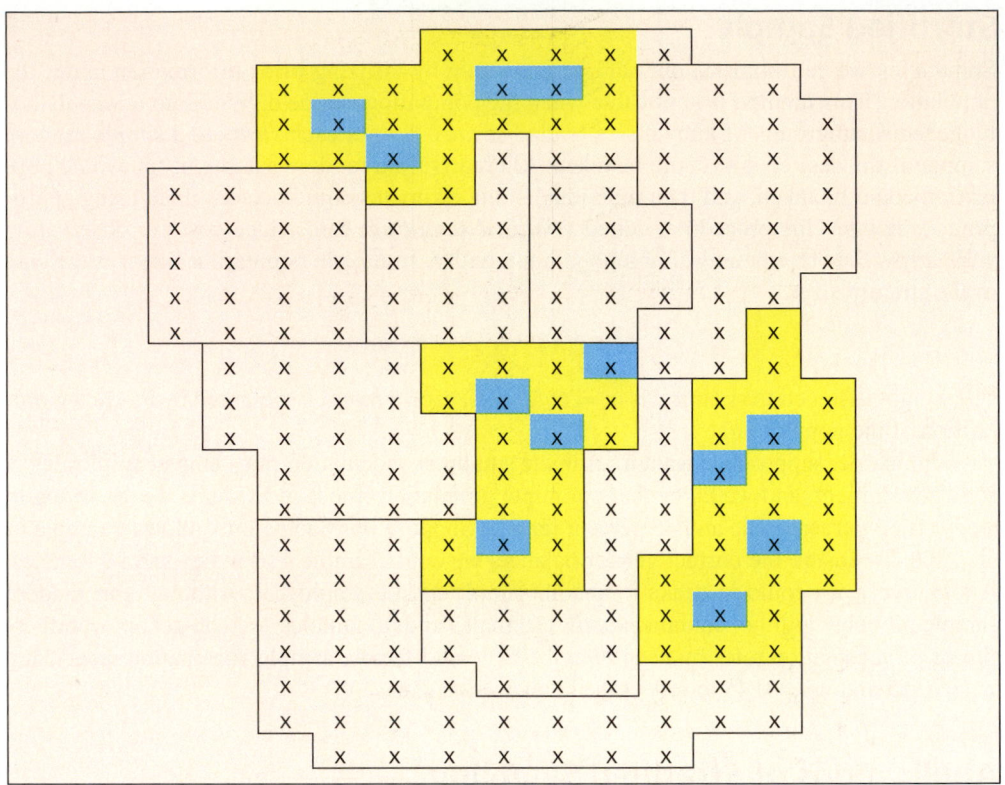

inventory parts. Forest sections may be viewed as clusters to be sampled for disease or timber growth rates.

Judgment Sample

Judgment sampling is a nonprobability sampling method that relies on the expertise of the sampler to choose items that are representative of the population. For example, to estimate the corporate spending on research and development (R&D) in the medical equipment industry, we might ask an industry expert to select several "typical" firms. Unfortunately, subconscious biases can affect experts, too. In this context, "bias" does not mean prejudice, but rather *nonrandomness* in the choice. Judgment samples may be the best alternative in some cases, but we can't be sure whether the sample was random. *Quota sampling* is a special kind of judgment sampling, in which the interviewer chooses a certain number of people in each category (e.g., men/women).

Convenience Sample

The sole virtue of *convenience sampling* is that it is quick. The idea is to grab whatever sample is handy. An accounting professor who wants to know how many MBA students would take a summer elective in international accounting can just survey the class she is currently teaching. The students polled may not be representative of all MBA students, but an answer (although imperfect) will be available immediately. A newspaper reporter doing a story on perceived airport security might interview co-workers who travel frequently. An executive might ask department heads if they think nonbusiness Web surfing is widespread.

You might think that convenience sampling is rarely used or, when it is, that the results are used with caution. However, this does not appear to be the case. Since convenience samples often sound the first alarm on a timely issue, their results have a way of attracting attention and have probably influenced quite a few business decisions. The mathematical properties of convenience samples are unknowable, but they do serve a purpose and their influence cannot be ignored.

Mini Case   2.2

Scanner Accuracy

Kmart was the first retailer fined in 1997 under Wisconsin's scanner accuracy law because the wrong prices were charged at some stores. A scanner reads a bar code, and then rings up the prices on the cash register. Nine of the 32 Kmart scanners failed random sampling tests. Samples of 50 items per store were taken, and failure was defined as 3 or more scanned at the wrong price. Although the number of overcharges and undercharges were nearly equal, the average overcharge ($2.85) exceeded the average undercharge ($1.00).

In Michigan, the Attorney General's office performs random scanner accuracy tests in 25 stores that represent six national chains. Over time, scanner accuracy has improved, as the error rate declined from 15.2 percent in 1998 to only 3.2 percent in 2001. Scanner errors ranged from zero percent in Target and Mervyn's to 1.8 percent in Sears, 3 percent in Kmart, 5.3 percent in Marshall Field's, and 6 percent in J. C. Penney. When a census is impossible, sampling is an essential tool in enforcing consumer protection laws.

Source: *Detroit Free Press,* October 23, 1997, p. 1E, and November 30, 2001, p. 1C.

Sample Size

The necessary sample size depends on the inherent variability of the quantity being measured and the desired precision of the estimate. For example, the caffeine content of Mountain Dew is fairly consistent because each can or bottle is filled at the factory, so a small sample size would suffice to estimate the mean. In contrast, the amount of caffeine in an individually brewed cup of Bigelow Raspberry Royale tea varies widely because people let it steep for varying lengths of time, so a larger sample would be needed to estimate the mean. The purposes of the investigation, the costs of sampling, the budget, and time constraints are also taken into account in deciding on sample size. Setting the sample size is worth a detailed discussion, found in later chapters.

SECTION EXERCISES

2.19 Suppose you want to know the ages of moviegoers who attend *Spiderman III*. What kind of sample is it if you (a) survey the first 20 persons to emerge from the theater, (b) survey every tenth person to emerge from the theater, and (c) survey everyone who is wearing an earring?

2.20 (a) Referring to the previous question, would a simple random sample be possible? Explain. (b) Identify possible flaws and/or strengths in each of the sampling methods suggested in the previous problem. (c) Why might a survey not work at all?

2.21 Below is a 6 × 8 array containing the ages of moviegoers (see file 🎬 **HarryPotter**). Treat this as a population. Select a random sample of 8 moviegoers' ages by using (a) simple random sampling with a random number table, (b) simple random sampling with Excel's =RANDBETWEEN() function, (c) systematic sampling, (d) judgment sampling, and (e) convenience sampling. Explain your methods.

32	34	33	12	57	13	58	16
23	23	62	65	35	15	17	20
14	11	51	33	31	13	11	58
23	10	63	34	12	15	62	13
40	11	18	62	64	30	42	20
21	56	11	51	38	49	15	21

2.22 (a) In the previous problem, what was the proportion of all 48 moviegoers who were under age 30? (b) For each of the samples of size $n = 8$ that you took, what was the proportion of moviegoers under age 30? (c) If your samples did not resemble the population, can you suggest why?

2.23 In Excel, type a list containing names for 10 of your friends into cells B1:B10. Choose three names at random by randomizing this list. To do this, enter =RAND( ) into cells A1:A10, copy the random column and paste it using Paste > Special > Values to fix the random numbers, and then sort the list by the random column. The first three names are the random sample.

2.6 DATA SOURCES

One goal of a statistics course is to help you learn where to find data that might be needed. Fortunately, many excellent sources are widely available, either in libraries or through private purchase. Table 2.11 summarizes a few of them.

The *Statistical Abstract of the United States* is the largest, most general, and widely available annual compendium of facts and figures from public sources. You can purchase it at government bookstores in major cities, order it by mail, or use it for free on the Web. It covers a wide range of cross-sectional data (e.g., states, cities) as well as time series data. Subjects include population, vital statistics, immigration, health, nutrition, education, law enforcement, geography, environment, parks, recreation, elections, government, national defense, social insurance, human services, labor force, income, prices, banking, finance, insurance, communications, energy, science, transportation, agriculture, forests, fisheries, mining, construction, housing, manufactures, and international statistics. No business statistician should be without this reference.

For annual and monthly time series economic data, try the *Economic Report of the President* (*ERP*), which is published every February. The tables in the *ERP* can be downloaded for free in Excel format. Data on cities, counties, and states can be found in the *State and Metropolitan Area Data Book,* published every few years by the Bureau of the Census and available on CD-ROM in many libraries.

Annual almanacs from several major publishers are sold at most bookstores. These include data reprinted from the above sources, but also information on recent events, sports, stock market, elections, Congress, world nations, states, and higher education. One of these almanacs should be on every informed citizen's shelf.

Annual surveys of major companies, markets, and topics of business or personal finance are found in magazines such as *BusinessWeek, Consumer Reports, Forbes, Fortune,* and *Money.* Indexes such as the *Business Periodical Index, The New York Times Index,* and *The Wall Street Journal Index* are useful for locating topics. Libraries have Web search engines that can access many of these periodicals in abstract or full-text form.

Specialized computer databases (e.g., CRSP, Compustat, Citibase, U.S. Census) are available (at a price) for research on stocks, companies, financial statistics, and census data. An excellent summary of sources is F. Patrick Butler's *Business Research Sources: A Reference Navigator*. The Web allows us to use search engines (e.g., Google, Yahoo!, MSN) to find information. Sometimes you may get lucky, but Web information is often undocumented, unreliable, or unverifiable. Better information is available through private companies or trade associations, though often at a steep price. Related Reading and Web Data Sources are listed at the end of this chapter.

Often overlooked sources of help are your university librarians. University librarians understand how to find databases and how to navigate databases quickly and accurately. Librarians can help you distinguish between valid and invalid Internet sources and then help you put the source citation in the proper format when writing reports.

TABLE 2.11
Useful Data Sources

Type of Data	Examples
U.S. general data	*Statistical Abstract of the United States*
U.S. economic data	*Economic Report of the President*
Almanacs	*World Almanac, Time Almanac*
Periodicals	*Economist, BusinessWeek, Fortune*
Indexes	*The New York Times, The Wall Street Journal*
Databases	*Compustat, Citibase, U.S. Census*
World data	*CIA World Factbook*
Web	*Google, Yahoo!, MSN*

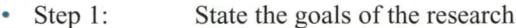

Most survey research follows the same basic steps. These steps may overlap in time:

- Step 1: State the goals of the research.
- Step 2: Develop the budget (time, money, staff).
- Step 3: Create a research design (target population, frame, sample size).
- Step 4: Choose a survey type and method of administration.
- Step 5: Design a data collection instrument (questionnaire).
- Step 6: Pretest the survey instrument and revise as needed.
- Step 7: Administer the survey (follow up if needed).
- Step 8: Code the data and analyze it.

Survey Types

Surveys fall into five general categories: mail, telephone, interview, Web, and direct observation. They differ in cost, response rate, data quality, time required, and survey staff training requirements. Table 2.12 lists some common types of surveys and a few of their salient strengths/weaknesses.

Response Rates

Consider the *cost per valid response*. A telephone survey might be cheapest to conduct, but bear in mind that over half the households in some metropolitan areas have unlisted phones,

Type of Survey	Characteristics
Mail	You need a well-targeted and current mailing list (people move a lot). Low response rates are typical and nonresponse bias is expected (nonrespondents differ from those who respond). Zip code lists (often costly) are an attractive option to define strata of similar income, education, and attitudes. To encourage participation, a cover letter should clearly explain the uses to which the data will be put. Plan for follow-up mailings.
Telephone	Random dialing yields very low response and is poorly targeted. Purchased phone lists help reach the target population, though a low response rate still is typical (disconnected phones, caller screening, answering machines, work hours, no-call lists). Other sources of nonresponse bias include the growing number of non-English speakers and distrust caused by scams and spams.
Interviews	Interviewing is expensive and time-consuming, yet a trade-off between sample size for high-quality results may still be worth it. Interviews must be carefully handled so interviewers must be well-trained—an added cost. But interviewers can obtain information on complex or sensitive topics (e.g., gender discrimination in companies, birth control practices, diet and exercise habits).
Web	Web surveys are growing in popularity but are subject to nonresponse bias because those who participate may differ from those who feel too busy, don't own computers, or distrust your motives (scams and spam are again to blame). This type of survey works best when targeted to a well-defined interest group on a question of self-interest (e.g., views of CPAs on new Sarbanes-Oxley accounting rules, frequent flyer views on airline security).
Direct Observation	This can be done in a controlled setting (e.g., psychology lab) but requires informed consent, which can change behavior. Unobtrusive observation is possible in some nonlab settings (e.g., what percentage of airline passengers carry on more than two bags, what percentage of SUVs carry no passengers, what percentage of drivers wear seat belts).

TABLE 2.12
Common Types of Surveys

TABLE 2.13
Survey Guidelines

Planning	What is the purpose of the survey? What do you really need to know? What staff expertise is available? What skills are best obtained externally? What degree of precision is required? How is your budget best spent?
Design	To ensure a good response and useful data, you must invest time and money in designing the survey. Take advantage of many useful books and references so that you do not make unnecessary errors.
Quality	Care in preparation is needed. Glossy printing and advertising have raised people's expectations about quality. A scruffy questionnaire will be ignored. Some surveys (e.g., Web-based) may require special software.
Pilot Test	Questions that are clear to you may be unclear to others. You can pretest the questionnaire on friends or co-workers, but using a small test panel of naive respondents who don't owe you anything is best.
Buy-In	Response rates may be improved by clearly stating the purpose of the survey, offering a token of appreciation (e.g., discount coupon, free gift) or paving the way with endorsements (e.g., from a trusted professional group).
Expertise	Consider working with an outside (or internal) consultant at the early stages, even if you plan to carry out the data collection and tabulation on your own. Early consultation is more cost-effective than waiting until you get in trouble.

and many have answering machines or call screening. The sample you get may not be very useful in terms of reaching the target population. Telephone surveys (even with random dialing) do lend themselves nicely to cluster sampling (e.g., using each three-digit area code as a cluster and each three-digit exchange as a cluster) to sample somewhat homogeneous populations. Similarly, mail surveys can be clustered by zip code, which is a significant attraction. Web surveys are cheap, but rather uncontrolled. Nonresponse bias is a problem with all of these. Interviews or observational experiments are expensive and labor-intensive, but they may provide higher quality data. Table 2.13 offers some tips to conduct successful surveys.

Getting Advice

You should consider hiring a consultant, at least in the early stages, to help you get your survey off the ground successfully. Alternatively, resources are available on the Web to help you plan a survey. The American Statistical Association (www.amstat.org) offers brochures *What Is a Survey* and *How to Plan a Survey*. Additional materials are available from the Research Industry Coalition, Inc., (www.researchindustry.org) and the Council of American Survey Research Organizations (www.casro.org). Entire books have been written to help you design and administer your own survey (see Related Reading).

Questionnaire Design

The layout must not be crowded (use lots of white space). Begin with very short, clear instructions, stating the purpose, assuring anonymity, and explaining how to submit the completed survey. Questions should be numbered. Divide the survey into sections if the topics fall naturally into distinct areas. Let respondents bypass sections that aren't relevant to them (e.g., "If you answered no to Question 7, skip directly to Question 15"). Include an "escape option" where it seems appropriate (e.g., "Don't know or Does not apply"). Use wording and response scales that match the reading ability and knowledge level of the intended respondents. Pretest and revise. Keep the questionnaire as short as possible. Table 2.14 lists a few common question formats and response scales.

Question Wording

The way a question is asked has a profound influence on the response. For example, in a *Wall Street Journal* editorial, Fred Barnes tells of a *Reader's Digest* poll that asked two similar questions:

> Version 1: I would be disappointed if Congress cut its funding for public television.
>
> Version 2: Cuts in funding for public television are justified to reduce federal spending.

Type of Question	*Example*
Open-ended	Briefly describe your job goals.
Fill-in-the-blank	How many times did you attend formal religious services during the last year? _____ times
Check boxes	Which of these statistics packages have you used? ❑ SAS ❑ Visual Statistics ❑ SPSS ❑ MegaStat ❑ Systat ❑ MINITAB
Ranked choices	Please evaluate your dining experience:
Pictograms	What do you think of the president's economic policies? (circle one) ☺ ☺ ☺ ☹ ☹
Likert scale	Statistics is a difficult subject.

TABLE 2.14
Question Format and Response Scale

Ranked choices — Please evaluate your dining experience:

	Excellent	Good	Fair	Poor
Food	❑	❑	❑	❑
Service	❑	❑	❑	❑
Ambiance	❑	❑	❑	❑
Cleanliness	❑	❑	❑	❑
Overall	❑	❑	❑	❑

Likert scale — Statistics is a difficult subject.

Strongly Agree	Slightly Agree	Neither Agree Nor Disagree	Slightly Disagree	Strongly Disagree
❑	❑	❑	❑	❑

The same 1,031 people were polled in both cases. Version 1 showed 40 percent in favor of cuts, while version 2 showed 52 percent in favor of cuts. The margin of error was ±3.5 percent (in "How to Rig a Poll," June 14, 1995, p. A18). To "rig" the poll, emotional overlays or "loaded" mental images can be attached to the question. In fact, it is often difficult to ask a neutral question without any context. For example:

Version 1:   Shall state taxes be cut?

Version 2:   Shall state taxes be cut, if it means reducing highway maintenance?

Version 3:   Shall state taxes be cut, if it means firing teachers and police?

An unconstrained choice (version 1) makes tax cuts appear to be a "free lunch," while versions 2 and 3 require the respondent to envision the consequences of a tax cut. An alternative is to use version 1 but then ask the respondent to list the state services that should be cut to balance the budget after the tax cut.

Another problem in wording is to make sure you have covered all the possibilities. For example, how does a widowed independent voter answer questions like these?

Are you married?   What is your party preference?

❑ Yes   ❑ Democrat

❑ No   ❑ Republican

Overlapping classes or unclear categories are a problem. What if your father is deceased or is 45 years old?

How old is your father?

❑ 35–45

❑ 45–55

❑ 55–65

❑ 65 or older

Coding and Data Screening

Survey responses usually are coded numerically (e.g., 1 = male, 2 = female) although some software packages can also tabulate text variables (nominal data) and use them in certain kinds of statistical tests. Most packages require you to denote missing values by a special character (e.g., blank, period, or asterisk). If too many entries on a given respondent's questionnaire are flawed or missing, you may decide to discard the entire response.

Other data screening issues include multiple responses (i.e., the respondent chose two responses where one was expected), outrageous replies on fill-in-the-blank questions (e.g., a respondent who claims to work 640 hours a week), "range" answers (e.g., 10–20 cigarettes smoked per day), or inconsistent replies (e.g., a 55-year-old respondent who claims to receive Medicare benefits). Sometimes a follow-up is possible, but in anonymous surveys you must make the best decisions you can about how to handle anomalous data. Be sure to document your data-coding decisions—not only for the benefit of others but also in case you are asked to explain how you did it (it is easy to forget after a month or two, when you have moved on to other projects).

Sources of Error

No matter how careful you are when conducting a survey, you will encounter potential sources of error. Let's briefly review a few, summarized in Table 2.15.

Nonresponse bias occurs when those who respond have characteristics different from those who don't respond. For example, people with caller ID, answering machines, blocked or unlisted numbers, or cell phones are likely to be missed in telephone surveys. Since these are generally more affluent individuals, their socioeconomic class may be underrepresented in the poll. A special case is *selection bias,* a self-selected sample. For example, a talk show host who invites viewers to take a Web survey about their sex lives will attract plenty of respondents. But those who are willing to reveal details of their personal lives (and who have time to complete the survey) are likely to differ substantially from those who dislike nosy surveys or are too busy (and probably weren't watching the show anyway).

Further, it is easy to imagine that hoax replies will be common to such a survey (e.g., a bunch of college dorm students giving silly answers on a Web survey). *Response error* occurs when respondents deliberately give false information to mimic socially acceptable answers, to avoid embarrassment, or to protect personal information.

Next, *coverage error* occurs when some important segment of the target population is systematically missed. For example, a survey of Notre Dame University alumni will fail to represent noncollege graduates or those who attended public universities. And *measurement error* results when the survey questions do not accurately reveal the construct being assessed, as discussed previously. When the interviewer's facial expressions, tone of voice, or appearance influences the responses data are subject to *interview error.*

Finally, *sampling error* is uncontrollable random error that is inherent in any survey. Even using a probability sampling method, it is possible that the sample will contain unusual responses. This cannot be prevented and is generally undetectable.

TABLE 2.15	Source of Error	Characteristics
Potential Sources of Survey Error	Nonresponse bias	Respondents differ from nonrespondents
	Selection bias	Self-selected respondents are atypical
	Response error	Respondents give false information
	Coverage error	Incorrect specification of frame or population
	Measurement error	Survey instrument wording is biased or unclear
	Interviewer error	Responses influenced by interviewer
	Sampling error	Random and unavoidable

Data File Format

Data usually are entered into a spreadsheet or database. A "flat file" is an $n \times m$ matrix. Specifically, each column is a variable (m columns) and each row is a subject (n rows).

Case	Variable 1	Variable 2	...	Variable m
1	XXX	XXX	...	XXX
2	XXX	XXX	...	XXX
3	XXX	XXX	...	XXX
...	...	...	...	...
n	XXX	XXX	...	XXX

Spreadsheets may offer enough statistical power to handle your needs (particularly if you have an add-in like MegaStat for Excel). But spreadsheets are a general tool with limited features. You may prefer to use a professional statistical package that is designed for statistical analysis (e.g., MINITAB, SPSS, SyStat, SAS, etc.). You can copy your spreadsheet data and paste it into columns in the statistical software package, which will store the data in its own proprietary format.

Advice on Copying Data

If your data set contains commas (e.g., 42,586), dollar signs (e.g., $14.88), or percents (e.g., 7.5%) your statistics package (e.g., MINITAB or SPSS) may treat the data as text. A numerical variable may only contain the digits 0–9, a decimal point, and a minus sign. Format the data column as plain numbers with the desired number of decimal places *before* you copy the data to whatever package you are using. Excel can display a value such as 32.8756 as 32.9 if you set only one decimal digit, but it is the *displayed* number that is copied, so your Excel statistics may not agree with the package you are using.

SECTION EXERCISES

2.24 What sources of error might you encounter if you want to know (a) about the dating habits of college men, so you go to a dorm meeting and ask students how many dates they have had in the last year; (b) how often people attend religious services, so you stand outside a particular church on Sunday and ask entering individuals how often they attend; (c) how often people eat at McDonald's, so you stand outside a particular McDonald's and ask entering customers how often they eat at McDonald's.

2.25 What kind of survey (mail, telephone, interview, Web, direct observation) would you recommend for each of the following purposes, and why? What problems might be encountered?
   a. To estimate the proportion of students at your university who would prefer a Web-based statistics class to a regular lecture.
   b. To estimate the proportion of students at your university who carry backpacks to class.
   c. To estimate the proportion of students at your university who would be interested in taking a two-month summer class in international business with tours of European factories.
   d. To estimate the proportion of U.S. business graduates who have taken a class in international business.

2.26 What kind of survey (mail, telephone, interview, Web, direct observation) would you recommend that a small laundry and dry cleaning business use for each of the following purposes, and why? What problems might be encountered?
   a. To estimate the proportion of customers preferring opening hours at 7 A.M. instead of 8 A.M.
   b. To estimate the proportion of customers who have only laundry and no dry cleaning.

c. To estimate the proportion of residents in the same zip code who spend more than $20 a month on dry cleaning.

d. To estimate the proportion of its seven employees who think it is too hot inside the building.

2.27   What would be the difference in student responses to the two questions shown?

Version 1:   I would prefer that tuition be reduced.

Version 2:   Cuts in tuition are a good idea even if some classes are canceled.

2.28   What problems are evident in the wording of these two questions?

What is your race?	What is your religious preference?
❑ White	❑ Christian
❑ Black	❑ Jewish

Mini Case   2.3

Roles of Colleges

A survey of public opinion on the role of colleges was conducted by *The Chronicle of Higher Education*. The survey utilized 1,000 telephone interviews of 20 minutes each, using a random selection of men and women aged 25 through 65. It was conducted February 25, 2004. The survey was administered by TMR Inc. of Broomall, Pennsylvania. Data were collected and analyzed by GDA Integrated Services, a market research firm in Old Saybrook, Connecticut. Table 2.16 shows selected results, indicating the top three and bottom three roles for colleges.

TABLE 2.16   Important Roles for a College to Perform ($n = 1,000$ interviews)

Role	Very Important	Important	Somewhat Important	Not Important	No Answer
Top three roles (percent of respondents)					
Prepare its undergraduate students for a career	70	22	7	1	0
Prepare students to be responsible citizens	67	18	11	3	0
Provide education for adults so they qualify for better jobs	66	21	11	2	0
Lowest three roles (percent of respondents)					
Promote international understanding by encouraging students to study in other countries	28	29	31	11	0
Provide cultural events for the community	27	29	33	11	0
Play athletics for the entertainment of the community	14	19	40	26	0

Source: *The Chronicle of Higher Education*, May 7, 2004. Copyright © 2004. Reprinted with permission. Percents may not sum to 100 due to rounding.

The Likert-type scale labels are weighted toward the positive, which is common when the survey items (roles for colleges in this case) are assumed to be potentially important and there is little likelihood of a strong negative response. Respondents were also asked for demographic information. Fifty-eight percent were women and 42 percent were men, coming from all states except Alaska and Hawaii. Eleven percent were African American (similar to the national average) but only 6 percent were Hispanic (about 8 percent below the national average). The under-representation of Hispanics was due to language barriers, illustrating one difficulty faced by surveys. However, the respondents' incomes, religious affiliations, and political views were similar to the general U.S. population. The random selection method was not specified. Note that firms that specialize in survey sampling generally have access to commercial lists and use their own proprietary methods.

Chapter Summary

A **data set** is an array with n rows and m columns. Data sets may be **univariate** (one variable), **bivariate** (two variables), or **multivariate** (three or more variables). There are two basic data types: **attribute data** (categories that are described by labels) or **numerical** (meaningful numbers). Numerical data are **discrete** if the values are integers or can be counted or **continuous** if any interval can contain more data values. **Nominal** measurements are names, **ordinal** measurements are ranks, **interval** measurements have meaningful distances between data values, and **ratio** measurements have meaningful ratios and a zero reference point. **Time series** data are observations measured at n different points in time or over sequential time intervals, while **cross-sectional** data are observations among n entities such as individuals, firms, or geographic regions. Among **probability samples, simple random** samples pick items from a list using random numbers, **systematic** samples take every kth item, **cluster** samples select geographic regions, and **stratified** samples take into account known population proportions. **Nonprobability** samples include convenience or judgment samples, gaining time but sacrificing randomness. **Survey design** requires attention to question **wording** and **scale definitions. Survey techniques** (mail, telephone, interview, Web, direct observation) depend on time, budget, and the nature of the questions and are subject to various sources of error.

Key Terms

attribute data, *24*
binary variable, *25*
bivariate data sets, *24*
census, *30*
cluster sample, *39*
coding, *24*
continuous data, *25*
convenience sampling, *40*
coverage error, *46*
cross-sectional data, *30*
data, *23*
data set, *23*
discrete data, *25*
individual, *23*
interval data, *27*

interviewer error, *46*
judgment sampling, *40*
Likert scale, *27*
measurement error, *46*
multivariate data sets, *24*
nominal data, *26*
nonprobability sampling, *33*
nonresponse bias, *46*
numerical data, *24*
observation, *23*
ordinal data, *27*
probability sampling, *33*
ratio data, *28*
response error, *46*
sample, *30*

sampling error, *46*
sampling frame, *32*
sampling with replacement, *35*
sampling without
    replacement, *35*
selection bias, *46*
simple random sample, *33*
stratified sampling, *39*
subject, *23*
systematic sampling, *37*
target population, *32*
time series data, *30*
univariate data sets, *24*
variable, *23*

Chapter Review

1. Define (a) data, (b) data set, (c) subject, and (d) variable.

2. How do business data differ from scientific experimental data?

3. Distinguish (a) univariate, bivariate, and multivariate data; (b) discrete and continuous data; (c) numerical and attribute data.

4. Define the four measurement levels and give an example of each.

5. Explain the difference between cross-sectional data and time series data.

6. (a) List three reasons why a census might be preferred to a sample; (b) List three reasons why a sample might be preferred to a census.

7. (a) What is the difference between a parameter and a statistic? (b) What is a target population?

8. (a) List four methods of probability sampling. (b) List two methods of nonprobability sampling. (c) Why would we ever use nonprobability sampling? (d) Why is sampling usually done without replacement?

9. List five (a) steps in a survey, (b) issues in survey design, (c) survey types, (d) question scale types, and (e) sources of error in surveys.

10. List advantages and disadvantages of the different types of surveys.

CHAPTER EXERCISES

DATA TYPES

2.29 Which type of data (attribute, discrete numerical, continuous numerical) is each of the following variables? Explain. If there is ambiguity, explain why.
a. Age of a randomly chosen tennis player in the Wimbledon tennis tournament.
b. Nationality of a randomly chosen tennis player in the Wimbledon tennis tournament.
c. Number of double-faults in a randomly chosen tennis game at Wimbledon.
d. Number of spectators at a randomly chosen Wimbledon tennis match.
e. Water consumption (liters) by a randomly chosen Wimbledon player during a match.

2.30 Which type of data (nominal, ordinal, interval, ratio) is each of the following variables? Explain.
a. "Seed" (e.g., 20 of 128) of a randomly chosen tennis player in the Wimbledon tournament.
b. Noise level 100 meters from the Dan Ryan Expressway at a randomly chosen moment.
c. Number of occupants in a randomly chosen commuter vehicle on the San Diego Freeway.
d. Number of annual office visits by a particular Medicare subscriber.
e. Daily caffeine consumption by a 6-year-old child.

2.31 (a) Give *two* original examples of discrete data. (b) Give *two* original examples of continuous data. In each case, explain and identify any ambiguities that might exist. *Hint:* Do not restrict yourself to published data. Consider data describing your own life (e.g., your sports performance or financial or academic data). You need *not* list all the data, merely describe them and show a few typical data values.

2.32 (a) Give *two* original examples of time series data. (b) Give *two* original examples of cross-sectional data. In each case, identify the unit of observation carefully. If the data is both cross-sectional and time series, explain why. *Hint:* Do not restrict yourself to published data, and consider data describing your own life (e.g., sports performance or financial data). You need *not* list any data, merely describe them and perhaps show a few typical data values.

2.33 Below are questions from a survey that was administered to a sample of MBA students (see *LearningStats,* Cross-Sectional Data, Surveys). Answers were recorded on paper in the blank at the left of each question. For each question, state the data type (attribute, discrete numerical, or continuous numerical) and measurement level (nominal, ordinal, interval, ratio). Explain your reasoning. If there is doubt, discuss the alternatives.

_____	Q1	What is your gender? (Male = 0, Female = 1)
_____	Q2	What is your approximate undergraduate college GPA? (1.0 to 4.0)
_____	Q3	Who was the U.S. President on March 3, 1944?
_____	Q4	About how many hours per week do you expect to work at an outside job this semester?
_____	Q5	What do you think is the ideal number of children for a married couple?
_____	Q6	Counting yourself, how many children did your parents have?
_____	Q7	On a 1 to 5 scale, which best describes your parents? 1 = Mother clearly dominant ↔ 5 = Father clearly dominant
_____	Q8	On a 1 to 5 scale, assess the current job market for your undergraduate major. 1 = Very bad ↔ 5 = Very good
_____	Q9	How far from campus do you live? (in miles, 0 if on campus)
_____	Q10	During the last month, how many times has your schedule been disrupted by car trouble?
_____	Q11	About how many years of college does the more-educated one of your parents have? (years)
_____	Q12	During the last year, how many traffic tickets (excluding parking) have you received?
_____	Q13	Which political orientation most nearly fits you? (1 = Liberal, 2 = Middle-of-Road, 3 = Conservative)

_____ Q14   What is the approximate population of Indonesia (in millions)?

_____ Q15   What is the age of the car you usually drive? (years)

_____ Q16   About how many times in the past year did you attend formal religious services?

_____ Q17   How often do you read a daily newspaper? (0 = Never, 1 = Occasionally, 2 = Regularly)

_____ Q18   Can you conduct simple transactions in a language other than English? (0 = No, 1 = Yes)

_____ Q19   How often do you exercise (aerobics, running, etc)? (0 = Not At All, 1 = Sometimes, 2 = Regularly)

_____ Q20   Do you like cats? (0 = No, 1 = Yes)

SAMPLING METHODS

2.34 Would you use a sample or a census to measure each of the following? Why? If you are uncertain, explain the issues.
a. The number of cans of Campbell's soup on your local supermarket's shelf today at 6:00 P.M.
b. The proportion of soup sales last week in Boston that was sold under the Campbell's brand.
c. The proportion of Campbell's brand soup cans in your family's pantry.
d. The number of workers currently employed by Campbell Soup Company.

2.35 Is each of the following a parameter or a statistic? If you are uncertain, explain the issues.
a. The number of cans of Campbell's soup sold last week at your local supermarket.
b. The proportion of all soup in the United States that was sold under the Campbell's brand last year.
c. The proportion of Campbell's brand soup cans in the family pantries of 10 students.
d. The total earnings of workers employed by Campbell Soup Company last year.

2.36 You can test Excel's algorithm for selecting random integers with a simple experiment. Enter =RANDBETWEEN(1,2) into cell A1 and then copy it to cells A1:E20. This creates a data block of 100 cells containing either a one or a two. In cell G1 type =COUNTIF(A1:E20,"=1") and in cell G2 type =COUNTIF(A1:E20,"=2"). Highlight cells G1 and G2 and use Excel's Chart Wizard to create a bar chart. Click on the vertical axis scale and set the lower limit to 0 and upper limit to 100. You will see something like the example shown below. Then hold down the F9 key and observe the chart. Are you convinced that, on average, you are getting about 50 ones and 50 twos? *Ambitious Students:* Generalize this experiment to integers 1 through 5.   **RandBetween**

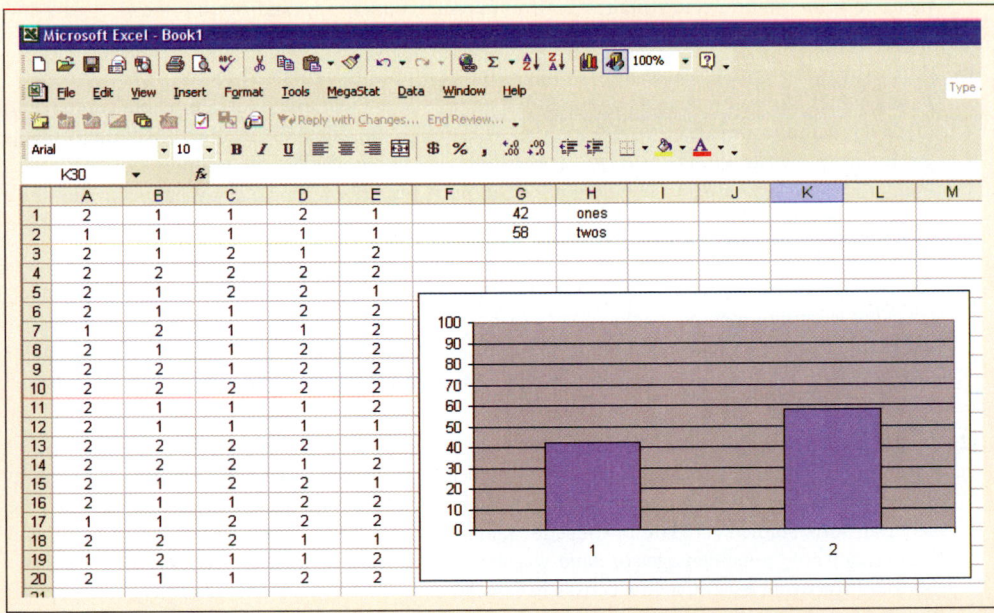

2.37 (a) To study profitability, which variables in the Fortune 1000 data set following could be used to *stratify* the sample? Name the strata for each. (b) Why might stratification be important if we wanted to study average profitability for both industries combined? (c) The Fortune 1000 list had 11 apparel companies and 39 chemical companies. If we just used the 20 companies here to estimate average profitability, what errors might we commit?

Profitability of 20 Selected Companies from the 2003 Fortune 1000 🐝 20Firms

Company	Profit as % of Revenue	Industry	Employees (000)
Ashland	1	Chemicals	15 and Up
Cabot	4	Chemicals	Under 15
Dow Chemical	5	Chemicals	15 and Up
DuPont	4	Chemicals	15 and Up
Jones Apparel Group	8	Apparel	15 and Up
Kellwood	3	Apparel	15 and Up
Levi Strauss	−9	Apparel	Under 15
Liz Claiborne	7	Apparel	15 and Up
Lubrizol	4	Chemicals	Under 15
Nike	4	Apparel	15 and Up
Phillips Van Heusen	1	Apparel	Under 15
Polo Ralph Lauren	7	Apparel	Under 15
PPG Industries	6	Chemicals	15 and Up
Reebok International	5	Apparel	Under 15
Rohm & Haas	4	Chemicals	15 and Up
Scotts	5	Chemicals	Under 15
Terra Industries	−1	Chemicals	Under 15
VF	8	Apparel	15 and Up
W.R. Grace	−3	Chemicals	Under 15
Warnaco Group	159	Apparel	Under 15

Source: *Fortune* 1000 list 149, no. 7 April 5, 2004 issue. Copyright © 2005 Time Inc. All rights reserved.

2.38 The General Accounting Office conducted random testing of retail gasoline in Michigan, Missouri, Oregon, and Tennessee. The study concluded that 49 percent of gasoline nationwide is mislabeled by more than one-half of an octane point. (a) What kind of sampling technique was most likely to have been used in this study? Why not the others? (b) Is the population finite or infinite? Listable or unlistable? (Data are from *Detroit Free Press,* April 27, 1990, p. 1A.)

2.39 What sampling method would you use to estimate the percent of automobile owners who have radar detectors nationwide? Suggest several alternative methods, and discuss the strengths and weaknesses of each. Is a census possible?

2.40 Aflatoxin is the generic name for a family of natural poisons produced by the mold *aspergillus flavus,* which grows on peanuts and grains. Lab tests show that aflatoxin is a potent carcinogen. (a) What sampling method would you use to estimate the aflatoxin in brand-name and fresh-ground peanut butter sold in grocery stores nationwide to see whether the samples violate the U.S. Food and Drug Administration guidelines of 20 parts per billion (ppb)? (b) What is the sampling frame? Is the population finite or infinite? Listable or unlistable? (c) Is a census possible? (See *Consumer Reports* 55, no. 9 [September 1990], p. 591.)

2.41 Arsenic (a naturally occurring, poisonous metal) in home water wells is a common threat. (a) What sampling method would you use to estimate the arsenic levels in wells in a rural county to see whether the samples violate the EPA limit of 10 parts per billion (ppb)? (b) Is the population finite or infinite? Listable or unlistable? (c) Is a census possible? (See *Popular Science,* February 2002, p. 24.)

2.42 In the aftermath of the 2003 SARS outbreak in Toronto, a survey firm Wirthlin Worldwide of Reston, Virginia, found that 95 percent of men and 97 percent of women using restrooms at Toronto International Airport during August 2003 washed their hands with soap and water. At the other airports studied (O'Hare in Chicago, Kennedy in New York, Dallas/Ft. Worth, Miami, and San Francisco) the percentages of hand-washers ranged from 62 to 80 percent for men and from 59 to 92 for women. (a) Could a census have been used for this type of study? (b) Is the population finite or infinite? Listable or unlistable? (c) Discuss what kind of sampling was probably used to study these questions. (d) How do you think the data were collected? (e) What biases or difficulties might be encountered? (Data are from *Science News* 164, no. 14 [October 2003], p. 222.)

2.43 How often are "fresh wild salmon" really farm-bred? Newspaper reporters visited eight stores in New York City and bought samples of salmon sold as "wild" to a laboratory. The results showed that 6 of the 8 samples were actually farm-bred, based on analysis of pigments known as carotenoids.

(a) What kind of sampling method would you suppose was used? (b) If it was not a true random sample, does this invalidate the conclusion? (See *New York Times,* April 10, 2005.)

2.44 The average American male wears a size 10 shoe and spends 4 hours a year tying a tie. The average American female college student owns 3.5 pairs of jeans. The average American laughs 15 times daily, swallows 215 aspirin tablets a year, and has a dog weighing 32 pounds. (a) Choose one of these estimates. How do you suppose it was derived? (b) What sampling method would *you* use to update each of these statistics? What problems would you anticipate? (c) Could a census be used? (d) Are the populations finite or infinite? Listable or unlistable? (Data are from Mike Feinsilber and William B. Mead, *American Averages: Amazing Facts of Everyday Life* [Doubleday-Dolphin, 1980].)

2.45 A survey by *The Economist* was taken to assess attitudes of randomly chosen 2,277 electors toward the proposed European Union constitution. (a) What kind of sampling technique was most likely to have been used in this study? Why not the others? (b) Is the population finite or infinite? Listable or unlistable? (Data are from *The Economist* 268, no. 8331 [July 5, 2003], p. 30.)

2.46 *Money Magazine* published an annual list of major stock funds. In 2003, the list contained 1,699 funds. What method would you recommend to obtain a sample of 20 stock funds to estimate the 10-year percent return? If more than one method is acceptable, discuss the strengths and weaknesses of each. (Data are from *Money* 32, no. 2 [February 2003], p. 166.)

2.47 From a list of 73 health care insurers, a sample of 11 was drawn by choosing every seventh company, starting from the third on the list. In this sample, 4 of the 11 selected companies (36 percent) charged the same annual premium for men and for women. A second random sample of 11 was drawn, using a random number table to select two-digit random numbers between 01 and 73. In the second sample, 7 of the 11 selected companies (64 percent) charged the same premium for men and women. (a) Are these methods equally appropriate for this situation? (b) How can you explain the different results?

2.48 According to a recent study, radar detector users have a lower accident rate than non-users. Moreover, detector users seem to be better citizens. The study found that detector users wear their seatbelts more and even vote more than non-users. (a) What sampling method do you suppose was used? (b) Can you suggest potential sources of coverage error? Nonresponse bias? Measurement error? (c) Do you agree with the conclusion that radar detector users are better citizens? Explain.

2.49 Prior to starting a recycling program, a city decides to measure the quantity of garbage produced by single-family homes in various neighborhoods. This experiment will require weighing garbage on the day it is set out. (a) What sampling method would you recommend, and why? (b) Why not the others? (c) What would be a potential source of sample error?

2.50 As a statistics project, a student examined every cigarette butt along the sidewalk and curb along one block near his home. Of 47 identifiable butts, 22 were Marlboro. (a) What sampling method is this (if any)? (b) Is it correct to infer that 47 percent of all smokers prefer Marlboro? (c) What inferences *would* be appropriate? (d) What potential sources of error are present in this sample?

2.51 Devise a practical sampling method (not necessarily one of those mentioned in this chapter) to collect data to estimate each parameter.
a. Mean length of TV commercials during Monday night NFL games.
b. Percentage of peanuts in cans of Planter's Mixed Nuts.
c. Percentage of bank mortgages issued to first-time borrowers.
d. Mean winner-loser margin in NCAA Division I regular season games.
e. Percentage of institutional holdings of publicly traded stocks in the United States.

2.52 Devise a practical sampling method (not necessarily one of those mentioned in this chapter) to collect data to estimate each parameter.
a. Percentage of an HMO's patients who make more than five office visits per year.
b. Percentage of commuters on your local freeway who drive alone.
c. Noise level (decibels) in neighborhoods 100 meters from a certain freeway.
d. Average flight departure delay for Northwest Airlines in Minneapolis.
e. Average price of gasoline in your area.

2.53 (a) If the goal is to estimate the price of a particular brand of soft drink at various stores in your county, suggest several strata that might be relevant to choose the stores. (b) Is the population of stores listable? (c) Suggest a feasible sampling method (not necessarily one of the standard ones).

2.54 What kind of bugs are killed by "mosquito zappers"? Prof. Douglas Tallamy, an entomologist at the University of Delaware, suspected that most of the carcasses were not mosquitoes. With the help of high school student volunteers, he analyzed 13,789 dead insects from six zappers from people's houses in suburban Newark, Delaware. The final count was only 18 mosquitoes and 13 other biting flies, or about 0.002 of the total. (a) Is there any alternative to sampling in this case? (b) What kind of stratification might be needed to generalize this experiment to the United States as a whole? (Data are from *Scientific American* 276, no. 6 [June 1997], p. 30.)

2.55   To protect baby scallops and ensure the survival of the species, the U.S. Fisheries and Wildlife Service requires that an average scallop must weigh at least 1/36 pound. The harbormaster at a Massachusetts port randomly selected 18 bags of scallops from 11,000 bags on an arriving vessel. From each bag, agents took a large scoop of scallops, separated and weighed the meat, and divided by the number of scallops in the scoop, finding a mean weight of 1/39 pound. (a) Is there any alternative to sampling in this case? (b) What kind of sampling method do you suppose was used to select the 18 bags? (Data are from *Interfaces* 25, no. 2 [March-April 1995], p. 18.)

2.56   *U.S. News & World Report* (March 17, 2003) reports that the U.S. Food and Drug Administration (FDA) estimates that swordfish contains about 1.00 parts per million (ppm) of mercury, which exceeds the FDA guideline of 0.20 ppm. What kind of sampling method do you suppose was used to arrive at the swordfish estimate? Would more than one method be appropriate? Could a census be done? Explain.

2.57   A survey of 500 potential customers for new vehicles across the United States indicated that 37 percent expected their next vehicle to be an SUV. What kind of sampling method do you suppose was used to arrive at this estimate? Why not the others? (Data are from *Detroit Free Press,* April 3, 2002, p. 3F.)

2.58   Blood lead levels exceeding 10 micrograms per deciliter have been shown to be harmful to mental and physical development in children. The U.S. Centers for Disease Control and Prevention in Atlanta say that about 500,000 children in the U.S. have blood concentrations of lead higher than this level. (a) Which sampling method do you suppose was used to measure blood levels of lead in U.S. children to reach this conclusion? (b) Which sampling methods would be infeasible in this case?

2.59   Households can sign up for a telemarketing "no-call list." How might households who sign up differ from those who don't? What biases might this create for telemarketers promoting (a) financial planning services, (b) carpet cleaning services, and (c) vacation travel packages?

2.60   "When we were kids, nobody wore seat belts or bike helmets. We used lead-based paint and didn't install ground-fault circuit protectors in our electrical circuits. Yet we survived." What kind of sampling bias(es) does this statement illustrate?

SURVEYS AND SCALES

2.61   Insurance companies are rated by several rating agencies. The Fitch 20-point scale is AAA, AA+, AA, AA−, A+, A, A−, BBB+, BBB, BBB−, BB+, BB, BB−, B+, B, B−, CCC+, CCC, CCC−, DD. (a) What level of measurement does this scale use? (b) To assume that the scale uses interval measurements, what assumption is required? (Scales are from *Weiss Ratings Guide to HMOs and Health Insurers,* Summer 2003, p. 15.)

2.62   Suggest response check boxes for these questions. In each case, what difficulties do you encounter as you try to think of appropriate check boxes?
a. Where are you employed?
b. What is the biggest issue facing the next U.S. president?
c. Are you happy?

2.63   Suggest both a Likert scale question and a response scale to measure the following:
a. A student's rating of a particular statistics professor.
b. A voter's satisfaction with the president's economic policy.
c. An HMO patient's perception of waiting time to see a doctor.

2.64   A survey by the National Abortion Rights Action League showed that 68 percent favored keeping abortion legal. A survey by the National Right to Life found that 53 percent opposed abortion. (a) How could these contradictory results be reconciled? (b) Write a question on abortion that favors a "yes" reply. Then write a question on abortion that favors a "no" reply. (c) Try to write a "neutral" question on abortion. (Data are from *Detroit Free Press,* February 18, 1992, p. 1C.)

2.65   A Web-based poll on newsweek.com asked *Newsweek* readers the question shown below. Do you consider the wording of the responses to be neutral? Can you suggest alternative response wording? (From *Newsweek,* May 8, 2002, p. 6.)

Should the Boy Scouts be allowed to exclude gays?
1. No, it is wrong to discriminate.
2. No, but they should have a "don't ask, don't tell" policy regarding gays.
3. Yes, as a private group, they can determine who they want to admit.
4. Yes, gays compromise the Scouts' moral code.

2.66 What level of measurement (nominal, ordinal, interval, ratio) is appropriate for the movie rating system that you see in *TV Guide* (☆, ☆☆, ☆☆☆, ☆☆☆☆)? Explain your reasoning.

2.67 A survey by the American Automobile Association is shown below. (a) What kind of response scale is this? (b) Suggest an alternative response scale. (Survey question from *Michigan Living,* Dec. 1994. Copyright © Automobile Association of America. Used with permission.)

> New drivers under 18 should be required to complete additional hours of supervised driving beyond that provided in driver education.
> ❏ Strongly agree
> ❏ Agree
> ❏ Disagree
> ❏ Strongly disagree
> ❏ Undecided

2.68 A tabletop survey by a restaurant asked the question shown below. (a) What kind of response scale is this? (b) Suggest an alternative response scale that would be more sensitive to differences in opinion. (c) Suggest possible sources of response bias in this type of survey.

> Were the food and beverage presentations appealing?
> ❏ Yes
> ❏ No

SAMPLING EXPERIMENTS

2.69 Below are 64 names of employees at NilCo. Colors denote different departments (finance, marketing, purchasing, engineering). Sample eight names from the display shown by using (a) simple random sampling, (b) sequential sampling, and (c) cluster sampling. Try to ensure that every name has an equal chance of being picked. Which sampling method seems most appropriate?

🦅 **PickEight**

Floyd	Sid	LaDonna	Tom	Mabel	Nicholas	Bonnie	Deepak
Nathan	Ginnie	Mario	Claudia	Dmitri	Kevin	Blythe	Dave
Lou	Tim	Peter	Jean	Mike	Jeremy	Chad	Doug
Loretta	Erik	Jackie	Juanita	Molly	Carl	Buck	Janet
Anne	Joel	Moira	Marnie	Ted	Greg	Duane	Amanda
Don	Gadis	Balaji	Al	Takisha	Dan	Ryan	Sam
Graham	Scott	Lorin	Vince	Jody	Brian	Tania	Ralph
Bernie	Karen	Ed	Liz	Erika	Marge	Gene	Pam

2.70 From the display below pick five cards (without replacement) by using random numbers. Explain your method. Why would the other sampling methods not work well in this case?

A ♠	A ♥	A ♣	A ♦
K ♠	K ♥	K ♣	K ♦
Q ♠	Q ♥	Q ♣	Q ♦
J ♠	J ♥	J ♣	J ♦
10 ♠	10 ♥	10 ♣	10 ♦
9 ♠	9 ♥	9 ♣	9 ♦
8 ♠	8 ♥	8 ♣	8 ♦
7 ♠	7 ♥	7 ♣	7 ♦
6 ♠	6 ♥	6 ♣	6 ♦
5 ♠	5 ♥	5 ♣	5 ♦
4 ♠	4 ♥	4 ♣	4 ♦
3 ♠	3 ♥	3 ♣	3 ♦
2 ♠	2 ♥	2 ♣	2 ♦

2.71 Treating this textbook as a population, select a sample of 10 pages at random by using (a) simple random sampling, (b) systematic sampling, (c) cluster sampling, and (d) judgment sampling. Explain your methodology carefully in each case. (e) Which method would you recommend to estimate the mean number of formulas per page? Why not the others?

2.72 Photocopy the exhibit below (omit these instructions) and show it to a friend or classmate. Ask him/her to choose a number at random and write it on a piece of paper. Collect the paper. Repeat for *at least* 20 friends/classmates. Tabulate the results. Were all the numbers chosen equally often? If not, which were favored or avoided? Why? *Hint:* Review section 2.6. 🐝 **PickOne**

0	11	17	22
8	36	14	18
19	28	6	41
12	3	5	0

2.73 Ask each of 20 friends or classmates to choose a whole number between 1 and 5. Tabulate the results. Do the results seem random? If not, can you think of any reasons?

Web Data Sources

Source	Web Site
Bureau of Economic Analysis	www.bea.gov
Bureau of Justice Statistics	www.ojp.usdoj.gov/bjs
Bureau of Labor Statistics	www.bls.gov
Central Intelligence Agency	www.cia.gov
Economic Report of the President	www.gpoaccess.gov/eop
Environmental Protection Agency	www.epa.gov
Federal Reserve System	www.federalreserve.gov
Financial Forecast Center	www.forecasts.org
National Agricultural Statistics Service	www.usda.gov/nass
National Center for Education Statistics	www.nces.ed.gov
National Center for Health Statistics	www.cdc.gov/nchs
National Science Foundation	www.nsf.gov
Population Reference Bureau	www.prb.org
State and Metropolitan Area Data Book	www.census.gov/statab/www/smadb.html
Statistical Abstract of the United States	www.census.gov/statab
Statistics Canada	www.statcan.ca
U.N. Dept of Economic and Social Affairs	www.un.org/depts/unsd
U.S. Bureau of the Census	www.census.gov
U.S. Federal Statistics	www.fedstats.gov
U.S. Government Printing Office	www.gpo.gov
World Bank	www.worldbank.org
World Demographics	www.demographia.com
World Health Organization	www.who.int/en

Related Reading

Guides to Data Sources

Butler, F. Patrick. *Business Research Sources: A Reference Navigator.* Irwin/McGraw-Hill, 1999.

Clayton, Gary E.; and Martin Giesbrecht. *A Guide to Everyday Economic Statistics.* 4th ed. Irwin/McGraw-Hill, 1997.

Sampling and Surveys

Cantwell, Patrick J.; Howard Hogan; and Kathleen M. Styles. "The Use of Statistical Methods in the U.S. Census: *Utah v. Evans.*" *The American Statistician* 58, no. 3 (August 2004), pp. 203–12.

Cochran, William G. *Sampling Techniques*. 3rd ed. Wiley, 1990.

Cooper, Donald R.; and Pamela S. Schindler. *Business Research Methods*. 7th ed. Irwin/McGraw-Hill, 2001.

Cox, Eli P. "The Optimal Number of Response Alternatives for a Scale: A Review," *Journal of Marketing Research* 17, pp. 407–22.

Dillman, Don A. *Mail and Internet Surveys*. Wiley, 2000.

Fowler, Floyd J. *Survey Research Methods*. 3rd ed. Sage, 2001.

Groves, Robert M. et al. *Survey Methodology*. Wiley, 2004.

Groves, Robert M.; Paul P. Biemer; and Lars E. Lyberg. *Telephone Survey Methodology*. Wiley, 2001.

Hahn, Gerald J.; and William Q. Meeker. "Assumptions for Statistical Inference." *The American Statistician* 47, no. 1 (February 1993), pp. 1–11.

Levy, Paul S.; and Stanley Lemeshow. *Sampling of Populations*. Wiley, 1999.

Lyberg, Lars; and Paul Blemer. *Introduction to Survey Quality*. Wiley Europe, 2003.

Peterson, Ivars. "Sampling and the Census: Improving the Accuracy of the Decennial Count." *Science News* 152 (October 11, 1997), pp. 238–39.

Salant, Priscilla; and Don A. Dillman. *Conducting Surveys: A Step-By-Step Guide to Getting the Information You Need*. Wiley, 1994.

Scheaffer, Richard L.; William Mendenhall; and Lyman Ott. *Elementary Survey Sampling*. 5th ed. Duxbury, 1996.

Singh, Ravindra; and Naurang Singh Mangat. *Elements of Survey Sampling*. Kluwer, 1996.

Som, R. K. *Practical Sampling Techniques*. 2nd ed. Marcel Dekker, 1995.

Thompson, Steven K. *Sampling*. 2nd ed. Wiley, 2002.

Velleman, Paul F.; and Leland Wilkinson. "Nominal, Ordinal, Interval, and Ratio Typologies Are Misleading." *The American Statistician* 47, no. 1 (February 1993), pp. 65–72.

LearningStats Unit 02   Manipulating Data   LS

LearningStats Unit 02 introduces data types, sampling, random numbers, and surveys. Modules are designed for self-study, so you can proceed at your own pace, concentrate on material that is new, and pass quickly over things that you already know. Your instructor may assign specific modules, or you may decide to check them out because the topic sounds interesting. In addition to helping you learn about statistics, they may be useful as references later on.

Topic	*LearningStats Modules*
Data types	Level of Measurement
Sampling	Sampling Methods—Overview Sampling Methods—Worksheet Who Gets Picked? Randomizing a File Sampling a Large Database*
Surveys	Survey Methods
Data sources	Web Data Sources

Key: = PowerPoint   = Word   = Excel

*Denotes a specialized topic.

Describing Data Visually

Chapter Learning Objectives

When you finish this chapter you should be able to

- Make a dot plot by hand or by computer.

- Create a frequency distribution for a data set.

- Make a histogram by hand or by computer.

- Recognize skewness, modes, and outliers in a histogram.

- Make and interpret a scatter plot by using the computer.

- Use line charts, bar charts, and pie charts appropriately.

- Use Excel to make effective charts.

- Recognize deceptive graphing techniques.

- Define the characteristics of good graphs in general.

Statisticians must organize, explore, and summarize data in a succinct way. Their methods may be *visual* (charts and graphs) or *numerical* (statistics or tables). In this chapter, you will see how visual displays can provide insight into the characteristics of a data set *without* using mathematics. We begin with a set of n observations $x_1, x_2, \ldots, x_n$ on one variable (univariate data). Such data can be discussed in terms of three characteristics: ***central tendency, dispersion,*** and ***shape.*** Table 3.1 summarizes these characteristics as *questions* that we will be asking about the data.

3.1
VISUAL DESCRIPTION

Characteristic	Interpretation
Measurement	What are the units of measurement? Are the data integer or continuous? Any missing observations? Any concerns with accuracy or sampling methods?
Central Tendency	Where are the data values concentrated? What seem to be typical or middle data values?
Dispersion	How much variation is there in the data? How spread out are the data values? Are there unusual values?
Shape	Are the data values distributed symmetrically? Skewed? Sharply peaked? Flat? Bimodal?

TABLE 3.1

Characteristics of Univariate Data

EXAMPLE

Price/Earnings Ratios

Price/earnings (P/E) ratios—current stock price divided by earnings per share in the last 12 months—show how much an investor is willing to pay for a stock based on the stock's earnings. P/E ratios are also used to determine how optimistic the market is for a stock's growth potential. Investors may be willing to pay more for a lower earning stock than a higher earning stock if they see potential for growth. Table 3.2 shows P/E ratios for a random sample of 30 companies from Standard & Poor's 500 index. We might be interested in learning how the P/E ratios of the companies in the S&P 500 compare to each other and what the overall distribution of P/E ratios looks like within the S&P 500. Visual displays can help us describe and summarize the main characteristics of this sample.

TABLE 3.2 P/E Ratios for 30 Companies  **PERatios**

Company	Symbol	P/E Ratio	Company	Symbol	P/E Ratio
Ace Ltd.	ACE	26	Goldman-Sachs Group	GS	19
AutoNation Inc.	AN	10	Jones Apparel	JNY	10
Baker Hughes Inc.	BHI	55	Lexmark Intl. Inc.	LXK	21
Bank New York	BK	29	Limited Brands	LTD	16
Bank One Corp.	ONE	14	Mellon Financial	MEL	19
Baxter Intl. Inc.	BAX	23	Northrop Grumman	NOC	26
Bemis Co.	BMS	15	Nucor Corp.	NUE	34
Burlington/Santa	BNI	14	Occidental Pete	OXY	8
Cinergy Corp.	CIN	13	PPG Inds. Inc.	PPG	20
Constellat Ener.	CEG	15	Radioshack Corp.	RSH	17
Emerson Elec. Co.	EMR	22	Rohm & Haas Co.	ROH	68
Family Dollar St.	FDO	27	SBC Communication	SBC	10
General Electric	GE	20	Symantec Corp.	SYMC	29
Genzyme-Genl. Div.	GENZ	48	Whirlpool Corp.	WHR	18
Golden West Fin.	GDW	13	Yum! Brands Inc.	YUM	16

Source: *The Wall Street Journal,* July 1, 2003.

Measurement

Before calculating any statistics or drawing any graphs, it is a good idea to *look at the data* and try to visualize how it was collected. Because the companies in the S&P 500 index are publicly traded, they are required to publish verified financial information, so the accuracy of the data is not an issue. Since the intent of the analysis is to study the S&P 500 companies at a *point in time,* these are *cross-sectional* data. (Financial analysts also study time series data on P/E ratios, which vary daily as stock prices change.) Although rounded by *The Wall Street Journal* to integers, the measurements are continuous. For example, a stock price of $43.22 divided by earnings per share of $2.17 gives a P/E ratio $(43.22)/(2.17) = 19.92$, which would be rounded to 20 for convenience. Since there is a true zero, we can speak meaningfully of ratios and can perform any standard mathematical operations. Finally, since the analysis is based on samples (not a census), we must allow for the possibility of *sampling error,* that is, the possibility that our sample is not representative of the population of all 500 S&P 500 firms, due to the nature of random sampling.

Sorting

As a first step, it is helpful to sort the data. This is a visual display, although a very simple one. From the sorted data, we can see the range $(68 - 8 = 60)$, the frequency of occurrence for each data value (the highest frequency is 3 for the value 10), and the data values that lie near the middle and ends (a low value of 8 and a high value of 68 with many values clustered around 19 or 20).

8	10	10	10	13	13	14	14	15	15
16	16	17	18	19	19	20	20	21	22
23	26	26	27	29	29	34	48	55	68

FIGURE 3.1

Histogram of P/E ratios

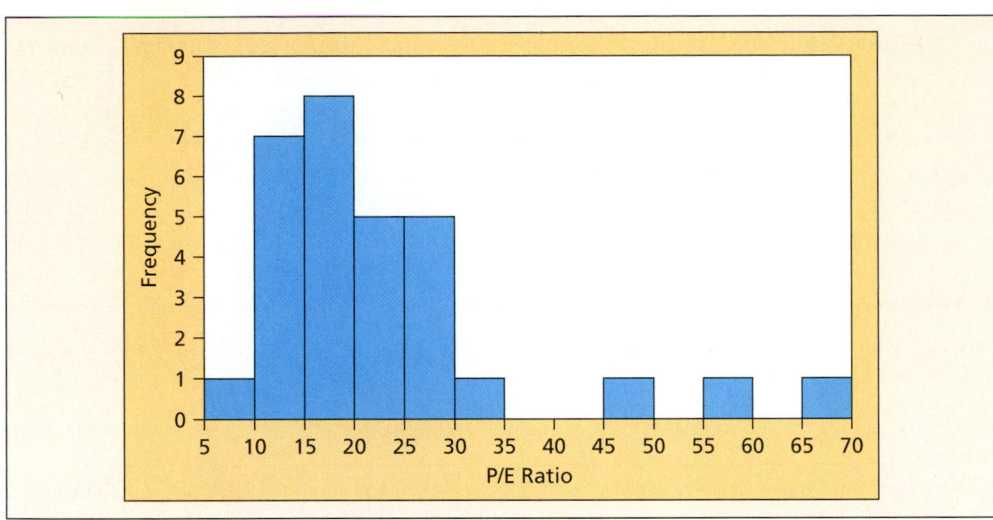

A sorted display of data values would be difficult to analyze if the number of observations were very large, say greater than 50. For this reason we typically summarize the data set in a graphical display. There are several different types of graphical displays that we can produce from this data set. One of the most common displays, a ***histogram,*** is shown in Figure 3.1. First, let's take a look at the histogram to see what kind of information it contains. Afterward we will learn how to construct various graphs and learn which ones are appropriate for the different types of data and measurement levels that exist.

The three characteristics discussed in the beginning of the chapter (central tendency, dispersion, and shape) can be seen in the *histogram.* We see that the highest frequency range is between 15 and 20. We also see that the range of the P/E ratios in this sample is approximately 65 (70 − 5). Finally, we can observe that while the majority of the values are less than 35, there are three observations that are much greater than 35. This last observation was not as apparent in the sorted display we looked at earlier.

It might be interesting to know which three companies have P/E ratios that appear much greater than the rest of the sample. Looking back at Table 3.2, we find that the companies are Genzyme-General, Baker Hughes Inc., and Rohm & Haas Co. These three companies represent the pharmaceutical industry, the oil industry, and the chemical industry, respectively. We might ask, "Do the values of these P/E ratios represent unusual observations?" Before we delve further into observations and questions about the graphs, we should learn how to create the graphical displays.

3.2

DOT PLOTS

A ***dot plot*** is the simplest graphical display of *n* individual values of numerical data. The basic steps in making a dot plot are to (1) make a scale that covers the data range, (2) mark the axes and label them, and (3) plot each data value as a dot above the scale at its approximate location. If more than one data value lies at approximately the same *X*-axis location, the dots are piled up vertically. Dot plots are an attractive tool for data exploration because they are easy to understand. A drawback is that they don't work well with large samples (e.g., *n* = 5,000).

Figure 3.2 shows the dot plot for the 30 P/E ratios. It shows *dispersion* by displaying the range of the data (from 8 to 68) and to some extent shows *central tendency* by revealing where the data values tend to cluster. However, unless the sample is large, a dot plot doesn't tell much about the *shape* of the distribution. We can add *annotations* (text boxes from Excel's Drawing Toolbar and arrows from Excel's AutoShapes) to call attention to interesting features of the dot plot (e.g., to identify the companies with the lowest and highest P/E ratios).

Small Sample: Home Prices

Even for a small data set, the dot plot makes it easier to *see* the data. For example, Figure 3.3 shows a dot plot of the data from Table 3.3 on median home prices for nine U.S. cities. This kind of display would be useful to realtors, as they discuss patterns in home selling prices within their community.

FIGURE 3.2

MegaStat dot plot for P/E ratios ($n = 30$)

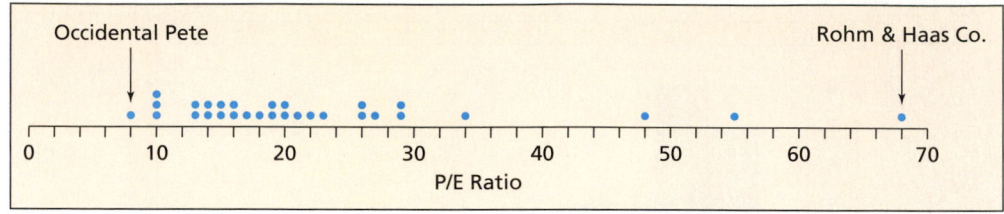

FIGURE 3.3

MegaStat dot plot of home prices ($n = 9$)

Homes

TABLE 3.3

Median Home Prices in Selected Cities ($n = 9$)

Homes-A

Source: National Association of Realtors, 2003.

Metropolitan Area	Median Home Price ($000)
Akron, OH	119.6
Bergen-Passaic, NJ	363.0
Bradenton, FL	170.4
Colorado Springs, CO	181.7
Hartford, CT	198.5
Milwaukee, WI	186.2
Raleigh-Durham, NC	173.8
San Francisco, CA	560.2
Topeka, KS	100.7

FIGURE 3.4

MegaStat menus for a dot plot

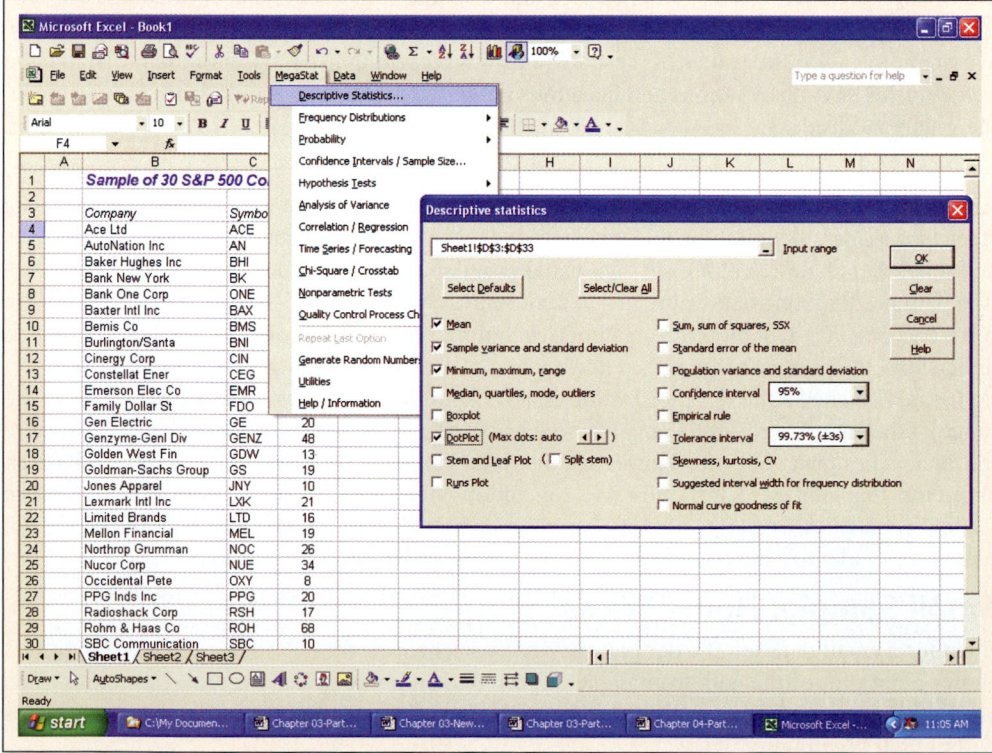

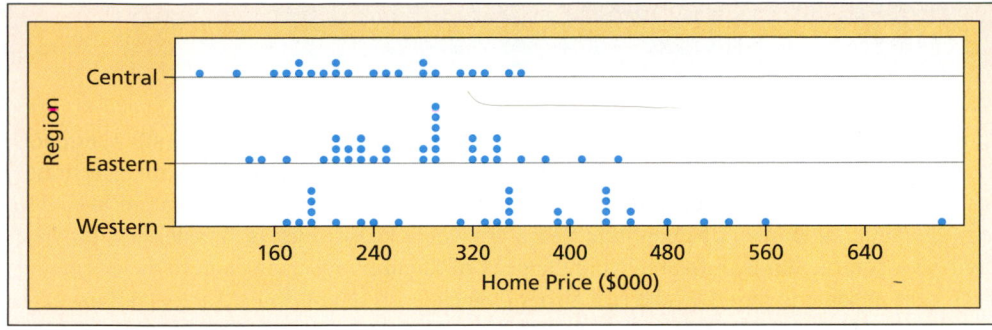

FIGURE 3.5

Minitab stacked dot plot
($n = 87$ cities)

🌐 **Homes-B**

Source: *Money Magazine,* vol. 32, no. 1
(January 2004), pp. 102–3.

Excel doesn't offer dot plots, but you can get them from MegaStat, Visual Statistics, or MINITAB. Figure 3.4 shows the MegaStat menus for a dot plot.

Comparing Groups

A *stacked dot plot* can be used to compare two or more groups. For example, Figure 3.5 shows a stacked dot plot for median home prices for 87 U.S. cities in three different regions. A common *X*-axis scale is used for all three dot plots. This stacked dot plot shows the range of data values and gives an idea of typical home values within each region. (MegaStat doesn't offer stacked dot plots, but MINITAB does.) Could a table show this amount of information as clearly?

SECTION EXERCISES

3.1   (a) Without using a computer, make a dot plot for these 32 observations on the number of customers to use a downtown CitiBank ATM during the noon hour on 32 consecutive workdays. (b) Describe its appearance.   🌐 **CitiBank**

25	37	23	26	30	40	25	26
39	32	21	26	19	27	32	25
18	26	34	18	31	35	21	33
33	9	16	32	35	42	15	24

3.2   Without using a computer, make a dot plot for the number of defects per 100 vehicles for these 12 randomly chosen brands from a list of 37 brands. Describe its appearance.   🌐 **JDPower**

Defects per 100 Vehicles			
Brand	**Defects**	**Brand**	**Defects**
Lexus	87	Subaru	123
Cadillac	93	Ford	130
Buick	100	Saab	133
Hyundai	102	Land Rover	148
Acura	117	Suzuki	149
Chrysler	120	Volkswagen	164

Source: J. D. Power and Associates 2004 Initial Quality Study™. Used with permission.

3.3   Sarah and Bob share a 1,000-minute cell phone calling plan. Without using a computer, make a *stacked dot plot* to compare the lengths of cell phone calls by Sarah and Bob during the last week. Describe what the dot plots tell you.   🌐 **PhoneCalls**

Sarah's calls: 1, 1, 1, 1, 2, 3, 3, 3, 5, 5, 6, 6, 7, 8, 8, 12, 14, 14, 22, 23, 29, 33, 38, 45, 66

Bob's calls: 5, 8, 9, 14, 17, 21, 23, 23, 24, 26, 27, 27, 28, 29, 31, 33, 35, 39, 41

Mini Case   3.1

U.S. Business Cycles

Although many businesses anticipated the 2001 recession that followed the long boom and stock market bubble of the 1990s, they needed to anticipate its probable length to form strategies for debt management and future product releases. Fortunately, good data are available from the National Bureau of Economic Research, which keeps track of business cycles. The length of a contraction is measured from the peak of the previous expansion to the beginning of the next expansion based on the real Gross Domestic Product (GDP). Table 3.4 shows the durations, in months, of 32 U.S. recessions.

TABLE 3.4   **U.S. Business Contractions, 1857–2001 (*n* = 32)**   **Recessions**

Peak	Trough	Months	Peak	Trough	Months
Jun 1857	Dec 1858	18	Jan 1920	Jul 1921	18
Oct 1860	Jun 1861	8	May 1923	Jul 1924	14
Apr 1865	Dec 1867	32	Oct 1926	Nov 1927	13
Jun 1869	Dec 1870	18	Aug 1929	Mar 1933	43
Oct 1873	Mar 1879	65	May 1937	Jun 1938	13
Mar 1882	May 1885	38	Feb 1945	Oct 1945	8
Mar 1887	Apr 1888	13	Nov 1948	Oct 1949	11
Jul 1890	May 1891	10	Jul 1953	May 1954	10
Jan 1893	Jun 1894	17	Aug 1957	Apr 1958	8
Dec 1895	Jun 1897	18	Apr 1960	Feb 1961	10
Jun 1899	Dec 1900	18	Dec 1969	Nov 1970	11
Sep 1902	Aug 1904	23	Nov 1973	Mar 1975	16
May 1907	Jun 1908	13	Jan 1980	Jul 1980	6
Jan 1910	Jan 1912	24	Jul 1981	Nov 1982	16
Jan 1913	Dec 1914	23	Jul 1990	Mar 1991	8
Aug 1918	Mar 1919	7	Mar 2001	Nov 2001	8

Source: U.S. Business Contractions found at www.nber.org. Copyright © 2005 National Bureau of Economic Research, Inc. Used with permission.

From the dot plot in Figure 3.6, we see that the 65-month contraction (1873–1879) was quite unusual, although four recessions did exceed 30 months. Most recessions have lasted less than 20 months. Only 7 of 32 lasted less than 10 months. The 8-month 2001 recession was therefore among the shortest, although its recovery phase was sluggish and inconsistent compared to most other recessions.

FIGURE 3.6

MegaStat dot plot of business cycle duration (*n* = 32)

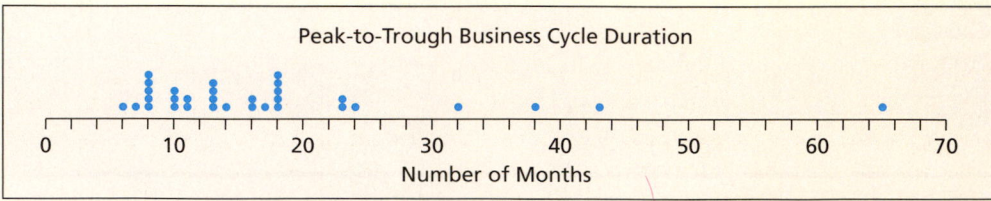

Still, the table supplies information that the dot plot cannot. For example, during the 1930s there were actually *two* major contractions (43 months from 1929 to 1933, 13 months from 1937 to 1938) which is one reason why that period seemed so terrible to those who lived through it. The Great Depression of the 1930s was so named because it lasted a long time and the economic decline was deeper than in most recessions.

Bins and Bin Limits

A *frequency distribution* is a table formed by classifying n data values into k classes called *bins* (we adopt this terminology from Excel). The *bin limits* define the values to be included in each bin. The bin widths must all be the same. The table shows the *frequency* of data values within each bin. Frequencies can also be expressed as *relative frequencies* or *percentages* of the total number of observations.

Frequency Distribution

A tabulation of n data values into k classes called *bins,* based on values of the data. The *bin limits* are cutoff points that define each bin. Bins must have equal widths and their limits cannot overlap.

The basic steps for constructing a frequency distribution are to (1) sort the data in ascending order, (2) choose the number of bins, (3) set the bin limits, (4) put the data values in the appropriate bin, and (5) create the table. Let's walk through these steps.

Constructing a Frequency Distribution

Step 1: Sort Data in Ascending Order

8	10	10	10	13	13	14	14	15	15
6	16	17	18	19	19	20	20	21	22
23	26	26	27	29	29	34	48	55	68

Step 2: Choose Number of Bins   Since a frequency distribution seeks to condense many data points into a small table, we expect the number of bins k to be much smaller than the sample size n. When you use *too many* bins some bins are likely to be sparsely populated, or even empty. With *too few* bins, dissimilar data values are lumped together. Left to their own devices, people tend to choose similar bin limits for a given data set. Generally, larger samples justify more bins. According to **Sturges's Rule,** a guideline proposed by statistician Herbert Sturges,* every time we double the sample size, we should add one bin, as shown in Table 3.5.

For sample sizes that you are likely to encounter, it suffices to use 5 to 11 classes. For example, for our data on P/E ratios ($n = 30$) Sturges would suggest about six bins. But, to get sensible bin limits, we decided to use seven bins. The choice of sensible or appropriate bin limits is an overriding consideration. If the sample is very small, we might not bother with bins, since we can just look at the entire data set.

Step 3: Set Bin Limits   Just as choosing the number of bins requires judgment, setting the bin limits also requires judgment. For guidance, find the approximate width of each bin by dividing the data range by the number of bins:

$$\text{Bin width} \approx \frac{x_{\max} - x_{\min}}{k} \tag{3.1}$$

Round the bin width *up* to an appropriate value, then set the lower limit for the first bin as a multiple of the bin width. What does "appropriate" mean? If the data are discrete, then it makes sense to have a width that is an integer value. If the data are continuous, then setting a bin width equal to a fractional value may be appropriate. Experiment until you get bins that cover the data range.

For example, for this data set, the smallest P/E ratio was 8 and the largest P/E ratio was 68, so if we want to use $k = 7$ bins, we calculate the approximate bin width as:

$$\text{Bin width} \approx \frac{68 - 8}{7} = \frac{60}{7} = 8.57$$

To obtain "nice" limits, we can round the bin width up to 10 and start the first bin at 0 to get bin limits 0, 10, 20, 30, 40, 50, 60, 70. Usually "nice" bin limits are 2, 5, or 10 multiplied by

---

*Sturges said that the number of classes to tabulate n items should be approximately $1 + \log_2(n)$.

TABLE 3.5

Sturges's Rule

Sample Size (n)	Suggested Number of Bins (k)
16	5
32	6
64	7
128	8
256	9
512	10
1,024	11

TABLE 3.6

Frequency Distribution for P/E Ratios Using Seven Bins

Bin Range	Frequency	Relative Frequency	Cumulative Relative Frequency
0 ≤ P/E Ratio < 10	1	0.0333	0.0333
10 ≤ P/E Ratio < 20	15	0.5000	0.5333
20 ≤ P/E Ratio < 30	10	0.3333	0.8666
30 ≤ P/E Ratio < 40	1	0.0333	0.8999
40 ≤ P/E Ratio < 50	1	0.0333	0.9332
50 ≤ P/E Ratio < 60	1	0.0333	0.9665
60 ≤ P/E Ratio < 70	1	0.0333	0.9998

an appropriate power of 10. As a starting point for the lowest bin, we choose the smallest multiple of the bin width smaller than the lowest data value.

Step 4: Put Data Values in Appropriate Bins In general, the lower limit is *included* in the bin, while the upper limit is *excluded*. MegaStat and MINITAB follow this convention. However, Excel's histogram option *includes* the upper limit and *excludes* the lower limit. There are advantages to either method. Our objective is to make sure none of the bins overlap and that data values are counted in only one bin.

Step 5: Create Table You can choose to show only the absolute frequencies, or counts, for each bin or also include the relative frequencies and the cumulative frequencies. Relative frequencies are calculated as the absolute frequency for a bin divided by the total number of data values. Cumulative relative frequencies accumulate relative frequency values as the bin limits increase. Table 3.6 shows the frequency distribution we've created for the P/E ratio data. Notice that the relative frequencies do not sum to 1. This can happen due to rounding.

Histograms

A *histogram* is a graphical representation of a frequency distribution. A histogram is a bar chart whose *Y*-axis shows the number of data values (or a percentage) within each bin of a frequency distribution and whose *X*-axis ticks show the end points of each bin. There should be no gaps between bars (except when there are no data in a particular bin).

As we discussed earlier, choosing the number of bins and bin limits requires judgment on our part. The process of creating a histogram is often an iterative process. Our first choice of bins and limits may not be our final choice for presentation. Figure 3.7 shows histograms for the P/E ratio sample using three different bin definitions. Our perception of the shape of the distribution depends on how the bins are chosen. The 4-bin histogram is too coarse to give a precise view of the data. The 7-bin histogram clearly shows concentration between 10 and 30. The 13-bin histogram reveals more detail in the right tail. You can use your own judgment to determine which histogram you would ultimately include in a report.

Excel Histograms

Excel will produce histograms. Click on the menu bar Tools > Data Analysis (if you don't see Data Analysis on the Tools menu, you must click Add-Ins and check Analysis Tool Pak). You can specify a range containing the bin limits (cells G23:G29 in Figure 3.8) or accept Excel's default. The result, shown in Figure 3.8, is not very attractive. Modifying an Excel histogram is possible, but you may prefer using software designed for drawing histograms.

FIGURE 3.7

Three histograms for P/E ratios

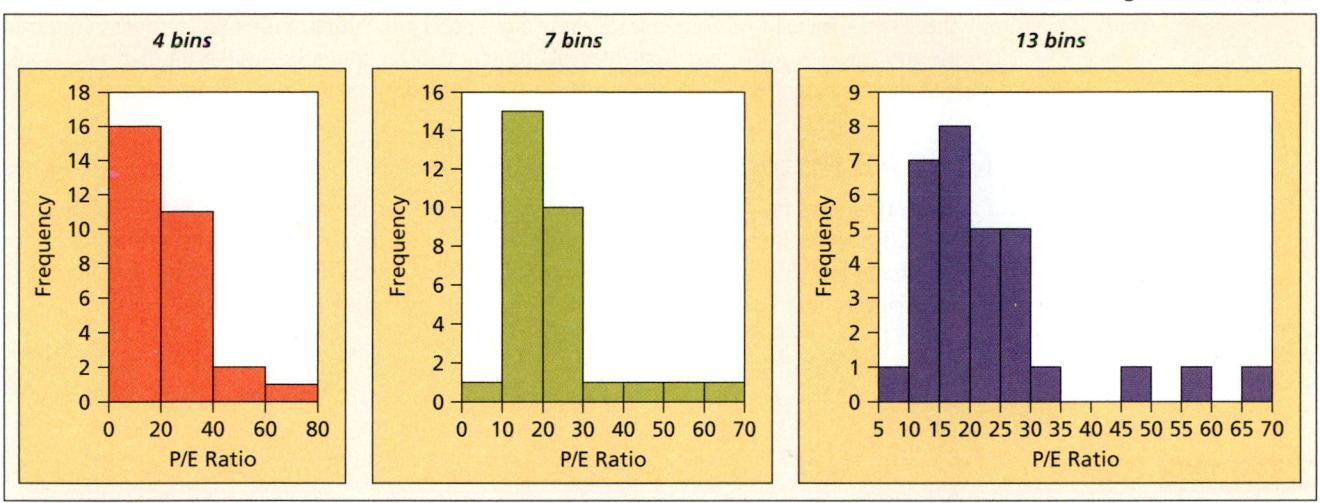

FIGURE 3.8

Excel's histogram
PERatios

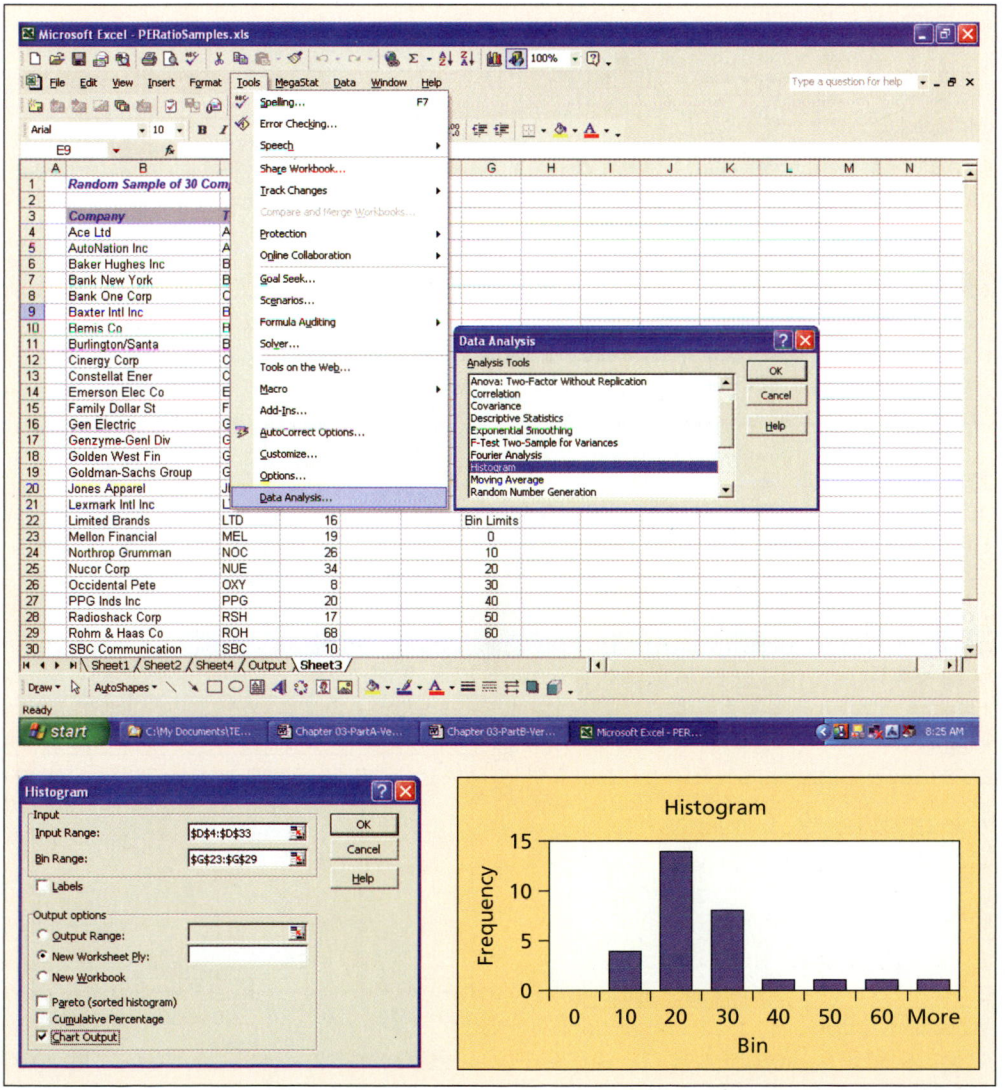

MegaStat Histograms

Figure 3.9 shows a histogram for the P/E ratios using seven bins. MegaStat shows percents on the *Y*-axis instead of frequencies. You can specify the bins with two numbers (interval width and lower limit of the first interval) or you can let MegaStat make its own decisions. MegaStat also provides a frequency distribution, including *cumulative* frequencies.

MINITAB Histograms

Figure 3.10 shows how MINITAB creates a histogram for the same data. Copy the data from the spreadsheet and paste it into MINITAB's worksheet, then choose Graphs > Histogram from the top menu bar. Let MINITAB use its default options. Once the histogram has been created, you can right-click the *X*-axis to adjust the bins, axis tick marks, and so on.

FIGURE 3.9

MegaStat frequency distribution and histogram   **PERatios**

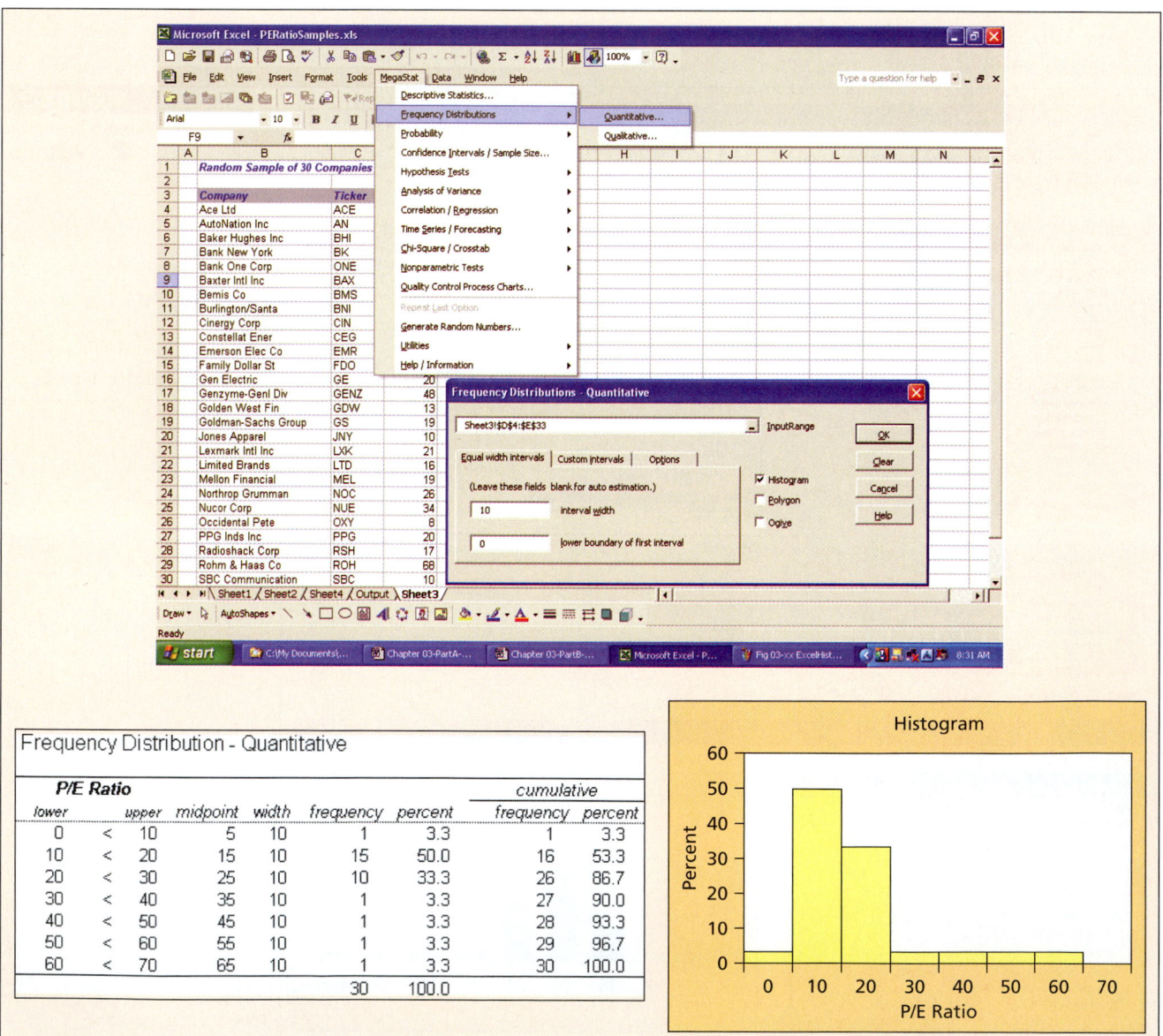

FIGURE 3.10

MINITAB histogram   🐝   **PERatios**

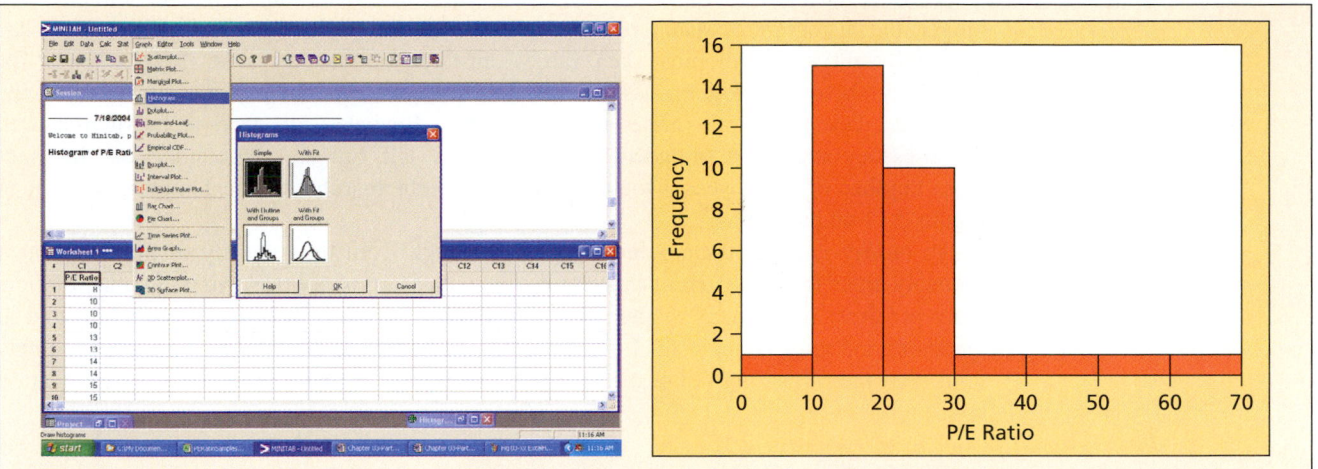

Modal Class

A *modal class* is a histogram bar that is higher than those on either side. A histogram with a single modal class is *unimodal,* one with two modal classes is *bimodal,* and one with more than two modes is *multimodal*. However, modal classes may be artifacts of the way the bin limits are chosen. It is wise to experiment with various ways of binning and to make cautious inferences about modality unless the modes are strong and invariant to binning. Figure 3.10 shows a single modal class for P/E ratios between 10 and 20.

Shape

A histogram suggests the *shape* of the population we are sampling, but, unless the sample is large, we must be cautious about making inferences. Our perception is also influenced by the

FIGURE 3.11

Prototype distribution shapes

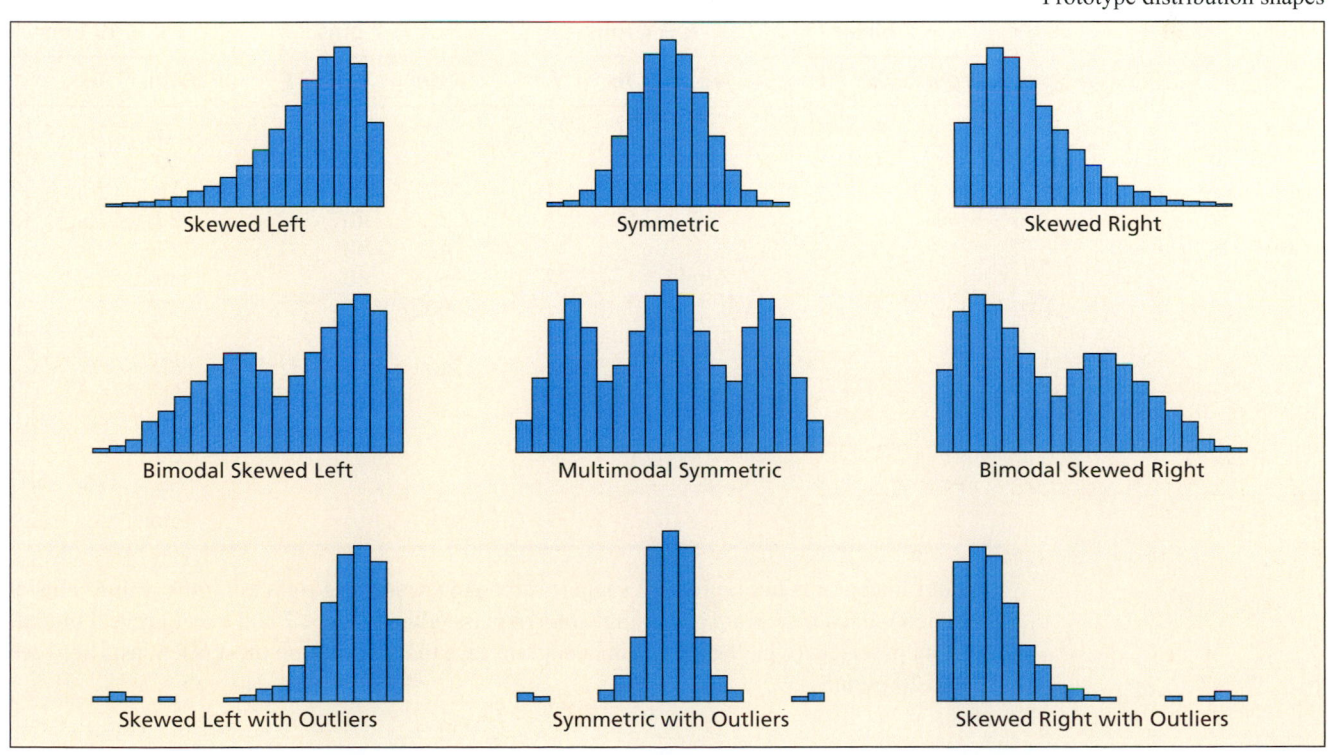

number of bins and the way the bin limits are chosen. The following terminology is helpful in discussing shape.

A histogram's *skewness* is indicated by the direction of its longer tail. If neither tail is longer, the histogram is **symmetric.** A **right-skewed** (or positively skewed) histogram has a longer right tail, with most data values clustered on the left side. A **left-skewed** (or negatively skewed) histogram has a longer left tail, with most data values clustered on the right side. Few histograms are exactly symmetric. Business data tend to be right-skewed because they are often bounded by zero on the left but are unbounded on the right (e.g., number of employees). You may find it helpful to refer to the templates shown in Figure 3.11 on page 69.

An **outlier** is an extreme value that is far enough from the majority of the data that it probably arose from a different cause or is due to measurement error. We will define outliers more precisely in the next chapter. For now, think of outliers as unusual points located in the histogram tails. None of the histograms shown so far has any obvious outliers (you may think that the 68 is "high" but it is not that much greater than the next lower observation at 55).

Mini Case   3.2

Duration of U.S. Recessions

Table 3.7 shows four "nice" ways to bin the data on the duration of 32 U.S. recessions (for details, see **Mini Case 3.1**). Most observers would think that $k = 2$ or $k = 4$ would be too few bins while $k = 13$ might be considered too many bins. Sturges would recommend using six bins, which suggests that seven bins would be the best choice. However, you can think of other valid possibilities.

TABLE 3.7   **Some Ways to Tabulate 32 Business Contractions**   **Recessions**

\(k = 2\) bins			\(k = 4\) bins			\(k = 7\) bins			\(k = 13\) bins		
From	*To*	*f*	*From*	*To*	*f*	*From*	*To*	*f*	*From*	*To*	*f*
0	35	29	0	20	25	0	10	7	5	10	7
35	70	3	20	40	5	10	20	18	10	15	10
			40	60	1	20	30	3	15	20	8
Total		32	60	80	1	30	40	2	20	25	3
						40	50	1	25	30	0
			Total		32	50	60	0	30	35	1
						60	70	1	35	40	1
									40	45	1
						Total		32	45	50	0
									50	55	0
									55	60	0
									60	65	0
									65	70	1
									Total		32

All four histograms in Figure 3.12 suggest right-skewness (long right tail, most values cluster to the left). Each histogram has a single modal class, although $k = 7$ and $k = 13$ reveal modality more precisely (e.g., the $k = 7$ bin histogram says that a recession most often lasts between 10 and 20 months).

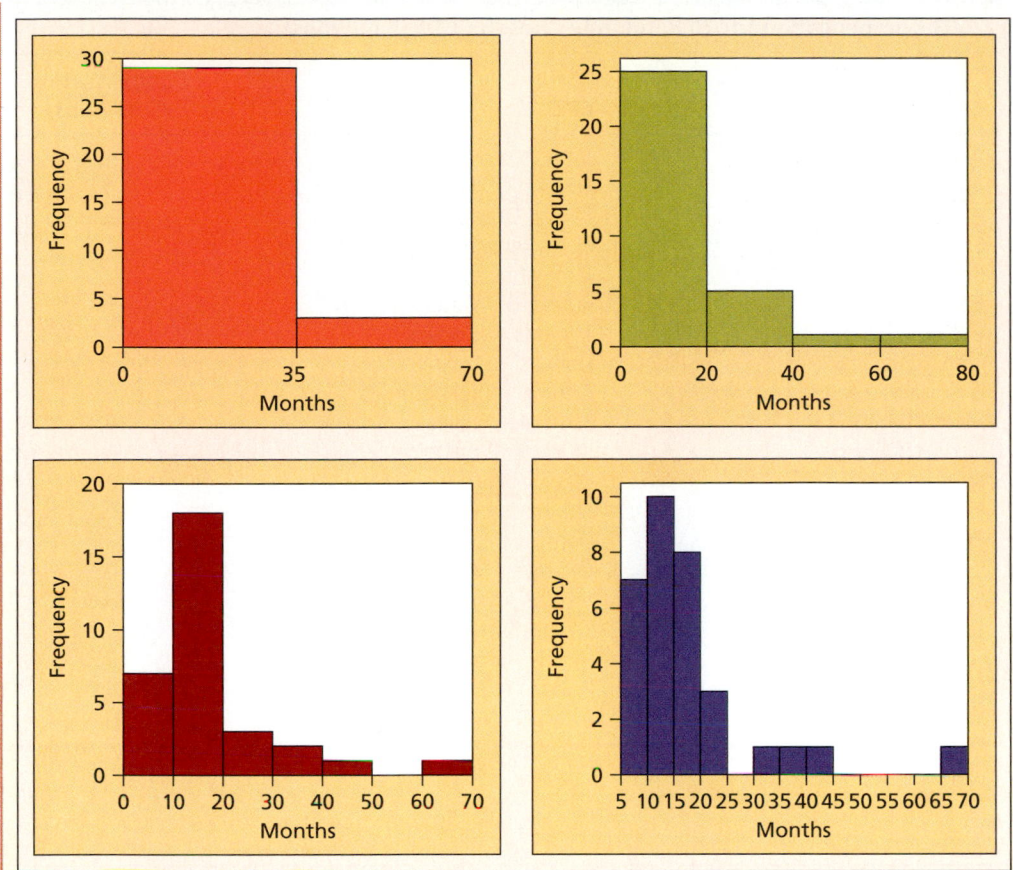

FIGURE 3.12

Histograms for 2, 4, 7, and 13 bins

SECTION EXERCISES

3.4   (a) Without using a computer, make a frequency distribution and histogram (using appropriate bins) for these 28 observations on the amount spent for dinner for four in downtown Chicago on Friday night. (b) Repeat the exercise, using a different number of bins. Which is preferred? Why?

Dinner

95	103	109	170	114	113	107
124	105	80	104	84	176	115
69	95	134	108	61	160	128
68	95	61	150	52	87	136

3.5   (a) Without using a computer, make a frequency distribution and histogram for the monthly off-campus rent paid by 30 students. (b) Repeat the exercise, using a different number of bins. Which is preferred? Why?   **Rents**

730	730	730	930	700	570
690	1030	740	620	720	670
560	740	650	660	850	930
600	620	760	690	710	500
730	800	820	840	720	700

3.6   (a) Without using a computer, make a frequency distribution and histogram for the 2003 annual compensation of these 20 randomly chosen CEO from a list of 200 top CEOs. (b) Repeat the exercise, using a different number of bins. Which is preferred? Why?   **CEOComp**

2003 Compensation for 20 Randomly Chosen CEOs ($ millions)

Company	CEO	Compensation ($ millions)
Aetna	John W. Rowe	16.9
Allstate	Edward M. Liddy	14.3
American Electric Power	E. Linn Draper, Jr.	2.1
Baxter International	H. M. Jansen Kraemer, Jr.	4.5
Bear Stearns	James E. Cayne	39.5
Cardinal Health	Robert D. Walter	13.4
Cooper Tire & Rubber	Thomas A. Dattilo	2.0
Family Dollar Stores	Howard R. Levine	2.1
Fifth Third Bancorp	George A. Schaefer, Jr.	6.0
Merrill Lynch	E. Stanley O'Neal	28.1
Harley-Davidson	Jeffrey L. Bleustein	6.7
NCR	Mark V. Hurd	2.6
PG&E	Robert D. Glynn, Jr.	20.1
Praxair	Dennis H. Reilley	5.6
Sara Lee	C. Steven McMillan	10.5
Sunoco	John G. Drosdick	8.6
Temple-Inland	Kenneth M. Jastrow II	2.5
U.S. Bancorp	Jerry A. Grundhofer	10.3
Union Pacific	Richard K. Davidson	18.6
Whirlpool	David R. Whitwam	6.6

Source: *The New York Times,* April 4, 2004, p. 8.

3.4
LINE CHARTS

Simple Line Charts

A *simple **line chart*** like the one shown in Figure 3.13 is used to display a time series, to spot trends, or to compare time periods. Line charts can be used to display several variables at once. If two variables are displayed, the right and left scales can differ, using the right scale for one variable and the left scale for the other. Excel's *two-scale line chart,* illustrated in Figure 3.14, lets you compare variables that *differ in magnitude* or are measured in *different units*. But keep in mind that someone who only glances at the chart may mistakenly conclude that both variables are of the same magnitude.

How many variables can be displayed at once on a line graph? Too much clutter ruins any visual display. If you try to display half a dozen time series variables at once, no matter how cleverly you choose symbols and graphing techniques, the result is likely to be unsatisfactory. You will have to use your judgment.

FIGURE 3.13

Line chart  **CableTV**

Source: *Statistical Abstract of the U.S., 2002,* p. 707.

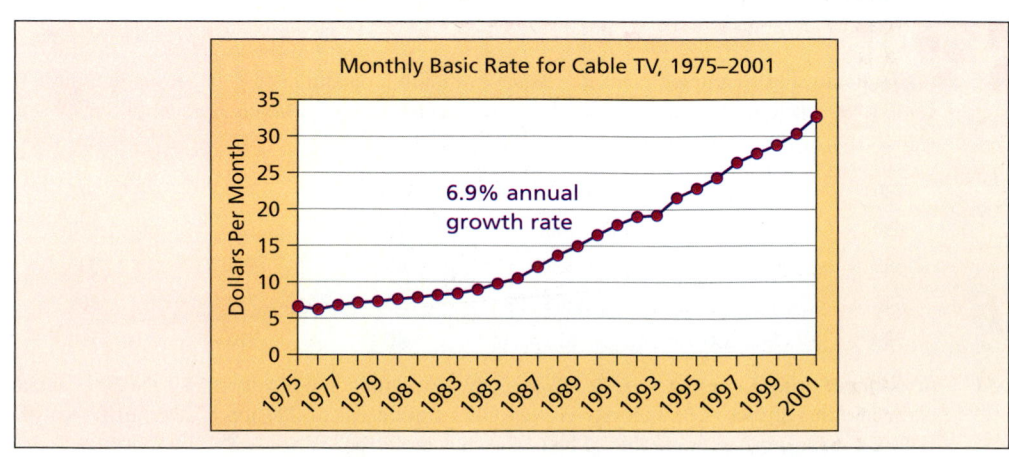

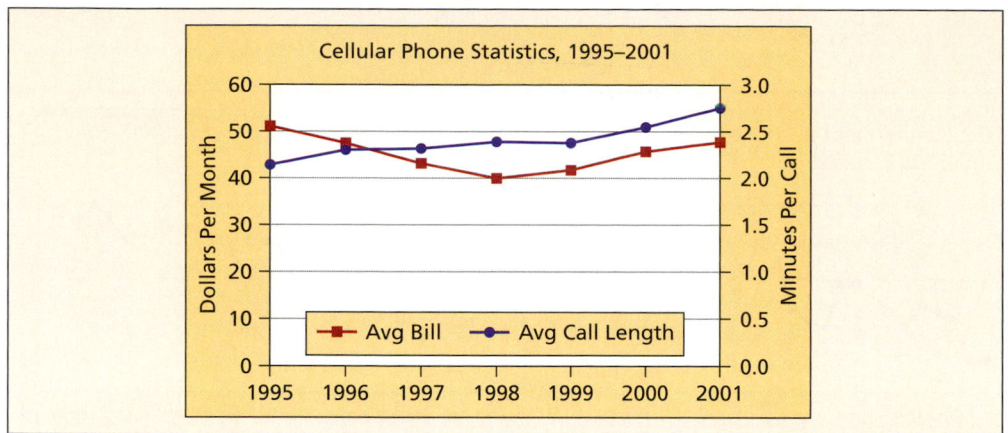

FIGURE 3.14

Two scales

CellPhones

Source: *Statistical Abstract of the U.S., 2002*, p. 710.

FIGURE 3.15

Different treatment of grid lines: (*a*) many heavy grid lines; (*b*) fewer, lighter grid lines

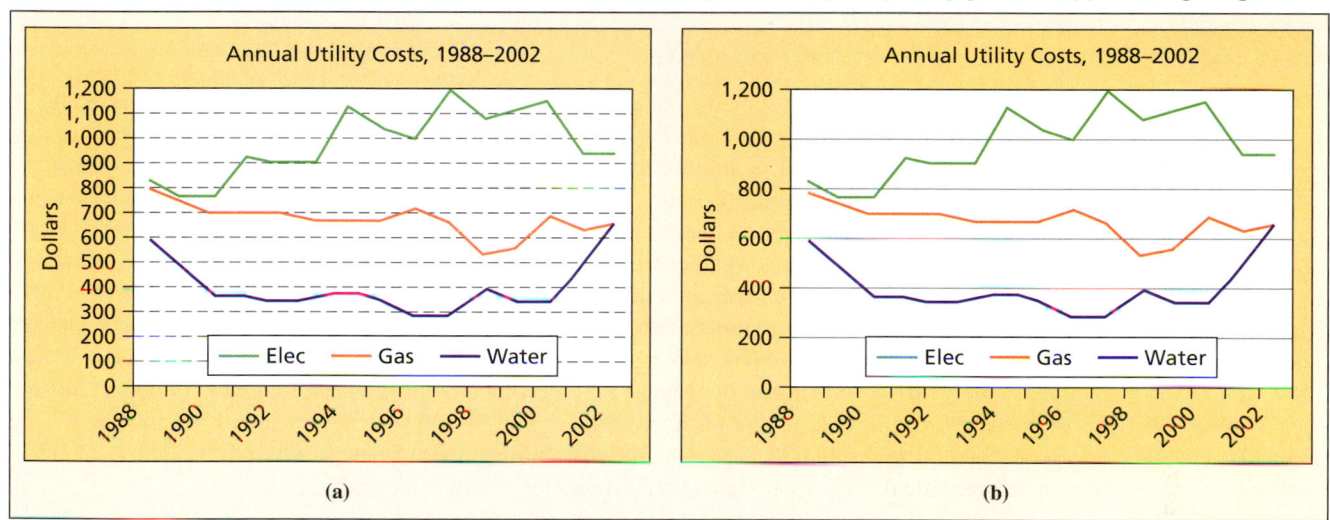

(a) (b)

Grid Lines   Utilities

A line graph usually has no vertical grid lines. What about horizontal grid lines? While grid lines do add background clutter, they make it easier to establish the *Y* value for a given year. One compromise is to use lightly colored dashed or dotted grid lines to minimize the clutter, and to increase grid line spacing, as illustrated in Figure 3.15. If the intent is to convey only a general sense of the data magnitudes, grid lines may be omitted.

Bar charts can also be used to portray time series data. Bars add a feeling of solidity and may hold the reader's attention, particularly if the reader is accustomed to bar charts. However, when you are displaying more than one time series, bar charts make it harder to see individual data values, so a line chart usually is preferred. In section 3.5 we discuss rules for bar charts. Exercise judgment to decide which type of display is most effective for the audience you are addressing.

Log Scales   BobsFunds

On the customary **arithmetic scale,** distances on the *Y*-axis are proportional to the magnitude of the variable being displayed. But on a **logarithmic scale,** equal distances represent equal *ratios* (for this reason, a log scale is sometimes called a *ratio scale*). When data vary over a wide range, say, by more than an order of magnitude (e.g., from 6 to 60), we might prefer a *log scale* for the vertical axis, to reveal more detail for small data values. For example, Figure 3.16 shows

FIGURE 3.16

Same data on different scales

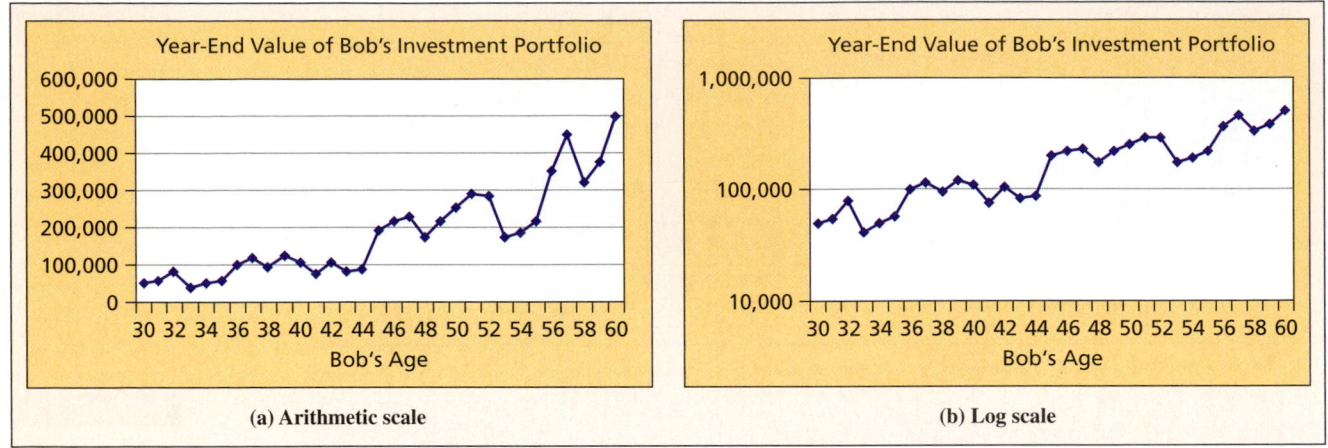

(a) Arithmetic scale   (b) Log scale

the value of an investment over a 30-year period. The data vary roughly from $50,000 to $500,000. The log scale reveals that there were substantial *relative* fluctuations in the first decade, which might go unnoticed on the arithmetic scale. The log scale also shows that the larger *absolute* fluctuations in the most recent decade are actually similar to those in the first decade in *relative* terms.

A log graph reveals whether the quantity is growing at an *increasing percent* (concave upward), *constant percent* (straight line), or *declining percent* (concave downward). On the arithmetic scale, Bob's investment appears to grow at an increasing rate, but on the log scale it is roughly a straight line. Thus, Bob's investment seems to be growing at a *constant percent rate* (the yearly average rate is actually 7.25 percent). On a log scale, *equal distances* represent *equal ratios*. That is, the distance from 10,000 to 100,000 is the same as the distance from 100,000 to 1,000,000. Since logarithms are undefined for negative or zero values (try it on your calculator), a log scale is only suited for positive data values.

When to Use Log Scales   A log scale is useful for time series data that might be expected to grow at a compound annual percentage rate (e.g., GDP, the national debt, or your future income). Log scales are common in financial charts that cover long periods of time or for data that grow rapidly (e.g., revenues for a start-up company). Some experts feel that corporate annual reports and stock prospectuses should avoid ratio scales, on the grounds that they may be misleading to uninformed individuals. But then how can we fairly portray data that vary by orders of magnitude? Should investors become better informed? The bottom line is that business students must understand log scales, because they are sure to run into them.

EXAMPLE

U.S. Trade

 **USTrade**

Figure 3-17 shows the U.S. balance of trade. The arithmetic scale shows that growth has been exponential. Yet, although exports and imports are increasing in absolute terms, the log graph suggests that the *growth rate* in both series may be slowing, because the log graph is slightly concave downward. On the log graph, the recently increasing trade deficit is not *relatively* as large. Regardless how it is displayed, the trade deficit remains a concern for policymakers, for fear that foreigners may no longer wish to purchase U.S. debt instruments to finance the trade deficit (see *The Wall Street Journal,* July 24, 2005, p. Cl).

FIGURE 3.17

Comparison of arithmetic and log scales

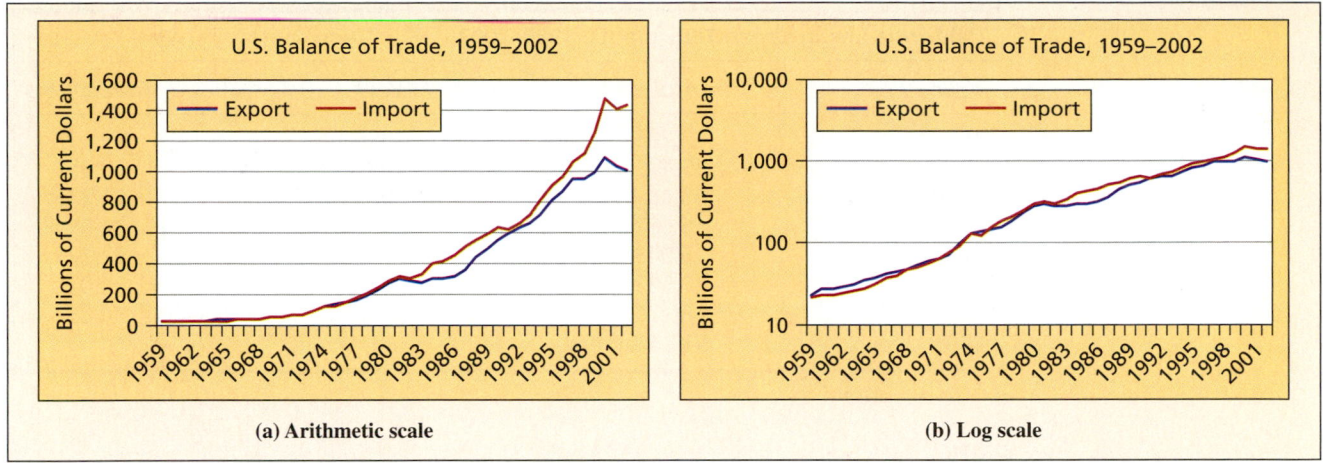

(a) Arithmetic scale   (b) Log scale

Tips for Effective Line Charts

Here are some general tips to keep in mind when creating line charts:

1. Line charts are used for *time series data* (never for cross-sectional data).

2. The numerical variable is shown on the *Y*-axis, while the time units go on the *X*-axis with time increasing from left to right. Business audiences expect this rule to be followed.

3. Except for log scales, use a zero origin on the *Y*-axis (this is the default in Excel) unless more detail is needed. The zero-origin rule is mandatory for a corporate annual report or investor stock prospectus.

4. To avoid graph clutter, numerical labels usually are *omitted* on a line chart, especially when the data cover many time periods. Use gridlines to help the reader read data values.

5. Data markers (squares, triangles, circles) are helpful. But when the series has many data values or when many variables are being displayed, they clutter the graph.

6. If the lines on the graph are too thick, the reader can't ascertain graph values.

SECTION EXERCISES

3.7 Use Excel to prepare a line chart to display the lightning death data. Modify the default colors, fonts, etc., as you judge appropriate to make the display effective.

U.S. Deaths by Lightning, 1940–2000   **Lightning**

Year	Deaths	Year	Deaths
1940	340	1975	91
1945	268	1980	74
1950	219	1985	74
1955	181	1990	74
1960	129	1995	85
1965	149	2000	51
1970	122		

Source: *Statistical Abstract of the United States, 2003.*

3.8   Use Excel to prepare a line chart to display the following transplant data. Modify the default colors, fonts, etc., to make the display effective.

California Living Organ Transplants, 1988–2002 🔆 Transplants			
Year	**Transplants**	**Year**	**Transplants**
1988	12,786	1996	19,518
1989	13,471	1997	20,052
1990	15,462	1998	21,223
1991	15,687	1999	21,594
1992	16,043	2000	22,773
1993	17,533	2001	24,076
1994	18,170	2002	24,851
1995	19,218		

Source: www.gsds.org.

3.5
BAR CHARTS

Plain Bar Charts 🔆 Tires

The *bar chart* is probably the most common type of data display in business. Attribute data is typically displayed using a bar chart. Each bar represents a category or attribute. The length of each bar reflects the frequency of that category. Each bar has a label showing a category or time period. Figure 3.18 shows simple bar charts comparing market shares among tire manufacturers. Each bar is separated from its neighbors by a slight gap to improve legibility (you can control gap width in Excel). *Vertical* bar charts are the most common, but *horizontal* bar charts can be useful when the axis labels are long or when there are many categories.

3-D and Novelty Bar Charts 🔆 Tires

This same data can be displayed in a *3-D bar chart,* shown in Figure 3.19. Many observers feel that the illusion of depth adds to the visual impact. The depth effect is mostly harmless in terms of bar proportions, but it does introduce ambiguity in bar height. Do we measure from the back of the bar or from the front? For a general readership (e.g., *USA Today*) 3-D charts are common, but in business they are rare. Novelty bar charts like the *pyramid chart* in Figure 3.20 are charming but should be avoided because they distort the bar volume and make it hard to measure bar height.

FIGURE 3.18

Same data displayed two ways

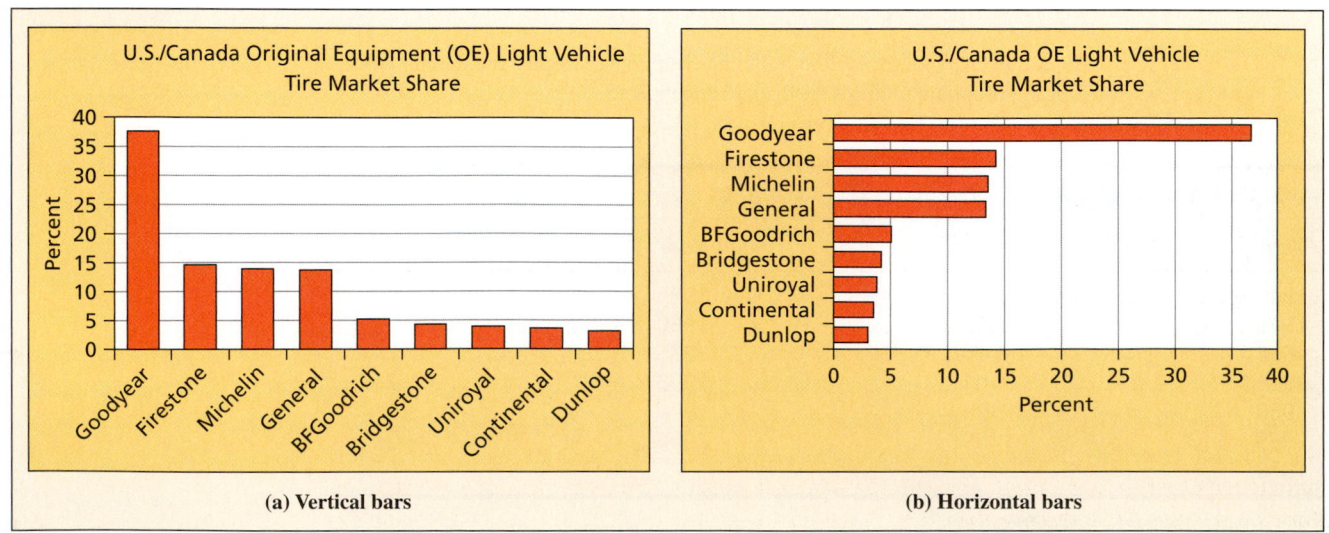

Source: www.mtdealer.com.

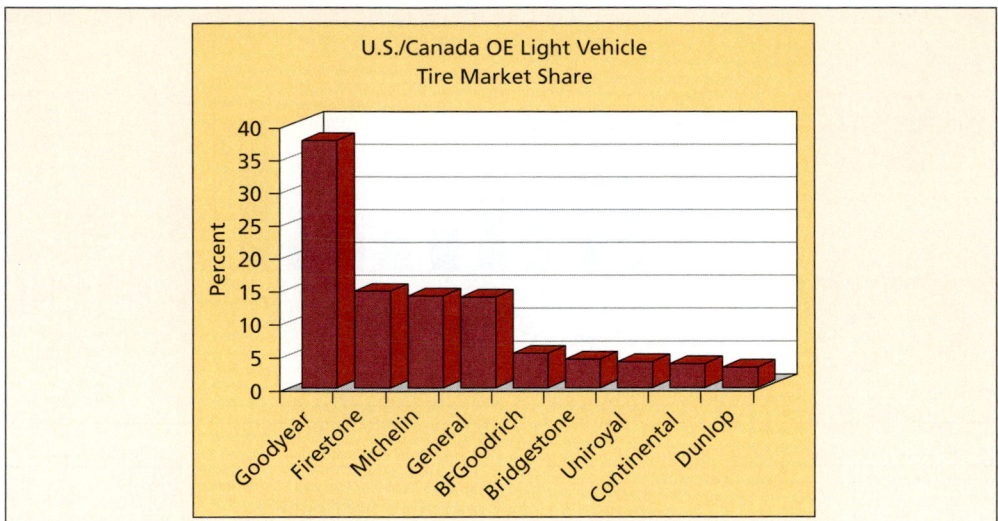

FIGURE 3.19

3-D bar chart

Source: www.mtdealer.com.

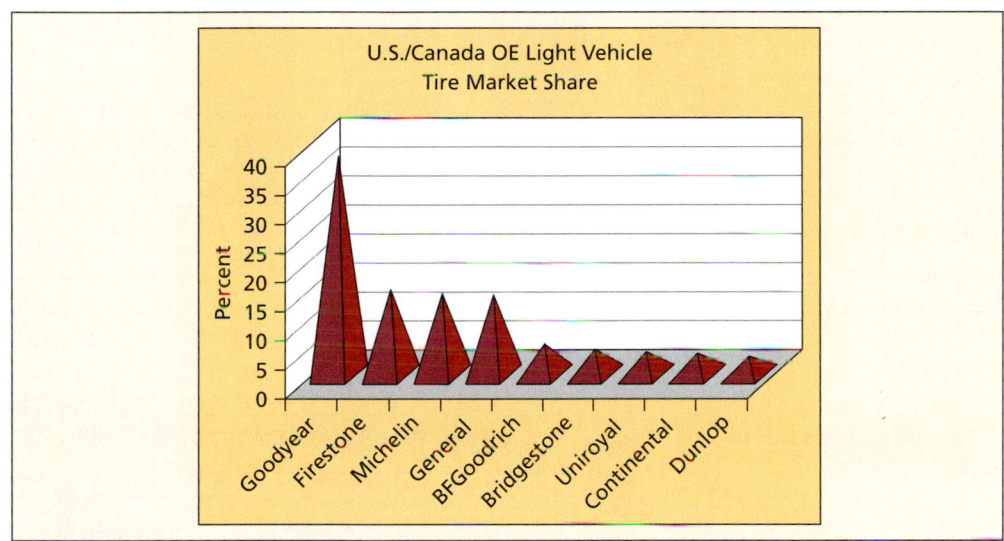

FIGURE 3.20

Pyramid chart (avoid it)

Source: www.mtdealer.com.

Pareto Charts

A special type of bar chart used frequently in business is the ***Pareto chart.*** Pareto charts are used in quality management to display the *frequency* of defects or errors of different types. Categories are displayed in descending order of frequency, so that the most common errors or defects appear first. This helps managers focus on the *significant few* (i.e., only a few categories typically account for most of the defects or errors).

Figure 3.21 shows a Pareto chart for paint and body defects in a sample of 50 new vehicles that were inspected. Defects were recorded by body location (e.g., right front door) using a checklist of 60 possible body locations. There were 44 defects altogether (many of them minor). The "top 9" locations accounted for 82 percent of the total defects (36 out of the 44 defects). The "Other" category contains 8 defects that each occurred once, spread out among the other 51 body locations. The company can concentrate its quality improvement efforts on the "top 9" body locations. The Pareto chart is attractive because it is easy to understand and is directly relevant to business tasks.

FIGURE 3.21

Pareto chart

👁 **BodyDefects**

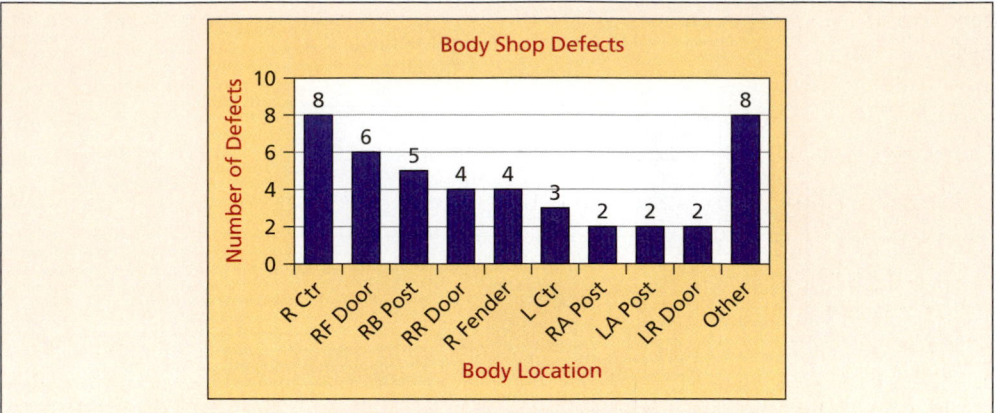

FIGURE 3.22

Stacked bar chart

👁 **MedSchools**

Source: *Modern Healthcare* 30, no. 45 (October 30, 2000), p. 16.

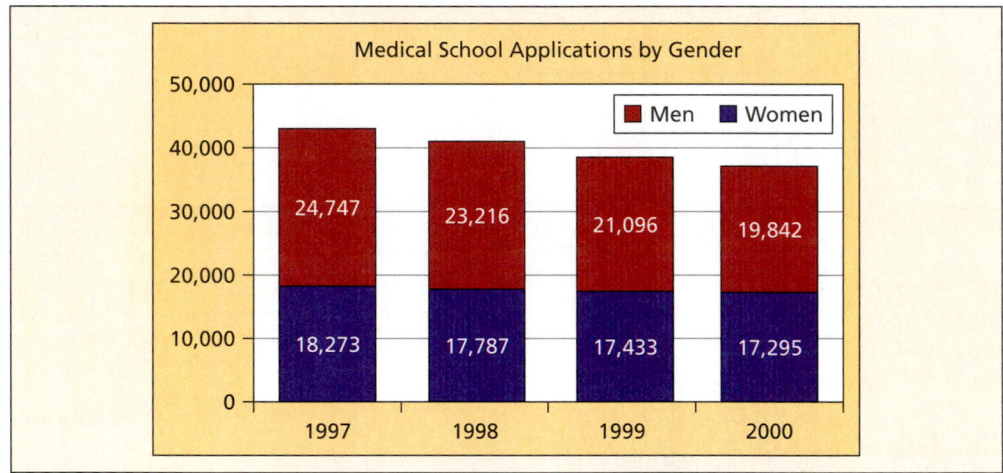

FIGURE 3.23

Same data on (*a*) line chart and (*b*) bar chart

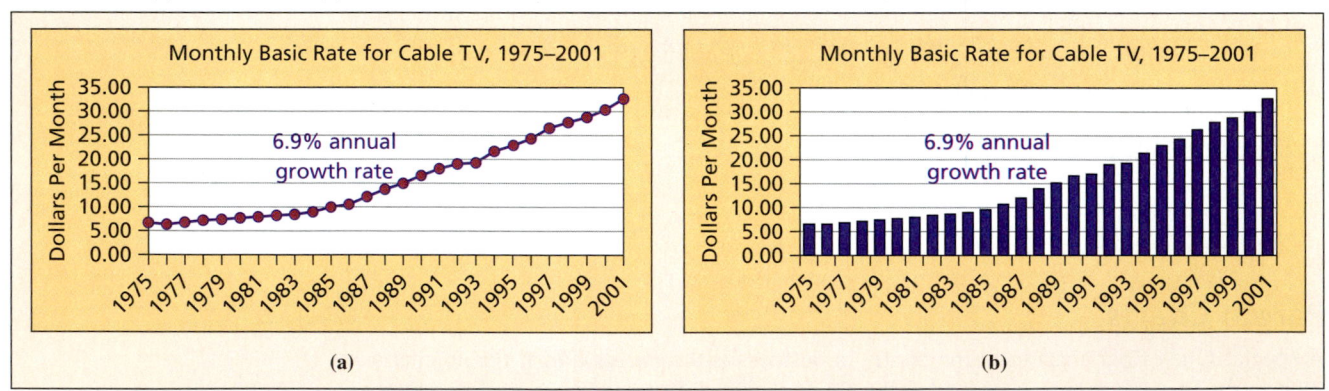

Source: *Statistical Abstract of the United States, 2002,* p. 707.

Stacked Bar Chart

In a ***stacked bar chart*** like Figure 3.22, the bar height is the sum of several subtotals. Areas may be compared by color to show patterns in the subgroups, as well as showing the total. Stacked bar charts can be effective for any number of groups but work best when you have only a few. Use numerical labels if exact data values are of importance.

Bar Charts for Time Series Data

You can use a bar chart for time series data. Figure 3.23 shows the same data, first in a line chart, and then in a bar chart. Some people feel that the solid bars give a clearer sense of the trend. However, if you have more than one time series, it is harder to compare trends on a bar chart.

Tips for Effective Bar Charts

The following guidelines will help you to create the most effective bar charts:

1. The numerical variable of interest usually is shown with vertical bars on the *Y*-axis, while the category labels go on the *X*-axis.

2. If the quantity displayed is a time series, the category labels (e.g., years) are displayed on the horizontal *X*-axis with time increasing from left to right.

3. The height or length of each bar should be proportional to the quantity displayed. This is easy, since most software packages default to a zero origin on a bar graph. The zero-origin rule is essential for a corporate annual report or investor stock prospectus (e.g., to avoid overstating earnings). However, nonzero origins may be justified to reveal sufficient detail.

4. Put numerical values at the top of each bar, except when labels would impair legibility (e.g., lots of bars) or when visual simplicity is needed (e.g., for a general audience).

SECTION EXERCISES

3.9 (a) Use Excel to prepare a line chart to display the following rural population data. Modify the default colors, fonts, etc., to make the display effective. (b) Right-click the chart area and change it to a *2-D bar chart*. Modify the display if necessary to make the display attractive. Do you prefer the line chart or bar chart? Why? *Hint:* Use years as *X*-axis labels. After the chart is completed, you can right-click the chart area, choose Source Data, and insert the range for the years in the Category (X) axis labels box.

U.S. Population in Rural Areas, 1800–2000	RuralPop
Year	**Percent**
1800	93.9
1850	84.6
1900	60.4
1950	36.0
2000	17.4

Source: U.S. Populations in rural areas table from *Scientific American* 291, no. 8 (August 2004), p. 27. Copyright © 2004 Rodger Doyle. Used with permission.

3.10 (a) Use Excel to prepare a *2-D vertical bar chart* for revenue per employee (the last column) for these four aerospace companies. Modify the colors, fonts, etc., to make the display effective. (b) Right-click the chart area, choose Chart Type, and change your graph to a *2-D horizontal bar chart*. Modify the chart if necessary to make it attractive. Do you prefer the vertical or horizontal bar chart? Why? (c) Right-click on your graph, choose Chart Type, and change your graph to a *3-D vertical bar chart*. Modify the chart if necessary to make it attractive. Is 3-D better than 2-D? Why? (d) Right-click the data series, choose Format Data Series, and add labels to the data. Do the labels help?

Revenue and Employees of the Four Largest Aerospace Companies			Aerospace
Company	**Revenues ($ millions)**	**Employees**	**Revenue per Employee ($)**
Boeing	50,485	157,000	321,560
Lockheed Martin	31,844	130,000	244,954
United Technologies	31,034	203,300	152,651
Northrop-Grumman	28,686	122,600	233,980

Source: *Fortune* 500 April 5, 2004 issue. Copyright © 2005 Time, Inc. All rights reserved.

3.11   (a) Use Excel to prepare a *stacked bar chart* for in-car use and noncar use of cell phones. Modify the colors, fonts, etc., to make the display effective. (b) Right-click the data series, choose Format Data Series, and add labels to the data. Do the labels help? *Hint:* Use only the first two data columns (not the total).

Annual U.S. Wireless Phone Usage (billions of minutes)  **Wireless**			
Year	In-Car Use	NonCar Use	Total
2000	187	87	274
2001	312	191	503
2002	324	346	670
2003	400	512	912

Source: © Dow Jones & Co., Inc. Used with permission.

3.6 SCATTER PLOTS

A *scatter plot* shows *n* pairs of observations $(x_1, y_1), (x_2, y_2), \ldots, (x_n, y_n)$ as dots (or some other symbol) on an *X-Y* graph. This type of display is so important in statistics that it deserves careful attention. A scatter plot is a starting point for bivariate data analysis. We create scatter plots to investigate the relationship between two variables. Typically, we would like to know if there is an *association* between two variables and if so, what kind of association exists. As we did with univariate data analysis, let's look at a scatter plot to see what we can observe.

EXAMPLE

Birth Rates and Life Expectancy

Table 3.8 shows the *birth rate* and *life expectancy* for nine randomly selected nations. Figure 3.24 shows a scatter plot with life expectancy on the *X*-axis and birth rates on the *Y*-axis. In this illustration, there seems to be an association between *X* and *Y*. That is, nations with higher birth rates tend to have lower life expectancy (and vice versa). No cause-and-effect relationship is implied, since in this example both variables could be influenced by a third variable that is not mentioned (e.g., GDP per capita). As with a dot plot, comments can be added. Here, nations with the lowest and highest life expectancy have been labeled. It is impractical to label all the data points.

TABLE 3.8 Birth Rates and Life Expectancy (*n* = 9 nations)  **LifeExp**		
Nation	Birth Rate (per 1,000)	Life Expectancy (years)
Afghanistan	41.03	46.60
Canada	11.09	79.70
Finland	10.60	77.80
Guatemala	34.17	66.90
Japan	10.03	80.90
Mexico	22.36	72.00
Pakistan	30.40	62.70
Spain	9.29	79.10
United States	14.10	77.40

Source: *The CIA World Factbook 2003*, www.cia.gov.

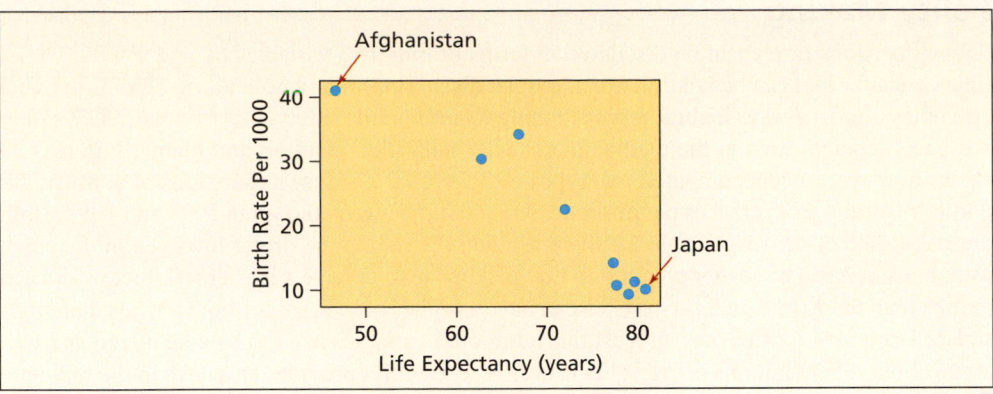

FIGURE 3.24

Scatter plot of birth rates and life expectancy ($n = 9$)

EXAMPLE

Aircraft Fuel Consumption

Table 3.9 shows five observations on flight time and fuel consumption for a twin-engine Piper Cheyenne aircraft. This time, a causal relationship between these two variables is assumed, since longer flights would consume more fuel.

TABLE 3.9	Flight Time and Fuel Consumption	Cheyenne
Trip Leg	**Flight Time (hours)**	**Fuel Used (pounds)**
1	2.3	145
2	4.2	258
3	3.6	219
4	4.7	276
5	4.9	283

Source: *Flying* 130, no. 4 (April 2003), p. 99.

Figure 3.25 shows a strong association. The pattern seen on the scatter plot appears to be a line. Because the linear pattern shows that, as flight time increases, fuel consumption increases, we say that the pattern is positive. Later, you will learn about describing this relationship by using statistics.

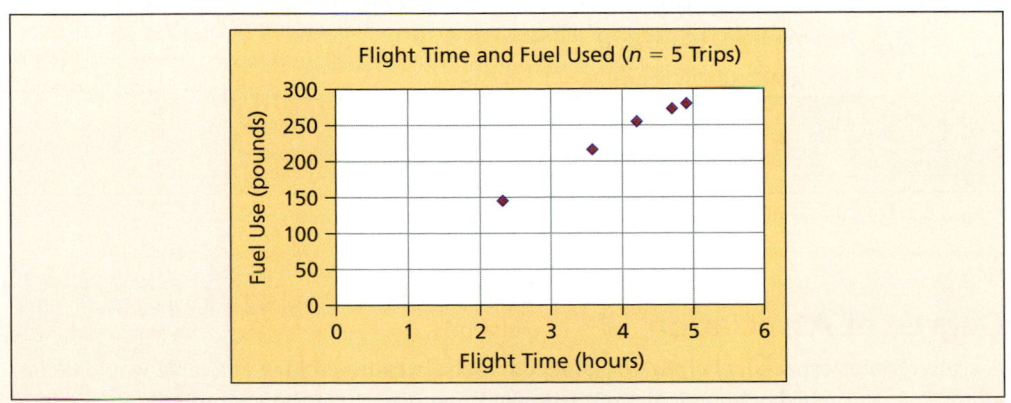

FIGURE 3.25

Excel scatter plot

Policy Making

Policy decisions rarely can be discussed in terms of only two variables (X and Y), but sometimes a scatter plot can be helpful. For example, discussions about policies on automotive fuel efficiency almost always include issues relating to automobile safety. In particular, SUV safety has been debated often in the media, and usually with high emotion and blame. Figure 3.26 shows how researchers compared two types of SUV risk. The researchers looked at traffic fatalities resulting from crashes per million vehicles sold between the years 1995 and 1999. Both the risk to the driver responsible for the crash and the risk to the driver involved in the crash were considered. The scatter plot shows that pickups tend to have a higher risk factor for both parties than many mid-size cars. SUVs can have a higher risk factor for both parties than mid-size or large cars. Critics may suggest that additional variables need to be considered and will argue about the definitions of "risk." However, a scatter plot provides structure to the dialogue and can serve as a step toward a rational analysis of the decisions being faced and the issues surrounding those decisions.

FIGURE 3.26

Automobile risks

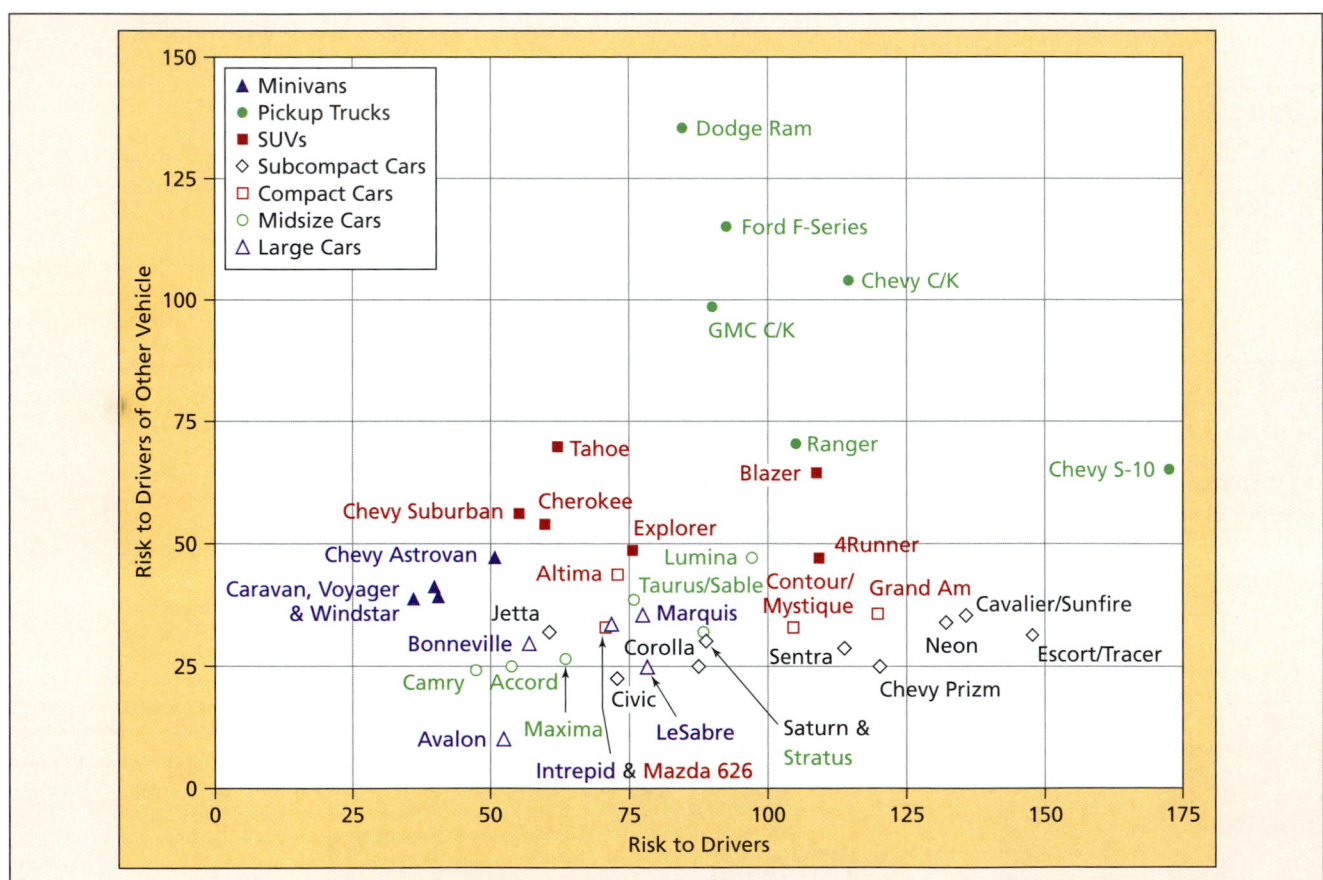

Source: http://enews.lbl.gov/Science-Articles/Archive/EETD-SUV-Safety-newWin.html.

Degree of Association 🐾 Correlations

A scatter plot is especially helpful for larger data sets, because looking at a table would be unlikely to reveal whether an association between Y and X exists or how strong the association might be. Figures 3.27 through 3.30 illustrate different degrees of association in larger data sets.

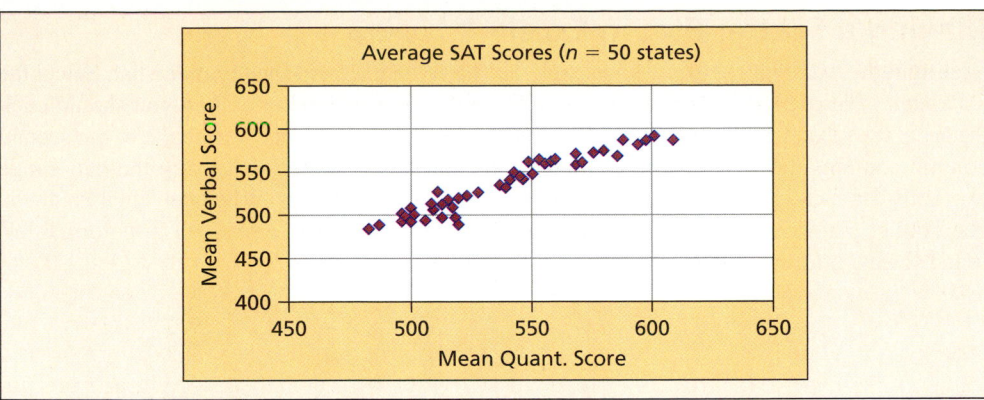

FIGURE 3.27

Very strong association

Source: *National Center for Education Statistics.*

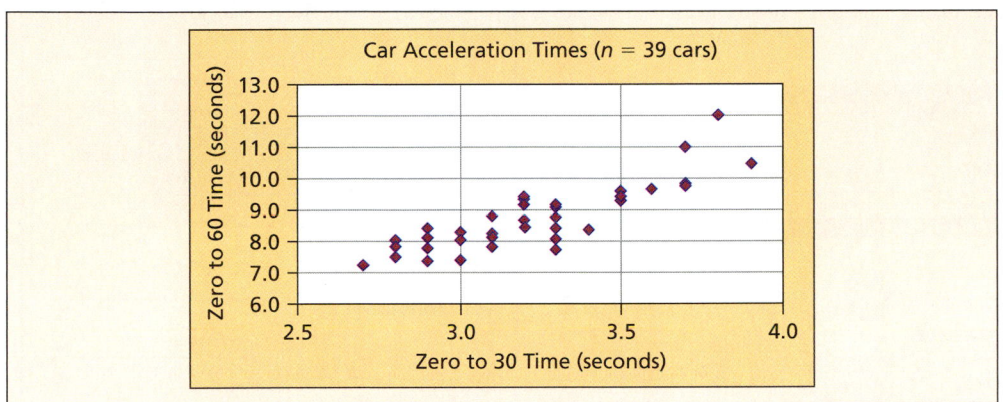

FIGURE 3.28

Strong association

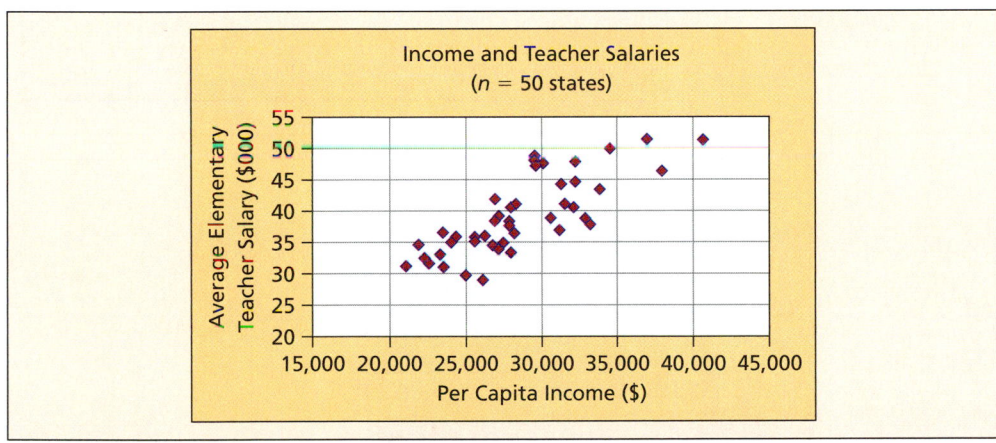

FIGURE 3.29

Moderate association

Source: *Statistical Abstract of the United States, 2001*, p. 151.

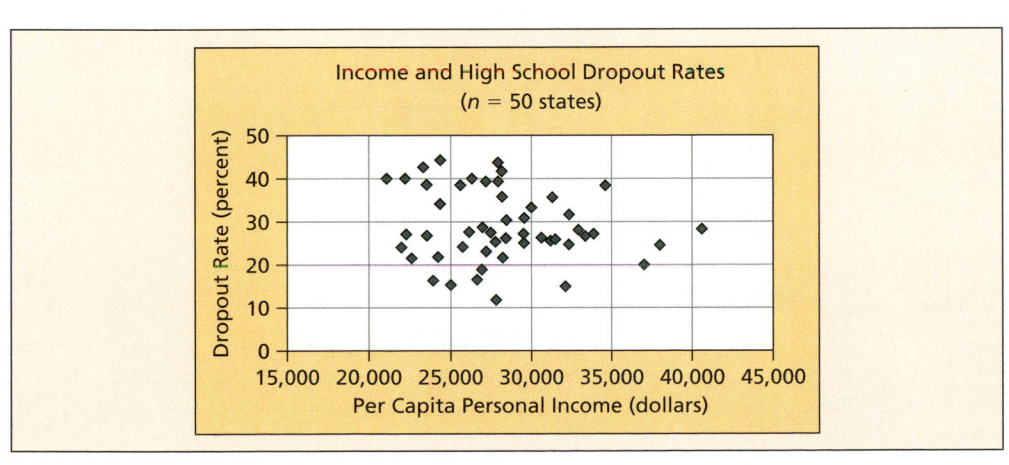

FIGURE 3.30

Little or no association

Source: *Statistical Abstract of the United States, 2001*, p. 141.

Making a Scatter Plot in Excel   LifeExp

Highlight the two data columns. Then click the Chart Wizard icon in the top menu bar. Select the XY(Scatter) (scatter plot) option, as shown in Figure 3.31. After you click Next you should click the Series tab. Excel assumes that the first column contains the *X*-axis variable and the second column contains the *Y*-axis variable. Since we want the opposite, we specify the data range explicitly for each variable in the X values and Y values dialogue boxes. When you click Finish you get a rather plain scatter plot (see Figure 3.32). However, you can embellish it (colors, titles, fonts, scales, gridlines, etc.) to your liking, as in Figure 3.33.

FIGURE 3.31

Setting up the Excel scatter plot

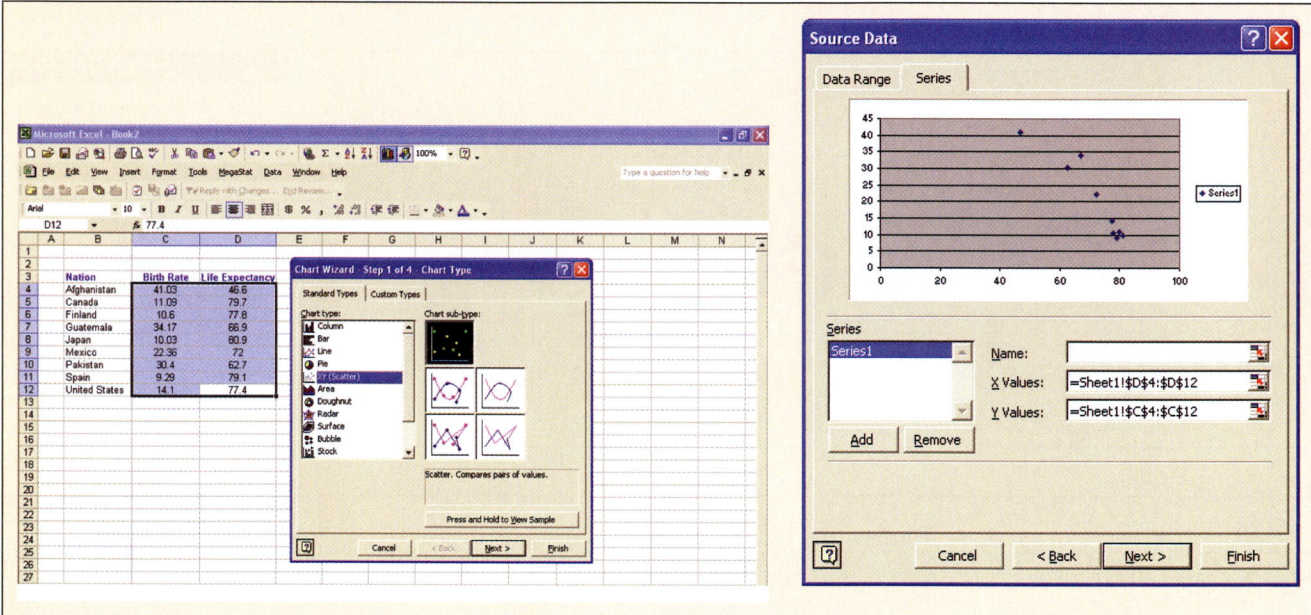

FIGURE 3.32

Excel's default graph

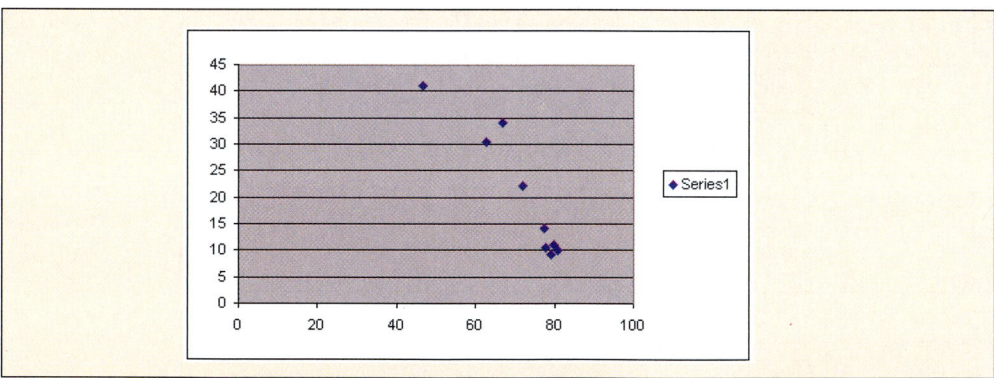

FIGURE 3.33

Embellished graph

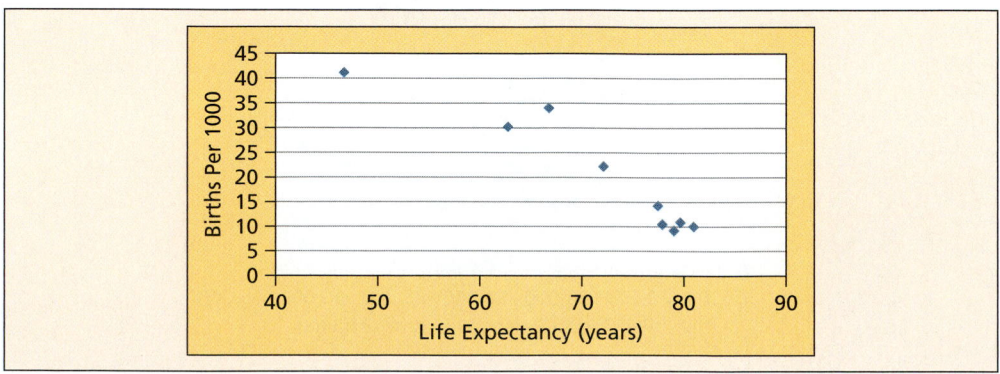

SECTION EXERCISES

3.12 (a) Use Excel to make a scatter plot of these vehicle data, placing Weight on the X-axis and City MPG on the Y-axis. Add titles and modify the default colors, fonts, etc., as you judge appropriate to make the scatter plot effective. (b) Describe the relationship (if any) between X and Y. Weak? Strong? Negative? Positive? Linear? Nonlinear?

Weight and MPG for 20 Randomly Selected Vehicles   **CityMPG**

Vehicle	City MPG	Weight (lbs.)
Acura TSX	23	3,320
BMW 3-Series	19	3,390
Chevrolet Corvette	19	3,255
Chevrolet Silverado 1500	14	4,935
Chrysler Pacifica	17	4,660
Dodge Caravan	18	4,210
Ford Focus	26	2,760
Infiniti FX	16	4,295
Jaguar XJ8	18	3,805
Lexus IS300	18	3,390
Lincoln Aviator	13	5,000
Mazda 6	19	3,355
Land Rover Freelander	17	3,640
Mercedes-Benz S-Class	17	4,195
Nissan 350Z	20	3,345
Nissan Xterra	16	4,315
Pontiac Vibe	28	2,805
Pontiac Grand Am	25	3,095
Toyota Sienna	19	4,120
Volvo C70	20	3,690

Source: © 2003 by Consumers Union of U.S., Inc. Yonkers, NY, a nonprofit organization. From *Consumer Reports New Car Buying Guide, 2003–2004.* Used with permission.

3.13 (a) Use Excel to make a scatter plot of the following exam score data, placing Midterm on the X-axis and Final on the Y-axis. Add titles and modify the default colors, fonts, etc., as you judge appropriate to make the scatter plot effective. (b) Describe the relationship (if any) between X and Y. Weak? Strong? Negative? Positive? Linear? Nonlinear?

Exam Scores for 18 Statistics Students   **ExamScores**

Name	Midterm Score	Final Score	Name	Midterm Score	Final Score
Aaron	50	30	Joe	68	83
Angela	95	83	Lisa	75	58
Brandon	75	90	Liz	70	83
Buck	60	83	Michele	60	73
Carole	60	75	Nancy	88	78
Cecilia	63	45	Ryan	93	100
Charles	90	100	Tania	73	83
Dmitri	88	90	Ursula	33	53
Ellie	75	68	Xiaodong	60	70

3.14 (a) Use Excel to make a scatter plot of the data, placing Floor Space on the X-axis and Weekly Sales on the Y-axis. Add titles and modify the default colors, fonts, etc., as you judge appropriate to make the scatter plot effective. (b) Describe the relationship (if any) between X and Y. Weak? Strong? Negative? Positive? Linear? Nonlinear?   **FloorSpace**

Floor Space (sq. ft.)	Weekly Sales (dollars)
6,060	16,380
5,230	14,400
4,280	13,820
5,580	18,230
5,670	14,200
5,020	12,800
5,410	15,840
4,990	16,610
4,220	13,610
4,160	10,050
4,870	15,320
5,470	13,270

3.15 (a) Use Excel to make a scatter plot of the data for bottled water sales for 10 weeks, placing **Price** on the X-axis and **Units Sold** on the Y-axis. Add titles and modify the default colors, fonts, etc., as you judge appropriate to make the scatter plot effective. (b) Describe the relationship (if any) between X and Y. Weak? Strong? Negative? Positive? Linear? Nonlinear?  **WaterSold**

Unit Price	Units Sold
1.15	186
0.94	216
1.04	173
1.05	182
1.08	183
1.33	150
0.99	190
1.25	165
1.16	190
1.11	201

3.7
TABLES

Tables are the simplest form of data display, yet creating effective tables is an acquired skill. By arranging numbers in rows and columns, their meaning can be enhanced so it can be understood at a glance.

EXAMPLE

School Expenditures

Table 3.10 is a *compound table* that contains time series data (going down the columns) on seven variables (going across the rows). The data can be viewed in several ways. We can focus on the time pattern (going down the columns) or on comparing public and private spending (between columns) for a given school level (elementary/secondary or college/ university). Or we can compare spending by school level (elementary/secondary or college/ university) for a given type of control (public or private). Figures are rounded to three or four significant digits to make it easier for the reader. Units of measurement are stated in the footnote to keep the column headings simple. Columns are grouped using merged heading cells (blank columns could be inserted to add vertical separation). Presentation tables can be linked dynamically to spreadsheets so that slides can be updated quickly, but take care that data changes do not adversely affect the table layout.

TABLE 3.10   School Expenditures by Control and Level, 1960–2000      **Schools**

Year	All Schools	Elementary and Secondary			Colleges and Universities		
		Total	Public	Private	Total	Public	Private
1960	142.2	99.6	93.0	6.6	42.6	23.3	19.3
1970	317.3	200.2	188.6	11.6	117.2	75.2	41.9
1980	373.6	232.7	216.4	16.2	140.9	93.4	47.4
1990	526.1	318.5	293.4	25.1	207.6	132.9	74.7
2000	691.9	418.2	387.8	30.3	273.8	168.8	105.0

Source: U.S. Census Bureau, *Statistical Abstract of the United States, 2002*, p. 133.

Note: All figures are in billions of constant 2000–2001 dollars.

Tips for Effective Tables

Here are some tips for creating effective tables:

1. Keep the table simple, consistent with its purpose. Put summary tables in the *main body* of the written report and detailed tables in an *appendix*. In a slide presentation, the main point of the table should be clear to the reader within *10 seconds*. If not, break the table into parts or aggregate the data.

2. Display the data to be compared in columns rather than rows. Research shows that people find it easier to compare across rather than down.

3. For presentation purposes, round off to three or four significant digits (e.g., 142 rather than 142.213). People mentally round numbers anyway. Exceptions: when accounting requirements supersede the desire for rounding or when the numbers are used in subsequent calculations.

4. Physical table layout should guide the eye toward the comparison you wish to emphasize. Spaces or shading may be used to separate rows or columns. Use lines sparingly.

5. Row and column headings should be simple yet descriptive.

6. Within a column, use a consistent number of decimal digits. Right-justify or decimal-align the data unless all field widths are the same within the column.

An Oft-Abused Chart   **PieCharts**

Many statisticians feel that a table or bar chart is a better choice than a *pie chart* for several reasons. But, because of their visual appeal, pie charts appear daily in company annual reports and the popular press (e.g., *USA Today, The Wall Street Journal, Scientific American*) so you must understand their uses and misuses. A pie chart can only convey a *general idea of the data* because it is hard to assess areas precisely. It should have only a few slices (e.g., two or three) and the slices should be labeled with data values or percents. The only correct use of a pie chart is to *portray data which sum to a total* (e.g., percent market shares). A simple 2-D pie chart is best, as in Figure 3.34. *The Wall Street Journal* used this chart to illustrate an article explaining that most small businesses do not plan to hire very many employees. A bar chart (Figure 3.35) could be used to display the same data.

Pie Chart Options   **PieCharts**

Exploded and *3-D* pie charts (Figures 3.36 and 3.37) add visual interest, but the sizes of pie slices are even harder to assess. Nonetheless, you will see 3-D charts in business publications because of their strong visual impact. Black-and-white charts may be used internally in business, but color is typically preferred for customers, stockholders, or investors. Practices may change as color copiers become more cost-effective.

3.8

PIE CHARTS

FIGURE 3.34

2-D pie with labels

Source: From *The Wall Street Journal*, July 27, 2004. © Dow Jones & Co., Inc. Used with permission.

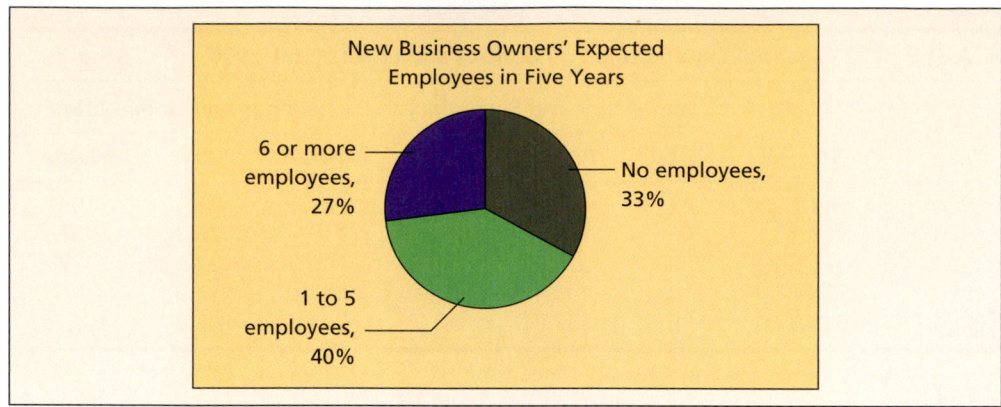

FIGURE 3.35

Bar chart alternative

Source: Based on data from *The Wall Street Journal*, July 27, 2004.

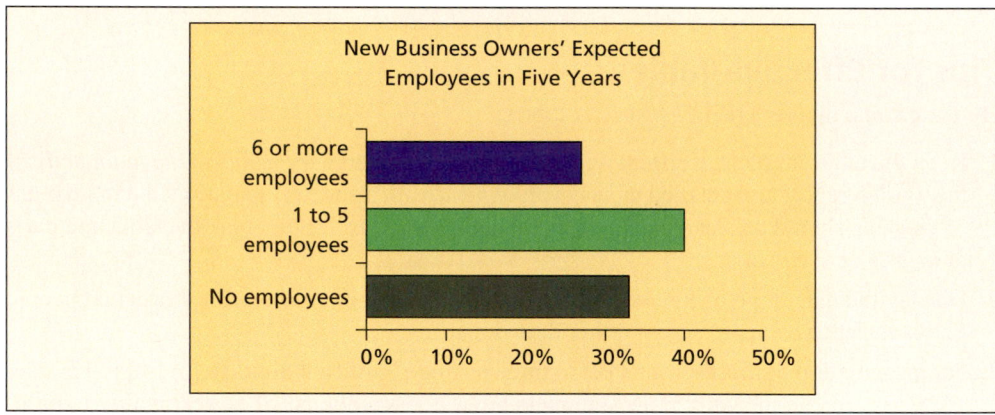

FIGURE 3.36

Exploded pie chart

Source: *PC Magazine* 22, no. 4 (March 11, 2003).

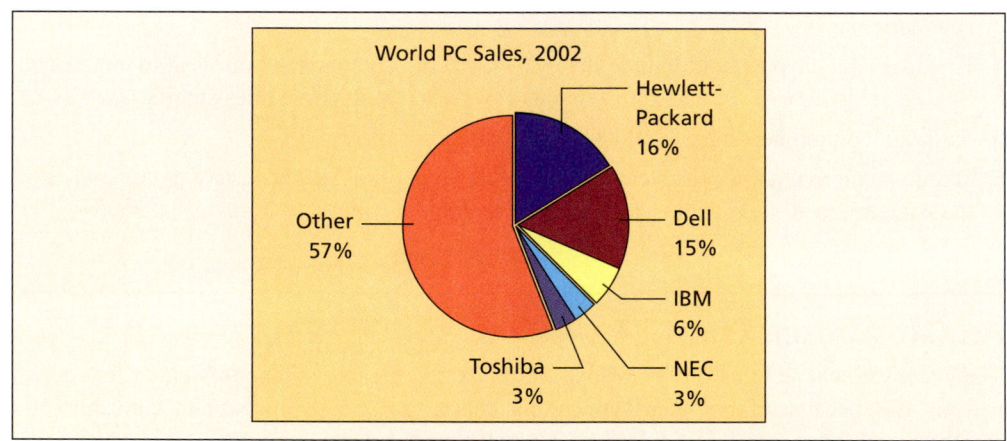

FIGURE 3.37

3-D exploded pie chart

Source: Based on data from www.tiaa-cref.org.

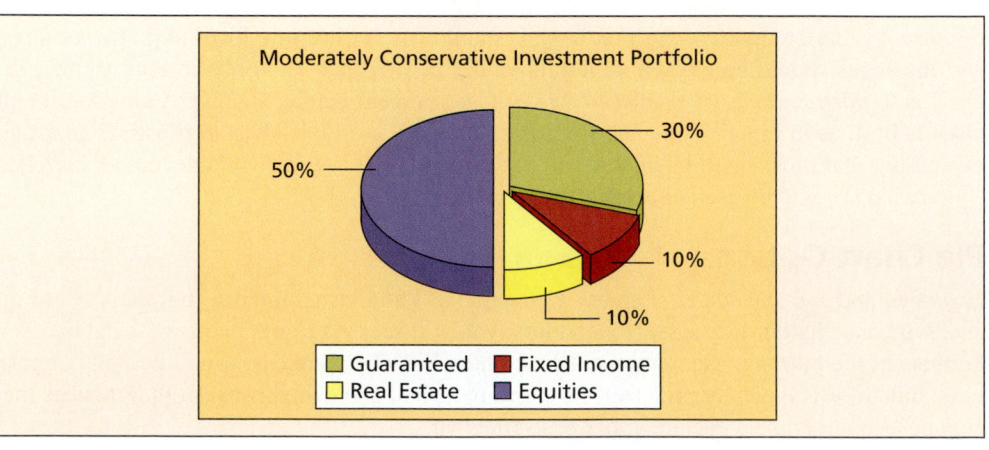

Common Errors in Pie Chart Usage

- Pie charts can only convey a general idea of the data values.
- Pie charts are ineffective when they have too many slices.
- Pie chart data must represent *parts of a whole* (e.g., percent market share).

SECTION EXERCISES

3.16 (a) Use Excel to prepare a *2-D pie chart* for these Web-surfing data. Modify the default colors, fonts, etc., as you judge appropriate to make the display effective. (b) Right-click the chart area, select Chart Type, and change to an *exploded 2-D pie chart*. (c) Right-click the chart area, select Chart Type, and change to a *bar chart*. Which do you prefer? Why? *Hint:* Include data labels with the percent *values*.

Are You Concerned About Being Tracked While Web Surfing?	**WebSurf**
Level of Concern	**Percent**
Very/extreme concern	68
Somewhat concerned	23
No/little concern	9
Total	100

Source: *PC Magazine* 21, no. 11 (November 2003), p. 146.

3.17 (a) Use Excel to prepare a *2-D pie chart* for the following Pitney-Bowes data. Modify the default colors, fonts, etc., as you judge appropriate to make the display effective. (b) Right-click the chart area, select Chart Type, and change to a *3-D pie chart*. (c) Right-click the chart area, select Chart Type, and change to a *bar chart*. Which do you prefer? Why? *Hint:* Include data labels with the percent *values*.

Pitney-Bowes Medical Claims in 2003	**PitneyBowes**
Spent On	**Percent of Total**
Hospital services	47.5
Physicians	27.0
Pharmaceuticals	19.5
Mental health	5.0
Other	1.0
Total	100.0

Source: *The Wall Street Journal,* July 13, 2004, p. A10. © Dow Jones & Co., Inc. Used with permission.

3.18 (a) Use Excel to prepare a *2-D pie chart* for these LCD (liquid crystal display) shipments data. Modify the default colors, fonts, etc., as you judge appropriate to make the display effective. (b) Do you feel that the chart has become too cluttered (i.e., are you displaying too many slices)? Would a bar chart be better? Explain. *Hint:* Include data labels with the percent *values*.

World Market Share of LCD Shipments in 2004   **LCDMarket**

Company	Percent
Sharp	34.6
Zenith	10.9
Sony	10.5
Samsung	9.6
Panasonic	8.7
Phillips	8.5
Others	17.3
Total	100.0

Source: *The Wall Street Journal,* July 15, 2004, p. B1. © Dow Jones & Co., Inc. Used with permission.
May not add to 100 due to rounding.

3.9
EFFECTIVE EXCEL CHARTS

You've heard it said that a picture is worth a thousand words. Effective visual displays help you get your point across and persuade others to listen to your point of view. Good visuals help your employer make better decisions, but they also make *you* a more desirable employee and help *you* see the facts more clearly. Powerful graphics stand out in business reports, to the career benefit of those who know how to create them. This means knowing which visual displays to use in different situations. If you can make complex data comprehensible, you stand to gain a reputation for clear thinking.

The good news is that it's fun to make Excel graphs. The skills to make good displays can be learned, and the information provided here builds on the basics of Excel graphical displays that you have already learned. Excel is used widely throughout business primarily because of its excellent graphics capabilities. You say you already know all about Excel charts? That would be surprising. Professionals who make charts say that they learn new things every day.

Chart Wizard

Excel's Chart Wizard offers a vast array of charts. Although only a few of them are likely to be used in business, it is a good idea to review the whole list and to become familiar with their uses (and abuses). For example, Figure 3.38 shows data on fractional shares of aircraft ownership from 1993 to 2002 in cells C4:C13. Use the mouse to select the data you want to plot, so the data are highlighted. When you click the Chart Wizard icon on Excel's upper menu bar, a sequence of pop-up menus will guide you through the steps of creating the chart. *Step 1* is to

FIGURE 3.38

Excel's Chart Wizard   **Fractional**

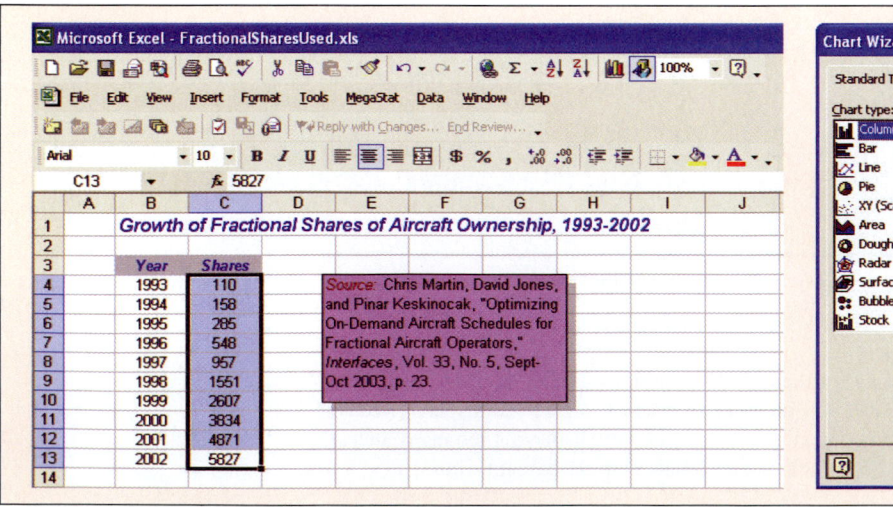
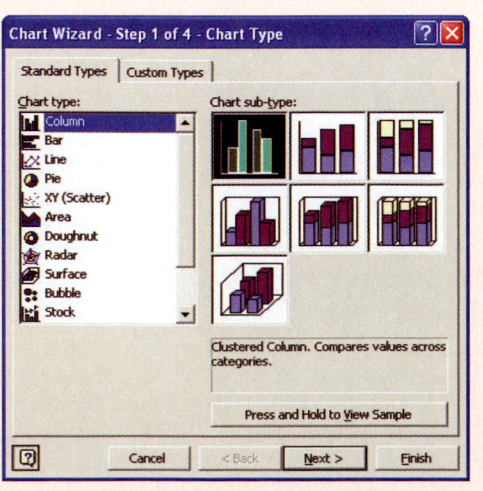

select the type of chart you want. The appropriate chart type depends on the data. Excel's default (a bar chart) is appropriate for the fractional share time series data set, so you can click the Next button.

As you proceed, sequential menus will let you add chart titles, axis labels, and so on. In *Step 2* you can add labels for years on the *X*-axis, so in Category (X) Axis Labels you enter cells B4:B13, as shown in Figure 3.39. A preview image of the chart appears on the menu, so you can see what you are going to get. In *Step 3* you can add a title, add axis labels, adjust the gridlines, or append a data table to the graph.

Embellished Charts

The finished chart, shown in Figure 3.40, is not very attractive. After the chart is created in Excel, you can edit the graph to:

- Improve the titles (main, *X*-axis, *Y*-axis).
- Change the axis scales (minimum, maximum, demarcations).
- Display the data values (on top of each bar).
- Add a data table underneath the graph.
- Change color or patterns in the plot area or chart area.
- Format the decimals (on the axes or data labels).
- Edit the gridlines (color, dotted or solid, patterns).
- Alter the appearance of the bars (color, pattern, gap width).

FIGURE 3.39

Adding *X*-axis labels and a chart title   **Fractional**

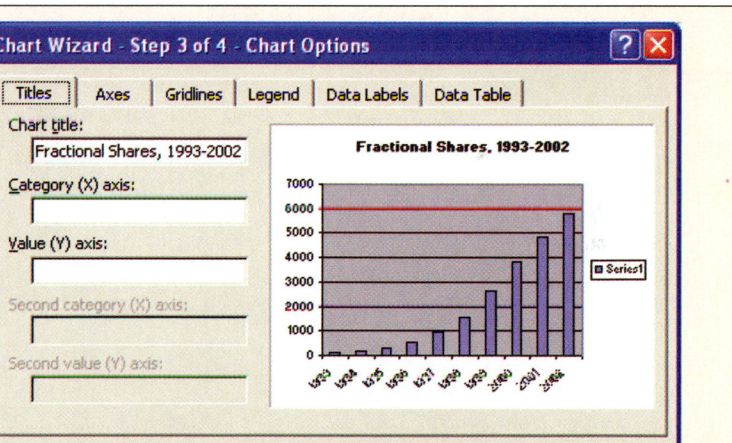

FIGURE 3.40

Format axis menu (scale tab)   **Fractional**

Source: *Interfaces* 33, no. 5 (2003), p. 23.

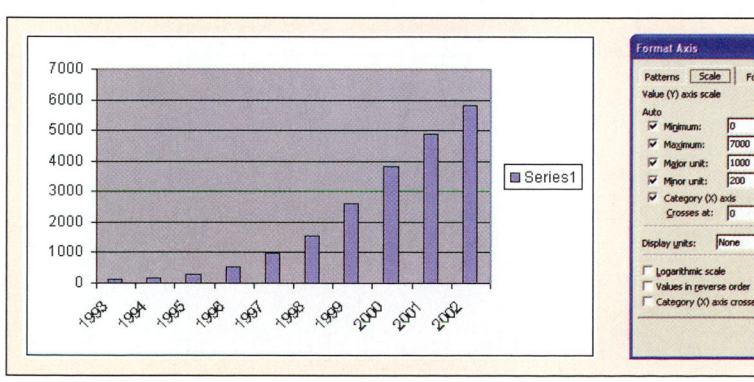

To alter a chart's appearance, click on any chart object (plot area, *X*-axis, *Y*-axis, gridlines, title, data series, chart area) to select the object, and then right-click to see a menu showing the *properties* that you can change. For example, in Figure 3.40 the *Y*-axis scale was selected (the black squares on the axis show that it has been selected) to bring up the Format Axis menu. The *Y*-axis format menu has five tabs (here, the Scale tab was selected). Other tabs allow you to change the Pattern (tick marks, labels, etc.), Font (color, size, etc.), Number (decimals displayed, etc.), and Alignment (horizontal, vertical, etc). *LearningStats* Unit 03 gives a step-by-step explanation of how to make and edit charts in Excel.

Business charts need not be dull. You can customize any graph to your taste. Figures 3.41 and 3.42 show embellished bar charts for the same data. Just don't let your artistic verve overwhelm the data.

Excel offers many other types of specialized charts. When data points are connected and the area is filled with color or shading, the result is an *area chart* (or *mountain chart*). This is basically a line chart. Its appeal is a feeling of solid dimensionality, which might make trends or patterns clearer to the reader. Figure 3.43 shows an example. A drawback is that, when plotting more than one variable (e.g., especially time series data), we can distinguish variables only if the data values "in back" are larger than the data values "in front." We might be better off using a multiple bar chart as in Figure 3.44 (or a line chart if we were showing time series data).

Excel offers other specialized charts, including:

- *Bubble* charts (to display three variables on a 2-dimensional scatter plot).
- *Stock* charts (for high/low/close stock prices).
- *Radar* or *spider* charts (to compare individual performance against a benchmark).
- *Floating bar* charts (to show a range of data values).

FIGURE 3.41

Embellished bar chart

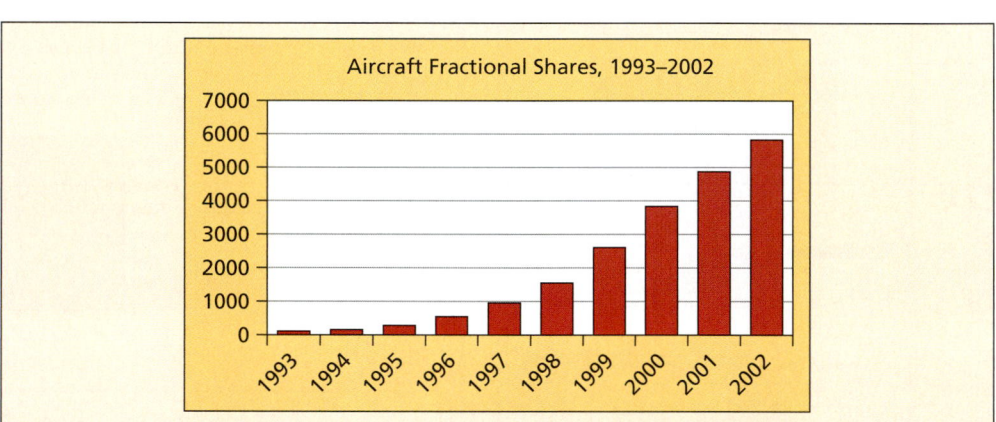

FIGURE 3.42

Over-embellished chart?

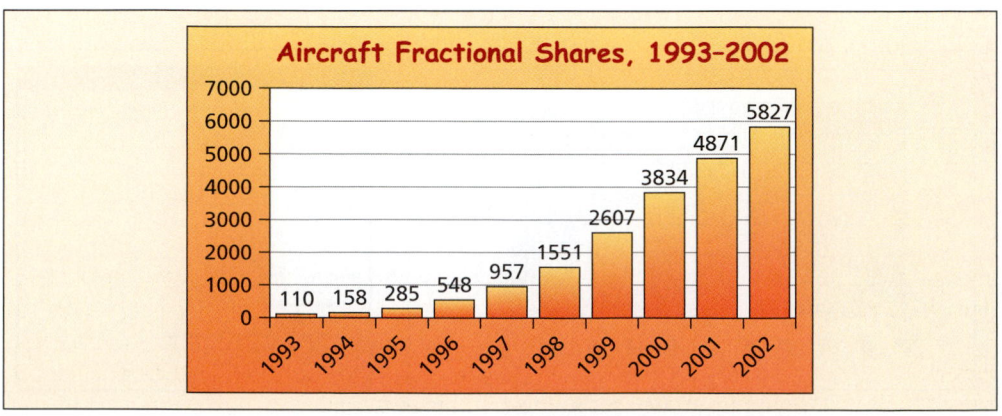

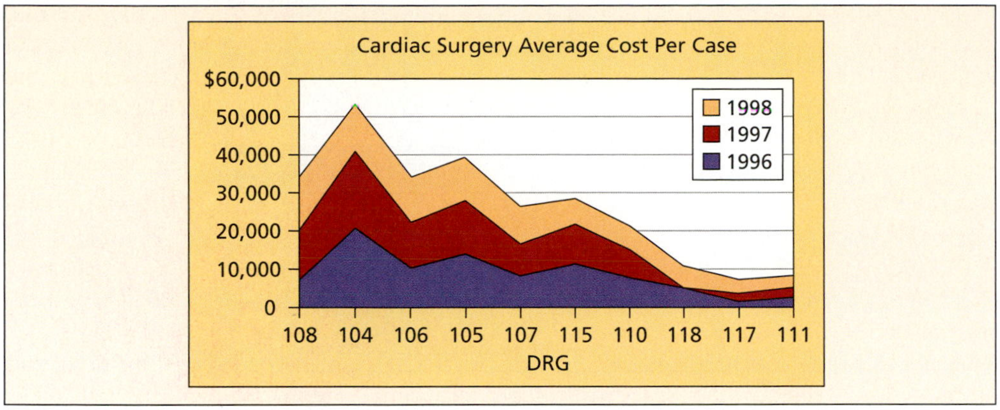

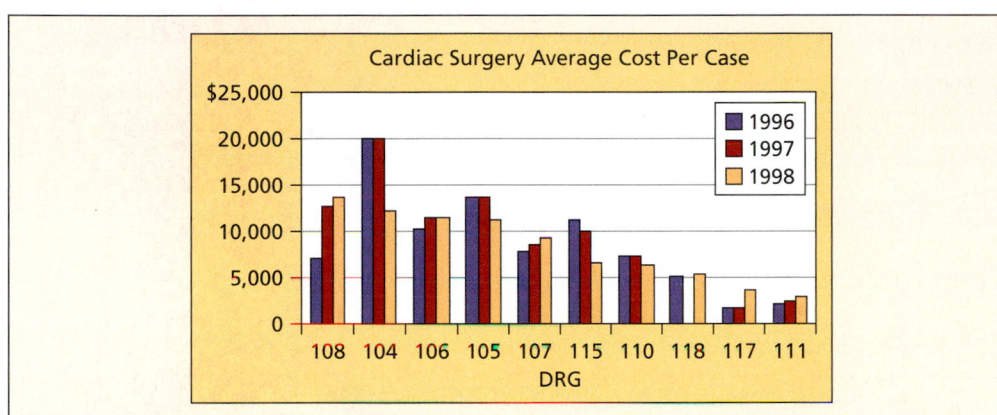

FIGURE 3.43

Area chart   **Cardiac**

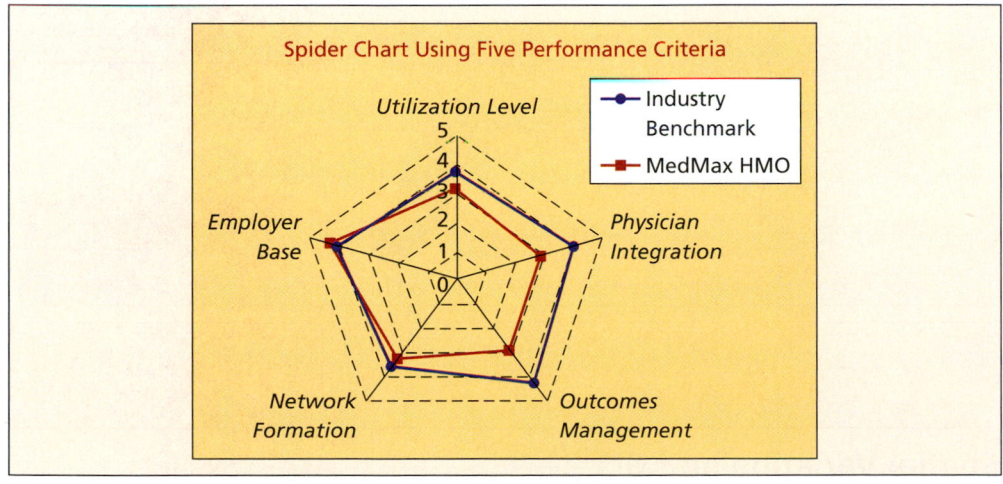

FIGURE 3.44

Multiple bar chart
Cardiac

FIGURE 3.45

Radar chart
MedMax

The last two are worth a closer look. Although ***radar charts*** are visually attractive, statisticians have reservations about them because they distort the data by emphasizing *areas*. In Figure 3.45, MedMax HMO seems farther below the industry benchmark on most criteria, because the eye sees *areas*. A ***floating bar chart*** can display low/high ranges (e.g., stock prices) as illustrated in Figure 3.46 for Maytag Company's stock.

FIGURE 3.46

Floating bar chart

🦅 **Maytag**

Source: *Standard and Poor's 500 Guide,*
2004.

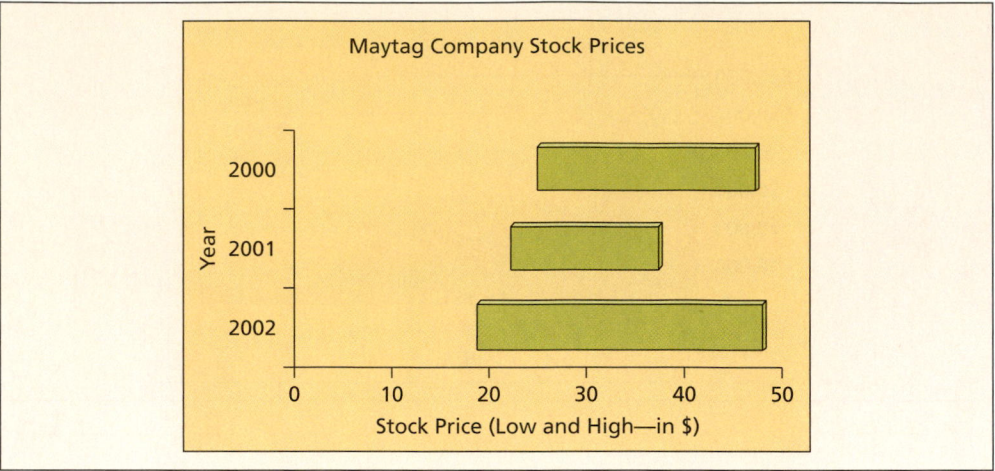

FIGURE 3.47

U.S. population change by county, 1990–2000

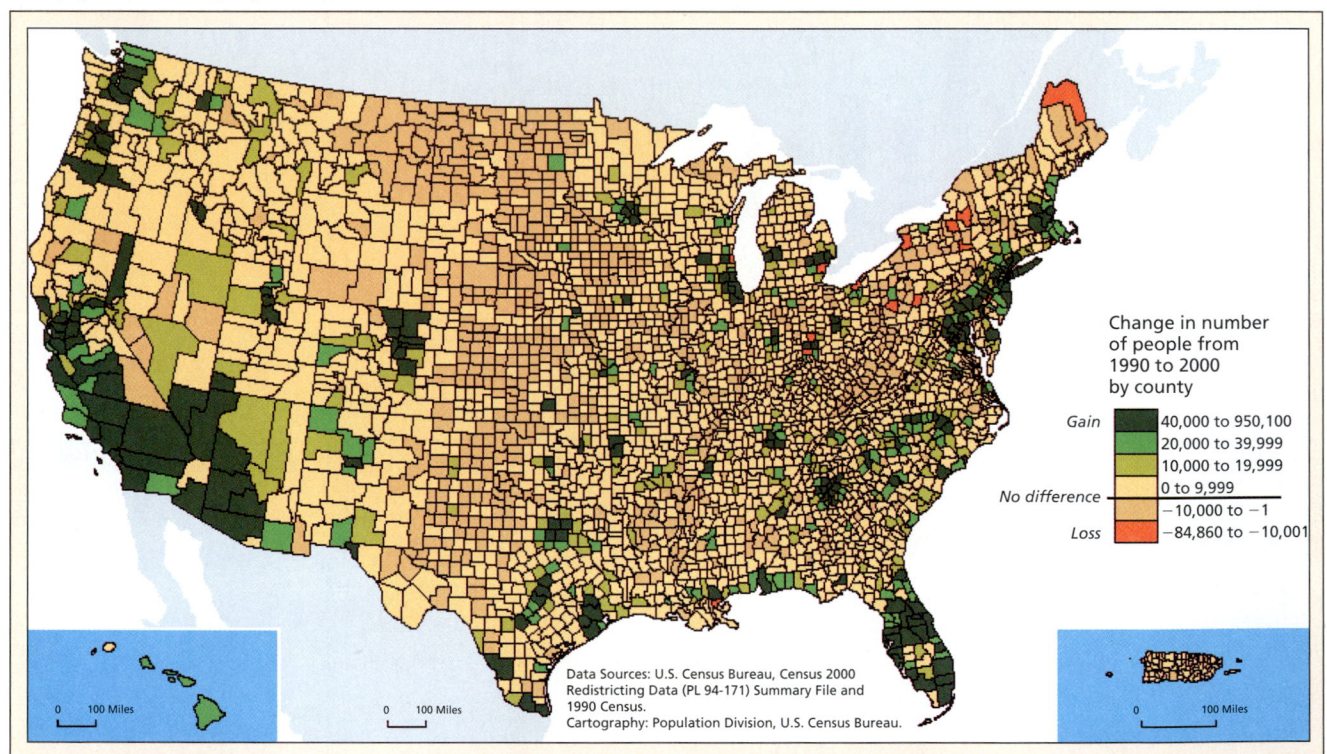

3.10

MAPS AND PICTOGRAMS

Spatial Variation and GIS

Maps can be used for displaying many kinds of data, such as health statistics, demographic information, and warranty claim patterns. They are appropriate when patterns of *variation across space* are of interest. The units of observation may be states, counties, zip codes, school districts, or any other regions. Maps are self-explanatory and may reveal more information than a table. The rapidly growing field of GIS (*geographic information systems*) combines statistics, geography, and graphics. Maps allow the reader to assess patterns based on geography. Figure 3.47 shows U.S. population change by county, based on the 1990 and 2000 censuses. Can you see where people came from, and where they went, in the past decade?

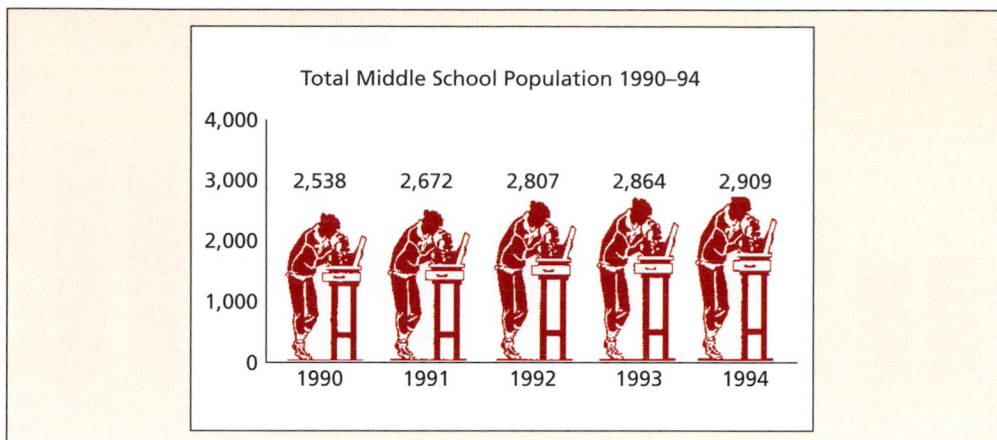

FIGURE 3.48

School pictogram

Source: Rochester Community Schools.

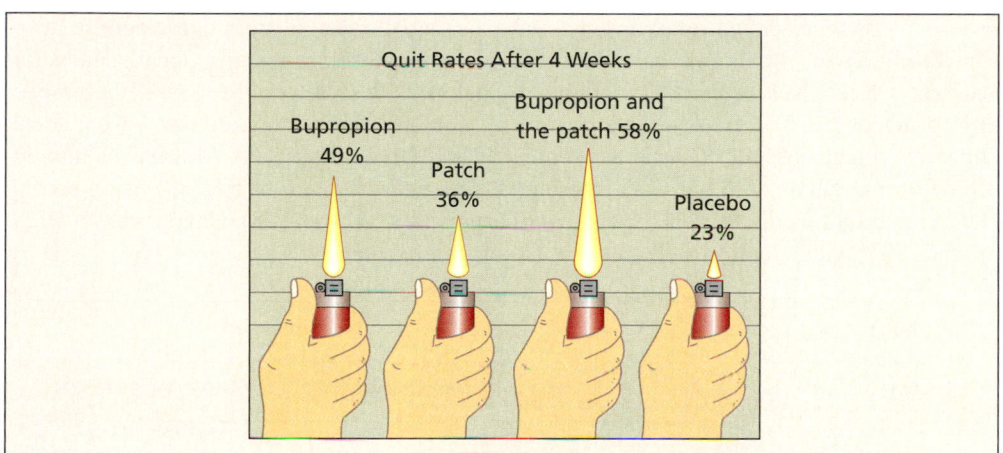

FIGURE 3.49

Cigarette pictogram

Source: St. Joseph Mercy Oakland.

Pictograms

A *pictogram* (Figures 3.48 and 3.49) is a visual display in which data values are replaced by pictures to add visual appeal for a general audience. If done carefully, pictograms can be innocuous, but they often create visual distortion. They are entertaining art, not really graphs. The print media (e.g., *USA Today*) use them often.

3.11 DECEPTIVE GRAPHS

We have explained how to create *good* graphs. Now, let's turn things around. As an impartial consumer of information, you need a checklist of errors to beware. Those who want to slant the facts may do these things deliberately, although most errors occur through ignorance. Use this list to protect yourself against ignorant or unscrupulous practitioners of the graphical arts.

Error 1: Nonzero Origin   NonZero

A nonzero origin will exaggerate the trend. Measured distances do not match the stated values or axis demarcations. The accounting profession is particularly aggressive in enforcing this rule. Although zero origins are preferred, sometimes a nonzero origin is needed to show sufficient detail.

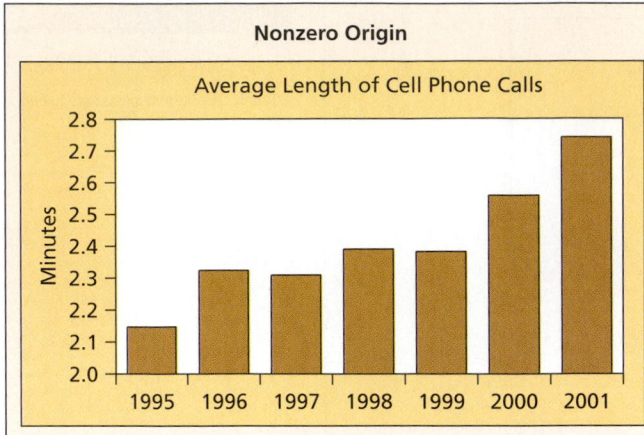

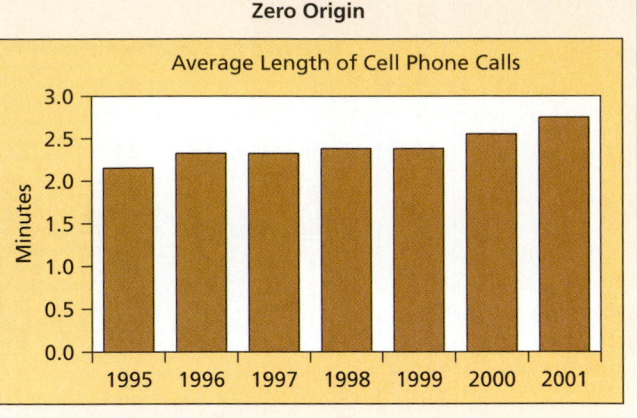

Error 2: Elastic Graph Proportions 🔊 Elastic

By shortening the *X*-axis in relation to the *Y*-axis, vertical change is exaggerated. For a time series (*X*-axis representing time) this can make a sluggish sales or profit curve appear steep. Conversely, a wide *X*-axis and short *Y*-axis can downplay alarming changes (recalls, industrial accidents). Keep the *aspect ratio* (width/height) below 2.00. Excel graphs use a default aspect ratio of about 1.8. The Golden Ratio you learned in art history suggests that 1.62 is ideal. Older TV screens use a 1:33 ratio as do older PCs (640 × 480 pixels). Movies use a wide-screen format (up to 2.55) but VHS tapes and DVDs may crop it to fit on a television screen. HDTV and multimedia computers use a 16:9 aspect ratio (about 1.78). Charts whose height exceeds their width don't fit well on pages or computer screens.

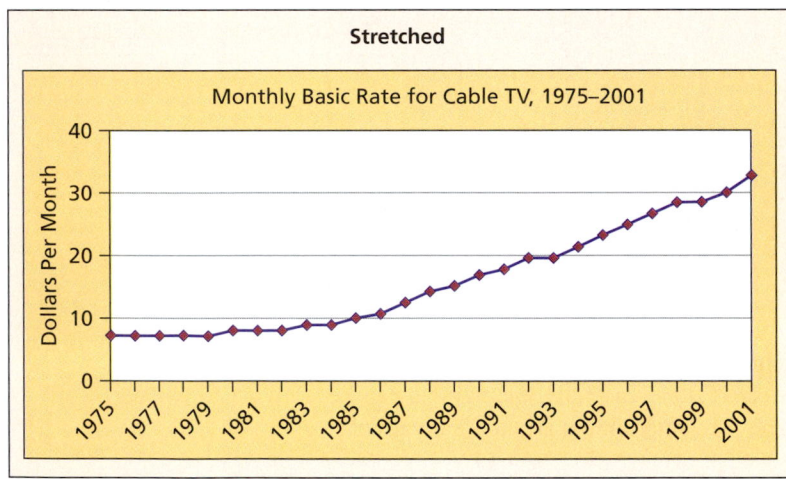

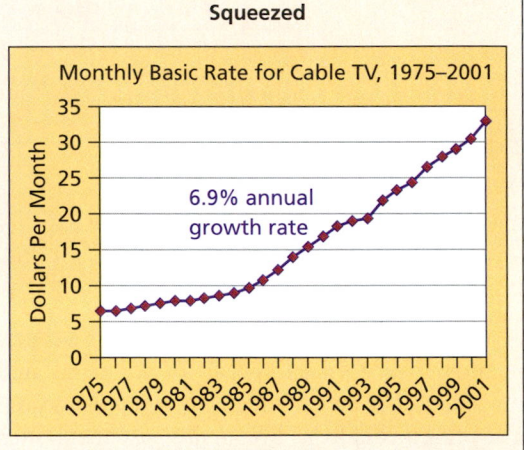

Source: *Statistical Abstract of the United States, 2002*, p. 707.

Error 3: Dramatic Title

The title often is designed more to grab the reader's attention than to convey the chart's content (Criminals on a Spree, Deficit Swamps Economy). Sometimes the title attempts to draw your conclusion for you (Inflation Wipes Out Savings, Imports Dwarf Exports). A title should be short but adequate for the purpose.

Error 4: Distracting Pictures

To add visual pizzazz, artists may superimpose the chart on a photograph (e.g., a gasoline price chart atop a photo of Middle East warfare) or add colorful cartoon figures, banners, or drawings. This is mostly harmless, but can distract the reader or impart an emotional slant (e.g., softening bad news about the home team's slide toward the cellar by drawing a sad-face team mascot cartoon).

Error 5: Authority Figures

Advertisements sometimes feature mature, attractive, conservatively attired actors portraying scientists, doctors, or business leaders examining scientific-looking charts. Because the public respects science's reputation, such displays impart credibility to self-serving commercial claims.

Error 6: 3-D and Rotated Graphs   MedSchool

By making a graph 3-dimensional and/or rotating it through space, the author can make trends appear to dwindle into the distance or loom alarmingly toward you. This example combines errors 1, 3, 4, 5, and 6 (nonzero origin, leading title, distracting picture, vague source, rotated 3-D look).

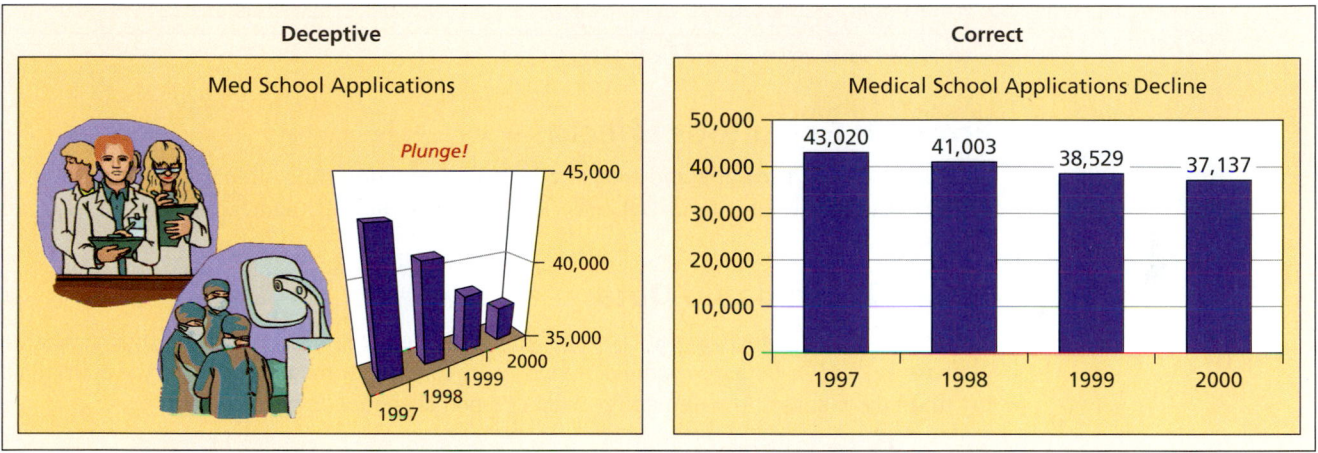

Source: American Medical Association.

Error 7: Missing Axis Demarcations

Without "tick" marks on the axis, the reader cannot identify individual data values. Grid lines help the viewer compare magnitudes but are often omitted for clarity. For maximum clarity in a bar graph, label each bar with its numerical value, unless the scale is clearly demarcated and labeled.

Error 8: Missing Measurement Units or Definitions

Missing or unclear units of measurement (dollars? percent?) can render a chart useless. Even if the vertical scale is in dollars, we must know whether the variable being plotted is sales, profits, assets, or whatever. If percent, indicate clearly *percentage of what*.

Error 9: Vague Source

Large federal agencies or corporations employ thousands of people and issue hundreds of reports per year. Vague sources like "Department of Commerce" may indicate that the author lost the citation, didn't know the data source, or mixed data from several sources. Scientific publications insist on complete source citations. Rules are less rigorous for publications aimed at a general audience.

Error 10: Complex Graphs

Complicated visual displays make the reader work harder. Keep your main objective in mind. Omit "bonus" detail or put it in the appendix. Apply the *10-second rule* to graphs. If the message really is complex, can it be broken into smaller parts? This example on the next page combines errors 3, 4, 7, 8, 9, and 10 (silly subtitle, distracting pictures, no data labels, no definitions, vague source, too much information).

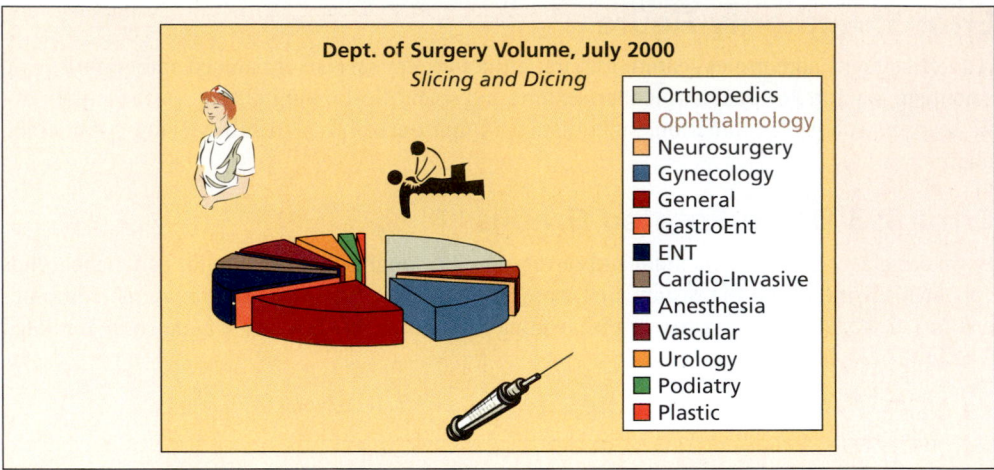

Source: Hospital reports.

Error 11: Gratuitous Effects

Slide shows often use color and special effects (sound, interesting slide transitions, spinning text, etc.) to attract attention. But once the novelty wears off, audiences may find special effects annoying.

Error 12: Estimated Data

In a spirit of zeal to include the "latest" figures, the last few data points in a time series are often estimated. Or perhaps a couple of years were missing or incompatible, so the author had to "fill in the blanks." At a minimum, estimated points should be noted.

Error 13: Area Trick 🐸 **AreaTrick**

One of the most pernicious visual tricks is simultaneously enlarging the width of the bars as their height increases, so the bar area misstates the true proportion (e.g., by replacing graph bars with figures like human beings, coins, or gas pumps). As figure height increases, so does width, distorting the area.

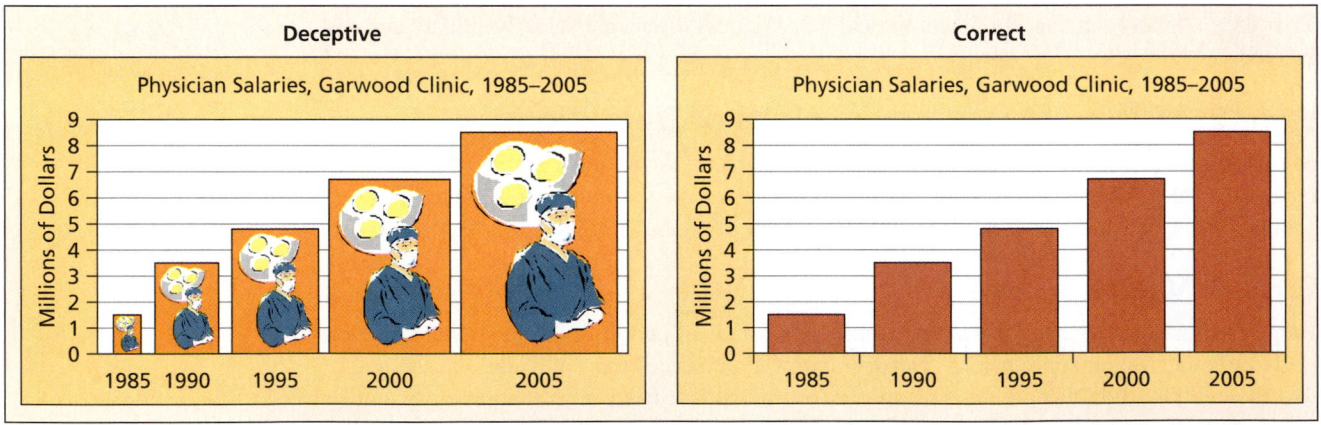

Final Advice

Can you trust any visual display (unless you created it yourself)? Be a skeptic, and be pleasantly surprised if the graph lives up to the best standards. Print media compete with TV and the Web, so newspapers and magazines must use colorful charts to attract reader interest. People enjoy visual displays, so we accept some artistic liberties. Mass-readership publications like *U.S. News & World Report, Maclean's, Time, Newsweek, USA Today,* or even the more specialized business-oriented publications like *Forbes, Fortune, BusinessWeek,* and *The Wall Street Journal* should not be judged by the same standards you would apply to an academic journal. Businesses want charts that follow the rules, because a deceptive chart may have serious consequences. Decisions may be made about products or services that affect lives, market share, and jobs (including yours). So know the rules, try to follow them, and expect your peers and subordinates to do the same. Catchy graphics have a place in selling your ideas but shouldn't dominate the data.

Further Challenges

If you enjoy playing with computers, try to learn these skills on your own:

- Copy and paste Excel charts into Word or PowerPoint.
- Copy and paste charts from other software (MINITAB, Visual Statistics).
- Use screen captures and edit the results in Paint if necessary.
- Use presentation software (e.g., PowerPoint) with transition effects.
- Know how (and when) to link Excel charts to spreadsheets.
- Use clip art and create your own simple graphics.

Chapter Summary

For a set of observations on a single numerical variable, a **dot plot** displays the individual data values, while a **frequency distribution** classifies the data into classes called **bins** for a **histogram** of **frequencies** for each bin. The number of bins and their limits are matters left to your judgment, though **Sturges's Rule** offers advice on the number of bins. The **line chart** shows values of one or more **time series** variables plotted against time. A **log scale** is sometimes used in time series charts when data vary by orders of magnitude. The **bar chart** shows a **numerical** data value for each category of an **attribute.** However, a bar chart can also be used for a time series. A **scatter plot** can reveal the association (or lack of association) between two variables X and Y. The **pie chart** (showing a **numerical** data value for each category of an **attribute** if the data values are parts of a whole) is common but should be used with caution. Sometimes a **simple table** is the best visual display. Creating effective visual displays is an acquired skill. Excel offers a wide range of charts from which to choose. Deceptive graphs are found frequently in both media and business presentations, and the consumer should be aware of common errors.

Key Terms

arithmetic scale, *73*	line chart, *72*	radar chart, *93*
bar chart, *76*	logarithmic scale, *73*	right-skewed, *70*
central tendency, *59*	maps, *94*	scatter plot, *80*
dispersion, *59*	modal class, *69*	shape, *59*
dot plot, *61*	outlier, *70*	stacked bar chart, *78*
floating bar chart, *93*	Pareto chart, *77*	stacked dot plot, *63*
frequency distribution, *65*	pictogram, *95*	Sturges's Rule, *65*
histogram, *61*	pie chart, *87*	symmetric, *70*
left-skewed, *70*	pyramid chart, *76*	

Chapter Review

1. (a) What is a dot plot? (b) Why are dot plots attractive? (c) What are their limitations?
2. (a) What is a frequency distribution? (b) What are the steps in creating one?
3. (a) What is a histogram? (b) What does it show?
4. (a) What is a bimodal histogram? (b) Explain the difference between left-skewed, symmetric, and right-skewed histograms. (c) What is an outlier?
5. (a) What is a scatter plot? (b) What do scatter plots reveal? (c) Sketch a scatter plot with a moderate positive correlation. (d) Sketch a scatter plot with a strong negative correlation.
6. For what kind of data would we use a bar chart? List three tips for creating effective bar charts.
7. For what kind of data would we use a line chart? List three tips for creating effective line charts.
8. (a) List the three most common types of charts in business, and sketch each type (no real data, just a sketch). (b) List three specialized charts that can be created in Excel, and sketch each type (no real data, just a sketch).

9. (a) For what kind of data would we use a pie chart? (b) Name two common pie chart errors. (c) Why are pie charts regarded with skepticism by some statisticians?

10. Which types of charts can be used for time series data?

11. (a) When might we need a log scale? (b) What do equal distances on a log scale represent? (c) State one drawback of a log scale graph.

12. (a) When might we use a stacked bar chart? An area chart? A radar chart? A floating bar chart? (b) Sketch one of each (no real data, just a sketch).

13. (a) Why do the media like pictograms? (b) Why aren't statisticians attracted to them?

14. List six deceptive graphical techniques.

CHAPTER EXERCISES

Note: In these exercises, you may use a software package. Use MegaStat's Descriptive Statistics for dot plots or Frequency Distributions for histograms. Use MINITAB's Graphs or a similar software package to create the dot plot or histogram.

3.19   A study of 40 U.S. cardiac care centers showed the following ratios of nurses to beds. (a) Prepare a dot plot. (b) Prepare a frequency distribution and histogram (you may either specify the bins yourself or use automatic bins). (c) Describe the distribution, based on these displays. 🐝 **Nurses**

1.48	1.16	1.24	1.52	1.30	1.28	1.68	1.40	1.12	0.98	0.93	2.76
1.34	1.58	1.72	1.38	1.44	1.41	1.34	1.96	1.29	1.21	2.00	1.50
1.68	1.39	1.62	1.17	1.07	2.11	2.40	1.35	1.48	1.59	1.81	1.15
1.35	1.42	1.33	1.41								

3.20   The first Rose Bowl (football) was played in 1902. The next was not played until 1916, but a Rose Bowl has been played every year since then. The margin of victory in each of the 87 Rose Bowls from 1902 through 2003 is shown below. (a) Prepare a dot plot. (b) Prepare a frequency distribution and histogram (you may either specify the bins yourself or use automatic bins). (c) Describe the distribution, based on these displays. (Data are from *Sports Illustrated 2004 Sports Almanac,* and www.cbs.sportsline.com.) 🐝 **RoseBowl**

49	14	14	1	28	0	11	0	17	1	0
1	1	33	24	9	35	7	16	7	21	13
4	14	8	4	9	29	25	20	31	49	6
3	8	33	7	8	13	3	16	3	26	36
10	18	5	10	27	2	1	11	11	7	10
1	25	21	1	13	8	7	7	1	17	28
10	36	3	17	7	3	8	7	12	20	7
5	18	9	3	5	7	8	10	23	20	

3.21   An executive's telephone log showed the following data for the length of 65 calls initiated during the last week of July. (a) Prepare a dot plot. (b) Prepare a frequency distribution and histogram (you may either specify the bins yourself or use automatic bins). (c) Describe the distribution, based on these displays. 🐝 **CallLength**

1	2	10	5	3	3	2	20	1	1
6	3	13	2	2	1	26	3	1	3
1	2	1	7	1	2	3	1	2	12
1	4	2	2	29	1	1	1	8	5
1	4	2	1	1	1	1	6	1	2
3	3	6	1	3	1	1	5	1	18
2	13	13	1	6					

3.22   As an independent project, a team of statistics students collected data on calories per gram for 14 different kinds of bread. (a) Prepare a dot plot with the following data. (b) Prepare a frequency distribution and histogram (you may either specify the bins yourself or use automatic bins). (c) Describe the distribution, based on these displays. Is the sample size large enough to draw valid inferences about shape? 🐝 **Bread**

Calories per Gram for 14 Breads

Manufacturer	Product Name	Type	Calories per Gram
Brownberry	Brownberry	Natural Wheat	2.50
Brownberry	Brownberry	Soft Wheat	2.50
Brownberry	Brownberry	Whole Wheat	2.37
Brownberry	Brownberry	Country Wheat	2.63
Compass Food	America's Choice	Light Wheat	1.86
Compass Food	America's Choice	Split-Top	2.50
Interstate Brand Co.	Home Pride	Butter Top Wheat	2.86
Interstate Brand Co.	Wonder	Whole Wheat	2.65
Koepplinger's Bakery	Koepplinger's	Natural Wheat	2.11
Koepplinger's Bakery	Koepplinger's	Whole Wheat	1.74
Metz Baking Co.	Taystee	Wheat	2.67
Metz Baking Co.	Roman Meal	Whole Wheat	2.19
Pepperidge Farm	Pepperidge Farm	Whole Wheat	2.40
Pepperidge Farm	Pepperidge Farm	Light Wheat	2.11

Source: Project by Madonna Klippstein, Nancy Kadarman, Katrina Gagnon, and Bryce Clark. Data are from sampled product labels.

3.23 Every year, J.D. Power and Associates issues its initial vehicle quality ratings, like those shown below. (a) Prepare a dot plot. (b) Prepare a frequency distribution and histogram (you may either specify the bins yourself or use automatic bins). (c) Describe the distribution, based on these displays. **JDPower**

Number of Defects per 100 Vehicles, 2004 Model Year

Brand	Defects	Brand	Defects	Brand	Defects
Acura	117	Infiniti	104	Oldsmobile	110
Audi	109	Jaguar	98	Pontiac	122
BMW	109	Jeep	136	Porsche	159
Buick	100	Kia	153	Saab	133
Cadillac	93	Land Rover	148	Saturn	149
Chevrolet	119	Lexus	87	Scion	158
Chrysler	120	Lincoln	121	Subaru	123
Dodge	121	Mazda	157	Suzuki	149
Ford	130	Mercedes-Benz	106	Toyota	104
GMC	127	Mercury	100	Volkswagen	164
Honda	99	Mini	142	Volvo	113
Hummer	173	Mitsubishi	130		
Hyundai	102	Nissan	154		

Source: J.D. Power and Associates 2004 Initial Quality Study[TM]. Ratings are intended for educational purposes only, and should not be used as a guide to consumer decisions.

3.24 (a) What kind of display is this? (b) Identify its strengths and weaknesses, using the tips and checklists shown in this chapter. (c) Can you suggest any improvements? Would a different type of display be better? **AHADues**

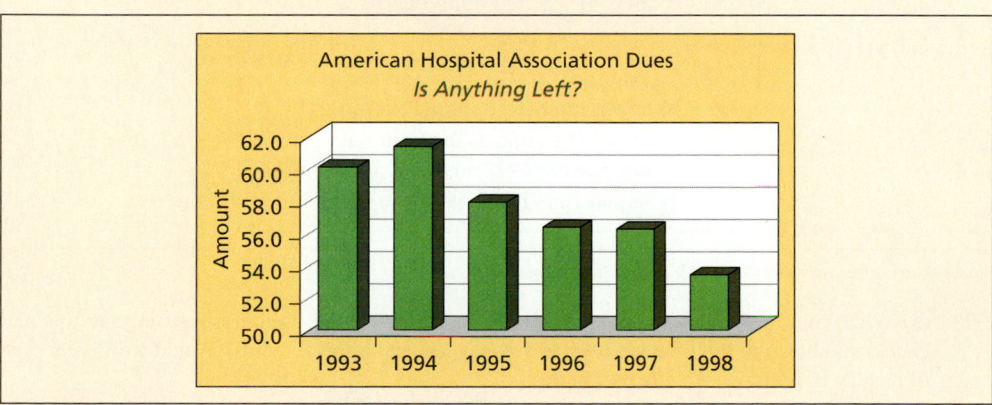

Source: *Modern Healthcare,* vol. 29, no. 34 (1999), p. 3.

3.25 (a) What kind of display is this? (b) Identify its strengths and weaknesses, using the tips and checklists shown in this chapter. (c) Can you suggest any improvements? Would a different type of display be better? **MedError**

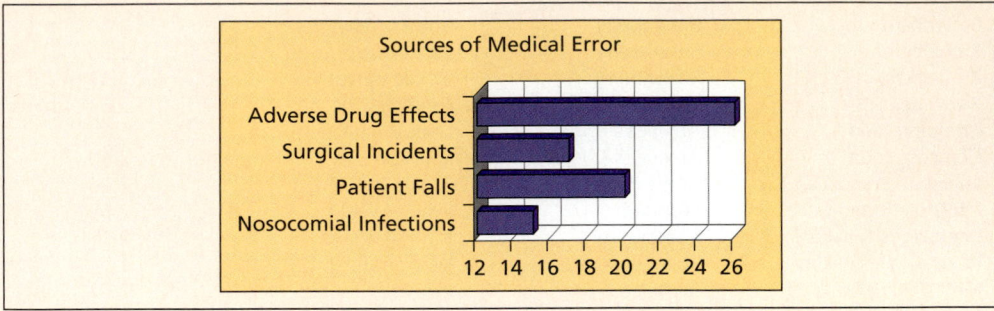

3.26 (a) What kind of display is this? (b) Identify its strengths and weaknesses, using the tips and checklists shown in this chapter. (c) Can you suggest any improvements? Would a different type of display be better? **Oxnard**

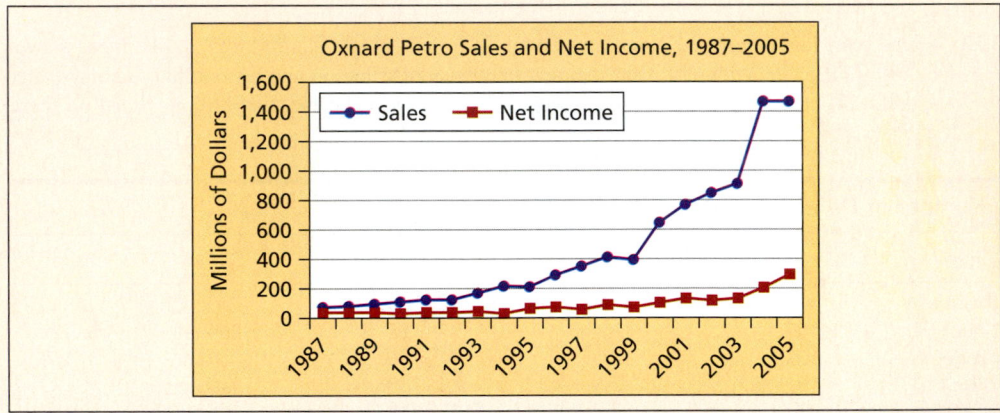

3.27 (a) What kind of display is this? (b) Identify its strengths and weaknesses, using the tips and checklists shown in this chapter. (c) Can you suggest any improvements? Would a different type of display be better?

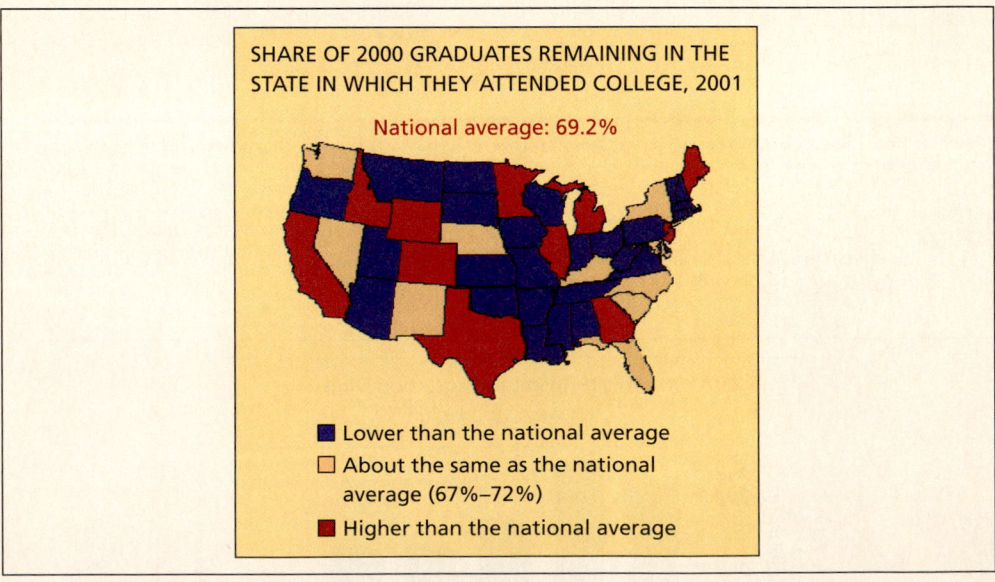

Source: Federal Reserve Bank of Cleveland, *Economic Trends,* January 2004, p. 15.

3.28 (a) What kind of display is this? (b) Identify its strengths and weaknesses, using the tips and checklists shown in this chapter. (c) Can you suggest any improvements? Would a different type of display be better? **Advertising**

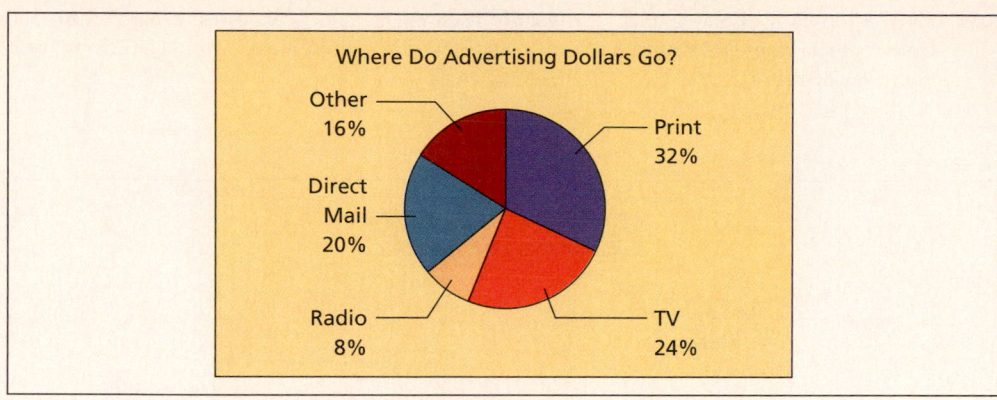

Source: *Statistical Abstract of the United States, 2002*, p. 772.

3.29   (a) What kind of display is this? (b) Identify its strengths and weaknesses, using the tips and checklists shown in this chapter. (c) Can you suggest any improvements? Would a different type of display be better?

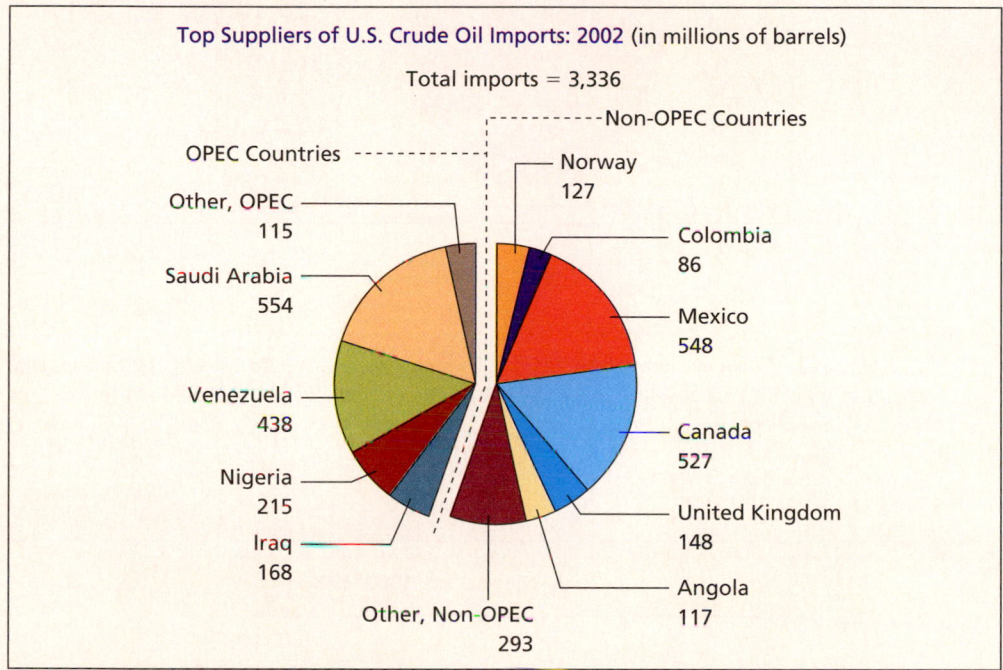

Source: *Statistical Abstract of the United States, 2003*.

3.30   (a) What kind of display is this? (b) Identify its strengths and weaknesses, using the tips and checklists shown in this chapter. (c) Can you suggest any improvements? Would a different type of display be better?   **BirthRate**

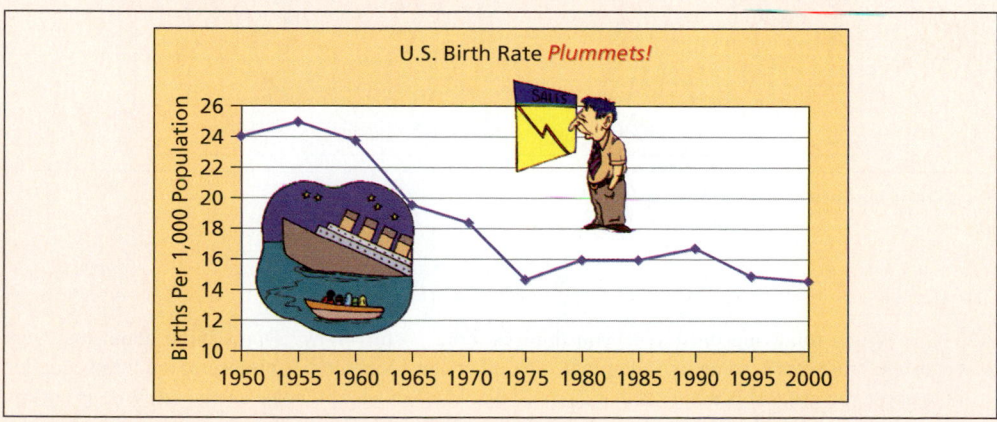

3.31 (a) What kind of display is this? (b) Identify its strengths and weaknesses, using the tips and checklists shown in this chapter. (c) Can you suggest any improvements? Would a different type of display be better?

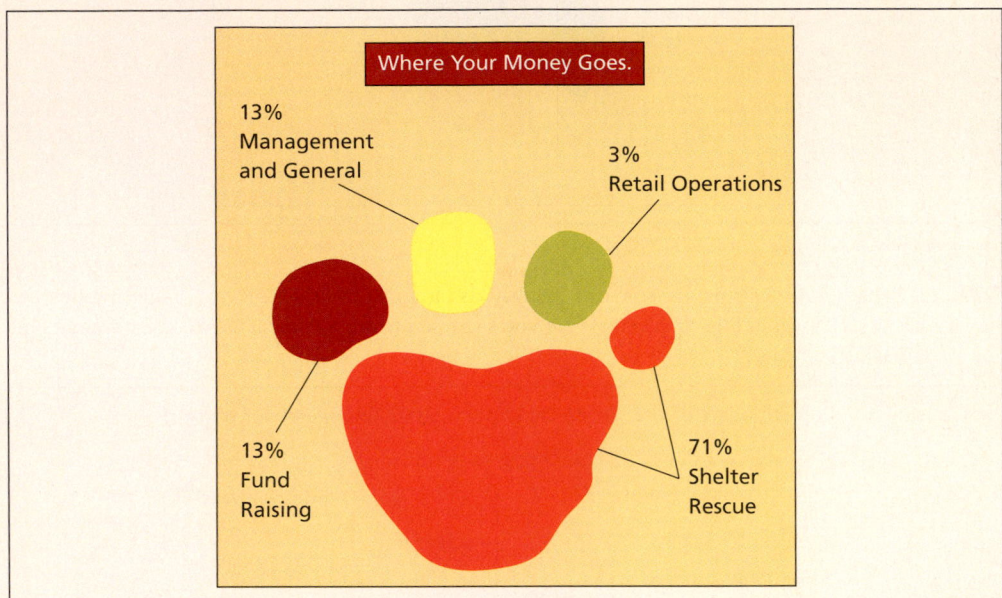

Source: Courtesy of Michigan Humane Society.

3.32 (a) What kind of display is this? (b) Identify its strengths and weaknesses, using the tips and checklists shown in this chapter. (c) Can you suggest any improvements? Would a different type of display be better?

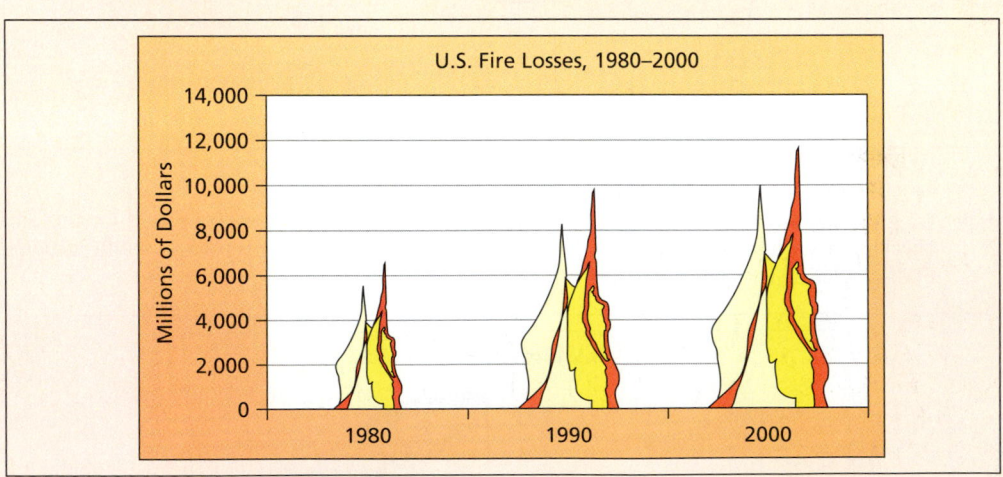

Source: *Statistical Abstract of the United States, 2001*, p. 340.

3.33 (a) Which following display do you think is more useful? Why? *Hint:* Think about the "zero origin" rule that is sometimes dominated by other considerations. (b) Interpret the fitted equation as best you can. (c) Is it logical that airspeed would affect cockpit noise levels? (d) Why is cockpit noise level a health issue for pilots (read the note below the figures before you answer). 🐦 **CockpitNoise**

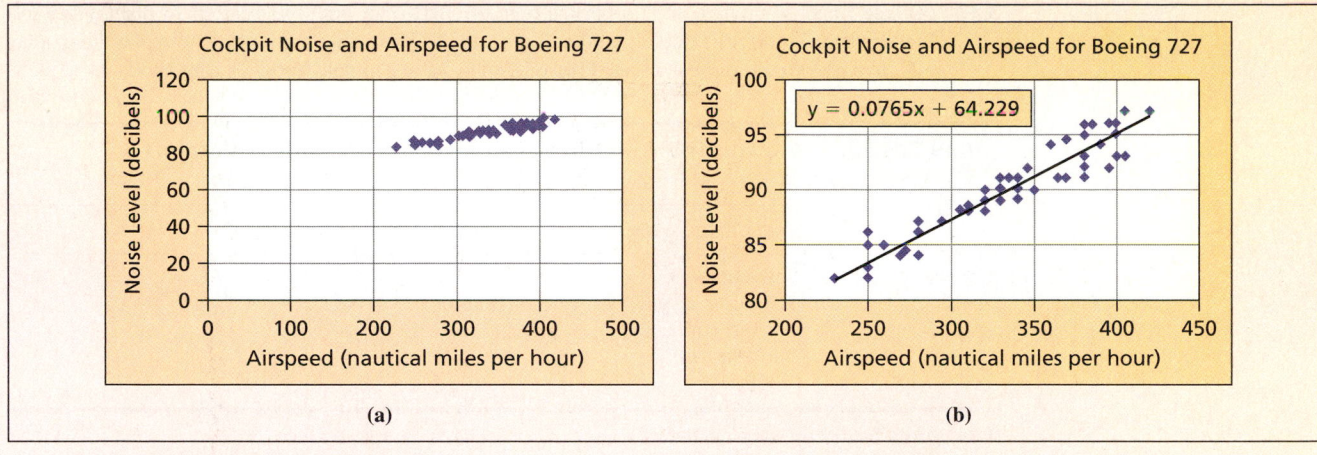

(a)   (b)

Source: Data are courtesy of Capt. Robert E. Hartl (retired).

Note: 60 decibels is a normal conversation, 75 is a typical vacuum cleaner, 85 is city traffic, 90 is a hair dryer, 110 is a chain saw.

3.34   (a) Use Excel to prepare an appropriate type of chart (bar, line, pie, scatter) to display the following data. Modify the default colors, fonts, etc., as you judge appropriate to make the display effective. (b) Would more than one kind of display be acceptable? Why or why not?

Per Capita Health Care Spending in Major Automobile Producing Nations (dollars)
HealthCare

Nation	1990	2000	Nation	1990	2000
U.S.	2,739	4,631	Japan	1,083	2,012
Germany	1,600	2,748	U.K.	972	1,763
Canada	1,676	2,535	Korea	355	893
Italy	1,321	2,032	Mexico	260	490

Source: *The Detroit News,* December 1, 2002, p. 10A.

3.35   (a) Use Excel to prepare an appropriate type of chart (bar, line, pie, scatter) to display the following data. Modify the default colors, fonts, etc., as you judge appropriate to make the display effective. (b) Would more than one kind of display be acceptable? Why or why not?

Outcomes of Medicare Appeals, 1999   **Medicare**

Outcome	Number of Appeals
Upheld	13,737
Overturned	3,578
Dismissed or withdrawn	2,465
Other	623
Total	20,403

Source: *Modern Healthcare* 30, no. 16 (April 17, 2000), p. 76.

3.36   (a) Use Excel to prepare an appropriate type of chart (bar, line, pie, scatter) to display the following data. Modify the default colors, fonts, etc., as you judge appropriate to make the display effective. (b) Would more than one kind of display be acceptable? Why or why not?

Method of Internet/Broadband Access   **Broadband**

Access Methods	2001	2002	2003
33K modem or slower	3	2	1
56K modem	49	32	24
Cable modem	30	42	50
DSL	17	21	22
Wireless local loop	1	1	1
ISDN	0	1	1
Total	100	100	100

Source: *PC Magazine* 22, no. 16 (September 16, 2003), p. 8.

Note: Columns may not sum to 100 due to rounding.

3.37 (a) Use Excel to prepare an appropriate type of chart (bar, line, pie, scatter) to display the following data. Modify the default colors, fonts, etc., as you judge appropriate to make the display effective. (b) Would more than one kind of display be acceptable? Why or why not?

How Confident Are You That You Have Saved Enough to Retire in Comfort?
🌑 **Retirement**

Confidence Level	1993 (%)	2003 (%)
Very confident	18	21
Somewhat confident	55	45
Not very confident	25	33
Don't know	2	1
Total	100	100

Source: *Detroit Free Press,* November 3, 2003.

3.38 (a) Use Excel to prepare an appropriate type of chart (bar, line, pie, scatter) to display the following data. Modify the default colors, fonts, etc., as you judge appropriate to make the display effective. (b) Would more than one kind of display be acceptable? Why or why not?

Distribution of Consumer Fraud Complaints by Age 🌑 **Fraud**

Age Group	Percent of Total*
19 and under	3
20 to 29	19
30 to 39	25
40 to 49	25
50 to 59	16
60 to 69	7
70 and over	6
Total	100

Source: *PC Magazine* 23, no. 4 (March 2, 2004), p. 76.

*Percentages are based on 140,763 consumer complaints to the FTC.

May not sum to 100 due to rounding.

3.39 (a) Use Excel to prepare an appropriate type of chart (bar, line, pie, scatter) to display the following data. Modify the default colors, fonts, etc., as you judge appropriate to make the display effective. (b) Would more than one kind of display be acceptable? Why or why not?

Bottled Water Industry Leaders, 1999 🌑 **Bottled**

Company	Market Share (%)
Perrier	28.9
Suntory	9.2
McKesson	7.6
Danone	7.2
Pepsi-Cola	5.5
Crystal Geyser	2.9
U.S. Filter	2.0
Coca-Cola	1.4
Aberfoyle Springs	1.4
Glacier	1.1
Others (900 brands)	32.8
Total	100.0

Source: © www.bottledwaterweb.com. Used with permission.

3.40 (a) Use Excel to prepare an appropriate type of chart (bar, line, pie, scatter) to display the following data. Modify the default colors, fonts, etc., as you judge appropriate to make the display effective. (b) Would more than one kind of display be acceptable? Why or why not?

U.S. and World Petroleum Usage (millions of barrels per day)   🛢   **Petroleum**

	1993	1994	1995	1996	1997	1998	1999	2000	2001	2002
U.S.	17.2	17.7	17.7	18.3	18.6	18.9	19.5	19.7	19.6	19.8
Non-U.S.	49.9	50.7	52.3	53.3	54.5	54.9	56.1	57.2	57.5	57.8

Source: U.S. Dept. of Transportation, www.bts.gov.

3.41   (a) Use Excel to prepare an appropriate type of chart (bar, line, pie, scatter) to display the following data. Modify the default colors, fonts, etc., as you judge appropriate to make the display effective. (b) Would more than one kind of display be acceptable? Why or why not?

2002 Cost Per Seat Mile for U.S. Airlines (cents)   🛢   **SeatMile**

Airline	Total	Labor
AirTran	8.64	3.64
Alaska Air	9.85	4.43
America West	8.20	2.21
American	10.78	4.87
Continental	9.22	3.69
Delta	10.32	4.35
JetBlue	7.71	1.97
Northwest	9.50	4.12
Southwest	7.41	2.89
United	11.33	4.78
US Airways	12.10	5.78

Source: *Detroit Free Press,* April 9, 2003, p. 4F.

3.42   (a) Use Excel to prepare an appropriate type of chart (bar, line, pie, scatter) to display the following data. Modify the default colors, fonts, etc., as you judge appropriate to make the display effective. (b) Would more than one kind of display be acceptable? Why or why not?

U.S. Fatal Crash Statistics, 2000   🛢   **Fatal**

Age Group	Percent of Drivers	Percent of Fatal Crashes
15–20	6.8	14.6
21–24	6.7	10.5
25–34	19.3	20.8
35–44	22.1	19.7
45–54	18.9	14.6
55–64	11.9	8.4
65–69	4.4	2.7
70+	9.9	8.4

Source: www-nrd.nhtsa.dot.gov.

Note: Columns may not sum to 100 due to rounding.

3.43   (a) Use Excel to prepare an appropriate type of chart (bar, line, pie, scatter) to display the following data. Modify the default colors, fonts, etc., as you judge appropriate to make the display effective. (b) Would more than one kind of display be acceptable? Why or why not?

Day Care Accidents by Time of Day   🛢   **Accidents**

Time of Day	Percent
Before 9	7.4
9 to 12	48.6
12 to 3	20.7
3 to 5	18.4
Unknown	4.9
Total	100.0

Source: R. Elardo, H. C. Solomons, and B. C. Snider, "An Analysis of Accidents at a Day Care Center," *American Journal of Orthopsy* 57, no. 1 (January 1987), pp. 60–65. Copyright © 1987 American Orthopsychiatric Association, Inc. Used with permission.

3.44 (a) Use Excel to prepare an appropriate type of chart (bar, line, pie, scatter) to display the following data. Modify the default colors, fonts, etc., as you judge appropriate to make the display effective. (b) Would more than one kind of display be acceptable? Why or why not?

Fatal Complications from Liposuction   Liposuc

Type of Complication	Percent of Total Fatalities
Blood clots	23.1
Abdominal perforation	14.6
Anesthesia complications	10.0
Fat embolism	8.5
Cardiorespiratory failure	5.4
Massive infection	5.4
Hemorrhage	4.6
Unknown/confidential	28.0
Total	100.0

Source: *San Francisco Chronicle,* June 30, 2002, p. A21.

Note: Details do not add to 100 percent due to rounding.

3.45 (a) Use Excel to prepare an appropriate type of chart (bar, line, pie, scatter) to display the following data. Modify the default colors, fonts, etc., as you judge appropriate to make the display effective. (b) Would more than one kind of display be acceptable? Why or why not?

2001 Average Assembly Productivity   Assembly

Firm	Hours per Vehicle
Nissan	17.92
Honda	19.78
Mitsubishi	21.82
Toyota	22.53
NUMMI	22.68
GM	26.10
Ford	26.87
CAMI	28.97
Auto Alliance	30.42
Chrysler Group	30.82

Source: *Detroit Free Press,* June 14, 2002, p. 1F.

3.46 (a) Use Excel to prepare an appropriate type of chart (bar, line, pie, scatter) to display the following data. Modify the default colors, fonts, etc., as you judge appropriate to make the display effective. (b) Would more than one kind of display be acceptable? Why or why not?

Average Age of Planes, 1999   Planes

Airline	Age (years)
Alaska	7.6
America West	11.0
American Airlines	10.7
Continental	11.3
Delta	12.3
Northwest	20.0
Southwest Airlines	8.3
TWA	16.2
United Airlines	9.0
US Airways	13.3

Source: *Detroit Free Press,* March 18, 1999, p. 1F.

3.47 (a) Use Excel to prepare an appropriate type of chart (bar, line, pie, scatter) to display the following data. Modify the default colors, fonts, etc., as you judge appropriate to make the display effective. (b) Would more than one kind of display be acceptable? Why or why not?

PC Shipments Worldwide, 2002   **PCShip**

Company	Units (000)
Hewlett-Packard	21,478
Dell	20,112
IBM	7,928
NEC	4,550
Toshiba	4,237
Others	74,046
Total	132,351

Source: *PC Magazine* 22, no. 4 (March 11, 2003), p. 27.

3.48 (a) Use Excel to prepare an appropriate type of chart (bar, line, pie, scatter) to display the following data. Modify the default colors, fonts, etc., as you judge appropriate to make the display effective. (b) Would more than one kind of display be acceptable? Why or why not?

Survey of 282,549 Freshmen at 437 Colleges and Universities   **Freshmen**

Year	Percent Who Study at Least 6 Hours/Week	Percent Who Plan to Major in Business
1995	31.6	17.6
1996	31.6	18.2
1997	32.7	17.0
1998	30.9	16.0
1999	28.9	16.2
2000	26.1	16.3
2001	21.8	15.6
2002	21.9	15.8

Source: *Chronical of Higher Education,* January 27, 2003; and UCLA's Higher Education Research Institute.

3.49 (a) Use Excel to prepare an appropriate type of chart (bar, line, pie, scatter) to display the following data. Modify the default colors, fonts, etc., as you judge appropriate to make the display effective. (b) Would more than one kind of display be acceptable? Why or why not?

Average Wedding Expenses in 2002   **Wedding**

Expense	$ Amount
Rings (engagement, wedding)	4,877
Photos	1,814
Flowers	967
Reception	7,630
Attire (except bride)	1,656
Bride's attire, makeup, hair	1,523
Rehearsal dinner	875
Music	900
Other	2,118

Source: *The New York Times,* July 13, 2003, p. 17.

3.50   Could the following table be made into an effective chart? If so, do it. If not, explain why not.

Average 401(k) Asset Allocations (percent of total assets)	Asset401K			
Investment Type	1996	1998	2000	2002
Equity funds	44	50	51	40
Company stock	19	18	19	16
Stable value funds	16	12	11	16
Bond funds	7	6	5	11
Balanced funds	8	8	8	9
Money market funds	5	5	4	6
Total	100	100	100	100

Source: *The Wall Street Journal,* July 19, 2004.

May not add to total due to rounding.

3.51   Could the following table be made into an effective chart? If so, do it. If not, explain why not.

Asset Allocation of European Pension Funds, 1999		AssetEur			
Nation	Domestic Equities	Domestic Bonds	Foreign Equities	Foreign Bonds	Real Estate	Cash/ Other
Austria	8	55	20	17	0	0
Belgium	9	15	46	23	3	4
Denmark	16	58	13	2	9	2
Finland	15	57	4	9	7	8
France	10	65	2	3	2	18
Germany	10	43	5	2	7	33
Ireland	25	12	44	10	5	4
Italy	16	35	0	0	48	1
Norway	13	50	11	16	6	4
Portugal	15	55	14	3	2	11
Spain	13	53	12	9	1	13
Sweden	24	44	14	8	5	5
Switzerland	18	26	9	13	25	9
U.K.	55	9	18	8	3	8

Source: R. Banz and S. Clough, "Globalization Reshaping World's Financial Markets," *Journal of Financial Planning* 15, no. 4 (April 2002), p. 74. Copyright © 2002. Used with permission.

Rows may not sum to 100 due to rounding.

DO-IT-YOURSELF

3.52   (a) On the Web, look up "geographical information systems" or "GIS." Do you find many references? (b) Suggest some potential applications of GIS (e.g., marketing, health care, government, military).

3.53   (a) Clip an example of a deceptive visual data presentation from a recent magazine or newspaper (if it is from a library, make a photocopy instead). Try to choose an outrageous example that violates many principles of ideal graphs. (b) Cite the exact source where you found the display. (c) What do you think is its presumed purpose? (d) Write a short, critical evaluation of its strengths and weaknesses. Be sure to attach the original clipping (or a good photocopy) to your analysis.

3.54   (a) Make a hand-drawn graph that presents some numerical data of your own (e.g., your GPA, earnings, work hours, golf scores) in a visual manner designed to dramatize or slant the facts. Violate the principles of ideal graphs *without actually changing any of the numbers*. (b) List each violation you tried to illustrate. (c) Now present the same data in an objective visual display that violates as few rules as possible. (d) Which took more time and effort, the deceptive display or the objective one?

Related Reading

Tables

Ehrenberg, A.S.C. "The Problem of Numeracy." *The American Statistician* 35, no. 2 (May 1981), pp. 67–71.

Sabin, William A. *The Gregg Reference Manual.* 9th ed. Glencoe/McGraw-Hill, 2000.

Charts

Chambers, J. M.; W. S. Cleveland; B. Kleiner; and P. A. Tukey. *Graphical Methods for Data Analysis*. Duxbury, 1983.

Cleveland, William S. *The Elements of Graphing Data*. Hobart Press, 1994.

Cleveland, William S. *Visualizing Data*. Hobart Press, 1993.

Huff, Darrell; and Irving Geiss. *How to Lie with Statistics*. W. W. Norton, 1954.

Jones, Gerald E. *How to Lie with Charts*. Sybex, 1995.

Koomey, Jonathan G. *Turning Numbers into Knowledge: Mastering the Art of Problem Solving*. Analytics Press, 2001.

"Market Spider: A New Tool Measures the Maturity of Managed Care Markets." *Hospitals & Health Networks* 71, no. 6 (March 20, 1997), pp. 74–75.

Monmonier, Mark. *How to Lie with Maps*. University of Chicago Press, 1996.

Steinbart, John P. "The Auditor's Responsibility for the Accuracy of Graphs in Annual Reports: Some Evidence of the Need for Additional Guidance." *Accounting Horizons* 3, no. 3 (1989), pp. 60–70.

Taylor, Barbara G.; and Lane K. Anderson. "Misleading Graphs: Guidelines for the Accountant." *Journal of Accountancy,* October 1986, pp. 126–35.

Tufte, Edward R. *The Visual Display of Quantitative Information*. Graphics Press, 1995.

Zelazny, Gene. *Say It with Charts: The Executive's Guide to Visual Communication*. Irwin Professional Publishers, 1995.

Zweig, Jason. "Chart Burn: The Mountain Charts in Fund Ads Can Be Confusing." *Money* 29, no. 4 (April 2000), pp. 67–68.

LearningStats Unit 03   Visual Displays   LS

LearningStats Unit 03 introduces tables, charts, and rules for visual displays. Modules are designed for self-study, so you can proceed at your own pace, concentrate on material that is new, and pass quickly over things that you already know. Your instructor may assign specific modules, or you may decide to check them out because the topic sounds interesting. In addition to helping you learn about statistics, they may be useful as references later on.

Topic	LearningStats Modules
Effective visual displays	Presenting Data—I
	Presenting Data—II
	EDA Graphics
How to make an Excel chart	Excel Charts: Step-by-Step
	Pivot Tables
	Using MegaStat
	Using Visual Statistics
	Using MINITAB
Types of Excel charts	Excel Charts: Bar, Pie, Line
	Excel Charts: Scatter, Pareto, Other
	Wrong Chart Type?
	Gallery of Charts—1
	Gallery of Charts—2
	Gallery of Charts—3
	Gallery of Charts—4
Applications	Adult Heights
	Bimodal Data
	Sturges's Rule
	Stem and Leaf Plots

Key: = PowerPoint   = Word   = Excel

Descriptive Statistics

Chapter Contents

Chapter Learning Objectives

When you finish this chapter you should be able to

- Explain the concepts of central tendency, dispersion, and shape.
- Use Excel to obtain descriptive statistics and visual displays.
- Calculate and interpret common descriptive statistics.
- Identify the properties of common measures of central tendency.
- Calculate and interpret common measures of dispersion.
- Transform a data set into standardized values.
- Apply the Empirical Rule and recognize outliers.
- Calculate quartiles and other percentiles.
- Make and interpret box plots.
- Calculate the mean and standard deviation from grouped data.
- Explain the concepts of skewness and kurtosis.

The last chapter explained *visual* descriptions of data (e.g., histograms, dot plots). This chapter explains *numerical* descriptions of data. Descriptive measures derived from a sample (*n* items) are *statistics,* while for a population (*N* items or infinite) they are *parameters.* As with visual data, numerical data have three key characteristics: central tendency, dispersion, and shape. Table 4.1 summarizes the questions that we will be asking about the data.

Chapter 1

Characteristic	Interpretation
Central Tendency	Where are the data values concentrated? What seem to be typical or middle data values?
Dispersion	How much variation is there in the data? How spread out are the data values? Are there unusual values?
Shape	Are the data values distributed symmetrically? Skewed? Sharply peaked? Flat? Bimodal?

TABLE 4.1

Characteristics of Numerical Data

EXAMPLE

Vehicle Quality

Every year, J.D. Power and Associates issues its initial vehicle quality ratings. These ratings are of interest to consumers, dealers, and manufacturers. Table 4.2 shows defect rates for 37 vehicle brands. We will demonstrate how numerical statistics can be used to summarize a data set like this. The brands represented are a random sample that we will use to illustrate certain calculations.

TABLE 4.2   Number of Defects per 100 Vehicles, 2004 Model Year   **JDPower**

Brand	Defects	Brand	Defects	Brand	Defects
Acura	117	Infiniti	104	Oldsmobile	110
Audi	109	Jaguar	98	Pontiac	122
BMW	109	Jeep	136	Porsche	159
Buick	100	Kia	153	Saab	133
Cadillac	93	Land Rover	148	Saturn	149
Chevrolet	119	Lexus	87	Scion	158
Chrysler	120	Lincoln	121	Subaru	123
Dodge	121	Mazda	157	Suzuki	149
Ford	130	Mercedes-Benz	106	Toyota	104
GMC	127	Mercury	100	Volkswagen	164
Honda	99	Mini	142	Volvo	113
Hummer	173	Mitsubishi	130		
Hyundai	102	Nissan	154		

Source: J.D. Power and Associates 2004 Initial Quality Study™. Used with permission.

Note: Ratings are intended for educational purposes only, and should not be used as a guide to consumer decisions.

Preliminary Analysis

Before calculating any statistics, we consider how the data were collected. A Web search reveals that J.D. Power and Associates is a well-established independent company whose methods are widely considered to be objective. Data on defects are obtained by inspecting randomly chosen vehicles for each brand, counting the defects, and dividing the number of defects by the number of vehicles inspected. J.D. Power multiplies the result by 100 to obtain defects per 100 vehicles, rounded to the nearest integer. However, the measurement scale is continuous (e.g., if 4 defects were found in 3 Saabs, the defect rate would be 1.333333, or 133 defects per 100 vehicles). Defect rates would vary from year to year, and perhaps even within a given model year, so the timing of the study could affect the results. Since the analysis is based on sampling, we must allow for the possibility of sampling error. With these cautions in mind, we look at the data. The dot plot, shown in Figure 4.1, offers a visual impression of the data.

FIGURE 4.1

Dot plot of J.D. Power data ($n = 37$ brands)

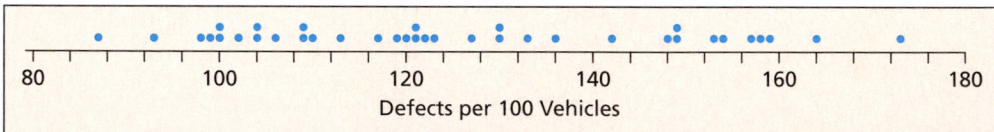

Sorting

A good first step is to sort the data. Except for tiny samples, this would be done in Excel, as illustrated in Figure 4.2. Highlight the data array (including the headings) and click on the menu bar's Data > Sort command, choose the column to sort, and click OK. Table 4.3 shows the sorted data for all 37 brands.

Chapter 1

Visual Displays

The sorted data in Table 4.3 provide insight into central tendency and dispersion. The values range from 87 (Lexus) to 173 (Hummer) and the middle values seem to be in the 120s.

The next visual step is a histogram, shown in Figure 4.3. Sturges's Rule suggests 5 bins, but 10 bins show more detail. The sample is too small to draw strong inferences about shape, but both histograms are roughly symmetric (maybe slightly right-skewed) with no extreme values. Both show a modal class toward the low end (100 < 120 for 5 bins, 100 < 110 for 10 bins).

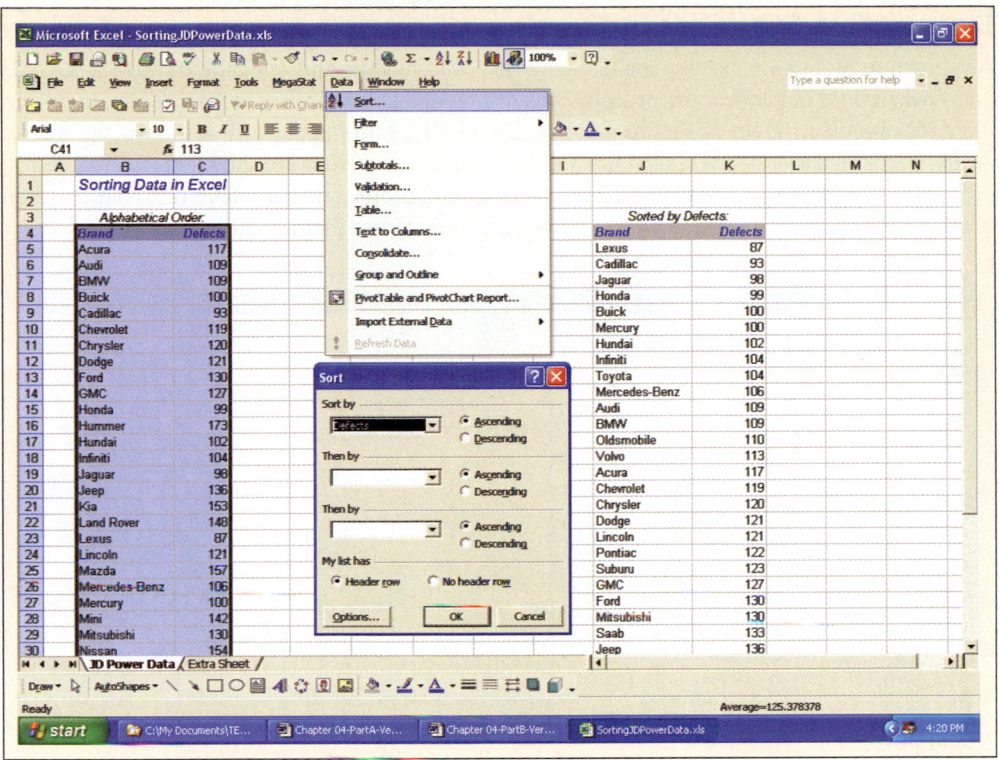

FIGURE 4.2

Sorting data in Excel
SortingInExcel

Brand	Defects	Brand	Defects	Brand	Defects
Lexus	87	Volvo	113	Mini	142
Cadillac	93	Acura	117	Land Rover	148
Jaguar	98	Chevrolet	119	Saturn	149
Honda	99	Chrysler	120	Suzuki	149
Buick	100	Dodge	121	Kia	153
Mercury	100	Lincoln	121	Nissan	154
Hyundai	102	Pontiac	122	Mazda	157
Infiniti	104	Subaru	123	Scion	158
Toyota	104	GMC	127	Porsche	159
Mercedes-Benz	106	Ford	130	Volkswagen	164
Audi	109	Mitsubishi	130	Hummer	173
BMW	109	Saab	133		
Oldsmobile	110	Jeep	136		

TABLE 4.3

Number of Defects per 100 Vehicles (2004 Model Year) Ranked Lowest to Highest **JDPower**

Source: J.D. Power and Associates 2004 Initial Quality Study[TM]. Used with permission.

FIGURE 4.3

Histograms of J.D. Power data ($n = 37$ brands)

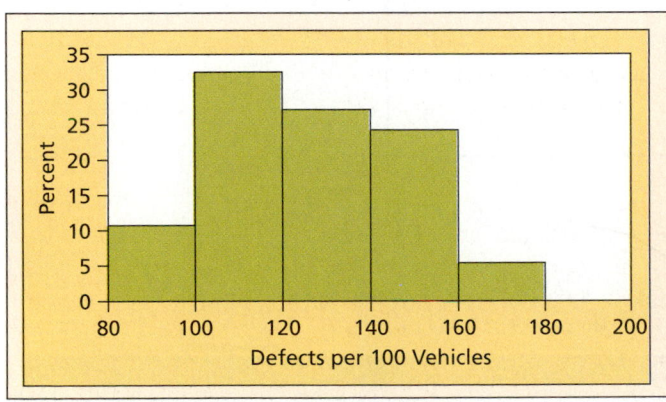

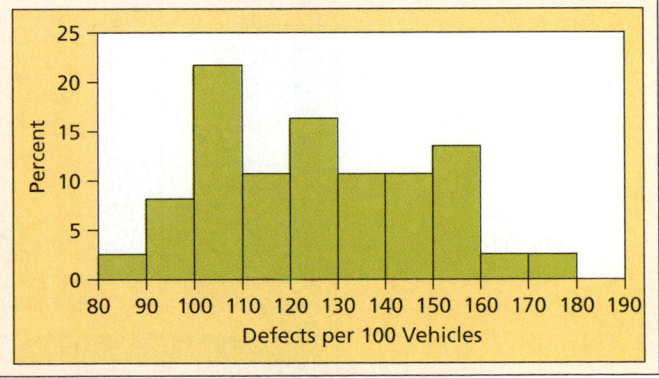

Descriptive Statistics in Excel

As shown in Figure 4.4, use the menu bar's Tools > Data Analysis and select Descriptive Statistics. (If Data Analysis does not appear under Tools, click Add-Ins and select Analysis ToolPak.) Then, highlight the data range as shown in Figure 4.5, specify a cell for the upper left corner of the output range, check Summary Statistics, and click OK. The resulting statistics are shown in Figure 4.6. You probably recognize some of them (e.g., mean, median, mode, standard deviation) but you also need to know exactly how they are calculated and how to use them to understand a data set.

FIGURE 4.4

Excel's data analysis

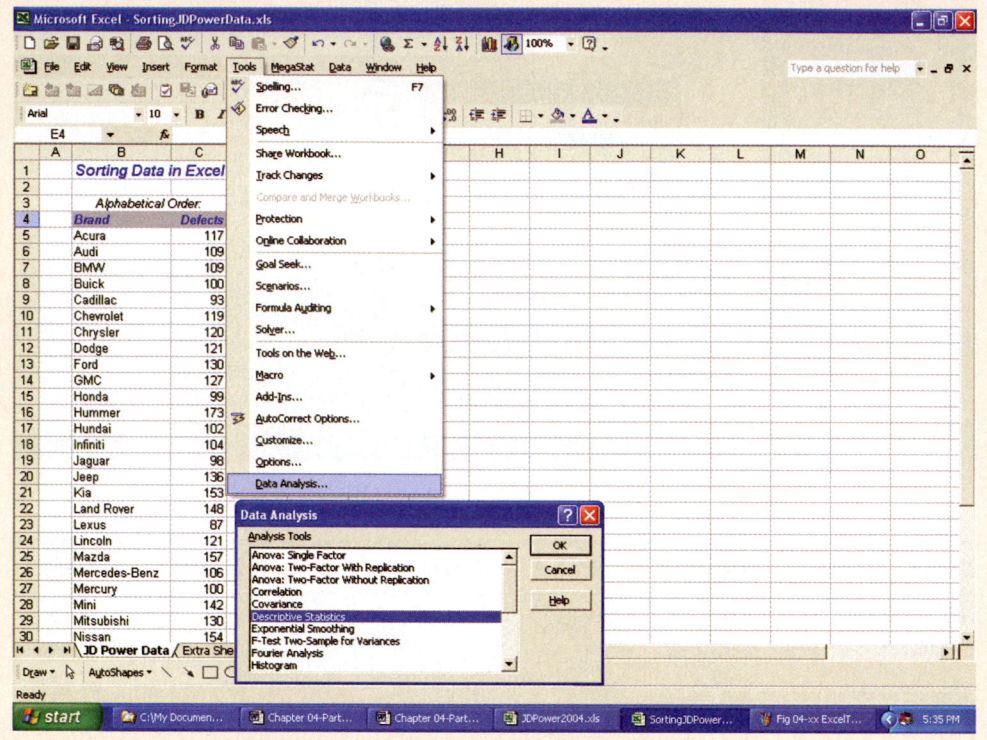

FIGURE 4.5

Specifying data range

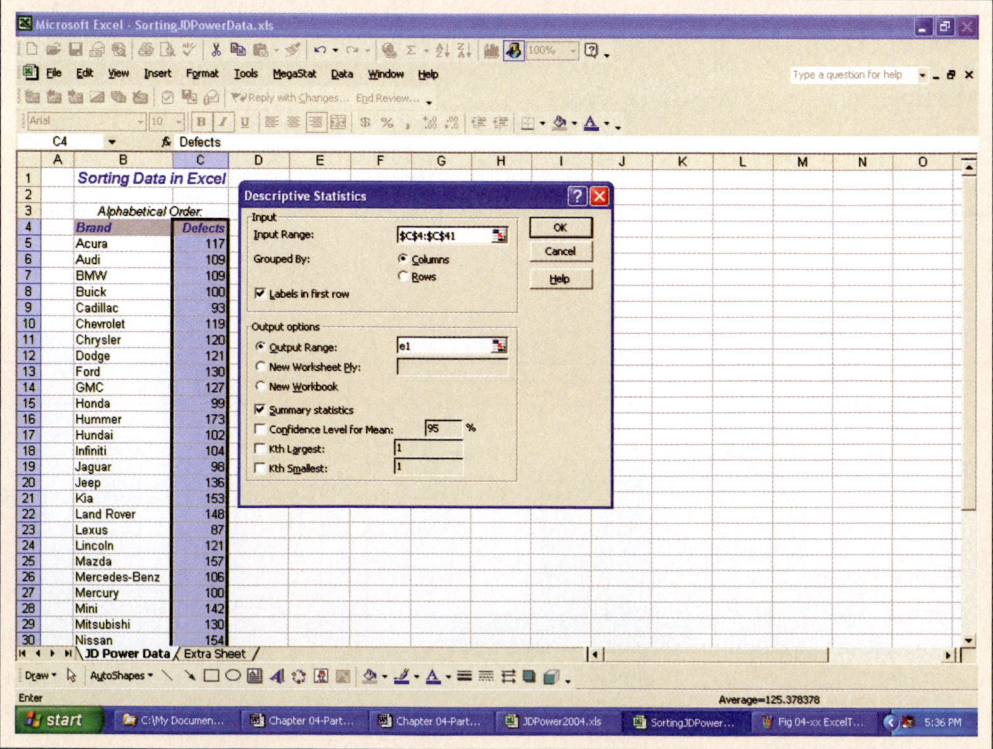

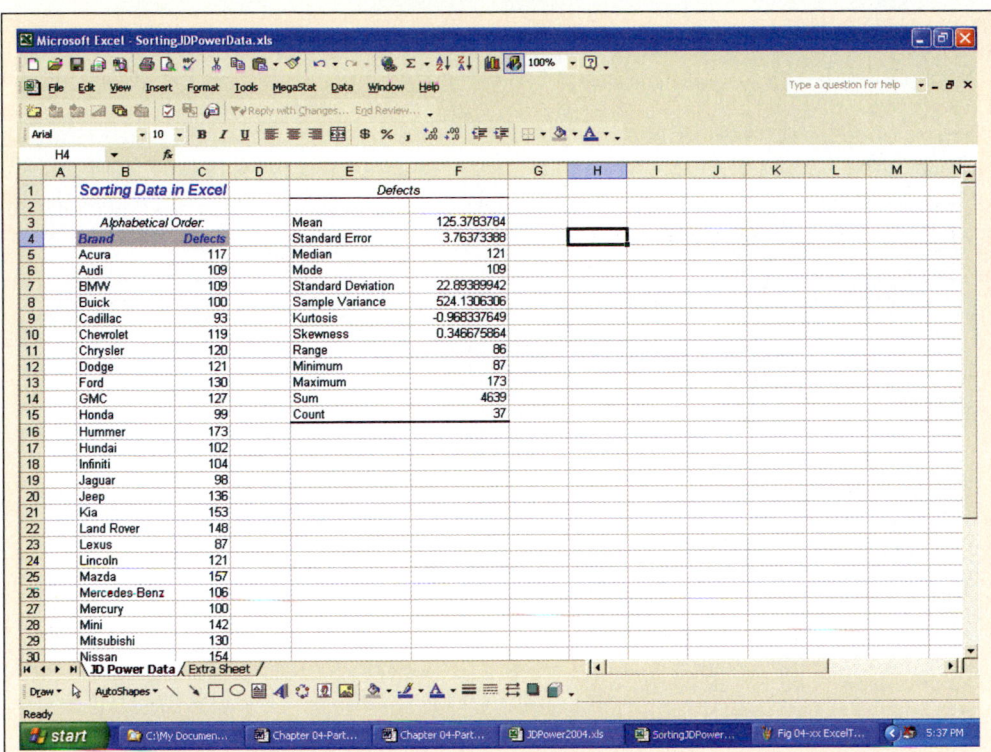

FIGURE 4.6

Excel's descriptive statistics

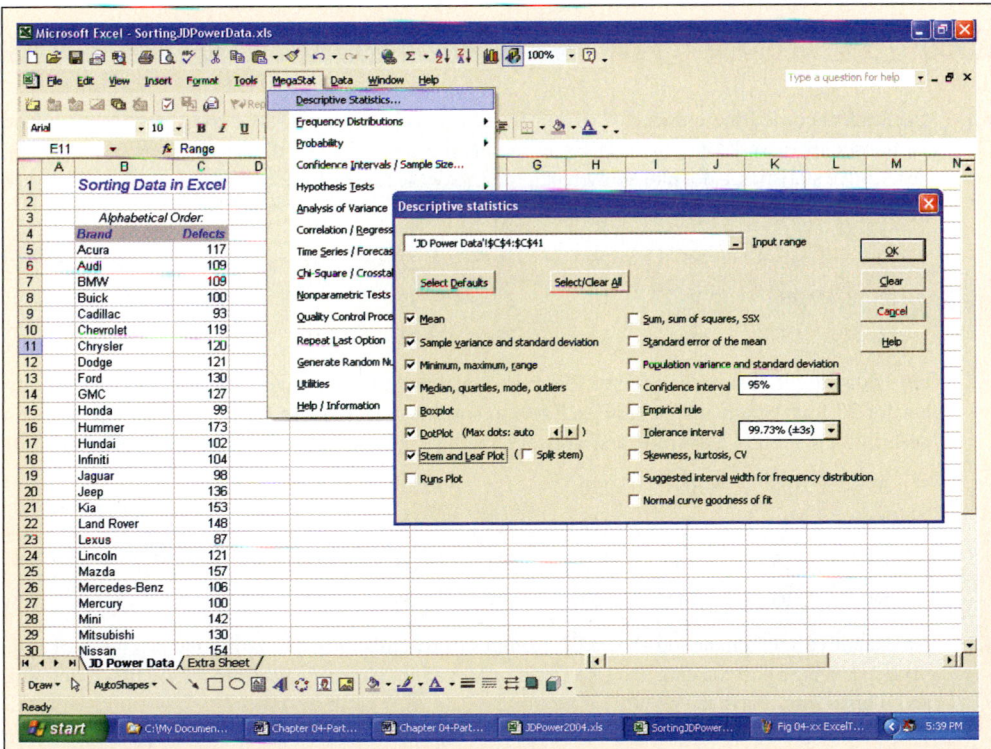

FIGURE 4.7

MegaStat's descriptive
statistics menu

Descriptive Statistics in MegaStat

You can get similar statistics from MegaStat, as illustrated in Figure 4.7. MegaStat will also give you a dot plot or a histogram. Results appear on a separate worksheet, as shown in Figure 4.8. Try using both Excel and MegaStat (or MINITAB) to see the similarities and differences in their interfaces and results. You could also refer to *LearningStats* 04 for PowerPoint demonstrations with more detailed explanations of how to use Excel and MINITAB for statistical data description.

FIGURE 4.8

MegaStat's descriptive statistics

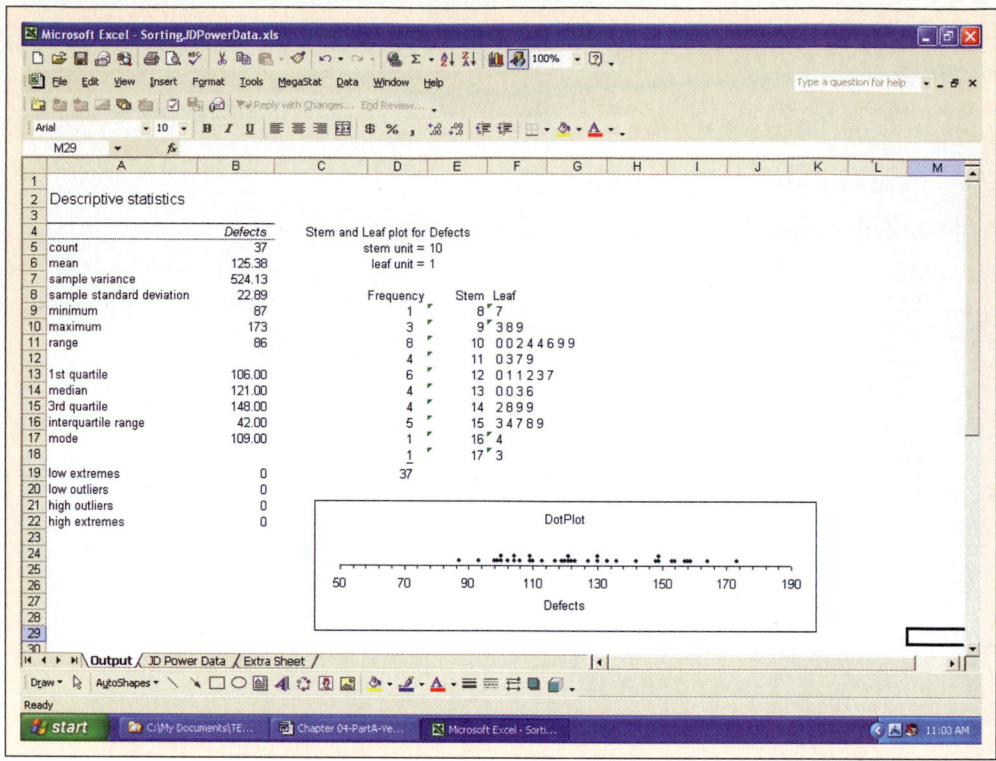

SECTION EXERCISES

4.1   CitiBank recorded the number of customers to use a downtown ATM during the noon hour on 32 consecutive workdays. (a) Use Excel to sort the data. (b) Use Excel or MegaStat to obtain descriptive statistics, a dot plot, and a histogram. Save the results for Exercise 4.5.   **CitiBank**

25	37	23	26	30	40	25	26
39	32	21	26	19	27	32	25
18	26	34	18	31	35	21	33
33	9	16	32	35	42	15	24

4.2   On Friday night, the owner of Chez Pierre in downtown Chicago noted the amount spent for dinner for 28 four-person tables. (a) Use Excel to sort the data. (b) Use Excel or MegaStat to obtain descriptive statistics, a dot plot, and a histogram. Save the results for Exercise 4.6.   **Dinner**

95	103	109	170	114	113	107
124	105	80	104	84	176	115
69	95	134	108	61	160	128
68	95	61	150	52	87	136

4.3   An executive's telephone log showed the lengths of 65 calls initiated during the last week of July. (a) Use Excel to sort the data. (b) Use Excel or MegaStat to obtain descriptive statistics, a dot plot, and a histogram. Save the results for Exercise 4.7.   **CallLength**

1	2	10	5	3	3	2	20	1	1
6	3	13	2	2	1	26	3	1	3
1	2	1	7	1	2	3	1	2	12
1	4	2	2	29	1	1	1	8	5
1	4	2	1	1	1	1	6	1	2
3	3	6	1	3	1	1	5	1	18
2	13	13	1	6					

When we speak of *central tendency* we are trying to describe the middle or typical values of a distribution. You can assess central tendency in a general way from a dot plot or histogram, but numerical statistics allow more precise statements. Table 4.4 lists six common measures of central tendency. Each has strengths and weaknesses. We need to look at several of them to obtain a clear picture of central tendency.

Chapter 1

Mean

The most familiar statistical measure of central tendency is the **mean.** It is the sum of the data values divided by number of data items. For a population we denote it μ, while for a sample we call it $\bar{x}$. We use equation 4.1 to calculate the mean of a population:

$$\mu = \frac{\sum\limits_{i=1}^{N} x_i}{N} \quad \text{(population definition)} \qquad (4.1)$$

Since we rarely deal with populations, the sample notation of equation 4.2 is more commonly seen:

$$\bar{x} = \frac{\sum\limits_{i=1}^{n} x_i}{n} \quad \text{(sample definition)} \qquad (4.2)$$

We calculate the mean by using Excel's function =AVERAGE(Data) where Data is an array containing the data. So for the sample of $n = 37$ car brands:

$$\bar{x} = \frac{\sum\limits_{i=1}^{n} x_i}{n} = \frac{87 + 93 + 98 + \cdots + 159 + 164 + 173}{37} = \frac{4639}{37} = 125.38$$

Characteristics of the Mean

The arithmetic mean is the "average" with which most of us are familiar. The mean is affected by every sample item. It is the balancing point or fulcrum in a distribution if we view the X-axis as a lever arm and represent each data item as a physical weight, as illustrated in Figure 4.9 for the J.D. Powers data.

TABLE 4.4   **Six Measures of Central Tendency**

Statistic	Formula	Excel Formula	Pro	Con
Mean	$\dfrac{1}{n}\sum\limits_{i=1}^{n} x_i$	=AVERAGE(Data)	Familiar and uses all the sample information.	Influenced by extreme values.
Median	Middle value in sorted array	=MEDIAN(Data)	Robust when extreme data values exist.	Ignores extremes and can be affected by gaps in data values.
Mode	Most frequently occurring data value	=MODE(Data)	Useful for attribute data or discrete data with a small range.	May not be unique, and is not helpful for continuous data.
Midrange	$\dfrac{x_{min} + x_{max}}{2}$	=0.5*(MIN(Data) +MAX(Data))	Easy to understand and calculate.	Influenced by extreme values and ignores most data values.
Geometric mean (G)	$\sqrt[n]{x_1 x_2 \cdots x_n}$	=GEOMEAN(Data)	Useful for growth rates and mitigates high extremes.	Less familiar and requires positive data.
Trimmed mean	Same as the mean except omit highest and lowest k% of data values (e.g., 5%)	=TRMEAN(Data, %)	Mitigates effects of extreme values.	Excludes some data values that could be relevant.

FIGURE 4.9

Mean as fulcrum
($n = 37$ vehicles)

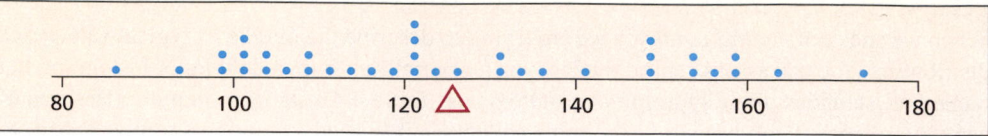

The mean is the balancing point because it has the property that distances from the mean to the data points *always* sum to zero:

(4.3)
$$\sum_{i=1}^{n} (x_i - \bar{x}) = 0$$

This statement is true for *any* sample or population, regardless of its shape (skewed, symmetric, bimodal, etc.). Even when there are extreme values, the distances below the mean are *exactly* counterbalanced by the distances above the mean. For example, Bob's scores on five quizzes were 42, 60, 70, 75, 78. His mean is pulled down to 65, mainly because of his poor showing on one quiz, as illustrated in Figure 4.10.

Although the data are asymmetric, the three scores above the mean exactly counterbalance the two scores below the mean:

$$\sum_{i=1}^{n} (x_i - \bar{x}) = (42 - 65) + (60 - 65) + (70 - 65) + (75 - 65) + (78 - 65)$$
$$= (-23) + (-5) + (5) + (10) + (13) = -28 + 28 = 0$$

FIGURE 4.10

Bob's quiz scores
($n = 5$ quizzes)

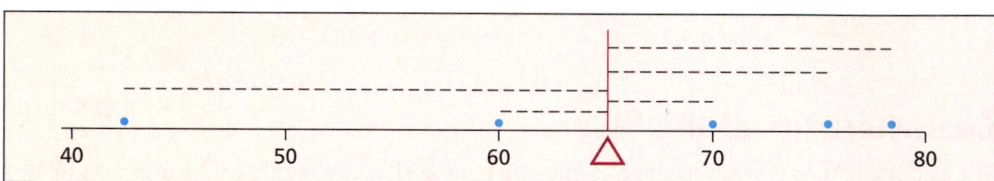

FIGURE 4.11

Illustration of the median

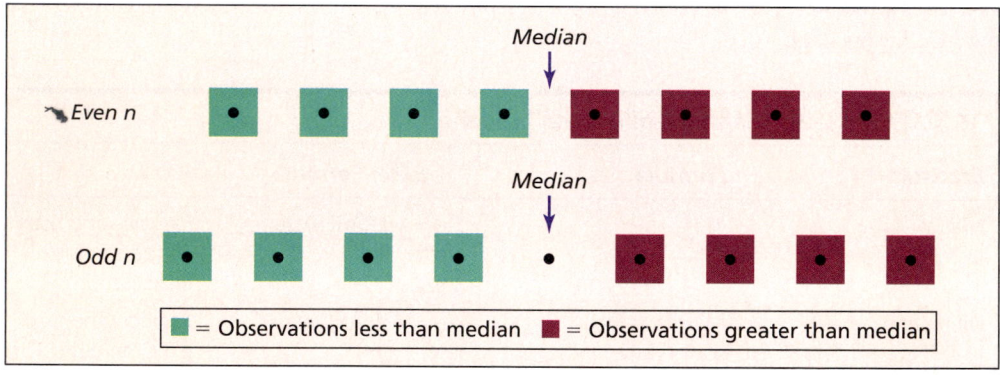

Median

The *median* (denoted M) is the 50th percentile or midpoint of the *sorted* sample data set $x_1, x_2, \ldots, x_n$. It separates the upper and lower half of the sorted observations:

Median
← Lower 50% | Upper 50% →

The median is the middle observation in the sorted array if n is odd, but is the average of the middle two observations if n is even, as illustrated in Figure 4.11.

For example, if we have an even n, say $n = 6$,

11   12   15   17   21   32

then the median is halfway *between* the third and fourth observation in the sorted array:

$$M = (x_3 + x_4)/2 = (15 + 17)/2 = 16$$

Similarly for an odd n, say $n = 7$,

$$12 \qquad 23 \qquad 23 \qquad \mathbf{25} \qquad 27 \qquad 34 \qquad 41$$

the median is the fourth observation in the sorted array:

$$M = x_4 = 25$$

The *position* of the median in the sorted array is $(n + 1)/2$ so we can write:

$$\text{Median} = x_{(n+1)/2} \quad \text{for } odd \ n \qquad \text{and} \qquad \text{Median} = \frac{x_{n/2} + x_{(n/2+1)}}{2} \quad \text{for even } n \qquad \textbf{(4.4)}$$

Excel's function for the median is =MEDIAN(Data) where Data is the data array. For the 37 vehicle quality ratings (odd n) the *position* of the median is $(n + 1)/2 = (37 + 1)/2 = 19$ so the median is:

$$M = x_{(n+1)/2} = x_{(37+1)/2} = x_{19} = 121$$

It is tempting to imagine that half the observations are less than the median, but this is not necessarily the case. For example, here are nine exam scores in ascending order:

$$51 \qquad 66 \qquad 71 \qquad 78 \qquad 78 \qquad \mathbf{78} \qquad 81 \qquad 82 \qquad 82 \qquad 91 \qquad 99$$

Their median is 78. But only three data values are *below* 78, while five data values are *above* 78. This median did not provide a clean "50-50 split" in the data, because there were several identical exam scores clustered at the middle of the distribution. This situation is not so unusual. In fact, we might expect it when there is strong central tendency in a data set.

Characteristics of the Median

The median is especially useful when there are extreme values. For example, government statistics use the median income, because a few very high incomes will render the mean atypical. The median's insensitivity to extremes may seem advantageous or not, depending on your point of view. Consider three students' scores on five quizzes:

Tom's scores: 20, 40, 70, 75, 80   Mean = 57, Median = 70, Total = 285

Jake's scores: 60, 65, 70, 90, 95   Mean = 76, Median = 70, Total = 380

Mary's scores: 50, 65, 70, 75, 90   Mean = 70, Median = 70, Total = 350

Each student has the same median quiz score (70). Tom, whose mean is pulled down by a few low scores, would rather have his grade based on the median. Jake, whose mean is pulled up by a few high scores, would prefer the mean. Mary is indifferent, since her measures of central tendency agree (she has symmetric scores).

The median lacks some of the mean's useful mathematical properties. For example, if we multiply the mean by the sample size, we always get the total of the data values. But this is not true for the median. For instance, Tom's total points on all five quizzes (285) are the product of the sample size times his mean ($5 \times 57 = 285$). But this is not true for his median ($5 \times 70 = 350$). That is one reason why instructors tend to base their semester grades on the mean. Otherwise, the lowest and highest scores would not "count."

Mode

The *mode* is the most frequently occurring data value. It may be similar to the mean and median, if data values near the center of the sorted array tend to occur often. But it may also be quite different from the mean and median. A data set may have multiple modes or no mode at all. For example, consider these four students' scores on five quizzes:

Lee's scores: 60, 70, 70, 70, 80   Mean = 70, Median = 70, Mode = 70

Pat's scores: 45, 45, 70, 90, 100   Mean = 70, Median = 70, Mode = 45

Sam's scores: 50, 60, 70, 80, 90   Mean = 70, Median = 70, Mode = none

Xiao's scores: 50, 50, 70, 90, 90   Mean = 70, Median = 70, Modes = 50, 90

Each student has the same mean (70) and median (70). Lee's mode (70) is the same as his mean and median, but Pat's mode (45) is nowhere near the "middle." Sam has no mode, while Xiao has two modes (50, 90). These examples illustrate some quirks of the mode.

The mode is easy to define, but is *not* easy to calculate (except in very small samples), because it requires tabulating the frequency of occurrence of every distinct data value. For example, the sample of $n = 37$ brands has six modes (100, 104, 109, 121, 130, 149), each occurring twice:

87	93	98	99	*100*	*100*	102	*104*	*104*	106	*109*	*109*	110
113	117	119	120	*121*	*121*	122	123	127	*130*	*130*	133	136
142	148	*149*	*149*	153	154	157	158	159	164	173		

Excel's function =MODE(Data) will return #N/A if there is no mode. If there are multiple modes, =MODE(Data) will return the first one it finds. In this example, since our data are already sorted, =MODE(Data) will return 100 as the mode. But if the data were in alphabetical order by car brand (as in Table 4.2) Excel would return 109 as the mode. Sometimes the mode is far from the "middle" of the distribution and may not be at all "typical." Indeed, for the car defects data, one has the feeling that the modes are merely a statistical fluke. For *continuous* data, the mode generally isn't useful, because continuous data values rarely repeat. To assess central tendency in continuous data, we would rely on the mean or median.

But the mode is good for describing central tendency in an *attribute* such as gender (male, female) or college major (accounting, finance, etc.). Indeed, the mode is the *only* useful measure of central tendency for attribute data. The mode is also useful to describe a *discrete* variable with a *small range* (e.g., responses to a five-point Likert scale).

EXAMPLE

Price/Earnings Ratios and Mode

Table 4.5 shows P/E ratios (current stock price divided by the last 12 months' earnings) for a random sample of 68 Standard & Poor's 500 stocks. Although P/E ratios are continuous data, *The Wall Street Journal* rounds the data to the nearest integer.

TABLE 4.5	P/E Ratios for 68 Randomly Chosen S&P 500 Stocks 	PERatios

7	8	8	10	10	10	10	12	13	13	13	13	13	13	13	14	14
14	15	15	15	15	15	16	16	16	17	18	18	18	18	19	19	19
19	19	20	20	20	21	21	21	22	22	23	23	23	24	25	26	26
26	26	27	29	29	30	31	34	36	37	40	41	45	48	55	68	91

Source: *The Wall Street Journal*, July 31, 2003.

Note: The data file has company names and ticker symbols.

Excel's Descriptive Statistics for this sample are:

Mean:	22.7206
Median:	19
Mode:	13
Range:	84
Minimum:	7
Maximum:	91
Sum:	1545
Count:	68

For these 68 observations, 13 is the mode (occurs 7 times) suggesting that it actually is somewhat "typical." However, the dot plot in Figure 4.12 also shows local modes at 10, 13, 15, 19, 23, 26, and 29 (a local mode is a "peak" with "valleys" on either side). These multiple "mini-modes" suggest that the mode is not a stable measure of central tendency and that these modes may not be very likely to recur if we took a different sample.

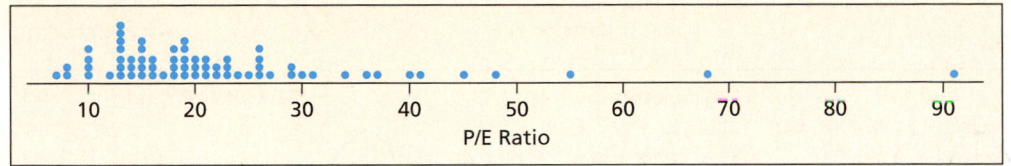

FIGURE 4.12

Dot plot for P/E ratios
($n = 68$ stocks)
PERatios

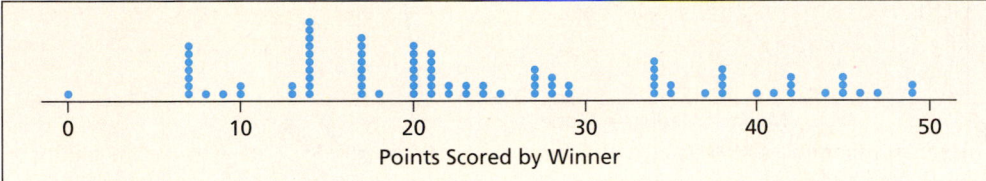

FIGURE 4.13

Dot plot of Rose Bowl
winners' points
($n = 87$ games)
RoseBowl

FIGURE 4.14

Heights of women, men, and both genders combined

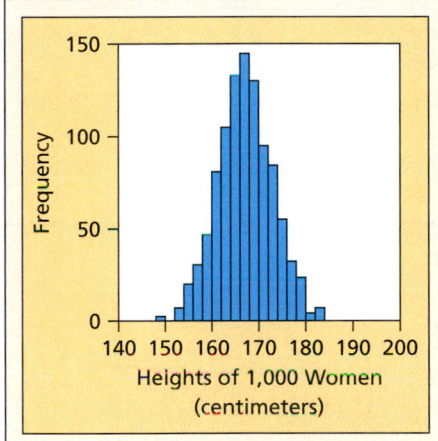
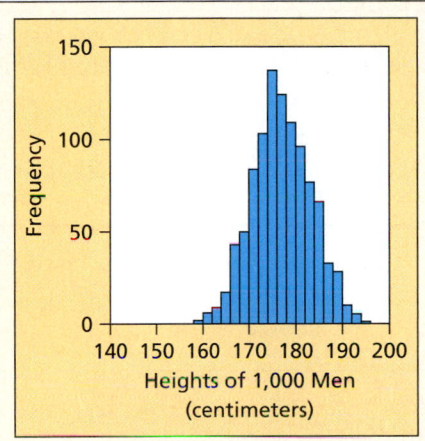
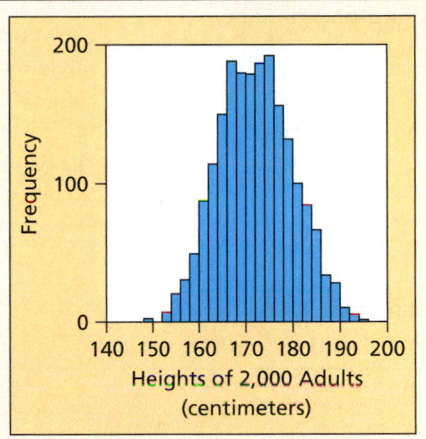

There may be a logical reason for the existence of modes. For example, points scored by winning college football teams on a given Saturday will tend to have modes at multiples of 7 (e.g., 7, 14, 21, etc.) because each touchdown yields 7 points (counting the extra point). Other mini-modes in football scores reflect commonly occurring combinations of scoring events. Figure 4.13 shows a dot plot of the points scored by the winning team in the first 87 Rose Bowl games (one game was a scoreless tie). *The* mode is 14, but there are several other local modes. If you are a football fan, you can figure out, for example, why 20 points occur so often.

When someone refers to a ***bimodal distribution,*** the reference probably is to the histogram rather than the mode of the raw data. A bimodal distribution occurs when dissimilar populations are combined in one sample. For example, if heights of 1,000 adult men and 1,000 adult women are combined into a single sample of 2,000 adults, we would get something like the third histogram in Figure 4.14.

In such a case, the mean of all 2,000 adults would not represent central tendency for either gender. When heterogeneity is known to exist, it would be better to create separate histograms and carry out the analysis on each group separately. Unfortunately, we don't always know when heterogeneous populations have been combined into one sample.

Skewness

The degree of ***skewness*** may be judged by looking at the histogram or by comparing the mean and median. In ***symmetric data,*** the mean and median are about the same. When the data are ***skewed right*** (or ***positively skewed***) the mean exceeds the median. When the data are ***skewed left*** (or ***negatively skewed***) the mean is below the median. Figure 4.15 shows prototype population shapes for each situation.

Chapter 3

FIGURE 4.15

Skewness prototype populations

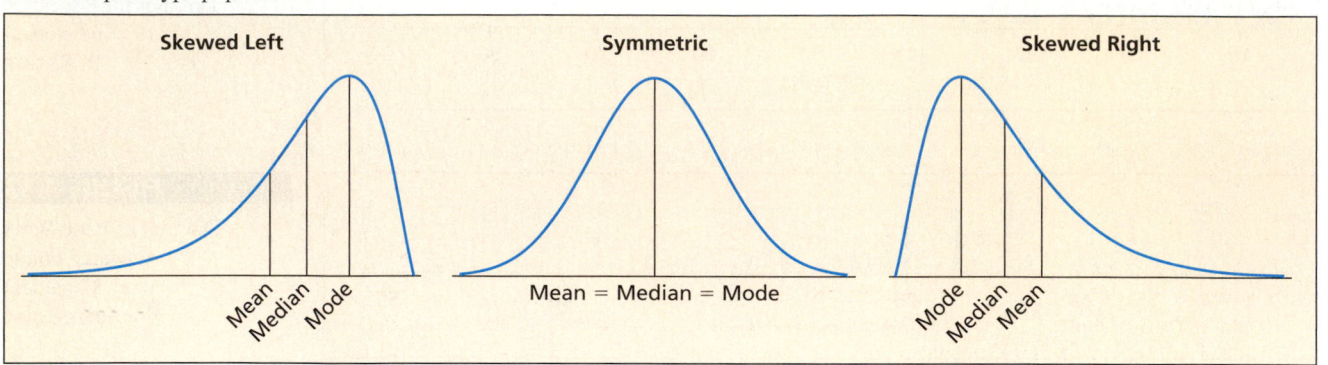

TABLE 4.6

Symptoms of Skewness

Distribution's Shape	Histogram Appearance	Statistics
Skewed left (negative skewness)	Long tail of histogram points left (a few low values but most data on right)	Mean < Median
Symmetric	Tails of histogram are balanced (low/high values offset)	Mean ≈ Median
Skewed right (positive skewness)	Long tail of histogram points right (most data on left but a few high values)	Mean > Median

FIGURE 4.16

Histograms of J.D. Power data ($n = 37$ brands)

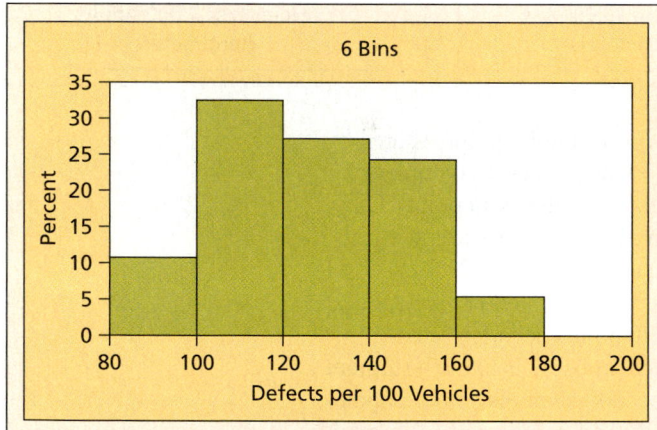
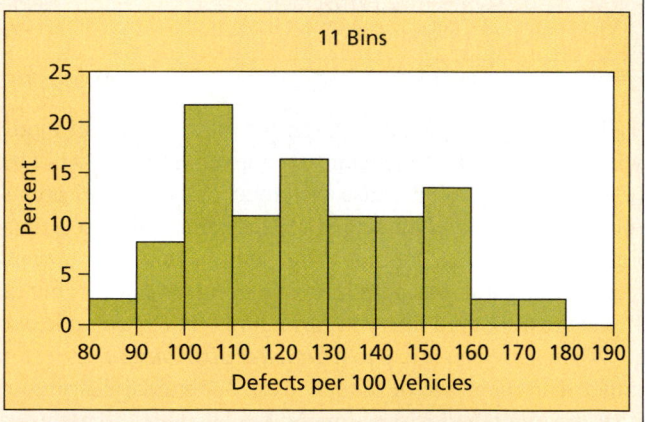

Table 4.6 summarizes the symptoms of skewness in a sample. Since few data sets are exactly symmetric, skewness is a matter of degree. Due to the nature of random sampling, the mean and median may differ, even when a symmetric population is being sampled. Small differences between the mean and median may not indicate significant skewness and may lack practical importance.

For the sample of J.D. Power quality ratings, the mean (125.38) exceeds the median (121), which suggests right-skewness. However, this small difference between the mean and median may lack practical importance, and the histograms in Figure 4.16 suggest that the skewness is minimal. In Section 4.8, we will introduce more precise tests for skewness.

Business data tend to be right-skewed because financial variables often are unlimited at the top but are bounded from below by zero (e.g., salaries, employees, inventory). This is also true for engineering data (e.g., time to failure, defect rates) and sports (e.g., scores in soccer). Even in a Likert scale (1, 2, 3, 4, 5) a few responses in the opposite tail can skew the mean if most replies are clustered toward the top or bottom of the scale.

SECTION EXERCISES

4.4 Prof. Hardtack gave four Friday quizzes last semester in his 10-student senior tax accounting class. (a) Without using Excel, find the mean, median, and mode for each quiz. (b) Do these measures of central tendency agree? Explain. (c) For each data set, note strengths or weaknesses of each statistic of central tendency. (d) Are the data symmetric or skewed? If skewed, which direction? (e) Briefly describe and compare student performance on each quiz.
Quizzes

Quiz 1: 60, 60, 60, 60, 71, 73, 74, 75, 88, 99

Quiz 2: 65, 65, 65, 65, 70, 74, 79, 79, 79, 79

Quiz 3: 66, 67, 70, 71, 72, 72, 74, 74, 95, 99

Quiz 4: 10, 49, 70, 80, 85, 88, 90, 93, 97, 98

4.5 CitiBank recorded the number of customers to use a downtown ATM during the noon hour on 32 consecutive workdays. (a) Use Excel or MegaStat to find the mean, median, and mode. (b) Do these measures of central tendency agree? Explain. (c) Are the data symmetric or skewed? If skewed, which direction? (d) Note strengths or weaknesses of each statistic of central tendency for the data. **CitiBank**

25	37	23	26	30	40	25	26
39	32	21	26	19	27	32	25
18	26	34	18	31	35	21	33
33	9	16	32	35	42	15	24

4.6 On Friday night, the owner of Chez Pierre in downtown Chicago noted the amount spent for dinner for 28 four-person tables. (a) Use Excel or MegaStat to find the mean, median, and mode. (b) Do these measures of central tendency agree? Explain. (c) Are the data symmetric or skewed? If skewed, which direction? (d) Note strengths or weaknesses of each statistic of central tendency for the data. **Dinner**

95	103	109	170	114	113	107
124	105	80	104	84	176	115
69	95	134	108	61	160	128
68	95	61	150	52	87	136

4.7 An executive's telephone log showed the lengths of 65 calls initiated during the last week of July. (a) Sort the data. (b) Use Excel or MegaStat to find the mean, median, and mode. (c) Do the measures of central tendency agree? Explain. (d) Are the data symmetric or skewed? If skewed, which direction? (e) Note strengths or weaknesses of each statistic of central tendency for the data. **CallLength**

1	2	10	5	3	3	2	20	1	1
6	3	13	2	2	1	26	3	1	3
1	2	1	7	1	2	3	1	2	12
1	4	2	2	29	1	1	1	8	5
1	4	2	1	1	1	1	6	1	2
3	3	6	1	3	1	1	5	1	18
2	13	13	1	6					

Mini Case   4.1

ATM Deposits

Table 4.7 shows a sorted random sample of 100 deposits at an ATM located in the student union on a college campus. The sample was selected at random from 1,459 deposits in one 30-day month. Deposits range from $3 to $1,341. The dot plot shown in Figure 4.17 indicates a right-skewed distribution with a few large values in the right tail and a strong clustering on the left (i.e., most ATM deposits are small). Excel's Descriptive Statistics indicate a very skewed distribution, since the mean (233.89) greatly exceeds the median (135). The mode (100) is somewhat "typical," occurring five times. However, 40, 50, and 200 each occur four times (mini-modes).

TABLE 4.7   100 ATM Deposits (dollars)   ATMDeposits

3	10	15	15	20	20	20	22	23	25	26	26
30	30	35	35	36	39	40	40	40	40	47	50
50	50	50	53	55	60	60	60	67	75	78	86
90	96	100	100	100	100	100	103	105	118	125	125
130	131	139	140	145	150	150	153	153	156	160	163
170	176	185	198	200	200	200	220	232	237	252	259
260	268	270	279	295	309	345	350	366	375	431	433
450	450	474	484	495	553	600	720	777	855	960	987
1,020	1,050	1,200	1,341								

Source: Michigan State University Federal Credit Union.

FIGURE 4.17

Dot plot for ATM deposits ($n = 100$)

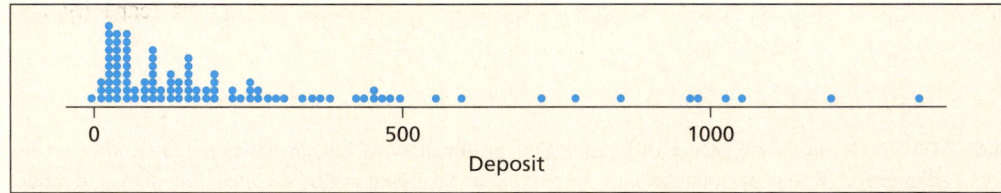

Figure 4.18 shows one possible histogram for this severely skewed data. Using seven equal bins (Sturges's Rule) with a nice bin width of 200, we don't get very much detail for the first bin. Figure 4.19 shows that even doubling the number of bins still does not show much detail in the first bin. This example illustrates some of the difficulties in making good frequency tabulations when the data are skewed (a very common situation in business and economic data).

FIGURE 4.18

Histogram with 7 bins

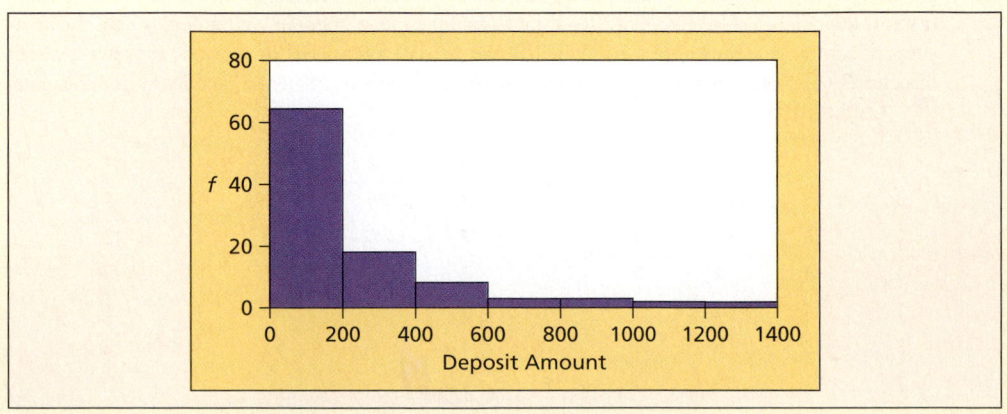

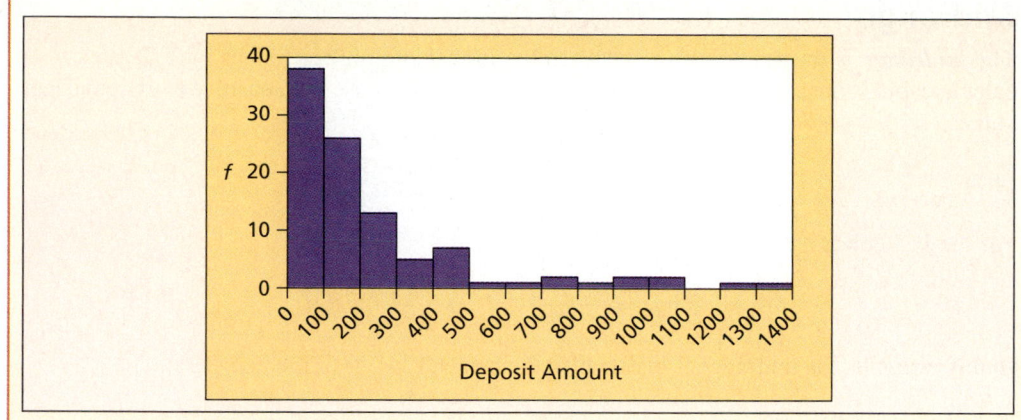

FIGURE 4.19

Histogram with 14 bins

Geometric Mean

The *geometric mean* (denoted G) is a multiplicative average, obtained by multiplying the data values and then taking the nth root of the product. This is a measure of central tendency used for highly skewed data that is positive (greater than zero).

$$G = \sqrt[n]{x_1 x_2 \cdots x_n} \quad \text{for the geometric mean} \tag{4.5}$$

For the J.D. Power quality data:

$$G = \sqrt[37]{(87)(93)(98)\cdots(164)(173)} = \sqrt[37]{2.37667 \times 10^{77}} = 123.38$$

The calculation is easy using Excel's function =GEOMEAN(Data). Scientific calculators have a y^x key whose inverse permits taking the nth root needed to calculate G. However, if the data values are large (or if the sample is large) the product can exceed the calculator's capacity. The geometric mean tends to mitigate the effects of high outliers.

Growth Rates

We can use a variation on the geometric mean to find the *average growth rate* for a time series (e.g., sales in a growing company):

$$G = \sqrt[n]{\frac{x_n}{x_1}} - 1 \quad \text{for the average growth rate of a time series} \tag{4.6}$$

For example, from 1998 to 2002, Spirit Airlines revenues grew dramatically, as shown in Table 4.8.

The *average growth rate* is given by taking the geometric mean of the ratios of each year's revenue to the preceding year. However, due to cancellations, only the first and last years are relevant:

$$G = \sqrt[5]{\left(\frac{227}{131}\right)\left(\frac{311}{227}\right)\left(\frac{354}{311}\right)\left(\frac{403}{354}\right)} - 1 = \sqrt[5]{\frac{403}{131}} - 1 = 1.252 - 1 = .252,$$

or 25.2% per year

In Excel, we could use the formula =(403/131)^(1/5)-1 to get this result.

Year	Revenue ($ millions)
1998	131
1999	227
2000	311
2001	354
2002	403

TABLE 4.8
Spirit Airlines Revenue
SpiritAir

Source: Spirit Airlines.

Midrange

The *midrange* is the point halfway between the lowest and highest values of X. It is easy to calculate, but is not a robust measure of central tendency because it is sensitive to extreme data values.

(4.7)
$$\text{Midrange} = \frac{x_{min} + x_{max}}{2}$$

For the J.D. Power data:

$$\text{Midrange} = \frac{x_1 + x_{37}}{2} = \frac{87 + 173}{2} = 130$$

In this example, the midrange is higher than the mean (125.38) or median (121).

Trimmed Mean

The *trimmed mean* is calculated like any other mean, except that the highest and lowest k percent of the observations are removed. For the 68 P/E ratios, the 5 percent trimmed mean will remove the three smallest and three largest ($0.05 \times 68 = 3.4$ observations). Excel's function for a 5 percent trimmed mean would be =TRIMMEAN(Data, 0.10) since $.05 + .05 = .10$. As shown below, the trimmed mean mitigates the effects of extremely high values, but still exceeds the median. The midrange is a poor measure of central tendency for the P/E data because of the high outlier ($x_{min} = 7, x_{max} = 91$).

Mean: 22.72	=AVERAGE(PERatio)
Median: 19.00	=MEDIAN(PERatio)
Mode: 13.00	=MODE(PERatio)
Geo Mean: 19.85	=GEOMEAN(PERatio)
Midrange: 49.00	=(MIN(PERatio)+MAX(PERatio))/2
5% Trim Mean: 21.10	=TRIMMEAN(PERatio,0.1)

The Federal Reserve uses a 16 percent trimmed mean to mitigate the effect of extremes in its analysis of trends in the Consumer Price Index, as illustrated in Figure 4.20.

FIGURE 4.20

16 percent trimmed mean for CPI

Source: Federal Reserve Bank of Cleveland, www.clevelandfed.org

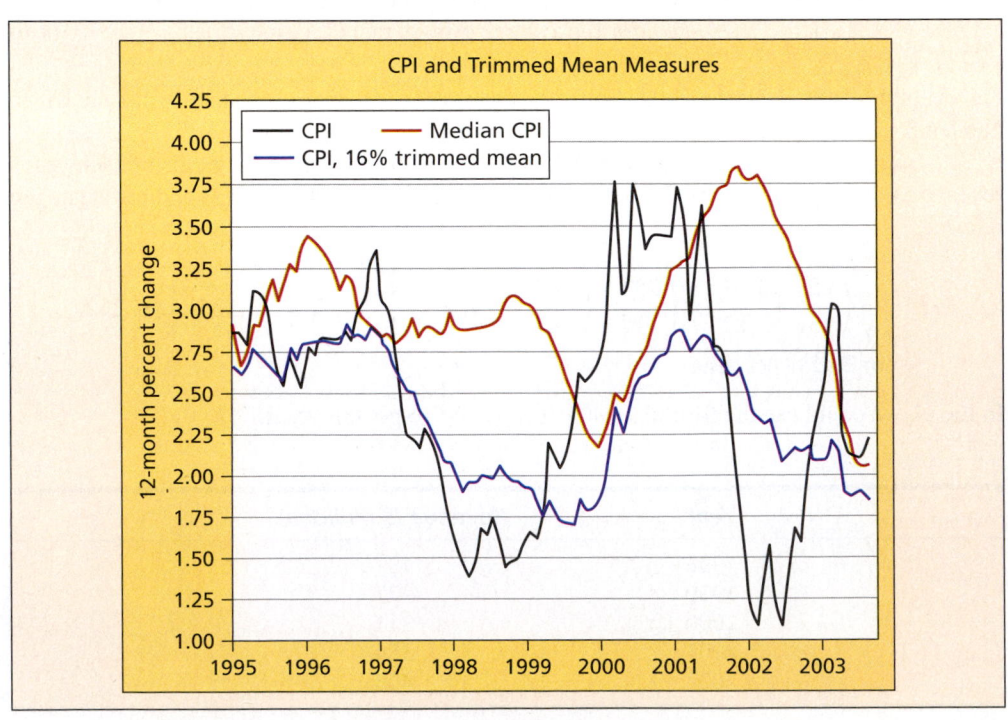

Mini Case   4.2

Prices of Lipitor®

Prescription drug prices vary across the United States and even among pharmacies in the same city. Table 4.9 shows prices for a 30-day supply of Lipitor® (a cholesterol-lowering prescription drug) in three U.S. cities from a random sample of pharmacies. Attention has recently been focused on prices of such drugs because recent medical research has suggested more aggressive treatment of high cholesterol levels in patients at risk for heart disease. This poses an economic issue for government because Medicare is expected to pay some of the cost of prescription drugs. It is also an issue for Pfizer, the maker of Lipitor®, who expects a fair return on its investments in research and patents. Finally, it is an issue for consumers who seek to shop wisely.

TABLE 4.9	Lipitor® Prices in Three Cities 🐿 **Lipitor**

New Orleans, LA (n = 12)	62.91	69.61	68.00	66.49	71.79	75.09	73.30	71.79	71.79	60.45
	73.57	66.49								
Providence, RI (n = 20)	71.99	78.50	67.15	79.79	80.00	80.00	76.00	76.00	77.00	83.69
	69.49	79.00	79.79	79.79	83.16	78.00	69.00	91.21	69.49	81.75
Grand Rapids, MI (n = 15)	77.99	69.19	71.98	72.91	71.56	65.73	76.89	76.89	61.33	64.84
	74.49	64.90	60.39	71.57	65.29					

Source: Survey by the Public Interest Research Group (www.pirg.org) in March/April 2003. Prices were studied for 10 drugs in 555 pharmacies in 48 cities in 19 states. Public Interest Research Groups are an alliance of state-based, citizen-funded advocacy organizations that seek to protect the environment, encourage a fair marketplace for consumers, and foster responsive, democratic government. Data used with permission.

From the dot plots in Figure 4.21, we gain an impression of the *dispersion* of the data (the *range* of prices for each drug) as well as the *central tendency* of the data (the middle or typical data values). Lipitor® prices vary from about $60 to about $91 and typically are in the $70s. The dot plots suggest that Providence tends to have higher prices, and New Orleans lower prices, though there is considerable variation among pharmacies.

In Table 4.10, the measures of central tendency unanimously say that Providence has higher prices. New Orleans and Grand Rapids are similar, although the measures of central tendency suggest that Grand Rapids has slightly higher prices than New Orleans. The means and medians within each city generally are similar, suggesting no significant skewness.

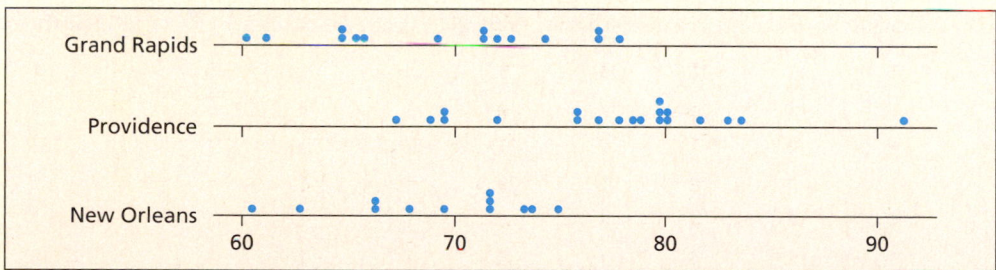

FIGURE 4.21

Dot plots for Lipitor® prices

TABLE 4.10	Measures of Central Tendency for Lipitor® Prices 🐿 **Lipitor**

Statistic	New Orleans	Providence	Grand Rapids
Sample size	12	20	15
Mean	69.27	77.54	69.73
Median	70.70	78.75	71.56
Mode	71.79	79.79	76.89
Geometric mean	69.14	77.33	69.51
Midrange	67.77	79.18	69.19
5% Trim mean	69.57	77.36	69.81

SECTION EXERCISES

4.8 Spirit Airlines kept track of the number of empty seats on flight 308 (DEN–DTW) for 10 consecutive trips on each weekday. (a) Sort the data for each weekday. (b) Without using Excel, find the mean, median, mode, midrange, geometric mean, and 10 percent trimmed mean (i.e., dropping the first and last observation) for each weekday. (c) Do the measures of central tendency agree? Explain. (d) Note strengths or weaknesses of each statistic of central tendency for the data. (e) Briefly describe and compare the number of empty seats on each weekday. 🌑 **EmptySeats**

Monday: 6, 1, 5, 9, 1, 1, 6, 5, 5, 1

Tuesday: 1, 3, 3, 1, 4, 6, 9, 7, 7, 6

Wednesday: 6, 0, 6, 0, 6, 10, 0, 0, 4, 6

Thursday: 1, 1, 10, 1, 1, 1, 1, 1, 1, 1

4.9 CitiBank recorded the number of customers to use a downtown ATM during the noon hour on 32 consecutive workdays. (a) Use Excel or MegaStat to find the mean, midrange, geometric mean, and 10 percent trimmed mean (i.e., dropping the first three and last three observations). (b) Do these measures of central tendency agree? Explain. 🌑 **CitiBank**

25	37	23	26	30	40	25	26
39	32	21	26	19	27	32	25
18	26	34	18	31	35	21	33
33	9	16	32	35	42	15	24

4.10 On Friday night, the owner of Chez Pierre in downtown Chicago noted the amount spent for dinner at 28 four-person tables. (a) Use Excel or MegaStat to find the mean, midrange, geometric mean, and 10 percent trimmed mean (i.e., dropping the first three and last three observations). (b) Do these measures of central tendency agree? Explain. 🌑 **Dinner**

95	103	109	170	114	113	107
124	105	80	104	84	176	115
69	95	134	108	61	160	128
68	95	61	150	52	87	136

4.11 An executive's telephone log showed the lengths of 65 calls initiated during the last week of July. (a) Use Excel to find the mean, midrange, geometric mean, and 10 percent trimmed mean (i.e., dropping the first seven and last seven observations). (b) Do the measures of central tendency agree? Explain. (c) Are the data symmetric or skewed? If skewed, which direction? (d) Note strengths or weaknesses of each statistic of central tendency for the data. 🌑 **CallLength**

1	2	10	5	3	3	2	20	1	1
6	3	13	2	2	1	26	3	1	3
1	2	1	7	1	2	3	1	2	12
1	4	2	2	29	1	1	1	8	5
1	4	2	1	1	1	1	6	1	2
3	3	6	1	3	1	1	5	1	18
2	13	13	1	6					

4.12 The number of Internet users in Latin America grew from 15.8 million in 2000 to 60.6 million in 2004. Use the geometric mean to estimate the mean annual growth rate. (Data are from George E. Belch and Michael A. Belch, *Advertising and Promotion* [Irwin, 2004], p. 488.)

4.3 DISPERSION

Histograms and dot plots tell us something about variation in a data set (the "spread" of data points about the center) but formal measures of dispersion are needed. Table 4.11 lists several common measures of dispersion. All formulas shown are for sample data sets.

TABLE 4.11	Five Measures of Dispersion for a Sample			
Statistic	**Formula**	**Excel**	**Pro**	**Con**
Range	$x_{max} - x_{min}$	=MAX(Data)-MIN(Data)	Easy to calculate.	Sensitive to extreme data values.
Sample variance (s^2)	$\dfrac{\sum\limits_{i=1}^{n}(x_i - \bar{x})^2}{n-1}$	=VAR(Data)	Plays a key role in mathematical statistics.	Nonintuitive meaning.
Sample standard deviation (s)	$\sqrt{\dfrac{\sum\limits_{i=1}^{n}(x_i - \bar{x})^2}{n-1}}$	=STDEV(Data)	Most common measure. Same units as the raw data ($, £, ¥, grams, etc.).	Nonintuitive meaning.
Coefficient of variation (CV)	$100 \times \dfrac{s}{\bar{x}}$	None	Measures relative variation in *percent* so can compare data sets.	Requires nonnegative data.
Mean absolute deviation (MAD)	$\dfrac{\sum\limits_{i=1}^{n}|x_i - \bar{x}|}{n}$	=AVEDEV(Data)	Easy to understand.	Lacks "nice" theoretical properties.

Range

The *range* is the difference between the largest and smallest observation:

$$\text{Range} = x_{max} - x_{min} \tag{4.8}$$

For the P/E data the range is:

$$\text{Range} = 91 - 7 = 84$$

Variance

Dispersion for a population is measured by the ***population variance*** (denoted σ^2) defined as the sum of squared deviations around the mean μ divided by the population size:

$$\sigma^2 = \frac{\sum\limits_{i=1}^{N}(x_i - \mu)^2}{N} \tag{4.9}$$

If we have a sample (i.e., most of the time), we replace μ with $\bar{x}$ to get the ***sample variance*** (denoted s^2):

$$s^2 = \frac{\sum\limits_{i=1}^{n}(x_i - \bar{x})^2}{n-1} \tag{4.10}$$

We divide the sum of squared deviations by $n-1$ instead of n because otherwise s^2 would tend to underestimate the unknown population variance σ^2.

Standard Deviation

In describing dispersion, we most often use the ***standard deviation*** (the square root of the variance). The standard deviation is a single number that helps us understand how individual values in a data set vary from the mean. Because the square root has been taken, its units of measurement are the same as X (e.g., dollars, kilograms, miles).

To find the standard deviation of a population we use:

$$\sigma = \sqrt{\frac{\sum\limits_{i=1}^{N}(x_i - \mu)^2}{N}} \tag{4.11}$$

and for the standard deviation of a sample:

$$(4.12) \qquad s = \sqrt{\frac{\sum_{i=1}^{n} (x_i - \bar{x})^2}{n - 1}}$$

Many inexpensive calculators have built-in formulas for the standard deviation. To distinguish between the population and sample formulas, some calculators have one function key labeled σ_x and another labeled s_x. Others have one key labeled σ_n and another labeled σ_{n-1}. The only question is whether to divide the numerator by the number of data items or the number of data items minus one. Computers and calculators don't know whether your data are a sample or a population. They will use whichever formula you request. It is up to you to know which is appropriate for your data. Excel has built-in functions for these calculations:

Statistic	*Excel population formula*	*Excel sample formula*
Variance	=VARP(Data)	=VAR(Data)
Standard deviation	=STDEVP(Data)	=STDEV(Data)

Calculating a Standard Deviation

Table 4.12 illustrates the calculation of a standard deviation using Stephanie's scores on five quizzes (40, 55, 75, 95, 95). Her mean is 72. Notice that the deviations around the mean (column three) sum to zero, an important property of the mean. Because the mean is rarely a "nice" number, such calculations typically require a spreadsheet or a calculator.

Stephanie's sample standard deviation is:

$$s = \sqrt{\frac{\sum_{i=1}^{n} (x_i - \bar{x})^2}{n - 1}} = \sqrt{\frac{2{,}380}{5 - 1}} = \sqrt{595} = 24.39$$

The **two-sum formula** can also be used to calculate the standard deviation:

$$(4.13) \qquad s^2 = \sqrt{\frac{\sum_{i=1}^{n} x_i^2 - \dfrac{\left(\sum_{i=1}^{n} x_i\right)^2}{n}}{n - 1}}$$

This formula avoids calculating the mean and subtracting it from each observation. Many calculators use this formula and also give the sums $\sum_{i=1}^{n} x_i$ and $\sum_{i=1}^{n} x_i^2$. For Stephanie's five quiz scores, using the sums shown in Table 4.12, we get the same result as from the definitional formula:

$$s^2 = \sqrt{\frac{\sum_{i=1}^{n} x_i^2 - \dfrac{\left(\sum_{i=1}^{n} x_i\right)^2}{n}}{n - 1}} = \sqrt{\frac{28{,}300 - \dfrac{(360)^2}{5}}{5 - 1}} = \sqrt{\frac{28{,}300 - 25{,}920}{5 - 1}} = \sqrt{595} = 24.39$$

TABLE 4.12
Worksheet for Standard Deviation
🐾 **Stephanie**

i	x_i	$x_i - \bar{x}$	$(x_i - \bar{x})^2$	x_i^2
1	40	$40 - 72 = -32$	$(-32)^2 = 1{,}024$	$40^2 = 1{,}600$
2	55	$55 - 72 = -17$	$(-17)^2 = 289$	$55^2 = 3{,}025$
3	75	$75 - 72 = +3$	$(3)^2 = 9$	$75^2 = 5{,}625$
4	95	$95 - 72 = +23$	$(23)^2 = 529$	$95^2 = 9{,}025$
5	95	$95 - 72 = +23$	$(23)^2 = 529$	$95^2 = 9{,}025$
Sum	360	0	2,380	28,300
Mean	72			

Because it is less intuitive (and because we usually rely on spreadsheets, calculators, statistical software) some textbooks omit the two-sum formula.*

Characteristics of the Standard Deviation

The standard deviation is nonnegative because the deviations around the mean are squared. When every observation is exactly equal to the mean, then the standard deviation is zero (i.e., there is no variation). For example, if every student received the same score on an exam, the numerators of formulas 4.9 through 4.13 would be zero because every student would be at the mean. At the other extreme, the greatest dispersion would be if the data were concentrated at x_{min} and x_{max} (e.g., if half the class scored 0 and the other half scored 100).

But the standard deviation can have any nonnegative value, depending on the unit of measurement. For example, yields on n randomly chosen investment bond funds (e.g., Westcore Plus at 0.052 in 2004) would have a small standard deviation compared to annual revenues of n randomly chosen Fortune 500 corporations (e.g., Wal-Mart at \$259 billion in 2003).

Standard deviations can be compared *only* for data sets measured in the same units. For example, prices of hotel rooms in Tokyo (yen) cannot be compared with prices of hotel rooms in Paris (euros). Also, standard deviations should not be compared if the means differ substantially, even when the units of measurement are the same. For instance, weights of apples (ounces) have a smaller mean than weights of watermelons (ounces).

Coefficient of Variation

To compare dispersion in data sets with dissimilar units of measurement (e.g., kilograms and ounces) or dissimilar means (e.g., home prices in two different cities) we define the ***coefficient of variation*** (CV), which is a unit-free measure of dispersion:

$$CV = 100 \times \frac{s}{\bar{x}} \qquad (4.14)$$

The CV is the standard deviation expressed as a percent of the mean. In some data sets, the standard deviation can actually exceed the mean so the CV can exceed 100 percent. The CV is useful for comparing variables measured in different units. For example:

Defect rates: $s = 22.89$, $\bar{x} = 125.38$ $\qquad CV = 100 \times (22.89)/(125.38) = 18\%$

ATM deposits: $s = 280.80$, $\bar{x} = 233.89$ $\qquad CV = 100 \times (280.80)/(233.89) = 120\%$

P/E ratios: $s = 14.08$, $\bar{x} = 22.72$ $\qquad CV = 100 \times (14.08)/(22.72) = 62\%$

Despite the different units of measurement, we can say that ATM deposits have much greater relative dispersion (120 percent) than either defect rates (18 percent) or P/E ratios (62 percent). The chief weakness of the CV is that it is undefined if the mean is zero or negative, so it is appropriate only for positive data.

Mean Absolute Deviation

An additional measure of dispersion is the ***mean absolute deviation*** (MAD). This statistic reveals the average distance from the center. Absolute values must be used since otherwise the deviations around the mean would sum to zero.

$$MAD = \frac{\sum\limits_{i=1}^{n} |x_i - \bar{x}|}{n} \qquad (4.15)$$

The MAD is appealing because of its simple, concrete interpretation. Using the lever analogy, the MAD tells us what the average distance is from an individual data point to the fulcrum. Excel's function =AVEDEV(Data) will calculate the MAD.

---

*The two-sum formula is sensitive to rounding of sums in some situations (e.g., poor data scaling or small range relative to the mean). However, the definitional formula can also give inaccurate results if you round off the mean before subtracting (a common error). For business data, either formula should be OK.

Mini Case   4.3

Bear Markets

Investors know that stock prices have extended cycles of downturns ("bear markets") or upturns ("bull markets"). But how long must an investor be prepared to wait for the cycle to end? Table 4.13 shows the duration of 14 bear markets since 1929 and the decline in the S&P 500 stock index.

TABLE 4.13   Duration of Bear Markets   🐻   **BearMarkets**

Peak	Trough	Duration (months)	S&P Loss (%)
Sep 1929	Jun 1932	34	83.4
Jun 1946	Apr 1947	11	21.0
Aug 1956	Feb 1957	7	10.2
Aug 1957	Dec 1957	5	15.0
Jan 1962	Jun 1962	6	22.3
Feb 1966	Sep 1966	8	15.6
Dec 1968	Jun 1970	19	29.3
Jan 1973	Sep 1974	21	42.6
Jan 1977	Feb 1978	14	14.1
Dec 1980	Jul 1982	20	16.9
Sep 1987	Nov 1987	3	29.5
Jun 1990	Oct 1990	5	14.7
Jul 1998	Aug 1998	2	15.4
Sep 2000	Mar 2003	31	42.0

Source: TIAA/CREF, *Balance,* Summer 2004, p. 15. Downturns are defined as a loss in value of 10 percent or more. Standard and Poor's 500 stock index and S&P 500 are registered trademarks.

Figure 4.22 shows that bear markets typically are short-lived (under 1 year) but may last nearly 3 years. S&P losses generally are in the 10–40 percent range, with one notable exception (the 1929 crash).

Table 4.14 shows that both duration (months) and S&P loss (percent) are right-skewed (mean substantially exceeding median) and have similar coefficients of variation. The other measures of central tendency and disperson cannot be compared because the units of measurement differ.

FIGURE 4.22

Dot plots of bear market measurements

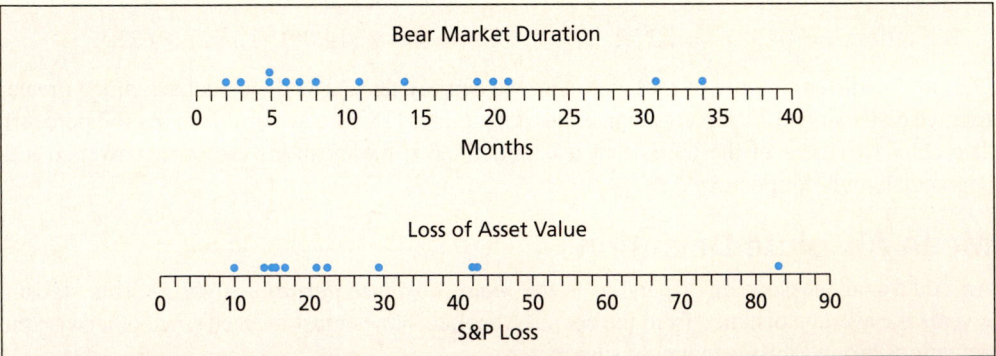

TABLE 4.14   Statistical Summary of Bear Markets

Statistic	Duration (months)	S&P Loss (%)
Count	14	14
Mean	13.29	26.57
Median	9.5	18.95
Standard deviation	10.29	19.27
Minimum	2	10.2
Maximum	34	83.4
Range	32	73.2
Coefficient of variation	77.4%	72.5%
Mean absolute deviation	8.47	13.42

SECTION EXERCISES

4.13   Without using Excel: (a) Find the mean and standard deviation for each sample. (b) What does this exercise show?

> *Sample A:* 6, 7, 8
>
> *Sample B:* 61, 62, 63
>
> *Sample C:* 1000, 1001, 1002

4.14   Without using Excel, for each data set: (a) Find the mean. (b) Find the standard deviation, treating the data as a sample. (c) Find the standard deviation, treating the data as a population. (d) What does this exercise show?

> *Data Set A:* 6, 7, 8
>
> *Data Set B:* 4, 5, 6, 7, 8, 9, 10
>
> *Data Set C:* 1, 2, 3, 4, 5, 6, 7, 8, 9, 10, 11, 12, 13

4.15   Find the coefficient of variation for prices of these three stocks. (a) Which stock has the greatest relative variation? (b) To measure variability, why not just compare the standard deviations?

> *Stock A:* $\bar{x} = \$24.50, s = 5.25$
>
> *Stock B:* $\bar{x} = \$147.25, s = 12.25$
>
> *Stock C:* $\bar{x} = \$5.75, s = 2.08$

4.16   Prof. Hardtack gave four Friday quizzes last semester in his 10-student senior tax accounting class. (a) Using Excel, find the mean, standard deviation, and coefficient of variation for each quiz. (b) How do these data sets differ in terms of central tendency and dispersion? (c) Briefly describe and compare student performance on each quiz.   **Quizzes**

> *Quiz 1:* 60, 60, 60, 60, 71, 73, 74, 75, 88, 99
>
> *Quiz 2:* 65, 65, 65, 65, 70, 74, 79, 79, 79, 79
>
> *Quiz 3:* 66, 67, 70, 71, 72, 72, 74, 74, 95, 99
>
> *Quiz 4:* 10, 49, 70, 80, 85, 88, 90, 93, 97, 98

4.17   An executive's telephone log showed the lengths of 65 calls initiated during the last week of July. Use Excel to find the sample standard deviation and mean absolute deviation.   **CallLength**

1	2	10	5	3	3	2	20	1	1
6	3	13	2	2	1	26	3	1	3
1	2	1	7	1	2	3	1	2	12
1	4	2	2	29	1	1	1	8	5
1	4	2	1	1	1	1	6	1	2
3	3	6	1	3	1	1	5	1	18
2	13	13	1	6					

Central Tendency versus Dispersion: Manufacturing

Figure 4.23 shows histograms of hole diameters drilled in a steel plate during a manufacturing process. The desired distribution is outlined. The samples from Machine *A* have the desired *mean* diameter (5 mm) but too much *variation* around the mean. It might be an older machine whose moving parts have become loose through normal wear, so there is greater variation in the holes drilled. Samples from Machine *B* have acceptable *variation* in hole diameter, but the *mean* is incorrectly adjusted (less than the desired 5 mm). To monitor quality, we would take frequent samples from the output of each machine, so that the process can be stopped and adjusted if the sample statistics indicate a problem.

Central Tendency and Dispersion: Job Performance

Table 4.15 shows how four professors were rated by students on eight teaching attributes (on a 10-point scale). Jones and Wu have identical means but different standard deviations. Smith and Gopal have different means but identical standard deviations. In teaching, a high mean

FIGURE 4.23

Central tendency versus dispersion

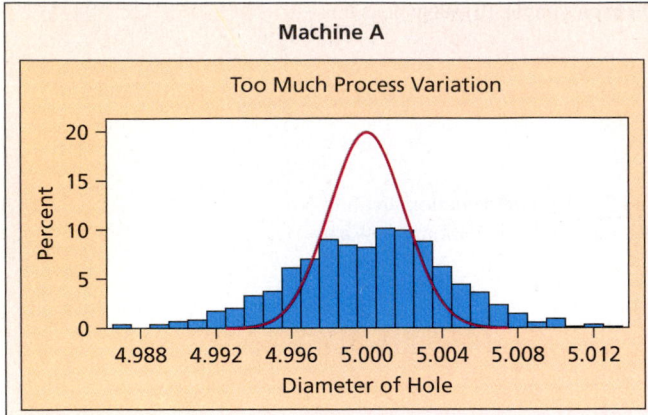
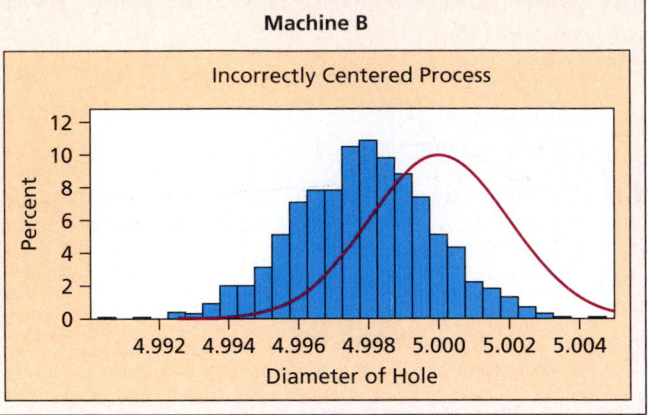

TABLE 4.15

Average Teaching Ratings for Four Professors

FourProfs

	Same Mean, Different Variance		Different Mean, Same Variance	
Attribute	**Prof. Wu**	**Prof. Jones**	**Prof. Smith**	**Prof. Gopal**
1. Challenging	8.4	5.1	7.5	7.8
2. Approachable	6.7	9.4	6.4	8.8
3. Enthusiastic	7.5	5.9	8.3	7.1
4. Helps students	7.0	9.2	6.8	7.3
5. Fair exams	7.4	7.8	7.3	7.8
6. Knowledge	6.9	8.3	7.3	6.9
7. Lecture ability	7.6	6.4	6.6	8.0
8. Organized	6.1	5.5	5.8	6.3
Mean	7.20	7.20	7.00	7.50
Std Dev	0.69	1.69	0.77	0.77
CV	9.6%	23.5%	11.0%	10.2%

(better rating) and a low standard deviation (more consistency) would presumably be preferred. How would *you* describe these professors?

4.4 STANDARDIZED DATA

The standard deviation is an important measure of dispersion because of its many roles in statistics. One of its main uses is to gauge the position of items within a data array.

Chebyshev's Theorem

The French mathematician Jules Bienaymé (1796–1878) and the Russian mathematician Pafnuty Chebyshev (1821–1894) proved that, for any data set, no matter how it is distributed, the percentage of observations that lie within k standard deviations of the mean (i.e., within $\mu \pm k\sigma$) must be at least $100 [1 - 1/k^2]$. Commonly called **Chebyshev's Theorem,** it says that for *any population* with mean μ and standard deviation σ:

$k = 2$ at least 75.0% will lie within $\mu \pm 2\sigma$.

$k = 3$ at least 88.9% will lie within $\mu \pm 3\sigma$.

Although applicable to any data set, these limits tend to be rather wide.

The Empirical Rule

More precise statements can be made about data from a normal or Gaussian distribution, named for its discoverer Karl Gauss (1777–1855). The Gaussian distribution is the well-known bell-shaped curve. Commonly called the **Empirical Rule,** it says that for data from a *normal distribution* we expect the interval $\mu \pm k\sigma$ to contain a known percentage of the data:

$k = 1$ about 68.26% will lie within $\mu \pm 1\sigma$.

$k = 2$ about 95.44% will lie within $\mu \pm 2\sigma$.

$k = 3$ about 99.73% will lie within $\mu \pm 3\sigma$.

The Empirical Rule is illustrated in Figure 4.24. The Empirical Rule does *not* give an upper bound, but merely describes what is *expected*. Rounding off a bit, we say that in samples from a normal distribution we expect 68 percent of the data within 1 standard deviation, 95 percent within 2 standard deviations, and virtually all of the data within 3 standard deviations. The last statement is imprecise, since 0.27 percent of the observations are expected outside 3 standard deviations, but it correctly conveys the idea that data values outside $\mu \pm 3\sigma$ are rare in a normal distribution.

EXAMPLE

Exam Scores

Suppose 80 students take an exam. How many students will score within 2 standard deviations of the mean? Assuming that exam scores follow a normal or bell-shaped curve, we might be willing to rely on the Empirical Rule, which predicts that 95.44% × 80 or approximately 76 students will score within 2 standard deviations from the mean. Since a normal distribution is symmetric about the mean, we further expect that about 2 students will score more than 2 standard deviations above the mean, and 2 below the mean. Using the Empirical Rule, we can further say that it is unlikely that any student will score more than 3 standard deviations from the mean (99.73% × 80 = 79.78 ≈ 80).

Unusual Observations

The Empirical Rule suggests criteria for detecting *unusual* observations (beyond $\mu \pm 2\sigma$) or *outliers* (beyond $\mu \pm 3\sigma$). Many variations on the criteria in Table 4.16 are possible.

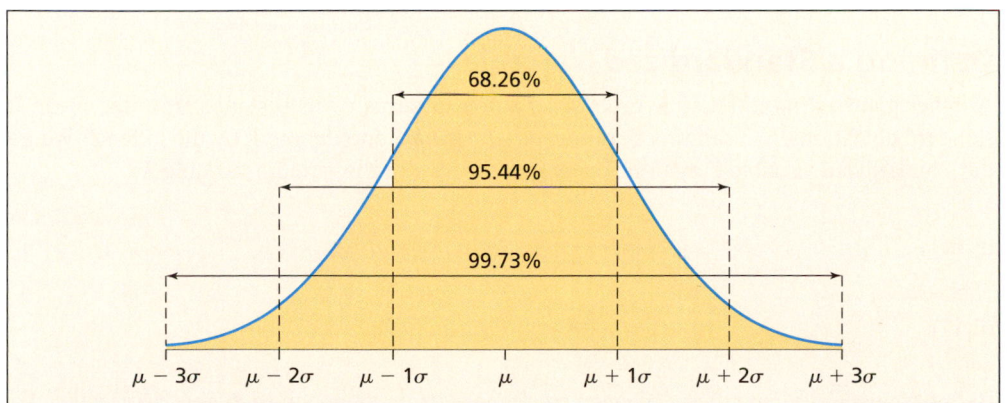

FIGURE 4.24

The Empirical Rule for a normal population

Term	Criterion	
Unusual	2 or more standard deviations from the mean	**TABLE 4.16**
Outlier	3 or more standard deviations from the mean	**Detecting Unusual Observations**

Note: These criteria are intended for small samples. For a large sample like $n = 1{,}000$ it would *not* be surprising to see a few data values outside the 3 standard deviation range, since 99.73% of 1,000 is only 997.

EXAMPLE

Unusual Observations

The P/E data set contains several large data values. Would we classify them as unusual or as outliers?

7	8	8	10	10	10	10	12	13	13	13	13
13	13	13	14	14	14	15	15	15	15	15	16
16	16	17	18	18	18	18	19	19	19	19	19
20	20	20	21	21	21	22	22	23	23	23	24
25	26	26	26	26	27	29	29	30	31	34	36
37	40	41	45	48	**55**	**68**	**91**				

For the P/E data, $\bar{x} = 22.72$ and $s = 14.08$. From these sample statistics, the Empirical Rule says that *if the sample came from a normal distribution:*

$\bar{x} \pm 1s$: $22.72 \pm 1(14.08)$ 68.26% of the P/E ratios would be within the interval 8.7 to 36.8.

$\bar{x} \pm 2s$: $22.72 \pm 2(14.08)$ 95.44% of the P/E ratios would be within the interval -5.4 to 50.9.

$\bar{x} \pm 3s$: $22.72 \pm 3(14.08)$ 99.73% of the P/E ratios would be within the interval -19.5 to 65.0.

We can ignore the negative lower limits, since negative P/E ratios are impossible. By these criteria, we have one *unusual* data value (55) and two *outliers* (68 and 91). In fact, our calculations suggest that the sample probably *isn't* from a normal population, because it does not match the Empirical Rule very well, as shown in Table 4.17. However, unless the sample is fairly large (say, 50 or more) comparing the tabulated sample frequencies with a normal distribution would not be very informative.

TABLE 4.17

P/E Sample versus Normal ($n = 68$)

 PERatios

Data Range	Sample	If Normal
Within $\bar{x} \pm 1s$	57/68, or 83.8%	68.26%
Within $\bar{x} \pm 2s$	65/68, or 95.59%	95.44
Within $\bar{x} \pm 3s$	66/68, or 97.06%	99.73

VS

Chapter 5

Defining a Standardized Variable

Another approach is to redefine each observation in terms of its distance from the mean in standard deviations. We call this a **standardized variable** and denote it by the letter Z. We get the standardized variable Z by transforming each value of the random variable X:

(4.16)
$$z_i = \frac{x_i - \mu}{\sigma} \quad \textit{for a population}$$

(4.17)
$$z_i = \frac{x_i - \bar{x}}{s} \quad \textit{for a sample}$$

By looking at z_i we can tell at a glance how far away from the mean each observation lies. For the P/E data the standardized values are:

-1.12	-1.05	-1.05	-0.90	-0.90	-0.90	-0.90	-0.76	-0.69	-0.69	-0.69	-0.69
-0.69	-0.69	-0.69	-0.62	-0.62	-0.62	-0.55	-0.55	-0.55	-0.55	-0.55	-0.48
-0.48	-0.48	-0.41	-0.34	-0.34	-0.34	-0.34	-0.26	-0.26	-0.26	-0.26	-0.26
-0.19	-0.19	-0.19	-0.12	-0.12	-0.12	-0.05	-0.05	0.02	0.02	0.02	0.09
0.16	0.23	0.23	0.23	0.23	0.30	0.45	0.45	0.52	0.59	0.80	0.94
1.01	1.23	1.30	1.58	1.80	*2.29*	*3.22*	*4.85*				

FIGURE 4.25

Empirical Rule using MegaStat (*n* = 37 cars)

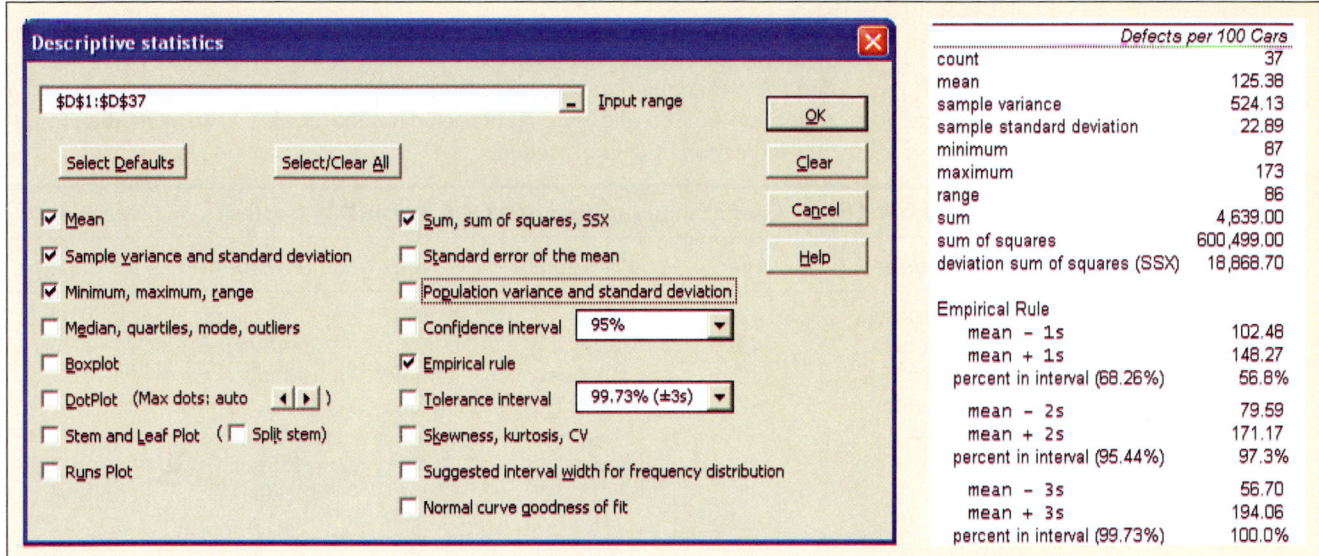

The standardizing calculations for the four largest data points (48, 55, 68, 91) are shown:

$$z_i = \frac{x_i - \bar{x}}{s} = \frac{48 - 22.72}{14.08} = 1.80 \qquad \text{Within 2 standard deviations (not unusual)}$$

$$z_i = \frac{x_i - \bar{x}}{s} = \frac{55 - 22.72}{14.08} = 2.29 \qquad \text{Beyond 2 standard deviations (unusual)}$$

$$z_i = \frac{x_i - \bar{x}}{s} = \frac{68 - 22.72}{14.08} = 3.22 \qquad \text{Beyond 3 standard deviations (outlier)}$$

$$z_i = \frac{x_i - \bar{x}}{s} = \frac{91 - 22.72}{14.08} = 4.85 \qquad \text{Beyond 4 standard deviations (extreme outlier)}$$

Excel's function =STANDARDIZE(XValue, Mean, StDev) makes it easy to calculate standardized values from a column of data. Visual Statistics calculates standardized values, sorts the data, checks for outliers, and tabulates the sample frequencies so you can apply the Empirical Rule. MegaStat does the same thing, as seen in Figure 4.25 for the J.D. Powers data.

Outliers

Extreme values of a variable are vexing, but what do we do about them? It is tempting to discard unusual data points. Discarding an outlier would be reasonable if we had reason to suppose it is erroneous data. For example, a blood pressure reading of 1200/80 seems impossible (probably was supposed to be 120/80). Perhaps the lab technician was distracted by a conversation while marking down the reading. An outrageous observation is almost certainly invalid. But how do we guard against self-deception? More than one scientist has been convinced to disregard data that didn't fit the pattern, when in fact the weird observation was trying to say something important. At this stage of your statistical training, it suffices to *recognize* unusual data points and outliers and their potential impact, and to know that there are entire books that cover the topic of outliers (see Related Reading).

Estimating Sigma

Since for a normal distribution essentially all the observations lie within $\mu \pm 3\sigma$, the range is approximately 6σ (from $\mu - 3\sigma$ to $\mu + 3\sigma$). Therefore, if you know the range R, you can estimate the standard deviation as $\sigma = R/6$. This rule can come in handy for approximating the standard deviation when all you know is the range. For example, the caffeine content of a cup of tea depends on the type of tea and length of time the tea steeps, with a range of 20 to 90 mg. Knowing only the range, we could estimate the standard deviation as $s = (90 - 20)/6$, or about 12 mg. This estimate assumes that the caffeine content of a cup of tea is normally distributed.

Mini Case   4.4

Presidential Ages

Table 4.18 shows the sorted ages at inauguration of the first 43 U.S. Presidents. There are two modes (age 51 and age 54) sorted that occur five times each. However, there are several other ages that occur four times (age 55 and age 57). In such data, the mean (54.86) or median (55.0) would give a better indication of central tendency.

TABLE 4.18		Ages at Inauguration of 43 U.S. Presidents (sorted)			Presidents
President	*Age*	*President*	*Age*	*President*	*Age*
T. Roosevelt	42	Lincoln	52	Washington	57
Kennedy	43	Carter	52	Jefferson	57
Grant	46	Van Buren	*54*	Madison	57
Cleveland	47	Hayes	*54*	J. Q. Adams	57
Clinton	47	McKinley	*54*	Monroe	58
Pierce	48	Hoover	*54*	Truman	60
Polk	49	G. W. Bush	*54*	J. Adams	61
Garfield	49	B. Harrison	55	Jackson	61
Fillmore	50	Cleveland	55	Ford	61
Tyler	*51*	Harding	55	Eisenhower	62
Arthur	*51*	L. Johnson	55	Taylor	64
Taft	*51*	A. Johnson	56	G. H. W. Bush	64
Coolidge	*51*	Wilson	56	Buchanan	65
F. Roosevelt	*51*	Nixon	56	W. H. Harrison	68
				Reagan	69

Source: Ken Parks, *The World Almanac and Book of Facts* 2002, p. 545. Copyright © 2005 The World Almanac Education Group, Inc.

The dot plot in Figure 4.26 shows the mode and several mini-modes. It also reveals the extremes on either end (Theodore Roosevelt and John Kennedy were the youngest presidents, while William Henry Harrison and Ronald Reagan were the oldest presidents).

FIGURE 4.26

Dot plot of presidents' ages at inauguration

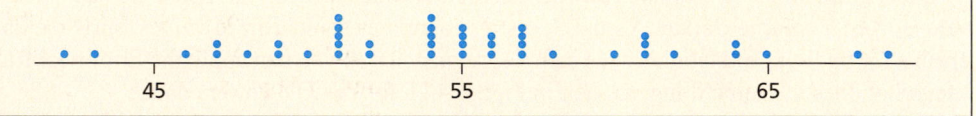

A histogram is more useful for revealing modality. Using six classes, based on Sturges's Rule, Figure 4.27 shows that the modal class is 50 to 55 (13 presidents are in that class). However, since the next higher class has almost as many observations, it might be more helpful to say that presidents tend to be between 50 and 59 years of age upon inauguration (25 presidents are within this range).

FIGURE 4.27

Histogram of presidents' ages at inauguration

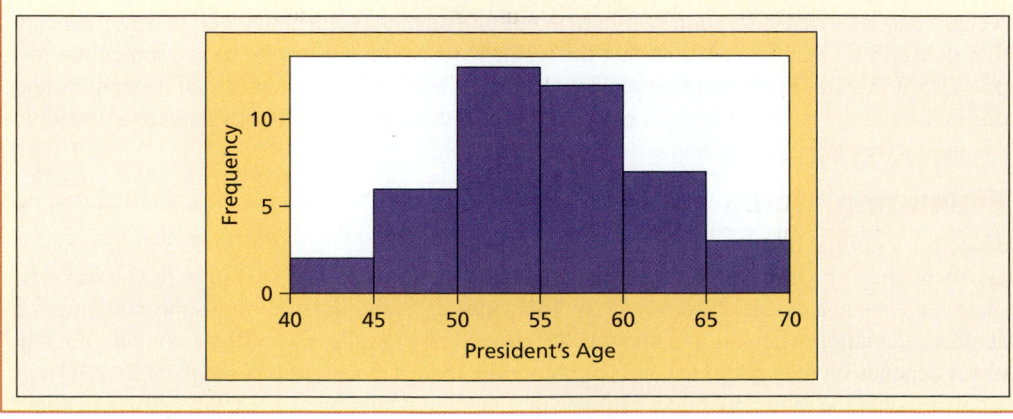

SECTION EXERCISES

4.18 CitiBank recorded the number of customers to use a downtown ATM during the noon hour on 32 consecutive workdays. (a) Use Excel or MegaStat to sort and standardize the data. (b) Based on the Empirical Rule, are there outliers? Unusual data values? (c) Compare the percent of observations that lie within 1 and 2 standard deviations of the mean with a normal distribution. What is your conclusion? (d) Do you feel the sample size is sufficient to assess normality?

CitiBank

25	37	23	26	30	40	25	26
39	32	21	26	19	27	32	25
18	26	34	18	31	35	21	33
33	9	16	32	35	42	15	24

4.19 An executive's telephone log showed the lengths of 65 calls initiated during the last week of July. (a) Use Excel or MegaStat to sort and standardize the data. (b) Based on the Empirical Rule, are there outliers? Unusual data values? (c) Compare the percent of observations that lie within 1 and 2 standard deviations of the mean with a normal distribution. What is your conclusion? (d) Do you feel the sample size is sufficient to assess normality? **CallLength**

1	2	10	5	3	3	2	20	1	1
6	3	13	2	2	1	26	3	1	3
1	2	1	7	1	2	3	1	2	12
1	4	2	2	29	1	1	1	8	5
1	4	2	1	1	1	1	6	1	2
3	3	6	1	3	1	1	5	1	18
2	13	13	1	6					

Percentiles

You are familiar with percentile scores of national educational tests such as ACT, SAT, and GMAT, which tell you where you stand in comparison with others. For example, if you are in the 83rd percentile, then 83 percent of the test-takers scored below you, and you are in the top 17 percent of all test-takers. However, only when the sample is large can we meaningfully divide the data into 100 groups (*percentiles*). Alternatively, we can divide the data into 10 groups (*deciles*), 5 groups (*quintiles*), or 4 groups (*quartiles*).

In health care, manufacturing, and banking, selected percentiles (e.g., 5, 25, 50, 75, and 95 percent) are calculated to establish *benchmarks* so that any firm can compare itself with similar firms (i.e., other firms in the same industry) in terms of profit margin, debt ratio, defect rate, or any other relevant performance measure. In finance, quartiles (25, 50, and 75 percent) are commonly used to assess financial performance of companies and stock portfolio performances. In human resources, percentiles are used in employee merit evaluations and salary benchmarking. The number of groups depends on the task at hand and the sample size, but quartiles deserve special attention because they are meaningful even for fairly small samples.

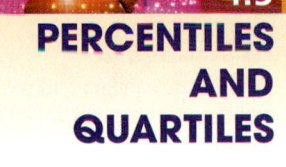

4.5
PERCENTILES AND QUARTILES

Quartiles

The **quartiles** (denoted Q_1, Q_2, Q_3) are scale points that divide the sorted data into four groups of approximately equal size, that is, the 25th, 50th, and 75th percentiles, respectively.

	Q_1		Q_2		Q_3	
⇐ Lower 25% ⇒		⇐ Second 25% ⇒		⇐ Third 25% ⇒		⇐ Upper 25% ⇒

The second quartile Q_2 is the *median*. Since equal numbers of data values lie below and above the median, it is an important indicator of *central tendency*.

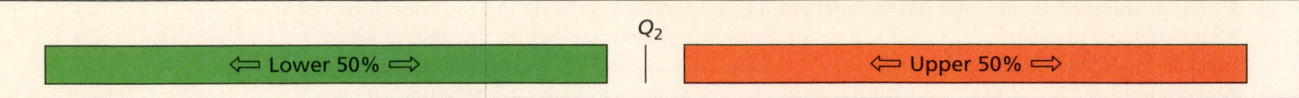

The first and third quartiles Q_1 and Q_3 indicate *central tendency* because they define the middle 50 percent of the data. But Q_1 and Q_3 also indicate *dispersion*, since the *interquartile range* Q_3–Q_1 measures the degree of spread in the data (the middle 50 percent).

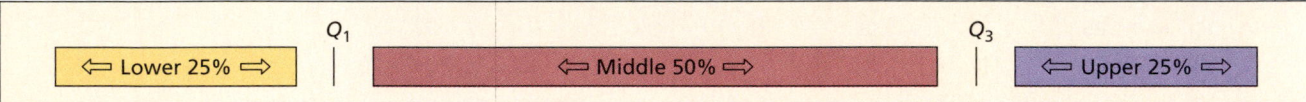

Conceptually, the first quartile Q_1 is the median of the data values below Q_2, and the third quartile Q_3 is the median of the data values above Q_2. Depending on n, the quartiles Q_1, Q_2, Q_3 may be members of the data set or may lie *between* two of the sorted data values. Figure 4.28 shows four possible situations.

Method of Medians

For small data sets, you can find the quartiles using the ***method of medians,*** as illustrated in Figure 4.28.

- Step 1:   Sort the observations.
- Step 2:   Find the median Q_2.
- Step 3:   Find the median of the data values that lie below Q_2.
- Step 4:   Find the median of the data values that lie above Q_2.

This method is attractive because it is quick and logical (see Freund 1987 in Related Reading). However, Excel uses a different method.

FIGURE 4.28

Possible quartile positions

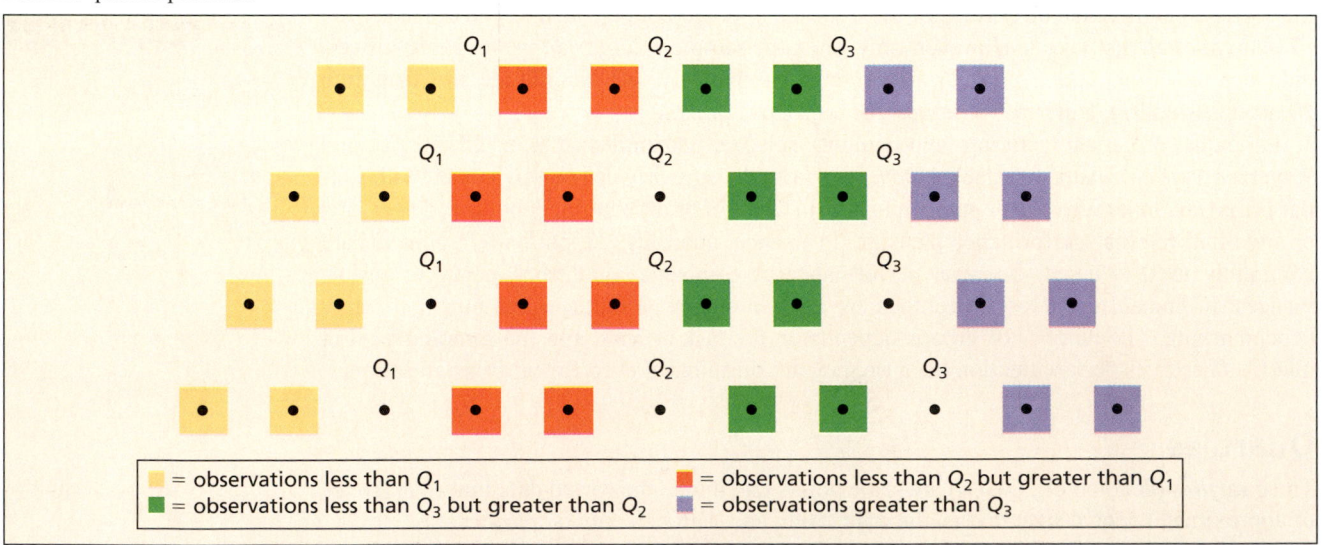

EXAMPLE

Method of Medians

A financial analyst has a portfolio of 12 energy equipment stocks. She has data on their recent price/earnings (P/E) ratios. To find the quartiles, she sorts the data, finds Q_2 (the median) halfway between the middle two data values, and then finds Q_1 and Q_3 (medians of the lower and upper halves, respectively) as illustrated in Figure 4.29.

FIGURE 4.29

Method of medians

Source: Data are from *BusinessWeek*, November 22, 2004, pp. 95–98.

Company	*Sorted P/E*
Maverick Tube	7
BJ Services	22
FMC Technologies	25
Nabors Industries	29
Baker Hughes	31
Varco International	35
National-Oilwell	36
Smith International	36
Cooper Cameron	39
Schlumberger	42
Halliburton	46
Transocean	49

Q_1 is between between x_3 and x_4 so $Q_1 = (x_3 + x_4)/2 = (25 + 29)/2 = 27.0$

Q_2 is between between x_6 and x_7 so $Q_2 = (x_6 + x_7)/2 = (35 + 36)/2 = 35.5$

Q_3 is between between x_9 and x_{10} so $Q_3 = (x_9 + x_{10})/2 = (39 + 42)/2 = 40.5$

Formula Method

Statistical software (e.g., Excel, MegaStat, MINITAB) will not use the method of medians, but instead will use a formula to calculate the quartile positions.* There are several possible ways of calculating the quartile positions. The two that you are most likely to use are:

	Method A (MINITAB)	*Method B (Excel or MegaStat)*
Position of Q_1	$0.25n + 0.25$	$0.25n + 0.75$
Position of Q_2	$0.50n + 0.50$	$0.50n + 0.50$
Position of Q_3	$0.75n + 0.75$	$0.75n + 0.25$

Q_2 is the same using either method, but Q_1 and Q_3 generally are not. It depends on the gap between data values when interpolation is necessary. Most textbooks prefer MINITAB's method, so it will be illustrated here.

EXAMPLE

Formula Method

Figure 4.30 illustrates the quartile calculations for the same sample of P/E ratios using *Method A*. The resulting quartiles are similar to those using the method of medians.

FIGURE 4.30

Formula interpolation method

Company	*Sorted P/E*
Maverick Tube	7
BJ Services	22
FMC Technologies	25
Nabors Industries	29
Baker Hughes	31
Varco International	35
National-Oilwell	36
Smith International	36
Cooper Cameron	39
Schlumberger	42
Halliburton	46
Transocean	49

Q_1 is at observation $0.25n + 0.25 = (0.25)(12) + 0.25 = 3.25$, so we interpolate between x_3 and x_4 to get $Q_1 = x_3 + (0.25)(x_4 - x_3) = 25 + (0.25)(29 - 25) = 26.00$

Q_2 is at observation $0.50n + 0.50 = (0.50)(12) + 0.50 = 6.50$, so we interpolate between x_6 and x_7 to get $Q_2 = x_6 + (0.50)(x_7 - x_6) = 35 + (0.50)(36 - 35) = 35.50$

Q_3 is at observation $0.75n + 0.75 = (0.75)(12) + 0.75 = 9.75$, so we interpolate between x_9 and x_{10} to get $Q_3 = x_9 + (0.75)(x_{10} - x_9) = 39 + (0.75)(42 - 39) = 41.25$

Source: Data are from *BusinessWeek*, November 22, 2004, pp. 95–98.

Excel Quartiles

Excel's function =QUARTILE(Data, k) returns the *k*th quartile, so =QUARTILE(Data, 1) would return Q_1 and =QUARTILE(Data, 3) would return Q_3. Excel treats quartiles as a special case of percentiles, so

*The quartiles (25th, 50th, and 75th percentiles) are a special case of percentiles. *Method A* defines the *P*th percentile position as $P(n + 1)/100$ while *Method B* defines it as $1 + P(n - 1)/100$.

you could get the same results by using the function =PERCENTILE(Data, Percent). For example, =PERCENTILE(Data, 0.75) would return the 75th percentile or Q_3.

EXAMPLE

P/E Ratios and Quartiles

A financial analyst has a diversified portfolio of 68 stocks. Their recent P/E ratios are shown. She wants to use the quartiles to define benchmarks for stocks that are low-priced (bottom quartile) or high-priced (top quartile).

7	8	8	10	10	10	10	12	13	13	13	13	13	13	13	14	14
14	15	15	15	15	15	16	16	16	17	18	18	18	18	19	19	19
19	19	20	20	20	21	21	21	22	22	23	23	23	24	25	26	26
26	26	27	29	29	30	31	34	36	37	40	41	45	48	55	68	91

Using Excel's method of interpolation (*Method B*), the quartile *positions* are:

Q_1 position: $0.25(68) + 0.75 = 17.75$ (interpolate between $x_{17} + x_{18}$)
Q_2 position: $0.50(68) + 0.50 = 34.50$ (interpolate between $x_{34} + x_{35}$)
Q_3 position: $0.75(68) + 0.25 = 51.25$ (interpolate between $x_{51} + x_{52}$)

The quartiles are:

First quartile: $Q_1 = x_{17} + 0.75(x_{18} - x_{17}) = 14 + 0.75(14 - 14) = 14$
Second quartile: $Q_2 = x_{34} + 0.50(x_{35} - x_{34}) = 19 + 0.50(19 - 19) = 19$
Third quartile: $Q_3 = x_{51} + 0.25(x_{52} - x_{51}) = 26 + 0.25(26 - 26) = 26$

The median stock has a P/E ratio of 19. A stock with a P/E ratio below 14 is in the bottom quartile, while a stock with a P/E ratio above 26 is in the upper quartile. These statements are easy to understand, and convey an impression both of central tendency *and* dispersion in the sample. But notice that the quartiles do not provide clean cut-points between groups of observations because of clustering of identical data values on either side of the quartiles (a common occurrence). Since stock prices vary with the stage of the economic cycle, portfolio analysts must revise their P/E benchmarks continually and would actually use a larger sample (perhaps even *all* publicly traded stocks).

Tip

Whether you use the method of medians or Excel, your quartiles will be about the same. Small differences in calculation techniques typically do not lead to different conclusions in business applications.

Caution   Quartiles are robust statistics that generally resist outliers. However, quartiles do not always provide clean cutpoints in the sorted data, particularly in small samples or when there are repeating data values. For example:

Data Set A: 1, 2, 4, 4, 8, 8, 8, 8 $Q_1 = 3, Q_2 = 6, Q_3 = 8$
Data Set B: 0, 3, 3, 6, 6, 6, 10, 15 $Q_1 = 3, Q_2 = 6, Q_3 = 8$

These two data sets have identical quartiles, but are not really similar. Because of the small sample size and "gaps" in the data, the quartiles do not represent either data set well.

Dispersion Using Quartiles

Quartiles can be used to define additional measures of central tendency and dispersion, some of which are shown in Table 4.19. They have the advantage of not being influenced by outliers. This makes them useful for analyzing changes over time, for example, in stock portfolios (which often contain extreme outliers).

Midhinge

The *midhinge* is the mean of the first and third quartiles:

(4.18)
$$\text{Midhinge} = \frac{Q_1 + Q_3}{2}$$

TABLE 4.19   **Some Robust Measures of Central Tendency and Dispersion**

Statistic	Formula	Excel	Pro	Con
Midhinge	$\dfrac{Q_1 + Q_3}{2}$	=0.5*(QUARTILE (Data,1) + QUARTILE (Data,3))	Robust to presence of extreme data values.	Less familiar to most people.
Midspread (interquartile range)	$Q_3 - Q_1$	=QUARTILE (Data,3) − QUARTILE (Data,1)	Stable when extreme data values exist.	Ignores magnitude of extreme data values.
Coefficient of quartile variation (CQV)	$100 \times \dfrac{Q_3 - Q_1}{Q_3 + Q_1}$	None	Relative variation in percent so we can compare data sets.	Less familiar to nonstatisticians.

For the 68 P/E ratios the midhinge is:

$$\text{Midhinge} = \frac{Q_1 + Q_3}{2} = \frac{14 + 26}{2} = 20$$

Unlike the mean and midrange, the midhinge is a relatively robust measure of central tendency because the quartiles ignore extreme values.

Midspread (Interquartile Range)

A robust measure of dispersion is the ***interquartile range*** or ***midspread,*** defined as the difference between the third and first quartiles:

$$\text{Midspread} = Q_3 - Q_1 \qquad\qquad (4.19)$$

For the P/E data the midspread is:

$$\text{Midspread} = 26 - 14 = 12$$

Coefficient of Quartile Variation

Relative dispersion may be measured by the ***coefficient of quartile variation*** (abbreviated *CQV*):

$$CQV = 100 \times \frac{Q_3 - Q_1}{Q_3 + Q_1} \qquad\qquad (4.20)$$

For the 68 P/E ratios:

$$CQV = 100 \times \frac{Q_3 - Q_1}{Q_3 + Q_1} = 100 \times \frac{26 - 14}{26 + 14} = 30.0\%$$

The *CQV* is an attractive statistic because it is expressed as a percent, and thus can be used to compare data sets measured in different units (e.g., euros and yen) or with different means (e.g., scores on two exams). In this role, the *CQV* resembles the *CV* discussed earlier.

A useful tool of ***exploratory data analysis*** (EDA) is the ***box plot*** (also called a *box-and-whisker plot*) based on the ***five-number summary:***

4.6

BOX PLOTS

$$x_{\min}, Q_1, Q_2, Q_3, x_{\max}$$

For example, the five-number summary for the 68 P/E ratios is:

7, 14, 19, 26, 91

Figure 4.31 shows a box plot of the P/E data. The vertical lines that define the ends of the box are located at Q_1 and Q_3 on the *X*-axis. The vertical line within the box is the median (Q_2). The "whiskers" are the horizontal lines that connect each side of the box to $x_{\min}$ and $x_{\max}$ and their length suggests the length of each tail of the distribution. The long right whisker suggests right-skewness in the P/E data, a conclusion also suggested by the fact that the median is to the left of the center of the box (the center of the box is the midhinge or average of Q_1 and Q_3).

FIGURE 4.31

Simple box plot of P/E ratios
($n = 68$ stocks) (Visual
Statistics)

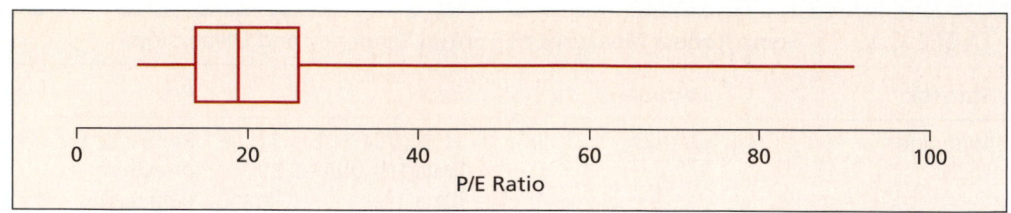

Fences and Unusual Data Values

We can use the quartiles to identify unusual data points. The idea is to detect data values that are far below Q_1 or far above Q_3. The *fences* are:

		Inner fences	*Outer fences*
(4.21)	Lower fence:	$Q_1 - 1.5(Q_3 - Q_1)$	$Q_1 - 3.0(Q_3 - Q_1)$
(4.22)	Upper fence:	$Q_3 + 1.5(Q_3 - Q_1)$	$Q_3 + 3.0(Q_3 - Q_1)$

Observations outside the inner fences are *unusual* while those outside the outer fences are *outliers*. For the P/E data:

	Inner fences	*Outer fences*
Lower fence:	$14 - 1.5(26 - 14) = -4$	$14 - 3.0(26 - 14) = -22$
Upper fence:	$26 + 1.5(26 - 14) = +44$	$26 + 3.0(26 - 14) = +62$

In this example, we can ignore the lower fences (since P/E ratios can't be negative) but in the right tail there are three unusual P/E values (45, 48, 55) that lie above the *inner* fence and two P/E values (68, 91) that are outliers because they exceed the *outer* fence. Unusual data points are shown on a box plot by truncating the whisker at the fences and displaying the unusual data points as dots or asterisks, as in Figure 4.32.

FIGURE 4.32

Box plot with fences
(MegaStat)

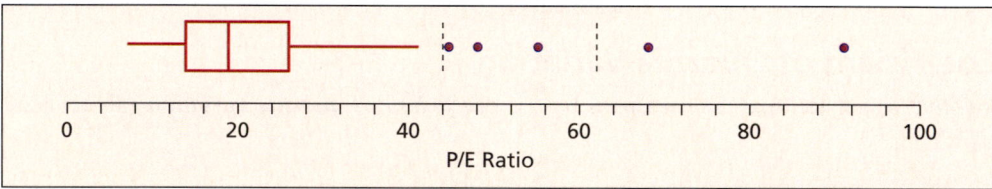

4.20   CitiBank recorded the number of customers to use a downtown ATM during the noon hour on 32 consecutive workdays. (a) Use Excel to find the quartiles. What do they tell you? (b) Find the midhinge. What does it tell you? (c) Make a box plot and interpret it.   **CitiBank**

25	37	23	26	30	40	25	26
39	32	21	26	19	27	32	25
18	26	34	18	31	35	21	33
33	9	16	32	35	42	15	24

4.21   An executive's telephone log showed the lengths of 65 calls initiated during the last week of July. (a) Use Excel to find the quartiles. What do they tell you? (b) Find the midhinge. What does it tell you? (c) Make a box plot and interpret it.   **CallLength**

1	2	10	5	3	3	2	20	1	1
6	3	13	2	2	1	26	3	1	3
1	2	1	7	1	2	3	1	2	12
1	4	2	2	29	1	1	1	8	5
1	4	2	1	1	1	1	6	1	2
3	3	6	1	3	1	1	5	1	18
2	13	13	1	6					

Mini Case 4.5

Airline Delays   UnitedAir

In 2005, United Airlines announced that it would award 500 frequent flier miles to every traveler on flights that arrived more than 30 minutes late on all flights departing from Chicago O'Hare to seven other hub airports (see *The Wall Street Journal,* June 14, 2005). What is the likelihood of such a delay? On a randomly chosen day (Tuesday, April 26, 2005) the Bureau of Transportation Statistics Web site (**www.bts.gov**) showed 278 United Airlines departures from O'Hare. The mean arrival delay was -7.45 minutes (i.e., flights arrived early, on average). The quartiles were $Q_1 = -19$ minutes, $Q_2 = -10$ minutes, and $Q_3 = -3$ minutes. While these statistics show that most of the flights arrive early, we must look further to estimate the probability of a frequent flier bonus.

In the box plot with fences (Figure 4.33) the "box" is entirely below zero. In the right tail, one flight was slightly above the inner fence (unusual) and eight flights were above the outer fence (outliers). An empirical estimate of the probability of a frequent flier award is 8/278 or about a 3% chance. A longer period of study might alter this estimate (e.g., if there were days of bad winter weather or traffic congestion).

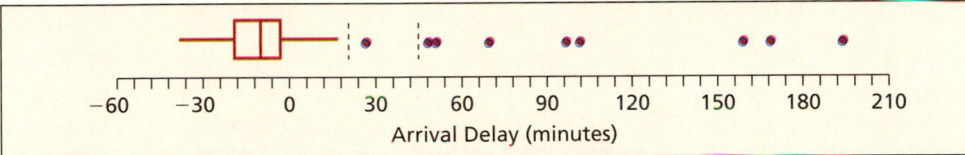

FIGURE 4.33

Box Plot of Flight Arrival Delays

The dot plot (Figure 4.34) shows that the distribution of arrival delays is rather bell-shaped, except for the unusual values in the right tail. This is consistent with the view that "normal" flight operations are predictable, with only random variation around the mean. While it is impossible for flights to arrive much earlier than planned, unusual factors could delay them by a lot.

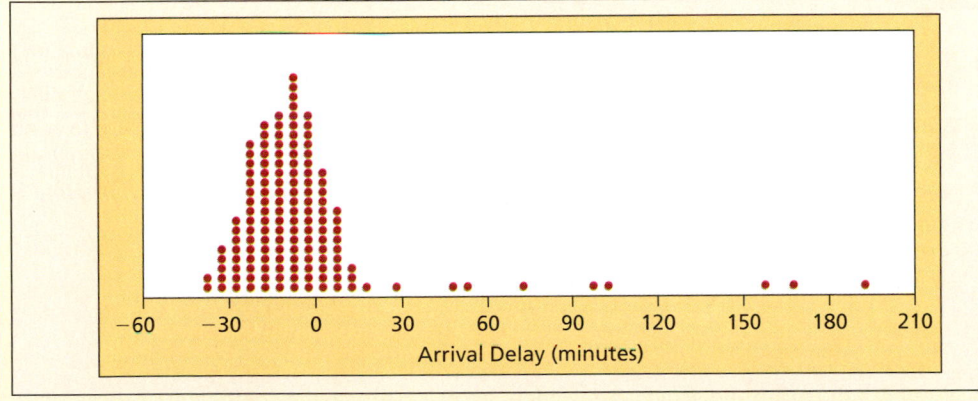

FIGURE 4.34

Dot Plot of Flight Arrival Delays

Nature of Grouped Data

Sometimes we must work with observations that have been grouped. When a data set is tabulated into bins, we lose information but gain clarity of presentation, because grouped data are often easier to display than raw data. As long as the bin limits are given, we can estimate the mean and standard deviation. The accuracy of the grouped estimates will depend on the number of bins, distribution of data within bins, and bin frequencies.

4.7

GROUPED DATA

Mean and Standard Deviation

Table 4.20 shows a frequency distribution for prices of Lipitor®, a cholesterol-lowering prescription drug, for three cities (see **Mini Case 4.2**). The observations are classified into bins of equal width 5. When calculating a mean or standard deviation from grouped data, we treat all observations within a bin *as if they were located at the midpoint*. For example, in the third class (70 but less than 75) we pretend that all 11 prices were equal to $72.50 (the interval midpoint). In reality, observations may be scattered within each interval, but we hope that *on average* they are located at the class midpoint.

TABLE 4.20	**Worksheet for Grouped Lipitor® Data ($n = 47$)**						**LipitorGrp**
From	*To*	f_j	m_j	$f_j m_j$	$m_j - \bar{x}$	$(m_j - \bar{x})^2$	$f(m - \bar{x})^2$
60	65	6	62.5	375	−10.42553	108.69172	652.15029
65	70	11	67.5	742.5	−5.42553	29.43640	323.80036
70	75	11	72.5	797.5	−0.42553	0.18108	1.99185
75	80	13	77.5	1,007.5	4.57447	20.92576	272.03486
80	85	5	82.5	412.5	9.57447	91.67044	458.35220
85	90	0	87.5	0	14.57447	212.41512	0.00000
90	95	1	92.5	92.5	19.57447	383.15980	383.15980
	Sum	47	Sum	3,427.5		Sum	2,091.48936
			Mean ($\bar{x}$)	72.925532		Std Dev (s)	6.74293408

Each interval j has a midpoint m_j and a frequency f_j. We calculate the estimated mean by multiplying the midpoint of each class by its class frequency, taking the sum over all k classes, and dividing by sample size n.

$$(4.23) \qquad \bar{x} = \sum_{j=1}^{k} \frac{f_j m_j}{n} = \frac{3,427.5}{47} = 72.925532$$

We then estimate the standard deviation by subtracting the estimated mean from each class midpoint, squaring the difference, multiplying by the class frequency, taking the sum over all classes to obtain the sum of squared deviations about the mean, dividing by $n - 1$, and taking the square root. *Avoid the common mistake of "rounding off" the mean before subtracting it from each midpoint.*

$$(4.24) \qquad s = \sqrt{\sum_{j=1}^{k} \frac{f_j (m_j - \bar{x})^2}{n - 1}} = \sqrt{\frac{2,091.48936}{47 - 1}} = 6.74293$$

Once we have the mean and standard deviation, we can estimate the coefficient of variation in the usual way:

$$CV = 100(s/\bar{x}) = 100\,(6.74293/72.925532) = 9.2\%$$

Accuracy Issues

How accurate are grouped estimates? In this example, they are very close to the ungrouped statistics (typically, we would have no way of knowing, but in this case we have the raw data from **Mini Case 4.2**). Table 4.21 shows that very little information was lost due to grouping. Of course, to the extent that observations are *not* evenly spaced within the bins, accuracy would be lost.

Statistic	Ungrouped	Grouped	
Mean	$72.94	$72.93	**TABLE 4.21**
Standard deviation	$6.71	$6.74	**Accuracy of Grouped**
Coefficient of variation	9.20%	9.24%	**Estimates**

The dot plot in Figure 4.35 does not reveal unevenness in the distribution of Lipitor® prices within the five-unit intervals. Unless there is systematic skewness (say, clustering at the low end of each class) the effects of uneven distributions within bins tend to average out.

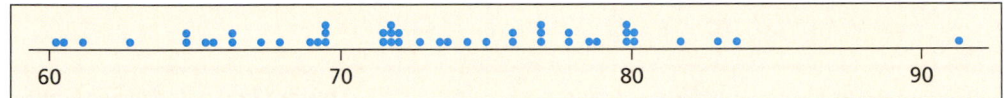

FIGURE 4.35

Dot plot of Lipitor® prices
($n = 47$)

Properties of Grouped Estimates

Accuracy tends to improve as the number of bins increases. If the first or last class is open-ended, there will be no class midpoint, and therefore no way to estimate the mean. For nonnegative data (e.g., GPA) we can assume a lower limit of zero when the first class is open-ended, although this assumption may make the first class too wide. Such an assumption may occasionally be possible for an open-ended top class (e.g., the upper limit of people's ages could be assumed to be 100) but many variables have no obvious upper limit (e.g., income). It is usually possible to estimate the median and quartiles from grouped data even with open-ended classes (see *LearningStats* Unit 04, which illustrates grouped quartile calculations).

Skewness

In a general way, *skewness* (as shown in Figure 4.36) may be judged by looking at the sample histogram, or by comparing the mean and median. However, this comparison is imprecise and does not take account of sample size. When more precision is needed, we look at the sample's ***skewness coefficient*** provided by Excel and MINITAB:

4.8

SKEWNESS AND KURTOSIS

$$\text{Skewness} = \frac{n}{(n-1)(n-2)} \sum_{i=1}^{n} \left(\frac{x_i - \bar{x}}{s} \right)^3 \qquad (4.25)$$

This unit-free statistic can be used to compare two samples measured in different units (say, dollars and yen) or to compare one sample with a known reference distribution such as the symmetric normal (bell-shaped) distribution. The skewness coefficient is obtained from Excel's Tools > Data Analysis > Descriptive Statistics or by the function =SKEW(Data).

FIGURE 4.36

Skewness prototype populations

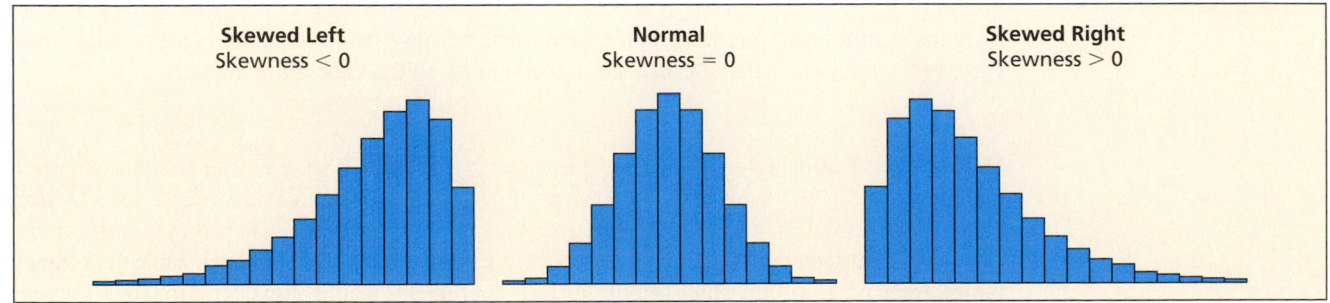

Skewed Left
Skewness < 0

Normal
Skewness $= 0$

Skewed Right
Skewness > 0

Table 4.22 shows the expected range within which the sample skewness coefficient would be expected to fall 90 percent of the time if the population being sampled were normal. A sample skewness statistic within the 90 percent range may be attributed to random variation, while coefficients outside the range would suggest that the sample came from a nonnormal population. As *n* increases, the range of chance variation narrows.

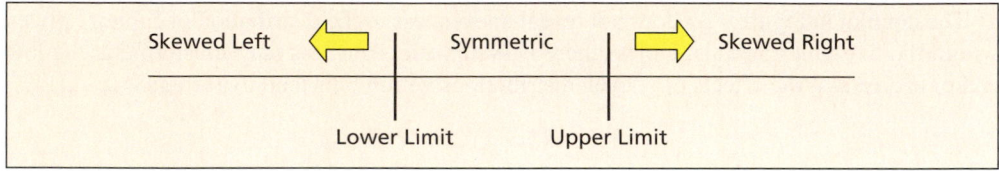

TABLE 4.22

90 Percent Range for Excel's Sample Skewness Coefficient

Source: Adapted from E. S. Pearson and H. O. Hartley, *Biometrika Tables for Statisticians,* 3rd ed. (Oxford University Press, 1970), pp. 207–8. Used with permission.

Note: Table and formula employ an adjustment for bias.

n	Lower Limit	Upper Limit	n	Lower Limit	Upper Limit
25	−0.726	0.726	90	−0.411	0.411
30	−0.673	0.673	100	−0.391	0.391
40	−0.594	0.594	150	−0.322	0.322
50	−0.539	0.539	200	−0.281	0.281
60	−0.496	0.496	300	−0.230	0.230
70	−0.462	0.462	400	−0.200	0.200
80	−0.435	0.435	500	−0.179	0.179

Kurtosis

Kurtosis refers to the relative length of the tails and the degree of concentration in the center. A normal bell-shaped population is called *mesokurtic* and serves as a benchmark (see Figure 4.37). A population that is flatter than a normal (i.e., has heavier tails) is called *platykurtic* while one that is more sharply peaked than a normal (i.e., has thinner tails) is *leptokurtic.* Kurtosis is *not* the same thing as dispersion, although the two are easily confused.

FIGURE 4.37

Kurtosis prototype shapes

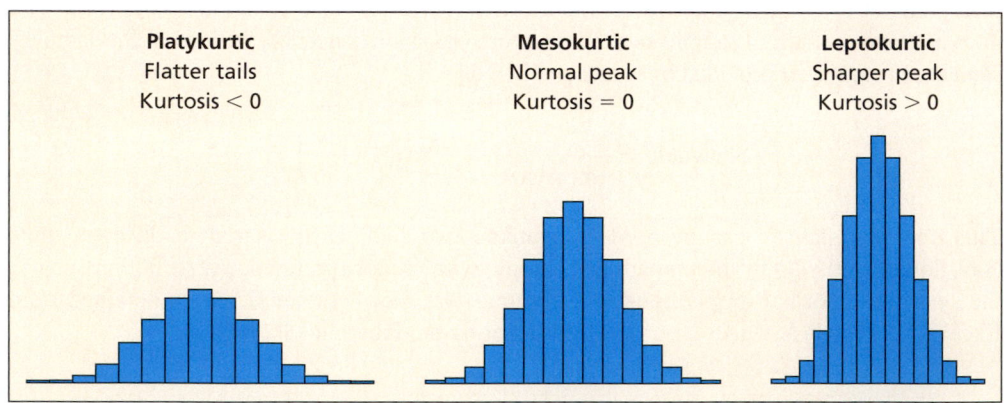

A histogram is an unreliable guide to kurtosis because its scale and axis proportions may vary, so a numerical statistic is needed. Excel and MINITAB use this statistic:

$$(4.26) \qquad \text{Kurtosis} = \frac{n(n+1)}{(n-1)(n-2)(n-3)} \sum_{i=1}^{n} \left(\frac{x_i - \bar{x}}{s} \right)^4 - \frac{3(n-1)^2}{(n-2)(n-3)}$$

The sample kurtosis coefficient is obtained from Excel's function =KURT(Data). Table 4.23 shows the expected range within which sample kurtosis coefficients would be expected to fall 90 percent

n	Lower Limit	Upper Limit
50	−0.81	1.23
75	−0.70	1.02
100	−0.62	0.87
150	−0.53	0.71
200	−0.47	0.62
300	−0.40	0.50
400	−0.35	0.43
500	−0.32	0.39

TABLE 4.23

90 Percent Range for Excel's Sample Kurtosis Coefficient

Source: Adapted from E. S. Pearson and H. O. Hartley, *Biometrika Tables for Statisticians,* 3rd ed. (Oxford University Press, 1970), pp. 207–8. Used with permission. Table and formula employ an adjustment for bias and subtract 3 so the statistic is centered at 0.

of the time if the population is normal. A sample coefficient within the ranges shown may be attributed to chance variation, while a coefficient outside this range would suggest that the sample differs from a normal population. As sample size increases, the chance range narrows. Unless you have at least 50 observations, inferences about kurtosis are risky.

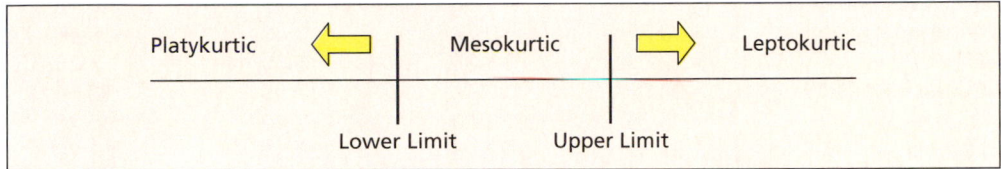

Mini Case   4.6

Stock Prices   **StockPrices**

An investor is tracking four stocks, two in the computer data services sector (IBM and EDS) and two in the consumer appliance sector (Maytag and Whirlpool). The analyst chose a two-month period of observation and recorded the closing price of each stock (42 trading days). Figure 4.38 shows MINITAB box plots for the stock prices (note that each has a different price scale).

FIGURE 4.38

Box Plots for Prices of Four Stocks

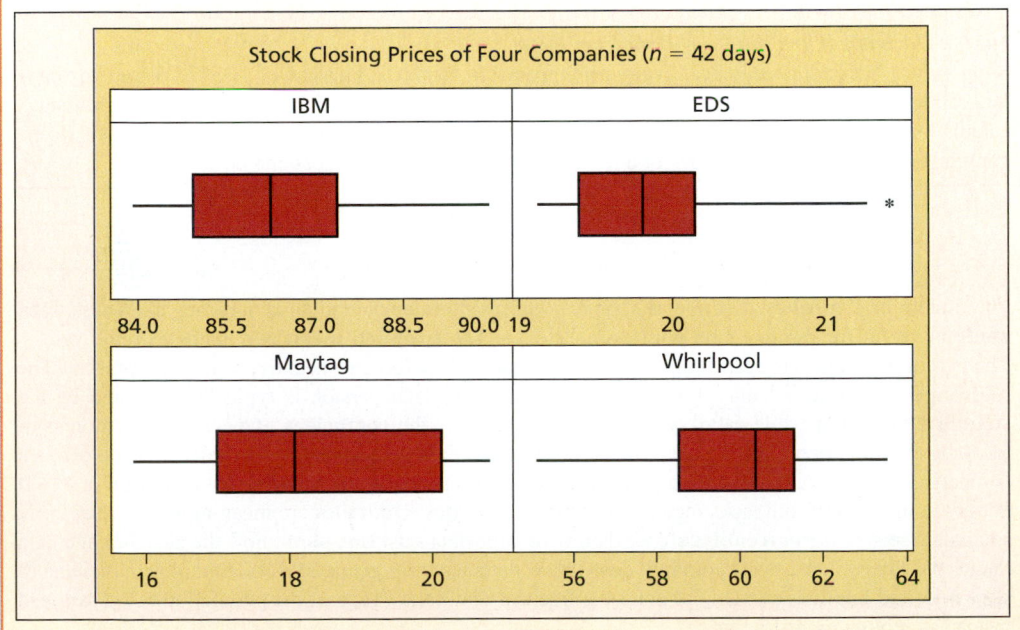

Looking at the numerical statistics (Table 4.24), EDS's skewness coefficient (1.04) suggests a right-skewed distribution (for $n = 40$, the normal skewness range is $-.594$ to $+.594$). This conclusion is supported by the EDS box plot, with its long right whisker and an outlier in the right tail. Maytag's kurtosis coefficient (-1.40) suggests a flatter-than-normal distribution (for $n = 50$, the kurtosis coefficient range is -0.81 to $+1.23$), although the sample size is too small to assess kurtosis reliably. Maytag's coefficient of variation (CV) and coefficient of quartile variation (CQV) are also high. The Maytag box plot supports the view of high relative variation. In addition to patterns in price variation, an investor would consider many other factors (e.g., prospects for growth, dividends, stability, etc.) in evaluating a portfolio.

TABLE 4.24   Four Companies' Stock Prices (September–October 2004)

Statistic	IBM	EDS	Maytag	Whirlpool
Mean	86.40	19.86	18.39	59.80
Standard deviation	1.70	0.59	1.59	1.94
Skewness	0.51	1.04	0.23	−0.48
Kurtosis	−0.62	0.72	−1.40	−0.16
CV (%)	2.0%	3.0%	8.6%	3.2%
Quartile 1	84.97	19.40	17.07	58.53
Quartile 2	86.25	19.80	18.10	60.20
Quartile 3	87.37	20.13	20.11	61.28
CQV (%)	1.4%	1.8%	8.2%	2.3%

Source: Data are from the Center for Research in Security Prices (CRSP®), a financial research center at the University of Chicago Graduate School of Business. Example is for statistical education only, and not as a guide to investment decisions.

Excel Hints

Hint 1: Formats When You Copy Data from Excel
Excel's dollar format (e.g., $214.07) or comma format (e.g., 12,417) will cause many statistical packages (e.g., MINITAB or Visual Statistics) to interpret the pasted data as text (because "$" and "," are not numbers). For example, in MINITAB a column heading C1-T indicates that the data column is text. Text cannot be analyzed numerically, so you can't get means, medians, etc. Check the format before you copy and paste.

Hint 2: Decimals When You Copy Data from Excel
Suppose you have adjusted Excel's decimal cell format to display 2.4 instead of 2.35477. When you copy this cell and paste it into MINITAB, the pasted cell contains 2.4 (not 2.35477). Thus, Excel's statistical calculations (based on 2.35477) will not agree with MINITAB (likewise for Visual Statistics). If you copy several columns of data (e.g., for a regression model), the differences can be serious.

Chapter Summary

The **mean** and **median** describe a sample's **central tendency** and also indicate **skewness**. The **mode** is useful for discrete data with a small range. The **trimmed mean** eliminates extreme values. The **geometric mean** mitigates high extremes but fails when zeros or negative values are present. The **midrange** is easy to calculate but is sensitive to extremes. Dispersion is typically measured by the **standard deviation** while **relative dispersion** is given by the **coefficient of variation** for nonnegative data. **Standardized data** reveal **outliers** or unusual data values, and the **Empirical Rule** offers a comparison with a normal distribution. In measuring dispersion, the **mean absolute deviation** or **MAD** is easy to understand, but lacks nice mathematical properties. **Quartiles** are meaningful even for fairly small data sets, while **percentiles** are used only for large data sets. **Box plots** show the quartiles and data range. We can estimate many common descriptive statistics from **grouped data**. Sample coefficients of **skewness** and **kurtosis** allow more precise inferences about the **shape** of the population being sampled instead of relying on histograms.

Key Terms

Central Tendency	Dispersion	Shape	Percentiles
geometric mean, *127*	Chebyshev's	bimodal	box plot, *145*
mean, *119*	Theorem, *136*	distribution, *123*	coefficient of quartile
median, *120*	coefficient of	kurtosis, *150*	variation, *145*
midrange, *128*	variation, *133*	leptokurtic, *150*	exploratory data
mode, *121*	Empirical Rule, *137*	mesokurtic, *150*	analysis, *145*
trimmed mean, *128*	mean absolute	negatively skewed, *123*	five-number
	deviation, *133*	platykurtic, *150*	summary, *145*
	outliers, *137*	positively skewed, *123*	interquartile
	population	skewed left, *123*	range, *145*
	variance, *131*	skewed right, *123*	method of
	range, *131*	skewness, *123*	medians, *142*
	sample variance, *131*	skewness	midhinge, *144*
	standard	coefficient, *149*	midspread, *145*
	deviation, *131*	symmetric data, *123*	quartiles, *141*
	standardized		
	variable, *138*		
	two-sum formula, *132*		

Commonly Used Formulas in Descriptive Statistics

Sample mean: $\bar{x} = \dfrac{1}{n}\sum_{i=1}^{n} x_i$

Geometric mean: $G = \sqrt[n]{x_1 x_2 \cdots x_n}$

Range: $\text{Range} = x_{\max} - x_{\min}$

Sample standard deviation: $s = \sqrt{\dfrac{\sum_{i=1}^{n}(x_i - \bar{x})^2}{n-1}}$

Coefficient of variation: $CV = 100 \times \dfrac{s}{\bar{x}}$

Standardized variable: $z_i = \dfrac{x_i - \mu}{\sigma}$

Grouped mean: $\bar{x} = \sum_{j=1}^{k} \dfrac{f_j m_j}{n}$

Chapter Review

1. What are descriptive statistics? How do they differ from visual displays of data?

2. Explain each concept: (a) central tendency, (b) dispersion, and (c) shape.

3. (a) Why is sorting usually the first step in data analysis? (b) Why is it useful to begin a data analysis by thinking about how the data were collected?

4. List strengths and weaknesses of each measure of central tendency and write its Excel function: (a) mean, (b) median, and (c) mode.

5. (a) Why must the deviations around the mean sum to zero? (b) What is the position of the median in the data array when *n* is even? When *n* is odd? (c) Why is the mode of little use in continuous data? For what type of data is the mode most useful?

6. (a) What is a bimodal distribution? (b) Explain two ways to detect skewness.

7. List strengths and weaknesses of each measure of central tendency and give its Excel function (if any): (a) midrange, (b) geometric mean, and (c) 10 percent trimmed mean.

8. (a) What is dispersion? (b) Name five measures of dispersion. List the main characteristics (strengths, weaknesses) of each measure.

9. (a) Which standard deviation formula (population, sample) is used most often? Why? (b) When is the coefficient of variation useful? When is it useless?

10. (a) To what kind of data does Chebyshev's Theorem apply? (b) To what kind of data does the Empirical Rule apply? (c) What is an outlier? An unusual data value?

11. (a) In a normal distribution, approximately what percent of observations are within 1, 2, and 3 standard deviations of the mean? (b) In a sample of 10,000 observations, about how many observations would you expect beyond 3 standard deviations of the mean?

12. (a) Write the mathematical formula for a standardized variable. (b) Write the Excel formula for standardizing a data value in cell F17 from an array with mean Mu and standard deviation Sigma.

13. (a) Why is it dangerous to delete an outlier? (b) When might it be acceptable to delete an outlier?

14. (a) Explain how quartiles can measure both centrality and dispersion. (b) Why don't we calculate percentiles for small samples?

15. (a) Explain the method of medians for calculating quartiles. (b) Write the Excel formula for the first quartile of an array named XData.

16. (a) What is a box plot? What does it tell us? (b) What is the role of fences in a box plot? (c) Define the midhinge and midspread (interquartile range).

17. (a) Why is some accuracy lost when we estimate the mean or standard deviation from grouped data? (b) Why do open-ended classes in a frequency distribution make it impossible to estimate the mean and standard deviation? (c) When would grouped data be presented instead of the entire sample of raw data?

18. *Optional* (a) What is the skewness coefficient of a normal distribution? A uniform distribution? (b) Why do we need a table for sample skewness coefficients that is based on sample size?

19. *Optional* (a) What is kurtosis? (b) Sketch a platykurtic population, a leptokurtic population, and a mesokurtic population. (c) Why can't we rely on a histogram to assess kurtosis?

CHAPTER EXERCISES

Note: Unless otherwise noted, you may use any desired statistical software for calculations and graphs in the following problems.

DESCRIBING DATA

4.22 Below are monthly rents paid by 30 students who live off campus. (a) Find the mean, median, mode, standard deviation, and quartiles. (b) Describe the "typical" rent paid by a student. (c) Do the measures of central tendency agree? Explain. (d) Sort and standardize the data. (e) Are there outliers or unusual data values? (f) Using the Empirical Rule, do you think the data could be from a normal population?   **Rents**

730	730	730	930	700	570
690	1,030	740	620	720	670
560	740	650	660	850	930
600	620	760	690	710	500
730	800	820	840	720	700

4.23 A random sample of 20 mail-order catalogs yielded the observations shown for the number of pages per catalog. (a) Calculate the mean, median, mode, and midrange. (b) Which is the best measure of central tendency, and why? (c) Describe the number of pages in a "typical" mail-order catalog. (d) Calculate the standard deviation. (e) Sort and standardize the data. (f) Are there outliers or unusual data values? (Data are from a project by MBA student Luanne Schonfeld.)   **Catalogs**

47	48	64	40	37	48	48	36	100	136
48	38	81	180	64	80	64	72	44	48

4.24 Weights (in pounds) of 29 stepladders sold in retail stores are shown. (a) Without using Excel, prepare a dot plot. (b) Without using Excel, calculate the mean, median, mode, midrange, and geometric mean. (c) Which is the best measure of central tendency, and why? (d) Describe a "typical" stepladder. (Data are from *Consumer Reports* 55, no. 9.) 🪓 **Ladders**

21	23	14	17	12	11	14	11	12	11	10	12	17	17	18
20	22	22	17	21	17	19	21	21	18	20	19	30	30	

4.25 How many days in advance do travelers purchase their airline tickets? Below are data showing the advance days for a sample of 28 passengers on United Airlines Flight 815 from Chicago to Los Angeles. (a) Prepare a dot plot and discuss it. (b) Calculate the mean, median, mode, and midrange. (c) Calculate the quartiles, midhinge, and coefficient of quartile variation. (d) Why can't you use the geometric mean for this data set? (e) Which is the best measure of central tendency? Why? (Data are from *The New York Times,* April 12, 1998.) 🪓 **Days**

11	7	11	4	15	14	71	29	8	7	16	28	17	249
0	20	77	18	14	3	15	52	20	0	9	9	21	3

4.26 In a particular week, the cable channel TCM (Turner Classic Movies) showed seven movies rated ****, nine movies rated ***, three movies rated **, and one movie rated *. Which measure of central tendency would you use to describe the "average" movie rating on TCM (assuming that week was typical)? (Data are from *TV Guide*.)

4.27 The "expense ratio" is a measure of the cost of managing the portfolio. Investors prefer a low expense ratio, all else equal. Below are expense ratios for 23 randomly chosen stock funds and 21 randomly chosen bond funds. (a) Calculate the mean, median, and mode for each sample. (b) Succinctly compare central tendency in expense ratios for stock funds and bond funds. (c) Calculate the standard deviation and coefficient of variation for each sample. Which type of fund has more variability? Explain. (d) Calculate the quartiles and midhinge. What do they tell you? (Data are from *Money* 32, no. 2 [February 2003]. Stock funds were selected from 1,699 funds by taking the 10th fund on each page in the list. Bond funds were selected from 499 funds by taking the 10th, 20th, and 30th fund on each page in the list.) 🪓 **Funds**

23 Stock Funds

1.12	1.44	1.27	1.75	0.99	1.45	1.19	1.22	0.99	3.18	1.21	1.89
0.60	2.10	0.73	0.90	1.79	1.35	1.08	1.28	1.20	1.68	0.15	

21 Bond Funds

1.96	0.51	1.12	0.64	0.69	0.20	1.44	0.68	0.40	0.94	0.75	1.77
0.93	1.25	0.85	0.99	0.95	0.35	0.64	0.41	0.90			

4.28 Statistics students were asked to fill a one-cup measure with raisin bran, tap the cup lightly on the counter three times to settle the contents, if necessary add more raisin bran to bring the contents exactly to the one-cup line, spread the contents on a large plate, and count the raisins. The 13 students who chose Kellogg's Raisin Bran obtained the results shown below. (a) Use Excel to calculate the mean, median, mode, and midrange. (b) Which is the best measure of central tendency, and why? (c) Calculate the standard deviation and coefficient of variation. (d) Why is there variation in the number of raisins in a cup of raisin bran? Why might it be difficult for Kellogg to reduce variation? 🪓 **Raisins**

23	33	44	36	29	42	31	33	61	36	34	23	24

4.29 Weights (in ounces) of 20 types of finishing sanders sold in retail stores are shown. (a) Calculate the mean, median, mode, and midrange. (b) Calculate the geometric mean. (c) Which is the best measure of central tendency, and why? (Data are from *Consumer Reports* 55, no. 9.) 🪓 **Sanders**

47	64	47	37	40	71	37	42	56	55
46	43	43	46	50	54	83	61	67	54

4.30 Salt-sensitive people must be careful of sodium content in foods. The sodium content (milligrams) in a 3-tablespoon serving of 33 brands of peanut butter is shown below. (a) Prepare a dot plot and discuss it. (b) Calculate the mean, median, mode, and midrange. (c) Which is the best measure of central tendency? The worst? Why? (d) Why would the geometric mean not work here? (e) Sort and standardize the data. (f) Are there outliers? Unusual data values? (Data are from *Consumer Reports* 67, no. 5.) 🪓 **Sodium**

98	225	225	225	23	0	210	0	210	225	210	165	180	240
225	8	375	225	270	285	180	210	180	195	195	188	173	
165	165	180	180	0	300								

4.31 Below are the lengths (in yards) of 27 18-hole golf courses in Oakland County, Michigan. (a) Prepare a dot plot and discuss it. (b) Calculate the mean, median, mode, and midrange. (c) Which is the best measure of central tendency? The worst? Why? (d) Why would the geometric mean pose a problem for this data set? (Data are from *Detroit Free Press,* April 13, 1995.)   **Golf**

5646	5767	5800	5820	6005	6078	6100	6110	6179
6186	6306	6366	6378	6400	6470	6474	6494	6500
6500	6554	6555	6572	6610	6620	6647	6845	7077

4.32 A false positive occurs when a radiologist who interprets a mammogram concludes that cancer is present, but a biopsy subsequently shows no breast cancer. False positives are unavoidable because mammogram results often are ambiguous. Below are false positive rates (percent) for 24 radiologists who interpreted a total of 8,734 mammograms. (a) Prepare a dot plot and interpret it. (b) Calculate the mean, median, mode, and midrange. (c) Which is the best measure of central tendency? The worst? Why? (Data are from Joann G. Elmore et al., "Screening Mammograms by Community Radiologists: Variability in False Positive Rates," *Journal of the National Cancer Institute* 94, no. 18 [September 18, 2002], p. 1376.)   **Cancer**

8.5	4.9	12.5	2.6	7.6	15.9	5.6	9.0	9.0	10.8	10.2	12.2
4.0	6.9	6.0	6.7	6.5	9.5	2.7	5.3	4.4	3.5	11.9	4.2

4.33 The table below shows percentiles of height (in cm) for 20-year-old males and females. (a) Calculate the midhinge and coefficient of quartile variation (*CQV*). Why are these statistics appropriate to measure centrality and dispersion in this situation? (b) Choose a 20 year old whose height you know and describe that person's height (*Note:* 1 in. = 2.54 cm) in comparison with these percentiles. (c) Do you suppose that height percentiles change over time for the population of a specified nation? Explain. (Data are from the National Center for Health Statistics, www.fedstats.gov.)

Selected Percentiles for Heights of 20 Year Olds (cm)

Gender	5%	25%	50%	75%	95%
Male	165	172	177	182	188
Female	153	159	163	168	174

4.34 Grace took a random sample of the number of steps per minute from the electronic readout of her aerobic climbing machine during a 1-hour workout. (a) Calculate the mean, median, and mode. (b) Which is the best measure of central tendency? The worst? Why? (Data are from a project by Grace Obringer, MBA student.)   **Steps**

90	110	97	144	54	60	156	86	82	64	100	47	80	164	93

4.35 How much revenue does it take to maintain a cricket club? The following table shows annual income for 18 first-class clubs that engage in league play. (a) Calculate the mean, median, and mode. Show your work carefully. (b) Describe a "typical" cricket club's income. (Data are from *The Economist* 367, no. 8329 [June 21, 2003], p. 47.)

Annual Income of First-Class Cricket Clubs in England   **Cricket**

Club	Income (£000)	Club	Income (£000)
Lancashire	5,366	Durham	3,009
Surrey	6,386	Worcestershire	2,446
Derbyshire	2,088	Gloucestershire	2,688
Middlesex	2,280	Northamptonshire	2,416
Somerset	2,544	Glamorgan	2,133
Nottinghamshire	3,669	Essex	2,417
Kent	2,894	Warwickshire	4,272
Leicestershire	2,000	Yorkshire	2,582
Sussex	2,477	Hampshire	2,557

4.36   A plumbing supplier's mean monthly demand for vinyl washers is 24,212 with a standard deviation of 6,053. The mean monthly demand for steam boilers is 6.8 with a standard deviation of 1.7. Compare the dispersion of these distributions. Which demand pattern has more relative variation? Explain.

4.37   On average, a laboratory mouse weighs 18 grams with a standard deviation of 0.9 grams, while a laboratory rat weighs 300 grams with a standard deviation of 20 grams. Compare the dispersion of these distributions. Which animal has more relative variation? Explain.

4.38   Analysis of portfolio returns over the period 1981–2000 showed the statistics below. (a) Calculate and compare the coefficients of variation. (b) Why would we use a coefficient of variation? Why not just compare the standard deviations? (c) What do the data tell you about risk and return at that time period?   **Returns**

Comparative Returns on Four Types of Investments

Investment	Mean Return	Standard Deviation	Coefficient of Variation
Venture funds (adjusted)	19.2	14.0	
All common stocks	15.6	14.0	
Real estate	11.5	16.8	
Federal short term paper	6.7	1.9	

Source: Dennis D. Spice and Stephen D. Hogan, "Venture Investing and the Role of Financial Advisors," *Journal of Financial Planning* 15, no. 3 (March 2002), p. 69. These statistics are for educational use only and should not be viewed as a guide to investing.

4.39   Analysis of annualized returns over the period 1991–2001 showed that prepaid tuition plans had a mean return of 6.3 percent with a standard deviation of 2.7 percent, while the Standard & Poor's 500 stock index had a mean return of 12.9 percent with a standard deviation of 15.8 percent. (a) Calculate and compare the coefficients of variation. (b) Why would we use a coefficient of variation? Why not just compare the standard deviations? (c) What do the data say about risk and return of these investments at that time? (Data are from Mark C. Neath, "Section 529 Prepaid Tuition Plans: A Low Risk Investment with Surprising Applications," *Journal of Financial Planning* 15, no. 4 [April 2002], p. 94.)

4.40   Caffeine content in a 5-ounce cup of brewed coffee ranges from 60 to 180 mg, depending on brew time, coffee bean type, and grind. (a) Use the midrange to estimate the mean. (b) Why is the assumption of a normal, bell-shaped distribution important in making these estimates? (c) Why might caffeine content of coffee *not* be normal? (Data are from *Popular Science* 254, no. 5 [May 1999].)

4.41   Chlorine is added to all city water to kill bacteria. In 2001, chlorine content in water from the Lake Huron Water Treatment plant ranged from 0.79 ppm (parts per million) to 0.92 ppm. (a) Use the midrange to estimate the mean. (b) Why is it reasonable to assume a normal distribution in this case? (Data are from City of Rochester Hills, Michigan, *2002 Water Quality Report*.)

THINKING ABOUT DISTRIBUTIONS

4.42   At the Midlothian Independent Bank, a study shows that the mean ATM transaction takes 74 seconds, the median 63 seconds, and the mode 51 seconds. (a) Sketch the distribution, based on these statistics. (b) What factors might cause the distribution to be like this?

4.43   At the Eureka library, the mean time a book is checked out is 13 days, the median is 10 days, and the mode is 7 days. (a) Sketch the distribution, based on these statistics. (b) What factors might cause the distribution to be like this?

4.44   On Professor Hardtack's last cost accounting exam, the mean score was 71, the median was 77, and the mode was 81. (a) Sketch the distribution, based on these statistics. (b) What factors might cause the distribution to be like this?

4.45   (a) Sketch the histogram you would expect for the number of DVDs owned by *n* randomly chosen families. (b) Describe the expected relationship between the mean, median, and mode. How could you test your ideas about these data?

4.46   (a) Sketch the histogram you would expect for the price of regular gasoline yesterday at *n* service stations in your area. (b) Guess the range and median. (c) How could you test your ideas about these data?

4.47 The median life span of a mouse is 118 weeks. (a) Would you expect the mean to be higher or lower than 118? (b) Would you expect the life spans of mice to be normally distributed? Explain. (Data are from *Science News* 161, no. 3 [January 19, 2002].)

4.48 The median waiting time for a liver transplant in the U.S. is 1,154 days for patients with type O blood (the most common blood type). (a) Would you expect the mean to be higher or lower than 1,154 days? Explain. (b) If someone dies while waiting for a transplant, how should that be counted in the average? (Data are from *The New York Times,* September 21, 2003.)

4.49 A small suburban community agreed to purchase police services from the county sheriff's department. The newspaper said, "In the past, the charge for police protection from the Sheriff's Department has been based on the median cost of the salary, fringe benefits, etc. That is, the cost per deputy was set halfway between the most expensive deputy and the least expensive." (a) Is this the median? If not, what is it? (b) Which would probably cost the city more, the midrange or the median? Why? (Data are from *Rochester Clarion,* March 20, 1986, p. 1.)

4.50 A company's contractual "trigger" point for a union absenteeism penalty is a certain distance above the *median* days missed by all workers. Now the company wants to switch the trigger to a certain distance above the *mean* days missed for all workers. (a) Visualize the distribution of missed days for all workers (symmetric, skewed left, skewed right). (b) Discuss the probable effect on the trigger point of switching from the mean to the median. (c) What position would the union be likely to take on the company's proposed switch?

EXCEL PROJECTS

4.51 (a) Use Excel functions to calculate the mean and standard deviation for weekend occupancy rates (percent) in nine resort hotels during the off-season. (b) What conclusion would a casual observer draw about centrality and dispersion, based on your statistics? (c) Now calculate the median for each sample. (d) Make a dot plot for each sample. (e) What did you learn from the medians and dot plots that was not apparent from the means and standard deviations? **Occupancy**

Observation	Week 1	Week 2	Week 3	Week 4
1	32	33	38	37
2	41	35	39	42
3	44	45	39	45
4	47	50	40	46
5	50	52	56	47
6	53	54	57	48
7	56	58	58	50
8	59	59	61	67
9	68	64	62	68

4.52 (a) Enter the Excel function =ROUND(NORMINV(RAND(),70,10),0) in cells B1:B100. This will create 100 random data points from a normal distribution using parameters $\mu = 70$ and $\sigma = 10$. Think of these numbers as exam scores for 100 students. (b) Use the Excel functions =AVERAGE(B1:B100) and =STDEV(B1:B100) to calculate the sample mean and standard deviation for your data array. (c) Every time you press F9 you will get a new sample. Watch the sample statistics and compare them with the desired parameters $\mu = 70$ and $\sigma = 10$. Do Excel's random samples have approximately the desired characteristics? (d) Use Excel's =MIN(B1:B100) and =MAX(B1:B100) to find the range of your samples. Do the sample ranges look as you would expect from the Empirical Rule?

GROUPED DATA (OPTIONAL)

Note: In each of the following tables, the upper bin limit is excluded from that bin, but is included as the lower limit of the next bin.

4.53 This table shows the fertility rate (children born per woman) in 191 world nations. (a) From the grouped data, calculate the mean, standard deviation, and coefficient of variation for each year. Show your calculations clearly in a worksheet. (b) Write a concise summary of central tendency and dispersion for fertility rates in world nations. (c) What additional information would you have gained by having the raw data? (d) What benefit arises from having only a summary table?

Fertility Rates in World Nations 🏵 **Fertile**

From	To	1990	2000
1.00	2.00	39	54
2.00	3.00	35	44
3.00	4.00	27	23
4.00	5.00	26	22
5.00	6.00	24	26
6.00	7.00	30	16
7.00	8.00	9	5
8.00	9.00	1	1
	Total	191	191

Source: World Health Organization. Raw data are available in *LearningStats* (Nations).

4.54 This table shows the distribution of winning times in the Kentucky Derby (a horse race) over 74 years. Times are recorded to the nearest 1/5 second (e.g., 121.4). (a) From the grouped data, calculate the mean, standard deviation, and coefficient of variation for each year. Show your calculations clearly in a worksheet. (b) Write a concise summary of central tendency and dispersion for Derby winning times. (c) What additional information would you have gained by having the raw data? (d) Do you think it likely that the distribution of times within each interval might not be uniform? Why would that matter?

Kentucky Derby Winning Times (seconds) 🏵 **Derby**

From	To	f
119	120	1
120	121	5
121	122	16
122	123	22
123	124	12
124	125	8
125	126	5
126	127	3
127	128	2
	Total	74

Source: *Sports Illustrated 2004 Sports Almanac.*

4.55 This table shows the number of heating degree-days in December in 35 U.S. cities. A heating degree-day is the sum over all days in the month of the difference between 65 degrees Fahrenheit and the daily mean temperature of each city. (a) From the grouped data, calculate the mean, standard deviation, and coefficient of variation for each year. Show your calculations clearly in a worksheet. (b) Write a concise summary of central tendency and dispersion for heating degree-days. (c) What additional information would you have gained by having the raw data? (d) Why do you suppose that unequal class intervals were used in this table? Does it affect the calculations you did?

December Heating Degree-Days in 35 Cities 🏵 **HeatGrp**

From	To	f
0	250	2
250	500	5
500	1,000	14
1,000	2,000	14
	Total	35

Source: U.S. Bureau of the Census, *Statistical Abstract of the United States, 1986*, p. 219.

4.56 This table shows the life expectancy at birth (in years) in 153 world nations. (a) From the grouped data, calculate the mean, standard deviation, and coefficient of variation for each year. Show your calculations clearly in a worksheet. (b) Write a concise summary of central tendency and dispersion for population increase in world nations. (c) What additional information would you have gained by having the raw data? (d) What is the advantage of having only a summary table?

Life Expectancy at Birth in Large Nations   **Life**

From	To	f
20	30	1
30	40	9
40	50	20
50	60	17
60	70	36
70	80	67
80	90	3
	Total	153

Source: U.S. Central Intelligence Agency, *The World Factbook, 2003*. Omits nations with population under 1 million. Raw data are available in *LearningStats* (Nations).

4.57   The self-reported number of hours worked per week by 204 top executives is given below. (a) Estimate the mean, standard deviation, and coefficient of variation, using an Excel worksheet to organize your calculations. (b) Do the unequal class sizes hamper your calculations? Why do you suppose that was done?

Weekly Hours of Work by Top Executives   **Work**

From	To	f
40	50	12
50	60	116
60	80	74
80	100	2
	Total	204

Source: Lamalie Associates, *Lamalie Report on Top Executives of the 1990s*, p. 11.

4.58   The table below shows the self-reported number of books read annually by 204 top executives. (a) Estimate the mean, standard deviation, and coefficient of variation, using an Excel worksheet to organize your calculations. (b) Do the unequal class sizes hamper your calculations? Why do you suppose that was done?

Books Read Annually by Top Executives   **Books**

From	To	f
0	3	23
3	6	46
6	10	37
10	20	44
20	30	31
30	50	23
	Total	204

Source: Lamalie Associates, *Lamalie Report on Top Executives of the 1990s*, p. 12.

4.59   (a) Which sample statistics, if any, can you obtain from the following data on farm size? Explain. (b) Why were unequal class intervals and open-end classes used?

Distribution of U.S. Farms by Size (acres)   **FarmSize**

From	To	Number of Farms (000)
0	10	154
10	50	411
50	100	295
100	180	298
180	260	165
260	500	238
500	1,000	176
1,000	2,000	101
2,000 and over		75
	Total	1,913

Source: U.S. Bureau of the Census, *Statistical Abstract of the United States, 2002*.

4.60 (a) Which sample statistics, if any, can you obtain from the data on CFP experience below? Explain. (b) Why were unequal class intervals and open-end classes used?

Years of Experience of 49 Certified Financial Planners 🏆 **Planners**

From	To	f
0	10	4
10	15	6
15	20	15
20	25	12
25	30	9
30	35	2
35 or more		1
	Total	49

Source: Tom L. Potts, et al., "Effective Retirement for Family Business Owner-Managers," *Journal of Financial Planning* 14, no. 6 (June 2001), p. 110. Copyright © 2001. Used with permission.

DO-IT-YOURSELF SAMPLING

4.61 (a) Record the points scored by the winning team in 50 college football games played last weekend (if it is not football season, do the same for basketball or another sport of your choice). If you can't find 50 scores, do the best you can. (b) Make a dot plot. What does it tell you? (c) Make a frequency distribution and histogram. Describe the histogram. (d) Calculate the mean, median, and mode. Which is the best measure of central tendency? Why? (e) Calculate standard deviation and coefficient of variation. (f) Standardize the data. Are there any outliers? (g) Find the quartiles. What do they tell you? (h) Make a box plot. What does it tell you?

4.62 (a) Record the length (in minutes) of 50 movies chosen at random from a movie guide (e.g., Leonard Maltin's *Movie and Video Guide*). Include the name of each movie. (b) Make a dot plot. What does it tell you? (c) Make a frequency distribution and histogram. Describe the histogram. (d) Calculate the mean, median, and mode. Which is the best measure of central tendency? Why? (e) Calculate the standard deviation and coefficient of variation. (f) Standardize the data. Are there any outliers? (g) Find the quartiles and coefficient of quartile variation. What do they tell you? (h) Make a box plot. What does it tell you?

MINI-PROJECTS

4.63 (a) Choose a data set and prepare a brief, descriptive report. You may use any computer software you wish (e.g., Excel, MegaStat, Visual Statistics, MINITAB). Include relevant worksheets or graphs in your report. If some questions do not apply to your data set, explain why not. (b) Discuss any possible weaknesses in the data. (c) Sort the data. (d) Make a dot plot. What does it tell you? (e) Make a histogram. Describe its shape. (f) Calculate the mean, median, and mode(s) and use them to describe central tendency for this data set. (g) Calculate the standard deviation and coefficient of variation. (h) Standardize the data and check for outliers. (i) Compare the data with the Empirical Rule. Discuss. (j) Calculate the quartiles and interpret them. (k) Make a box plot. Describe its appearance.

DATA SET A **Advertising Dollars as Percent of Sales in Selected Industries (*n* = 30)** 🏆 **Ads**

Industry	Percent	Industry	Percent
Accident and health insurance	0.9	Jewelry stores	4.6
Apparel and other finished products	5.5	Management services	1.0
Beverages	7.4	Millwork, veneer, and plywood	3.5
Cable and pay TV services	1.3	Misc. furniture and fixtures	2.3
Computer data processing	1.1	Mortgage bankers and loans	4.9
Computer storage devices	1.8	Motorcycles, bicycles, and parts	1.7
Cookies and crackers	3.5	Paints, varnishes, lacquers	3.1
Drug and proprietary stores	0.9	Perfume and cosmetics	11.9
Electric housewares and fans	6.4	Photographic equipment	4.3
Equipment rental and leasing	2.0	Racing and track operations	2.5
Footwear except rubber	4.5	Real estate investment trusts	3.8
Greeting cards	3.5	Shoe stores	3.0
Grocery stores	1.1	Steel works and blast furnaces	1.9
Hobby, toy, and games shops	3.0	Tires and inner tubes	1.8
Ice cream and frozen desserts	2.0	Wine, brandy, and spirits	11.3

Source: George E. Belch and Michael A. Belch, *Advertising and Promotion*, pp. 219–220. Copyright © 2004 Richard D. Irwin. Used with permission of McGraw-Hill Companies, Inc.

DATA SET B   Maximum Rate of Climb for Selected Piston Aircraft (*n* = 54)
🐾 ClimbRate

Manufacturer/Model	Year	Climb (ft./min.)	Manufacturer/Model	Year	Climb (ft./min.)
AMD CH 2000	2000	820	Diamond C1 Eclipse	2002	1,000
Beech Baron 58	1984	1,750	Extra Extra 400	2000	1,400
Beech Baron 58P	1984	1,475	Lancair Columbia 300	1998	1,340
Beech Baron D55	1968	1,670	Liberty XL-2	2003	1,150
Beech Bonanza B36 TC	1982	1,030	Maule Comet	1996	920
Beech Duchess	1982	1,248	Mooney 231	1982	1,080
Beech Sierra	1972	862	Mooney Eagle M205	1999	1,050
Bellanca Super Viking	1973	1,840	Mooney M20C	1965	800
Cessna 152	1978	715	Mooney Ovation 2 M20R	2000	1,150
Cessna 170B	1953	690	OMF Aircraft Symphony	2002	850
Cessna 172 R Skyhawk	1997	720	Piper 125 Tri Pacer	1951	810
Cessna 172 RG Cutlass	1982	800	Piper Archer III	1997	667
Cessna 1825 Skylane	1997	865	Piper Aztec F	1980	1,480
Cessna 182Q Skylane	1977	1,010	Piper Dakota	1979	965
Cessna 310 R	1975	1,662	Piper Malibu Mirage	1998	1,218
Cessna 337G Skymotor II	1975	1,100	Piper Malibu Mirage	1989	1,218
Cessna 414A	1985	1,520	Piper Saratoga II TC	1998	818
Cessna 421B	1974	1,850	Piper Satatoga SP	1980	1,010
Cessna Cardinal	1970	840	Piper Seneca III	1982	1,400
Cessna P210	1982	945	Piper Seneca V	1997	1,455
Cessna T210K	1970	930	Piper Seneca V	2002	1,455
Cessna T303 Crusader	1983	1,480	Piper Super Cab	1975	960
Cessna Turbo Skylane RG	1979	1,040	Piper Turbo Lance	1979	1,000
Cessna Turbo Skylane T182T	2001	1,060	Rockwell Commander 114	1976	1,054
Cessna Turbo Stationair TU206	1981	1,010	Sky Arrow 650 TC	1998	750
Cessna U206H	1998	1,010	Socata TB20 Trinidad	1999	1,200
Cirrus SR20	1999	946	Tiger AG-5B	2002	850

Source: *Flying Magazine* (various issues from 1997 to 2002).

DATA SET C   December Heating Degree-Days for Selected U.S. Cities (*n* = 35)
🐾 Heating

City	Degree-Days	City	Degree-Days	City	Degree-Days
Albuquerque	911	El Paso	639	Omaha	1,172
Baltimore	884	Hartford	1,113	Philadelphia	915
Bismarck	1,538	Honolulu	0	Phoenix	368
Buffalo	1,122	Indianapolis	1,039	Providence	1,014
Charleston	871	Jackson	513	Salt Lake City	1,076
Charlotte	694	Los Angeles	255	San Francisco	490
Cheyenne	1,107	Miami	42	Seattle	744
Chicago	1,156	Mobile	382	Sioux Falls	1,404
Cleveland	1,051	Nashville	747	St. Louis	955
Concord	1,256	New Orleans	336	Washington, D.C.	809
Detroit	1,132	Norfolk	667	Wichita	949
Duluth	1,587	Oklahoma City	778		

Source: U.S. Bureau of the Census, *Statistical Abstract of the United States.*

Note: A degree-day is the sum over all days in the month of the difference between 65 degrees Fahrenheit and the daily mean temperature of each city.

DATA SET D   Commercial Bank Profit as Percent of Revenue, 2003   🐦 **Banks**

Bank	Percent	Bank	Percent
AmSouth Bancorp	21	Mellon Financial Group	15
Bank of America Corp.	22	National City Corp.	22
Bank of New York Co.	18	National Commerce Finan	20
Bank One Corp.	16	North Fork Bancorp	31
BankNorth Group	22	Northern Trust Corp.	16
BB&T Corp.	17	PNC Financial Services Group	17
Charter One Financial	22	Popular	18
Citigroup	19	Provident Financial Group	6
Comerica	20	Providian Financial	7
Compass Bancshares	19	Regions Financial	18
Fifth Third Bancorp	27	SouthTrust Corp.	23
First Tenn. Natl. Corp.	18	State St. Corp.	13
FleetBoston	18	SunTrust Banks	19
Hibernia Corp.	20	Synovus Financial Corp.	16
Huntington Bancshares	16	U.S. Bancorp	24
J. P. Morgan Chase	15	Union Planters Corp.	21
KeyCorp	16	Wachovia Corp.	19
M&T Bank Corp.	19	Wells Fargo	20
Marshall & Ilsley Corp.	20	Zions Bancorp	18
MBNA	20		

Source: *Fortune* 149, no. 7 (April 5, 2004). Copyright © 2004 Time Inc. All rights reserved.

Note: These banks are in the Fortune 1000 companies.

DATA SET E   Caffeine Content of Randomly Selected Beverages ($n = 32$)   🐦 **Caffeine**

Company/Brand	mg/oz.	Company/Brand	mg/oz.
Barq's Root Beer	1.83	Mountain Dew	4.58
Coca-Cola Classic	2.83	Mr. Pibb	3.33
Cool from Nestea	1.33	Nestea Earl Grey	4.17
Cool from Nestea Rasberry Cooler	0.50	Nestea Peach	1.33
Diet A&W Cream Soda	1.83	Nestea Rasberry	1.33
Diet Ale 8	3.67	Nestea Sweet	2.17
Diet Code Red	4.42	Pepsi One	4.58
Diet Dr. Pepper	3.42	RC Edge	5.85
Diet Inca Kola	3.08	Royal Crown Cola	3.60
Diet Mountain Dew	4.58	Snapple Diet Peach Tea	2.63
Diet Mr. Pibb	3.33	Snapple Lemon Tea	2.63
Diet Pepsi-Cola	3.00	Snapple Lightning (Black Tea)	1.75
Inca Kola	3.08	Snapple Sun Tea	0.63
KMX (Blue)	0.00	Snapple Sweet Tea	1.00
Mello Yello Cherry	4.25	Sunkist Orange Soda	3.42
Mello Yello Melon	4.25	Vanilla Coke	2.83

Source: National Soft Drink Association (www.nsda.org).

DATA SET F   Super Bowl Scores 1967–2005 (*n* = 37 games)   🏈 **SuperBowl**

Year	Teams and Scores	Year	Teams and Scores
1967	Green Bay 35, Kansas City 10	1986	Chicago 46, New England 10
1968	Green Bay 33, Oakland 14	1987	NY Giants 39, Denver 20
1969	NY Jets 16, Baltimore 7	1988	Washington 42, Denver 10
1970	Kansas City 23, Minnesota 7	1989	San Francisco 20, Cincinnati 16
1971	Baltimore 16, Dallas 13	1990	San Francisco 55, Denver 10
1972	Dallas 24, Miami 3	1991	NY Giants 20, Buffalo 19
1973	Miami 14, Washington 7	1992	Washington 37, Buffalo 24
1974	Miami 24, Minnesota 7	1993	Dallas 52, Buffalo 17
1975	Pittsburgh 16, Minnesota 6	1994	Dallas 30, Buffalo 13
1976	Pittsburgh 21, Dallas 17	1995	San Francisco 49, San Diego 26
1977	Oakland 32, Minnesota 14	1996	Dallas 27, Pittsburgh 17
1978	Dallas 27, Denver 10	1997	Green Bay 35, New England 21
1979	Pittsburgh 35, Dallas 31	1998	Denver 31, Green Bay 24
1980	Pittsburgh 31, LA Rams 19	1999	Denver 34, Atlanta 19
1981	Oakland 27, Philadelphia 10	2000	St. Louis 23, Tennessee 16
1982	San Francisco 26, Cincinnati 21	2001	Baltimore 34, New York 7
1983	Washington 27, Miami 17	2002	New England 20, St. Louis 17
1984	LA Raiders 38, Washington 9	2003	Tampa Bay 48, Oakland 21
1985	San Francisco 38, Miami 16	2004	New England 32, Carolina 29
		2005	New England 24, Philadelphia 21

Source: *Sports Illustrated 2004 Sports Almanac, Detroit Free Press,* and www.cbs.sportsline.com.

DATA SET G   Property Crimes Per 100,000 Residents (*n* = 68 cities)   🏙 **Crime**

City and State	Crime	City and State	Crime	City and State	Crime
Albuquerque, NM	8,515	Honolulu, HI	4,671	Phoenix, AZ	6,888
Anaheim, CA	2,827	Houston, TX	6,084	Pittsburgh, PA	5,246
Anchorage, AK	4,370	Indianapolis, IN	4,306	Portland, OR	6,897
Arlington, TX	5,615	Jacksonville, FL	6,118	Raleigh, NC	6,327
Atlanta, GA	10,759	Kansas City, MO	9,882	Riverside, CA	3,610
Aurora, CO	5,079	Las Vegas, NV	4,520	Sacramento, CA	5,859
Austin, TX	6,406	Lexington, KY	5,315	San Antonio, TX	6,232
Birmingham, AL	7,030	Long Beach, CA	3,407	San Diego, CA	3,405
Boston, MA	4,986	Los Angeles, CA	3,306	San Francisco, CA	4,859
Buffalo, NY	5,791	Louisville, KY	5,102	San Jose, CA	2,363
Charlotte, NC	7,484	Memphis, TN	6,958	Santa Ana, CA	3,008
Chicago, IL	6,333	Mesa, AZ	5,590	Seattle, WA	8,397
Cincinnati, OH	5,694	Miami, FL	8,619	St. Louis, MO	11,765
Cleveland, OH	5,528	Milwaukee, WI	6,886	St. Paul, MN	6,215
Colorado Springs, CO	4,665	Minneapolis, MN	7,247	Stockton, CA	5,638
Columbus, OH	8,247	Nashville, TN	7,276	Tampa, FL	8,675
Corpus Christi, TX	6,266	New Orleans, LA	6,404	Toledo, OH	6,721
Dallas, TX	8,201	New York, NY	2,968	Tucson, AZ	8,079
Denver, CO	4,685	Newark, NJ	6,068	Tulsa, OK	6,234
Detroit, MI	8,163	Oakland, CA	6,820	Virginia Beach, VA	3,438
El Paso, TX	5,106	Oklahoma City, OK	8,464	Washington, DC	6,434
Fort Worth, TX	6,636	Omaha, NE	5,809	Wichita, KS	5,733
Fresno, CA	6,145	Philadelphia, PA	5,687		

Source: *Statistical Abstract of the United States, 2002.*

Related Reading

Barnett, Vic; and Toby Lewis. *Outliers in Statistical Data.* 3rd ed. John Wiley and Sons, 1994.

Blyth, C. R. "Minimizing the Sum of Absolute Deviations." *The American Statistician* 44, no. 4 (November 1990), p. 329.

Chebyshev, P. L. "Des Valeurs Moyennes." *Journal de Mathématiques Pures et Appliquées, 2 Série* 12 (1967), pp. 177–84.

Freund, John E.; and Benjamin M. Perles. "A New Look at Quartiles of Ungrouped Data." *The American Statistician* 41, no. 3 (August 1987), pp. 200–203.

Hoaglin, David C.; Frederick Mosteller; and John W. Tukey. *Understanding Robust and Exploratory Data Analysis.* John Wiley and Sons, 1983.

Pukelsheim, Friedrich. "The Three Sigma Rule." *The American Statistician* 48, no. 2 (May 1994), pp. 88–91.

Roderick, J. A.; A. Little; and Donald B. Rubin. *Statistical Analysis with Missing Data.* 2nd ed. John Wiley and Sons, 2002.

Tukey, John W. *Exploratory Data Analysis.* Addison-Wesley, 1977.

LearningStats Unit 04   Describing Data   **LS**

LearningStats Unit 04 uses interesting data sets, samples, and simulations to illustrate the tools of data analysis. Your instructor may assign a specific project, but you can work on the others if they sound interesting.

Topic	LearningStats Modules
Overview	Describing Data
	Using MegaStat
	Using Visual Statistics
	Using MINITAB
Descriptive statistics	Basic Statistics
	Quartiles
	Box Plots
	Coefficient of Variation
	Grouped Data
	Data Format
	Skewness and Kurtosis
Case studies	Brad's Bowling Scores
	Aircraft Cockpit Noise
	Batting Averages
	Bridget Jones's Diary
	Sample Variation
	Sampling NYSE Stocks
Sampling methods	Simple Random Sampling
	Systematic Sampling
	Cluster Sampling
Student projects	College Tuition
	NHL Player Performance
	Per Capita Income
Formulas	Table of Formulas

Key: = PowerPoint   = Word   = Excel

Visual Statistics

Visual Statistics is a software tool that is included on your CD, to be installed on your own computer. The CD will guide you through the installation process. Visual Statistics consists of 21 learning modules. Its purpose is to help you learn *concepts* on your own, through experimentation, individual learning exercises, and team projects. It consists of software with graphical displays, customized experiments, well-indexed help files (definitions, formulas, examples), and a complete textbook (in .PDF format). Each chapter has learning exercises (basic, intermediate, advanced), learning projects (individual, team), a self-evaluation quiz, a glossary of terms, and solutions.

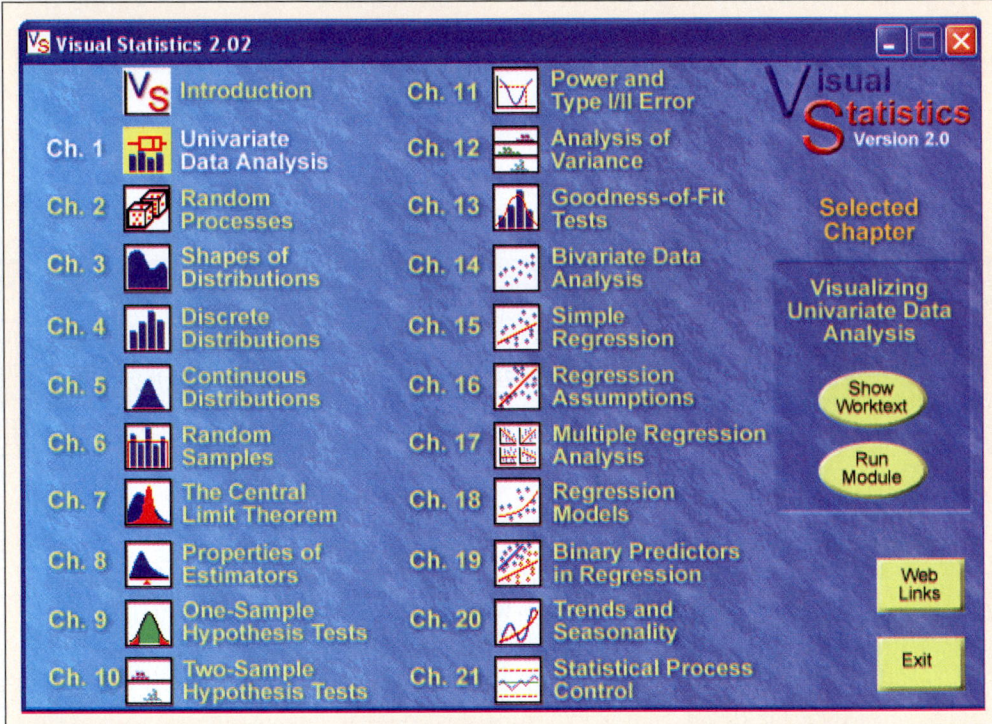

Visual Statistics modules 1, 3, and 6 are designed to help you

- Recognize and interpret different types of histograms (frequency, cumulative, relative).
- Realize how histogram setup can affect one's perception of the data.
- Be able to visualize common shape measures (centrality, dispersion, skewness, kurtosis).
- Recognize discrete and continuous random variables.
- Learn to infer a population's shape, mean, and standard deviation from a sample.
- See how outliers affect histograms.

Visual Statistics Modules on Describing Data

Module	Module Name
1	Univariate Data Analysis
3	Shapes of Distributions
6	Random Samples

MegaStat for Excel by J. B. Orris of Butler University is an Excel add-in that is included on the CD, to be installed on your own computer. The CD will guide you through the installation process. MegaStat goes beyond Excel's built-in statistical functions to offer a full range of statistical tools to help you analyze data, create graphs, and perform difficult calculations. MegaStat examples are shown throughout this textbook.

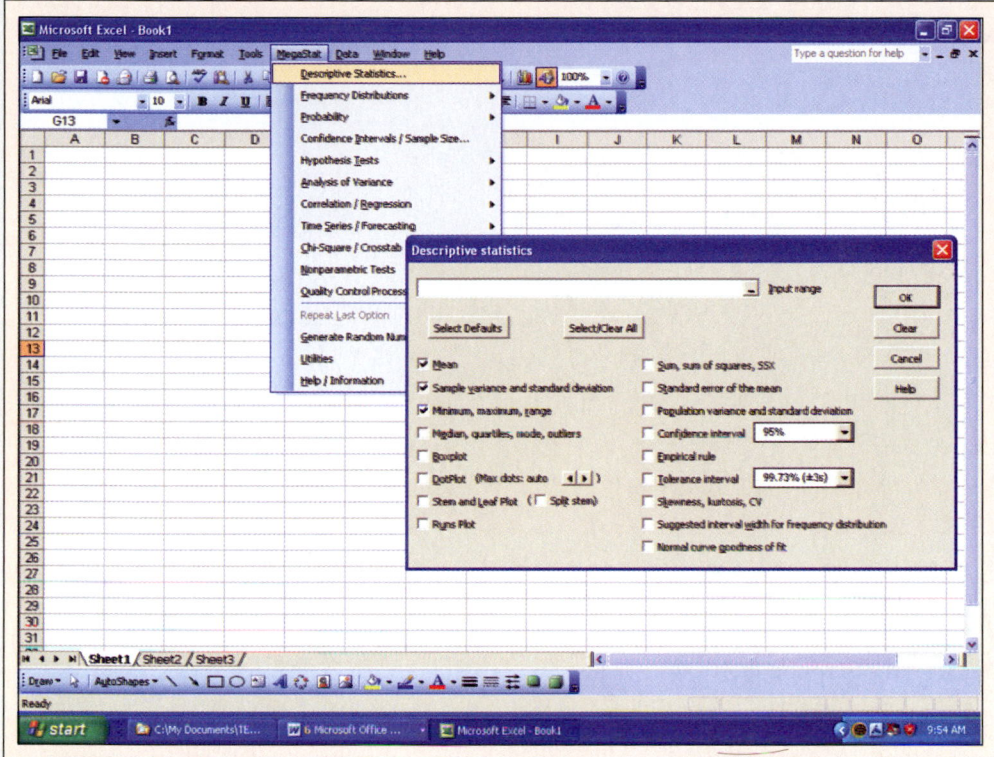

On File Download Screen, click Open. After installing MegaStat for the first time, you will need to select Tools > Add-Ins in Excel and check the box for MegaStat.

Attention Excel 2003 Users: After installing MegaStat and opening Excel, you will need to do the following steps: In Excel, select Tools > Add-Ins. Click on the Browse button and go to the default location: C:\Program Files\Microsoft Office\Office\Library, select MegaStat, and the MegaStat add-in will appear in the Add-Ins available window as a checked item.

CHAPTER

5

Probability

Chapter Learning Objectives

When you finish this chapter you should be able to

- Describe the sample space of a random experiment.

- Distinguish among the three views of probability.

- Apply the definitions and rules of probability.

- Calculate odds from given probabilities.

- Determine when events are independent.

- Apply the concepts of probability to contingency tables.

- Interpret a tree diagram.

- Use Bayes's theorem to calculate revised probabilities (optional).

- Apply counting rules to calculate possible event arrangements (optional).

Sample Space

A *random experiment* is an observational process whose results cannot be known in advance. For example, when a customer enters a Lexus dealership, will the customer buy a car or not? How much will the customer spend? The set of all possible *outcomes* (denoted S) is the *sample space* for the experiment. A sample space with a countable number of outcomes is *discrete*. Some discrete sample spaces can be enumerated easily, while others may be immense or impossible to enumerate. For example, when CitiBank makes a consumer loan, we might define a sample space with only two outcomes:

$$S = \{\text{default, no default}\}$$

The sample space describing a Wal-Mart customer's payment method might have four outcomes:

$$S = \{\text{cash, debit card, credit card, check}\}$$

The sample space to describe rolling a die has six outcomes:

$$S = \{1, 2, 3, 4, 5, 6\}$$

When two dice are rolled, the sample space consists of 36 outcomes, each of which is a pair:

$$S = \{(1, 1), (1, 2), (1, 3), (1, 4), (1, 5), (1, 6), (2, 1), (2, 2), (2, 3), (2, 4), (2, 5), (2, 6),$$
$$(3, 1), (3, 2), (3, 3), (3, 4), (3, 5), (3, 6), (4, 1), (4, 2), (4, 3), (4, 4), (4, 5), (4, 6)$$
$$(5, 1), (5, 2), (5, 3), (5, 4), (5, 5), (5, 6), (6, 1), (6, 2), (6, 3), (6, 4), (6, 5), (6, 6)\}$$

The sample space to describe a randomly chosen United Airlines employee by gender (2 genders), job classification (21 jobs), home base (6 major hubs), and education (4 levels) has 1,008 possible distinct outcomes. It would be possible but impractical to enumerate such a sample space.

FIGURE 5.1

Venn diagram for a sample space

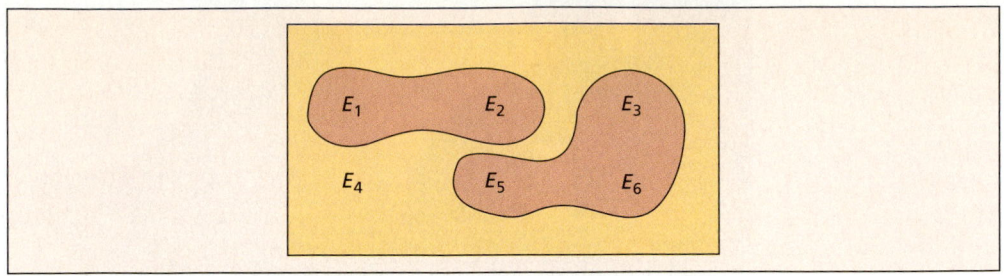

If the outcome of the experiment is a *continuous* measurement, the sample space cannot be enumerated, but can be described by a rule. For example, the sample space for the length of a randomly chosen cell phone call would be

$$S = \{\text{all } X \text{ such that } X \geq 0\}$$

and the sample space to describe a randomly chosen student's GPA would be

$$S = \{\text{all } X \text{ such that } 0.00 \leq X \leq 4.00\}$$

Events

An *event* is any subset of outcomes in the sample space. A *simple event,* or *elementary event,* is a single outcome. A discrete sample space S consists of all the simple events, denoted $E_1, E_2, \ldots, E_n$.

(5.1) $S = \{E_1, E_2, \ldots, E_n\}$

Consider the random experiment of tossing a balanced coin. The sample space for this experiment would be $S = \{H, T\}$. The chance of observing a head is the same as the chance of observing a tail. We say that these two elementary events are *equally likely*. When you buy a lottery ticket, the sample space $S = \{\text{win, lose}\}$ also has two elementary events; however, these events are not equally likely.

A *compound event* consists of two or more simple events. For example, in a sample space of six simple events we could define compound events $A = \{E_1, E_2\}$ and $B = \{E_3, E_5, E_6\}$ and display them in a *Venn diagram* like Figure 5.1.

Many different compound events could be defined. Often, a compound event can be described by a rule. For example, when you throw two dice, the compound event $A =$ "rolling a seven" consists of six simple events, each of which is a pair:

$$A = \{(1, 6), (2, 5), (3, 4), (4, 3), (5, 2), (6, 1)\}$$

For a Wal-Mart customer's purchase, the event $A =$ "spends less than \$25" can be written:

$$A = \{X \mid X < 25\}$$

SECTION EXERCISES

5.1   A credit card customer at Border's can use Visa (V), MasterCard (M), or American Express (A). The merchandise may be books (B), electronic media (E), or other (O). (a) Enumerate the elementary events in the sample space describing a customer's purchase. (b) Would each elementary event be equally likely? Explain.

5.2   A survey asked tax accounting firms their business form ($S =$ sole proprietorship, $P =$ partnership, $C =$ corporation) and type of risk insurance they carry ($L =$ liability only, $T =$ property loss only, $B =$ both liability and property). (a) Enumerate the elementary events in the sample space. (b) Would each elementary event be equally likely? Explain.

5.3   A baseball player bats either left-handed (L) or right-handed (R). The player either gets on base (B) or does not get on base (B'). (a) Enumerate the elementary events in the sample space. (b) Would these elementary events be equally likely? Explain.

5.4   A die is thrown (1, 2, 3, 4, 5, 6) and a coin is tossed (H, T). (a) Enumerate the elementary events in the sample space for the die/coin combination. (b) Are the elementary events equally likely? Explain.

Recall that in Chapter 1 we defined a statistic as a measurement that describes a sample data set of observations. It is also important to be able to describe the future. Businesses want to be able to quantify the *uncertainty* of future events. What are the chances that our revenue next month will exceed last year's average? How likely is it that our new production system will help us decrease our product defect rate? Businesses also want to understand how they can increase the chance of positive future events (increasing market share) and decrease the chance of negative future events (failing to meet forecasted sales). We use a field of study called *probability* to help us understand and quantify the uncertainty surrounding the future.

Definitions

The **probability** of an event is a number that measures the relative likelihood that the event will occur. The probability of an event A, denoted $P(A)$, must lie within the interval from 0 to 1:

$$0 \leq P(A) \leq 1 \tag{5.2}$$

$P(A) = 0$ means the event cannot occur (e.g., a naturalized citizen becoming president of the United States) while $P(A) = 1$ means the event is certain to occur (e.g., rain occurring in Hilo, Hawaii, sometime this year). In a discrete sample space, the probabilities of all simple events must sum to 1, since it is certain that one of them will occur:

$$P(S) = P(E_1) + P(E_2) + \cdots + P(E_n) = 1 \tag{5.3}$$

For example, if 32 percent of purchases are made by credit card, 15 percent by debit card, 35 percent by cash, and 18 percent by check, then:

$$P(\text{credit card}) + P(\text{debit card}) + P(\text{cash}) + P(\text{check}) = .32 + .15 + .35 + .18 = 1$$

What Is "Probability"?

There are three distinct ways of assigning probability, listed in Table 5.1. Many people mix them up or use them interchangeably; however, each approach must be considered separately.

CLOSE TO HOME By John McPherson

WELL, THAT'S PRETTY CONCLUSIVE. 182 CARTS HIT THE CORVETTE, 11 HIT THE PINTO, AND 7 WENT STRAIGHT UP THE MIDDLE.

Researchers at MIT prove that rolling shopping carts will almost invariably hit the most expensive car in their vicinity.

	Approach	Example
TABLE 5.1 Three Views of Probability	Empirical	There is a 2 percent chance of twins in a randomly chosen birth.
	Classical	There is a 50 percent chance of heads on a coin flip.
	Subjective	There is a 75 percent chance that England will adopt the euro currency by 2010.

Empirical Approach

Sometimes we can collect empirical data through observations or experiments. We can use the *empirical* or *relative frequency approach* to assign probabilities by counting the frequency of observed outcomes (f) defined in our experimental sample space and dividing by the number of observations (n).

For example, we could estimate the reliability of a bar code scanner:

$$P(\text{a missed scan}) = \frac{\text{number of missed scans}}{\text{number of items scanned}}$$

or the default rate on student loans:

$$P(\text{a student defaults}) = \frac{\text{number of defaults}}{\text{number of loans}}$$

Empirical estimation is necessary when we have no prior knowledge of the events. As we increase the number of observations (n) or the number of times we perform the experiment, our estimate will become more and more accurate. We use the ratio f/n to represent the probability.

Law of Large Numbers

An important probability theorem is the *law of large numbers.* Imagine flipping a coin 50 times. You know that the proportion of heads should be near .50. But in any finite sample it will be some ratio such as 1/3, 7/13, 10/22, or 28/50. Coin flip experiments show that a large n may be needed to get close to .50. As you can see in Figure 5.2, even after many flips, the ratio is likely to still differ from .50.

The law of large numbers says that as the number of trials increases, the empirical probability approaches its theoretical limit. Gamblers are aware of this principle, although they sometimes misconstrue it to imply that a streak of bad luck is "bound to change." But the probability of rolling a seven is always 6/36, even if you have rolled the dice 20 times previously without getting a seven.

Practical Issues for Actuaries

You may know that *actuarial science* is a high-paying career that involves estimating empirical probabilities. Actuaries help companies calculate payout rates on life insurance, pension plans, and health care plans. Actuaries created the tables that guide IRA withdrawal rates for individuals from age 70 to 99. Here are a few challenges that actuaries face:

- Is n "large enough" to say that f/n has become a good approximation to the probability of the event of interest? Data collection costs money, and decisions must be made. The sample should be large enough but not larger than necessary for a given level of precision.

- Was the experiment repeated identically? Subtle variations may exist in the experimental conditions and data collection procedures.

- Is the underlying process invariant over time? For example, default rates on 1997 student loans may not apply in 2007, due to changes in attitudes and interest rates.

- Do nonstatistical factors override data collection? Drug companies want clinical trials of a promising AIDS treatment to last long enough to ascertain its adverse side effects, yet ethical considerations forbid withholding a drug that could be beneficial.

FIGURE 5.2

Results of 10, 20, 50, and 500 coin flips **CoinFlips**

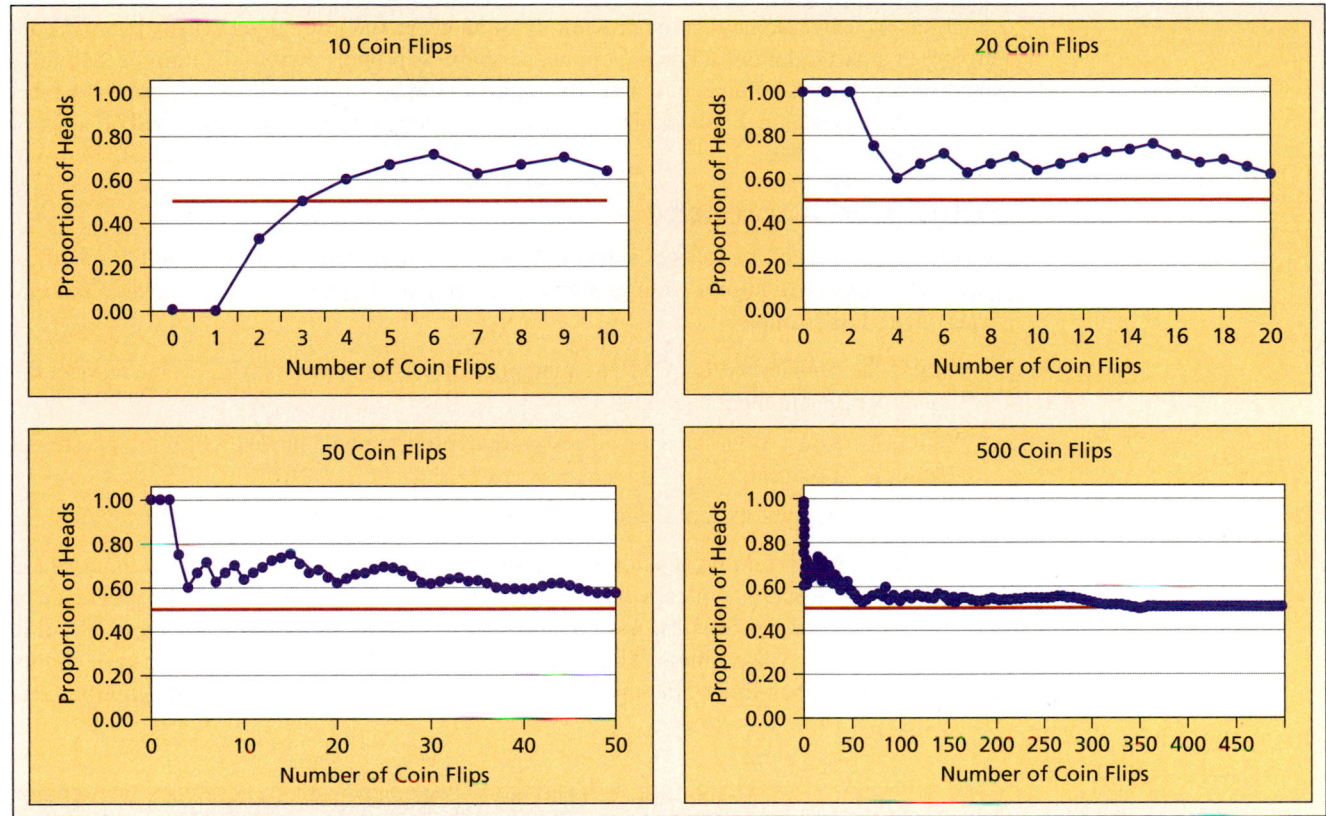

FIGURE 5.3

Venn diagram for two dice
DiceRolls

(1,1)	(1,2)	(1,3)	(1,4)	(1,5)	**(1,6)**
(2,1)	(2,2)	(2,3)	(2,4)	**(2,5)**	(2,6)
(3,1)	(3,2)	(3,3)	**(3,4)**	(3,5)	(3,6)
(4,1)	(4,2)	**(4,3)**	(4,4)	(4,5)	(4,6)
(5,1)	**(5,2)**	(5,3)	(5,4)	(5,5)	(5,6)
(6,1)	(6,2)	(6,3)	(6,4)	(6,5)	(6,6)

- What if repeated trials are impossible? A good example occurred when Lloyd's of London was asked to insure a traveling exhibition of Monet paintings that was sent on a tour of the United States. Such an event only occurs once, so we have no f/n to help us.

Classical Approach

When flipping a coin or rolling a pair of dice, we do not actually have to perform an experiment, because the nature of the process allows us to envision the entire sample space as a collection of equally likely outcomes. We can use deduction to determine $P(A)$. Statisticians use the term *a priori* to refer to the process of assigning probabilities *before* we actually observe the event. For example, the two dice experiment shown in Figure 5.3 has 36 equally likely simple events, so the probability of rolling a seven is:

$$P(A) = \frac{\text{number of outcomes with 7 dots}}{\text{number of outcomes in sample space}} = \frac{6}{36} = .1667$$

The probability is obtained *a priori* without actually doing an experiment. This is the ***classical approach*** to probability. Such calculations are rarely possible in business situations.

We can apply pure reason to cards, lottery numbers, and roulette. Also, in some physical situations we can assume that the probability of an event such as a defect (leak, blemish) occurring in a particular unit of area, volume, or length is proportional to the ratio of that unit's size to the total area, volume, or length. Examples would be pits on rolled steel, stress fractures in concrete, or leaks in pipelines. These are *a priori* probabilities if they are based on logic or theory, not experience.

Subjective Approach

A *subjective* probability reflects someone's personal judgment about the likelihood of an event. The ***subjective approach*** to probability is needed when there is no repeatable random experiment. For example:

- What is the probability that GM's new supplier of plastic fasteners will be able to meet the September 23 shipment deadline?

- What is the probability that a new truck product program will show a return on investment of at least 10 percent?

- What is the probability that the price of GM stock will rise within the next 30 days?

In such cases, we rely on personal judgment or expert opinion. However, such a judgment is not random, because it is typically based on experience with similar events and knowledge of the underlying causal processes. Assessing the New York Knicks's chances of an NBA title next year would be an example. Thus, subjective probabilities have something in common with empirical probabilities, although their empirical basis is informal and not quantified.

SECTION EXERCISES

5.5   "There is a 20% chance that a new stock offered in an initial public offering (IPO) will reach or exceed its target price on the first day." (a) What kind of probability is this? (b) How would it have been derived?

5.6   "There is a 50% chance that AT&T Wireless and Cingular will merge." (a) What kind of probability is this? (b) How would it have been derived?

5.7   "Commercial rocket launches have a 95% success rate." (a) What kind of probability is this? (b) How would it have been derived?

5.8   "The probability of rolling three sevens in a row with dice is .0046." (a) What kind of probability is this? (b) How would it have been derived?

5.3 RULES OF PROBABILITY

Complement of an Event

The ***complement*** of an event A is denoted A' and consists of everything in the sample space S except event A, as illustrated in the Venn diagram in Figure 5.4.

Since A and A' together comprise the sample space, their probabilities sum to 1:

(5.4)
$$P(A) + P(A') = 1$$

The probability of the complement of A is found by subtracting the probability of A from 1:

(5.5)
$$P(A') = 1 - P(A)$$

For example, *The Wall Street Journal* reports that about 33 percent of all new small businesses fail within the first 2 years (July 12, 2004). From this we can determine that the probability that a new small business will survive at least 2 years is:

$$P(\text{survival}) = 1 - P(\text{failure}) = 1 - .33 = .67, \text{ or } 67\%$$

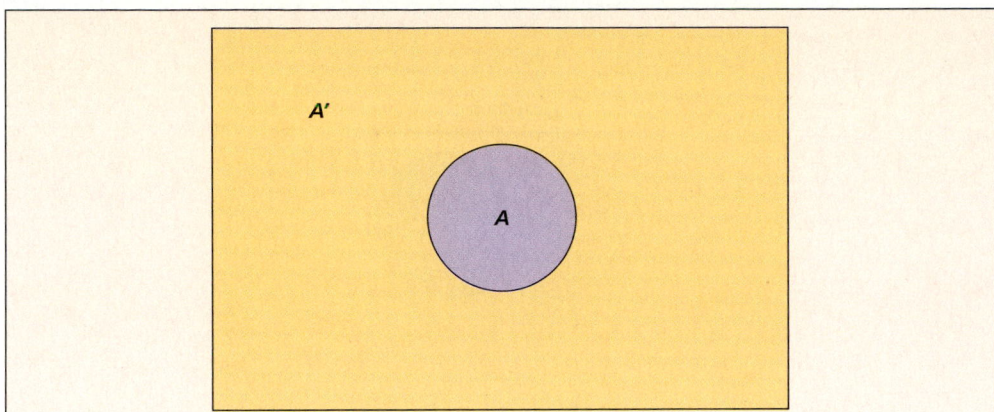

FIGURE 5.4

Complement of event *A*

Odds of an Event

We define the **odds** in favor of an event A as the ratio of the probability that A occurs to the probability that A does not occur, that is, the ratio of $P(A)$ to $P(A')$:

$$\text{Odds} = \frac{P(A)}{P(A')} = \frac{P(A)}{1 - P(A)} \tag{5.6}$$

Statisticians usually speak of probabilities rather than odds, but in sports and games of chance, we often hear odds quoted. For a pair of fair dice, the probability of rolling a seven is 6/36 or 1/6, so the odds in favor of rolling a seven would be:

$$\text{Odds} = \frac{P(\text{rolling seven})}{1 - P(\text{rolling seven})} = \frac{1/6}{1 - 1/6} = \frac{1/6}{5/6} = \frac{1}{5}$$

This means that on the average for every time we roll seven there will be five times that we do not roll seven. The odds are 1 to 5 *in favor* of rolling a seven (or 5 to 1 *against* rolling a seven). In horse racing and other sports, odds usually are quoted *against* winning. If the odds against event A are quoted as b to a, then the implied probability of event A is:

$$P(A) = \frac{a}{a + b} \tag{5.7}$$

For example, if a race horse has 4 to 1 odds *against* winning, this is equivalent to saying that the odds-makers assign the horse a 20 percent chance of winning:

$$P(\text{win}) = \frac{a}{a + b} = \frac{1}{4 + 1} = \frac{1}{5} = .20, \text{ or } 20\%$$

Union of Two Events

The **union** of two events consists of all outcomes in the sample space S that are contained either in event A or in event B or in both. The union of A and B is sometimes denoted $A \cup B$ or "A or B" as illustrated in the Venn diagram in Figure 5.5. The symbol $\cup$ may be read "or" since it means that either or both events occur. For example, when we choose a card at random from a deck of playing cards, if Q is the event that we draw a queen and R is the event that we draw a red card, $Q \cup R$ consists of getting *either* a queen (4 possibilities in 52) *or* a red card (26 possibilities in 52) or *both* a queen and a red card (2 possibilities in 52).

Intersection of Two Events

The **intersection** of two events A and B is the event consisting of all outcomes in the sample space S that are contained in both event A and event B. The intersection of A and B is denoted $A \cap B$ or "A and B" as illustrated in a Venn diagram in Figure 5.6. The probability of $A \cap B$ is called the **joint probability** and is denoted $P(A \cap B)$.

FIGURE 5.5

Union of two events

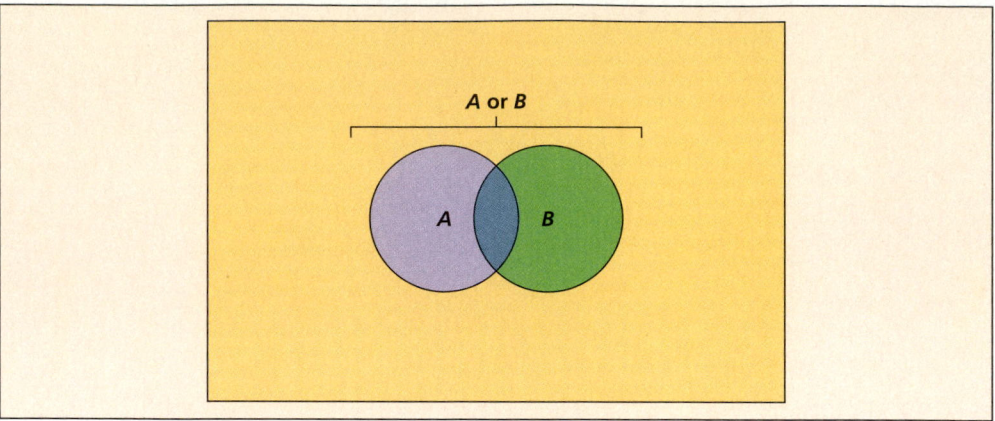

FIGURE 5.6

Intersection of two events

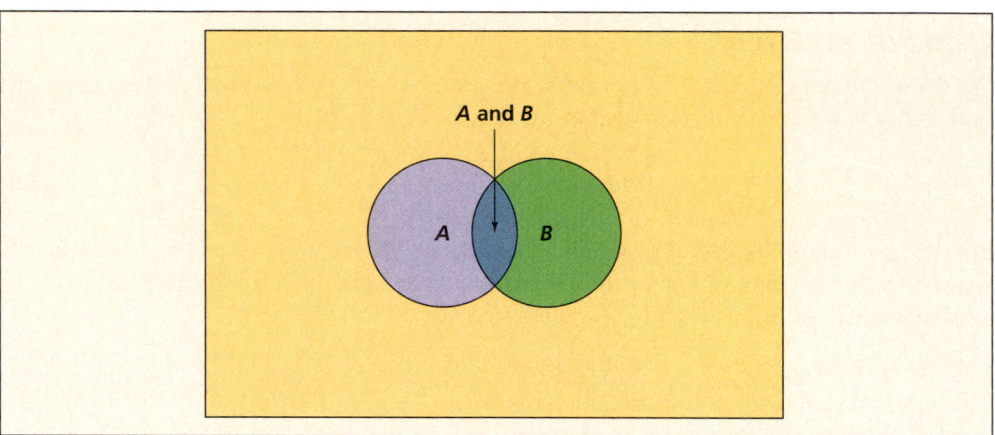

The symbol ∩ may be read "and" since the intersection means that both events occur. For example, if Q is the event that we draw a queen and R is the event that we draw a red card, then, $Q \cap R$ is the event that we get a card that is both a queen and red. That is, the intersection of sets Q and R consists of two cards (Q♥ and Q♦).

General Law of Addition

The *general law of addition* says that the probability of the union of two events A and B is the sum of their probabilities less the probability of their intersection:

(5.8)
$$P(A \cup B) = P(A) + P(B) - P(A \cap B)$$

The rationale for this formula is apparent from an examination of Figure 5.6. If we just add the probabilities of A and B, we would count the intersection twice, so we must subtract the probability of $A \cap B$ to avoid overstating the probability of $A \cup B$. For the card example:

Queen: $P(Q) = 4/52$	(there are 4 queens in a deck)
Red: $P(R) = 26/52$	(there are 26 red cards in a deck)
Queen and Red: $P(Q \cap R) = 2/52$	(there are 2 red queens in a deck)

Therefore,

$$\text{Queen or Red:} \quad P(Q \cup R) = P(Q) + P(R) - P(Q \cap R)$$

$$= 4/52 + 26/52 - 2/52$$

$$= 28/52 = .5385, \text{ or a } 53.85\% \text{ chance}$$

This result, while simple to calculate, is not obvious.

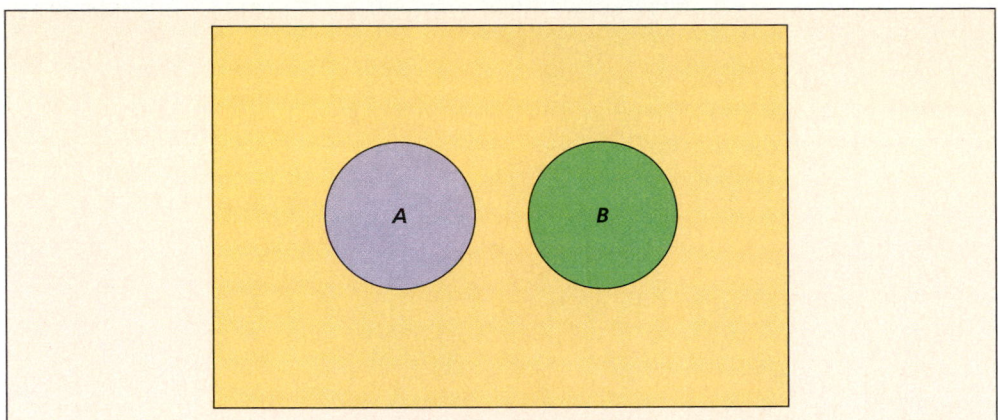

FIGURE 5.7

Mutually exclusive events

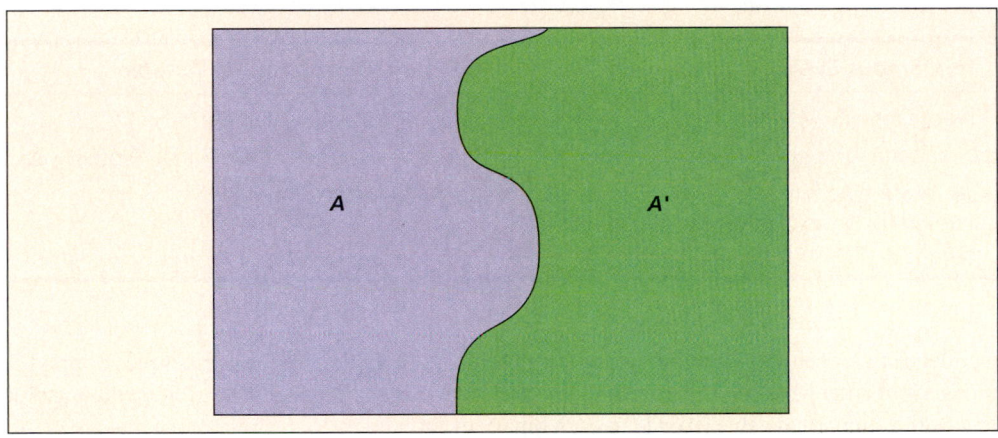

FIGURE 5.8

Dichotomous events

Mutually Exclusive Events

Events A and B are **mutually exclusive** (or **disjoint**) if their intersection is the **null set** (a set that contains no elements). The null set is denoted ϕ.

$$\text{If } A \cap B = \phi, \text{ then } P(A \cap B) = 0 \qquad (5.9)$$

As illustrated in Figure 5.7, the probability of $A \cap B$ is zero when the events do not overlap. For example, if A is the event that an Applebee's customer finishes her lunch in less than 30 minutes and B is the event that she takes 30 minutes or more, then $P(A \cap B) = P(\phi) = 0$.

Special Law of Addition

If A and B are mutually exclusive events, then $P(A \cap B) = 0$ and the addition law reduces to

$$P(A \cap B) = P(A) + P(B) \qquad \text{(addition law for mutually exclusive events)} \quad (5.10)$$

Collectively Exhaustive Events

Events are **collectively exhaustive** if their union is the entire sample space S. Two mutually exclusive, collectively exhaustive events are **dichotomous** (or *binary*) **events,** as illustrated in Figure 5.8. For example, a car repair is either covered by the warranty (A) or is not covered by the warranty (A'). More than two mutually exclusive, collectively exhaustive events are **polytomous events,** as illustrated in Figure 5.9. For example, a Wal-Mart customer can pay by credit card (A), debit card (B), cash (C), or check (D).

Forced Dichotomy

Polytomous events (e.g., freshman, sophomore, junior, senior) can be collapsed into dichotomous events by defining the second category as everything *not* in the first category. For example,

FIGURE 5.9

Polytomous events

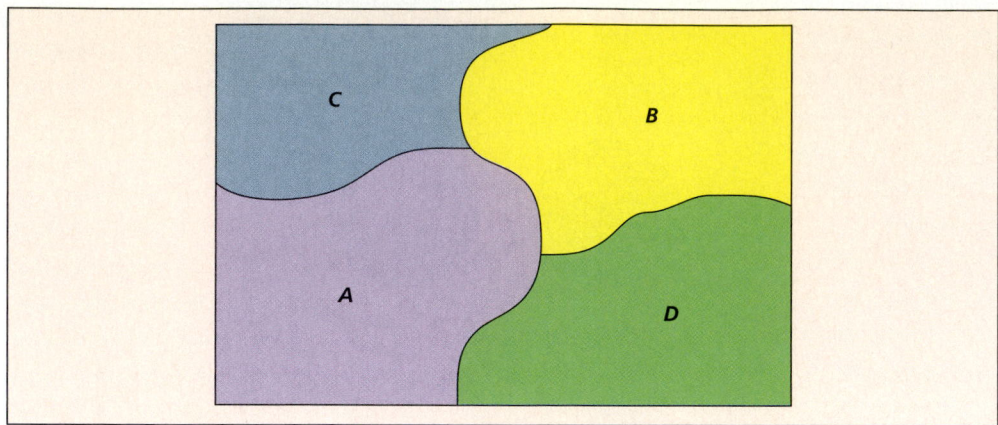

TABLE 5.2

Examples of Forced Dichotomy

Polytomous Events	Binary (Dichotomous) Variable
Vehicle type (SUV, sedan, truck, motorcycle)	$X = 1$ if SUV, 0 otherwise
A randomly chosen NBA player's height	$X = 1$ if height exceeds 7 feet, 0 otherwise
Tax return type (single, married filing jointly, married filing separately, head of household, qualifying widower)	$X = 1$ if single, 0 otherwise

a college student either *is* a senior (A) or *isn't* a senior (A'). Table 5.2 shows examples of polytomous events that have been "binarized" into dichotomous events. In statistics, it is often useful to assign a numerical value (0 or 1) to each binary event.

Conditional Probability

The probability of event A *given* that event B has occurred is a ***conditional probability,*** denoted $P(A \mid B)$ which is read "the probability of A given B." The vertical line is read as "given." The conditional probability is the joint probability of A and B divided by the probability of B.

(5.11) $$P(A \mid B) = \frac{P(A \cap B)}{P(B)} \quad \text{for } P(B) > 0 \text{ and undefined otherwise}$$

The logic of formula 5.11 is apparent by looking at the Venn diagram in Figure 5.10. The sample space is restricted to B, an event that we know has occurred (the lightly shaded circle). The intersection, $A \cap B$, is the part of B that is also in A (the heavily shaded area). The ratio of the relative size of set $A \cap B$ to set B is the conditional probability $P(A \mid B)$.

FIGURE 5.10

Conditional probability

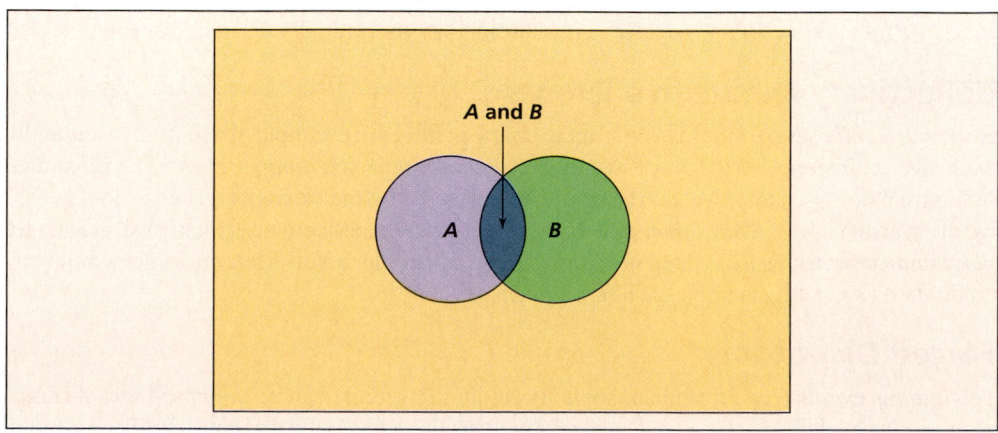

EXAMPLE

High School Dropouts

Of the population aged 16–21 and not in college, 13.50 percent are unemployed, 29.05 percent are high school dropouts, and 5.32 percent are unemployed high school dropouts. What is the conditional probability that a member of this population is unemployed, given that the person is a high school dropout? To answer this question, define:

U = the event that the person is unemployed

D = the event that the person is a high school dropout

This "story problem" contains three facts:

$$P(U) = .1350 \qquad P(D) = .2905 \qquad P(U \cap D) = .0532$$

So by formula 5.11 the conditional probability of an unemployed youth given that the person dropped out of high school is:

$$P(U \mid D) = \frac{P(U \cap D)}{P(D)} = \frac{.0532}{.2905} = .1831, \text{ or } 18.31\%$$

The *conditional* probability of being unemployed is $P(U \mid D) = .1831$ (18.31 percent), which is greater than the *unconditional probability* of being unemployed $P(U) = .1350$ (13.50 percent). In other words, knowing that someone is a high school dropout alters the probability that the person is unemployed.

SECTION EXERCISES

5.9 Given $P(A) = .40$, $P(B) = .50$, and $P(A \cap B) = .05$, find (a) $P(A \cup B)$, (b) $P(A \mid B)$, and (c) $P(B \mid A)$. (d) Sketch a Venn diagram.

5.10 Given $P(A) = .70$, $P(B) = .30$, and $P(A \cap B) = .00$, find (a) $P(A \cup B)$ and (b) $P(A \mid B)$. (c) Sketch a Venn diagram and describe it in words.

5.11 Samsung ships 21.7 percent of the liquid crystal displays (LCDs) in the world. Let S be the event that a randomly selected LCD was made by Samsung. Find (a) $P(S)$, (b) $P(S')$, (c) the odds *in favor* of event S, and (d) the odds *against* event S. (Data are from *The Economist* 372, no. 8385 [July 24, 2004], p. 59.)

5.12 In 1997, the probability of an IRS audit was 1.7 percent for U.S. taxpayers who filed form 1040 and who earned $100,000 or more. (a) What are the odds that such a taxpayer will be audited? (b) What are the odds *against* such a taxpayer being audited? (Data are from *The New York Times*, April 12, 1998, p. I-17.)

5.13 List *two* dichotomous events that describe the outcome of each situation.
a. A pharmaceutical firm seeks FDA approval for a new drug.
b. A baseball batter goes to bat.
c. A woman has a mammogram test.

5.14 List *more than two* events (i.e., polytomous events) that might describe the outcome of each situation.
a. A student applies for admission to Oxnard University.
b. A football quarterback throws a pass.
c. A bank customer makes a certain type of ATM transaction.

5.15 Let S be the event that a randomly chosen female aged 18–24 is a smoker. Let C be the event that a randomly chosen female aged 18–24 is a Caucasian. Given $P(S) = .246$, $P(C) = .830$, and $P(S \cap C) = .232$, find each probability and express the event in words. (Data are from *Statistical Abstract of the United States, 2001.*)
a. $P(S')$.
b. $P(S \cup C)$.
c. $P(S \mid C)$.
d. $P(S \mid C')$.

5.4
INDEPENDENT EVENTS

Event A is **independent** of event B if the conditional probability $P(A \mid B)$ is the same as the unconditional probability $P(A)$, that is, if the probability of event A is the same whether event B occurs or not. To check for independence, we apply this test:

(5.12)   If $P(A \mid B) = P(A)$, then event A is *independent* of event B.

Another way to check for independence is to ask whether the product of the event probabilities equals the probability of their intersection:

(5.13)   If $P(A \cap B) = P(A)P(B)$, then event A is *independent* of event B.

This is so because, it $P(A \cap B) = P(A)P(B)$, then by the definition of conditional probability in formula 5.11:

$$P(A \mid B) = \frac{P(A \cap B)}{P(B)} = \frac{P(A)P(B)}{P(B)} = P(A).$$

EXAMPLE

Television Ads

The target audience is 2,000,000 viewers. Ad A reaches 500,000 viewers, ad B reaches 300,000 viewers, and both ads reach 100,000 viewers. That is:

$$P(A) = \frac{500,000}{2,000,000} = .25 \quad P(B) = \frac{300,000}{2,000,000} = .15 \quad P(A \cap B) = \frac{100,000}{2,000,000} = .05$$

Applying the definition of conditional probability from formula 5.11, the conditional probability that ad A reaches a viewer *given* that ad B reaches the viewer is:

$$P(A \mid B) = \frac{P(A \cap B)}{P(B)} = \frac{.05}{.15} = .3333 \text{ or } 33.3\%$$

We see that A and B are not independent because $P(A) = .25$ is not equal to $P(A \mid B) = .3333$. That is, knowing that ad B reached the viewer raises the probability that ad A reached the viewer from $P(A) = .25$ to $P(A \mid B) = .3333$. Alternatively, since $P(A)P(B) = (.25)(.15) = .0375$ is not equal to $P(A \cap B) = .05$, we know that events A and B are not independent.

Dependent Events

When $P(A)$ differs from $P(A \mid B)$ the events are **dependent.** Dependent events may be causally related, but statistical dependence does *not* prove cause-and-effect. It only means that knowing that event B has occurred will affect the *probability* that event A will occur. You can easily think of examples of dependence. For example, cell phone text messaging is more common among young people, while arteriosclerosis is more common among older people. Therefore, knowing a person's age would affect the *probability* that the individual uses text messaging or has arteriosclerosis, but causation would have to be proven in other ways.

EXAMPLE

Loans and Insurance

Banks and credit unions know that the probability that a customer will default on a car loan is dependent on his/her past record of unpaid credit obligations. That is why lenders consult credit bureaus (e.g., Equifax, Experian, and TransUnion) before they make a loan. Your credit score is based on factors such as the ratio of your credit card balance to your credit limit, length of your credit history, number of accounts with balances, and frequency of requests for credit. Your score can be compared with a national average to see what percentile you are in. The lender can then decide whether your loan is worth the risk.

Automobile insurance companies (e.g., AAA, Allstate, State Farm) know that the probability that a driver will be involved in an accident depends on the driver's age, past traffic convictions, and similar factors. This actuarial information is used in deciding whether to accept you as a new customer and to set your insurance premium. The situation is similar for life insurance. Can you think of factors that might affect a person's life insurance premium?

Actuaries Again

In each of these loan and insurance examples, knowing B will affect our estimate of the likelihood of A. Obviously, bankers and insurance companies need to quantify these conditional probabilities precisely. An *actuary* studies conditional probabilities empirically, using accident statistics, mortality tables, and insurance claims records. Although few people undergo the extensive training to become actuaries, many businesses rely on actuarial services, so a business student needs to understand the concepts of conditional probability and statistical independence.

Multiplication Law for Independent Events

The probability of several independent events occurring simultaneously is the product of their separate probabilities, as shown in formula 5.14 for n independent events $A_1, A_2, \ldots, A_n$.

$$P(A_1 \cap A_2 \cap \cdots \cap A_n) = P(A_1)P(A_2) \cdots P(A_n) \quad \text{if the events are independent} \quad \textbf{(5.14)}$$

The ***multiplication law*** for independent events can be applied to system reliability. To illustrate, suppose a Web site has two independent file servers (i.e., no shared power or other components). Each server has 99 percent reliability (i.e., is "up" 99 percent of the time). What is the total system reliability? Let F_1 be the event that server 1 fails, and F_2 be the event that server 2 fails. Then

$$P(F_1) = 1 - 0.99 = .01$$
$$P(F_2) = 1 - 0.99 = .01$$

Applying the rule of independence:

$$P(F_1 \cap F_2) = P(F_1)P(F_2) = (.01)(.01) = .0001$$

The probability that at least one server is up is 1 minus the probability that both servers are down, or $1 - .0001 = .9999$. Dual file servers dramatically improve reliability to 99.99 percent.

EXAMPLE

Space Shuttle

↘   ***Redundancy*** can increase system reliability even when individual component reliability is low. For example, the NASA space shuttle has three flight computers. Suppose that they function independently but that each has an unacceptable .03 chance of failure (3 failures in 100 missions). Let F_j = event that computer j fails. Then

$$
\begin{aligned}
P(\text{all 3 fail}) &= P(F_1 \cap F_2 \cap F_3) \\
&= P(F_1)P(F_2)P(F_3) \quad \text{(presuming that failures are independent)} \\
&= (.03)(.03)(.03) \\
&= .000027, \text{ or 27 in } 1,000,000 \text{ missions}
\end{aligned}
$$

Triple redundancy can reduce the probability of computer failure to .000027 (27 failures in 1,000,000 missions). Of course, in practice, it is very difficult to have truly independent computers, since they may share electrical buses or cables. On one shuttle mission, two of the three computers actually did fail, which proved the value of redundancy. ↖

The Five Nines Rule

How high must reliability be? Prime business customers expect public carrier-class telecommunications data links to be available 99.999 percent of the time. This so-called five nines rule implies only 5 minutes of downtime per year. Such high reliability is needed not only in telecommunications but also for mission-critical systems such as airline reservation systems or banking funds transfers. Table 5.3 shows some expected system reliabilities in contemporary applications.

	Type of System	Typical Reliability (%)
TABLE 5.3 Typical System Reliabilities in Various Applications	Commercial fiber-optic cable systems	99.999
	Cellular-radio base stations with mobile switches connected to public-switched telephone networks	99.99
See *Scientific American* 287, no. 1 (July 2002), p. 52, and 288, no. 6, p. 56.	Private-enterprise networking (e.g., connecting two company offices)	99.9
	Airline luggage systems	99
	Excellent student exam-taking	90

How Much Redundancy Is Needed?

Suppose a certain network Web server is up only 94 percent of the time (i.e., its probability of being down is .06). How many independent servers are needed to ensure that the system is up at least 99.99 percent of the time? This is equivalent to requiring that the probability of all the servers being down is .0001 (i.e., $1 - .9999$). Four servers will accomplish the goal*:

2 servers: $P(F_1 \cap F_2) = (.06)(.06) = .0036$

3 servers: $P(F_1 \cap F_2 \cap F_3) = (.06)(.06)(.06) = .000216$

4 servers: $P(F_1 \cap F_2 \cap F_3 \cap F_4) = (.06)(.06)(.06)(.06) = .00001296$

Applications of Redundancy

The principle of redundancy is found in many places. Basketball teams have more than five players, even though only five can play at once. You set two alarm clocks in case the first doesn't wake you up. The Embraer Legacy 13-passenger jet ($21.2 million) has two identical generators on each of its two engines to allow the plane to be used as a commercial regional jet (requiring 99.5 percent dispatch reliability) as well as for private corporate travel. With four generators, plus an auxiliary power unit that can be started and run in flight, the Legacy can fly even after the failure of a generator or two (*Flying* 131, no. 9 [September 2004], p. 50).

Older airliners (e.g., Boeing 747) had four engines, not only because older engine designs were less powerful but also because they were less reliable. Particularly for transoceanic flights, four-engine planes could fly even if one engine failed (or maybe even two). Modern airliners (e.g., Boeing 777) have only two engines because newer engines are more powerful and more reliable. At first, two-engine airliners were not certified for lengthy over-water operations under the international rules for ETOPS (Extended Twin-engine OPerationS). Improved engine reliability has led to relaxation of ETOPS rules to allow twin-engine commercial transport to fly routes further than 60 minutes' flying time from any diversion airports. This new definition allows twin-engine airliners like Boeing 757, 767, and 777, and Airbus A300, A320 series, and A330 to fly routes that were previously off-limits to twin-engine airliners.

It is not just a matter of individual component reliability but also of cost and consequence. Cars have only one battery because the consequence of battery failure (walking home or calling AAA) does not justify the expense of having a backup battery. But spare tires are cheap enough that all cars carry one (maybe two, if you are driving in Alaska).

Redundancy is not required when components are highly reliable, cost per component is high, and consequences of system failure are tolerable (e.g., cell phone, alarm clock). Unfortunately, true component independence is difficult to achieve. The same catastrophe (fire, flood, etc.) that damages one component may well damage the backup system. On August 24, 2001, a twin-engine Air Transat Airbus A330 transiting the Atlantic Ocean did have a double engine shutdown with 293 passengers aboard. Fortunately, the pilot was able to glide 85 miles to a landing in the Azores, resulting in only minor injuries (*Aviation Week and Space Technology,* September 3, 2001, p. 34).

---

*In general, if p is the probability of failure, we can set $p^k = .0001$, plug in $p = .06$, take the log of both sides, and solve for k. In this case, $k = 3.27$, so we can then round up to the next higher integer.

SECTION EXERCISES

5.16 Given $P(A) = .40$, $P(B) = .50$. If A and B are independent, find $P(A \cap B)$.

5.17 Given $P(A) = .40$, $P(B) = .50$, and $P(A \cap B) = .05$. (a) Find $P(A \mid B)$. (b) In this problem, are A and B independent? Explain.

5.18 Which pairs of events are independent?
a. $P(A) = .60$, $P(B) = .40$, $(A \cap B) = .24$.
b. $P(A) = .90$, $P(B) = .20$, $(A \cap B) = .18$.
c. $P(A) = .50$, $P(B) = .70$, $(A \cap B) = .25$.

5.19 The probability that a student has a Visa card (event V) is .70. The probability that a student has a MasterCard (event M) is .60. The probability that a student has both cards is .50. (a) Find the probability that a student has either a Visa card or a MasterCard. (b) In this problem, are V and M independent? Explain.

5.20 Bob sets two alarm clocks (battery-powered) to be sure he arises for his Monday 8:00 A.M. accounting exam. There is a 75 percent chance that either clock will wake Bob. (a) What is the probability that Bob will oversleep? (b) If Bob had three clocks, would he have a 99 percent chance of waking up?

5.21 A hospital's backup power system has three independent emergency electrical generators, each with uptime averaging 95 percent (some downtime is necessary for maintenance). Any of the generators can handle the hospital's power needs. Does the overall reliability of the backup power system meet the five nines test?

What Is a Contingency Table?

5.5
CONTINGENCY TABLES

To better understand dependent events and conditional probability, let's look at some real data. A *contingency table* is a cross-tabulation of frequencies into rows and columns. The intersection of each row and column is a *cell*. A contingency table is like a frequency distribution for a single variable, except it has *two* variables (rows and columns).

Table 5.4 shows a cross-tabulation of tuition cost versus 5-year net salary gains for MBA degree recipients at 67 top-tier graduate schools of business. Here, salary gain is compensation after graduation, minus the sum of tuition and forgone compensation. Are large salary gains more likely for graduates of high-tuition MBA programs?

EXAMPLE

Salary Gains and MBA Tuition

TABLE 5.4   **Cross-Tabulation of Frequencies ($n = 67$ MBA programs)**
MBASalary

| | Salary Gain | | | |
Tuition	Small (S_1) Under $50K	Medium (S_2) $50K–$100K	Large (S_3) $100K+	Row Total
Low (T_1) Under $40K	5	10	1	16
Medium (T_2) $40K–$50K	7	11	1	19
High (T_3) $50K+	5	12	15	32
Column Total	17	33	17	67

Source: Data are from *Forbes* 172, no. 8 (October 13, 2003), p. 78. Copyright © 2005 Forbes, Inc. Reprinted with permission.

Inspection of this table reveals that MBA graduates of the high-tuition schools do tend to have large salary gains (15 of the 67 schools) and that about half of the top-tier schools charge high tuition (32 of 67 schools). We can make more precise interpretations of this data by applying the concepts of probability.

Marginal Probabilities

The *marginal probability* of an event is found by dividing a row or column total by the total sample size. For example, using the column totals, 33 out of 67 schools had medium salary gains, so the marginal probability of a medium salary gain is $P(S_2) = 33/67 = .4925$. In other words, salary gains at about 49 percent of the top-tier schools were between \$50,000 and \$100,000. This calculation is shown in Table 5.5.

TABLE 5.5

Marginal Probability of Event S_2

| | Salary Gain | | | |
Tuition	Small (S_1)	Medium (S_2)	Large (S_3)	Row Total
Low (T_1)	5	10	1	16
Medium (T_2)	7	11	1	19
High (T_3)	5	12	15	32
Column Total	17	33	17	67

Using the row totals, for example, we see that 16 of the 67 schools had low tuition so the marginal probability of low tuition is $P(T_1) = 16/67 = .2388$. In other words, there is a 24 percent chance that a top-tier school's MBA tuition is under \$40,000. This calculation is illustrated in Table 5.6.

TABLE 5.6

Marginal Probability of Event T_1

| | Salary Gain | | | |
Tuition	Small (S_1)	Medium (S_2)	Large (S_3)	Row Total
Low (T_1)	5	10	1	16
Medium (T_2)	7	11	1	19
High (T_3)	5	12	15	32
Column Total	17	33	17	67

Joint Probabilities

Each of the six main cells is used to calculate a *joint probability* representing the intersection of *two* events. For example, the upper right-hand cell is the joint event that the school has low tuition (T_1) *and* has large salary gains (S_3). We can write this event either as $P(T_1$ and $S_3)$ or as $P(T_1 \cap S_3)$. Since only 1 out of 67 schools is in this category, the joint probability is $P(T_1$ and $S_3) = 1/67 = .0149$. In other words, there is less than a 2 percent chance that a top-tier school has *both* low tuition *and* high salary gains. This calculation is illustrated in Table 5.7.

TABLE 5.7

Joint Probability of Event $T_1 \cap S_3$

| | Salary Gain | | | |
Tuition	Small (S_1)	Medium (S_2)	Large (S_3)	Row Total
Low (T_1)	5	10	1	16
Medium (T_2)	7	11	1	19
High (T_3)	5	12	15	32
Column Total	17	33	17	67

	Salary Gain			
Tuition	Small (S_1)	Medium (S_2)	Large (S_3)	Row Total
Low (T_1)	5	10	1	16
Medium (T_2)	7	11	1	19
High (T_3)	5	12	15	32
Column Total	17	33	17	67

TABLE 5.8
Conditional Probability
$P(S_1 \mid T_3)$

Conditional Probabilities

Conditional probabilities may be found by *restricting* ourselves to a single row or column (the *condition*). For example, suppose we know that a school's MBA tuition is high (T_3). When we restrict ourselves to the 32 schools in the third row (those with high tuition) the conditional probabilities of any event may be calculated. For example, Table 5.8 illustrates the calculation of the conditional probability that salary gains are small (S_1) *given* that the MBA tuition is large (T_3). This conditional probability may be written $P(S_1 \mid T_3)$. We see that $P(S_1 \mid T_3) = 5/32 = .1563$, so there is about a 16 percent chance that a top-tier school's salary gains will be small despite its high tuition because there were 5 small-gain schools out of the 32 high-tuition schools.

Here are some other conditional probabilities and their interpretations:

Low Tuition MBA Program

$P(S_1 \mid T_1) = 5/16 = .3125$ There is a 31 percent probability that schools whose tuition is low will have small MBA salary gains.

$P(S_2 \mid T_1) = 10/16 = .6250$ There is a 63 percent probability that schools whose tuition is low will have medium MBA salary gains.

$P(S_3 \mid T_1) = 1/16 = .0625$ There is a 6 percent probability that schools whose tuition is low will have large MBA salary gains.

High Tuition MBA Program

$P(S_1 \mid T_3) = 5/32 = .1563$ There is a 16 percent probability that schools whose tuition is high will have small MBA salary gains.

$P(S_2 \mid T_3) = 12/32 = .3750$ There is a 38 percent probability that schools whose tuition is high will have medium MBA salary gains.

$P(S_3 \mid T_3) = 15/32 = .4688$ There is a 47 percent probability that schools whose tuition is high will have large MBA salary gains.

Caveat   Conditional probabilities show, as we would expect, that higher tuition is associated with higher MBA salary gains (and conversely). But these results pertain only to a set of elite universities at a particular point in time, and few MBA students actually have access to such schools. Data from different universities or at a different point in time might show a different pattern.

Independence

To check whether events in a contingency table are independent, we can look at *conditional probabilities*. For example, if large salary gains (S_3) were independent of low tuition (T_1), then the conditional probability $P(S_3 \mid T_1)$ would be the same as the marginal probability $P(S_3)$. But this is not the case:

Conditional   *Marginal*

$P(S_3 \mid T_1) = 1/16 = .0625$ $P(S_3) = 17/67 = .2537$

Thus, large salary gains (S_3) is *not* independent of low tuition (T_1). Alternatively, we could ask whether $P(S_3 \text{ and } T_1) = P(S_3) P(T_1)$ is a necessary condition for independence. But

$$P(S_3)P(T_1) = (17/67)(16/67) = .0606$$

TABLE 5.9
Relative Frequency Table

Tuition	Salary Gains			Row Total
	Small (S_1)	Medium (S_2)	Large (S_3)	
Low (T_1)	.0746	.1493	.0149	.2388
Medium (T_2)	.1045	.1642	.0149	.2836
High (T_3)	.0746	.1791	.2239	.4776
Column Total	.2537	.4926	.2537	1.0000

TABLE 5.10
Symbolic Notation for Relative Frequencies

Tuition	Salary Gains			Row Total
	Small (S_1)	Medium (S_2)	Large (S_3)	
Low (T_1)	$P(T_1$ and $S_1)$	$P(T_1$ and $S_2)$	$P(T_1$ and $S_3)$	$P(T_1)$
Medium (T_2)	$P(T_2$ and $S_1)$	$P(T_2$ and $S_2)$	$P(T_2$ and $S_3)$	$P(T_2)$
High (T_3)	$P(T_3$ and $S_1)$	$P(T_3$ and $S_2)$	$P(T_3$ and $S_3)$	$P(T_3)$
Column Total	$P(S_1)$	$P(S_2)$	$P(S_3)$	1.0000

which is *not* equal to the observed joint probability

$$P(S_3 \text{ and } T_1) = 1/67 = .0149$$

Therefore, large salary gains (S_3) are *not* independent of low tuition (T_1).

Relative Frequencies

To facilitate probability calculations, we can divide each table frequency by the total sample size ($n = 67$) to get the *relative frequencies* shown in Table 5.9. For example, the upper left-hand cell becomes $5/67 = .0746$.

Joint probabilities show everything in one table. In symbolic terms, Table 5.9 of relative frequencies may be written as shown in Table 5.10.

The nine joint probabilities sum to 1.0000 since these are all the possible intersections:

$$.0746 + .1045 + .0746 + .1493 + .1642 + .1791 + .0149 + .0149 + .2239 = 1.0000$$

Except for rounding, summing the joint probabilities across a row or down a column gives *marginal* (or *unconditional*) probabilities for the respective row or column:

Adding Across Rows

In symbolic form

$P(T_1$ and $S_1) + P(T_1$ and $S_2) + P(T_1$ and $S_3) = P(T_1)$

$P(T_2$ and $S_1) + P(T_2$ and $S_2) + P(T_2$ and $S_3) = P(T_2)$

$P(T_3$ and $S_1) + P(T_3$ and $S_2) + P(T_3$ and $S_3) = P(T_3)$

In numerical form

$.0746 + .1493 + .0149 = .2388$

$.1045 + .1642 + .0149 = .2836$

$.0746 + .1791 + .2239 = .4776$

Adding Down Columns

In symbolic form

$P(T_1$ and $S_1)$ $P(T_1$ and $S_2)$ $P(T_1$ and $S_3)$

$+ P(T_2$ and $S_1)$ $+ P(T_2$ and $S_2)$ $+ P(T_2$ and $S_3)$

$+ P(T_3$ and $S_1)$ $+ P(T_3$ and $S_2)$ $+ P(T_3$ and $S_3)$

$= P(S_1)$ $= P(S_2)$ $= P(S_3)$

In numerical form

.0746   .1493   .0149

$+ .1045$ $+ .1642$ $+ .0149$

$+ .0746$ $+ .1791$ $+ .2239$

$= .2537$ $= .4926$ $= .2537$

The marginal row and column probabilities sum to 1.0000 (except for rounding):

Columns (Salary): $P(S_1) + P(S_2) + P(S_3) = .2537 + .4926 + .2537 = 1.0000$
Rows (Tuition): $P(T_1) + P(T_2) + P(T_3) = .2388 + .2836 + .4776 = 1.0000$

A small grocery store would like to know if the number of items purchased by a customer is independent of the type of payment method the customer chooses to use. Having this information can help the store manager determine how to set up his/her various checkout lanes. The manager collected a random sample of 368 customer transactions. The results are shown in Table 5.11.

TABLE 5.11   Contingency Table for Payment Method by Number of Items Purchased

| Number of Items Purchased | Payment Method | | | |
	Cash	Check	Credit/ Debit Card	Row Total
1–5	30	15	43	88
6–10	46	23	66	135
10–20	31	15	43	89
20+	19	10	27	56
Column Total	126	63	179	368

Looking at the frequency data presented in the table we can calculate the marginal probability that a customer will use cash to make the payment. Let C be the event that the customer chose cash as the payment method.

$$P(C) = \frac{126}{368} = .3424$$

Is $P(C)$ the same if we condition on number of items purchased?

$$P(C \mid 1-5) = \frac{30}{88} = .3409 \qquad P(C \mid 6-10) = \frac{46}{135} = .3407$$

$$P(C \mid 10-20) = \frac{31}{89} = .3483 \qquad P(C \mid 20+) = \frac{19}{56} = .3393$$

Notice that there is little difference in these probabilities. If we perform the same type of analysis for the next two payment methods we find that *payment method* and *number of items purchased* are essentially independent. Based on this study, the manager might decide to offer a cash-only checkout lane that is *not* restricted to the number of items purchased.

How Do We Get a Contingency Table?

Contingency tables do not just "happen" but require careful data organization and forethought. They are created from raw data. In this example, numerical values were mapped into discrete codes, as shown in Table 5.12. If the data were already categorical (e.g., a survey with discrete responses) this step would have been unnecessary. Once the data are coded, we tabulate the frequency in each cell of the contingency table. The tabulation would be done by a software package (e.g., MINITAB's Stat > Tables > Cross Tabulation).

TABLE 5.12

Data Coding for MBA Data 🐢 **MBASalary**

Note: S_1 is salary gain under $50K, $S_2 =$ salary gain $50K–$100K, and S_3 is salary gain $100K+. T_1 is tuition under $40K, T_2 is tuition from $40K–$50K, and T_3 is tuition of $50K+. Data are provided for educational purposes and not as a guide to financial gains.

Source: *Forbes* 172, no. 8 (October 13, 2003), p. 78. Copyright © 2005 Forbes, Inc. Reprinted by permission of Forbes magazine.

School	Original Data ($000) Tuition	Gain	Coded Data Tuition	Gain
Alabama (Manderson)	67	21	T_3	S_1
Arizona (Eller)	69	42	T_3	S_1
Arizona State (Carey)	70	41	T_3	S_1
Auburn	46	18	T_2	S_1
Babson (Olin)	22	53	T_1	S_2
⋮	⋮	⋮	⋮	⋮
Wake Forest (Babcock)	91	50	T_3	S_2
Washington U.—St. Louis (Olin)	120	61	T_3	S_2
William & Mary	94	45	T_3	S_1
Wisconsin—Madison	81	48	T_3	S_1
Yale	137	65	T_3	S_2

Mini Case   5.1

Smoking and Gender

Table 5.13 shows that the proportion of women over age 65 who have never smoked is much higher than for men, that a higher proportion of men than women used to smoke but have quit, and that the number of current smokers over 65 is about the same for men and women.

TABLE 5.13   Smoking and Gender for Persons Age 65 and Over (Thousands)
🐢 **Smoking1**

Gender	Never Smoked (N)	Former Smoker (R)	Current Smoker (S)	Total
Male (M)	3,160	5,087	2,320	10,567
Female (F)	10,437	2,861	2,007	15,305
Total	13,597	7,948	4,327	25,872

Source: U.S. Department of Commerce, *Statistical Abstract of the United States, 1986*, p. 119.

Conditional probabilities may be found from Table 5.13 by restricting ourselves to a single row or column (the *condition*). For example, for males we get:

$P(N \mid M) = 3{,}160/10{,}567 = .2990$ There is a 29.9% probability that an individual never smoked *given* that the person is male.

$P(R \mid M) = 5{,}087/10{,}567 = .4814$ There is a 48.1% probability that an individual is a former smoker *given* that the person is male.

$P(S \mid M) = 2{,}320/10{,}567 = .2196$ There is a 22.0% probability that an individual currently smokes *given* that the person is male.

On the other hand, for females we get:

$P(N \mid F) = 10{,}437/15{,}305 = .6819$ There is a 68.2% probability that an individual never smoked *given* that the person is female.

$P(R \mid F) = 2{,}861/15{,}305 = .1869$ There is an 18.7% probability that an individual is a former smoker *given* that the person is female.

$P(S \mid F) = 2{,}007/15{,}305 = .1311$ There is a 13.1% probability that an individual currently smokes *given* that the person is female.

These conditional probabilities show that a female is over twice as likely as a male never to have smoked. However, the number of *former* smokers is higher among males (you can't be a former smoker unless you once smoked).

Table 5.14 shows the *relative frequencies* obtained by dividing each table frequency by the sample size ($n = 25,872$).

TABLE 5.14 **Smoking and Gender for Persons Age 65 and Over (Thousands)**

Gender	Never Smoked (N)	Former Smoker (R)	Current Smoker (S)	Total
Male (M)	.1221	.1966	.0897	0.4084
Female (F)	.4034	.1106	.0776	0.5916
Total	.5256	.3072	.1673	1.0000

For example, the joint probability $P(M \cap N)$ is .1221 (i.e., about 12.2 percent of the sample were males who had never smoked). The six joint probabilities sum to 1.0000, as they should.

SECTION EXERCISES

5.22 This contingency table describes 200 business students. Find each probability and interpret it in words. **GenderMajor**

    a. $P(A)$ b. $P(M)$ c. $P(A \cap M)$ d. $P(F \cap S)$
    e. $P(A \mid M)$ f. $P(A \mid F)$ g. $P(F \mid S)$ h. $P(E \cup F)$

Gender	Major Accounting (A)	Economics (E)	Statistics (S)	Row Total
Female (F)	44	30	24	98
Male (M)	56	30	16	102
Column Total	100	60	40	200

5.23 Based on the previous problem, is major independent of gender? Explain the basis for your conclusion.

5.24 This contingency table shows average yield (rows) and average duration (columns) for 38 bond funds. For a randomly chosen bond fund, find the probability that:
    a. The bond fund is long duration.
    b. The bond fund has high yield.
    c. The bond fund has high yield given that it is of short duration.
    d. The bond fund is of short duration given that it has high yield.

Yield	Average Portfolio Duration Short (D_1)	Intermediate (D_2)	Long (D_3)	Row Total
Small (Y_1)	8	2	0	10
Medium (Y_2)	1	6	6	13
High (Y_3)	2	4	9	15
Column Total	11	12	15	38

Source: Data are from *Forbes* 173, no. 2 (February 2, 2004). **BondFunds**

5.6
TREE DIAGRAMS

Chapter 2

What Is a Tree?

Events and probabilities can be displayed in the form of a *tree diagram* or *decision tree* to help visualize all possible outcomes. This is a common business planning activity. We begin with a contingency table. Table 5.15 shows a cross-tabulation of expense ratios (low, medium, high) by fund type (bond, stock) for a sample of 21 bond funds and 23 stock funds. For purposes of this analysis, a fund's expense ratio is defined as "low" if it is in the lowest 1/3 of the sample, "medium" if it is in the middle 1/3 of the sample, and "high" if it is in the upper 1/3 of the sample.

To label the tree, we need to calculate *conditional probabilities*. Table 5.16 shows conditional probabilities by fund type (i.e., dividing each cell frequency by its column total). For example, $P(L \mid B) = 11/21 = .5238$. This says there is about a 52 percent chance that a fund has a low expense ratio if it is a bond fund. In contrast, $P(L \mid S) = 3/23 = .1304$. This says there is about a 13 percent chance that a fund has a low expense ratio if it is a stock fund.

The tree diagram in Figure 5.11 shows all events along with their marginal, conditional, and joint probabilities. To illustrate the calculation of joint probabilities, we make a slight modification of the formula for conditional probability for events A and B:

$$P(A \mid B) = \frac{P(A \cap B)}{P(B)} \qquad \text{or} \qquad P(A \cap B) = P(B)\,P(A \mid B)$$

Thus, the joint probability of each terminal event on the tree can be obtained by multiplying the probabilities along its branch. For example, following the top branch of the tree, the joint probability of a bond fund (B) with low expenses (L) is

$$P(B \cap L) = P(B)\,P(L \mid B) = (.4773)(.5238) = .2500$$

The conditional probabilities sum to 1 *within* each branch, and the joint probabilities also sum to 1 *down all six terminal events*.

SECTION EXERCISES

5.25 Of grocery shoppers who have a shopping cart, 70 percent pay by credit/debit card (event C_1), 20 percent pay cash (event C_2), and 10 percent pay by check (event C_3). Of shoppers without a grocery cart, 50 percent pay by credit/debit card (event C_1), 40 percent pay cash (event C_2), and 10 percent pay by check (event C_3). On Saturday morning, 80 percent of the shoppers take a

TABLE 5.15
Frequency Tabulation of Expense Ratios by Fund Type **BondFunds**

Source: *Money* 32, no. 2 (February 2003).

	Fund Type		
Expense Ratio	Bond Fund (B)	Stock Fund (S)	Row Total
Low (L)	11	3	14
Medium (M)	7	9	16
High (H)	3	11	14
Column Total	21	23	44

TABLE 5.16
Conditional Probabilities by Fund Type **BondFund**

	Fund Type	
Expense Ratio	Bond Fund (B)	Stock Fund (S)
Low (L)	.5238	.1304
Medium (M)	.3333	.3913
High (H)	.1429	.4783
Column Total	1.0000	1.0000

FIGURE 5.11

Tree diagram for fund type and expense ratios BondFund

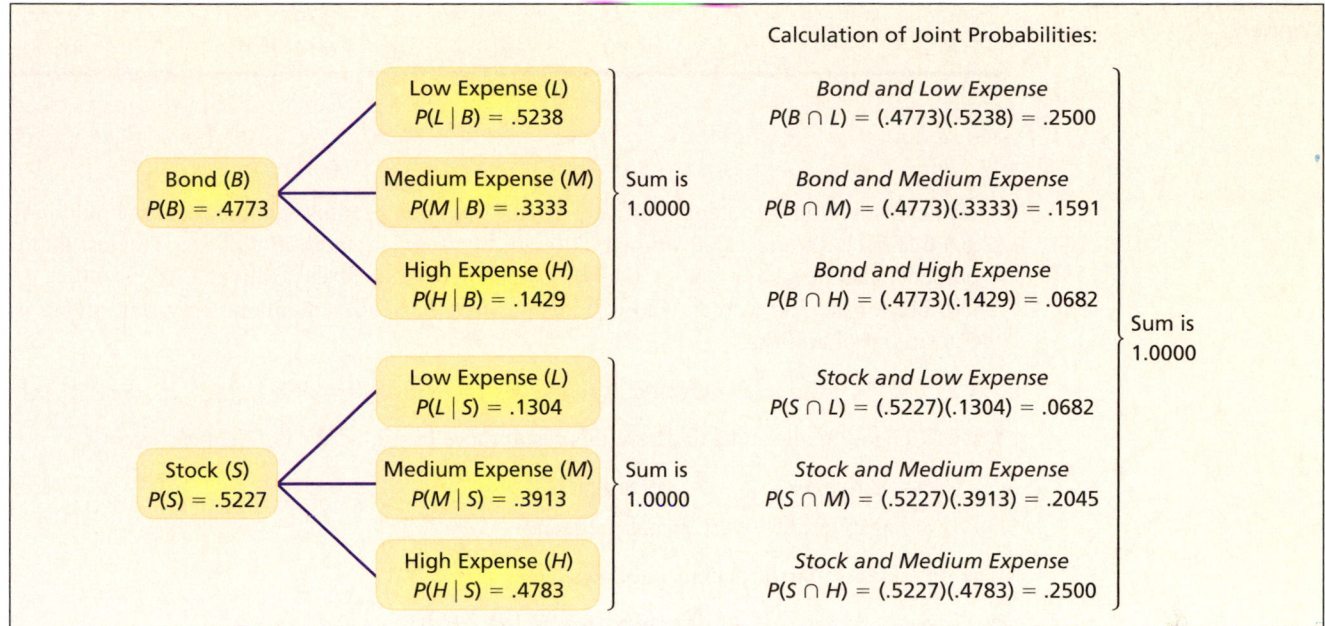

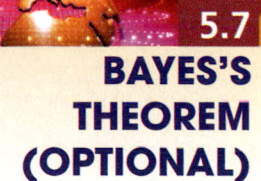

shopping cart (event S_1) and 20 percent do not (event S_2). (a) Sketch a tree based on this data. (b) Calculate the probability of all joint probabilities (e.g., $S_1 \cap C_1$). (c) Verify that the joint probabilities sum to 1.

5.26 A study showed that 60 percent of *The Wall Street Journal* subscribers watch CNBC every day. Of these, 70 percent watch it outside the home. Only 20 percent of those who don't watch CNBC every day watch it outside the home. Let D be the event "watches CNBC daily" and O be the event "watches CNBC outside the home." Sketch a tree based on this data. (b) Calculate the probability of all joint probabilities (e.g., $D \cap O$). (c) Verify that the joint probabilities sum to 1.

5.7 BAYES'S THEOREM (OPTIONAL)

An important theorem published by Thomas Bayes (1702–1761) provides a method of revising probabilities to reflect new information. The ***prior*** (unconditional) ***probability*** of an event B is revised after event A has been considered to yield a ***posterior*** (conditional) ***probability***. We begin with a formula slightly different from the standard definition of conditional probability:

$$P(B \mid A) = \frac{P(A \mid B)P(B)}{P(A)} \tag{5.15}$$

Unfortunately, in some situations $P(A)$ is not given. The most useful and common form of ***Bayes's Theorem*** replaces $P(A)$ with an expanded formula:

$$P(B \mid A) = \frac{P(A \mid B)P(B)}{P(A \mid B)P(B) + P(A \mid B')P(B')} \tag{5.16}$$

How Bayes's Theorem Works

Bayes's Theorem is best understood by example. Suppose that 60 percent of the women who purchase over-the-counter pregnancy testing kits are actually pregnant. For a particular brand of kit, if a woman is pregnant, the test will yield a positive result 96 percent of the time and a negative result 4 percent of the time (called a "false negative"). If she is not pregnant, the test will yield a positive result 1 percent of the time (called a "false positive") and a negative result 99 percent of the time. Suppose the test comes up positive. What is the probability that she is really pregnant?

TABLE 5.17

Pregnancy Test Frequencies for 1,000 Women   **Pregnancy**

Actual	Positive Test	Negative Test	Total
Pregnant	576	24	600
Not Pregnant	4	396	400
Total	580	420	1,000

We can solve this problem intuitively. If 1,000 women use this test, the results should look like Table 5.17. Of the 1,000 women, 600 will be pregnant and 400 will not. The test yields 4 percent false negatives ($.04 \times 600 = 24$) and 1 percent false positives ($.01 \times 400 = 4$). Therefore, of the 580 women who will test positive, 576 will actually be pregnant, giving us the desired probability:

$$P(pregnant \mid positive\ test) = 576/580 = .9931$$

Bayes's Theorem allows us to derive this result more formally. We define these events:

A = positive test B = pregnant

A' = negative test B' = not pregnant

The given facts may be stated as follows:

$$P(A \mid B) = .96 \qquad P(A \mid B') = .01 \qquad P(B) = .60$$

The complement of each event is found by subtracting from 1:

$$P(A' \mid B) = .04 \qquad P(A' \mid B') = .99 \qquad P(B') = .40$$

Applying Bayes's Theorem:

$$P(B \mid A) = \frac{P(A \mid B)P(B)}{P(A \mid B)P(B) + P(A \mid B')P(B')} = \frac{(.96)(.60)}{(.96)(.60) + (.01)(.40)}$$

$$= \frac{.576}{.576 + .004} = \frac{.576}{.580} = .9931$$

There is a 99.31 percent chance that a woman is pregnant, given that the test is positive. A common error is to feel that the probability should be 96 percent. But 96 percent is the probability of a positive test *if* the woman is pregnant, while many of the women who take the test are *not* pregnant.

What Bayes's Theorem does is to show us how to revise our *prior* probability of pregnancy (60 percent) to get the *posterior* probability (99.31 percent) after the results of the pregnancy test are known:

Prior (before the test)   *Posterior (after positive test result)*

$P(B) = .60$ $P(B \mid A) = .9931$

The given information did not permit a direct calculation of $P(B \mid A)$ since we only knew the conditional probabilities $P(A \mid B)$ and $P(A \mid B')$. Bayes's Theorem is useful in situations like this.

A tree diagram (Figure 5.12) is helpful in visualizing the situation. Only branches 1 and 3 have a positive test, and only in branch 1 is the woman actually pregnant, so $P(B \mid A) = .576/(.576 + .004) = .9931$. The conditional probabilities for each branch sum to 1.

General Form of Bayes's Theorem

A generalization of Bayes's Theorem allows event B to have as many categories as we wish ($B_1, B_2, \ldots, B_n$) rather than just the dichotomous categories B and B':

(5.17) $\qquad P(B_i \mid A) = \dfrac{P(A \mid B_i)P(B_i)}{P(A \mid B_1)P(B_1) + P(A \mid B_2)P(B_2) + \cdots + P(A \mid B_n)P(B_n)}$

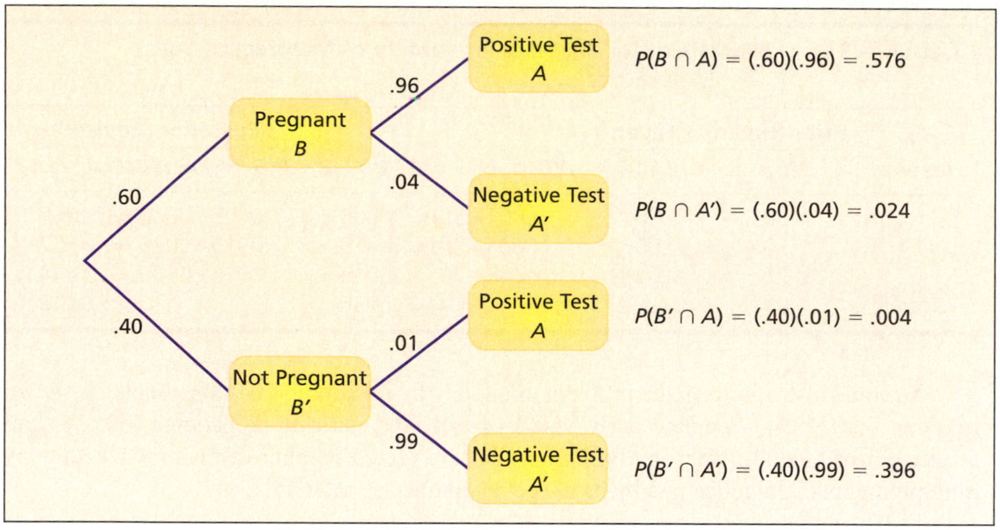

FIGURE 5.12

Tree diagram for home
pregnancy test
Pregnancy

Based on historical data, three hospital trauma centers have 50, 30, and 20 percent of the cases, respectively. The probability of a case resulting in a malpractice suit in each of the three hospitals is .001, .005, and .008, respectively. If a malpractice suit is filed, what is the probability that it originated in hospital 1? This problem is solved as follows. We define:

EXAMPLE

*Hospital Trauma
Centers*

Event A = event that a malpractice suit is filed by patient

Event B_i = event that the patient was treated at trauma center i ($i = 1, 2, 3$)

The given information can be presented in a table like Table 5.18.

TABLE 5.18   **Given Information for Hospital Trauma Centers**   **Malpractice**

Hospital	Marginal	Conditional: Suit Filed
1	$P(B_1) = .50$	$P(A \mid B_1) = .001$
2	$P(B_2) = .30$	$P(A \mid B_2) = .005$
3	$P(B_3) = .20$	$P(A \mid B_3) = .008$

Applying formula 5.17, we can find $P(B_1 \mid A)$ as follows:

$$P(B_1 \mid A) = \frac{P(A \mid B_1)P(B_1)}{P(A \mid B_1)P(B_1) + P(A \mid B_2)P(B_2) + P(A \mid B_3)P(B_3)}$$

$$= \frac{(.001)(.50)}{(.001)(.50) + (.005)(.30) + (.008)(.20)}$$

$$= \frac{.0005}{.0005 + .0015 + .0016} = \frac{.0005}{.0036} = .1389$$

The probability that the malpractice suit was filed in hospital 1 is .1389, or 13.89 percent. Although hospital 1 sees 50 percent of the trauma patients, it is expected to generate less than half the malpractice suits, since the other two hospitals have much higher incidence of malpractice suits.

There is nothing special about $P(B_1 \mid A)$. In fact, it is easy to calculate *all* the posterior probabilities at once by using a worksheet, as shown in Table 5.19:

$P(B_1 \mid A) = .1389$ (probability that a malpractice lawsuit originated in hospital 1)

$P(B_2 \mid A) = .4167$ (probability that a malpractice lawsuit originated in hospital 2)

$P(B_3 \mid A) = .4444$ (probability that a malpractice lawsuit originated in hospital 3)

TABLE 5.19   **Worksheet for Bayesian Probability of Malpractice Suit**
        🦠 **Malpractice**

Hospital	Prior (Given) $P(B_i)$	Given $P(A \mid B_i)$	$P(B_i \cap A) = P(A \mid B_i) P(B_i)$	Posterior (Revised) $P(B_i \mid A) = P(B_i \cap A)/P(A)$
1	.50	.001	(.001)(.50) = .0005	.0005/.0036 = .1389
2	.30	.005	(.005)(.30) = .0015	.0015/.0036 = .4167
3	.20	.008	(.008)(.20) = .0016	.0016/.0036 = .4444
Total	1.00		$P(A) = .0036$	1.0000

We could also approach the problem intuitively by imagining 10,000 patients, as shown in Table 5.20. First, calculate each hospital's expected number of patients (50, 30, and 20 percent of 10,000). Next, find each hospital's expected number of malpractice suits by multiplying its malpractice rate by its expected number of patients:

Hospital 1: $.001 \times 5,000 = 5$ (expected malpractice suits at hospital 1)

Hospital 2: $.005 \times 3,000 = 15$ (expected malpractice suits at hospital 2)

Hospital 3: $.008 \times 2,000 = 16$ (expected malpractice suits at hospital 3)

Adding down, the total number of malpractice suits is 36. Hence, $P(B_1 \mid A) = 5/36 = .1389$, $P(B_2 \mid A) = 15/36 = .4167$, and $P(B_3 \mid A) = 16/36 = .4444$. These three probabilities add to 1. Overall, there are 36 malpractice suits, so we can also calculate $P(A) = 36/10,000 = .0036$. Many people find the table method easier to understand than the formulas. Do you agree?

TABLE 5.20   **Malpractice Frequencies for 10,000 Hypothetical Patients**
        🦠 **Malpractice**

Hospital	Malpractice Suit Filed	No Malpractice Suit Filed	Total
1	5	4,995	5,000
2	15	2,985	3,000
3	16	1,984	2,000
Total	36	9,964	10,000

We could visualize this situation as shown in Figure 5.13. The initial sample space consists of three mutually exclusive and collectively exhaustive events (hospitals B_1, B_2, B_3). As indicated by their relative areas, B_1 is 50 percent of the sample space, B_2 is 30 percent of the

FIGURE 5.13

Illustration of hospital trauma center example

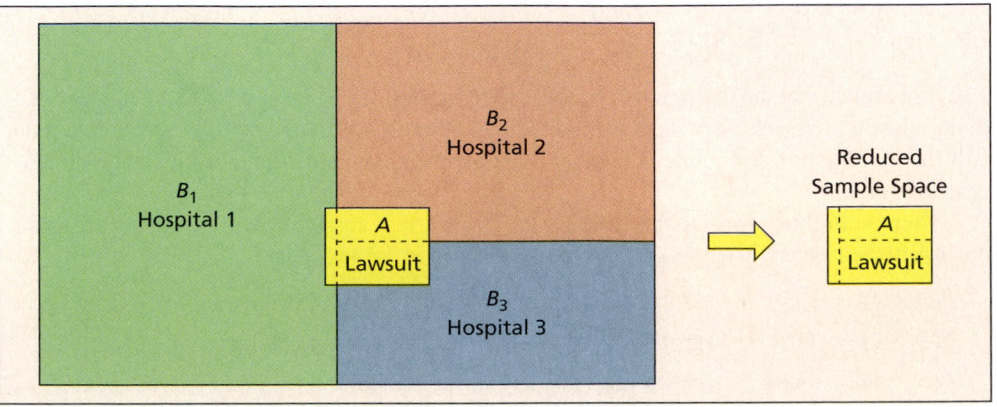

sample space, and B_3 is 20 percent of the sample space. But *given* that a malpractice case has been filed (event A), then the relevant sample space is *reduced* to that of event A.

The revised (posterior) probabilities are the relative areas *within* event A:

$P(B_1 \mid A)$ is the proportion of A that lies within $B_1 = 13.89\%$

$P(B_2 \mid A)$ is the proportion of A that lies within $B_2 = 41.67\%$

$P(B_3 \mid A)$ is the proportion of A that lies within $B_3 = 44.44\%$

These percentages were calculated in the previous worksheets. A worksheet is still needed to calculate $P(A)$ for the denominator.

SECTION EXERCISES

5.27   A drug test for athletes has a 5 percent false positive rate and a 10 percent false negative rate. Of the athletes tested, 4 percent have actually been using the prohibited drug. If an athlete tests positive, what is the probability that the athlete has actually been using the prohibited drug? Explain your reasoning clearly.

5.28   Half of a set of the parts are manufactured by machine A and half by machine B. Four percent of all the parts are defective. Six percent of the parts manufactured on machine A are defective. Find the probability that a part was manufactured on machine A, given that it is defective. Explain your reasoning clearly.

5.29   An airport gamma ray luggage scanner coupled with a neural net artificial intelligence program can detect a weapon in suitcases with a false positive rate of 2 percent and a false negative rate of 2 percent. Assume a .001 probability that a suitcase contains a weapon. If a suitcase triggers the alarm, what is the probability that it contains a weapon? Explain your reasoning.

Mini Case   5.2

Smoking and Gender Again

Table 5.21 shows that the proportion of women over age 65 who have never smoked is much higher than for men, that a higher proportion of men than women used to smoke but have quit, and that the number of current smokers over 65 is about the same for men and women.

TABLE 5.21   Smoking and Gender for Persons Age 65 and Over (Thousands)
🐀   **Smoking1**

Gender	Never Smoked (N)	Former Smoker (R)	Current Smoker (S)	Total
Male (M)	3,160	5,087	2,320	10,567
Female (F)	10,437	2,861	2,007	15,305
Total	13,597	7,948	4,327	25,872

Source: U.S. Department of Commerce, *Statistical Abstract of the United States, 1986,* p. 119.

We see from Table 5.21 that $P(M) = 10{,}567/25{,}872 = .4084$ and $P(F) = 15{,}305/25{,}872 = .5916$. We also have these conditional probabilities:

$P(N \mid M) = 3{,}160/10{,}567 = .2990$ There is a 29.9 percent chance that an individual never smoked *given* that the person is male.

$P(R \mid M) = 5{,}087/10{,}567 = .4814$ There is a 48.1 percent chance that an individual is a former smoker *given* that the person is male.

$P(S \mid M) = 2,320/10,567 = .2196$ There is a 22.0 percent chance that an individual currently smokes *given* that the person is male.

$P(N \mid F) = 10,437/15,305 = .6819$ There is a 68.2 percent chance that an individual never smoked *given* that the person is female.

$P(R \mid F) = 2,861/15,305 = .1869$ There is an 18.7 percent chance that an individual is a former smoker *given* that the person is female.

$P(S \mid F) = 2,007/15,305 = .1311$ There is a 13.1 percent chance that an individual currently smokes *given* that the person is female.

The tree is shown in Figure 5.14.

FIGURE 5.14

Tree for smoking and gender   **Smoking1**

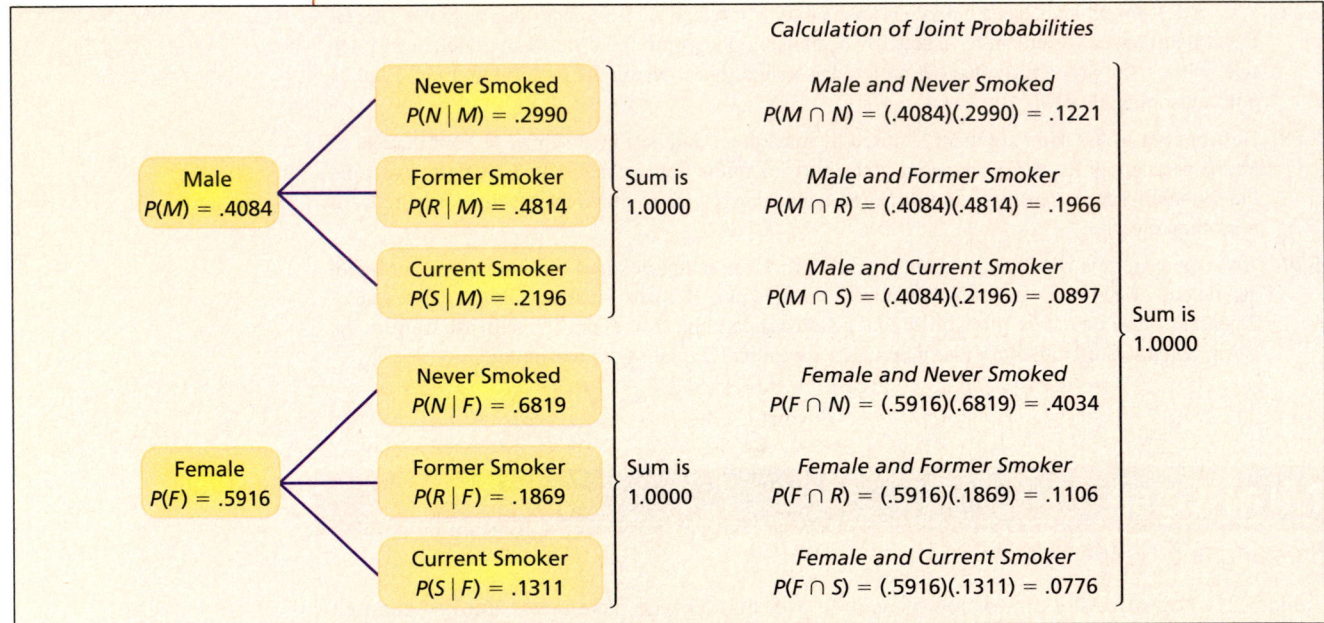

Applying Bayes's Theorem, the probability that a 65-year-old person is male, given that a person is a smoker, is 53.62 percent (even though only 40.84 percent of 65 year olds are males):

$$P(M \mid S) = \frac{P(S \mid M)P(M)}{P(S \mid M)P(M) + P(S \mid M')P(M')}$$

$$= \frac{(.2196)(.4084)}{(.2196)(.4084) + (.1311)(.5916)}$$

$$= \frac{.0897}{.0897 + .0776} = \frac{.0897}{.1673} = .5362$$

5.8
COUNTING RULES (OPTIONAL)

Fundamental Rule of Counting

If event A can occur in n_1 ways and event B can occur in n_2 ways, then events A and B can occur in $n_1 \times n_2$ ways. In general, the number of ways that m events can occur is $n_1 \times n_2 \times \cdots \times n_m$.

EXAMPLE

Stock-Keeping Labels

How many unique stock-keeping unit (SKU) labels can a chain of hardware stores create by using two letters (ranging from *AA* to *ZZ*) followed by four numbers (digits 0 through 9)? For example:

AF1078: hex-head 6 cm bolts—box of 12

RT4855: Lime-A-Way cleaner—16 ounce

LL3119: Rust-Oleum Professional primer—gray 15 ounce

This problem may be viewed as filling six empty boxes, as shown in Figure 5.15.

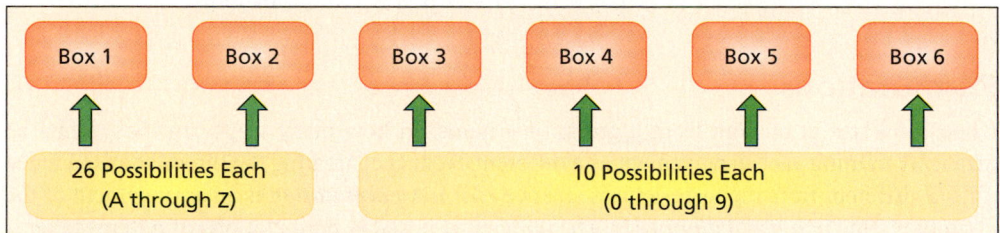

FIGURE 5.15

Creating SKU labels

There are 26 ways (letters A through Z) to fill either the first or second box. There are 10 ways (digits 0 through 9) to fill the third through sixth boxes. The number of unique inventory labels is therefore $26 \times 26 \times 10 \times 10 \times 10 \times 10 = 6{,}760{,}000$. Such a system should suffice for a moderately large retail store.

EXAMPLE

Shirt Inventory

The number of possibilities can be large, even for a very simple counting problem. For example, the L.L. Bean men's cotton chambray shirt comes in six colors (blue, stone, rust, green, plum, indigo), five sizes (*S, M, L, XL, XXL*), and two styles (short sleeve, long sleeve). Their stock, therefore, might include $6 \times 5 \times 2 = 60$ possible shirts. The number of shirts of each type to be stocked will depend on prior demand experience. Counting the outcomes is easy with the counting formula, but even for this simple problem, a tree diagram would be impossible to fit on one page, and the enumeration of them all would be tedious (but necessary for L.L. Bean).

Factorials

The number of ways that *n* items can be arranged in a particular order is *n* **factorial,** the product of all integers from 1 to *n*.

$$n! = n(n-1)(n-2) \cdots 1 \tag{5.18}$$

This rule is useful for counting the possible arrangements of any *n* items. There are *n* ways to choose the first item, $n - 1$ ways to choose the second item, and so on until we reach the last item, as illustrated in Figure 5.16.

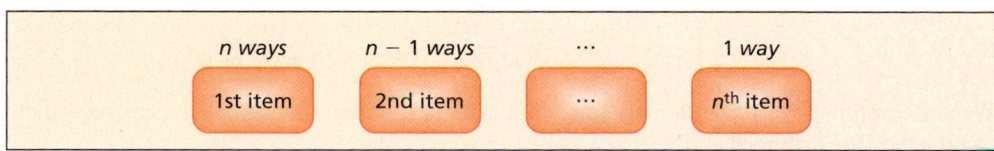

FIGURE 5.16

Choosing *n* items

EXAMPLE

Truck Routing

In very small problems we can actually count the possibilities. For example, a home appliance service truck must make three stops (A, B, C). In how many ways could the three stops be arranged? There are six possible arrangements: {ABC, ACB, BAC, BCA, CAB, CBA}. But if all we want is the *number of possibilities* without listing them all:

$$3! = 3 \times 2 \times 1 = 6$$

Even in moderate-sized problems, listing all the possibilities is not feasible. For example, the number of possible arrangements of nine baseball players in a batting order rotation is:

$$9! = 9 \times 8 \times 7 \times 6 \times 5 \times 4 \times 3 \times 2 \times 1 = 362,880$$

Permutations

Choose r items at random from a group of n items. In how many ways can the r items be arranged, treating each arrangement as a different event (i.e., treating the three-letter sequence XYZ as different from the three-letter sequence ZYX). A *permutation* is an arrangement of the r sample items *in a particular order*. The number of possible permutations of n items taken r at a time is denoted $_nP_r$.

(5.19)
$$_nP_r = \frac{n!}{(n-r)!}$$

Permutations are used when we are interested in finding how many different ways we can select r items from n items, when each possible arrangement of items is a distinct event.

EXAMPLE

Appliance Service Calls

Five home appliance customers (A, B, C, D, E) need service calls, but the field technician can service only three of them before noon. The order in which they are serviced is important (to the customers, anyway) so each possible arrangement of three service calls is different. The dispatcher must assign the sequence. The number of possible permutations is

$$_nP_r = \frac{n!}{(n-r)!} = \frac{5!}{(5-3)!} = \frac{5 \cdot 4 \cdot 3 \cdot 2 \cdot 1}{2!} = \frac{120}{2} = 60$$

This may seem a surprisingly large number, but it can be enumerated. There are 10 distinct groups of three customers (two customers must be omitted):

   ABC ABD ABE ACD ACE ADE BCD BCE BDE CDE

In turn, each group of three customers can be arranged in six possible orders. For example, the first distinct set of customers {A, B, C} could be arranged in six distinct ways:

   ABC ACB CAB CBA BAC BCA

We could do the same for each of the other nine groups of three customers. Since there are 10 distinct groups of three customers and six possible arrangements per group, there are $10 \times 6 = 60$ permutations. Clearly, we would prefer not to enumerate sequences like this very often.

Combinations

A *combination* is an arrangement of r items chosen at random from n items where the order of the selected items is *not* important (i.e., treating the three-letter sequence XYZ as being the same as the three-letter sequence ZYX). The number of possible combinations of r items chosen from n items is denoted $_nC_r$.

(5.20)
$$_nC_r = \frac{n!}{r!(n-r)!}$$

We use combinations when the only thing that matters is which r items are chosen, regardless of how they are arranged.

Suppose that five customers (*A, B, C, D, E*) need service calls and the maintenance worker can only service three of them this morning. The customers don't care when they are serviced as long as it's before noon, so the dispatcher does not care who is serviced first, second, or third. In other words, the dispatcher regards *ABC, ACB, BAC, BCA, CAB,* or *CBA* as being the same event because the same three customers (*A, B, C*) get serviced. The number of combinations is:

$$_nC_r = \frac{n!}{r!(n-r)!} = \frac{5!}{3!(5-3)!} = \frac{5 \cdot 4 \cdot 3 \cdot 2 \cdot 1}{(3 \cdot 2 \cdot 1)(2 \cdot 1)} = \frac{120}{12} = 10$$

This is much smaller than the number of permutations in the previous example where order was important. In fact, the possible combinations can be enumerated easily since there are only 10 distinct groups of three customers:

ABC ABD ABE ACD ACE ADE BCD BCE BDE CDE

Permutations or Combinations?

Permutations and combinations both calculate the number of ways we could choose *r* items from *n* items. But in permutations *order is important* while in combinations *order does not matter*. The number of permutations generally is greater than the number of combinations.

MegaStat offers computational assistance with factorials, permutations, and combinations. It is exceptionally fast and accurate, even for very large factorials.

SECTION EXERCISES

5.30 At Oxnard University, a student ID consists of two letters (26 possibilities) followed by four digits (10 possibilities). (a) How many unique student IDs can be created? (b) Would one letter followed by three digits suffice for a university with 40,000 students? (c) Why is extra capacity in student IDs a good idea?

5.31 Until 2005, the UPC bar code had 12 digits (0–9). The first six digits represent the manufacturer, the next five represent the product, and the last is a check digit. (a) How many different manufacturers could be encoded? (b) How many different products could be encoded? (c) In 2005, the EAN bar code replaced the UPC bar code, adding a 13th digit. If this new digit is used for product identification, how many different products could now be encoded?

5.32 Bob has to study for four final exams: accounting (*A*), biology (*B*), communications (*C*), and drama (*D*). (a) If he studies one subject at a time, in how many different ways could he arrange them? (b) List the possible arrangements in the sample space.

5.33 (a) In how many ways could you arrange seven books on a shelf? (b) Would it be feasible to list the possible arrangements?

5.34 Find the following permutations $_nP_r$:
   a. $n = 8$ and $r = 3$.
   b. $n = 8$ and $r = 5$.
   c. $n = 8$ and $r = 1$.
   d. $n = 8$ and $r = 8$.

5.35 Find the following combinations $_nC_r$:
   a. $n = 8$ and $r = 3$.
   b. $n = 8$ and $r = 5$.
   c. $n = 8$ and $r = 1$.
   d. $n = 8$ and $r = 8$.

5.36 A real estate office has 10 sales agents. Each of four new customers must be assigned an agent. (a) Find the number of agent arrangements where order *is* important. (b) Find the number of agent arrangements where order is *not* important. (c) Why is the number of combinations smaller than the number of permutations?

Chapter Summary

The **sample space** for a **random experiment** describes all possible outcomes. **Simple events** in a **discrete** sample space can be enumerated, while outcomes of a **continuous** sample space can only be described by a rule. An **empirical** probability is based on relative frequencies, a **classical** probability can be deduced from the nature of the experiment, and a **subjective** probability is based on judgment. An event's **complement** is every outcome except the event. The **odds** are the ratio of an event's probability to the probability of its complement. The **union** of two events is all outcomes in either or both, while the intersection is only those events in both. **Mutually exclusive** events cannot both occur, and **collectively exhaustive** events cover all possibilities. **Dichotomous** or **polytomous** events are mutually exclusive and collectively exhaustive. The **conditional probability** of an event is its probability given that another event has occurred. Two events are **independent** if the conditional probability of one is the same as its **unconditional** probability. The **joint probability** of independent events is the product of their probabilities. A **contingency table** is a cross-tabulation of frequencies for two variables with categorical outcomes and can be used to calculate probabilities. A **tree** visualizes events in a sequential diagram. **Bayes's Theorem** shows how to revise a **prior** probability to obtain a **conditional** or **posterior** probability when another event's occurrence is known. The number of arrangements of sampled items drawn from a population is found with the formula for **permutations** (if order is important) or **combinations** (if order does not matter).

Key Terms

actuarial science, *172*
Bayes's Theorem, *191*
classical approach, *174*
collectively exhaustive, *177*
combination, *198*
complement, *174*
compound event, *170*
conditional probability, *178*
contingency table, *183*
dependent, *180*
dichotomous events, *177*
disjoint, *177*
empirical approach, *172*

event, *170*
factorial, *197*
general law of addition, *176*
independent, *180*
intersection, *175*
joint probability, *175*
law of large numbers, *172*
marginal probability, *184*
multiplication law, *181*
mutually exclusive, *177*
null set, *177*
odds, *175*
permutation, *198*

polytomous events, *177*
posterior probability, *191*
prior probability, *191*
probability, *171*
random experiment, *169*
redundancy, *181*
relative frequency approach, *172*
sample space, *169*
simple event, *170*
subjective approach, *174*
tree diagram, *190*
union, *175*
Venn diagram, *170*

Commonly Used Formulas in Probability

Odds: $\dfrac{P(A)}{1 - P(A)}$

General Law of Addition: $P(A \cup B) = P(A) + P(B) - P(A \cap B)$

Conditional probability: $P(A \mid B) = \dfrac{P(A \cap B)}{P(B)}$

Independence property: $P(A \cap B) = P(A)P(B)$

Bayes's Theorem: $P(B \mid A) = \dfrac{P(A \mid B)P(B)}{P(A \mid B)P(B) + P(A \mid B')P(B')}$

Permutation: $_nP_r = \dfrac{n!}{(n - r)!}$

Combination: $_nC_r = \dfrac{n!}{r!(n - r)!}$

Chapter Review

1. Define (a) random experiment, (b) sample space, (c) simple event, and (d) compound event.
2. What are the three approaches to determining probability? Explain the differences among them.
3. Sketch a Venn diagram to illustrate (a) complement of an event, (b) union of two events, (c) intersection of two events, (d) mutually exclusive events, and (e) dichotomous events.
4. Define *odds*. What does it mean to say that odds are usually quoted against an event?

5. (a) State the additive law. (b) Why do we subtract the intersection?

6. (a) Write the formula for conditional probability. (b) When are two events independent?

7. (a) What is a contingency table? (b) How do we convert a contingency table into a table of relative frequencies?

8. In a contingency table, explain the concepts of (a) marginal probability and (b) joint probability.

9. Why are tree diagrams useful? Why are they not always practical?

10. What is the main point of Bayes's Theorem?

11. Define (a) fundamental rule of counting, (b) factorial, (c) permutation, and (d) combination.

CHAPTER EXERCISES

Note: Explain answers and show your work clearly. Problems marked * are more difficult or rely on optional material.

EMPIRICAL PROBABILITY EXPERIMENTS

5.37   (a) Make your own empirical estimate of the probability that a car is parked "nose first" (as opposed to "backed in"). Choose a local parking lot, such as a grocery store. Let A be the event that a car is parked nose first. Out of n cars examined, let f be the number of cars parked nose first. Then $P(A) = f/n$. (b) Do you feel your sample is large enough to have a reliable empirical probability? (c) If you had chosen a different parking lot (such as a church or a police station) would you expect the estimate of $P(A)$ to be similar? That is, would $P(A \mid \text{church}) = P(A \mid \text{police station})$? Explain.

5.38   (a) Make your own empirical estimate of the probability that a page in this book contains a figure. For n pages sampled (chosen using random numbers or some other random method) let f be the number of pages with a figure. Then $P(A) = f/n$. (b) Do you feel your sample is large enough to have a reliable empirical probability? (c) If you had chosen a different textbook (such as a biology book or an art history book), would you expect $P(A)$ to be similar? That is, would $P(A \mid \text{biology}) = P(A \mid \text{art history})$? Explain.

5.39   (a) Make your own empirical estimate of the probability that a DVD movie from your collection is longer than 2 hours (120 minutes). For the n DVDs in your sample, let f be the number that exceed 2 hours. Then $P(A) = f/n$. (b) Do you feel your sample is large enough to have a reliable empirical probability? (c) If you had chosen a different DVD collection (say, your best friend's), would you expect $P(A)$ to be similar? Explain.

5.40   M&Ms are blended in a ratio of 13 percent brown, 14 percent yellow, 13 percent red, 24 percent blue, 20 percent orange, and 16 percent green. Suppose you choose a sample of two M&Ms at random from a large bag. (a) Show the sample space. (b) What is the probability that both are brown? (c) Both blue? (d) Both green? (e) Find the probability of one brown and one green M&M. (f) Actually take 100 samples of two M&Ms (with replacement) and record the frequency of each outcome listed in (b) and (c) above. How close did your empirical results come to your predictions? (g) Which definition of probability applies in this situation? (Data are from www.mmmars.com.)

PROBLEMS

5.41   A survey showed that 44 percent of online Internet shoppers experience some kind of technical failure at checkout (e.g., when submitting a credit card) after loading their shopping cart. (a) What kind of probability is this? Explain. (b) What are the odds *for* a technical failure? (See J. Paul Peter and Jerry C. Olson, *Consumer Behavior and Marketing Strategy,* 7th ed. [McGraw-Hill-Irwin], p. 278.)

5.42   A Johnson Space Center analysis estimated a 1 in 71 chance of losing the International Space Station to space debris or a meteoroid hit. (a) What kind of probability is this? Explain. (b) What is the probability of losing the station in this way? (See *Aviation Week & Space Technology* 149, no. 16 [October 19, 1998], p. 11.)

5.43   Baseball player Tom Brookens once commented on his low batting average of .176: "I figure the law of averages has got to come into play sooner or later." A batting average is the ratio of hits to times at bat. Do you think the law of large numbers can be counted on to save Tom's batting average?

5.44   Bob says he is 50 percent sure he could swim across the Thames River. (a) What kind of probability is this? (b) On what facts might Bob have based his assertion?

5.45 In the first year after its release, 83 percent of emergency room doctors were estimated to have tried Dermabond glue (an alternative to sutures in some situations). (a) What kind of probability is this? (b) How was it probably estimated? (c) Why might the estimate be inaccurate? (Data are from *Modern Healthcare* 29, no. 32 [August 9, 1999], p. 70.)

5.46 The U.S. Cesarean section delivery rate in a recent year was estimated at 20.6 percent. (a) What kind of probability is this? (b) How was it probably estimated? (c) How accurate would you say this estimate is? (Data are from *Modern Healthcare* 27, no. 40 [October 6, 1997], p. 60.)

5.47 A recent article states that there is a 2 percent chance that an asteroid 100 meters or more in diameter will strike the earth before 2100. (a) What kind of probability is this? (b) How was it probably estimated? (c) How accurate would you say this estimate is? (Data are from *Scientific American* 289, no. 5 [November 2003], p. 56.)

5.48 If Punxsutawney Phil sees his shadow on the first Monday in February, then legend says that winter will last 6 more weeks. In 118 years, Phil has seen his shadow 104 times. (a) What is the probability that Phil will see his shadow on a randomly chosen Groundhog Day? (b) What kind of probability is this? (Data are from www.groundhog.org.)

5.49 "On Los Angeles freeways during the rush hour, there is an 18 percent probability that a driver is using a hand-held cell phone." (a) What kind of probability would you say this is? (b) How might it have been estimated? (c) How might the estimate be inaccurate?

5.50 Of all U.S. retail transactions in 2005, 22.7 percent were paid by debit card. (a) What are the odds that a given transaction will be paid by a debit card? (b) That it will not? (Data are from *Statistical Abstract of the United States, 2004–2005,* p. 746.)

5.51 Ten percent of fourth-graders tested for cholesterol show a dangerously high level (over 200 mg/dl). Three fourth-graders are chosen at random and checked sequentially for high (*H*) or normal (*N*) cholesterol. (a) Make a tree for this experiment. (b) What is the probability that none will have dangerously high cholesterol? One student? Two? All three?

5.52 Many youths dream of playing basketball in the NBA. Data show that each year about 475,000 fourth-grade boys play basketball, about 87,000 end up playing high school senior varsity basketball, about 4,310 receive college basketball scholarships (1,560 Division I, 1,350 Division II, 1,400 Division III), and about 30 are eventually drafted by the NBA (and another 130 play pro basketball in Europe). (a) Make a tree diagram for this experiment. (b) What is the probability that a fourth-grade boy who plays basketball will end up in the NBA? (c) What is the probability that a fourth-grade boy who plays basketball will receive a Division I college basketball scholarship? (d) What is the probability that a fourth-grade boy who plays basketball will receive a Division I college basketball scholarship given that he plays senior varsity basketball in high school? (Data are from *U.S. News and World Report* 136, no. 20 [June 7, 2004], p. 52.)

5.53 During 2002, the theft probability of an Acura Integra was estimated as 1.3 percent. Find the odds against an Acura Integra being stolen. (Data are from *Popular Science* 261, no. 3 [September 2002], p. 30.)

5.54 A person hit by lightning has a 33 percent chance of being killed (event *K*). (a) Find the odds that a person will be killed if struck by lightning. (b) Find the odds *against* a person being killed if struck by lightning (event *K′*). (Data are from Martin A. Uman, *Understanding Lightning* [Bek Technical Publications, 1971], p. 19.)

5.55 During the 2003 NBA playoffs, the Caesar's Palace Race and Sports Book gave the Detroit Pistons 50–1 odds against winning the NBA championship, and the New Jersey Nets 5–1 odds against winning the NBA championship. What is the implied probability of each team's victory? (Data are from *Detroit Free Press,* May 22, 2003, p. 1E.)

5.56 A certain model of remote-control Stanley garage door opener has nine binary (off/on) switches. The homeowner can set any code sequence. (a) How many separate codes can be programmed? (b) A newer model has 10 binary switches. How many codes can be programmed? (c) If you try to use your door opener on 1,000 other garages, how many times would you expect to succeed? What assumptions are you making in your answer?

5.57 (a) In a certain state, license plates consist of three letters (A–Z) followed by three digits (0–9). How many different plates can be issued? (b) If the state allows any six-character mix (in any order) of 26 letters and 10 digits, how many unique plates are possible? (c) Why might some combinations of numbers and letters be disallowed? *(d) Would the system described in (b) permit a unique license number for every car in the United States? For every car in the world? Explain your assumptions. *(e) If the letters O and I are not used because they look too much like the numerals 0 and 1, how many different plates can be issued?

5.58 Bob, Mary, and Jen go to dinner. Each orders a different meal. The waiter forgets who ordered which meal, so he randomly places the meals before the three diners. Let C be the event that a diner gets the correct meal and let N be the event that a diner gets an incorrect meal. Enumerate the sample space and then find the probability that:
  a. No diner gets the correct meal.
  b. Exactly one diner gets the correct meal.
  c. Exactly two diners get the correct meal.
  d. All three diners get the correct meal.

5.59 An MBA program offers seven concentrations: accounting (A), finance (F), human resources (H), information systems (I), international business (B), marketing (M), and operations management (O). Students in the capstone business policy class are assigned to teams of three. In how many different ways could a team contain exactly one student from each concentration?

5.60 A poker hand (5 cards) is drawn from an ordinary deck of 52 cards. Find the probability of each event, showing your reasoning carefully.
  a. The first four cards are the four aces.
  b. Any four cards are the four aces.

5.61 Two cards are drawn from an ordinary deck of 52 cards. Find the probability of each event, showing your reasoning carefully.
  a. Two aces.
  b. Two red cards.
  c. Two red aces.
  d. Two honor cards (A, K, Q, J, 10).

5.62 A certain airplane has two independent alternators to provide electrical power. The probability that a given alternator will fail on a 1-hour flight is .02. What is the probability that (a) both will fail? (b) Neither will fail? (c) One or the other will fail? Show all steps carefully.

5.63 There is a 30 percent chance that a bidding firm will get contract A and a 40 percent chance they will get contract B. There is a 5 percent chance that they will get both. Are the events independent?

5.64 A couple has two children. What is the probability that both are boys, given that the first is a boy?

5.65 On July 14, 2004, a power outage in the Northwest Airlines operations center near Minneapolis forced the airline's computer systems to shut down, leading to cancellation of 200 flights and delays in scores of other flights. (a) Explain how the concept of statistical independence might be applicable here. (b) How would the airline decide whether, say, expenditure of $100,000 would be justified for a backup system to prevent future occurrences? (Data are from *The Wall Street Journal,* July 15, 2004.)

5.66 Which are likely to be independent events? For those you think are not, suggest reasons why.
  a. Gender of two consecutive babies born in a hospital.
  b. Car accident rates and the driver's gender.
  c. Phone call arrival rates at a university admissions office and time of day.

5.67 In child-custody cases, about 70 percent of the fathers win the case if they contest it. In the next three custody cases, what is the probability that all three win? What assumption(s) are you making?

5.68 RackSpace-managed hosting advertises 99.999 percent guaranteed network uptime. (a) How many independent network servers would be needed if each has 99 percent reliability? (b) If each has 90 percent reliability? (Data are from www.rackspace.com.)

5.69 Fifty-six percent of American adults eat at a table-service restaurant at least once a week. Suppose that four American adults are asked if they ate at table-service restaurants last week. What is the probability that all of them say yes?

*5.70 The probability is 1 in 4,000,000 that a single auto trip in the United States will result in a fatality. Over a lifetime, an average U.S. driver takes 50,000 trips. (a) What is the probability of a fatal accident over a lifetime? Explain your reasoning carefully. *Hint:* Assume independent events. Why might the assumption of independence be violated? (b) Why might a driver be tempted not to use a seat belt "just on this trip"?

*5.71 If there are two riders on a city bus, what is the probability that no two have the same birthday? What if there are 10 riders? 20 riders? 50 riders? Hint: Use *LearningStats*.

*5.72 How many riders would there have to be on a bus to yield (a) a 50 percent probability that at least two will have the same birthday? (b) A 75 percent probability? Hint: Use *LearningStats*.

5.73 Four students divided the task of surveying the types of vehicles in parking lots of four different shopping malls. Each student examined 100 cars in each of three large suburban Detroit malls and one suburban Jamestown, New York, mall, resulting in the 5×4 contingency table shown below. (a) Calculate each probability (i–ix) and explain in words what it means. (b) Do you see evidence that vehicle type is not independent of mall location? Explain. (c) Do the row-total vehicle percentages correspond roughly to your experience in your own city and state? If not, discuss possible reasons for the difference. (Data are from an independent project by MBA students Steve Bennett, Alicia Morais, Steve Olson, and Greg Corda.) 🐝 **Malls**

i. $P(C)$ ii. $P(G)$ iii. $P(T)$
iv. $P(V \mid S)$ v. $P(C \mid J)$ vi. $P(J \mid C)$
vii. $P(C \text{ and } G)$ viii. $P(T \text{ and } O)$ ix. $P(M \text{ and } J)$

Number of Vehicles of Each Type in Four Shopping Malls

Vehicle Type	Somerset (S)	Oakland (O)	Great Lakes (G)	Jamestown, NY (J)	Row Total
Car (C)	44	49	36	64	193
Minivan (M)	21	15	18	13	67
Full-size van (F)	2	3	3	2	10
SUV (V)	19	27	26	12	84
Truck (T)	14	6	17	9	46
Column Total	100	100	100	100	400

5.74 Refer to the contingency table shown below. (a) Calculate each probability (i–vi) and explain in words what it means. (b) Do you see evidence that smoking and race are *not* independent? Explain. (c) Do the smoking rates shown here correspond to your experience? (d) Why might public health officials be interested in this type of data? (Data are from *Statistical Abstract of the United States, 2001*, pp. 12 and 16. Note: Actual statistics are applied to a hypothetical sample of 1,000.) 🐝 **Smoking2**

i. $P(S)$ ii. $P(W)$ iii. $P(S \mid W)$
iv. $P(S \mid B)$ v. $P(S \text{ and } W)$ vi. $P(N \text{ and } B)$

Smoking by Race for Males Aged 18–24

	Smoker (S)	Nonsmoker (N)	Row Total
White (W)	290	560	850
Black (B)	30	120	150
Column Total	320	680	1,000

5.75 Analysis of forecasters' interest rate predictions over the period 1982–1990 was intended to see whether the predictions corresponded to what actually happened. The 2×2 contingency table below shows the frequencies of actual and predicted interest rate movements. (a) Calculate each probability (i–vi) and explain in words what it means. (b*) Do you think that the forecasters' predictions were accurate? Explain. (Data are from R. A. Kolb and H. O. Steckler, "How Well Do Analysts Forecast Interest Rates?" *Journal of Forecasting* 15, no. 15 [1996], pp. 385–394.)

🐝 **Forecasts**

i. $P(F-)$ ii. $P(A+)$ iii. $P(A- \mid F-)$
iv. $P(A+ \mid F+)$ v. $P(A+ \text{ and } F+)$ vi. $P(A- \text{ and } F-)$

Interest Rate Forecast Accuracy

	Actual Change		
Forecast Change	Decline (A−)	Rise (A+)	Row Total
Decline (F−)	7	12	19
Rise (F+)	9	6	15
Column Total	16	18	34

5.76 High levels of cockpit noise in an aircraft can damage the hearing of pilots who are exposed to this hazard for many hours. Cockpit noise in a jet aircraft is mostly due to airflow at hundreds of miles per hour. This 3×3 contingency table shows 61 observations of data collected by an airline pilot using a handheld sound meter in a Boeing 727 cockpit. Noise level is defined as "low" (under 88 decibels), "medium" (88 to 91 decibels), or "high" (92 decibels or more). There are three flight phases (climb, cruise, descent). (a) Calculate each probability (i–ix) and explain in words what it means. (b) Do you see evidence that noise level depends on flight phase? Explain. (c) Where else might ambient noise be an ergonomic issue? (*Hint*: search the Web). (Data are from Capt. Robert E. Hartl, retired.) **Cockpit**

i. $P(B)$	ii. $P(L)$	iii. $P(H)$
iv. $P(H \mid C)$	v. $P(H \mid D)$	vi. $P(D \mid L)$
vii. $P(L \text{ and } B)$	viii. $P(L \text{ and } C)$	ix. $P(H \text{ and } C)$

Cockpit Noise

	Flight Phase			
Noise Level	Climb (B)	Cruise (C)	Descent (D)	Row Total
Low (L)	6	2	6	14
Medium (M)	18	3	8	29
High (H)	1	3	14	18
Column Total	25	8	28	61

5.77 In a study of childhood asthma, 4,317 observations were collected on education and smoking during pregnancy, shown in the 4×3 contingency table below. (a) Calculate each probability (i–ix) and explain in words what it means. (b) Create a table of relative frequencies. (c) Do you see evidence that smoking during pregnancy is related to education? Explain. (Data are from Michael Weitzman and Deborah Klein Walker, "Maternal Smoking and Asthma," *Pediatrics* 85, no. 4 [April 1990], p. 507.) **Smoking3**

i. $P(N)$	ii. $P(V)$	iii. $P(C)$
iv. $P(N \mid G)$	v. $P(N \mid H)$	vi. $P(N \mid C)$
vii. $P(N \text{ and } G)$	viii. $P(N \text{ and } C)$	ix. $P(V \text{ and } C)$

Mothers Smoking During Pregnancy

Education	No Smoking (N)	$< 1/2$ Pack (M)	$\geq 1/2$ Pack (V)	Row Total
<High school (G)	641	196	196	1,033
High school (H)	1,370	290	270	1,930
Some college (S)	635	68	53	756
College (C)	550	30	18	598
Column Total	3,196	584	537	4,317

5.78 Refer to the cross-tabulation of response frequencies for 159 business statistics students who answered questions about their political views and parent dominance on an anonymous survey. Find the following probabilities. (*Note:* The full 20-question survey of statistics students is in *LearningStats*.) **Politics**

a. $P(L)$	b. $P(C)$	c. $P(M)$
d. $P(F)$	e. $P(C \mid F)$	f. $P(C \mid M)$

Student Survey Responses

	Dominant Parent			
Political Views	Mother (M)	Neither (N)	Father (F)	Row Total
Liberal (L)	8	9	4	21
Middle (D)	32	44	29	105
Conservative (C)	11	7	15	33
Column Total	51	60	48	159

*5.79   A test for ovarian cancer has a 5 percent rate of false positives and a 0 percent rate of false negatives. On average, 1 in every 2,500 American women over age 35 actually has ovarian cancer. If a woman over 35 tests positive, what is the probability that she actually has cancer? Hint: Make a contingency table for a hypothetical sample of 1,000 women. Explain your reasoning. (Data are from *Scientific American* 287, no. 4 [October 2002], p. 12.)

*5.80   A biometric security device using fingerprints erroneously refuses to admit 1 in 1,000 authorized persons from a facility containing classified information. The device will erroneously admit 1 in 1,000,000 unauthorized persons. Assume that 95 percent of those who seek access are authorized. If the alarm goes off and a person is refused admission, what is the probability that the person was really authorized? (Data are from *High Technology,* February 1987, p. 54.)

*5.81   A study of university students revealed that 52 percent of left-handed students had suffered an accident requiring medical attention during the last 2 years, compared with 36 percent of right-handed students. At the university, 10 percent of all the students are left-handed. Given that a student has suffered an accident, what is the probability that the student is left-handed? Explain your reasoning clearly. (Data are from "Los Zurdos son más Propensos a Accidentarse, Según Estudio," *El Mundo,* 13 Julio 1990, p. 5.)

Related Reading

Albert, James H. "College Students' Conceptions of Probability." *The American Statistician* 57, no. 1 (February 2001), pp. 37–45.

LearningStats Unit 05   Probability

LS

LearningStats Unit 05 reviews set notation, introduces probability concepts, illustrates decision trees and Bayes's Theorem, and explains counting rules. Modules are designed for self-study, so you can proceed at your own pace, concentrate on material that is new, and pass quickly over things that you already know. Your instructor may assign specific modules, or you may decide to check them out because the topic sounds interesting. In addition to helping you learn about statistics, they may be useful as references later on.

Topic	*LearningStats Modules*
Events and probability	Probability Basics Empirical Probability
Contingency tables	Contingency Tables Cross-Tabulations Independent Events
Life tables and expected value	Mortality Rates Using Life Tables Survival Curves Retirement Planning
Independent events	Birthday Problem Four-Leaf Clover System Reliability Organ Transplants
Random processes	Law of Large Numbers Dice Rolls Pick a Card Random Names
Bayes's Theorem	Bayes's Theorem
Life insurance	Life Insurance Terminology

Key: = PowerPoint   = Word   = Excel

Visual Statistics

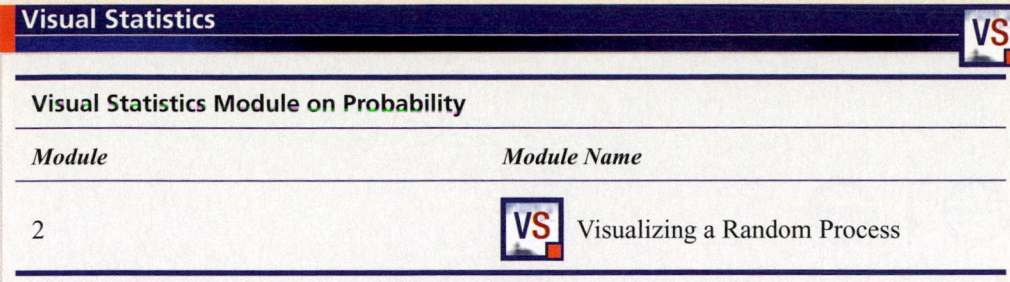

Visual Statistics Module on Probability

Module	Module Name
2	**VS** Visualizing a Random Process

Visual Statistics Module 2 is designed to help you

- Recognize that outcomes of a random process exhibit regularity even through the process is random.
- Learn through experimentation how the parameters affect the outcomes of an experiment.
- Learn how a histogram can summarize the results of an experiment.
- Visualize data-generating processes that give rise to common probability distributions.
- Understand how relative frequencies can be used to estimate the probability of an event.

The worktext chapter (included on the CD as a .PDF file) contains a list of concepts, objectives of the module, overview of concepts, illustration of concepts, orientation to module features, learning exercises (basic, intermediate, advanced), learning projects (individual, team), self-evaluation quiz, glossary of terms, and solutions to self-evaluation quiz.

Discrete Distributions

Chapter Learning Objectives

When you finish this chapter you should be able to

- Define a discrete random variable and a probability distribution.

- Solve problems by using the concepts of expected value and variance.

- Explain common discrete probability models and their parameters.

- Recognize the appropriate discrete model to use from the problem context.

- Find event probabilities for discrete models by using Excel, formulas, or tables.

This chapter shows how probability can be used to analyze *random processes* and to understand business processes. A random process is also called a **stochastic process** and is defined as a repeatable random experiment. Almost any business process can be thought of as a stochastic process. For example, consider cars being serviced in a quick oil change shop or calls arriving at the L.L. Bean order center. Think of each car or call as a random experiment. The variable of interest associated with the car might be service time. The variable of interest associated with the call might be amount of order.

We use **probability models** to depict the essential characteristics of a stochastic process, to guide decisions or make predictions. How many service technicians do we need from noon to 1 P.M. on Friday afternoon? To answer this we need to model the process of servicing cars during the lunch hour. Can L.L. Bean predict its total order amount from the next 50 callers? To answer this question L.L. Bean needs to model the process of call orders to its call center. Probability models must be reasonably realistic yet simple enough to be analyzed.

Many stochastic processes can be described by using common probability models whose properties are well known. To correctly use these probability models it is important that you understand their development. In the following sections we will explain how probability models are developed and describe several commonly used models.

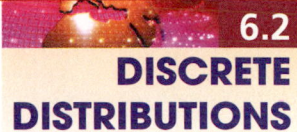

6.1
PROBABILITY MODELS

Random Variables

6.2
DISCRETE DISTRIBUTIONS

A **random variable** is a function or rule that assigns a numerical value to each outcome in the sample space of a random experiment. We use X when referring to a random variable in general, while specific values of X are shown in lowercase (e.g., x_1). The random variable often is a direct result of an observational experiment (e.g., counting the number of takeoffs in a given hour at O'Hare Airport). A **discrete random variable** has a countable number of distinct values. Some random variables have a clear upper limit (e.g., number of absences in a class of

40 students) while others do not (e.g., number of text messages you receive in a given hour). Here are some examples of decision problems involving discrete random variables.

Decision Problem	*Discrete Random Variable (Range)*
• Oxnard University has space in its MBA program for 65 new students. In the past, 75 percent of those who are admitted actually enroll. The decision is made to admit 80 students. What is the probability that more than 65 admitted students will actually enroll?	• $X =$ number of admitted MBA students who actually enroll ($X = 0, 1, 2, \ldots, 80$)
• On the late morning (9 to 12) work shift, L.L. Bean's order processing center staff can handle up to 5 orders per minute. The mean arrival rate is 3.5 orders per minute. What is the probability that more than 5 orders will arrive in a given minute?	• $X =$ number of phone calls that arrive in a given minute at the L.L. Bean order processing center ($X = 0, 1, 2, \ldots$)
• Rolled steel from a certain supplier averages 0.01 defects per linear meter. Toyota will reject a shipment of 500 linear meters if it has more than 10 defects. What is the probability that the order will be rejected?	• $X =$ number of defects in 500 meters of rolled steel ($X = 0, 1, 2, \ldots$)

Probability Distributions

A *discrete probability distribution* assigns a probability to each value of a discrete random variable X. Each probability is between 0 and 1, and all the probabilities must sum to 1. If there are n distinct values of X ($x_1, x_2, \ldots, x_n$):

(6.1) $0 \leq P(x_i) \leq 1$ (the probability for any given value of X)

(6.2) $\sum_{i=1}^{n} P(x_i) = 1$ (the sum over all values of X)

EXAMPLE

Coin Flips

ThreeCoins

When you flip a coin three times, the sample space has eight equally likely simple events: {HHH, HHT, HTH, THH, HTT, THT, TTH, TTT}. If X is the number of heads, then X is a random variable whose probability distribution is shown in Table 6.1 and Figure 6.1.

TABLE 6.1   Probability Distribution for Three Coin Flips

Possible Events	*x*	*P(x)*
TTT	0	1/8
HTT, THT, TTH	1	3/8
HHT, HTH, THH	2	3/8
HHH	3	1/8
Total		1

The values of X need not be equally likely. In this example, $X = 1$ and $X = 2$ are more likely than $X = 0$ or $X = 3$. However, the probabilities sum to 1, as in any probability distribution.

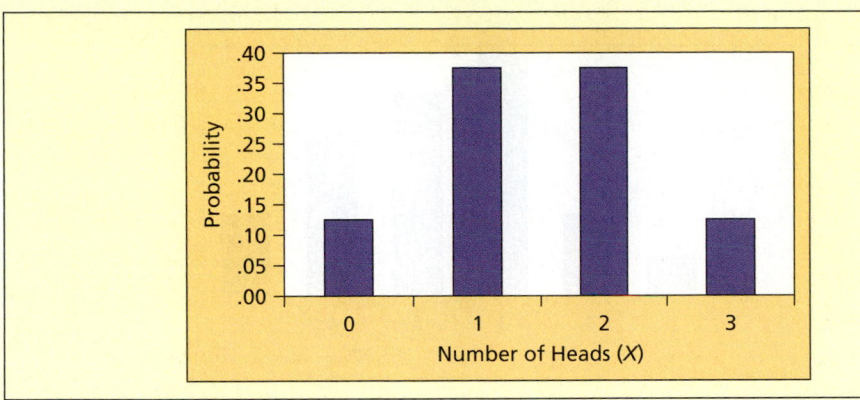

FIGURE 6.1

Probability distribution
for three coin flips

Expected Value

As shown in Figure 6.1, a discrete probability distribution is defined only at specific points on the X-axis. The **expected value** $E(X)$ of a discrete random variable is the sum of all X-values weighted by their respective probabilities.* It is a measure of *central tendency*. If there are n distinct values of X $(x_1, x_2, \ldots, x_n)$, the expected value is

$$E(X) = \mu = \sum_{i=1}^{n} x_i P(x_i) \tag{6.3}$$

The expected value is a weighted average. We usually call $E(X)$ the *mean* and use the symbol μ.

EXAMPLE

Service Calls

 **ServiceCalls**

The distribution of Sunday emergency service calls by Ace Appliance Repair is shown in Table 6.2. The probabilities sum to 1, as must be true for any probability distribution.

TABLE 6.2   **Probability Distribution of Service Calls**

x	P(x)	xP(x)
0	.05	0.00
1	.10	0.10
2	.30	0.60
3	.25	0.75
4	.20	0.80
5	.10	0.50
Total	1.00	2.75

The mode (most likely value of X) is 2, but the *expected* number of service calls $E(X)$ is 2.75, that is, $\mu = 2.75$. In other words, the "average" number of service calls is 2.75 on Sunday:

$$E(X) = \mu = \sum_{i=1}^{5} x_i P(x_i) = 0P(0) + 1P(1) + 2P(2) + 3P(3) + 4P(4) + 5P(5)$$

$$= 0(.05) + 1(.10) + 2(.30) + 3(.25) + 4(.20) + 5(.10) = 2.75$$

In Figure 6.2, we see that this particular probability distribution is not symmetric around the mean $\mu = 2.75$. However, the mean $\mu = 2.75$ is still the balancing point, or fulcrum.

---

*For a population of N data values, $P(x_i) = 1/N$ and the formula becomes the usual definition of a population mean. However, in this chapter we are not referring to data sets or samples.

FIGURE 6.2

Probability distribution for service calls

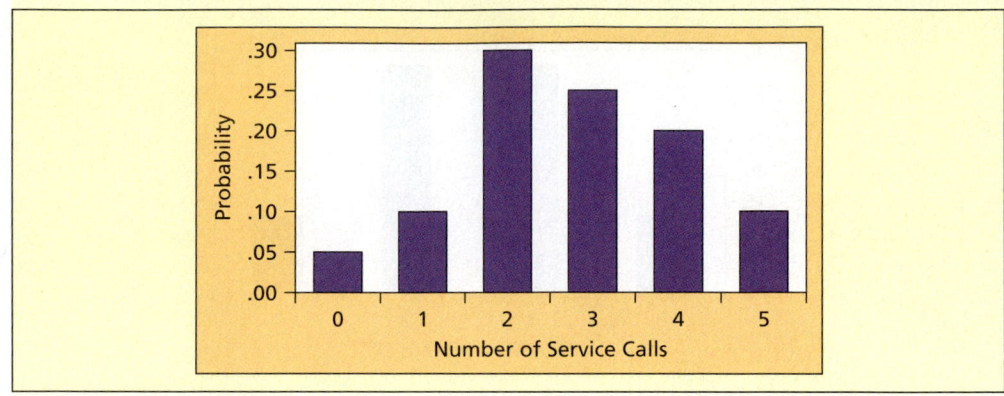

Note that $E(X)$ need not be an observable event. For example, you could have 2 service calls or 3 service calls, but not 2.75 service calls. This makes sense because $E(X)$ is an *average*. It is like saying that "the average American family has 2.1 children" (even though families come only in integer sizes) or "Barry Bonds's batting average is .275" (even though the number of hits by Bonds in a particular game must be an integer).

Application: Life Insurance

Expected value is the basis of life insurance, a purchase that almost everyone makes. For example, based on U.S. mortality statistics, the probability that a 30-year-old white female will die within the next year is .00059 (see *LearningStats* Unit 05) so the probability of living another year is $1 - .00059 = .99941$. What premium should a life insurance company charge to break even on a \$500,000 1-year term insurance policy (that is, to achieve zero expected payout)? This situation is shown in Table 6.3. Let X be the amount paid by the company to settle the policy. The expected payout is \$295, so the premium should be \$295 plus whatever return the company needs to cover its administrative overhead and profit.

TABLE 6.3

Expected Payout for a 1-Year Term Life Policy

Source: Centers for Disease Control and Prevention, *National Vital Statistics Reports* 47, no. 28 (1999).

Event	x	P(x)	xP(x)
Live	0	.99941	.00
Die	500,000	.00059	295.00
Total		1.00000	295.00

The mortality rate shown here is for *all* 30-year-old women. An insurance quote (e.g., from the Web) is likely to yield a lower premium, as long as you are a healthy, educated, nonsmoker in a nonrisky occupation. Insurance companies make money by knowing the actuarial probabilities and using them to set their premiums.

Application: Raffle Tickets

Expected value can be applied to raffles and lotteries. If it costs \$2 to buy a ticket in a raffle to win a new luxury automobile worth \$55,000 and 29,346 raffle tickets are sold, the expected value of a lottery ticket is

$$E(X) = (\text{value if you win})P(\text{win}) + (\text{value if you lose})P(\text{lose})$$

$$= (55{,}000)\left(\frac{1}{29{,}346}\right) + (0)\left(\frac{29{,}345}{29{,}346}\right)$$

$$= (55{,}000)(.000034076) + (0)(.999965924) = \$1.87$$

The raffle ticket is actually worth \$1.87. So why would you pay \$2.00 for it? Partly because you hope to beat the odds, but also because you know that your ticket purchase helps the charity. Since the idea of a raffle is to raise money, the sponsor tries to sell enough tickets to push the expected value of the ticket below its price (otherwise, the charity would lose money on the raffle). If the raffle prize is donated (or partially donated) by a well-wisher, the break-even point may be much less than the full value of the prize.

Actuarial Fairness

Like a lottery, an ***actuarially fair*** insurance program must collect as much in overall revenue as it pays out in claims. This is accomplished by setting the premiums to reflect empirical experience with the insured group. Individuals may gain or lose, but if the pool of insured persons is large enough, the total payout is predictable. Of course, many insurance policies have exclusionary clauses for war, natural disaster, and so on, to deal with cases where the events are not independent. Actuarial analysis is critical for corporate pension fund planning. Group health insurance is another major application.

Variance and Standard Deviation

The ***variance*** $V(X)$ of a discrete random variable is the sum of the squared deviations about its expected value, weighted by the probability of each X-value. If there are n distinct values of X, the variance is

$$V(X) = \sigma^2 = \sum_{i=1}^{n} [x_i - \mu]^2 P(x_i) \tag{6.4}$$

Just as the expected value $E(X)$ is a weighted average that measures *central tendency,* the variance $V(X)$ is a weighted average that measures *dispersion* about the mean. And just as we interchangeably use μ or $E(X)$ to denote the mean of a distribution, we use either σ^2 or $V(X)$ to denote its variance.

The *standard deviation* is the square root of the variance and is denoted σ:

$$\sigma = \sqrt{\sigma^2} = \sqrt{V(X)} \tag{6.5}$$

The Bay Street Inn is a seven-room bed-and-breakfast in the sunny California coastal city of Santa Theresa. Demand for rooms generally is strong during February, a prime month for tourists. However, experience shows that demand is quite variable. The probability distribution of room rentals during February is shown in Table 6.4 where $X =$ the number of rooms rented ($X = 0, 1, 2, 3, 4, 5, 6, 7$). The worksheet shows the calculation of $E(X)$ and $V(X)$.

EXAMPLE

Bed and Breakfast

RoomRent

TABLE 6.4   **Worksheet for $E(X)$ and $V(X)$ for February Room Rentals**

x	$P(x)$	$xP(x)$	$x - \mu$	$[x - \mu]^2$	$[x - \mu]^2 P(x)$
0	.05	0.00	−4.71	22.1841	1.109205
1	.05	0.05	−3.71	13.7641	0.688205
2	.06	0.12	−2.71	7.3441	0.440646
3	.10	0.30	−1.71	2.9241	0.292410
4	.13	0.52	−0.71	0.5041	0.065533
5	.20	1.00	+0.29	0.0841	0.016820
6	.15	0.90	+1.29	1.6641	0.249615
7	.26	1.82	+2.29	5.2441	1.363466
Total	1.00	$\mu = 4.71$			$\sigma^2 = 4.225900$

The formulas are:

$$E(X) = \mu = \sum_{i=1}^{7} x_i P(x_i) = 4.71$$

$$V(X) = \sigma^2 = \sum_{i=1}^{7} [x_i - \mu]^2 P(x_i) = 4.2259$$

$$\sigma = \sqrt{4.2259} = 2.0557$$

FIGURE 6.3

Probability distribution of
room rentals

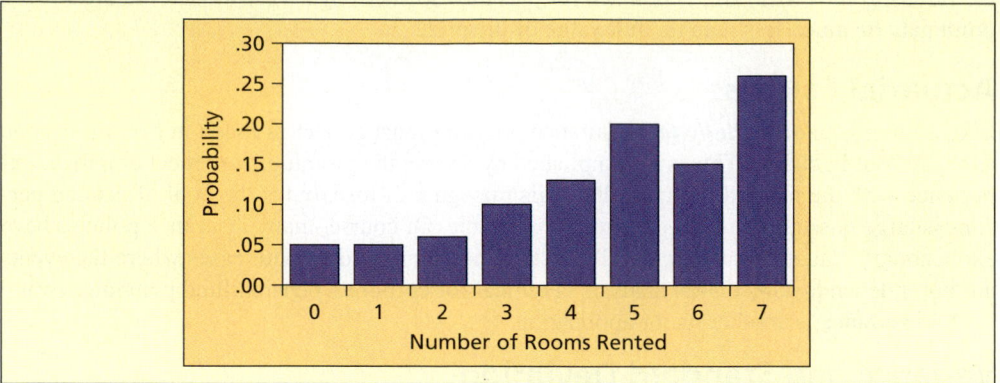

This distribution is skewed to the left and bimodal. The mode (most likely value) is 7 rooms
rented, but the average is only 4.71 room rentals in February. The standard deviation of 2.06
indicates that there is considerable variation around the mean, as seen in Figure 6.3.

What Is a PDF or CDF?

The rest of this chapter explains several well-known discrete distributions and their practical
applications. A known distribution can be described either by its ***probability distribution
function*** (PDF) or by its ***cumulative distribution function*** (CDF). The PDF shows the probability of each X-value, while the CDF shows the cumulative sum of probabilities, adding from the
smallest to the largest X-value, approaching 1. Figure 6.4 illustrates a discrete PDF, while
Figure 6.5 shows its corresponding CDF. The PDF or CDF are *mathematical functions* (not to be

FIGURE 6.4

Illustrative PDF

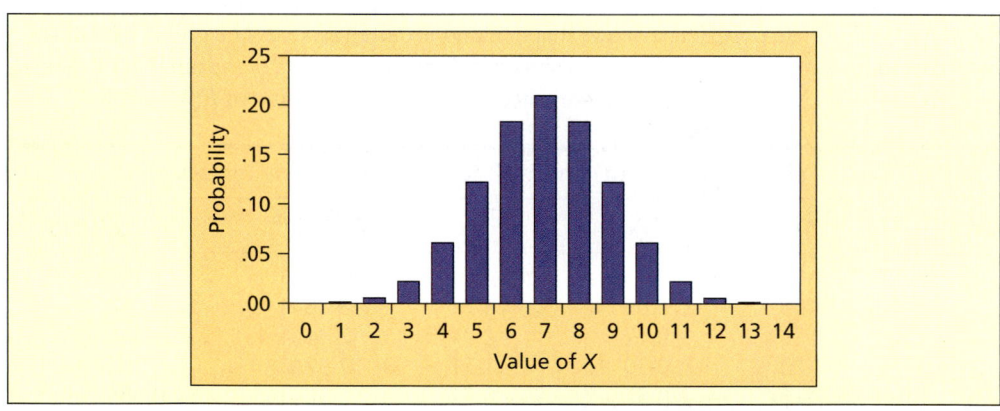

FIGURE 6.5

Illustrative CDF

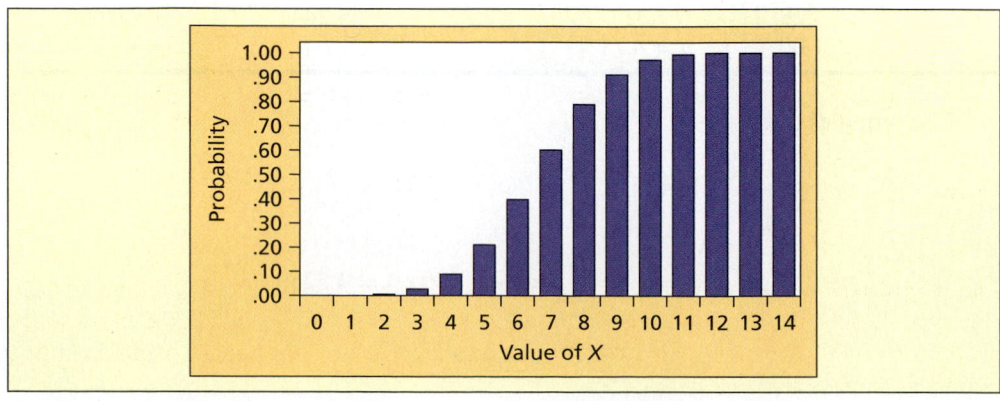

confused with a histogram, which describes a data set). The equations for the PDF and CDF and its characteristics (such as the mean and variance) depend on the *parameter(s)* of the distribution. The parameters, in turn, depend on the situation being described.

SECTION EXERCISES

6.1 Which of the following could *not* be probability distributions? Explain.

Example A		Example B		Example C	
x	P(x)	x	P(x)	x	P(x)
0	.80	1	.05	50	.30
1	.20	2	.15	60	.60
		3	.25	70	.40
		4	.40		
		5	.10		

6.2 (a) Calculate the expected value and standard deviation of this random variable *X* by using the PDF shown. (b) Describe the shape of this distribution.

x	60	70	80	90	Total
P(x)	.40	.30	.20	.10	1.00

6.3 On the midnight shift, the number of patients with head trauma in an emergency room has the probability distribution shown below. (a) Calculate the mean and standard deviation. (b) Describe the shape of this distribution.

x	0	1	2	3	4	5	Total
P(x)	.05	.30	.25	.20	.15	.05	1.00

6.4 Pepsi and Mountain Dew products sponsored a contest giving away a Lamborghini sports car worth $215,000. The probability of winning from a single bottle purchase was .00000884. Find the expected value. Show your calculations clearly. (Data are from J. Paul Peter and Jerry C. Olson, *Consumer Behavior and Marketing Strategy*, 7th ed. [McGraw-Hill/Irwin, 2005], p. 226.)

6.5 Student Life Insurance Company wants to offer a $1,000 student personal property plan for dorm students to cover theft of certain items. Past experience suggests that the probability of a total loss claim is .01. What premium should be charged if the company wants to make a profit of $25 per policy (assume total loss with no deductible)? Show your calculations clearly.

6.6 A lottery ticket costs $1 and the prize is $28,000,000. The probability of winning is .000000023. Find the expected value of a ticket, arranging your calculations clearly.

6.7 Oxnard Petro Ltd. is buying hurricane insurance for its off-coast oil drilling platform. During the next 5 years, the probability of total loss of only the above-water superstructure ($250 million) is .30, the probability of total loss of the facility ($950 million) is .30, and the probability of no loss is .40. Find the expected loss.

Characteristics of the Uniform Distribution

6.3

UNIFORM DISTRIBUTION

The **uniform distribution** is one of the simplest discrete models. It describes a random variable with a finite number of integer values from *a* to *b*. That is, the entire distribution depends only on the two parameters *a* and *b*. Each value is equally likely. Table 6.5 summarizes the characteristics of the uniform discrete distribution.

TABLE 6.5

Uniform Discrete Distribution

Parameters	a = lower limit b = upper limit
PDF	$P(x) = \dfrac{1}{b - a + 1}$
Range	$a \leq X \leq b$ (for integer x only)
Mean	$\dfrac{a + b}{2}$
Standard deviation	$\sqrt{\dfrac{[(b - a) + 1]^2 - 1}{12}}$
Random data generation in Excel	=a+INT((b-a+1)*RAND( ))
Comments	Used mainly as a benchmark, to generate random integers, or to create other distributions.

EXAMPLE

Rolling a Die

DieRoll

When you roll one die, the number of dots forms a uniform discrete random variable with six equally likely integer values 1, 2, 3, 4, 5, 6, shown in Figure 6.6. The CDF is shown in Figure 6.7.

FIGURE 6.6

PDF for one die

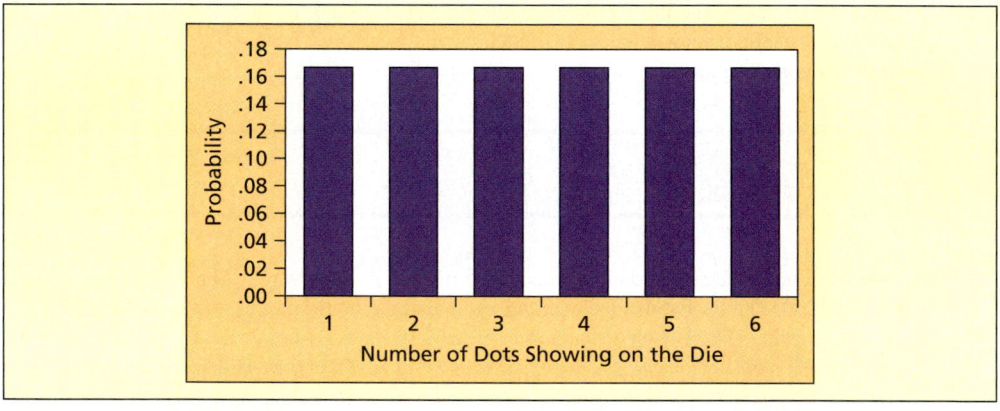

FIGURE 6.7

CDF for one die

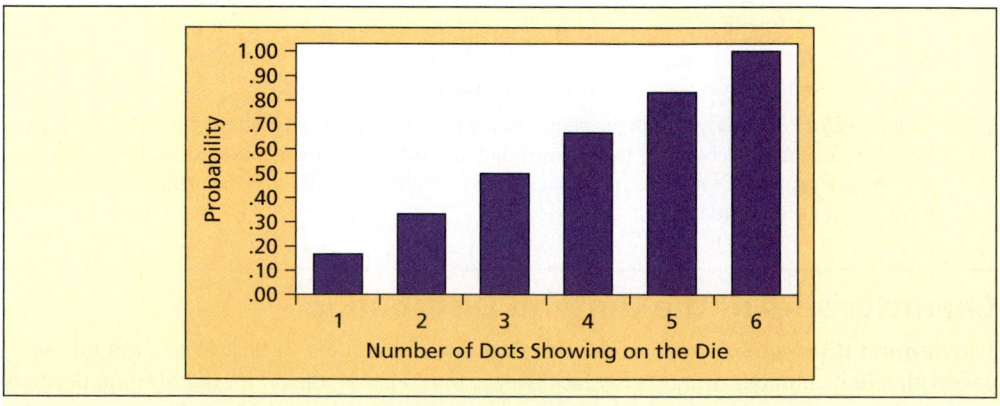

For this example, the mean and standard deviation are:

$$\text{PDF} = P(x) = \frac{1}{b - a + 1} = \frac{1}{6 - 1 + 1} = \frac{1}{6} \quad \text{for } x = 1, 2, \ldots, 6$$

$$\text{Mean} = \frac{a + b}{2} = \frac{1 + 6}{2} = 3.5$$

$$\text{Std. Dev.} = \sqrt{\frac{[(b - a) + 1]^2 - 1}{12}} = \sqrt{\frac{[(6 - 1) + 1]^2 - 1}{12}} = 1.708$$

You can see that the mean (3.5) must be halfway between 1 and 6, but there is no way you could anticipate the standard deviation without using a formula. Try rolling a die many times, or use Excel to simulate the rolling of a die by generating random integers from 1 through 6. Compare the mean and standard deviation from your random experiment to the values we calculated above.

Application: Pumping Gas **Petrol**

The last two digits (pennies) showing on a fill-up will be a uniform random integer (assuming you don't "top off" but just let the pump stop automatically) ranging from $a = 00$ to $b = 99$. Figure 6.8 shows the PDF for this uniform distribution. You could verify the predicted mean and standard deviation shown here by looking at a large sample of fill-ups on your own car:

$$\text{PDF} = P(x) = \frac{1}{b - a + 1} = \frac{1}{99 - 0 + 1} = \frac{1}{100} = .010 \quad \text{for all } x$$

$$\text{Mean} = \frac{a + b}{2} = \frac{0 + 99}{2} = 49.5$$

$$\text{Std. Dev.} = \sqrt{\frac{[(b - a) + 1]^2 - 1}{12}} = \sqrt{\frac{[(99 - 0) + 1]^2 - 1}{12}} = 28.87$$

FIGURE 6.8

Uniform PDF and CDF with $a = 00$ and $b = 99$

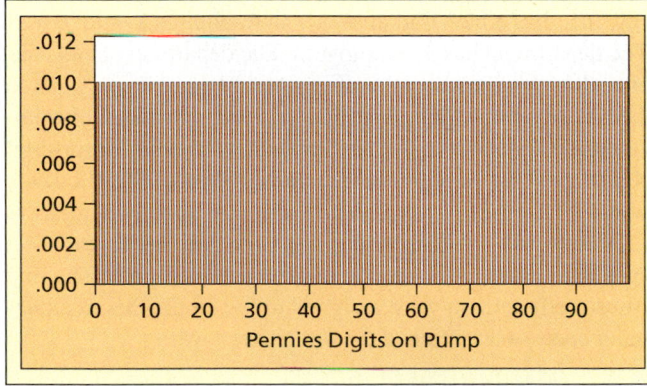

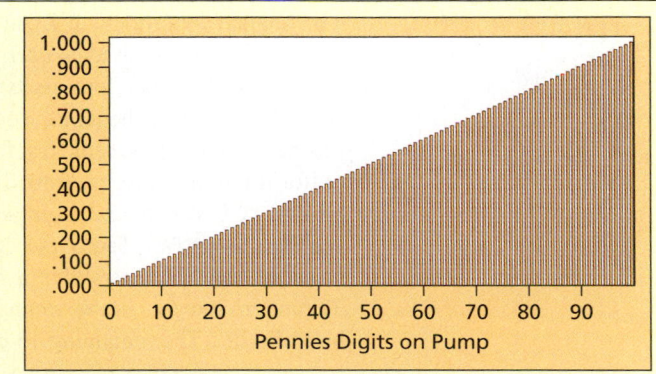

Mini Case   6.1

The "Daily 3" Lottery

Many states have a "daily 3" lottery. The daily 3 is a uniformly distributed discrete random variable whose values range from 000 through 999. There are 1,000 equally likely outcomes, so the probability of any given three-digit number is 1/1,000. The theoretical characteristics of this lottery are:

$$P(x) = \frac{1}{b - a + 1} = \frac{1}{999 - 0 + 1} = \frac{1}{1,000} = .001$$

$$\mu = \frac{a + b}{2} = \frac{0 + 999}{2} = 499.5$$

$$\sigma = \sqrt{\frac{(b - a + 1)^2 - 1}{12}} = \sqrt{\frac{(999 - 0 + 1)^2 - 1}{12}} = 288.67$$

In a large sample of three-digit lottery numbers, you would expect the sample mean and standard deviation to be very close to 499.5 and 288.67, respectively. For example, in Michigan's daily three-digit lottery, from January 1, 1999, through October 5, 2002, there were 1,180 evening drawings. The mean of all the three-digit numbers drawn over that period was 502.1 with a standard deviation of 287.6. These sample results are extremely close to what would be expected. It is the nature of random samples to vary, so no sample is expected to yield statistics identical with the population parameters.

In Michigan, randomization is achieved by drawing a numbered ping-pong ball from each of three bins. Within each bin, the balls are agitated using air flow. Each bin contains 10 ping-pong balls. Each ball has a single digit (0, 1, 2, 3, 4, 5, 6, 7, 8, 9). The drawing is televised, so there is no possibility of bias or manipulation. Lotteries are studied frequently to make sure that they are truly random, using statistical comparisons like these, as well as tests for overall shape and patterns over time.

Uniform Random Integers

To generate random integers from a discrete uniform distribution we can use the Excel function =a+INT((b-a+1)*RAND( )). For example, to generate a random integer from 5 through 10, the Excel function would be =5+INT((10-5+1)*RAND( )). To create random integers 1 through N, set $a = 1$ and $b = N$ and use the Excel function =1+INT(N*RAND( )). The same integer may come up more than once, so to obtain n distinct random integers you would have to generate a few extras and then eliminate the duplicates. This method is useful in accounting and auditing (e.g., to allow the auditor to choose numbered invoices at random).*

Application: Copier Codes

The finance department at Zymurgy, Inc., has a new digital copier that requires a unique user ID code for each individual user. The department has 37 employees. The department head considered using the last four digits of each employee's social security number, but it was pointed out to her that it is illegal to use the SSN for individual identification (and more than one employee could have the same last four digits). Instead, the department generated unique four-digit uniform random integers from 1000 to 9999 by copying the function =1000+INT(9000*RAND( )) into 50 cells on an Excel spreadsheet. The 50 cells were copied and pasted to two adjacent columns using Paste Special (so the value would not keep changing every time the spreadsheet was updated). The first column was sorted to check for duplicates (none was found). The first 37 random integers in the second (unsorted) column were assigned to the employees in alphabetical order. The remaining 13 copier codes were retained for future employees.

---

*Excel's function =RANDBETWEEN(a,b) is even easier to use, but it is not available unless the Analysis ToolPak Add-In is installed. If not, go to Tools > Add-In and check the box for Analysis ToolPak.

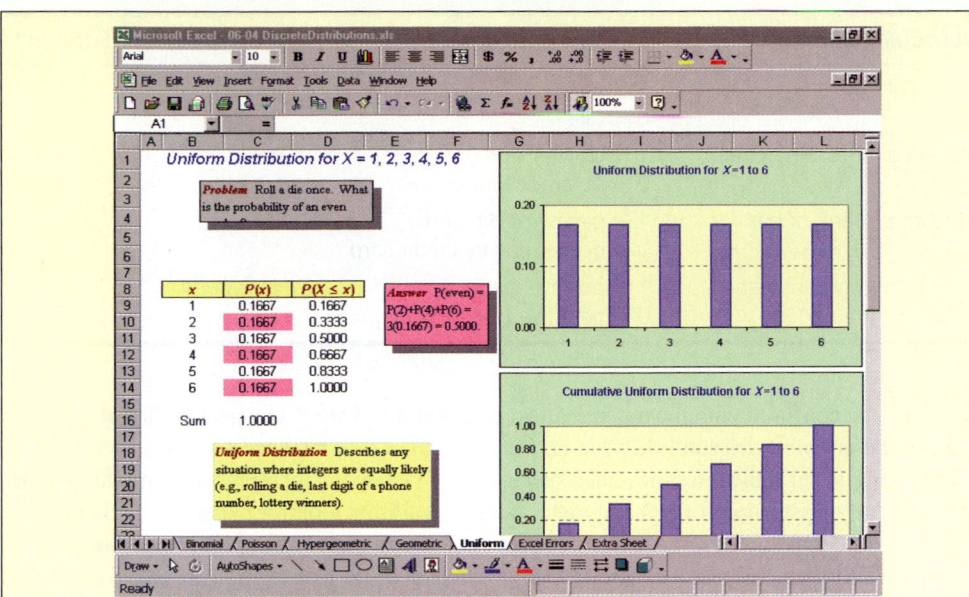

FIGURE 6.9

LearningStats uniform display

Uniform Model in *LearningStats*

Figure 6.9 shows the *uniform distribution* for one die from *LearningStats*. The distribution is visually apparent. The uniform distribution is so simple that you really don't need a spreadsheet. *LearningStats* also has demonstrations of uniform random number generation.

SECTION EXERCISES

6.8 Find the mean and standard deviation of four-digit uniformly distributed lottery numbers (0000 through 9999).

6.9 The ages of Java programmers at SynFlex Corp. range from 20 to 60. (a) If their ages are uniformly distributed, what would be the mean and standard deviation? (b) What is the probability that a randomly selected programmer's age is at least 40? At least 30? *Hint:* Treat employee ages as integers.

6.10 An auditor for a medical insurance company selects a random sample of prescription drug claims for evaluation of correct payment by company experts. The claims were selected at random from a database of 500,000 claims by using uniform random numbers between 1 and 500,000. To verify that the random numbers really were from a uniform distribution, the auditor calculated the mean and standard deviation of the random numbers. What should the mean and standard deviation be if these were uniformly distributed random integers?

6.11 (a) If the birthdays of students born in January are uniformly distributed, what would be their expected mean and standard deviation? (b) Do you think that birthdays in January really are uniformly distributed?

6.12 Use Excel to generate 100 random integers from (a) 1 through 2, inclusive; (b) 1 through 5, inclusive; and (c) 0 through 99, inclusive. (d) In each case, write the Excel formula. (e) In each case, calculate the mean and standard deviation of the sample of 100 integers you generated, and compare them with their theoretical values.

Bernoulli Experiments

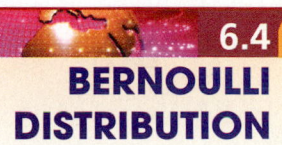

6.4
BERNOULLI DISTRIBUTION

A random experiment that has only two outcomes is called a ***Bernoulli experiment,*** named after Jakob Bernoulli (1654–1705). We arbitrarily call one outcome a "success" (denoted $X = 1$) and the other a "failure" (denoted $X = 0$). The probability of success is denoted π (the Greek letter

TABLE 6.6

Examples of Bernoulli Experiments

Bernoulli Experiment	Possible Outcomes	Probability of "Success"
Flip a coin	1 = heads 0 = tails	$\pi = .50$
Inspect a jet turbine blade	1 = crack found 0 = no crack found	$\pi = .001$
Purchase a tank of gas	1 = pay by credit card 0 = do not pay by credit card	$\pi = .78$
Do a mammogram test	1 = positive test 0 = negative test	$\pi = .0004$

"pi", *not* to be confused with the mathematical constant 3.14159).* The probability of failure is $1 - \pi$, so the probabilities sum to 1, that is, $P(0) + P(1) = (1 - \pi) + \pi = 1$.

The examples in Table 6.6 show that a success ($X = 1$) may in fact represent something undesirable. Metallurgists look for signs of metal fatigue. Auditors look for expense voucher errors. Bank loan officers look for loan defaults. A success, then, is merely an event of interest.

The probability of success π can be any value between 0 and 1. In flipping a coin, π is .50. But in other applications π could be close to 1 (e.g., the probability that a customer's Visa purchase will be approved) or close to 0 (e.g., the probability that an adult male is HIV positive). Table 6.6 is only intended to suggest the possibilities. The definitions of success and failure are arbitrary and can be switched, although for convenience we usually define success as the less likely outcome so that π is less than .5. A Bernoulli experiment has mean π and variance $\pi(1 - \pi)$ as we see from the definitions of $E(X)$ and $V(X)$:

$$(6.6) \quad E(X) = \sum_{i=1}^{2} x_i P(x_i) = (0)(1 - \pi) + (1)(\pi) = \pi \qquad \text{(Bernoulli mean)}$$

$$V(X) = \sum_{i=1}^{2} [x_i - E(X)]^2 P(x_i)$$

$$(6.7) \qquad = (0 - \pi)^2 (1 - \pi) + (1 - \pi)^2 (\pi) = \pi(1 - \pi) \qquad \text{(Bernoulli variance)}$$

We are not interested in any other properties of the Bernoulli distribution, but its mean and variance are useful in developing the next model.

SECTION EXERCISES

6.13 Define a Bernoulli variable for (a) guessing on a true-false exam question; (b) checking to see whether an ER patient has health insurance; (c) dialing a talkative friend's cell phone; (d) going on a 10-day diet.

6.14 (a) In the previous exercise, suggest the approximate probability of success in each scenario. (b) Is success a desirable or undesirable thing in each of these scenarios?

6.5
BINOMIAL DISTRIBUTION

Chapter 4

Characteristics of the Binomial Distribution

Bernoulli experiments lead to an important and more interesting model. The **binomial distribution** arises when a Bernoulli experiment is repeated n times. Each Bernoulli trial is independent so that the probability of success π remains constant on each trial. In a binomial experiment, we are interested in $X = $ the number of successes in n trials, so the binomial random variable X is the sum of n independent Bernoulli random variables:

$$X = x_1 + x_2 + \cdots + x_n$$

---

*Some textbooks denote the probability of success p. However, in this textbook, we prefer to use Greek letters for population parameters. Later, p will be used to denote a sample estimate of π.

Parameters	n = number of trials π = probability of success	**TABLE 6.7** **Binomial Distribution**
PDF	$P(x) = \dfrac{n!}{x!(n-x)!}\pi^x(1-\pi)^{n-x}$	
Excel function	=BINOMDIST(x, n, π, 0)	
Range	$X = 0, 1, 2, \ldots, n$	
Mean	$n\pi$	
Standard deviation	$\sqrt{n\pi(1-\pi)}$	
Random data generation in Excel	Sum n values of =1+INT(2*RAND( )) or use Excel's **Tools > Data Analysis**	
Comments	Skewed right if $\pi < .50$, skewed left if $\pi > .50$, and symmetric if $\pi = .50$.	

We can add the n identical Bernoulli means $(\pi + \pi + \cdots + \pi)$ to get the binomial mean $n\pi$. Since the n Bernoulli events are independent, we can add* the n identical Bernoulli variances $\pi(1-\pi) + \pi(1-\pi) + \cdots + \pi(1-\pi)$ to obtain the binomial variance $n\pi(1-\pi)$ and hence its standard deviation $\sqrt{n\pi(1-\pi)}$. The range of the binomial is $X = 0, 1, 2, \ldots, n$. The binomial probability of a particular number of successes $P(x)$ is determined by the two parameters n and π. The characteristics of the binomial distribution are summarized in Table 6.7.

EXAMPLE

Servicing Cars at a Quick Oil Change Shop

Consider a shop that specializes in quick oil changes. It is important to this type of business to ensure that a car's service time is not considered "late" by the customer. Therefore, to study this process, we can define service times as being either *late* or *not late* and define the random variable X to be the number of cars that are late out of the total number of cars serviced. We further assume that cars are independent of each other and the chance of a car being late stays the same for each car. Based on our knowledge of the process we know that P(car is late) $= \pi = .10$.

Now, think of each car as a Bernoulli experiment and let's apply the binomial distribution. Suppose we would like to know the probability that exactly 2 of the next 12 cars serviced are late. In this case, $n = 12$, and we want to know $P(X = 2)$:

$$P(X = 2) = \frac{12!}{2!(12-2)!}(.10)^2(1-.10)^{12-2} = .2301$$

Alternatively, we could calculate this by using the Excel function =BINOMDIST(2,12,.1,0). The fourth parameter, 0, means that we want Excel to calculate $P(X = 2)$ rather than $P(X \leq 2)$.

Binomial Shape

A binomial distribution is skewed right if $\pi < .50$, skewed left if $\pi > .50$, and symmetric only if $\pi = .50$. However, skewness decreases as n increases, regardless of the value of π, as illustrated in Figure 6.10. Notice that $\pi = .20$ and $\pi = .80$ have the same shape, except reversed from left to right. This is true for any values of π and $1 - \pi$.

Binomial Shape

$\pi < .50$	skewed right
$\pi = .50$	symmetric
$\pi > .50$	skewed left

*The last section in this chapter (optional) explains the rules for transforming and summing random variables.

FIGURE 6.10

Binomial distributions

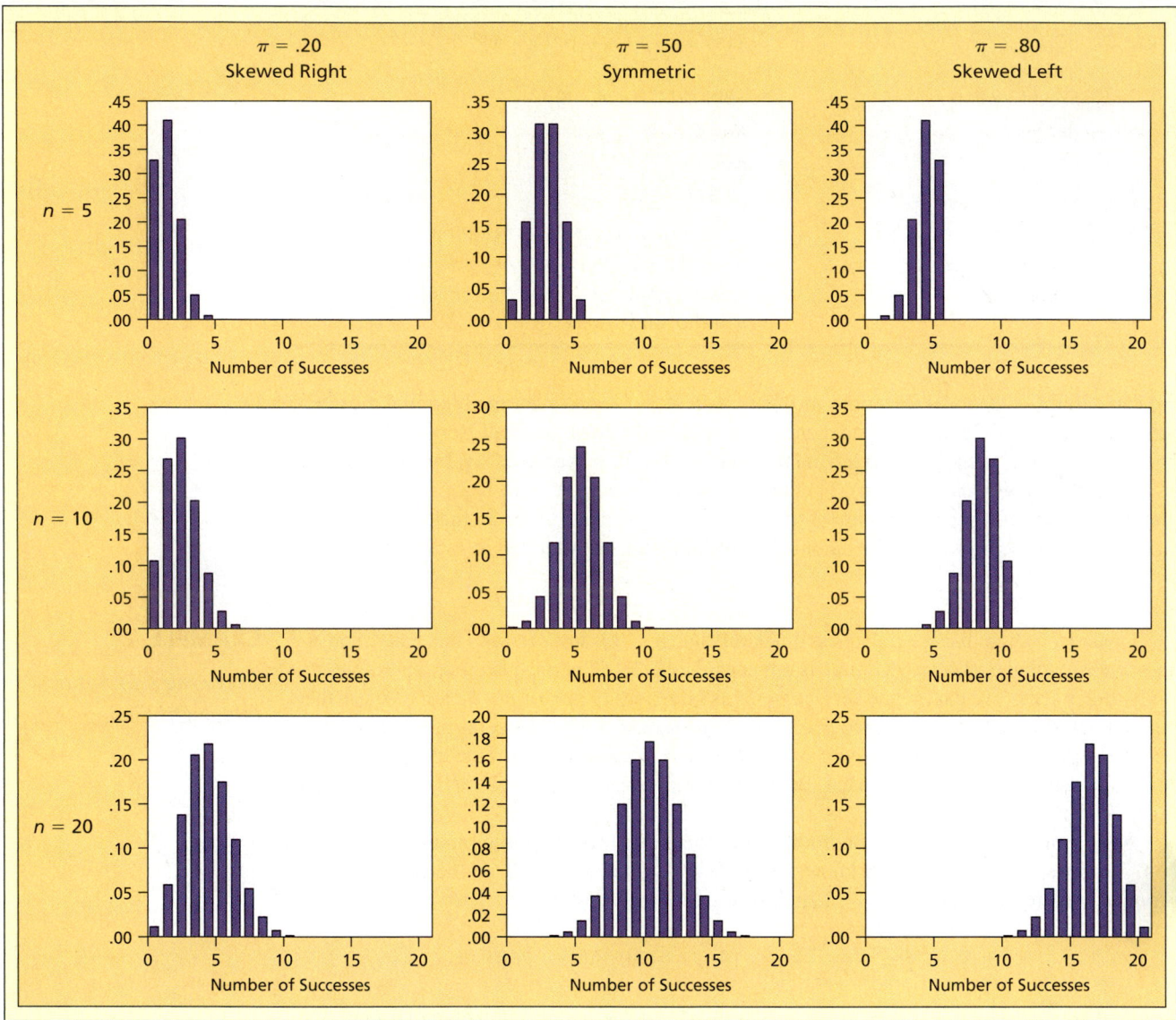

Application: Uninsured Patients   Uninsured

On average, 20 percent of the emergency room patients at Greenwood General Hospital lack health insurance. In a random sample of four patients, what is the probability that two will be uninsured? Define X = number of uninsured patients and set $\pi = .20$ (i.e., a 20 percent chance that a given patient will be uninsured) and $1 - \pi = .80$ (i.e., an 80 percent chance that a patient will be insured). The range is $X = 0, 1, 2, 3, 4$ patients. Applying the binomial formulas, the mean and standard deviation are:

$$\text{Mean} = \mu = n\pi = (4)(.20) = 0.8 \text{ patients}$$

$$\text{Standard deviation} = \sigma = \sqrt{n\pi(1 - \pi)} = \sqrt{(4)(.20)(1 - .20)} = 0.8 \text{ patients}$$

Using the Binomial Formula

The PDF and CDF are shown in Table 6.8. We can calculate these probabilities by using Excel's binomial formula =BINOMDIST(x, n, π, cumulative) where cumulative is 0 (if you want a PDF)

X	PDF	CDF
0	.4096	.4096
1	.4096	.8192
2	.1536	.9728
3	.0256	.9984
4	.0016	1.0000

TABLE 6.8

Binomial Distribution for $n = 4, \pi = .20$

or 1 (if you want a CDF). We can also use a calculator to work it out from the mathematical formula with $n = 4$ and $\pi = .20$. For example:

PDF Formula   *Excel Function*

$$P(0) = \frac{4!}{0!(4-0)!}(.20)^0(1-.20)^{4-0} = 1 \times .20^0 \times .80^4 = .4096 \qquad \text{=BINOMDIST(0,4,.20,0)}$$

$$P(1) = \frac{4!}{1!(4-1)!}(.20)^1(1-.20)^{4-1} = 4 \times .20^1 \times .80^3 = .4096 \qquad \text{=BINOMDIST(1,4,.20,0)}$$

$$P(2) = \frac{4!}{2!(4-2)!}(.20)^2(1-.20)^{4-2} = 6 \times .20^2 \times .80^2 = .1536 \qquad \text{=BINOMDIST(2,4,.20,0)}$$

$$P(3) = \frac{4!}{3!(4-3)!}(.20)^3(1-.20)^{4-3} = 4 \times .20^3 \times .80^1 = .0256 \qquad \text{=BINOMDIST(3,4,.20,0)}$$

$$P(4) = \frac{4!}{4!(4-4)!}(.20)^4(1-.20)^{4-4} = 1 \times .20^4 \times .80^0 = .0016 \qquad \text{=BINOMDIST(4,4,.20,0)}$$

As for any discrete probability distribution, the probabilities sum to unity. That is, $P(0) + P(1) + P(2) + P(3) + P(4) = .4096 + .4096 + .1536 + .0256 + .0016 = 1.0000$. Figure 6.11 shows the PDF. Since $\pi < .50$, the distribution is right-skewed. The mean $\mu = n\pi = 0.8$ would be the balancing point or fulcrum of the PDF. Figure 6.12 shows the corresponding CDF.

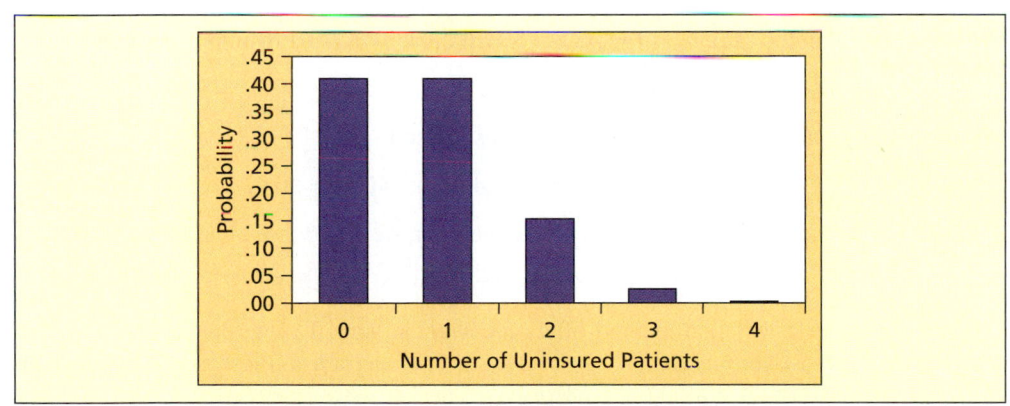

FIGURE 6.11

Binomial PDF for $n = 4$, $\pi = .20$

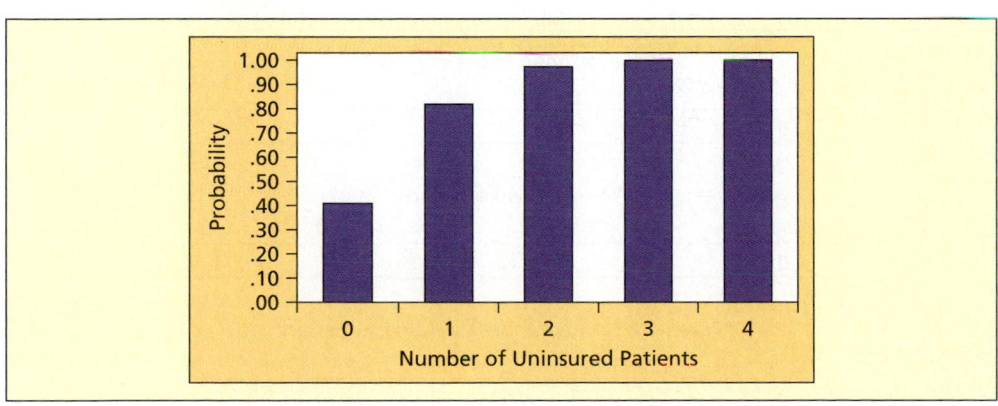

FIGURE 6.12

Binomial CDF for $n = 4$, $\pi = .20$

Using Tables: Appendix A

The binomial formula is cumbersome, even for small n, so we prefer to use a computer program (Excel, MINITAB, MegaStat, Visual Statistics, or *LearningStats*) or a calculator with a built-in binomial function. When you have no access to a computer (e.g., taking an exam) you can use Appendix A to look up binomial probabilities for selected values of n and π. An abbreviated portion of Appendix A is shown in Figure 6.13. The probabilities for $n = 4$ and $\pi = .20$ are highlighted. Probabilities that round to less than .0001 are suppressed.

FIGURE 6.13

Binomial probabilities from Appendix A

								π										
n	X	.01	.02	.05	.10	.15	.20	.30	.40	.50	.60	.70	.80	.85	.90	.95	.98	.99
2	0	.9801	.9604	.9025	.8100	.7225	.6400	.4900	.3600	.2500	.1600	.0900	.0400	.0225	.0100	.0025	.0004	.0001
	1	.0198	.0392	.0950	.1800	.2550	.3200	.4200	.4800	.5000	.4800	.4200	.3200	.2550	.1800	.0950	.0392	.0198
	2	.0001	.0004	.0025	.0100	.0225	.0400	.0900	.1600	.2500	.3600	.4900	.6400	.7225	.8100	.9025	.9604	.9801
3	0	.9703	.9412	.8574	.7290	.6141	.5120	.3430	.2160	.1250	.0640	.0270	.0080	.0034	.0010	.0001	—	—
	1	.0294	.0576	.1354	.2430	.3251	.3840	.4410	.4320	.3750	.2880	.1890	.0960	.0574	.0270	.0071	.0012	.0003
	2	.0003	.0012	.0071	.0270	.0574	.0960	.1890	.2880	.3750	.4320	.4410	.3840	.3251	.2430	.1354	.0576	.0294
	3	—	—	.0001	.0010	.0034	.0080	.0270	.0640	.1250	.2160	.3430	.5120	.6141	.7290	.8574	.9412	.9703
4	0	.9606	.9224	.8145	.6561	.5220	.4096	.2401	.1296	.0625	.0256	.0081	.0016	.0005	.0001	—	—	—
	1	.0388	.0753	.1715	.2916	.3685	.4096	.4116	.3456	.2500	.1536	.0756	.0256	.0115	.0036	.0005	—	—
	2	.0006	.0023	.0135	.0486	.0975	.1536	.2646	.3456	.3750	.3456	.2646	.1536	.0975	.0486	.0135	.0023	.0006
	3	—	—	.0005	.0036	.0115	.0256	.0756	.1536	.2500	.3456	.4116	.4096	.3685	.2916	.1715	.0753	.0388
	4	—	—	—	.0001	.0005	.0016	.0081	.0256	.0625	.1296	.2401	.4096	.5220	.6561	.8145	.9224	.9606

Compound Events

We can add the individual probabilities to obtain any desired event probability. For example, the probability that the sample of four patients will contain *at least* two uninsured patients is

$$P(X \geq 2) = P(2) + P(3) + P(4) = .1536 + .0256 + .0016 = .1808$$

The probability that *fewer than 2* patients have insurance is

$$P(X < 2) = P(0) + P(1) = .4096 + .4096 = .8192$$

Since $P(X \geq 2)$ and $P(X < 2)$ are complementary events, we could also obtain $P(X < 2)$:

$$P(X < 2) = 1 - P(X \geq 2) = 1 - .1808 = .8192$$

Choose whichever calculation method offers the shortest sum. To interpret phrases such as "more than," "at most," or "at least," it is helpful to sketch a diagram, as illustrated in Figure 6.14.

FIGURE 6.14

Diagrams to illustrate events

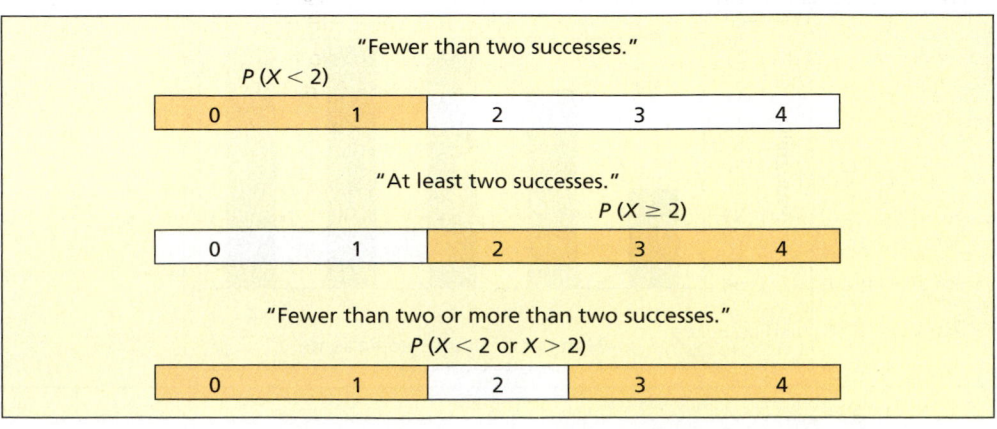

FIGURE 6.15

Excel's binomial function

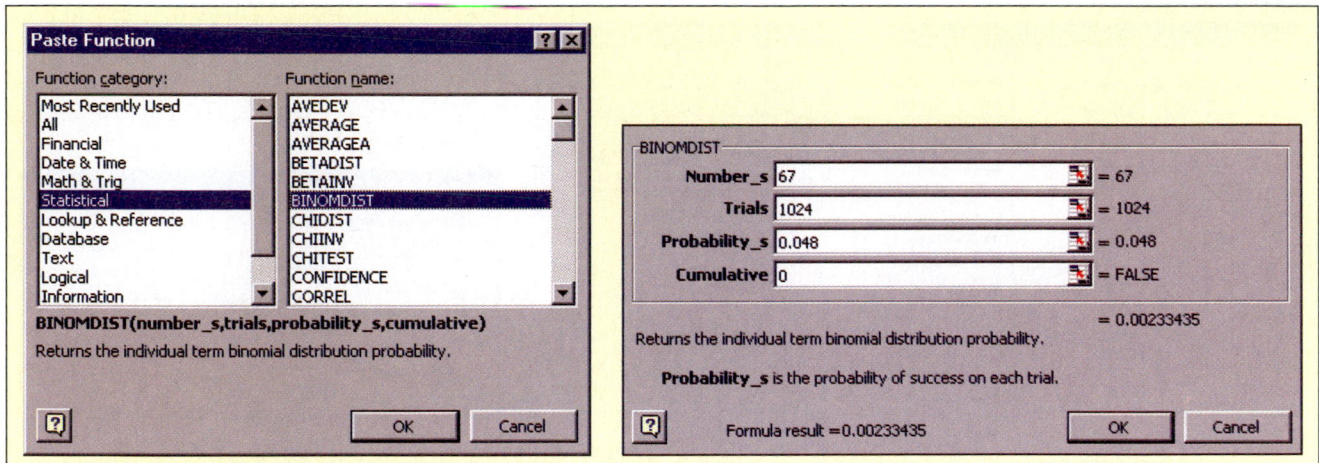

Binomial Probabilities: Excel

Figure 6.15 shows Excel's Insert > Function menu to calculate the probability of $x = 67$ successes in $n = 1,024$ trials with success probability $\pi = .048$. Alternatively, you could just enter the formula =BINOMDIST(67,1024,0.048,0) in the spreadsheet cell.

Binomial Probabilities: MegaStat

MegaStat will compute an entire binomial PDF (not just a single point probability) for any n and π that you specify, as illustrated in Figure 6.16 for $n = 10$, $\pi = .50$. Optionally, you can see a graph of the PDF. This is even easier than entering your own Excel functions.

Binomial Probabilities: Visual Statistics

Figure 6.17 shows a binomial distribution for $n = 10$, $\pi = .50$ from *Visual Statistics* **Module 4.** Numerical probabilities are shown in a table in the lower left (both PDF and CDF). The graph can be copied and pasted as a bitmap, and the tab-delimited table probabilities can be copied and pasted into Excel. An attractive feature of Visual Statistics is that you can "spin" both n and π and can superimpose a normal curve on your binomial distribution to see if it is bell-shaped.

Chapter 4

Binomial Probabilities: *LearningStats*

Figure 6.18 shows a *LearningStats* binomial screen using $n = 50$ and $\pi = .095$ with graphs and a table of probabilities. The spin buttons let you vary n and π.

Binomial Random Data

You could generate a single binomial random number by summing n Bernoulli random variables (0 or 1) created with Excel's function =IF(RAND( )< , 1, 0). However, that only creates a single random data value and is tedious. Why not rely on Excel's Tools > Data Analysis to generate binomial random data? Figure 6.19 shows how to use the Excel menu to generate 20 binomial random data values (1, 1, 2, 3, 0, 0, 0, 1, 0, 0, 3, 0, 2, 1, 2, 1, 1, 0, 1, 2) using $n = 4$ and $\pi = .20$.

Recognizing Binomial Applications

Can you recognize a binomial situation? Look for n independent Bernoulli trials with constant probability of success.

In a sample of 20 friends:

- How many are left-handed?
- How many have ever worked on a factory floor?
- How many own a motorcycle?

FIGURE 6.16

MegaStat's binomial distribution

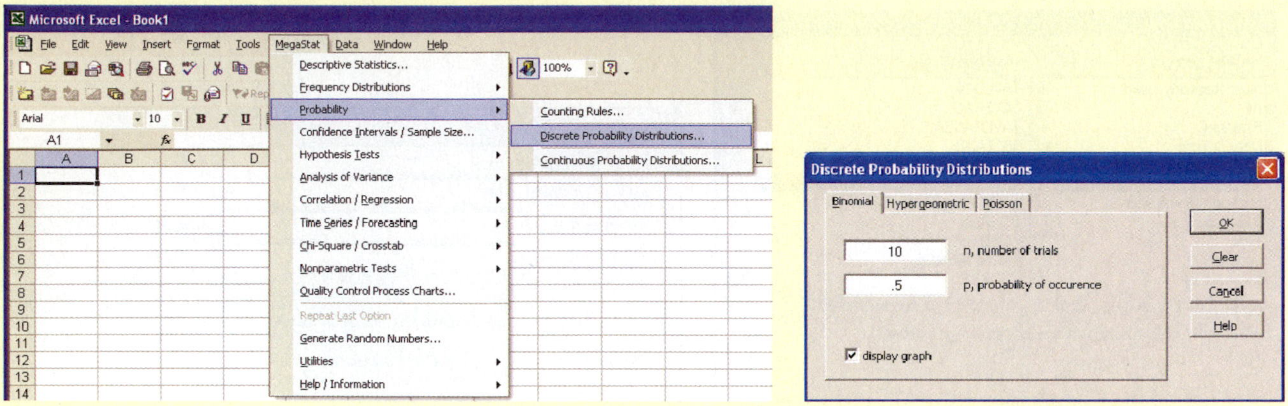

Binomial distribution

		cumulative
	10 n	
	0.5 p	
X	p(X)	probability
0	0.00098	0.00098
1	0.00977	0.01074
2	0.04395	0.05469
3	0.11719	0.17188
4	0.20508	0.37695
5	0.24609	0.62305
6	0.20508	0.82813
7	0.11719	0.94531
8	0.04395	0.98926
9	0.00977	0.99902
10	0.00098	1.00000
	1.00000	

5.000 expected value
2.500 variance
1.581 standard deviation

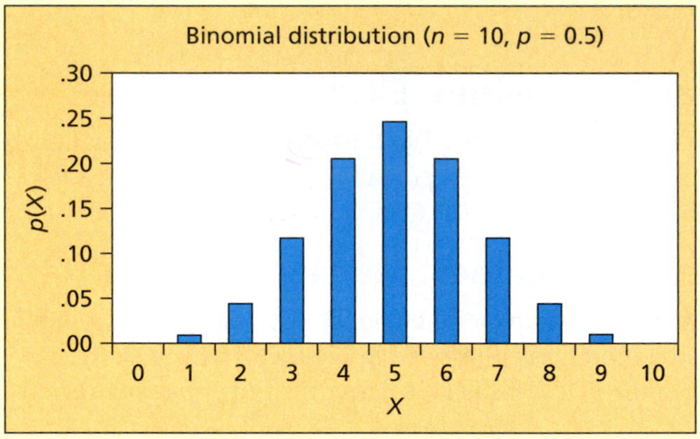

FIGURE 6.17

Visual Statistics binomial display

VS

Chapter 4

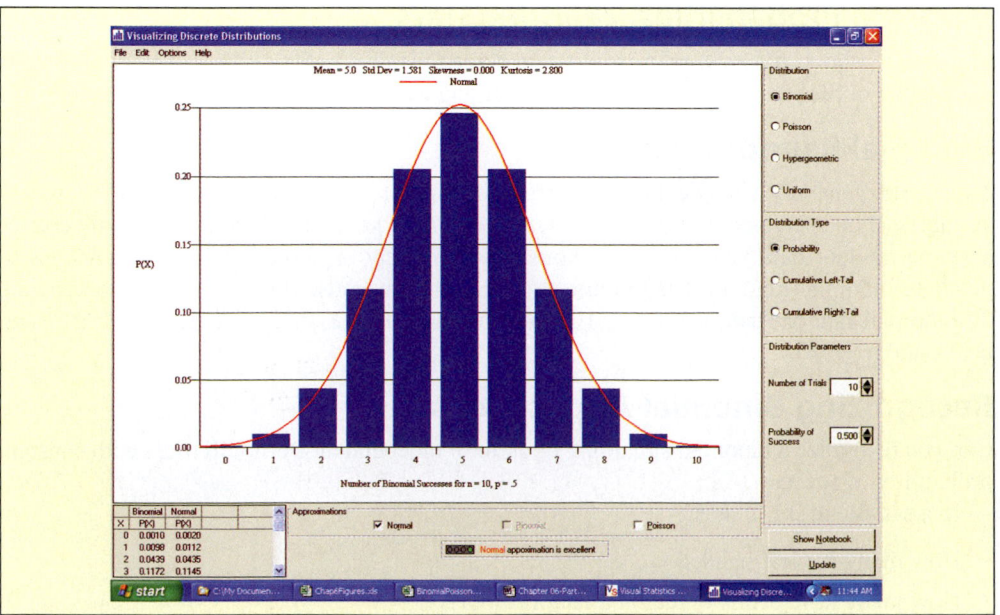

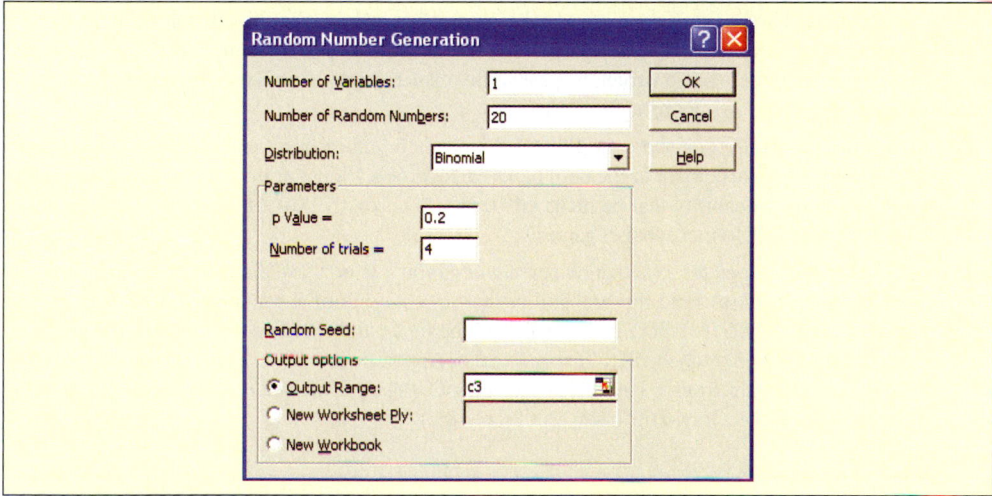

FIGURE 6.18

LearningStats binomial display

FIGURE 6.19

Excel's binomial random number menu

In a sample of 50 cars in a parking lot:

- How many are parked end-first?
- How many are blue?
- How many have hybrid engines?

In a sample of 10 emergency patients with chest pain:

- How many will be admitted?
- How many will need bypass surgery?
- How many will be uninsured?

Even if you don't know π, you may have a binomial experiment. In practice, the value of π would be estimated from experience, but in this chapter it will be given.

SECTION EXERCISES

6.15 Find the mean and standard deviation for each binomial random variable:

a. $n = 8, \pi = .10$	b. $n = 10, \pi = .40$	c. $n = 12, \pi = .50$
d. $n = 30, \pi = .90$	e. $n = 80, \pi = .70$	f. $n = 20, \pi = .80$

6.16 Calculate each binomial probability:
a. $X = 2, n = 8, \pi = .10$
b. $X = 1, n = 10, \pi = .40$
c. $X = 3, n = 12, \pi = .70$
d. $X = 5, n = 9, \pi = .90$

6.17 Calculate each compound event probability:
a. $X \leq 3, n = 8, \pi = .20$
b. $X > 7, n = 10, \pi = .50$
c. $X < 3, n = 6, \pi = .70$
d. $X \leq 10, n = 14, \pi = .95$

6.18 Calculate each binomial probability:
a. Fewer than 4 successes in 12 trials with a 10 percent chance of success.
b. At least 3 successes in 7 trials with a 40 percent chance of success.
c. At most 9 successes in 14 trials with a 60 percent chance of success.
d. More than 10 successes in 16 trials with an 80 percent chance of success.

6.19 In the Ardmore Hotel, 20 percent of the customers pay by American Express credit card. (a) Of the next 10 customers, what is the probability that none pay by American Express? (b) At least two? (c) Fewer than three? (d) What is the expected number who pay by American Express? (e) Find the standard deviation. (f) Construct the probability distribution (using Excel or Appendix A). (g) Make a graph of its PDF, and describe its shape.

6.20 Historically, 5 percent of a mail-order firm's repeat charge-account customers have an incorrect current address in the firm's computer database. (a) What is the probability that none of the next 12 repeat customers who call will have an incorrect address? (b) One customer? (c) Two customers? (d) Fewer than three? (e) Construct the probability distribution (using Excel or Appendix A), make a graph of its PDF, and describe its shape.

6.21 In an office football pool, there are 10 closely matched games this week (i.e., either team has a 50-50 chance). A participant in the pool picks each game's winner at random by using a coin flip. (a) What is the probability that he picks all 10 games correctly? (b) At least 5 games? (c) Fewer than 3 games? (d) No more than 6 games?

6.22 J.D. Power and Associates says that 60 percent of car buyers now use the Internet for research and price comparisons. (a) Find the probability that in a sample of 8 car buyers, all 8 will use the Internet; (b) at least 5; (c) more than 4. (d) Find the mean and standard deviation of the probability distribution. (e) Sketch the PDF (using Excel or Appendix A) and describe its appearance (e.g., skewness). (Data are from J. Paul Peter and Jerry C. Olson, *Consumer Behavior and Marketing Strategy,* 7th ed. [McGraw-Hill/Irwin, 2005], p. 188.)

6.6
POISSON DISTRIBUTION

Poisson Processes

Named for the French mathematician Siméon-Denis Poisson (1781–1840), the **Poisson distribution** describes the number of occurrences within a randomly chosen unit of time (e.g., minute, hour) or space (e.g., square foot, linear mile). For the Poisson distribution to apply, the events must occur randomly and independently over a continuum of time or space, as illustrated in Figure 6.20. We will call the continuum "time" since the most common Poisson application is modeling **arrivals** *per unit of time.* Each dot (•) is an occurrence of the event of interest.

FIGURE 6.20

Poisson events distributed over time

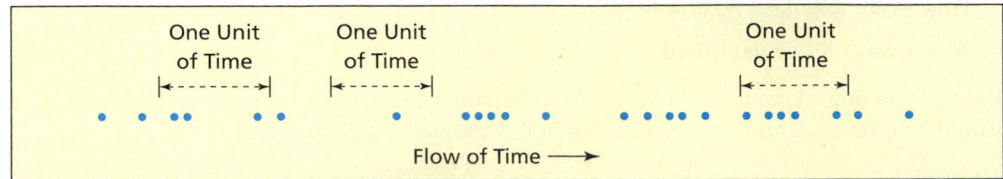

Let $X =$ the number of events per unit of time. The value of X is a random variable that depends on when the unit of time is observed. Figure 6.20 shows that we could get $X = 3$ or $X = 1$ or $X = 5$ events, depending on where the randomly chosen unit of time happens to fall.

We often call the Poisson distribution the *model of arrivals* (customers, defects, accidents). Arrivals can reasonably be regarded as Poisson events if each event is **independent** (i.e., each event's occurrence has no effect on the probability of other events occurring). Some situations lack this characteristic. For example, computer users know that a power interruption often presages another within seconds or minutes. But, as a practical matter, the Poisson assumptions often are met sufficiently to make it a useful model of reality. For example:

- X = number of customers arriving at a bank ATM in a given minute.
- X = number of file server virus infections at a data center during a 24-hour period.
- X = number of asthma patient arrivals in a given hour at a walk-in clinic.
- X = number of Airbus 330 aircraft engine shutdowns per 100,000 flight hours.
- X = number of blemishes per sheet of white bond paper.

The Poisson model has only one parameter denoted λ (the Greek letter "lambda") representing the *mean number of events per unit of time or space*. The unit of time should be short enough that the mean arrival rate is not large (typically $\lambda < 20$). For this reason, the Poisson distribution is sometimes called the *model of **rare events.*** If the mean is large, we can reformulate the time units to yield a smaller mean. For example, $\lambda = 90$ events per hour is the same as $\lambda = 1.5$ events per minute.

Characteristics of the Poisson Distribution

All characteristics of the Poisson model are determined by its mean λ, as shown in Table 6.9. The constant e (the base of the natural logarithm system) is approximately 2.71828 (to see a more precise value of e, use your calculator's e^x function with $x = 1$). The mean of the Poisson distribution is λ, and its standard deviation is the square root of the mean. The simplicity of the Poisson formulas makes it an attractive model (easier than the binomial, for example). Unlike the binomial, X has no obvious limit, that is, the number of events that can occur in a given unit of time is not bounded. However, Poisson probabilities taper off toward zero as X increases, so the effective range is usually small.

Table 6.10 shows some Poisson PDFs. Going down each column, the probabilities must sum to 1.0000 (except for rounding, since these probabilities are only accurate to four decimals).

Poisson distributions are always right-skewed (long right tail) but become less skewed and more bell-shaped as λ increases, as illustrated in Figure 6.21.

VS

Chapter 4

Parameters	λ = mean arrivals per unit of time or space	**TABLE 6.9**
PDF	$P(x) = \dfrac{\lambda^x e^{-\lambda}}{x!}$	**Poisson Distribution**
Range	$X = 0, 1, 2, \ldots$ (no obvious upper limit)	
Mean	λ	
Standard deviation	$\sqrt{\lambda}$	
Random data	Use Excel's **Tools > Data Analysis > Random Number Generation**	
Comments	Always right-skewed, but less so for larger λ.	

x	$\lambda = 0.1$	$\lambda = 0.5$	$\lambda = 0.8$	$\lambda = 1.6$	$\lambda = 2.0$	**TABLE 6.10**
0	.9048	.6065	.4493	.2019	.1353	**Poisson PDFs for Various Values of λ**
1	.0905	.3033	.3595	.3230	.2707	
2	.0045	.0758	.1438	.2584	.2707	
3	.0002	.0126	.0383	.1378	.1804	
4	—	.0016	.0077	.0551	.0902	
5	—	.0002	.0012	.0176	.0361	
6	—	—	.0002	.0047	.0120	
7	—	—	—	.0011	.0034	
8	—	—	—	.0002	.0009	
9	—	—	—	—	.0002	
Sum	1.0000	1.0000	1.0000	1.0000	1.0000	

Note: Probabilities less than .0001 have been omitted. Columns may not sum to 1 due to rounding.

FIGURE 6.21

Poisson becomes less skewed for larger λ

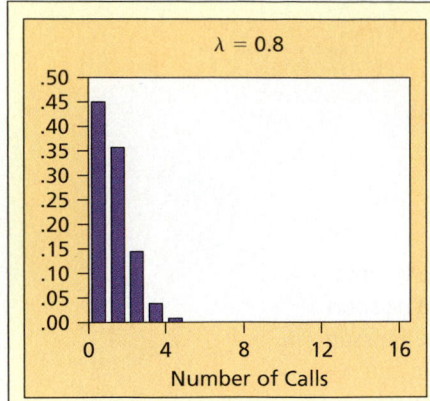 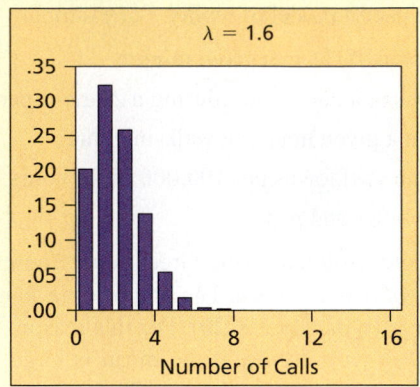 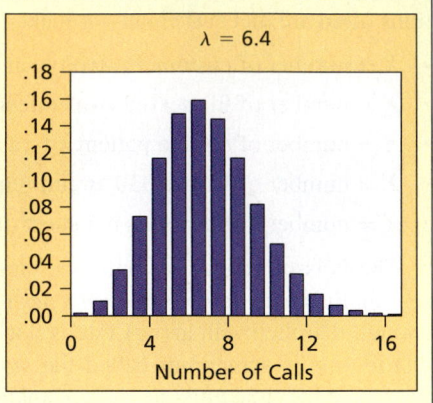

EXAMPLE

Credit Union Customers

CreditUnion

On Thursday morning between 9 A.M. and 10 A.M. customers arrive at a mean rate of 1.7 customers per minute at the Oxnard University Credit Union and enter the queue (if any) for the teller windows. Using the Poisson formulas with λ = 1.7, the equations for the PDF, mean, and standard deviation are:

$$\text{PDF: } P(x) = \frac{\lambda^x e^{-\lambda}}{x!} = \frac{(1.7)^x e^{-1.7}}{x!}$$

$$\text{Mean: } \lambda = 1.7$$

$$\text{Standard deviation: } \sigma = \sqrt{\lambda} = \sqrt{1.7} = 1.304$$

TABLE 6.11
Probability Distribution for λ = 1.7

x	PDF P(X = x)	CDF P(X ≤ x)
0	.1827	.1827
1	.3106	.4932
2	.2640	.7572
3	.1496	.9068
4	.0636	.9704
5	.0216	.9920
6	.0061	.9981
7	.0015	.9996
8	.0003	.9999
9	.0001	1.0000

Using the Poisson Formula

Table 6.11 shows the probabilities for each value of *X*. The probabilities for individual *X*-values can be calculated by inserting λ = 1.7 into the Poisson PDF or by using Excel's Poisson function =POISSON(x, λ, cumulative) where cumulative is 0 (if you want a PDF) or 1 (if you want a CDF).

PDF Formula   *Excel Function*

$$P(0) = \frac{1.7^0 e^{-1.7}}{0!} = .1827$$ =POISSON(0,1.7,0)

$$P(1) = \frac{1.7^1 e^{-1.7}}{1!} = .3106$$ =POISSON(1,1.7,0)

$$P(2) = \frac{1.7^2 e^{-1.7}}{2!} = .2640 \qquad \text{=POISSON(2,1.7,0)}$$

$$P(3) = \frac{1.7^3 e^{-1.7}}{3!} = .1496 \qquad \text{=POISSON(3,1.7,0)}$$

$$P(4) = \frac{1.7^4 e^{-1.7}}{4!} = .0636 \qquad \text{=POISSON(4,1.7,0)}$$

$$P(5) = \frac{1.7^5 e^{-1.7}}{5!} = .0216 \qquad \text{=POISSON(5,1.7,0)}$$

$$P(6) = \frac{1.7^6 e^{-1.7}}{6!} = .0061 \qquad \text{=POISSON(6,1.7,0)}$$

$$P(7) = \frac{1.7^7 e^{-1.7}}{7!} = .0015 \qquad \text{=POISSON(7,1.7,0)}$$

$$P(8) = \frac{1.7^8 e^{-1.7}}{8!} = .0003 \qquad \text{=POISSON(8,1.7,0)}$$

$$P(9) = \frac{1.7^9 e^{-1.7}}{9!} = .0001 \qquad \text{=POISSON(9,1.7,0)}$$

Poisson probabilities must sum to 1 (except due to rounding) as with any discrete probability distribution. Beyond $X = 9$, the probabilities are below .0001. Graphs of the PDF and CDF are shown in Figures 6.22 and 6.23. The most likely event is one arrival (probability .3106, or a

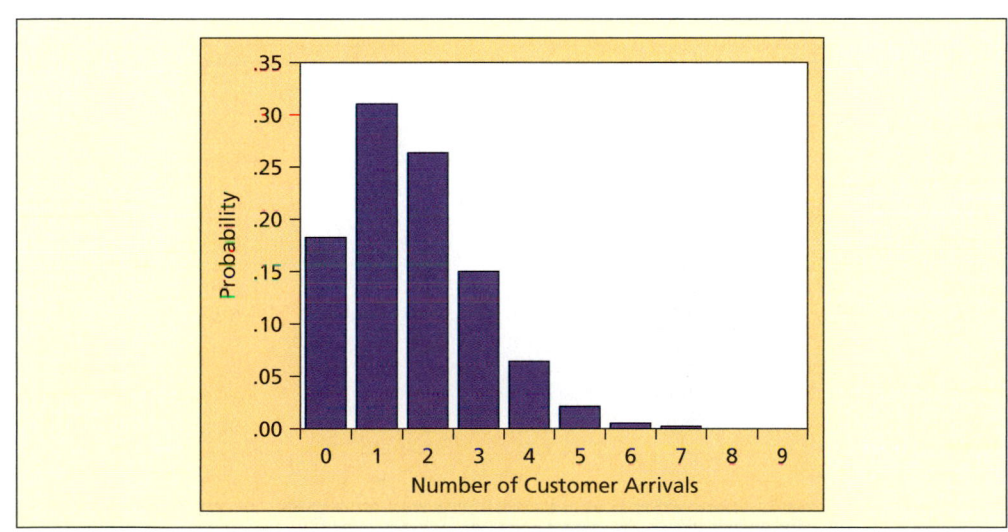

FIGURE 6.22

Poisson PDF for $\lambda = 1.7$

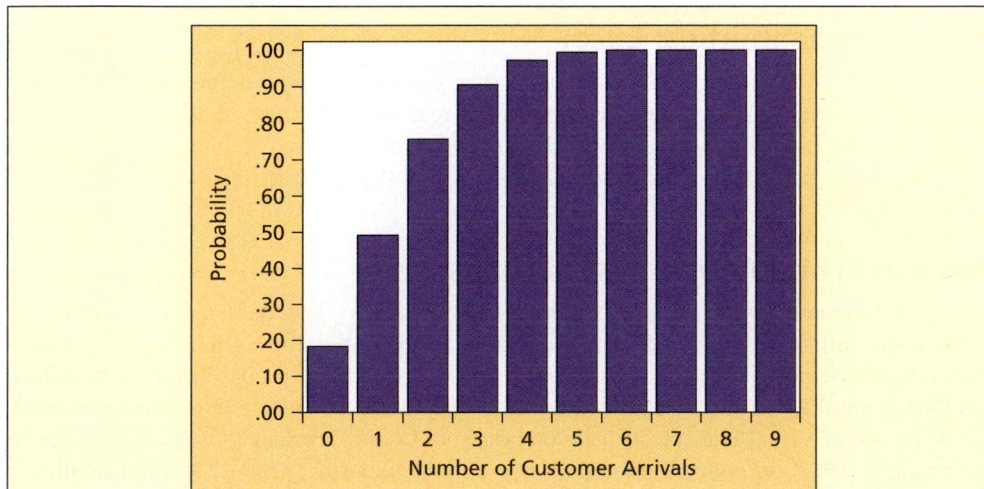

FIGURE 6.23

Poisson CDF for $\lambda = 1.7$

31.1 percent chance), although two arrivals is almost as likely (probability .2640, or a 26.4 percent chance). This PDF would help the credit union schedule its tellers for the Thursday morning work shift.

Compound Events

Cumulative probabilities can be evaluated by summing individual X probabilities. For example, the probability that two or fewer customers will arrive in a given minute is the sum of probabilities for several events:

$$P(X \leq 2) = P(0) + P(1) + P(2)$$
$$= .1827 + .3106 + .2640 = .7573$$

We could then calculate the probability of at least three customers (the complementary event):

$$P(X \geq 3) = 1 - P(X \leq 2) = 1 - [P(0) + P(1) + P(2)]$$
$$= 1 - [.1827 + .3106 + .2640] = 1 - .7573 = .2427$$

The cumulative probability $P(X \leq 2)$ can also be obtained by using the Excel function =POISSON(2,1.7,1).

Poisson Probabilities: Tables (Appendix B)

Appendix B facilitates Poisson calculations, as illustrated in Figure 6.24 with highlighted probabilities for the terms in the sum for $P(X \geq 3)$. Appendix B doesn't go beyond $\lambda = 20$, partly because the table would become huge, but mainly because we have Excel.

FIGURE 6.24

Poisson probabilities for $P(X \geq 3)$ from Appendix B

				λ		
X	**1.6**	**1.7**	**1.8**	**1.9**	**2.0**	**2.1**
0	.2019	.1827	.1653	.1496	.1353	.1225
1	.3230	.3106	.2975	.2842	.2707	.2572
2	.2584	.2640	.2678	.2700	.2707	.2700
3	.1378	.1496	.1607	.1710	.1804	.1890
4	.0551	.0636	.0723	.0812	.0902	.0992
5	.0176	.0216	.0260	.0309	.0361	.0417
6	.0047	.0061	.0078	.0098	.0120	.0146
7	.0011	.0015	.0020	.0027	.0034	.0044
8	.0002	.0003	.0005	.0006	.0009	.0011
9	—	.0001	.0001	.0001	.0002	.0003
10	—	—	—	—	—	.0001
11	—	—	—	—	—	—

Poisson Probabilities: Excel

Tables are helpful for taking statistics exams (when you may not have access to Excel). However, tables contain only selected λ values, and in real-world problems, we cannot expect λ always to be a nice round number. Excel's menus are illustrated in Figure 6.25. In this example, Excel calculates =POISSON(11,17,0) as .035544812, which is more accurate than Appendix B.

Poisson Probabilities: Visual Statistics

Figure 6.26 shows *Visual Statistics Module 4* using $\lambda = 1.7$. A table of probabilities is in the lower left. You can also display cumulative probabilities from either tail. The Visual Statistics graph can be copied and pasted into a report, and its table probabilities can be copied and pasted into Excel (they are tab-delimited, so they will paste nicely into Excel columns). An advantage of Visual Statistics is that you can "spin" λ and can display a normal overlay. In this example, the Poisson distribution does not resemble a normal because λ is too small.

Chapter 4

FIGURE 6.25

Excel's Poisson function

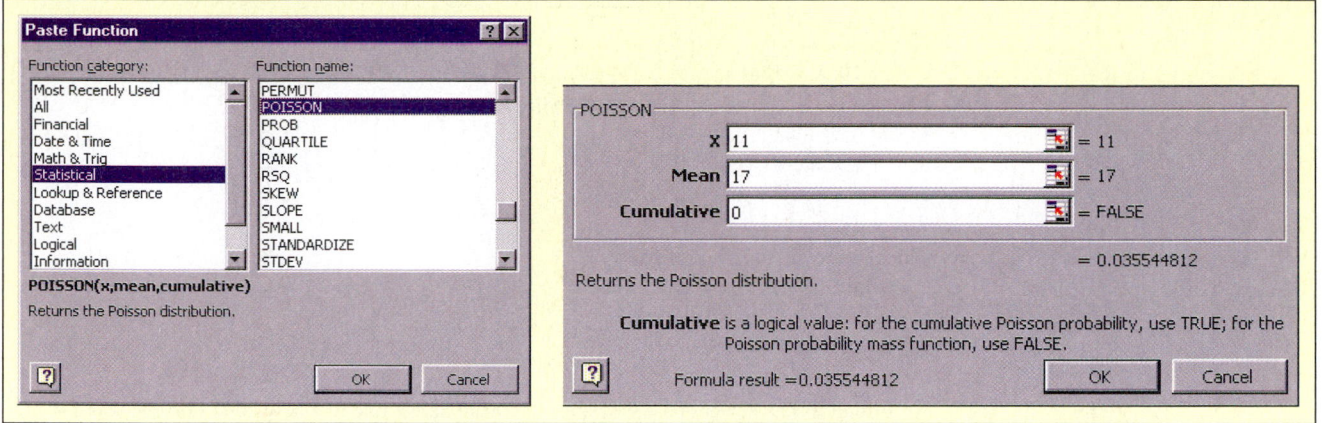

FIGURE 6.26

Visual Statistics
Poisson display

Chapter 4

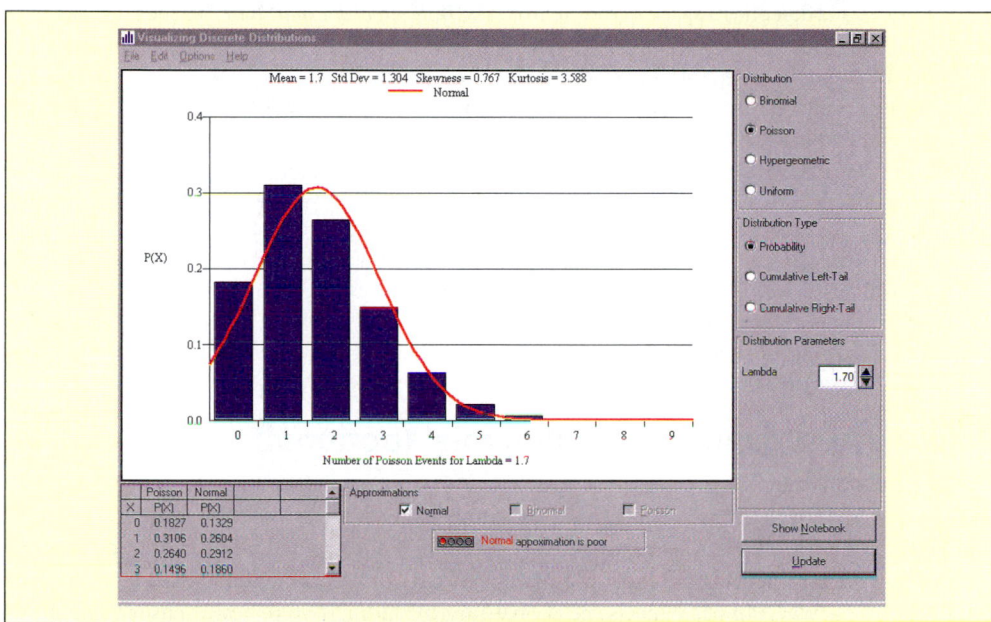

Recognizing Poisson Applications

Can you recognize a Poisson situation? Look for arrivals of "rare" independent events with *no obvious upper limit*.

- In the last week, how many credit card applications did you receive by mail?
- In the last week, how many checks did you write?
- In the last week, how many e-mail viruses did your firewall deflect?

It may be a Poisson process, even if you don't know the mean (λ). In business applications, the value of λ would have to be estimated from experience, but in this chapter λ will be given.

SECTION EXERCISES

6.23   Find the mean and standard deviation for each Poisson:

a. $\lambda = 1.0$ b. $\lambda = 2.0$ c. $\lambda = 4.0$ d. $\lambda = 9.0$ e. $\lambda = 12.0$

6.24   Calculate each Poisson probability:
  a. $X = 2$, $\lambda = 0.1$
  b. $X = 1$, $\lambda = 2.2$
  c. $X = 3$, $\lambda = 1.6$
  d. $X = 6$, $\lambda = 4.0$
  e. $X = 10$, $\lambda = 12.0$

6.25   Calculate each compound event probability:
  a. $X \leq 3$, $\lambda = 4.3$
  b. $X > 7$, $\lambda = 5.2$
  c. $X < 3$, $\lambda = 2.7$
  d. $X \leq 10$, $\lambda = 11.0$

6.26   Calculate each Poisson probability:
  a. Fewer than 4 arrivals with $\lambda = 5.8$.
  b. At least 3 arrivals with $\lambda = 4.8$.
  c. At most 9 arrivals with $\lambda = 7.0$.
  d. More than 10 arrivals with $\lambda = 8.0$.

6.27   According to J.D. Power and Associates, the mean defect rate in a new 2004 Porsche was 2.4. In a randomly selected new Porsche, find the probability of (a) at least one defect; (b) no defects; (c) more than three defects. (d) Construct the probability distribution (Excel or Appendix B), make a graph of its PDF, and describe its shape. (Data are from *The Wall Street Journal*, June 30, 2004, p. D3.)

6.28   At an outpatient mental health clinic, appointment cancellations occur at a mean rate of 1.5 per day on a typical Wednesday. Let X be the number of cancellations on a particular Wednesday. (a) Justify the use of the Poisson model. (b) What is the probability that no cancellations will occur on a particular Wednesday? (c) One? (d) More than two? (e) Five or more?

6.29   In the World Cup soccer match, the average is 2.7 goals per game. In a particular game, let X be the number of goals. (a) Justify the use of the Poisson model. (b) What is the probability of at least one goal? (c) More than three goals? (d) Construct the probability distribution (Excel or Appendix B), make a graph of its PDF, and describe its shape. (Data are from *USA Today*, July 2, 1998, p. 1C.)

6.30   (a) Why might the number of yawns per minute by students in a warm classroom not be a Poisson event? (b) Give two additional examples of events per unit of time that might violate the assumptions of the Poisson model, and explain why.

Poisson Approximation to Binomial (optional)

The binomial and Poisson are close cousins. The Poisson distribution may be used to approximate a binomial by setting $\lambda = n\pi$. This approximation is helpful when the binomial calculation is difficult (e.g., when n is large) and when Excel is not available. For example, suppose 1,000 women are screened for a rare type of cancer that has a nationwide incidence of 6 cases per 10,000 (i.e., $\pi = .0006$). What is the probability of finding two or fewer cases? The number of cancer cases would follow a binomial distribution with $n = 1,000$ and $\pi = .0006$. However, the binomial formula would involve awkward factorials. To use a Poisson approximation, we set the Poisson mean (λ) equal to the binomial mean ($n\pi$):

$$\lambda = n\pi = (1000)(.0006) = 0.6$$

To calculate the probability of x successes, we can then use Appendix B or the Poisson PDF $P(x) = \lambda^x e^{-\lambda}/x!$ which is simpler than the binomial PDF $P(x) = \dfrac{n!}{x!(n-x)!}\pi^x(1-\pi)^{n-x}$.

The Poisson approximation of the desired probability is $P(X \leq 2) = P(0) + P(1) + P(2) = .5488 + .3293 + .0988 = .9769$.

Poisson Approximation	*Actual Binomial Probability*
$P(0) = 0.6^0 e^{-0.6}/0! = .5488$	$P(0) = \dfrac{1000!}{0!(1000-0)!}.0006^0(1-.0006)^{1000-0} = .5487$
$P(1) = 0.6^1 e^{-0.6}/1! = .3293$	$P(1) = \dfrac{1000!}{1!(1000-1)!}.0006^1(1-.0006)^{1000-1} = .3294$
$P(2) = 0.6^2 e^{-0.6}/2! = .0988$	$P(2) = \dfrac{1000!}{2!(1000-2)!}.0006^2(1-.0006)^{1000-2} = .0988$

The Poisson calculations are easy and (at least in this example) the Poisson approximation is accurate. The Poisson approximation does a good job in this example, but when is it "good enough" in other situations? The general rule is that n should be "large" and π should be "small." A common rule of thumb says the approximation is adequate if $n \geq 20$ and $\pi \leq .05$.

SECTION EXERCISES

*6.31   An experienced order taker at the L.L. Bean call center has a .003 chance of error on each keystroke (i.e., $\pi = .003$). In 500 keystrokes, find the approximate probability of (a) at least two errors and (b) fewer than four errors. (c) Why not use the binomial? (d) Is the Poisson approximation justified?

*6.32   The probability of a manufacturing defect in an aluminum beverage can is .00002. If 100,000 cans are produced, find the approximate probability of (a) at least one defective can and (b) two or more defective cans. (c) Why not use the binomial? (d) Is the Poisson approximation justified? (See *Scientific American* 271, no. 3 [September 1994], pp. 48–53.)

*6.33   Three percent of the letters placed in a certain postal drop box have incorrect postage. Suppose 200 letters are mailed. (a) For this binomial, what is the expected number with incorrect postage? (b) For this binomial, what is the standard deviation? (c) What is the approximate probability that at least 10 letters will have incorrect postage? (d) Fewer than five? (e) Why not use the binomial? (f) Is the Poisson approximation justified?

Characteristics of the Hypergeometric Distribution

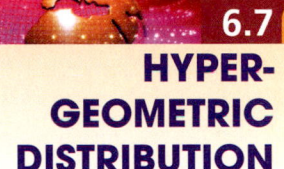

6.7
HYPER-GEOMETRIC DISTRIBUTION

The **hypergeometric distribution** is similar to the binomial except that sampling is *without replacement* from a finite population of N items. The hypergeometric distribution has three parameters: N (the number of items in the population), n (the number of items in the sample), and s (the number of successes in the population). The distribution of X (the number of successes in the sample) is hypergeometric, with the characteristics shown in Table 6.12. The hypergeometric distribution may be skewed right or left, and is symmetric only if $s/N = .50$ (i.e., if the proportion of successes in the population is 50 percent).

The hypergeometric PDF uses the formula for combinations:

$$P(x) = \frac{\binom{s}{x}\binom{N-s}{n-x}}{\binom{N}{n}}$$

Chapter 4

Parameters	N = number of items in the population n = sample size s = number of successes in population
PDF	$P(x) = \dfrac{\binom{s}{x}\binom{N-s}{n-x}}{\binom{N}{n}}$
Range	$\max(0, n - N + s) \leq X \leq \min(s, n)$
Mean	$n\pi$ where $\pi = s/N$
Standard deviation	$\sqrt{n\pi(1-\pi)}\sqrt{\dfrac{N-n}{N-1}}$
Comments	Similar to binomial, but sampling is without replacement from a finite population. Can be approximated by binomial with $\pi = s/N$ if $n/N < 0.05$ (i.e., less than 5 percent sample).

TABLE 6.12
Hypergeometric Distribution

where

$$\binom{s}{x} = \text{the number of ways to choose } x \text{ successes from } s \text{ successes in the population}$$

$$\binom{N-s}{n-x} = \text{the number of ways to choose } n-x \text{ failures from } N-s \text{ failures in the population}$$

$$\binom{N}{n} = \text{the number of ways to choose } n \text{ items from } N \text{ items in the population}$$

and $N - s$ is the number of failures in the population, x is the number of successes in the sample, and $n - x$ is the number of failures in the sample.

EXAMPLE

Damaged iPods

In a shipment of 10 iPods, 2 are damaged and 8 are good. The receiving department at Best Buy tests a sample of 3 iPods at random to see if they are defective. The number of damaged iPods in the sample is a random variable X. The problem description is:

$N = 10$	(number of iPods in the shipment)
$n = 3$	(sample size drawn from the shipment)
$s = 2$	(number of damaged iPods in the shipment, i.e., successes in population)
$N - s = 8$	(number of nondamaged iPods in the shipment)
$x = ?$	(number of damaged iPods in the sample, i.e., successes in sample)
$n - x = ?$	(number of nondamaged iPods in the sample)

It is tempting to think of this as a binomial problem with $n = 3$ and $\pi = s/N = 2/10 = .20$. But π is not constant. On the first draw, the probability of a damaged iPod is indeed $\pi_1 = 2/10$. But on the second draw, the probability of a damaged iPod could be $\pi_2 = 1/9$ (if the first draw contained a damaged iPod) or $\pi_2 = 2/9$ (if the first draw did not contain a damaged iPod). On the third draw, the probability of a damaged iPod could be $\pi_3 = 0/8$, $\pi_3 = 1/8$, or $\pi_3 = 2/8$ depending on what happened in the first two draws.

Using the Hypergeometric Formula

For the iPod example, the only possible values of x are 0, 1, and 2 since there are only 2 damaged iPods in the population. The probabilities are:

PDF Formula   *Excel Function*

$$P(0) = \frac{\binom{2}{0}\binom{8}{3}}{\binom{10}{3}} = \frac{\left(\frac{2!}{0!2!}\right)\left(\frac{8!}{3!5!}\right)}{\left(\frac{10!}{3!7!}\right)} = \frac{56}{120} = \frac{7}{15} = .4667 \qquad \text{=HYPGEOMDIST(0, 3, 2, 10)}$$

$$P(1) = \frac{\binom{2}{1}\binom{8}{2}}{\binom{10}{3}} = \frac{\left(\frac{2!}{1!1!}\right)\left(\frac{8!}{2!6!}\right)}{\left(\frac{10!}{3!7!}\right)} = \frac{56}{120} = \frac{7}{15} = .4667 \qquad \text{=HYPGEOMDIST(1, 3, 2, 10)}$$

$$P(2) = \frac{\binom{2}{2}\binom{8}{1}}{\binom{10}{3}} = \frac{\left(\frac{2!}{2!0!}\right)\left(\frac{8!}{1!7!}\right)}{\left(\frac{10!}{3!7!}\right)} = \frac{8}{120} = \frac{1}{15} = .0667 \qquad \text{=HYPGEOMDIST(2, 3, 2, 10)}$$

The values of $P(X)$ sum to 1, as they should: $P(0) + P(1) + P(2) = 7/15 + 7/15 + 1/15 = 1$. We can also find the probability of compound events. For example, the probability of at least one damaged iPod is $P(X \geq 1) = P(1) + P(2) = 7/15 + 1/15 = 8/15 = .533$, or 53.3 percent.

Hypergeometric Probabilities: Excel

The hypergeometric formula is tedious and tables are impractical because there are three parameters, so we prefer Excel's hypergeometric function =HYPGEOMDIST(x, n, s, N). For example, using $X = 5$, $n = 10$, $s = 82$, $N = 194$ the formula =HYPGEOMDIST(5,10,82,194) gives .222690589, as illustrated in Figure 6.27. You can also get hypergeometric probabilities from MegaStat (menus not shown).

FIGURE 6.27

Excel's hypergeometric function (where $N = 194$, $n = 10$, $s = 82$)

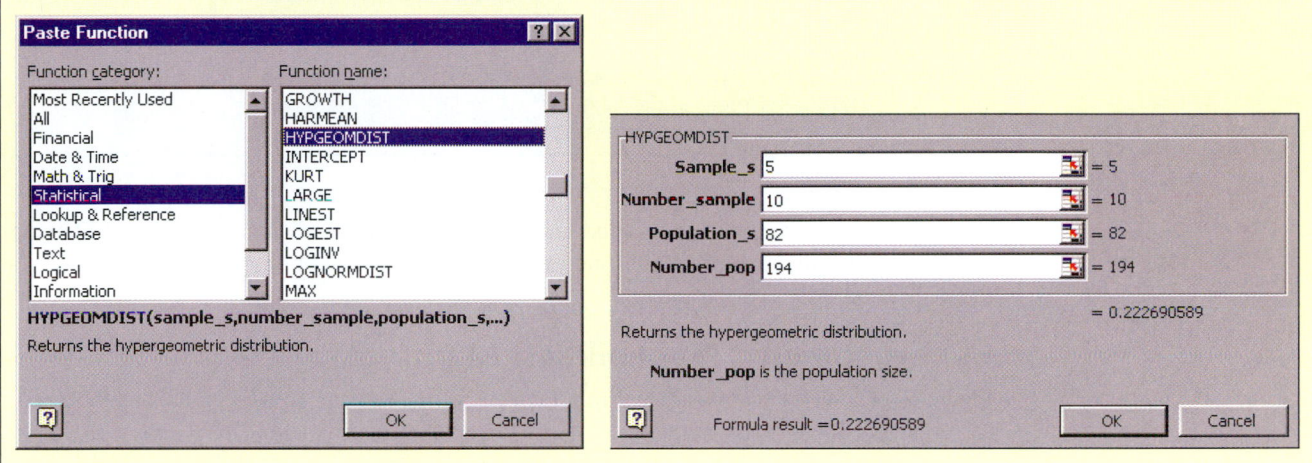

Hypergeometric Probabilities: Visual Statistics

Figure 6.28 shows a screen from Visual Statistics **Module 4.** Numerical probabilities are shown in a table in the lower left. The graph can be copied and pasted as a bitmap and the table

Chapter 4

FIGURE 6.28

Visual Statistics hypergeometric display (where $N = 50$, $n = 10$, $s = 25$)

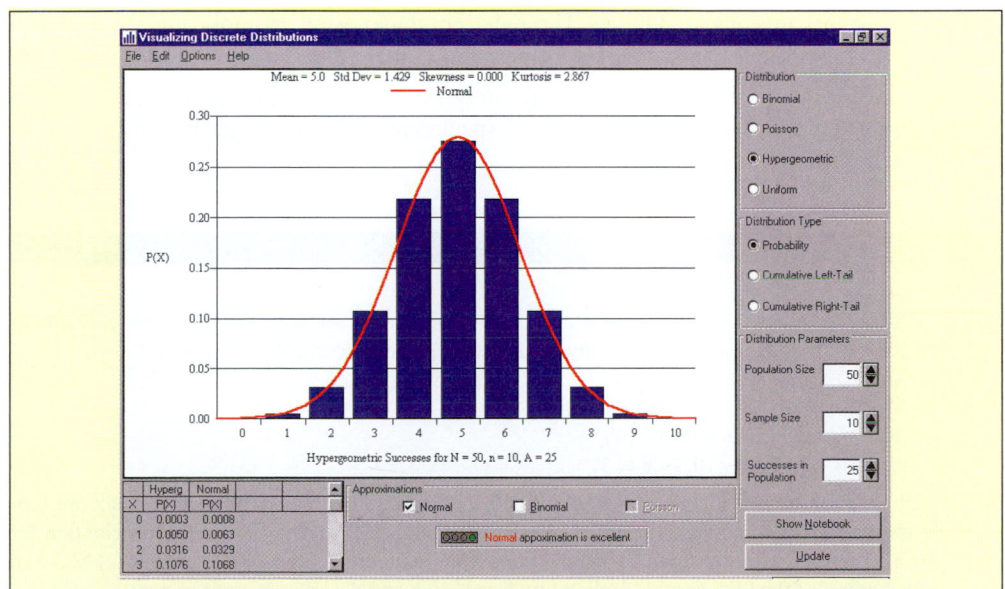

FIGURE 6.29

LearningStats hypergeometric display

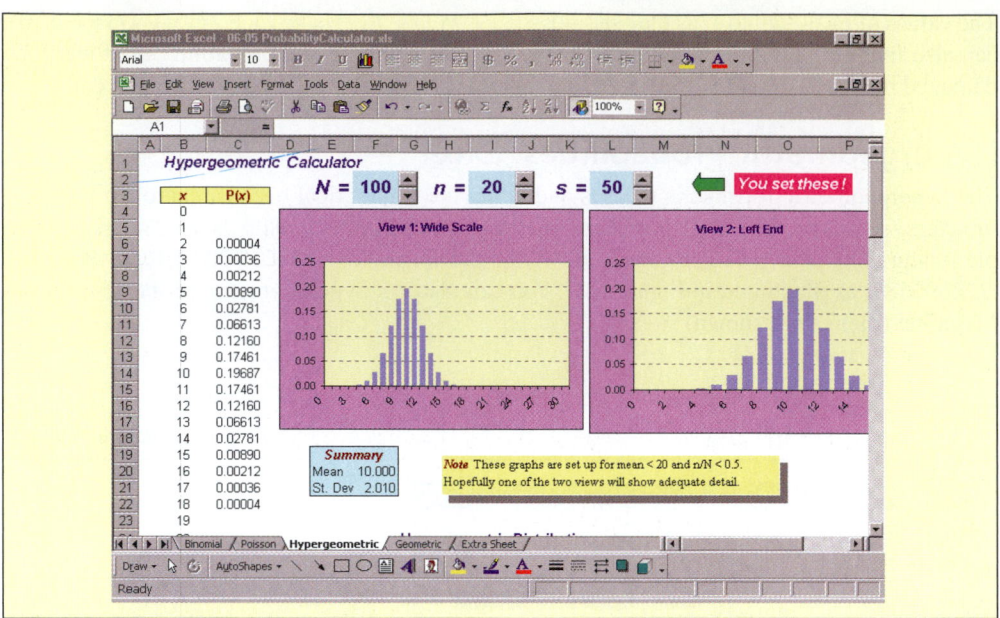

probabilities can be copied and pasted into Excel columns. An advantage of Visual Statistics is that you can spin N, n, and s and superimpose either a normal or binomial approximation on the hypergeometric distribution.

Hypergeometric Probabilities: *LearningStats*

Figure 6.29 shows a sample screen from *LearningStats*. You can spin the values of N, n, and s to get the probability you want.

Recognizing Hypergeometric Applications

Look for a finite population (N) containing a known number of successes (s) and *sampling without replacement* (n items in the sample). For example:

- Forty automobiles are to be inspected for California emissions compliance. Thirty-two are compliant but 8 are not. A sample of 7 cars is chosen at random. What is the probability that all are compliant? At least 5?

- A law enforcement agency must process 500 background checks for firearms purchasers. Fifty applicants are convicted felons. Through a computer error, 10 applicants are approved without a background check. What is the probability that none is a felon? At least two are?

- A medical laboratory receives 40 blood specimens to check for HIV. Eight actually contain HIV. A worker is accidentally exposed to 5 specimens. What is the probability that none contained HIV?

SECTION EXERCISES

6.34 (a) State the values that X can assume in each hypergeometric scenario. (b) Use the hypergeometric PDF formula to find the probability requested. (c) Check your answer by using Excel.
  i. $N = 10$, $n = 3$, $s = 4$, $P(X = 3)$
  ii. $N = 20$, $n = 5$, $s = 3$, $P(X = 2)$
  iii. $N = 36$, $n = 4$, $s = 9$, $P(X = 1)$
  iv. $N = 50$, $n = 7$, $s = 10$, $P(X = 3)$

6.35 ABC Warehouse has eight refrigerators in stock. Two are side-by-side models and six are top-freezer models. (a) Using Excel, calculate the entire hypergeometric probability distribution for the number of top-freezer models in a sample of four refrigerators chosen at random. (b) Make an Excel graph of the PDF for this probability distribution and describe its appearance.

6.36   A statistics textbook chapter contains 60 exercises, 6 of which contain incorrect answers. A student is assigned 10 problems. (a) Use Excel to calculate the entire hypergeometric probability distribution. (b) What is the probability that all the answers are correct? (c) That at least one is incorrect? (d) That two or more are incorrect? (e) Make an Excel graph of the PDF of the hypergeometric distribution and describe its appearance.

6.37   Fifty employee travel expense reimbursement vouchers were filed last quarter in the finance department at Ramjac Corporation. Of these, 20 contained errors. A corporate auditor inspects five vouchers at random. Let X be the number of incorrect vouchers in the sample. (a) Use Excel to calculate the entire hypergeometric probability distribution. (b) Find $P(X = 0)$. (c) Find $P(X = 1)$. (d) Find $P(X \geq 3)$. (e) Make an Excel graph of the PDF of the hypergeometric distribution and describe its appearance.

6.38   A medical laboratory receives 40 blood specimens to check for HIV. Eight actually contain HIV. A worker is accidentally exposed to five specimens. (a) Use Excel to calculate the entire hypergeometric probability distribution. (b) What is the probability that none contained HIV? (c) Fewer than three? (d) At least two? (e) Make an Excel graph of the PDF of the hypergeometric distribution and describe its appearance.

Binomial Approximation to the Hypergeometric (optional)

There is a strong similarity between the binomial and hypergeometric models. Both involve samples of size n and both treat X as the number of successes in the sample. If you replaced each item after it was selected, then you would have a binomial distribution instead of a hypergeometric distribution. If the size of the sample (n) is small in relation to the population (N), then the probability of success is nearly constant on each draw, so the two models are almost the same if we set $\pi = s/N$. A common *rule of thumb* is that the binomial is a safe approximation to the hypergeometric whenever $n/N < 0.05$. In other words, if we sample less than 5 percent of the population, π will remain essentially constant, even if we sample without replacement. For example, suppose we want $P(X = 6)$ for a hypergeometric with $N = 400$, $n = 10$, and $s = 200$. Since $n/N = 10/400 = .025$, the binomial approximation would be acceptable. Set $\pi = s/N = 200/400 = .50$ and use Appendix A to obtain $P(X = 6) = .2051$. But in the iPod example, the binomial approximation would be unacceptable, because we sampled more than 5 percent of the population (i.e., $n/N = 3/10 = .30$ for the iPod problem).

Rule of Thumb

If $n/N < .05$ it is safe to use the binomial approximation to the hypergeometric, using sample size n and success probability $\pi = s/N$.

SECTION EXERCISES

*6.39   (a) Check whether the binomial approximation is acceptable in each of the following hypergeometric situations. (b) Find the binomial approximation (using Appendix A) for each probability requested. (c) Check the accuracy of your approximation by using Excel to find the actual hypergeometric probability.

   a. $N = 100, n = 3, s = 40, P(X = 3)$
   b. $N = 200, n = 10, s = 60, P(X = 2)$
   c. $N = 160, n = 12, s = 16, P(X = 1)$
   d. $N = 500, n = 7, s = 350, P(X = 5)$

*6.40   Two hundred employee travel expense reimbursement vouchers were filed last year in the finance department at Ramjac Corporation. Of these, 20 contained errors. A corporate auditor audits a sample of five vouchers. Let X be the number of incorrect vouchers in the sample. (a) Find the probability that the sample contains no erroneous vouchers. (b) Find the probability that the sample contains at least two erroneous vouchers. (c) Justify the use of the binomial approximation.

*6.41   A law enforcement agency processes 500 background checks for firearms purchasers. Fifty applicants are convicted felons. Through a clerk's error, 10 applicants are approved without checking for felony convictions. (a) What is the probability that none of the 10 is a felon? (b) That at least two of the 10 are convicted felons? (c) That fewer than 4 of the 10 are convicted felons? (d) Justify the use of the binomial approximation.

*6.42 Four hundred automobiles are to be inspected for California emissions compliance. Of these, 320 actually are compliant but 80 are not. A random sample of 6 cars is chosen. (a) What is the probability that all are compliant? (b) At least 4? (c) Justify the use of the binomial approximation.

6.8
GEOMETRIC DISTRIBUTION (OPTIONAL)

Characteristics of the Geometric Distribution

The *geometric distribution* is related to the binomial. It describes the number of Bernoulli trials until the first success is observed. But the number of trials is not fixed. We define X as the number of trials until the first success, and π as the constant *probability* of a success on each trial. The geometric distribution depends only on π (i.e., it is a one-parameter model). The range of X is $\{1, 2, \ldots\}$ since we must have at least one trial to obtain our first success, but there is no limit on how many trials may be necessary. The characteristics of the geometric distribution are shown in Table 6.13. It is always skewed to the right. It can be shown that the geometric probabilities sum to 1 and that the mean and standard deviation are nearly the same when π is small. Probabilities diminish as X increases, but not rapidly.

TABLE 6.13
Geometric Distribution

Parameters	π = probability of success
PDF	$P(x) = \pi(1 - \pi)^{x-1}$
CDF	$P(X \leq x) = 1 - (1 - \pi)^x$
Range	$X = 1, 2, \ldots$
Mean	$1/\pi$
Standard deviation	$\sqrt{\dfrac{1 - \pi}{\pi^2}}$
Comments	Describes the number of trials before the first success. Highly skewed.

EXAMPLE

Telefund Calling

At Faber University, 15 percent of the alumni (the historical average) make a donation or pledge during the annual telefund. What is the probability that the first donation will come within the first five calls? To calculate this geometric probability, we would set $\pi = .15$, apply the PDF formula $P(x) = \pi(1 - \pi)^{x-1}$, and then sum the probabilities:

$$P(1) = (.15)(1 - .15)^{1-1} = (.15)(.85)^0 = .1500$$
$$P(2) = (.15)(1 - .15)^{2-1} = (.15)(.85)^1 = .1275$$
$$P(3) = (.15)(1 - .15)^{3-1} = (.15)(.85)^2 = .1084$$
$$P(4) = (.15)(1 - .15)^{4-1} = (.15)(.85)^3 = .0921$$
$$P(5) = (.15)(1 - .15)^{5-1} = (.15)(.85)^4 = .0783$$

Then $P(X \leq 5) = P(1) + P(2) + P(3) + P(4) + P(5) = .5563$. Alternately, we can use the CDF to get $P(X \leq 5) = 1 - (1 - .15)^5 = 1 - .4437 = .5563$. The CDF is a much easier method when sums are required. The expected number of phone calls until the first donation is

$$\mu = 1/\pi = 1/(.15) = 6.67 \text{ calls}$$

On the average, we expect to call between 6 and 7 alumni until the first donation. However, the standard deviation is rather large:

$$\sigma = [(1 - \pi)/\pi^2]^{1/2} = [(1 - .15)/(.15)^2]^{1/2} = 6.15 \text{ calls}$$

The large standard deviation is a signal that it would be unwise to regard the mean as a good prediction of how many trials will be needed until the first donation.

Using *LearningStats*

Figure 6.30 shows a sample screen from *LearningStats*. You can see the distribution visually or obtain the numerical probabilities from the table. The extreme skewness of the geometric distribution for $\pi = .15$ is evident. You might have to wait a lot longer than the mean.

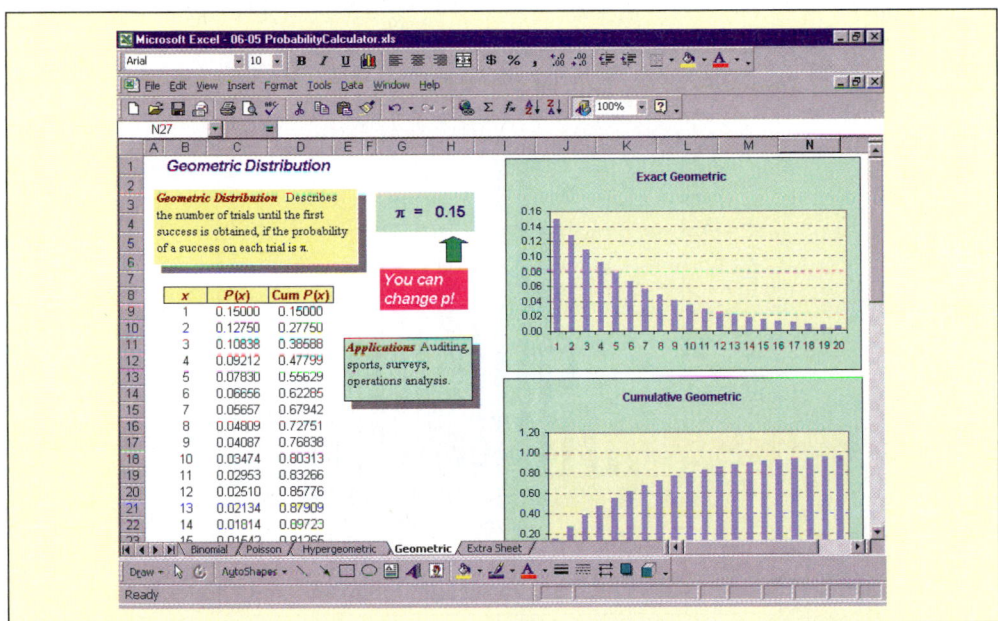

FIGURE 6.30

LearningStats geometric display

SECTION EXERCISES

*6.43 Find each geometric probability.

  a. $P(X = 5)$ when $\pi = .50$
  b. $P(X = 3)$ when $\pi = .25$
  c. $P(X = 4)$ when $\pi = .60$

*6.44 In the Ardmore Hotel, 20 percent of the guests (a historical average) pay by American Express credit card. (a) What is the expected number of guests until the next one pays by American Express credit card? (b) What is the probability that 10 or fewer guests will pay before the first one uses an American Express card?

*6.45 In a certain Kentucky Fried Chicken franchise, half of the customers request "crispy" instead of "original," on average. (a) What is the expected number of customers before the next customer requests "crispy"? (b) What is the probability of serving more than 10 customers before the first request for "crispy"?

6.9

TRANSFORMA-TIONS OF RANDOM VARIABLES (OPTIONAL)

Linear Transformation

A *linear transformation* of a random variable X is performed by adding a constant or multiplying by a constant. Below are two useful rules about the mean and variance of a transformed random variable $aX + b$, where a and b are any constants ($a \geq 0$). Adding a constant shifts the mean but does not affect the standard deviation. Multiplying by a constant affects both the mean and the standard deviation.

Rule 1:	$\mu_{aX+b} = a\mu_X + b$	(mean of a transformed variable)
Rule 2:	$\sigma_{aX+b} = a\sigma_X$	(standard deviation of a transformed variable)

Application: Exam Scores

Professor Hardtack gave a tough exam whose raw scores had $\mu = 40$ and $\sigma = 10$, so he decided to raise the mean by 20 points. One way to increase the mean to 60 is to shift the curve by adding 20 points to every student's score. Rule 1 says that adding a constant to all X-values will *shift the mean* but will leave the standard deviation unchanged, as illustrated in Figure 6.31 using $a = 1$ and $b = 20$.

FIGURE 6.31

Effect of adding a constant to X

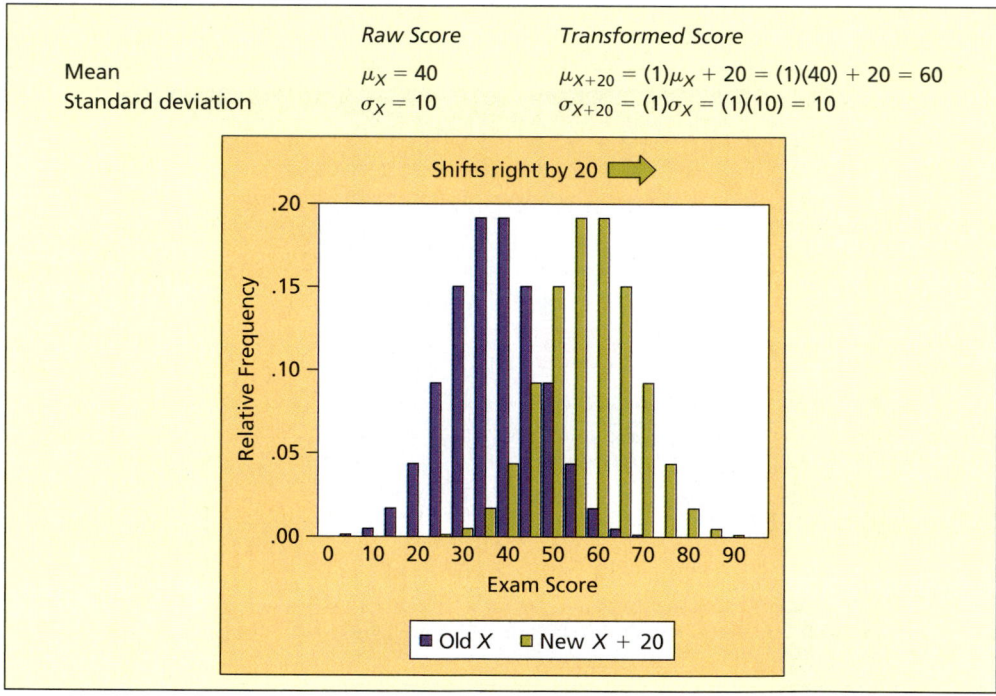

	Raw Score	Transformed Score
Mean	$\mu_X = 40$	$\mu_{X+20} = (1)\mu_X + 20 = (1)(40) + 20 = 60$
Standard deviation	$\sigma_X = 10$	$\sigma_{X+20} = (1)\sigma_X = (1)(10) = 10$

Alternatively, Professor Hardtack could multiply every exam score by 1.5, which would also accomplish the goal of raising the mean from 40 to 60. However, Rule 2 says that the standard deviation would rise from 10 to 15, thereby also *increasing the dispersion*. In other words, this policy would "spread out" the students' exam scores, as shown in Figure 6.32. Some scores might even exceed 100. Shifting the scale by adding 20 points seems a less distorting alternative.

Application: Total Cost

A linear transformation useful in business is the calculation of total cost as a function of quantity produced: $C = vQ + F$, where C is total cost, v is variable cost per unit, Q is the number of units produced, and F is fixed cost. Sonoro Ltd. is a small firm that manufactures kortholts. Its variable cost per unit is $v = \$35$, its annual fixed cost is $F = \$24,000$, and its monthly order quantity Q is a random variable with mean $\mu_Q = 500$ units and standard deviation $\sigma_Q = 40$.

FIGURE 6.32

Effect of multiplying X
by a constant

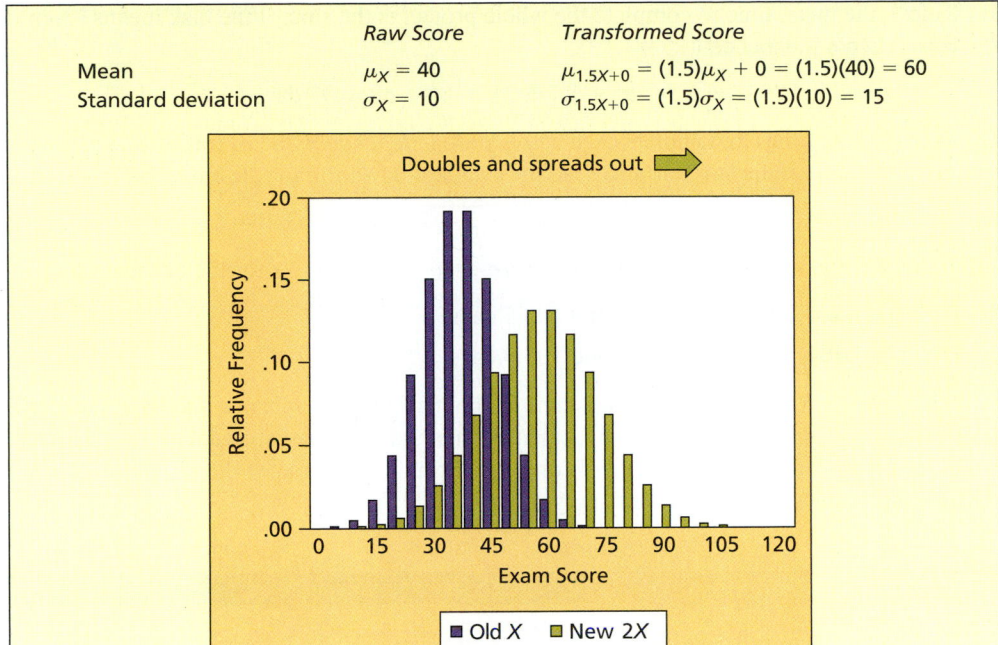

	Raw Score	Transformed Score
Mean	$\mu_X = 40$	$\mu_{1.5X+0} = (1.5)\mu_X + 0 = (1.5)(40) = 60$
Standard deviation	$\sigma_X = 10$	$\sigma_{1.5X+0} = (1.5)\sigma_X = (1.5)(10) = 15$

Total cost C is a random variable $C = vQ + F$ so we can apply Rules 1 and 2:

$$\text{Mean of total cost: } \mu_{vQ+F} = v\mu_Q + F = (35)(500) + 24{,}000 = \$41{,}500$$
$$\text{Std. Dev. of total cost: } \sigma_{vQ+F} = v\sigma_Q = (35)(40) = \$1{,}400$$

Sums of Random Variables

Below are two more useful rules that apply to *sums of random variables.* Rule 3 says that the means can be added. Rule 4 says that the variances can be added *if* the variables are independent. These rules apply to the sum of any number of variables and are useful for analyzing situations where we must combine random variables. For example, if a firm has k different products, each with a known stochastic demand, then total revenue R is the sum of the revenue for each of the k products: $R = R_1 + R_2 + R_3 + \cdots + R_k$.

Rule 3: $\mu_{X+Y} = \mu_X + \mu_Y$ (mean of sum of two random variables X and Y)

Rule 4: $\sigma_{X+Y} = \sqrt{\sigma_X{}^2 + \sigma_Y{}^2}$ (standard deviation of sum *if* X and Y are independent)

Application: Gasoline Expenses

The daily gasoline expense of Apex Movers, Inc., is a random variable with mean $\mu = \$125$ and standard deviation $\sigma = \$35$ ($\sigma^2 = 1225$). If we define Y to be the gasoline expense *per year,* and there are 250 working days per year at Apex Movers, then

$$Y = \sum_{i=1}^{250} X_i \qquad \mu_Y = 250 \times 125 = \$31{,}250 \qquad \sigma_Y = \sqrt{250 \times 1225} = \$553$$

This assumes that daily gasoline expenses are independent of each other.

Application: Project Scheduling

The initial phase of a construction project entails three activities that must be undertaken sequentially (that is, the second activity cannot begin until the first is complete, and so on) and the time to complete each activity is a random variable with a known mean and variance:

Excavation	*Foundations*	*Structural Steel*
$\mu_1 = 25$ days	$\mu_2 = 14$ days	$\mu_3 = 58$ days
$\sigma_1{}^2 = 3$ days^2	$\sigma_2{}^2 = 2$ days^2	$\sigma_3{}^2 = 7$ days^2

By Rule 3, the mean time to complete the whole project is the sum of the task means (even if the tasks are not independent):

$$\mu = \mu_1 + \mu_2 + \mu_3 = 25 + 14 + 58 = 97 \text{ days}$$

By Rule 4, if the times to complete each activity are *independent,* the overall variance for the project is the sum of the task variances, so the standard deviation for the entire project is:

$$\sigma = \sqrt{\sigma_1{}^2 + \sigma_2{}^2 + \sigma_3{}^2} = \sqrt{3 + 2 + 7} = \sqrt{12} = 3.464 \text{ days}$$

From this information, we can construct $\mu \pm 1\sigma$ or $\mu \pm 2\sigma$ intervals for the entire project:

$97 \pm (1)(3.464)$, or between 93.5 and 100.5 days

$97 \pm (2)(3.464)$, or between 90.1 and 103.9 days

So the *Empirical Rule* would imply that there is about a 95 percent chance that the project will take between 90.1 and 103.9 days. This calculation could help the construction firm estimate upper and lower bounds for the project completion time. Of course, if the distribution is not normal, the Empirical Rule may not apply.

SECTION EXERCISES

*6.46 The height of a Los Angeles Lakers basketball player averages 6 feet 7.6 inches (i.e., 79.6 inches) with a standard deviation of 3.24 inches. To convert from inches to centimeters, we multiply by 2.54. (a) In centimeters, what is the mean? (b) In centimeters, what is the standard deviation? (c) Which rules did you use? (Data are from www.cnnsi.com/basketball/nba/rosters.)

*6.47 July sales for Melodic Kortholt, Ltd., average $\mu_1 = \$9,500$ with $\sigma_1{}^2 = \$1,250$. August sales average $\mu_2 = \$7,400$ with $\sigma_2{}^2 = \$1,425$. September sales average $\mu_3 = \$8,600$ with $\sigma_3{}^2 = \$1,610$. (a) Find the mean and standard deviation of total sales for the third quarter. (b) What assumptions are you making?

Chapter Summary

A **random variable** assigns a numerical value to each outcome in the sample space of a **stochastic process**. A **discrete random variable** has a countable number of distinct values. Probabilities in a **discrete probability distribution** must be between zero and one, and must sum to one. The **expected value** is the mean of the distribution, measuring central tendency, and its **variance** is a measure of dispersion. A known distribution is described by its **parameters**, which imply its **probability distribution function** (PDF) and its **cumulative distribution function** (CDF).

As summarized in Table 6.14 the **uniform distribution** has two parameters (a, b) that define its range $a \leq X \leq b$. The **Bernoulli distribution** has one parameter $(\pi$, the probability of success) and two outcomes (0 or 1). The **binomial distribution** has two parameters (n, π). It describes the sum of n independent Bernoulli random experiments with constant probability of success. It may be skewed left $(\pi > .50)$ or right $(\pi < .50)$ or symmetric $(\pi = .50)$ but becomes less skewed as n increases. The **Poisson distribution** has one parameter $(\lambda$, the mean arrival rate). It describes arrivals of independent events per unit of time or space. It is always right-skewed, becoming less so as λ increases. The **hypergeometric distribution** has three parameters (N, n, s). It is like a binomial, except that sampling of n items is without replacement from

TABLE 6.14 **Comparison of Models**

Model	Parameters	Mean $E(X)$	Variance $V(X)$	Characteristics
Bernoulli	π	π	$\pi(1 - \pi)$	Used to generate the binomial.
Binomial	n, π	$n\pi$	$n\pi(1 - \pi)$	Skewed right if $\pi < .50$, left if $\pi > .50$.
Geometric	π	$1/\pi$	$(1 - \pi)/\pi^2$	Always skewed right and leptokurtic.
Hypergeometric	N, n, s	$n\pi$ where $\pi = s/N$	$n\pi(1 - \pi)[(N - n)/(N - 1)]$	Like binomial except sampling without replacement from a finite population.
Poisson	λ	λ	λ	Always skewed right and leptokurtic.
Uniform	a, b	$(a + b)/2$	$[(b - a + 1)^2 - 1]/12$	Always symmetric and platykurtic.

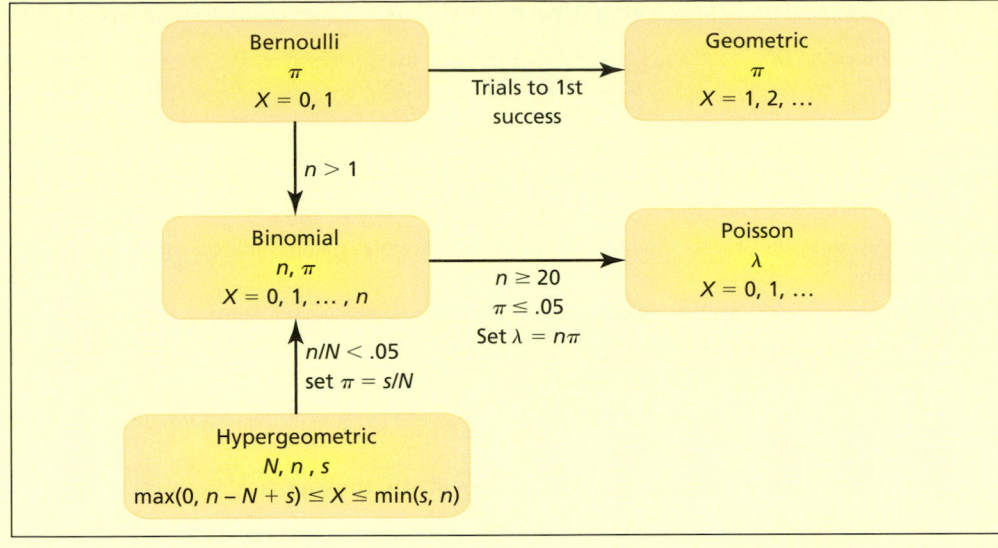

FIGURE 6.33

Relationships among discrete models

a finite population of N items containing s successes. The **geometric distribution** is a one-parameter model (π, the probability of success) that describes the number of trials until the first success. Figure 6.33 shows the relationships among these five discrete models.

Rules for **linear transformations** of random variables say that adding a constant to a random variable shifts the distribution, but does not changes its variance, while multiplying a random variable by a constant changes both its mean and its variance. Rules for summing random variables permit adding of their means, but their variances can be summed only if the random variables are independent.

Key Terms

Commonly Used Formulas in Discrete Distributions

Total probability: $\displaystyle\sum_{i=1}^{n} P(x_i) = 1$

Expected value: $\displaystyle E(X) = \mu = \sum_{i=1}^{n} x_i P(x_i)$ if there are n distinct values $x_1, x_2, \ldots, x_n$

Variance: $\displaystyle V(X) = \sigma^2 = \sum_{i=1}^{n} [x_i - \mu]^2 P(x_i)$

Uniform PDF: $\displaystyle P(x) = \frac{1}{b - a + 1}$ $X = a, a + 1, \ldots, b$

Binomial PDF: $\displaystyle P(x) = \frac{n!}{x!(n - x)!} \pi^x (1 - \pi)^{n - x}$ $X = 0, 1, 2, \ldots, n$

Poisson PDF: $\displaystyle P(x) = \frac{\lambda^x e^{-\lambda}}{x!}$ $X = 0, 1, 2, \ldots$

Hypergeometric PDF: $$P(x) = \frac{\binom{s}{x}\binom{N-s}{n-x}}{\binom{N}{n}} \qquad \max(0, n-N+s) \leq X \leq \min(s, n)$$

Geometric PDF: $$P(x) = \pi(1-\pi)^{x-1} \qquad X = 1, 2, \ldots$$

Chapter Review

1. Define (a) stochastic process; (b) random variable; (c) discrete random variable; and (d) probability distribution.

2. Without using formulas, explain the meaning of (a) expected value of a random variable; (b) actuarial fairness; and (c) variance of a random variable.

3. What is the difference between a PDF and a CDF? Sketch a picture of each.

4. (a) What are the two parameters of a uniform distribution? (b) Why is the uniform distribution the first one considered in this chapter?

5. (a) Describe a Bernoulli experiment and give two examples. (b) What is the connection between a Bernoulli experiment and a binomial distribution?

6. (a) What are the parameters of a binomial distribution? (b) What is the mean of a binomial distribution? The standard deviation? (c) When is a binomial skewed right? Skewed left? Symmetric? (d) Suggest a data-generating situation that might be binomial.

7. (a) What are the parameters of a Poisson distribution? (b) What is the mean of a Poisson distribution? The standard deviation? (c) Is a Poisson ever symmetric? (d) Suggest a data-generating situation that might be Poisson.

8. In the binomial and Poisson models, why is the assumption of independent events important?

*9. (a) When are we justified in using the Poisson approximation to the binomial? (b) Why would we want to do this approximation?

10. (a) Explain a situation when we would need the hypergeometric distribution. (b) What are the three parameters of the hypergeometric distribution? (c) How does it differ from a binomial distribution?

*11. When are we justified in using (a) the Poisson approximation to the binomial? (b) The binomial approximation to the hypergeometric?

12. (a) Name a situation when we would need the (a) hypergeometric distribution; (b)* geometric distribution; (c) uniform distribution.

*13. What do Rules 1 and 2 say about transforming a random variable?

*14. What do Rules 3 and 4 say about sums of several random variables?

CHAPTER EXERCISES

Note: Show your work clearly. Problems marked * are harder or rely on optional material from this chapter.

6.48 The probability that a 30-year-old white male will live another year is .99842. What premium would an insurance company charge to break even on a 1-year $1 million term life insurance policy? (Data are from National Center for Health Statistics, *National Vital Statistics Reports* 47, no. 28 [December 13, 1999], p. 8.)

6.49 If a fair die rolled once comes up 6 you win $100. Otherwise, you lose $15. Would a rational person play this game? Justify your answer, using the definition of $E(X)$.

6.50 As a birthday gift, you are mailing a new personal digital assistant (PDA) to your cousin in Toledo. The PDA cost $250. There is a 2 percent chance it will be lost or damaged in the mail. Is it worth $4 to insure the mailing? Explain, using the concept of expected value.

6.51 A large sample of two-digit lottery numbers between 01 and 44 shows a mean of 29.22 and a standard deviation of 18.71. (a) To what extent do these results differ from a uniform distribution? (b) What else would you want to know to decide whether the random number generator was working correctly?

6.52 Use Excel to generate 1,000 random integers in the range 1 through 5. (a) What is the expected mean and standard deviation? (b) What is your sample mean and standard deviation? (c) Is your sample consistent with the uniform model? Discuss. (d) Show the Excel formula you used.

6.53   Consider the Bernoulli model. What would be a typical probability of success (π) for (a) free throw shooting by a good college basketball player? (b) Hits by a good baseball batter? (c) Passes completed by a good college football quarterback? (d) Incorrect answers on a five-part multiple choice exam if you are guessing? (e) Can you suggest reasons why independent events might not be assumed in some of these situations? Explain.

6.54   For patients over age 80, the probability is .05 that a coronary bypass patient will die soon after the surgery. (a) If a hospital performs eight such operations, what is the probability of no fatalities? (b) Two or more fatalities? (c) What is the expected number of fatalities? (d) Find the standard deviation. (e) Is the distribution skewed right, skewed left, or symmetric? (See *Scientific American* 283, no. 4 [October 2000], p. 60.)

6.55   In a certain year, on average 10 percent of the vehicles tested for emissions failed the test. Suppose that five vehicles are tested. (a) What is the probability that all pass? (b) All but one pass? (c) Sketch the probability distribution and discuss its shape.

6.56   The probability that an American CEO can transact business in a foreign language is .20. Ten American CEOs are chosen at random. (a) What is the probability that none can transact business in a foreign language? (b) That at least two can? (c) That all 10 can? (d) Sketch the probability distribution and discuss its appearance. (See Lamalie Associates, *The Lamalie Report on Top Executives of the 1990's,* p. 11.)

6.57   In a certain Kentucky Fried Chicken franchise, half of the customers typically request "crispy" instead of "original." (a) What is the probability that none of the next four customers will request "crispy?" (b) At least two? (c) At most two? (d) Construct the probability distribution (Excel or Appendix A), make a graph of its PDF, and describe its shape.

6.58   On average, 40 percent of U.S. beer drinkers order light beer. (a) What is the probability that none of the next eight customers who order beer will order light beer? (b) That one customer will? (c) Two customers? (d) Fewer than three? (e) Construct the probability distribution (Excel or Appendix A), make a graph of its PDF, and describe its shape. (See George E. Belch and Michael A. Belch, *Advertising & Promotion,* 6th ed. [McGraw-Hill, 2004], p. 43.)

6.59   Write the Excel binomial formula for each probability.
a. Three successes in 20 trials with a 30 percent chance of success.
b. Seven successes in 50 trials with a 10 percent chance of success.
c. Six or fewer successes in 80 trials with a 5 percent chance of success.
d. At least 30 successes in 120 trials with a 20 percent chance of success.

6.60   Tired of careless spelling and grammar, a company decides to administer a test to all job applicants. The test consists of 20 sentences. Applicants must state whether each sentence contains any grammar or spelling errors. Half the sentences contain errors. The company requires a score of 14 or more. (a) If an applicant guesses randomly, what is the probability of passing? (b) What minimum score would be required to reduce the probability "passing by guessing" to 5 percent or less?

6.61   The default rate on government-guaranteed student loans at a certain private 4-year institution is 7 percent. The college extends 10 such loans. (a) What is the probability that none of them will default? (b) That at least three will default? (c) What is the expected number of defaults?

6.62   Experience indicates that 8 percent of the pairs of men's trousers dropped off for dry cleaning will have an object in the pocket that should be removed before cleaning. Suppose that 14 pairs of pants are dropped off and the cleaner forgets to check the pockets. What is the probability that none have an object in the pocket?

6.63   A study by the Parents' Television Council showed that 80 percent of movie commercials aired on network television between 8 and 9 P.M. (the prime family viewing hour) were for R-rated films. (a) Find the probability that in 16 commercials during this time slot at least 10 will be for R-rated films. (b) Find the probability of fewer than 8 R-rated films.

6.64   Write the Excel formula for each Poisson probability, using a mean arrival rate of 10 arrivals per hour.
a. Seven arrivals.
b. Three arrivals.
c. Fewer than five arrivals.
d. At least 11 arrivals.

6.65   A small feeder airline knows that the probability is .10 that a reservation holder will not show up for its daily 7:15 A.M. flight into a hub airport. The flight carries 10 passengers. (a) If the flight is fully booked, what is the probability that all those with reservations will show up? (b) If the airline overbooks by selling 11 seats, what is the probability that no one will have to be bumped? (c) That more than one passenger will be bumped? *(d) The airline wants to overbook the flight by enough seats to ensure a 95 percent chance that the flight will be full, even if some passengers may be bumped. How many seats would it sell?

6.66 Although television HDTV converters are tested before they are placed in the installer's truck, the installer knows that 20 percent of them still won't work properly. The driver must install eight converters today in an apartment building. (a) Ten converters are placed in the truck. What is the probability that the driver will have enough working converters? *(b) How many boxes should the driver load to ensure a 95 percent probability of having enough working converters?

6.67 (a) Why might the number of calls received per minute at a fire station not be a Poisson event? (b) Name two other events per unit of time that might violate the assumptions of the Poisson model.

6.68 The U.S. mint, which produces billions of coins annually, has a mean daily defect rate of 5.2 coins. Let X be the number of defective coins produced on a given day. (a) Justify the use of the Poisson model. (b) On a given day, what is the probability of exactly five defective coins? (c) More than 10? (d) Construct the probability distribution (Excel or Appendix B) and make a graph of its PDF. (Data are from *Scientific American* 271, no. 3 [September 1994], pp. 48–53.)

6.69 Tampa, Florida, receives an average of 14 lightning strikes per square kilometer a year. Let X be the number of lightning strikes on a particular square kilometer in a given year. (a) Justify the use of the Poisson model. (b) What is the probability of at least five strikes? (c) More than 20 strikes? (d) Construct the probability distribution (Excel or Appendix B) and make a graph of its PDF. (Data are from *Detroit Free Press,* September 11, 1990, p. 1C.)

6.70 In the U.K. in a recent year, potentially dangerous commercial aircraft incidents (e.g., near collisions) averaged 1.2 per 100,000 flying hours. Let X be the number of incidents in a 100,000-hour period. (a) Justify the use of the Poisson model. (b) What is the probability of at least one incident? (c) More than three incidents? (d) Construct the probability distribution (Excel or Appendix B) and make a graph of its PDF. (Data are from *Aviation Week and Space Technology* 151, no. 13 [September 27, 1999], p. 17.)

6.71 At an outpatient mental health clinic, appointment cancellations occur at a mean rate of 1.5 per day on a typical Wednesday. Let X be the number of cancellations on a particular Wednesday. (a) Justify the use of the Poisson model. (b) What is the probability that no cancellations will occur on a particular Wednesday? (c) That one will? (d) More than two? (e) Five or more?

6.72 During the period 1975–1984, the mean number of fatal airline crashes was 2.8 crashes per year. In 1985 there were four fatal airline crashes. A news story appeared, entitled "Trouble in Our Skies," suggesting inadequate FAA surveillance. (a) Justify the use of the Poisson model. (b) Based on the historical average, what was the probability of at least four fatal crashes? (c) Of fewer than four crashes? (d) In your opinion, how unusual was 1985? (Data are from *Detroit Free Press,* September 15, 1985, p. 1A.)

6.73 In a certain automobile manufacturing paint shop, paint defects on the hood occur at a mean rate of 0.8 defects per square meter. A hood on a certain car has an area of 3 square meters. (a) Justify the use of the Poisson model. (b) If a customer inspects a hood at random, what is the probability that there will be no defects? (c) One defect? (d) Fewer than two defects?

6.74 In the manufacture of gallium arsenide wafers for computer chips, defects average 10 per square centimeter. Let X be the number of defects on a given square centimeter. (a) Justify the use of the Poisson model. (b) What is the probability of fewer than five defects? (c) More than 15 defects? (d) Construct the probability distribution (Excel or Appendix B) and make a graph of its PDF. (Data are from *Scientific American* 266, no. 2 [February 1992], p. 102.)

*6.75 In our Milky Way galaxy, supernovas occur at a mean rate of 1 every 30 years. Let X be the number of supernovas in a given year. (a) Find the mean and standard deviation of X. (b) Using the probability density function formula, what is the probability of at least one supernova in a given year? Show your work. (c) Why not use Appendix B instead of the formula? (Data are from *Scientific American* 269, no. 6 [December 1993], p. 75.)

6.76 In Northern Yellowstone Lake, earthquakes occur at a mean rate of 1.2 quakes per year. Let X be the number of quakes in a given year. (a) Justify the use of the Poisson model. (b) What is the probability of fewer than three quakes? (c) More than five quakes? (d) Construct the probability distribution (Excel or Appendix B) and make a graph of its PDF. (Data are from *Scientific American* 288, no. 3 [March 2003], p. 33.)

6.77 On New York's Verrazano Narrows bridge, traffic accidents occur at a mean rate of 2.0 crashes per day. Let X be the number of crashes in a given day. (a) Justify the use of the Poisson model.

(b) What is the probability of at least one crash? (c) Fewer than five crashes? (d) Construct the probability distribution (Excel or Appendix B), make a graph of its PDF, and describe its shape. (Data are from *New Yorker,* December 2, 2002, p. 64.)

APPROXIMATIONS

*6.78   Leaks occur in a pipeline at a mean rate of 1 leak per 1,000 meters. In a 2,500-meter section of pipe, what is the probability of (a) no leaks? (b) Three or more leaks? (c) Sketch the probability distribution. (d) What is the expected number of leaks? (e) Why not use the binomial? (f) Will the approximation be good?

*6.79   Among live deliveries, the probability of a twin birth is .02. (a) In 200 live deliveries, how many would be expected to have twin births? (b) What is the probability of no twin births? (c) One twin birth? (d) Calculate these probabilities both with and without an approximation. (e) Is the approximation justified? Discuss fully.

*6.80   The probability is .03 that a passenger on American Airlines flight 2458 is a Platinum flyer (50,000 miles per year). If 200 passengers take this flight, use Excel to find the binomial probability of (a) no Platinum flyers. (b) One Platinum flyer. (c) Two Platinum flyers. (d) Calculate the same probabilities using a Poisson approximation. (e) Is the Poisson approximation justified? Explain.

*6.81   The National Safety Council reports that over a 5-year period the probability is .00114 that a hang glider participant will be killed. Suppose that 4,386 hang glider fans participate in this sport over a 5-year period. (a) What is the expected number of fatalities? (b) What is the standard deviation? (c) What is the approximate probability of fewer than five fatalities? (d) More than 10 fatalities? (e) Explain any assumptions that are needed to solve this problem. (See *U.S. News & World Report,* January 15, 1990, p. 67.)

*6.82   On average, 2 percent of all persons who are given a breathalyzer test by the State Police pass the test (blood alcohol under .08 percent). Suppose that 500 breathalyzer tests are given. (a) What is the expected number who pass the test? (b) What is the approximate Poisson probability that 5 or fewer will pass the test?

6.83   From a deck of 52 cards, 5 cards are dealt at random. Let X be the number of hearts in the sample. (a) Use the hypergeometric formula to find the probability that all 5 cards are hearts. (b) Would a binomial approximation be appropriate here? Discuss.

6.84   A turbine has 50 blades of which 2 have microscopic cracks. An inspector examines 10 blades at random. Let X be the number of cracked blades in the sample. (a) Justify the use of the hypergeometric distribution and state its parameters. (b) What is the range of X? (c) What is the probability that $X = 0$? $X = 1$? $X = 2$? *Hint:* Use Excel to check your work.

GEOMETRIC

*6.85   In a certain city, 8 percent of the cars have a burned-out headlight. (a) What is the expected number that must be inspected before the first one with a burned-out headlight is found? (b) What is the standard deviation? (c) What is the probability of finding the first one within the first five cars? *Hint:* use the CDF.

*6.86   For patients aged 81 to 90, the probability is .07 that a coronary bypass patient will die soon after the surgery. (a) What is the expected number of operations until the next fatality? (b) What is the probability of conducting 20 or more operations before the first fatality? (See *Scientific American* 283, no. 4 [October 2000], p. 60.) *Hint:* use the CDF.

*6.87   Historically, 5 percent of a mail-order firm's regular charge-account customers have an incorrect current address in the firm's computer database. (a) What is the expected number of customers until the next one with an incorrect current address places an order? (b) What is the probability of mailing 30 bills or more until the next one is returned with a wrong address? *Hint:* use the CDF.

*6.88   At a certain clinic, 2 percent of all pap smears show signs of abnormality. (a) What is the expected number of pap smears that must be inspected before the next abnormal one is found? (b) What is the standard deviation? (c) Based on your answers to (a) and (b), why would it be difficult for a technician to maintain vigilance while inspecting pap smears?

*6.89   For the uniform discrete distribution, prove that the $P(X)$ sum to 1. Show your reasoning clearly.

6.90   A lottery consists of uniformly distributed random numbers from 0000 to 9999. Find the mean and standard deviation. Show your reasoning clearly.

TRANSFORMATIONS

*6.91 The weight of a Los Angeles Lakers basketball player averages 233.1 pounds with a standard deviation of 34.95 pounds. To express these measurements in terms a European would understand, we could convert from pounds to kilograms by multiplying by .4536. (a) In kilograms, what is the mean? (b) In kilograms, what is the standard deviation? (Data are from **www.cnnsi.com/basketball/nba/rosters.**)

*6.92 The Rejuvo Corp. manufactures granite countertop cleaner and polish. Quarterly sales Q is a random variable with a mean of 25,000 bottles and a standard deviation of 2,000 bottles. Variable cost is $8 per unit and fixed cost is $150,000. (a) Find the mean and standard deviation of Rejuvo's total cost. (b) If all bottles are sold, what would the selling price have to be to break even, on average? To make a profit of $20,000?

*6.93 The scores on Professor Lazare's first exam have a mean of 70 with a standard deviation of 8. On the second exam, the mean is 80 with a standard deviation of 6. Each student's scores are summed. (a) What is the expected value (mean) of the sum of a student's scores on both exams? (b) What is the standard deviation of the sum? (c) What assumption was made in your answer to the previous question? Do you think it is valid?

*6.94 A manufacturing project has five independent phases whose completion must be sequential. The time to complete each phase is a random variable. The mean and standard deviation of the time for each phase is shown below. Find the expected completion time and make a 2-sigma interval around the mean ($\mu \pm 2\sigma$). State your assumptions.

Phase	Mean (hours)	Std. Dev. (hours)
Set up dies and other tools	20	4
Milling and machining	10	2
Finishing and painting	14	3
Packing and crating	6	2
Shipping	48	6

*6.95 In September, demand for industrial furnace boilers at a large plumbing supply warehouse has a mean of 7 boilers with a standard deviation of 2 boilers. The warehouse pays a unit cost of $2,225 per boiler plus a fee of $500 per month to act as dealer for these boilers. Boilers are sold for $2,850 each. (a) Find the mean and standard deviation of September profit (revenue minus cost). (b) Which rules did you use?

*6.96 Professor Hardtack gave an exam with a mean score of 25 and a standard deviation of 6. After looking at the distribution, he felt the scores were too low and asked two colleagues for advice on how to raise the mean to 75. Professor Senex suggested adding 50 to everyone's score, while Professor Juven suggested tripling everyone's score. Explain carefully the effects of these alternatives on the distribution of scores.

*6.97 A commuter passes a certain traffic light every day on her way to work. On a randomly chosen day there is a 25 percent chance that the light will be red. (a) If she commutes to work 240 days a year, what is the expected number of times the light will be red? (b) What is the variance? (c) Construct $\mu \pm 1\sigma$ and $\mu \pm 2\sigma$ intervals about the mean and interpret them. Under what circumstances would the Empirical Rule apply?

Related Reading

Evans, Merran; Nicholas Hastings; and Brian Peacock. *Statistical Distributions.* 3rd ed. John Wiley & Sons, 2000.

LearningStats Unit 06   Discrete Distribution

LearningStats Unit 06 covers expected value and discrete distributions. Modules are designed for self-study, so you can proceed at your own pace, concentrate on material that is new, and pass quickly over things that you already know. Your instructor may assign specific modules, or you may decide to check them out because the topic sounds interesting.

Topic	LearningStats Modules
Discrete distributions	⬛ Distributions: An Overview ⬛ Discrete Distributions ⬛ Discrete Distributions: Examples ⬛ Probability Calculator ⬛ Random Discrete Data
Expected value	⬛ Life Insurance
Approximations	⬛ Binomial/Poisson Approximation
Equations	⬛ Discrete Models: Characteristics
Tables	⬛ Table A—Binomial Probabilities ⬛ Table B—Poisson Probabilities
Applications	⬛ Hypergeometric Probabilities

Key: ⬛ = PowerPoint   ⬛ = Word   ⬛ = Excel

Visual Statistics

Visual Statistics Modules on Discrete Distributions

Module	Module Name
2	**VS** Visualizing a Random Process
4	**VS** Visualizing Discrete Distributions

Visual Statistics Modules 2 and 4 (included on your CD) are designed to help you

- Recognize that outcomes of a stochastic process may exhibit regularity even though the process is random.
- Learn through experimentation how changing the parameters can affect the outcomes of an experiment.
- Visualize data-generating situations that give rise to common probability distributions.
- Recognize common discrete distributions and their cumulative distribution functions.
- Identify the parameters of common discrete distributions and how they affect its shape.
- Understand when to apply approximations and learn to assess their accuracy.

The worktext chapter (included on the CD in .PDF format) contains a list of concepts covered, objectives of the module, overview of concepts, illustration of concepts, orientation to module features, learning exercises (basic, intermediate, advanced), learning projects (individual, team), self-evaluation quiz, glossary of terms, and solutions to the self-evaluation quiz.

CHAPTER

7

Continuous Distributions

Chapter Contents

Chapter Learning Objectives

When you finish this chapter you should be able to

- Distinguish between discrete and continuous random variables.
- State the parameters and uses of the uniform, normal, and exponential distributions.
- Select, in a problem context, the appropriate continuous distribution.
- Sketch uniform, normal, and exponential probability density functions and areas.
- Use a table or spreadsheet to find uniform, normal, or exponential areas for a given X.
- Solve for X for a given area from a uniform, normal, or exponential model.
- Know how and when a normal distribution can approximate a binomial or a Poisson.
- Know how a triangular distribution is used in "what-if" analysis.

Events as Intervals

If *X* is a *discrete variable,* each value of *X* has its own probability $P(X)$ and the probability function looks like a stair-step bar graph. But when *X* is a *continuous variable,* it is impossible to speak of the probability of a point, because the values of *X* are not a set of discrete points. Instead, events are *intervals,* and probabilities are areas underneath smooth curves. For example, if *X* is the length of a phone call (in seconds) we might want to find $P(60 \leq X \leq 120)$, the probability that a call lasts between 60 and 120 seconds. An interval could be open-ended, such as $X \geq 45$ (the event that a call lasts at least 45 seconds) or $X < 30$ (the event that a call lasts less than 30 seconds). In fact, open-ended events are quite common.

For a continuous variable, it doesn't matter (except for aesthetics) whether we include the end point or not, since *a point has no probability.* That is, for a continuous variable $P(52 < X < 56)$ is the same as $P(52 \leq X \leq 56)$, as shown in Figure 7.1. Unlike a discrete random variable, a point such as $X = 52$ has no probability because no call will last *exactly* 52 seconds (if you measured very precisely, *X* would always be a number like 52.0061 seconds or 51.9873 seconds).

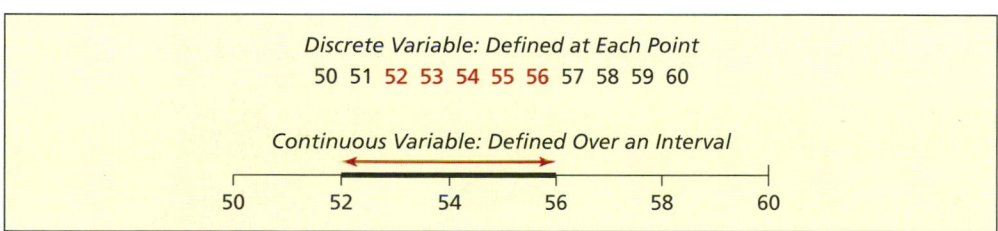

Discrete Variable: Defined at Each Point
50 51 52 53 54 55 56 57 58 59 60

Continuous Variable: Defined Over an Interval
50   52   54   56   58   60

FIGURE 7.1

Discrete and continuous events

PDFs and CDFs

A known distribution can be described either by its *probability density function (PDF)* or by its *cumulative distribution function (CDF).* For a continuous random variable, the PDF is an equation that shows the height of the curve $f(x)$ at each possible value of *X* over the *range* of *X.* Any continuous PDF must be nonnegative and the area under the entire PDF must be 1. The

253

mean, variance, and shape of the distribution depend on the PDF and its *parameters*. The CDF is denoted $F(x)$ and shows $P(X \leq x)$, the cumulative *area* to the left of a given value of X. The CDF is useful for probabilities, while the PDF reveals the *shape* of the distribution. There are Excel functions for most common PDFs or CDFs.

For example, Figure 7.2 shows a hypothetical PDF for a distribution of exam scores. It is a smooth curve showing the probability density at points along the X-axis. The CDF in Figure 7.3 shows the *cumulative* proportion of scores, gradually approaching 1 as X approaches 90. In this illustration, the distribution is symmetric and bell-shaped (Gaussian) with a mean of 75 and a standard deviation of 5.

FIGURE 7.2

Normal PDF

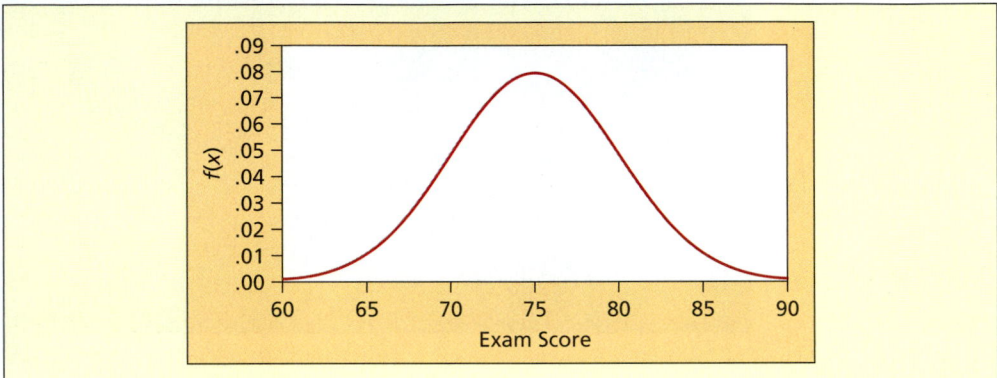

FIGURE 7.3

Normal CDF

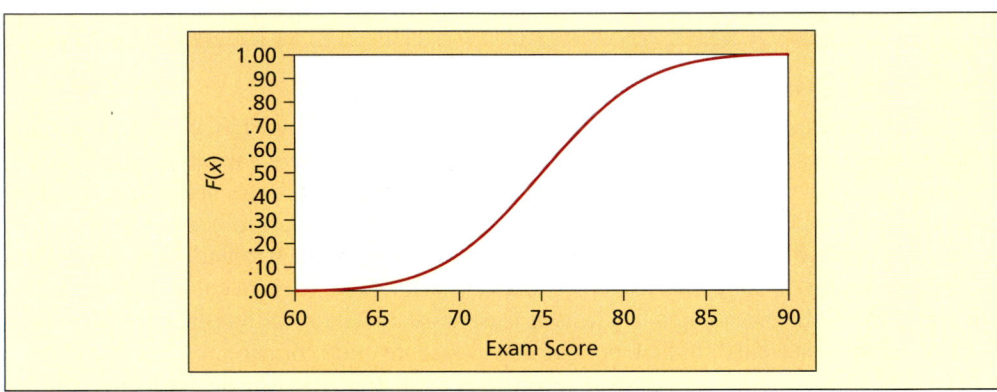

Probabilities as Areas

With discrete variables, we take sums of probabilities over groups of points. But continuous probability functions are smooth curves, so the area *at* any point would be zero. Instead of taking sums of probabilities, we speak of *areas under curves*. In calculus terms, we would say that $P(a < X < b)$ is the **integral** of the probability density function $f(x)$ over the interval from a to b. Figure 7.4 shows the area under a continuous PDF. The entire area under any PDF must be 1.

FIGURE 7.4

Probability as an area

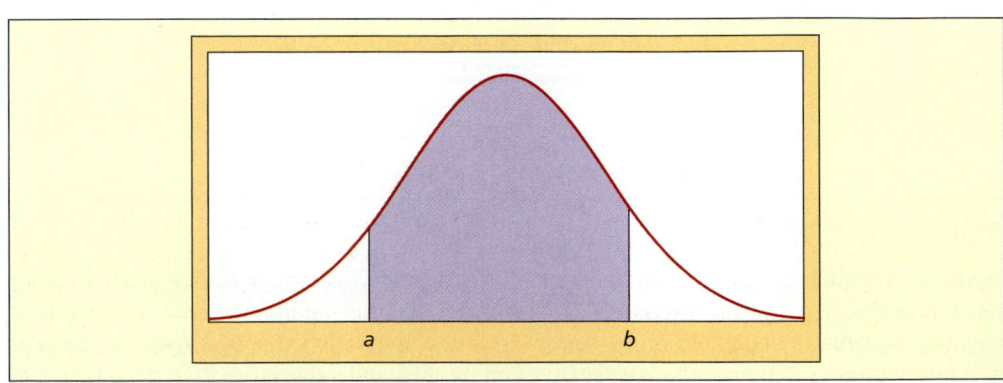

Expected Value and Variance

The mean and variance of a continuous random variable are analogous to $E(X)$ and $V(X)$ for a discrete random variable, except that the integral sign $\int$ replaces the summation sign Σ. Integrals are taken over all X-values. The mean is still the balancing point or fulcrum for the entire distribution, and the variance is still a measure of dispersion about the mean. The mean is still the average of all X-values weighted by their probabilities, and the variance is still the weighted average of all squared deviations around the mean. The standard deviation is still the square root of the variance.

	Continuous Variable	*Discrete Variable*	
Mean	$E(X) = \mu = \displaystyle\int_{-\infty}^{+\infty} x f(x)\, dx$	$E(X) = \mu = \displaystyle\sum_{\text{all } x} x P(x)$	**(7.1)**
Variance	$V(X) = \sigma^2 = \displaystyle\int_{-\infty}^{+\infty} (x - \mu)^2 f(x)\, dx$	$V(X) = \sigma^2 = \displaystyle\sum_{\text{all } x} [x - \mu]^2 P(x)$	**(7.2)**

Oh My, Calculus?

Calculus notation is used occasionally for the benefit of those who have studied it. But statistics can be taught without calculus, if you are willing to accept that others have worked out the details by using calculus. If you decide to become an actuary, you *will* use calculus (so don't sell your calculus book). However, in this chapter, the means and variances are presented *without* proof for the distributions that you are most likely to see applied to business situations.

SECTION EXERCISES

7.1   Flight 202 is departing Los Angeles. Is each random variable discrete (D) or continuous (C)?
a. Number of airline passengers traveling with children under age 3.
b. Proportion of passengers traveling without checked luggage.
c. Weight of a randomly chosen passenger on Flight 202.

7.2   It is Saturday morning at Starbucks. Is each random variable discrete (D) or continuous (C)?
a. Temperature of the coffee served to a randomly chosen customer.
b. Number of customers who order only coffee with no food.
c. Waiting time before a randomly chosen customer is handed the order.

7.3   Which of the following could *not* be probability density functions for a continuous random variable? Explain. *Hint:* Find the area under the function $f(x)$.
a. $f(x) = .25$ for $0 \le x \le 1$
b. $f(x) = .25$ for $0 \le x \le 4$
c. $f(x) = x$ for $0 \le x \le 2$

7.4   For a continuous PDF, why can't we sum the probabilities of all x-values to get the total area under the curve?

Characteristics of the Uniform Distribution

7.3
UNIFORM CONTINUOUS DISTRIBUTION

The **uniform continuous distribution** is perhaps the simplest model one can imagine. If X is a random variable that is uniformly distributed between a and b, its PDF has constant height, as shown in Figure 7.5. The uniform continuous distribution is sometimes denoted $U(a, b)$ for short. Its mean and standard deviation are shown in Table 7.1.

Since the PDF is rectangular, you can easily verify that the area under the curve is 1 by multiplying its base $(b - a)$ by its height $1/(b - a)$. Its CDF increases linearly to 1, as shown in

FIGURE 7.5

Uniform PDF

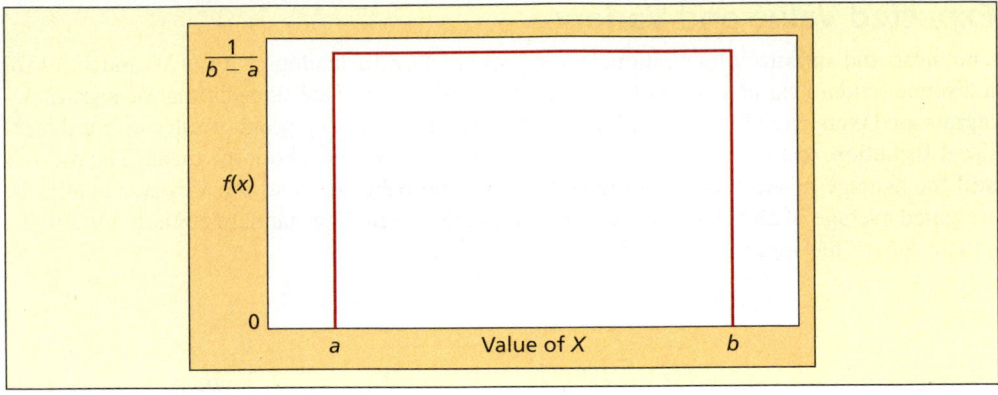

TABLE 7.1

Uniform Continuous Distribution

Parameters	a = lower limit b = upper limit
PDF	$f(x) = \dfrac{1}{b-a}$
CDF	$P(X \le x) = \dfrac{x-a}{b-a}$
Range	$a \le X \le b$
Mean	$\dfrac{a+b}{2}$
Standard deviation	$\sqrt{\dfrac{(b-a)^2}{12}}$
Shape	Symmetric with no mode.
Random data in Excel	=a+b*RAND()
Comments	Used as a conservative what-if benchmark.

FIGURE 7.6

Uniform CDF

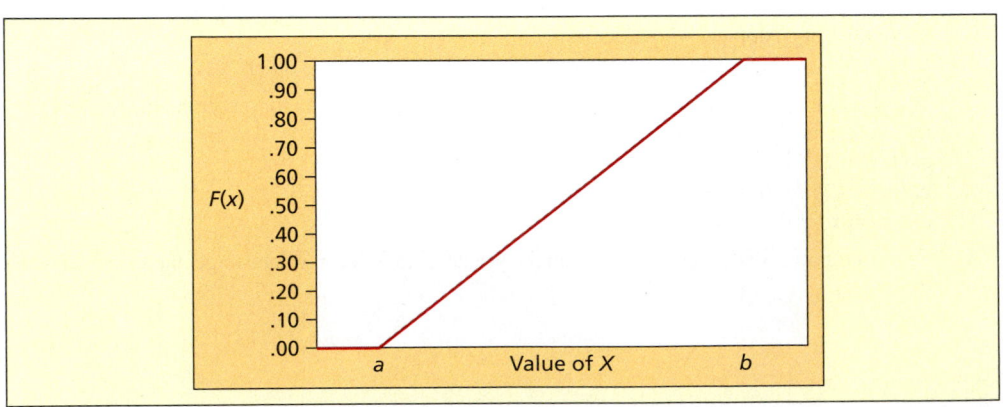

Figure 7.6. Since events can easily be shown as rectangular areas, we rarely need to refer to the CDF, whose formula is just $P(X \le x) = (x - a)/(b - a)$.

The continuous uniform distribution is similar to the discrete uniform distribution if the range is large. For example, three-digit lottery numbers ranging from 000 to 999 would closely resemble a continuous uniform with $a = 0$ and $b = 999$.

An oral surgeon injects a painkiller prior to extracting a tooth. Given the varying characteristics of patients, the dentist views the time for anesthesia effectiveness as a uniform random variable that takes between 15 minutes and 30 minutes. In short notation, we could say that X is $U(15, 30)$. Setting $a = 15$ and $b = 30$ we obtain the mean and standard deviation:

$$\mu = \frac{a+b}{2} = \frac{15+30}{2} = 22.5 \text{ minutes}$$

$$\sigma = \sqrt{\frac{(b-a)^2}{12}} = \sqrt{\frac{(30-15)^2}{12}} = 4.33 \text{ minutes}$$

An event probability is simply an interval width expressed as a proportion of the total. Thus, the probability of taking between c and d minutes is

$$P(c < X < d) = (d-c)/(b-a) \qquad \text{(area between } c \text{ and } d \text{ in a uniform model)} \qquad \textbf{(7.3)}$$

For example, the probability that the anesthetic takes between 20 and 25 minutes is

$$P(20 < X < 25) = (25 - 20)/(30 - 15) = 5/15 = 0.3333, \text{ or } 33.3\%.$$

This situation is illustrated in Figure 7.7.

EXAMPLE

Anesthesia Effectiveness

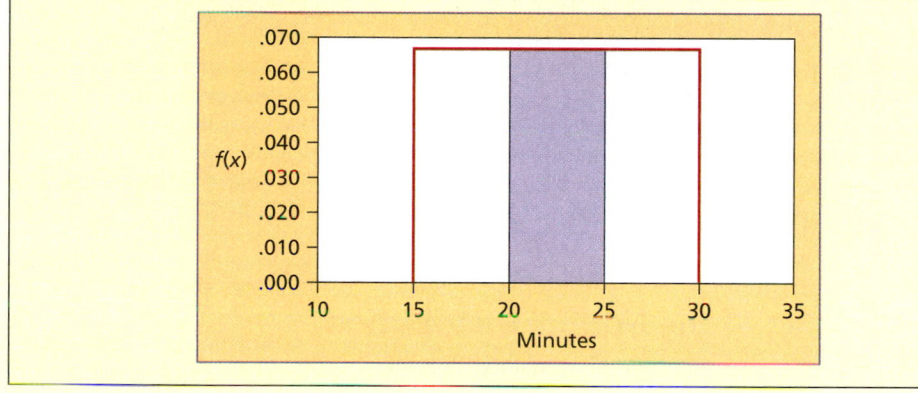

FIGURE 7.7

Uniform probability
$P(20 < X < 25)$

Special Case: Unit Rectangular

The ***unit rectangular distribution,*** denoted $U(0, 1)$, has limits $a = 0$ and $b = 1$, as shown in Figure 7.8. Using the formulas for the mean and standard deviation, you can easily show that this distribution has $\mu = 0.5$ and $\sigma = 0.2887$. This special case is important because Excel's function =RAND() uses this distribution. If you create random numbers by using =RAND() you know what their mean and standard deviation should be. This important distribution is discussed in more detail in later chapters on simulation and goodness-of-fit tests.

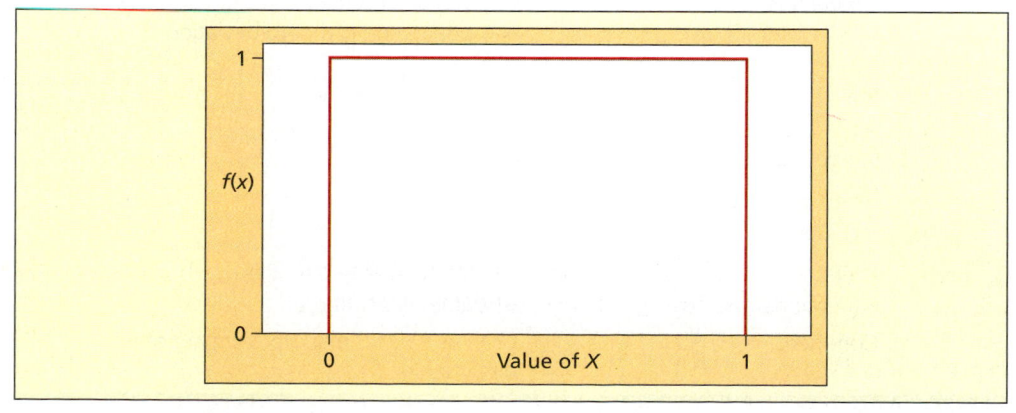

FIGURE 7.8

Unit rectangular distribution

Uses of the Uniform Model

The uniform model $U(a, b)$ is used only when you have no reason to imagine that any values in the range are more likely than others. In reality, this would be a rare situation. However, the uniform distribution can be useful in business for what-if analysis, in situations where you know the "worst" and "best" range, but don't want to make any assumptions about the distribution in between. That may sound like a conservative approach. But bear in mind that if the data-generating situation has any central tendency at all, the assumption of a uniform distribution would lead to a higher standard deviation than might be appropriate. Still, the uniform is often used in business planning, partly because it is easy to understand.

SECTION EXERCISES

7.5 Find the mean and standard deviation for each uniform continuous model.
a. $U(0, 10)$ b. $U(100, 200)$ c. $U(1, 99)$

7.6 Find each uniform continuous probability and sketch a graph showing it as a shaded area.
a. $P(X < 10)$ for $U(0, 50)$
b. $P(X > 500)$ for $U(0, 1,000)$
c. $P(25 < X < 45)$ for $U(15, 65)$

7.7 For a continuous uniform distribution, why is $P(25 < X < 45)$ the same as $P(25 \leq X \leq 45)$?

7.8 The weight of a randomly chosen American passenger car is a uniformly distributed random variable ranging from 2,500 pounds to 4,500 pounds. (a) What is the mean weight of a randomly chosen vehicle? (b) The standard deviation? (c) The quartiles? (d) What is the probability that a vehicle will weigh less than 3,000 pounds? (e) More than 4,000 pounds? (f) Between 3,000 and 4,000 pounds? (Data are from *Popular Science* 254–258 [selected issues]. Parameters are based on actual weights of 1997 through 2002 vehicles.)

7.4 NORMAL DISTRIBUTION

Chapter 5

Characteristics of the Normal Distribution

The ***normal*** or ***Gaussian distribution,*** named for German mathematician Karl Gauss (1777–1855), has already been mentioned several times. Its importance gives it a major role in our discussion of continuous models. A normal probability distribution is defined by two parameters, μ and σ. It is often denoted $N(\mu, \sigma)$. The domain of a normal random variable is $-\infty < X < +\infty$; however, as a practical matter, $\mu - 3\sigma < X < \mu + 3\sigma$ includes almost all the area (as you know from the Empirical Rule in Chapter 4). Besides μ and σ, the normal probability density function $f(x)$ depends on the constants e (approximately 2.71828) and π (approximately 3.14159). It may be shown that the expected value of a normal random variable is μ and that its variance is σ^2. The normal distribution is always symmetric. Table 7.2 summarizes its main characteristics.

TABLE 7.2
Normal Distribution

Parameters	μ = population mean σ = population standard deviation
PDF	$f(x) = \dfrac{1}{\sigma\sqrt{2\pi}} e^{-\frac{1}{2}\left(\frac{x-\mu}{\sigma}\right)^2}$
Range	$-\infty < X < +\infty$
Mean	μ
Std. Dev.	σ
Shape	Symmetric and bell-shaped.
Random data in Excel	=NORMINV(RAND(),μ,σ)
Comment	Used as a benchmark to compare other distributions.

The normal probability density function $f(x)$ reaches a maximum at μ and has points of inflection at $\mu \pm \sigma$ as shown in Figure 7.9. Despite its appearance, $f(x)$ does not reach the X-axis beyond $\mu \pm 3\sigma$, but is merely asymptotic to it. Its single peak and symmetry cause some observers to call it "mound-shaped" or "bell-shaped." Its CDF has a "lazy-S" shape, as shown in Figure 7.10. It approaches, but never reaches, 1.

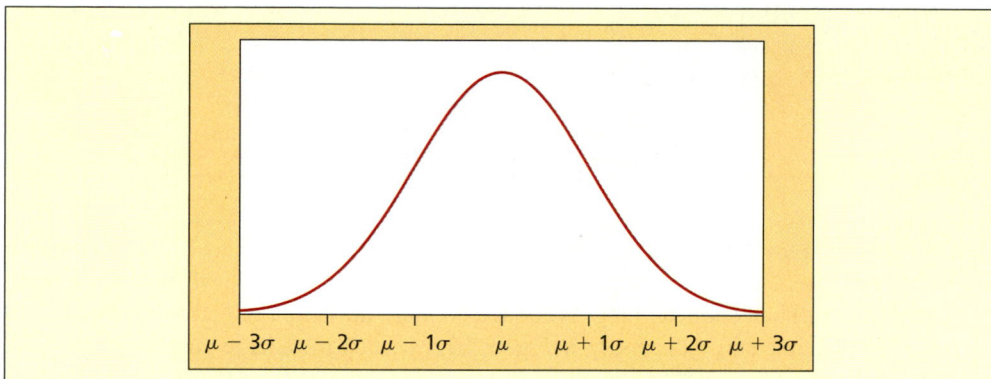

FIGURE 7.9

Normal PDF

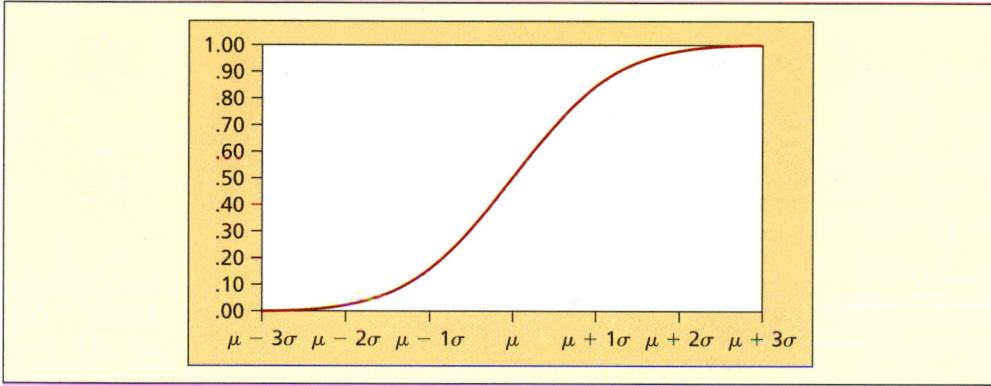

FIGURE 7.10

Normal CDF

A normal distribution with mean μ and standard deviation σ is sometimes denoted $N(\mu, \sigma)$ for short. All normal distributions have the same shape, differing only in the axis scales. For example, Figure 7.11 shows the distribution of diameters of golf balls from a manufacturing process that produces normally distributed diameters with a mean diameter of $\mu = 42.70$ mm and a standard deviation $\sigma = 0.01$ mm, or $N(42.70, 0.01)$ in short notation. Figure 7.12 shows the distribution of scores on the CPA theory exam, assumed to be normal with a mean of $\mu = 70$ and a standard deviation $\sigma = 10$, or $N(70, 10)$ in short notation. Although the shape of each PDF is the same, notice that the horizontal and vertical axis scales differ.

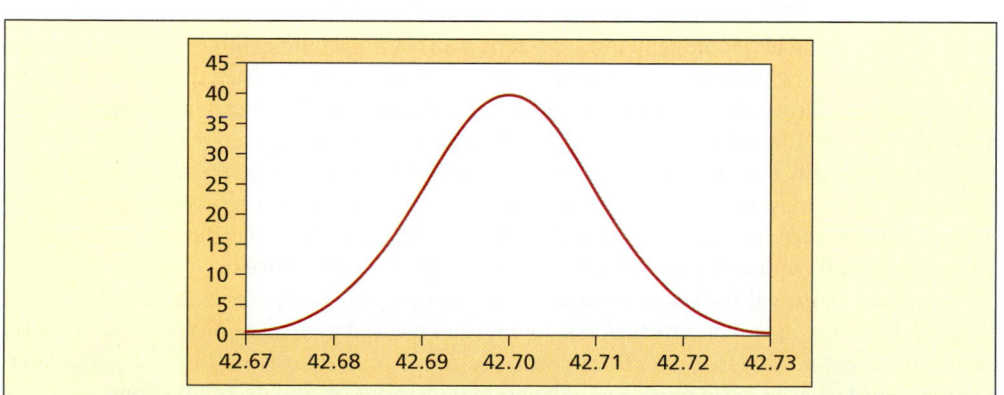

FIGURE 7.11

Golf ball diameter (mm)

FIGURE 7.12

CPA exam scores (percent)

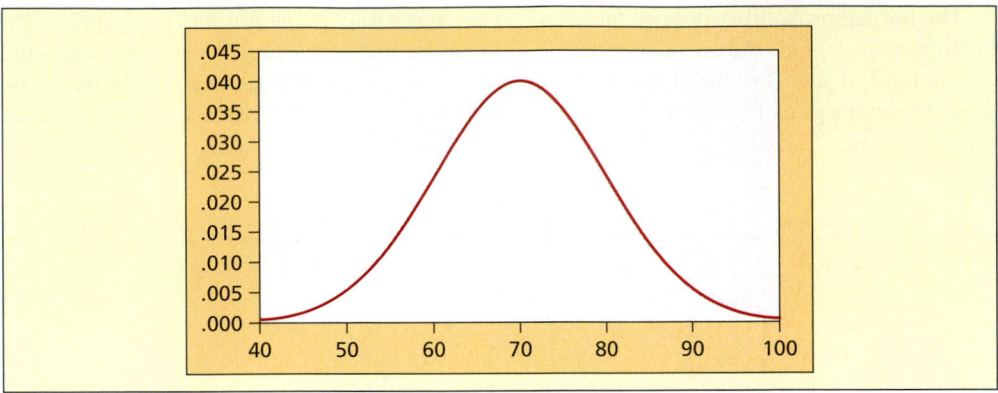

It is a common myth that $f(x)$ must be smaller than 1, but in Figure 7.11 you can see that this is not the case. Because the area under the entire curve must be 1, when X has a small range (e.g., the golf ball diameter range is about 0.06 mm), the height of $f(x)$ is large (about 40 for the golf ball diameters). Conversely, in Figure 7.12, when X has a large range (e.g., the CPA exam range is about 60 points), the height of $f(x)$ is small (about 0.40 for the exam scores). You could roughly verify that the area under each curve is 1 by treating them as triangles (area = ½ base × height).

What Is Normal?

Many physical measurements in engineering and the sciences resemble normal distributions. Normal random variables can also be found in economic and financial data, behavioral measurement scales, marketing research, and operations analysis. The normal distribution is especially important as a sampling distribution for estimation and hypothesis testing. To be regarded as a candidate for normality, a random variable should:

- Be measured on a continuous scale.
- Possess clear central tendency.
- Have only one peak (unimodal).
- Exhibit tapering tails.
- Be symmetric about the mean (equal tails).

When the range is large, we often treat a discrete variable as continuous. For example, exam scores are discrete (range from 0 to 100) but are often treated as continuous data. Here are some variables that *might* be expected to be approximately normally distributed:

- $X =$ quantity of beverage in a 2-liter bottle of Diet Pepsi.
- $X =$ absentee percent for skilled nursing staff at a large urban hospital on Tuesday.
- $X =$ cockpit noise level in a Boeing 777 at the captain's left ear during cruise.
- $X =$ diameter in millimeters of a manufactured steel ball bearing.

Each of these variables would tend toward a certain mean but would exhibit random variation. For example, even with excellent quality control, not every bottle of a soft drink will have exactly the same fill (even if the variation is only a few milliliters). The mean and standard deviation depend on the nature of the data-generating process. Precision manufacturing can achieve very small σ in relation to μ (e.g., steel ball bearing diameter) while other data-generating situations produce relatively large σ in relation to μ (e.g., your driving fuel mileage). Thus, each normally distributed random variable may have a different coefficient of variation, even though they may share a common shape.

There are statistical tests to see whether a sample came from a normal population. In Chapter 4, for example, you saw that a histogram can be used to assess normality. Visual tests suffice to detect gross departures from normality. More precise tests will be discussed later. For now, our task is to learn more about the normal distribution and its applications.

SECTION EXERCISES

7.9   If all normal distributions have the same shape, how do they differ?

7.10   (a) Where is the maximum of a normal distribution $N(75,5)$? (b) Does $f(x)$ touch the X-axis at $\mu \pm 3\sigma$?

7.11   State the Empirical Rule for a normal distribution (see Chapter 4).

7.12   Discuss why you would or would not expect each of the following variables to be normally distributed. *Hint:* Would you expect a single central mode and tapering tails? Would the distribution be roughly symmetric? Would one tail be longer than the other?
a. Shoe size of adult males.
b. Years of education of 30-year-old employed women.
c. Days from mailing home utility bills to receipt of payment.
d. Time to process insurance claims for residential fire damage.

Characteristics of the Standard Normal

7.5
STANDARD NORMAL DISTRIBUTION

Since there is a different normal distribution for every value of μ and σ, we often transform the variable by subtracting the mean and dividing by the standard deviation to produce a *standardized variable,* just as in Chapter 4, except that now we are talking about a population distribution instead of sample data. This important transformation is shown in formula 7.4.

$$z = \frac{x - \mu}{\sigma} \qquad \text{(transformation of each } x\text{-value to a } z\text{-value)} \qquad (7.4)$$

Chapter 5

If X is normally distributed, the transformed variable Z has a **standard normal distribution** with mean 0 and standard deviation 1, denoted $N(0, 1)$. The peak of $f(z)$ is at 0 (the mean) and its points of inflection are at ± 1 (the standard deviation). The shape of the distribution is unaffected by the z transformation. Table 7.3 summarizes the main characteristics of the standard normal distribution.

Parameters	μ = population mean
	σ = population standard deviation
PDF	$f(z) = \dfrac{1}{\sqrt{2\pi}} e^{-z^2/2}$ where $z = \dfrac{x-\mu}{\sigma}$
Range	$-\infty < Z < +\infty$
Mean	0
Standard deviation	1
Shape	Symmetric and bell-shaped.
Random data in Excel	=NORMSINV(RAND())
Comment	There is no simple formula for a normal CDF, so we need normal tables or Excel to find areas.

TABLE 7.3
Standard Normal Distribution

Notation

Use an uppercase variable name like Z or X when speaking in general, and a lowercase variable name like z or x to denote a particular value of Z or X.

Since every transformed normal distribution will look the same, we can use a common scale, usually labeled from -3 to $+3$, as shown in Figures 7.13 and 7.14. Since $f(z)$ is a probability density function, the entire area under the curve is 1, as you can approximately verify by treating

FIGURE 7.13

Standard normal PDF

FIGURE 7.13

Standard normal PDF

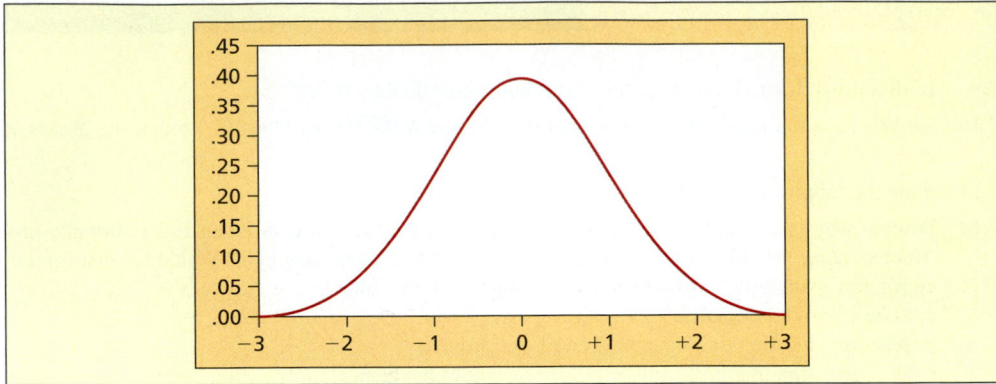

FIGURE 7.14

Standard normal CDF

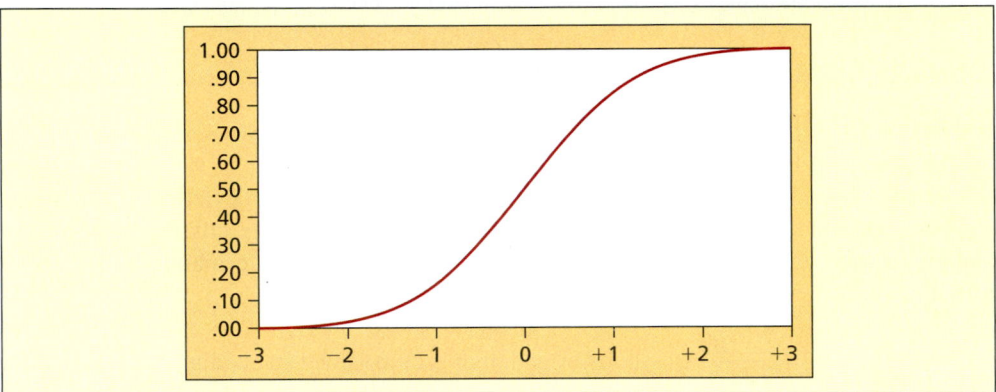

it as a triangle (area = ½ base × height). As a rule, we are not interested in the height of the function $f(z)$ but rather in areas under the curve (although Excel will provide either). The probability of an event $P(z_1 < Z < z_2)$ is a definite integral of $f(z)$. Although there is no simple integral for $f(z)$, a normal area can be approximated to any desired degree of accuracy using various methods (e.g., covering the area from 0 to $f(z)$ with many narrow rectangles and summing their areas). You do not need to worry about this, because tables or Excel functions are available.

Normal Areas from Appendix C-1

Tables of normal probabilities have been prepared so you can look up any desired normal area. Such tables have many forms. Table 7.4 illustrates Appendix C-1 which shows areas from 0 to z using increments of 0.01 from $Z = 0$ to $Z = 3.69$ (beyond this range, areas are very small). For example, to calculate $P(0 < Z < 1.96)$, you select the row for $z = 1.9$ and the column for 0.06 (since $1.96 = 1.90 + 0.06$). This row and column are shaded in Table 7.4. At the intersection of the shaded row and column, we see $P(0 < Z < 1.96) = .4750$. This area is illustrated in Figure 7.15. Since half the area lies to the right of the mean, we can find a right-tail area by subtraction. For example, $P(Z > 1.96) = .5000 - P(0 < Z < 1.96) = .5000 - .4750 = .0250$ as illustrated in Figure 7.15.

FIGURE 7.15

Finding areas using Appendix C-1

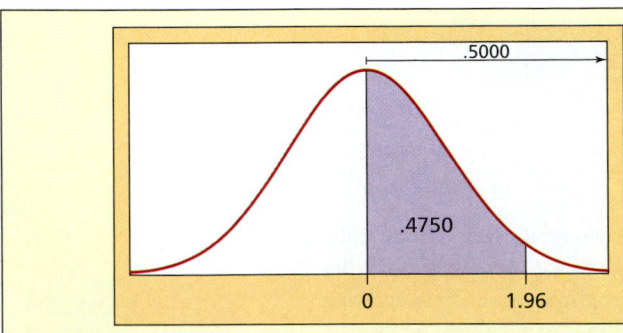

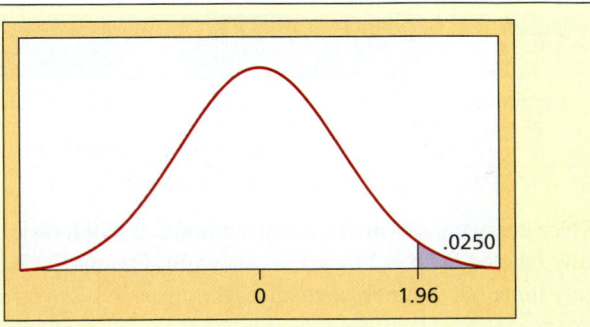

TABLE 7.4
Normal Area from 0 to *z*
(from Appendix C-1)

z	0.00	0.01	0.02	0.03	0.04	0.05	0.06	0.07	0.08	0.09
0.0	.0000	.0040	.0080	.0120	.0160	.0199	.0239	.0279	.0319	.0359
0.1	.0398	.0438	.0478	.0517	.0557	.0596	.0636	.0675	.0714	.0753
0.2	.0793	.0832	.0871	.0910	.0948	.0987	.1026	.1064	.1103	.1141
⋮	⋮	⋮	⋮	⋮	⋮	⋮	⋮	⋮	⋮	⋮
1.6	.4452	.4463	.4474	.4484	.4495	.4505	.4515	.4525	.4535	.4545
1.7	.4554	.4564	.4573	.4582	.4591	.4599	.4608	.4616	.4625	.4633
1.8	.4641	.4649	.4656	.4664	.4671	.4678	.4686	.4693	.4699	.4706
1.9	.4713	.4719	.4726	.4732	.4738	.4744	**.4750**	.4756	.4761	.4767
2.0	.4772	.4778	.4783	.4788	.4793	.4798	.4803	.4808	.4812	.4817
2.1	.4821	.4826	.4830	.4834	.4838	.4842	.4846	.4850	.4854	.4857
2.2	.4861	.4864	.4868	.4871	.4875	.4878	.4881	.4884	.4887	.4890
2.3	.4893	.4896	.4898	.4901	.4904	.4906	.4909	.4911	.4913	.4916
⋮	⋮	⋮	⋮	⋮	⋮	⋮	⋮	⋮	⋮	⋮
3.6	.49984	.49985	.49985	.49986	.49986	.49987	.49987	.49988	.49988	.49989
3.7	.49989	.49990	.49990	.49990	.49991	.49991	.49992	.49992	.49992	.49992

Suppose we want a middle area such as $P(-1.96 < Z < +1.96)$. Because the normal distribution is symmetric, we also know that $P(-1.96 < Z < 0) = .4750$. Adding these areas, we get

$$P(-1.96 < Z < +1.96) = P(-1.96 < Z < 0) + P(0 < Z < 1.96)$$
$$= .4750 + .4750 = .9500$$

So the interval $-1.96 < Z < 1.96$ encloses 95 percent of the area under the normal curve. Figure 7.16 illustrates this calculation. Since a point has no area in a continuous distribution, the probability $P(-1.96 \leq Z \leq +1.96)$ is the same as $P(-1.96 < Z < +1.96)$, so, for simplicity, we omit the equality.

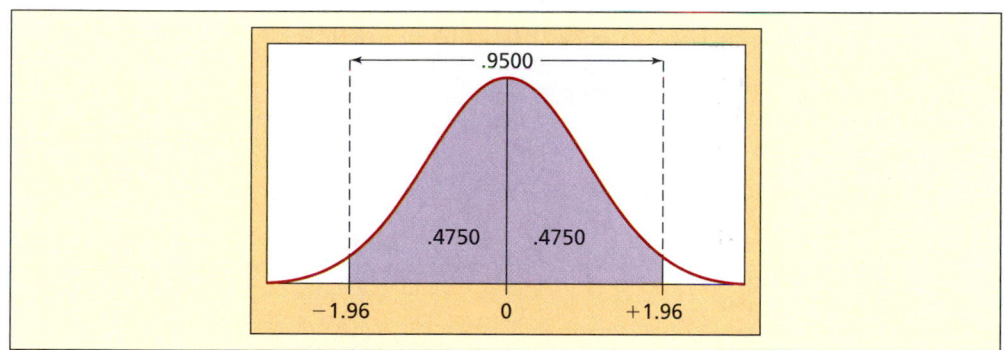

FIGURE 7.16

Finding areas by using
Appendix C-1

Basis for the Empirical Rule

From Appendix C-1 we can see the basis for the Empirical Rule, illustrated in Figure 7.17. These are the "*k*-sigma" intervals mentioned in Chapter 4 and used by statisticians for quick reference to the normal distribution. Thus, it is *approximately* correct to say that a "2-sigma interval" contains 95 percent of the area (actually $z = 1.96$ would yield a 95 percent area):

$$P(-1.00 < Z < +1.00) = 2 \times P(0 < Z < 1.00) = 2 \times .3413 = .6826, \text{ or } 68.26\%$$

$$P(-2.00 < Z < +2.00) = 2 \times P(0 < Z < 2.00) = 2 \times .4772 = .9544, \text{ or } 95.44\%$$

$$P(-3.00 < Z < +3.00) = 2 \times P(0 < Z < 3.00) = 2 \times .49865 = .9973, \text{ or } 99.73\%$$

FIGURE 7.17

Normal areas within $\mu \pm k\sigma$

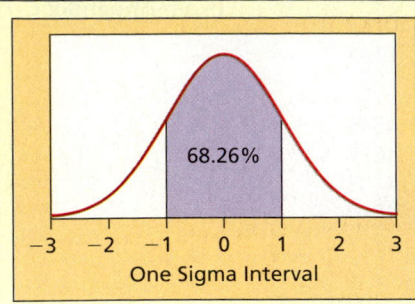
68.26%
One Sigma Interval

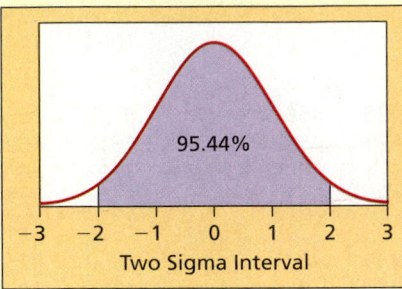
95.44%
Two Sigma Interval

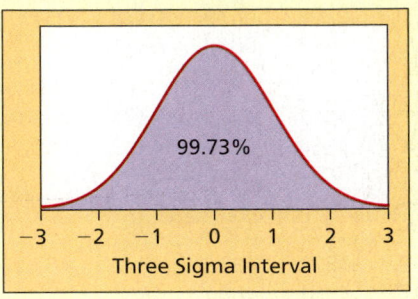
99.73%
Three Sigma Interval

Normal Areas from Appendix C-2

Table 7.5 illustrates another kind of table. Appendix C-2 shows cumulative normal areas from the left to z. This second table corresponds to the way Excel calculates normal areas. Using this approach, we see that $P(Z < -1.96) = .0250$ and $P(Z < +1.96) = .9750$. By subtraction, we get

$$P(-1.96 < Z < +1.96) = P(Z < +1.96) - P(Z < -1.96) = .9750 - .0250 = .9500$$

The result is identical to that obtained previously. The interval $-1.96 < Z < 1.96$ encloses 95 percent of the area under the normal curve. This calculation is illustrated in Figure 7.18.

TABLE 7.5

Cumulative Normal Area from Left to z (from Appendix C-2)

z	0.00	0.01	0.02	0.03	0.04	0.05	0.06	0.07	0.08	0.09
−3.7	.00011	.00010	.00010	.00010	.00009	.00009	.00008	.00008	.00008	.00008
−3.6	.00016	.00015	.00015	.00014	.00014	.00013	.00013	.00012	.00012	.00011
⋮	⋮	⋮	⋮	⋮	⋮	⋮	⋮	⋮	⋮	⋮
−2.3	.0107	.0104	.0102	.0099	.0096	.0094	.0091	.0089	.0087	.0084
−2.2	.0139	.0136	.0132	.0129	.0125	.0122	.0119	.0116	.0113	.0110
−2.1	.0179	.0174	.0170	.0166	.0162	.0158	.0154	.0150	.0146	.0143
−2.0	.0228	.0222	.0217	.0212	.0207	.0202	.0197	.0192	.0188	.0183
−1.9	.0287	.0281	.0274	.0268	.0262	.0256	.0250	.0244	.0239	.0233
−1.8	.0359	.0351	.0344	.0336	.0329	.0322	.0314	.0307	.0301	.0294
−1.7	.0446	.0436	.0427	.0418	.0409	.0401	.0392	.0384	.0375	.0367
−1.6	.0548	.0537	.0526	.0516	.0505	.0495	.0485	.0475	.0465	.0455
⋮	⋮	⋮	⋮	⋮	⋮	⋮	⋮	⋮	⋮	⋮
0.0	.5000	.5040	.5080	.5120	.5160	.5199	.5239	.5279	.5319	.5359
0.1	.5398	.5438	.5478	.5517	.5557	.5596	.5636	.5675	.5714	.5753
0.2	.5793	.5832	.5871	.5910	.5948	.5987	.6026	.6064	.6103	.6141
⋮	⋮	⋮	⋮	⋮	⋮	⋮	⋮	⋮	⋮	⋮
1.6	.9452	.9463	.9474	.9484	.9495	.9505	.9515	.9525	.9535	.9545
1.7	.9554	.9564	.9573	.9582	.9591	.9599	.9608	.9616	.9625	.9633
1.8	.9641	.9649	.9656	.9664	.9671	.9678	.9686	.9693	.9699	.9706
1.9	.9713	.9719	.9726	.9732	.9738	.9744	.9750	.9756	.9761	.9767
2.0	.9772	.9778	.9783	.9788	.9793	.9798	.9803	.9808	.9812	.9817
2.1	.9821	.9826	.9830	.9834	.9838	.9842	.9846	.9850	.9854	.9857
2.2	.9861	.9864	.9868	.9871	.9875	.9878	.9881	.9884	.9887	.9890
2.3	.9893	.9896	.9898	.9901	.9904	.9906	.9909	.9911	.9913	.9916
⋮	⋮	⋮	⋮	⋮	⋮	⋮	⋮	⋮	⋮	⋮
3.6	.99984	.99985	.99985	.99986	.99986	.99987	.99987	.99988	.99988	.99989
3.7	.99989	.99990	.99990	.99990	.99991	.99991	.99992	.99992	.99992	.99992

FIGURE 7.18

Finding areas by using Appendix C-2

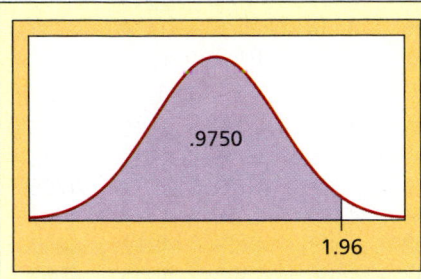
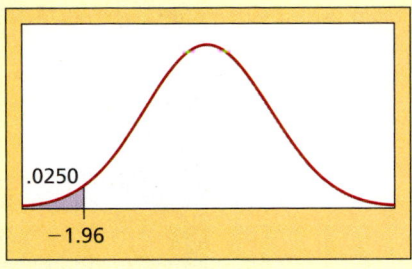
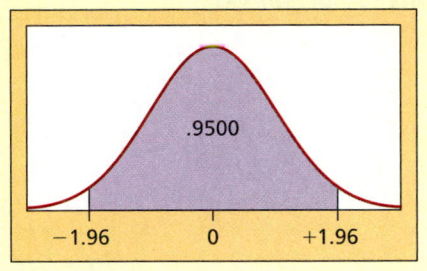

Since Appendix C-1 and Appendix C-2 yield identical results, you should use whichever table is easier for the area you are trying to find. Appendix C-1 is often easier for "middle areas." It also has the advantage of being more compact (it fits on one page) which is one reason why it has traditionally been used for statistics exams and in other textbooks (e.g., marketing). But Appendix C-2 is easier for left-tail areas and some complex areas. Further, Appendix C-2 corresponds to the way Excel calculates normal areas. When subtraction is required for a right-tail or middle area, either table is equally convenient.

SECTION EXERCISES

Note: Use Appendix C-1 or C-2 for these exercises.

7.13 Find the standard normal area for each of the following, showing your reasoning clearly and indicating which table you used.
   a. $P(0 < Z < 0.50)$ b. $P(-0.50 < Z < 0)$ c. $P(Z > 0)$ d. $P(Z = 0)$

7.14 Find the standard normal area for each of the following, showing your reasoning clearly and indicating which table you used.
   a. $P(1.22 < Z < 2.15)$ b. $P(2.00 < Z < 3.00)$ c. $P(-2.00 < Z < 2.00)$ d. $P(Z > 0.50)$

7.15 Find the standard normal area for each of the following, showing your reasoning clearly and indicating which table you used.
   a. $P(-1.22 < Z < 2.15)$ b. $P(-3.00 < Z < 2.00)$ c. $P(Z < 2.00)$ d. $P(Z = 0)$

7.16 Daily output of Marathon's Garyville, Lousiana, refinery is normally distributed with a mean of 232,000 barrels of crude oil per day with a standard deviation of 7,000 barrels. (a) What is the probability of producing at least 232,000 barrels? (b) Between 232,000 and 239,000 barrels? (c) Less than 239,000 barrels? (d) Less than 245,000 barrels? (e) More than 225,000 barrels?

7.17 Assume that the number of calories in a McDonald's Egg McMuffin is a normally distributed random variable with a mean of 290 calories and a standard deviation of 14 calories. (a) What is the probability that a particular serving contains fewer than 300 calories? (b) More than 250 calories? (c) Between 275 and 310 calories? Show all work clearly. (Data are from McDonalds.com)

7.18 The weight of a miniature Tootsie Roll is normally distributed with a mean of 3.30 grams and standard deviation of 0.13 grams. (a) Within what weight range will the middle 95 percent of all miniature Tootsie Rolls fall? (b) What is the probability that a randomly chosen miniature Tootsie Roll will weigh more than 3.50 grams? (Data are from a project by MBA student Henry Scussel.)

Finding *z* for a Given Area

We can also use the tables to find the *z*-value that corresponds to a given area. For example, what *z*-value defines the top 1 percent of a normal distribution? Since half the area lies above the mean, an upper area of 1 percent implies that 49 percent of the area must lie between 0 and *z*. Searching Appendix C-1 for an area of .4900 we see that $z = 2.33$ yields an area of .4901. Without interpolation, that is as close as we can get to 49 percent. This is illustrated in Table 7.6 and Figure 7.19.

TABLE 7.6

Normal Area from 0 to z (from Appendix C-1)

z	0.00	0.01	0.02	0.03	0.04	0.05	0.06	0.07	0.08	0.09
0.0	.0000	.0040	.0080	.0120	.0160	.0199	.0239	.0279	.0319	.0359
0.1	.0398	.0438	.0478	.0517	.0557	.0596	.0636	.0675	.0714	.0753
0.2	.0793	.0832	.0871	.0910	.0948	.0987	.1026	.1064	.1103	.1141
⋮	⋮	⋮	⋮	⋮	⋮	⋮	⋮	⋮	⋮	⋮
1.6	.4452	.4463	.4474	.4484	.4495	.4505	.4515	.4525	.4535	.4545
1.7	.4554	.4564	.4573	.4582	.4591	.4599	.4608	.4616	.4625	.4633
1.8	.4641	.4649	.4656	.4664	.4671	.4678	.4686	.4693	.4699	.4706
1.9	.4713	.4719	.4726	.4732	.4738	.4744	.4750	.4756	.4761	.4767
2.0	.4772	.4778	.4783	.4788	.4793	.4798	.4803	.4808	.4812	.4817
2.1	.4821	.4826	.4830	.4834	.4838	.4842	.4846	.4850	.4854	.4857
2.2	.4861	.4864	.4868	.4871	.4875	.4878	.4881	.4884	.4887	.4890
2.3	.4893	.4896	.4898	.4901	.4904	.4906	.4909	.4911	.4913	.4916
⋮	⋮	⋮	⋮	⋮	⋮	⋮	⋮	⋮	⋮	⋮
3.6	.49984	.49985	.49985	.49986	.49986	.49987	.49987	.49988	.49988	.49989
3.7	.49989	.49990	.49990	.49990	.49991	.49991	.49992	.49992	.49992	.49992

FIGURE 7.19

Finding areas by using Appendix C-1

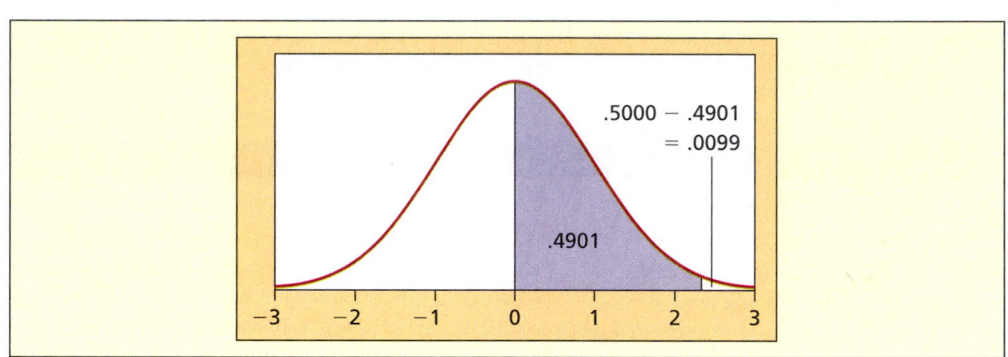

.5000 − .4901 = .0099

.4901

We can find other important areas in the same way. Since we are often interested in the top 25 percent, 10 percent, 5 percent, 1 percent, etc., or the middle 50 percent, 90 percent, 95 percent, 99 percent, etc., it is convenient to record these important z-values for quick reference. Table 7.7 summarizes some important normal areas. For greater accuracy, these z-values are shown to three decimals (they were obtained from Excel).

TABLE 7.7

Some Important Normal Areas

Upper Tail Areas		Middle Areas	
z	Upper Tail Area	Z Range	Middle Area
0.675	0.25, or 25%	−0.675 < Z < 0.675	0.50, or 50%
1.282	0.10, or 10%	−1.282 < Z < 1.282	0.80, or 80%
1.645	0.05, or 5%	−1.645 < Z < 1.645	0.90, or 90%
1.960	0.025, or 2.5%	−1.960 < Z < 1.960	0.95, or 95%
2.326	0.01, or 1%	−2.326 < Z < 2.326	0.98, or 98%
2.576	0.005, or 0.5%	−2.576 < Z < 2.576	0.99, or 99%

SECTION EXERCISES

7.19 The time required to verify and fill a common prescription at a neighborhood pharmacy is normally distributed with a mean of 10 minutes and a standard deviation of 3 minutes. Find the time for each event. Show your work.

a. Highest 10 percent   b. Highest 50 percent   c. Highest 5 percent

d. Highest 80 percent   e. Lowest 10 percent   f. Middle 50 percent

g. Lowest 93 percent   h. Middle 95 percent   i. Lowest 7 percent

7.20 The weight of a small Starbucks coffee is a normally distributed random variable with a mean of 360 grams and a standard deviation of 9 grams. Find the weight that corresponds to each event. Show your work.

a. Highest 10 percent   b. Highest 50 percent   c. Highest 5 percent
d. Highest 80 percent   e. Lowest 10 percent   f. Middle 50 percent
g. Lowest 90 percent   h. Middle 95 percent   i. Highest 4 percent

7.21 The weight of newborn babies in Foxboro Hospital is normally distributed with a mean of 6.9 pounds and a standard deviation of 1.2 pounds. (a) How unusual is a baby weighing 8.0 pounds or more? (b) What would be the 90th percentile for birth weight? (c) Within what range would the middle 95 percent of birth weights lie?

7.22 The credit score of a 35 year old applying for a mortgage at Ulysses Mortgage Associates is normally distributed with a mean of 600 and a standard deviation of 100. (a) Find the credit score that defines the upper 5 percent. (b) Seventy-five percent of the customers will have a credit score higher than what value? (c) Within what range would the middle 80 percent of credit scores lie?

Finding Normal Areas with Excel

Table 7.8 and Figure 7.20 show four Excel functions that provide normal areas or z-values. Excel is more accurate than a table; however, you still have to be careful of syntax. It is a good idea to *visualize* the answer you expect, so that you will recognize if you are getting the wrong answer from Excel.

TABLE 7.8 Four Excel Functions for Normal Areas

Syntax of Function	Example	What It Does
=NORMDIST(x,μ,σ,cumulative)	=NORMDIST(80,70,10,1) = 0.84134475	Area to the left of x for given μ and σ. Here, 84.13% of the CPA exam-takers score 80 or less if μ = 70 and σ = 10.
=NORMINV(area,μ,σ)	=NORMINV(0.99,70,10) = 93.2634699	Value of x corresponding to a given left-tail area. Here, the 99th percentile for CPA exam-takers is a score of 93.26 or 93 to nearest integer.
=NORMSDIST(z)	=NORMSDIST(1.96) = 0.975002175	Area to the left of z in a standard normal. Here, we see that 97.50% of the area is to the left of z = 1.96.
=NORMSINV(area)	=NORMSINV(0.75) = 0.674489526	Value of z corresponding to a given left-tail area. Here, the 75th percentile (third quartile) of a standard normal is at z = 0.675.

Finding Areas by Using Standardized Variables

John took an economics exam and scored 86 points. The class mean was 75 with a standard deviation of 7. What percentile is John in? That is, what is $P(X < 86)$? We need first to calculate John's standardized Z-score:

$$z_{John} = \frac{z_{John} - \mu}{\sigma} = \frac{86 - 75}{7} = \frac{11}{7} = 1.57$$

This says that John's score is 1.57 standard deviations above the mean. From Appendix C-2 we get $P(X < 86) = P(Z < 1.57) = .9418$, so John is approximately in the 94th percentile. That

FIGURE 7.20

Four useful normal functions in Excel

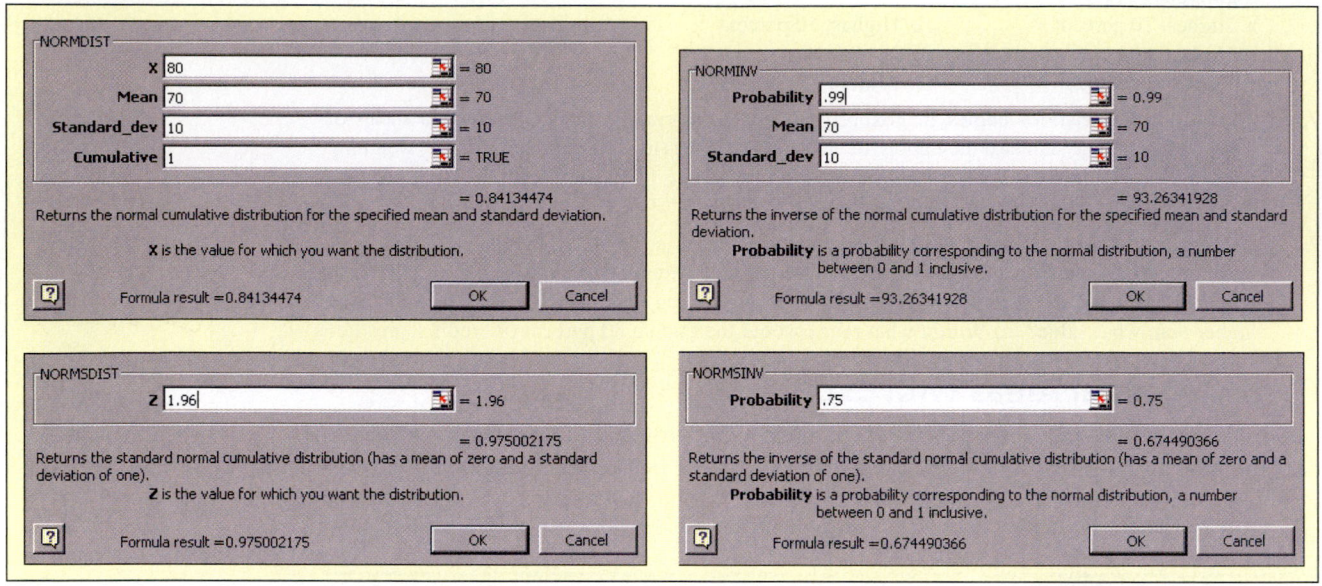

FIGURE 7.21

Original scale $P(X < 86)$

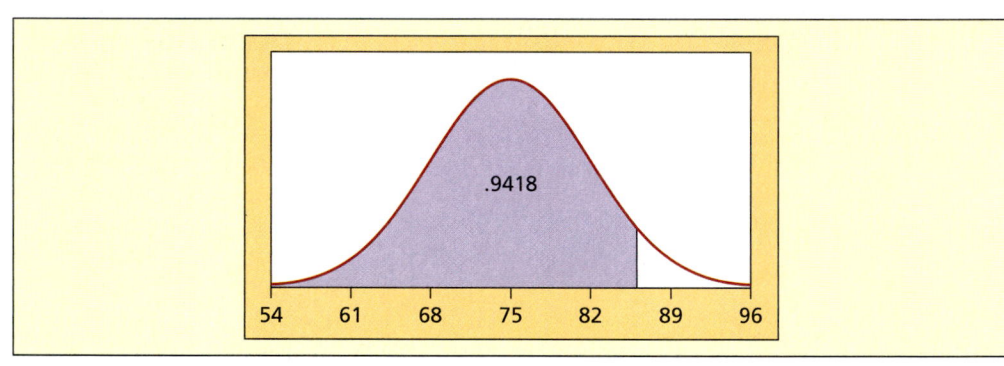

FIGURE 7.22

Standard scale $P(Z < 1.57)$

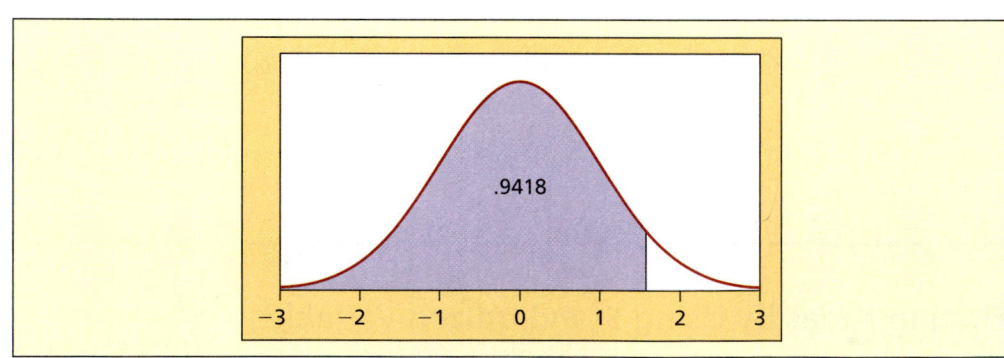

means that his score was better than 94 percent of the class, as illustrated in Figures 7.21 and 7.22.

On this exam, what is the probability that a randomly chosen test-taker would have a score of at least 65? We begin by standardizing:

$$z = \frac{x - \mu}{\sigma} = \frac{65 - 75}{7} = \frac{-10}{7} = -1.43$$

Using Appendix C-1 we can calculate $P(X \geq 65) = P(Z \geq -1.43)$ as

$$P(Z \geq -1.43) = P(-1.43 < Z < 0) + .5000$$
$$= .4236 + .5000 = .9236, \text{ or } 92.4\%$$

Using Appendix C-2 we can calculate $P(X \geq 65) = P(Z \geq -1.43)$ as

$$P(Z \geq -1.43) = 1 - P(Z < -1.43) = 1 - .0764 = .9236, \text{ or } 92.4\%$$

Using either method, there is a 92.4 percent chance that a student scores 65 or above on this exam. These calculations are illustrated in Figures 7.23 and 7.24.

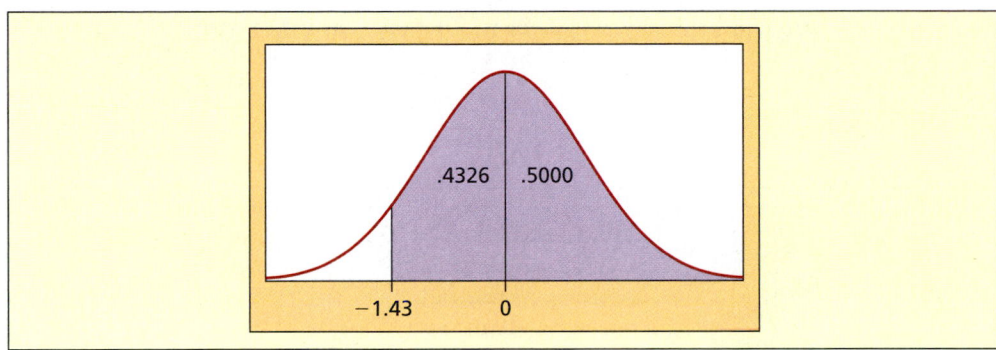

FIGURE 7.23

Using Appendix C-1

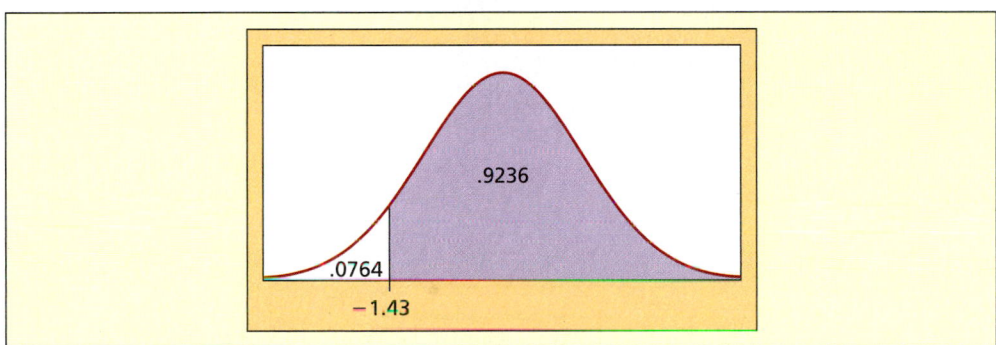

FIGURE 7.24

Using Appendix C-2

Inverse Normal

How can we find the various normal percentiles (5th, 10th, 25th, 75th, 90th, 95th, etc.) known as the *inverse normal*? That is, how can we find X for a given area? We simply turn the standardizing transformation around:

$$x = \mu + z\sigma \qquad \left(\text{solving for } x \text{ in } z = \frac{x - \mu}{\sigma}\right) \qquad (7.5)$$

Using Table 7.7 (or looking up the areas in Excel) we obtain the results shown in Table 7.9. Note that to find a lower tail area (such as the lowest 5 percent) we must use negative Z-values.

Percentile	z	$x = \mu + z\sigma$	x (to nearest integer)
95th (highest 5%)	1.645	$x = 75 + (1.645)(7)$	86.52, or 87 (rounded)
90th (highest 10%)	1.282	$x = 75 + (1.282)(7)$	83.97, or 84 (rounded)
75th (highest 25%)	0.675	$x = 75 + (0.675)(7)$	79.73, or 80 (rounded)
25th (lowest 25%)	−0.675	$x = 75 - (0.675)(7)$	70.28, or 70 (rounded)
10th (lowest 10%)	−1.282	$x = 75 - (1.282)(7)$	66.03, or 66 (rounded)
5th (lowest 5%)	−1.645	$x = 75 - (1.645)(7)$	63.49, or 63 (rounded)

TABLE 7.9

Percentiles for Desired Normal Area

Using Excel Without Standardizing

Excel's NORMDIST and NORMINV functions let us evaluate areas and inverse areas *without* standardizing. For example, let X be the diameter of a manufactured steel ball bearing whose mean diameter is $\mu = 2.040$ cm and whose standard deviation $\sigma = .001$ cm. What is the probability that a given steel bearing will have a diameter between 2.039 and 2.042 cm? We use Excel's function =NORMDIST(x, μ, σ, cumulative) where cumulative is TRUE.

Since Excel gives left-tail areas, we first calculate $P(X < 2.039)$ and $P(X < 2.042)$ as in Figures 7.25 and 7.26. We then obtain the area between by subtraction, as illustrated in Figure 7.27. The desired area is approximately 81.9 percent. Of course, we could do exactly the same thing by using Appendix C-2:

$$P(2.039 < X < 2.042) = P(X < 2.042) - P(X < 2.039)$$

$$= .9773 - .1587 = .8186, \text{ or } 81.9\%$$

FIGURE 7.25

Excel's $P(X < 2.039)$

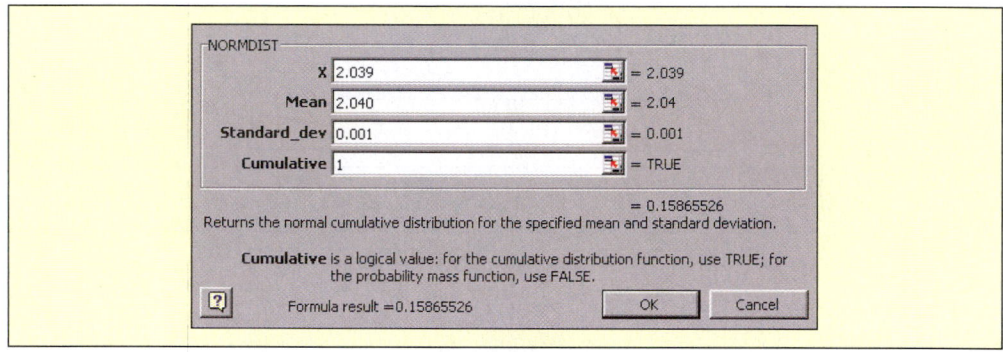

FIGURE 7.26

Excel's $P(X < 2.042)$

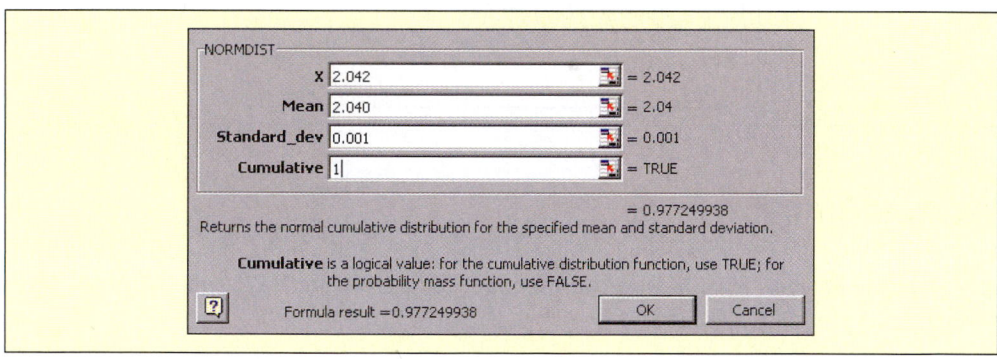

FIGURE 7.27

Cumulative areas from Excel's NORMDIST

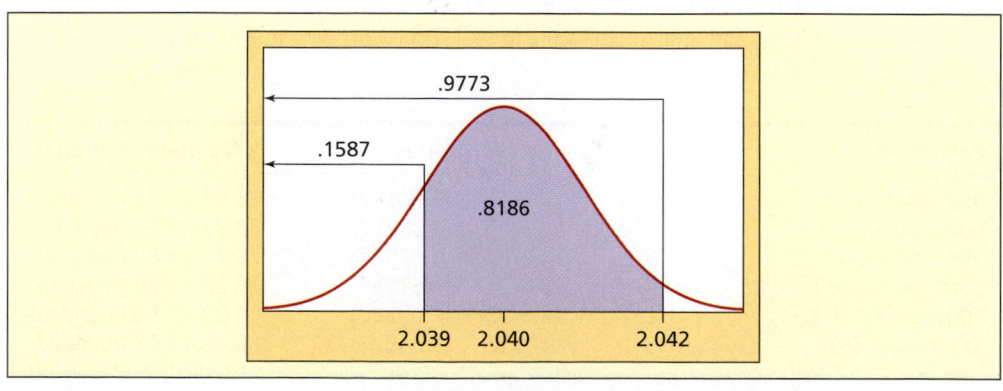

Normal Random Data (Optional)

You can generate random data from a normal distribution $N(\mu, \sigma)$ by using Excel's function =NORMINV(RAND(),μ,σ). Copy this formula to *n* cells to get a sample of *n* random data values. Every time you press F9 you will get a different sample. For example, =NORMINV(RAND(),25,3) will generate a random data point from a normal distribution with mean $\mu = 25$ and standard deviation $\sigma = 3$. This technique is useful in what-if simulation experiments.

EXAMPLE

Service Times in a
Quick Oil Change Shop

After studying the process of changing oil, the shop's manager has found that the distribution of service times, X, is normal with a mean $\mu = 28$ minutes and a standard deviation $\sigma = 5$ minutes, that is, $X \sim N(28, 5)$. This information can now be used to answer questions such as "What proportion of cars will be finished in less than half an hour?," "What is the chance that a randomly selected car will take longer than 40 minutes to service?," or "What service time corresponds to the 90th percentile?"

To answer these types of questions it is helpful to follow a few basic steps. (1) Draw a picture and label the picture with the information you know. (2) Shade in the area that will answer your question. (3) Standardize the random variable. (4) Find the area by using one of the tables or Excel.

What proportion of cars will be finished in less than half an hour?

- **Steps 1 and 2:**   Draw a picture and shade the desired area.

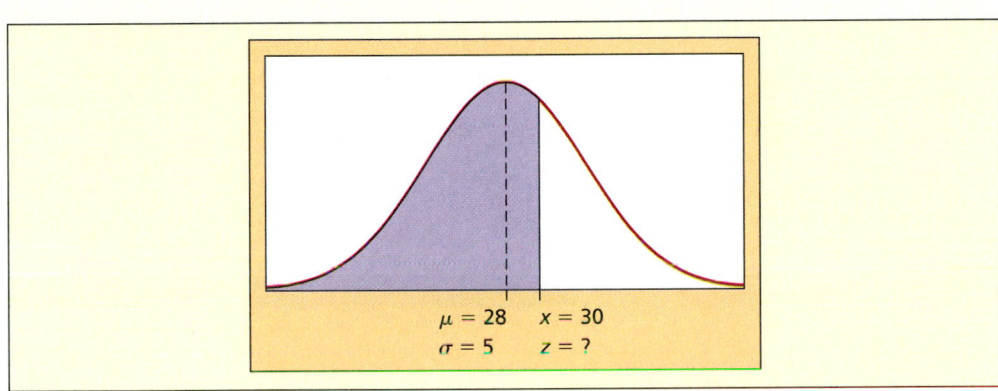

$\mu = 28$ $x = 30$
$\sigma = 5$ $z = ?$

- **Step 3:** $z = \dfrac{30 - 28}{5} = 0.40$

- **Step 4:**   Using Appendix C-2 or Excel we find that $P(Z < 0.40) = .6554$.

Approximately 66 percent of the cars will be finished in less than half an hour.

What is the chance that a randomly selected car will take longer than 40 minutes to complete?

- **Steps 1 and 2:**   Draw a picture and shade the desired area.

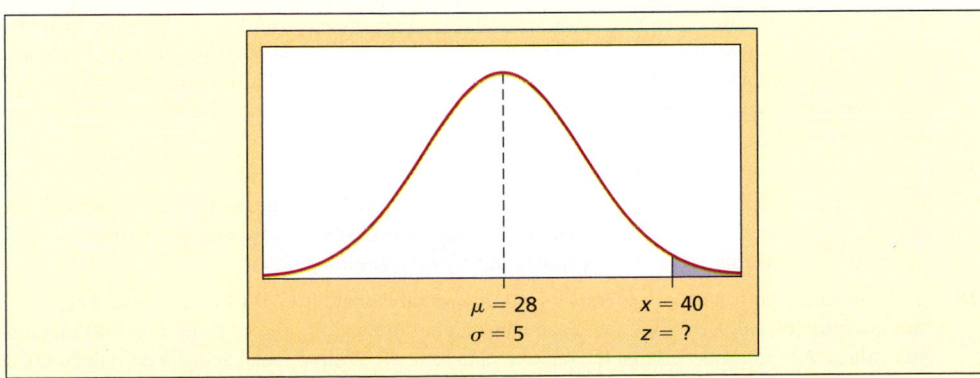

$\mu = 28$ $x = 40$
$\sigma = 5$ $z = ?$

- **Step 3:** $z = \dfrac{40 - 28}{5} = 2.4$

- **Step 4:** Using Appendix C-2 or Excel we find that $P(Z > 2.4) = 1 - P(Z \le 2.4) = 1 - .9918 = .0082.$

There is less than a 1 percent chance that a car will take longer than 40 minutes to complete. *What service time corresponds to the 90th percentile?*

Steps 1 and 2: Draw a picture and shade the desired area.

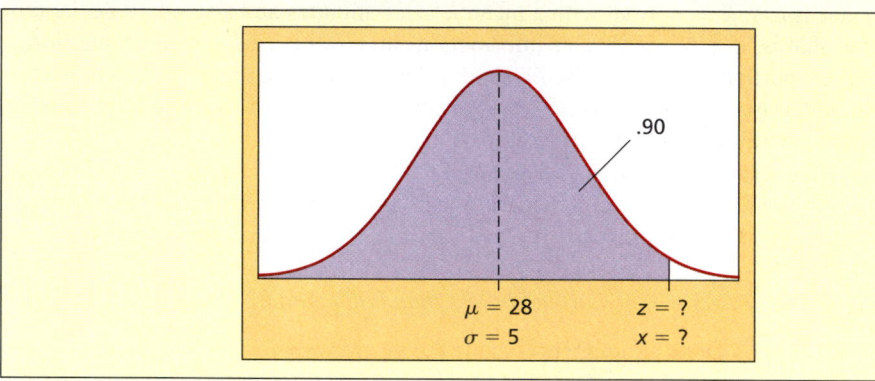

In this case, steps 3 and 4 need to be reversed.

- **Step 3:** Find $z = 1.28$ by using the tables or Excel.

- **Step 4:** $1.28 = \dfrac{x - 28}{5}$, so $x = 28 + 5(1.28) = 34.4$ minutes.

Ninety percent of the cars will be finished in 34.4 minutes or less.

SECTION EXERCISES

7.23 Use Excel to find each probability.
a. $P(Z < 110)$ for $N(100, 15)$
b. $P(Z < 2.00)$ for $N(0, 1)$
c. $P(Z < 5,000)$ for $N(6000, 1000)$
d. $P(Z < 450)$ for $N(600, 100)$

7.24 Use Excel to find each probability.
a. $P(80 < Z < 110)$ for $N(100, 15)$
b. $P(1.50 < Z < 2.00)$ for $N(0, 1)$
c. $P(4, 500 < Z < 7, 000)$ for $N(6000, 1000)$
d. $P(225 < Z < 450)$ for $N(600, 100)$

7.25 The weight of a small Starbucks coffee is a random variable with a mean of 360 g and a standard deviation of 9 g. Use Excel to find the weight corresponding to each percentile of weight.
a. 10th percentile
b. 32nd percentile
c. 75th percentile
d. 90th percentile
e. 99.9th percentile
f. 99.99th percentile

7.26 A study found that the mean waiting time to see a physician at an outpatient clinic was 40 minutes with a standard deviation of 28 minutes. Use Excel to find each probability. (a) What is the probability of more than an hour's wait? (b) Less than 20 minutes? (c) At least 10 minutes. (Data are from J. C. Bennett and D. J. Worthington, "An Example of Good but Partially Successful OR Engagement: Improving Outpatient Clinic Operations," *Interfaces* 28, no. 5 [September–October 1998], pp. 56–69.)

*7.27 (a) Write an Excel formula to generate a random normal deviate from $N(0, 1)$ and copy the formula into 10 cells. (b) Find the mean and standard deviation of your sample of 10 random data values. Are you satisfied that the random data have the desired mean and standard deviation? (c) Press F9 to generate 10 more data values and repeat question (b).

*7.28 (a) Write an Excel formula to generate a random normal deviate from $N(4000, 200)$ and copy the formula into 100 cells. (b) Find the mean and standard deviation of your sample of 100 random data values. Are you satisfied that the random data have the desired mean and standard deviation? (c) Make a histogram of your sample. Does it appear normal?

When Is Approximation Needed?

We have seen that (unless we are using Excel) binomial probabilities may be difficult to calculate when n is large, particularly when many terms must be summed. Instead, we can use a normal approximation. The logic of this approximation is that as n becomes large, the discrete binomial bars become more like a smooth, continuous, normal curve. Figure 7.28 illustrates this idea for 4, 8, and 16 flips of a fair coin with X defined as the number of heads in n tries. As sample size increases it becomes easier to visualize a smooth, bell-shaped curve overlaid on the bars in Figure 7.28.

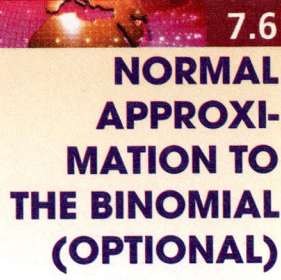

7.6
NORMAL APPROXIMATION TO THE BINOMIAL (OPTIONAL)

Chapter 4

FIGURE 7.28

Binomial with $n = 4$, $n = 8$, and $n = 16$

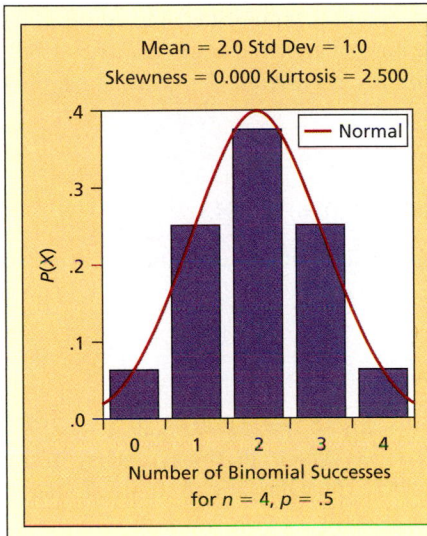
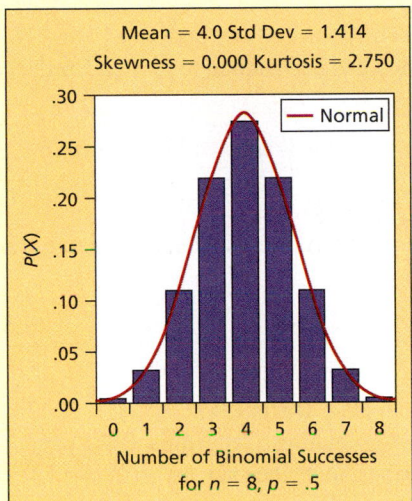
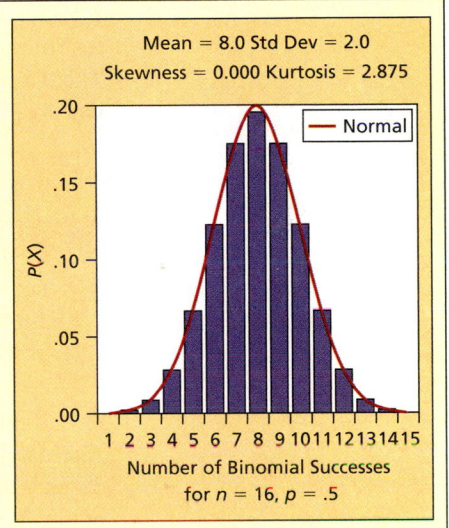

As a rule of thumb, when $n\pi \geq 10$ and $n(1 - \pi) \geq 10$ it is appropriate to use the normal approximation to the binomial, setting the normal μ and σ equal to the binomial mean and standard deviation:

$$\mu = n\pi \tag{7.6}$$

$$\sigma = \sqrt{n\pi(1 - \pi)} \tag{7.7}$$

EXAMPLE

Coin Flips

What is the probability of more than 17 heads in 32 flips of a fair coin? In binomial terms, this would be $P(X \geq 18) = P(18) + P(19) + \cdots + P(32)$, which would be a tedious sum even if we had a table. Could the normal approximation be used? With $n = 32$ and $\pi = .50$ we clearly meet the requirement that $n\pi \geq 10$ and $n(1 - \pi) \geq 10$. However, when translating a discrete scale into a continuous scale we must be careful about individual points. The event "more than 17" actually falls halfway *between* 17 and 18 on a discrete scale, as shown in Figure 7.29.

You don't need to draw the entire distribution. All you need is a little diagram (ignoring the low and high ends of the scale since they are not relevant) to show the event "more than 17" visually:

$$\ldots 14 \quad 15 \quad 16 \quad 17 \quad | \quad \mathbf{18} \quad \mathbf{19} \quad \mathbf{20} \quad \mathbf{21} \quad \mathbf{22} \quad \mathbf{23} \ldots \longrightarrow$$

FIGURE 7.29

Normal approximation to
$P(X \geq 18)$

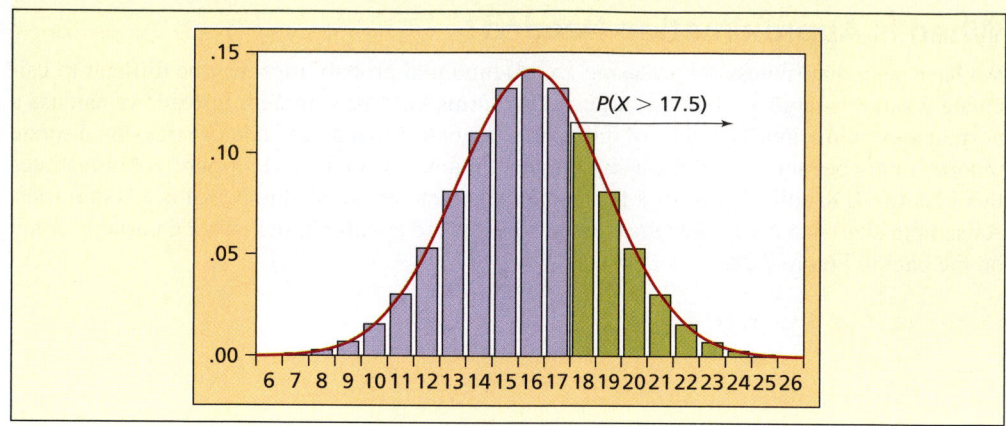

If you make a diagram like this, you can *see* the correct cutoff point. Since the cutoff point for "more than 17" is halfway between 17 and 18, the normal approximation is $P(X > 17.5)$. The 0.5 which has been added to X is called the ***continuity correction.*** The normal parameters are

$$\mu = n\pi = (32)(0.5) = 16$$

$$\sigma = \sqrt{n\pi(1 - \pi)} = \sqrt{(32)(0.5)(1 - 0.5)} = 2.82843$$

We then perform the usual standardizing transformation with the continuity-corrected X-value:

$$z = \frac{x - \mu}{\sigma} = \frac{17.5 - 16}{2.82843} = .53$$

From Appendix C-1 we find $P(Z > .53) = .5000 - P(0 < Z < .53) = .5000 - .2019 = .2981$. Alternately, we could use Appendix C-2 to get $P(Z > .53)$ which, by the symmetry of the normal distribution, is the same as $P(Z < -.53) = .2981$. The calculations are illustrated in Figure 7.30.

FIGURE 7.30

Normal area for $P(Z > .53)$

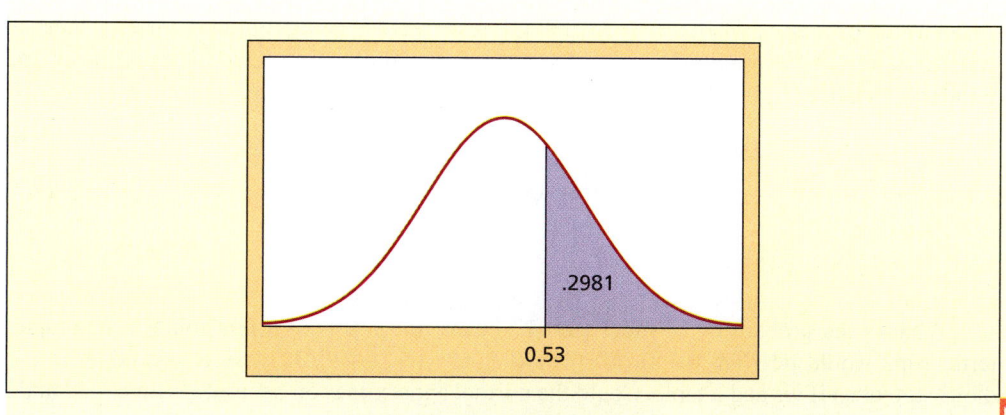

How accurate is this normal approximation to the binomial $P(X \geq 18)$ in our coin flip example? We can check it by using Excel. Since Excel's function is cumulative to the left, we find $P(X \leq 17)$ with the Excel function =BINOMDIST(17,32,0.5,1) and then subtract from 1:

$$P(X \geq 18) = 1 - P(X \leq 17) = 1 - .7017 = .2983$$

In this case, the normal approximation (.2981) is very close to the binomial probability, partly because this binomial is roughly symmetric (π is near .50).

What about when a binomial distribution is badly skewed (π near 0 or 1)? When n is large, the normal approximation improves, regardless of π. But sample size alone does not guarantee a good approximation. For example, if $n = 80$ and $\pi = .03$, we have a severely right-skewed binomial distribution even though n is fairly large, as shown in Figure 7.31. The normal approximation is inadvisable in this example since $n\pi = (80)(.03) = 2.4$, which violates our rule of thumb that $n\pi \geq 10$ and $n(1 - \pi) \geq 10$. When we fit a normal distribution to this binomial, the left tail of the normal is truncated at the origin. In a *right-skewed* binomial (when $\pi < .50$) the rule $n\pi \geq 10$ ensures that the mean $\mu = n\pi$ is far enough above 0 to prevent severe truncation. In a *left-skewed* binomial distribution (when $\pi > .50$) the rule that $n(1 - \pi) \geq 10$ guards against severe truncation at the upper end of the scale by making sure that the mean is well below n. That is why both rules are needed.

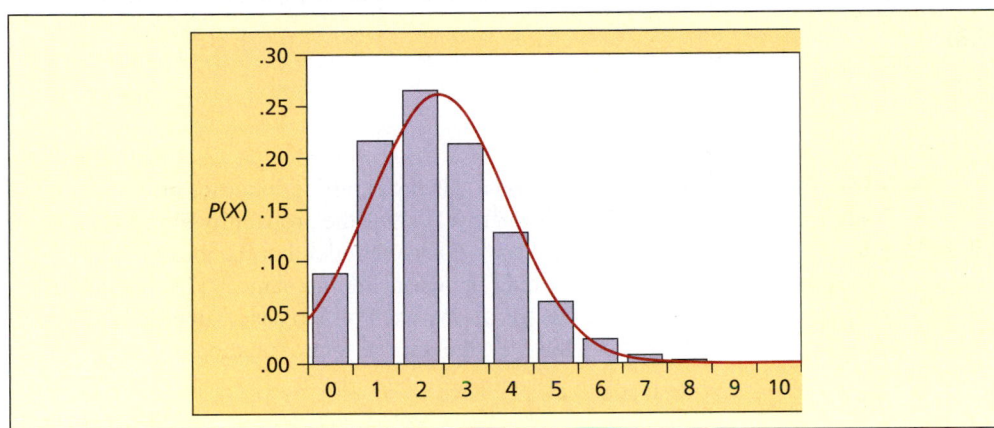

FIGURE 7.31

Poor normal approximation

To be sure you understand the continuity correction, consider the events in the table below. We sketch a diagram to find the correct cutoff point to approximate a discrete model with a continuous one.

Event	Relevant Range of X	Normal Cutoff
At least 17	. . . 14 15 16 *17 18 19 20* . . .	Use $x = 16.5$
More than 15	. . . 14 15 *16 17 18 19 20* . . .	Use $x = 15.5$
Fewer than 19	. . . *14 15 16 17 18* 19 20 . . .	Use $x = 18.5$

SECTION EXERCISES

Note: Use Appendix C-2 for these exercises.

*7.29   The default rate on government-guaranteed student loans at a certain public 4-year institution is 7 percent. (a) If 1,000 student loans are made, what is the probability of fewer than 50 defaults? (b) More than 100? Show your work carefully.

*7.30   In a certain store, there is a .03 probability that the scanned price in the bar code scanner will not match the advertised price. The cashier scans 800 items. (a) What is the expected number of mismatches? The standard deviation? (b) What is the probability of at least 20 mismatches? (c) What is the probability of more than 30 mismatches? Show your calculations clearly.

*7.31   The probability that a vending machine in the Oxnard University Student Center will dispense the desired item when correct change is inserted is .90. If 200 customers try the machine, find the probability that (a) at least 175 will receive the desired item and (b) that fewer than 190 will receive the desired item. Explain.

*7.32   When confronted with an in-flight medical emergency, pilots and crew can consult staff physicians at MedAire, an emergency facility in Tempe, Arizona. If MedAire is called, there is a

4.8 percent chance that the flight will be diverted for an immediate landing. (a) If MedAire is called 8,465 times (as it was in 2002), what is the expected number of diversions? (b) What is the probability of at least 400 diversions? (c) Fewer than 450 diversions? Show your work carefully. (Data are from *Popular Science* 263, no. 5 [November 2003], p. 70.)

7.7

NORMAL APPROXI- MATION TO THE POISSON (OPTIONAL)

When Is Approximation Needed?

The normal approximation for the Poisson works best when λ is fairly large. If you can't find λ in Appendix B (which only goes up to $\lambda = 20$), you are reasonably safe in using the normal approximation. Some textbooks allow the approximation when $\lambda \geq 10$, which is comparable to the rule that the binomial mean must be at least 10. To use the normal approximation to the Poisson we set the normal μ and σ equal to the Poisson mean and standard deviation:

(7.8) $$\mu = \lambda$$

(7.9) $$\sigma = \sqrt{\lambda}$$

EXAMPLE

Utility Bills

On Wednesday between 10 A.M. and noon, customer billing inquiries arrive at a mean rate of 42 inquiries per hour at Consumers Energy. What is the probability of receiving more than 50 calls? Call arrivals presumably follow a Poisson model, but the mean $\lambda = 42$ is too large to use Appendix B. The formula would entail an infinite sum $P(51) + P(52) + \cdots$ whose terms gradually become negligible (recall that the Poisson has no upper limit) but the calculation would be tedious at best. However, the normal approximation is simple. We set

$$\mu = \lambda = 42$$
$$\sigma = \sqrt{\lambda} = \sqrt{42} = 6.48074$$

The continuity-corrected cutoff point for $X \geq 51$ is $X = 50.5$ (halfway between 50 and 51):

$$\ldots 46\ 47\ 48\ 49\ 50\ \overline{51\ 52\ 53} \ldots \longrightarrow$$

The standardized Z-value for the event "more than 50" is $P(X > 50.5) = P(Z > 1.31)$ since

$$z = \frac{x - \mu}{\sigma} = \frac{50.5 - 42}{6.48074} \cong 1.31$$

Using Appendix C-2 we look up $P(Z < -1.31) = .0951$, which is the same as $P(Z > 1.31)$ because the normal distribution is symmetric. We can check the actual Poisson probability by using Excel's cumulative function =POISSON(50,42,1) and subtracting from 1:

$$P(X \geq 51) = 1 - P(X \leq 50) = 1 - .9025 = .0975$$

In this case, the normal approximation comes fairly close to the actual Poisson result. This example gives us confidence in the approximation. Of course, if you have access to Excel, you don't need the approximation at all.

SECTION EXERCISES

Note: Use Appendix C-2 for these exercises.

*7.33 On average, 28 patients per hour arrive in the Foxboro 24-Hour Walk-in Clinic on Friday between 6 P.M. and midnight. (a) What is the approximate probability of more than 35 arrivals? (b) What is the approximate probability of fewer than 25 arrivals? (c) Is the normal approximation justified? Show all calculations. (d) Use Excel to calculate the actual Poisson probabilities. How close were your approximations?

*7.34 For a large Internet service provider (ISP), Web virus attacks occur at a mean rate of 150 per day. (a) Estimate the probability of at least 175 attacks in a given day. (b) Estimate the probability of fewer than 125 attacks. (c) Is the normal approximation justified? Show all calculations. (d) Use Excel to calculate the actual Poisson probabilities. How close were your approximations?

Characteristics of the Exponential Distribution

If events per unit of time follow a Poisson distribution, the waiting time until the next event follows the **exponential distribution,** detailed in Table 7.10. In the exponential model, the focus is on the waiting time until the next event, a continuous variable. The exponential probability function approaches zero as x increases, and is very skewed, as shown in Figures 7.32 and 7.33.

Parameters	λ = mean arrival rate per unit of time or space (same as Poisson mean)	
PDF	$f(x) = \lambda e^{-\lambda x}$	
CDF	$P(X \le x) = 1 - e^{-\lambda x}$	
Range	$X \ge 0$	
Mean	$1/\lambda$	
Standard deviation	$1/\lambda$	
Shape	Always right-skewed.	
Comments	Waiting time is exponential when arrivals follow a Poisson model. Often $1/\lambda$ is given (mean time between events) rather than λ.	

TABLE 7.10
Exponential Distribution

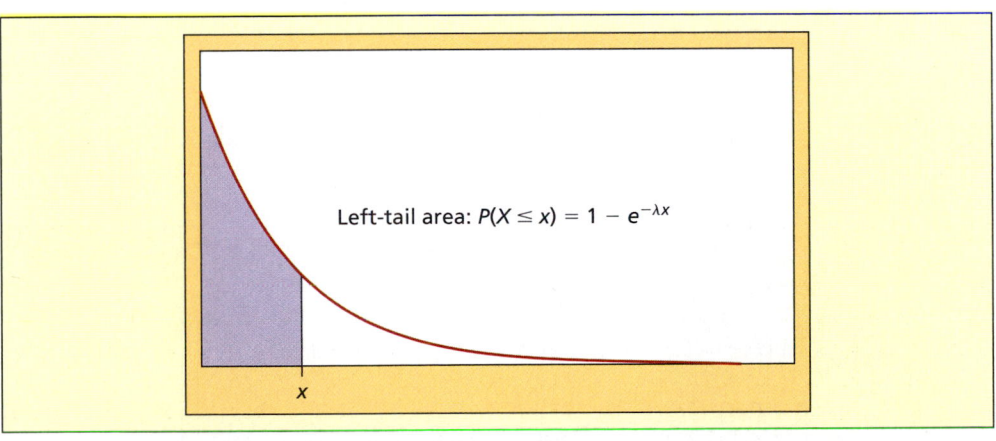

FIGURE 7.32
Right-tail exponential area

Right-tail area: $P(X > x) = e^{-\lambda x}$

FIGURE 7.33
Left-tail exponential area

Left-tail area: $P(X \le x) = 1 - e^{-\lambda x}$

We are usually not interested in the height of the function $f(x)$ but rather in areas under the curve. Fortunately, the CDF is simple; no tables are needed, just a calculator that has the e^x function key. The probability of waiting more than x units of time until the next arrival is $e^{-\lambda x}$, while the probability of waiting x units of time or less is $1 - e^{-\lambda x}$.

(7.10)   Right-tail area: $P(X > x) = e^{-\lambda x}$ (probability of waiting *more* than x)

(7.11)   Left-tail area: $P(X \le x) = 1 - e^{-\lambda x}$ (probability of waiting x or less)

Recall that $P(X \le x)$ is the same as $P(X < x)$ since the point x has no area. For this reason, we could use either $<$ or $\le$ in formula 7.11.

EXAMPLE

Customer Waiting Time

Between 2 P.M. and 4 P.M. on Wednesday, patient insurance inquiries arrive at Blue Choice insurance at a mean rate of 2.2 calls per minute. What is the probability of waiting more than 30 seconds for the next call? We set $\lambda = 2.2$ events per minute and $x = 0.50$ minutes. Note that we must convert 30 seconds to 0.50 minutes since λ is expressed in minutes, and the units of measurement must be the same. We have

$$P(X > 0.50) = e^{-\lambda x} = e^{-(2.2)(0.50)} = .3329, \text{ or } 33.29\%$$

There is about a 33 percent chance of waiting more than 30 seconds before the next call arrives. Since $x = 0.50$ is a *point* that has no area in a continuous model, $P(X \ge 0.50)$ and $P(X > 0.50)$ refer to the same event (unlike, say, a binomial model, in which a point *does* have a probability). The probability that 30 seconds or less (0.50 minutes) will be needed before the next call arrives is

$$P(X \le 0.50) = 1 - e^{-(2.2)(0.50)} = 1 - .3329 = .6671$$

These calculations are illustrated in Figures 7.34 and 7.35.

FIGURE 7.34

$P(X > 0.50)$ for $\lambda = 2.2$

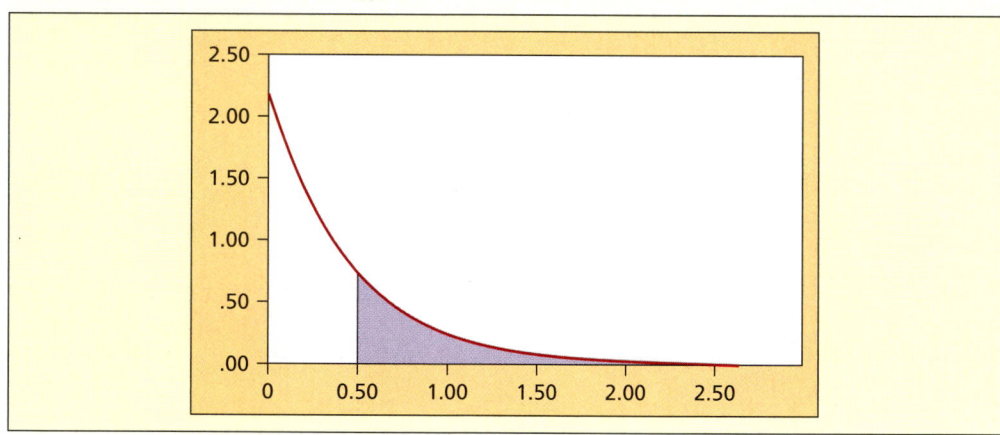

FIGURE 7.35

$P(X \le 0.50)$ for $\lambda = 2.2$

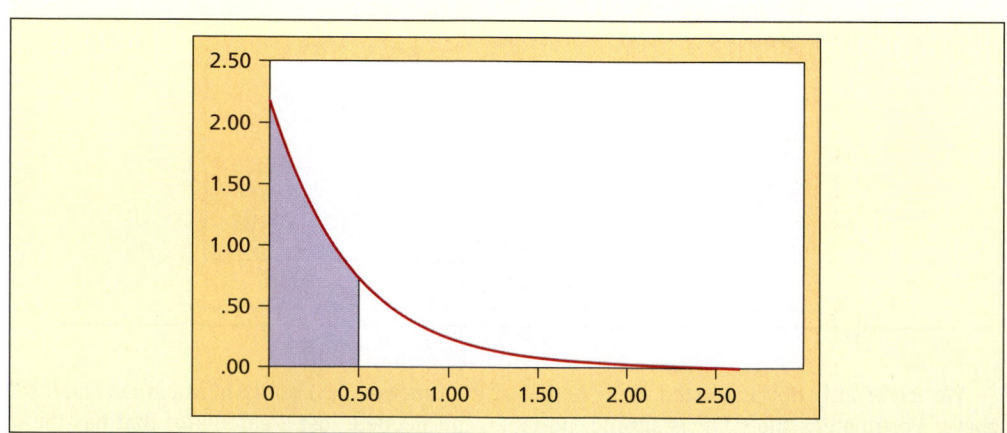

SECTION EXERCISES

7.35 In Santa Theresa, false alarms are received at the downtown fire station at a mean rate of 0.3 per day. (a) What is the probability that more than 7 days will pass before the next false alarm arrives? (b) Less than 2 days? (c) Explain fully.

7.36 Between 11 P.M. and midnight on Thursday night, Mystery Pizza gets an average of 4.2 telephone orders per hour. Find the probability that (a) at least 30 minutes will elapse before the next telephone order; (b) less than 15 minutes will elapse; and (c) between 15 and 30 minutes will elapse.

7.37 A passenger metal detector at Chicago's Midway Airport gives an alarm 6.0 times a minute. What is the probability that (a) less than 60 seconds will pass before the next alarm? (b) More than 30 seconds? (c) At least 45 seconds?

7.38 A Seagate IDE hard drive advertised a 250,000 hour MTBF (mean time between failure) with a 3-year warranty. What is the probability of a warranty claim, assuming continuous drive use? (Data are from *PC Connection* 191E [1997], p. 111.)

Inverse Exponential

We can use the exponential area formula in reverse. If the mean arrival rate is 2.2 calls per minute, we want the 90th percentile for waiting time (the top 10 percent of waiting time) as illustrated in Figure 7.36. We want to find the *x*-value that defines the upper 10 percent.

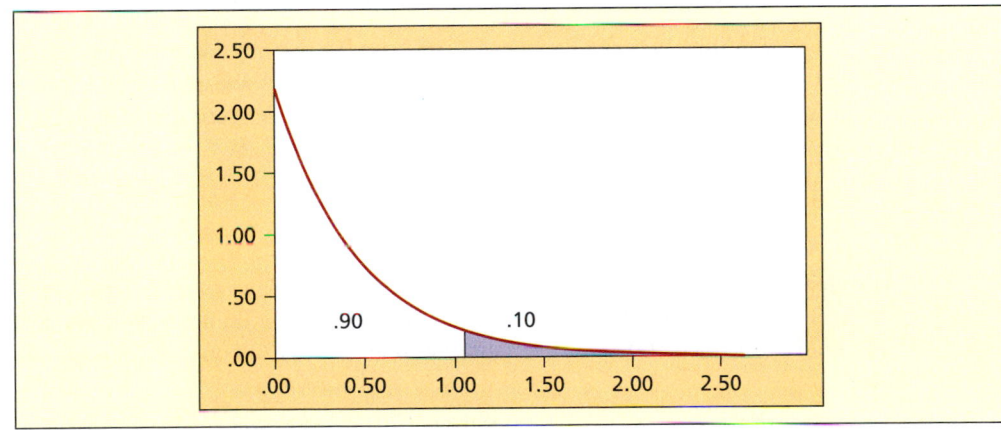

FIGURE 7.36

Finding *x* for the upper 10 percent

Call the unknown time *x*. Since $P(X \le x) = .90$ implies $P(X > x) = .10$, we set the right-tail area to .10, take the natural logarithm of both sides, and solve for *x*:

$$e^{-\lambda x} = .10$$

$$-\lambda x = \ln(.10)$$

$$-\lambda x = -2.302585$$

$$x = 2.302585/\lambda$$

$$x = 2.302585/2.2$$

$$x = 1.0466 \text{ minutes}$$

So 90 percent of the calls will arrive within 1.0466 minutes (or 62.8 seconds). We can find any percentile in the same way. For example, Table 7.11 illustrates similar calculations to find the quartiles (25 percent, 50 percent, 75 percent) of waiting time.

TABLE 7.11	Quartiles for Exponential with $\lambda = 2.2$	
First Quartile Q_1	**Second Quartile Q_2 (median)**	**Third Quartile Q_3**
$e^{-\lambda x} = .75$	$e^{-\lambda x} = .50$	$e^{-\lambda x} = .25$
$-\lambda x = \ln(.75)$	$-\lambda x = \ln(.50)$	$-\lambda x = \ln(.25)$
$-\lambda x = -0.2876821$	$-\lambda x = -0.6931472$	$-\lambda x = -1.386294$
$x = 0.2876821/\lambda$	$x = 0.6931472/\lambda$	$x = 1.386294/\lambda$
$x = 0.2876821/2.2$	$x = 0.6931472/2.2$	$x = 1.386294/2.2$
$x = 0.1308$ minutes, or 7.9 seconds	$x = 0.3151$ minutes, or 18.9 seconds	$x = 0.6301$ minutes, or 37.8 seconds

The calculations in Table 7.11 show that the mean waiting time is $1/\lambda = 1/2.2 = 0.4545$ minutes, or 27 seconds. It is instructive to note that the median waiting time (18.9 seconds) is less than the mean. Since the exponential distribution is highly right-skewed, we would expect the mean waiting time to be above the median, which it is.

Mean Time Between Events

Exponential waiting times are often described in terms of the *mean time between events (MTBE)* rather than in terms of Poisson arrivals per unit of time. In other words, we might be given $1/\lambda$ instead of λ.

$$\text{MTBE} = 1/\lambda = \textit{mean time between events (units of time per event)}$$
$$1/\text{MTBE} = \lambda = \text{mean } \textit{events per unit of time} \text{ (events per unit of time)}$$

For example, if the mean time between patient arrivals in an emergency room is 20 minutes, then $\lambda = 1/20 = 0.05$ arrivals per minute (or $\lambda = 3.0$ arrivals per hour). We could work a problem either using hours or minutes, as long as we are careful to make sure that x and λ are expressed in the same units when we calculate $e^{-\lambda x}$. For example, $P(X > 12 \text{ minutes}) = e^{-(0.05)(12)} = e^{-0.60}$ is the same as $P(X > 0.20 \text{ hour}) = e^{-(3)(0.20)} = e^{-0.60}$.

EXAMPLE

Flat-Panel Displays

The NexGenCo color flat-panel display in an aircraft cockpit has a mean time between failures (MTBF) of 22,500 flight hours. What is the probability of a failure within the next 10,000 flight hours? Since 22,500 hours per failure implies $\lambda = 1/22,500$ failures per hour, we calculate:

$$P(X < 10,000) = 1 - e^{-\lambda x} = 1 - e^{-(1/22,500)(10,000)} = 1 - e^{-0.4444} = 1 - .6412 = .3588$$

There is a 35.88 percent chance of failure within the next 10,000 hours of flight. This assumes that failures follow the Poisson model.

EXAMPLE

Warranty Period

A manufacturer of GPS navigation receivers for boats knows that their mean life under typical maritime conditions is 7 years. What warranty should be offered in order that not more than 30 percent of the GPS units will fail before the warranty expires? The situation is illustrated in Figure 7.37.

Let x be the length of the warranty. To solve this problem, we note that if 30 percent fail before the warranty expires, 70 percent will fail afterward. That is, $P(X > x) = 1 - P(X \leq x) = 1 - 0.30 = .70$.

We set $P(X > x) = e^{-\lambda x} = .70$ and solve for x by taking the natural log of both sides of the equation:

$$e^{-\lambda x} = .70$$
$$-\lambda x = \ln(.70)$$

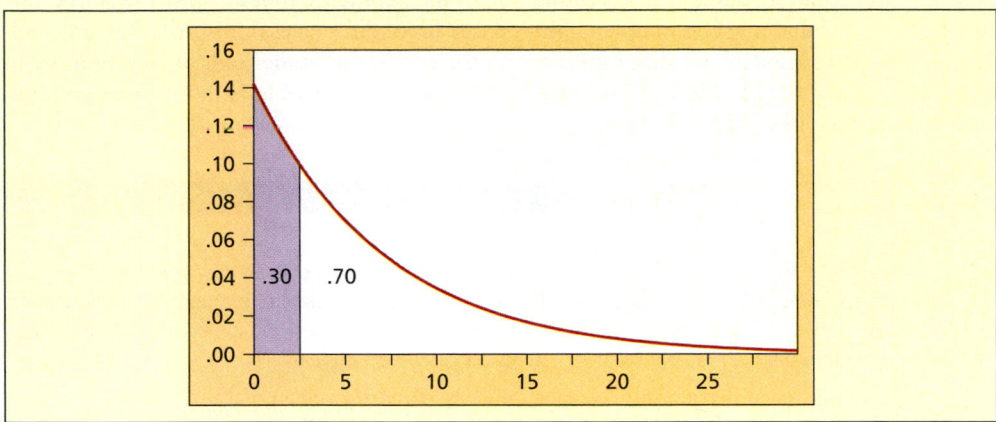

FIGURE 7.37

Finding *x* for the lower 30 percent

$$-\lambda x = -0.356675$$

$$x = (0.356675)/\lambda$$

But in this case, we are not given λ but rather its reciprocal MTBF $= 1/\lambda$. Seven years *mean time between failures* is the same as saying $\lambda = 1/7$ *failures per year*. So we plug in $\lambda = 1/7 = 0.1428571$ to finish solving for *x*:

$$x = (0.356675)/(0.142857) = 2.497 \text{ years}$$

Thus, the firm would offer a 30-month warranty.

It may seem paradoxical that such a short warranty would be offered for something that lasts 7 years. However, the right tail is very long. A few long-lived GPS units will pull up the mean. This is typical of electronic equipment, which helps explain why your laptop computer may have only a 1-year warranty when we know that laptops often last for many years. Similarly, automobiles typically outlast their warranty period (although competitive pressures have recently led to warranties of 5 years or more, even though it may result in a loss on the warranty). In general, warranty periods are a policy tool used by business to balance costs of expected claims against the competitive need to offer contract protection to consumers.

Using Excel

The Excel function =EXPONDIST(x,Lambda,1) will return the left-tail area $P(X \leq x)$. The "1" indicates a cumulative area. If you enter 0 instead of 1, you will get the height of the PDF instead of the left-tail area for the CDF.

Every situation with Poisson arrivals over time is associated with an exponential waiting time. Both models depend solely on the parameter $\lambda =$ mean arrival rate per unit of time. These two closely related distributions are summarized in Table 7.12.

TABLE 7.12	**Relation Between Exponential and Poisson Models**			
Model	*Random Variable*	*Parameter*	*Range*	*Variable Type*
Poisson	$X =$ number of arrivals per unit of time	$\lambda = \dfrac{\text{(mean arrivals)}}{\text{(unit of time)}}$	$X = 0, 1, 2, \ldots$	Discrete
Exponential	$X =$ waiting time until next arrival	$\lambda = \dfrac{\text{(mean arrivals)}}{\text{(unit of time)}}$	$X \geq 0$	Continuous

The exponential model may also remind you of the geometric model, which describes the number of items that must be sampled until the first binomial success. In spirit, they are similar. However, the models are different because the geometric model tells us the number of *discrete* events until the next success, while the exponential model tells the *continuous* waiting time until the next arrival of an event.

7.39   Between 11 P.M. and midnight on Thursday night, Mystery Pizza gets an average of 4.2 telephone orders per hour. (a) Find the median waiting time until the next telephone order. (b) Find the upper quartile of waiting time before the next telephone order. (c) What is the upper 10 percent of waiting time until the next telephone order? Show all calculations clearly.

7.40   A passenger metal detector at Chicago's Midway Airport gives an alarm 0.5 times a minute. (a) Find the median waiting time until the next alarm. (b) Find the first quartile of waiting time before the next alarm. (c) Find the 30th percentile waiting time until the next alarm. Show all calculations clearly.

7.41   Between 2 A.M. and 4 A.M. at an all-night pizza parlor the mean time between arrival of telephone pizza orders is 20 minutes. (a) Find the median wait for pizza order arrivals. (b) Explain why the median is not equal to the mean. (c) Find the upper quartile.

7.42   The mean life of a certain computer hard disk in continual use is 8 years. (a) How long a warranty should be offered if the vendor wants to ensure that not more than 10 percent of the hard disks will fail within the warranty period? (b) Not more than 20 percent?

7.9 TRIANGULAR DISTRIBUTION (OPTIONAL)

Characteristics of the Triangular Distribution

Table 7.13 shows the characteristics of the *triangular distribution.* Visually, it is a simple distribution, as you can see in Figure 7.38. It can be symmetric or skewed. Like the uniform, it has a range from a to b. But unlike the uniform, it has a mode or "peak" at c. The peak is reminiscent of a normal, which also has a single maximum. But unlike the normal, the triangular does not go on forever, being confined to the range between a and b. The triangular distribution is sometimes denoted $T(a, c, b)$ or $T(\text{min, mode, max})$.

TABLE 7.13
Triangular Distribution

Parameters	a = lower limit b = upper limit c = mode
PDF	$f(x) = \dfrac{2(x-a)}{(b-a)(c-a)}$ for $a \leq x \leq c$ $f(x) = \dfrac{2(b-x)}{(b-a)(b-c)}$ for $c \leq x \leq b$
CDF	$P(X \leq x) = \dfrac{(x-a)^2}{(b-a)(c-a)}$ for $a \leq x \leq c$ $P(X \leq x) = 1 - \dfrac{(b-x)^2}{(b-a)(b-c)}$ for $c \leq x \leq b$
Range	$a \leq X \leq b$
Mean	$\dfrac{a+b+c}{3}$
Standard deviation	$\sqrt{\dfrac{a^2+b^2+c^2-ab-ac-bc}{18}}$
Shape	Positively skewed if $c < (a+b)/2$. Negatively skewed if $c > (a+b)/2$.
Comments	Practical model, useful in business what-if analysis. A symmetric triangular is the sum of two uniform variates.

FIGURE 7.38

Triangular PDFs

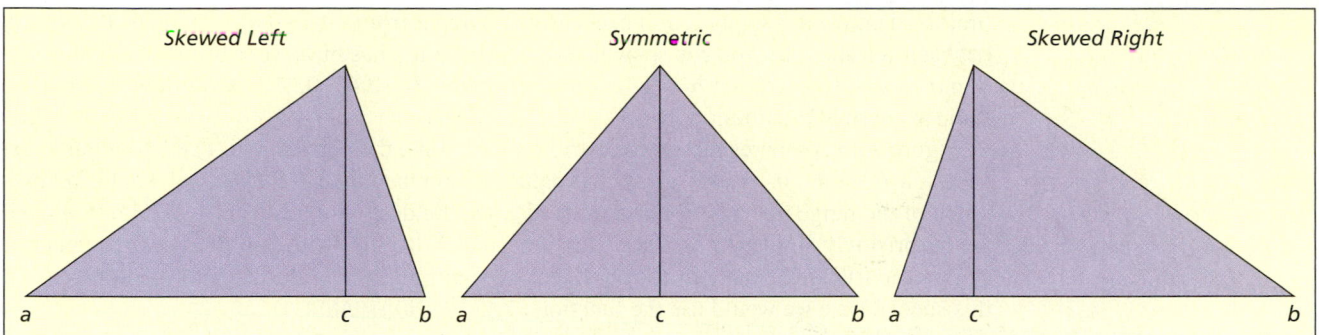

Skewed Left   Symmetric   Skewed Right

An oral surgeon injects a painkiller prior to extracting a tooth. Given the varying characteristics of patients, the dentist views the time for anesthesia effectiveness as a triangular random variable that takes between 15 minutes and 30 minutes, with 20 minutes as the most likely time. Setting $a = 15$, $b = 30$, and $c = 20$, we obtain

EXAMPLE

Anesthetic Effectiveness Using Triangular Distribution

$$\mu = \frac{a+b+c}{3} = \frac{15+30+20}{3} = 21.7 \text{ minutes}$$

$$\sigma = \sqrt{\frac{a^2+b^2+c^2-ab-ac-bc}{18}}$$

$$= \sqrt{\frac{15^2+30^2+20^2-(15)(30)-(15)(20)-(30)(20)}{18}}$$

$$= 3.12 \text{ minutes}$$

Using the cumulative distribution function or CDF (the integral of the PDF, whose derivation is not shown here) we can calculate the probability of taking less than x minutes:

$$P(X \leq x) = \frac{(x-a)^2}{(b-a)(c-a)} \quad \text{for } a \leq x \leq c \tag{7.12}$$

$$P(X \leq x) = 1 - \frac{(b-x)^2}{(b-a)(b-c)} \quad \text{for } c \leq x \leq b \tag{7.13}$$

For example, the probability that the anesthetic takes less than 25 minutes is

$$P(X \leq 25) = 1 - \frac{(30-25)^2}{(30-15)(30-20)} = .8333$$

Basically, we are finding the small triangle's area (½ base × height) and then subtracting from 1. This situation is illustrated in Figure 7.39. In contrast, assuming a uniform distribution with parameters $a = 15$ and $b = 30$ would yield $P(X \leq 25) = .6667$. Why is it different? Because the triangular, with mode 20, has more probability on the low end, making it more likely that a patient will be fully anesthetized within 25 minutes. Assuming a uniform distribution may seem conservative, but could lead to patients sitting around longer waiting to be sure the anesthetic has taken effect. Only experience could tell us which model is more realistic.

FIGURE 7.39

Triangular $P(X \leq 25)$

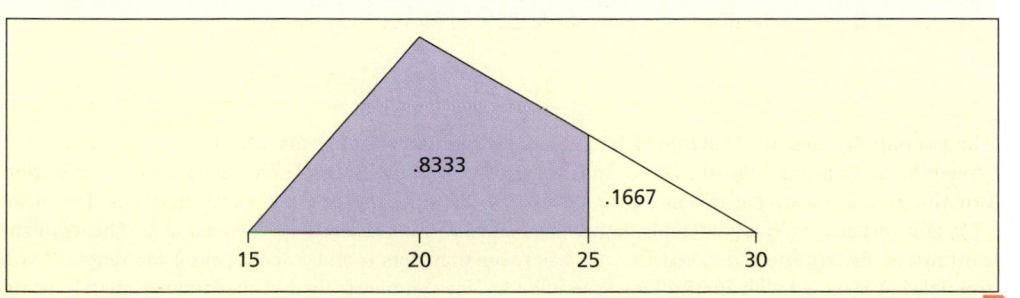

.8333   .1667

15   20   25   30

Special Case: Symmetric Triangular

An interesting special case is a **symmetric triangular distribution** centered at 0, whose lower limit is identical to its upper limit except for sign (e.g., from $-b$ to $+b$) with mode 0 (halfway between $-b$ and $+b$). You can show that this distribution has mean $\mu = 0$ and standard deviation $\sigma = b/\sqrt{6}$. If you set $b = 2.45$, the distribution $T(-2.45, 0, +2.45)$ closely resembles a standard normal distribution $N(0, 1)$.

Figure 7.40 compares these two distributions. Unlike the normal $N(0, 1)$ the triangular distribution $T(-2.45, 0, +2.45)$ always has values within the range $-2.45 \leq X \leq +2.45$. Yet over much of the range, the distributions are alike, and random samples from $T(-2.45, 0, +2.45)$ are surprisingly similar to samples from a normal $N(0, 1)$ distribution. It is easy to generate symmetric triangular random data in Excel by summing two uniforms RAND()+RAND(), so for this special case we would use the function =2.45 *(RAND()+RAND()-1).

FIGURE 7.40

Symmetric triangular

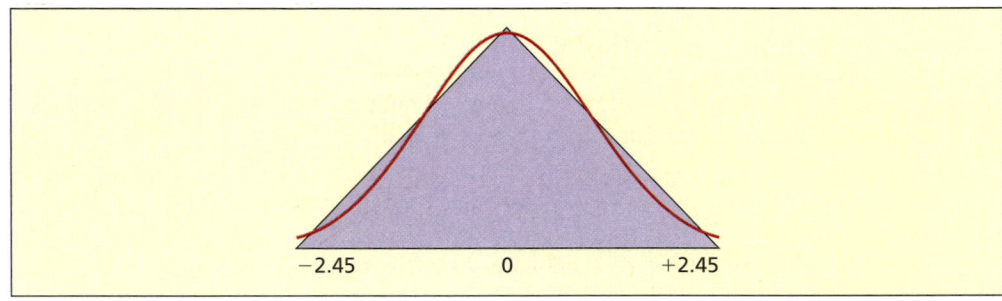

$-2.45 \qquad 0 \qquad +2.45$

Uses of the Triangular

The triangular distribution is a way of thinking about variation that corresponds rather well to what-if analysis in business. It is not surprising that business analysts are attracted to the triangular model. Its finite range and simple form are more understandable than a normal distribution. It is more versatile than a normal, because it can be skewed in either direction. Yet it has some of the nice properties of a normal, such as a distinct mode. The triangular model is especially handy for what-if analysis when the business case depends on predicting a stochastic variable (e.g., the price of a raw material, an interest rate, a sales volume). If the analyst can anticipate the range (a to b) and most likely value (c), it will be possible to calculate probabilities of various financial outcomes. Many times, such distributions will be skewed, so a normal wouldn't be much help. Later, we will explore what-if analysis using the triangular $T(a, c, b)$ model in simulations.

SECTION EXERCISES

*7.43 Suppose that the distribution of order sizes (in dollars) at L.L. Bean has a distribution that is $T(0, 25, 75)$. (a) Find the mean. (b) Find the standard deviation. (c) Find the probability that an order will be less than $25. (d) Sketch the distribution and shade the area for the event in part (c).

*7.44 Suppose that the distribution of oil prices ($/bbl) is forecast to be $T(50, 65, 105)$. (a) Find the mean. (b) Find the standard deviation. (c) Find the probability that the price will be greater than $75. (d) Sketch the distribution and shade the area for the event in part (c).

Chapter Summary

The **probability density function (PDF)** of a **continuous random variable** is a smooth curve, and probabilities are **areas** under the curve. The area under the entire PDF is 1. The **cumulative distribution function (CDF)** shows the area under the PDF to the left of X, approaching 1 as X increases. The mean $E(X)$ and variance $V(X)$ are integrals, rather than sums, as for a discrete random variable. The **uniform continuous distribution,** denoted $U(a, b)$, has two parameters a and b that enclose the range. It is a simple what-if model with applications in simulation. The symmetric, bell-shaped **normal distribution,** denoted $N(\mu, \sigma)$, has two parameters, the mean μ and standard deviation σ. It serves as a benchmark. Because there is a different normal distribution for every possible μ and σ, we apply the transformation $z = (x - \mu)/\sigma$ to get a new random variable that follows a **standard normal distribution,** denoted $N(0, 1)$, with mean 0 and standard deviation 1. There is no simple formula for normal areas, but tables or Excel functions are available to find an area under the curve for given z-values or to find z-values that give a specified area (the "inverse normal"). As shown in Figure 7.41, a **normal approximation** for a binomial or Poisson probability is acceptable when the mean is at least 5. The **exponential distribution** describes **waiting time** until the next Poisson arrival. Its one parameter is λ (the mean) and its right tail area is $e^{-\lambda x}$ (the probability of waiting at least x time units for the next arrival). It is strongly right-skewed and is used to predict warranty claims or to schedule facilities. The **triangular distribution** $T(a, c, b)$ has three parameters (a and b enclose the range, and c is the mode). It may be symmetric or skewed in either direction. It is easy to visualize and is a useful model for what-if simulation. Table 7.14 compares these five models.

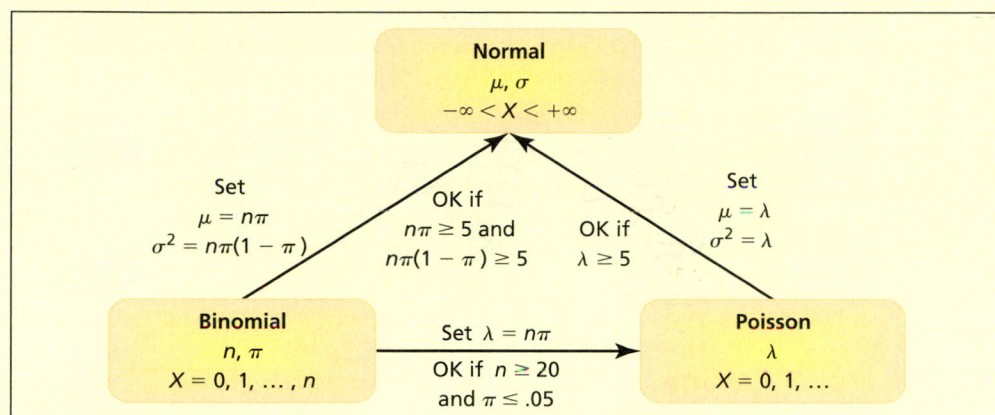

FIGURE 7.41

Relationships among three models

TABLE 7.14   **Comparison of Models**

Model	Parameters	Mean E(X)	Variance V(X)	Characteristics
Uniform	a, b	$(a+b)/2$	$(b-a)^2/12$	Always symmetric
Normal	μ, σ	μ	σ^2	Symmetric. Useful as reference benchmark.
Standard normal	μ, σ	0	1	Special case of the normal with $z = (x - \mu)/\sigma$
Exponential	λ	$1/\lambda$	$1/\lambda$	Always skewed right. Right-tail area is $e^{-\lambda x}$ for waiting times.
Triangular	a, b, c	$(a+b+c)/3$	$(a^2 + b^2 + c^2 - ab - ac - bc)/18$	Useful for what-if business modeling.

Commonly Used Formulas in Continuous Distributions ———•

Uniform CDF: $P(X \leq x) = \dfrac{x-a}{b-a}$ for $a \leq X \leq b$

Exponential CDF: $P(X \leq x) = 1 - e^{-\lambda x}$ for $X \geq 0$

Standard Normal Random Variable: $z = \dfrac{x-\mu}{\sigma}$ for $-\infty < X < +\infty$

Normal Approximation to Binomial: $\mu = n\pi$ $\sigma = \sqrt{n\pi(1-\pi)}$ for $n\pi \geq 10$ and $n(1-\pi) \geq 10$

Normal Approximation to Poisson: $\mu = \lambda$ $\sigma = \sqrt{\lambda}$ for $\lambda \geq 10$

Chapter Review

1. (a) Why does a point have no probability in a continuous distribution? (b) Why are probabilities areas under curves in a continuous distribution?

2. Define (a) parameter, (b) PDF, and (c) CDF.

3. For the uniform distribution: (a) tell how many parameters it has; (b) indicate what the parameters represent; (c) describe its shape; and (d) explain when it would be used.

4. For the normal distribution: (a) tell how many parameters it has; (b) indicate what the parameters represent; (c) describe its shape; and (d) explain why all normal distributions are alike despite having different μ and σ.

5. (a) What features of a stochastic process might lead you to anticipate a normal distribution? (b) Give two examples of random variables that might be considered normal.

6. (a) What is the transformation to standardize a normal random variable? (b) Why do we standardize a variable to find normal areas? (c) How does a standard normal distribution differ from any other normal distribution, and how is it similar?

7. (a) Explain the difference between Appendix C-1 and Appendix C-2. (b) List advantages of each type of table. (c) Which table do you expect to use, and why? (d) Why not always use Excel?

8. (a) Why does Excel rely on the cumulative to find normal areas? (b) Write an example of each of the four normal functions in Excel and tell what each function does.

9. List the standard normal z-values for several common areas (tail and/or middle). *You will use them often.*

10. For the exponential distribution: (a) tell how many parameters it has; (b) indicate what the parameters represent; (c) describe its shape; and (d) explain when it would be used.

*11. When does the normal give an acceptable approximation (a) to a binomial and (b) to a Poisson? (c) Why might you never need these approximations? (d) When might you need them?

*12. For the triangular distribution: (a) tell how many parameters it has; (b) indicate what the parameters represent; (c) describe its shape in a general way (e.g., skewness); and (d) explain when it would be used.

*13. Why is calculus needed to find probabilities for continuous distributions, but not for discrete distributions?

CHAPTER EXERCISES

Note: Show your work clearly. Problems marked * are harder or rely on optional material.

7.45 Which of the following is a continuous random variable?
   a. Number of Honda Civics sold in a given day at a car dealership.
   b. Gallons of gasoline used for a 200-mile trip in a Honda Civic.
   c. Miles driven on a particular Thursday by the owner of a Honda Civic.

7.46 Which of the following could be probability density functions for a continuous random variable? Explain.
   a. $f(x) = .50$ for $0 \leq x \leq 2$ b. $f(x) = 2 - x$ for $0 \leq x \leq 2$ c. $f(x) = .5x$ for $0 \leq x \leq 2$

7.47   Applicants for a night caretaker position are uniformly distributed in age between 25 and 65. (a) What is the mean age of an applicant? (b) The standard deviation? (c) What is the probability that an applicant will be over 45? (d) Over 55? (e) Between 30 and 60?

7.48   Passengers using New York's MetroCard system must swipe the card at a rate between 10 and 40 inches per second, or else the card must be re-swiped through the card reader. Research shows that actual swipe rates by subway riders are uniformly distributed between 5 and 50 inches per second. (a) What is the mean swipe rate? (b) What is the standard deviation of the swipe rate? (c) What are the quartiles? (d) What percentage of subway riders must re-swipe the card because they were outside the acceptable range? (Data are from *The New York Times,* July 18, 2004, p. 23.)

7.49   Discuss why you would or would not expect each of the following variables to be normally distributed. *Hint:* Would you expect a single central mode and tapering tails? Would the distribution be roughly symmetric? Would one tail be longer than the other?
a. Time for households to complete the U.S. Census short form.
b. Size of automobile collision damage claims.
c. Diameters of randomly chosen circulated quarters.
d. Weight of contents of 16-ounce boxes of elbow macaroni.

7.50   Chlorine concentration in a municipal water supply is a uniformly distributed random variable that ranges between 0.74 ppm and 0.98 ppm. (a) What is the mean chlorine concentration? (b) The standard deviation? (c) What is the probability that the chlorine concentration will exceed 0.80 ppm on a given day? (d) Will be under 0.85 ppm? (e) Will be between 0.80 ppm and 0.90 ppm? (f) Why is chlorine added to municipal water? What if there is too much? Too little? *Hint:* Use the Internet. (Data are from *Annual Water Quality Report,* City of Rochester Hills, MI.)

7.51   The weekly demand for Baked Lay's potato chips at a certain Subway sandwich shop is a random variable with mean 450 and standard deviation 80. Find the value of X for each event. Show your work.
a. Highest 50 percent   b. Lowest 25 percent   c. 90th percentile
d. Highest 80 percent   e. Highest 5 percent   f. Middle 50 percent
g. 20th percentile   h. Middle 95 percent   i. Highest 1 percent

7.52   The length of a Colorado brook trout is normally distributed. (a) What is the probability that a brook trout's length exceeds the mean? (b) Exceeds the mean by at least 1 standard deviation? (c) Exceeds the mean by at least 2 standard deviations? (d) Is within 2 standard deviations?

7.53   The caffeine content of a cup of home-brewed coffee is a normally distributed random variable with a mean of 115 mg with a standard deviation of 20 mg. (a) What is the probability that a randomly chosen cup of home-brewed coffee will have more than 130 mg of caffeine? (b) Less than 100 mg? (c) A very strong cup of tea has a caffeine content of 91 mg. What is the probability that a cup of coffee will have less caffeine than a very strong cup of tea? (Data are from *Popular Science* 254, no. 5 [May 1999], p. 95.)

7.54   The fracture strength of a certain type of manufactured glass is normally distributed with a mean of 579 MPa with a standard deviation of 14 MPa. (a) What is the probability that a randomly chosen sample of glass will break at less than 579 MPa? (b) More than 590 MPa? (c) Less than 600 MPa? (Data are from *Science* 283 [February 26, 1999], p. 1296.)

7.55   Tire pressure in a certain car is a normally distributed random variable with mean 30 psi (pounds per square inch) and standard deviation 2 psi. The manufacturer's recommended correct inflation range is 28 psi to 32 psi. A motorist's tire is inspected at random. (a) What is the probability that the tire's inflation is within the recommended range? (b) What is the probability that the tire is under-inflated? *(c) The Alliance of Automotive Manufacturers has developed a microchip that will warn when a tire is 25 percent below the recommended mean, to warn of dangerously low tire pressure. How often would such an alarm be triggered? (See *The Wall Street Journal,* July 14, 2004.)

7.56   In a certain microwave oven on the high power setting, the time it takes a randomly chosen kernel of popcorn to pop is normally distributed with a mean of 140 seconds and a standard deviation of 25 seconds. What percentage of the kernels will fail to pop if the popcorn is cooked for (a) 2 minutes? (b) Three minutes? (c) If you wanted 95 percent of the kernels to pop, what time would you allow? (d) If you wanted 99 percent to pop?

7.57   Procyon Manufacturing produces tennis balls. Their manufacturing process has a mean ball weight of 2.035 ounces with a standard deviation of 0.003 ounces. Regulation tennis balls are required to have a weight between 1.975 ounces and 2.095 ounces. What proportion of Procyon's production will fail to meet these specifications? (See *Scientific American* 292, no. 4 [April 2005], p. 95.)

7.58 Manufacturers of HRT (hormone replacement therapy) drugs need to know the potential market for their products that relieve side effects of menopause. For women without hysterectomy, the average age at menopause is 51.4 years. Assume a standard deviation of 3.8 years. (a) What is the probability that menopause will occur before age 40? (b) After age 55? (c) What assumptions did you make? *(d) Among the 73.1 million American women between ages 30 and 75, how many would be potential users of HRT? *Hint:* Assume equal numbers of women in all ages from 30 to 75, and compute the $\mu \pm 3\sigma$ range for menopause age. (Data are from *Statistical Abstract of the United States, 2001.*)

7.59 In a study of e-mail consultations with physicians at the University of Virginia Children's Medical Center, the monthly average was 37.6 requests with a standard deviation of 15.9 requests. (a) What is the probability of more than 50 requests in a given month? (b) Fewer than 29? (c) Between 40 and 50 requests? (d) What assumptions did you make? (Data are from S. M. Borowitz and J. Wyatt, "The Origin, Content, and Workload of E-Mail Consultations," *Journal of the American Medical Association* 280, no. 15 [October 1998], p. 1321.)

7.60 The time it takes to give a man a shampoo and haircut is normally distributed with mean 22 minutes and standard deviation 3 minutes. Customers are scheduled every 30 minutes. (a) What is the probability that a male customer will take longer than the allotted time? *(b) If three male customers are scheduled sequentially on the half-hour, what is the probability that all three will be finished within their allotted half-hour times?

7.61 The length of a time-out during a televised professional football game is normally distributed with a mean of 84 seconds and a standard deviation of 10 seconds. If the network runs consecutive commercials totaling 90 seconds, what is the probability that play will resume before the commercials are over? What assumption(s) did you make in answering this question?

7.62 In Rivendell Memorial Hospital the time to complete surgery in a routine tubal ligation without complications is normally distributed with a mean of 30 minutes and a standard deviation of 8 minutes. The next procedure has been scheduled in the same operating room 60 minutes after the beginning of a tubal ligation procedure. Allowing 20 minutes to vacate and prepare the operating room between procedures, what is the probability that the next procedure will have to be delayed? Explain carefully.

7.63 Demand for residential electricity at 6:00 P.M. on the first Monday in October in Santa Theresa County is normally distributed with a mean of 4,905 MW (megawatts) and a standard deviation of 355 MW. Due to scheduled maintenance and unexpected system failures in a generating station the utility can supply a maximum of 5,200 MW at that time. What is the probability that the utility will have to purchase electricity from other utilities or allow brownouts?

7.64 Jim's systolic blood pressure is a random variable with a mean of 145 mmHg and a standard deviation of 20 mmHg. For Jim's age group, 140 is the cutoff for high blood pressure. (a) If Jim's systolic blood pressure is taken at a randomly chosen moment, what is the probability that it will be 135 or less? (b) 175 or more? (c) Between 125 and 165? (d) Discuss the implications of variability for physicians who are trying to identify patients with high blood pressure.

7.65 A statistics exam was given. Explain the meaning of each z-value.
a. John's z-score was -1.62.
b. Mary's z-score was 0.50.
c. Zak's z-score was 1.79.
d. Frieda's z-score was 2.48.

7.66 Are the following statements true or false? Explain your reasoning.
a. "If we see a standardized z-value beyond ± 3, the variable cannot be normally distributed."
b. "If X and Y are two normally distributed random variables measured in different units (e.g., X is in pounds and Y is in kilograms), then it is not meaningful to compare the standardized z-values."
c. "Two machines fill 2-liter soft drink bottles by using a similar process. Machine A has $\mu = 1,990$ ml and $\sigma = 5$ ml while Machine B has $\mu = 1,995$ ml and $\sigma = 3$ ml. The variables cannot both be normally distributed since they have different standard deviations."

*7.67 John can take either of two routes (A or B) to LAX airport. At midday on a typical Wednesday the travel time on either route is normally distributed with parameters $\mu_A = 54$ minutes, $\sigma_A = 6$ minutes, $\mu_B = 60$ minutes, and $\sigma_B = 3$ minutes. (a) Which route should he choose if he must be at the airport in 54 minutes to pick up his spouse? (b) Sixty minutes? (c) Sixty-six minutes? Explain carefully.

7.68 The amount of fill in a half-liter (500 ml) soft drink bottle is normally distributed. The process has a standard deviation of 5 ml. The mean is adjustable. (a) Where should the mean be set to ensure a 95 percent probability that a half-liter bottle will not be underfilled? (b) A 99 percent probability? (c) A 99.9 percent probability? Explain.

7.69 The length of a certain kind of Colorado brook trout is normally distributed with a mean of 12.5 inches and a standard deviation of 1.2 inch. What minimum size limit should the Department of Natural Resources set if it wishes to allow people to keep 80 percent of the trout they catch?

*7.70 Times for a surgical procedure are normally distributed. There are two methods. Method *A* has a mean of 28 minutes and a standard deviation of 4 minutes, while method *B* has a mean of 32 minutes and a standard deviation of 2 minutes. (a) Which procedure is preferred if the procedure must be completed within 28 minutes? (b) Thirty-eight minutes? (c) Thirty-six minutes? Explain your reasoning fully.

*7.71 The length of a brook trout is normally distributed. Two brook trout are caught. (a) What is the probability that both exceed the mean? (b) Neither exceeds the mean? (c) One is above the mean and one is below? (d) Both are equal to the mean?

APPROXIMATIONS

*7.72 Among live deliveries, the probability of a twin birth is .02. (a) In 2,000 live deliveries what is the probability of at least 50 twin births? (b) Fewer than 35? Explain carefully.

*7.73 Nationwide, the probability that a rental car is from Hertz is 25 percent. In a sample of 100 rental cars, what is the probability that fewer than 20 are from Hertz? Explain.

*7.74 When a needle biopsy is ordered, there is an 85 percent chance that the test will indicate no breast cancer. In a given week, 20,000 such tests are performed. Find the quartiles for the number of such biopsies that will indicate no cancer. Explain fully and show all steps. (Data are from *The Economist Technology Quarterly* 367, no. 8329 [June 21, 2003], p. 8.)

*7.75 A multiple-choice exam has 100 questions. Each question has four choices. (a) What minimum score should be required to reduce the chance of passing by random guessing to 5 percent? (b) To 1 percent? (c) Find the quartiles for a guesser. Explain fully.

*7.76 The probability that a certain kind of flower seed will germinate is .80. (a) If 200 seeds are planted, what is the probability that fewer than 150 will germinate? (b) That at least 150 will germinate?

*7.77 On a cold morning the probability is .02 that a given car will not start. In the small town of Eureka 1,500 cars are started each cold morning. (a) What is the probability that at least 25 cars will not start? (b) More than 40?

*7.78 At a certain fire station, false alarms are received at a mean rate of 0.2 per day. In a year, what is the probability that fewer than 60 false alarms are received? Explain fully and show all steps.

EXPONENTIAL DISTRIBUTION

7.79 The Rockwell-Collins AHS-3000 quartz tuning-fork gyro for civil aviation has a mean time between failure (MTBF) of 10,000 hours. (a) What is the probability of failure within the first 10,000 flight hours? (b) Why is your answer more than 50 percent? Shouldn't exactly half the area be below the mean? Explain. (Data are from *Aviation Week & Space Technology* 149, no. 6 [August 10, 1998], p. 68.)

7.80 Automobile warranty claims for engine mount failure in a Troppo Malo 2000 SE are rare at a certain dealership, occurring at a mean rate of 0.1 claims per month. (a) What is the probability that the dealership will wait at least 6 months until the next claim? (b) At least a year? (c) At least 2 years? (d) At least 6 months but not more than 1 year?

7.81 The BF Goodrich Aerospace Avionics System fully color LCD digital flat-panel GH-3000 altitude indicator has no moving parts. Its MTBF is 25,000 hours. (a) What is the probability that the altitude indicator will last more than 15,000 hours? (b) If the altitude indicator is installed in an airplane that is flown 25 percent of the time, what is the probability of failure within 10 years? Explain any assumptions you make. (Data are from *Aviation Week & Space Technology* 143, no. 14 [October 2, 1995], p. 23.)

7.82 In 1982, the in-flight shutdown rate for the Garrett TFE731 turbofan engine was 6.0 shutdowns per 100,000 hours. In 1992, with improvements, the in-flight shutdown rate for this same engine dropped to 1.5 shutdowns per 100,000 hours. (a) Find the probability that at least 50,000 hours would elapse before the next in-flight shutdown in 1982. Calculate the same probability in 1992. (b) How would you characterize the degree of improvement in reliability? (Data are from *Flying*, 122, no. 4 [April 1995], p. 61.)

TRIANGULAR DISTRIBUTION

7.83 The price (dollars per 1,000 board feet) of Douglas fir from western Washington and Oregon varies according to a triangular distribution $T(300, 350, 490)$. (a) Find the mean. (b) Find the standard deviation. (c) What is the probability that the price will exceed 400?

*7.84 The distribution of scores on a statistics exam is $T(50, 60, 95)$. (a) Find the mean. (b) Find the standard deviation. (c) Find the probability that a score will be less than 75. (d) Sketch the distribution and shade the area for the event in part (c).

*7.85 The distribution of beach condominium prices in Santa Theresa ($ thousands) is $T(500, 700, 2,100)$. (a) Find the mean. (b) Find the standard deviation. (c) Find the probability that a condo price will be greater than $750K. (d) Sketch the distribution and shade the area for the event in part (c).

DISCUSSION QUESTION

7.86 On a police sergeant's examination, the historical mean score was 80 with a standard deviation of 20. Four officers who were alleged to be cronies of the police chief scored 195, 171, 191, and 189, respectively, on the test. This led to allegations of irregularity in the exam. (a) Convert these four officers' scores to standardized z-values. (b) Do you think there was sufficient reason to question these four exam scores? What assumptions are you making? (Data are from *Detroit Free Press*, March 19, 1999, p. 10A.)

Related Reading

Balakrishnan, N.; and V. B. Nevzorov. *A Primer on Statistical Distributions*. Wiley, 2003.

Evans, Merran; Nicholas Hastings; and Brian Peacock. *Statistical Distributions*. 3rd ed. Wiley, 2000.

International Organization for Standardization. *Guide to the Expression of Uncertainty in Measurement*. 1995.

LearningStats Unit 07   Continuous Distributions   LS

LearningStats Unit 07 lets you work with continuous distributions, particularly the normal distribution, demonstrating how to calculate areas and showing the shapes of the distributions. Modules are designed for self-study, so you can proceed at your own pace.

Topic	LearningStats Modules
Overview	Continuous Distributions
Calculations	Continuous Distributions: Examples
	Normal Areas
	Probability Calculator
Normal approximations	Evaluating Rules of Thumb
Random data	Random Continuous Data
Tables	Table C—Normal Probabilities
Applications	Formulas for Continuous PDFs
	Exponential Model and Problems

Key: = PowerPoint   = Word   = Excel

Visual Statistics

Visual Statistics Modules on Continuous Distributions

Module	*Module Name*
5	Visualizing Continuous Distributions

Visual Statistics Module 5 (included on your CD) is designed to help you

- Recognize common continuous distributions and their distribution functions.
- Identify the parameters of common continuous distributions and how they affect shape.
- Recognize shape measures for common distributions.
- Understand when common continuous distributions can be approximated by a normal.
- Understand the relation between a value of a distribution and its tail area.

The worktext chapter (included on the CD in .PDF format) contains a list of concepts covered, objectives of the module, overview of concepts, illustration of concepts, orientation to module features, learning exercises (basic, intermediate, advanced), learning projects (individual, team), self-evaluation quiz, glossary of terms, and solutions to a self-evaluation quiz.

Sampling Distributions and Estimation

Chapter Learning Objectives

When you finish this chapter you should be able to

- Define sampling variation, sampling error, parameter, and estimator.
- Explain why it is desirable that an estimator be unbiased, consistent, and efficient.
- State the Central Limit Theorem for a mean or proportion.
- Explain how the standard error is affected by sample size.
- Construct a 90, 95, or 99 percent confidence interval for a mean or proportion.
- Describe similarities and differences between z and Student's t.
- Find t-values in tables or Excel for a desired confidence level.
- Calculate sample size for a given precision and confidence level to estimate μ or π.
- Construct a confidence interval for a difference of two means or proportions (optional).
- Construct a confidence interval for a variance (optional).

A sample statistic is a *random variable* whose value depends on which population items happen to be included in the *random sample*. Some samples may represent the population well, while other samples could differ greatly from the population (particularly if the sample size is small). To illustrate **sampling variation,** let's draw some random samples from a large population of GMAT scores for MBA applicants. The population *parameters* are $\mu = 520.78$ and $\sigma = 86.80$. Figure 8.1 shows a dot plot of the entire population, which resembles a normal distribution.

FIGURE 8.1

Dot plot of GMAT population
 **GMAT**

Source: Data for 2,637 MBA applicants at a medium-sized public university located in the Midwest.

VS

Chapter 6

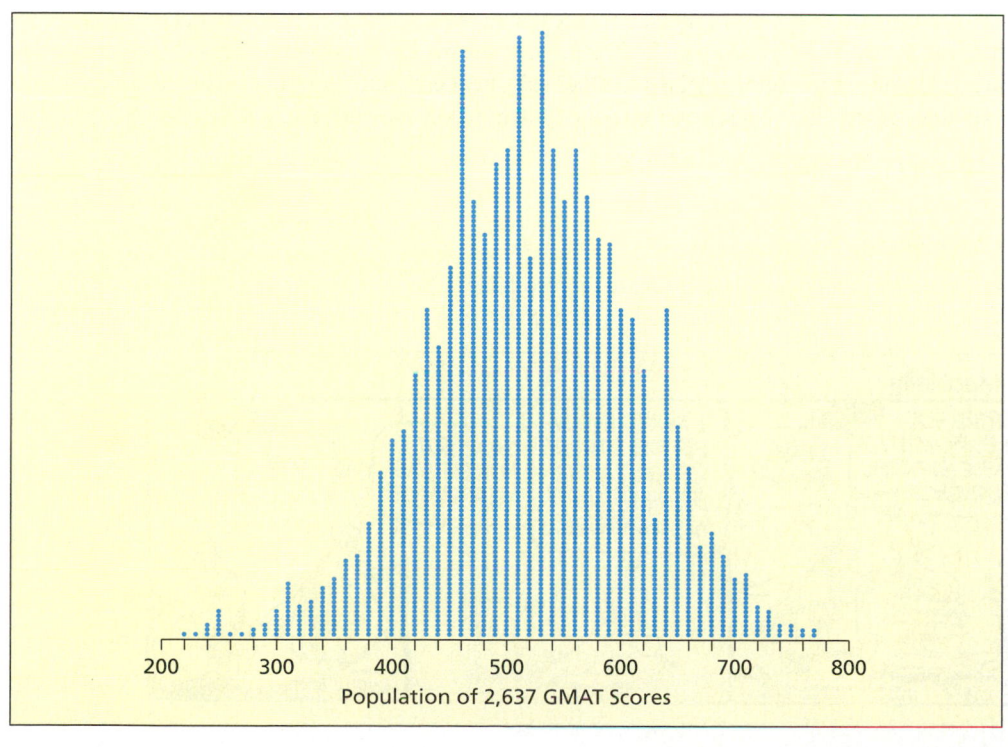

Population of 2,637 GMAT Scores

The table below shows eight random samples of $n = 5$ from this population. The samples vary because of the variability of GMAT scores in the population. Sampling variation is inevitable, yet there is a tendency for the sample means to be close to the population mean ($\mu = 520.78$), as shown in Figure 8.2. In larger samples, the sample means would tend to be even closer to μ. This phenomenon is the basis for *statistical estimation.*

Random Samples ($n = 5$) from the GMAT Score Population

Sample 1	Sample 2	Sample 3	Sample 4	Sample 5	Sample 6	Sample 7	Sample 8
490	310	500	450	420	450	490	670
580	590	450	590	640	670	450	610
440	730	510	710	470	390	590	550
580	710	570	240	530	500	640	540
430	540	610	510	640	470	650	540
$\bar{x}_1 = 504.0$	$\bar{x}_2 = 576.0$	$\bar{x}_3 = 528.0$	$\bar{x}_4 = 500.0$	$\bar{x}_5 = 540.0$	$\bar{x}_6 = 496.0$	$\bar{x}_7 = 564.0$	$\bar{x}_8 = 582.0$

FIGURE 8.2

Dot plots of eight sample means

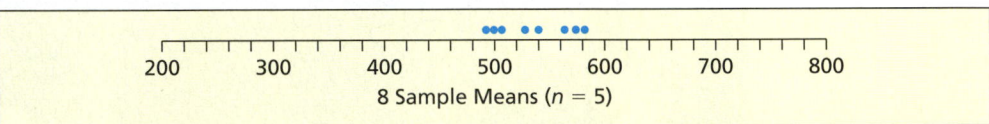

8 Sample Means ($n = 5$)

FIGURE 8.3

Dot plots of eight samples of size $n = 5$

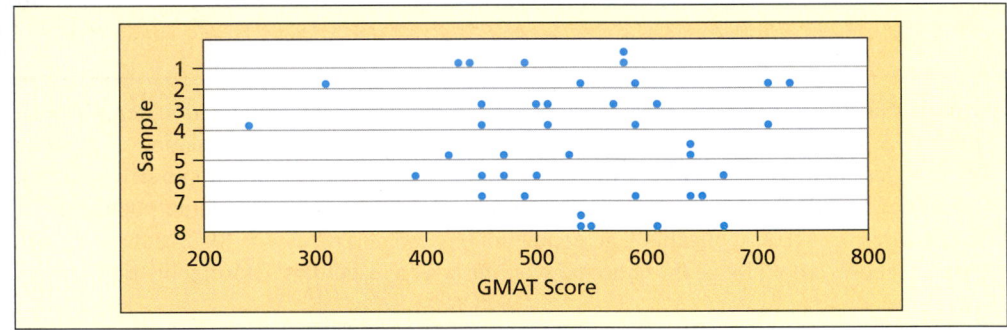

By comparing Figures 8.2 and 8.3 we see that the sample *means* also have much less variation than the *individual* sample items. This is because the mean is an *average*. This chapter describes the behavior of the sample mean and other statistical estimators of population parameters, and explains how to make *inferences* about a population that take into account four factors:

- Sampling variation (uncontrollable).
- Population variation (uncontrollable).
- Sample size (controllable).
- Desired *confidence* in the estimate (controllable).

Distributed by Tribune Media Services. Used with permission.

Some Terminology

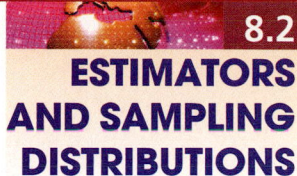

An *estimator* is a statistic derived from a sample to infer the value of a population *parameter.* An *estimate* is the value of the estimator in a particular sample. Table 8.1 and Figure 8.4 show some common estimators. We usually denote a population parameter by a Greek letter (e.g., μ, σ, or π). The corresponding sample estimator is usually a Roman letter (e.g., $\bar{x}$, s, or p) or a Greek letter with a "hat" (e.g., $\hat{\mu}$, $\hat{\sigma}$, or $\hat{\pi}$). Statistics books may use different symbols for these things. That's because the science of statistics developed over many decades and its founders had various ways of expressing their ideas.

Estimator	Formula	Population Parameter
Sample mean	$\bar{x} = \dfrac{1}{n}\displaystyle\sum_{i=1}^{n} x_i$ where x_i is the ith data value and n is the sample size	μ
Sample proportion	$p = x/n$ where x is the number of successes in the sample and n is the sample size	π
Sample standard deviation	$s = \sqrt{\dfrac{\displaystyle\sum_{i=1}^{n}(x_i - \bar{x})^2}{n-1}}$ where x_i is the ith data value and n is the sample size	σ

TABLE 8.1
Examples of Estimators

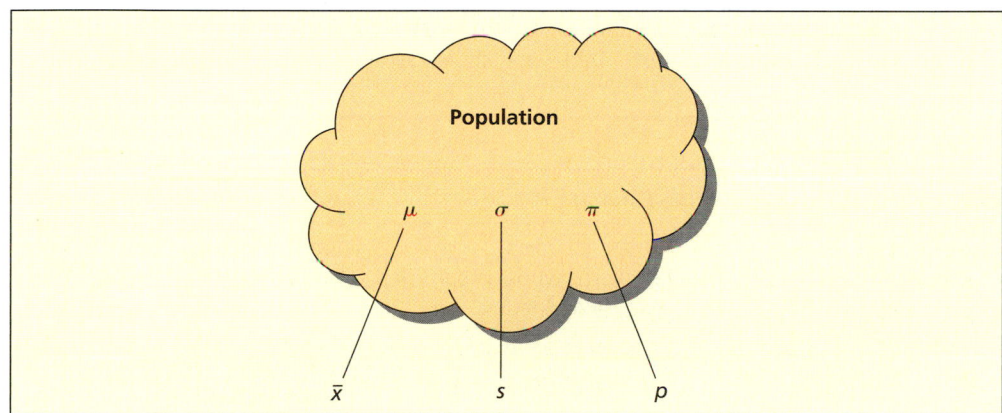

FIGURE 8.4

Sample estimators of population parameters

Sampling Distributions

The *sampling distribution* of an estimator is the probability distribution of all possible values the statistic may assume when a random sample of size *n* is taken. Samples vary, so an estimator is a *random variable*. It has a probability distribution, mean, and variance. The *sampling error* is the difference between an estimate $\hat{\theta}$ and the corresponding population parameter θ:

$$\text{Sampling Error} = \hat{\theta} - \theta \qquad (8.1)$$

Sampling error exists because different samples will yield varying values for $\hat{\theta}$, depending on which population items happen to be included in the sample.

Bias

The *bias* is the difference between the expected value (i.e., the average value) of the estimator and the true parameter:

$$\text{Bias} = E(\hat{\theta}) - \theta \qquad (8.2)$$

An estimator is *unbiased* if $E(\hat{\theta}) = \theta$. There can be sampling error in a particular sample, but an **unbiased estimator** neither overstates nor understates the true parameter *on average*.

Sampling error is *random* whereas bias is *systematic*. Consider an analogy with target shooting, illustrated in Figure 8.5. An expert whose rifle sights are correctly aligned will produce a target pattern like one on the left. The same expert shooting a rifle with misaligned sights might produce the pattern on the right. There is sample variation, but the unbiased estimator is correctly *aimed*.

FIGURE 8.5

Illustration of bias

Chapter 8

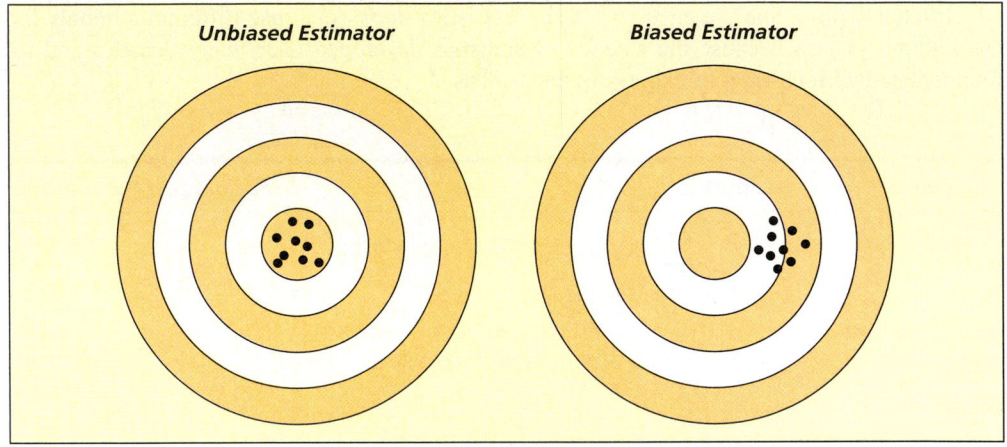

Some samples may happen to hit closer to the bull's-eye than others, but at least an unbiased estimator avoids *systematic* error. You cannot observe bias in a sample because you do not know the true population parameter, but bias can be studied mathematically or by simulation experiments (e.g., Visual Statistics). Statisticians have shown that the sample mean $\bar{x}$ and the sample proportion p are unbiased estimators for μ and π, respectively. Similarly, s^2 is an unbiased estimate of σ^2. Table 8.2 shows examples of estimates from *known*

TABLE 8.2   **Sample Estimates**

Estimator	True Parameter	Sample Estimate	Interpretation
Sample mean	William Shakespeare's play *All's Well That Ends Well* has $N = 24,261$ words whose mean length is $\mu = 4.349$ letters.	Act II, Scene I, contains $n = 1,796$ words whose mean length is $\bar{x} = 4.404$ letters.	Since the sample mean is an unbiased estimator of the true mean, the difference between $\bar{x}$ and μ is *sampling error* (we are assuming that Act II, Scene I, is a random sample of the entire play). Another sample could yield a different estimate of μ.
Sample proportion	In 1998, the proportion of all Fortune 500 companies that reported negative profit (i.e., a loss) was $\pi = 65/498 = .1305$, or about 13% (two firms didn't report their profit).	In a random sample of 50 of these firms, the proportion reporting negative profit was $p = 7/50 = .14$, or 14%.	In this case, the sample proportion p happens to be very close to the true proportion π. The low *sampling error* was partly luck. Another sample could yield a different estimate of π.
Sample standard deviation	In 2001, CEO compensation in $N = 200$ large U.S. companies averaged $\mu = \$15,520,349$ with $\sigma = \$20,647,358$ (σ is huge because of outliers and skewed data).	In a random sample of 20 of these companies, the average CEO compensation was $\bar{x} = \$9,136,229$ with $s = \$5,479,936$.	This sample gave poor estimates of μ and σ, due to *sampling error*. In the population, a dozen CEOs earned over $50 million, but none showed up in our sample, so we got a smaller mean and smaller standard deviation.

populations. It is interesting to see that some of the estimates came very close to the population values, while others did not. While it is helpful in visualizing the process of estimation, Table 8.2 is unusual because most of the time you wouldn't *know* the true population parameters (if you had the population, why would you take a sample?). As you think about Table 8.2, you might ask yourself how *you* would take a "random sample" from each of these populations.

Bias is not a concern for the sample mean ($\bar{x}$) and sample proportion (p). But we can find examples of biased estimators. For example, you will get a slightly biased estimate of σ if you use Excel's population standard deviation formula =STDEVP(Data) instead of its sample standard deviation formula =STDEV(Data) for a sample array named Data. But why would you do that? Further, there is no reason to *worry* about sampling error, because it is an inevitable risk in statistical sampling. Anyway, you cannot *know* whether you have sampling error without knowing the population parameter (and if you knew it, you wouldn't be taking a sample). It is more important to take a large enough sample to obtain a reliable estimate and to take the sample scientifically (see Chapter 2, "Data Collection").

Efficiency

Efficiency refers to the variance of the estimator's sampling distribution. Smaller variance means a more efficient estimator. We prefer an estimator with a small variance, other things being equal. Furthermore, we prefer a ***minimum variance estimator*** that is also unbiased. Statisticians refer to this estimator as MVUE (minimum variance unbiased estimator). Figure 8.6 shows two unbiased estimators. Both patterns are centered on the bull's-eye, but the estimator on the left has less variation. You cannot assess efficiency from one sample, but it can be studied either mathematically or by simulation (e.g., Visual Statistics). While an MVUE does not exist for every parameter of every type of distribution, statisticians have proved that, for a normal distribution, $\bar{x}$ and p and s^2 are minimum variance estimators of μ and π and σ^2, respectively (i.e., no other estimators can have smaller variance). That is one reason these statistics are widely used.

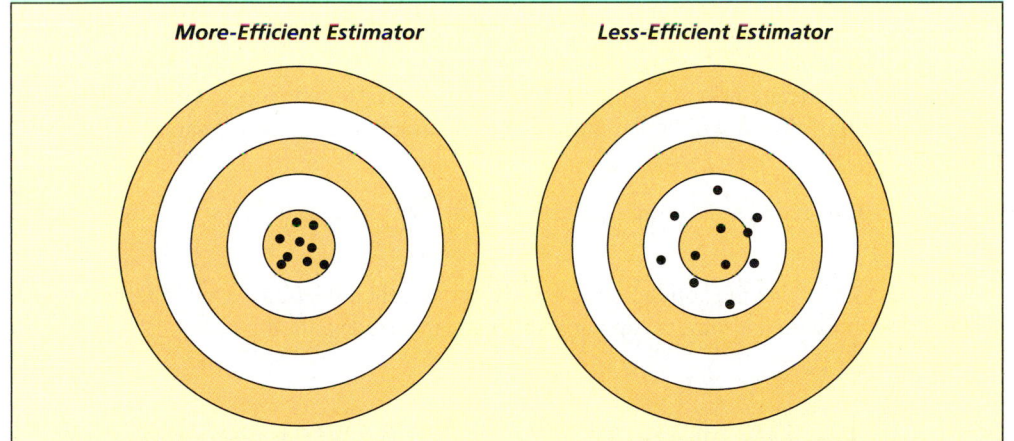

More-Efficient Estimator **Less-Efficient Estimator**

FIGURE 8.6

Illustration of efficiency

Consistency

A ***consistent estimator*** converges toward the parameter being estimated as the sample size increases. That is, the sample distribution collapses on the true parameter, as illustrated in Figure 8.7. It seems logical that in larger samples $\bar{x}$ ought to be closer to μ, p ought to be closer to π, and s ought to be closer to σ. In fact, it can be shown that the variances of these three estimators diminish as n increases, so all are consistent estimators. Figure 8.7 illustrates the importance of a large sample, because in a large sample your estimate is likely to be closer to θ.

FIGURE 8.7

Illustration of consistency

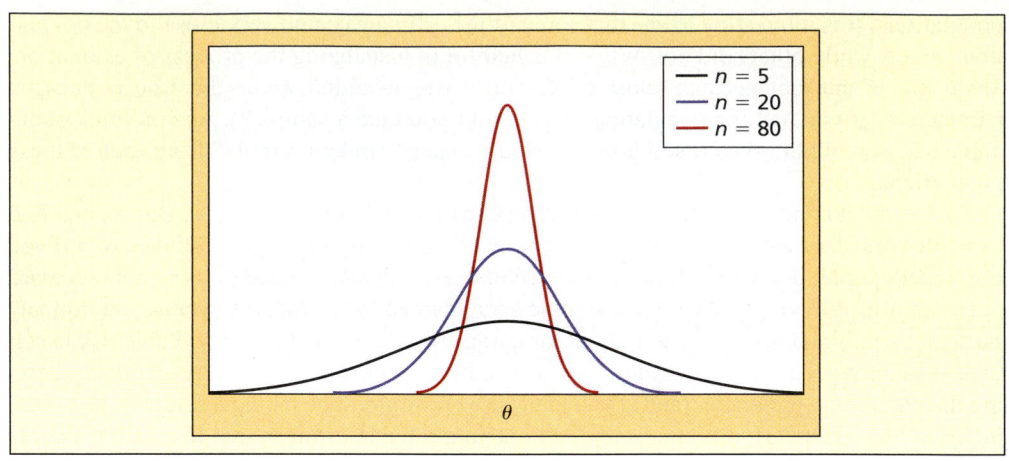

8.3

SAMPLE MEAN AND THE CENTRAL LIMIT THEOREM

VS

Chapter 7

Consider the sample mean $\bar{X}$ used to estimate the population mean μ. Our ultimate objective is to use the sampling distribution of $\bar{X}$ to say something about the population that we are studying. To describe the sampling distribution we need to know the mean, variance, and shape of the distribution. As we've already learned, the sample mean is an unbiased estimator for μ; therefore,

$$(8.3) \qquad E(\bar{X}) = \mu \qquad \text{(expected value of the mean)}$$

We've also learned that the value of $\bar{X}$ will change whenever we take a different sample. And as long as our samples are *random samples*, we should feel confident that the only type of error we will have in our estimating process is *sampling error*. The sampling error of the sample mean is described by its standard deviation. This value has a special name, the ***standard error of the mean.*** Notice that the standard error of the mean decreases as the sample size increases:

$$(8.4) \qquad \sigma_{\bar{x}} = \frac{\sigma}{\sqrt{n}} \qquad \text{(standard error of the mean)}$$

Suppose the average price, μ, of a 5 GB MP3 player is $80.00 with a standard deviation, σ, equal to $10.00. What will be the mean and standard error of $\bar{x}$ from a sample of 20 MP3 players?

$$\mu_{\bar{x}} = \$80.00, \qquad \sigma_{\bar{x}} = \frac{\$10.00}{\sqrt{20}} = \$2.236$$

If we also know that the population is exactly normal, then the sample mean follows a normal distribution with the same mean but a smaller standard deviation $\sigma/\sqrt{n}$.

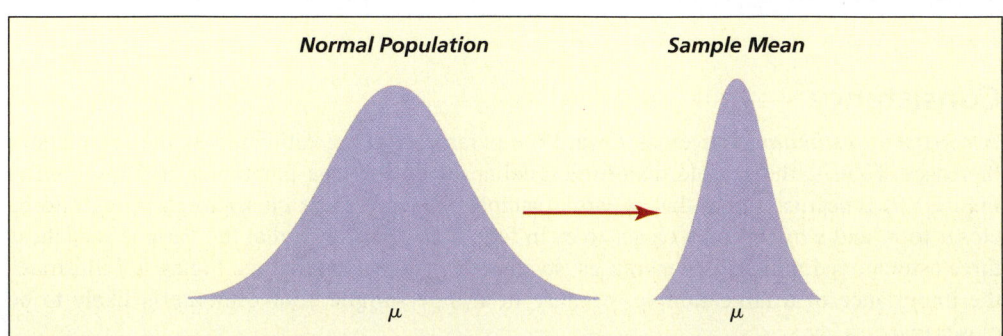

If the distribution of prices of 5 GB MP3 players is $N(80, 10)$, then we now know that the sampling distribution of $\bar{X}$ is $N(80, 2.236)$.

Unfortunately, it is not always the case that the population has exactly a normal distribution, or we may simply not know *what* the population distribution looks like. What can we do in these circumstances? We can use one of the most fundamental laws of statistics, the Central Limit Theorem.

Central Limit Theorem for a Mean

The ***Central Limit Theorem*** (CLT) is a powerful result that allows us to *approximate* the shape of the sampling distribution of $\bar{X}$ even when we don't know the shape of the population distribution. If the sample is large enough, the sample means will have approximately a normal distribution even if your population is *not* normal:

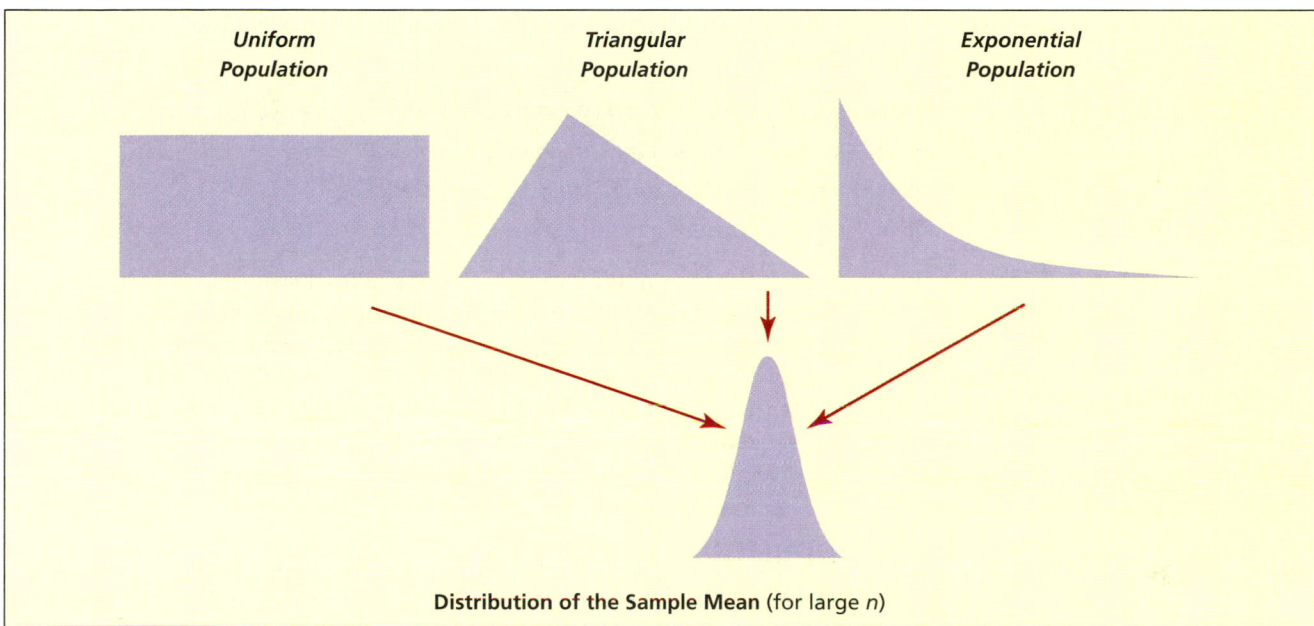

Distribution of the Sample Mean (for large *n*)

Central Limit Theorem for a Mean

If a random sample of size n is drawn from a population with mean μ and standard deviation σ, the distribution of the sample mean $\bar{x}$ approaches a normal distribution with mean μ and standard deviation $\sigma_{\bar{x}} = \sigma/\sqrt{n}$ as the sample size increases. If the population is normal, the distribution of the sample mean is normal regardless of sample size.

Symmetric Population: Uniform Distribution

You may have heard the rule of thumb that $n \geq 30$ to obtain a normal distribution for the sample mean, but a much smaller n will suffice if the population is symmetric. You can demonstrate this by performing your own simulations in *LearningStats* or Visual Statistics. For example, consider a uniform population $U(500, 1500)$ with parameters $\mu = 1,000$ and $\sigma = 288.7$, as shown in Figure 8.8.

FIGURE 8.8

Uniform population with $\mu = 1{,}000$ and $\sigma = 288.7$

🐾 **CLTPopulations**

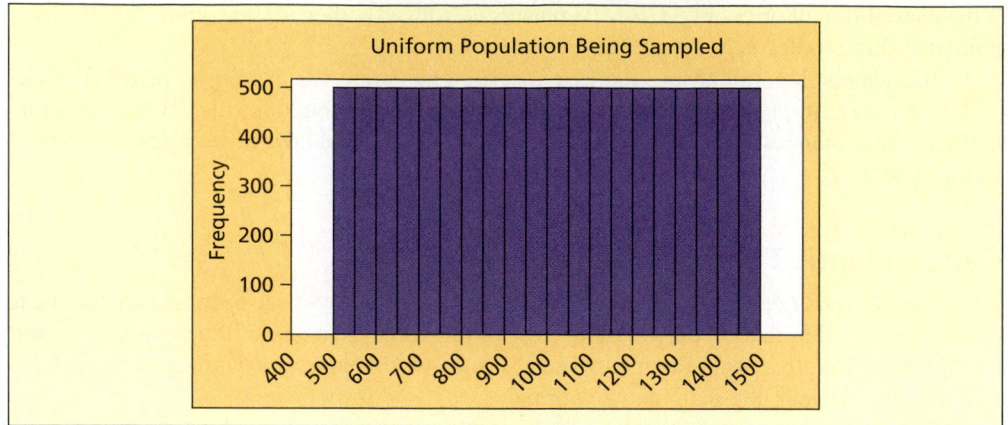

The Central Limit Theorem predicts that samples drawn from this population will have a mean of 1,000 and that the standard error of the mean for samples of $n = 1$, $n = 2$, $n = 4$, and $n = 16$ will be:

Predicted standard error for $n = 1$: $\sigma_{\bar{x}} = \sigma/\sqrt{n} = 288.7/\sqrt{1} = 288.7$

Predicted standard error for $n = 2$: $\sigma_{\bar{x}} = \sigma/\sqrt{n} = 288.7/\sqrt{2} = 204.1$

Predicted standard error for $n = 4$: $\sigma_{\bar{x}} = \sigma/\sqrt{n} = 288.7/\sqrt{4} = 144.3$

Predicted standard error for $n = 16$: $\sigma_{\bar{x}} = \sigma/\sqrt{n} = 288.7/\sqrt{16} = 72.2$

Figure 8.9 shows histograms of the means of 1,000 samples drawn from this uniform population. There is sampling variation, but the mean of the 1,000 sample means $\bar{\bar{x}}$ and standard deviation of the 1,000 sample means $s_{\bar{x}}$ shown above each histogram are close to the CLT's predictions. When $n = 1$, the "means" are simply individual population items, so the histogram looks like the population and is not normal. But even for $n = 2$, we see the approach to a bell-shaped histogram and decreasing variance of the mean as sample size increases. For $n = 4$ and $n = 16$ the reduced variation and normal fit are obvious.

Skewed Population: Waiting Time

A symmetric, uniform population does not pose much of a challenge for the Central Limit Theorem. But what if the population is severely skewed? For example, consider the strongly skewed population for waiting times at airport security screening, shown in Figure 8.10.

The Central Limit Theorem predicts that samples drawn from this population will have a mean of 2.983 minutes (the same as the population) and that the standard error of the mean for samples of $n = 1$, $n = 2$, $n = 4$, and $n = 16$ will be:

Predicted standard error for $n = 1$: $\sigma_{\bar{x}} = \sigma/\sqrt{n} = 2.451/\sqrt{1} = 2.451$

Predicted standard error for $n = 2$: $\sigma_{\bar{x}} = \sigma/\sqrt{n} = 2.451/\sqrt{2} = 1.733$

Predicted standard error for $n = 4$: $\sigma_{\bar{x}} = \sigma/\sqrt{n} = 2.451/\sqrt{4} = 1.225$

Predicted standard error for $n = 16$: $\sigma_{\bar{x}} = \sigma/\sqrt{n} = 2.451/\sqrt{16} = 0.613$

Figure 8.11 shows histograms of the means of 1,000 samples drawn from this skewed population. Despite the skewness, the mean of the 1,000 sample means $\bar{\bar{x}}$ and standard deviation of the 1,000 sample means $s_{\bar{x}}$ shown above each histogram are very close to the CLT's predictions. When $n = 1$, the "means" are simply individual population items, so the histogram of means looks like the skewed parent population. In contrast to the uniform population example, $n = 2$ and $n = 4$ do *not* produce bell-shaped histograms, although the variance does decrease. Only when $n = 16$ does the histogram begin to look normal. A still larger sample might be preferable. In some populations, even $n \geq 30$ will not ensure normality, though in general it is not a bad rule. However, in severely skewed populations, the mean is a poor measure of central tendency to begin with.

FIGURE 8.9

Histograms of sample means from uniform population

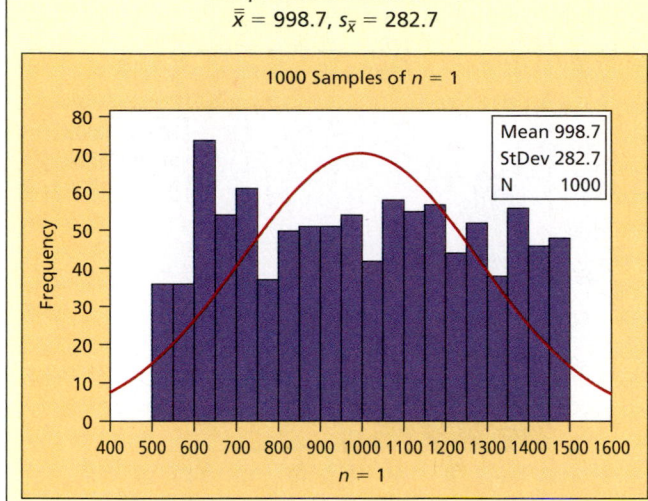

Sample Means with n = 1
$\bar{\bar{x}} = 998.7$, $s_{\bar{x}} = 282.7$

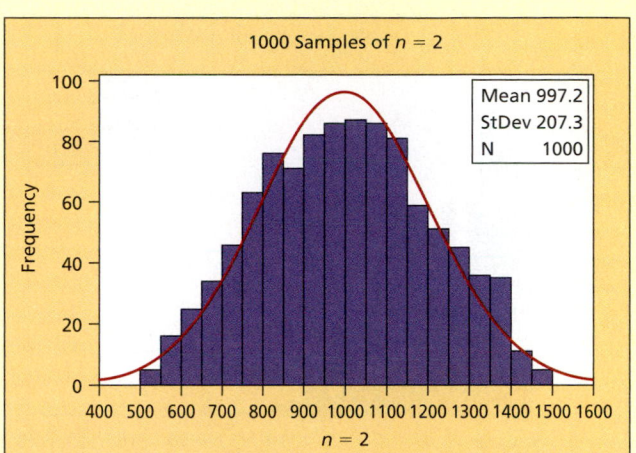

Sample Means with n = 2
$\bar{\bar{x}} = 997.2$, $s_{\bar{x}} = 207.3$

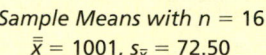

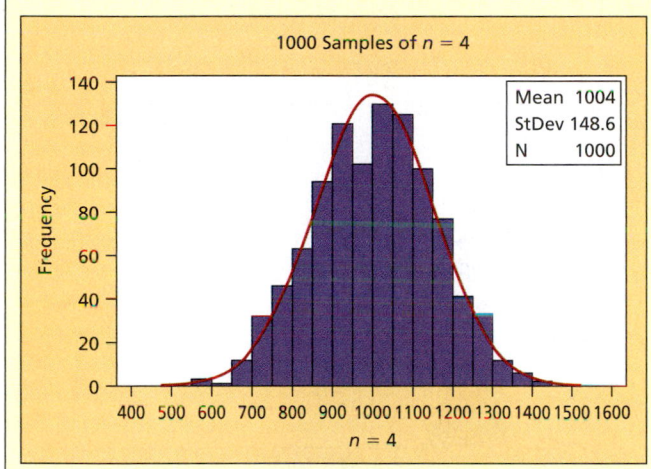

Sample Means with n = 4
$\bar{\bar{x}} = 1004$, $s_{\bar{x}} = 148.6$

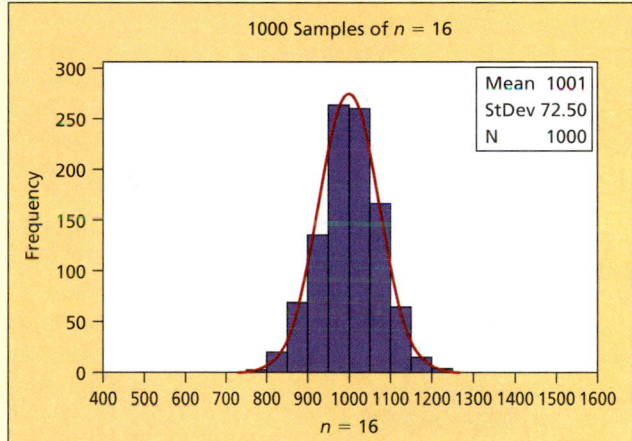

Sample Means with n = 16
$\bar{\bar{x}} = 1001$, $s_{\bar{x}} = 72.50$

FIGURE 8.10

Skewed population with
$\mu = 2.983$, $\sigma = 2.451$
CLTPopulations

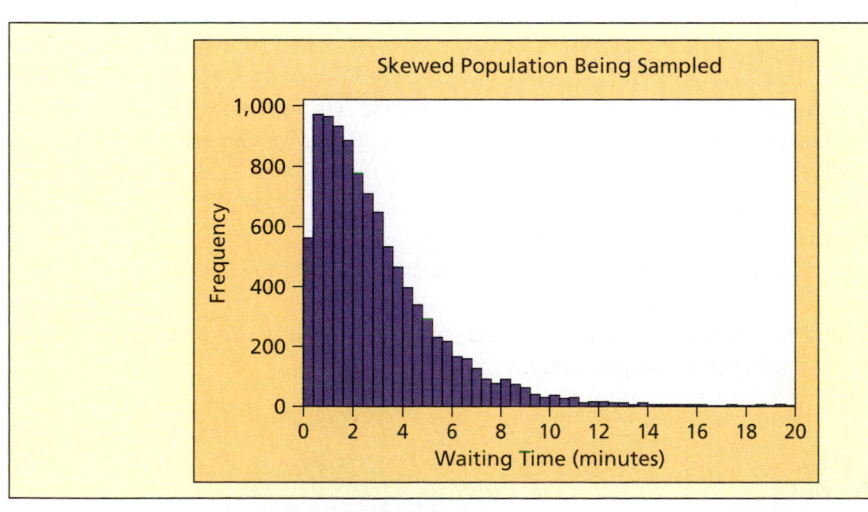

FIGURE 8.11

Histograms of sample means from skewed population

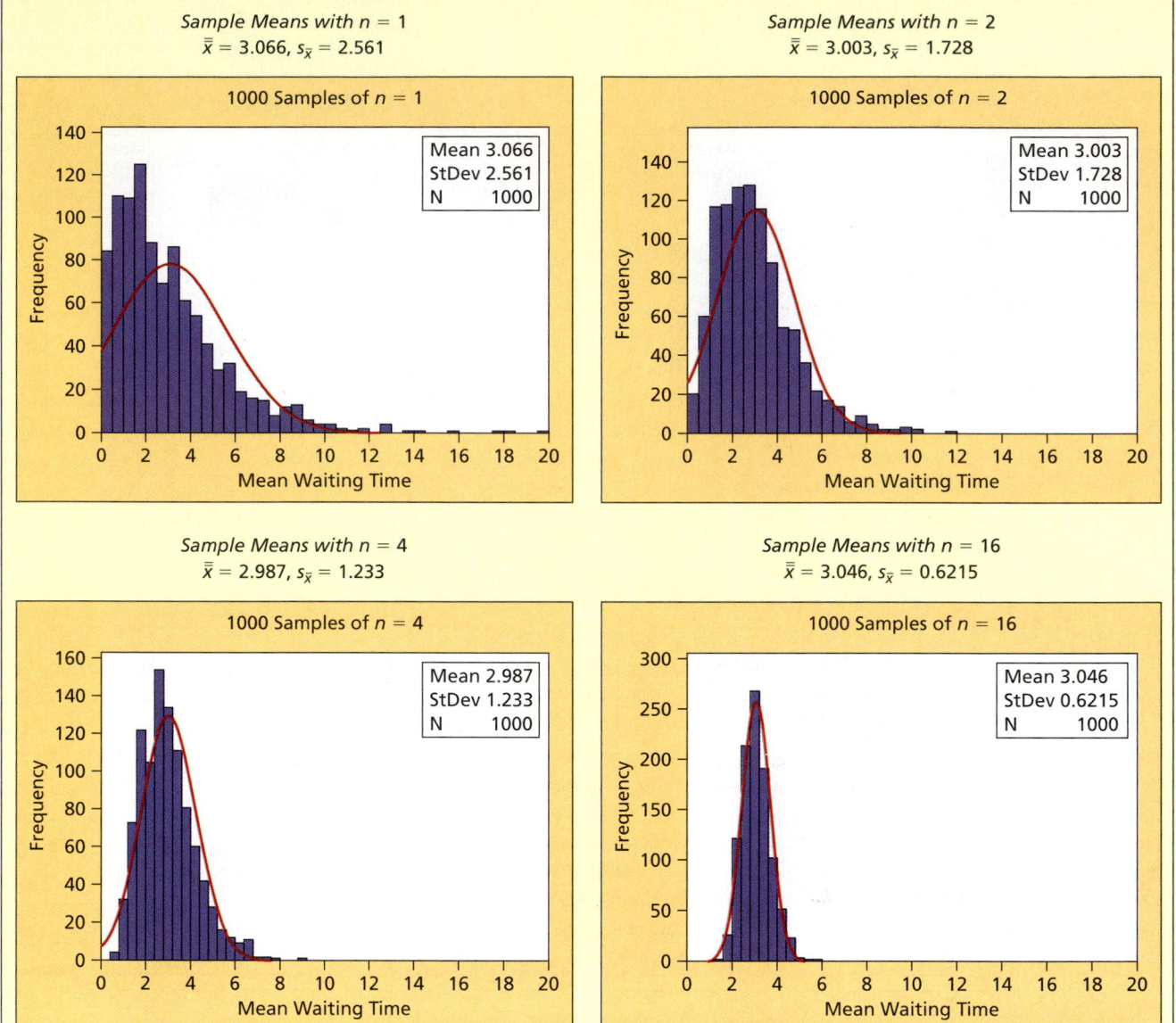

Range of Sample Means

The Central Limit Theorem permits us to define an interval within which the sample means are expected to fall. As long as the sample size n is large enough, we can use the normal distribution regardless of the population shape (or any n if the population is normal to begin with):

(8.5) $$\mu \pm z\frac{\sigma}{\sqrt{n}}$$ (range of sample means according to CLT)

We use the familiar z-values for the standard normal distribution. If we know μ and σ, we can predict the range of sample means for samples of size n:

90% Interval	95% Interval	99% Interval
$\mu \pm 1.645\dfrac{\sigma}{\sqrt{n}}$	$\mu \pm 1.960\dfrac{\sigma}{\sqrt{n}}$	$\mu \pm 2.576\dfrac{\sigma}{\sqrt{n}}$

Illustration: GMAT Scores

Within what range would we expect GMAT means to fall for samples of $n = 5$ applicants (see Figure 8.1)? The population is approximately normal with parameters $\mu = 520.78$ and $\sigma = 86.80$, so the predicted range for 95 percent of the sample means is

$$\mu \pm 1.960\frac{\sigma}{\sqrt{n}} = 520.78 \pm 1.960\frac{86.80}{\sqrt{5}} = 520.78 \pm 76.08$$

Our eight sample means for $n = 5$ (see Figure 8.2) drawn from this population fall comfortably within this range (roughly 444 to 597), as predicted by the Central Limit Theorem.

EXAMPLE

Bottle Filling: Variation in $\bar{X}$

The amount of fill in a half-liter (500 ml) bottle of Diet Coke is normally distributed with mean $\mu = 505$ ml and standard deviation $\sigma = 1.2$ ml. Since the population is normal, the sample mean $\bar{X}$ will be a normally distributed random variable for any sample size. If we sample a single bottle (i.e., $n = 1$) and measure its fill, the sample "mean" is just X, which should lie within the ranges shown in Table 8.3. It appears that the company has set the mean far enough above 500 ml that essentially all bottles contain at least the advertised half-liter quantity.

TABLE 8.3   Range of Means for $n = 1$

90% Range for $\bar{X}$	95% Range for $\bar{X}$	99% Range for $\bar{X}$
$\mu \pm 1.645\frac{\sigma}{\sqrt{n}}$	$\mu \pm 1.960\frac{\sigma}{\sqrt{n}}$	$\mu \pm 2.576\frac{\sigma}{\sqrt{n}}$
$= 505 \pm 1.645\frac{1.2}{\sqrt{1}}$	$= 505 \pm 1.960\frac{1.2}{\sqrt{1}}$	$= 505 \pm 2.576\frac{1.2}{\sqrt{1}}$
$= 505 \pm 1.974$	$= 505 \pm 2.352$	$= 505 \pm 3.091$

What happens if we increase the sample size to $n = 4$ bottles? We expect the sample means to lie within the ranges shown in Table 8.4. The ranges are much narrower, because when we average four items, we *reduce the variability* in the sample mean.

TABLE 8.4   Range of Means for $n = 4$

90% Range for $\bar{X}$	95% Range for $\bar{X}$	99% Range for $\bar{X}$
$\mu \pm 1.645\frac{\sigma}{\sqrt{n}}$	$\mu \pm 1.960\frac{\sigma}{\sqrt{n}}$	$\mu \pm 2.576\frac{\sigma}{\sqrt{n}}$
$= 505 \pm 1.645\frac{1.2}{\sqrt{4}}$	$= 505 \pm 1.960\frac{1.2}{\sqrt{4}}$	$= 505 \pm 2.576\frac{1.2}{\sqrt{4}}$
$= 505 \pm 0.987$	$= 505 \pm 1.176$	$= 505 \pm 1.546$

Interpretation If the bottle-filling experiment were repeated a large number of times, we would expect that the sample means would lie within the limits shown above. For example, if we took 1,000 samples and computed the mean fill for each sample, we would expect that approximately 900 of the sample means would lie within the 90 percent limits, 950 within the 95 percent limits, and 990 within the 99 percent limits. But we don't really take 1,000 samples (except in a computer simulation). We actually take only *one* sample. The importance of the CLT is that it *predicts* what will happen with that *one* sample.

Sample Size and Standard Error

Even if the population standard deviation σ is large, the sample means will fall within a narrow interval as long as n is large. The key is the *standard error of the mean:* $\sigma_{\bar{x}} = \sigma/\sqrt{n}$. The standard error declines as n increases, but at a decreasing rate. Figure 8.12 illustrates how enlarging n reduces the standard error (expressed in this diagram as a fraction of σ). This phenomenon is the key to obtaining precise predictions for $\bar{X}$.

FIGURE 8.12

Standard error declines as n increases

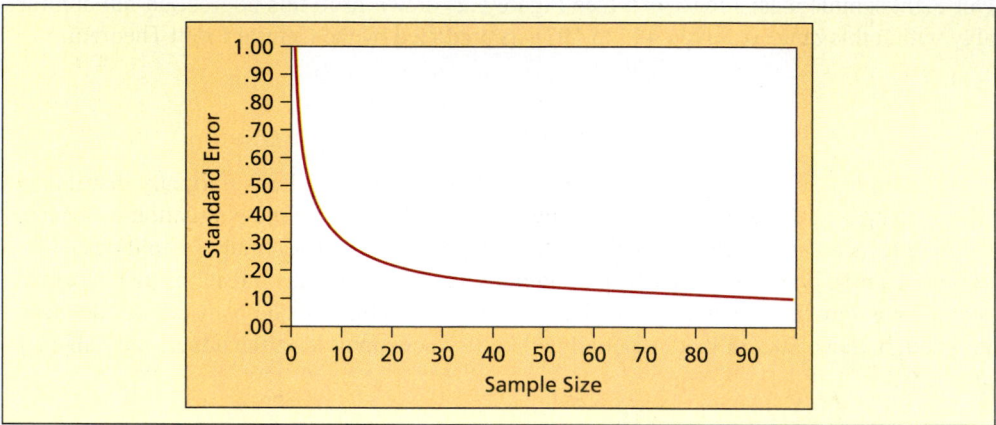

For example, when $n = 4$ the standard error is halved. To halve it again requires $n = 16$, and to halve it again requires $n = 64$. To *halve* the standard error, you must *quadruple* the sample size (the law of diminishing returns).

Sample Size	Standard Error
$n = 4$	$\sigma_{\bar{x}} = \sigma/2$
$n = 16$	$\sigma_{\bar{x}} = \sigma/4$
$n = 64$	$\sigma_{\bar{x}} = \sigma/8$

You can make the interval $\mu \pm z\sigma/\sqrt{n}$ as small as you want by increasing n. Thus, the distribution of sample means collapses at the true population mean μ as n increases.

Illustration: All Possible Samples from a Uniform Population

To help visualize the meaning of the Central Limit Theorem, consider a small discrete uniform population consisting of the integers $\{0, 1, 2, 3\}$. The population parameters are $\mu = 1.5$ and $\sigma = 1.118$ (using the population definition of σ).

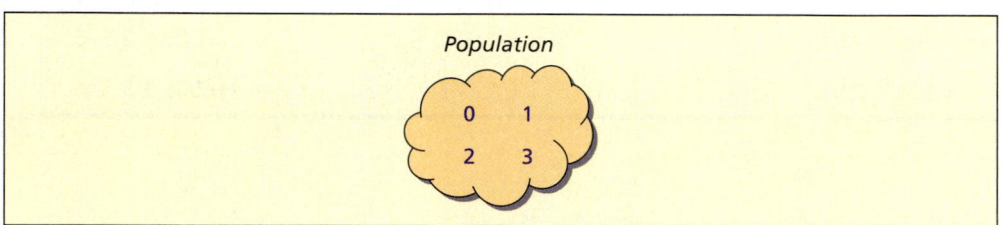

Population

$$\mu = \frac{1}{N}\sum_{i=1}^{N}x_i = \frac{0+1+2+3}{4} = 1.5$$

$$\sigma = \sqrt{\frac{\sum_{i=1}^{n}(x_i - \mu)^2}{N}} = \sqrt{\frac{(0-1.5)^2 + (1-1.5)^2 + (2-1.5)^2 + (3-1.5)^2}{4}} = 1.118$$

Take all possible random samples of $n = 2$ items *with replacement*. There are 16 equally likely outcomes (x_1, x_2). Each sample mean is $\bar{x} = (x_1 + x_2)/2$:

Possible Values of x_2	Possible Values of x_1			
	0	**1**	**2**	**3**
0	$\bar{x} = (0+0)/2 = 0.0$	$\bar{x} = (1+0)/2 = 0.5$	$\bar{x} = (2+0)/2 = 1.0$	$\bar{x} = (3+0)/2 = 1.5$
1	$\bar{x} = (0+1)/2 = 0.5$	$\bar{x} = (1+1)/2 = 1.0$	$\bar{x} = (2+1)/2 = 1.5$	$\bar{x} = (3+1)/2 = 2.0$
2	$\bar{x} = (0+2)/2 = 1.0$	$\bar{x} = (1+2)/2 = 1.5$	$\bar{x} = (2+2)/2 = 2.0$	$\bar{x} = (3+2)/2 = 2.5$
3	$\bar{x} = (0+3)/2 = 1.5$	$\bar{x} = (1+3)/2 = 2.0$	$\bar{x} = (2+3)/2 = 2.5$	$\bar{x} = (3+3)/2 = 3.0$

The population is uniform (0, 1, 2, 3 are equally likely) yet the distribution of all possible sample means has a peaked triangular shape, as shown in Table 8.5 and Figure 8.13. The distribution of sample means has distinct central tendency, as predicted by the Central Limit Theorem.

Sample Mean	Frequency	Relative Frequency
0.0	1	0.0625
0.5	2	0.1250
1.0	3	0.1875
1.5	4	0.2500
2.0	3	0.1875
2.5	2	0.1250
3.0	1	0.0625
Total	16	1.0000

TABLE 8.5

All Possible Sample Means for $n = 2$

FIGURE 8.13

Population and sampling distribution of means for $n = 2$

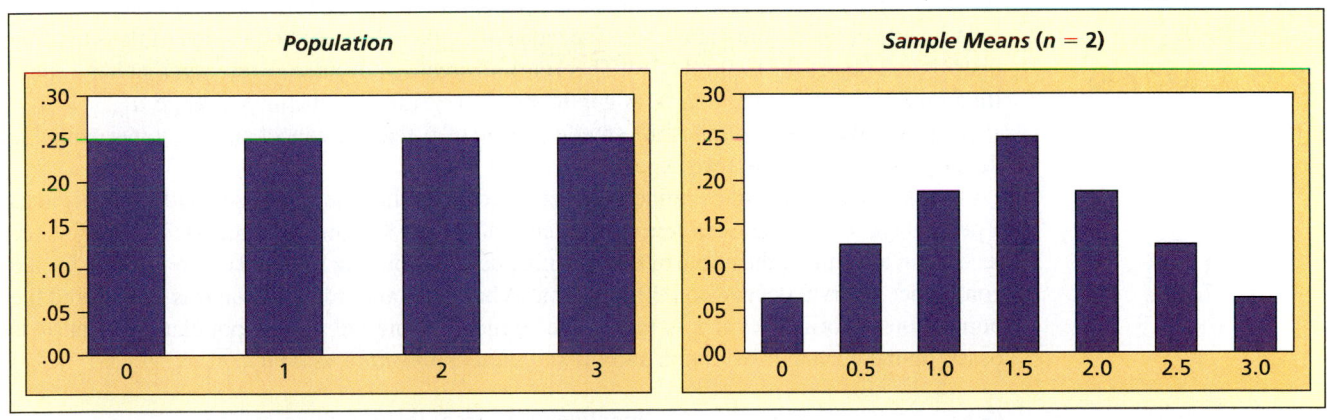

The Central Limit Theorem's predictions for the mean and standard error are

$$\mu_{\bar{x}} = \mu = 1.5 \quad \text{and} \quad \sigma_{\bar{x}} = \frac{\sigma}{\sqrt{n}} = \frac{1.118}{\sqrt{2}} = 0.7905$$

These theoretical predictions are borne out exactly for all 16 possible sample means. The mean of *means* $\bar{\bar{x}}$ is

$$\bar{\bar{x}} = \frac{1(0.0) + 2(0.5) + 3(1.0) + 4(1.5) + 3(2.0) + 2(2.5) + 1(3.0)}{16} = 1.5$$

As predicted by the CLT, the standard deviation of the *sample means* is

$$\sigma_{\bar{x}} = \sqrt{\frac{\left[\begin{array}{l} 1(0.0-1.5)^2 + 2(0.5-1.5)^2 + 3(1.0-1.5)^2 + 4(1.5-1.5)^2 \\ + 3(2.0-1.5)^2 + 2(2.5-1.5)^2 + 1(3.0-1.5)^2 \end{array}\right]}{16}} = 0.7906$$

SECTION EXERCISES

8.1 Find the standard error of the mean for each sampling situation (assuming a normal population). What happens to the standard error each time you quadruple the sample size?
   a. $\sigma = 32, n = 4$
   b. $\sigma = 32, n = 16$
   c. $\sigma = 32, n = 64$

8.2 Find the 95 percent range for the sample mean, assuming that each sample is from a normal population.
   a. $\mu = 200, \sigma = 12, n = 36$
   b. $\mu = 1,000, \sigma = 15, n = 9$
   c. $\mu = 50, \sigma = 1, n = 25$

8.3 The diameter of bushings turned out by a manufacturing process is a normally distributed random variable with a mean of 4.035 mm and a standard deviation of 0.005 mm. The inspection procedure requires a sample of 25 bushings once an hour. (a) Within what range should 95 percent of the bushing diameters fall? (b) Within what range should 95 percent of the sample *means* fall? (c) What conclusion would you reach if you saw a sample mean of 4.020? A sample mean of 4.055?

8.4 For this exercise, you will use *LearningStats* Unit 08 "CLT Demonstration." (a) Use the first worksheet (uniform distribution) to complete exercises 1–4 (shown on the worksheet) to study the behavior of 100 sample means with sample sizes of $n = 1, 2, 4, 8, 16, 32, 64$. (b) Repeat, using the second worksheet (skewed distribution). (c) Do you prefer computer simulation or mathematical discussion to clarify the meaning of the Central Limit Theorem?

8.4
CONFIDENCE INTERVAL FOR A MEAN (μ) WITH KNOWN σ

Chapter 9

What Is a Confidence Interval?

A sample mean $\bar{x}$ is a **point estimate** of the population mean μ. Since samples vary, we need to indicate our uncertainty about the true value of μ. Based on our knowledge of the sampling distribution (using the Central Limit Theorem) we create a **confidence interval** that has a specified *probability* of containing μ. A confidence interval for the mean is a range $\mu_{\text{lower}} < \mu < \mu_{\text{upper}}$ where the lower bound is the smallest value of μ that we expect and the upper bound is the largest value of μ that we expect.

The probability that the confidence interval contains the true mean is usually expressed as a percentage, called the **confidence level** (commonly 90, 95, and 99 percent). The confidence level is an area under the curve of the sampling distribution (e.g., normal). The formula for the confidence interval depends on the situation. When the standard deviation σ is known and the population is normal (or if n is large), the confidence interval for the population mean μ is based on the normal distribution and the *standard error of the mean* $\sigma/\sqrt{n}$.

(8.6)
$$\bar{x} \pm z\frac{\sigma}{\sqrt{n}}$$
(confidence interval for μ with known σ)

Table 8.6 shows z-values for common confidence levels.

TABLE 8.6
Common *z*-Values

Confidence Level	z
90	1.645
95	1.960
98	2.326
99	2.576

Confidence Interval for μ (known σ)

$$\bar{x} - z\frac{\sigma}{\sqrt{n}} < \mu < \bar{x} + z\frac{\sigma}{\sqrt{n}}$$

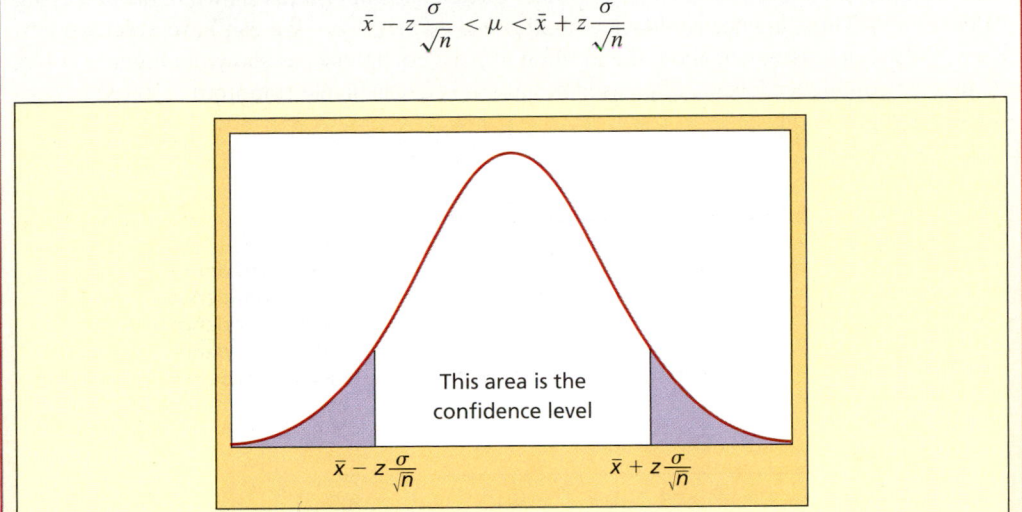

This area is the confidence level

$\bar{x} - z\dfrac{\sigma}{\sqrt{n}}$ $\bar{x} + z\dfrac{\sigma}{\sqrt{n}}$

This method applies to a sample from a normal population or from a nonnormal population if the sample is large enough for the CLT to apply. The rule of thumb that $n \geq 30$ to assume normality is sufficient for a symmetric population without outliers. However, a larger n may be needed if you are sampling a skewed population or one with outliers.

EXAMPLE

Bottle Filling: Confidence Intervals for μ

The amount of fill in a half-liter bottle of Diet Coke is normally distributed. From past experience, the process standard deviation is known to be $\sigma = 1.20$ ml. The mean amount of fill can be adjusted. A sample of 10 bottles gives a sample mean $\bar{x} = 503.4$ ml. Since the population is normal, the sample mean is a normally distributed random variable for any sample size, so we can use the z distribution to construct a confidence interval.

For a 90 percent confidence *interval estimate* for the μ, we insert $z = 1.645$ in the formula along with the sample mean $\bar{x} = 503.4$ and the known standard deviation $\sigma = 1.20$:

$$90\% \text{ confidence interval:} \quad \bar{x} \pm z\frac{\sigma}{\sqrt{n}} = 503.4 \pm 1.645\frac{1.20}{\sqrt{10}} = 503.4 \pm 0.62$$

The 90 percent confidence interval for the true mean is $502.78 < \mu < 504.02$. An interval constructed this way has a probability of .90 of containing μ. For a 95 percent confidence interval, we would use $z = 1.960$, keeping everything else the same:

$$95\% \text{ confidence interval:} \quad \bar{x} \pm z\frac{\sigma}{\sqrt{n}} = 503.4 \pm 1.96\frac{1.20}{\sqrt{10}} = 503.4 \pm 0.74$$

The 95 percent confidence interval for μ is $502.66 < \mu < 504.14$. There is a probability of .95 that an interval constructed this way will contain μ. For a 99 percent confidence interval, we would use $z = 2.576$ in the formula, keeping everything else the same:

$$99\% \text{ confidence interval:} \quad \bar{x} \pm z\frac{\sigma}{\sqrt{n}} = 503.4 \pm 2.576\frac{1.2}{\sqrt{10}} = 503.4 \pm 0.98$$

The 99 percent confidence interval for μ is $502.42 < \mu < 504.38$. There is a probability of .99 that an interval created in this manner will enclose μ.

Choosing a Confidence Level

You might be tempted to assume that a higher confidence level gives a "better" estimate. However, *a higher confidence level leads to a wider confidence interval* (as shown in the preceding calculations). Thus, greater confidence implies *loss of precision*. We can have greater confidence only if our statement about the location of μ is less precise, as shown in Figure 8.14. A 95 percent confidence level is often used because it is a reasonable compromise between confidence and precision.

FIGURE 8.14

Confidence intervals for true mean μ

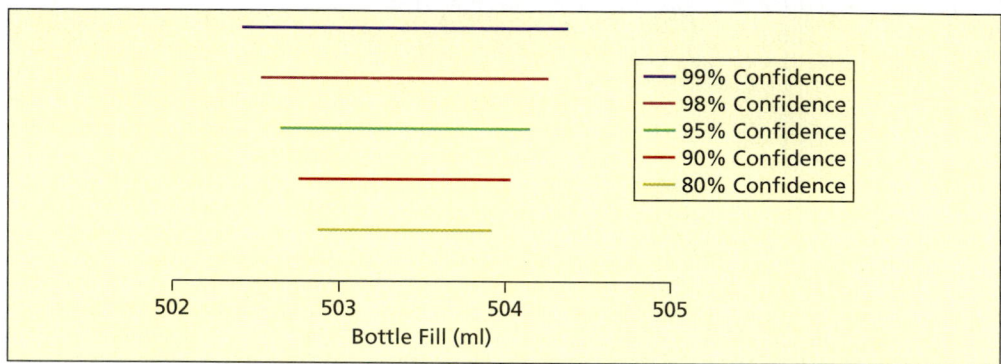

Interpretation A confidence interval either *does* or *does not* contain μ. But the confidence level quantifies the *risk*. If 100 statisticians were to use exactly this procedure to create 95 percent confidence intervals, approximately 95 of their intervals *would* contain μ, while approximately 5 unlucky ones *would not* contain μ. Since you only do it once, you don't know if you captured the true mean or not. For the bottle-filling example, lower bounds all five of the confidence intervals shown in Figure 8.14 are well above 500, indicating that the mean of the bottle-filling process is safely above the required minimum half-liter (500 ml).

Is σ Ever Known?

Yes, but not very often. In quality control applications with ongoing manufacturing processes, it may be reasonable to assume that σ stays the same over time. The type of confidence interval just seen is therefore important because it is used to construct *control charts* to track the mean of a process (such as bottle filling) over time. However, the case of unknown σ is more typical, and will be examined in the next section.

SECTION EXERCISES

8.5 Find a confidence interval for μ assuming that each sample is from a normal population.
  a. $\bar{x} = 14$, $\sigma = 4$, $n = 5$, 90 percent confidence
  b. $\bar{x} = 37$, $\sigma = 5$, $n = 15$, 99 percent confidence
  c. $\bar{x} = 121$, $\sigma = 15$, $n = 25$, 95 percent confidence

8.6 Prof. Hardtack gave three exams last semester in a large lecture class. The standard deviation $\sigma = 7$ was the same on all three exams, and scores were normally distributed. Below are scores for 10 randomly chosen students on each exam. Find the 95 percent confidence interval for the mean score on each exam. Do the confidence intervals overlap? If so, what does this suggest?
  Exams1
  Exam 1: 71, 69, 78, 80, 72, 76, 70, 82, 76, 76
  Exam 2: 77, 66, 71, 73, 94, 85, 83, 72, 89, 80
  Exam 3: 67, 69, 64, 65, 72, 59, 64, 70, 64, 56

8.7 In a certain manufacturing process, the diameter of holes drilled in a steel plate is a normally distributed random variable. The process standard deviation is known to be $\sigma = 0.005$ cm. A sample of 15 plates shows a mean hole diameter of 2.475 cm. Find the 95 percent confidence interval for μ.

Student's *t* Distribution

In situations where the population is normal but its standard deviation σ is unknown, the **Student's *t* distribution** should be used instead of the normal z distribution. This is particularly important when the sample size is small. When σ is unknown, the formula for a confidence interval resembles the formula for known σ except that t replaces z and s replaces σ:

$$\bar{x} \pm t \frac{s}{\sqrt{n}} \qquad \text{(confidence interval for } \mu \text{ with unknown } \sigma) \qquad \textbf{(8.7)}$$

Confidence Interval for μ (unknown σ)

$$\bar{x} - t \frac{s}{\sqrt{n}} < \mu < \bar{x} + t \frac{s}{\sqrt{n}}$$

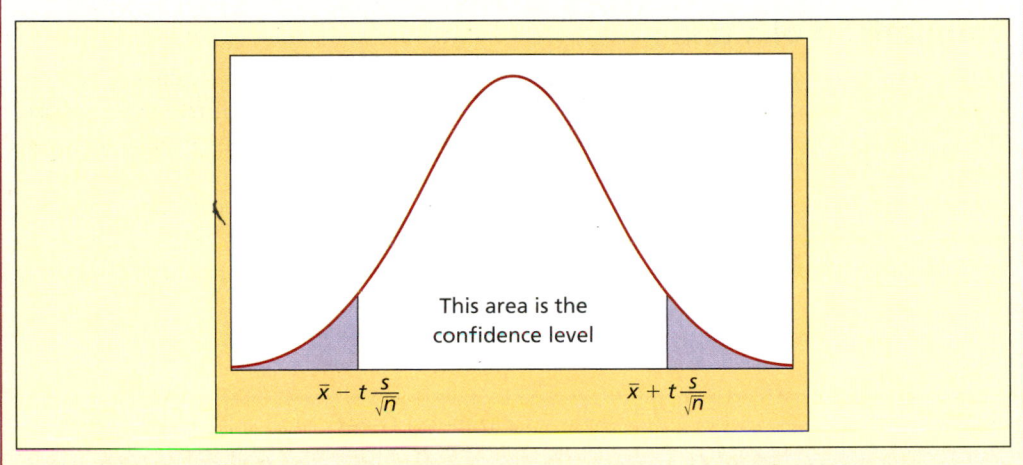

This area is the confidence level

$$\bar{x} - t \frac{s}{\sqrt{n}} \qquad \bar{x} + t \frac{s}{\sqrt{n}}$$

The Student's *t* distributions were proposed by a Dublin brewer named W. S. Gossett (1876–1937) who published his research under the name "Student" because his employer did not approve of publishing research based on company data. The *t* distributions are symmetric and shaped very much like the standard normal distribution, except they are somewhat less peaked and have thicker tails. Note that the *t* distributions are a class of distributions, each of which is dependent on the size of the sample we are using. Figure 8.15 shows how the tails of the distributions change as the sample size increases. A closer look reveals that the *t* distribution's tails lie *above* the normal.

FIGURE 8.15

Comparison of normal and Student's *t*

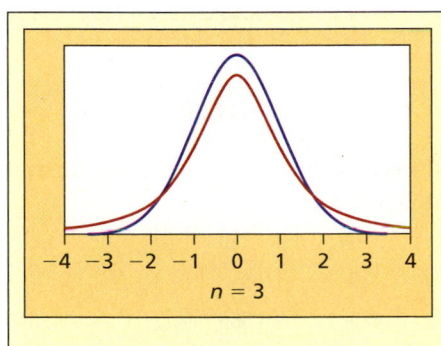
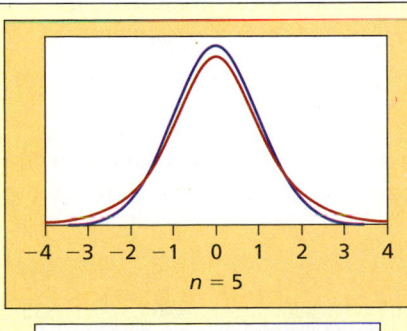
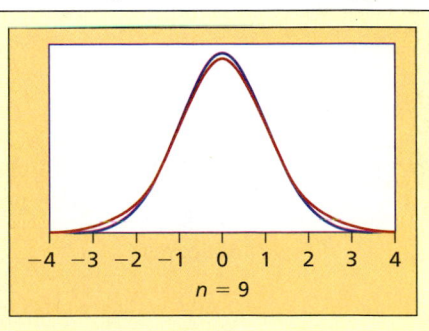

$n = 3$ $n = 5$ $n = 9$

— Student's *t*   — Std Normal

Degrees of Freedom

Knowing the sample size allows us to calculate a parameter called **degrees of freedom** (sometimes abbreviated d.f.). This parameter is used to determine the value of the t statistic used in the confidence interval formula. The degrees of freedom tell us how many observations we used to calculate s, the sample standard deviation, less the number of intermediate estimates we used in our calculation. Recall that the formula for s uses all n individual values from the sample and also $\bar{x}$, the sample mean. Therefore, the degrees of freedom are equal to the sample size minus 1. We will use the symbol ν (the Greek letter "nu"), to represent degrees of freedom.

(8.8) $\nu = n - 1$ (degrees of freedom for a confidence interval for μ)

For large degrees of freedom the t distribution approaches the shape of the normal distribution, as illustrated in Figure 8.15. However, in small samples, the difference is important. For example, in Figure 8.15 the lower axis scale range extends out to ± 4, while a range of ± 3 would cover most of the area for a standard normal distribution. We have to go out further into the tails of the t distribution to enclose a given area, so for a given confidence level, t *is always larger than* z so the confidence interval is always *wider* than if z were used.

Comparison of *z* and *t*

Table 8.7 (taken from Appendix D) shows that for very small samples the t-values differ substantially from the normal. But for a given confidence level, as degrees of freedom increase, the t-values approach the familiar normal z-values (shown at the bottom of each column corresponding to an infinitely large sample). For example, for $n = 31$, we would have degrees of freedom $\nu = 31 - 1 = 30$, so for a 90 percent confidence interval, we would use $t = 1.697$, which is only slightly larger than $z = 1.645$. It might seem tempting to use the z-values to avoid having to look up the correct degrees of freedom, but this would not be conservative (because the resulting confidence interval would be slightly too narrow).

TABLE 8.7

Student's *t*-values for Selected Degrees of Freedom

ν	Confidence Level				
	80%	**90%**	**95%**	**98%**	**99%**
1	3.078	6.314	12.706	31.821	63.656
2	1.886	2.920	4.303	6.965	9.925
3	1.638	2.353	3.182	4.541	5.841
4	1.533	2.132	2.776	3.747	4.604
5	1.476	2.015	2.571	3.365	4.032
10	1.372	1.812	2.228	2.764	3.169
20	1.325	1.725	2.086	2.528	2.845
30	1.310	1.697	2.042	2.457	2.750
40	1.303	1.684	2.021	2.423	2.704
60	1.296	1.671	2.000	2.390	2.660
100	1.290	1.660	1.984	2.364	2.626
∞	1.282	1.645	1.960	2.326	2.576

Note: The bottom row shows the z-values for each confidence level.

EXAMPLE

GMAT Scores, Again

GMATScores

Let's look again at the random sample of GMAT scores submitted by 20 applicants to an MBA program. A dot plot of this sample is shown in Figure 8.16.

530	450	600	570	360
550	640	490	460	550
480	440	530	470	560
500	430	640	420	530

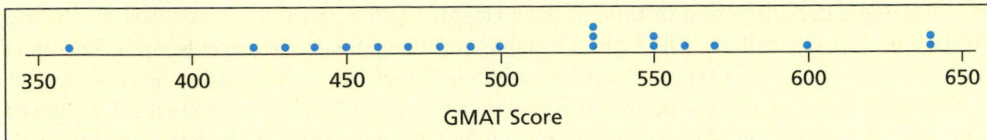

FIGURE 8.16

Dot plot for sample
GMATScores

We will construct a 90 percent confidence interval for the mean GMAT score of all MBA applicants. The sample mean is $\bar{x} = 510$ and the sample standard deviation is $s = 73.77$. Since the population standard deviation σ is unknown, we will use the Student's t for our confidence interval with 19 degrees of freedom:

$$\nu = n - 1 = 20 - 1 = 19 \qquad \text{(degrees of freedom for } n = 20\text{)}$$

For a 90 percent confidence interval, we consult Appendix D and find $t_{0.90} = 1.729$:

			Confidence Level		
	0.80	**0.90**	**0.95**	**0.98**	**0.99**
			Upper Tail Area		
ν	**0.10**	**0.05**	**0.03 .025**	**0.01**	**0.005**
1	3.078	6.314	12.706	31.821	63.656
2	1.886	2.920	4.303	6.965	9.925
3	1.638	2.353	3.182	4.541	5.841
4	1.533	2.132	2.776	3.747	4.604
5	1.476	2.015	2.571	3.365	4.032
6	1.440	1.943	2.447	3.143	3.707
7	1.415	1.895	2.365	2.998	3.499
8	1.397	1.860	2.306	2.896	3.355
9	1.383	1.833	2.262	2.821	3.250
10	1.372	1.812	2.228	2.764	3.169
11	1.363	1.796	2.201	2.718	3.106
12	1.356	1.782	2.179	2.681	3.055
13	1.350	1.771	2.160	2.650	3.012
14	1.345	1.761	2.145	2.624	2.977
15	1.341	1.753	2.131	2.602	2.947
16	1.337	1.746	2.120	2.583	2.921
17	1.333	1.740	2.110	2.567	2.898
18	1.330	1.734	2.101	2.552	2.878
19	1.328	1.729	2.093	2.539	2.861
20	1.325	1.725	2.086	2.528	2.845

The 90 percent confidence interval is

$$\bar{x} \pm t \frac{s}{\sqrt{n}} = 510 \pm (1.729)\frac{73.77}{\sqrt{20}} = 510 \pm 28.52$$

We are 90 percent confident that the true mean GMAT score is within the interval $481.48 < \mu < 538.52$. There is a 90 percent chance that an interval constructed in this manner contains μ (but a 10 percent chance that it does not). If we wanted a narrower confidence interval, we would need a larger sample size to reduce the right-hand side of $\bar{x} \pm t \frac{s}{\sqrt{n}}$.

EXAMPLE

Hospital Stays

   **Maternity**

During a certain period of time, Balzac Hospital had 8,261 maternity cases. Each case is assigned a code called a DRG (which stands for "Diagnostic Related Group"). The most common DRG was 373 (simple delivery without complicating diagnoses), accounting for 4,409 cases during the study period. Hospital management needs to know the mean length of stay (LOS) so they can plan the maternity unit bed capacity and schedule the nursing staff. For DRG 373, a random sample of hospital records for $n = 25$ births, the mean length of stay was $\bar{x} = 39.144$ hours with a standard deviation of $s = 16.204$ hours. What is the 95 percent confidence interval for the true mean?

To justify using the Student's t distribution we will assume that the population is normal (we will examine this assumption later). Since the population standard deviation is unknown, we use the Student's t for our confidence interval with 24 degrees of freedom:

$$v = n - 1 = 25 - 1 = 24 \qquad \text{(degrees of freedom for } n = 25\text{)}$$

For a 95 percent confidence interval, we consult Appendix D and find $t_{.025} = 2.064$:

	Confidence Level				
	0.80	**0.90**	**0.95**	**0.98**	**0.99**
			Upper Tail Area		
v	**0.10**	**0.05**	**0.025**	**0.01**	**0.005**
1	3.078	6.314	12.706	31.821	63.656
2	1.886	2.920	4.303	6.965	9.925
3	1.638	2.353	3.182	4.541	5.841
4	1.533	2.132	2.776	3.747	4.604
5	1.476	2.015	2.571	3.365	4.032
6	1.440	1.943	2.447	3.143	3.707
7	1.415	1.895	2.365	2.998	3.499
8	1.397	1.860	2.306	2.896	3.355
9	1.383	1.833	2.262	2.821	3.250
10	1.372	1.812	2.228	2.764	3.169
11	1.363	1.796	2.201	2.718	3.106
12	1.356	1.782	2.179	2.681	3.055
13	1.350	1.771	2.160	2.650	3.012
14	1.345	1.761	2.145	2.624	2.977
15	1.341	1.753	2.131	2.602	2.947
16	1.337	1.746	2.120	2.583	2.921
17	1.333	1.740	2.110	2.567	2.898
18	1.330	1.734	2.101	2.552	2.878
19	1.328	1.729	2.093	2.539	2.861
20	1.325	1.725	2.086	2.528	2.845
21	1.323	1.721	2.080	2.518	2.831
22	1.321	1.717	2.074	2.508	2.819
23	1.319	1.714	2.069	2.500	2.807
24	1.318	1.711	2.064	2.492	2.797
25	1.316	1.708	2.060	2.485	2.787

The 95 percent confidence interval is

$$\bar{x} \pm t \frac{s}{\sqrt{n}} = 39.144 \pm (2.064) \frac{16.204}{\sqrt{25}} = 39.144 \pm 6.689$$

With 95 percent confidence, the true mean LOS is within the interval $32.455 < \mu < 45.833$, so our best guess is that a simple maternity stay averages between 32.5 hours and 45.8 hours. A dot plot of this sample is shown in Figure 8.17.

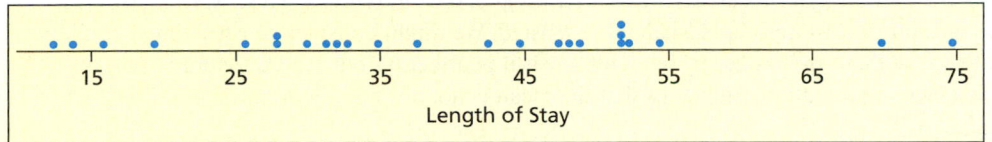

Length of Stay

FIGURE 8.17

Dot plot for sample of 25 births 🐣 **Maternity**

Confidence Interval Width

Our confidence interval width reflects the sample size, the confidence level, and the standard deviation. If we wanted a narrower interval (i.e., more precision) we could either increase the sample size or lower the confidence level (e.g., to 90 percent or even 80 percent). But we cannot do anything about the standard deviation, because it is an aspect of the sample. In fact, some samples could have larger standard deviations than this one.

A "Good" Sample?

Was our sample of 25 births typical? If we took a different sample, would we get a different confidence interval? Let's take a few new samples and see what happens. Table 8.8 shows 95 percent confidence intervals using five *different* random samples of 25 births (the samples are from a very large population of $N = 4,409$ births). Samples 1 through 4 give similar results. However, sample 5 has a much higher mean and standard deviation, and a very wide confidence interval, as shown in Figure 8.18.

Sample Statistics	Sample 1	Sample 2	Sample 3	Sample 4	Sample 5
Mean	39.144	37.717	38.462	38.478	48.058
Std. dev.	16.204	19.811	17.676	16.979	45.689
Standard error	3.241	3.962	3.535	3.396	9.138
t-value	2.064	2.064	2.064	2.064	2.064
Lower 95%	32.455	29.539	31.166	31.469	29.197
Upper 95%	45.833	45.895	45.759	45.487	66.918

TABLE 8.8

Comparing Five Different Samples of 25 Births 🐣 **Maternity**

Note: Calculations were done in Excel. Samples are from actual hospital records.

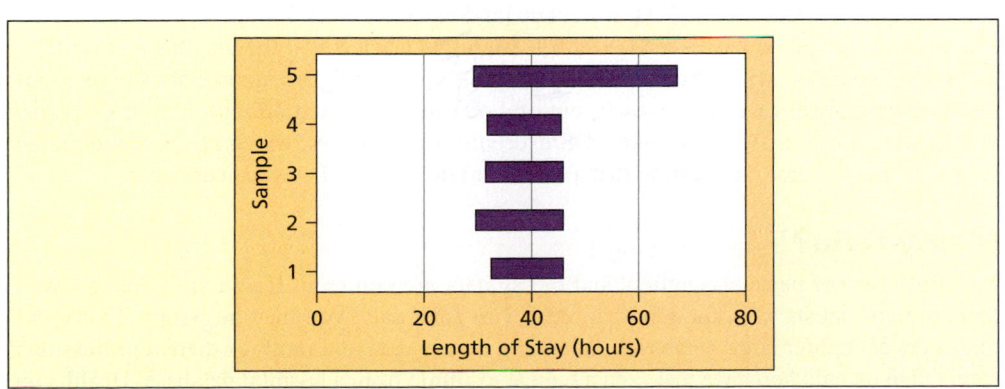

Length of Stay (hours)

FIGURE 8.18

Five sample confidence intervals

What happened? Well, sample 5 included one patient who stayed in the hospital for 254 hours (more than 10 days), skewing the sample severely. This outlier's effects are best seen visually in Figure 8.19. Yet an observer might still conclude that a "typical" length of stay is around 40 hours. It is just a matter of luck which sample you get. However, the statistician who obtains sample 5 is not helpless. He/she would know that the sample contained a severe outlier, as shown in Figure 8.19. This might suggest taking a larger sample. It would certainly be a warning that the confidence interval from sample 5 cannot be trusted. We might consider constructing a confidence interval without the outlier to see how much it is affecting our results. More importantly, the existence of an outlier reminds us that the mean is not always a good measure of the "typical" value of X.

FIGURE 8.19

Dot plot for sample 5
Maternity

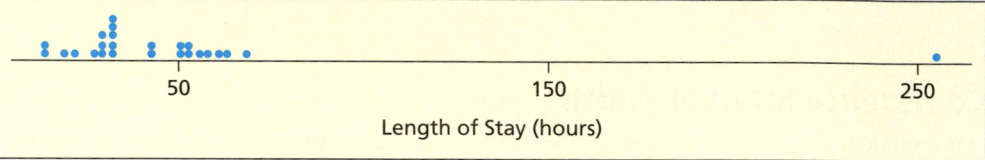

Length of Stay (hours)

More Analysis Needed

Preoccupation with mathematics could make us forget the purpose of the research. The statistician is expected to help the client understand the problem, not to use a particular formula. We should ask: (1) Are there outliers that might invalidate the assumption of normality? (2) Is a sample of 25 cases large enough for the Central Limit Theorem to apply? (3) Is a confidence interval really needed? Figure 8.20 shows a large random sample of LOS for 200 births from the same population. Its quartiles are $Q_1 = 29.1$ hours, $Q_2 = 40.3$ hours, and $Q_3 = 54.8$ hours. Instead of constructing a confidence interval, we could simply define 55 hours or more (the third quartile) as "long" stay, 29 hours or less (the first quartile) as "short" stay, and 40 hours as "typical" stay. Maybe that's all the hospital wants to know.

FIGURE 8.20

LOS dot plot for sample of $n = 200$ Births
Maternity

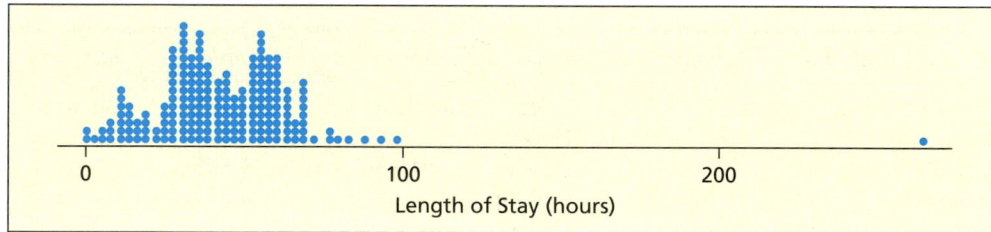

Length of Stay (hours)

Yet, from the point of view of staffing, the mean *does* matter. Although outliers can render confidence intervals useless, that does not imply that the hospital can ignore them. If a handful of maternity patients stay 10 days (240 hours) instead of 2 days (48 hours), real resources will be required to treat them. What we can do (and must do) is ask some deeper questions. For example, if a length of stay exceeds 10 days, we might suspect that the diagnostic code DRG 373 (simple delivery without complicating diagnoses) was assigned incorrectly. In this example, further analysis revealed 23 cases out of 4,409 in the population with LOS greater than 240 hours (10 days). Two cases had LOS exceeding 1,000 hours, which are almost certainly errors in classification, suggesting that a different DRG should have been assigned.

Messy Data?

Yes. But also not unusual. Outliers and messy data are common. If you are thinking, Well, there are specialists who know how to deal with such data, you may be wrong. Every day, managers encounter large databases containing unruly data and rarely is there a professional statistician on call. You have just seen a typical example from a hospital database. Health care managers in hospitals, clinics, insurers, state and federal agencies all spend a lot of time working with messy data just like this. In the United States, health care spending is nearly 1/6 of the GDP, suggesting that 1 job out of every 6 (perhaps yours) is tied directly or indirectly to health care, so examples like this are not unusual. You need to be ready to deal with messy data.

Must the Population Be Normal?

The *t* distribution assumes a normal population, but in practice, this assumption can be relaxed, as long as the population is not badly skewed. Large sample size offers further protection if the normality assumption is questionable.

Using Appendix D

Beyond $v = 50$, Appendix D shows v in steps of 5 or 10. If Appendix D does not show the exact degrees of freedom that you want, use the *t*-value for the *next lower* v. For example, if $v = 54$, you would use $v = 50$. Using the next lower degrees of freedom is a conservative procedure because it widens the interval slightly so that confidence is increased (not decreased). Since *t*-values change very slowly as v rises beyond $v = 50$, rounding down will make little difference. In fact, Appendix D only goes up to 150 degrees of freedom, so if you have a sample larger than that, go ahead and use *z*.

Can I Ever Use *z* Instead of *t*?

In large samples, *z* and *t* give similar results. But a conservative statistician always uses the *t* distribution for confidence intervals when σ is unknown. Using *z* decreases the confidence level slightly. Since *t* tables are easy to use (or we can get *t*-values from Excel) there isn't much justification for using *z* when σ is unknown.

Using Excel

If you have access to Excel, you don't need tables. Excel's function =TINV(probability,degrees of freedom) gives a two-tailed value of *t*, where probability is 1 minus the confidence level. For example, for a 95 percent confidence interval with 60 degrees of freedom, the function =TINV(0.05,60) yields $t = 2.000298$. Since Excel wants the *two-tailed area* outside the confidence interval, we would use 0.05 for 95 percent, 0.01 for 99 percent, etc. The output from Excel's Tools > Data Analysis > Descriptive Statistics does not give the confidence interval limits, but it does give the standard error and width of the confidence interval $ts/\sqrt{n}$ (the oddly labeled last line in the table). Figure 8.21 shows Excel's results for sample 1 (maternity LOS).

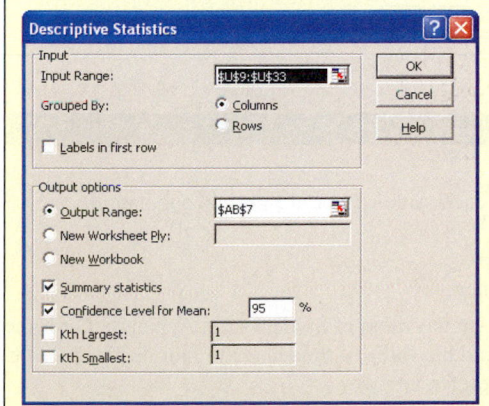

FIGURE 8.21

Excel's confidence interval

Mean	39.144
Standard Error	3.240769405
Median	37.37
Mode	#N/A
Standard Deviation	16.20384702
Sample Variance	262.5646583
Kurtosis	-0.28780002
Skewness	0.263313568
Range	61.92
Minimum	12.59
Maximum	74.51
Sum	978.6
Count	25
Confidence Level(95.0%)	6.688617936

Using MegaStat

If you really want to make the calculations easy, MegaStat gives you a choice of z or t, and does all the calculations for you, as illustrated in Figure 8.22 for sample 1 (maternity LOS). Notice the Preview button. If you click OK you will also see the t-value and other details.

FIGURE 8.22

MegaStat's confidence interval

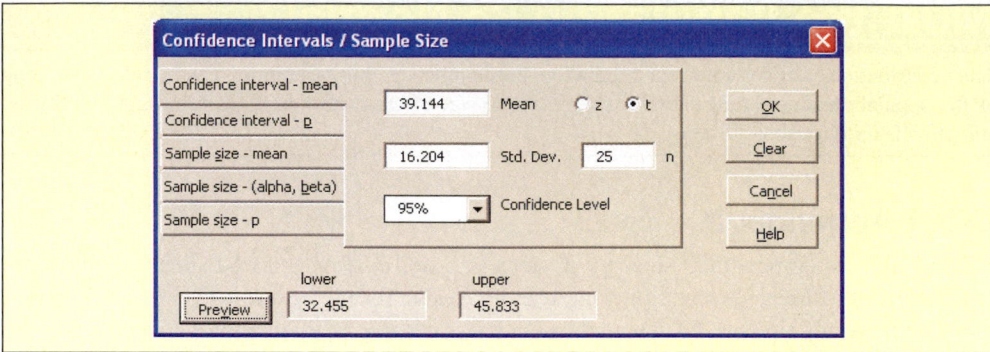

Using MINITAB

Use MINITAB's Stat > Basic Statistics > Graphical Summary to get confidence intervals, as well as a histogram and box plot. MINITAB uses the Student's t for the confidence interval for the mean. It also gives confidence intervals for the median and standard deviation. Figure 8.23 shows the MINITAB Graphical Summary for sample 1 (maternity LOS).

FIGURE 8.23

MINITAB's confidence interval

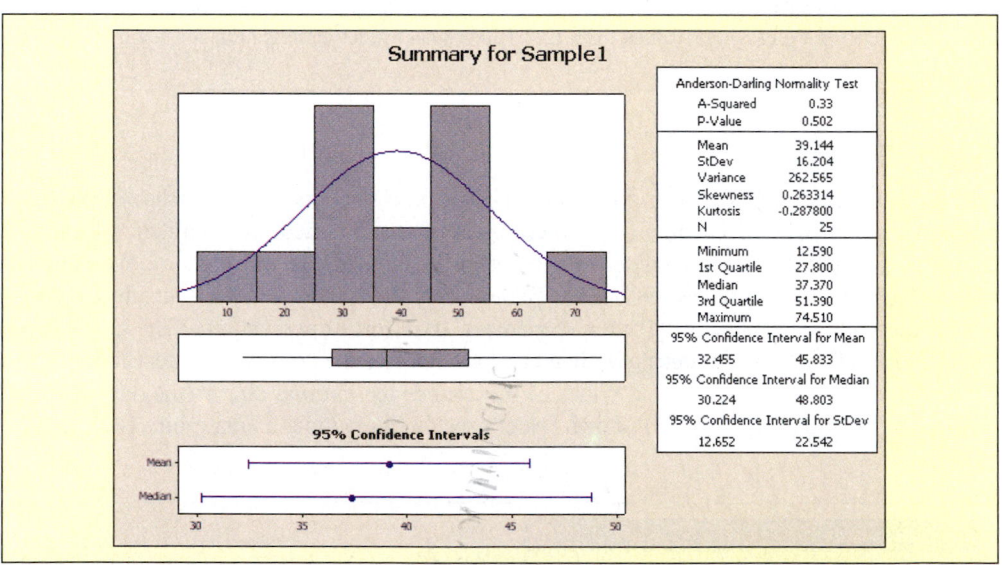

SECTION EXERCISES

8.8 Find a confidence interval for μ assuming that each sample is from a normal population.
a. $\bar{x} = 24$, $s = 3$, $n = 7$, 90 percent confidence
b. $\bar{x} = 42$, $s = 6$, $n = 18$, 99 percent confidence
c. $\bar{x} = 119$, $s = 14$, $n = 28$, 95 percent confidence

8.9 For each value of v (degrees of freedom) look up the value of Student's t in Appendix D for the stated level of confidence. Then use Excel to find the value of Student's t to four decimal places. Which method (Appendix D or Excel) do you prefer, and why?

a. $v = 9$, 95 percent confidence
b. $v = 15$, 98 percent confidence
c. $v = 47$, 90 percent confidence

8.10 For each value of v look up the value of Student's t in Appendix D for the stated level of confidence. How close is the t-value to the corresponding z-value (at the bottom of the column for $v = \infty$).
a. $v = 40$, 95 percent confidence
b. $v = 80$, 95 percent confidence
c. $v = 100$, 95 percent confidence

8.11 A sample of 21 minivan electrical warranty repairs for "loose, not attached" wires (one of several electrical failure categories the dealership mechanic can select) showed a mean repair cost of $45.66 with a standard deviation of $27.79. (a) Construct a 95 percent confidence interval for the true mean repair cost. (b) How could the confidence interval be made narrower? (Data are from a project by MBA student Tim Polulak.)

8.12 A random sample of 16 pharmacy customers showed the waiting times below (in minutes). Find a 90 percent confidence interval for μ, assuming that the sample is from a normal population.
Pharmacy

21	22	22	17	21	17	23	20
20	24	9	22	16	21	22	21

8.13 A random sample of monthly rent paid by 12 college seniors living off campus gave the results below (in dollars). Find a 99 percent confidence interval for μ, assuming that the sample is from a normal population. **Rents**

900	810	770	860	850	790
810	800	890	720	910	640

8.14 A random sample of 10 shipments of stick-on labels showed the following order sizes. (a) Construct a 95 percent confidence interval for the true mean order size. (b) How could the confidence interval be made narrower? (c) Do you think the population is normal? (Data are from a project by MBA student Henry Olthof, Jr.) **OrderSize**

| 12,000 | 18,000 | 30,000 | 60,000 | 14,000 | 10,500 | 52,000 | 14,000 | 15,700 | 19,000 |

8.15 Prof. SoftTouch gave three exams last semester. Scores were normally distributed on each exam. Below are scores for 10 randomly chosen students on each exam. (a) Find the 95 percent confidence interval for the mean score on each exam. (b) Do the confidence intervals overlap? What inference might you draw by comparing the three confidence intervals? (c) How is this problem different from Exercise 8.6? **Exams2**
Exam 1: 81, 79, 88, 90, 82, 86, 80, 92, 86, 86
Exam 2: 87, 76, 81, 83, 100, 95, 93, 82, 99, 90
Exam 3: 77, 79, 74, 75, 82, 69, 74, 80, 74, 76

8.6 CONFIDENCE INTERVAL FOR A PROPORTION (π)

The Central Limit Theorem (CLT) also applies to a sample proportion, since a proportion is just a mean of data whose only values are 0 or 1. For a proportion, the CLT says that the distribution of a sample proportion $p = x/n$ tends toward normality and collapses at the population proportion π as n increases. Its standard error σ_p can be made as small as you want by increasing n (in other words, $p = x/n$ is a *consistent* estimator of π).

Central Limit Theorem for a Proportion

As sample size increases, the distribution of the sample proportion $p = x/n$ approaches a normal distribution with mean π and standard deviation $\sigma_p = \sqrt{\dfrac{\pi(1-\pi)}{n}}$.

Illustration: Internet Hotel Reservations   Hotel

Management of the Pan-Asian Hotel System tracks the percent of hotel reservations made over the Internet to adjust its advertising and Web reservation system. Such data are binary: Either a reservation is made on the Internet (1) or not (0). A week's data set looks like this:

```
01000000101000000000000001000001001100000100000001000000001000000000010000000001
10000000000001000000000000000000011001000100001000000000000000000001000000000001000
10000111000000010001111000000000000101001000001100010000001001000101000000000000
01001001000000000010001010000001000000100100000001000110000000000001000000000000
00000010000100000000001001101000000000000100000100000000011001000010010000000000100
01001111110000100001001100000000000001001100000000000001000000000001000000000010
01000010100011000100000000100000101001000001110001000000000000000001010010001100
10001000100000000000000100000000010011100001000000000001000110010000110000000001
00000000000100000001111000000000001000010000000000000001000011111100000000110000
00000001001010001010010001000000000000001001000000101000001111010000100001000000
00000010000000001000000011000000001110010100011100000000001101001101001101000000
00010000100000000000000000000011000000101100000000000010100000000000001000000000
00100000000000010000110100000100000001010000000000000000001000001000000000000101
00000001000000010010100011100010000111000100001010010000000000010000000100000000
01000000011001010001010010000100000100000000001000100000000000100010000000000000
00000001100010001001010000001001101100000000001000110000000000001000000000111011
01000100000001000000001001010001000000010000010100100000000001001000000000000000
10000000000001000010010100000001000111001000000010101000001001100000110001110000
00000010000000000100010000110110010000010100001010001000000011000100100000010101
00011100000001000001000000000000000000000001100000010100001000010001000100010010
10110010000010000010000000001000101100001100100000000001000000001001000000010000
10100010000000000000010100100011010100000000010000000000001001001011001010010
00001000000010010100011100000000000000010000010001000010000000010001000011000
00100000110000001010000000011000000100000100001000001000100000000010100110100101
00000000001100000010000001000000010100100101001001000000001001000000100001000000
```

Treating this as a population, the proportion of Internet reservations is $\pi = .20$ (as you can verify if you have the time). Here are five random samples of $n = 20$ hotel reservations. Each p is a *point estimate* of π. Some sample p-values are close to $\pi = .20$ while others are not.

Sample 1: 00010000100010010000 $p = x/n = 4/20 = .20$

Sample 2: 00001000100000000001 $p = x/n = 3/20 = .15$

Sample 3: 00111000010000001000 $p = x/n = 5/20 = .25$

Sample 4: 00000000000110000110 $p = x/n = 4/20 = .20$

Sample 5: 00101000000000000000 $p = x/n = 2/20 = .10$

There is sampling variation in the value of p. If we took many such samples, we could empirically study the *sampling distribution* of p. But even for one sample, we can still apply the CLT to *predict* the behavior of p.

Applying the CLT

In Chapter 6, you learned that the binomial model describes the number of successes in a sample of n items from a population with constant probability of success π. A binomial distribution is symmetric if $\pi = .50$ but, regardless of π, approaches symmetry as n increases. The same is true for the distribution of the sample proportion $p = x/n$. Figure 8.24 shows histograms of $p = x/n$ for 1,000 samples of various sizes with $\pi = .20$. For small n, the distribution is quite discrete. For example:

Sample Size	Possible Values of $p = x/n$
$n = 5$	0/5, 1/5, 2/5, 3/5, 4/5, 5/5
$n = 10$	0/10, 1/10, 2/10, 3/10, 4/10, 5/10, 6/10, 7/10, 8/10, 9/10, 10/10

As n increases, the statistic $p = x/n$ more closely resembles a continuous random variable and its distribution becomes more symmetric and bell-shaped.

FIGURE 8.24

Histograms of $p = x/n$ when $\pi = .20$ **Hotel**

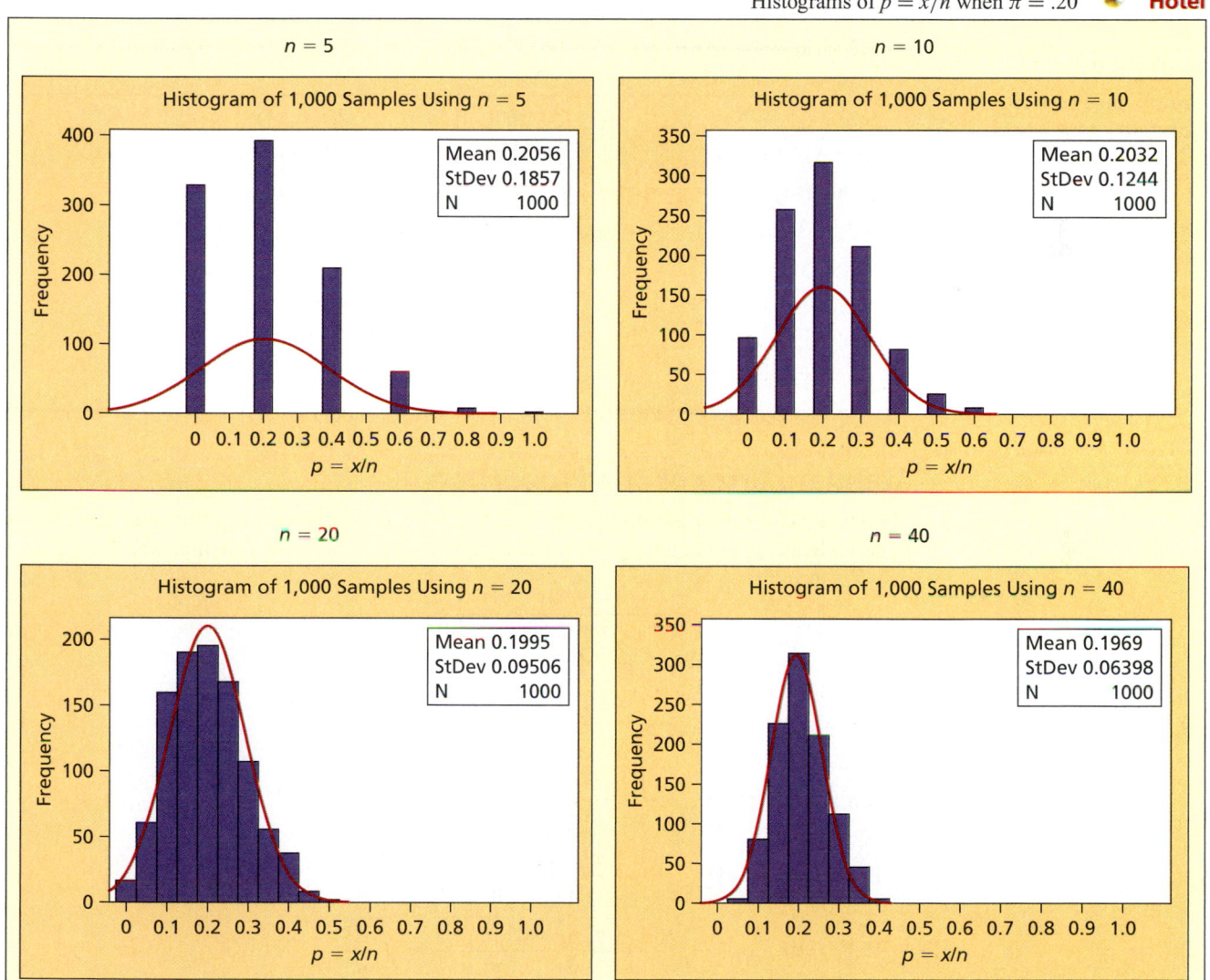

As n increases, the range of the sample proportion $p = x/n$ narrows, because n appears in the denominator of the *standard error:*

$$\sigma_p = \sqrt{\frac{\pi(1 - \pi)}{n}} \qquad \text{(standard error of the sample proportion)} \qquad \textbf{(8.9)}$$

Therefore, the sampling variation can be reduced by increasing the sample size. Larger samples also help justify the use of the normal distribution.

When Is It Safe to Assume Normality?

The statistic $p = x/n$ may be assumed normally distributed when the sample is "large." How large must n be? Table 8.9 illustrates a conservative rule of thumb that normality may be assumed whenever $n\pi \geq 10$ and $n(1 - \pi) \geq 10$. By this rule, a very large sample may be needed to assume normality of the sample proportion when π differs greatly from .50.*

Rule of Thumb

The sample proportion $p = x/n$ may be assumed normal if both $n\pi \geq 10$ and $n(1 - \pi) \geq 10$.

TABLE 8.9

Sample Size to Assume Normality of $p = x/n$

π	n
.50	20
.40 or .60	25
.30 or .70	33
.20 or .80	50
.10 or .90	100
.05 or .95	200
.02 or .98	500
.01 or .99	1,000
.005 or .995	2,000
.002 or .998	5,000
.001 or .999	10,000

Standard Error of the Proportion

The **standard error of the proportion** is denoted σ_p. It depends on π, as well as on n, being largest when the population proportion is near $\pi = .50$ and becoming smaller when π is near 0 or 1. For example:

$$\text{If } \pi = .50: \quad \sigma_p = \sqrt{\frac{\pi(1 - \pi)}{n}} \quad \sqrt{\frac{.50(1 - .50)}{n}} = \sqrt{\frac{.25}{n}}$$

$$\text{If } \pi = .40: \quad \sigma_p = \sqrt{\frac{\pi(1 - \pi)}{n}} \quad \sqrt{\frac{.40(1 - .40)}{n}} = \sqrt{\frac{.24}{n}}$$

$$\text{If } \pi = .30: \quad \sigma_p = \sqrt{\frac{\pi(1 - \pi)}{n}} \quad \sqrt{\frac{.30(1 - .30)}{n}} = \sqrt{\frac{.21}{n}}$$

$$\text{If } \pi = .20: \quad \sigma_p = \sqrt{\frac{\pi(1 - \pi)}{n}} \quad \sqrt{\frac{.20(1 - .20)}{n}} = \sqrt{\frac{.16}{n}}$$

$$\text{If } \pi = .10: \quad \sigma_p = \sqrt{\frac{\pi(1 - \pi)}{n}} \quad \sqrt{\frac{.10(1 - .10)}{n}} = \sqrt{\frac{.09}{n}}$$

The formula is symmetric (i.e., $\pi = .20$ gives the same standard error as $\pi = .80$). Figure 8.25 shows the *relative* size of the standard error of the proportion σ_p for different values of π. Figure 8.26 shows that enlarging n reduces the standard error σ_p but at a diminishing rate (e.g., you have to *quadruple* the sample size to *halve* σ_p).

---

*An alternative rule is to require $n > 9(1 - \pi)/\pi$ and $n > 9\pi/(1 - \pi)$. See Merran Evans, Nicholas Hastings, and Brian Peacock, *Statistical Distributions,* 3rd ed. (Wiley, 2000). Later on, we will discuss what to do when normality cannot be assumed.

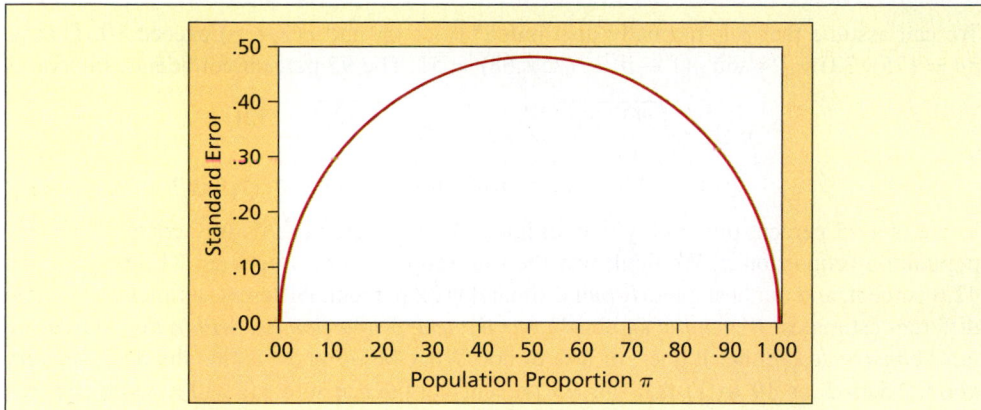

FIGURE 8.25

Effect of π on σ_p

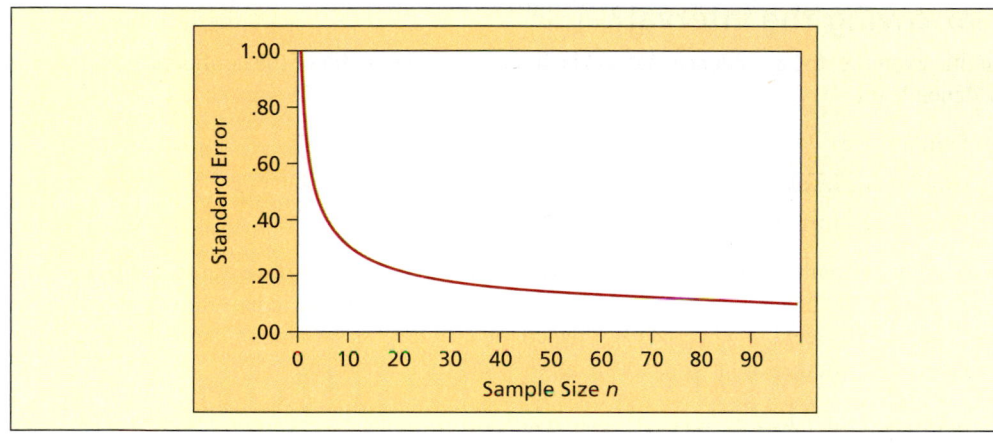

FIGURE 8.26

Effect of n on σ_p

Confidence Interval for π

By the Central Limit Theorem, we can state the probability that a sample proportion will fall within a given interval. For example, there is a 95 percent chance that p will fall within the range $\pi \pm z_{.025}\sqrt{\frac{\pi(1-\pi)}{n}}$ where $z_{.025} = 1.96$ and similarly for other values of z. This is the basis for a confidence interval estimate of π. Replacing π with $p = x/n$ (since π is unknown) and assuming a large sample (to justify the assumption of normality), the confidence interval for π is

$$p \pm z\sqrt{\frac{p(1-p)}{n}} \qquad \text{(confidence interval for } \pi\text{)} \qquad \textbf{(8.10)}$$

We can choose z for any confidence level we want. For example:

$z_{.05} = 1.645$, for 90 percent confidence

$z_{.025} = 1.960$, for 95 percent confidence

$z_{.01} = 2.326$, for 98 percent confidence

$z_{.005} = 2.576$, for 99 percent confidence

↘ A sample of 75 retail in-store purchases showed that 24 were paid in cash. We will construct a 95 percent confidence interval for the proportion of all retail in-store purchases that are paid in cash. The sample proportion is

$$p = x/n = 24/75 = .32 \qquad \text{(proportion of in-store cash transactions)}$$

EXAMPLE

Auditing

We can assume that p is normally distributed* since np and $n(1 - p)$ exceed 10. That is, $np = (75)(.32) = 24$ and $n(1 - p) = (75)(.68) = 51$. The 95 percent confidence interval is

$$p \pm z\sqrt{\frac{p(1 - p)}{n}} = .32 \pm 1.960\sqrt{\frac{.32(1 - .32)}{75}}$$
$$= .32 \pm .106 = .214 < \pi < .426$$

There is a 95 percent probability that an interval constructed in this way contains the true population proportion π. We think that the true proportion π is between 21.4 percent and 42.6 percent, and our best guess (point estimate) is 32 percent. Different samples could yield different estimates. *We cannot know whether the true proportion lies within the interval we have constructed.* Either it does, or it does not. What we *do* know is that the odds are very good (95 to 5 or 19 to 1) that our 95 percent confidence interval will contain the true proportion π.

Narrowing the Interval?

In this example, the confidence interval is fairly wide. The width of the confidence interval for π depends on

- Sample size
- Confidence level
- Sample proportion p

We cannot do anything about p because it is an aspect of the sample. If we want a narrower interval (i.e., more precision), we could either increase the sample size or reduce the confidence level (e.g., from 95 percent to 90 percent). If the confidence level is sacrosanct, our only choice is to increase n. Of course, larger samples are more costly (or even impossible).

EXAMPLE

Display Ads

A random sample of 200 pages from the *Ameritech Pages Plus Yellow Pages* telephone directory revealed that 30 of the selected pages contained at least one multicolored display ad (large blocks with illustrations, maps, and text). What is the 90 percent confidence interval for the proportion of all pages with at least one such display ad? The sample proportion is

$$p = x/n = 30/200 = .15 \qquad \text{(proportion of pages with at least one display ad)}$$

The normality test is easily met because $np = (200)(.15) = 30$ and $n(1 - p) = (200)(.85) = 170$. The 90 percent confidence interval requires $z = 1.645$:

$$p \pm z\sqrt{\frac{p(1 - p)}{n}} = .15 \pm 1.645\sqrt{\frac{.15(1 - .15)}{200}}$$
$$= .15 \pm .042 = .108 < \pi < .192$$

With 90 percent confidence, between 10.8 percent and 19.2 percent of the pages have multicolor display ads. This confidence interval is narrower than the previous example because the sample is larger and the confidence level is lower.

An increase in confidence decreases the precision of the estimate. Further, the law of diminishing returns applies: A given increment in confidence widens the confidence interval disproportionately, as we must go farther out into the tails of the normal distribution to enclose the desired area. A wider confidence interval is less helpful in visualizing the location of the true value π. In the limit, we can be 100 percent confident that π lies somewhere between 0 and 100 percent, but such a statement is useless. Given its common use, it appears that many people feel that 95 percent confidence strikes a good balance between confidence and precision for common applications.

---

*When constructing a confidence interval, we use p instead of π in our rule of thumb to test whether n is large enough to assure normality because π is unknown. The test is therefore equivalent to asking if $x \geq 10$ and $n - x \geq 10$.

To illustrate the trade-off between *confidence* and *precision* (the interval half-width), here are some alternatives that could have been used in the display ad example:

Confidence Level	z	Interval Width
80%	$z = 1.282$	$.15 \pm .032$
90%	$z = 1.645$	$.15 \pm .042$
95%	$z = 1.960$	$.15 \pm .049$
98%	$z = 2.326$	$.15 \pm .059$
99%	$z = 2.576$	$.15 \pm .065$

Using Excel and MegaStat

Excel's Tools > Data Analysis does not offer a confidence interval for a proportion, presumably because the calculations are easy. For example:

=0.15–NORMSINV(.95)*SQRT(0.15*(1-0.15)/200)   for the lower 95% confidence limit

=0.15+NORMSINV(.95)*SQRT(0.15*(1-0.15)/200)   for the upper 95% confidence limit

However, MegaStat makes it even easier, as shown in Figure 8.27. You only need to enter p and n. A convenient feature is that, if you enter p larger than 1, MegaStat assumes that it is the x-value in $p = x/n$ so you don't even have to calculate p. Click the Preview button to see the confidence interval. This example verifies the Ameritech calculations shown previously (click OK for additional details). MegaStat always assumes normality, even when it is not justified, so you need to check this assumption for yourself.

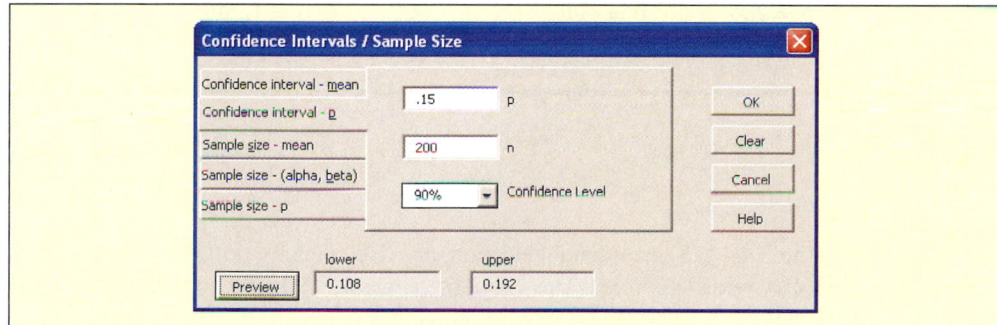

FIGURE 8.27

MegaStat's confidence interval

Small Samples: MINITAB

If the sample is small (i.e., if we cannot meet the requirement that $n\pi \geq 10$ and $n(1 - \pi) \geq 10$), the distribution of p may not be well approximated by the normal. Instead of assuming a continuous normal model, confidence limits around p can be constructed by using the binomial distribution. MINITAB uses this method by default, since it works for any n (you have to press the Options button to assume normality). Although the underlying calculations are a bit complex, MINITAB does all the work and the resulting interval is correct for any n and p.

For example, *The New York Times Magazine* reported that, in a sample of 14 purchasers of the *Spider-Man 2* DVD, 11 watched only the film and never even looked at the "extras" (November 14, 2004, p. 107). The sample proportion is $p = 11/14$. What is the 95 percent confidence interval for the proportion of purchasers who never viewed the "extras"? We have $np = 11$ but $n(1 - p) = 3$, which is less than 5, so we should not assume normality. Figure 8.28 shows a sample of MINITAB's confidence interval using the binomial distribution with Stat > Basic Statistics > One Proportion. MINITAB's binomial confidence interval (.492, .953) is quite different from the normal confidence interval (.571, 1.000). MINITAB includes a warning about the normal confidence interval.

FIGURE 8.28

MINITAB's confidence interval

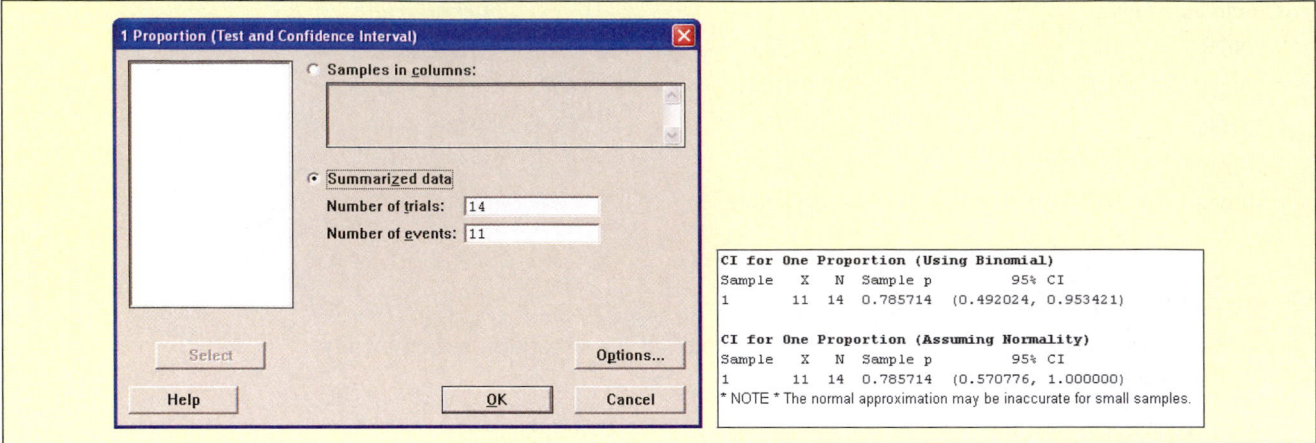

Polls and Margin of Error

In polls and survey research, the confidence interval half-width when $\pi = .50$ is called the *margin of error.* This is a conservative assumption since σ_p is at its maximum when $\pi = .50$. Table 8.10 shows the margin of error for various sample sizes. The law of diminishing returns is apparent. Greater accuracy is possible, but each reduction in the margin of error requires a disproportionately larger sample size.

TABLE 8.10

Margin of Error for 95 percent Confidence Interval Assuming $\pi = .50$

n = 100	n = 200	n = 400	n = 800	n = 1,200	n = 1,600
± 9.8%	± 6.9%	± 4.9%	± 3.5%	± 2.8%	± 2.5%

EXAMPLE

The 2004 Election

Just before the 2004 U.S. presidential election, an ABC tracking poll showed Bush with 50 percent and Kerry with 46 percent. The sample size was 1,589 likely adult voters, and the reported accuracy was ±2.5 percent, exactly as shown in Table 8.10. At about the same time, a Reuters/Zogby poll showed Kerry with 46 percent and Bush with 45 percent, based on 1,216 likely voters, with a reported accuracy of ±2.9 percent. These are typical sample sizes for national opinion polls on major issues such as a presidential election, foreign policy, or a Supreme Court decision. Tracking polls do vary, but if several different independent polls show the same candidate ahead, and if the margin is stable over time, they usually get it right. Of course, the opinions being tracked may be changing continuously from day to day.

The margin of error is sometimes referred to as the *sample accuracy*. Popular media sometimes use statistical terminology loosely, but the idea is the same. Statewide political polls, such as a gubernatorial race, typically have 800 respondents (margin of error ±3.5 percent) while a mayoral or local political poll might have 400 respondents (margin of error ±4.9 percent). Private market research or customer mail surveys may rely on even smaller samples, while Internet surveys can yield very large samples.

Rule of Three

A useful quick rule is the *Rule of Three*. If in n independent trials no events occur, the upper 95 percent confidence bound is approximately $3/n$. For example, if no medical complications arise in 17 prenatal fetal surgeries, the upper bound on such complications is roughly

$3/17 = .18$, or about 18 percent. This rule is sometimes used by health care practitioners when limited data are available.*

Very Quick Rule

The ubiquity of the 95 percent confidence interval has led consulting statisticians to create various quick rules.** For example, a *Very Quick Rule* (VQR) for a 95 percent confidence interval when p is near .50 is

$$p \pm \frac{1}{\sqrt{n}} \qquad \text{(very quick 95\% confidence interval if } p \text{ is near .50)} \qquad \textbf{(8.11)}$$

By trying a few values of p near .50 in Formula 8.10 you can verify the VQR. However, the VQR begins to fail when p is outside the range $.40 < p < .60$. For example, it works poorly for the Ameritech example because $p = .15$. However, the VQR may be useful in making a quick assessment.

Advice on Proportions

Proportions are easy to work with, and they occur frequently. In many ways, estimating π is simpler than estimating μ because you are just counting things.

Sample Proportions Are Important

Statisticians are fond of talking about means, but proportions (i.e., percents) are more common in business.

SECTION EXERCISES

8.16 Calculate the standard error. May normality be assumed?
  a. $n = 30, \pi = .50$ b. $n = 50, \pi = .20$ c. $n = 100, \pi = .10$ d. $n = 500, \pi = .005$

8.17 A car dealer is taking a customer satisfaction survey. Find the margin of error (i.e., assuming 95% confidence and $\pi = .50$) for (a) 250 respondents, (b) 125 respondents, and (c) 65 respondents.

8.18 In a sample of 500 new Web sites registered on the Internet, 24 were anonymous (i.e., they shielded their name and contact information). (a) Construct a 95 percent confidence interval for the proportion of all new Web sites that were anonymous. (b) May normality be assumed? Explain. (c) Would the *Very Quick Rule* work here? (Data are from "New Services Are Making It Easier to Hide Who Is Behind Web Sites," *The Wall Street Journal,* September 30, 2004.)

8.19 From a list of stock mutual funds, 52 funds were selected at random. Of the funds chosen, it was found that 19 required a minimum initial investment under $1,000. (a) Construct a 90 percent confidence interval for the true proportion requiring an initial investment under $1,000. (b) May normality be assumed? Explain.

8.20 Of 43 bank customers depositing a check, 18 received some cash back. (a) Construct a 90 percent confidence interval for the proportion of all depositors who ask for cash back. (b) Check the normality assumption.

8.21 A 2003 survey showed that 4.6 percent of the 250 Americans surveyed had suffered some kind of identify theft in the past 12 months. (a) Construct a 98 percent confidence interval for the true proportion of Americans who had suffered identify theft in the past 12 months. (b) May normality be assumed? Explain. (Data are from *Scientific American* 291, no. 6, p. 33.)

8.22 A sample of 50 homes in a subdivision revealed that 24 were ranch style (as opposed to colonial, tri-level, or Cape Cod). (a) Construct a 98 percent confidence interval for the true proportion of ranch style homes. (b) Check the normality assumption.

---

*For further details, see B. D. Jovanovic and P. S. Levy, "A Look at the Rule of Three," *The American Statistician* 51, no. 2 (May 1997), pp. 137–39.
**See James R. Boen and Douglas A. Zahn, *The Human Side of Statistical Consulting* (Wadsworth, 1982), p. 171.

8.23   In a grocery parking lot 32 of 136 cars selected at random were white. (a) Construct a 98 percent confidence interval for the true proportion of white cars. (b) May normality be assumed? Explain. (c) What sample size would be needed to estimate the true proportion of white cars with an error of ± 0.06 and 90 percent confidence? With an error of ± 0.03 and 95 percent confidence? (d) Why are the sample sizes in (c) so different?

Mini Case   8.1

Airline Water Quality

Is the water on your airline flight safe to drink? It isn't feasible to analyze the water on every flight, so sampling is necessary. In August and September 2004, the Environmental Protection Agency (EPA) found bacterial contamination in water samples from the lavatories and galley water taps on 20 of 158 randomly selected U.S. flights (12.7 percent of the flights). Alarmed by the data, the EPA ordered sanitation improvements and then tested water samples again in November and December 2004. In the second sample, bacterial contamination was found in 29 of 169 randomly sampled flights (17.2 percent of the flights).

Aug./Sep. sample: $p = 20/158 = .12658$, or 12.7% contaminated

Nov./Dec. sample: $p = 29/169 = .17160$, or 17.2% contaminated

Is the problem getting worse instead of better? From these samples, we can construct confidence intervals for the true proportion of flights with contaminated water. We begin with the 95 percent confidence interval for π based on the August/September water sample:

$$p \pm z\sqrt{\frac{p(1-p)}{n}} = .12658 \pm 1.96\sqrt{\frac{.12658(1-.12658)}{158}}$$
$$= .12658 \pm .05185, \text{ or } 7.5\% \text{ to } 17.8\%$$

Next we determine the 95 percent confidence interval for π based on the November/December water sample:

$$p \pm z\sqrt{\frac{p(1-p)}{n}} = .17160 \pm 1.96\sqrt{\frac{.17160(1-.17160)}{169}}$$
$$= .17160 \pm .05684, \text{ or } 11.5\% \text{ to } 22.8\%$$

Although the sample percentage (a point estimate of π) did rise, the margin of error is a little over 5 percent in each sample. Since the confidence intervals overlap, we cannot rule out the possibility that there has been no change in water contamination on airline flights; that is, the difference could be due to sampling variation. Nonetheless, the EPA is taking further steps to encourage airlines to improve water quality.

The Wall Street Journal, November 10, 2004, and January 20, 2005.

8.7

SAMPLE SIZE DETERMINATION FOR A MEAN

A Myth

Many people feel that when the population is large, you need a larger sample to obtain a given level of precision in the estimate. This is incorrect. For a given level of precision, it is the sample size that matters, even if the population is a million or a billion. This is apparent from the confidence interval formula, which includes n but not N.*

Sample Size to Estimate μ

Suppose we wish to estimate a population mean with an allowable error $\pm E$. What sample size is required? We start with the general form of the confidence interval:

General Form	*What We Want*
$\bar{x} \pm z\dfrac{\sigma}{\sqrt{n}}$	$\bar{x} \pm E$

---

*The special case of sampling finite populations is discussed in *LearningStats*.

In this confidence interval, we use z instead of t because we are going to solve for n, and degrees of freedom cannot be determined unless we know n. Equating the allowable error E to half of the confidence interval width and solving for n,

$$E = z\frac{\sigma}{\sqrt{n}} \quad \rightarrow \quad E^2 = z^2\frac{\sigma^2}{n} \quad \rightarrow \quad n = z^2\frac{\sigma^2}{E^2}$$

Thus, the formula for the sample size can be written:

$$n = \left(\frac{z\sigma}{E}\right)^2 \qquad \text{(sample size to estimate } \mu) \qquad \textbf{(8.12)}$$

Always round n to the next higher integer.

How to Estimate σ?

Into this formula, we can plug our desired precision E and the appropriate z for the desired confidence level. However, σ poses a problem since it is usually unknown. Table 8.11 shows several ways to approximate the value of σ. You can always try more than one method and see how much difference it makes. But until you take the sample, you will not know for sure if you have achieved your goal (i.e., the desired precision E).

TABLE 8.11
Four Ways to Estimate σ

Method 1: Take a Preliminary Sample
Take a small preliminary sample and use the sample estimate s in place of σ. This method is the most common, though its logic is somewhat circular (i.e., take a sample to plan a sample).

Method 2: Assume Uniform Population
Estimate rough upper and lower limits a and b and set $\sigma = [(b - a)^2/12]^{1/2}$. For example, we might guess the weight of a light-duty truck to range from 1,500 pounds to 3,500 pounds, implying a standard deviation of $\sigma = [(3,500 - 1,500)^2/12]^{1/2} = 577$ pounds. Since a uniform distribution has no central tendency, the actual σ is probably smaller than our guess, so we get a larger n than necessary (a conservative result).

Method 3: Assume Normal Population
Estimate rough upper and lower bounds a and b, and set $\sigma = (b - a)/4$. This assumes normality with most of the data within $\mu + 2\sigma$ and $\mu - 2\sigma$ so the range is 4σ. For example, we might guess the weight of a light truck to range from 1,500 pounds to 3,500 pounds, implying $\sigma = (3,500 - 1,500)/4 = 500$ pounds. Some books suggest $\sigma = R/6$ based on the Empirical Rule, but recent research shows that rule is not conservative enough (see Related Reading).

Method 4: Poisson Arrivals
In the special case when μ is a Poisson arrival rate, then $\sigma = \sqrt{\mu}$. For example, if you think the arrival rate is about 20 customers per hour, then you would estimate $\sigma = \sqrt{20} = 4.47$.

EXAMPLE

Onion Weight

A produce manager wants to estimate the mean weight of Spanish onions being delivered by a supplier, with 95 percent confidence and an error of ± 1 ounce. A preliminary sample of 12 onions shows a sample standard deviation of 3.60 ounces. For a 95 percent confidence interval, we will set $z = 1.96$. We use $s = 3.60$ in place of σ and set the desired error $E = 1$ to obtain the required sample size:

$$n = [(1.96)(3.60)/(1)]^2 = 49.79, \text{ or } 50 \text{ onions}$$

We would round to the next higher integer and take a sample of 50 Spanish onions. This should ensure an estimate of the true mean weight with an error not exceeding ± 1 ounce.

A seemingly modest change in E can have a major effect on the sample size because it is squared. Suppose we reduce the allowable error to $E = 0.5$ ounce to obtain a more precise estimate. The required sample size would then be

$$n = [(1.96)(3.60)/(0.5)]^2 = 199.1, \text{ or } 200 \text{ onions}$$

Using *LearningStats*

There is a sample size calculator in *LearningStats* that makes these calculations easy, as illustrated in Figure 8.29 for $E = 1$ and $E = 0.5$.

FIGURE 8.29

LearningStats's sample size for a mean

Assuming E = ±1 and σ = 1					
	Desired Confidence Level				
	90%	**95%**	**98%**	**99%**	**99.9%**
z	1.645	1.960	2.326	2.576	3.291
n	36	50	71	86	141

Assuming E = ±1 and σ = .5					
	Desired Confidence Level				
	90%	**95%**	**98%**	**99%**	**99.9%**
z	1.645	1.960	2.326	2.576	3.291
n	141	200	281	344	562

Using MegaStat

There is also a sample size calculator in MegaStat, as illustrated in Figure 8.30. The Preview button lets you change the setup and see the result immediately.

FIGURE 8.30

MegaStat's sample size for a mean

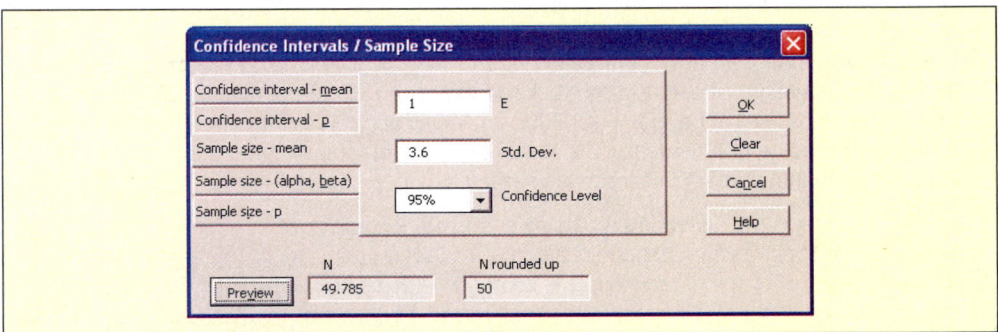

Caution 1: Units of Measure

When estimating a mean, the allowable error E is expressed in the same units as X and σ. For example, E would be expressed in dollars when estimating the mean order size for mail-order customers (e.g., $E = \$2$) or in minutes to estimate the mean wait time for patients at a clinic (e.g., $E = 10$ minutes). To estimate last year's starting salaries for MBA graduates from a university, the allowable error could be large (e.g., $E = \$2,000$) because a $2,000 error in estimating μ might still be a reasonably accurate estimate.

Caution 2: Using *z*

Using z in the sample size formula for a mean is necessary but not conservative. Since t always exceeds z for a given confidence level, your actual interval may be wider than $\pm E$ as intended. As long as the required sample size is large (say 30 or more), the difference will be acceptable.

Caution 3: Larger *n* Is Better

The sample size formulas for a mean are not conservative, that is, they tend to underestimate the required sample size.* Therefore, the sample size formulas for a mean should be

---

*See Lawrence L. Kupper and Kerry B. Hafner, "How Appropriate Are Popular Sample Size Formulas?" *The American Statistician* 43, no. 2 (May 1989), pp. 101–105.

regarded only as a minimum guideline. Whenever possible, samples should exceed this minimum.*

SECTION EXERCISES

8.24 For each level of precision, find the required sample size to estimate the mean starting salary for a new CPA with 95 percent confidence, assuming a population standard deviation of $7,500 (same as last year).
a. $E = \$2,000$ b. $E = \$1,000$ c. $E = \$500$

8.25 Last year, a study showed that the average ATM cash withdrawal took 65 seconds with a standard deviation of 10 seconds. The study is to be repeated this year. How large a sample would be needed to estimate this year's mean with 95 percent confidence and an error of ± 4 seconds?

8.26 The EPA city/hwy mpg range for a 2005 Saturn Vue FWD automatic 5-speed transmission is 20 to 28 mpg. If you owned this vehicle, how large a sample (e.g., how many tanks of gas) would be required to estimate your mean mpg with an error of ± 1 mpg and 90 percent confidence? Explain your assumption about σ.

8.27 Popcorn kernels are believed to take between 100 and 200 seconds to pop in a certain microwave. What sample size (number of kernels) would be needed to estimate the true mean seconds to pop with an error of ± 5 seconds and 95 percent confidence? Explain your assumption about σ.

8.28 Analysis showed that the mean arrival rate for vehicles at a certain Shell station on Friday afternoon last year was 4.5 vehicles per minute. How large a sample would be needed to estimate this year's mean arrival rate with 98 percent confidence and an error of ± 0.5?

8.29 Dave the jogger runs the same route every day. On several consecutive days, he recorded the number of steps he took using a pedometer, which ranged from 3,103 to 3,450. What sample size would you need to estimate Dave's mean steps with 95 percent confidence and an error of ± 25 steps? Explain your assumption about σ.

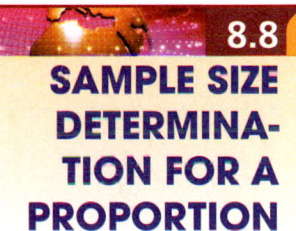

8.8 SAMPLE SIZE DETERMINATION FOR A PROPORTION

Suppose we wish to estimate a population proportion with a precision (allowable error) of $\pm E$. What sample size is required? We start with the general form of the confidence interval:

General Form   *What We Want*

$$p \pm z\sqrt{\frac{\pi(1-\pi)}{n}} \qquad\qquad p \pm E$$

We equate the allowable error E to half of the confidence interval width and solve for n:

$$E = z\sqrt{\frac{\pi(1-\pi)}{n}} \quad\rightarrow\quad E^2 = z^2\frac{\pi(1-\pi)}{n} \quad\rightarrow\quad n = z^2\frac{\pi(1-\pi)}{E^2}$$

Thus, the formula for the sample size for a proportion can be written:

$$n = \left(\frac{z}{E}\right)^2 \pi(1-\pi) \qquad \text{(sample size to estimate } \pi) \qquad\qquad \textbf{(8.13)}$$

Always round n to the next higher integer.

Since a proportion is a number between 0 and 1, the precision allowable error E is also between 0 and 1. For example, if we want an allowable error of ± 7 percent we would specify $E = 0.07$.

Since π is unknown (that's why we are taking the sample) we need to make an assumption about π to plan our sample size. If we have a prior estimate of π (e.g., from last year or a comparable application), we can plug it in the formula. Or we could take a small preliminary sample. Some experts recommend using $\pi = .50$ because the resulting sample size will guarantee the desired precision for any π. However, this conservative assumption may lead to a larger sample

---

*If you are sampling a finite population without replacement and your required sample size (n) exceeds 5 percent of the population size (N), you can adjust the sample size by using $n' = \frac{nN}{n+(N-1)}$. This adjustment will guarantee that the sample size never exceeds the population size. See *LearningStats* for details.

than necessary. Sampling costs money, so if a prior estimate of π is available, it might be advisable to use it, especially if you think that π differs greatly from .50. For example, in estimating the proportion of home equity loans that result in default, we would expect π to be much smaller than .50, while in estimating the proportion of motorists who use seat belts, we would hope that π would be much larger than .50. Table 8.12 details three ways to estimate π.

TABLE 8.12

Three Ways to Estimate π

Method 1: Take a Preliminary Sample

Take a small preliminary sample and insert p into the sample size formula in place of π. This method is appropriate if π is believed to differ greatly from .50, as is often the case, though its logic is somewhat circular (i.e., we must take a sample to plan our sample).

Method 2: Use a Prior Sample or Historical Data

A reasonable approach, but how often are such data available? And might π have changed enough to make it a questionable assumption?

Method 3: Assume That $\pi = .50$

This method is conservative and ensures the desired precision. It is therefore a sound choice. However, the sample may end up being larger than necessary.

EXAMPLE

ATM Withdrawals

A university credit union wants to know the proportion of cash withdrawals that exceed $50 at its ATM located in the student union building. With an error of ± 2 percent and a confidence level of 95 percent, how large a sample is needed to estimate the proportion of withdrawals exceeding $50? The z-value for 95 percent confidence is $z = 1.960$. Using $E = 0.02$ and assuming conservatively that $\pi = .50$, the required sample size is

$$n = \left(\frac{z}{E}\right)^2 \pi(1-\pi) = \left(\frac{1.960}{0.02}\right)^2 (.50)(1 - .50) = 2{,}401$$

We would need to examine $n = 2{,}401$ withdrawals to estimate π within ± 2 percent and with 95 percent confidence. In this case, last year's proportion of ATM withdrawals over $50 was 27 percent. If we had used this estimate in our calculation, the required sample size would be

$$n = \left(\frac{z}{E}\right)^2 p(1-p) = \left(\frac{1.960}{0.02}\right)^2 (.27)(1 - .27) = 1{,}893 \qquad \text{(rounded to next higher integer)}$$

We would need to examine $n = 1{,}893$ withdrawals to estimate π within ± 0.02. The required sample size is smaller than when we make the conservative assumption $\pi = .50$.

Alternatives

Suppose that our research budget will not permit a large sample. In the previous example, we could reduce the confidence interval level from 95 to 90 percent and increase the allowable error to ± 4 percent. Assuming $\pi = .50$, the required sample size is

$$n = \left(\frac{z}{E}\right)^2 \pi(1-\pi) = \left(\frac{1.645}{0.04}\right)^2 (.50)(1 - .50) = 423 \qquad \text{(rounded to next higher integer)}$$

These seemingly modest changes make a huge difference in the sample size.

Practical Advice

Choosing a sample size is a common problem. Clients who take samples are constrained by time and money. Naturally, they prefer the highest possible confidence level and the lowest possible error. But when a statistical consultant shows them the required sample size, they may find it infeasible. A better way to look at it is that the formula for sample size provides a structure for a dialogue between statistician and client. A good consultant can propose several possible confidence levels and errors, and let the client choose the combination that best balances the need for accuracy against the available time and budget. The statistician can offer advice about these trade-offs, so the client's objectives are met. Other issues include nonresponse rates, dropout rates from ongoing studies, and possibly incorrect assumptions used in the calculation.

Using *LearningStats*

The sample size calculator in *LearningStats* makes these calculations easy, as illustrated in Figure 8.31 for $\pi = .50$ and $E = 0.02$.

	Desired Confidence Level				
	90%	**95%**	**98%**	**99%**	**99.9%**
z	1.645	1.960	2.326	2.576	3.291
n	1691	2401	3383	4147	6768

FIGURE 8.31

LearningStats's sample size for a mean

Caution 1: Units of Measure

A common error is to insert $E = 2$ in the formula when you want an error of ± 2 percent. Because we are dealing with a *proportion,* a 2% error is $E = 0.02$. In other words, when estimating a proportion, E is always between 0 and 1.

Caution 2: Finite Population

If you are sampling a ***finite population*** without replacement and your required sample size (n) exceeds 5 percent of the population size (N), you can adjust the sample size by using $n' = \frac{nN}{n + (N - 1)}$. This adjustment will guarantee that the sample size never exceeds the population size. See *LearningStats* for details.

SECTION EXERCISES

8.30 (a) What sample size would be required to estimate the true proportion of American female business executives who prefer the title "Ms.", with an error of ± 0.025 and 98 percent confidence? (b) What sampling method would you recommend? Explain.

8.31 (a) What sample size would be needed to estimate the true proportion of American households that own more than one DVD player, with 90 percent confidence and an error of ± 0.02? (b) What sampling method would you recommend? Why?

8.32 (a) What sample size would be needed to estimate the true proportion of students at your college (if you are a student) who are wearing backpacks, with 95 percent confidence and an error of ± 0.04? (c) What sampling method would you recommend? Why?

8.33 (a) What sample size would be needed to estimate the true proportion of American adults who know their cholesterol level, using 95 percent confidence and an error of ± 0.02? (b) What sampling method would you recommend, and why?

If the confidence interval for the ***difference of two means*** includes zero, we could conclude that there is no significant difference in means. When the population variances are unknown (the usual situation) the procedure for constructing a confidence interval for $\mu_1 - \mu_2$ depends on our assumption about the unknown variances. If the population is normal and the population variances can be assumed equal, the difference of means follows a Student's t distribution with $(n_1 - 1) + (n_2 - 1)$ degrees of freedom. The pooled variance is a weighted average of the sample variances with weights $n_1 - 1$ and $n_2 - 1$ (the respective degrees of freedom for each sample).

   Assuming equal variances:

$$(\bar{x}_1 - \bar{x}_2) \pm t \sqrt{\frac{(n_1 - 1)s_1^2 + (n_2 - 1)s_2^2}{n_1 + n_2 - 2}} \sqrt{\frac{1}{n_1} + \frac{1}{n_2}} \quad \text{with } \nu = (n_1 - 1) + (n_2 - 1) \quad \textbf{(8.14)}$$

8.9

CONFIDENCE INTERVAL FOR THE DIFFERENCE OF TWO MEANS,

$\mu_1 - \mu_2$

(OPTIONAL)

If the population variances are unknown and are likely to be unequal, we should not pool the variances. A practical alternative is to use the t distribution, adding the variances and using *Welch's formula* for the degrees of freedom (denoted ν').

Assuming unequal variances:

(8.15) $$(\bar{x}_1 - \bar{x}_2) \pm t\sqrt{\frac{s_1^2}{n_1} + \frac{s_2^2}{n_2}} \quad \text{with } \nu' = \frac{\left[s_1^2/n_1 + s_2^2/n_2\right]^2}{\dfrac{\left(s_1^2/n_1\right)^2}{n_1 - 1} + \dfrac{\left(s_1^2/n_1\right)^2}{n_2 - 1}}$$

If you wish to avoid the complex algebra of the Welch formula for ν', you can just use degrees of freedom equal to $\nu^* = \min(n_1 - 1, n_2 - 1)$. This conservative quick rule allows fewer degrees of freedom than Welch's formula yet generally gives reasonable results.*

EXAMPLE

Marketing Teams

Senior marketing majors were randomly assigned to a virtual team that met only electronically or to a face-to-face team that met in person. Both teams were presented with the task of analyzing eight complex marketing cases. After completing the project, they were asked to respond on a 1–5 Likert scale to this question:

"As compared to other teams, the members got along together."

TABLE 8.13   **Means and Standard Deviations for the Two Marketing Teams**

Statistic	Virtual Team	Face-to-Face Team
Sample Mean	$\bar{x}_1 = 2.48$	$\bar{x}_2 = 1.83$
Sample Std. Dev.	$s_1 = 0.76$	$s_2 = 0.82$
Sample Size	$n_1 = 44$	$n_2 = 42$

Source: Roger W. Berry, "The Efficacy of Electronic Communication in the Business School: Marketing Students' Perception of Virtual Teams," *Marketing Education Review* 12, no. 2 (Summer 2002), pp. 73–78. Copyright © 2002. Reprinted with permission, CTC Press. All rights reserved.

Table 8.13 shows the means and standard deviations for the two groups. The population variances are unknown, but will be assumed equal (note the similar standard deviations). For a confidence level of 90 percent we use Student's t with $\nu = 44 + 42 - 2 = 84$. From Appendix D we obtain $t_{.05} = 1.664$ (using 80 degrees of freedom, the next lower value). The confidence interval is

$$(\bar{x}_1 - \bar{x}_2) \pm t\sqrt{\frac{(n_1 - 1)s_1^2 + (n_2 - 1)s_2^2}{n_1 + n_2 - 2}}\sqrt{\frac{1}{n_1} + \frac{1}{n_2}}$$

$$= (2.48 - 1.83) \pm (1.664)\sqrt{\frac{(44 - 1)(0.76)^2 + (42 - 1)(0.82)^2}{44 + 42 - 2}}\sqrt{\frac{1}{44} + \frac{1}{42}}$$

$$= 0.65 \pm 0.284, \quad 0.366 < \mu_1 - \mu_2 < 0.934$$

Since this confidence interval does not include zero, we can say with 90 percent confidence that there is a significant difference between the means (i.e., the virtual team's mean differs from the face-to-face team's mean).

In Chapter 10, you will learn more about the comparison of two sample means. Because the calculations are rather complex, it is helpful to use software. Figure 8.32 shows a MINITAB menu that gives the option to assume equal variances or not. If we had not assumed equal variances, the results would be the same in this case because the samples are large and of similar

---

*See P. Leaverton and J. J. Birch, "Small Sample Power Curves for the Two Sample Location Problem," *Technometrics* 11 (1969), pp. 299–307. For degrees of freedom, the relationship is $\nu^* \leq \nu' \leq \nu$. That is, Welch's formula generally allows fewer d.f. than if variances are pooled, and the quick rule allows even fewer. For large samples with similar variances and near-equal sample sizes, the methods give similar results.

size, and the variances do not differ greatly. But when you have small, unequal sample sizes or unequal variances, the methods can yield different results.

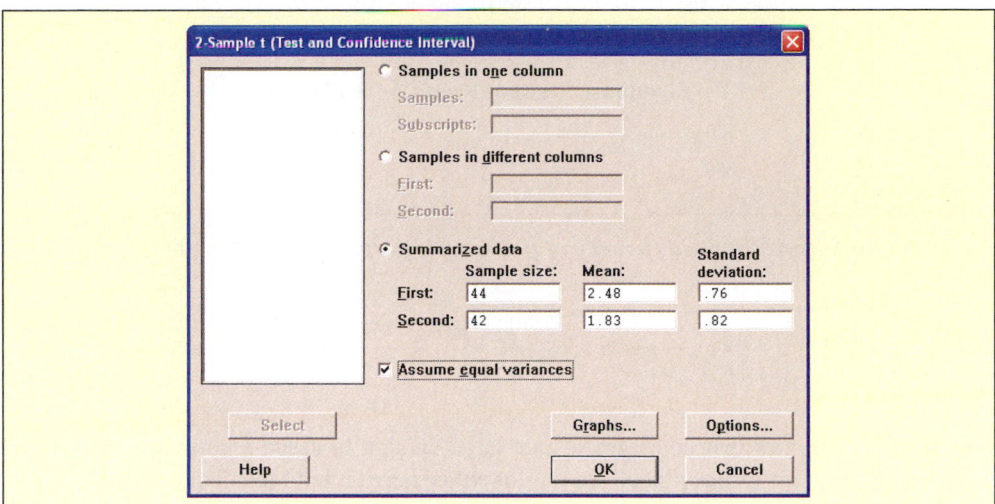

FIGURE 8.32

MINITAB's menu for comparing two sample means

Should Sample Sizes Be Equal?

Many people instinctively try to choose equal sample sizes for tests of means. It is preferable to avoid unbalanced sample sizes, but it is not necessary. Unequal sample sizes are common, and the formulas still apply.

SECTION EXERCISES

8.34 A special bumper was installed on selected vehicles in a large fleet. The dollar cost of body repairs was recorded for all vehicles that were involved in accidents over a 1-year period. Those with the special bumper are the test group and the other vehicles are the control group, shown below. Each "repair incident" is defined as an invoice (which might include more than one separate type of damage).

Statistic	Test Group	Control Group
Mean Damage	$\bar{x}_1 = \$1,101$	$\bar{x}_2 = \$1,766$
Sample Std. Dev.	$s_1 = \$696$	$s_2 = \$838$
Repair Incidents	$n_1 = 12$	$n_2 = 9$

Source: Unpublished study by Thomas W. Lauer and Floyd G. Willoughby.

(a) Construct a 90 percent confidence interval for the true difference of the means assuming equal variances. Show all work clearly. (b) Repeat, using the assumption of unequal variances with either Welch's formula for ν' or the quick rule for $\nu*$ degrees of freedom. Did the assumption about variances make a major difference, in your opinion? (c) Construct separate confidence intervals for each mean. Do they overlap? (d) What conclusions can you draw?

8.35 In trials of an experimental Internet-based method of learning statistics, pre-tests and post-tests were given to two groups: traditional instruction (22 students) and Internet-based (17 students). Pre-test scores were not significantly different. On the post-test, the first group (traditional instruction) had a mean score of 8.64 with a standard deviation of 1.88, while the second group (experimental instruction) had a mean score of 8.82 with a standard deviation of 1.70. (a) Construct a 90 percent confidence interval for the true difference of the means assuming equal variances. Show all work clearly. (b) Repeat, using the assumption of unequal variances with either Welch's formula for ν' or the quick rule for $\nu*$ degrees of freedom. Did the assumption about variances make a major difference, in your opinion? (c) Construct separate confidence intervals for each mean. Do they overlap? (d) What conclusions can you draw?

8.36 Construct a 95 percent confidence interval for the difference of mean monthly rent paid by undergraduates and graduate students. What do you conclude? 🐷 **Rent2**

Undergraduate Student Rents ($n = 10$)

820	780	870	670	800
790	810	680	1,000	730

Graduate Student Rents ($n = 12$)

1,130	920	930	880	780	910
790	840	930	910	860	850

8.10
CONFIDENCE INTERVAL FOR THE DIFFERENCE OF TWO PROPORTIONS, $\pi_1 - \pi_2$ (OPTIONAL)

A confidence interval for the **difference of two sample proportions** is given by

(8.16)
$$(p_1 - p_2) \pm z \sqrt{\frac{p_1(1 - p_1)}{n_1} + \frac{p_2(1 - p_2)}{n_2}}$$

This formula assumes that both samples are large enough to assume normality. MINITAB gives a warning if $np < 5$ or if $n(1 - p) < 5$ for either sample, but MegaStat does not.

EXAMPLE

Fire Truck Color

Compared to a traditional red fire truck, does a bright yellow fire truck have a lower accident rate? Proponents of the brighter yellow color argued that its enhanced visibility allowed other traffic to see the trucks and avoid them during fire runs. A 4-year study in Dallas, Texas, produced the statistics shown in Table 8.14.

TABLE 8.14   **Accident Rate for Dallas Fire Trucks**

Statistic	Red Fire Trucks	Yellow Fire Trucks
Number of accidents	$x_1 = 20$ accidents	$x_2 = 4$ accidents
Number of fire runs	$n_1 = 153{,}348$ runs	$n_2 = 135{,}035$ runs
Accident rate	$p_1 = \dfrac{20}{153{,}348}$ $= .000130422$	$p_2 = \dfrac{4}{135{,}035}$ $= .000029622$

Source: *The Wall Street Journal,* June 26, 1995, p. B1.

Although the second sample is small ($np < 10$), we will use it to illustrate the confidence interval formula. The 95 percent confidence interval for the difference between the proportions is

$$(p_1 - p_2) \pm z \sqrt{\frac{p_1(1 - p_1)}{n_1} + \frac{p_2(1 - p_2)}{n_2}}$$

$$= (.000130422 - .000029622)$$

$$\pm (1.960) \sqrt{\frac{(.000130422)(.999869578)}{153{,}348} + \frac{(.000029622)(.999970378)}{135{,}035}}$$

$$= .0000366959 < \pi_1 - \pi_2 < .000164905$$

Since the confidence interval for $\pi_1 - \pi_2$ does not include zero, it appears that the accident rates are significantly different. Should all fire trucks be painted yellow? With such large samples, no one could say that this was a "small sample" fluke. However, both accident rates are quite small to begin with, an argument used by those who favor the traditional red color. A greater problem, the critics say, is that the public has become inured to sirens and flashing lights. As often happens, statistics may play only a small part in the policy decision. ↖

SECTION EXERCISES

8.37 The American Bankers Association reports that, in a sample of 120 consumer purchases in France, 60 were made with cash, compared with 26 in a sample of 50 consumer purchases in the United States. Construct a 90 percent confidence interval for the difference in proportions. (Data are from *The Wall Street Journal,* July 27, 2004.)

8.38 A study showed that 12 of 24 cell phone users with a headset missed their exit, compared with 3 of 24 talking to a passenger. Construct a 95 percent confidence interval for the difference in proportions. (Data are from *The Wall Street Journal,* September 24, 2004.)

8.39 A survey of 100 cigarette smokers showed that 71 were loyal to one brand, compared to 122 of 200 toothpaste users. Construct a 90 percent confidence interval for the difference in proportions. (Data are from J. Paul Peter and Jerry C. Olson, *Consumer Behavior and Marketing Strategy,* 7th ed. [McGraw-Hill, 2005], p. 97.)

Chi-Square Distribution

If the population is normal, the sample variance s^2 follows the **chi-square distribution** (the Greek letter χ is pronounced "kye") with degrees of freedom equal to $v = n - 1$. Lower tail and upper tail percentiles for the chi-square distribution (denoted χ_L^2 and χ_U^2, respectively) can be found in Appendix E. Using the sample variance s^2, the confidence interval is

$$\frac{(n-1)s^2}{\chi_U^2} < \sigma^2 < \frac{(n-1)s^2}{\chi_L^2} \qquad \text{(confidence interval for } \sigma^2 \text{ from sample variance } s^2 \text{)} \qquad \text{(8.17)}$$

8.11
CONFIDENCE INTERVAL FOR A POPULATION VARIANCE, σ^2 (OPTIONAL)

EXAMPLE

DVD Prices   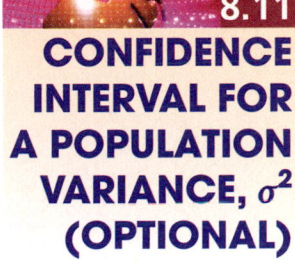 **DVD**

In a particular week, the prices of the top 40 DVD movies at Blockbuster showed a mean of $\bar{x} = 24.76$ with a sample variance $s^2 = 12.77$.

29.51	21.09	29.98	29.95	21.07	29.52	21.07	24.95	21.07	24.95
24.98	29.95	24.95	21.07	25.30	25.30	29.95	29.99	29.95	24.95
24.95	21.07	24.98	21.09	21.07	24.98	21.07	25.30	29.95	25.30
25.30	24.98	16.86	25.30	25.30	16.86	24.95	24.98	25.30	21.07

Source: From a project by statistics students Robyn Freeman, Sarah Jespersen, and Jennifer Pritchett.

The sample data were nearly symmetric (median $24.98) with no outliers. Normality of the prices will be assumed. From Appendix E, using 39 degrees of freedom ($v = n - 1 = 40 - 1 = 39$) we obtain bounds for the 95 percent middle area, as illustrated in Figure 8.33.

FIGURE 8.33

Using the chi-square table for 95 percent confidence with $v = 39$

Appendix E: Chi-Square Critical Values

This table shows the critical value for the tail areas for the stated degrees of freedom (v).

	Left Tail Area						Right Tail Area				
v	0.005	0.01	0.025	0.05	0.10		0.10	0.05	0.025	0.01	0.005
1	0.000	0.000	0.001	0.004	0.016		2.706	3.841	5.024	6.635	7.879
2	0.010	0.020	0.051	0.103	0.211		4.605	5.991	7.378	9.210	10.60
3	0.072	0.115	0.216	0.352	0.584		6.251	7.815	9.348	11.34	12.84
4	0.207	0.297	0.484	0.711	1.064		7.779	9.488	11.14	13.28	14.86
5	0.412	0.554	0.831	1.145	1.610		9.236	11.07	12.83	15.09	16.75
6	0.676	0.872	1.237	1.635	2.204		10.64	12.59	14.45	16.81	18.55
7	0.989	1.239	1.690	2.167	2.833		12.02	14.07	16.01	18.48	20.28
8	1.344	1.647	2.180	2.733	3.490		13.36	15.51	17.53	20.09	21.95
9	1.735	2.088	2.700	3.325	4.168		14.68	16.92	19.02	21.67	23.59
10	2.156	2.558	3.247	3.940	4.865		15.99	18.31	20.48	23.21	25.19
...	...	...	...	...	...		...	...	...	...	...
36	17.89	19.23	21.34	23.27	25.64		47.21	51.00	54.44	58.62	61.58
37	18.59	19.96	22.11	24.07	26.49		48.36	52.19	55.67	59.89	62.88
38	19.29	20.69	22.88	24.88	27.34		49.51	53.38	56.90	61.16	64.18
39	20.00	21.43	23.65	25.70	28.20		50.66	54.57	58.12	62.43	65.48
40	20.71	22.16	24.43	26.51	29.05		51.81	55.76	59.34	63.69	66.77

$\chi_L^2 = 23.65$ (lower 2.5 percent)

$\chi_U^2 = 58.12$ (upper 2.5 percent)

The 95 percent confidence interval for the population variance σ^2 is

$$\text{Lower bound: } \frac{(n-1)s^2}{\chi_U^2} = \frac{(40-1)(12.77)}{58.12} = 8.569$$

$$\text{Upper bound: } \frac{(n-1)s^2}{\chi_L^2} = \frac{(40-1)(12.77)}{23.65} = 21.058$$

With 95 percent confidence, we believe that $8.569 < \sigma^2 < 21.058$.

Confidence Interval for σ

If you want a confidence interval for the standard deviation, just take the square root of the interval bounds. In the DVD example, we get $2.93 < \sigma < 4.59$. If you have raw data, MINITAB's Stats > Basic Statistics > Graphical Summary gives nice confidence intervals for the mean, median, and standard deviation for a column of raw data, as well as a histogram and box plot. MINITAB uses Student's t for the confidence interval for the mean and calculates the confidence interval for σ, as illustrated in Figure 8.34.

FIGURE 8.34

MINITAB's confidence intervals

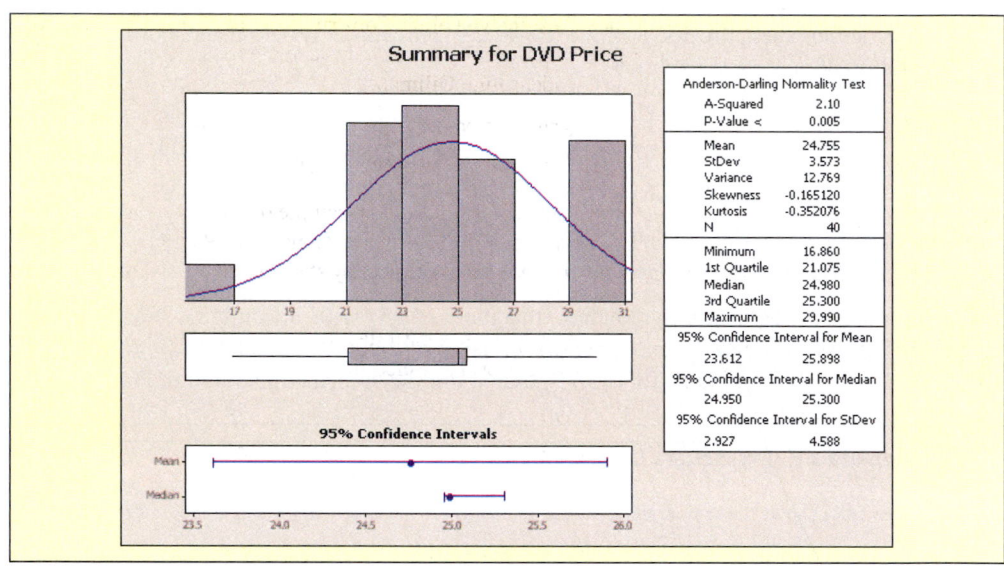

Using *LearningStats*

Figure 8.35 shows the chi-square distribution for $v = 39$. The sample screen is from *LearningStats*. Although the chi-square distribution is always right-skewed, this one is somewhat bell-shaped because the sample size is large (i.e., large degrees of freedom). In smaller samples, its skewness would be more apparent.

Caution: Assumption of Normality

The methods just described for confidence interval estimation of the variance and standard deviation are highly dependent on the population having a normal distribution. There is not a CLT that can be used for the statistic s^2. If the population does not have a normal distribution, then the confidence interval should not be considered accurate.

FIGURE 8.35

LearningStats's chi-square distribution

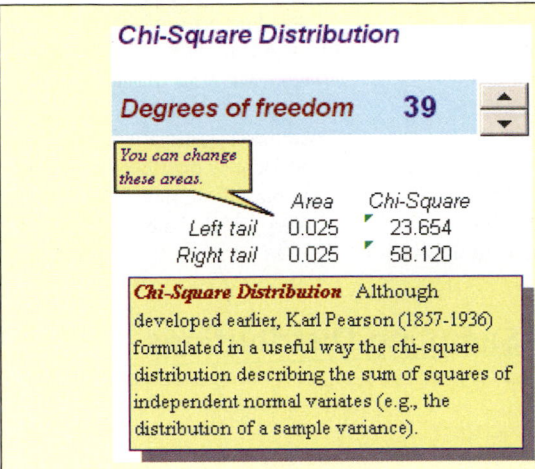

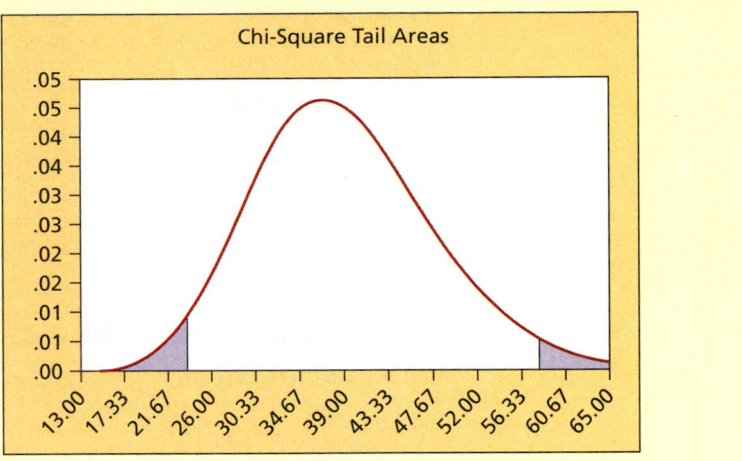

SECTION EXERCISES

8.40 Find the 95 percent confidence interval for the population variance from these samples.
a. $n = 15$ commuters, $s = 10$ miles driven   b. $n = 18$ students, $s = 12$ study hours

8.41 The weights of 20 oranges (in ounces) are shown below. Construct a 95 percent confidence interval for the population standard deviation. *Note:* Scale was only accurate to the nearest 1/4 ounce. (Data are from a project by statistics student Julie Gillman.) **Oranges**

5.50	6.25	6.25	6.50	6.50	7.00	7.00	7.00	7.50	7.50
7.75	8.00	8.00	8.50	8.50	9.00	9.00	9.25	10.00	10.50

8.42 A pediatrician's records showed the mean height of a random sample of 25 girls at age 12 months to be 29.530 inches with a standard deviation of 1.0953 inches. Construct a 95 percent confidence interval for the population variance. (Data are from a project by statistics students Lori Bossardet, Shannon Wegner, and Stephanie Rader.)

8.43 Find the 90 percent confidence interval for the standard deviation of gasoline mileage mpg for these 16 San Francisco commuters driving hybrid gas-electric vehicles. **Hybrid**

38.8	48.9	28.5	40.0	38.8	29.2	29.1	38.5
34.4	46.1	51.8	30.7	36.9	25.6	42.7	38.3

Chapter Summary

An **estimator** is a sample statistic ($\bar{x}$, s, p) that is used to estimate an unknown population **parameter** (μ, σ, π). A desirable estimator is **unbiased** (correctly centered), **efficient** (minimum variance), and **consistent** (variance goes to zero as n increases). **Sampling error** (the difference between an estimator and its parameter) is inevitable, but a larger sample size yields estimates that are closer to the unknown parameter. The **Central Limit Theorem** (CLT) states that the sample mean $\bar{x}$ is centered at μ and follows a normal distribution if n is large, regardless of the population shape. A **confidence interval** for μ consists of lower and upper bounds that have a specified probability (called the **confidence level**) of enclosing μ. Any confidence level may be used, but 90, 95, and 99 percent are common. If the population variance is unknown, we replace z in the confidence interval formula for μ with **Student's** t using $n - 1$ degrees of freedom. The CLT also applies to the sample proportion (p) as an estimator of π, using a rule of thumb to decide if normality may be assumed. The **margin of error** is the half-width of the confidence interval for π. Formulas exist for the required **sample size** for a given level of precision in a confidence interval for μ or π, although they entail assumptions and are only approximate. Confidence intervals and sample sizes may be adjusted for finite populations, but often the adjustments are not material. Confidence intervals may be created for differences of means or proportions, or for a variance.

Key Terms

bias, *295*
Central Limit Theorem, *299*
chi-square distribution, *335*
confidence interval, *306*
confidence level, *306*
consistent estimator, *297*
degrees of freedom, *310*
difference of two means, *331*
difference of two sample
    proportions, *334*

efficiency (efficient
    estimator), *297*
estimate, *295*
estimator, *295*
finite population, *331*
interval estimate, *307*
margin of error, *324*
minimum variance
    estimator, *297*
point estimate, *306*
sampling distribution, *295*

sampling error, *295*
sampling variation, *293*
standard error of the
    mean, *298*
standard error of the
    proportion, *320*
statistical estimation, *294*
Student's *t* distribution, *309*
unbiased estimator, *295*
Very Quick Rule, *325*

Commonly Used Formulas in Sampling Distributions and Estimation

Sample Proportion: $p = \dfrac{x}{n}$

Standard Error of the Sample Mean: $\sigma_{\bar{x}} = \dfrac{\sigma}{\sqrt{n}}$

Confidence Interval for μ, known σ: $\bar{x} \pm z\dfrac{\sigma}{\sqrt{n}}$

Confidence Interval for μ, unknown σ: $\bar{x} \pm t\dfrac{s}{\sqrt{n}}$

Degrees of Freedom: $\nu = n - 1$

Standard Error of the Sample Proportion: $\sigma_p = \sqrt{\dfrac{\pi(1 - \pi)}{n}}$

Confidence Interval for π: $p \pm z\sqrt{\dfrac{p(1 - p)}{n}}$

Sample Size to Estimate μ: $n = \left(\dfrac{z\sigma}{E}\right)^2$

Sample Size to Estimate π: $n = \left(\dfrac{z}{E}\right)^2 \pi(1 - \pi)$

Confidence Interval; Difference of Two Means: $(\bar{x}_1 - \bar{x}_2) \pm t\sqrt{\dfrac{s_1^2}{n_1} + \dfrac{s_2^2}{n_2}}$

Confidence Interval; Difference of Two Proportions: $(p_1 - p_2) \pm z\sqrt{\dfrac{p_1(1 - p_1)}{n_1} + \dfrac{p_2(1 - p_2)}{n_2}}$

Chapter Review

1. Define (a) parameter, (b) estimator, (c) sampling error, and (d) sampling distribution.

2. Explain the difference between sampling error and bias. Can they be controlled?

3. Name three estimators. Which ones are unbiased?

4. Explain what it means to say an estimator is (a) unbiased, (b) efficient, and (c) consistent.

5. State the main points of the Central Limit Theorem for a mean.

6. Why is population shape of concern when estimating a mean? What does sample size have to do with it?

7. (a) Define the standard error of the mean. (b) What happens to the standard error as sample size increases? (c) How does the law of diminishing returns apply to the standard error?

8. Define (a) point estimate, (b) interval estimate, (c) confidence interval, and (d) confidence level.

9. List some common confidence levels. Why not use other confidence levels?

10. List differences and similarities between Student's *t* and the standard normal distribution.

11. Give an example to show that (a) for a given confidence level, the Student's *t* confidence interval for the mean is wider than if we use a *z*-value; and (b) it makes little difference in a large sample whether we use Student's *t* or *z*.

12. Why do outliers and skewed populations pose a problem for estimating a sample mean?

13. (a) State the Central Limit Theorem for a proportion. (b) When is it safe to assume normality for a sample proportion?

14. (a) Define the standard error of the proportion. (b) What happens to the standard error as sample size increases? (c) Why does a larger sample improve a confidence interval?

15. (a) What is the Rule of Three? (b) What is the Very Quick Rule? When does it not work well?

16. (a) Why does σ pose a problem for sample size calculation for a mean? (b) How can σ be approximated when it is unknown?

17. (a) When doing a sample size calculation for a proportion, why is it conservative to assume that $\pi = .50$? (b) When might we not want to assume that $\pi = .50$, and why?

*18. Why would we be interested in a confidence interval for a difference of two means or two proportions? Give an example.

CHAPTER EXERCISES

Note: Explain answers and show your work clearly. Problems marked * rely on optional material.

8.44 This is an exercise using Excel. (a) Use =RANDBETWEEN(0,99) to create 20 samples of size $n = 4$ by choosing two-digit random numbers between 00 and 99 (see illustration below). (b) For each sample, calculate the mean. (c) Make a histogram of the 80 *individual X-values* using bins 10 units wide (i.e., 0, 10, 20, . . . , 100). Describe the shape of the histogram. (d) Make a histogram of your 20 *sample means* using bins 10 units wide. (e) Discuss the histogram shape. Does the Central Limit Theorem seem to be working? (f) Find the mean of the sample means. Was it what you would expect by the CLT? Explain. (g) Find the average standard deviation of the sample means. Was it what you would expect by the CLT? (h) What was the point of this exercise? *Hint:* Here is an example of a data set. 🐿 **ExamSim**

Sample	x_1	x_2	x_3	x_4	Mean
1	37	0	13	34	21.00
2	62	50	9	99	55.00
3	34	98	12	32	44.00
4	59	92	95	6	63.00
5	70	81	74	81	76.50
6	45	85	91	15	59.00
7	35	95	28	65	55.75
8	15	49	86	97	61.75
9	87	23	2	16	32.00
10	3	83	6	74	41.50
11	52	29	63	48	48.00
12	95	75	49	92	77.75
13	25	40	19	90	43.50
14	32	14	4	31	20.25
15	45	8	7	96	39.00
16	32	29	54	11	31.50
17	88	72	8	46	53.50
18	55	24	7	59	36.25
19	29	22	93	98	60.50
20	15	52	9	16	23.00

8.45 A random sample of 21 nickels measured with a very accurate micrometer showed a mean diameter of 0.834343 inches with a standard deviation of 0.001886 inches. (a) Why would nickel diameters vary? (b) Construct a 99 percent confidence interval for the true mean diameter of a nickel. (c) Discuss any assumptions that are needed. (d) What sample size would ensure an error of ± 0.0005 inches with 99 percent confidence? (Data are from a project by MBA student Bob Tindall.)

8.46 A random sample of 10 miniature Tootsie Rolls was taken from a bag. Each piece was weighed on a very accurate scale. The results in grams were

3.087	3.131	3.241	3.241	3.270	3.353	3.400	3.411	3.437	3.477

(a) Construct a 90 percent confidence interval for the true mean weight. (b) What sample size would be necessary to estimate the true weight with an error of ± 0.03 grams with 90 percent confidence? (c) Discuss the factors which might cause variation in the weight of Tootsie Rolls during manufacture. (Data are from a project by MBA student Henry Scussel.) 🍫 **Tootsie**

8.47 Statistics students were asked to go home and fill a 1-cup measure with raisin bran, tap the cup lightly on the counter three times to settle the contents, if necessary add more raisin bran to bring the contents exactly up to the 1-cup line, spread the contents on a large plate, and count the raisins. For the 13 students who chose Kellogg's brand the reported results were

23	33	44	36	29	42	31	33	61	36	34	23	24

(a) Construct a 90 percent confidence interval for the mean number of raisins per cup. Show your work clearly. (b) Can you think of features of the sample or data-gathering method that might create problems? If so, how could they be improved? (c) Identify factors that might prevent Kellogg's from achieving uniformity in the number of raisins per cup of raisin bran. (d) How might a quality control system work to produce more uniform quantities of raisins, assuming that improvement is desired? 🥣 **Raisins**

8.48 A sample of 20 pages was taken without replacement from the 1,591-page phone directory *Ameritech Pages Plus Yellow Pages*. On each page, the mean area devoted to display ads was measured (a display ad is a large block of multicolored illustrations, maps, and text). The data (in square millimeters) are shown below:

0	260	356	403	536	0	268	369	428	536
268	396	469	536	162	338	403	536	536	130

(a) Construct a 95 percent confidence interval for the true mean. (b) Why might normality be an issue here? (c) What sample size would be needed to obtain an error of ±10 square millimeters with 99 percent confidence? (d) If this is not a reasonable requirement, suggest one that is. (Data are from a project by MBA student Daniel R. Dalach.) 📒 **DisplayAds**

8.49 Sixteen owners of 2005 Chrysler Pacifica 2WD vehicles kept track of their average fuel economy for a month. The results are shown below. (a) Construct a 95 percent confidence interval for the mean. (b) What factor(s) limit the conclusions that can be drawn about the true mean? (Data are from www.fueleconomy.gov.) 🚗 **MPG**

20.8	20.0	19.4	19.7	21.1	22.6	18.3	20.1
20.5	19.5	17.4	22.4	18.9	20.2	19.6	19.0

8.50 Twenty-five blood samples were selected by taking every seventh blood sample from racks holding 187 blood samples from the morning draw at a medical center. The white blood count (WBC) was measured using a Coulter Counter Model S. The mean WBC was 8.636 with a standard deviation of 3.9265. (a) Construct a 90 percent confidence interval for the true mean. (b) Why might normality be an issue here? (c) What sample size would be needed for an error of ± 1.5 with 98 percent confidence? (Data are from a project by MBA student Wendy Blomquist.)

8.51 Twenty-one warranty repairs were selected from a population of 126 by selecting every sixth item. The population consisted of "loose, not attached" minivan electrical wires (one of several electrical failure categories the dealership mechanic can select). The mean repair cost was $45.664 with a standard deviation of $27.793. (a) Construct a 95 percent confidence interval for the true mean repair cost. (b) Why might normality be an issue here? Explain. (c) What sample size would be needed to obtain an error of ±$5 with 95 percent confidence? *(d) Construct a 95 percent confidence interval for the true standard deviation. (Data are from a project by MBA student Tim Polulak.)

8.52 Dave the jogger runs the same route every day (about 2.2 miles). On 18 consecutive days, he recorded the number of steps using a pedometer. The results were

3,450	3,363	3,228	3,360	3,304	3,407	3,324	3,365	3,290
3,289	3,346	3,252	3,237	3,210	3,140	3,220	3,103	3,129

(a) Construct a 95 percent confidence interval for the true mean number of steps Dave takes on his run. (b) What sample size would be needed to obtain an error of ± 20 steps with 95 percent confidence? (c) Using Excel, plot a line chart of the data. What does the data suggest about the pattern over time?   **DaveSteps**

8.53 A pediatrician's records showed the mean height of a random sample of 25 girls at age 12 months to be 29.530 inches with a standard deviation of 1.0953 inches. (a) Construct a 95 percent confidence interval for the true mean height. (b) Could normality reasonably be assumed for this population? (c) What sample size would be needed for 95 percent confidence and an error of ± .20 inch? (Data are from a project by statistics students Lori Bossardet, Shannon Wegner, and Stephanie Rader.)

8.54 During the Rose Bowl, the length (in seconds) of 12 randomly chosen commercial breaks during timeouts (following touchdown, turnover, field goal, or punt) were

65	75	85	95	80	100	90	80	85	85	60	65

(a) Assuming a normal population, construct a 90 percent confidence interval for the mean length of a commercial break during the Rose Bowl. (b) What are the limitations on your estimate? How could they be overcome?   **TimeOuts**

8.55 A sample of 40 CDs from a student's collection showed a mean length of 52.74 minutes with a standard deviation of 13.21 minutes. (a) Construct a 95 percent confidence interval for the mean. (b) Why might the normality assumption be an issue here? (c) What sample size would be needed for 95 percent confidence and an error of ± 3 minutes? (Data are from a project by statistics students Michael Evatz, Nancy Petack, and Jennifer Skladanowski.)

8.56 The Environmental Protection Agency (EPA) requires that cities monitor over 80 contaminants in their drinking water. Samples from the Lake Huron Water Treatment Plant gave the results shown here. Only the range is reported, not the mean (presumably the mean would be the midrange). (a) For each substance, estimate the *standard deviation* σ by using the methods shown in Table 8.11 in section 8.7. (b) Why might an estimate of σ be helpful in planning future water sample testing?

Substance	MCLG Range Detected	Allowable MCLG	Origin of Substance
Chromium	0.47 to 0.69	100	Discharge for steel and pulp mills, natural erosion
Selenium	0 to 0.0014	50	Corrosion of household plumbing, leaching from wood preservatives, natural erosion
Barium	0.004 to 0.019	2	Discharge from drilling wastes, metal refineries, natural erosion
Fluoride	1.07 to 1.17	4.0	Natural erosion, water additive, discharge from fertilizer and aluminum factories

MCLG = Maximum contaminant level goal

8.57 In a sample of 100 Planter's Mixed Nuts, 19 were found to be almonds. (a) Construct a 90 percent confidence interval for the true proportion of almonds. (b) May normality be assumed? Explain. (c) What sample size would be needed for 90 percent confidence and an error of ± 0.03? (d) Why would a quality control manager at Planter's need to understand sampling?

8.58 Fourteen of 180 publicly traded business services companies failed a test for compliance with Sarbanes-Oxley requirements for financial records and fraud protection. (a) Assuming that these are a random sample of all publicly traded companies, construct a 95 percent confidence interval for the overall noncompliance proportion. (b) Why might this statistic not apply to all sectors of publicly traded companies (e.g., aerospace and defense)? See *The New York Times,* April 27, 2005, p. BU5.

8.59 In a California study, 69 of 612 fourth-graders had blood cholesterol above 200 mg/dl, a level that is dangerously high for children. (a) Construct a 90 percent confidence interval for the true proportion with dangerously high blood cholesterol. (b) May normality be assumed? (c) What sample size is required for an error of ± 0.02 with 90 percent confidence? (e) This study was done 15 years ago. Would you expect the results today to be different? Explain. (Data are from *Psychology Today,* September 1989, p. 28.)

8.60 A certain brand of dry noodles contains a mixture of beet, spinach, carrot, and plain. A random sample of 200 dry noodles contained 47 beet noodles. (a) Construct a 95 percent confidence interval for the true proportion of beet noodles. (b) Check the normality assumption. Show your work. (c) Does the *Very Quick Rule* work well here? Explain. (d) What sample size would be needed to obtain an error of ± 0.04 with 90 percent confidence? (e) How might a manufacturer design a quality control program to monitor the proportions of each type of noodles so as to produce a consistent mix?

8.61 NBC asked a sample of VCR owners to record "Late Night with David Letterman" on their VCRs. Of the 125 VCR owners surveyed, 83 either "gave up or screwed up" because they did not understand how to program the VCR. (a) Construct a 90 percent confidence interval for the true proportion of VCR owners who cannot program their VCRs. (b) Would viewers of this program be typical of all television viewers? Explain. (Data are from *Popular Science* 237, no. 5, p. 63.)

8.62 In 1992, the FAA conducted 86,991 pre-employment drug tests on job applicants who were to be engaged in safety and security-related jobs, and found that 1,143 were positive. (a) Construct a 95 percent confidence interval for the population proportion of positive drug tests. (b) Why is the normality assumption not a problem, despite the very small value of p? (Data are from *Flying* 120, no. 11 [November 1993], p. 31.)

8.63 The State of Michigan tested 766 water samples from private wells in Lapeer County, Michigan, and found that 112 exceeded the EPA guidelines of 50 ppb. (a) Find the standard error of the estimated proportion. (b) Find the 95 percent confidence interval width for the true proportion. (c) Is normality an issue here? Explain. (d) Try the *Very Quick Rule*. Does it work well here? Explain. (Data are from *Detroit Free Press,* November 27, 1997, p. 8A.)

8.64 Biting an unpopped kernel of popcorn hurts! As an experiment, a self-confessed connoisseur of cheap popcorn carefully counted 773 kernels and put them in a popper. After popping, the unpopped kernels were counted. There were 86. (a) Construct a 90 percent confidence interval for the proportion of all kernels that would not pop. (b) Check the normality assumption. (c) Try the *Very Quick Rule*. Does it work well here? Why, or why not? (d) Why might this sample not be typical?

8.65 A careful count of 13,789 carcasses of bugs killed by "mosquito zappers" used in homes near water showed that only 18 were mosquitoes. (a) Construct a 90 percent confidence interval for the proportion of all zapped bugs that are mosquitoes. (b) Is a confidence interval really helpful in deciding whether the devices fulfill their purpose? Explain. (Data are from *Scientific American* 276, no. 4 [June 1997].)

8.66 The U.S. Customs Service conducted a random check of Miami longshoremen and found that 36 of 50 had arrest records. (a) Construct a 90 percent confidence interval for the true proportion. (b) Is the sample size large enough to be convincing? Explain. (c) How would *you* select a random sample of longshoremen? (See *U.S. News & World Report* 123, no. 22 [December 8, 1997].)

*8.67 Of 123 raisins taken from a box, 6 were found to have stems attached. Use MINITAB to obtain a 95 percent confidence interval for the population proportion with attached stems, both assuming normality and without assuming normality. Does it make a difference?

*8.68 Of 15 F/A-18E Super Hornet fighter engines inspected, 3 had cracked turbine blades. Use MINITAB to obtain a 95 percent confidence interval for the population proportion with cracked turbine blades, both assuming normality and without assuming normality. Is normality justified? (See *Aviation Week & Space Technology* 149, no. 24 [December 14, 1998], p. 18.)

*8.69 Acoustomagnetic surveillance antitheft portals (the kind used to prevent shoplifting) temporarily affected the pacemakers in 48 out of 50 subjects tested. (a) Construct a 90 percent confidence interval for the proportion of all subjects whose pacemakers would be affected. (b) What problems of interpretation arise? (c) Check the normality assumption. If not met, what could we do? (d) Use MINITAB to estimate a confidence interval without assuming normality. (Data are from *Science News* 154, no. 19, p. 294.)

8.70 (a) A poll of 2,277 voters throughout Britain on the proposed EU constitution would have approximately what margin of error? (b) The poll showed that 44 percent opposed Britain's signing the proposed constitution. Construct a 90 percent confidence interval for the true proportion opposed to signing it. (c) Would you say that the percentage of all voters opposed could be 50 percent? Explain. (Data are from *The Economist* 268, no. 8331 [July 5, 2003], p. 30.)

8.71 To determine the percentage of taxpayers who prefer filing tax returns electronically, a survey of 600 taxpayers was conducted by EPIC/ERA, a marketing research firm in Lansing, Michigan. What is the margin of error of this survey? What assumptions are required to find the margin of error?

8.72 A sample of 40 CDs from a student's collection showed a mean length of 52.74 minutes with a standard deviation of 13.21 minutes. Construct a 95 percent confidence interval for the population standard deviation. (Data are from a project by statistics students Michael Evatz, Nancy Petack, and Jennifer Skladanowski.)

TWO-SAMPLE COMPARISONS

*8.73 One group of accounting students used simulation programs, while another group received a tutorial. Scores on an exam were compared. (a) Construct a 90 percent confidence interval for the true difference in mean scores, explaining any assumptions that are necessary. (b) Do you think the learning methods have significantly different results? Explain.

Statistic	Simulation	Tutorial
Mean score	$\bar{x}_1 = 9.1$	$\bar{x}_2 = 10.3$
Sample std. dev.	$s_1 = 2.4$	$s_2 = 2.5$
Number of students	$n_1 = 20$	$n_2 = 20$

*8.74 One day in December, 16 babies were born in Colorado Springs. Eleven baby boys had a mean birth weight of 7.381 pounds with a standard deviation of 0.931 pounds, while five baby girls had a mean weight of 6.225 pounds with a standard deviation of 1.236 pounds. (a) Construct a 90 percent confidence interval for the difference in mean weight. (b) Discuss any assumptions that are necessary. Show all work clearly. (Data are from *Colorado Springs Gazette-Telegraph,* December 25, 1981, p. 3B.)

*8.75 In one group of 132 youths, 5 suffered head injuries. In a second group of 138 youths, 12 suffered head injuries. Construct a 95 percent confidence interval for the difference in proportions. Do you conclude that the incidence of head injuries is the same? (Data are from H. L. Needleman, et al., "The Long-Term Effects of Exposure to Low Doses of Lead in Childhood," *The New England Journal of Medicine* 322, no. 2 [January 11, 1990], pp. 83–88.)

*8.76 During a post-MI (myocardial infarction) monitoring program it was found that among the 375 married men there were 25 cardiac deaths within a 1-year period, compared with 9 cardiac deaths among the 78 unmarried men in the sample. Construct a 95 percent confidence interval for the difference in proportions. What is your conclusion? Explain carefully. (Data are from Nancy Frasure-Smith and Raymond Prince, "Long-term Follow-up of the Ischemic Heart Disease Life Stress Monitoring Program," *Psychosomatic Medicine* 51, 1989, pp. 485–513.)

EXPERIMENTS

8.77 For 10 tanks of gas for your car, calculate the miles per gallon. (a) Construct a 95 percent confidence interval for the true mean mpg for your car. (b) Discuss the normality assumption. (c) How many tanks of gas would you need to obtain an error of ± 0.2 mpg with 95 percent confidence?

8.78 (a) Take a random sample of 50 members of the U.S. House of Representatives. Explain your sampling methodology. (b) Count the number whose surname begins with "S." (c) Construct a 95 percent confidence interval for the true proportion of U.S. representatives whose surname begins with "S." (d) Is normality assured?

8.79 (a) Look at 50 vehicles in a parking lot near you. Count the number that are SUVs (state your definition of SUV). Use any sampling method you like (e.g., the first 50 you see). (b) Construct a 95 percent confidence interval for the true population proportion of SUVs. (c) What sample size would be needed to ensure an error of ± 0.025 with 98 percent confidence? (d) Would the proportion be the same if this experiment were repeated in a university parking lot?

8.80 (a) From a sports almanac or Web site, take a random sample of 50 NBA players and calculate the proportion who are at least 7 feet in height. (b) Make a 90 percent confidence interval for the population proportion of all NBA players who are at least 7 feet tall.

8.81   (a) Look at 50 vehicles from a college or university student parking lot. Count the number of two-door vehicles. Use any sampling method you like (e.g., the first 50 you see). (b) Do the same for a grocery store that is not very close to the college or university. (c) Construct a 95 percent confidence interval for the difference in population proportions. Is there a significant difference? Discuss.

Related Reading

Albert, James H. "College Students' Conceptions of Probability." *The American Statistician* 57, no. 1 (February 2001), pp. 37–45.

Boos, Dennis D.; and Jacqueline M. Hughes-Oliver. "How Large Does *n* Have to be for *z* and *t* Intervals?" *The American Statistician* 54, no. 2 (May 2000), pp. 121–28.

Browne, Richard H. "Using the Sample Range as a Basis for Calculating Sample Size in Power Calculations." *The American Statistician* 55, no. 4 (November 2001), pp. 293–98.

Efron, Bradley. "The Bootstrap and Modern Statistics." *Journal of the American Statistical Association* 95, no. 452 (December 2000), pp. 1293–1300.

Efron, Bradley; and Rob Tibshirani. *An Introduction to the Bootstrap.* CRC Press, 1994.

Kupper, Lawrence L.; and Kerry B. Hafner. "How Appropriate Are Popular Sample Size Formulas?" *The American Statistician* 43, no. 2 (May 1989), pp. 101–105.

Lenth, Russell V. "Some Practical Guidelines for Effective Sample Size Determination." *The American Statistician* 55, no. 3 (August 2001), pp. 187–93.

Parker, Robert A. "Sample Size: More Than Calculations." *The American Statistician* 57, no. 3 (August 2003), pp. 166–70.

van Belle, Gerald. *Statistical Rules of Thumb.* Wiley, 2002.

LearningStats Unit 08   Estimation

LS

LearningStats Unit 08 illustrates the idea of sample variation, the Central Limit Theorem, and confidence intervals. Your instructor may assign specific units, or you may decide to check them out because the topic sounds interesting.

Topic	*LearningStats Modules*
Overview	Survey Guidelines Sampling Methods Confidence Intervals Sample Size
Central Limit Theorem	CLT Demonstration
Sampling distributions	Sampling Distributions Critical Values (z, t, χ^2)
Confidence intervals	Confidence Interval: Means Confidence Interval: Proportions Confidence Interval: Variances Confidence Interval: Simulation Confidence Interval: Bootstrap
Sample size	Sample Size Calculator
Student projects	Coffee Drinking Habits Office Chairs with Wheels
Applications and case studies	Sample Variation Finite Populations Bootstrap Explained
Tables	Appendix C—Normal Appendix D—Student's t Appendix E—Chi-Square
Equations	Equations: Confidence Intervals Equations: PDFs

Key: = PowerPoint   = Word   = Excel

Visual Statistics

Visual Statistics Modules on Estimation

Module	Module Name
6	Visualizing Random Samples
7	Visualizing the Central Limit Theorem
8	Visualizing Properties of Estimators
9	Visualizing One-Sample Hypothesis Tests

Visual Statistics Modules 6, 7, 8, and 9 (included on your CD) are designed to help you

- Understand variability in samples.
- Learn to infer a population's shape from samples.
- Recognize outliers and their effects.
- Distinguish between the population sampled and the sampling distribution of the mean.
- Understand how sample size affects the standard error.
- Understand unbiasedness, efficiency, and consistency.
- Learn what a confidence interval represents.

The worktext (included on the CD in .PDF format) contains lists of concepts covered, objectives of the modules, overviews of concepts, illustrations of concepts, orientations to module features, learning exercises (basic, intermediate, advanced), learning projects (individual, team), self-evaluation quizzes, glossaries of terms, and solutions to self-evaluation quizzes.

One-Sample Hypothesis Tests

Chapter Learning Objectives

When you finish this chapter you should be able to

- Formulate a null and alternative hypothesis for a mean or proportion.
- Define Type I error, Type II error, and power.
- List the steps in testing hypotheses.
- Do a hypothesis test for a proportion.
- Find the p-value for a test statistic using z.
- Do a hypothesis test for a mean with known or unknown σ.
- Explain similarities and differences between Student's t and z.
- Find critical values of z or t in tables or by using Excel.
- Find the p-value for a test statistic using t.
- Interpret a power curve or OC curve.
- Do a hypothesis test for a variance (optional).

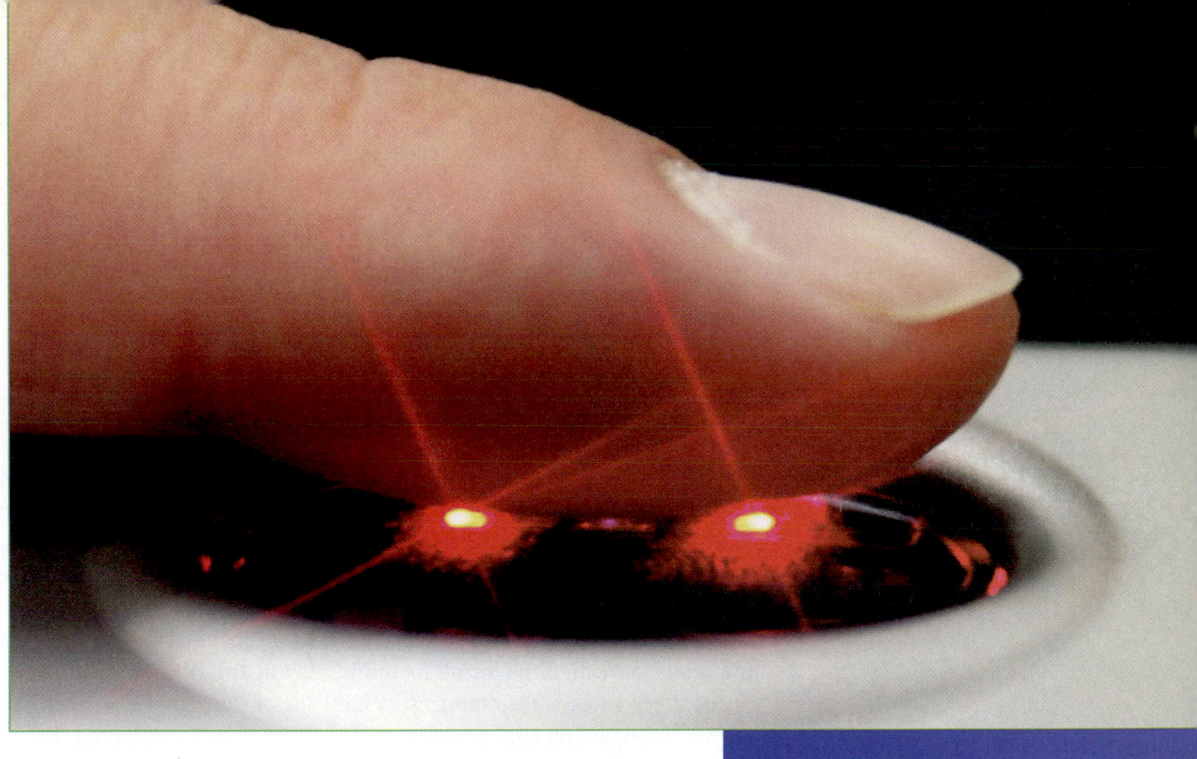

Every day in business, whether the business is small or large, profit or nonprofit, managers are faced with decisions. Should a school district hire a full-time staff member to perform background checks on substitute teachers or should that task be outsourced? Does a large car dealership need to provide better training for its maintenance department employees? Should a local ice cream shop raise the price on single-scoop ice cream cones?

Today's managers also have to constantly show improvement in their business processes. Has a ski resort decreased its response time to accidents since last year? Does a new manufacturing process produce items with fewer defects? Did customer satisfaction increase after the automated phone system was installed?

Savvy businesspeople use many of the statistical tools that you've already learned to answer these types of questions. We will build on these tools in this chapter and learn about one of the most widely used statistical tools—*hypothesis testing.* Hypothesis testing is used in both science and business to test assumptions and theories and ultimately guide managers when facing decisions. First we will learn how science has developed the process of hypothesis testing and then how business has adapted this procedure for decision making.

Process of Science

Scientific inquiry requires that theories be tested rigorously and under various conditions. A theory that survives tests that could have led to its rejection is a strong theory. Sometimes scientific progress consists of identifying the conditions under which a theory holds or fails. The theory's testable implications are *hypotheses.* Received knowledge is the collection of hypotheses that have not been rejected even though rigorous efforts have been made to do so. Hypothesis testing often begins with a hunch and leads to an iterative loop of testing which continues until the theory is either rejected or satisfactorily reformulated.

Steps in Hypothesis Testing

- Step 1   Get an idea or hunch
- Step 2   Formulate testable hypotheses

- Step 3   Design the experiment
- Step 4   Set up a decision rule
- Step 5   Collect some data
- Step 6   Make a decision
- Step 7   Revise your ideas (back to step 2).

Who Tests Hypotheses?

Anyone who does research in science, engineering, social science, education, or medicine needs strong training in hypothesis testing. Further, all managers need at least a basic understanding of hypothesis testing. Although managerial responsibilities are not strictly speaking "research," managers often interact with specialists and deal with technical reports. Managers in accounting, finance, and human resources must know enough not to be intimidated. Those involved in marketing, operations analysis, or quality management need somewhat stronger skills.

Why? Because the innovative vigor of our economy is largely based on technology: new materials, new manufacturing methods, new distribution systems, new information strategies. A manager must understand especially the meaning of concepts such as *significance* and *power,* because financial or strategic decisions often are required. For example, if a redesigned process could improve a truck engine's mpg rating *significantly,* but requires spending $250 million, is it worth doing? Such a decision requires clear understanding not only of **significance,** but also of the **importance** of the potential improvement: the magnitude of the effect, and its implications for product durability, customer satisfaction, budgets, cash flow, and staffing. Sound business decisions cannot be made without understanding the basic ideas of hypothesis tests.

Good News

You are already halfway there, if you understand the previous chapter. A confidence interval often gives enough information to assist decision-making. Knowing the 95 percent range of likely values for a key decision parameter (e.g., the proportion of repeat customers under age 30) may be all you need. This chapter extends the idea of confidence intervals by showing how to test a sample against a benchmark, and how to assess the risk of incorrect decisions. The next chapter discusses two-sample comparisons.

Hypothesis Formulation

We formulate a pair of mutually exclusive, collectively exhaustive statements about the world. One statement or the other must be true, but they cannot both be true.

H_0: Null Hypothesis

H_1: Alternative Hypothesis

The two statements are *hypotheses* because the truth is unknown. Efforts will be made to reject the **null hypothesis** (sometimes called the *maintained hypothesis*). If H_0 happens to be a favorite theory, we might not really wish to reject it, but we try anyway. If we reject H_0, we tentatively conclude that the **alternative hypothesis** H_1 is the case. Whereas H_0 represents the *status quo* (e.g., the current state of affairs) H_1 is sometimes called the *action alternative* because action may be required if we reject H_0 in favor of H_1.

Can Hypotheses Be Proved?

No, we cannot prove a null hypothesis—we can only *fail to reject* it. A null hypothesis that survives repeated tests without rejection is "true" only in the limited sense that it has been thoroughly scrutinized. Today's "true" hypothesis could be falsified tomorrow. If we fail to reject H_0, we provisionally accept H_0. However, an "accepted" hypothesis may be retested. That is how scientific inquiry works. Einstein's theories, for example, are over 100 years old but are still being subjected to rigorous tests. Yet few scientists really think that Einstein's theories are "wrong." It's in the nature of science to keep trying to refute accepted theories, especially when a new test is possible or when new data become available. Similarly, the safety of commonly used prescription drugs is continually being studied. Sometimes, "safe" drugs are revealed to have serious side effects only after large-scale, long-term use by consumers (e.g., the Vioxx arthritis drug that was shown to be safe in clinical trials, but later showed a dangerous association with heart attack after years of use by millions of people).

Role of Evidence

A hypothesis is tested by contrasting its implications against empirical evidence. The null hypothesis is *assumed true* and a contradiction is sought. To make an analogy, a defendant in a criminal trial is assumed innocent. The prosecutor collects and presents evidence according to the rules of law in an attempt to convince the jury to reject the hypothesis of the defendant's innocence. If the evidence sufficiently contradicts the hypothesis of innocence, the jury will vote to convict. Similarly, statisticians collect and assess sample evidence according to the rules of statistics. More complete evidence (a larger sample) will make a correct decision more likely. However, the time and effort a prosecutor (or statistician) can devote to collecting sample evidence is finite. At some point, a decision must be made based on whatever data are available.

Types of Error

The true situation determines whether our decision was correct, as shown in Table 9.1. If the decision about the null hypothesis matches the true situation, there is no error. Rejecting the null hypothesis when it is true is **Type I error,** with probability α. Failure to reject the null hypothesis when it is false is **Type II error,** with probability β. Since the true situation is usually unknown, statisticians do not know whether they have committed an error. For jurors as well as for statisticians, there is no way to prevent error, although the probability of either type of error can be reduced by gathering more evidence.

Decision	If H_0 is True	If H_0 is False
Reject H_0	Type I error (α risk)	Correct decision
Fail to reject H_0	Correct decision	Type II error (β risk)

TABLE 9.1

Type I and Type II Error

The consequences of these two errors are quite different, and the costs are borne by different parties. Depending on the situation, decision-makers may fear one error more than the other. It would be nice if both types of error could be avoided. Unfortunately, when making a decision based on a fixed body of sample evidence, reducing the risk of one type of error necessarily increases the risk of the other. Consider a few examples. In each case H_0 is the status quo, the normal, expected state of affairs.

Criminal Trial   In a criminal trial, the hypotheses are

H_0: Defendant is innocent

H_1: Defendant is guilty

Type I error is convicting an innocent defendant, so the cost is borne by the defendant. Type II error is failing to convict a guilty defendant, so the cost is borne by society if the guilty person returns to the streets. Concern for the rights of the accused and stricter rules of evidence during the 1960s and 70s led American courts to try to reduce the risk of Type I error, which probably increased the risk of Type II error. But during the 1980s and 90s, amid growing concern over the social costs of crime and victims' rights, courts began closing loopholes to reduce Type II error, presumably at the expense of Type I error. Both risks can be reduced only by devoting more effort to gathering evidence and strengthening the legal process (expediting trials, improving jury quality, increasing investigative work).

Drug Testing   When an Olympic athlete is tested for performance-enhancing drugs like steroids, the presumption is that the athlete is in compliance with the rules. Samples of urine or blood are taken as evidence. The hypotheses are

H_0: No illegal steroid use

H_1: Illegal steroid use

Type I error is unfairly disqualifying an athlete who is "clean." Type II error is letting the drug user get away with it and have an unfair competitive advantage. The cost of Type I error is hard feelings and unnecessary embarrassment. The cost of Type II error is tarnishing the Olympic image and rewarding those who break the rules. Over time, improved tests have reduced the risk of both types of error. However, for a given technology, the threshold can be set lower or higher, balancing Type I and Type II error. Which error is more to be feared?

Biometric Security   This rapidly growing application of hypothesis testing seeks ways to identify authorized and unauthorized persons for computer access, ATM withdrawals, entry into secure facilities, and so on, using the person's physical characteristics (e.g., fingerprints, facial structure, iris patterns). The intent is to get rid of paper and plastic IDs, which can be forged. The hypotheses are

H_0: User is authorized

H_1: User is unauthorized

Type I error means denying a legitimate user access to a facility or funds. Type II error is letting an unauthorized user have access to facilities or money. Technology has progressed to the point where Type II errors have become very rare, though Type I errors remain a problem. The error rates depend on how much is spent on the equipment and software.

Statistical Hypothesis Testing

A *statistical hypothesis* is a statement about the value of a population parameter that we are interested in (call it θ). For example, the parameter θ could be a mean, a proportion, or a variance. A *hypothesis test* is a decision between two competing, mutually exclusive, and collectively exhaustive hypotheses about the value of θ:

Left-Sided Test	*Two-Sided Test*	*Right-Sided Test*
$H_0: \theta \geq \theta_0$	$H_0: \theta = \theta_0$	$H_0: \theta \leq \theta_0$
$H_1: \theta < \theta_0$	$H_1: \theta \neq \theta_0$	$H_1: \theta > \theta_0$

The *direction of the test* is indicated by H_1:

> indicates a ***right-tailed test***

< indicates a ***left-tailed test***

$\neq$ indicates a ***two-tailed test***

Some particular value θ_0 is the center of interest. If the true value of θ is θ_0, then a sample estimate should not differ greatly from θ_0. We rely on our knowledge of the *sampling distribution* and the *standard error of the estimate* to decide if the sample estimate is far enough away from θ_0 to contradict the assumption that $\theta = \theta_0$, as illustrated in Figure 9.1.

FIGURE 9.1

Outcomes in a sampling distribution

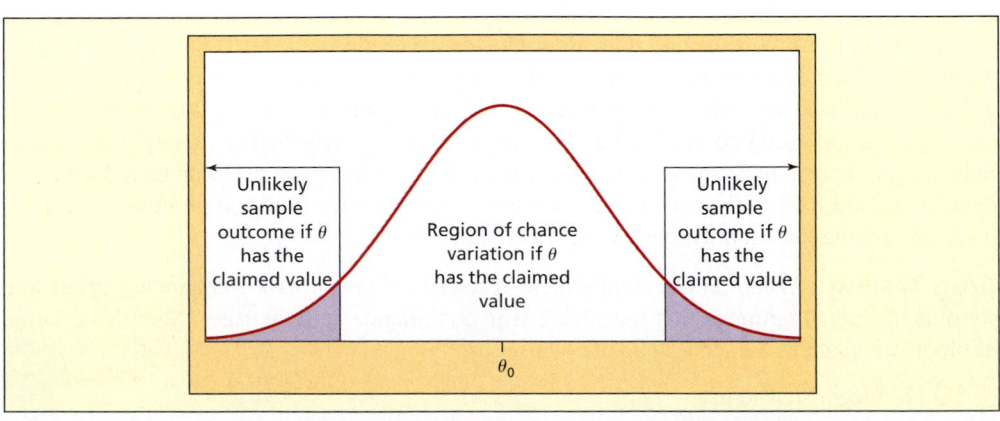

Infections that are acquired while a patient is in a hospital are called *nosocomial infections*. In one recent year, it is estimated that nosocomial infections in the United States cost $4.5 billion and contributed to more than 88,000 deaths. While some deaths are preventable in principle, others are inevitable due to practical and cost constraints faced by hospitals. The Centers for Disease Control's National Nosocomial Infections Surveillance system receives monthly reports of nosocomial infections from a nonrandom sampling of more than 270 hospitals in the United States. Based on recent experience, the current level of nosocomial infection is 9.8 per 1,000 patient days, or .0098. This is a *proportion* (ratio of number of infections to number of patient days). Every time a monthly sample is received, we test a hypothesis about the proportion of nosocomial infections. Has the rate risen? Fallen? Stayed the same? The possible pairs of hypotheses are

Left-Sided Test	Two-Sided Test	Right-Sided Test
$H_0: \pi \geq .0098$	$H_0: \pi = .0098$	$H_0: \pi \leq .0098$
$H_1: \pi < .0098$	$H_1: \pi \neq .0098$	$H_1: \pi > .0098$

If we suspect that the rate has fallen ($\pi < .0098$), we might choose a *left-sided test*. If we are only concerned whether the rate has changed ($\pi \neq .0098$), a *two-sided test* would be appropriate (i.e., if we do not care about the direction of change). If we are worried that the rate has risen ($\pi > .0098$), we might choose a *right-sided test*. If H_0 is rejected, action may be required. For example, a statistically significant *rise* in the rate might trigger tightened enforcement of rules or new procedures for controlling infections. The decision depends on the sample size, the severity of the departure from H_0, the test type, and our tolerance for making the wrong decision.

The width of a sheet of standard size copier paper should be $\mu = 216$ mm (i.e., 8.5 inches). There is some variation in paper width due to the nature of the production process, so the width of a sheet of paper is a random variable. However, per strict industry standards only 34 nonconforming sheets per million would be allowable. For this reason, samples are taken from the production process, the width is measured with extreme accuracy, and the mean is calculated. Each time a sample is taken, we use its mean to test a hypothesis. Has the mean decreased? Increased? Stayed the same? The possible pairs of hypotheses are

Left-Sided Test	Two-Sided Test	Right-Sided Test
$H_0: \mu \geq 216$	$H_0: \mu = 216$	$H_0: \mu \leq 216$
$H_1: \mu < 216$	$H_1: \mu \neq 216$	$H_1: \mu > 216$

If the paper is too narrow ($\mu < 216$ mm), the pages might not be well-centered in the feeder. If this is our main concern, we might choose a *left-sided test*. If the pages are too wide ($\mu > 216$ mm), sheets could jam in the feeder or paper trays. If this is our main concern, we might choose a *right-sided test*. Since either violation poses a quality problem ($\mu \neq 216$ mm) we would probably choose a two-sided test. If the null hypothesis is rejected, the manufacturing process should be corrected, that is, action is required. Our decision depends on the severity of the departure from H_0, the test type, and our tolerance for making the wrong decision.

One-Sided Tests

In a left-sided or right-sided test, the inequality in H_0 comprises an *infinite* number of hypotheses. But we can only test *one* value of the hypothesized parameter at a time. To handle this problem, we test the null hypothesis H_0 *only* at the point of equality $H_0: \theta = \theta_0$. That is, we temporarily ignore the infinite possibilities in H_0. If we reject $\theta = \theta_0$ in favor of the alternative, then we implicitly reject the *entire class* of H_0 possibilities. For example, suppose we want a right-sided test for the paper size problem (i.e., we are checking only for oversized paper). We take a sample of 100 sheets and measure them carefully. If the sample mean is far enough above 216 mm to cause us to reject the null hypothesis H_0: $\mu = 216$ mm in favor of the alternative hypothesis H_1: $\mu > 216$ mm, the same sample would also permit rejection of any value of μ *less than* $\mu = 216$ mm. If we reject $\mu = 216$ mm, we actually can reject $\mu \leq 216$ mm.

When to Use a One-Sided Test

In quality control, any deviation from specifications indicates that something may be wrong with the process, so a two-sided test is common. In a two-sided test, direction is of no interest to the decision-maker. Or maybe the researcher simply has no *a priori* reason to expect rejection in one direction. In such cases, it is reasonable to use a two-sided test. As you'll soon see, rejection in a two-sided test guarantees rejection in a one-sided test, other things being equal.

However, when the consequences of rejecting H_0 are asymmetric, or where one tail is of special importance to the researcher, we might prefer a one-sided test. For example, suppose that a machine is supposed to bore holes with a 3.5-mm diameter in a piece of sheet metal. Although any deviation from 3.5 mm is a violation of the specification, the consequences of rejecting H_0 may be different. Suppose an attachment pin is to be inserted into the hole. If the hole is too small, the pin cannot be inserted, but the metal piece could probably be reworked to enlarge the hole so the pin does fit. On the other hand, if the hole is too large, the pin will fit too loosely and may fall out. The piece may have to be discarded since an oversized hole cannot be made smaller. This is illustrated in Figure 9.2.

FIGURE 9.2

Asymmetric effects of nonconformance

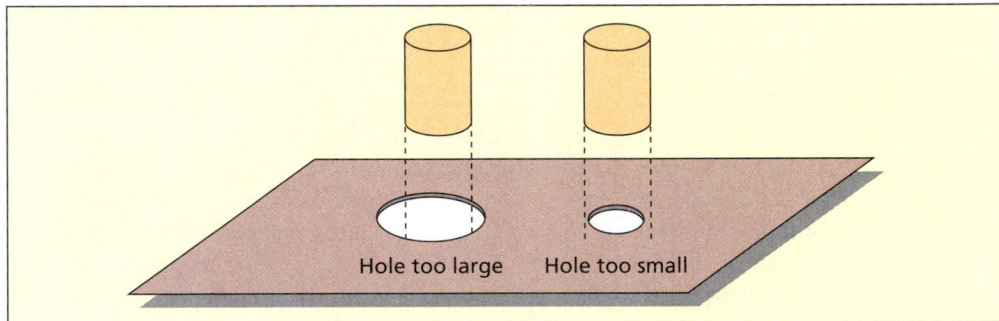

Hole too large   Hole too small

Decision Rule

To test for departure from a specified value of an unknown population parameter, we rely on a *test statistic* showing how far the sample estimate is from its expected value, in terms of its own standard error. The *decision rule* uses the known sampling distribution of the test statistic to establish a threshold called the *critical value.* The critical value divides the sampling distribution into two regions. If the test statistic lies in the *rejection region,* we will reject H_0. Otherwise, we will not reject H_0. For example, we might reject H_0 if the sample mean is more than 1.96 standard errors away from the hypothesized mean.

Since rejection occurs in the *tails* of the sampling distribution, these are usually called *left-tailed, right-tailed,* or *two-tailed* tests. The three decision rules defined in Table 9.2 are illustrated in Figures 9.3 through 9.5. Although these illustrations show bell-shaped distributions, you saw in the last chapter that some sample estimators do not follow a z or t distribution. For example, later in this chapter, you will revisit the chi-square distribution, which is skewed. However, the basic idea is the same.

Type I Error

The probability of Type I error is denoted α and is commonly called the *level of significance.* It is the risk that we will wrongly reject a true H_0:

(9.1)
$$\alpha = P(\text{reject } H_0 \mid H_0 \text{ is true})$$

Test Type	Decision Rule
Two-tailed	Reject H_0 if the test statistic < left-tail critical value or if the test statistic > right-tail critical value
Left-tailed	Reject H_0 if the test statistic < left-tail critical value
Right-tailed	Reject H_0 if the test statistic > right-tail critical value

TABLE 9.2

Three Types of Decision Rules

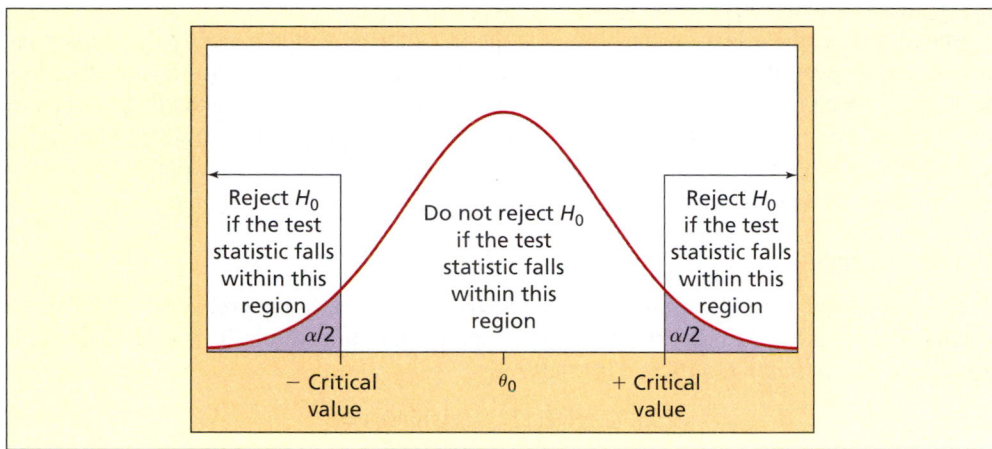

FIGURE 9.3

Two-tailed test

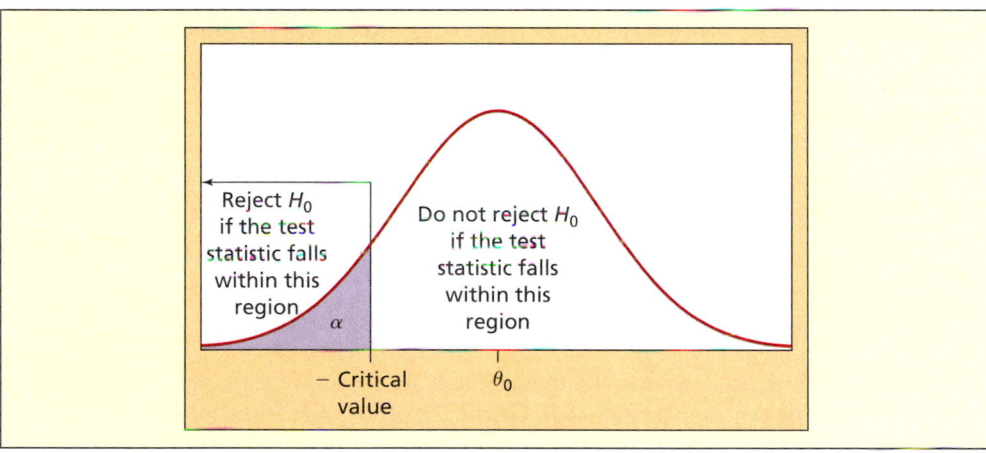

FIGURE 9.4

Left-tailed test

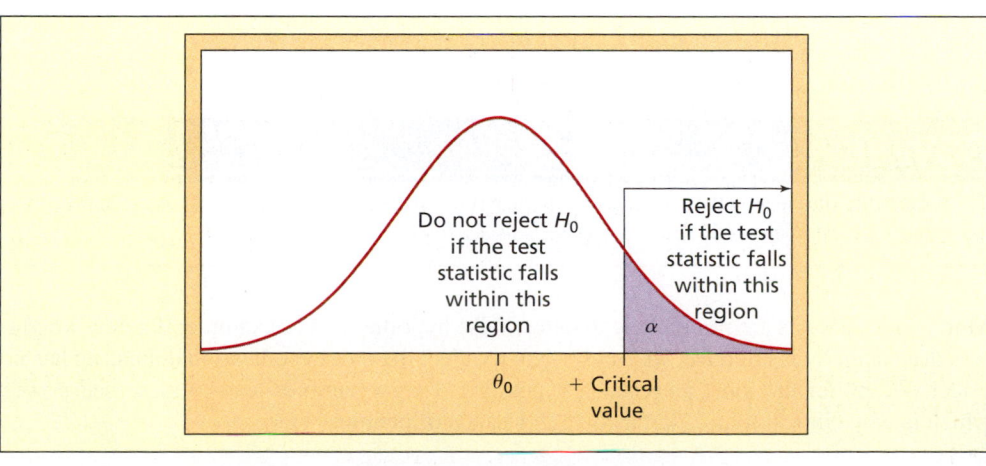

FIGURE 9.5

Right-tailed test

Type I Error

The probability of rejecting the null hypothesis when it is true is denoted α and is called the *level of significance*. A Type I error is sometimes called a *false positive*.

If we choose a decision rule using $\alpha = .05$, we would expect to commit a Type I error about 5 times in 100. We would like α to be small, other things being equal. Common choices for α are .10, .05, .025, .01, and .005. The level of significance is usually expressed as a percent, that is, 10, 5, 2.5, 1, and 0.5 percent.

Stated differently, α is the probability that the test statistic would happen to fall in the rejection region even though H_0 is true. Since we don't want to reject a true hypothesis, this would be a Type I error. This α risk is the area under the tail(s) of the sampling distribution. In a two-sided test, the α risk is split with $\alpha/2$ in each tail, since there are two ways to reject H_0 (if the test statistic is too far above or below the expected value). Thus, in a two-sided test using $\alpha = .10$ we would put half the risk ($\alpha/2 = .05$) in each tail, as shown in Figure 9.3.

Type II Error

The probability of Type II error, sometimes referred to as β risk, is the probability that the test statistic falls in the acceptance region, even though the null hypothesis H_0 is actually false. It is the risk that we will wrongly accept a false H_0:

(9.2) $$P(\text{fail to reject } H_0 \mid H_0 \text{ is false}) = \beta$$

Type II Error

The probability of accepting the null hypothesis when it is false is denoted β. A Type II error is sometimes called a *false negative*.

Unlike α, we cannot choose β in advance. The reason is that β depends on several things, including our choice for α and the size of the sample. Other things being equal, we would like β to be small. However, for a given sample, there is a trade-off between α and β. We will discuss this trade-off in more detail shortly.

Power of a Test

If the null hypothesis is false, we ought to reject it. If we do so, we have done the right thing, and there is no Type II error. The ***power*** of a test is the probability that a false hypothesis will be rejected. More power is good, because power is the probability of doing the right thing. Power is the complement of beta risk ($1 - \beta$). If we have low β risk, we have high power:

(9.3) $$\text{Power} = P(\text{reject } H_0 \mid H_0 \text{ is false}) = 1 - \beta$$

Power

The probability of rejecting the null hypothesis when it is false is $1 - \beta$ and is called *power*. In medicine, the power of a test to correctly detect a disease is its *sensitivity*.

More powerful tests are more likely to detect false hypotheses. For example, if a new weight-loss drug actually is effective, we would want to reject the null hypothesis that the drug has no effect. We prefer the most powerful test possible. Larger samples lead to increased power, which is why clinical trials often involve thousands of people.

Relationship Between α and β

We desire tests that avoid false negatives (small β risk) yet we also want to avoid false positives (small α risk). Given two acceptable tests, we will choose the more powerful one. But for a given type of test and fixed sample size, there is a trade-off between α and β. The larger critical value needed to reduce α risk makes it harder to reject H_0, thereby increasing β risk. The proper balance between α and β can be elusive. Consider these examples:

- If your household carbon monoxide detector's sensitivity threshold is increased to reduce the risk of overlooking danger (reduced β), there will be more false alarms (increased α).

- A doctor who is conservative about admitting patients with symptoms of myocardial infarction to the ICU (reduced β) will admit more patients without myocardial infarction (increased α).

- Reducing the threshold for dangerously high blood pressure from 140/90 to 130/80 will reduce the chance of missing the diagnosis of hypertension (reduced β), but some patients may incorrectly be given medication that is not needed (increased α).

Both α and β risk can be reduced simultaneously only by increasing the sample size (gathering more evidence), which is not always feasible or cost-effective.

Consequences of Type II Error

Firms typically recall defective products as soon as flaws are discovered (e.g., Verizon's 2004 recall of 50,000 cell phone batteries after one exploded and another caused a car fire) or even *before* anything bad happens (e.g., Intel's 2004 recall of its 915 G/P and 925X chip sets from OEMs, before the chips actually reached any consumers). Failure to act swiftly can generate liability and adverse publicity as with the spate of Ford Explorer rollover accidents and eventual recall of certain 15-inch Firestone radial tires. Ford and Firestone believed they had found an engineering work-around to make the tire design safe, until accumulating accident data, lawsuits, and NHTSA pressure forced recognition that there was a problem. In 2004, certain COX_2 inhibitor drugs that had previously been thought effective and safe, based on extensive clinical trials, were found to be associated with increased risk of heart attack. The makers' stock price plunged (e.g., Merck). Lawyers, of course, have an incentive to claim product defects, even when the evidence is doubtful (e.g., Dow's silicone breast implants). The courts, therefore, often must use statistical evidence to adjudicate product liability claims.

Choice of α

By choosing a small α (say $\alpha = .01$) the decision-maker can make it harder to reject the null hypothesis. By choosing a larger α (say $\alpha = .05$) it is easier to reject the null hypothesis. This raises the possibility of manipulating the decision. For this reason, the choice of α should precede the calculation of the test statistic, thereby minimizing the temptation to select α so as to favor one conclusion over the other.

Statistical Significance versus Practical Importance

The standard error of most sample estimators approaches zero as sample size increases (if they are consistent estimators), so almost any difference between θ and θ_0, no matter how tiny, will be significant if the sample size is large enough. Researchers who deal with large samples must expect "significant" effects, even when an effect is too slight to have any *practical importance*. Is an improvement of 0.2 mpg in fuel economy *important* to Toyota buyers? Is a 0.5 percent loss of market share *important* to Hertz? Is a laptop battery life increase of 15 minutes *important* to Dell customers? Such questions depend not so much on statistics as on the cost/benefit calculation. Since resources are always scarce, a dollar spent on a quality improvement always has an opportunity cost (the foregone alternative). If we spend money to make a certain product improvement, then some other project may have to be shelved. Since we can't do everything, we must ask whether the proposed product improvement is the best use of our scarce resources. These are questions that must be answered by experts in medicine, marketing, product safety, or engineering, rather than by statisticians.

9.1   Sketch a diagram of the decision rule for each pair of hypotheses.
   a. H_0: $\mu \geq 80$ versus H_1: $\mu < 80$
   b. H_0: $\mu = 80$ versus H_1: $\mu \neq 80$
   c. H_0: $\mu \leq 80$ versus H_1: $\mu > 80$

9.2   In 1,000 samples, assuming that H_0 is true, how many times would you expect to commit Type I error if (a) $\alpha = .05$, (b) $\alpha = .01$, and (c) $\alpha = .001$.

9.3   Define Type I and Type II error for each scenario, and discuss the cost(s) of each type of error.
   a. A 25-year-old ER patient in Minneapolis complains of chest pain. Heart attacks in 25 year olds are rare, and beds are scarce in the hospital. The null hypothesis is that there is no heart attack (probably muscle pain due to shoveling snow).
   b. Approaching O'Hare for landing, a British Air flight from London has been in a holding pattern for 45 minutes due to bad weather. Landing is expected within 15 minutes. The flight crew could declare an emergency and land immediately, but an FAA investigation would be launched. The null hypothesis is that there is enough fuel to stay aloft for 15 more minutes.
   c. You are trying to finish a lengthy statistics report and print it for your evening class. Your color printer is very low on ink, and you just have time to get to Staples for a new cartridge. But it is snowing and you need every minute to finish the report. The null hypothesis is that you have enough ink.

9.4   Discuss the issues of *statistical significance* and *practical importance* in each scenario.
   a. A process for producing I-beams of oriented strand board used as main support beams in new houses has a mean breaking strength of 2,000 lbs./ft. A sample of boards from a new process has a mean breaking strength of 2,150 lbs./ft. The improvement is statistically significant, but the per-unit cost is higher.
   b. Under continuous use, the mean battery life in a certain cell phone is 45 hours. In tests of a new type of battery, the sample mean battery life is 46 hours. The improvement is statistically significant, but the new battery costs more to produce.
   c. For a wide-screen HDTV LCD unit, the mean half-life (i.e., to lose 50 percent of its brightness) is 32,000 hours. A new process is developed. In tests of the new display, the sample mean half-life is 35,000 hours. The improvement is statistically significant, though the new process is more costly.

9.5   A firm decides to test its employees for illegal drugs. (a) State the null and alternative hypotheses. (b) Define Type I and II error. (c) What are the consequences of each? Which is more to be feared, and by whom?

9.6   A hotel installs smoke detectors with adjustable sensitivity in all public guest rooms. (a) State the null and alternative hypotheses. (b) Define Type I and II error. What are the consequences of each? (c) Which is more to be feared, and by whom? (d) If the hotel decides to reduce β risk, what would be the consequences? Who would be affected?

Mini Case   9.1

Type I and Type II Error

We generally call a Type I error, rejecting a true H_0, a "false positive" or a "false rejection." A Type II error, failing to reject a false H_0, is often called a "false negative" or a "false acceptance." Technology is always changing, but this mini case shows some actual rates of Type I error and Type II error in real applications. In each application, ask: What is the cost of a false positive or a false negative? Who bears these costs? This way of thinking will help you decide whether Type I or Type II error is more to be feared, and why.

BIOMETRIC SECURITY

This is a hot area for business. If your ATM could recognize your physical characteristics (e.g., fingerprint, face, palm, iris) you wouldn't need an ATM card or a PIN. A reliable biometric ID system could also reduce the risk of ID theft, eliminate computer passwords, and speed airport security screening. The hypotheses are

   H_0: User is authorized

   H_1: User is not authorized

Fujitsu Laboratories has tested a palm ID system on 700 people, ranging from children to seniors. It achieved a false rejection rate of 1 percent and a false acceptance rate of 0.5 percent. Bank of Tokyo-Mitsubishi introduced palm-scanning at its ATM machines in 2004. DigitalPersona of Redwood City, California, has developed a fingerprint scanner (called *U.Are.U*) that is able to recognize fingerprints in 200 milliseconds with a 1 percent false rejection rate and a 0.002 percent false acceptance rate. In some high-end devices, false acceptance rates as low as 25 per million have been achieved. False rejection rates (Type I error) are higher, but merely cause user inconvenience. The low rates of false acceptance (Type II error) are encouraging, since they mean that others cannot easily impersonate you. Fingerprint scanning is the most popular because it is cheaper and easier to implement, though many experts believe that iris scanning has better long-run potential to reduce both error rates (especially important in airport security screening). Any such system requires a stored database of biometric data.

Sources: *BusinessWeek*, November 22, 2004, p. 127; *Scientific American* 290, no. 6 (June 2004), p. 108, and 289, no. 4 (April 2003), p. 74; and *PC Magazine*, April 22, 2003, p. 74.

MEDICAL TESTS

Cancer-screening tests have become routine. Unfortunately, they have fairly high rates of Type I error (unnecessary alarm, risk of biopsy) and Type II error (missed cancer). The hypotheses are

H_0: No cancer exists

H_1: Cancer exists

Consider these examples. Up to 25 percent of men with prostate cancer have normal PSA levels, while 50 percent of those with no cancer have elevated PSA levels and 70 percent of men with high PSA levels do not have cancer. Up to 33 percent of the PAP smears for ovarian cancer give false positives—a rate that may soon be reduced by applying computer pattern recognition to the 50 million tests done every year by human technicians. MRI scanning for breast cancer detects about 80 percent of invasive growths in women (power $= 1 - \beta$) compared with only 33 percent for standard mammography. In other medical testing, of the 250,000 people treated annually for appendicitis, from 15 percent to 40 percent have a healthy appendix removed, while about 20 percent of the time the appendicitis diagnosis is missed.

Sources: *Scientific American* 284, no. 12 (December 1998), p. 75; *Technology Review* 107, no. 6, p. 64; *Popular Science* 247, no. 6, p. 76; *The Wall Street Journal*, July 29, 2004; and *Science News* 153 (January 31, 1998), p. 78.

OTHER APPLICATIONS

Tests for "mad cow" disease have a 1 in 10,000 chance of a false positive. Most computer virus-detection software packages have very low rates of false positives (e.g., McAfee and Norton Antivirus had only 1 false positive in 3,700,000 files tested). But in spam detection, the results are not as good (e.g., in one test, ZoneAlarm misidentified less than 1 percent of legitimate e-mails as spam but failed to detect 4 percent of actual spam). Accuracy will improve over time in most of these applications.

Sources: www.npr.org, accessed July 3, 2004; *PC Magazine* 23, no. 10 (June 8, 2004), p. 116, and 24, no. 2 (February 8, 2005), p. 40.

9.2
TESTING A PROPORTION

As we've already learned, a hypothesis test tests claims about population parameters such as π, μ, and σ. We will first learn how to test a proportion π.

Proportions are used frequently in business situations because collecting proportion data is straightforward. For example, it is easier to ask a customer if he or she likes (or dislikes) this year's new automobile color than to quantify an individual customer's degree of satisfaction with the new color. Also, many business performance indicators such as market share, employee retention rates, and employee accident rates are expressed as proportions.

To conduct a hypothesis test we need to know the parameter being tested, the sample statistic used to estimate the parameter, and the sampling distribution of the sample statistic. The sampling distribution tells us which test statistic to use. A sample proportion p estimates the population proportion π. We know from chapter 8 that for a sufficiently large sample the sample proportion can be assumed to follow a normal distribution. If we can assume a normal sampling distribution, then the test statistic would be the z-score. Recall that the sample proportion is

(9.4)
$$p = \frac{x}{n} = \frac{\text{number of successes}}{\text{sample size}}$$

The test statistic, calculated from sample data, is the difference between the sample proportion p and the hypothesized proportion π_0 divided by the *estimated standard error of the proportion* (sometimes denoted σ_p):

(9.5)
$$z = \frac{p - \pi_0}{\sqrt{\dfrac{\pi_0(1 - \pi_0)}{n}}} \quad \text{or} \quad z = \frac{p - \pi_0}{\sigma_p} \quad \text{if } n\pi_0 \geq 10 \text{ and } n(1 - \pi_0) \geq 10$$

How do we choose π_0? The value of π_0 that we are testing is a **benchmark,** such as past performance, an industry standard, or a product specification. The value of π_0 does *not* come from a sample.

Where Do We Get π_0?

The value of π_0 that we are testing is a *benchmark,* such as past experience, an industry standard, or a product specification. The value of π_0 does *not* come from a sample.

In checking for normality, we use the hypothesized proportion π_0 rather than the sample proportion p. We can choose whichever type of test the situation requires:

Left-Tailed Test	*Two-Tailed Test*	*Right-Tailed Test*
$H_0: \pi \geq \pi_0$	$H_0: \pi = \pi_0$	$H_0: \pi \leq \pi_0$
$H_1: \pi < \pi_0$	$H_1: \pi \neq \pi_0$	$H_1: \pi > \pi_0$

Critical Value

The test statistic is compared with a *critical value* from a table. The critical value shows the range of values for the test statistic that would be expected by chance if the null hypothesis were true. For a two-tailed test (but *not* for a one-tailed test) the hypothesis test is equivalent to asking whether the confidence interval on z includes zero. In a two-tailed test, half the risk of Type I error (i.e., $\alpha/2$) goes in each tail, as shown in Table 9.3, so the z-values are the same as for a confidence interval. You can verify these z-values from Appendix C.

TABLE 9.3
Some Common z-Values

Level of Significance (α)	Two-Tailed Test	Right-Tailed Test	Left-Tailed Test
.10	±1.645	1.282	−1.282
.05	±1.960	1.645	−1.645
.01	±2.576	2.326	−2.326

EXAMPLE

Return Policy

Retailers such as Guess, Staples, Sports Authority, and Limited Brands are employing new technology to crack down on "serial exchangers"—customers who abuse their return and exchange policies (*The Wall Street Journal*, November 29, 2004). For example, some customers buy an outfit, wear it once or twice, and then return it. Software called *Verify-1*, a product of a California-based company Return Exchange, tracks a shopper's record of bringing back items. The historical return rate for merchandise at department stores is 13.0 percent. At one department store, after implementing the new software, there were 22 returns in a sample of 250 purchases. At $\alpha = .05$, does this sample prove that the true return rate has fallen?

Step 1: State the Hypotheses

The hypotheses are

$H_0: \pi \geq .13$ (return rate is the same or greater than the historical rate)

$H_1: \pi < .13$ (return rate has fallen below the historical rate)

Step 2: Specify the Decision Rule

For $\alpha = .05$ in a left-tailed test, the critical value is $z_{.05} = -1.645$, so the decision rule is

Reject H_0 if $z < -1.645$

Otherwise do not reject H_0

This decision rule is illustrated in Figure 9.6.

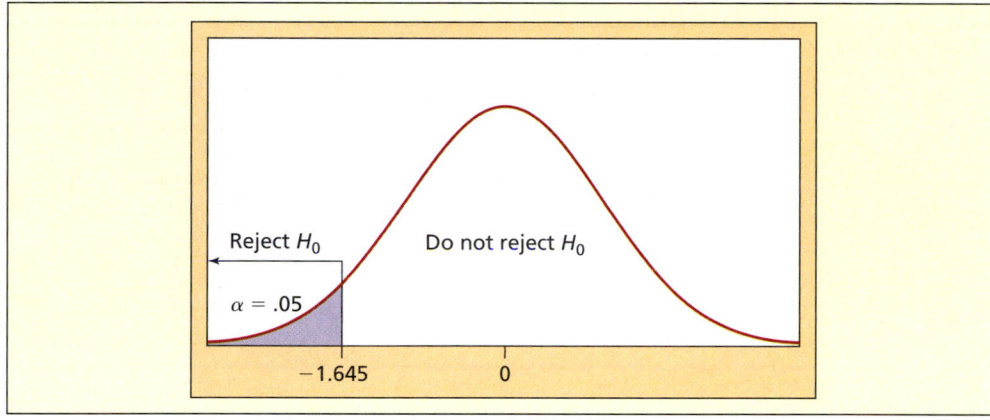

FIGURE 9.6

Left-tailed z test using $\alpha = .05$

Before using z we should check the normality assumption. To assume normality we require that $n\pi_0 \geq 10$ and $n(1 - \pi_0) \geq 10$. Note that we use the hypothesized proportion π_0 (not p) to check normality, because we are assuming H_0 to be the truth about the population. Inserting $\pi_0 = .13$ and $n = 250$ we see that these conditions are easily met: $(250)(.13) = 32.5$ and $(250)(1 - .13) = 217.5$.

Step 3: Calculate the Test Statistic

Since $p = x/n = 22/250 = .088$, the sample seems to favor H_1. But we will assume that H_0 is true and see if the test statistic contradicts this assumption. We test the hypothesis at $\pi = .13$. If we can reject $\pi = .13$ in favor of $\pi < .13$, then we implicitly reject the class of hypotheses $\pi \geq .13$. The test statistic is the difference between the sample proportion $p = x/n$ and the hypothesized parameter π_0 divided by the standard error of p:

$$z = \frac{p - \pi_0}{\sqrt{\dfrac{\pi_0(1 - \pi_0)}{n}}} = \frac{.088 - .13}{\sqrt{\dfrac{.13(1 - .13)}{250}}} = \frac{-.042}{.02127} = -1.975$$

Step 4: Make the Decision

The test statistic falls in the left-tail rejection region, so we conclude that π is less than .13 at the 5 percent level of significance.

p-Value Method

The critical value method described above requires that you determine your rejection criteria in terms of the test statistic before you take a sample. The ***p-value method*** is a different and more useful approach to hypothesis testing. It requires that you express the strength of your evidence (i.e., your sample) against the null hypothesis in terms of a probability. The *p*-value answers the following question: What is the probability that we would observe our particular sample mean (or something more extreme) if, in fact, the null hypothesis is true? The *p*-value gives us more information than a test using one particular value of α.

p-Value

The *p-value* is the probability of the sample result (or one more extreme) assuming that H_0 is true.

For our test statistic $z = -1.975$, the *p*-value can be obtained from Excel's cumulative standard normal =NORMSDIST(–1.975), which yields $p = .02413$. Alternatively, we can use the cumulative normal table in Appendix C-2 if we round off the test statistic to two decimals, $p = .02442$ if $z = -1.97$ or $p = .02385$ if $z = -1.98$ as shown in Table 9.4. Using the *p*-value, we reject H_0 at $\alpha = .05$, but the decision would be very close if we had used $\alpha = .025$. Figure 9.7 illustrates the *p*-value.

TABLE 9.4   Finding the *p*-Value for *z* = 1.975 in Appendix C-2

z	.00	.01	.02	.03	.04	.05	.06	.07	.08	.09
−3.7	.00011	.00010	.00010	.00010	.00009	.00009	.00008	.00008	.00008	.00008
−3.6	.00016	.00015	.00015	.00014	.00014	.00013	.00013	.00012	.00012	.00011
−3.5	.00023	.00022	.00022	.00021	.00020	.00019	.00019	.00018	.00017	.00017
⋮	⋮	⋮	⋮	⋮	⋮	⋮	⋮	⋮	⋮	⋮
−2.0	.02275	.02222	.02169	.02118	.02068	.02018	.01970	.01923	.01876	.01831
−1.9	.02872	.02807	.02743	.02680	.02619	.02559	.02500	*.02442*	*.02385*	.02330
−1.8	.03593	.03515	.03438	.03362	.03288	.03216	.03144	.03074	.03005	.02938

FIGURE 9.7

Left-tail *p*-value for $z = -1.975$

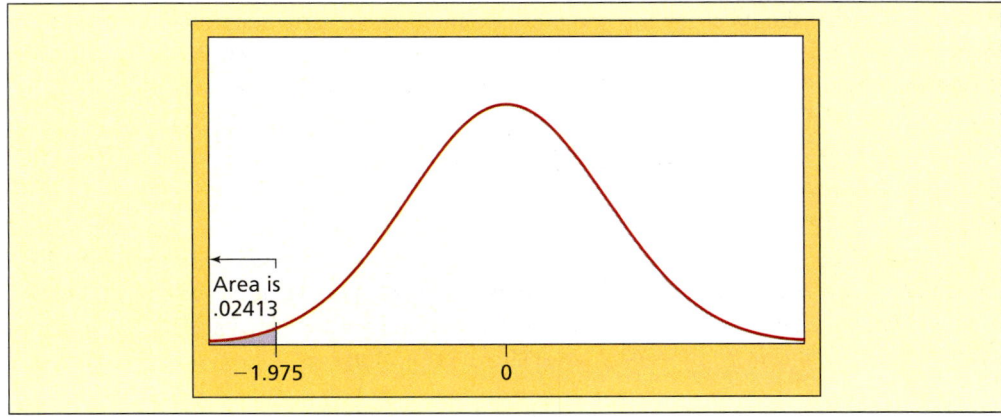

Interpreting a *p*-Value

The *smaller* the *p*-value, the more we want to *reject H_0*. Does this seem backward? You might think a large *p*-value would be "more significant" than a small one. But the *p*-value is a direct measure of the level of significance at which we could reject H_0, so *a smaller* p-*value is more convincing*. For the left-tailed test, the *p*-value tells us that there is a .02413 probability of getting a sample proportion of .088 or less if the true proportion is .13; that is, such a sample would arise by chance only about 24 times in 1,000 tests if the null hypothesis is true. In our left-tailed test, we would reject H_0 because the *p*-value (.02413) is smaller than α (.05). In fact, we could reject H_0 at *any* α greater than .02413.

Two-Tailed Test

What if we used a two-tailed test? This might be appropriate if the objective is to detect a change in the return rate in *either* direction. In fact, two-tailed tests are used more often, because rejection in a two-tailed test always implies rejection in a one-tailed test, other things being equal. The same sample can be used for either a one-tailed or two-tailed test. The type of hypothesis test is up to the statistician.

Step 1: State the Hypotheses   The hypotheses are

H_0: $\pi = .13$ (return rate is the same as the historical rate)

H_1: $\pi \neq .13$ (return rate is different from the historical rate)

Step 2: Specify the Decision Rule   For a two-tailed test, we split the risk of Type I error by putting $\alpha/2 = .05/2 = .025$ in each tail (as we would for a confidence interval). For $\alpha = .05$ in a two-tailed test, the critical value is $z_{.025} = 1.96$ so the decision rule is

Reject H_0 if $z > +1.96$ or if $z < -1.96$

Otherwise do not reject H_0

The decision rule is illustrated in Figure 9.8.

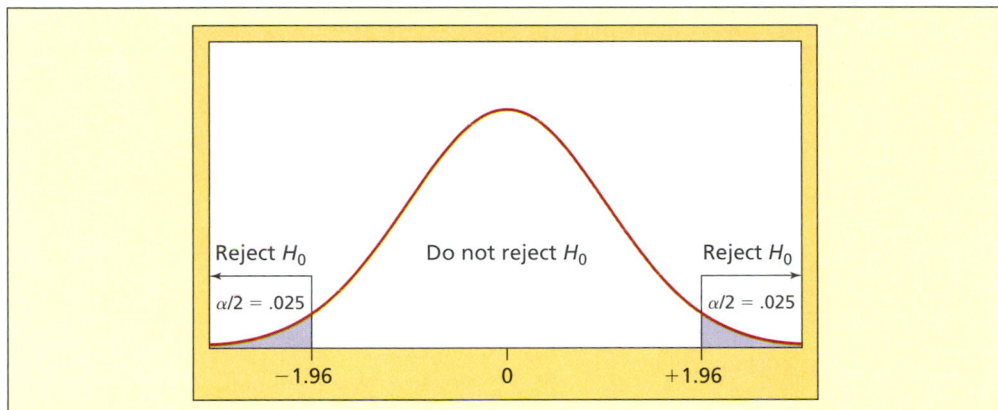

FIGURE 9.8

Two-tailed z test for $\alpha = .05$

Step 3: Calculate the Test Statistic   The test statistic is *unaffected by the hypotheses or the level of significance*. The value of the test statistic is the same as for the one-tailed test:

$$z = \frac{p - \pi_0}{\sqrt{\dfrac{\pi_0(1 - \pi_0)}{n}}} = \frac{.088 - .13}{\sqrt{\dfrac{.13(1 - .13)}{250}}} = \frac{-.042}{.02127} = -1.975$$

Step 4: Make the Decision   Since the test statistic falls in the left tail of the rejection region, we reject the null hypothesis H_0: $\pi = .13$ and conclude H_1: $\pi \neq .13$ at the 5 percent level of significance. Another way to say this is that the sample proportion *differs significantly* from the historical return rate at $\alpha = .05$ in a two-tailed test. Note that this decision is rather a close one, since the test statistic just barely falls into the rejection region.

Notice also that the rejection was stronger in a one-tailed test, that is, the test statistic is farther from the critical value. *Holding α constant, rejection in a two-tailed test always implies rejection in a one-tailed test.* This reinforces the logic of choosing a two-tailed test unless there is a specific reason to prefer a one-tailed test.

Calculating a *p*-Value for a Two-Tailed Test

In a two-tailed test, we divide the risk into equal tails, one on the left and one on the right, to allow for the possibility that we will reject H_0 whenever the sample statistic is very small or very large. With the *p*-value approach in a two-tailed test, we find the tail area associated with our sample test statistic, multiply this by two, and then compare that probability to α. Our z statistic was calculated to be -1.975. The p-value would then be

$$2 \times P(z < -1.975) = 2 \times .02413 = .04826$$

We would reject the null hypothesis because the p-value .04826 is less than α (.05).

Effect of α

Would the decision be the same if we had used a different level of significance? Table 9.5 shows some possibilities. *The test statistic is the same regardless of α.* While we can reject the null hypothesis at $\alpha = .10$ or $\alpha = .05$, we cannot reject at $\alpha = .01$. Therefore, we would say that the sample proportion differs from the historical return rate at the 10 percent and 5 percent levels of significance, but not at the 1 percent level of significance.

TABLE 9.5
Effect of Varying α

α	Test Statistic	Two-Tailed Critical Values	Decision
.10	$z = -1.975$	$z_{.05} = \pm 1.645$	Reject H_0
.05	$z = -1.975$	$z_{.025} = \pm 1.960$	Reject H_0
.01	$z = -1.975$	$z_{.005} = \pm 2.576$	Don't reject H_0

Which level of significance is the "right" one? They all are. It depends on how much Type I error we are willing to allow. Before concluding that $\alpha = .01$ is "better" than the others because it allows less Type I error, you should remember that smaller Type I error leads to increased Type II error. In this case, Type I error would imply that there has been a change in return rates when in reality nothing has changed, while Type II error implies that the software had no effect on the return rate, when in reality the software did decrease the return rate.

EXAMPLE

Length of Hospital Stay

A hospital is comparing its performance against an industry benchmark that no more than 50 percent of normal births should result in a hospital stay exceeding 2 days (48 hours). Thirty-one births in a sample of 50 normal births had a length of stay (LOS) greater than 48 hours. At $\alpha = .025$, does this sample prove that the hospital exceeds the benchmark? This question requires a right-tailed test.

Step 1: State the Hypotheses
The hypotheses are

H_0: $\pi \leq .50$ (the hospital is compliant with the benchmark)

H_1: $\pi > .50$ (the hospital is exceeding the benchmark)

Step 2: Specify the Decision Rule
For $\alpha = .025$ in a right-tailed test, the critical value is $z_{.025} = 1.96$, so the decision rule is

Reject H_0 if $z > 1.960$

Otherwise do not reject H_0

This decision rule is illustrated in Figure 9.9.

Before using z we should check the normality assumption. To assume normality we require that $n\pi_0 \geq 10$ and $n(1 - \pi_0) \geq 10$. Inserting $\pi_0 = .50$ and $n = 50$ we see that the normality conditions are easily met: $(50)(.50) = 25$ and $(50)(1 - .50) = 25$.

Step 3: Calculate the Test Statistic
Since $p = x/n = 31/50 = .62$, the sample seems to favor H_1. But we will assume that H_0 is true and see if the test statistic contradicts this assumption. We test the hypothesis at $\pi = .50$.

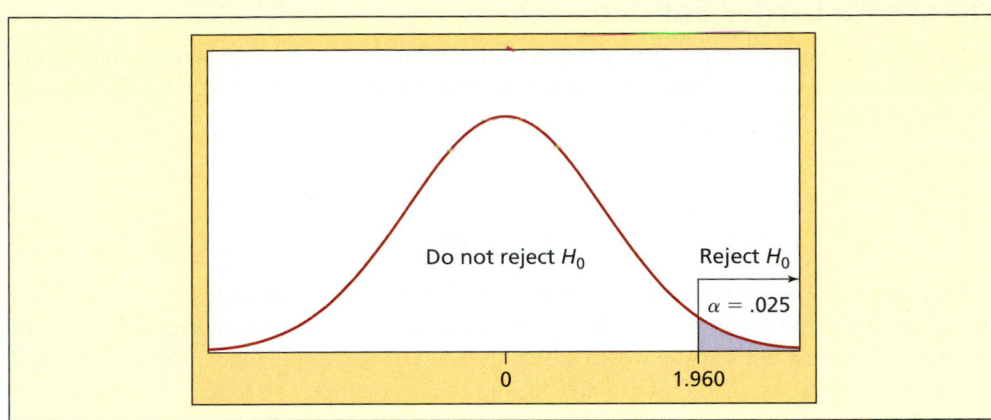

FIGURE 9.9

Right-tailed z test using
$\alpha = .025$

If we can reject $\pi = .50$ in favor of $\pi > .50$, then we can reject the class of hypotheses $\pi \leq .50$. The test statistic is the difference between the sample proportion $p = x/n$ and the hypothesized parameter π_0 divided by the standard error of p:

$$z = \frac{p - \pi_0}{\sqrt{\dfrac{\pi_0(1 - \pi_0)}{n}}} = \frac{.62 - .50}{\sqrt{\dfrac{.50(1 - .50)}{50}}} = \frac{.12}{.07071068} = 1.697$$

Step 4: Make the Decision
The test statistic does not fall in the right-tail rejection region, so we cannot reject the hypothesis that $\pi \leq .50$ at the 2.5 percent level of significance. In other words, the test statistic is within the realm of chance at $\alpha = .025$.

Using the *p*-Value

In this case, the *p*-value can be obtained from Excel's cumulative standard normal function =1−NORMSDIST(1.697)=.04485 or from Appendix C-2 (using $z = 1.70$ we get $p = 1 - .9554 = .0446$). Excel's accuracy is greater because $z = 1.697$ is not rounded to $z = 1.70$. Since we want a right-tail area, we must subtract the cumulative distribution function from 1. The *p*-value is not less than .025 so we cannot reject the null hypothesis in a right-tailed test at $\alpha = .05$. We could (barely) reject at $\alpha = .05$. This demonstrates that the level of significance can affect our decision. The advantage of the *p*-value is that it tells you exactly the point of indecision between rejecting or not rejecting H_0. The *p*-value is illustrated in Figure 9.10.

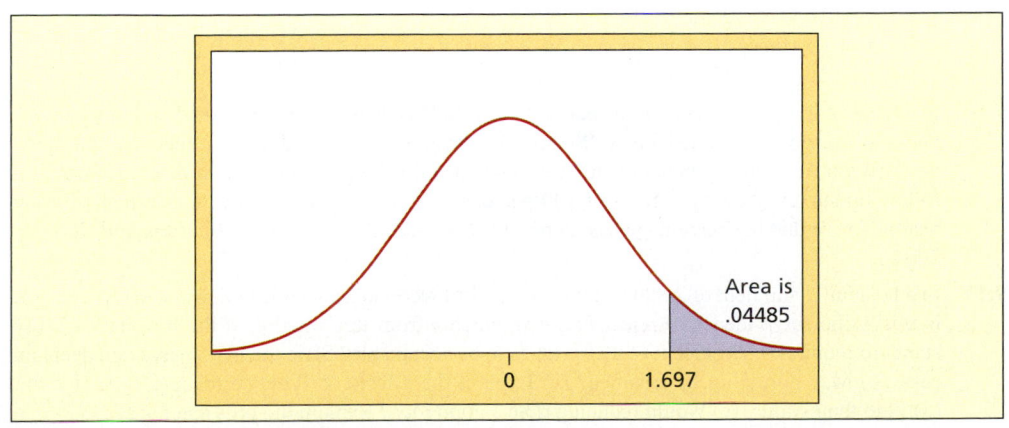

FIGURE 9.10

Right-tail *p*-value for
$z = 1.697$

Effect of a Larger Sample

In this case, a larger sample was possible. Fifty more births were examined, increasing the sample size to $n = 100$ births. In this new sample, 61 had an LOS exceeding 48 hours, or $p = 61/100 = .61$. The new test statistic is

$$z = \frac{p - \pi_0}{\sqrt{\dfrac{\pi_0(1 - \pi_0)}{n}}} = \frac{.61 - .50}{\sqrt{\dfrac{.50(1 - .50)}{100}}} = \frac{.11}{.05} = 2.20$$

This time we obtain a rejection since $z = 2.20$ exceeds the critical value $z_{.025} = 1.96$. With the larger sample, the rejection is decisive. The new p-value ($p = .0139$) shown in Figure 9.11 indicates that such a test statistic would arise only 1.39 percent of the time by chance alone, if the true proportion were .50. This example illustrates the fact that *sample size increases power* (our ability to detect a false hypothesis).

FIGURE 9.11

Right-tail p-value for $n = 100$

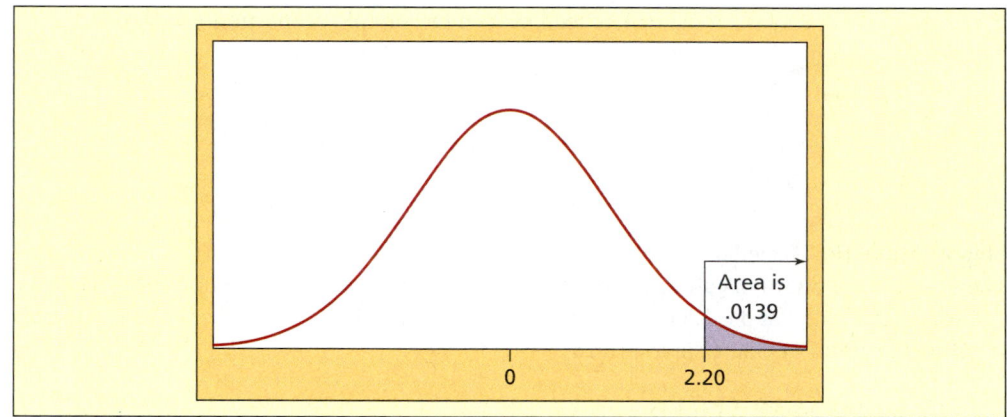

Area is .0139

0   2.20

SECTION EXERCISES

9.7   Calculate the test statistic and p-value for each sample.
   a. $H_0\colon \pi = .20$ versus $H_1\colon \pi \neq .20$, $\alpha = .025$, $p = .28$, $n = 100$
   b. $H_0\colon \pi \geq .50$ versus $H_1\colon \pi < .50$, $\alpha = .025$, $p = .60$, $n = 90$
   c. $H_0\colon \pi \leq .75$ versus $H_1\colon \pi > .75$, $\alpha = .10$, $p = .82$, $n = 50$

9.8   Calculate the test statistic and p-value for each sample.
   a. $H_0\colon \pi \leq .60$ versus $H_1\colon \pi > .60$, $\alpha = .05$, $x = 56$, $n = 80$
   b. $H_0\colon \pi = .30$ versus $H_1\colon \pi \neq .30$, $\alpha = .05$, $x = 18$, $n = 40$
   c. $H_0\colon \pi \geq .10$ versus $H_1\colon \pi < .10$, $\alpha = .01$, $x = 3$, $n = 100$

9.9   May normality be assumed? Show your work.
   a. $H_0\colon \pi = .30$ versus $H_1\colon \pi \neq .30$, $n = 20$
   b. $H_0\colon \pi = .05$ versus $H_1\colon \pi \neq .05$, $n = 50$
   c. $H_0\colon \pi = .10$ versus $H_1\colon \pi \neq .10$, $n = 400$

9.10 In a recent survey, 10 percent of the participants rated Pepsi as being "concerned with my health." PepsiCo's response included a new "Smart Spot" symbol on its products that meet certain nutrition criteria, to help consumers who seek more healthful eating options. At $\alpha = .05$, would a follow-up survey showing that 18 of 100 persons now rate Pepsi as being "concerned with my health" prove that the percentage has increased? (Data are from *The Wall Street Journal*, July 30, 2004.)

9.11 In a hospital's shipment of 2,880 insulin syringes, 14 were unusable due to defects. (a) At $\alpha = .05$, is this sufficient evidence to reject future shipments from this supplier if the hospital's quality standard requires 99.7 percent of the syringes to be acceptable? State the hypotheses and decision rule. (b) May normality be assumed? (c) Explain the effects of Type I error and Type II error. (d) Find the p-value. (e) Would reducing α be a good idea? Explain the pros and cons.

9.12   The Tri-Cities Tobacco Coalition sent three underage teenagers into various stores in Detroit and Highland Park to see if they could purchase cigarettes. Of 320 stores checked, 82 sold cigarettes to teens between 15 and 17 years old. (a) If the goal is to reduce the percent to 20 percent or less, does this sample show that the goal is *not* being achieved at $\alpha = .05$ in a right-tailed test? (b) Construct a 95 percent confidence interval for the true percent of sellers who allow teens to purchase tobacco. (c) Explain how the confidence interval is equivalent to a two-tailed test at $\alpha = .05$. (Data are from *Detroit Free Press,* March 19, 2001, p. 2C.)

9.13   To encourage telephone efficiency, a catalog call center issues a guideline that at least half of all telephone orders should be completed within 2 minutes. Subsequently, a random sample of 64 telephone calls showed that 40 calls lasted over 2 minutes. (a) At $\alpha = .05$ is this a significant departure from the guideline in a right-tailed test? State your hypotheses and decision rule. (b) Find the *p*-value. (c) Is the difference important (as opposed to significant)?

9.14   The recent default rate on all student loans is 5.2 percent. In a recent random sample of 300 loans at private universities there were 9 defaults. (a) Does this sample show sufficient evidence that the private university loan default rate is below the rate for all universities, using a left-tailed test at $\alpha = .01$? (b) Calculate the *p*-value. (c) Verify that the assumption of normality is justified.

9.15   The Association of Flight Attendants/Communication Workers of America and National Consumers League conducted a poll of 702 frequent and occasional fliers and found that 442 respondents favored a ban on cell phones in flight, even if technology permits it. At $\alpha = .05$, can we conclude that more than half the sampled population supports a ban? (Data are from *Aviation Week and Space Technology* 182, no. 15 [April 11, 2005], p. 14.)

Mini Case   9.2

Every Minute Counts

As more company business is transacted by telephone or Internet, there is a considerable premium to reduce customer time spent with human operators. Verizon recently installed a new speech recognition system for its repair calls. In the old system, the user had to press keys on the numeric keypad to answer questions, which led many callers to opt to talk to an operator instead. Under the old system, 94 percent of the customers had to talk to an operator to get their needs met. Suppose that, using the new system, a sample of 150 calls showed that 120 required an operator. The hypotheses are

$H_0: \pi \geq .94$ (the new system is no better than the old system)

$H_1: \pi < .94$ (the new system has reduced the proportion of operator calls)

These hypotheses call for a left-tailed test. Using $\alpha = .01$, the left-tail critical value is $z_{.01} = -2.326$, as illustrated in Figure 9.12.

FIGURE 9.12

Decision rule for left-tailed test

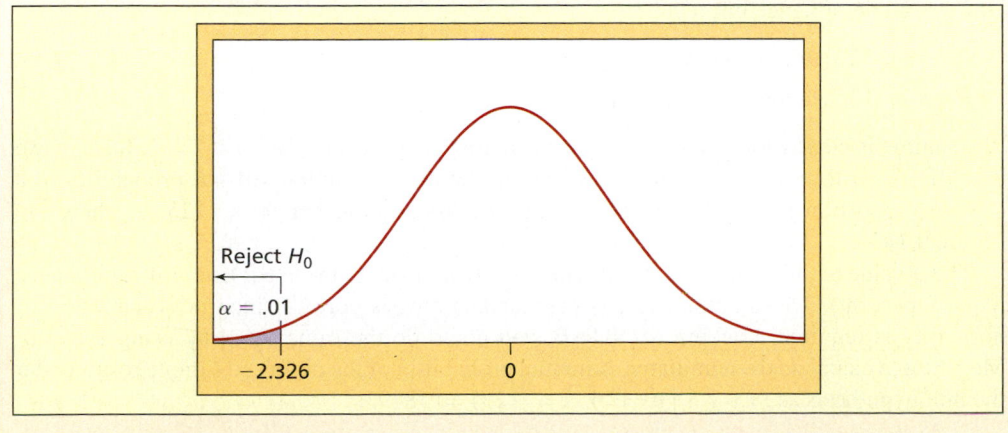

For normality, we want $n\pi_0 \geq 10$ and $n(1 - \pi_0) \geq 10$. The condition for normality is not quite met, since $(150)(.94) = 141$ but $(150)(.06) = 9$. Since this is only a rule of thumb, we will proceed, bearing in mind this possible concern. The sample proportion is $p = 120/150 = .80$ so the test statistic is

$$z = \frac{p - \pi_0}{\sqrt{\dfrac{\pi_0(1 - \pi_0)}{n}}} = \frac{.80 - .94}{\sqrt{\dfrac{.94(1 - .94)}{150}}} = \frac{-.14}{.01939} = -7.22$$

The test statistic is far below the critical value, so we conclude that the percentage of customers who require an operator has declined. MINITAB verifies this calculation and also gives the p-value (.000) as shown in Figure 9.13. In view of this strong rejection, the question of normality is of secondary interest.

FIGURE 9.13

MINITAB results for one-sample proportion

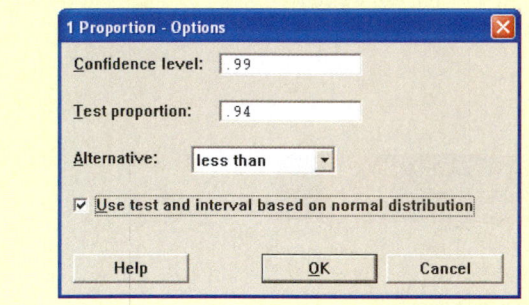

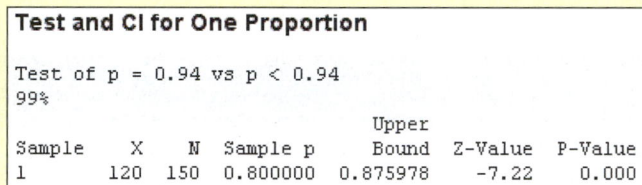

Test and CI for One Proportion

```
Test of p = 0.94 vs p < 0.94
99%
                                     Upper
Sample     X     N   Sample p       Bound   Z-Value   P-Value
1        120   150   0.800000    0.875978     -7.22     0.000
```

Besides being significant, such savings are important. For example, Boston Financial Data Services, a company that provides record-keeping services for mutual funds, shaved a minute off the mean time to process a customer request. Since its call centers process 1.7 million calls a year, the savings are very large.

See *The Wall Street Journal,* July 26, 2004.

Small Samples and Non-Normality (Optional)

In random tests by the FAA, 12.5 percent of all passenger flights failed the agency's test for bacterial count in water served to passengers (*The Wall Street Journal,* November 10, 2004, p. D1). Airlines now are trying to improve their compliance with water quality standards. Random inspection of 16 recent flights showed that only 1 flight failed the water quality test. Has overall compliance improved?

H_0: $\pi \geq .125$ (failure rate has not improved)

H_1: $\pi < .125$ (failure rate has declined)

The sample is clearly too small to assume normality since $n\pi_0 = (16)(.125) = 2$. Instead, we use MINITAB to test the hypotheses by finding the exact binomial left-tail probability of a sample proportion $p = 1/16 = .0625$ under the assumption that $\pi = .125$, as shown in Figure 9.14.

The p-value of .388 does not permit rejection of H_0 at any of the usual levels of significance (e.g., 5 percent). The binomial test is easy and is always correct since no assumption of normality is required. Lacking MINITAB, you could do the same thing by using Excel or MegaStat to calculate the cumulative binomial probability of the observed sample result under the null hypothesis as $P(X \leq 1 \mid n = 16, \pi = .125) = .38793$.

FIGURE 9.14

MINITAB small-sample test
of a proportion

1 Proportion - Options

Confidence level: 95.0

Test proportion: .125

Alternative: less than

☐ Use test and interval based on normal distribution

Help   OK   Cancel

Test and CI for One Proportion

Test of p = 0.125 vs p < 0.125

Sample	X	N	Sample p	95% Upper Bound	Exact P-Value
1	1	16	0.062500	0.263957	0.388

SECTION EXERCISES

*9.16 A coin was flipped 12 times and came up heads 10 times. (a) Is the assumption of normality justified? Explain. (b) Calculate a *p*-value for the observed sample outcome, using the normal distribution. At the .05 level of significance in a right-tailed test, is the coin biased toward heads? (c) Use Excel to calculate the binomial probability $P(X \geq 10 \mid n = 12, \pi = .50) = 1 - P(X \leq 9 \mid n = 12, \pi = .50)$. (d) Why is the binomial probability not exactly the same as the *p*-value you calculated under the assumption of normality?

*9.17 BriteScreen, a manufacturer of 19-inch LCD computer screens, requires that on average 99.9 percent of all LCDs conform to its quality standard. In a day's production of 2,000 units, 4 are defective. (a) Assuming this is a random sample, is the standard being met, using the 10 percent level of significance? *Hint:* Use MegaStat or Excel to find the binomial probability $P(X \geq 4 \mid n = 2000, \pi = .001) = 1 - P(X \leq 3 \mid n = 2000, \pi = .001)$. Alternatively, use MINITAB. (b) Show that normality should not be assumed.

*9.18 Perfect pitch is the ability to identify musical notes correctly without hearing another note as a reference. The probability that a randomly chosen person has perfect pitch is .0005. (a) If 20 students at Julliard School of Music are tested, and 2 are found to have perfect pitch, would you conclude that Julliard students are more likely than the general population to have perfect pitch? *Hint:* Use MegaStat or Excel to find the right-tailed binomial probability $P(X \geq 2 \mid n = 20, \pi = .0005)$. Alternatively, use MINITAB. (b) Show that normality should not be assumed.

The hypothesis testing procedure for a sample mean depends on whether the population variance σ^2 is known. We begin with the case of known σ^2 before turning to the more common case when σ^2 is estimated. The procedures are similar, yet there are important differences.

9.3

TESTING A MEAN: KNOWN POPULATION VARIANCE

Test Statistic

The hypothesized mean is denoted μ_0. Recall that the value of μ_0 that we are testing is a *benchmark*, such as a national average or an industry standard. The value of μ_0 does *not* come from a sample. The *test statistic* compares the sample mean $\bar{x}$ with the hypothesized mean μ_0. The difference between $\bar{x}$ and μ_0 is divided by the *estimated standard error of the mean* (denoted $\sigma_{\bar{x}}$). The test statistic is

$$z = \frac{\bar{x} - \mu_0}{\frac{\sigma}{\sqrt{n}}} \quad \text{or} \quad z = \frac{\bar{x} - \mu_0}{\sigma_{\bar{x}}} \qquad \text{(test statistic for a mean with known } \sigma) \qquad \textbf{(9.6)}$$

Chapter 9

If the true mean is μ_0 then $\bar{x}$ should be near μ_0 and the test statistic should be near zero. The test statistic is based on the Central Limit Theorem, using the same standard error that we used for confidence intervals in the last chapter. If the population is normal or if the sample is very large, the sample mean (a random variable) may be assumed normal.

EXAMPLE

Paper Manufacturing

The Hammermill Company produces paper for laser printers. Standard paper width is supposed to be 216 mm, or 8.5 inches. Suppose that the actual width is a random variable that is normally distributed with a known standard deviation of .023 mm. This standard deviation reflects the manufacturing technology currently in use and is known from long experience with this type of equipment. The standard deviation is small, due to the company's considerable effort to maintain precise control over paper width. However, variation still arises during manufacturing because of slight differences in the paper stock, vibration in the rollers and cutting tools, and wear and tear on the equipment. The cutters can be adjusted if the paper width drifts from the correct mean. A quality control inspector chooses 50 sheets at random and measures them with a precise instrument, showing a mean width of 216.007 mm. Using a 5 percent level of significance ($\alpha = .05$), does this sample show that the process mean exceeds the specification?   **Paper**

One-Tailed Test

Let's apply the one-tailed test to our paper manufacturing example.

Step 1: Choose the Hypotheses   For a right-tailed test, the hypotheses would be

$H_0: \mu \leq 216$ (process mean does not exceed the specification)

$H_1: \mu > 216$ (process mean has risen above the specification)

Step 2: Specify the Decision Rule   For a right-tailed test, we want the right-tail area to be $\alpha = .05$. The critical value of z that accomplishes this is $z_{.05} = 1.645$. As illustrated in Figure 9.15, the decision rule is

Reject H_0 if $z > 1.645$

Otherwise do not reject H_0

FIGURE 9.15

Right-tailed z test for $\alpha = .05$

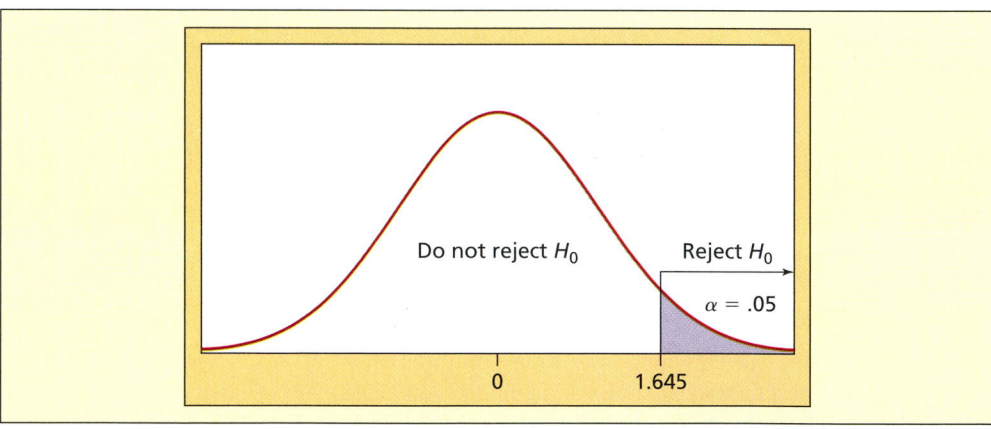

Step 3: Calculate the Test Statistic   If H_0 is true, then the test statistic should be near 0 because $\bar{x}$ should be near μ_0. The value of the test statistic is

$$z = \frac{\bar{x} - \mu_0}{\frac{\sigma}{\sqrt{n}}} = \frac{216.007 - 216.000}{\frac{0.023}{\sqrt{50}}} = \frac{0.007}{0.00325269} = 2.152$$

Step 4: Make the Decision   The test statistic falls in the right rejection region, so we reject the null hypothesis $H_0: \mu \leq 216$ and conclude the alternative hypothesis $H_1: \mu > 216$ at the 5 percent level of significance. Although the difference is slight, it is statistically significant.

p-Value Method

To find the *p*-value for the test statistic $z = 2.152$, we use Excel's function =NORMSDIST(2.152) to obtain the left-tail area for the cumulative *z* distribution (see Figure 9.16). Since $P(z < 2.152) = .9843$ the right-tail area is $P(z > 2.152) = 1 - .9843 = .0157$. This is the *p*-value for the right-tailed test, as illustrated in Figure 9.16. The *p*-value diagram does not show α. The *p*-value of .0157 says that in a right-tailed test a test statistic of $z = 2.152$ (or a more extreme test statistic) would happen by chance about 1.57 percent of the time if the null hypothesis were true.

FIGURE 9.16

Right-tail *p*-value for $z = 2.152$, using Excel

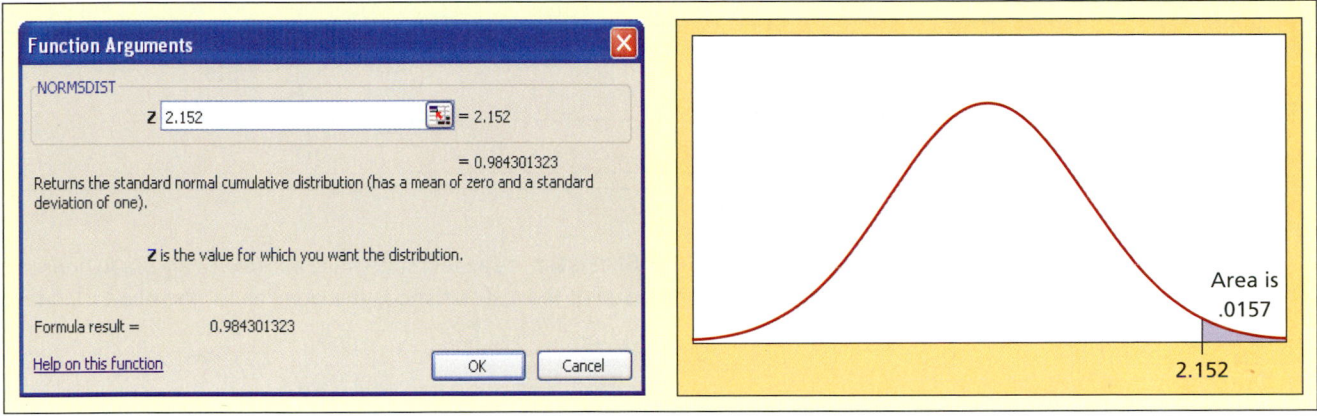

We could also obtain the *p*-value from Appendix C-2, which shows cumulative standard normal areas less than *z*, as illustrated in Table 9.6. The cumulative area is not exactly the same as Excel, because Appendix C-2 requires that we round the test statistic to two decimals ($z = 2.15$).

TABLE 9.6

Finding the *p*-Value for $z = 2.15$ in Appendix C-2

z	.00	.01	.02	.03	.04	.05	.06	.07	.08	.09
−3.7	.00011	.00010	.00010	.00010	.00009	.00009	.00008	.00008	.00008	.00008
−3.6	.00016	.00015	.00015	.00014	.00014	.00013	.00013	.00012	.00012	.00011
−3.5	.00023	.00022	.00022	.00021	.00020	.00019	.00019	.00018	.00017	.00017
⋮	⋮	⋮	⋮	⋮	⋮	⋮	⋮	⋮	⋮	⋮
2.0	.97725	.97778	.97831	.97882	.97932	.97982	.98030	.98077	.98124	.98169
2.1	.98214	.98257	.98300	.98341	.98382	*.98422*	.98461	.98500	.98537	.98574
2.2	.98610	.98645	.98679	.98713	.98745	.98778	.98809	.98840	.98870	.98899

Two-Tailed Test

What if we used a two-tailed test? This might be appropriate if the objective is to detect a deviation from the desired mean in *either* direction.

Step 1: Choose the Hypotheses   For a two-tailed test, the hypotheses are

H_0: $\mu = 216$ (process mean is what it is supposed to be)

H_1: $\mu \neq 216$ (process mean is not what it is supposed to be)

Step 2: Specify the Decision Rule   We will use the same $\alpha = .05$ as in the right-tailed test. But for a two-tailed test, we split the risk of Type I error by putting $\alpha/2 = .05/2 = .025$ in each tail. For $\alpha = .05$ in a two-tailed test, the critical value is $z_{.025} = \pm 1.96$ so the decision rule is

Reject H_0 if $z > +1.96$ or if $z < -1.96$

Otherwise do no reject H_0

The decision rule is illustrated in Figure 9.17.

FIGURE 9.17

Two-tailed z test for $\alpha = .05$

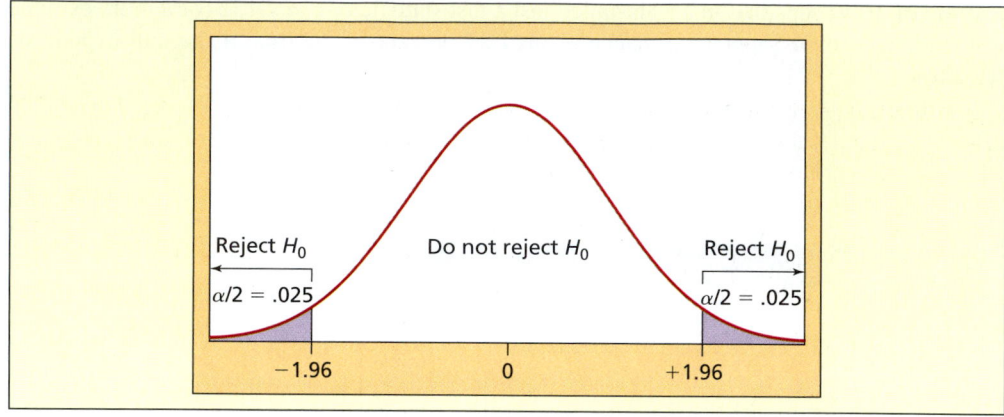

Step 3: Calculate the Test Statistic The test statistic is *unaffected by the hypotheses or the level of significance.* The value of the test statistic is the same as for the one-tailed test:

$$z = \frac{\bar{x} - \mu_0}{\frac{\sigma}{\sqrt{n}}} = \frac{216.007 - 216.000}{\frac{.023}{\sqrt{50}}} = \frac{.007}{.00325269} = 2.152$$

Step 4: Make the Decision Since the test statistic falls in the right tail of the rejection region, we reject the null hypothesis H_0: $\mu = 216$ and conclude H_1: $\mu \neq 216$ at the 5 percent level of significance. Another way to say this is that the sample mean *differs significantly* from the desired specification at $\alpha = .05$ in a two-tailed test. Note that this decision is rather a close one, since the test statistic just barely falls into the rejection region.

Using the *p*-Value

As for a right-tailed test, to find the *p*-value for the test statistic $z = 2.152$, we use Excel's function =NORMSDIST(2.152) to obtain the left-tail area for the cumulative z distribution. Since $P(z < 2.152) = .9843$ we know that the right-tail area is $P(z > 2.152) = 1 - .9843 = .0157$. But for a two-tailed test, we must *double* the one-tail area to get a *p*-value of $2 \times .0157 = .0314$. See Figure 9.18. This says that in a two-tailed test a result as extreme as 2.152 would arise about 3.14 percent of the time by chance alone (i.e., about 31 times in 1,000 samples).

FIGURE 9.18

Two-tail *p*-value for $z = 2.152$

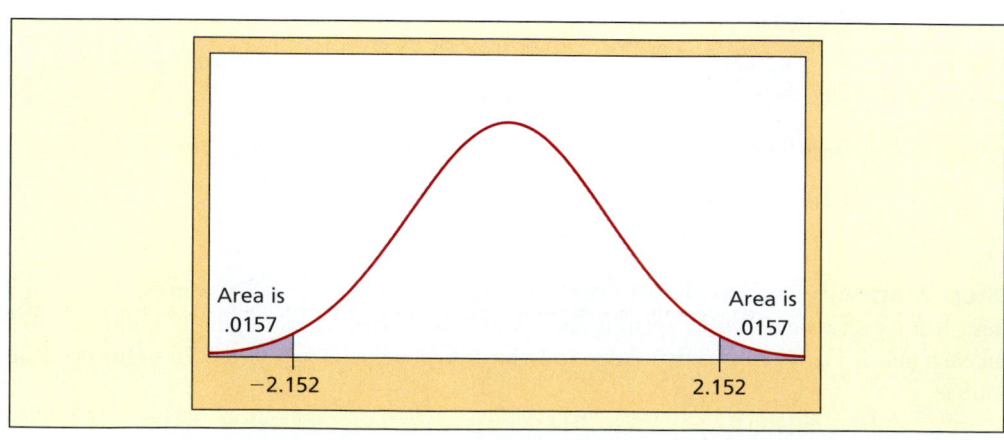

Analogy to Confidence Intervals

A two-tailed hypothesis test at the 5 percent level of significance ($\alpha = .05$) is exactly equivalent to asking whether the 95 percent confidence interval for the mean includes the hypothesized mean. If the confidence interval includes the hypothesized mean H_0: $\mu = 216$, then we cannot reject the null hypothesis. In this case the 95 percent confidence interval would be

$$\bar{x} \pm z\frac{\sigma}{\sqrt{n}} = 216.007 \pm 1.96\frac{.023}{\sqrt{50}} = 216.001 < \mu < 216.013$$

Since this confidence interval does not include 216, we reject the null hypothesis H_0: $\mu = 216$. However, the decision is rather a close one as it was with the two-tailed hypothesis test, since the lower limit of the confidence interval almost includes 216.

Interpretation   Although the sample mean 216.007 might seem very close to 216, it is more than two standard deviations from the desired mean. This example shows that even a small difference can be significant. It all depends on σ and n, that is, on the standard error of the mean in the denominator of the test statistic. In this case, there is a high degree of precision in the manufacturing process ($\sigma = .023$ is very small) so the standard error (and hence the allowable variation) is extremely small. Such a tiny difference in means would not be noticeable to consumers, but stringent quality control standards are applied to ensure that no shipment goes out with any noticeable nonconformance.

Significance versus Importance

Our statistical tests show that there is a *significant* departure from the desired mean for paper width at $\alpha = .05$. But is the difference *important?* Is 216.007 so close to 216 that nobody could tell the difference? The question of whether to adjust the process is up to the engineers or business managers, not statisticians.

SECTION EXERCISES

9.19   Calculate the test statistic and *p*-value for each sample.
  a. H_0: $\mu = 60$ versus H_1: $\mu \neq 60$, $\alpha = .025$, $\bar{x} = 63$, $\sigma = 8$, $n = 16$
  b. H_0: $\mu \geq 60$ versus H_1: $\mu < 60$, $\alpha = .05$, $\bar{x} = 58$, $\sigma = 5$, $n = 25$
  c. H_0: $\mu \leq 60$ versus H_1: $\mu > 60$, $\alpha = .05$, $\bar{x} = 65$, $\sigma = 8$, $n = 36$

9.20   Find the *p*-value for each test statistic.
  a. Right-tailed test, $z = +1.34$ b. Left-tailed test, $z = -2.07$ c. Two-tailed test, $z = -1.69$

9.21   Procyon Mfg. produces tennis balls. Weights are supposed to be normally distributed with a mean of 2.035 ounces and a standard deviation of 0.002 ounces. A sample of 25 tennis balls shows a mean weight of 2.036 ounces. At $\alpha = .025$ in a right-tailed test, is the mean weight heavier than it is supposed to be?

9.22   The mean arrival rate of flights at O'Hare Airport in marginal weather is 195 flights per hour with a historical standard deviation of 13 flights. To increase arrivals, a new air traffic control procedure is implemented. In the next 30 days of marginal weather the mean arrival rate is 200 flights per hour. (a) Set up a right-tailed decision rule at $\alpha = .025$ to decide whether there has been a significant increase in the mean number of arrivals per hour. (b) Carry out the test and make the decision. Is it close? Would the decision be different if you used $\alpha = .01$? (c) What assumptions are you making, if any?   **Flights**

210	215	200	189	200	213	202	181	197	199
193	209	215	192	179	196	225	199	196	210
199	188	174	176	202	195	195	208	222	221

9.23   An airline serves bottles of Galena Spring Water that are supposed to contain an average of 10 ounces. The filling process follows a normal distribution with process standard deviation 0.07 ounce. Twelve randomly chosen bottles had the weights shown below (in ounces). (a) Set up a two-tailed decision rule to detect quality control violations using the 5 percent level of significance. (b) Carry out the test. (c) What assumptions are you making, if any?   **BottleFill**

| 10.02 | 9.95 | 10.11 | 10.10 | 10.08 | 10.04 | 10.06 | 10.03 | 9.98 | 10.01 | 9.92 | 9.89 |

9.4

TESTING A MEAN: UNKNOWN POPULATION VARIANCE

Chapter 9

If the population variance σ^2 must be estimated from the sample, the hypothesis testing procedure is modified. There is a loss of information when s replaces σ in the formulas, and it is no longer appropriate to use the normal distribution. However, the basic hypothesis testing steps are the same.

Using Student's t

When the population standard deviation σ is unknown (as it usually is) and the population may be assumed normal (or generally symmetric with no outliers) the test statistic follows the Student's t distribution with $n-1$ degrees of freedom. Since σ is rarely known, we generally expect to use Student's t instead of z, as you saw for confidence intervals in the previous chapter.

(9.7)
$$t = \frac{\bar{x} - \mu_0}{\frac{s}{\sqrt{n}}} \quad \text{if } \sigma \text{ is unknown}$$

EXAMPLE

Hot Chocolate

In addition to its core business of bagels and coffee, Bruegger's Bagels also sells hot chocolate for the noncoffee crowd. Customer research shows that the ideal temperature for hot chocolate is 142°F ("hot" but not "too hot"). A random sample of 24 cups of hot chocolate is taken at various times, and the temperature of each cup is measured using an ordinary kitchen thermometer that is accurate to the nearest whole degree. 🐝 **HotChoc**

140	140	141	145	143	144	142	140
145	143	140	140	141	141	137	142
143	141	142	142	143	141	138	139

The sample mean is 141.375 with a sample standard deviation of 1.99592. At $\alpha = .10$, does this sample evidence show that the true mean differs from 142?

Step 1: Choose the Hypotheses
We use a two-tailed test. The null hypothesis is in conformance with the desired standard.

$H_0: \mu = 142$ (mean temperature is correct)

$H_1: \mu \neq 142$ (mean temperature is incorrect)

Step 2: Specify the Decision Rule
For $\alpha = .10$, using Excel, the critical value for $v = n - 1 = 24 - 1 = 23$ degrees of freedom is =TINV(0.10,23) = 1.714 (note that Excel's inverse t assumes a two-tailed test). The same value can be obtained from Appendix D, shown here in abbreviated form:

			Upper Tail Area		
v	.10	.05	.025	.01	.005
1	3.078	6.314	12.706	31.821	63.657
2	1.886	2.920	4.303	6.965	9.925
3	1.638	2.353	3.182	4.541	5.841
⋮	⋮	⋮	⋮	⋮	⋮
21	1.323	1.721	2.080	2.518	2.831
22	1.321	1.717	2.074	2.508	2.819
23	1.319	*1.714*	2.069	2.500	2.807
24	1.318	1.711	2.064	2.492	2.797
25	1.316	1.708	2.060	2.485	2.787

We will reject H_0 if $t > 1.714$ or if $t < -1.714$, as illustrated in Figure 9.19.

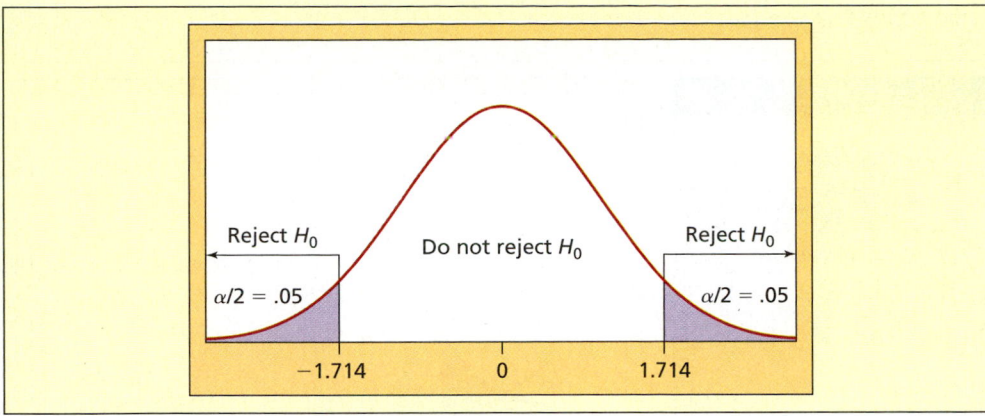

FIGURE 9.19

Two-tailed test for a mean
using *t* for $\nu = 23$

Step 3: Calculate the Test Statistic
Plugging in the sample information, the test statistic is

$$t = \frac{\bar{x} - \mu_0}{\frac{s}{\sqrt{n}}} = \frac{141.375 - 142}{\frac{1.99592}{\sqrt{24}}} = \frac{-.6250}{.40742} = -1.534$$

Step 4: Make the Decision
Since the test statistic lies within the range of chance variation, we cannot reject the null
hypothesis H_0: $\mu = 142$.

Sensitivity to α

Is our conclusion sensitive to the choice of level of significance? Table 9.7 shows several critical values of Student's *t*. At $\alpha = .20$ we could we reject H_0, but not at the other α values shown.
This table is not to suggest that experimenting with various α values is desirable, but merely
to illustrate that our decision may depend on the choice of α.

	$\alpha = .20$	$\alpha = .10$	$\alpha = .05$	$\alpha = .01$
Critical value	$t_{.10} = \pm 1.319$	$t_{.05} = \pm 1.714$	$t_{.025} = \pm 2.069$	$t_{.005} = \pm 2.807$
Decision	Reject H_0	Don't reject H_0	Don't reject H_0	Don't reject H_0

TABLE 9.7
**Effect of α on the
Decision (Two-Tailed *t*
Test with $\nu = 23$)**

Using the *p*-Value

A more general approach favored by researchers is to find the *p*-value. We want to determine
the tail area less than $t = -1.534$ or greater than $t = +1.534$. However, from Appendix D we
can only get a range for the *p*-value. From Appendix D, we see that the two-tail *p*-value must
lie between .20 and .10 (it's a two-tailed test, so we double the right-tail area). It is easier and
more precise to use Excel's function =TDIST(t test statistic,degrees of freedom, tails). In this case the
formula =TDIST(1.534,23,2) gives the two-tailed *p*-value of .13867. The area of each tail is half
that, or .06934, as shown in Figure 9.20. A sample mean as extreme in either tail would occur
by chance about 139 times in 1,000 two-tailed tests if H_0 were true, so the sample's departure
from H_0 is not very convincing.

FIGURE 9.20

Two-tail *p*-value for $t = 1.534$

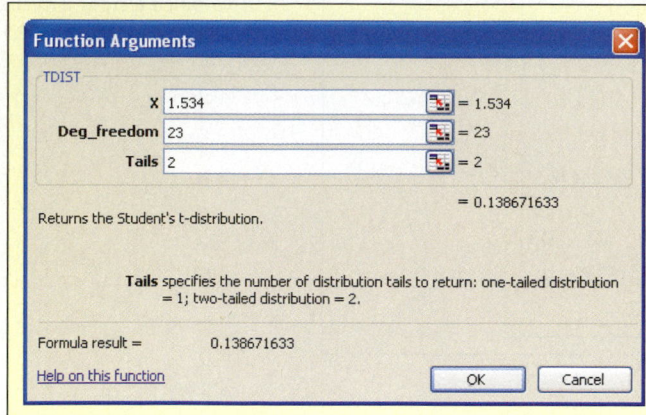
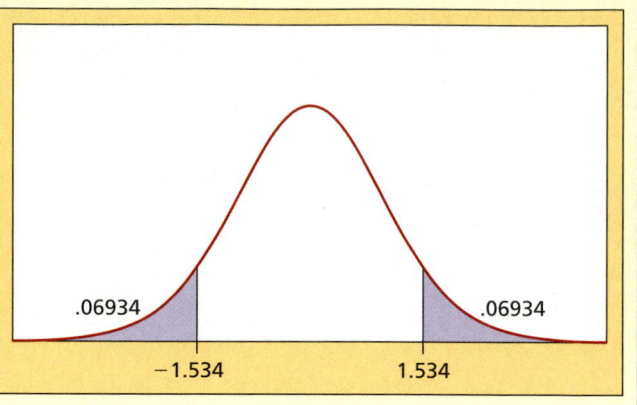

Significance versus Importance

It is doubtful whether a consumer could tell the difference in hot chocolate temperature within a few degrees of 142°F, so a tiny difference in means might lack *practical importance* even if it were *statistically significant*. Importance must be judged by management, not by the statistician.

Normality Assumption

In the hot chocolate example, there are no outliers and something of a bell-shape (see Figure 9.21). Even if not, the *t* test is reasonably robust to mild non-normality. However, outliers or extreme skewness can affect the test, just as when we construct confidence intervals.

FIGURE 9.21

Dot plot of hot chocolate temperatures ($n = 24$)

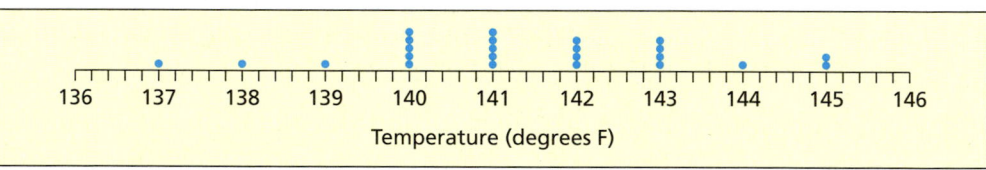

Confidence Interval versus Hypothesis Test

The two-tailed test at the 10 percent level of significance is equivalent to a two-sided 90 percent confidence interval. If the confidence interval does not contain μ_0, we reject H_0. For the hot chocolate, the sample mean is 141.375 with a sample standard deviation of 1.99592. Using Appendix D we find $t_{.05} = 1.714$ so the 90 percent confidence interval for μ is

$$\bar{x} \pm t\frac{s}{\sqrt{n}} = 141.375 \pm (1.714)\frac{1.99592}{\sqrt{24}} = 141.375 \pm .6983$$

Since $\mu = 142$ lies within the 90 percent confidence interval $140.677 < \mu < 142.073$, we cannot reject the hypothesis $H_0: \mu = 142$ at $\alpha = .10$ in a two-tailed test. Many decisions can be handled either as hypothesis tests or using confidence intervals. The confidence interval has the appeal of providing a graphic feeling for the location of the hypothesized mean within the confidence interval, as shown in Figure 9.22. We can see that 142 is near the upper end of the confidence interval, nearly (but not quite) leading to a rejection of $H_0: \mu = 142$.

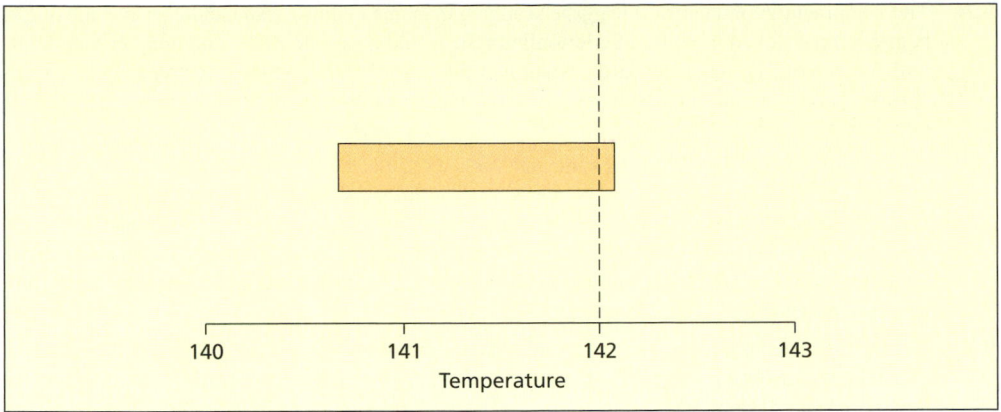

FIGURE 9.22

90 percent confidence
interval for μ

Using MegaStat

You can get tests for one mean, including a confidence interval, using MegaStat. Figure 9.23 shows its setup screen and output for the test of one mean for the hot chocolate data. You enter the data range and everything else is automatic. It gives a choice of z or t, but to use z you must know σ.

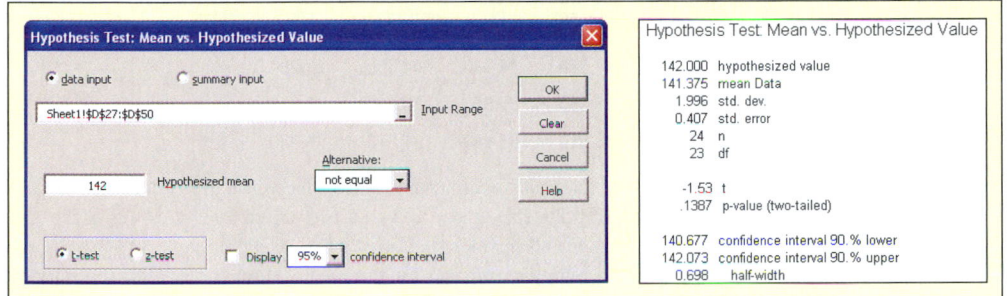

FIGURE 9.23

MegaStat test for one mean

Large Samples

From Appendix D you can verify that when n is large, there is little difference between critical values of t and z (the last line in Appendix D, for $\nu = \infty$). For this reason, it is unlikely that harm will result if you use z instead of t, as long as the sample size is not small. The test statistic is

$$z = \frac{\bar{x} - \mu_0}{\dfrac{s}{\sqrt{n}}} \qquad \text{(large sample, unknown } \sigma \text{)} \qquad \textbf{(9.8)}$$

However, using z instead of t is not conservative, because it will increase Type I error somewhat. Therefore, statisticians recommend that we always apply t when σ is unknown. We then can use Excel or Appendix D to get the critical value.

9.24 Use Excel to find the *p*-value for each test statistic.
   a. Right-tailed test, $t = +1.677$, $n = 13$ b. Left-tailed test, $t = -2.107$, $n = 5$ c. Two-tailed test, $t = -1.865$, $n = 34$

9.25 Calculate the test statistic and *p*-value for each sample. State the conclusion for the specified α.
   a. H_0: $\mu = 200$ versus H_1: $\mu \neq 200$, $\alpha = .025$, $\bar{x} = 203$, $s = 8$, $n = 16$
   b. H_0: $\mu \geq 200$ versus H_1: $\mu < 200$, $\alpha = .05$, $\bar{x} = 198$, $s = 5$, $n = 25$
   c. H_0: $\mu \leq 200$ versus H_1: $\mu > 200$, $\alpha = .05$, $\bar{x} = 205$, $s = 8$, $n = 36$

9.26   The manufacturer of an airport baggage scanning machine claims it can handle an average of 530 bags per hour. (a) At $\alpha = .05$ in a left-tailed test, would a sample of 16 randomly chosen hours with a mean of 510 and a standard deviation of 50 indicate that the manufacturer's claim is overstated? (b) Why might the assumption of a normal population be doubtful? (See *Aviation Week and Space Technology* 162, no. 4 (January 24, 2005), p. 42.)

9.27   The manufacturer of Glo-More flat white interior latex paint claims one-coat coverage of 400 square feet per gallon on interior walls. A painter keeps careful track of 6 gallons and finds coverage (in square feet) of 360, 410, 380, 360, 390, 400. (a) At $\alpha = .10$ does this evidence contradict the claim? State your hypotheses and decision rule. (b) Is this conclusion sensitive to the choice of α? (c) Use Excel to find the *p*-value. Interpret it. (d) Discuss the distinction between importance and significance in this example.   🐝 **Paint**

9.28   The average weight of a package of rolled oats is supposed to be at least 18 ounces. A sample of 18 packages shows a mean of 17.78 ounces with a standard deviation of 0.41 ounces. (a) At the 5 percent level of significance, is the true mean smaller than the specification? Clearly state your hypotheses and decision rule. (b) Is this conclusion sensitive to the choice of α? (c) Use Excel to find the *p*-value. Interpret it.

9.29   According to J.D. Power & Associates, the mean wait for an airport rental car shuttle bus in 2004 was 19 minutes. In 2005, a random sample of 20 business travelers showed a mean wait of 15 minutes with a standard deviation of 7 minutes. (a) At $\alpha = .05$, has the mean wait decreased? State the hypotheses and decision rule clearly. (b) Use Excel to find the *p*-value. Interpret it.

9.30   In 2004, a small dealership leased 21 Chevrolet Impalas on 2-year leases. When the cars were returned in 2006, the mileage was recorded (see below). Is the dealer's mean significantly greater than the national average of 30,000 miles for 2-year leased vehicles, using the 10 percent level of significance?   🐝 **Mileage**

40,060	24,960	14,310	17,370	44,740	44,550	20,250
33,380	24,270	41,740	58,630	35,830	25,750	28,910
25,090	43,380	23,940	43,510	53,680	31,810	36,780

9.31   At Oxnard University, a sample of 18 senior accounting majors showed a mean cumulative GPA of 3.35 with a standard deviation of 0.25. (a) At $\alpha = .05$ in a two-tailed test, does this differ significantly from 3.25 (the mean GPA for all business school seniors at the university)? (b) Use the sample to construct a 95 percent confidence interval for the mean. Does the confidence interval include 3.25? (c) Explain how the hypothesis test and confidence interval are equivalent.

Mini Case   9.3

Beauty Products and Small Business

Lisa has been working at a beauty counter in a department store for 5 years. In her spare time she's also been creating lotions and fragrances using all natural products. After receiving positive feedback from her friends and family about her beauty products, Lisa decides to open her own store. Lisa knows that convincing a bank to help fund her new business will require more than a few positive testimonials from family. Based on her experience working at the department store, Lisa believes women in her area spend more than the national average on fragrance products. This fact could help make her business successful.

Lisa would like to be able to support her belief with data to include in a business plan proposal that she would then use to obtain a small business loan. Lisa took a business statistics course while in college and decides to use the hypothesis testing tool she learned. After conducting research she learns that the national average spending by women on fragrance products is $59 every 3 months.

The hypothesis test is based on this survey result:

H_0: $\mu \leq \$59$

H_1: $\mu > \$59$

In other words, she will assume the average spending in her town is the same as the national average *unless she has strong evidence that says otherwise.* Lisa takes a random sample of 25 women and finds that the sample mean $\bar{x}$ is $68 and the sample standard deviation s is $15. Lisa uses a t statistic because she doesn't know the population standard deviation. Her calculated t statistic is

$$t = \frac{68 - 59}{\frac{15}{\sqrt{25}}} = 3.00 \quad \text{with 24 degrees of freedom}$$

Using the Excel formula =TDIST(3,24,1), Lisa finds that the one-tail p-value is .003103. This p-value is quite small and she can safely reject her null hypothesis. Rejecting the null hypothesis says that Lisa now has strong evidence to conclude that over a 3-month period women in her area spend more than $59 on average.

Lisa would also like to include an estimate for the average amount women in her area *do* spend. Calculating a confidence interval would be her next step. Lisa chooses a 95 percent confidence level and finds the t statistic to use in her calculations by using the Excel formula =TINV(0.05,24). The result is $t = 2.0639$. Her 95 percent confidence interval for μ is

$$\$68 \pm 2.0639 \frac{15}{\sqrt{25}} = \$68 \pm \$6.19$$

Lisa's business plan proposal can confidently claim that women in her town spend more than the national average on fragrance products and that she estimates the average spending is between $62 and $74 every 3 months. Hopefully the bank will see not only that Lisa creates excellent beauty products, but she also will be a smart businessperson!

Source: For national average spending see The NPD Group press release, "New NPD Beauty Study Identifies Key Consumer Differences and Preferences," March 28, 2005.

Recall that *power* is the probability of correctly rejecting a false null hypothesis. While we cannot always attain the power we desire in a statistical test, we can at least calculate what the power would be in various possible situations. We will show step by step how to calculate power for tests of a mean or proportion, and how to draw *power curves* that show how power depends on the true value of the parameter we are estimating.

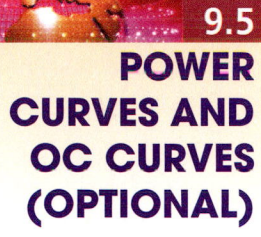

9.5
POWER CURVES AND OC CURVES (OPTIONAL)

Chapter 11

Power Curve for a Mean: An Example

Power depends on how far the true value of the parameter is from the null hypothesis value. The further away the true population value is from the assumed value, the easier it is for your hypothesis test to detect and the more power it has. To illustrate the calculation of β risk and power, consider a utility that is installing underground PVC pipe as a cable conduit. The specifications call for a mean strength of 12,000 psi (pounds per square inch). A sample of 25 pieces of pipe is tested under laboratory conditions to ascertain the compressive pressure that causes the pipe to collapse. The standard deviation is known from past experience to be $\sigma = 500$ psi. If the pipe proves stronger than the specification, there is no problem, so the utility requires a left-tailed test:

H_0: $\mu \geq 12,000$

H_1: $\mu < 12,000$

If the true mean strength is 11,900 psi, what is the probability that the utility will accept the null hypothesis and mistakenly conclude that $\mu = 12,000$? At $\alpha = .05$, what is the power of the test? Recall that β is the risk of Type II error, the probability of incorrectly accepting a false hypothesis. Type II error is bad, so we want β to be small.

$$\beta = P(\text{accept } H_0 \mid H_0 \text{ is false}) \tag{9.9}$$

In this example, $\beta = P(\text{conclude } \mu = 12{,}000 \,|\, \mu = 11{,}900)$.

Conversely, power is the probability that we correctly reject a false hypothesis. More power is better, so we want power to be as close to 1 as possible:

(9.10) $$\text{Power} = P(\text{reject } H_0 \,|\, H_0 \text{ is false}) = 1 - \beta$$

The values of β and power will vary, depending on the difference between the true mean μ and the hypothesized mean μ_0, the standard deviation σ, the sample size n, and the level of significance α.

(9.11) $$\text{Power} = f(\mu - \mu_0, \sigma, n, \alpha) \qquad \text{(determinants of power for a mean)}$$

Table 9.8 summarizes their effects. While we cannot change μ and σ, the sample size and level of significance often are under our control. We can get more power by increasing α, but would we really want to increase Type I error in order to reduce Type II error? Probably not, so the way we usually increase power is by choosing a larger sample size. We will discuss each of these effects in turn.

TABLE 9.8

Determinants of Power in Testing One Mean

Parameter	*If . . .*	*then . . .*
True mean (μ)	$|\mu - \mu_0| \uparrow$	Power $\uparrow$
True standard deviation (σ)	$\sigma \uparrow$	Power $\downarrow$
Sample size (n)	$n \uparrow$	Power $\uparrow$
Level of significance (α)	$\alpha \uparrow$	Power $\uparrow$

Calculating Power

To calculate β and power, we follow a simple sequence of steps for any given values of μ, σ, n, and α. We assume a normal population (or a large sample) so that the sample mean $\bar{X}$ may be assumed normally distributed.

Step 1   Find the left-tail *critical value* for the sample mean. At $\alpha = .05$ in a left-tailed test, we know that $z_{.05} = -1.645$. Using the formula for a z-score,

$$z_{\text{critical}} = \frac{\bar{x}_{\text{critical}} - \mu_0}{\dfrac{\sigma}{\sqrt{n}}}$$

we can solve algebraically for $\bar{x}_{\text{critical}}$:

$$\bar{x}_{\text{critical}} = \mu_0 + z_{\text{critical}} \frac{\sigma}{\sqrt{n}} = 12{,}000 - 1.645 \left(\frac{500}{\sqrt{25}} \right) = 11{,}835.5$$

In terms of the data units of measurement (pounds per square inch) the decision rule is

Reject H_0: $\mu \geq 12{,}000$ if $\bar{X} < 11{,}835.5$ psi

Otherwise do not reject H_0

Now suppose that the true mean is $\mu = 11{,}900$. Then the sampling distribution of $\bar{X}$ would be centered at 11,900 instead of 12,000 as we hypothesized. The probability of β error is the area to the right of the critical value $\bar{x}_{\text{critical}} = 11{,}835.5$ (the acceptance region) representing $P(\bar{X} > \bar{x}_{\text{critical}} \,|\, \mu = 11{,}900)$. Figure 9.24 illustrates this situation.

Step 2   Express the difference between the critical value $\bar{x}_{\text{critical}}$ and the true mean μ as a z-value:

$$z = \frac{\bar{x}_{\text{critical}} - \mu}{\dfrac{\sigma}{\sqrt{n}}} = \frac{11{,}835.5 - 11{,}900}{\dfrac{500}{\sqrt{25}}} = -0.645$$

FIGURE 9.24

Finding β when $\mu = 11{,}900$

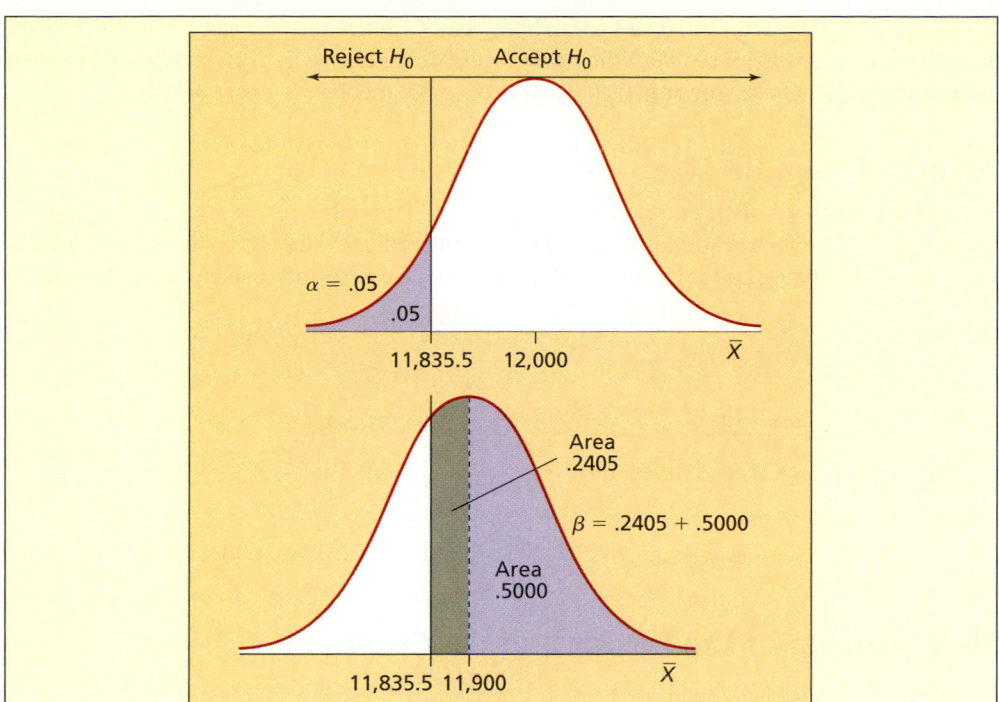

Step 3   Find the β risk and power as areas under the normal curve, using Appendix C-2 or Excel:

Calculation of β

$$\beta = P(\bar{X} > \bar{x}_{critical} \mid \mu = 11{,}900)$$
$$= P(z > -0.645)$$
$$= 0.2405 + 0.5000$$
$$= 0.7405, \text{ or } 74.1\%$$

Calculation of Power

$$\text{Power} = P(\bar{X} < \bar{x}_{critical} \mid \mu = 11{,}900)$$
$$= 1 - \beta$$
$$= 1 - 0.7405$$
$$= 0.2595, \text{ or } 26.0\%$$

This calculation shows that if the true mean is $\mu = 11{,}900$, then there is a 74.05 percent chance that we will commit β error by failing to reject $\mu = 12{,}000$. Since 11,900 is not very far from 12,000 in terms of the standard error, our test has relatively low power. Although our test may not be sensitive enough to reject the null hypothesis reliably if μ is only *slightly* less than 12,000, we would expect that if μ is *far* below 12,000 our test would be more likely to lead to rejection of H_0. Although we cannot know the true mean, we *can* repeat our power calculation for as many values of μ and n as we wish. These calculations may appear tedious, but they are straightforward in a spreadsheet. Table 9.9 shows β and power for samples of $n = 25$, 50, and 100 over a range of μ values from 12,000 down to 11,600.

TABLE 9.9

β and Power for $\mu_0 = 12{,}000$

	n = 25			n = 50			n = 100		
True μ	z	β	Power	z	β	Power	z	β	Power
12000	−1.645	0.9500	0.0500	−1.645	0.9500	0.0500	−1.645	0.9500	0.0500
11950	−1.145	0.8739	0.1261	−0.938	0.8258	0.1742	−0.645	0.7405	0.2595
11900	−0.645	0.7405	0.2595	−0.231	0.5912	0.4088	0.355	0.3612	0.6388
11850	−0.145	0.5576	0.4424	0.476	0.3169	0.6831	1.355	0.0877	0.9123
11800	0.355	0.3612	0.6388	1.184	0.1183	0.8817	2.355	0.0093	0.9907
11750	0.855	0.1962	0.8038	1.891	0.0293	0.9707	3.355	0.0004	0.9996
11700	1.355	0.0877	0.9123	2.598	0.0047	0.9953	4.355	0.0000	1.0000
11650	1.855	0.0318	0.9682	3.305	0.0005	0.9995	5.355	0.0000	1.0000
11600	2.355	0.0093	0.9907	4.012	0.0000	1.0000	6.355	0.0000	1.0000

Notice that β drops toward 0 and power approaches 1 when the true value μ is far from the hypothesized mean $\mu_0 = 12,000$. When $\mu = 12,000$ there can be no β error, since β error can only occur if H_0 is false. Power is then equal to $\alpha = .05$, the lowest power possible.

Effect of Sample Size

Table 9.9 also shows that, other things being equal, if sample size were to increase, β risk would decline and power would increase because the critical value $\bar{x}_{\text{critical}}$ would be closer to the hypothesized mean μ. For example, if the sample size were increased to $n = 50$, then

$$\bar{x}_{\text{critical}} = \mu_0 + z_{\text{critical}}\frac{\sigma}{\sqrt{n}} = 12,000 - 1.645\left(\frac{500}{\sqrt{50}}\right) = 11,883.68$$

$$z = \frac{\bar{x}_{\text{critical}} - \mu}{\frac{\sigma}{\sqrt{n}}} = \frac{11,883.68 - 11,900}{\frac{500}{\sqrt{25}}} = -0.231$$

$$\text{Power} = P(\bar{X} < \bar{x}_{\text{critical}} \mid \mu = 11,900) = P(z < -.231) = .4088, \text{ or } 40.9\%$$

Relationship of the Power and OC Curves

Power is much easier to understand when it is made into a graph. A ***power curve*** is a graph whose Y-axis shows the power of the test $(1 - \beta)$ and whose X-axis shows the various possible true values of the parameter while holding the sample size constant. Figure 9.25 shows the power curve for this example, using three different sample sizes. You can see that power increases as the departure of μ from 12,000 becomes greater and that each larger sample size creates a higher power curve. In other words, larger samples have more power. Since the power curve approaches $\alpha = .05$ as the true mean approaches the hypothesized mean of 12,000, we can see that α also affects the power curve. If we increase α, the power curve will shift up. Although it is not illustrated here, power also rises if the standard deviation is smaller, because a small σ gives the test more precision.

FIGURE 9.25

Power curves for H_0: $\mu = 12,000$

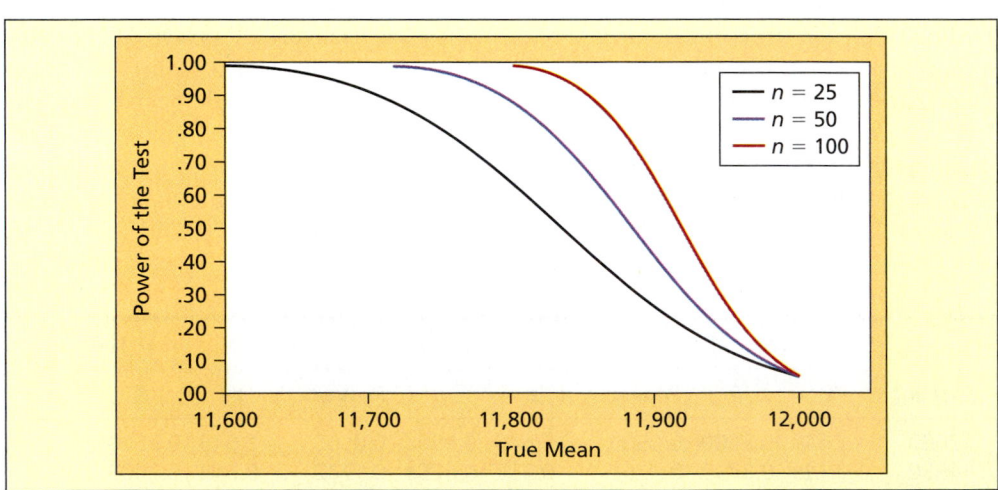

The graph of β risk against this same X-axis is called the ***operating characteristic*** or ***OC curve.*** Figure 9.26 shows the OC curve for this example. It is simply the converse of the power curve, so it is redundant if you already have the power curve.

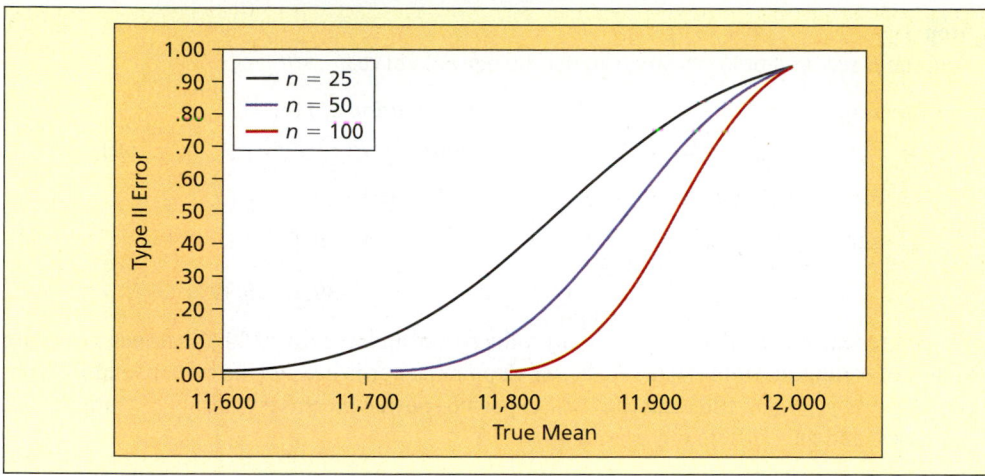

FIGURE 9.26

OC Curves for
$H_0: \mu = 12,000$

Power Curve for Tests of a Proportion

For tests of a proportion, power depends on the true proportion π, the hypothesized proportion π_0, the sample size n, and the level of significance α. Table 9.10 summarizes their effects on power. As with a mean, enlarging the sample size is the most common method of increasing power, unless we are willing to raise the level of significance (that is, trade off Type I error against Type II error).

Parameter	If . . .	then . . .
True proportion π	$|\pi - \pi_0| \uparrow$	Power $\uparrow$
Sample size n	$n \uparrow$	Power $\uparrow$
Level of significance α	$\alpha \uparrow$	Power $\uparrow$

TABLE 9.10

Determinants of Power in Testing a Proportion

EXAMPLE

*Length of Hospital
Stay: Power Curve*

A sample is taken of 50 births in a major hospital. We are interested in knowing whether at least half of all mothers have a length of stay (LOS) less than 48 hours. We will do a right-tailed test using $\alpha = .10$. The hypotheses are

$H_0: \pi \leq .50$

$H_1: \pi > .50$

To find the power curve, we follow the same procedure as for a mean—actually, it is easier than a mean, because we don't have to worry about σ. For example, what would be the power of the test if the true proportion were $\pi = .60$ and the sample size were $n = 50$?

Step 1
Find the left-tail *critical value* for the sample proportion. At $\alpha = .10$ in a right-tailed test, we would use $z_{.10} = 1.282$ (actually, $z = 1.28155$ if we use Excel) so

$$p_{\text{critical}} = \pi_0 + 1.28155\sqrt{\frac{\pi_0(1 - \pi_0)}{n}} = .50 + 1.28155\sqrt{\frac{(.50)(1 - .50)}{50}} = .590619$$

Step 2
Express the difference between the critical value p_{critical} and the true proportion π as a z-value:

$$z = \frac{p_{\text{critical}} - \pi}{\sqrt{\frac{\pi(1 - \pi)}{n}}} = \frac{.590619 - .600000}{\sqrt{\frac{(.60)(1 - .60)}{50}}} = -0.1354$$

Step 3

Find the β risk and power as areas under the normal curve:

Calculation of β	Calculation of Power
$\beta = P(p < p_{\text{critical}} \mid \pi = .60)$	Power $= P(p > p_{\text{critical}} \mid \pi = .60)$
$= P(z < -0.1354)$	$= 1 - \beta$
$= .4461$, or 44.61%	$= 1 - 0.4461$
	$= .5539$, or 55.39%

We can repeat these calculations for any values of π and n. Table 9.11 illustrates power for values of π ranging from .50 to .70, at which point power is near its maximum, and for sample sizes of $n = 50$, 100, and 200. As expected, power increases sharply as sample size increases, and as π differs more from $\pi_0 = .50$.

TABLE 9.11 β and Power for $\pi_0 = .50$

	n = 50			n = 100			n = 200		
π	z	β	Power	z	β	Power	z	β	Power
0.50	1.282	0.9000	0.1000	1.282	0.9000	0.1000	1.282	0.9000	0.1000
0.52	1.000	0.8412	0.1588	0.882	0.8112	0.1888	0.716	0.7631	0.2369
0.54	0.718	0.7637	0.2363	0.483	0.6855	0.3145	0.151	0.5599	0.4401
0.56	0.436	0.6686	0.3314	0.082	0.5327	0.4673	−0.419	0.3378	0.6622
0.58	0.152	0.5605	0.4395	−0.323	0.3735	0.6265	−0.994	0.1601	0.8399
0.60	−0.135	0.4461	0.5539	−0.733	0.2317	0.7683	−1.579	0.0572	0.9428
0.62	−0.428	0.3343	0.6657	−1.152	0.1246	0.8754	−2.176	0.0148	0.9852
0.64	−0.727	0.2335	0.7665	−1.582	0.0569	0.9431	−2.790	0.0026	0.9974
0.66	−1.036	0.1502	0.8498	−2.025	0.0214	0.9786	−3.424	0.0003	0.9997
0.68	−1.355	0.0877	0.9123	−2.485	0.0065	0.9935	−4.083	0.0000	1.0000
0.70	−1.688	0.0457	0.9543	−2.966	0.0015	0.9985	−4.774	0.0000	1.0000

Interpretation   Figure 9.27 presents the results for our LOS example visually. As would be expected, the power curves for the larger sample sizes are higher, and the power of each curve is lowest when π is near the hypothesized value of $\pi_0 = .50$. The lowest point on the curve has power equal to $\alpha = .10$. Thus, if we increase α, the power curve would shift up. Otherwise, we can only decrease β (and thereby raise power) by increasing the chance of Type I error, a trade-off we might not wish to make.

FIGURE 9.27

Power curve families for right-tailed test of $\pi = .50$

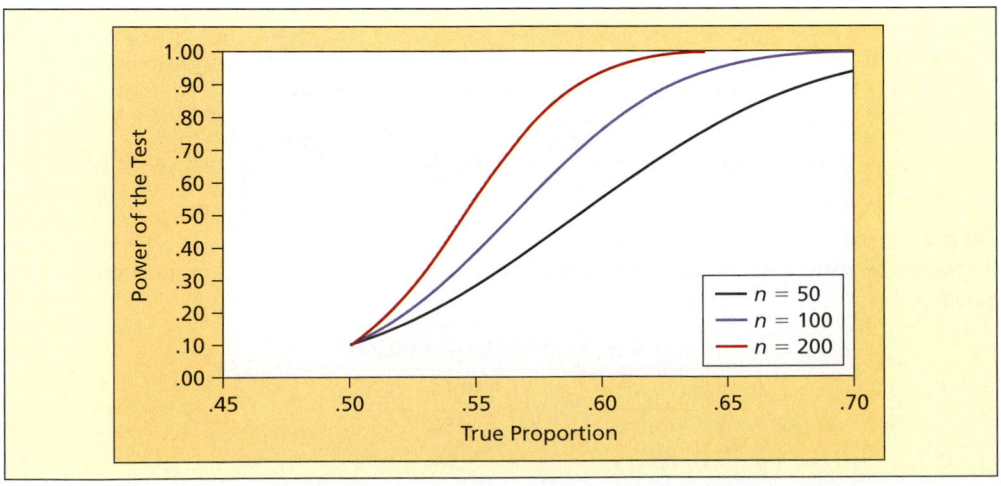

Using *LearningStats*

There are do-it-yourself demonstrations in *LearningStats* that let you create power curves for a mean or a proportion without tedious calculations. An example is shown in Figure 9.28.

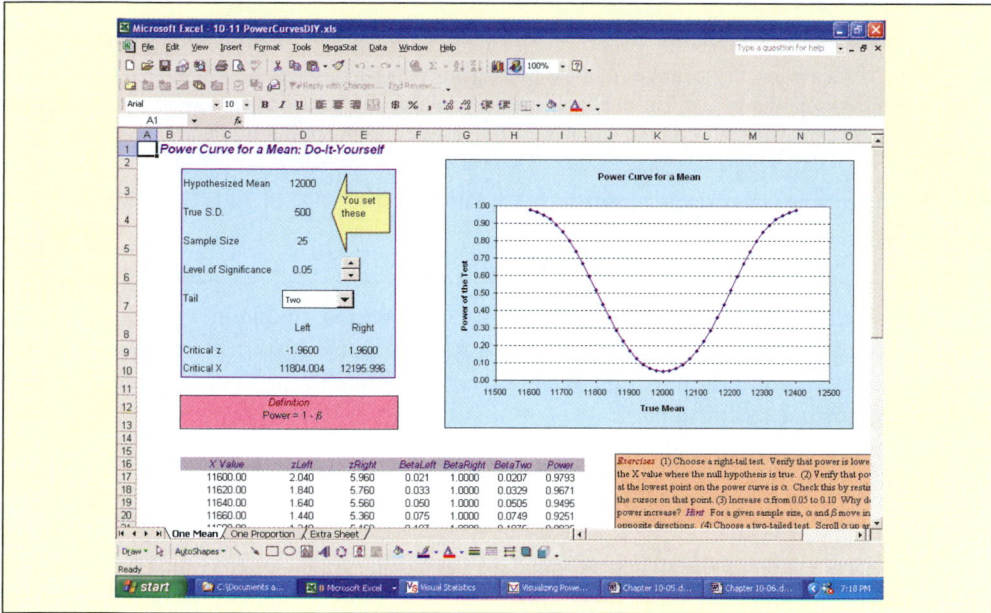

FIGURE 9.28

LearningStats's two-tail power curve for a mean

Using Visual Statistics

There is a demonstration in Visual Statistics that allows you to create power curves for a mean or a proportion, including families of curves based on sample size (e.g., $n/2$, n, $2n$), without tedious calculations. An example is shown in Figure 9.29.

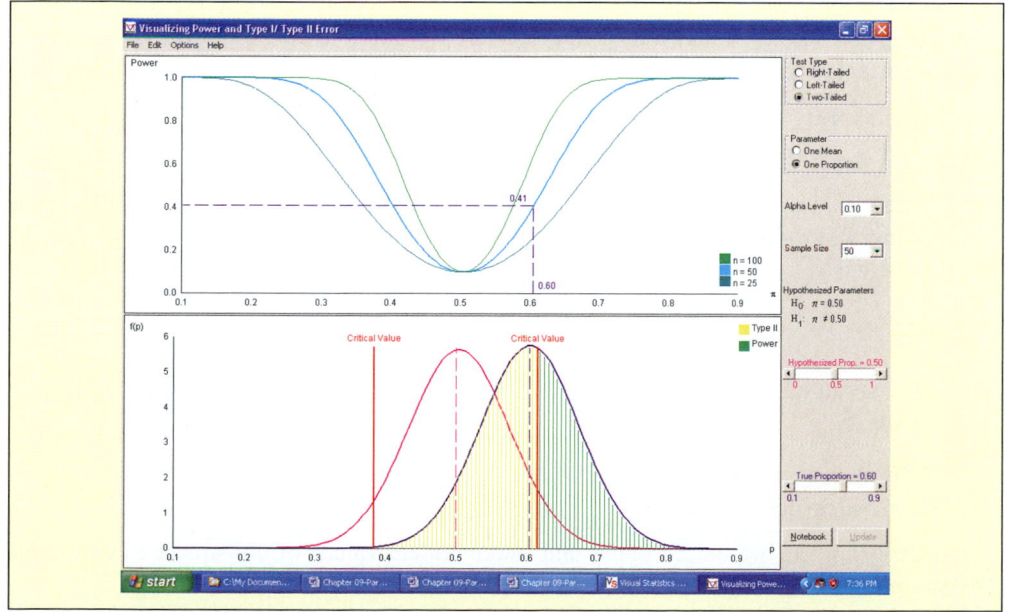

FIGURE 9.29

Visual Statistics's power curve families for a proportion

SECTION EXERCISES

Note: Check your answers using *LearningStats*.

9.32 A quality expert inspects 400 items to test whether the population proportion of defectives exceeds .03, using a right-tailed test at $\alpha = .10$. (a) What is the power of this test if the true proportion of defectives is $\pi = .04$? (b) If the true proportion is $\pi = .05$? (c) If the true proportion of defectives is $\pi = .06$?

9.33 Repeat the previous exercise, using $\alpha = .05$. For each true value of π, is the power higher or lower?

9.34 For a certain wine, the mean pH (a measure of acidity) is supposed to be 3.50 with a known standard deviation of $\sigma = .10$. The quality inspector examines 25 bottles at random to test whether the pH is too low, using a left-tailed test at $\alpha = .01$. (a) What is the power of this test if the true mean is $\mu = 3.48$? (b) If the true mean is $\mu = 3.46$? (c) If the true mean is $\mu = 3.44$?

9.35 Repeat the previous exercise, using $\alpha = .05$. For each true value of μ, is the power higher or lower?

9.6
TESTS FOR ONE VARIANCE (OPTIONAL)

Not all business hypothesis tests involve proportions or means. In quality control, for example, it is important to compare the variance of a process with a historical benchmark, to see whether variance reduction has been achieved, or to compare a process standard deviation with an engineering specification.

EXAMPLE

Attachment Times

Chapter 9

Historical statistics show that the standard deviation of attachment times for an instrument panel in an automotive assembly line is $\sigma = 7$ seconds. Observations on 20 randomly chosen attachment times are shown in Table 9.12. At $\alpha = .05$, does the variance in attachment times differ from the historical variance ($\sigma^2 = 7^2 = 49$)?

TABLE 9.12	Panel Attachment Times (seconds)	🐞 Attachment		
120	143	136	126	122
140	133	133	131	131
129	128	131	123	119
135	137	134	115	122

The sample mean is $\bar{x} = 129.400$ with a standard deviation of $s = 7.44382$. We ignore the sample mean since it is irrelevant to this test. For a two-tailed test, the hypotheses are

$H_0: \sigma^2 = 49$

$H_1: \sigma^2 \neq 49$

For a test of one variance, assuming a normal population, the statistic s^2 follows the ***chi-square distribution*** with degrees of freedom equal to $v = n - 1 = 20 - 1 = 19$. The test statistic is

(9.12)
$$\chi^2 = \frac{(n-1)s^2}{\sigma^2} \qquad \text{(test for one variance)}$$

For our two-tailed test, the decision rule based on the upper and lower critical values of chi-square is

Reject H_0 if $\chi^2 < \chi^2_{\text{lower}}$ or if $\chi^2 > \chi^2_{\text{upper}}$

Otherwise do not reject H_0

From Appendix E, we obtain upper and lower critical values of chi-square to define the rejection region, as illustrated in Figures 9.30 and 9.31.

FIGURE 9.30

Two-tail chi-square values for
$v = 19$ and $\alpha = .05$

Appendix E: Chi-Square Critical Values

This table shows the critical value for the tail areas for the stated degrees of freedom (v).

	Left Tail Area						Right Tail Area				
v	0.005	0.01	0.025	0.05	0.10		0.10	0.05	0.025	0.01	0.005
1	0.000	0.000	0.001	0.004	0.016		2.706	3.841	5.024	6.635	7.879
2	0.010	0.020	0.051	0.103	0.211		4.605	5.991	7.378	9.210	10.60
3	0.072	0.115	0.216	0.352	0.584		6.251	7.815	9.348	11.34	12.84
4	0.207	0.297	0.484	0.711	1.064		7.779	9.488	11.14	13.28	14.86
5	0.412	0.554	0.831	1.145	1.610		9.236	11.07	12.83	15.09	16.75
6	0.676	0.872	1.237	1.635	2.204		10.64	12.59	14.45	16.81	18.55
7	0.989	1.239	1.690	2.167	2.833		12.02	14.07	16.01	18.48	20.28
8	1.344	1.647	2.180	2.733	3.490		13.36	15.51	17.53	20.09	21.95
9	1.735	2.088	2.700	3.325	4.168		14.68	16.92	19.02	21.67	23.59
10	2.156	2.558	3.247	3.940	4.865		15.99	18.31	20.48	23.21	25.19
11	2.603	3.053	3.816	4.575	5.578		17.28	19.68	21.92	24.73	26.76
12	3.074	3.571	4.404	5.226	6.304		18.55	21.03	23.34	26.22	28.30
13	3.565	4.107	5.009	5.892	7.041		19.81	22.36	24.74	27.69	29.82
14	4.075	4.660	5.629	6.571	7.790		21.06	23.68	26.12	29.14	31.32
15	4.601	5.229	6.262	7.261	8.547		22.31	25.00	27.49	30.58	32.80
16	5.142	5.812	6.908	7.962	9.312		23.54	26.30	28.85	32.00	34.27
17	5.697	6.408	7.564	8.672	10.09		24.77	27.59	30.19	33.41	35.72
18	6.265	7.015	8.231	9.390	10.86		25.99	28.87	31.53	34.81	37.16
19	6.844	7.633	8.907	10.12	11.65		27.20	30.14	32.85	36.19	38.58
20	7.434	8.260	9.591	10.85	12.44		28.41	31.41	34.17	37.57	40.00

FIGURE 9.31

Decision rule for chi-square
test

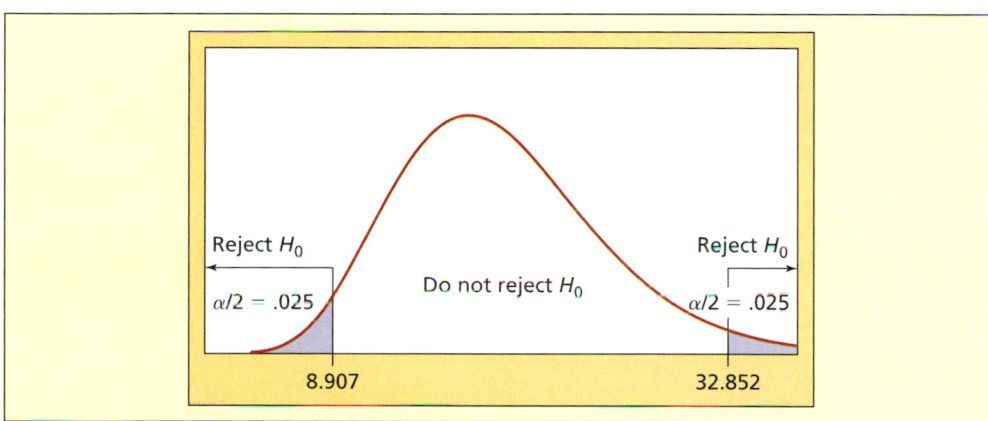

The critical values are $\chi^2_{\text{lower}} = 8.907$ and $\chi^2_{\text{upper}} = 32.852$. The value test statistic is

$$\chi^2 = \frac{(n-1)s^2}{\sigma^2} = \frac{(20-1)(7.44382)^2}{7^2} = 21.49$$

Since the test statistic is within the middle range, we conclude that the sample variance does not differ significantly from 49; that is, the assembly process variance is unchanged.

Using MegaStat

MegaStat does tests for one variance, including a confidence interval. Figure 9.32 shows its setup screen and output for the variance test.

FIGURE 9.32

MegaStat test for one variance

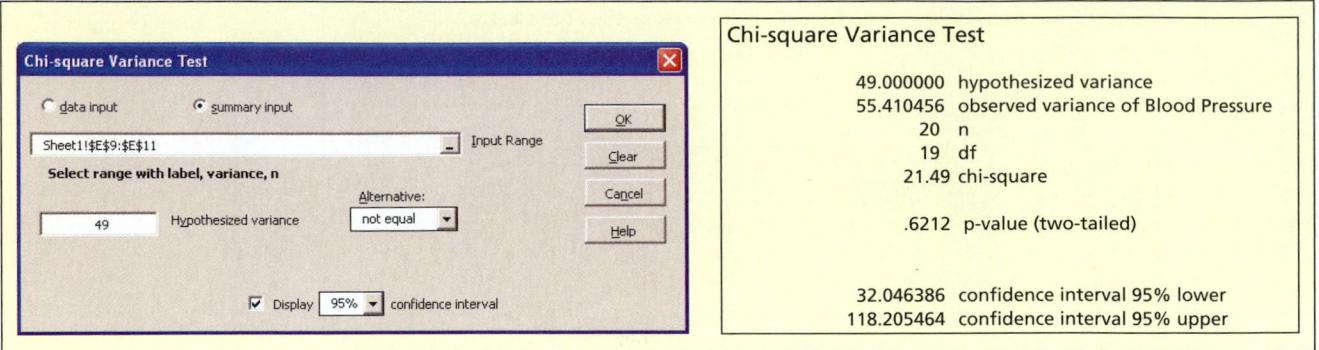

When to Use Tests for One Variance

In general, we would be interested in a test of variances when it is not the *center* of the distribution, but rather the *variability* of the process that matters. More variation implies a more erratic data-generating process. For example, variance tests are important in manufacturing processes, because increased variation around the mean can be a sign of wear and tear on equipment that would require attention.

Caution   The chi-square test for a variance is not robust to non-normality of the population. If normality cannot be assumed (e.g., if the data set has outliers or severe skewness), you might need to use a bootstrap method (see *LearningStats* Unit 08) to test the hypothesis, using specialized software. In such a situation, it is best to consult a statistician.

SECTION EXERCISES

9.36   A sample of size $n = 10$ has variance $s^2 = 16$. At $\alpha = .10$ in a two-tailed test, does this sample contradict the hypothesis that $\sigma^2 = 24$?

9.37   A sample of size $n = 19$ has variance $s^2 = 1.96$. At $\alpha = .05$ in a right-tailed test, does this sample contradict the hypothesis that $\sigma^2 = 1.21$?

9.38   pH is a measure of acidity that winemakers must watch. A "healthy wine" should have a pH in the range 3.1 to 3.7. The acceptable standard deviation is $\sigma = 0.10$ (i.e., $\sigma^2 = 0.01$). The pH measurements for a sample of 16 bottles of wine are shown below. At $\alpha = .05$ in a two-tailed test, is the sample variance either too high or too low? Show all steps, including the hypotheses and critical values from Appendix E. *Hint:* Ignore the mean. (See www.winemakermag.com.)
🍷   **WinePH**

3.49	3.54	3.58	3.57	3.54	3.34	3.48	3.60
3.48	3.27	3.46	3.32	3.51	3.43	3.56	3.39

9.39   In a U.S. hospital, the average length of stay (LOS) for a diagnosis of pneumonia is 137 hours with a standard deviation of 25 hours. The LOS (in hours) for a sample of 12 pneumonia patients at Santa Theresa Memorial Hospital is shown below. In a two-tailed test at $\alpha = .05$, is this sample variance consistent with the national norms? Show all steps, including the hypotheses and critical values from Appendix E. *Hint:* Ignore the mean. (See National Center for Health Statistics, *Advance Data from Vital and Health Statistics,* no. 332 [April 9, 2003], p. 13.)
🐛   **Pneumonia**

132	143	143	120	124	116
130	165	100	83	115	141

The **null hypothesis (H_0)** represents the status quo or a benchmark. We try to reject H_0 in favor of the **alternative hypothesis (H_1)** on the basis of the sample evidence. The alternative hypothesis points to the tail of the test ($<$ for a left-tailed test, $>$ for a right-tailed test, $\neq$ for a two-tailed test). Rejecting a true H_0 is **Type I error,** while failing to reject a false H_0 is **Type II error.** The **power** of the test is the probability of correctly rejecting a false H_0. The probability of Type I error is denoted α (often called **the level of significance**) and can be set by the researcher. The probability of Type II error is denoted β and is dependent on the true parameter value, sample size, and α. In general, lowering α increases β, and vice versa. The **test statistic** compares the sample statistic with the hypothesized parameter. For a mean, the **decision rule** tells us whether to reject H_0 by comparing the test statistic with the **critical value** of z (known σ) or t (unknown σ) from a table or from Excel. Tests of a proportion are based on the normal distribution (if the sample is large enough, according to a rule of thumb), although in small samples the binomial is required. In any hypothesis test, the **p-value** shows the probability that the test statistic (or one more extreme) would be observed by chance, assuming that H_0 is true. If the p-value is smaller than α, we reject H_0 (i.e., a small p-value indicates a **significant** departure from H_0). A two-sided test is analogous to a confidence interval seen in the last chapter. Power is greater the further away the true parameter is from the null hypothesis value. A **power curve** is a graph that plots the power of the test against possible values of the true parameter. Tests of a variance use the **chi-square distribution** and suffer if the data are badly skewed.

alternative hypothesis, *348*
benchmark, *358*
chi-square distribution, *384*
critical value, *352*
decision rule, *352*
hypotheses, *347*
hypothesis test, *350*
hypothesis testing, *347*

importance, *348*
left-tailed test, *350*
level of significance, *352*
null hypothesis, *348*
OC curve, *380*
power, *354*
power curve, *380*
p-value method, *359*

rejection region, *352*
right-tailed test, *350*
significance, *348*
statistical hypothesis, *350*
test statistic, *352*
two-tailed test, *350*
Type I error, *349*
Type II error, *349*

Commonly Used Formulas in One-Sample Hypothesis Tests

Type I error: $\alpha = P(\text{reject } H_0 \mid H_0 \text{ is true})$

Type II error: $\beta = P(\text{fail to reject } H_0 \mid H_0 \text{ is false})$

Power: $1 - \beta = P(\text{reject } H_0 \mid H_0 \text{ is false})$

Test statistic for sample mean, σ known: $z = \dfrac{\bar{x} - \mu_0}{\dfrac{\sigma}{\sqrt{n}}}$

Test statistic for sample mean, σ unknown: $t = \dfrac{\bar{x} - \mu_0}{\dfrac{s}{\sqrt{n}}}$

Test statistic for sample proportion: $z = \dfrac{p - \pi_0}{\sqrt{\dfrac{\pi_0(1 - \pi_0)}{n}}}$

1. (a) List the steps in testing a hypothesis. (b) Why can't a hypothesis ever be proven?
2. (a) Explain the difference between the null hypothesis and the alternative hypothesis. (b) How is the null hypothesis chosen (why is it "null")?
3. (a) Why do we say "fail to reject H_0" instead of "accept H_0"? (b) What does it mean to "provisionally accept a hypothesis"?
4. (a) Define Type I error and Type II error. (b) Give an original example to illustrate.
5. (a) Explain the difference between a left-sided test, two-sided test, and right-sided test. (b) When would we choose a two-sided test? (c) How can we tell the direction of the test by looking at a pair of hypotheses?

6. (a) Explain the meaning of the rejection region in a decision rule. (b) Why do we need to know the sampling distribution of a statistic before we can do a hypothesis test?

7. (a) Define level of significance. (b) Define power.

8. (a) Why do we prefer low values for α and β? (b) For a given sample size, why is there a trade-off between α and β? (c) How could we decrease both α and β?

9. (a) Why is a "statistically significant difference" not necessarily a "practically important difference"? Give an illustration. (b) Why do statisticians play only a limited role in deciding whether a significant difference requires action?

10. (a) In a hypothesis test for a proportion, when can normality be assumed? *Optional* (b) If the sample is too small to assume normality, what can we do?

11. (a) In a hypothesis test of one mean, what assumptions do we make? (b) When do we use t instead of z? (c) When is the difference between z and t immaterial?

12. (a) Explain what a p-value means. Give an example and interpret it. (b) Why is the p-value method an attractive alternative to specifying α in advance?

13. Why is a confidence interval similar to a two-sided test?

*14. (a) What does a power curve show? (b) What factors affect power for a test of a mean? (c) What factors affect power for a proportion? (d) What is the most commonly used method of increasing power?

*15. (a) In testing a hypothesis about a variance, what distribution do we use? (b) When would a test of a variance be needed? (c) If the population is not normal, what can we do?

CHAPTER EXERCISES

Note: Explain answers and show your work clearly. Problems marked * rely on optional material from this chapter.

TYPE I AND II ERROR

9.40   Suppose you always reject the null hypothesis, regardless of any sample evidence. (a) What is the probability of Type II error? (b) Why might this be a bad policy?

9.41   Suppose the judge decides to acquit all defendants, regardless of the evidence. (a) What is the probability of Type I error? (b) Why might this be a bad policy?

9.42   High blood pressure, if untreated, can lead to increased risk of stroke and heart attack. A common definition of hypertension is diastolic blood pressure of 90 or more. (a) State the null and alternative hypotheses for a physician who checks your blood pressure. (b) Define Type I and II error. What are the consequences of each? (c) Which type of error is more to be feared, and by whom?

9.43   A nuclear power plant replaces its ID card facility access system cards with a biometric security system that scans the iris pattern of the employee and compares it with a data bank. Users are classified as authorized or unauthorized. (a) State the null and alternative hypotheses. (b) Define Type I and II error. What are the consequences of each? (c) Which is more to be feared, and by whom?

9.44   If the true mean is 50 and we reject the hypothesis that $\mu = 50$, what is the probability of Type II error? *Hint:* This is a trick question.

9.45   If the null hypothesis that $\pi = .50$ is accepted even though the true proportion is .60, what is the probability of Type I error? *Hint:* This is a trick question.

9.46   Pap smears are a test for abnormal cancerous and precancerous cells taken from the cervix. (a) State a pair of hypotheses and then explain the meaning of a false negative and a false positive. (b) Why is the null hypothesis "null"? (c) Who bears the cost of each type of error?

9.47   About 250,000 patients are treated for appendicitis each year. The chance of removing a healthy appendix is estimated to be between .15 and .40. The probability of failing to diagnose appendicitis in a timely way is estimated at about .20. (a) For a given patient, set up a pair of hypotheses about appendicitis to be considered by the physician. Explain the consequences of the Type I and II error. (b) Why do you suppose the error rates are so high? (Data are from *Science News* 53 [January 31, 1998], p. 78.)

9.48   In a commercially available fingerprint scanner (e.g., for your home or office PC) false acceptances are 1 in 25 million for high-end devices, with false rejection rates of around 3 percent.

(a) Define Type I and II error. (b) Why do you suppose the false rejection rate is so high compared with the false acceptance rate? (Data are from *Scientific American* 288, no. 3 [March 2003], p. 98.)

9.49 The prostate-specific antigen (PSA) test for prostate cancer has a Type I error rate of about 25 percent. Explain in words what this means and who is affected. (See *Scientific American* 279, no. 6 [December 1998], p. 75.)

9.50 When told that over a 10-year period a mammogram test has a false positive rate of 50 percent, Bob said, "That means that about half the women tested actually have no cancer." Correct Bob's mistaken interpretation.

TESTS OF MEANS AND PROPORTIONS

9.51 A can of peeled whole tomatoes is supposed to contain an average of 19 ounces of tomatoes (excluding the juice). The actual weight is a normally distributed random variable whose standard deviation is known to be 0.25 ounces. (a) In quality control, would a one-tailed or two-tailed test be used? Why? (b) Explain the consequences of departure from the mean in either direction. (c) Which sampling distribution would you use if samples of four cans are weighed? Why? (d) Set up a two-tailed decision rule for $\alpha = .01$.

9.52 At Ajax Spring Water, a half-liter bottle of soft drink is supposed to contain a mean of 520 ml. The filling process follows a normal distribution with a known process standard deviation of 4 ml. (a) Which sampling distribution would you use if random samples of 10 bottles are to be weighed? Why? (b) Set up hypotheses and a two-tailed decision rule for the correct mean using the 5 percent level of significance. (c) If a sample of 16 bottles shows a mean fill of 515 ml, does this contradict the hypothesis that the true mean is 520 ml?

9.53 On eight Friday quizzes, Bob received scores of 80, 85, 95, 92, 89, 84, 90, 92. He tells Prof. Hardtack that he is really a 90+ performer but this sample just happened to fall below his true performance level. (a) State an appropriate pair of hypotheses. (b) State the formula for the test statistic and show your decision rule using the 1 percent level of significance. (c) Carry out the test. Show your work. (d) What assumptions are required? (e) Use Excel to find the *p*-value and interpret it.   **BobQuiz**

9.54 Faced with rising fax costs, a firm issued a guideline that transmissions of 10 pages or more should be sent by 2-day mail instead. Exceptions are allowed, but they want the average to be 10 or below. The firm examined 35 randomly chosen fax transmissions during the next year, yielding a sample mean of 14.44 with a standard deviation of 4.45 pages. (a) At the .01 level of significance, is the true mean greater than 10? (b) Use Excel to find the right-tail *p*-value.

9.55 A U.S. dime is supposed to weigh 2.268 grams. A random sample of 15 circulated dimes showed a mean weight of 2.256 grams with a standard deviation of .026 grams. (a) Using $\alpha = .05$, is the mean weight of all circulated dimes lower than the specification? State your hypotheses and decision rule. (b) Why might circulated dimes weigh less than the mint specification? (See *Science News* 157, no. 14 [April 1, 2000], p. 216.)

9.56 A coin was flipped 60 times and came up heads 38 times. (a) At the .10 level of significance, is the coin biased toward heads? Show your decision rule and calculations. (b) Calculate a *p*-value and interpret it.

9.57 A sample of 100 one-dollar bills from the Subway cash register revealed that 16 had something written on them besides the normal printing (e.g., "Bob ♥ Mary"). (a) At $\alpha = .05$, is this sample evidence consistent with the hypothesis that 10 percent or fewer of all dollar bills have anything written on them besides the normal printing? Include a sketch of your decision rule and show all calculations. (b) Is your decision sensitive to the choice of α? (c) Find the *p*-value.

9.58 A sample of 100 mortgages approved during the current year showed that 31 were issued to a single-earner family or individual. The historical average is 25 percent. (a) At the .05 level of significance in a right-tailed test, has the percentage of single-earner or individual mortgages risen? Include a sketch of your decision rule and show all work. (b) Is this a close decision? (c) State any assumptions that are required.

9.59 A state weights-and-measures standard requires that no more than 5 percent of bags of Halloween candy be underweight. A random sample of 200 bags showed that 16 were underweight. (a) At $\alpha = .025$, is the standard being violated? Use a right-tailed test and show your work. (b) Find the *p*-value.

9.60 Ages for the 2005 Boston Red Sox pitchers are shown below. (a) Assuming this is a random sample of major league pitchers, at the 5 percent level of significance does this sample show that the true mean age of all American League pitchers is over 30 years? State your hypotheses and decision rule and show all work. (b) If there is a difference, is it important? (c) Find the *p*-value and interpret it. (Data are from http://boston.redsox.mlb.com.)   **RedSox**

Ages of Boston Red Sox Pitchers, October 2005

Arroyo	28	Foulke	33	Mantei	32	Timlin	39
Clement	31	Gonzalez	30	Miller	29	Wakefield	39
Embree	35	Halama	33	Myers	36	Wells	42

9.61   The EPA is concerned about the quality of drinking water served on airline flights. In September 2004, a sample of 158 flights found unacceptable bacterial contamination on 20 flights. (a) At $\alpha = .05$, does this sample show that more than 10 percent of all flights have contaminated water? (b) Find the *p*-value. (Data are from *The Wall Street Journal,* November 10, 2004, p. D1.)

9.62   The Web-based company *Oh Baby! Gifts* has a goal of processing 95 percent of its orders on the same day they are received. If 485 out of the next 500 orders are processed on the same day, would this prove that they are exceeding their goal, using $\alpha = .025$? (See story.news.yahoo.com accessed June 25, 2004.)

9.63   In the Big Ten (the NCAA sports league) a sample showed that only 267 out of 584 freshmen football players graduated within 6 years. (a) At $\alpha = .05$ does this sample contradict the claim that at least half graduate within 6 years? State your hypotheses and decision rule. (b) Calculate the *p*-value and interpret it. (c) Do you think the difference is important, as opposed to significant?

9.64   An auditor reviewed 25 oral surgery insurance claims from a particular surgical office, determining that the mean out-of-pocket patient billing above the reimbursed amount was $275.66 with a standard deviation of $78.11. (a) At the 5 percent level of significance, does this sample prove a violation of the guideline that the average patient should pay no more than $250 out-of-pocket? State your hypotheses and decision rule. (b) Is this a close decision?

9.65   A consumer agency tested 290 hams, finding that 64 were underweight. (a) Construct a 95 percent confidence interval for the true percent of underweight hams. (b) If the goal is to reduce the incidence of underweight hams to 25 percent or less, does this sample show that the goal is being achieved? (c) Explain how this confidence interval is equivalent to a two-tailed test at $\alpha = .05$. (Data are from *Detroit Free Press,* March 9, 1999, p. 2A.)

9.66   A digital camcorder repair service has set a goal not to exceed an average of 5 working days from the time the unit is brought in to the time repairs are completed. A random sample of 12 repair records showed the following repair times (in days): 9, 2, 5, 1, 5, 4, 7, 5, 11, 3, 7, 2. At $\alpha = .05$ is the goal being met?   🎲 **Repair**

9.67   (a) At the .025 level of significance, does the random sample below show that the average NBA player gets over 300 rebounds per season? State your hypotheses and decision rule, and show all work. (b) Why might non-normality be a problem?   🎲 **Rebounds**

Rebounds by 12 Randomly Chosen NBA Players in 2000–2001 Season

Player	Rebounds	Player	Rebounds
Lorenzen Wright	535	Hersey Hawkins	80
Nazr Mohammed	307	Lamond Murray	340
Chris Crawford	110	Greg Buckner	157
Paul Pierce	522	Maurice Taylor	378
Baron Davis	408	Jalen Rose	359
Jamaal Magloire	295	Zan Tabak	213

Source: *The World Almanac and Book of Facts, 2002*, pp. 938–40.

9.68   A process is supposed to produce aluminum castings with a mean weight of 1.223 kg. The weights follow a normal distribution with known standard deviation 0.084 kg. (a) Set up hypotheses and a two-tailed decision rule to detect quality control violations using the .05 level of significance. (b) From the following sample of 12 castings, what conclusion can you draw?   🎲 **Aluminum**

1.067	1.204	1.047	1.167	1.368	1.251
1.274	1.185	1.261	1.345	1.077	1.335

PROPORTIONS: SMALL SAMPLES

*9.69   An automaker states that its cars equipped with electronic fuel injection and computerized engine controls will start on the first try (hot or cold) 99 percent of the time. A survey of 100 new car owners revealed that 3 had not started on the first try during a recent cold snap. (a) At $\alpha = .025$ does this demonstrate that the automaker's claim is incorrect? (b) Calculate the *p*-value and interpret it. *Hint:* Use MINITAB, or use Excel to calculate the cumulative binomial probability $P(X \geq 3 \mid n = 100, \pi = .01) = 1 - P(X \leq 2 \mid n = 100, \pi = .01)$.

*9.70 A quality standard says that no more than 2 percent of the eggs sold in a store may be cracked (not broken, just cracked). In 3 cartons (12 eggs each carton) 2 eggs are cracked. (a) At the .10 level of significance, does this prove that the standard is exceeded? (b) Calculate a *p*-value for the observed sample result. *Hint:* Use Excel to calculate the binomial probability $P(X \geq 2 \mid n = 36, \pi = .02) = 1 - P(X \leq 1 \mid n = 36, \pi = .02)$.

*9.71 An experimental medication is administered to 16 people who suffer from migraines. After an hour, 10 say they feel better. Is the medication effective (i.e., is the percent who feel better greater than 50 percent)? Use $\alpha = .10$, explain fully, and show all steps.

9.72 The historical on-time percentage for Amtrak's Sunset Limited is 10 percent. In July 2004, the train was on time 0 times in 31 runs. Has the on-time percentage fallen? Explain clearly. *Hint:* Use Excel to calculate the cumulative binomial probability $P(X \leq 0 \mid n = 31, \pi = .10)$. (Data are from *The Wall Street Journal,* August 10, 2004.)

*9.73 After 7 months, none of 238 angioplasty patients who received a drug-coated stent to keep their arteries open had experienced restenosis (re-blocking of the arteries). (a) Use MINITAB to construct a 95 percent binomial confidence interval for the proportion of all angioplasty patients who experience restenosis. (b) Why is it necessary to use a binomial in this case? (c) If the goal is to reduce the occurrence of restenosis to 5 percent or less, does this sample show that the goal is being achieved? (Data are from *Detroit Free Press,* March 18, 2002, p. 1A.)

9.74 (a) A statistical study reported that a drug was effective with a *p*-value of .042. Explain in words what this tells you. (b) How would that compare to a drug that had a *p*-value of .087?

9.75 Bob said, "Why is a small *p*-value significant, when a large one isn't? That seems backwards." Try to explain it to Bob, giving an example to make your point.

POWER

Hint: In the power problems, use *LearningStats* to check your answers.

*9.76 A certain brand of flat white interior latex paint claims one-coat coverage of 400 square feet per gallon. The standard deviation is known to be 20. A sample of 16 gallons is tested. (a) At $\alpha = .05$ in a left-sided test, find the β risk and power assuming that the true mean is really 380 square feet per gallon. (b) Construct a left-sided power curve, using increments of 5 square feet (400, 395, 390, 385, 380).

*9.77 A process is normally distributed with standard deviation 12. Samples of size 4 are taken. Suppose that you wish to test the hypothesis that $\mu = 500$ at $\alpha = .05$ in a left-tailed test. (a) What is the β risk if the true mean is 495? If the true mean is 490? If the true mean is 485? If the true mean is 480? (b) Calculate the power for each of the preceding values of μ and sketch a power curve. (c) Repeat the previous exercises using $n = 16$.

TESTS OF VARIANCES

Hint: Use MegaStat to check your work.

*9.78 Is this sample of 25 exam scores inconsistent with the hypothesis that the true variance is 64 (i.e., $\sigma = 8$)? Use the 5 percent level of significance in a two-sided test. Show all steps, including the hypotheses and critical values from Appendix E. 🏃 **Exams**

80	79	69	71	74
73	77	75	65	52
81	84	84	79	70
78	62	77	68	77
88	70	75	85	84

*9.79 Hammermill Premium Inkjet 24 lb. paper has a specified brightness of 106. (a) At $\alpha = .005$, does this sample of 24 randomly chosen test sheets from a day's production run show that the mean brightness exceeds the specification? (b) Does the sample show that $\sigma^2 < 0.0025$? State the hypotheses and critical value for the left-tailed test from Appendix E. 🏃 **Brightness**

106.98	107.02	106.99	106.98	107.06	107.05	107.03	107.04
107.01	107.00	107.02	107.04	107.00	106.98	106.91	106.93
107.01	106.98	106.97	106.99	106.94	106.98	107.03	106.98

SHORT ESSAY

9.80 Read the passage below, and then consider the following scenario. A physician is trying to decide whether to prescribe medication for cholesterol reduction in a 45-year-old female patient. The null hypothesis is that the patient's cholesterol is less than the threshold of treatable hypercholesterolemia. However, a sample of readings over a 2-year time period shows considerable variation, usually below but sometimes above the threshold. (a) Define Type I and Type II error. (b) List the costs of each type of error (in general terms). Who bears the cost of each? (c) How might the patient's point of view differ from the HMO's or doctor's? (d) In what sense is this a business problem? A societal problem? An individual problem?

> Hypercholesterolemia is a known risk factor for coronary artery disease. The risk of death from coronary artery disease has a continuous and graded relation to total serum cholesterol levels higher than 180 mg/dl. However, the ratio of total cholesterol to HDL cholesterol is a better predictor of coronary artery disease than the level of either fraction alone. . . . After menopause, plasma LDL cholesterol concentrations rise to equal, and then to exceed, those of men, at the same time HDL cholesterol concentrations fall slightly. . . . This puts women at equal or greater risk for cardiovascular disease. According to the results of medical trials, there is compelling evidence that a reduction in the level of cholesterol leads to a significant decrease in the rate of cardiovascular events. . . . Therefore, screening for high blood cholesterol is an important clinical intervention. The National Heart, Lung, and Blood Institute . . . recommends that all persons aged 20 and above have a cholesterol determination at least once every five years. . . . Timely identification of high-risk individuals allows consideration of various treatment alternatives. For patients who do not have coronary heart disease or peripheral vascular disease, emphasis should be placed on non-pharmacologic approaches, mainly changes in diet and exercise. Drug therapy should be reserved for those at highest risk of coronary heart disease: men above 35 years of age and postmenopausal women. (Source: www.dakotacare.com.)

LearningStats Unit 09   One-Sample Hypothesis Tests   LS

LearningStats Unit 09 explains the logic of hypothesis testing, gives examples of the most common one-sample hypothesis tests (one mean, one proportion, one variance), and discusses Type I and II error. Your instructor may assign specific modules, or you may decide to check them out because the topic sounds interesting.

Topic	LearningStats Modules
Hypothesis testing	Overview of Hypothesis Testing
	One-Sample Hypothesis Tests
Common hypothesis tests	One-Sample Tests
	Do-It-Yourself Simulation
	Sampling Distribution Examples
Type I error and power	Type I Error
	p-Value Illustration
	Power Curves: Examples
	Power Curves: Do-It-Yourself
	Power Curve Families: μ
	Power Curve Families: π
Optional topics	Probability Plots
	Finite Population Correction
Equations	One-Sample Formulas
	Sampling Distributions
Tables	Appendix C—Normal
	Appendix D—Student's *t*
	Appendix E—Chi-Square

Key: = PowerPoint   = Word   = Excel

Visual Statistics

Visual Statistics Modules on One-Sample Tests

Module	*Module Name*
6	**VS** Visualizing Random Samples
9	**VS** Visualizing One-Sample Hypothesis Tests

Visual Statistics Modules 6 and 9 (included on your CD) are designed to help you

- Understand variability in samples.
- Learn to distinguish between one-tailed and two-tailed tests.
- Be able to explain the meaning of significance and power.
- Interpret decision rules, critical values, and *p*-values.
- Know the role of the normality assumption and the effects of violating it.

The worktext (included on the CD in .PDF format) contains lists of concepts covered, objectives of the modules, overviews of concepts, illustrations of concepts, orientations to module features, learning exercises (basic, intermediate, advanced), learning projects (individual, team), self-evaluation quizzes, glossaries of terms, and solutions to self-evaluation quizzes.

Two-Sample Hypothesis Tests

Chapter Learning Objectives

When you finish this chapter you should be able to

- Recognize when a two-sample test for proportions is required.

- Carry out a two-sample test for proportions and know its assumptions.

- Check whether normality may be assumed for two proportions.

- Explain the analogy between confidence intervals and two-tailed tests.

- Recognize when a two-sample test for means is required.

- Choose the correct formulas for a two-sample comparison for means.

- Explain the assumptions underlying the two-sample test of means.

- Know when a two-sample test of means should not be performed.

- Recognize paired data and be able to perform a paired t test.

- List the main characteristics of the F distribution and why it is used.

- Perform a one-tailed or two-tailed test to compare two variances.

- Recognize the assumptions underlying the F test and when they are violated.

- Be able to use one or more computer software packages to do two-sample tests.

The logic and applications of hypothesis testing that you learned in Chapter 9 will continue here, but now we consider two-sample tests. The use of these techniques is widespread in science and engineering as well as social sciences. Drug companies use sophisticated versions called clinical trials to determine the effectiveness of new drugs, agricultural science continually uses these methods to compare yields to improve productivity, and a wide variety of businesses use them to test or compare things.

What Is a Two-Sample Test?

Two-sample tests compare two sample estimates *with each other,* whereas one-sample tests compare a sample estimate with a nonsample benchmark (a claim or prior belief about a population parameter). Here are some actual two-sample tests from this chapter:

Automotive   A new bumper is installed on selected vehicles in a corporate fleet. During a 1-year test period, 12 vehicles with the new bumper were involved in accidents, incurring mean damage of $1,101 with a standard deviation of $696. During the same year, 9 vehicles with the old bumpers were involved in accidents, incurring mean damage of $1,766 with a standard deviation of $838. Did the new bumper significantly reduce damage? Did it reduce variation?

Marketing   At a matinee performance of *Bride of Chucky,* a random sample of 25 concession purchases showed a mean of $5.29 with a standard deviation of $3.02. For the evening performance a random sample of 25 concession purchases showed a mean of $5.12 with a standard deviation of $2.14. Is there less variation in the evenings?

Safety   In Dallas, some fire trucks were painted yellow (instead of red) to heighten their visibility. During a test period, the fleet of red fire trucks made 153,348 runs and had 20 accidents, while the fleet of yellow fire trucks made 135,035 runs and had 4 accidents. Is the difference in accident rates significant?

Medicine   Half of a group of 18,882 healthy men with no sign of prostate cancer were given an experimental drug called finasteride, while half were given a placebo, based on a random selection process. Participants underwent annual exams and blood tests. Over the next 7 years, 571 men in the placebo group developed prostate cancer, compared with only 435 in the finasteride group. Is the difference in cancer rates significant?

Education   In a certain college class, 20 randomly chosen students were given a tutorial, while 20 others used a self-study computer simulation. On the same 20-point quiz, the tutorial students' mean score was 16.7 with a standard deviation of 2.5, compared with a mean of 14.5 and a standard deviation of 3.2 for the simulation students. Did the tutorial students do better, or is it just due to chance? Is there any significant difference in the degree of variation in the two groups?

Basis of Two-Sample Tests

Two-sample tests are especially useful because they possess a built-in point of comparison. You can think of many situations where two groups are to be compared (e.g., before and after, old and new, experimental and control). Sometimes we don't really care about the actual value of the population parameter, but only whether the parameter is the same for both populations. Usually, the null hypothesis is that both samples were drawn from populations with the same parameter value, but we can also test for a given degree of difference.

The logic of two-sample tests is based on the fact that two samples drawn from the *same population* may yield *different estimates* of a parameter due to chance. For example, exhaust emission tests could yield different results for two vehicles of the same type. Only if the two sample statistics differ by more than the amount attributable to chance can we conclude that the samples came from populations with different parameter values, as illustrated in Figure 10.1.

FIGURE 10.1

Same population or different?

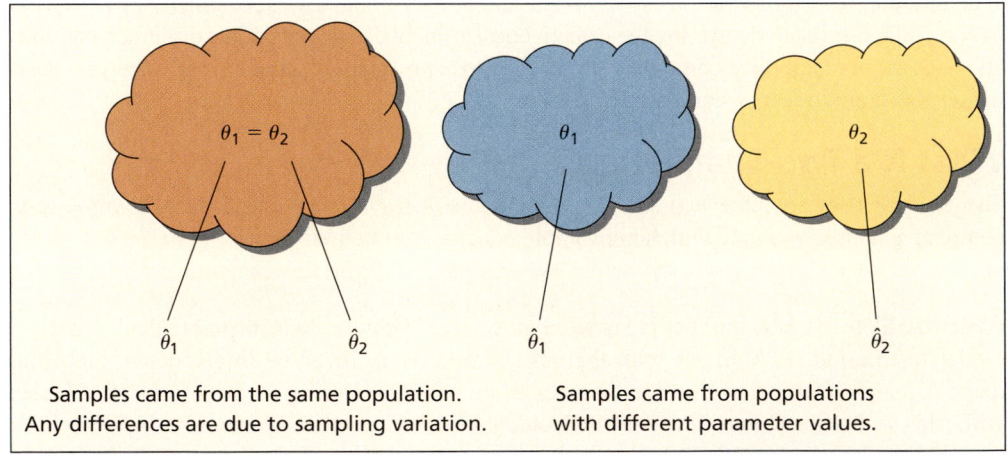

Samples came from the same population. Any differences are due to sampling variation.

Samples came from populations with different parameter values.

Test Procedure

The testing procedure is like that of one-sample tests. We state our hypotheses, set up a decision rule, insert the sample statistics, and make a decision, or we can use *p-values.* Since the true parameters are unknown, we rely on statistical theory to help us reach a defensible conclusion about our hypotheses. Our decision could be wrong—we could commit a *Type I* or *Type II error*—but at least we can specify our acceptable risk levels. Larger samples are always desirable because they permit us to reduce either Type I error or Type II error (i.e., increase the power of the test) or some combination, as we choose.

The test for two proportions is the simplest and perhaps most commonly used two-sample test, because percents are ubiquitous. Is the president's approval rating greater, lower, or the same as last month? Is the proportion of satisfied Dell customers greater than Gateway's? Is the annual nursing turnover percentage at Mayo Clinic higher, lower, or the same as Johns Hopkins? To answer such questions, we would compare two sample proportions.

Testing for Zero Difference: $\pi_1 = \pi_2$

Let the true proportions in the two populations be denoted π_1 and π_2. To compare the two population proportions, the pairs of possible hypotheses are

Left-Tailed Test	Two-Tailed Test	Right-Tailed Test
$H_0: \pi_1 \geq \pi_2$	$H_0: \pi_1 = \pi_2$	$H_0: \pi_1 \leq \pi_2$
$H_1: \pi_1 < \pi_2$	$H_1: \pi_1 \neq \pi_2$	$H_1: \pi_1 > \pi_2$

Sample Proportions

The sample proportion p_1 is a point estimate of π_1, and the sample proportion p_2 is a point estimate of π_2. A "success" is any event of interest (not necessarily something desirable).

$$p_1 = \frac{x_1}{n_1} = \frac{\text{number of "successes" in sample 1}}{\text{number of items in sample 1}} \qquad (10.1)$$

$$p_2 = \frac{x_2}{n_2} = \frac{\text{number of "successes" in sample 2}}{\text{number of items in sample 2}} \qquad (10.2)$$

Pooled Proportion

If H_0 is true, there is no difference between π_1 and π_2, so the samples can logically be *pooled* or averaged into one "big" sample to estimate the common population proportion:

$$\bar{p} = \frac{x_1 + x_2}{n_1 + n_2} = \frac{\text{number of successes in combined samples}}{\text{combined sample size}} \qquad \textit{(pooled proportion)} \quad (10.3)$$

Test Statistic

If the samples are large, the difference of proportions $p_1 - p_2$ may be assumed normally distributed. The **test statistic** is the difference of the sample proportions $p_1 - p_2$ divided by the standard error of the difference $p_1 - p_2$. The standard error is calculated by using the pooled proportion. If we are testing the hypothesis that $\pi_1 = \pi_2$, the test statistic is

$$z = \frac{p_1 - p_2}{\sqrt{\dfrac{\bar{p}(1 - \bar{p})}{n_1} + \dfrac{\bar{p}(1 - \bar{p})}{n_2}}} \qquad \text{(test statistic for equality of proportions)} \quad (10.4)$$

If you find it easier for computation, the test statistic may also be written

$$z = \frac{p_1 - p_2}{\sqrt{\bar{p}(1 - \bar{p})\left[\dfrac{1}{n_1} + \dfrac{1}{n_2}\right]}} \qquad \text{(test statistic for equality of proportions)} \quad (10.5)$$

↘ A study showed 118 instances of breast cancer among 3,033 mothers who used diethylstilbestrol (DES), an estrogen-like substance formerly used to prevent miscarriage, compared with 80 cases in 3,033 unexposed women comprising a control group (See Table 10.1). At the .01 level of significance, was the incidence of cancer greater in the DES users?

EXAMPLE

DES and Cancer

TABLE 10.1   Cancer Study Results

Statistic	DES Takers	Non-DES Takers
Number of cancers	$x_1 = 118$ cancers	$x_2 = 80$ cancers
Number of mothers	$n_1 = 3{,}033$ women	$n_2 = 3{,}033$ women
Cancer rate	$p_1 = \dfrac{118}{3{,}033} = .03891$	$p_2 = \dfrac{80}{3{,}033} = .02638$

Source: *Science News* 126, no. 22 (1984), p. 343.

Step 1: State the Hypotheses

Because it is suspected that DES increases the cancer risk, we will do a right-tailed test for equality of proportions. We test *only at the equality* because rejecting $H_0: \pi_1 = \pi_2$ would imply rejecting the entire class of hypotheses $H_0: \pi_1 \leq \pi_2$. We can state the pair of hypotheses in either of two equivalent ways:

$$H_0: \pi_1 = \pi_2 \quad \text{or} \quad H_0: \pi_1 - \pi_2 = 0$$
$$H_1: \pi_1 > \pi_2 \quad \text{or} \quad H_1: \pi_1 - \pi_2 > 0$$

Step 2: State the Decision Rule

At $\alpha = .01$ the right-tail critical value is $z_{.01} = 2.326$, which yields the decision rule

Reject H_0 if $z > 2.326$

Otherwise do not reject H_0

The decision rule is illustrated in Figure 10.2.

FIGURE 10.2

Right-tailed test for two proportions

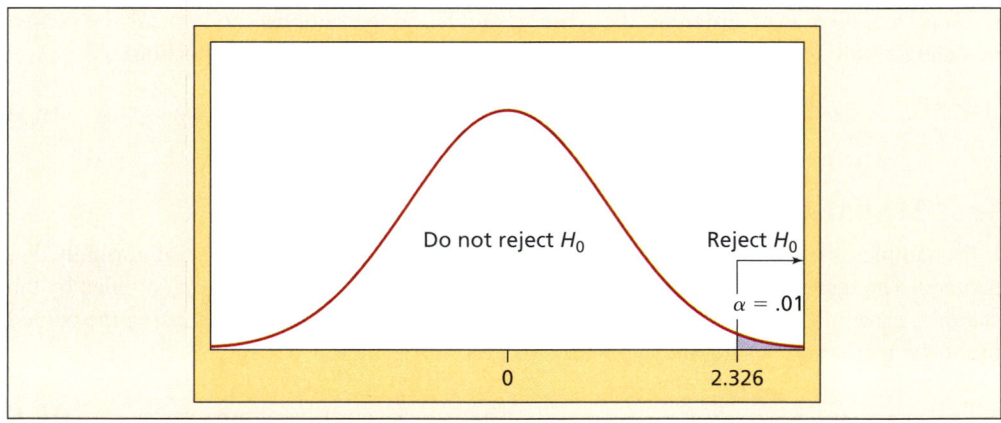

Step 3: Calculate the Test Statistic

The sample proportions indicate that DES-users have a higher incidence of breast cancer (.03891) than non-DES users (.02638). We assume that $\pi_1 = \pi_2$ and see if a contradiction stems from this assumption. Assuming that $\pi_1 = \pi_2$, we can pool the two samples to obtain a **pooled estimate** of the common proportion by dividing the combined number of breast cancer cases by the combined sample size:

$$\bar{p} = \frac{x_1 + x_2}{n_1 + n_2} = \frac{118 + 80}{3{,}033 + 3{,}033} = \frac{198}{6{,}066} = .03264, \text{ or } 3.26\%$$

Assuming normality (i.e., large samples) the test statistic is

$$z = \frac{p_1 - p_2}{\sqrt{\bar{p}(1 - \bar{p})\left[\dfrac{1}{n_1} + \dfrac{1}{n_2}\right]}} = \frac{.03891 - .02638}{\sqrt{.03264(1 - .03264)\left[\dfrac{1}{3{,}033} + \dfrac{1}{3{,}033}\right]}} = 2.746$$

Step 4: Make the Decision

If H_0 were true, the test statistic should be near zero. Since the test statistic ($z = 2.746$) exceeds the critical value ($z_{.01} = 2.326$) we reject the null hypothesis and conclude that $\pi_1 > \pi_2$. Since we are able to reject the hypothesis $\pi_1 = \pi_2$, we can also reject the entire class of hypotheses $\pi_1 \leq \pi_2$ at $\alpha = .01$, that is, DES users have a significantly higher cancer rate than do non-DES users.

Using the *p*-Value

We can find the right-tail area for $z = 2.746$ by using the function =1-NORMSDIST(2.746) in Excel:

$$P(z > 2.746) = 1 - .9970 = .0030 \qquad \text{(from Excel)}$$

This *p*-value of .003 is the level of significance which would allow us to reject H_0. The *p*-value says that if H_0 were true, a sample result as extreme as ours would happen by chance approximately 3 times in 1,000 decisions. If we don't have Excel, we can obtain the same result from Appendix C-2 even though it requires rounding the *z*-value slightly to two digits:

$$P(z > 2.75) = 1 - .9970 = .0030 \qquad \text{(from Appendix C-2)}$$

Since the *p*-value (.0030) is less than the chosen level of significance ($\alpha = .01$) we would reject H_0 in a right-tailed test. The advantage of the *p*-value approach is that it gives more information and lets different researchers choose their own α values. For example, the FDA might have a different view of Type I error than a cancer patient. The *p*-value directly shows our chance of Type I error if we reject H_0. *A smaller p-value indicates a more significant difference.* Figure 10.3 illustrates the *p*-value.

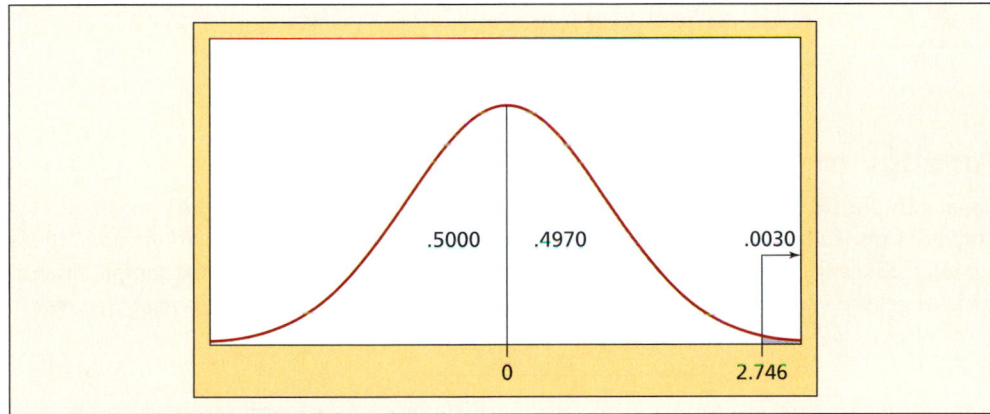

FIGURE 10.3

Right-tail *p*-value for DES and non-DES users

Checking Normality

We have assumed a normal distribution for the statistic $p_1 - p_2$. This assumption can be checked. For a test of two proportions, the criterion for normality is $n\pi \geq 10$ and $n(1 - \pi) \geq 10$ for *each* sample, using each sample proportion in place of π:

$$n_1 p_1 = (3,033)(118/3,033) = 118 \quad n_1(1 - p_1) = (3,033)(1 - 118/3,033) = 2,915$$
$$n_2 p_2 = (3,033)(80/3,033) = 80 \quad n_2(1 - p_2) = (3,033)(1 - 80/3,033) = 2,953$$

The normality requirement is comfortably fulfilled in this case. Ideally, these numbers should exceed 10 by a comfortable margin, as they do in this example. Since the samples are pooled, this guarantees that the pooled proportion $(n_1 + n_2)\bar{p} \geq 10$. Note that when using sample data, the sample size rule of thumb is equivalent to requiring that each sample contains at least 10 "successes" and at least 10 "failures."

Small Samples

If sample sizes do not justify the normality assumption, each sample should be treated as a binomial experiment. Unless you have good computational software, this may not be worthwhile. If the samples are small, the test is likely to have low power.

Must Sample Sizes Be Equal?

No. Although sample sizes happen to be equal in our example, balanced sample sizes are not necessary. Unequal sample sizes are common, and the formulas still apply.

Using Software for Calculations

Given the tedium of the calculations, it is desirable to use software. MegaStat gives you the option of entering sample proportions or the fractions. MINITAB gives you the option of nonpooled proportions, which we will discuss shortly. Figure 10.4 illustrates their data-entry screens using the DES data.

FIGURE 10.4

Two proportion tests using MegaStat and MINITAB

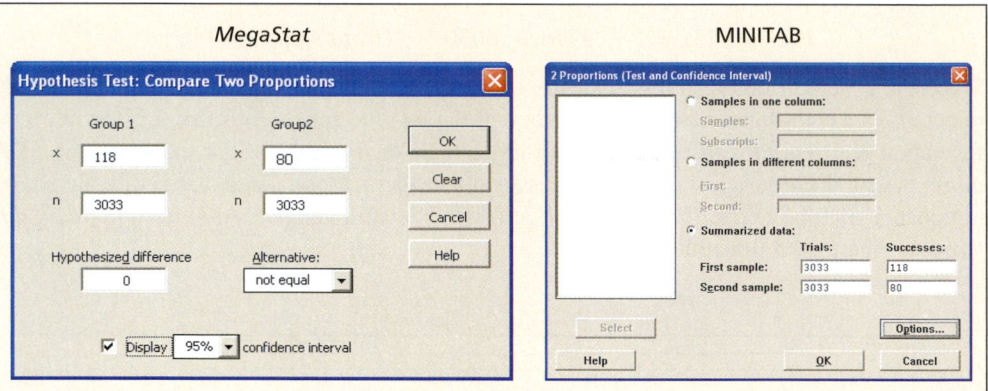

Analogy to Confidence Intervals

Especially for two-tailed tests, the analogy between confidence intervals and two sample hypothesis tests is very strong. We create the confidence interval for $\pi_1 - \pi_2$ *without pooling the samples*. Since the samples are treated separately, we add the variances of the sample proportions to get the variance of $p_1 - p_2$ and take the square root to obtain the *estimated standard error* of $p_1 - p_2$. The confidence interval is

$$(10.6) \quad (p_1 - p_2) \pm z \sqrt{\frac{p_1(1 - p_1)}{n_1} + \frac{p_2(1 - p_2)}{n_2}} \quad \text{(confidence interval for } \pi_1 - \pi_2\text{)}$$

Plugging in $p_1 = 118/3{,}033$ and $p_2 = 80/3{,}033$ we obtain confidence intervals for $\pi_1 - \pi_2$, shown below (calculations not shown).

Confidence Level	Confidence Interval for $\pi_1 - \pi_2$
90% ($z = \pm1.645$)	$.00503 < \pi_1 - \pi_2 < .02003$
95% ($z = \pm1.960$)	$.00359 < \pi_1 - \pi_2 < .02147$
99% ($z = \pm2.576$)	$.00078 < \pi_1 - \pi_2 < .02428$

All three confidence intervals for the difference of proportions fail to include zero, suggesting rejection of H_0: $\pi_1 - \pi_2 = 0$. These confidence intervals are more vivid if displayed graphically, as in Figure 10.5. Although none of the confidence intervals includes zero, the 99 percent confidence interval *almost* does, so our rejection of H_0: $\pi_1 - \pi_2 = 0$ would be a close call for 99 percent confidence and a two-tailed test.

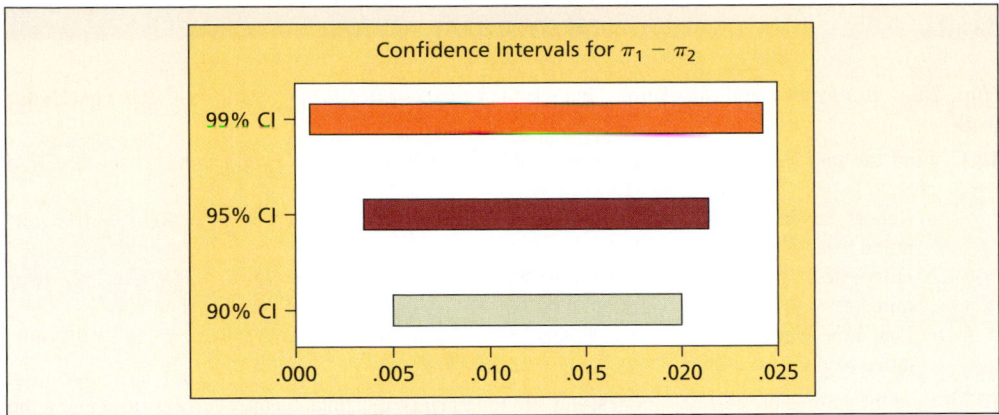

FIGURE 10.5

Confidence intervals for difference of proportions

Separate Confidence Intervals?

We could also construct a separate confidence interval for each proportion. For DES users and non-DES users, by using the formula you learned in Chapter 9:

$$p \pm z\sqrt{\frac{p(1-p)}{n}} \qquad \text{(confidence interval for one proportion)} \qquad \textbf{(10.7)}$$

If the resulting confidence intervals do not overlap, we would expect to conclude that the population proportions differ. However, researchers have found that comparing two confidence intervals does not maintain the desired Type I error we obtain when we construct one confidence interval for the difference $\pi_1 - \pi_2$. A possible way around this problem is to divide each z value by $\sqrt{2}$ in order to reduce the confidence level:*

Desired Confidence	*DES Users*	*Non-DES Users*
90% (use $z = 1.163$)	$.03482 < \pi_1 < .04299$	$.02299 < \pi_2 < .02976$
95% (use $z = 1.386$)	$.03404 < \pi_1 < .04377$	$.02234 < \pi_2 < .03041$
99% (use $z = 1.821$)	$.03251 < \pi_1 < .04530$	$.02108 < \pi_2 < .03168$

It is easier to see the implications if we graph the confidence intervals, as shown in Figure 10.6. Since the intervals do not overlap, we conclude that the proportions differ.

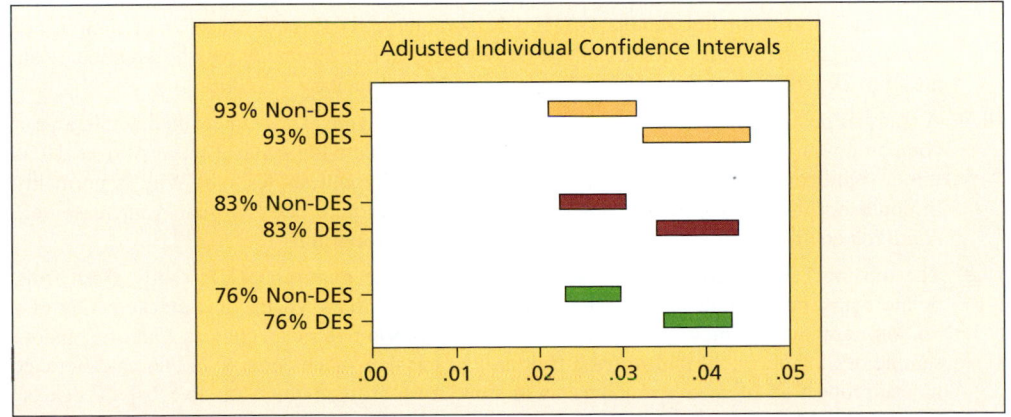

---

*90, 95, and 99 percent confidence levels are reduced roughly to 76, 83, and 93%. For explanation, see end of chapter reference by Payton, Greenstone, and Schenker (2003).

SECTION EXERCISES

Hint: Show all formulas and calculations, but use the calculator in *LearningStats* Unit 10 to check your work.

10.1 Find the test statistic and do the two-sample test for equality of proportions. Is the decision close?
a. Repeat buyers at two car dealerships: $p_1 = .30$, $n_1 = 50$, $p_2 = .54$, $n_2 = 50$, $\alpha = .01$, left-tailed test.
b. Honor roll students in two sororities: $p_1 = .45$, $n_1 = 80$, $p_2 = .25$, $n_2 = 48$, $\alpha = .10$, two-tailed test.
c. First-time Hawaii visitors at two hotels: $p_1 = .20$, $n_1 = 80$, $p_2 = .32$, $n_2 = 75$, $\alpha = .05$, left-tailed test.

10.2 Find the sample proportions and test statistic for equal proportions. Is the decision close? Find the *p*-value.
a. Dissatisfied workers in two companies: $x_1 = 40$, $n_1 = 100$, $x_2 = 30$, $n_2 = 100$, $\alpha = .05$, two-tailed test.
b. Rooms rented at least a week in advance at two hotels: $x_1 = 24$, $n_1 = 200$, $x_2 = 12$, $n_2 = 50$, $\alpha = .01$, left-tailed test.
c. Home equity loan default rates in two banks: $x_1 = 36$, $n_1 = 480$, $x_2 = 26$, $n_2 = 520$, $\alpha = .05$, right-tailed test.

10.3 In 1999, a sample of 200 in-store shoppers showed that 42 paid by debit card. In 2004, a sample of the same size showed that 62 paid by debit card. (a) Formulate appropriate hypotheses to test whether the percentage of debit card shoppers increased. (b) Carry out the test at $\alpha = .01$. (c) Find the *p*-value. (d) Test whether normality may be assumed.

10.4 A survey of 100 mayonnaise purchasers showed that 65 were loyal to one brand. For 100 bath soap purchasers, only 53 were loyal to one brand. (a) Perform a two-tailed test comparing the proportion of brand-loyal customers at $\alpha = .05$. (b) Form a confidence interval for the difference of proportions, without pooling the samples. Does it include zero?

10.5 A 20-minute consumer survey mailed to 500 adults aged 25–34 included a $5 Starbucks gift certificate. The same survey was mailed to 500 adults aged 25–34 without the gift certificate. There were 65 responses from the first group and 45 from the second group. (a) Perform a two-tailed test comparing the response rates (proportions) at $\alpha = .05$. (b) Form a confidence interval for the difference of proportions, without pooling the samples. Does it include zero?

10.6 Is the water on your airline flight safe to drink? It is not feasible to analyze the water on every flight, so sampling is necessary. In August and September 2004, the Environmental Protection Agency (EPA) found bacterial contamination in water samples from the lavatories and galley water taps on 20 of 158 randomly selected U.S. flights. Alarmed by the data, the EPA ordered sanitation improvements, and then tested water samples again in November and December 2004. In the second sample, bacterial contamination was found in 29 of 169 randomly sampled flights. (a) Use a left-tailed test at $\alpha = .05$ to check whether the percent of all flights with contaminated water was lower in the first sample. (b) Find the *p*-value. (c) Discuss the question of significance versus importance in this specific application. (d) Test whether normality may be assumed. (Data are from *The Wall Street Journal,* November 10, 2004, and January 20, 2005.)

10.7 A study of post-coronary recovery showed that 11 of 39 patients without pets died within a year, compared with only 3 of 53 pet-owning patients. (a) Calculate the survival rates. At $\alpha = .10$, is this a significant difference? Explain the steps in your hypothesis test. (b) Why is normality in doubt in this test? (c) Should post-coronary patients acquire pets? Explain your reasoning. *Hint:* You could use the *LearningStats* calculator for two proportions.

10.8 The top food snacks consumed by adults aged 18–54 are gum, chocolate candy, fresh fruit, potato chips, breath mints/candy, ice cream, nuts, cookies, bars, yogurt, and crackers. Out of a random sample of 25 men, 15 ranked fresh fruit in their top five snack choices. Out of a random sample of 32 women, 22 ranked fresh fruit in their top five snack choices. Is there a difference in the proportion of men and women who rank fresh fruit in their top five list of snacks? (a) State the hypotheses and a decision rule for $\alpha = .10$. (b) Calculate the sample proportions. (c) Find the test statistic and its *p*-value. What is your conclusion? (d) Is normality assured? (Data are from The NPD Group press release, "Fruit #1 Snack Food Consumed by Kids," June 16, 2005.)

10.9   When tested for compliance with Sarbanes-Oxley requirements for financial records and fraud protection, 14 of 180 publicly traded business services companies failed, compared with 7 of 67 computer hardware, software and telecommunications companies. (a) Is this a statistically significant difference at $\alpha = .05$? (b) Can normality be assumed? (Data are from *The New York Times,* April 27, 2005, p. BU5.)

Testing for Nonzero Difference (Optional)

Testing for equality of π_1 and π_2 is a special case of testing for a specified difference D_0 between the two proportions:

Left-Tailed Test	*Two-Tailed Test*	*Right-Tailed Test*
$H_0: (\pi_1 - \pi_2) - D_0 \geq 0$	$H_0: (\pi_1 - \pi_2) - D_0 = 0$	$H_0: (\pi_1 - \pi_2) - D_0 \leq 0$
$H_1: (\pi_1 - \pi_2) - D_0 < 0$	$H_1: (\pi_1 - \pi_2) - D_0 \neq 0$	$H_1: (\pi_1 - \pi_2) - D_0 > 0$

We have shown how to test for $D_0 = 0$, that is, $\pi_1 = \pi_2$. If the hypothesized difference D_0 is nonzero, we do not pool the sample proportions, but instead use the test statistic shown in formula 10.8.

$$z = \frac{p_1 - p_2 - D_0}{\sqrt{\dfrac{p_1(1 - p_1)}{n_1} + \dfrac{p_2(1 - p_2)}{n_2}}} \qquad \text{(test statistic for nonzero difference } D_0) \quad \textbf{(10.8)}$$

A sample of 111 magazine advertisements in *Good Housekeeping* showed 70 that listed a Web site. In *Fortune,* a sample of 145 advertisements showed 131 that listed a Web site. At $\alpha = .05$ level of significance, does the *Fortune* proportion differ from the *Good Housekeeping* proportion by at least 20 percent? Table 10.2 shows the data.

EXAMPLE

Magazine Ads

TABLE 10.2 Magazine Ads with Web Sites		
Statistic	**Fortune**	**Good Housekeeping**
Number with Web sites	$x_1 = 131$ with Web site	$x_2 = 70$ with Web site
Number of ads examined	$n_1 = 145$ ads	$n_2 = 111$ ads
Proportion	$p_1 = \dfrac{131}{145} = .90345$	$p_2 = \dfrac{70}{111} = .63063$

Source: Project by MBA students Frank George, Karen Orso, and Lincy Zachariah.

Test Statistic

We will do a two-tailed test for $D_0 = .20$. The hypotheses are

$$H_0: (\pi_1 - \pi_2) - .20 = 0$$
$$H_1: (\pi_1 - \pi_2) - .20 \neq 0$$

The test statistic is

$$z = \frac{p_1 - p_2 - D_0}{\sqrt{\dfrac{p_1(1 - p_1)}{n_1} + \dfrac{p_2(1 - p_2)}{n_2}}}$$

$$= \frac{.90345 - .63063 - .20}{\sqrt{\dfrac{.90345(1 - .90345)}{145} + \dfrac{.63063(1 - .63063)}{111}}} = 1.401$$

At $\alpha = .05$ the two-tail critical values are $z_{.025} = \pm 1.960$, so the difference of proportions is insufficient to reject the hypothesis that the difference is .20 or more. The decision rule is illustrated in Figure 10.7.

FIGURE 10.7

Two-tailed test for magazine ads at $\alpha = .05$

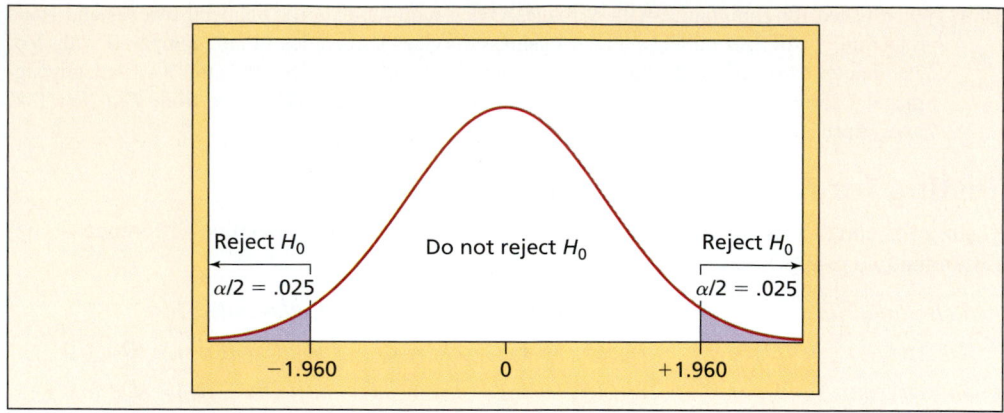

Using the *p*-Value

Using the *p*-value approach, we would insert the test statistic $z = 1.401$ into Excel's cumulative normal =1-NORMSDIST(1.401) to obtain a right-tail area of .0806. Since we want a two-tailed test, we must double this area to obtain $2 \times .0806 = .1612$, as illustrated in Figure 10.8. This *p*-value says that if we were to reject the hypothesis of a difference $D_0 = .20$, we would face a Type I error of about 16 percent. Therefore, if we used a 5 percent level of significance, we would not reject H_0.

FIGURE 10.8

p-Value for magazine proportions differing by $D_0 = .20$

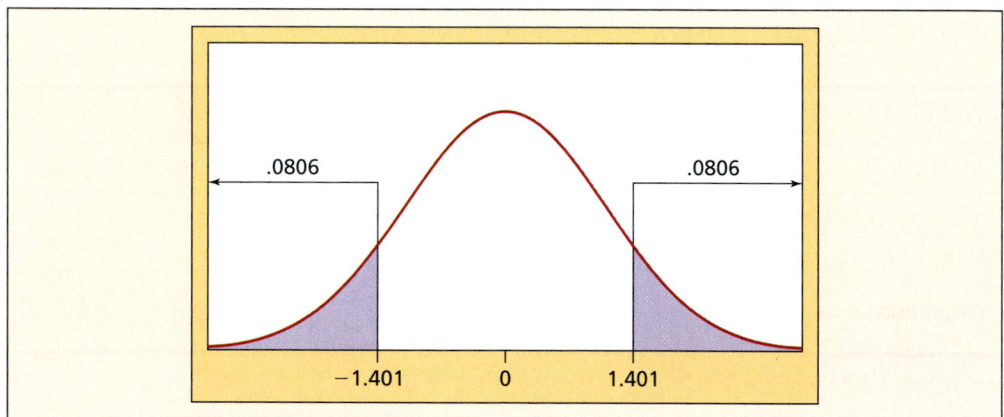

SECTION EXERCISES

Note: Use *LearningStats*, MINITAB, or MegaStat for calculations.

*10.10 In 1999, a sample of 200 in-store shoppers showed that 42 paid by debit card. In 2004, a sample of the same size showed that 62 paid by debit card. (a) Formulate appropriate hypotheses to test whether the percentage of debit card shoppers increased by at least 5 percent, using $\alpha = .10$. (b) Find the *p*-value.

*10.11 From a telephone log, an executive finds that 36 of 128 incoming telephone calls last week lasted at least 5 minutes. She vows to make an effort to reduce the length of time spent on calls. The phone log for the next week shows that 14 of 96 incoming calls lasted at least 5 minutes. (a) At $\alpha = .05$, has the proportion of 5-minute phone calls declined by at least 10 percent? (b) Find the *p*-value.

*10.12 A 30-minute consumer survey mailed to 500 adults aged 25–34 included a $10 gift certificate to Borders. The same survey was mailed to 500 adults aged 25–34 without the gift certificate. There were 185 responses from the first group and 45 from the second group. (a) At $\alpha = .025$, did the gift certificate increase the response rate by at least 20 percent? (b) Find the *p*-value.

Mini Case

10.1

Automated Parking Lot Entry/Exit Gate System

Large universities have many different parking lots. Delivery trucks travel between various buildings all day long to deliver food, mail, and other items. Automated entry/exit gates make travel time much faster for the trucks and cars entering and exiting the different parking lots because the drivers do not have to stop to activate the gate manually. The gate is electronically activated as the truck or car approaches the parking lot.

One large university with two campuses recently negotiated with a company to install a new automated system. One requirement of the contract stated that the proportion of failed gate activations on one campus would be no different from the proportion of failed gate activations on the second campus. (A failed activation was one in which the driver had to manually activate the gate.) The university facilities operations manager designed and conducted a test to establish whether the gate company had violated this requirement of the contract. The university could renegotiate the contract if there was significant evidence showing that the two proportions were different.

The test was set up as a two-tailed test and the hypotheses tested were

$H_0: \pi_1 = \pi_2$

$H_1: \pi_1 \neq \pi_2$

Both the university and the gate company agreed on a 5 percent level of significance. Random samples from each campus were collected. The data are shown in Table 10.3.

TABLE 10.3	Proportion of Failed Gate Activations	
Statistic	**Campus 1**	**Campus 2**
Number of failed activations	$x_1 = 52$	$x_2 = 63$
Sample size (number of entry/exit attempts)	$n_1 = 1{,}000$	$n_2 = 1{,}000$
Proportion	$p_1 = \dfrac{52}{1{,}000} = .052$	$p_2 = \dfrac{63}{1{,}000} = .063$

The pooled proportion is

$$\bar{p} = \frac{x_1 + x_2}{n_2 + n_2} = \frac{52 + 63}{1{,}000 + 1{,}000} = \frac{115}{2{,}000} = .0575$$

The test statistic is

$$z = \frac{p_1 - p_2}{\sqrt{\bar{p}(1 - \bar{p})\left[\dfrac{1}{n_1} + \dfrac{1}{n_2}\right]}} = \frac{.052 - .063}{\sqrt{.0575(1 - .0575)\left[\dfrac{1}{1{,}000} + \dfrac{1}{1{,}000}\right]}} = -1.057$$

Using the 5 percent level of significance the critical value is $z_{.025} = 1.96$ so it is clear that there is no significant difference between these two proportions. This conclusion is reinforced by Excel's cumulative normal function =NORMSDIST(−1.057) which gives the area to the left of −1.057 as .1453. Because this is a two-tailed test the *p*-value is .2906.

Was it reasonable to assume normality of the test statistic? Yes, the criterion was met.

$n_1 p_1 = 1{,}000(52/1{,}000) = 52$ $\qquad n_1(1 - p_1) = 1{,}000(1 - 52/1{,}000) = 948$

$n_2 p_2 = 1{,}000(63/1{,}000) = 63$ $\qquad n_2(1 - p_2) = 1{,}000(1 - 63/1{,}000) = 937$

Based on this sample, the university had no evidence to refute the gate company's claim that the failed activation proportions were the same for each campus.

Source: This case was based on a real contract negotiation between a large western university and a private company. The contract was still being negotiated as of the publication of this text.

10.3 COMPARING TWO MEANS: INDEPENDENT SAMPLES

VS.

Chapter 10

Comparing two means is a common business problem. Is the average customer purchase at Starbucks the same on Saturday and Sunday morning? Is the average customer waiting time the same at two different branches of Chase Bank? Do male and female Wal-Mart employees work the same average overtime hours?

Format of Hypotheses

The population means are denoted μ_1 and μ_2. The possible pairs of hypotheses are

Left-Tailed Test	*Two-Tailed Test*	*Right-Tailed Test*
$H_0: \mu_1 \geq \mu_2$	$H_0: \mu_1 = \mu_2$	$H_0: \mu_1 \leq \mu_2$
$H_1: \mu_1 < \mu_2$	$H_1: \mu_1 \neq \mu_2$	$H_1: \mu_1 > \mu_2$

Test Statistic

The test statistic is the difference of the sample means divided by its standard error. If the population variances σ_1^2 and σ_2^2 are known (a rarity), we can use the normal distribution. If the variances are estimated using s_1^2 and s_2^2, we must use Student's t (the typical situation). There are three cases, shown in Table 10.4. Although the formulas may appear different, the same reasoning is used in each. Each test statistic divides the difference of sample means by its standard error. All the formulas presume a normal population, although in practice they are robust to non-normality as long as the samples are not too small and the population is not too skewed.

TABLE 10.4
Test Statistic for Difference of Means

Case 1	Case 2	Case 3
Known Variances	Unknown Variances, Assumed Equal	Unknown Variances, Assumed Unequal
$$z = \frac{\bar{x}_1 - \bar{x}_2}{\sqrt{\dfrac{\sigma_1^2}{n_1} + \dfrac{\sigma_2^2}{n_2}}}$$	$$t = \frac{\bar{x}_1 - \bar{x}_2}{\sqrt{\dfrac{s_p^2}{n_1} + \dfrac{s_p^2}{n_2}}} \text{ where}$$ $$s_p^2 = \frac{(n_1 - 1)s_1^2 + (n_2 - 1)s_2^2}{n_1 + n_2 - 2}$$	$$t = \frac{\bar{x}_1 - \bar{x}_2}{\sqrt{\dfrac{s_1^2}{n_1} + \dfrac{s_2^2}{n_2}}}$$
For critical value, use normal distribution	For critical value, use Student's t with $n_1 + n_2 - 2$ degrees of freedom	For critical value, use Student's t with Welch's degrees of freedom

The formulas in Table 10.4 require some calculations, but most of the time you will be using a computer. As long as you have raw data (i.e., the original samples of n_1 and n_2 observations) Excel's Tools > Data Analysis menu handles all three cases, as shown in Figure 10.9. *MegaStat* and *MINITAB* also perform these tests. *LearningStats* also provides a calculator for summarized data (i.e., when you have $\bar{x}_1, \bar{x}_2, s_1, s_2$ instead of the n_1 and n_2 data columns).

FIGURE 10.9

Excel's Tools > Data Analysis Menu

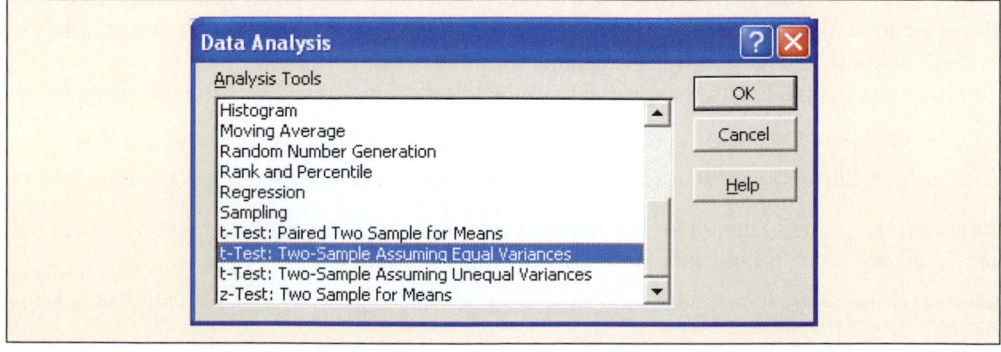

Case 1: Known Variances

In all three cases, the numerator is the *difference* of the sample means and the denominator is the *standard error* of the difference of the means. In *Case 1, σ_1^2* and *σ_2^2* are known (an unlikely situation) so the standard error is the square root of the sum of the variances of $\bar{x}_1$ and $\bar{x}_2$, and we use the normal distribution for the test (assuming a normal population):

$$z = \frac{\bar{x}_1 - \bar{x}_2}{\sqrt{\dfrac{\sigma_1^2}{n_1} + \dfrac{\sigma_2^2}{n_2}}} \qquad \text{(Case 1: known population variances)} \qquad \textbf{(10.9)}$$

Case 2: Unknown Variances, Assumed Equal

In *Case 2,* the variances are unknown (as they usually are) so we must estimate them and use the Student's *t* distribution. If we assume that the population variances are equal, we can take a weighted average of the sample variances s_1^2 and s_2^2 to create an *estimate* of the common variance. Weights are assigned to s_1^2 and s_2^2 based on their respective degrees of freedom $(n_1 - 1)$ and $(n_2 - 1)$. Because we are pooling the sample variances, the common variance estimate is called the **pooled variance** and is denoted s_p^2. *Case 2* is often called the *pooled t test.*

$$s_p^2 = \frac{(n_1 - 1)s_1^2 + (n_2 - 1)s_2^2}{n_1 + n_2 - 2} \qquad \text{(pooled estimate of common variance)} \qquad \textbf{(10.10)}$$

Since the variances are assumed equal, s_p^2 replaces both σ_1^2 and σ_2^2, so the test statistic is

$$t = \frac{\bar{x}_1 - \bar{x}_2}{\sqrt{\dfrac{s_p^2}{n_1} + \dfrac{s_p^2}{n_2}}} \qquad \text{(Case 2: unknown variances, assumed equal)} \qquad \textbf{(10.11)}$$

When the sample variances are pooled, we add their degrees of freedom $(n_1 - 1) + (n_2 - 1)$:

$$\nu = n_1 + n_2 - 2 \qquad \text{(degrees of freedom for pooled } t \text{ test)} \qquad \textbf{(10.12)}$$

Case 3: Unknown Variances, Assumed Unequal

If the unknown variances σ_1^2 and σ_2^2 are assumed *unequal,* we do not pool the variances (a safer assumption than Case 2). Statisticians have shown that under these conditions the distribution of the random variable $\bar{x}_1 - \bar{x}_2$ is no longer certain, a difficulty known as the **Behrens-Fisher problem.** One solution to this problem is the **Welch-Satterthwaite test** which replaces σ_1^2 and σ_2^2 with s_1^2 and s_2^2 in the known variance z formula, but then uses a Student's *t* test with **Welch's adjusted degrees of freedom.**

$$t = \frac{\bar{x}_1 - \bar{x}_2}{\sqrt{\dfrac{s_1^2}{n_1} + \dfrac{s_2^2}{n_2}}} \qquad \text{(unknown variances, assumed unequal)} \qquad \textbf{(10.13)}$$

$$\nu' = \frac{\left[\dfrac{s_1^2}{n_1} + \dfrac{s_2^2}{n_2}\right]^2}{\dfrac{\left(\dfrac{s_1^2}{n_1}\right)^2}{n_1 - 1} + \dfrac{\left(\dfrac{s_2^2}{n_2}\right)^2}{n_2 - 1}} \qquad \text{(Welch's adjusted degrees of freedom)} \qquad \textbf{(10.14)}$$

If, the variances are similar, Welch's adjusted degrees of freedom ν' (i.e., *Case 3*) will be almost the same as the unadjusted degrees of freedom $\nu = n_1 + n_2 - 2$ (i.e., *Case 2*). Finding Welch's adjusted degrees of freedom requires a tedious calculation, but this is easily handled by Excel, MegaStat, or MINITAB. Welch's adjusted degrees of freedom ν' is always between $\min(n_1 - 1, n_2 - 1)$ and $n_1 + n_2 - 2$. To avoid calculating ν', a conservative quick rule for degrees of freedom is to use $\nu^* = \min(n_1 - 1, n_2 - 1)$.

EXAMPLE

*Drug Prices
in Two States*

The price of prescription drugs is an ongoing national issue in the United States. Zocor is a common prescription cholesterol-reducing drug prescribed for people who are at risk for heart disease. Table 10.5 shows Zocor prices from 15 randomly selected pharmacies in two states. At $\alpha = .05$, is there a difference in the mean for all pharmacies in Colorado and Texas? From the dot plots shown in Figure 10.10, it seems unlikely that there is a significant difference, but we will do a test of means to see whether our intuition is correct.

TABLE 10.5   Zocor Prices (30-Day Supply) in Two States   Zocor

Colorado Pharmacies		Texas Pharmacies	
City	*Price ($)*	*City*	*Price ($)*
Alamosa	125.05	Austin	145.32
Avon	137.56	Austin	131.19
Broomfield	142.50	Austin	151.65
Buena Vista	145.95	Austin	141.55
Colorado Springs	117.49	Austin	125.99
Colorado Springs	142.75	Dallas	126.29
Denver	121.99	Dallas	139.19
Denver	117.49	Dallas	156.00
Eaton	141.64	Dallas	137.56
Fort Collins	128.69	Houston	154.10
Gunnison	130.29	Houston	126.41
Pueblo	142.39	Houston	114.00
Pueblo	121.99	Houston	144.99
Pueblo	141.30		
Sterling	153.43		
Walsenburg	133.39		

$$\bar{x}_1 = \$133.994 \qquad\qquad\qquad \bar{x}_2 = \$138.018$$
$$s_1 = \$11.015 \qquad\qquad\qquad\quad s_2 = \$12.663$$
$$n_1 = 16 \text{ pharmacies} \qquad\qquad n_2 = 13 \text{ pharmacies}$$

Source: Public Research Interest Group (www.pirg.org). Surveyed pharmacies were chosen from the telephone directory in 2004. Data used with permission.

FIGURE 10.10

Zocor prices in two states

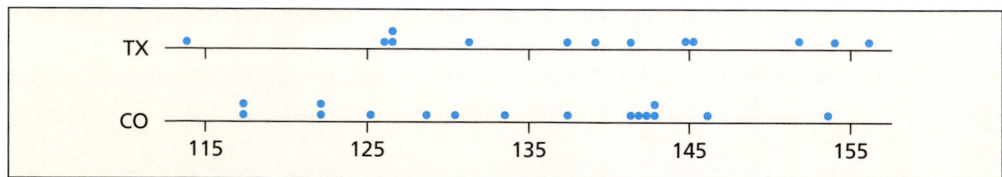

Step 1: Formulate the Hypotheses

To check for a significant difference without regard for its direction, we choose a two-tailed test. The hypotheses to be tested are

$$H_0: \mu_1 = \mu_2$$
$$H_1: \mu_1 \neq \mu_2$$

Step 2: State the Decision Rule

We will assume equal variances. For the pooled-variance t test, degrees of freedom are $v = n_1 + n_2 - 2 = 16 + 13 - 2 = 27$. From Appendix D we get the two-tail critical value $t = \pm 2.052$. The decision rule is illustrated in Figure 10.11.

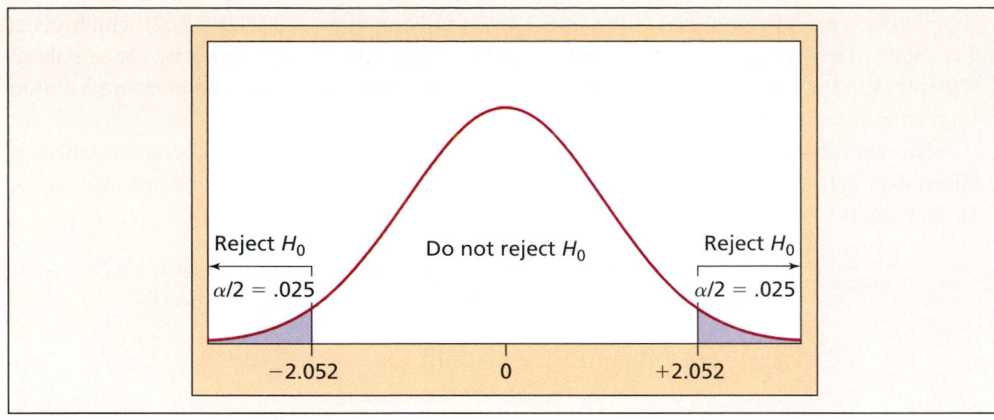

FIGURE 10.11

Two-tailed decision rule for Student's *t* with $\alpha = .05$ and d.f. = 27

Step 3: Calculate the Test Statistic

The sample statistics are

$$\bar{x}_1 = 133.994 \qquad \bar{x}_2 = 138.018$$
$$s_1 = 11.015 \qquad s_2 = 12.663$$
$$n_1 = 16 \qquad n_2 = 13$$

The pooled variance s_p^2 is

$$s_p^2 = \frac{(n_1 - 1)s_1^2 + (n_2 - 1)s_2^2}{n_1 + n_2 - 2} = \frac{(16 - 1)(11.015)^2 + (13 - 1)(12.663)^2}{16 + 13 - 2} = 138.6737$$

Using s_p^2 the test statistic is

$$t = \frac{\bar{x}_1 - \bar{x}_2}{\sqrt{\dfrac{s_p^2}{n_1} + \dfrac{s_p^2}{n_2}}} = \frac{133.994 - 138.018}{\sqrt{\dfrac{138.6737}{16} + \dfrac{138.6737}{13}}} = \frac{-4.024}{4.39708} = -0.915$$

The pooled standard deviation is $s_p = \sqrt{138.6737} = 11.776$. Notice that s_p always lies between s_1 and s_2 (if not, you have an arithmetic error). This is because s_p^2 is an average of s_1^2 and s_2^2.

Step 4: Make the Decision

The test statistic $t = -0.915$ does not fall in the rejection region so we cannot reject the hypothesis of equal means. Excel's menu and output are shown in Figure 10.12. Both one-tailed and two-tailed tests are shown.

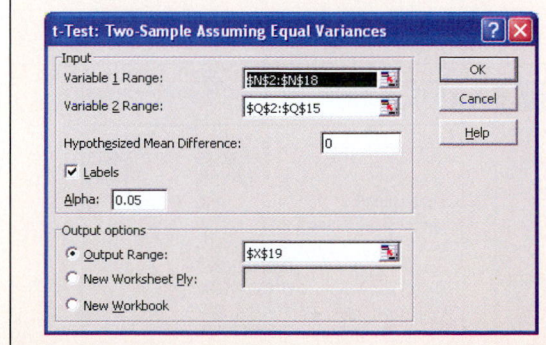

t-Test: Two-Sample Assuming Equal Variances

	Colorado	Texas
Mean	133.99375	138.0184615
Variance	121.3293183	160.3542641
Observations	16	13
Pooled Variance	138.6737387	
Hypothesized Mean	0	
df	27	
t Stat	-0.915314443	
P(T<=t) one-tail	0.184064721	
t Critical one-tail	1.703288423	
P(T<=t) two-tail	0.368129443	
t Critical two-tail	2.051830493	

FIGURE 10.12

Excel's **Tools > Data Analysis** with unknown but equal variances

The *p*-value can be calculated using Excel's two-tail function =TDIST(.915,27,2) which gives $p = .3681$. This large *p*-value says that a result this extreme would happen by chance about 37 percent of the time if $\mu_1 = \mu_2$. The difference in sample means seems to be well within the realm of chance.

The sample variances in this example are similar, so the assumption of equal variances is reasonable. But if we instead use the formulas for *Case 3* (assuming *unequal* variances) the test statistic is

$$t = \frac{\bar{x}_1 - \bar{x}_2}{\sqrt{\dfrac{s_1^2}{n_1} + \dfrac{s_2^2}{n_2}}} = \frac{133.994 - 138.018}{\sqrt{\dfrac{(11.015)^2}{16} + \dfrac{(12.663)^2}{13}}} = \frac{-4.024}{4.4629} = -0.902$$

The formula for adjusted degrees of freedom for the Welch-Satterthwaite test is

$$\nu' = \frac{\left[\dfrac{s_1^2}{n_1} + \dfrac{s_2^2}{n_2}\right]^2}{\dfrac{\left(\dfrac{s_1^2}{n_1}\right)^2}{n_1 - 1} + \dfrac{\left(\dfrac{s_2^2}{n_2}\right)^2}{n_2 - 1}} = \frac{\left[\dfrac{(11.015)^2}{16} + \dfrac{(12.663)^2}{13}\right]^2}{\dfrac{\left(\dfrac{(11.015)^2}{16}\right)^2}{16 - 1} + \dfrac{\left(\dfrac{(12.663)^2}{13}\right)^2}{13 - 1}} = 24$$

The adjusted degrees of freedom are rounded to the next lower integer, to be conservative.

For the unequal-variance *t* test with degrees of freedom $\nu' = 24$, Appendix D gives the two-tail critical value $t = \pm2.064$. The decision rule is illustrated in Figure 10.13.

FIGURE 10.13

Two-tail decision rule for Student's *t* with $\alpha = .05$ and d.f. = 24

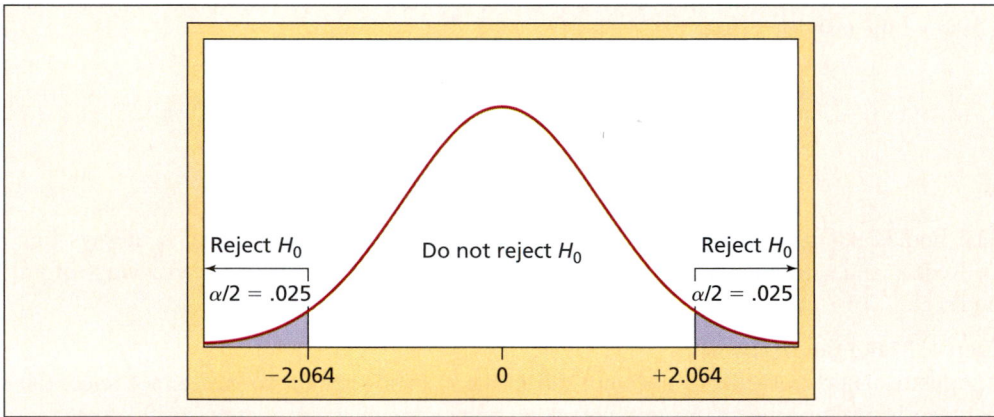

The calculations are best done by computer. Excel's menu and output are shown in Figure 10.14. Both one-tailed and two-tailed tests are shown.

FIGURE 10.14

Excel's Tools > Data Analysis with unknown but equal variances

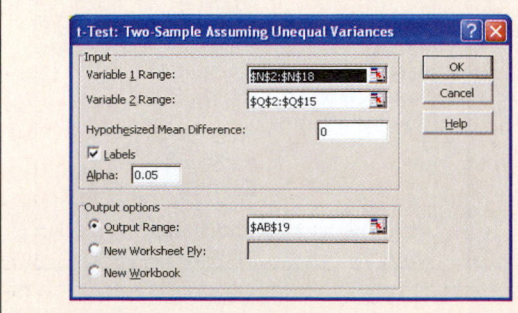

t-Test: Two-Sample Assuming Unequal Variances		
	Colorado	Texas
Mean	133.99375	138.0184615
Variance	121.3293183	160.3542641
Observations	16	13
Hypothesized Mean	0	
df	24	
t Stat	-0.901802871	
P(T<=t) one-tail	0.188061598	
t Critical one-tail	1.710882067	
P(T<=t) two-tail	0.376123196	
t Critical two-tail	2.063898547	

For the Zocor data, either assumption leads to the same conclusion:

Assumption	Test Statistic	d.f.	Critical Value	Decision
Case 2 (equal variances)	$t = -0.915$	27	$t = \pm 2.052$	Don't reject
Case 3 (unequal variances)	$t = -0.902$	24	$t = \pm 2.064$	Don't reject

Which Assumption Is Best?

If the *sample sizes are equal,* the *Case 2* and *Case 3* test statistics will be identical, although the degrees of freedom may differ. If the *variances are similar,* the two tests usually agree. If you have no information about the population variances, then the best choice is *Case 3.* The fewer assumptions you make about your populations, the less likely you are to make a mistake in your conclusions. Case 1 (known population variances) is not explored further here because it is so uncommon in business.

Must Sample Sizes Be Equal?

Unequal sample sizes are common, and the formulas still apply. However, there are advantages to equal sample sizes. We avoid unbalanced sample sizes when possible. But many times, we have to take the samples as they come.

Large Samples

For unknown variances, if both samples are large ($n_1 \geq 30$ and $n_2 \geq 30$) and you have reason to think the population isn't badly skewed (look at the histograms or dot plots of the samples), it is permissible to use formula 10.15 with Appendix C. Even though it usually gives results very close to the "proper" *t* tests, this approach is not conservative (i.e., it may increase Type I risk).

$$z = \frac{\bar{x}_1 - \bar{x}_2}{\sqrt{\dfrac{s_1^2}{n_1} + \dfrac{s_2^2}{n_2}}} \qquad \text{(large samples, symmetric populations)} \qquad (10.15)$$

Caution: Three Issues

Bear in mind three questions when you are comparing two sample means:

- Are the populations skewed? Are there outliers?
- Are the sample sizes large ($n \geq 30$)?
- Is the difference *important* as well as significant?

Skewness or outliers can usually be seen in a histogram or dot plot of each sample. The *t* tests (*Case 2* and *Case 3*) are probably OK in the face of moderate skewness, especially if the samples are large (e.g., sample sizes of at least 30). Outliers are more serious and might require consultation with a statistician. In such cases, you might ask yourself whether a test of means is appropriate. With small samples or skewed data, the mean may not be a very reliable indicator of central tendency, and your test may lack power. In such situations, it may be better merely to describe the samples, comment on similarities or differences in the data, and skip the formal *t*-tests.

   Regarding importance, note that a small difference in means or proportions could be significant if the sample size is large, because the standard error gets smaller as the sample size gets larger. So, we must separately ask if the difference is *important.* The answer depends on the data magnitude and the consequences to the decision-maker. How large must a price differential be to make it worthwhile for a consumer to drive from *A* to *B* to save 10 percent on a loaf of bread? A DVD player? A new car? Research suggests, for example, that some cancer victims will travel far and pay much for treatments that offer only small improvement in their chances of survival, because life is so precious. But few consumers compare prices or drive far to save money on a gallon of milk or other items that are unimportant in their overall budget.

Mini Case 10.2

Length of Statistics Articles

Are articles in leading statistics journals getting longer? It appears so, based on a comparison of the June 2000 and June 1990 issues of the *Journal of the American Statistical Association* (*JASA*), shown in Table 10.6.

TABLE 10.6   Article Length in *JASA*

June 1990 JASA	June 2000 JASA
$\bar{x}_1 = 7.1333$ pages	$\bar{x}_2 = 11.8333$ pages
$s_1 = 1.9250$ pages	$s_2 = 2.5166$ pages
$n_1 = 30$ articles	$n_2 = 12$ articles

Source: *Journal of the American Statistical Association* 85, no. 410, and 95, no. 450.

We will do a left-tailed test at $\alpha = .01$. The hypotheses are

$H_0: \mu_1 \geq \mu_2$

$H_1: \mu_1 < \mu_2$

Since the variances are unknown, we will use a *t* test (both equal and unequal variances) checking the results with Excel. The pooled-variance test (*Case 2*) requires degrees of freedom $\nu = n_1 + n_2 - 2 = 30 + 12 - 2 = 40$, yielding a left-tail critical value of $t_{.01} = -2.423$. The estimate of the pooled variance is

$$s_p = \sqrt{\frac{(n_1 - 1)s_1^2 + (n_2 - 1)s_2^2}{n_1 + n_2 - 2}} = \sqrt{\frac{(30 - 1)(1.9250)^2 + (12 - 1)(2.5166)^2}{30 + 12 - 2}}$$

$$= \sqrt{4.428333} = 2.10436$$

The test statistic is $t = -6.539$, indicating a very strong rejection of the hypothesis of equal means:

$$t = \frac{\bar{x}_1 - \bar{x}_2}{s_p\sqrt{\frac{1}{n_1} + \frac{1}{n_2}}} = \frac{7.1333 - 11.8333}{(2.10436)\sqrt{\frac{1}{30} + \frac{1}{12}}} = \frac{-4.70000}{0.718776} = -6.539$$

Using the Welch-Sattherwaite *t* test (assuming unequal variances) the test statistic is

$$t = \frac{\bar{x}_1 - \bar{x}_2}{\sqrt{\frac{s_1^2}{n_1} + \frac{s_2^2}{n_2}}} = \frac{7.1333 - 11.8333}{\sqrt{\frac{(1.9250)^2}{30} + \frac{(2.5166)^2}{12}}} = \frac{-4.7000}{0.80703} = -5.824$$

The formula for adjusted degrees of freedom for the Welch-Satterthwaite test is

$$\nu' = \frac{\left[\frac{s_1^2}{n_1} + \frac{s_2^2}{n_2}\right]^2}{\frac{\left(\frac{s_1^2}{n_1}\right)^2}{n_1 - 1} + \frac{\left(\frac{s_2^2}{n_2}\right)^2}{n_2 - 1}} = \frac{\left[\frac{(1.9250)^2}{30} + \frac{(2.5166)^2}{12}\right]^2}{\frac{\left(\frac{(1.9250)^2}{30}\right)^2}{30 - 1} + \frac{\left(\frac{(2.5166)^2}{12}\right)^2}{12 - 1}} = 16$$

so the critical value is $t_{.01} = -2.583$. If we use the Quick Rule for degrees of freedom, instead of wading through this tedious calculation, we get $\nu^* = \min(n_1 - 1 \text{ or } n_2 - 1) =$

min(30 − 1 or 12 − 1) = 11 or $t_{.01} = -2.718$, which leads to the same conclusion. Regardless of our assumption about variances, we conclude that articles in *JASA* are getting longer. The decision is clear-cut. Our conviction about the conclusion depends on whether these samples are truly representative of *JASA* articles. This question might be probed further, and more articles could be examined. However, this result seems reasonable *a priori,* due to the growing use of graphics and computer simulation that could lengthen the articles. Is a difference of 4.7 pages of practical importance? Well, editors must find room for articles, so if articles are getting longer, journals must contain more pages or publish fewer articles. A difference of 5 pages over 20 or 30 articles might indeed be important.

SECTION EXERCISES

Hint: Show all formulas and calculations, but use the calculator in *LearningStats* Unit 10 to check your work. Calculate the *p*-values using Excel, and show each Excel formula you used (note that Excel's TDIST function requires that you omit the sign if the test statistic is negative).

10.13 Do a two-sample test for equality of means assuming equal variances. Calculate the *p*-value.
  a. Comparison of GPA for randomly chosen college juniors and seniors: $\bar{x}_1 = 3.05$, $s_1 = .20$, $n_1 = 15$, $\bar{x}_2 = 3.25$, $s_2 = .30$, $n_2 = 15$, $\alpha = .025$, left-tailed test.
  b. Comparison of average commute miles for randomly chosen students at two community colleges: $\bar{x}_1 = 15$, $s_1 = 5$, $n_1 = 22$, $\bar{x}_2 = 18$, $s_2 = 7$, $n_2 = 19$, $\alpha = .05$, two-tailed test.
  c. Comparison of credits at time of graduation for randomly chosen accounting and economics students: $\bar{x}_1 = 139$, $s_1 = 2.8$, $n_1 = 12$, $\bar{x}_2 = 137$, $s_2 = 2.7$, $n_2 = 17$, $\alpha = .05$, right-tailed test.

10.14 Repeat the previous exercise, assuming unequal variances. Calculate the *p*-value using Excel, and show the Excel formula you used.

10.15 The average length of stay (LOS) from U.S. short-stay hospitals for a sample of 25 male pneumonia patients was 5.5 days with a standard deviation of 1.2 days. For a sample of 25 females, the average LOS was 5.9 days with a standard deviation of 2.2 days. (a) Assuming equal variances, is there a significant difference at $\alpha = .10$? (b) Calculate the *p*-value using Excel. (See Department of Health and Human Services, *Advance Data from Vital and Health Statistics,* no. 332 [April 9, 2003], p. 13.)

10.16 The average mpg usage for a 2004 Ford Expedition 2WD for a sample of 10 tanks of gas was 17.0 with a standard deviation of 0.8. For a Ford Explorer 2WD, the average mpg usage for a sample of 10 tanks of gas was 18.5 with a standard deviation of 1.0. (a) Assuming equal variances, at $\alpha = .01$, is the true mean mpg lower for the Ford Expedition? (b) Calculate the *p*-value using Excel. (Data are from www.fueleconomy.gov.)

10.17 When the background music was slow, the mean amount of bar purchases for a sample of 17 restaurant patrons was $30.47 with a standard deviation of $15.10. When the background music was fast, the mean amount of bar purchases for a sample of 14 patrons in the same restaurant was $21.62 with a standard deviation of $9.50. (a) Assuming unequal variances, at $\alpha = .01$, is the true mean higher when the music is slow? (b) Calculate the *p*-value using Excel.

10.18 Are women's feet getting bigger? Retailers in the last 20 years have had to increase their stock of larger sizes. Wal-Mart Stores, Inc., and Payless ShoeSource, Inc., have been aggressive in stocking larger sizes, and Nordstrom's reports that its larger sizes typically sell out first. Assuming equal variances, at $\alpha = .025$, do these random shoe size samples of 12 randomly chosen women in each age group show that women's shoe sizes have increased? (See *The Wall Street Journal,* July 17, 2004.) **ShoeSize1**

Born in 1980:	8	7.5	8.5	8.5	8	7.5	9.5	7.5	8	8	8.5	9
Born in 1960:	8.5	7.5	8	8	7.5	7.5	7.5	8	7	8	7	8

10.19 A new drug is being tested to see if it reduces the number of migraine headaches. Assuming equal variances, at $\alpha = .025$, do these samples of number of monthly migraines from eight volunteers who are taking the drug and eight who are not show a significant reduction in the mean number of monthly migraine headaches? (See *Science News* 165, no. 9 [February 28, 2004].) **Migraine1**

Topiramate:	3	3	2	4	3	4	3	5
Control:	3	3	5	5	7	5	5	4

10.4

COMPARING TWO MEANS: PAIRED SAMPLES

Paired Data

When sample data consist of n matched pairs, a different approach is required. If the *same* individuals are observed twice but under different circumstances, we have a **paired comparison.** For example:

- Fifteen retirees with diagnosed hypertension are assigned a program of diet, exercise, and meditation. A baseline measurement of blood pressure is taken *before* the program begins and again *after* 2 months. Was the program effective in reducing blood pressure?
- Ten cutting tools use lubricant A for 10 minutes. The blade temperatures are taken. When the machine has cooled, it is run with lubricant B for 10 minutes and the blade temperatures are again measured. Which lubricant makes the blades run cooler?
- Weekly sales of Snapple at 12 Wal-Mart stores are compared *before* and *after* installing a new eye-catching display. Did the new display increase sales?

Paired data typically come from a *before-after* experiment. If we treat the data as two independent samples, ignoring the *dependence* between the data pairs, the test is less powerful.

Paired t Test

In the **paired t test** we define a new variable $d = X_1 - X_2$ as the *difference* between X_1 and X_2. We usually present the n observed differences in column form:

Obs	X_1	X_2	$d = X_1 - X_2$
1	XXX	XXX	XXX
2	XXX	XXX	XXX
3	XXX	XXX	XXX
. . .	. . .	. . .	. . .
. . .	. . .	. . .	. . .
n	XXX	XXX	XXX

The same sample data could also be presented in row form:

Obs	1	2	3	. . .	. . .	n
X_1	XXX	XXX	XXX	. . .	. . .	XXX
X_2	XXX	XXX	XXX	. . .	. . .	XXX
$d = X_1 - X_2$	XXX	XXX	XXX	. . .	. . .	XXX

The mean $\bar{d}$ and standard deviation s_d of the sample of n differences are calculated with the usual formulas for a mean and standard deviation. We call the mean $\bar{d}$ instead of $\bar{x}$ merely to remind ourselves that we are dealing with *differences*.

$$(10.16) \qquad \bar{d} = \frac{\sum_{i=1}^{n} d_i}{n} \qquad \text{(mean of } n \text{ differences)}$$

$$(10.17) \qquad s_d = \sqrt{\sum_{i=1}^{n} \frac{(d_i - \bar{d})^2}{n-1}} \qquad \text{(Std. Dev. of } n \text{ differences)}$$

Since the population variance of d is unknown, we will do a paired t test using Student's t with $n - 1$ degrees of freedom to compare the sample mean difference $\bar{d}$ with a hypothesized difference μ_d (usually $\mu_d = 0$). The test statistic is really a one-sample t test, just like those in Chapter 9.

$$(10.18) \qquad t = \frac{\bar{d} - \mu_d}{\dfrac{s_d}{\sqrt{n}}} \qquad \text{(test statistic for } \textbf{paired samples}\text{)}$$

↘   An insurance company's procedure in settling a claim under $10,000 for fire or water damage to a home owner is to require two estimates for cleanup and repair of structural damage before allowing the insured to proceed with the work. The insurance company compares estimates from two contractors who most frequently handle this type of work in this geographical area. Table 10.7 shows the 10 most recent claims for which damage estimates were provided by both contractors. At the .05 level of significance, is there a difference between the two contractors?

TABLE 10.7   **Damage Repair Estimates ($) for 10 Claims**   **Repair**

	X_1	X_2	$d = X_1 - X_2$
Claim	*Contractor A*	*Contractor B*	*Difference*
1. Jones, C.	5,500	6,000	−500
2. Smith, R.	1,000	900	100
3. Xia, Y.	2,500	2,500	0
4. Gallo, J.	7,800	8,300	−500
5. Carson, R.	6,400	6,200	200
6. Petty, M.	8,800	9,400	−600
7. Tracy, L.	600	500	100
8. Barnes, J.	3,300	3,500	−200
9. Rodriguez, J.	4,500	5,200	−700
10. Van Dyke, P.	6,500	6,800	−300

$$\bar{d} = -240.00$$
$$s_d = 327.28$$
$$n = 10$$

Step 1: Formulate the Hypotheses
Since we have no reason to be interested in directionality, we will choose a two-tailed test using these hypotheses:

$H_0: \mu_d = 0$

$H_1: \mu_d \neq 0$

Step 2: State the Decision Rule
Our test statistic will follow a Student's t distribution with d.f. $= n - 1 = 10 - 1 = 9$, so from Appendix D with $\alpha = .05$ the two-tail critical value is $t_{.025} = \pm 2.262$, as illustrated in Figure 10.15. The decision rule is

Reject H_0 if $t < -2.262$ or if $t > +2.262$

Otherwise accept H_0

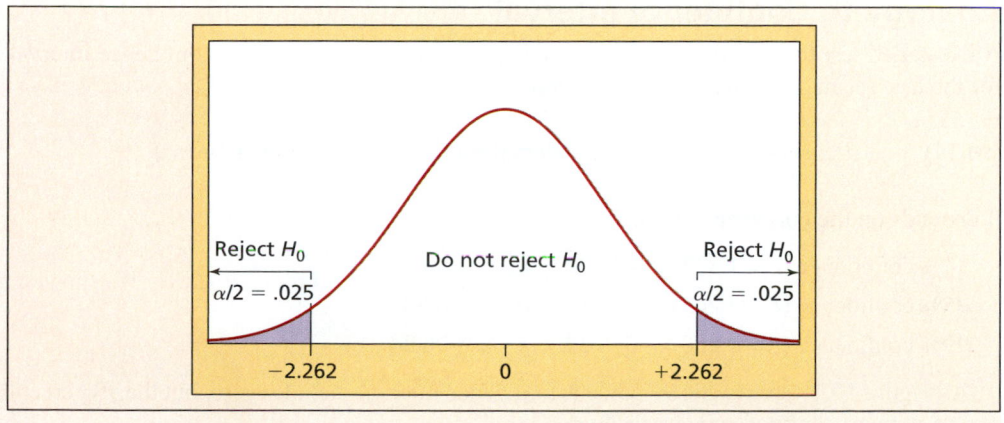

Reject H_0
$\alpha/2 = .025$

Do not reject H_0

Reject H_0
$\alpha/2 = .025$

−2.262   0   +2.262

Step 3: Calculate the Test Statistic
The mean and standard deviation are calculated in the usual way, as shown in Table 10.7, so the test statistic is

$$t = \frac{\bar{d} - \mu_d}{\frac{s_d}{\sqrt{n}}} = \frac{-240 - 0}{\left(\frac{327.28}{\sqrt{10}}\right)} = \frac{-240}{103.495} = -2.319$$

Step 4: Make the Decision
Since $t = -2.319$ falls in the left-tail critical region (below -2.262), we reject the null hypothesis, and conclude that there is a significant difference between the two contractors. However, it is a *very* close decision.

Excel's Paired Difference Test

The calculations for our repair estimates example are easy in Excel, as illustrated in Figure 10.16. Excel gives you the option of choosing either a one-tailed or two-tailed test, and also shows the *p*-value. For a two-tailed test, the *p*-value is $p = .0456$, which would barely lead to rejection of the hypothesis of zero difference of means at $\alpha = .05$. The borderline *p*-value reinforces our conclusion that the decision is sensitive to our choice of α. MegaStat and MINITAB also provide a paired *t* test.

FIGURE 10.16

Results of Excel's paired *t* test at $\alpha = .05$

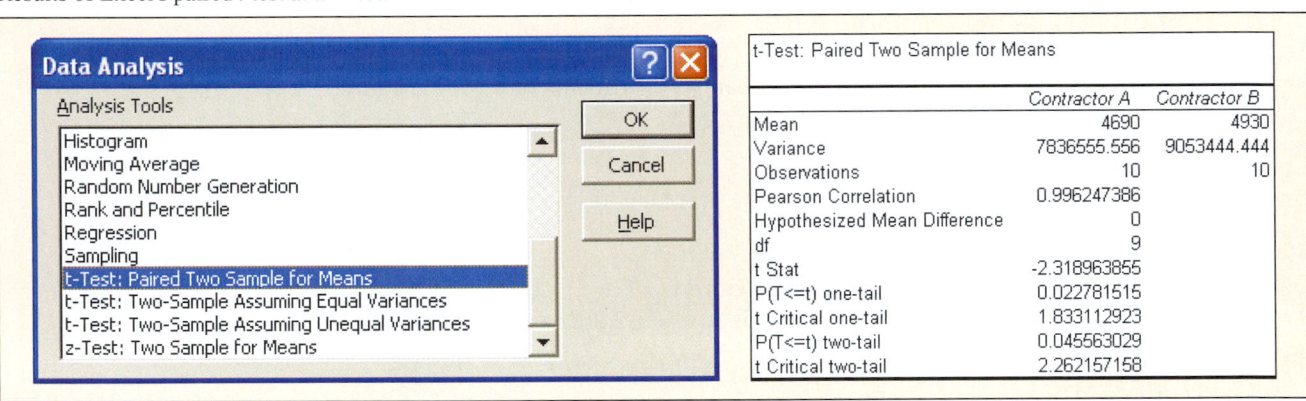

Analogy to Confidence Interval

A two-tailed test for a zero difference is equivalent to asking whether the confidence interval for the true mean difference μ_d includes zero.

(10.19) $\bar{d} \pm t\dfrac{s_d}{\sqrt{n}}$ (confidence interval for difference of paired means)

It depends on the confidence level:

90% confidence ($t = 1.833$): $-429.72 < \mu_d < -50.28$

95% confidence ($t = 2.262$): $-474.12 < \mu_d < -5.88$

99% confidence ($t = 3.250$): $-576.34 < \mu_d < +96.34$

As Figure 10.17 shows, the 99 percent confidence interval includes zero, but the 90 percent and 95 percent confidence intervals do not.

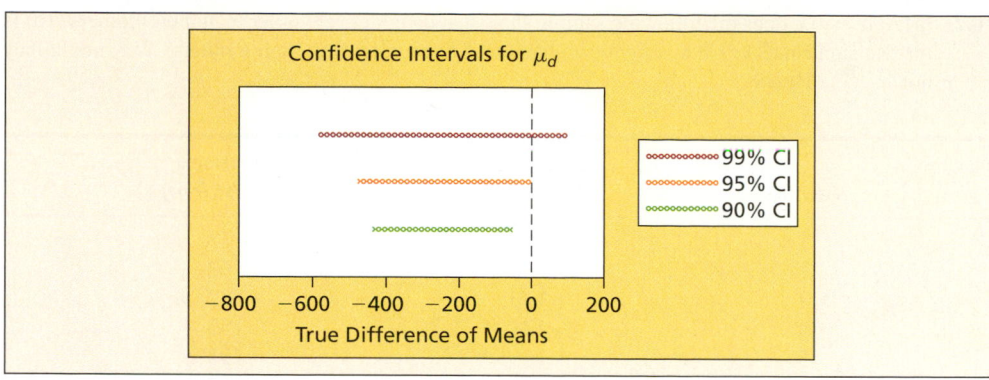

FIGURE 10.17

Confidence intervals for difference of means

Why Not Treat Paired Data As Independent Samples?

When observations are matched pairs, the paired *t* test is more powerful, because it utilizes information that is ignored if we treat the samples separately. To show this, let's treat each data column as an ***independent sample.*** We get the results shown in Figure 10.18. The *p*-values (one tail or two-tail) are not even close to being significant at the usual α levels.* By ignoring the dependence between the samples, we unnecessarily *sacrifice the power of the test.* If the two data columns are paired, do *not* treat them independently.

$$\bar{x}_1 = 4{,}690.00 \qquad \bar{x}_2 = 4{,}930.00$$
$$s_1 = 2{,}799.38 \qquad s_2 = 3{,}008.89$$
$$n_1 = 10 \qquad n_2 = 10$$

FIGURE 10.18

Excel's independent sample *t* tests

t-Test: Two-Sample Assuming Equal Variances		
	Contractor A	Contractor B
Mean	4690	4930
Variance	7836555.556	9053444.444
Observations	10	10
Pooled Variance	8445000	
Hypothesized Mean Difference	0	
df	18	
t Stat	-0.184670029	
P(T<=t) one-tail	0.427776285	
t Critical one-tail	1.734063592	
P(T<=t) two-tail	0.855552569	
t Critical two-tail	2.100922037	

t-Test: Two-Sample Assuming Unequal Variances		
	Contractor A	Contractor B
Mean	4690	4930
Variance	7836555.556	9053444.444
Observations	10	10
Hypothesized Mean Difference	0	
df	18	
t Stat	-0.184670029	
P(T<=t) one-tail	0.427776285	
t Critical one-tail	1.734063592	
P(T<=t) two-tail	0.855552569	
t Critical two-tail	2.100922037	

SECTION EXERCISES

10.20 A new cell phone battery is being considered as a replacement for the current one. Ten college student cell phone users are selected to try each battery in their usual mix of "talk" and "standby" and to record the number of hours until recharge was needed. (a) Do these results show that the new battery has significantly longer life at $\alpha = .05$? State your hypotheses and show all steps clearly. (b) Is the decision close? (c) Are you convinced?   **Battery**

	Bob	May	Deno	Sri	Pat	Alexis	Scott	Aretha	Jen	Ben
New battery	45	41	53	40	43	43	49	39	41	43
Old battery	52	34	40	38	38	44	34	45	28	33

*Since the sample sizes are equal, the test statistics are identical for *Case 2* (equal variances) and *Case 3* (unequal variances).

10.21 (a) At $\alpha = .05$, does the following sample show that daughters are taller than their mothers? (b) Is the decision close? (c) Why might daughters tend to be taller than their mothers? Why might they not? 🐛 **Height**

Family	Daughter's Height (cm)	Mother's Height (cm)
1	167	172
2	166	162
3	176	157
4	171	159
5	165	157
6	181	177
7	173	174

10.22 An experimental surgical procedure is being studied as an alternative to the old method. Both methods are considered safe. Five surgeons perform the operation on two patients matched by age, sex, and other relevant factors, with the results shown. The time to complete the surgery (in minutes) is recorded. (a) At the 5 percent significance level, is the new way faster? State your hypotheses and show all steps clearly. (b) Is the decision close? 🐛 **Surgery**

	Surgeon 1	Surgeon 2	Surgeon 3	Surgeon 4	Surgeon 5
Old way	36	55	28	40	62
New way	29	42	30	32	56

10.23 Blockbuster is testing a new policy of waiving all late fees on DVD rentals using a sample of 10 randomly chosen customers. (a) At $\alpha = .10$, does the data show that the mean number of monthly rentals has increased? (b) Is the decision close? (c) Are you convinced? 🐛 **DVDRental**

Customer	No Late Fee	Late Fee
1	14	10
2	12	7
3	14	10
4	13	13
5	10	9
6	13	14
7	12	12
8	10	7
9	13	13
10	13	9

10.24 Below is a random sample of shoe sizes for 12 mothers and their daughters. (a) At $\alpha = .01$, does this sample show that women's shoe sizes have increased? State your hypotheses and show all steps clearly. (b) Is the decision close? (c) Are you convinced? (d) Why might shoe sizes change over time? (See *The Wall Street Journal,* July 17, 2004.) 🐛 **ShoeSize2**

	1	2	3	4	5	6	7	8	9	10	11	12
Daughter	8	8	7.5	8	9	9	8.5	9	9	8	7	8
Mother	7	7	7.5	8	8.5	8.5	7.5	7.5	6	8	7	7

10.25 A newly installed automatic gate system was being tested to see if the number of failures in 1,000 entry attempts was the same as the number of failures in 1,000 exit attempts. A random sample of eight delivery trucks was selected for data collection. Do these sample results show that there is a significant difference between entry and exit gate failures? Use $\alpha = .01$.

	Truck 1	Truck 2	Truck 3	Truck 4	Truck 5	Truck 6	Truck 7	Truck 8
Entry failures	43	45	53	56	61	51	48	44
Exit failures	48	51	60	58	58	45	55	50

Mini Case   10.3

Detroit's Weight-Loss Contest

Table 10.8 shows the results of a weight-loss contest sponsored by a local newspaper. Partici-pants came from the East Side and West Side, and were encouraged to compete over a 1-month period. At $\alpha = .01$, was there a significant weight loss? The hypotheses are $H_0: \mu_d \geq 0$ and $H_1: \mu_d < 0$.

TABLE 10.8   **Results of Detroit's Weight-Loss Contest**   🏋   **WeightLoss**

Obs	Name	After	Before	Difference
1	Michael M.	202.5	217.0	−14.5
2	Tracy S.	178.0	188.0	−10.0
3	Gregg G.	210.0	225.0	−15.0
4	Boydea P.	157.0	168.0	−11.0
5	Donna I.	169.0	178.0	−9.0
6	Elizabeth C.	173.5	182.0	−8.5
7	Carole K.	163.5	174.5	−11.0
8	Candace G.	153.0	161.5	−8.5
9	Jo Anne M.	170.5	177.5	−7.0
10	Willis B.	336.0	358.5	−22.5
11	Marilyn S.	174.0	181.0	−7.0
12	Tim B.	197.5	210.0	−12.5

$$\bar{d} = -11.375$$
$$s_d = 4.37516$$

Source: *Detroit Free Press*, February 12, 2002, pp. 10H–11H.

The test statistic is over nine standard errors from zero, a highly significant difference:

$$t = \frac{\bar{d} - 0}{\frac{s_d}{\sqrt{n}}} = \frac{-11.375 - 0}{\frac{4.37516}{\sqrt{12}}} = -9.006$$

Excel's *p*-value for the paired *t* test in Figure 10.19 is $p = .0000$ for a one-tailed test (a signif-icant result at any α). Therefore, the mean weight loss of 11.375 pounds was *significant* at $\alpha = .01$. Moreover, to most people, a weight loss of 11.375 pounds would also be *important*.

t-Test: Paired Two Sample for Means

	After	Before
Mean	190.375	201.75
Variance	2416.4148	2825.0227
Observations	12	12
Hypothesized Mean Diff	0	
df	11	
t Stat	−9.006	
P(T < t) one-tail	0.0000	
t Critical one-tail	1.796	

FIGURE 10.19

Excel output for paired *t* test

10.5

COMPARING TWO VARIANCES

VS
Chapter 10

Just as it is often important to test whether two population *means* are equal, we may also need to test whether two population *variances* are equal. The focus is on variation around the mean. Is the *variance* in Ford Mustang assembly times the same this month as last month? Is the *variability* in customer waiting times the same at two Tim Horton's franchises? Is the *variation* the same for customer concession purchases at a movie theater on Friday and Saturday nights?

Format of Hypotheses

We may test the null hypothesis against a left-tailed, two-tailed, or right-tailed alternative:

Left-Tailed Test	*Two-Tailed Test*	*Right-Tailed Test*
$H_0: \sigma_1^2 \geq \sigma_2^2$	$H_0: \sigma_1^2 = \sigma_2^2$	$H_0: \sigma_1^2 \leq \sigma_2^2$
$H_1: \sigma_1^2 < \sigma_2^2$	$H_1: \sigma_1^2 \neq \sigma_2^2$	$H_1: \sigma_1^2 > \sigma_2^2$

An equivalent way to state these hypotheses is to look at the *ratio* of the two variances. A ratio near 1 would indicate equal variances.

Left-Tailed Test	*Two-Tailed Test*	*Right-Tailed Test*
$H_0: \dfrac{\sigma_1^2}{\sigma_2^2} \geq 1$	$H_0: \dfrac{\sigma_1^2}{\sigma_2^2} = 1$	$H_0: \dfrac{\sigma_1^2}{\sigma_2^2} \leq 1$
$H_1: \dfrac{\sigma_1^2}{\sigma_2^2} < 1$	$H_1: \dfrac{\sigma_1^2}{\sigma_2^2} \neq 1$	$H_1: \dfrac{\sigma_1^2}{\sigma_2^2} > 1$

The *F* Test

In a left-tailed or right-tailed test, we actually test only at the equality, with the understanding that rejection of H_0 would imply rejecting values more extreme. The test statistic is the ratio of the sample variances. The test statistic follows the **F distribution,** named for Ronald A. Fisher (1890–1962), one of the most famous statisticians of all time.

(10.20)

$$F = \frac{s_1^2}{s_2^2} \qquad \begin{array}{l} \text{d.f.} = n_1 - 1 \\[2mm] \text{d.f.} = n_2 - 1 \end{array}$$

If the null hypothesis of equal variances is true, this ratio should be near 1:

$$F \approx 1 \qquad (\text{if } H_0 \text{ is true})$$

If the test statistic F is much less than 1 or much greater than 1, we would reject the hypothesis of equal population variances. The numerator s_1^2 has degrees of freedom $\nu_1 = n_1 - 1$, while the denominator s_2^2 has degrees of freedom $\nu_2 = n_2 - 1$. The F distribution is skewed. Its mean is always greater than 1 and its mode (the "peak" of the distribution) is always less than 1, but both the mean and mode tend to be near 1 for large samples. F cannot be negative, since s_1^2 and s_2^2 cannot be negative. (See *LearningStats* Unit 10 for details.)

Critical Values

Critical values for the **F test** are denoted F_L (left tail) and F_R (right tail). The form of the two-tailed F test is shown in Figure 10.20. Notice that the rejection regions are asymmetric. A right-tail critical value F_R may be found from Appendix F using ν_1 and ν_2 degrees of freedom. It is written

(10.21)

$$F_R = F_{\nu_1, \nu_2} \qquad (\text{right-tail critical } F)$$

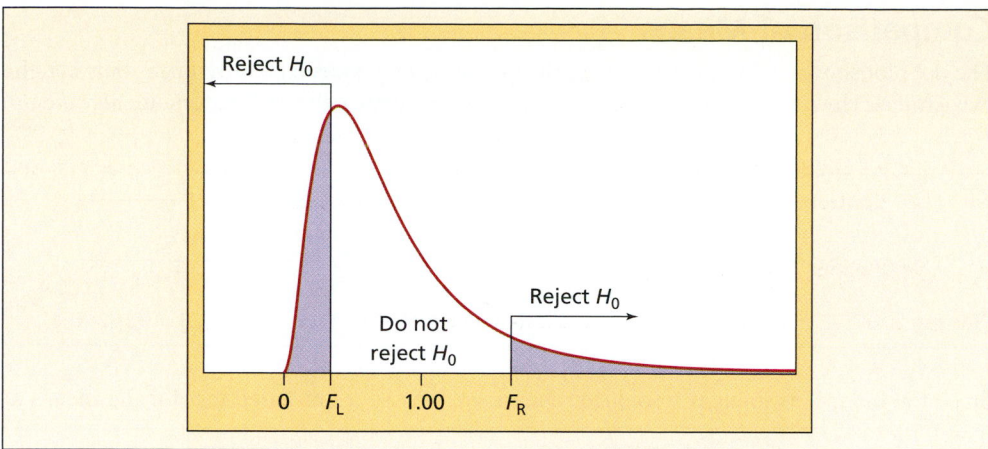

FIGURE 10.20

Critical values for *F* test for variances

To obtain a left-tail critical value F_L we reverse the numerator and denominator degrees of freedom, find the critical value from Appendix F, and take its reciprocal:

$$F_L = \frac{1}{F_{v_2,v_1}} \qquad \text{(left-tail critical } F \text{ with switched } v_1 \text{ and } v_2\text{)} \qquad \textbf{(10.22)}$$

Excel will give F_R using the function =FINV(α, v_1, v_2) or F_L using =FINV(1-α, v_1, v_2).

Illustration: Collision Damage

An experimental bumper was designed to reduce damage in low-speed collisions. This bumper was installed on an experimental group of vans in a large fleet, but not on a control group. At the end of a trial period, accident data showed 12 repair incidents (a "repair incident" is a repair invoice) for the experimental vehicles and 9 repair incidents for the control group vehicles. Table 10.9 shows the dollar cost of the repair incidents. At the .05 significance level, we could ask:

- Did the experimental bumper affect the *mean* repair cost?
- Did the experimental bumper affect the *variance* in repair cost?

Tests of variances are often linked to tests of means, since the same sample could be used to answer either question. The comparison of *means* is related to the firm's *overall cost,* while the comparison of *variances* is related to the firm's ability to *predict* individual repair cost. We will look at both questions, but will examine the means only briefly while focusing on comparing the variances.

Experimental Vehicles	Control Vehicles
1,973	1,185
403	885
509	2,955
2,103	815
1,153	2,852
292	1,217
1,916	1,762
1,602	2,592
1,559	1,632
547	
801	
359	
$\bar{x}_1 = \$1{,}101.42$	$\bar{x}_2 = \$1{,}766.11$
$s_1 = \$696.20$	$s_2 = \$837.62$
$n_1 = 12$ incidents	$n_2 = 9$ incidents

TABLE 10.9

Repair Cost ($) for Accident Damage

Damage

Source: Unpublished study by Floyd G. Willoughby and Thomas W. Lauer, Oakland University.

Comparison of Means

The dot plot shown in Figure 10.21 suggests that there may indeed be differences between the two groups. However, a formal test is needed to see whether the differences are *significant*.

FIGURE 10.21

Dot plots for collision repair costs ✏ **Damage**

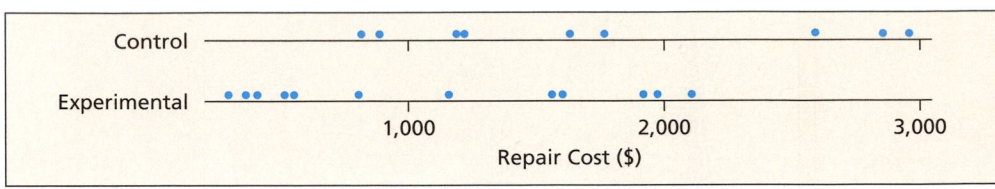

Since the bumper is thought to reduce repair cost, we use a left-tailed test for the means at $\alpha = .05$:

$$H_0: \mu_1 \geq \mu_2$$
$$H_1: \mu_1 < \mu_2$$

Independent sample t tests (calculations from Excel are not shown) indicate a significant reduction in mean repair cost at $\alpha = .05$ (since the p-value is approximately .03). Either assumption about variances gives the same result:

	Test Statistic	d.f.	$t_{.05}$	Decision	Left-tail p-Value
Case 2: Equal variances	$t = -1.986$	19	$t = -1.729$	Reject	$p = .031$
Case 3: Unequal variances	$t = -1.932$	15	$t = -1.753$	Reject	$p = .036$

Comparison of Variances: Two-Tailed Test

Do the sample variances support the idea of equal variances in the population? We will perform a two-tailed test.

Step 1: Formulate the Hypotheses   For a two-tailed test for equality of variances, the hypotheses are

$$H_0: \sigma_1^2 = \sigma_2^2 \quad \text{or} \quad H_0: \sigma_1^2 / \sigma_2^2 = 1$$
$$H_1: \sigma_1^2 \neq \sigma_2^2 \qquad\quad H_1: \sigma_1^2 / \sigma_2^2 \neq 1$$

Step 2: State the Decision Rule   Degrees of freedom for the F test are

Numerator: $v_1 = n_1 - 1 = 12 - 1 = 11$

Denominator: $v_2 = n_2 - 1 = 9 - 1 = 8$

For a two-tailed test, we split the α risk and put $\alpha/2$ in each tail. For $\alpha = .05$ we use Appendix F with $\alpha/2 = .025$. To avoid interpolating, we use the next lower degrees of freedom when the required entry is not found in Appendix F. This conservative practice will not increase the probability of Type I error. For example, since $F_{11,8}$ is not in the table we use $F_{10,8}$, as shown in Figure 10.22.

$$F_R = F_{v_1, v_2} = F_{11,8} \approx F_{10,8} = 4.30 \qquad \text{(right-tail critical value)}$$

To find the left-tail critical value we reverse the numerator and denominator degrees of freedom, find the critical value from Appendix F, and take its reciprocal, as shown in Figure 10.23.

$$F_L = \frac{1}{F_{v_2, v_1}} = \frac{1}{F_{8,11}} = \frac{1}{3.66} = 0.273 \qquad \text{(left-tail critical value)}$$

As shown in Figure 10.24, the two-sided decision rule is

Reject H_0 if $F < 0.273$ or if $F > 4.30$

Otherwise do not reject H_0

Appendix F: Critical Values of $F_{0.025}$

This table shows the 2.5% right-tail critical values of F for the stated degrees of freedom (ν).

		1	2	3	4	5	6	7	8	9	10	12
						Numerator Degrees of Freedom (ν_1)						
	1	647.8	799.5	864.2	899.6	921.8	937.1	948.2	956.6	963.3	968.6	976.7
	2	38.51	39.00	39.17	39.25	39.30	39.33	39.36	39.37	39.39	39.40	39.41
	3	17.44	16.04	15.44	15.10	14.88	14.73	14.62	14.54	14.47	14.42	14.34
	4	12.22	10.65	9.98	9.60	9.36	9.20	9.07	8.98	8.90	8.84	8.75
	5	10.01	8.43	7.76	7.39	7.15	6.98	6.85	6.76	6.68	6.62	6.52
	6	8.81	7.26	6.60	6.23	5.99	5.82	5.70	5.60	5.52	5.46	5.37
	7	8.07	6.54	5.89	5.52	5.29	5.12	4.99	4.90	4.82	4.76	4.67
Denominator Degrees of Freedom (ν_2)	8	7.57	6.06	5.42	5.05	4.82	4.65	4.53	4.43	4.36	4.30	4.20
	9	7.21	5.71	5.08	4.72	4.48	4.32	4.20	4.10	4.03	3.96	3.87
	10	6.94	5.46	4.83	4.47	4.24	4.07	3.95	3.85	3.78	3.72	3.62
	11	6.72	5.26	4.63	4.28	4.04	3.88	3.76	3.66	3.59	3.53	3.43
	12	6.55	5.10	4.47	4.12	3.89	3.73	3.61	3.51	3.44	3.37	3.28
	13	6.41	4.97	4.35	4.00	3.77	3.60	3.48	3.39	3.31	3.25	3.15
	14	6.30	4.86	4.24	3.89	3.66	3.50	3.38	3.29	3.21	3.15	3.05
	15	6.20	4.77	4.15	3.80	3.58	3.41	3.29	3.20	3.12	3.06	2.96
	16	6.12	4.69	4.08	3.73	3.50	3.34	3.22	3.12	3.05	2.99	2.89
	17	6.04	4.62	4.01	3.66	3.44	3.28	3.16	3.06	2.98	2.92	2.82
	18	5.98	4.56	3.95	3.61	3.38	3.22	3.10	3.01	2.93	2.87	2.77

FIGURE 10.22

Critical value for right-tail F_R for $\alpha/2 = .025$

Appendix F: Critical Values of $F_{0.025}$

This table shows the 2.5% right-tail critical values of F for the stated degrees of freedom (ν).

		1	2	3	4	5	6	7	8	9	10	12
						Numerator Degrees of Freedom (ν_1)						
	1	647.8	799.5	864.2	899.6	921.8	937.1	948.2	956.6	963.3	968.6	976.7
	2	38.51	39.00	39.17	39.25	39.30	39.33	39.36	39.37	39.39	39.40	39.41
	3	17.44	16.04	15.44	15.10	14.88	14.73	14.62	14.54	14.47	14.42	14.34
	4	12.22	10.65	9.98	9.60	9.36	9.20	9.07	8.98	8.90	8.84	8.75
	5	10.01	8.43	7.76	7.39	7.15	6.98	6.85	6.76	6.68	6.62	6.52
	6	8.81	7.26	6.60	6.23	5.99	5.82	5.70	5.60	5.52	5.46	5.37
	7	8.07	6.54	5.89	5.52	5.29	5.12	4.99	4.90	4.82	4.76	4.67
Denominator Degrees of Freedom (ν_2)	8	7.57	6.06	5.42	5.05	4.82	4.65	4.53	4.43	4.36	4.30	4.20
	9	7.21	5.71	5.08	4.72	4.48	4.32	4.20	4.10	4.03	3.96	3.87
	10	6.94	5.46	4.83	4.47	4.24	4.07	3.95	3.85	3.78	3.72	3.62
	11	6.72	5.26	4.63	4.28	4.04	3.88	3.76	3.66	3.59	3.53	3.43
	12	6.55	5.10	4.47	4.12	3.89	3.73	3.61	3.51	3.44	3.37	3.28
	13	6.41	4.97	4.35	4.00	3.77	3.60	3.48	3.39	3.31	3.25	3.15
	14	6.30	4.86	4.24	3.89	3.66	3.50	3.38	3.29	3.21	3.15	3.05
	15	6.20	4.77	4.15	3.80	3.58	3.41	3.29	3.20	3.12	3.06	2.96
	16	6.12	4.69	4.08	3.73	3.50	3.34	3.22	3.12	3.05	2.99	2.89
	17	6.04	4.62	4.01	3.66	3.44	3.28	3.16	3.06	2.98	2.92	2.82
	18	5.98	4.56	3.95	3.61	3.38	3.22	3.10	3.01	2.93	2.87	2.77

FIGURE 10.23

Critical value for left-tail F_L for $\alpha/2 = .025$

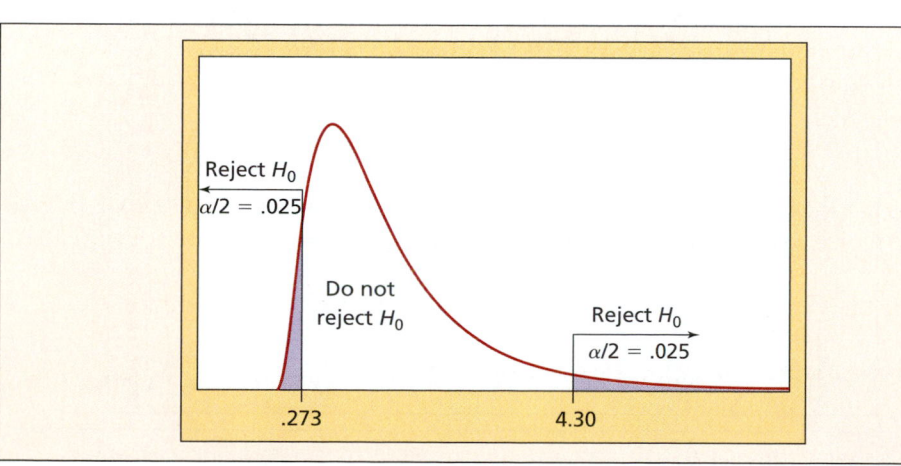

FIGURE 10.24

Two-tailed F test at $\alpha = .05$

Step 3: Calculate the Test Statistic The test statistic is

$$F = \frac{s_1^2}{s_2^2} = \frac{(696.20)^2}{(837.62)^2} = 0.691$$

Step 4: Make the Decision Since $F = 0.691$, we cannot reject the hypothesis of equal variances in a two-tailed test at $\alpha = .05$. In other words, the ratio of the sample variances does not differ significantly from 1.

Comparison of Variances: One-Tailed Test

Although we cannot reject the hypothesis of equal variances in a two-tailed test, we might be able to do so in a one-tailed test. In this case, the firm was interested in knowing whether the new bumper had *reduced* the variance in collision damage cost, so the consultant was asked to do a left-tailed test.

Step 1: Formulate the Hypotheses The hypotheses for a left-tailed test are

$$H_0: \sigma_1^2 \geq \sigma_2^2$$
$$H_1: \sigma_1^2 < \sigma_2^2$$

Step 2: State the Decision Rule Degrees of freedom for the F test are the same as for a two-tailed test (the hypothesis doesn't affect the degrees of freedom):

Numerator: $v_1 = n_1 - 1 = 12 - 1 = 11$

Denominator: $v_2 = n_2 - 1 = 9 - 1 = 8$

However, now the entire $\alpha = .05$ goes in the left tail. We reverse the degrees of freedom and find the left-tail critical value from Appendix F as the reciprocal of the table value, as illustrated in Figures 10.25 and 10.26. Notice that the asymmetry of the F distribution causes the left-tail area to be compressed in the horizontal direction.

$$F_L = \frac{1}{F_{v_2, v_1}} = \frac{1}{F_{8,11}} = \frac{1}{2.95} = 0.339 \qquad \text{(left-tail critical value)}$$

FIGURE 10.25

Right-tail F_R for $\alpha = .05$

Appendix F: Critical Values of F₀.₀₅

This table shows the 5% right-tail critical values of F for the stated degrees of freedom (ν).

		1	2	3	4	5	6	7	8	9	10	12
	1	161.4	199.5	215.7	224.6	230.2	234.0	236.8	238.9	240.5	241.9	243.9
	2	18.51	19.00	19.16	19.25	19.30	19.33	19.35	19.37	19.38	19.40	19.41
	3	10.13	9.55	9.28	9.12	9.01	8.94	8.89	8.85	8.81	8.79	8.74
	4	7.71	6.94	6.59	6.39	6.26	6.16	6.09	6.04	6.00	5.96	5.91
	5	6.61	5.79	5.41	5.19	5.05	4.95	4.88	4.82	4.77	4.74	4.68
	6	5.99	5.14	4.76	4.53	4.39	4.28	4.21	4.15	4.10	4.06	4.00
	7	5.59	4.74	4.35	4.12	3.97	3.87	3.79	3.73	3.68	3.64	3.57
	8	5.32	4.46	4.07	3.84	3.69	3.58	3.50	3.44	3.39	3.35	3.28
	9	5.12	4.26	3.86	3.63	3.48	3.37	3.29	3.23	3.18	3.14	3.07
	10	4.96	4.10	3.71	3.48	3.33	3.22	3.14	3.07	3.02	2.98	2.91
	11	4.84	3.98	3.59	3.36	3.20	3.09	3.01	2.95	2.90	2.85	2.79
	12	4.75	3.89	3.49	3.26	3.11	3.00	2.91	2.85	2.80	2.75	2.69
	13	4.67	3.81	3.41	3.18	3.03	2.92	2.83	2.77	2.71	2.67	2.60
	14	4.60	3.74	3.34	3.11	2.96	2.85	2.76	2.70	2.65	2.60	2.53
	15	4.54	3.68	3.29	3.06	2.90	2.79	2.71	2.64	2.59	2.54	2.48
	16	4.49	3.63	3.24	3.01	2.85	2.74	2.66	2.59	2.54	2.49	2.42
	17	4.45	3.59	3.20	2.96	2.81	2.70	2.61	2.55	2.49	2.45	2.38
	18	4.41	3.55	3.16	2.93	2.77	2.66	2.58	2.51	2.46	2.41	2.34

Numerator Degrees of Freedom (v₁)

Denominator Degrees of Freedom (v₂)

FIGURE 10.26

Left-tail F_L for $\alpha = .05$

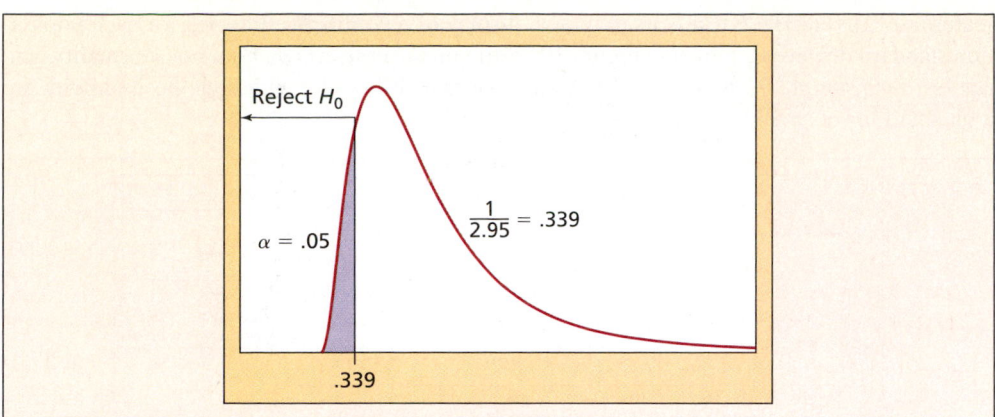

The decision rule is

Reject H_0 if $F < 0.339$

Otherwise do not reject H_0

Step 3: Calculate the Test Statistic   The test statistic is the same as for a two-tailed test (the hypothesis doesn't affect the test statistic):

$$F = \frac{s_1^2}{s_2^2} = \frac{(696.20)^2}{(837.62)^2} = 0.691$$

Step 4: Make the Decision   Since the test statistic $F = 0.691$ is not in the critical region, we cannot reject the hypothesis of equal variances in a one-tailed test. The bumpers did not significantly decrease the variance in collision repair cost.

Excel's *F* Test

Excel makes it quite easy to do the F test for variances. Figure 10.27 shows Excel's left-tailed test. One advantage of using Excel is that you also get a p-value. For the bumper data, the large p-value of .279 indicates that we would face a Type I error risk of about 28 percent if we were to reject H_0. In other words, a sample variance ratio as extreme as $F = 0.691$ would occur by chance about 28 percent of the time if the population variances were in fact equal. The sample evidence does not indicate that the variances differ.

FIGURE 10.27

Excel's *F* test of variances

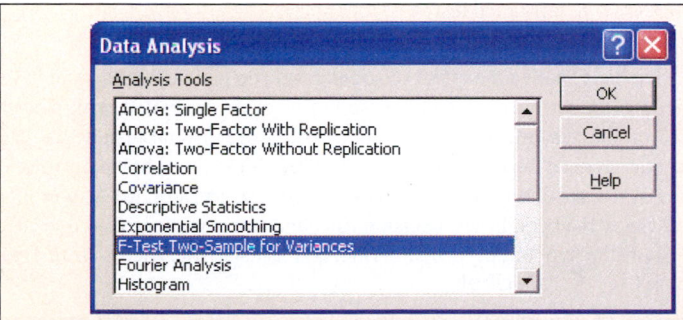

Assumptions of the *F* Test

The F test assumes that the populations being sampled are normal. Unfortunately, the test is rather sensitive to non-normality of the sampled populations. Alternative tests are available, but they tend to be rather complex and nonintuitive. MINITAB reports both the F test and a robust alternative known as *Levene's test* along with their p-values. As long as you know how to interpret a p-value, you really don't need to know the details of Levene's test. An attractive feature of MINITAB's F test is its graphical display of a confidence interval for each population standard deviation, shown in Figure 10.28. If you are concerned about non-normality, you can test each sample for non-normality by using a probability plot, although these samples are a bit small for normality tests.

FIGURE 10.28

MINITAB's test for variances

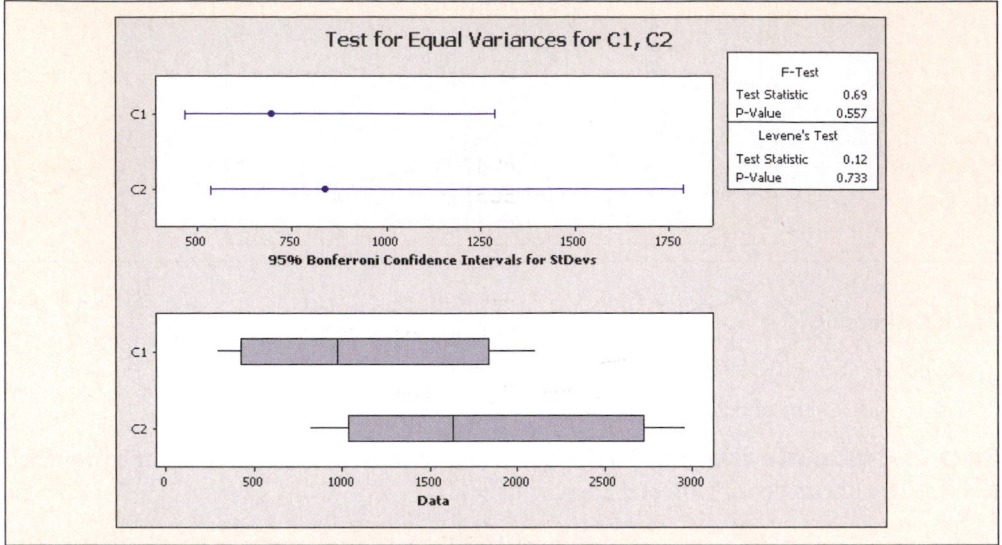

Significance versus Importance

The test of means showed a mean difference of $665 per repair incident. That is large enough that it might be important. The incremental cost per vehicle of the new bumper would have to be compared with the present discounted value of the expected annual savings per vehicle over its useful life. In a large fleet of vehicles, the payback period could be calculated. Most firms require that a change pay for itself in a fairly short period of time. *Importance* is a question to be answered ultimately by financial experts, not statisticians.

SECTION EXERCISES

Hint: Use Excel or MegaStat.

10.26 Which samples show unequal variances? Use $\alpha = .05$ in all tests. Show the critical values and degrees of freedom clearly and illustrate the decision rule.
a. $s_1 = 5.1$, $n_1 = 11$, $s_2 = 3.2$, $n_2 = 8$, two-tailed test
b. $s_1 = 221$, $n_1 = 8$, $s_2 = 445$, $n_2 = 8$, left-tailed test
c. $s_1 = 67$, $n_1 = 10$, $s_2 = 15$, $n_2 = 13$, right-tailed test

10.27 Researchers at the Mayo Clinic have studied the effect of sound levels on patient healing and have found a significant association (louder hospital ambient sound level is associated with slower postsurgical healing). Based on the Mayo Clinic's experience, Ardmore Hospital installed a new vinyl flooring that is supposed to reduce the mean sound level (decibels) in the hospital corridors. The sound level is measured at five randomly selected times in the main corridor. (a) At $\alpha = .05$, has the mean been reduced? Show the hypotheses, decision rule, and test statistic. (b) At $\alpha = .05$, has the variance changed? Show the hypotheses, decision rule, and test statistic. (See *Detroit Free Press*, February 2, 2004, p. 8H.) **Decibels**

New Flooring	Old Flooring
42	48
41	51
40	44
37	48
44	52

10.28 A manufacturing process drills holes in sheet metal that are supposed to be .5000 cm in diameter. Before and after a new drill press is installed, the hole diameter is carefully measured (in cm) for 12 randomly chosen parts. At $\alpha = .05$, do these independent random samples prove that the new process has smaller variance? Show the hypotheses, decision rule, and test statistic. *Hint:* Use Excel =FINV(1-α, v_1, v_2) to get F_L.   **Diameter**

New drill:	.5005	.5010	.5024	.4988	.4997	.4995
	.4976	.5042	.5014	.4995	.4988	.4992
Old drill:	.5052	.5053	.4947	.4907	.5031	.4923
	.5040	.5035	.5061	.4956	.5035	.4962

10.29 Examine the data below showing the weights (in pounds) of randomly selected checked bags for an airline's flights on the same day. (a) At $\alpha = .05$, is the mean weight of an international bag greater? Show the hypotheses, decision rule, and test statistic. (b) At $\alpha = .05$, is the variance greater for bags on an international flight? Show the hypotheses, decision rule, and test statistic.   **Luggage**

International (10 bags)		Domestic (15 bags)		
39	47	29	37	43
54	48	36	33	42
46	28	33	29	32
39	54	34	43	35
69	62	38	39	39

Chapter Summary

A **two-sample test** compares samples with each other rather than comparing with a benchmark, as in a one-sample test. For two proportions, the samples may be **pooled** if the population proportions are assumed equal, and the test statistic is the difference of proportions divided by the standard error, the square root of the sum of the sample variances. For proportions, **normality** may be assumed if both samples are large, that is, if they each contain at least 10 successes and 10 failures. For **independent samples,** the comparison of means generally utilizes the Student's *t* distribution, because the population variances are almost always unknown. If the unknown variances are **assumed equal,** we use a **pooled variance** estimate and **add the degrees of freedom.** If the unknown variances are **assumed unequal,** we do not pool the variances and we reduce the degrees of freedom by using **Welch's formula.** The test statistic is the difference of means divided by their standard error. For tests of means or proportions, **equal sample sizes** are desirable, but not necessary. The *t* **test for paired samples** uses the differences of *n* paired observations, thereby being a **one-sample** *t* test. The *F* **test** for equality of **two variances** is named after Sir Ronald Fisher. Its test statistic is the **ratio** of the sample variances. We want to see if the ratio differs significantly from 1. The *F* table shows critical values based on both **numerator** and **denominator** degrees of freedom.

Key Terms

Behrens-Fisher problem, *407*
F distribution, *420*
F test, *420*
independent sample, *417*
paired comparison, *414*
paired samples, *414*

paired *t* test, *414*
pooled estimate, *398*
pooled proportion, *397*
pooled variance, *407*
p-values, *396*
test statistic, *397*
two-sample tests, *395*

Type I error, *396*
Type II error, *396*
Welch-Satterthwaite test, *407*
Welch's adjusted degrees of freedom, *407*

Commonly Used Formulas in Two-Sample Hypothesis Tests

Pooled Sample Proportion: $\bar{p} = \dfrac{x_1 + x_2}{n_1 + n_2}$

Test Statistic (Equality of Proportions): $z = \dfrac{p_1 - p_2}{\sqrt{\bar{p}(1 - \bar{p})\left[\dfrac{1}{n_1} + \dfrac{1}{n_2}\right]}}$

Confidence Interval for $\pi_1 - \pi_2$: $(p_1 - p_2) \pm z\sqrt{\dfrac{p_1(1 - p_1)}{n_1} + \dfrac{p_2(1 - p_2)}{n_2}}$

Test Statistic (Difference of Means, Equal Variances): $t = \dfrac{\bar{x}_1 - \bar{x}_2}{\sqrt{\dfrac{s_p^2}{n_1} + \dfrac{s_p^2}{n_2}}}$

Pooled Variance Estimate: $s_p^2 = \dfrac{(n_1 - 1)s_1^2 + (n_2 - 1)s_2^2}{n_1 + n_2 - 2}$

Test Statistic (Difference of Means, Unequal Variances): $t = \dfrac{\bar{x}_1 - \bar{x}_2}{\sqrt{\dfrac{s_1^2}{n_1} + \dfrac{s_2^2}{n_2}}}$

Test Statistic (Paired Differences): $t = \dfrac{\bar{d} - \mu_d}{\dfrac{s_d}{\sqrt{n}}}$

Test Statistic (Two Variances): $F = \dfrac{s_1^2}{s_2^2}$

Chapter Review

1. (a) Explain why two samples from the same population could appear different. (b) Why do we say that two-sample tests have a built-in point of reference?

2. (a) In a two-sample test of proportions, what is a pooled proportion? (b) Why is the test for normality important for a two-sample test of proportions? (c) What is the criterion for assuming normality of the test statistic?

3. (a) Is it necessary that sample sizes be equal for a two-sample test of proportions? Is it desirable? (b) Explain the analogy between overlapping confidence intervals and testing for equality of two proportions.

4. List the three cases for a test comparing two means. Explain carefully how they differ.

5. Consider *Case 1* (known variances) in the test comparing two means. (a) Why is *Case 1* unusual and not used very often? (b) What distribution is used for the test statistic? (c) Write the formula for the test statistic.

6. Consider *Case 2* (unknown but equal variances) in the test comparing two means. (a) Why is *Case 2* common? (b) What distribution is used for the test statistic? (c) State the degrees of freedom used in this test. (d) Write the formula for the pooled variance and interpret it. (e) Write the formula for the test statistic.

7. Consider *Case 3* (unknown and unequal variances) in the test comparing two means. (a) What complication arises in degrees of freedom for *Case 3*? (b) What distribution is used for the test statistic? (c) Write the formula for the test statistic.

8. (a) Is it ever acceptable to use a normal distribution in a test of means with unknown variances? (b) If we assume normality, what is gained? What is lost?

9. Why is it a good idea to use a computer program like Excel to do tests of means?

10. (a) Explain why the paired *t* test for dependent samples is really a one-sample test. (b) State the degrees of freedom for the paired *t* test. (c) Why not treat two paired samples as if they were independent?

11. Explain how a difference in means could be statistically *significant* but not *important*.

12. (a) Why do we use an F test? (b) Where did it get its name? (c) When two population variances are equal, what value would you expect of the F test statistic?

13. (a) In an F test for two variances, explain how to obtain left- and right-tail critical values. (b) What are the assumptions underlying the F test?

CHAPTER EXERCISES

Note: For tests on two proportions, two means, or two variances it is a good idea to check your work by using MINITAB, MegaStat, or the *LearningStats* two-sample calculators in Unit 10.

10.30 In Dallas, some fire trucks were painted yellow (instead of red) to heighten their visibility. During a test period, the fleet of red fire trucks made 153,348 runs and had 20 accidents, while the fleet of yellow fire trucks made 135,035 runs and had 4 accidents. At $\alpha = .01$, did the yellow fire trucks have a significantly lower accident rate? (a) State the hypotheses. (b) State the decision rule and sketch it. (c) Find the sample proportions and z test statistic. (d) Make a decision. (e) Find the p-value and interpret it. (f) If statistically significant, do you think the difference is large enough to be important? If so, to whom, and why? (g) Is the normality assumption fulfilled? Explain.

Accident Rate for Dallas Fire Trucks

Statistic	Red Fire Trucks	Yellow Fire Trucks
Number of accidents	$x_1 = 20$ accidents	$x_2 = 4$ accidents
Number of fire runs	$n_1 = 153,348$ runs	$n_2 = 135,035$ runs

Source: *The Wall Street Journal,* June 26, 1995, p. B1.

10.31 Do a larger proportion of college students than young children eat cereal? Researchers surveyed both age groups to find the answer. The results are shown in the table below. (a) State the hypotheses used to answer the question. (b) Using $\alpha = .05$, state the decision rule and sketch it. (c) Find the sample proportions and z statistic. (d) Make a decision. (e) Find the p-value and interpret it. (f) Is the normality assumption fulfilled? Explain.

Statistic	College Students (ages 18–25)	Young Children (ages 6–11)
Number who eat cereal	$x_1 = 833$	$x_2 = 692$
Number surveyed	$n_1 = 850$	$n_2 = 740$

10.32 A 2005 study found that 202 women held board seats out of a total of 1,195 seats in the Fortune 100 companies. A 2003 study found that 779 women held board seats out of a total of 5,727 seats in the Fortune 500 companies. Treating these as random samples (since board seat assignments change often), can we conclude that Fortune 100 companies have a greater proportion of women board members than the Fortune 500? (a) State the hypotheses. (b) Calculate the sample proportions. (c) Find the test statistic and its p-value. What is your conclusion at $\alpha = .05$? (d) If statistically significant, can you suggest factors that might explain the increase? (Data are from *The 2003 Catalyst Census of Women Board Directors of the Fortune 500,* and "Women and Minorities on Fortune 100 Boards," *The Alliance for Board Diversity*, May 17, 2005.)

10.33 A study of the Fortune 100 board of director members showed that there were 36 minority women holding board seats out of 202 total female board members. There were 142 minority men holding board seats out of 993 total male board members. (a) Treating the findings from this study as samples, calculate the sample proportions. (b) Find the test statistic and its p-value. (c) At the 5 percent level of significance, is there a difference in the percentage of minority women board directors and minority men board directors? (Data are from "Women and Minorities on Fortune 100 Boards," *The Alliance for Board Diversity,* May 17, 2005.)

10.34 To test his hypothesis that students who finish an exam first get better grades, a professor kept track of the order in which papers were handed in. Of the first 25 papers, 10 received a B or better compared with 8 of the last 24 papers handed in. Is the first group better, at $\alpha = .10$? (a) State your hypotheses and obtain a test statistic and p-value. Interpret the results. (b) Are the samples large enough to assure normality? (c) Make an argument that early-finishers should do better. Then make the opposite argument. Which is more convincing?

10.35 How many full-page advertisements are found in a magazine? In an October issue of *Muscle and Fitness,* there were 252 ads, of which 97 were full-page. For the same month, the magazine *Glamour* had 342 ads, of which 167 were full-page. (a) Is the difference significant at $\alpha = .01$? (b) Find the *p*-value. (c) Is normality assured? (d) Based on what you know of these magazines, why might the proportions of full-page ads differ? (Data are from a project by MBA students Amy DeGuire and Don Finney.)

10.36 In Utica, Michigan, 205 of 226 school buses passed the annual safety inspection. In Detroit, Michigan, only 151 of 296 buses passed the inspection. (a) State the hypotheses for a right-tailed test. (b) Obtain a test statistic and *p*-value. (c) Is normality assured? (d) If *significant,* is the difference also large enough to be *important?* (Data are from *Detroit Free Press,* August 19, 2000, p. 8A.)

10.37 After John F. Kennedy, Jr., was killed in an airplane crash at night, a survey was taken, asking whether a noninstrument-rated pilot should be allowed to fly at night. Of 409 New York State residents, 61 said yes. Of 70 aviation experts who were asked the same question, 40 said yes. (a) At $\alpha = .01$, did a larger proportion of experts say yes compared with the general public, or is the difference within the realm of chance? (b) Find the *p*-value and interpret it. (b) Is normality assured? (Data are from www.siena.edu/sri.)

10.38 A ski company in Vail owns two ski shops, one on the east side and one on the west side. Sales data showed that at the eastern location there were 56 pairs of large gloves sold out of 304 total pairs sold. At the western location there were 145 pairs of large gloves sold out of 562 total pairs sold. (a) Calculate the sample proportion of large gloves for each location. (b) At $\alpha = .05$, is there a significant difference in the proportion of large gloves sold? (c) Can you suggest any reasons why a difference might exist? (*Note:* Problem is based on actual sales data).

10.39 Does hormone replacement therapy (HRT) cause breast cancer? Researchers studied women ages 50 to 79 who used either HRT or a dummy pill over a 5-year period. Of the 8,304 HRT women, 245 cancers were reported, compared with 185 cancers for the 8,304 women who got the dummy pill. Assume that the participants were randomly assigned to two equal groups. (a) State the hypotheses for a one-tailed test to see if HRT was associated with increased cancer risk. (b) Obtain a test statistic and *p*-value. Interpret the results. (c) Is normality assured? (d) Is the difference large enough to be important? Explain. (e) What else would you need to know to assess this research? (Data are from www.cbsnews.com, accessed June 25, 2003.)

10.40 A sample of high school seniors showed that 18 of 60 who owned PlayStation 3 spent more than an hour a day playing games, compared with 32 of 80 who owned Xbox 360. Is there a significant difference in the population proportions at $\alpha = .10$?

10.41 A survey of 117,156 women who were free of heart disease showed that 31,101 had at least one parent who had suffered a heart attack before age 60. Four years later, 133 of those with a positive family history of heart attack themselves had signs of heart disease, compared with 141 of those whose parent had not suffered a heart attack. (a) State the hypotheses for a one-tailed test to see if positive family history is associated with increased risk. (b) Obtain a test statistic and *p*-value. Interpret the results. (c) Is normality assured? (d) Is the difference large enough to be important? (Data are from *Science News* 126, no. 22, p. 351.)

10.42 A study of people in a driving simulator showed that 12 of 24 using a cell phone with a headset (group 1) missed their freeway exit, 3 of 24 talking to a passenger (group 2) missed their freeway exit, and 2 of 48 driving unaccompanied and not talking (group 3) missed their freeway exit. (a) For each sample, construct a 95 percent confidence interval for the true proportion. Do they overlap? So what? (b) Do a two-tailed hypothesis test at $\alpha = .05$ to compare group 1 and group 2. What is your conclusion? (c) Did you find the confidence intervals or the hypothesis test more helpful in visualizing the situation? (d) Is normality assured? (Data are from *The Wall Street Journal,* September 24, 2004, p. B1.)

10.43 In a marketing class, 44 student members of virtual (Internet) project teams (group 1) and 42 members of face-to-face project teams (group 2) were asked to respond on a 1–5 scale to the question: "As compared to other teams, the members helped each other." For group 1 the mean was 2.73 with a standard deviation of 0.97, while for group 2 the mean was 1.90 with a standard deviation of 0.91. At $\alpha = .01$, is the virtual team mean significantly higher? (Data are from Roger W. Berry, *Marketing Education Review* 12, no. 2 [2002], pp. 73–78.)

10.44 Does lovastatin (a cholesterol-lowering drug) reduce the risk of heart attack? In a Texas study, researchers gave lovastatin to 2,325 people and an inactive substitute to 2,081 people (average age 58). After 5 years, 57 of the lovastatin group had suffered a heart attack, compared with 97 for the inactive pill. (a) State the appropriate hypotheses. (b) Obtain a test statistic and *p*-value. Interpret the results at $\alpha = .01$. (c) Is normality assured? (d) Is the difference large enough to be important? (e) What else would medical researchers need to know before prescribing this drug widely? (Data are from *Science News* 153 [May 30, 1998], p. 343.)

10.45 U.S. Vice President Dick Cheney received a lot of publicity after his fourth heart attack. A portable defibrillator was surgically implanted in his chest to deliver an electric shock to restore his heart rhythm whenever another attack was threatening. Researchers at the University of Rochester (NY) Medical Center implanted defibrillators in 742 patients after a heart attack and compared them with 490 similar patients without the implant. Over the next 2 years, 98 of those without defibrillators had died, compared with 104 of those with defibrillators. (a) State the hypotheses for a one-tailed test to see if the defibrillators reduced the death rate. (b) Obtain a test statistic and *p*-value. (c) Is normality assured? (d) Why might such devices not be widely implanted in heart attack patients? (Data are from *Science News* 161 [April 27, 2002], p. 270.)

10.46 To test the hypothesis that students who finish an exam first get better grades, Professor Hardtack kept track of the order in which papers were handed in. The first 25 papers showed a mean score of 77.1 with a standard deviation of 19.6, while the last 24 papers handed in showed a mean score of 69.3 with a standard deviation of 24.9. Is this a significant difference at $\alpha = .05$? (a) State the hypotheses for a right-tailed test. (b) Obtain a test statistic and *p*-value assuming equal variances. Interpret these results. (c) Is the difference in mean scores large enough to be important? (d) Is it reasonable to assume equal variances? (e) Carry out a formal test for equal variances at $\alpha = .05$, showing all steps clearly.

10.47 Has the cost to outsource a standard employee background check changed from 2005 to 2006? A random sample of 10 companies in spring 2005 showed a sample average of $105 with a sample standard deviation equal to $32. A random sample of 10 different companies in spring 2006 resulted in a sample average of $75 with a sample standard deviation equal to $45. (a) Conduct a hypothesis test to test the difference in sample means with a level of significance equal to .05. Assume the population variances are not equal. (b) Discuss why a paired sample design might have made more sense in this case.

10.48 From her firm's computer telephone log, an executive found that the mean length of 64 telephone calls during July was 4.48 minutes with a standard deviation of 5.87 minutes. She vowed to make an effort to reduce the length of calls. The August phone log showed 48 telephone calls whose mean was 2.396 minutes with a standard deviation of 2.018 minutes. (a) State the hypotheses for a right-tailed test. (b) Obtain a test statistic and *p*-value assuming unequal variances. Interpret these results using $\alpha = .01$. (c) Why might the sample data *not* follow a normal, bell-shaped curve? If not, how might this affect your conclusions?

10.49 An experimental bumper was designed to reduce damage in low-speed collisions. This bumper was installed on an experimental group of vans in a large fleet, but not on a control group. At the end of a trial period, accident data showed 12 repair incidents for the experimental group and 9 repair incidents for the control group. Vehicle downtime (in days per repair incident) is shown below. At $\alpha = .05$, did the new bumper reduce downtime? (a) Make stacked dot plots of the data (a sketch is OK). (b) State the hypotheses. (c) State the decision rule and sketch it. (d) Find the test statistic. (e) Make a decision. (f) Find the *p*-value and interpret it. (g) Do you think the difference is large enough to be important? Explain. (Data are from an unpublished study by Floyd G. Willoughby and Thomas W. Lauer, Oakland University.) **DownTime**

New bumper (12 repair incidents): 9, 2, 5, 12, 5, 4, 7, 5, 11, 3, 7, 1

Control group (9 repair incidents): 7, 5, 7, 4, 18, 4, 8, 14, 13

10.50 Medicare spending per patient in different U.S. metropolitan areas may differ. Based on the sample data below, is the average spending in the northern region significantly less than the average spending in the southern region at the 1 percent level? (a) State the hypotheses and decision rule. (b) Find the test statistic assuming unequal variances. (c) State your conclusion. Is this a strong conclusion? (d) Can you suggest reasons why a difference might exist? (See *The New Yorker* [May 30, 2005], p. 38).

Medicare Spending per Patient (adjusted for age, sex, and race)

Statistic	Northern Region	Southern Region
Sample mean	$3,123	$8,456
Sample standard deviation	$1,546	$3,678
Sample size	14 patients	16 patients

10.51 A statistics professor compared the scores of her morning class and afternoon class on the same quiz. The 42 morning students' average score was 83.52 with a standard deviation of 7.81, while the 46 afternoon students' average score was 79.44 with a standard deviation of 6.62. (a) Which test would you use to compare the means? (b) State the hypotheses to see if there was a difference. (c) Obtain a test statistic and p-value. (d) Why might there be a difference between morning and afternoon scores? Explain. (e) Is it reasonable to assume equal variances? (f) Carry out a formal test for equal variances at $\alpha = .05$, showing all steps clearly.

10.52 One group of accounting students took a distance learning class, while another group took the same course in a traditional classroom. At $\alpha = .10$, is there a significant difference in the mean scores listed below? (a) State the hypotheses. (b) State the decision rule and sketch it. (c) Find the test statistic. (d) Make a decision. (e) Use Excel to find the p-value and interpret it.

Exam Scores for Accounting Students

Statistic	Distance	Classroom
Mean scores	$\bar{x}_1 = 9.1$	$\bar{x}_2 = 10.3$
Sample std. dev.	$s_1 = 2.4$	$s_2 = 2.5$
Number of students	$n_1 = 20$	$n_2 = 20$

10.53 Do male and female school superintendents earn the same pay? Salaries for 20 males and 17 females in a certain metropolitan area are shown below. At $\alpha = .01$, were the mean superintendent salaries greater for men than for women? (a) Make stacked dot plots of the sample data (a sketch will do). (b) State the hypotheses. (c) State the decision rule and sketch it. (d) Find the test statistic. (e) Make a decision. (f) Estimate the p-value and interpret it. (g) If statistically significant, do you think the difference is large enough to be important? Explain.   **Paycheck**

School Superintendent Pay

Men (n = 20)		Women (n = 17)	
114,000	121,421	94,675	96,000
115,024	112,187	123,484	112,455
115,598	110,160	99,703	120,118
108,400	128,322	86,000	124,163
109,900	128,041	108,000	76,340
120,352	125,462	94,940	89,600
118,000	113,611	83,933	91,993
108,209	123,814	102,181	
110,000	111,280	86,840	
151,008	112,280	85,000	

10.54 The average take-out order size for Ashoka Curry House restaurant is shown. Assuming equal variances, at $\alpha = .05$, is there a significant difference in the order sizes? (a) State the hypotheses. (b) State the decision rule and sketch it. (c) Find the test statistic. (d) Make a decision. (e) Use Excel to find the p-value and interpret it.

Customer Order Size

Statistic	Friday Night	Saturday Night
Mean order size	$\bar{x}_1 = 22.32$	$\bar{x}_2 = 25.56$
Standard deviation	$s_1 = 4.35$	$s_2 = 6.16$
Number of orders	$n_1 = 13$	$n_2 = 18$

10.55 Cash withdrawals (in multiples of $20) at an on-campus ATM for a random sample of 30 Fridays and 30 Mondays are shown following. At $\alpha = .01$, is there a difference in the mean ATM withdrawal on Monday and Friday? (a) Make stacked dot plots of the data (a sketch is OK). (b) State the hypotheses. (c) State the decision rule and sketch it. (d) Find the test statistic. (e) Make a decision. (f) Find the *p*-value and interpret it.   **ATM**

Randomly Chosen ATM Withdrawals ($)

Friday			Monday		
250	10	10	40	30	10
20	10	30	100	70	370
110	20	10	20	20	10
40	20	40	30	50	30
70	10	10	200	20	40
20	20	400	20	30	20
10	20	10	10	20	100
50	20	10	30	40	20
100	20	20	50	10	20
20	60	70	60	10	20

10.56 A sample of 25 concession stand purchases at the October 22 matinee of *Bride of Chucky* showed a mean purchase of $5.29 with a standard deviation of $3.02. For the October 26 evening showing of the same movie, for a sample of 25 purchases the mean was $5.12 with a standard deviation of $2.14. The means appear to be very close, but not the variances. At $\alpha = .05$, is there a difference in variances? Show all steps clearly, including an illustration of the decision rule. (Data are from a project by statistics students Kim Dyer, Amy Pease, and Lyndsey Smith.)

10.57 A ski company in Vail owns two ski shops, one on the west side and one on the east side of Vail. Is there a difference in daily average goggle sales between the two stores? Assume equal variances. (a) State the hypotheses for a two-tailed test. (b) State the decision rule for a level of significance equal to 5 percent and sketch it. (c) Find the test statistic and state your conclusion.

Sales Data for Ski Goggles

Statistic	East Side Shop	West Side Shop
Mean sales	$328	$435
Sample std. dev.	$104	$147
Sample size	28 days	29 days

10.58 A ski company in Vail owns two ski shops, one on the west side and one on the east side of Vail. Ski hat sales data (in dollars) for a random sample of 5 Saturdays during the 2004 season showed the following results. Is there a significant difference in sales dollars of hats between the west side and east side stores at the 5 percent level of significance? (a) State the hypotheses. (b) State the decision rule and sketch it. (c) Find the test statistic and state your conclusion.   **Hats**

Saturday Sales Data ($) for Ski Hats

Saturday	East Side Shop	West Side Shop
1	548	523
2	493	721
3	609	695
4	567	510
5	432	532

10.59 Emergency room arrivals in a large hospital showed the statistics below for 2 months. At $\alpha = .05$, has the variance changed? Show all steps clearly, including an illustration of the decision rule.

Statistic	October	November
Mean arrivals	177.0323	171.7333
Standard deviation	13.48205	15.4271
Days	31	30

10.60 Here are heart rates for a sample of 30 students before and after a class break. At $\alpha = .05$, was there a significant difference in the mean heart rate? (a) State the hypotheses. (b) State the decision rule and sketch it. (c) Find the test statistic. (d) Make a decision. (e) Estimate the p-value and interpret it. 🐢 **HeartRate**

Heart Rate Before and After Class Break

Student	Before	After	Student	Before	After
1	60	62	16	70	64
2	70	76	17	69	66
3	77	78	18	64	69
4	80	83	19	70	73
5	82	82	20	59	58
6	82	83	21	62	65
7	41	66	22	66	68
8	65	63	23	81	77
9	58	60	24	56	57
10	50	54	25	64	62
11	82	93	26	78	79
12	56	55	27	75	74
13	71	67	28	66	67
14	67	68	29	59	63
15	66	75	30	98	82

Note: Thanks to colleague Gene Fliedner for having his evening students take their own pulses before and after the 10-minute class break.

10.61 A certain company will purchase the house of any employee who is transferred out of state and will handle all details of reselling the house. The purchase price is based on two assessments, one assessor being chosen by the employee and one by the company. Based on the sample of eight assessments shown, do the two assessors agree? Use the .01 level of significance, state hypotheses clearly, and show all steps. 🐢 **HomeValue**

Assessments of Eight Homes ($ thousands)

Assessed By	Home 1	Home 2	Home 3	Home 4	Home 5	Home 6	Home 7	Home 8
Company	328	350	455	278	290	285	535	745
Employee	318	345	470	285	310	280	525	765

10.62 Nine homes are chosen at random from real estate listings in two suburban neighborhoods, and the square footage of each home is noted following. At the .10 level of significance, is there a difference between the sizes of homes in the two neighborhoods? State your hypotheses and show all steps clearly. 🐢 **HomeSize**

Size of Homes in Two Subdivisions

Subdivision	Square Footage								
Greenwood	2,320	2,450	2,270	2,200	2,850	2,150	2,400	2,800	2,430
Pinewood	2,850	2,560	2,300	2,100	2,750	2,450	2,550	2,750	3,150

10.63 Two labs produce 1280 × 1024 LCD displays. Twelve displays are chosen at random from each lab, and the number of bad pixels is noted for each display. At the .01 level of significance, is there a difference in the defect rate between the two labs? State your hypotheses and assumptions clearly.   **LCDDefects**

Defects in Randomly Inspected LCD Displays

Facility	Number of Bad Pixels											
Lab *A*	2	0	5	0	1	2	0	5	0	4	1	2
Lab *B*	0	1	2	3	1	0	0	1	2	2	1	0

10.64 A cognitive retraining clinic assists outpatient victims of head injury, anoxia, or other conditions that result in cognitive impairment. Each incoming patient is evaluated to establish an appropriate treatment program and estimated length of stay. To see if the evaluation teams are consistent, 12 randomly chosen patients are separately evaluated by two expert teams (*A* and *B*) as shown. At the .10 level of significance, are the evaluator teams consistent in their estimates? State your hypotheses and show all steps clearly.   **LengthStay**

Estimated Length of Stay in Weeks

Team	Patient											
	1	2	3	4	5	6	7	8	9	10	11	12
A	24	24	52	30	40	30	18	30	18	40	24	12
B	24	20	52	36	36	36	24	36	16	52	24	16

10.65 Rates of return (annualized) in two investment portfolios are compared over the last 12 quarters. They are considered similar in safety, but portfolio *B* is advertised as being "less volatile." (a) At $\alpha = .025$, does the sample show that portfolio *A* has significantly greater variance in rates of return than portfolio *B*? (b) At $\alpha = .025$, is there a significant difference in the means?   **Portfolio**

Portfolio A	Portfolio B
5.23	8.96
10.91	8.60
12.49	7.61
4.17	6.60
5.54	7.77
8.68	7.06
7.89	7.68
9.82	7.62
9.62	8.71
4.93	8.97
11.66	7.71
11.49	9.91

DO-IT-YOURSELF

10.66 Count the number of two-door vehicles among 50 vehicles from a college or university student parking lot. Use any sampling method you like (e.g., the first 50 you see). Do the same for a grocery store that is not very close to the college or university. At $\alpha = .10$, is there a significant difference in the proportion of two-door vehicles in these two locations? (a) State the hypotheses. (b) State the decision rule and sketch it. (c) Find the sample proportions and z test statistic. (d) Make a decision. (e) Find the p-value and interpret it. (f) Is the normality assumption fulfilled? Explain.

10.67 Choose 40 words at random from this book (use a systematic sampling method, such as every fifth word on every tenth page). Then do the same for a novel of your choice. List the words and count the syllables in each. Find the mean and standard deviation. Is there a significant difference in the number of syllables at the .05 level? If so, is the difference important, as well as significant? To whom, and why? Show all work carefully.

10.68 Choose 100 words at random from this book (use a systematic sampling method, such as every tenth word on every fifth page). Then do the same for a novel of your choice. List the words and count the syllables in each. For each sample, find the proportion of words with more than three syllables. Is there a significant difference in the mean number of syllables at the .05 level? How does this analysis differ from the preceding exercise?

10.69 Use the *LearningStats* MBA database for this exercise. Choose either year (1990 or 1998) and sort the data on any variable you wish (sex, GPA, major, etc.). Then split the data into two groups based on the sorted list (e.g., male or female, high GPA or low GPA). For each group, calculate the mean and standard deviation for a quantitative variable of your choice (number of siblings, hours of work, number of traffic tickets, etc.). Test for significant difference of two means, choosing any level of significance you wish. State your hypotheses clearly and tell why you might expect a difference (or not, if none is expected). Show work and explain.

10.70 Use the *LearningStats* MBA database for this exercise. Choose either year (1990 or 1998) and sort the data on any variable you wish (sex, GPA, major, etc.). Then split the data into two groups based on the sorted list (e.g., male or female, high GPA or low GPA). For each group, calculate a proportion of your choice (proportion who read a daily newspaper, proportion who can conduct transactions in a foreign language, etc.). Choose any level of significance you wish. State your hypotheses clearly and tell why you might expect a difference (or not, if none is expected). Show all work and explain fully.

10.71 Use the *LearningStats* miscellaneous data for this exercise. Compare the age at inauguration of the first 21 U.S. presidents (George Washington through Chester Alan Arthur) with the second set of 22 U.S. presidents (Grover Cleveland through George W. Bush). (a) At the .05 level of significance, is there a significant difference in mean age at inauguration? Explain clearly and intrepret the results. (b) At the .05 level of significance, should equal variances be assumed? Explain your reasoning fully.

10.72 Use the *LearningStats* state data for this exercise. Choose a database for any year (1990, 1997, or 2000). (a) Copy three data columns into a new worksheet: State, Income, and Urban%. (b) Sort the data on Urban% and then split the states into two roughly equal groups (low urban, high urban). (c) For each group, calculate the mean and standard deviation for Income and carry out a test for difference of means at $\alpha = .05$. Explain fully. (d) Perform a test for equal variances in the two groups at $\alpha = .05$. Explain fully. (e) Does urbanization seem to be related to income? (f) Make a scatter plot of Urban% and Income. What does it suggest?

10.73 Use the *LearningStats* nations data for this exercise. Choose a database for any year (1995, 1999, or 2002). (a) Copy three data columns into a new worksheet: Nation, BirthRate, and InfMort. (b) Sort the data on BirthRate and then split the nations into two roughly equal groups (low births, high births). (c) For each group, calculate the mean and standard deviation for InfMort and carry out a test for difference of means at $\alpha = .05$. Explain fully. (d) Perform a test for equal variances in the two groups at $\alpha = .05$. Explain fully. (e) Does birth rate seem to be related to infant mortality? (f) Make a scatter plot of BirthRate and InfMort. What does it suggest?

Related Reading

Best, D. J.; and J. C. W. Rayner. "Welch's Approximate Solution for the Behrens-Fisher Problem." *Technometrics* 29 (1987), pp. 205–10.

Payton, Mark E.; Matthew H. Greenstone; and Nathan Schenker. "Overlapping Confidence Intervals or Standard Error Intervals: What Do They Mean in terms of Statistical Significance?" *Journal of Insect Science* 3, no. 34.

Posten, H. O. "Robustness of the Two-Sample *t*-Test under Violations of the Homogeneity of Variance Assumption, Part II." *Communications in Statistics—Theory and Methods* 21 (1995), pp. 2169–84.

Scheffé, H. "Practical Solutions of the Behrens-Fisher Problem." *Journal of the American Statistical Association* 65 (1970), pp. 1501–08.

Shoemaker, Lewis F. "Fixing the *F* Test for Equal Variances." *The American Statistician* 57, no. 2 (May 2003), pp. 105–14.

Wang, Y. "Probabilities of the Type I Errors of the Welch Tests for the Behrens-Fisher Problem." *Journal of the American Statistical Association* 66 (1971), pp. 605–08.

LearningStats Unit 10   Two-Sample Hypothesis Tests

LearningStats Unit 10 gives examples of the most common two-sample hypothesis tests (two means, two proportions, two variances) and offers tables of critical values. Your instructor may assign specific modules, or you may pursue those that sound interesting.

Topic	LearningStats Modules
Hypothesis testing	Two-Sample Hypothesis Tests
Common hypothesis tests	Two-Sample Tests Calculator for Two Means Calculator for Two Proportions
Simulations	Two-Sample Generator Paired Data Generator Two-Sample Bootstrap Welch Correction Demo
Case studies	Case—Exam Scores Case—Weight-Loss Paired Data Case—Heart Rate Paired Case—Right-Handed Desks
Equations	Formulas for Two-Sample Tests Sampling Distribution PDFs
Tables	Appendix C—Normal Appendix D—Student's *t* Appendix F—*F* Distribution

Key: = PowerPoint   = Word   = Excel

Visual Statistics

Visual Statistics Modules on Two-Sample Tests

Module	Module Name
10	Visualizing Two-Sample Hypothesis Tests

Visual Statistics Module 10 (included on your CD) is designed to help you

- Become familiar with the sampling distributions used in tests of two means or two variances.
- Understand the relationship between a confidence interval and a two-sample test.
- Be able to explain Type I error, Type II error, and power for two-sample tests.
- Know the assumptions underlying two-sample tests and the effects of violating them.

The worktext (included on the CD in .PDF format) contains lists of concepts covered, objectives of the modules, overviews of concepts, illustrations of concepts, orientations to module features, learning exercises (basic, intermediate, advanced), learning projects (individual, team), self-evaluation quizzes, glossaries of terms, and solutions to self-evaluation quizzes.

Analysis of Variance

**Chapter Learning
Objectives**

When you finish this chapter you should be able to

- Use basic ANOVA terminology correctly (e.g., response variable, factors, treatments).

- Use a table or Excel to find critical values for the F distribution.

- Recognize from the data format which type of ANOVA is appropriate.

- Use Excel or another software package to perform ANOVA calculations.

- Explain the assumptions of ANOVA and why they are important.

- Understand and perform Tukey's test for differences in pairs of group means.

- Use the F_{max} or other tests for equal variances in c treatment groups.

- Interpret main effects and interaction effects in two-factor ANOVA.

- Explain the advantages of replication in two-factor ANOVA.

- Recognize when higher-order ANOVA models are needed and why Excel is insufficient.

- Explain why experimental design is important and list a few common designs.

Chapter 12

You have already learned to compare the means of two samples. In this chapter, you will learn to compare more than two means *simultaneously* and how to trace sources of variation to potential explanatory factors by using ***analysis of variance*** (commonly referred to as ***ANOVA***). Proper *experimental design* can make efficient use of limited data to draw the strongest possible inferences. Although analysis of variance has a relatively short history, it is one of the richest and most thoroughly explored fields of statistics. Originally developed by the English statistician Ronald A. Fisher (1890–1962) in connection with agricultural research (factors affecting crop growth), it was quickly applied in biology and medicine. Because of its versatility, it is now used in engineering, psychology, marketing, and many other areas. In this chapter, we will only illustrate a few kinds of problems where ANOVA may be utilized (see Related Reading if you need to go further).

The Goal: Explaining Variation

Analysis of variance seeks to identify *sources of variation* in a numerical *dependent* variable Y (the ***response variable***). Variation in the response variable about its mean either is ***explained*** by one or more categorical *independent* variables (the ***factors***) or is ***unexplained*** (random error):

$$\begin{array}{ccccc} \text{Variation in } Y & = & \text{Explained Variation} & + & \text{Unexplained Variation} \\ \text{(around its mean)} & & \text{(due to factors)} & & \text{(random error)} \end{array}$$

ANOVA is a *comparison of means*. Each possible value of a factor or combination of factors is a ***treatment.*** Sample observations within each treatment are viewed as coming from populations with possibly different means. We test whether each factor has a significant effect on Y, and sometimes we test for interaction between factors. The test uses the F distribution, which was introduced in Chapter 10. ANOVA can handle any number of factors, but the researcher often is interested only in a few. Also, data collection costs may impose practical limits on the number of factors or treatments we can choose. This chapter concentrates on ANOVA models with one or two factors, although more complex models are briefly mentioned at the end of the chapter.

Illustration: Manufacturing Defect Rates

Figure 11.1 shows a dot plot of daily defect rates for automotive computer chips manufactured at four plant locations. Samples of 10 days' production were taken at each plant. Are the observed differences in the plants' sample mean defect rates merely due to random variation? Or are the observed differences between the plants' defect rates too great to be attributed to chance? This is the kind of question that ANOVA is designed to answer.

FIGURE 11.1

Chip defect rates at four plants. The treatment means are significantly different ($p = .02$). Note that the confidence interval for Lee's Bluff falls to the right of the dotted vertical line, which represents the overall mean.

VS
Chapter 12

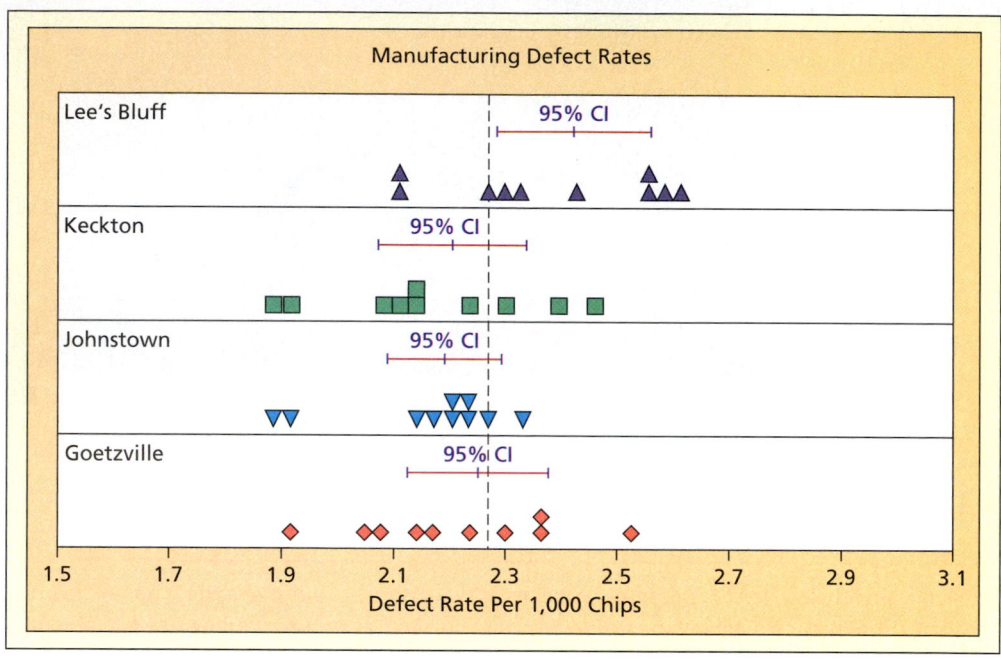

A simple way to state the ANOVA hypothesis is

H_0: $\mu_1 = \mu_2 = \mu_3 = \mu_4$ (mean defect rates are the same at all four plants)

H_1: Not all the means are equal (at least one mean differs from the others)

If we cannot reject H_0, then we conclude that the observations within each treatment or group actually have a common mean μ (represented by a dashed line in Figure 11.1). This one-factor ANOVA model may be visualized as in Figure 11.2.

FIGURE 11.2

ANOVA model for chip defect rate

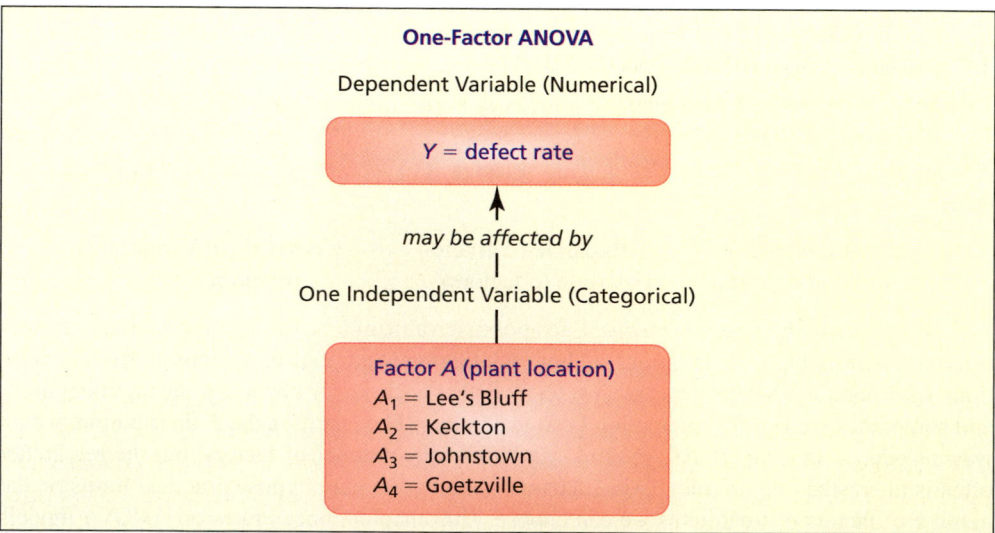

Illustration: Hospital Length of Stay

To allocate resources and fixed costs correctly, hospital management needs to test whether a patient's length of a stay (LOS) depends on the diagnostic-related group (DRG) code and the patient's age group. Consider the case of a bone fracture. LOS is a *numerical* response variable (measured in hours). The hospital organizes the data by using five diagnostic codes for type of fracture (facial, radius or ulna, hip or femur, other lower extremity, all other) and three age groups (under 18, 18 to 64, 65 and over). Although patient age is a numerical variable, it is coded into three categories based on stages of bone growth. Figure 11.3 illustrates two possible ANOVA models (one-factor or two-factor). We could also test for *interaction* between factors, as you will see later on.

One factor: Length of stay $= f$(Type of Fracture)

Two factors: Length of stay $= f$(Type of Fracture, Age Group)

FIGURE 11.3

ANOVA models for hospital length of stay

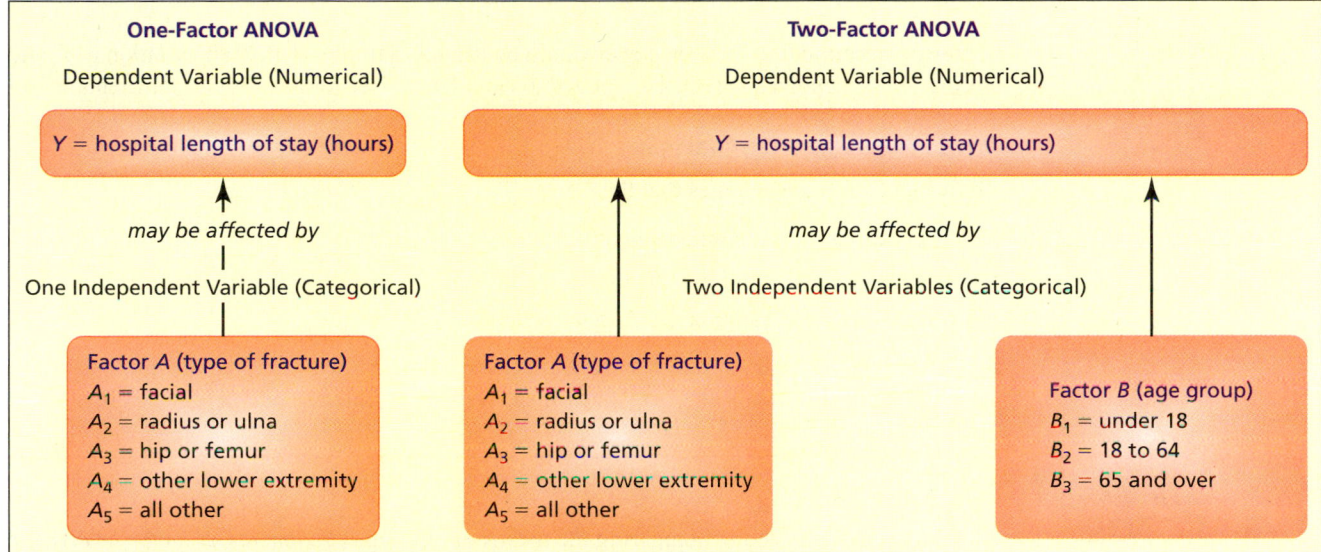

Illustration: Automobile Painting

Paint quality is a major concern of car makers. A key characteristic of paint is its viscosity, a continuous *numerical* variable. Viscosity is to be tested for dependence on application temperature (low, medium, high) and/or the supplier of the paint (Sasnak Inc., Etaoin Ltd., or Shrdlu Inc.). Although temperature is a numerical variable, it has been coded into *categories* that represent the test conditions of the experiment. Figure 11.4 illustrates two potential ANOVA models:

One factor: Viscosity $= f$(temperature)

Two factors: Viscosity $= f$(temperature, supplier)

ANOVA Calculations

ANOVA calculations usually are too tedious to do by calculator, so after we choose an ANOVA model and collect the data, we rely on software (e.g., Excel, MegaStat, MINITAB, SPSS) to do the calculations. In some applications (accounting, finance, human resources, marketing) large samples can easily be taken from existing records, while in others (engineering, manufacturing, computer systems) experimental data collection is so expensive that small samples are used. Large samples increase the power of the test, but power also depends on the

FIGURE 11.4

Several ANOVA models for paint viscosity

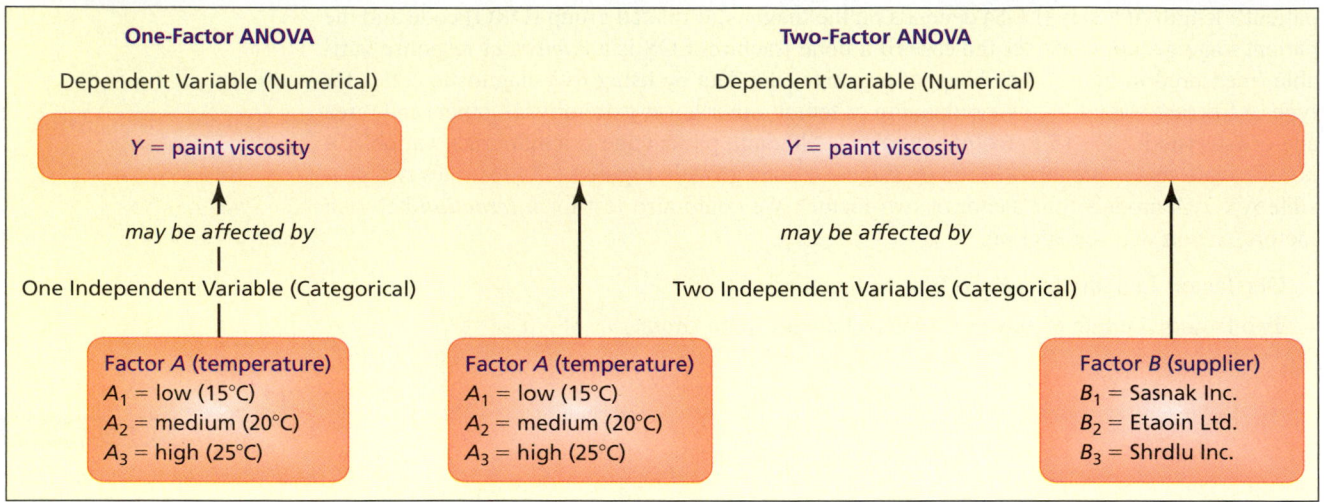

degree of variation in Y. Lowest power would be in small samples with high variation in Y, and conversely. Specialized software is needed to calculate power for ANOVA experiments.

ANOVA Assumptions

Analysis of variance assumes that the

- Observations on Y are independent.
- Populations being sampled are normal.
- Populations being sampled have equal variances.

Fortunately, ANOVA is somewhat robust to departures from the normality and equal variance assumptions. Later in this chapter, you will see tests for equal variances and normality.

11.2

ONE-FACTOR ANOVA (COMPLETELY RANDOMIZED MODEL)

Data Format

If we are only interested in comparing the means of c groups (*treatments* or *factor levels*), we have a ***one-factor ANOVA.**** This is by far the most common ANOVA model that covers many business problems. The one-factor ANOVA is usually viewed as a comparison between several columns of data, although the data could also be presented in rows. Table 11.1 illustrates the data format for a one-factor ANOVA with c treatments, denoted $A_1, A_2, \ldots, A_c$. The group means are $\bar{y}_1, \bar{y}_2, \ldots, \bar{y}_c$.

TABLE 11.1

Format of One-Factor ANOVA Data

One-Factor ANOVA: Data in Columns

A_1	A_2	...	A_c
y_{11}	y_{12}	...	y_{1c}
y_{21}	y_{22}	...	y_{2c}
y_{31}	y_{32}	...	y_{3c}
...	...	...	...
etc.	etc.	...	etc.
n_1 obs.	n_2 obs.	...	n_c obs.
$\bar{y}_1$	$\bar{y}_2$	...	$\bar{y}_c$

One-Factor ANOVA: Data in Rows

A_1	y_{11}	y_{21}	y_{31}	...	etc.	n_1 obs.	$\bar{y}_1$
A_2	y_{12}	y_{22}	y_{32}	...	etc.	n_2 obs.	$\bar{y}_2$
...					...	...	...
A_c	y_{1c}	y_{2c}	y_{3c}	...	etc.	n_c obs.	$\bar{y}_c$

*If subjects (or individuals) are assigned randomly to treatments, then we call this the *completely randomized model*.

Within treatment j we have n_j observations on Y. Sample sizes within each treatment do *not* need to be equal, although there are advantages to having balanced sample sizes. The total number of observations is the sum of the sample sizes for each treatment:

$$n = n_1 + n_2 + \cdots + n_c \tag{11.1}$$

Hypotheses to Be Tested

The question of interest is whether the mean of Y varies from treatment to treatment. The hypotheses to be tested are

H_0: $\mu_1 = \mu_2 = \cdots = \mu_c$ (all the means are equal)

H_1: Not all the means are equal (at least one mean is different)

Since one-factor ANOVA is a generalization of the test for equality of two means, why not just compare all possible pairs of means by using repeated two-sample t tests (as in Chapter 10)? Consider our experiment comparing the four manufacturing plant average defect rates. To compare pairs of plant averages we would have to perform six different t tests. If each t test has a Type I error probability equal to .05, then the probability that at least one of those tests results in a Type I error is $1 - (.95)^6 = .2649$. ANOVA tests all the means *simultaneously* and therefore does not inflate our Type I error.

One-Factor ANOVA as a Linear Model

An equivalent way to express the one-factor model is to say that observations in treatment j came from a population with a common mean (μ) plus a treatment effect (A_j) plus random error (ε_{ij}):

$$y_{ij} = \mu + A_j + \varepsilon_{ij} \qquad j = 1, 2, \ldots, c \quad \text{and} \quad i = 1, 2, \ldots, n_j \tag{11.2}$$

The random error is assumed to be normally distributed with zero mean and the same variance for all treatments. If we are interested only in what happens to the response for the particular **levels** of the factor that were selected (a ***fixed-effects model***), then the hypotheses to be tested are

H_0: $A_1 = A_2 = \cdots = A_c = 0$ (all treatment effects are zero)

H_1: Not all A_j are zero (some treatment effects are nonzero)

If the null hypothesis is true ($A_j = 0$ for all j), then knowing that an observation x came from treatment j does not help explain the variation in Y and the ANOVA model collapses to

$$y_{ij} = \mu + \varepsilon_{ij} \tag{11.3}$$

Group Means

The *mean of each group* is calculated in the usual way by summing the observations in the treatment and dividing by the sample size:

$$\bar{y}_j = \frac{1}{n_j} \sum_{i=1}^{n_j} y_{ij} \tag{11.4}$$

The *overall sample mean* or *grand mean* $\bar{y}$ can be calculated either by summing *all* the observations and dividing by n or by taking a weighted average of the c sample means:

$$\bar{y} = \frac{1}{n} \sum_{j=1}^{c} \sum_{i=1}^{n_j} y_{ij} = \frac{1}{n} \sum_{j=1}^{c} n_j \bar{y}_j \tag{11.5}$$

Partitioned Sum of Squares

To understand the logic of ANOVA, consider that for a given observation y_{ij} the following relationship must hold (on the right-hand side we just add and subtract $\bar{y}_j$):

$$(y_{ij} - \bar{y}) = (\bar{y}_j - \bar{y}) + (y_{ij} - \bar{y}_j) \tag{11.6}$$

This says that any deviation of an observation from the grand mean $\bar{y}$ may be expressed in two parts: the deviation of the column mean ($\bar{y}_j$) from the grand mean ($\bar{y}$), or *between* treatments, and the deviation of the observation (y_{ij}) from its own column mean ($\bar{y}_j$), or *within* treatments. We can show that this relationship also holds for *sums* of squared deviations, yielding the **partitioned sum of squares:**

$$\textbf{(11.7)} \qquad \sum_{j=1}^{c}\sum_{i=1}^{n_j}(y_{ij}-\bar{y})^2 = \sum_{j=1}^{c}n_j(\bar{y}_j-\bar{y})^2 + \sum_{j=1}^{c}\sum_{i=1}^{n_j}(y_{ij}-\bar{y}_j)^2$$

This important relationship may be expressed simply as

$$\textbf{(11.8)} \qquad SST = SSA + SSE \qquad \text{(partitioned sum of squares)}$$

Partitioned Sum of Squares

Sum of Squares Total (*SST*)	=	Sum of Squares Between Treatments (*SSA*)	+	Sum of Squares Within Treatments (*SSE*)
		↑ Explained by Factor *A*		↑ Unexplained Random Error

If the treatment means do not differ greatly from the grand mean, *SSA* will be small and *SSE* will be large (and conversely). The sums *SSA* and *SSE* may be used to test the hypothesis that the treatment means differ from the grand mean. However, we first divide each sum of squares by its *degrees of freedom* (to adjust for group sizes). The *test statistic* is the ratio of the resulting *mean squares.* These calculations can be arranged in the tabular format shown in Table 11.2.

TABLE 11.2
One-Factor ANOVA Table

Source of Variation	Sum of Squares	Degrees of Freedom	Mean Square	F Statistic
Treatment (between groups)	$SSA = \sum_{j=1}^{c} n_j(\bar{y}_j - \bar{y})^2$	$c-1$	$MSA = \dfrac{SSA}{c-1}$	$F = \dfrac{MSA}{MSE}$
Error (within groups)	$SSE = \sum_{j=1}^{c}\sum_{i=1}^{n_j}(y_{ij} - \bar{y}_j)^2$	$n-c$	$MSE = \dfrac{SSE}{n-c}$	
Total	$SST = \sum_{j=1}^{c}\sum_{i=1}^{n_j}(y_{ij} - \bar{y})^2$	$n-1$		

FIGURE 11.5

Excel's ANOVA menu

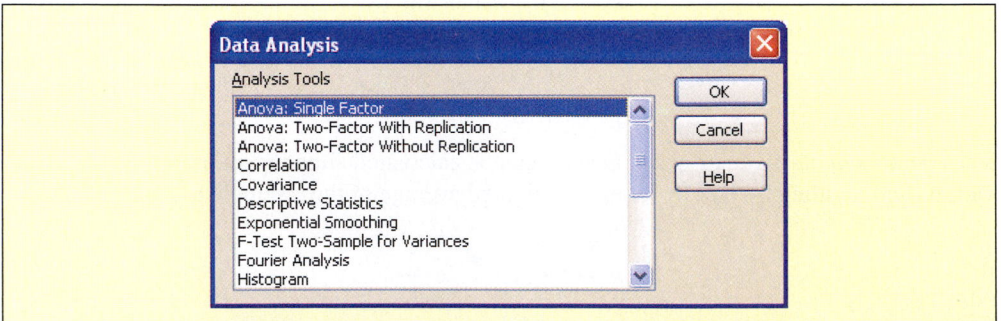

The ANOVA calculations are mathematically simple but involve tedious sums. These calculations are almost always done on a computer.* For example, Excel's one-factor ANOVA menu using Tools > Data Analysis is shown in Figure 11.5. MegaStat uses a similar menu.

*Detailed examples of ANOVA calculations can be found in the case studies in *LearningStats* Unit 11.

Test Statistic

At the beginning of this chapter we described the variation in Y as consisting of explained variation and unexplained variation. To test whether the independent variable explains a significant proportion of the variation in Y, we need to compare the explained (due to treatments) and unexplained (due to error) variation. Recall that the F distribution describes the *ratio of two variances*. Therefore it makes sense that the ANOVA test statistic is the F test statistic. The F statistic is the ratio of the variance due to treatments to the variance due to error. MSA is the mean square due to treatments and MSE is the mean square within treatments. Equation 11.9 shows the F statistic and its degrees of freedom.

$$F = \frac{MSA}{MSE} = \frac{\left(\dfrac{SSA}{c-1}\right)\longleftarrow \text{d.f.}_1 = c - 1 \ (\text{numerator})}{\left(\dfrac{SSE}{n-c}\right)\longleftarrow \text{d.f.}_2 = n - c \ (\text{denominator})} \qquad (11.9)$$

If there is little difference among treatments, we would expect MSA to be near zero because the treatment means $\bar{y}_j$ would be near the overall mean $\bar{y}$. Thus, when F is near zero we would not expect to reject the hypothesis of equal group means. The larger the F statistic, the more we are inclined to reject the hypothesis of equal means. But how large must F be to convince us that the means differ? Just as with a z test or a t test, we need a *decision rule*.

Decision Rule

The F distribution is a right-skewed distribution that starts at zero (F cannot be negative since variances are sums of squares) and has no upper limit (since the variances could be of any magnitude). For ANOVA, the F test is a right-tailed test. For a given level of significance α, we can use Appendix F to obtain the right-tail critical value of F. Alternatively, we can use Excel's function =FINV(α,df$_1$,df$_2$). The decision rule is illustrated in Figure 11.6. This critical value is denoted $F_{\text{df}_1,\text{df}_2}$ or $F_{c-1,n-c}$.

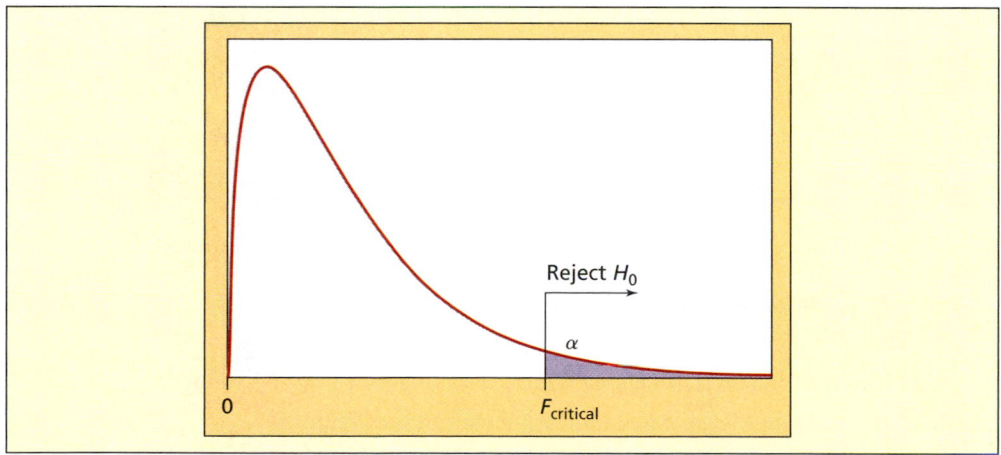

FIGURE 11.6

Decision rule for an F test

A cosmetics manufacturer's regional distribution center has four workstations that are responsible for packing cartons for shipment to small retailers. Each workstation is staffed by two workers. The task involves assembling each order, placing it in a shipping carton, inserting packing material, taping the carton, and placing a computer-generated shipping label on each carton. Generally, each station can pack 200 cartons a day, and often more. However, there is variability, due to differences in orders, labels, and cartons. Table 11.3 shows the

EXAMPLE

Carton Packing

number of cartons packed per day during a recent week. Is the variation among stations within the range attributable to chance, or do these samples indicate actual differences in the means?

TABLE 11.3 **Number of Cartons Packed** 🂠 **Cartons**

	Station 1	Station 2	Station 3	Station 4
	236	238	220	241
	250	239	236	233
	252	262	232	212
	233	247	243	231
	239	246	213	213
Sum	1,210	1,232	1,144	1,130
Mean	242.0	246.4	228.8	226.0
St. Dev.	8.515	9.607	12.153	12.884
n	5	5	5	5

As a preliminary step, we plot the data (Figure 11.7) to check for any time pattern and just to visualize the data. We see some potential differences in means, but no obvious time pattern (otherwise we would have to consider observation order as a second factor). We proceed with the hypothesis test.

FIGURE 11.7

Plot of the data

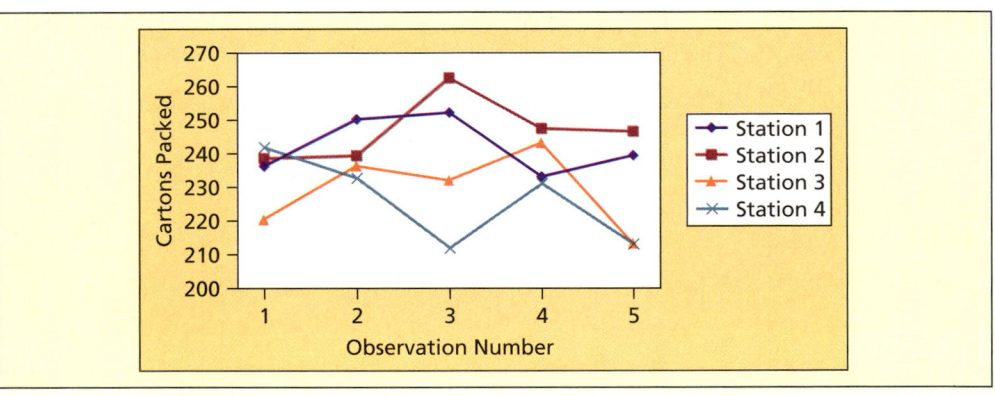

Step 1: State the Hypotheses
The hypotheses to be tested are

$H_0: \mu_1 = \mu_2 = \mu_3 = \mu_4$ (the means are the same)

H_1: Not all the means are equal (at least one mean is different)

Step 2: State the Decision Rule
There are $c = 4$ groups and $n = 20$ observations, so degrees of freedom for the F test are

Numerator: $\text{d.f.}_1 = c - 1 = 4 - 1 = 3$ (between treatments, factor)

Denominator: $\text{d.f.}_2 = n - c = 20 - 4 = 16$ (within treatments, error)

We will use $\alpha = .05$ for the test. The 5 percent right-tail critical value from Appendix F is $F_{3,16} = 3.24$. Instead of Appendix F we could use Excel's function =FINV(0.05,3,16) which yields $F_{.05} = 3.238872$. This decision rule is illustrated in Figure 11.8.

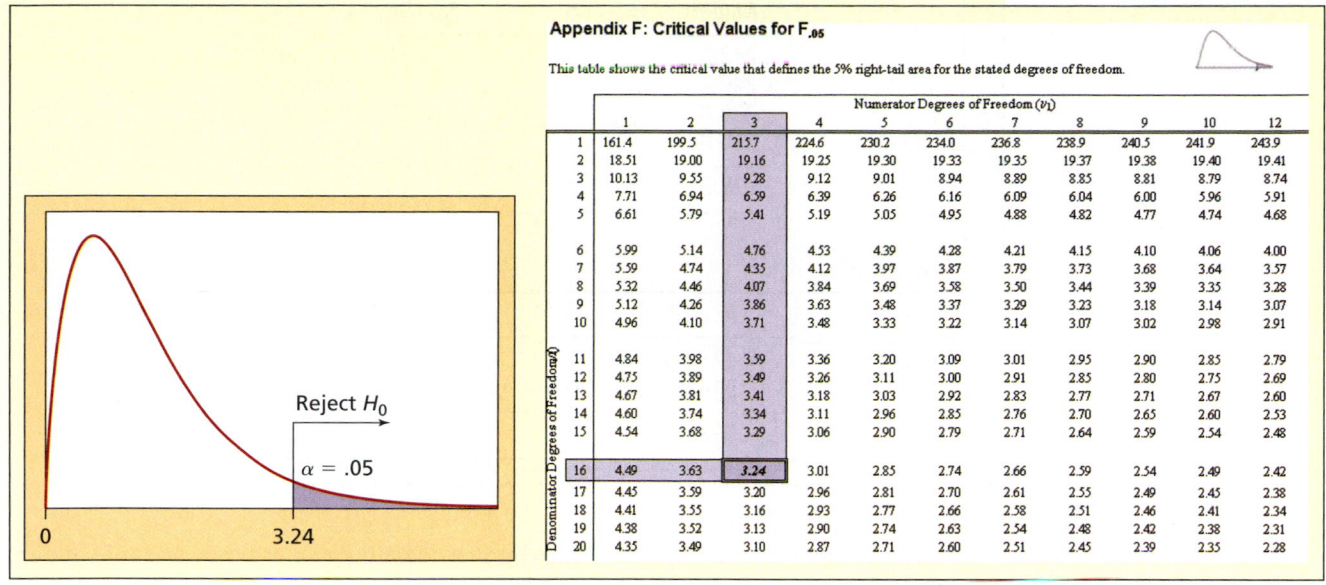

FIGURE 11.8

F test using $\alpha = .05$ with $F_{3,16}$

Step 3: Perform the Calculations

Using Excel for the calculations, we obtain the results shown in Figure 11.9. You can specify the desired level of significance (Excel's default is $\alpha = .05$). Note that Excel labels *SSA* "between groups" and *SSE* "within groups." This is an intuitive and attractive way to describe the variation.

FIGURE 11.9

Excel's one-factor ANOVA results

Anova: Single Factor

SUMMARY

Groups	Count	Sum	Average	Variance
Station 1	5	1210	242	72.5
Station 2	5	1232	246.4	92.3
Station 3	5	1144	228.8	147.7
Station 4	5	1130	226	166

ANOVA

Source of Variation	SS	df	MS	F	P-value	F crit
Between Groups	1479.2	3	493.0667	4.121769	0.024124	3.238872
Within Groups	1914	16	119.625			
Total	3393.2	19				

Step 4: Make the Decision

Since the test statistic $F = 4.12$ exceeds the critical value $F_{.05} = 3.24$, we can reject the hypothesis of equal means. Since Excel gives the *p*-value, you don't actually need Excel's critical value. The *p*-value ($p = .024124$) is less than the level of significance ($\alpha = .05$) which confirms that we should reject the hypothesis of equal treatment means. For comparison, Figure 11.10 shows MegaStat's ANOVA table for the same data. The results are the same, although MegaStat rounds things off, highlights significant *p*-values, and gives standard deviations instead of variances for each treatment.

FIGURE 11.10

MegaStat's one-factor
ANOVA results

One factor ANOVA

Mean	n	Std. Dev	
242.0	5	8.51	Station 1
246.4	5	9.61	Station 2
228.8	5	12.15	Station 3
226.0	5	12.88	Station 4
235.8	20	13.36	Total

ANOVA table

Source	SS	df	MS	F	p-value
Treatment	1,479.20	3	493.067	4.12	.0241
Error	1,914.00	16	119.625		
Total	3,393.20	19			

MegaStat provides additional insights by showing a dot plot of observations by group, shown in Figure 11.11. The display includes group means (shown as short horizontal tick marks) and the overall mean (shown as a dashed line). The dot plot suggests that stations 3 and 4 have means below the overall mean, while stations 1 and 2 are above the overall mean.

FIGURE 11.11

Dot plot of four samples
Cartons

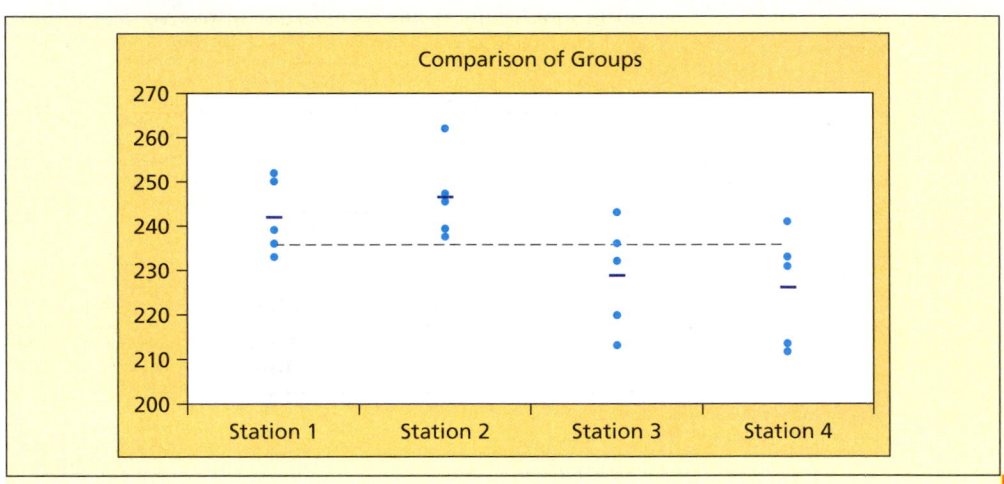

Using MINITAB

MINITAB's output, shown in Figure 11.12, is the same as Excel's except that MINITAB rounds off the results and displays a confidence interval for each group mean, an attractive feature.* In our carton example, the confidence intervals overlap, except possibly stations 2 and 4.

---

*MINITAB and most other statistical packages prefer the data in *stacked* format. Each variable has its own column (e.g., column one contains all the Y values, while column two contains group labels like "Station 1"). MINITAB will convert *unstacked* data to *stacked* data for one-factor ANOVA, but not for other ANOVA models. See *LearningStats* Unit 11 for examples of *stacked* versus *unstacked* data.

FIGURE 11.12

MINITAB's one-factor ANOVA

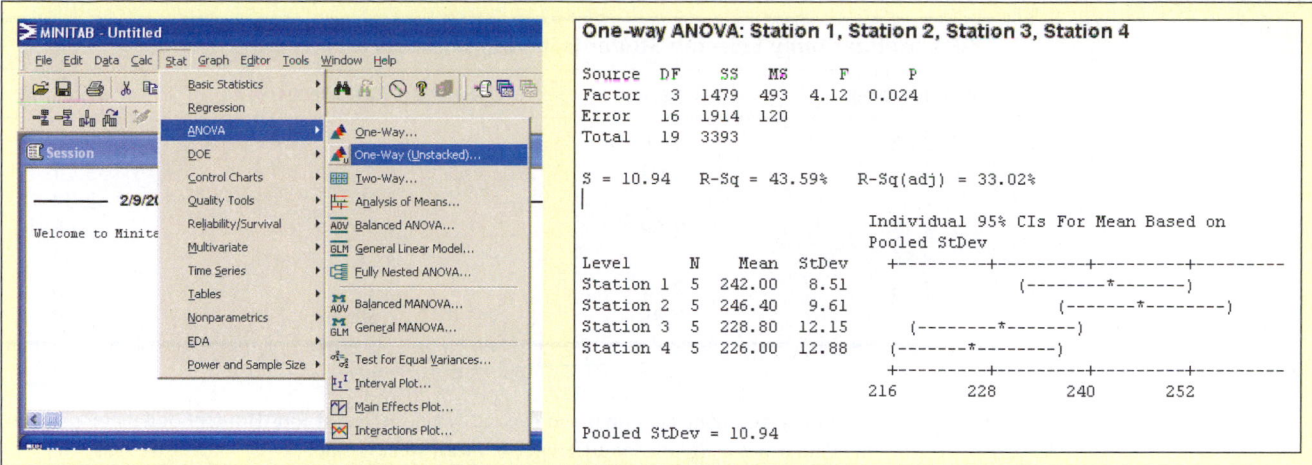

SECTION EXERCISES

Instructions: For each data set: (a) State the hypotheses. (b) Use Excel's Tools > Data Analysis (or MegaStat or MINITAB) to perform the one-factor ANOVA, using $\alpha = .05$. (c) State your conclusion about the population means. Was the decision close? (d) Interpret the *p*-value carefully. (e) Include a plot of the data for each group if you are using MegaStat, and confidence intervals for the group means if you are using MINITAB. What do the plots show?

11.1   Scrap rates per thousand (parts whose defects cannot be reworked) are compared for 5 randomly selected days at three plants. Does the data prove a significant difference in mean scrap rates?   **ScrapRate**

Scrap Rate (Per Thousand Units)

	Plant A	Plant B	Plant C
	11.4	11.1	10.2
	12.5	14.1	9.5
	10.1	16.8	9.0
	13.8	13.2	13.3
	13.7	14.6	5.9

11.2   One particular morning, the length of time spent in the examination rooms is recorded for each patient seen by each physician at an orthopedic clinic. Does the data prove a significant difference in mean times?   **Physicians**

Time in Examination Rooms (minutes)

Physician 1	Physician 2	Physician 3	Physician 4
34	33	17	28
25	35	30	33
27	31	30	31
31	31	26	27
26	42	32	32
34	33	28	33
21		26	40
		29	

11.3 Semester GPAs are compared for seven randomly chosen students in each class level at Oxnard University. Does the data prove a significant difference in mean GPAs? **GPA1**

GPA for Randomly Selected Students in Four Business Majors

Accounting	Finance	Human Resources	Marketing
2.48	3.16	2.93	3.54
2.19	3.01	2.89	3.71
2.62	3.07	3.48	2.94
3.15	2.88	3.33	3.46
3.56	3.33	3.53	3.50
2.53	2.87	2.95	3.25
3.31	2.85	3.58	3.20

11.4 Sales of *People* magazine are compared over a 5-week period at four Borders outlets in Chicago. Does the data prove a significant difference in mean weekly sales? **Magazines**

Weekly Sales

Store 1	Store 2	Store 3	Store 4
102	97	89	100
106	77	91	116
105	82	75	87
115	80	106	102
112	101	94	100

11.3
MULTIPLE COMPARISONS

Tukey's Test

In Figure 11.12, we naturally want to compare the confidence intervals to see whether they overlap. In so doing, we are trying to answer the question, Which means differ significantly? However, to maintain the desired overall probability of Type I error, we need to create a *simultaneous confidence interval* for the difference of means and then see which pairs exclude zero. For c groups, there are $c(c-1)/2$ distinct pairs of means to be compared.

Several *multiple comparison* tests are available. Their logic is similar. We will discuss only one, called *Tukey's studentized range test* (sometimes called the *HSD* or "honestly significant difference" test). It has good power and is widely used. We will refer to it as *Tukey's test,* named for statistician John Wilder Tukey (1915–2000). This test is available in most statistical packages (but not in Excel's Tools > Data Analysis). It is a two-tailed test for equality of paired means from c groups compared simultaneously and is a natural follow-up when the results of the one-factor ANOVA test show a significant difference in at least one mean. The hypotheses are

$H_0: \mu_j = \mu_k$

$H_1: \mu_j \neq \mu_k$

The decision rule is

(11.10) $\qquad$ Reject H_0 if $\dfrac{|\bar{y}_j - \bar{y}_k|}{\sqrt{MSE\left[\dfrac{1}{n_j} + \dfrac{1}{n_k}\right]}} > T_\alpha$

where $T_\alpha = 0.707 q_{c,n-c}$ and $q_{c,n-c}$ is a critical value of the *studentized range* for the desired level of significance. Table 11.4 shows 5 percent critical values of $q_{c,n-c}$. If the desired degrees of freedom cannot be found, we could interpolate or better yet rely on a computer package like MegaStat to provide the exact critical value. We take *MSE* directly from the ANOVA calculations (see Table 11.2).

Denominator d.f.	Numerator d.f.								
	2	**3**	**4**	**5**	**6**	**7**	**8**	**9**	**10**
5	3.64	4.60	5.22	5.67	6.03	6.33	6.58	6.80	6.99
6	3.36	4.34	4.90	5.30	5.63	5.90	6.12	6.32	6.49
7	3.34	4.16	4.68	5.06	5.36	5.61	5.82	6.00	6.16
8	3.26	4.04	4.53	4.89	5.17	5.40	5.60	5.77	5.92
9	3.20	3.95	4.41	4.76	5.02	5.24	5.43	5.59	5.74
10	3.15	3.88	4.33	4.65	4.91	5.12	5.30	5.46	5.60
15	3.01	3.67	4.08	4.37	4.59	4.78	4.94	5.08	5.20
20	2.95	3.58	3.96	4.23	4.45	4.62	4.77	4.90	5.01
30	2.89	3.49	3.85	4.10	4.30	4.46	4.60	4.72	4.82
40	2.86	3.44	3.79	4.04	4.23	4.39	4.52	4.63	4.73
60	2.83	3.40	3.74	3.98	4.16	4.31	4.44	4.55	4.65
120	2.80	3.36	3.68	3.92	4.10	4.24	4.36	4.47	4.56
∞	2.77	3.31	3.63	3.86	4.03	4.17	4.29	4.39	4.47

TABLE 11.4

Upper 5 Percent Points of Studentized Range

Source: E. S. Pearson and H. O. Hartley, *Biometrika Tables for Statisticians*, 3rd ed. (Oxford University Press, 1970), p. 192. Copyright © 1970 Oxford University Press. Used with permission.

We will illustrate the Tukey test for the carton-packing data. We assume that a one-factor ANOVA has already been performed and the results showed that at least one mean was significantly different. We will use the *MSE* from the ANOVA. For the carton-packing data there are 4 groups and 20 observations, so $c = 4$ and $n - c = 20 - 4 = 16$. From Table 11.4 we must interpolate between $q_{4,15} = 4.08$ and $q_{4,20} = 3.96$ to get $q_{4,16} = 4.056$ so the approximate critical value is $T_\alpha = (0.707)(4.056) = 2.87$ and the decision rule for any pair of means is

$$\text{Reject } H_0 \text{ if } \frac{|\bar{y}_j - \bar{y}_k|}{\sqrt{MSE\left[\frac{1}{n_j} + \frac{1}{n_k}\right]}} > 2.87$$

There may be a different decision rule for every pair of cities unless the sample sizes n_j and n_k are identical (in our example, the group sizes are the same). For example, to compare groups 2 and 4 the test statistic is

$$\frac{|\bar{y}_2 - \bar{y}_4|}{\sqrt{MSE\left[\frac{1}{n_2} + \frac{1}{n_4}\right]}} = \frac{|246.4 - 226.0|}{\sqrt{119.625\left[\frac{1}{5} + \frac{1}{5}\right]}} = 2.95$$

Since 2.95 exceeds 2.87, we reject the hypothesis of equal means for station 2 and station 4. We conclude that there is a significant difference between the mean output of stations 2 and 4. A similar test must be performed for every possible pair of means.

Using MegaStat

MegaStat includes all six possible comparisons of means, as shown in Figure 11.13. Only stations 2 and 4 differ at $\alpha = .05$. However, if we use the independent sample t test (as in Chapter 10) shown in MegaStat's lower table, we obtain two p-values smaller than $\alpha = .05$ (stations 1, 4 and stations 2, 3) and one that is below $\alpha = .01$ (stations 2, 4). This demonstrates that a *simultaneous* Tukey t test is not the same as comparing individual pairs of means. As noted in section 11.2, using multiple independent t tests results in a greater probability of making a Type I error. An attractive feature of MegaStat's Tukey test is that it highlights significant results using color-coding for $\alpha = .05$ and $\alpha = .01$. Note that MegaStat's Tukey critical value T_α is slightly more accurate than our interpolated $T_\alpha = 2.87$ from Table 11.4.

FIGURE 11.13

MegaStat's Tukey tests and independent sample *t* tests 🐞 **Cartons**

Tukey simultaneous comparison *t*-values (d.f. = 16)

		Station 4 226.0	Station 3 228.8	Station 1 242.0	Station 2 246.4
Station 4	226.0				
Station 3	228.8	0.40			
Station 1	242.0	2.31	1.91		
Station 2	246.4	2.95	2.54	0.64	

critical values for experimentwise error rate:

0.05	2.86
0.01	3.67

p-values for pairwise *t*-tests

		Station 4 226.0	Station 3 228.8	Station 1 242.0	Station 2 246.4
Station 4	226.0				
Station 3	228.8	.6910			
Station 1	242.0	.0344	.0745		
Station 2	246.4	.0094	.0217	.5337	

SECTION EXERCISES

Instructions: Use MegaStat, MINITAB, or another software package to perform Tukey's test for significant pairwise differences. Perform the test using both the 5 percent and 1 percent levels of significance.

11.5 Refer to Exercise 11.1. Which pairs of mean scrap rates differ significantly (3 plants)? 🐞 **ScrapRate**

11.6 Refer to Exercise 11.2. Which pairs of mean examination times differ significantly (4 physicians)? 🐞 **Physicians**

11.7 Refer to Exercise 11.3. Which pairs of mean GPAs differ significantly (4 majors)? 🐞 **GPA1**

11.8 Refer to Exercise 11.4. Which pairs of mean weekly sales differ significantly (4 stores)? 🐞 **Magazines**

11.4

TESTS FOR HOMOGENEITY OF VARIANCES (OPTIONAL)

ANOVA Assumptions

Analysis of variance assumes that observations on the response variable are from normally distributed populations that have the same variance. We have noted that few populations meet these requirements perfectly and unless the sample is quite large, a test for normality is impractical. However, we can easily test the assumption of *homogeneous* (equal) *variances.* Although the one-factor ANOVA test is only slightly affected by inequality of variance when group sizes are equal or nearly so, it is still a good idea to test this assumption. In general, surprisingly large differences in variances must exist to conclude that the population variances are unequal.

Hartley's F_{max} Test

If we had only two groups, we could use the *F* test you learned in Chapter 10 to compare the variances. But for *c* groups, a more general test is required. One such test is *Hartley's F_{max} test,* named for statistician H. O. Hartley (1912–1980). The hypotheses are

$H_0: \sigma_1^2 = \sigma_2^2 = \cdots = \sigma_c^2$

H_1: Not all the σ_j^2 are equal

The test statistic is the ratio of the largest sample variance to the smallest sample variance:

$$F_{max} = \frac{s_{max}^2}{s_{min}^2} \qquad (11.11)$$

Critical values of F_{max} may be found in Table 11.5 using degrees of freedom given by

Numerator: $\text{d.f.}_1 = c$

Denominator: $\text{d.f.}_2 = \dfrac{n}{c} - 1$

where n is the total number of observations. This test assumes equal group sizes, so d.f._2 would be an integer. For group sizes that are not drastically unequal, this procedure will still be approximately correct, using the next lower integer if d.f._2 is not an integer. Note that this is *not* the same table as the F table you have used previously.

Denominator d.f.	Numerator d.f.								
	2	3	4	5	6	7	8	9	10
2	39.0	87.5	142	202	266	333	403	475	550
3	15.4	27.8	39.2	50.7	62.0	72.9	83.5	93.9	104
4	9.60	15.5	20.6	25.2	29.5	33.6	37.5	41.1	44.6
5	7.15	10.8	13.7	16.3	18.7	20.8	22.9	24.7	26.5
6	5.82	8.38	10.4	12.1	13.7	15.0	16.3	17.5	18.6
7	4.99	6.94	8.44	9.7	10.8	11.8	12.7	13.5	14.3
8	4.43	6.00	7.18	8.12	9.03	9.78	10.5	11.1	11.7
9	4.03	5.34	6.31	7.11	7.80	8.41	8.95	9.45	9.91
10	3.72	4.85	5.67	6.34	6.92	7.42	7.87	8.28	8.66
12	3.28	4.16	4.79	5.30	5.72	6.09	6.42	6.72	7.00
15	2.86	3.54	4.01	4.37	4.68	4.95	5.19	5.40	5.59
20	2.46	2.95	3.29	3.54	3.76	3.94	4.10	4.24	4.37
30	2.07	2.40	2.61	2.78	2.91	3.02	3.12	3.21	3.29
60	1.67	1.85	1.96	2.04	2.11	2.17	2.22	2.26	2.30
∞	1.00	1.00	1.00	1.00	1.00	1.00	1.00	1.00	1.00

TABLE 11.5

Critical 5 Percent Values of Hartley's

$F_{max} = s_{max}^2 / s_{min}^2$

Source: E. S. Pearson and H. O. Hartley, *Biometrika Tables for Statisticians,* 3rd. ed. (Oxford University Press, 1970), p. 202. Copyright © 1970 Oxford University Press. Used with permission.

EXAMPLE

Carton Packing: Tukey Test 🐝 **Cartons**

Using the carton-packing data in Table 11.3, there are 4 groups and 20 total observations, so we have

Numerator: $\text{d.f.}_1 = c = 4$

Denominator: $\text{d.f.}_2 = n/c - 1 = 20/4 - 1 = 5 - 1 = 4$

From Table 11.5 we choose the critical value $F_{max} = 20.6$ using $\text{d.f.}_1 = 4$ and $\text{d.f.}_2 = 4$. The sample statistics (from Excel) for our workstations are

Work Station	n	Mean	Variance
Station 1	15	242.0	72.5
Station 2	17	246.4	92.3
Station 3	15	228.8	147.7
Station 4	12	226.0	166.0

The test statistic is

$$F_{max} = \frac{s_{max}^2}{s_{min}^2} = \frac{166.0}{72.5} = 2.29$$

In this case, we cannot reject the hypothesis of equal variances. Indeed, Table 11.5 makes it clear that unless the sample size is very large, the variance ratio would have to be quite large to reject the hypothesis of equal population variances. If the F_{max} test is significant, we prefer an alternative* to one-factor ANOVA, which does not require this assumption.   ↖

Levene's Test

The F_{max} test relies on the assumption of normality in the populations from which the sample observations are drawn. A more robust alternative is **Levene's test,** which does not assume a normal distribution. This test requires a computer package. It is not necessary to discuss the computational procedure except to say that Levene's test is based on the distances of the observations from their sample *medians* rather than their sample *means*. As long as you know how to interpret a *p*-value, Levene's test is easy to use. Figure 11.14 shows MINITAB's output for the test of homogeneity of variance for the carton-packing data using Levene's test, with the added attraction of confidence intervals for each population standard deviation. Since the confidence intervals overlap and the *p*-value (.823) is large, we cannot reject the hypothesis of equal population variances. This confirms that the one-factor ANOVA procedure was appropriate for the carton-packing data.

FIGURE 11.14

MINITAB's equal-variance test   🐾   **Cartons**

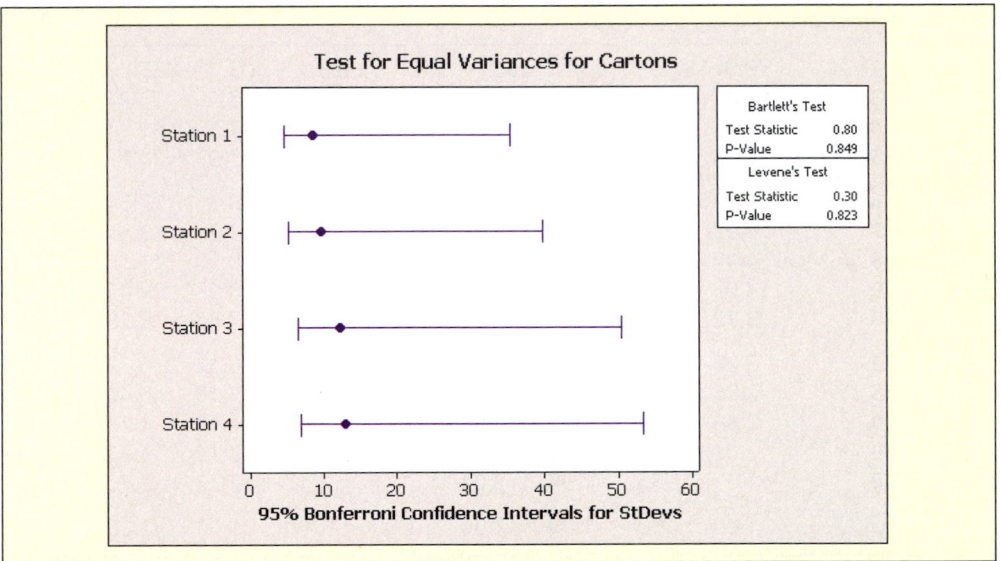

11.9   Refer to Exercise 11.1. Are the population variances the same for scrap rates (3 plants)?
🐾   **ScrapRate**

SECTION EXERCISES

Instructions: For each data set, use Hartley's F_{max} test to test the hypothesis of equal variances, using the 5 percent table of critical values from this section and the largest and smallest sample variances from your previous ANOVA. Alternatively, if you have access to MINITAB or another software package, perform Levene's test for equal group variances, discuss the *p*-value, and interpret the graphical display of confidence intervals for standard deviations.

11.9   Refer to Exercise 11.1. Are the population variances the same for scrap rates (3 plants)?
🐾   **ScrapRate**

11.10   Refer to Exercise 11.2. Are the population variances the same for examination times (4 physicians)?   🐾   **Physicians**

11.11   Refer to Exercise 11.3. Are the population variances the same for the GPAs (4 majors)?
🐾   **GPA1**

11.12   Refer to Exercise 11.4. Are the population variances the same for weekly sales (4 stores)?
🐾   **Magazines**

*For one-factor ANOVA, we could use the nonparametric *Kruskal-Wallis* test described in Chapter 15.

Mini Case

11.1

Hospital Emergency Arrivals

To plan its staffing schedule, a large urban hospital examined the number of arrivals per day over a 3-month period, as shown in Table 11.6. Each day has 13 observations except Tuesday, which has 14. Data are shown in rows rather than in columns to make a more compact table.

TABLE 11.6 **Number of Emergency Arrivals by Day of the Week** **Emergency**

Mon	188	175	208	176	179	184	191	194	174	191	198	213	217	
Tue	174	167	165	164	169	164	150	175	178	164	202	175	191	180
Wed	177	169	180	173	182	181	168	165	174	175	174	177	182	
Thu	170	164	190	169	164	170	153	150	156	173	177	183	208	
Fri	177	167	172	185	185	170	170	193	212	171	175	177	209	
Sat	162	184	173	175	144	170	163	157	181	185	199	203	198	
Sun	182	176	183	228	148	178	175	174	188	179	220	207	193	

We perform a one-factor ANOVA to test the model *Arrivals* = *f*(*Weekday*). The single factor (*Weekday*) has 7 treatments. The Excel results, shown in Figure 11.15, indicate that *Weekday* does have a significant effect on *Arrivals,* since the test statistic $F = 3.257$ exceeds the 5 percent critical value $F_{6,85} = 2.207$. The *p*-value (.006) indicates that a test statistic this large would arise by chance only about 6 times in 1,000 samples if the hypothesis of equal daily means were true.

FIGURE 11.15

One-factor ANOVA for
emergency arrivals
and sample plot

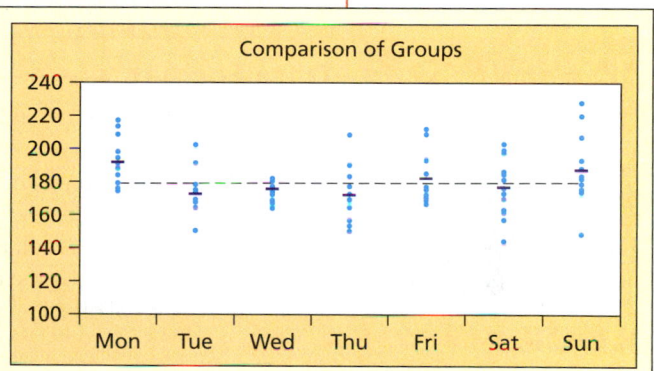

SUMMARY

Groups	Count	Sum	Average	Variance
Mon	13	2488	191.385	206.423
Tue	14	2418	172.714	164.220
Wed	13	2277	175.154	29.808
Thu	13	2227	171.308	250.564
Fri	13	2363	181.769	216.692
Sat	13	2294	176.462	300.769
Sun	13	2431	187.000	445.667

ANOVA: Single Factor

Source of Variation	SS	df	MS	F	P-value	F crit
Between Groups	4514.283	6	752.3806	3.257899	0.006238	2.20723
Within Groups	19629.93	85	230.9404			
Total	24144.22	91				

The Tukey multiple comparison test (Figure 11.16) shows that the only pairs of *significantly* different means at $\alpha = .05$ are (*Mon, Tue*) and (*Mon, Thu*). In testing for equal variances, we get

FIGURE 11.16

MegaStat's Tukey test
for $\mu_j - \mu_k$

Tukey simultaneous comparison *t*-values (d.f. = 84)

		Thu	Tue	Wed	Sat	Fri	Sun	Mon
		171.3	172.2	175.2	176.5	181.8	187.0	191.4
Thu	171.3							
Tue	172.2	0.14						
Wed	175.2	0.64	0.50					
Sat	176.5	0.86	0.72	0.22				
Fri	181.8	1.75	1.61	1.10	0.89			
Sun	187.0	2.62	2.48	1.98	1.76	0.87		
Mon	191.4	3.35	3.21	2.71	2.49	1.61	0.73	

critical values for experimentwise error rate:

0.05	3.03
0.01	3.59

conflicting conclusions, depending on which test we use. Hartley's test gives $F_{max} = (445.667)/(29.808) = 14.95$, which exceeds the critical value $F_{7,12} = 6.09$ (note that *Wed* has a *very* small variance). But Levene's test for homogeneity of variances (Figure 11.17) has a *p*-value of .221, which at $\alpha = .05$ does not allow us to reject the equal-variance assumption that underlies the ANOVA test. When it is available, we prefer Levene's test because it does not depend on the assumption of normality.

FIGURE 11.17

MINITAB test for equal variances

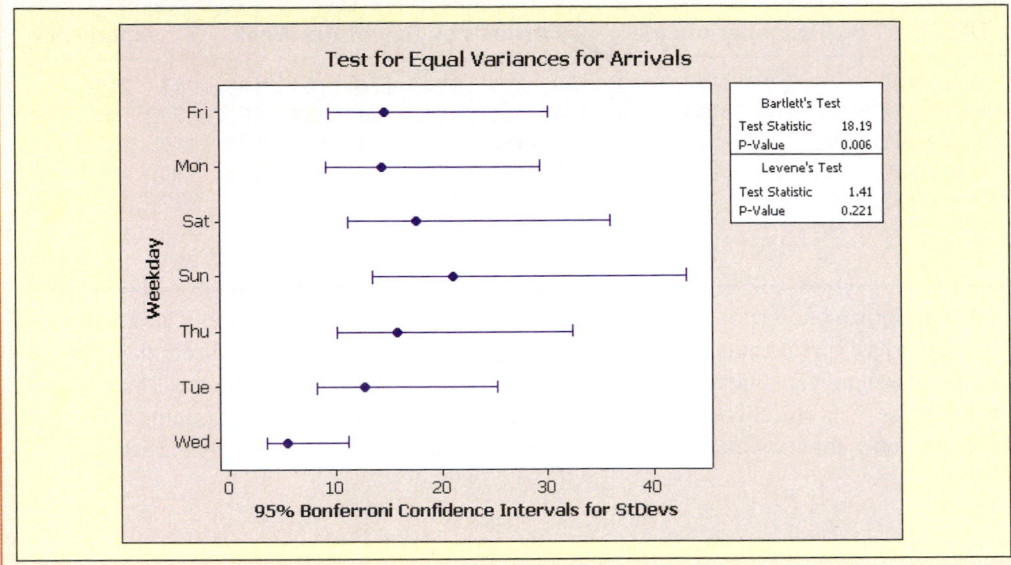

11.5

TWO-FACTOR ANOVA WITHOUT REPLICATION (RANDOMIZED BLOCK MODEL)

Data Format

Suppose that two factors A and B may affect Y. One way to visualize this is to imagine a data matrix with r rows and c columns. Each row is a level of factor A, while each column is a level of factor B. Initially, we will consider the case where all levels of both factors occur, and each cell contains only one observation. In this ***two-factor ANOVA without replication*** (or *nonrepeated measures design*) each factor combination is observed exactly once. The mean of Y can be computed either across the rows or down the columns, as shown in Table 11.7. The grand mean $\bar{y}$ is the sum of all data values divided by the sample size rc.

TABLE 11.7

Format of Two-Factor ANOVA Data Set Without Replication

Levels of Factor A	Levels of Factor B				Row Mean
	B_1	B_2	. . .	B_c	
A_1	y_{11}	y_{12}	. . .	y_{1c}	$\bar{y}_{1.}$
A_2	y_{21}	y_{22}	. . .	y_{2c}	$\bar{y}_{2.}$
. . .	. . .	. . .	. . .	. . .	. . .
A_r	y_{r1}	y_{r2}	. . .	y_{rc}	$\bar{y}_{r.}$
Col Mean	$\bar{y}_{.1}$	$\bar{y}_{.2}$	. . .	$\bar{y}_{.c}$	$\bar{y}$

For example, Y might be computer chip defects per thousand for three different deposition techniques (A_1, A_2, A_3) on four different types of silicon substrate (B_1, B_2, B_3, B_4) yielding a table with $3 \times 4 = 12$ cells. Each factor combination is a *treatment*. With only one observation per treatment, no interaction between the two factors is included.*

---

*There are not enough degrees of freedom to estimate an interaction unless the experiment is replicated.

Two-Factor ANOVA Model

Expressed in linear form, the two-factor ANOVA model is

$$y_{jk} = \mu + A_j + B_k + \varepsilon_{jk} \qquad (11.12)$$

where

y_{jk} = observed data value in row j and column k

μ = common mean for all treatments

A_j = effect of row factor A ($j = 1, 2, \ldots, r$)

B_k = effect of column factor B ($k = 1, 2, \ldots, c$)

ε_{jk} = random error

The random error is assumed to be normally distributed with zero mean and the same variance for all treatments.

Hypotheses to Be Tested

If we are interested only in what happens to the response for the particular levels of the factors that were selected (a *fixed-effects* **model**) then the hypotheses to be tested are

Factor *A*

H_0: $A_1 = A_2 = \cdots = A_r = 0$ (row factor has no effect)

H_1: Not all the A_j are equal to zero (row factor has an effect)

Factor *B*

H_0: $B_1 = B_2 = \cdots = B_c = 0$ (column factor has no effect)

H_1: Not all the B_k are equal to zero (column factor has an effect)

If we are unable to reject either null hypothesis, all variation in Y is just a random disturbance around the mean μ:

$$y_{jk} = \mu + \varepsilon_{jk} \qquad (11.13)$$

Randomized Block Model

A special terminology is used when only one factor is of research interest and the other factor is merely used to control for potential confounding influences. In this case, the two-factor ANOVA model with one observation per cell is sometimes called the **randomized block model.** In the randomized block model, it is customary to call the column effects *treatments* (as in one-factor ANOVA to signify that they are the effect of interest) while the row effects are called *blocks*.* For example, a North Dakota agribusiness might want to study the effect of four kinds of fertilizer (F_1, F_2, F_3, F_4) in promoting wheat growth (Y) on three soil types (S_1, S_2, S_3). To control for the effects of soil type, we could define three blocks (rows) each containing one soil type, as shown in Table 11.8. Subjects within each block (soil type) would be randomly assigned to the treatments (fertilizer).

Block	Treatment (Fertilizer)			
(Soil Type)	F_1	F_2	F_3	F_4
S_1				
S_2				
S_3				

TABLE 11.8
Format of Randomized Block Experiment: Two Factors

*In principle, either rows or columns could be the blocking factor, but it is customary to put the blocking factor in rows.

A randomized block model looks like a two-factor ANOVA and is computed exactly like a two-factor ANOVA. However, its interpretation by the researcher may resemble a one-factor ANOVA since only the column effects (treatments) are of interest. The blocks exist only to reduce variance. The effect of the blocks will show up in the hypothesis test, but is of no interest to the researcher as a separate factor. In short, the difference between a randomized block model and a standard two-way ANOVA model lies in the mind of the researcher. Since calculations for a randomized block design are identical to the two-factor ANOVA with one observation per cell, we will not call the row factor a "block" and the column factor a "treatment." Instead, we just call them *factor A* and *factor B*. Interpretation of the factors is not a mathematical issue. If only the column effect is of interest, you may call the column effect the "treatment."

Format of Calculation of Nonreplicated Two-Factor ANOVA

Calculations for the unreplicated two-factor ANOVA may be arranged as in Table 11.9. Degrees of freedom sum to $n - 1$. For a data set with r rows and c columns, notice that $n = rc$. The total sum of squares shown in Table 11.9 has three components:

(11.14) $$SST = SSA + SSB + SSE$$

where

$SST =$ total sum of squared deviations about the mean

$SSA =$ between rows sum of squares (effect of factor A)

$SSB =$ between columns sum of squares (effect of factor B)

$SSE =$ error sum of squares (residual variation)

SSE is a measure of unexplained variation. If SSE is relatively high, we would fail to reject the null hypothesis that the factor effects do not differ significantly from zero. Conversely, if SSE is relatively small, it is a sign that at least one factor is a relevant predictor of Y, and we would expect either SSA or SSB (or both) to be relatively large. Before doing the F test, each sum of squares must be divided by its degrees of freedom to obtain the *mean square*. Calculations are almost always done by a computer. For details of two-factor calculation methods see *LearningStats* Unit 11. There are case studies for each ANOVA.

TABLE 11.9 **Format of Two-Factor ANOVA with One Observation per Cell**

Source of Variation	Sum of Squares	Degrees of Freedom	Mean Square	F Ratio
Factor A (row effect)	$SSA = c \sum_{j=1}^{r} (\bar{y}_{j.} - \bar{y})^2$	$r - 1$	$MSA = \dfrac{SSA}{r - 1}$	$F_A = \dfrac{MSA}{MSE}$
Factor B (column effect)	$SSB = r \sum_{k=1}^{c} (\bar{y}_{.k} - \bar{y})^2$	$c - 1$	$MSB = \dfrac{SSB}{c - 1}$	$F_B = \dfrac{MSB}{MSE}$
Error	$SSE = \sum_{j=1}^{r} \sum_{k=1}^{c} (y_{jk} - \bar{y}_{j.} - \bar{y}_{.k} + \bar{y})^2$	$(r - 1)(c - 1)$	$MSE = \dfrac{SSE}{(c - 1)(r - 1)}$	
Total	$SST = \sum_{j=1}^{c} \sum_{k=1}^{r} (y_{jk} - \bar{y})^2$	$rc - 1$		

↘   Drivers expect a car to have good acceleration. A driver is coasting on the highway, with his foot off the accelerator. He steps on the gas to speed up. What is the peak acceleration to a final speed of 80 mph? Tests were carried out on one vehicle at 4 different initial speeds (10, 25, 40, 55 mph) and three different levels of rotation of accelerator pedal (5, 8, 10 degrees). The acceleration results are shown in Table 11.10. Does this sample show that the two experimental factors (pedal rotation, initial speed) are significant predictors of acceleration? Bear in mind that a different sample could yield different results; this is an *unreplicated* experiment.

TABLE 11.10   **Maximum Acceleration Under Test Conditions**   🚗   **Acceleration**

	Initial Speed			
Pedal Rotation	**10 mph**	**25 mph**	**40 mph**	**55 mph**
5 degrees	0.35	0.19	0.14	0.10
8 degrees	0.37	0.28	0.19	0.19
10 degrees	0.42	0.30	0.29	0.23

Note: Maximum acceleration is measured as a fraction of acceleration due to gravity (32 ft./sec.^{2}).

Step 1: State the Hypotheses

It is helpful to assign short, descriptive variable names to each factor. The general form of the model is

$$Acceleration = f(PedalRotation, InitialSpeed)$$

Stated as a linear model:

$$y_{jk} = \mu + A_j + B_k + \varepsilon_{jk}$$

The hypotheses are

Factor *A* (*PedalRotation*)

$H_0: A_1 = A_2 = A_3 = 0$ (pedal rotation has no effect)

$H_1:$ Not all the A_j are equal to zero

Factor *B* (*InitialSpeed*)

$H_0: B_1 = B_2 = B_3 = B_4 = 0$ (initial speed has no effect)

$H_1:$ Not all the B_k are equal to zero

Step 2: State the Decision Rule

Each *F* test may require a different right-tail critical value because the numerator degrees of freedom depend on the number of factor levels, while denominator degrees of freedom (error *SSE*) are the same for all three tests:

Factor A: d.f.$_1 = r - 1 = 3 - 1 = 2$ ($r = 3$ pedal rotations)

Factor B: d.f.$_1 = c - 1 = 4 - 1 = 3$ ($c = 4$ initial speeds)

Error: d.f.$_2 = (r - 1)(c - 1) = (3 - 1)(4 - 1) = 6$

From Appendix F, the 5 percent critical values in a right-tailed test (all ANOVA tests are right-tailed tests) are

$F_{2,6} = 5.14$ for factor *A*

$F_{3,6} = 4.76$ for factor *B*

We will reject the null hypothesis (no factor effect) if the *F* test statistic exceeds the critical value.

Step 3: Perform the Calculations

Calculations are done by using Excel's Tools > Data Analysis. The menu and results are shown in Figure 11.18. There is a table of means and variances, followed by the ANOVA table.

FIGURE 11.18

Excel's ANOVA: two-factor without replication 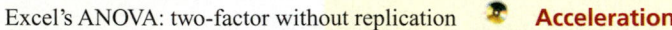 **Acceleration**

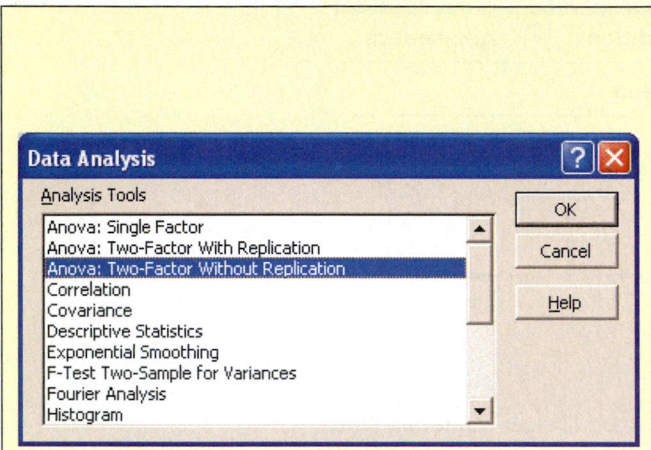

Anova: Two-Factor Without Replication

SUMMARY	Count	Sum	Average	Variance
5 degrees	4	0.78	0.1950	0.0120
8 degrees	4	1.03	0.2575	0.0074
10 degrees	4	1.24	0.3100	0.0063
10 mph	3	1.14	0.3800	0.0013
25 mph	3	0.77	0.2567	0.0034
40 mph	3	0.62	0.2067	0.0058
55 mph	3	0.52	0.1733	0.0044

ANOVA

Source of Variation	SS	df	MS	F	P-value	F crit
Rows	0.026517	2	0.013258	22.83732	0.001565	5.143253
Columns	0.073892	3	0.024631	42.42584	0.000196	4.757063
Error	0.003483	6	0.000581			
Total	0.103892	11				

Data Analysis dialog box:

Analysis Tools:
- Anova: Single Factor
- Anova: Two-Factor With Replication
- Anova: Two-Factor Without Replication
- Correlation
- Covariance
- Descriptive Statistics
- Exponential Smoothing
- F-Test Two-Sample for Variances
- Fourier Analysis
- Histogram

[OK] [Cancel] [Help]

Step 4: Make the Decision

Since $F_A = 22.84$ (rows) exceeds $F_{2,6} = 5.14$, we see that factor A (pedal rotation) has a significant effect on acceleration. The p-value for pedal rotation is very small ($p = .001565$), which says that the F statistic is not due to chance. Similarly, $F_B = 42.43$ exceeds $F_{3,6} = 4.76$, so we see that factor B (initial speed) also has a significant effect on acceleration. Its tiny p-value (.000196) is unlikely to be a chance result. In short, we conclude that

- Acceleration is significantly affected by pedal rotation ($p = .001565$).
- Acceleration is significantly affected by initial speed ($p = .000196$).

The p-values suggest that initial speed is a more significant predictor than pedal rotation, although both are highly significant. These results conform to your own experience. Maximum acceleration ("pushing you back in your seat") from a low speed or standing stop is greater than when you are driving down the freeway, and of course the harder you press the accelerator pedal, the faster you will accelerate. In fact, you might think of the pedal rotation as a blocking factor since its relationship to acceleration is tautological and of little research interest. Nonetheless, omitting pedal rotation and using a one-factor model would not be a correct model specification. Further, the engineers who did this experiment were actually interested in both effects.

Using MegaStat

Figure 11.19 shows MegaStat's dot plot and ANOVA table. The dot plot shows the column factor (presumed to be the factor of research interest) on the horizontal axis, while the row factor (presumed to be a blocking factor) is only used to define the line graphs. MegaStat rounds its ANOVA results more than Excel and highlights significant p-values. MegaStat does not provide critical F values, which are basically redundant since you have the p-values.

FIGURE 11.19

MegaStat's two-factor ANOVA (randomized block model)   **Acceleration**

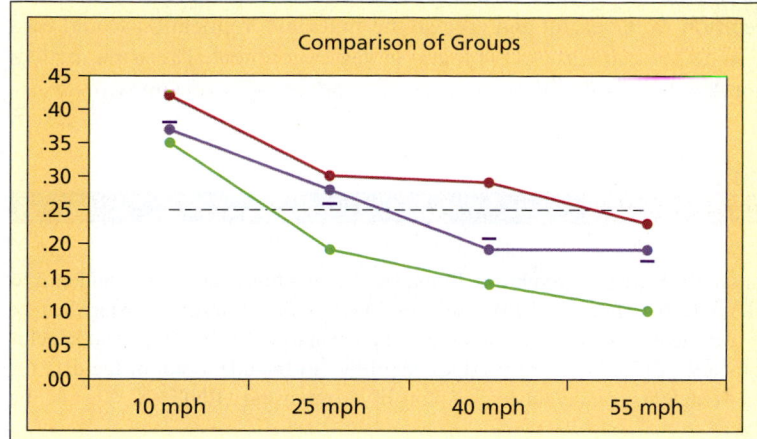

Randomized blocks ANOVA

	Mean	n	Std. Dev	
	0.38000	3	0.03606	10 mph
	0.25667	3	0.05859	25 mph
	0.20667	3	0.07638	40 mph
	0.17333	3	0.06658	55 mph
	0.19500	4	0.10970	5 degrees
	0.25750	4	0.08617	8 degrees
	0.31000	4	0.07958	10 degrees
	0.25417	12	0.09718	Total

ANOVA table

Source	SS	df	MS	F	p-value
Treatments	0.0739	3	0.02463	42.43	.0002
Blocks	0.0265	2	0.01326	22.84	.0016
Error	0.0035	6	0.00058		
Total	0.1039	11			

Multiple Comparisons

Figure 11.20 shows MegaStat's Tukey simultaneous comparisons of the treatment pairs using a pooled variance. There are also *p*-values for corresponding independent two-sample *t* tests. However, MegaStat presents Tukey comparisons *only for the column factor* (the row factor is presumed merely to be a blocking factor). For this data, the Tukey *t* tests and independent sample *t* tests agree on all comparisons except for 25 mph versus 40 mph. (The *t* test shows a significant difference between 25 mph and 40 mph at the .05 level of significance.) Both tests show no significant difference in acceleration between 40 mph and 55 mph.

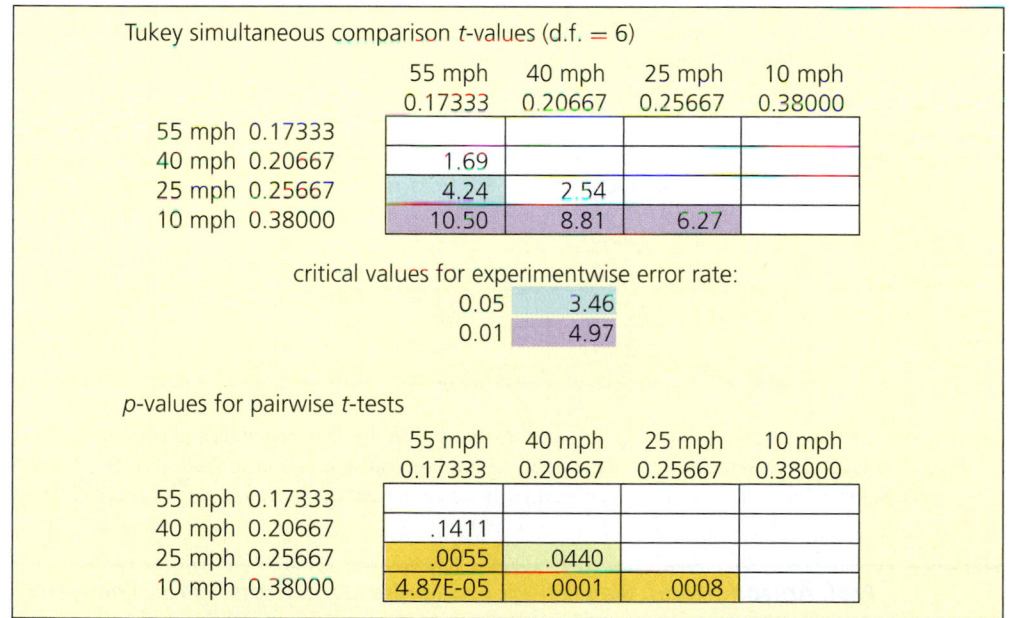

FIGURE 11.20

MegaStat's Tukey and independent sample *t* tests

 Acceleration

Tukey simultaneous comparison *t*-values (d.f. = 6)

	55 mph 0.17333	40 mph 0.20667	25 mph 0.25667	10 mph 0.38000
55 mph 0.17333				
40 mph 0.20667	1.69			
25 mph 0.25667	4.24	2.54		
10 mph 0.38000	10.50	8.81	6.27	

critical values for experimentwise error rate:

0.05	3.46
0.01	4.97

p-values for pairwise *t*-tests

	55 mph 0.17333	40 mph 0.20667	25 mph 0.25667	10 mph 0.38000
55 mph 0.17333				
40 mph 0.20667	.1411			
25 mph 0.25667	.0055	.0440		
10 mph 0.38000	4.87E-05	.0001	.0008	

Limitations of Two-Factor ANOVA Without Replication

When replication is impossible or extremely expensive, two-factor ANOVA without replication must suffice. For example, crash-testing of automobiles to estimate collision damage is very costly. However, whenever possible, there is a strong incentive to replicate the experiment to add power to the tests. Would different results have been obtained if the car had been tested not once but several times at each speed? Or if several different cars had been tested? For testing acceleration, there would seem to be no major cost impediment to replication except the time and effort required to take the measurements. Of course, it could be argued that if the measurements of acceleration were careful and precise the first time, replication would be a waste of time. And yet, some random variation is found in any experiment. These are matters to ponder. But two-factor ANOVA *with replication* does offer advantages, as you will see.

SECTION EXERCISES

Instructions: For each data set: (a) State the hypotheses. If you are viewing this data set as a randomized block, which is the blocking factor, and why? (b) Use Excel's Tools > Data Analysis (or MegaStat or MINITAB) to perform the two-factor ANOVA without replication, using $\alpha = .05$. (c) State your conclusions about the treatment means. (d) Interpret the *p*-values carefully. (e) Include a plot of the data for each group if you are using MegaStat, or individual value plots if you are using MINITAB. What do the plots show?

11.13 Concerned about Friday absenteeism, management examined absenteeism rates for the last three Fridays in four assembly plants. Does this sample prove that there is a significant difference in treatment means? 🐝 **Absences**

	Plant 1	Plant 2	Plant 3	Plant 4
March 4	19	18	27	22
March 11	22	20	32	27
March 18	20	16	28	26

11.14 Engineers are testing company fleet vehicle fuel economy (miles per gallon) performance by using different types of fuel. One vehicle of each size is tested. Does this sample prove that there is a significant difference in treatment means? 🐝 **MPG2**

	87 Octane	89 Octane	91 Octane	Ethanol 5%	Ethanol 10%
Compact	27.2	30.0	30.3	26.8	25.8
Mid-Size	23.0	25.6	28.6	26.6	23.3
Full-Size	21.4	22.5	22.2	18.9	20.8
SUV	18.7	24.1	22.1	18.7	17.4

11.15 Five statistics professors are using the same textbook with the same syllabus and common exams. At the end of the semester, the department committee on instruction looked at average exam scores. Does this sample prove a significant difference in treatment means? 🐝 **ExamScores**

	Prof. Argand	Prof. Blague	Prof. Clagmire	Prof. Dross	Prof. Ennuyeux
Exam 1	80.9	72.3	84.9	81.2	70.9
Exam 2	75.5	74.6	78.7	76.5	70.3
Exam 3	79.0	76.0	79.6	75.0	73.7
Final	69.9	78.0	77.8	74.1	73.9

11.16 A beer distributor is comparing quarterly sales of Coors Light (number of six-packs sold) at three convenience stores. Does this sample prove a significant difference in treatment means? 🐝 **BeerSales**

	Store 1	Store 2	Store 3
Qtr 1	1,521	1,298	1,708
Qtr 2	1,396	1,492	1,382
Qtr 3	1,178	1,052	1,132
Qtr 4	1,730	1,659	1,851

Mini Case 11.2

Automobile Interior Noise Level

Most consumers prefer quieter cars. Table 11.11 shows interior noise level for five vehicles se-lected from tests performed by a popular magazine. Noise level (in decibels) was measured at idle, at 60 miles per hour, and under hard acceleration from 0 to 60 mph. For reference, 60 dB is a normal conversation, 75 dB is a typical vacuum cleaner, 85 dB is city traffic, 90 dB is a typical hair dryer, and 110 dB is a chain saw. Two questions may be asked: (1) Does noise level vary significantly among the vehicles? (2) Does noise level vary significantly with speed? If you wish to think of this as a randomized block experiment, the column variable (*vehicle type*) is the research question, while the row variable (*speed*) is the blocking factor.

TABLE 11.11   **Interior Noise Levels in Five Randomly Selected Vehicles**
NoiseLevel

Speed	Chrysler 300M	BMW 528i Sport Wagon	Ford Explorer Sport Trac	Chevy Malibu LS	Subaru Outback H6-3.0
Idle	41	45	44	45	46
60 mph	65	67	66	66	76
0–60 mph	76	72	76	77	64

Source: Popular Science 254–258 (selected issues).

Note: Data are a random sample to be used for educational purposes only and should not be viewed as a guide to vehicle performance.

The general form of the model is *NoiseLevel* $= f(CarSpeed, CarType)$. Degrees of freedom for *CarSpeed* (rows) will be $r - 1 = 3 - 1 = 2$, while degrees of freedom for *CarType* (columns) will be $c - 1 = 5 - 1 = 4$. Denominator degrees of freedom will be the same for both factors since *SSE* has degrees of freedom $(r - 1)(c - 1) = (3 - 1)(5 - 1) = 8$. Excel's ANOVA results and MegaStat's dot plot are shown in Figure 11.21.

FIGURE 11.21

Results of two-factor ANOVA without replication for car noise

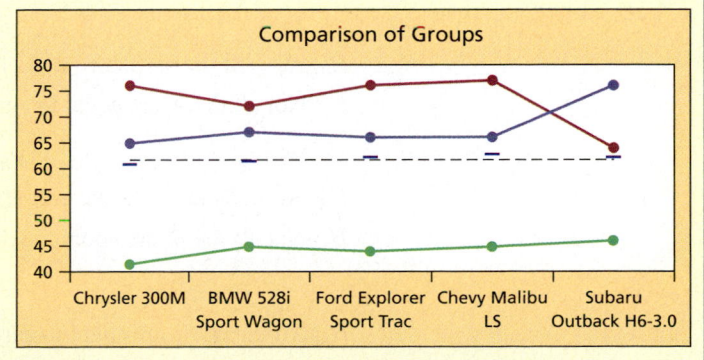

SUMMARY	Count	Sum	Average	Variance
Idle	5	221	44.200	3.700
60 mph	5	340	68.000	20.500
0-60 mph	5	365	73.000	29.000
Chrysler 300M	3	182	60.667	320.333
BMW 528i Sport Wagon	3	184	61.333	206.333
Ford Explorer Sport Trac	3	186	62.000	268.000
Chevy Malibu LS	3	188	62.667	264.333
Subaru Outback H6-3.0	3	186	62.000	228.000

ANOVA: Two-Factor Without Replication

Source of Variation	SS	df	MS	F	P-value	F crit
Rows	2368.133	2	1184.067	46.01295	0.00004	4.45897
Columns	6.933333	4	1.733333	0.06736	0.99006	3.83785
Error	205.8667	8	25.73333			
Total	2580.933	14				

Since $F = 46.01$ exceeds $F_{2,8} = 4.46$, we see that *CarSpeed* (row factor) does have a highly significant effect on noise level. Its very small *p*-value ($p = .00004$) is unlikely to be a chance result. But *CarType* (column factor) has no significant effect on noise level since $F = 0.07$ does not exceed $F_{4,8} = 3.84$. The *p*-value for *CarType* ($p = .99006$) says that its F statistic could easily have arisen by chance. In short, we conclude that

- Interior noise *is* significantly affected by car speed ($p = .00004$).

- Interior noise *is not* significantly affected by car type ($p = .9901$).

We do not bother with Tukey multiple comparisons of means since we know that car type has no significant effect on noise level (the research hypothesis) and the effect of initial speed is of less research interest (a blocking factor).

11.6 TWO-FACTOR ANOVA WITH REPLICATION (FULL FACTORIAL MODEL)

What Does Replication Accomplish?

In a two-factor model, suppose that each factor combination is observed m times. With an equal number of observations in each cell (*balanced data*) we have a two-factor ANOVA model *with replication.* Replication allows us to test not only the factors' **main effects** but also an **interaction effect.** This model is often called the **full factorial** model. In linear model format it may be written

(11.15) $$y_{ijk} = \mu + A_j + B_k + AB_{jk} + \varepsilon_{ijk}$$

where

$y_{ijk} =$ observation i for row j and column $k(i = 1, 2, \ldots, m)$

$\mu =$ common mean for all treatments

$A_j =$ effect attributed to factor A in row $j(j = 1, 2, \ldots, r)$

$B_k =$ effect attributed to factor B in column $k(k = 1, 2, \ldots, c)$

$AB_{jk} =$ effect attributed to interaction between factors A and B

$\varepsilon_{ijk} =$ random error (normally distributed, zero mean, same variance for all treatments)

Interaction effects can be important. For example, an agribusiness researcher might postulate that corn yield is related to seed type (A), soil type (B), interaction between seed type and soil type (AB), or all three. In the absence of any factor effects, all variation about the mean μ is purely random.

Format of Hypotheses

For a fixed-effects ANOVA model, the hypotheses that could be tested in the two-factor ANOVA model with replicated observations are

Factor A: Row Effect

H_0: $A_1 = A_2 = \cdots = A_r = 0$ (factor A has no effect)

H_1: Not all the A_j are equal to zero (factor A has an effect)

Factor B: Column Effect

H_0: $B_1 = B_2 = \cdots = B_c = 0$ (factor B has no effect)

H_1: Not all the B_k are equal to zero (factor B has an effect)

Interaction Effect

H_0: All the AB_{jk} are equal to zero (there is no interaction effect)

H_1: Not all AB_{jk} are equal to zero (there is an interaction effect)

If none of the proposed factors has anything to do with Y, then the model collapses to

$$y_{ijk} = \mu + \varepsilon_{ijk} \qquad (11.16)$$

Format of Data

Table 11.12 shows the format of a data set with two factors and a balanced (equal) number of observations per treatment (each row/column intersection is a treatment). To avoid needless subscripts, the m observations in each treatment are represented simply as yyy. Except for the replication within cells, the format is the same as the unreplicated two-factor ANOVA.

TABLE 11.12
Data Format of Replicated Two-Factor ANOVA

	Levels of Factor B				
Levels of Factor A	B_1	B_2	$\ldots$	B_c	**Row Mean**
A_1	yyy yyy $\ldots$ yyy	yyy yyy $\ldots$ yyy	$\ldots$ $\ldots$ $\ldots$ $\ldots$	yyy yyy $\ldots$ yyy	$\bar{y}_{1.}$
A_2	yyy yyy $\ldots$ yyy	yyy yyy $\ldots$ yyy	$\ldots$ $\ldots$ $\ldots$ $\ldots$	yyy yyy $\ldots$ yyy	$\bar{y}_{2.}$
$\ldots$	$\ldots$	$\ldots$	$\ldots$	$\ldots$	$\ldots$
A_r	yyy yyy $\ldots$ yyy	yyy yyy $\ldots$ yyy	$\ldots$ $\ldots$ $\ldots$ $\ldots$	yyy yyy $\ldots$ yyy	$\bar{y}_{r.}$
Col Mean	$\bar{y}_{.1}$	$\bar{y}_{.2}$	$\ldots$	$\bar{y}_{.c}$	$\bar{y}$

Sources of Variation

There are now three F tests that could be performed: one for each main effect (factors A and B) and a third F test for interaction. The total sum of squares is partitioned into four components:

$$SST = SSA + SSB + SSI + SSE \qquad (11.17)$$

where

SST = total sum of squared deviations about the mean

SSA = between rows sum of squares (effect of factor A)

SSB = between columns sum of squares (effect of factor B)

SSI = interaction sum of squares (effect of AB)

SSE = error sum of squares (residual variation)

For an experiment with r rows, c columns, and m replications per treatment, the sums of squares and ANOVA calculations may be presented in a table, shown in Table 11.13.

If SSE is relatively high, we expect that we would fail to reject H_0 for the various hypotheses. Conversely, if SSE is relatively small, it is likely that at least one of the factors (row effect, column effect, or interaction) is a relevant predictor of Y. Before doing the F test, each sum of squares must be divided by its degrees of freedom to obtain its *mean square*. Degrees of freedom sum to $n - 1$ (note that $n = rcm$).

TABLE 11.13   Two-Factor ANOVA with Replication

Source of Variation	Sum of Squares	Degrees of Freedom	Mean Square	F Ratio
Factor A (row effect)	$SSA = cm \sum_{j=1}^{r} (\bar{y}_{j.} - \bar{y})^2$	$r - 1$	$MSA = \dfrac{SSA}{r-1}$	$F_A = \dfrac{MSA}{MSE}$
Factor B (column effect)	$SSB = rm \sum_{k=1}^{c} (\bar{y}_{.k} - \bar{y})^2$	$c - 1$	$MSB = \dfrac{SSB}{c-1}$	$F_B = \dfrac{MSB}{MSE}$
Interaction $(A \times B)$	$SSI = m \sum_{j=1}^{r} \sum_{k=1}^{c} (\bar{y}_{jk} - \bar{y}_{j.} - \bar{y}_{.k} + \bar{y})^2$	$(r-1)(c-1)$	$MSI = \dfrac{SSI}{(r-1)(c-1)}$	$F_I = \dfrac{MSI}{MSE}$
Error	$SSE = \sum_{i=1}^{m} \sum_{j=1}^{r} \sum_{k=1}^{c} (y_{ijk} - \bar{y}_{jk})^2$	$rc(m-1)$	$MSE = \dfrac{SSE}{rc(m-1)}$	
Total	$SST = \sum_{i=1}^{m} \sum_{j=1}^{r} \sum_{k=1}^{c} (y_{ijk} - \bar{y})^2$	$rcm - 1$		

EXAMPLE

Delivery Time

A health maintenance organization orders weekly medical supplies for its four clinics from five different suppliers. Delivery times (in days) for 4 recent weeks are shown in Table 11.14.

TABLE 11.14   Delivery Times (in days) 🐝 **Deliveries**

	Supplier 1	Supplier 2	Supplier 3	Supplier 4	Supplier 5
Clinic A	8	14	10	8	17
	8	9	15	7	12
	10	14	10	13	9
	13	11	7	10	10
Clinic B	13	9	12	6	15
	14	9	10	10	12
	12	7	10	12	12
	13	8	11	8	10
Clinic C	11	8	12	10	14
	10	9	10	11	13
	12	11	13	7	10
	14	12	10	10	12
Clinic D	7	8	7	8	14
	10	13	5	5	13
	10	9	6	11	8
	13	12	5	4	11

Using short variable names, the two-factor ANOVA model has the general form

$$DeliveryTime = f(Clinic, Supplier, Clinic \times Supplier)$$

The effects are assumed additive. The linear model is

$$y_{ijk} = \mu + A_j + B_k + AB_{jk} + \varepsilon_{ijk}$$

Step 1: State the Hypotheses
The hypotheses are

Factor *A*: Row Effect (*Clinic*)

$H_0: A_1 = A_2 = \cdots = A_r = 0$ (clinic means are the same)

$H_1:$ Not all the A_j are equal to zero (clinic means differ)

Factor *B*: Column Effect (*Supplier*)

$H_0: B_1 = B_2 = \cdots = B_c = 0$ (supplier means are the same)

$H_1:$ Not all the B_k are equal to zero (supplier means differ)

Interaction Effect (*Clinic × Supplier*)

$H_0:$ All the AB_{jk} are equal to zero (there is no interaction effect)

$H_1:$ Not all AB_{jk} are equal to zero (there is an interaction effect)

Step 2: State the Decision Rule
Each F test may require a different right-tail critical value because the numerator degrees of freedom depend on the number of factor levels, while denominator degrees of freedom (error *SSE*) are the same for all three tests:

Factor A: $\text{d.f.}_1 = r - 1 = 4 - 1 = 3$ ($r = 4$ clinics)

Factor B: $\text{d.f.}_1 = c - 1 = 5 - 1 = 4$ ($c = 5$ suppliers)

Interaction (AB): $\text{d.f.}_1 = (r - 1)(c - 1) = (4 - 1)(5 - 1) = 12$

Error $\text{d.f.}_2 = rc(m - 1) = 4 \times 5 \times (4 - 1) = 60$

Excel provides the right-tail F critical values for $\alpha = .05$, which we can verify using Appendix F:

$F_{3,60} = 2.76$ for Factor *A*

$F_{4,60} = 2.53$ for Factor *B*

$F_{12,60} = 1.92$ for Factor *AB*

We reject the null hypothesis if an F test statistic exceeds its critical value.

Step 3: Perform the Calculations
Excel provides tables of row and column sums and means (not shown here because they are lengthy). The ANOVA table in Figure 11.22 summarizes the partitioning of variation into its component sums of squares, degrees of freedom, mean squares, F test statistics, *p*-values, and critical *F*-values for $\alpha = .05$.

FIGURE 11.22

Excel's two-factor ANOVA with replication  **Deliveries**

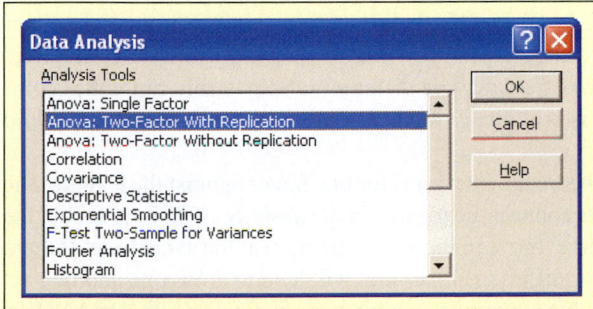

ANOVA						
Source of Variation	*SS*	*df*	*MS*	*F*	*P-value*	*F crit*
Sample	51.350	3	17.1167	3.434783	0.022424	2.758078
Columns	104.425	4	26.1063	5.238712	0.001097	2.525215
Interaction	102.775	12	8.5646	1.718645	0.085176	1.917396
Within	299.000	60	4.9833			
Total	557.550	79				

Step 4: Make the Decision
For the row variable (*Clinic*) the test statistic $F = 3.435$ and its *p*-value ($p = .0224$) lead us to conclude that the mean delivery times among clinics are not the same at $\alpha = .05$. For the

column variable (*Supplier*) the test statistic $F = 5.239$ and its *p*-value ($p = .0011$) lead us to conclude that the mean delivery times from suppliers are not the same at $\alpha = .05$. For the interaction effect, the test statistic $F = 1.719$ and its *p*-value ($p = .0852$) lack significance at $\alpha = .05$. The *p*-values permit a more flexible interpretation since α need not be specified in advance. In summary:

Variable	p-Value	Interpretation
Clinic	.0224	Clinic means differ (significant at $\alpha = .05$)
Supplier	.0011	Supplier means differ (significant at $\alpha = .01$)
Clinic × Supplier	.0852	Weak interaction effect (significant at $\alpha = .10$)

Using MegaStat

MegaStat's two-factor ANOVA results, shown in Figure 11.23, are similar to Excel's except that the table of treatment means is more compact, the results are rounded, and significant *p*-values are highlighted (bright yellow for $\alpha = .01$, light green for $\alpha = .05$).

FIGURE 11.23

MegaStat's two-factor ANOVA 🐝 **Deliveries**

Two factor ANOVA

Means: Factor 2

		Supplier 1	Supplier 2	Supplier 3	Supplier 4	Supplier 5	
	Clinic A	9.8	12.0	10.5	9.5	12.0	10.8
Factor 1	Clinic B	13.0	8.3	10.8	9.0	12.3	10.7
	Clinic C	11.8	10.0	11.3	9.5	12.3	11.0
	Clinic D	10.0	10.5	5.8	7.0	11.5	9.0
		11.1	10.2	9.6	8.8	12.0	10.3

ANOVA table

Source	SS	df	MS	F	p-value
Factor 1	51.35	3	17.117	3.43	.0224
Factor 2	104.43	4	26.106	5.24	.0011
Interaction	102.78	12	8.565	1.72	.0852
Error	299.00	60	4.983		
Total	557.56	79			

Interaction Effect

The statistical test for interaction is just like any other *F* test. But you might still wonder, What *is* an interaction, anyway? You may be familiar with the idea of drug interaction. If you consume a few ounces of vodka, it has an effect on you. If you take an allergy pill, it has an effect on you. But if you combine the two, the effect may be different (and possibly dramatic) compared with either drug by itself. That is why many medications carry a warning like "Avoid alcohol while using this medication."

To visualize an interaction, we plot the treatment means for one factor against the levels of the other factor. Within each factor level, we connect the means. In the absence of an interaction, the lines will be roughly parallel or will tend to move in the same direction at the same time. If there is a strong interaction, the lines will have differing slopes and will tend to cross one another.

Figure 11.24 illustrates several possible situations, using a hypothetical two-factor ANOVA model in which factor *A* has three levels and factor *B* has two levels. For the delivery time example, a significant *interaction effect* would mean that suppliers have different mean delivery times for different clinics. However, Figure 11.25 shows that, while the interaction plot lines do cross, there is no consistent pattern, and the lines tend to be parallel more than crossing. The visual indications of interaction are, therefore, weak for the delivery time data. This conclusion is consistent with the interaction *p*-value ($p = .085$) for the *F* test of $A \times B$.

FIGURE 11.24

Possible interaction patterns

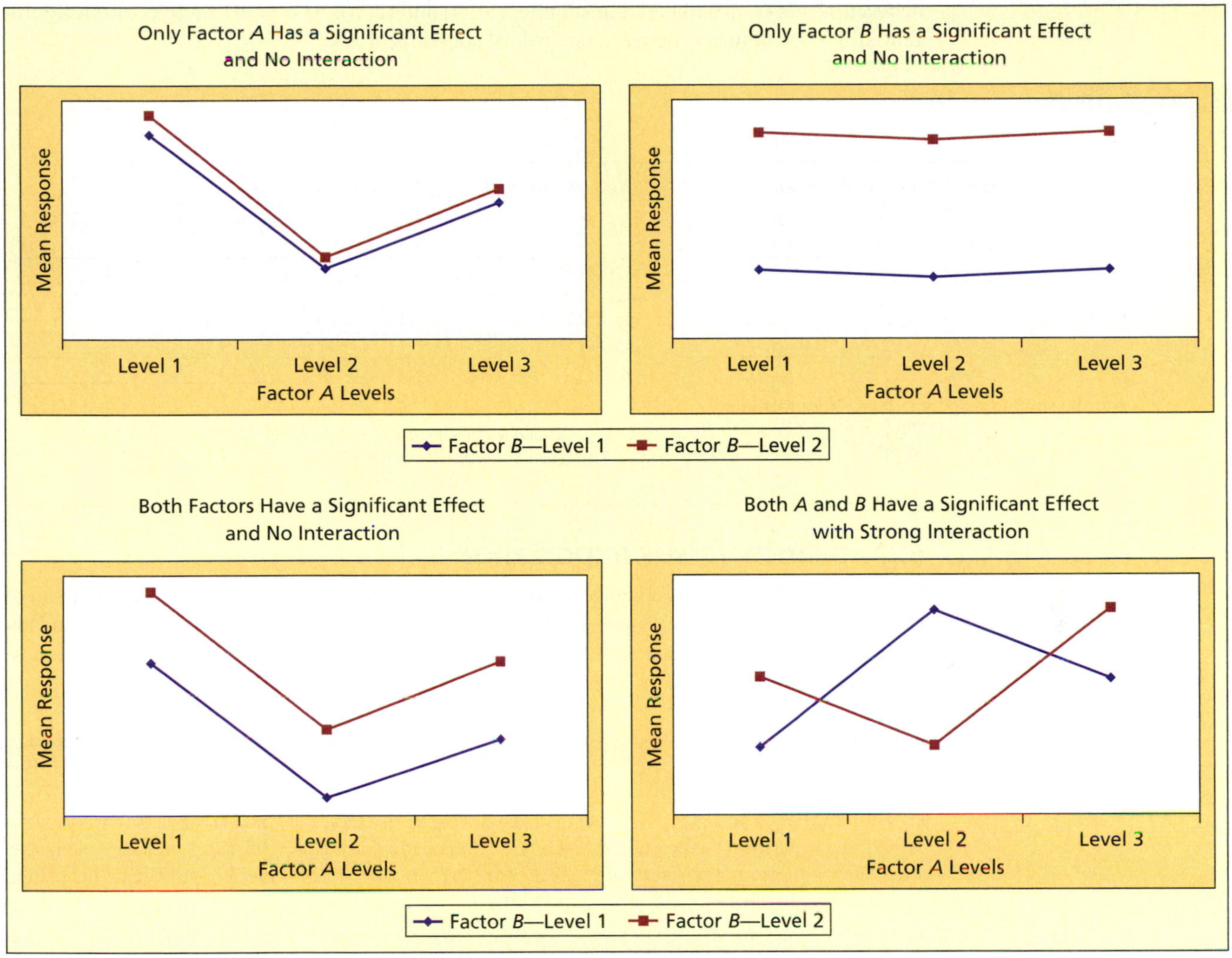

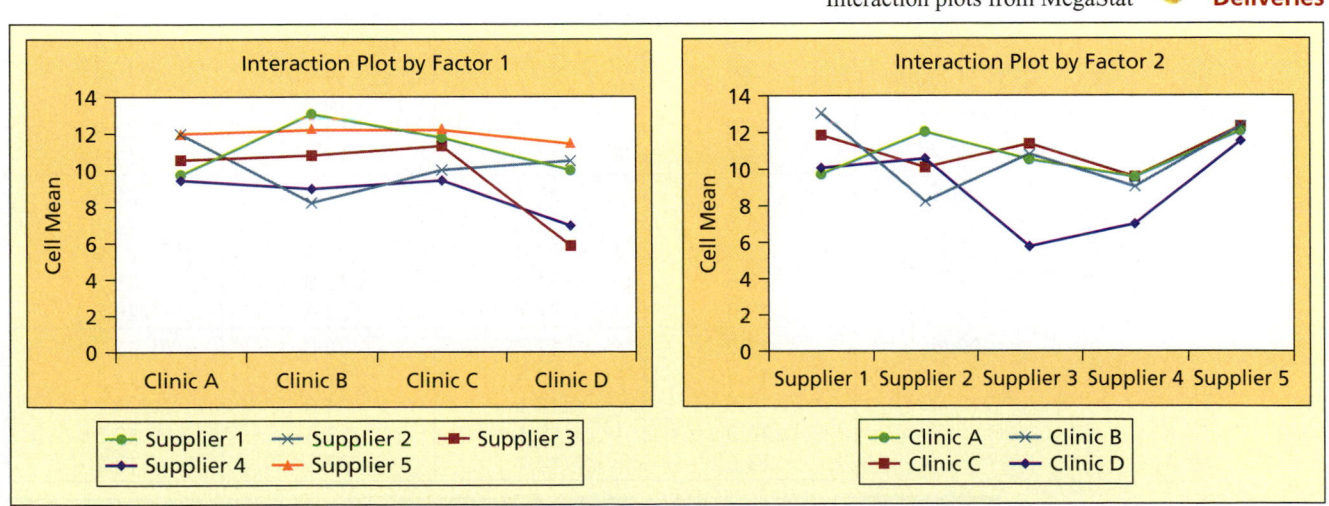

FIGURE 11.25

Interaction plots from MegaStat   **Deliveries**

Tukey Tests of Pairs of Means

MegaStat's Tukey comparisons, shown in Figure 11.26, reveal significant differences at $\alpha = .05$ between plants C, D and between suppliers (1, 4) and (3, 5). At $\alpha = .01$ there is also a significant difference in means between one pair of suppliers (4, 5).

FIGURE 11.26

MegaStat table of Tukey comparisons   **Deliveries**

Tukey simultaneous comparison t-values (d.f. = 60)

		Clinic D 9.0	Clinic B 10.7	Clinic A 10.8	Clinic C 11.0
Clinic D	9.0				
Clinic B	10.7	2.41			
Clinic A	10.8	2.55	0.14		
Clinic C	11.0	2.83	0.42	0.28	

critical values for experimentwise error rate:
0.05   2.64
0.01   3.25

Tukey simultaneous comparison t-values (d.f. = 60)

		Supplier 4 8.8	Supplier 3 9.6	Supplier 2 10.2	Supplier 1 11.1	Supplier 5 12.0
Supplier 4	8.8					
Supplier 3	9.6	1.03				
Supplier 2	10.2	1.82	0.79			
Supplier 1	11.1	3.01	1.98	1.19		
Supplier 5	12.0	4.12	3.09	2.30	1.11	

critical values for experimentwise error rate:
0.05   2.81
0.01   3.41

Significance versus Importance

MegaStat's table of means (Figure 11.23) allows us to explore these differences further and to assess the question of *importance* as well as *significance*. The largest differences in means between clinics or suppliers are about 2 days. Such a small difference might be unimportant most of the time. However, if their inventory is low, a 2-day difference could be important.

SECTION EXERCISES

Instructions: For each data set: (a) State the hypotheses. (b) Use Excel's Tools > Data Analysis (or MegaStat or MINITAB) to perform the two-factor ANOVA with replication, using $\alpha = .05$. (c) State your conclusions about the main effects and interaction effects. (d) Interpret the p-values carefully. (e) Create interaction plots and interpret them.

11.17 A small independent stock broker has created four sector portfolios for her clients. Each portfolio always has five stocks that may change from year to year. The volatility (coefficient of variation) of each stock is recorded for each year. Are the main effects significant? Is there an interaction?
    Volatility

Year	Health	Energy	Retail	Leisure
	Stock Portfolio Type			
2004	14.5	23.0	19.4	17.6
	18.4	19.9	20.7	18.1
	13.7	24.5	18.5	16.1
	15.9	24.2	15.5	23.2
	16.2	19.4	17.7	17.6
2005	21.6	22.1	21.4	25.5
	25.6	31.6	26.5	24.1
	21.4	22.4	21.5	25.9
	26.6	31.3	22.8	25.5
	19.0	32.5	27.4	26.3
2006	12.6	12.8	22.0	12.9
	13.5	14.4	17.1	11.1
	13.5	13.1	24.8	4.9
	13.0	8.1	13.4	13.3
	13.6	14.7	22.2	12.7

11.18 Oxnard Petro, Ltd., has three interdisciplinary project development teams that function on an on-going basis. Team members rotate from time to time. Every 4 months (three times a year) each department head rates the performance of each project team (using a 0 to 100 scale, where 100 is the best rating). Are the main effects significant? Is there an interaction? 🐝 **Ratings**

Year	Marketing	Engineering	Finance
2004	90	69	96
	84	72	86
	80	78	86
2005	72	73	89
	83	77	87
	82	81	93
2006	92	84	91
	87	75	85
	87	80	78

11.19 A market research firm is testing consumer reaction to a new shampoo on four age groups in four regions. There are five consumers in each test panel. Each consumer completes a 10-question product satisfaction instrument with a 5-point scale (5 is the highest rating) and the average score is recorded. Are the main effects significant? Is there an interaction? 🐝 **Satisfaction**

	Northeast	Southeast	Midwest	West
Youth (under 18)	3.9	3.9	3.6	3.9
	4.0	4.2	3.9	4.4
	3.7	4.4	3.9	4.0
	4.1	4.1	3.7	4.1
	4.3	4.0	3.3	3.9
College (18–25)	4.0	3.8	3.6	3.8
	4.0	3.7	4.1	3.8
	3.7	3.7	3.8	3.6
	3.8	3.6	3.9	3.6
	3.8	3.7	4.0	4.1
Adult (26–64)	3.2	3.5	3.5	3.8
	3.8	3.3	3.8	3.6
	3.7	3.4	3.8	3.4
	3.4	3.5	4.0	3.7
	3.4	3.4	3.7	3.1
Senior (65+)	3.4	3.6	3.3	3.4
	2.9	3.4	3.3	3.2
	3.6	3.6	3.1	3.5
	3.7	3.6	3.1	3.3
	3.5	3.4	3.1	3.4

11.20 Oxnard Petro, Ltd., has three suppliers of catalysts. Orders are placed with each supplier every 15 working days, or about once every 3 weeks. The delivery time (days) is recorded for each order over 1 year. Are the main effects significant? Is there an interaction? 🐝 **Deliveries2**

	Supplier 1	Supplier 2	Supplier 3
Qtr 1	12	10	16
	15	13	13
	11	11	14
	11	9	14
Qtr 2	13	10	14
	11	10	11
	13	13	12
	12	11	12
Qtr 3	12	11	13
	8	9	8
	8	8	13
	13	6	6
Qtr 4	8	8	11
	10	10	11
	13	10	10
	11	10	11

Mini Case

11.3

Turbine Engine Thrust

Engineers testing turbofan aircraft engines wanted to know if oil pressure and turbine temperature are related to engine thrust (pounds). They chose four levels for each factor and observed each combination five times, using the two-factor replicated ANOVA model *Thrust = f(OilPres, TurbTemp, OilPres×TurbTemp)*. The test data are shown in Table 11.15.

TABLE 11.15 **Turbofan Engine Thrust Test Results** 🦃 **Turbines**

	Turbine Temperature			
Oil Pressure	**T1**	**T2**	**T3**	**T4**
P1	1,945.0	1,942.3	1,934.2	1,916.7
	1,933.0	1,931.7	1,930.0	1,943.0
	1,942.4	1,946.0	1,944.0	1,948.8
	1,948.0	1,959.0	1,941.0	1,928.0
	1,930.0	1,939.9	1,942.0	1,946.0
P2	1,939.4	1,922.0	1,950.6	1,929.6
	1,952.8	1,936.8	1,947.9	1,930.0
	1,940.0	1,928.0	1,950.0	1,934.0
	1,948.0	1,930.7	1,922.0	1,923.0
	1,925.0	1,939.0	1,918.0	1,914.0
P3	1,932.0	1,939.0	1,952.0	1,960.4
	1,955.0	1,932.0	1,963.0	1,946.0
	1,949.7	1,933.1	1,923.0	1,931.0
	1,933.0	1,952.0	1,965.0	1,949.0
	1,936.5	1,943.0	1,944.0	1,906.0
P4	1,960.2	1,937.0	1,940.0	1,924.0
	1,909.3	1,941.0	1,984.0	1,906.0
	1,950.0	1,928.2	1,971.0	1,925.8
	1,920.0	1,938.9	1,930.0	1,923.0
	1,964.9	1,919.0	1,944.0	1,916.7

Source: Research project by three engineering students enrolled in an MBA program. Data are disguised.

The ANOVA results in Figure 11.27 indicate that only turbine temperature is significantly related to thrust. The table of means suggests that, because mean thrust varies only over a tiny range, the effect may not be very important. The lack of interaction is revealed by the nearly parallel ***interaction plots.*** Levene's test for equal variances (not shown) shows a p-value of $p = .42$ indicating that variances may be assumed equal, as is desirable for an ANOVA test.

FIGURE 11.27

MegaStat two-factor
ANOVA results

Means:		Temperature				
		T1	T2	T3	T4	
	P1	1,939.68	1,943.78	1,938.24	1,936.50	1,939.55
Pressure	P2	1,941.04	1,931.30	1,937.70	1,926.12	1,934.04
	P3	1,941.24	1,939.82	1,949.40	1,938.48	1,942.24
	P4	1,940.88	1,932.82	1,953.80	1,919.10	1,936.65
		1,940.71	1,936.93	1,944.79	1,930.05	1,938.12

ANOVA table: Two-Factor with Replication

Source	SS	df	MS	F	p-value
Pressure	755.708	3	251.9028	1.32	.2756
Temperature	2,353.426	3	784.4755	4.11	.0099
Interaction	1,989.095	9	221.0106	1.16	.3367
Error	12,212.052	64	190.8133		
Total	17,310.282	79			

Interaction Plot by Factor 1

Legend: T1, T2, T3, T4

(Cell Mean vs P1, P2, P3, P4)

Interaction Plot by Factor 2

Legend: P1, P2, P3, P4

(Cell Mean vs T1, T2, T3, T4)

Higher-Order ANOVA Models

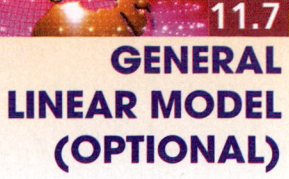

**11.7
GENERAL
LINEAR MODEL
(OPTIONAL)**

Why limit ourselves to two factors? Although a three-factor data set cannot be shown in a two-dimensional table, the idea of a three-factor ANOVA is not difficult to grasp. Consider the hospital LOS and paint viscosity problems introduced at the beginning of this chapter. Figure 11.28 adds a third factor (gender) to the hospital model and Figure 11.29 adds a third factor (solvent ratio) to the paint viscosity model.

FIGURE 11.28

Three-factor ANOVA model for hospital length of stay

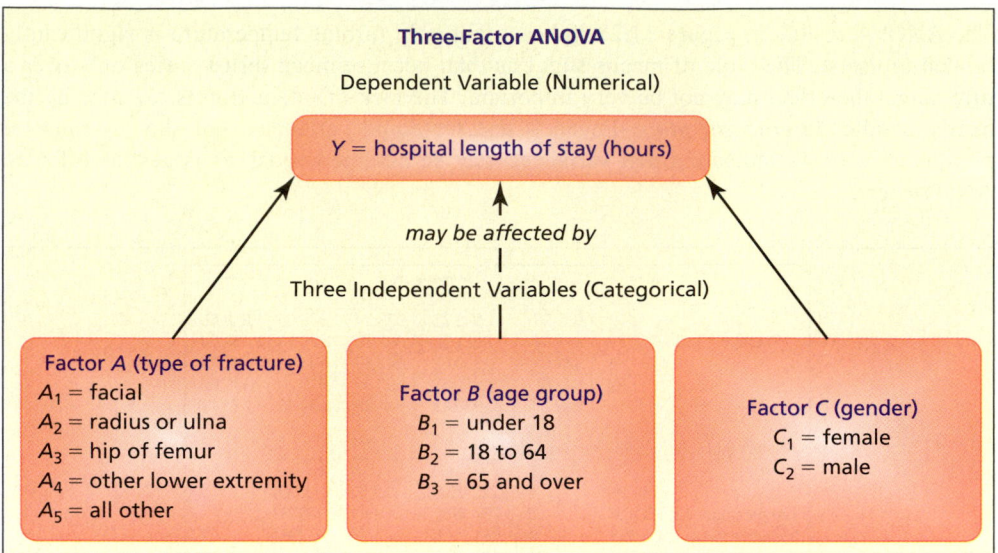

FIGURE 11.29

Three-factor ANOVA model for paint viscosity

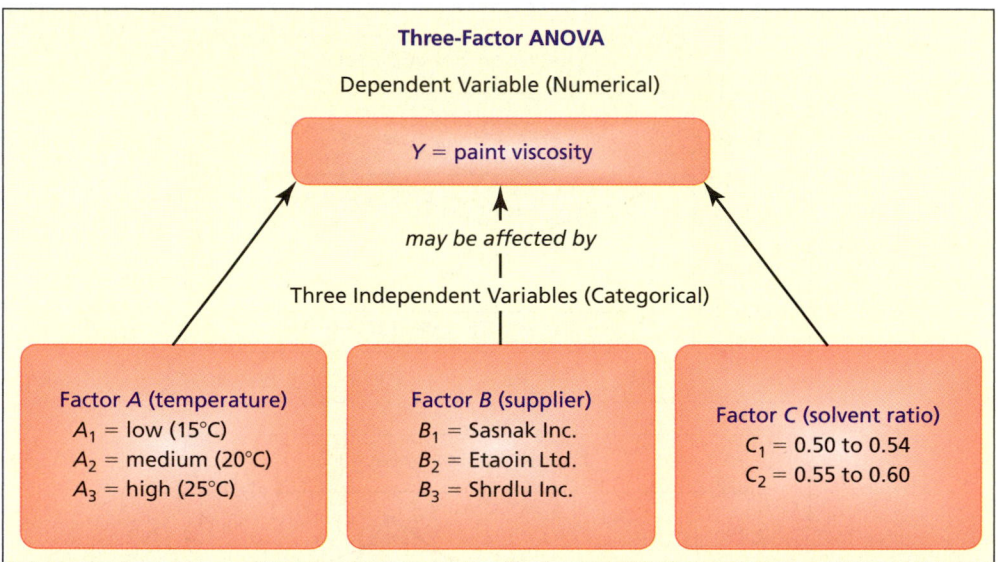

A three-factor ANOVA allows more two-factor interactions ($A \times B$, $A \times C$, $B \times C$) and even a three-factor interaction ($A \times B \times C$). However, since the computations are already done by computer, the analysis would be no harder than a two-factor ANOVA. The "catch" is that higher-order ANOVA models are beyond Excel's capabilities, so you will need fancier software. Fortunately, any general-purpose statistical package (e.g., MINITAB, SPSS, SAS) can handle ANOVA with *any* number of factors with *any* number of levels (subject to computer software limitations).

What Is GLM?

The *general linear model* (GLM) is a versatile tool for estimating large and complex ANOVA models. Besides allowing more than two factors, GLM permits unbalanced data (unequal sample size within treatments) and any desired subset of interactions among factors (including three-way interactions or higher) as long as you have enough observations (i.e., enough degrees of freedom) to compute the effects. GLM can also provide predictions and identify unusual observations. GLM does not require equal variances, although care must be taken to avoid sparse or empty cells in the data matrix. Data are expected to be in stacked format (one column for *Y* and one column for each factor *A*, *B*, *C*, etc.). The output of GLM is easily understood by anyone who is familiar with ANOVA, as you can see in Mini Case 11.4.

Mini Case   11.4

Hospital Maternity Stay   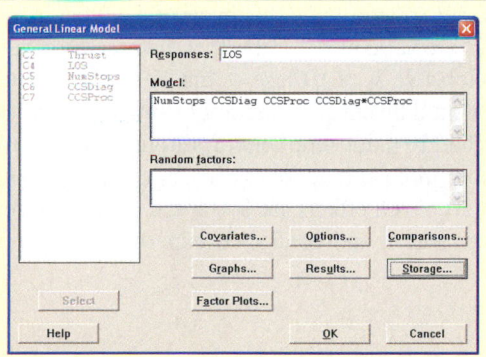 MaternityLOS

The data set consists of 4,409 maternity hospital visits whose DRG (diagnostic-related group) code is 373 (simple delivery without complicating diagnoses). The dependent variable of interest is the length of stay (LOS) in the hospital. The model contains one discrete numerical factor and two categorical factors: the number of surgical stops (*NumStops*), the CCS diagnostic code (*CCSDiag*), and the CCS procedure code (*CCSProc*). CCS codes are a medical classification scheme developed by the American Hospital Research Council to help hospitals and researchers organize medical information. The proposed model is

$$LOS = f(NumStops, CCSDiag, CCSProc)$$

Before starting the GLM analysis, a frequency tabulation was prepared for each factor. The tabulation (not shown) revealed that some factor levels were observed too rarely to be useful. Cross-tabulations (not shown) also revealed that some treatments would be empty or very sparse. Based on this preliminary data screening, the factors were recoded to avoid GLM estimation problems. *NumStops* was recoded as a binary variable (2 if there were 1 or 2 stops, 3 if there were 3 or more stops). *CCSDiag* codes with a frequency less than 100 were recoded as 999. Patients whose *CCSProc* code occurred less than 10 times (19 patients) were deleted from the sample, leaving a sample of 4,390 patients.

MINITAB's menu and GLM results are shown in Figure 11.30. You can select a variable by clicking on it, but if you want an interaction, you must type it in the Model window. The first thing shown is the number of levels for each factor and the discrete values of each factor. Frequencies of the factor values are not shown, but can be obtained from MINITAB's Tables command.

FIGURE 11.30

MINITAB menu and GLM results   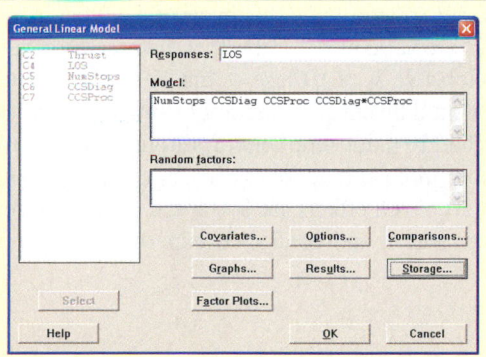 **MaternityLOS**

```
General Linear Model
  C2   Thrust      Responses: LOS
  C4   LOS
  C5   NumStops    Model:
  C6   CCSDiag     NumStops CCSDiag CCSProc CCSDiag*CCSProc
  C7   CCSProc

               Random factors:


     Covariates...   Options...   Comparisons...
     Graphs...       Results...   Storage...
  Select           Factor Plots...
  Help                          OK    Cancel
```

```
Factor      Type  Levels  Values
NumStops    fixed      2  2 3
CCSDiag     fixed      9  181 184 185 190 191 193 195 196 999
CCSProc     fixed      6  133 135 136 137 139 140

Analysis of Variance for LOS, using Adjusted SS for Tests

Source          DF     Seq SS     Adj SS   Adj MS      F      P
NumStops         1       1340       7385     7385   3.25  0.072
CCSDiag          8     446299      94498    11812   5.19  0.000
CCSProc          5      37139      45061     9012   3.96  0.001
CCSDiag*CCSProc 40     194618     194618     4865   2.14  0.000
Error         4335    9865440    9865440     2276
Total         4389   10544837
```

The *p*-values from the ANOVA table suggest that *NumStops* is significant at $\alpha = .10$ ($p = .072$) while the other two main effects *CCSDiag* and *CCSProc* ($p = .000$ and $p = .001$) are highly significant (such small *p*-values would arise less than once in 1,000 samples if there were no relationship). The interaction *CCSDiag×CCSProc* is also highly significant ($p = .000$). Because the sample size is large, even slight effects could be *significant*, so further analysis may be needed to see if the effects are also *important*. Unfortunately, there are outliers in the data (a violation of the normality assumption) that show up clearly on the residual normality plot in Figure 11.31. Thus, we must regard the ANOVA results with caution.

FIGURE 11.31

MINITAB normality plot

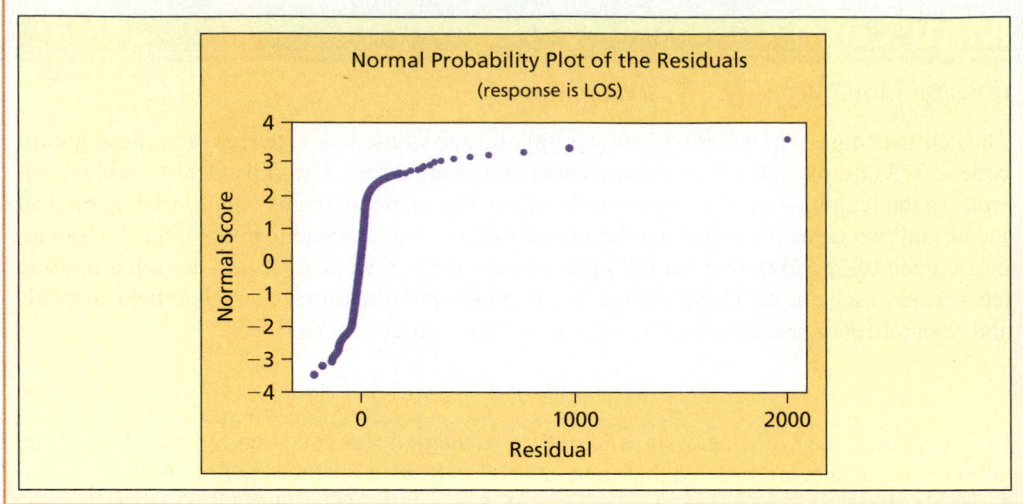

11.8 EXPERIMENTAL DESIGN: AN OVERVIEW (OPTIONAL)

Experimental design is a specialized topic that goes far beyond this textbook. However, you may need to interact professionally with engineers or quality improvement teams that are working on product design, reliability, and product performance. It is therefore helpful to have a general idea of what experimental design is all about and to learn some of the basic terminology. If you become more deeply involved, you can ask your employer to send you to a 3-day training class in experimental design to boost your skills.

What Is Experimental Design?

Experimental design refers to the number of factors under investigation, the number of levels assigned to each factor, the way factor levels are defined, and the way observations are obtained. *Fully crossed* or *full factorial* designs include all possible combinations of factor levels. *Fractional factorial* designs, for reasons of economy, limit data collection to a subset of possible factor combinations. If all levels of one factor are fully contained in another, the design is **nested** or **hierarchical.** **Balanced designs** are characterized by an equal number of observations for each factor combination. In a *fixed-effects model* the levels of each factor are predetermined, which implies that our inferences are valid only for the specified factor levels. For example, if a firm has only three paint suppliers (S_1, S_2, S_3), these would be our factor levels. In a *random effects model* the factor levels would be chosen randomly from a population of potential factor levels. For example, if a firm has 20 paint suppliers (S_1 through S_{20}) but we only want to study three of them, we might choose three at random (say S_7, S_{11}, and S_{18}) from the 6,840 possible ways to choose 3 items from 20. Fixed effects are by far the most common models used in business analysis, where randomization and controlled experiments are not practical.

2^k Models

When there are k factors, each with two levels, we have a *2^k factorial design*. Reducing a factor to two levels is a useful simplification that reduces the data requirements in a replicated experiment, because the data matrix will have fewer cells. Even a continuous factor (e.g., *Pressure*) can be "binarized" into roughly equal groups (*Low, High*) by cutting the data array at the median. The 2^k design is especially useful when the number of factors is very large. In automotive engineering, for example, it is not uncommon to study more than a dozen factors that are predictive of exhaust emissions. Even when each factor is limited to only two levels, full factorial 2^k experiments with replication can require substantial data-collection effort.

Fractional Factorial Designs

Unlike a full factorial design, a *fractional factorial* design, for reasons of economy, limits data collection to a subset of the possible factor combinations. Fractional factorial designs are extremely important in real-life situations where many factors exist. For example, suppose that automobile combustion engineers are investigating 10 factors, each with two levels, to determine their effect on emissions. This would yield $2^{10} = 1,024$ possible factor combinations. It would be impractical and uneconomical to gather data for all 1,024 factor combinations.

By excluding some factor combinations, a fractional factorial model necessarily sacrifices some of the interaction effects. If the most important objective is to study the *main effects* (which is frequently the case, or is at least an acceptable compromise), it is possible to get by with a much smaller number of observations. It often is possible to estimate some, though not all, interaction effects in a fractional factorial experiment. Templates are published to guide experimenters in choosing the correct design and sample size for the desired number of factors (see Related Reading). The American Supplier Institute sponsors training seminars on *robust engineering* utilizing *Taguchi designs* to make efficient use of data.

Nested or Hierarchical Design

If all levels of one factor are fully contained within another, the design is *nested* or *hierarchical*. Using most computer packages, nested designs can be represented using simple notation like

$$Defects = f(Experience, Method (Machine))$$

In this model, *Machine* is nested within *Method* so the effect of *Machine* cannot appear as a main effect. Presumably the nature of the manufacturing process dictates that *Machine* depends on *Method*. Although the model is easy to state, this example is not intended to suggest that estimates of nested models are easy to interpret.

Random Effects Models

In a *fixed-effects model* the levels of each factor are predetermined, which implies that our inferences are valid only for the specified factor levels. In a *random effects model* the factor levels are chosen randomly from a population of potential factor levels. Computation and interpretation of random effects are more complicated, and not all tests may be feasible. Novices are advised that estimation of random effects models should be preceded by further study (see Related Reading).

Chapter Summary

ANOVA tests whether a numerical dependent variable (**response variable**) is associated with one or more categorical independent variables (**factors**) with several **levels**. Each level or combination of levels is a treatment. A **one-factor ANOVA** compares means in c columns of data. It is a generalization of a two-tailed t test for two independent sample means. Fisher's **F statistic** is a ratio of two variances (treatment versus error). It is compared with a right-tailed critical value from an F table or from Excel for appropriate numerator and denominator degrees of freedom. Alternatively, we compare the p-value for the F test statistic with the desired level of significance (p less than α is significant). An **unreplicated two-factor ANOVA** can be viewed as a **randomized block model** if only one factor is of research interest. A **replicated two-factor ANOVA** (or full factorial model) has more than one observation per treatment, permitting inclusion of an interaction test in addition to tests for the **main effects. Interaction effects** can be seen as crossing lines on plots of factor means. The **Tukey test** compares individual treatment means. We test for homogeneous variances (an assumption of ANOVA) using **Hartley's F_{max} test** or **Levene's test.** The **general linear model** (GLM) can be used when there are more than two factors. **Experimental design** helps make efficient use of limited data. Other general advice:

- ANOVA may be helpful even if those who collected the data did not utilize a formal experimental design (often the case in real-world business situations).

- ANOVA calculations are tedious because of the sums required, so computers are generally used.

- One-factor ANOVA is the most common and suffices for many business situations.

- ANOVA is an overall test. To tell which specific pairs of treatment means differ, use the Tukey test.

- Although real-life data may not perfectly meet the normality and equal-variance assumptions, ANOVA is reasonably robust (and alternative tests do exist).

- Experimental design books usually can show you an example of exactly the design you need for parsimonious use of data. Call for expert advice when you are in doubt, to save a lot of rework.

Key Terms

analysis of variance (ANOVA), *439*	hierarchical design, *476*	partitioned sum of squares, *444*
balanced designs, *476*	homogeneous variances, *452*	randomized block model, *457*
experimental design, *476*	interaction, *441*	replication, *464*
explained variance, *439*	interaction effect, *464*	response variable, *439*
factors, *439*	interaction plots, *473*	treatment, *439*
fixed-effects model, *457*	Levene's test, *454*	Tukey's studentized range test, *450*
fractional factorial, *476*	main effects, *464*	
full factorial, *464*	mean squares, *444*	two-factor ANOVA without replication, *456*
general linear model, *474*	multiple comparison, *450*	
	nested design, *476*	unexplained variance, *439*
Hartley's F_{max} test, *452*	one-factor ANOVA, *442*	

Chapter Review

Note: Questions labeled * are based on optional material from this chapter.

1. Explain each term: (a) explained variation; (b) unexplained variation; (c) factor; (d) treatment.

2. (a) Explain the difference between one-factor and two-factor ANOVA. (b) Write the linear model form of one-factor ANOVA. (c) State the hypotheses for a one-factor ANOVA in two different ways. (d) Why is one-factor ANOVA used a lot?

3. (a) State three assumptions of ANOVA. (b) What do we mean when we say that ANOVA is fairly robust to violations of these assumptions?

4. (a) Sketch the format of a one-factor ANOVA data set (completely randomized model). (b) Must group sizes be the same for one-factor ANOVA? Is it better if they are? (c) Explain the concepts of variation *between treatments* and variation *within treatments*. (d) What is the F statistic? (e) State the degrees of freedom for the F test in one-factor ANOVA.

5. (a) Sketch the format of a two-factor ANOVA data set without replication. (b) State the hypotheses for a two-factor ANOVA without replication. (c) What is the difference between a randomized block model and a two-factor ANOVA without replication? (d) What do the two F statistics represent in a two-factor ANOVA without replication? (e) What are their degrees of freedom?

6. (a) Sketch the format of a two-factor ANOVA data set with replication. (b) What is gained by replication? (c) State the hypotheses for a two-factor ANOVA with replication. (d) What do the three F statistics represent in a two-factor ANOVA with replication? (e) What are their degrees of freedom?

7. (a) What is the purpose of the Tukey test? (b) Why can't we just compare all possible pairs of group means using the two-sample t test?

*8. (a) What does a test for homogeneity of variances tell us? (b) Why should we test for homogeneity of variances? (c) Explain what Hartley's F_{max} test measures. (d) Why might we use Levene's test instead of the F_{max} test?

*9. What is the general linear model and why is it useful?

*10. (a) What is a 2^k design, and what are its advantages? (b) What is a fractional factorial design, and what are its advantages? (c) What is a nested or hierarchical design? (d) How is a random effects model different than a fixed-effects model?

CHAPTER EXERCISES

Instructions: You may use Excel, MegaStat, MINITAB, or another computer package of your choice. Attach appropriate copies of the output or capture the screens, tables, and relevant graphs and include them in a written report. Try to state your conclusions succinctly in language that would be clear to a decision maker who is a nonstatistician. Exercises marked * are based on optional material. Answer the following questions, or those your instructor assigns.

a. Choose an appropriate ANOVA model. State the hypotheses to be tested.

b. Display the data visually (e.g., dot plots or MegaStat's line plots). What do the displays show?

c. Do the ANOVA calculations using the computer.

d. State the decision rule for $\alpha = .05$ and make the decision. Interpret the p-value.

e. In your judgment, are the observed differences in treatment means (if any) large enough to be of practical importance?

f. Do you think the sample size is sufficient? Explain. Could it be increased? Given the nature of the data, would more data collection be costly?

g. Perform Tukey multiple comparison tests and discuss the results.

*h. Perform a test for homogeneity of variances. Explain fully.

11.21 Below are grade point averages for 25 randomly chosen university business students during a recent semester. *Research question:* Are the mean grade point averages the same for students in these four class levels? **GPA2**

Grade Point Averages of 25 Business Students

Freshman (5 students)	Sophomore (7 students)	Junior (7 students)	Senior (6 students)
1.91	3.89	3.01	3.32
2.14	2.02	2.89	2.45
3.47	2.96	3.45	3.81
2.19	3.32	3.67	3.02
2.71	2.29	3.33	3.01
	2.82	2.98	3.17
	3.11	3.26	

11.22 The XYZ Corporation is interested in possible differences in days worked by salaried employees in three departments in the financial area. A survey of 23 randomly chosen employees reveals the data shown below. Because of the casual sampling methodology in this survey, the sample sizes are unequal. *Research question:* Are the mean annual attendance rates the same for employees in these three departments? **DaysWorked**

Days Worked Last Year by 23 Employees

Department	Days Worked									
Budgets (5 workers)	278	260	265	245	258					
Payables (10 workers)	205	270	220	240	255	217	266	239	240	228
Pricing (8 workers)	240	258	233	256	233	242	244	249		

11.23 Mean output of solar cells of three types are measured six times under random light intensity over a period of 5 minutes, yielding the results shown. *Research question:* Is the mean solar cell output the same for all cell types? **SolarWatts**

Solar Cell Output (watts)

Cell Type	Output (watts)					
A	123	121	123	124	125	127
B	125	122	122	121	122	126
C	126	128	125	129	131	128

11.24 In a bumper test, three types of autos were deliberately crashed into a barrier at 5 mph, and the resulting damage (in dollars) was estimated. Five test vehicles of each type were crashed, with the results shown below. *Research question:* Are the mean crash damages the same for these three vehicles?   **Crash1**

Crash Damage ($)

Goliath	Varmint	Weasel
1,600	1,290	1,090
760	1,400	2,100
880	1,390	1,830
1,950	1,850	1,250
1,220	950	1,920

11.25 The waiting time (in minutes) for emergency room patients with non-life-threatening injuries was measured at four hospitals for all patients who arrived between 6:00 and 6:30 PM on a certain Wednesday. The results are shown below. *Research question:* Are the mean waiting times the same for emergency patients in these four hospitals?   **ERWait**

Emergency Room Waiting Time (minutes)

Hospital A (5 patients)	Hospital B (4 patients)	Hospital C (7 patients)	Hospital D (6 patients)
10	8	5	0
19	25	11	20
5	17	24	9
26	36	16	5
11		18	10
		29	12
		15	

11.26 The results shown below are mean productivity measurements (average number of assemblies completed per hour) for a random sample of workers at each of three plants. *Research question:* Are the mean hourly productivity levels the same for workers in these three plants?   **Productivity**

Hourly Productivity of Assemblers in Plants

Plant	Finished Units Produced Per Hour									
A (9 workers)	3.6	5.1	2.8	4.6	4.7	4.1	3.4	2.9	4.5	
B (6 workers)	2.7	3.1	5.0	1.9	2.2	3.2				
C (10 workers)	6.8	2.5	5.4	6.7	4.6	3.9	5.4	4.9	7.1	8.4

11.27 Below are results of braking tests of the Ford Explorer on glare ice, packed snow, and split traction (one set of wheels on ice, the other on dry pavement), using three braking methods. *Research questions:* Is the mean stopping distance affected by braking method and/or by surface type?   **Brake2**

Stopping Distance from 40 mph to 0 mph

Method	Ice	Split Traction	Packed Snow
Pumping	441	223	149
Locked	455	148	146
ABS	460	183	167

Source: *Popular Science* 252, no. 6 (June 1998), p. 78.

11.28 As an independent project, students went to grocery stores and noted the fat grams per serving of various types of bread (from the product label). This was a convenience sample. Manufacturers with only one product are omitted. *Research question:* Are there differences in the mean fat content (fat per gram) among these seven manufacturers? **BreadFat**

Fat Content of Various Bread Products

Manufacturer	Product Name	Serving Size (grams)	Fat Grams Per Serving	Fat Grams Per Gram
Aunt Millie's	ButterMilk—White	34	1	0.0294
Aunt Millie's	Split Top—White	28	1	0.0357
Brownberry	Natural Wheat	36	1	0.0278
Brownberry	Soft Wheat	32	2	0.0625
Brownberry	Whole Wheat	38	1	0.0263
Brownberry	Country Wheat	38	1.5	0.0395
Brownberry	White	38	1	0.0263
Compass Food	America's Choice Light Wheat	21.5	0.5	0.0233
Compass Food	America's Choice Split Top	28	1	0.0357
Interstate Brand Co.	Home Pride Butter Top Wheat	28	1	0.0357
Interstate Brand Co.	Wonder Whole Wheat	34	1.5	0.0441
Interstate Brand Co.	Wonder White	26	1	0.0385
Koepplinger's Bakery	Natural Wheat	38	0	0.0000
Koepplinger's Bakery	Whole Wheat	23	0.5	0.0217
Koepplinger's Bakery	White	26	1	0.0385
Metz Baking Co.	Taystee Wheat	22.5	0.75	0.0333
Metz Baking Co.	Roman Meal Whole Wheat	32	1	0.0313
Metz Baking Co.	Taystee White	26	1	0.0385
Pepperidge Farm	Whole Wheat A	25	1	0.0400
Pepperidge Farm	Light Wheat	19	1	0.0526
Pepperidge Farm	Whole Wheat B	34	1	0.0294
Pepperidge Farm	Pepperidge Farm	32	1.5	0.0469

Source: Class project by statistics students Madonna Klippstein, Nancy Kadarman, Katrina Gagnon, and Bryce Clark.

Note: Data are for educational use and should not be viewed as a guide to current products.

11.29 Is a state's income related to its high school dropout rate? *Research question:* Do the high school dropout rates differ among the five income quintiles? **Dropout**

State High School Dropout Rates by Income Groups

Lowest Income Quintile		2nd Income Quintile		3rd Income Quintile		4th Income Quintile		Highest Income Quintile	
State	Dropout %	State	Dropout %	State	Dropout %	State	Dropout %	State	Dropout %
Mississippi	40.0	Kentucky	34.3	N. Carolina	39.5	Oregon	26.0	Minnesota	15.3
W. Virginia	24.2	S. Carolina	44.5	Wyoming	23.3	Ohio	30.5	Illinois	24.6
New Mexico	39.8	N. Dakota	15.5	Missouri	27.6	Pennsylvania	25.1	California	31.7
Arkansas	27.3	Arizona	39.2	Kansas	25.5	Michigan	27.2	Colorado	28.0
Montana	21.5	Maine	24.4	Nebraska	12.1	Rhode Island	31.3	N. Hampshire	27.0
Louisiana	43.0	S. Dakota	28.1	Texas	39.4	Alaska	33.2	Maryland	27.4
Alabama	39.0	Tennessee	40.1	Georgia	44.2	Nevada	26.3	New York	39.0
Oklahoma	26.9	Iowa	16.8	Florida	42.2	Virginia	25.7	New Jersey	20.4
Utah	16.3	Vermont	19.5	Hawaii	36.0	Delaware	35.9	Massachusetts	25.0
Idaho	22.0	Indiana	28.8	Wisconsin	21.9	Washington	25.9	Connecticut	28.2

Source: *Statistical Abstract of the United States, 2002.*

11.30 In a bumper test, three test vehicles of each of three types of autos were crashed into a barrier at 5 mph, and the resulting damage was estimated. Crashes were from three angles: head-on, slanted, and rear-end. The results are shown on page 482. *Research questions:* Is the mean repair cost affected by crash type and/or vehicle type? Are the observed effects (if any) large enough to be of practical importance (as opposed to statistical significance)? **Crash2**

5 mph Collision Damage ($)

Crash Type	Goliath	Varmint	Weasel
Head-On	700	1,700	2,280
	1,400	1,650	1,670
	850	1,630	1,740
Slant	1,430	1,850	2,000
	1,740	1,700	1,510
	1,240	1,650	2,480
Rear-end	700	860	1,650
	1,250	1,550	1,650
	970	1,250	1,240

11.31 Repeat exercise 11.30 using 6 crashes (not 3) of each type of vehicle and crash angle, as shown below. This is an exact "doubling" of the data set. What effect does doubling the sample size have on your test statistics and conclusions, *ceteris paribus?* Explain fully. **Crash3**

5 mph Collision Damage ($)

Crash Type	Goliath	Varmint	Weasel
Head-On	700	1,700	2,280
	1,400	1,650	1,670
	850	1,630	1,740
	700	1,700	2,280
	1,400	1,650	1,670
	850	1,630	1,740
Slant	1,430	1,850	2,000
	1,740	1,700	1,510
	1,240	1,650	2,480
	1,430	1,850	2,000
	1,740	1,700	1,510
	1,240	1,650	2,480
Rear-end	700	860	1,650
	1,250	1,550	1,650
	970	1,250	1,240
	700	860	1,650
	1,250	1,550	1,650
	970	1,250	1,240

11.32 Three samples of each of three types of PVC pipe of equal wall thickness are tested to failure under three temperature conditions, yielding the results shown below. *Research questions:* Is mean burst strength affected by temperature and/or by pipe type? Is there a "best" brand of PVC pipe? Explain. **PVCPipe**

Burst Strength of PVC Pipes (psi)

Temperature	PVC1	PVC2	PVC3
Hot (70° C)	250	301	235
	273	285	260
	281	275	279
Warm (40° C)	321	342	302
	322	322	315
	299	339	301
Cool (10° C)	358	375	328
	363	355	336
	341	354	342

11.33 The percent of tax returns audited by income taxpayer class is shown below for 6 years. *Research question:* Is the mean tax audit rate affected by taxpayer class and/or by year?   🐛 **Audits**

IRS Audit Rates by Taxpayer Class

Taxpayer Class	1990	1991	1992	1993	1994	1995
1040A TPI	0.55	0.94	0.78	0.74	1.04	1.96
1040 TPI < $25,000	0.91	1.03	0.92	0.66	0.88	1.30
1040 TPI $25,000–49,999	0.97	0.77	0.70	0.58	0.53	0.90
1040 TPI $50,000–100,000	1.38	1.24	1.10	0.88	0.72	1.05
1040 TPI > $100,000	5.55	5.64	5.28	4.03	2.94	2.79
C-GR < $25,000	1.84	1.91	1.89	2.24	4.39	5.85
C-GR $25,000–100,000	2.35	2.22	2.28	2.41	3.01	3.08
C-GR > $100,000	3.84	3.92	4.17	3.91	3.57	3.47
F-GR < $100,000	1.67	1.53	1.28	1.06	1.16	1.23
F-GR > $100,000	3.09	3.98	2.40	2.06	1.74	2.51

Source: H. Cecil Wayne, "The Real Audit Rates for Individual Taxpayers," 75 *Tax Notes* 831, May 12, 1997.

11.34 To check pain-relieving medications for potential side effects on blood pressure, it is decided to give equal doses of each of four medications to test subjects. To control for the potential effect of weight, subjects are classified by weight groups. Subjects are approximately the same age and are in general good health. Two subjects in each category are chosen at random from a large group of male prison volunteers. Subjects' blood pressures 15 minutes after the dose are shown below. *Research question:* Is mean blood pressure affected by body weight and/or by medication type?   🐛 **Systolic**

Systolic Blood Pressure of Subjects (mmHg)

Percent of Normal Weight	Medication M1	Medication M2	Medication M3	Medication M4
Under 1.1	131	146	140	130
	135	136	132	125
1.1 to 1.3	136	138	134	131
	145	145	147	133
1.3 to 1.5	145	149	146	139
	152	157	151	141

11.35 To assess the effects of instructor and student gender on student course scores, an experiment was conducted in 11 sections of managerial accounting classes ranging in size from 25 to 66 students. The factors were instructor gender (M, F) and student gender (M, F). There were 11 instructors (7 male, 4 female). Steps were taken to eliminate subjectivity in grading, such as common exams and sharing exam grading responsibility among all instructors so no one instructor could influence exam grades unduly. (a) What type of ANOVA is this? (b) What conclusions can you draw? (c) Discuss sample size and raise any questions you think may be important.

Analysis of Variance for Students' Course Scores

Source of Variation	Sum of Squares	Degrees of Freedom	Mean Square	F Ratio	p-Value
Instructor gender (I)	97.84	1	97.84	0.61	0.43
Student gender (S)	218.23	1	218.23	1.37	0.24
Interaction ($I \times S$)	743.84	1	743.84	4.66	0.03
Error	63,358.90	397	159.59		
Total	64,418.81	400			

Source: Marlys Gascho Lipe, "Further Evidence on the Performance of Female Versus Male Accounting Students," *Issues in Accounting Education* 4, no. 1 (Spring 1989), pp. 144–50.

11.36 In a market research study, members of a consumer test panel are asked to rate the visual appeal (on a 1 to 10 scale) of the texture of dashboard plastic trim in a mockup of a new fuel cell car. The manufacturer is testing four finish textures. Panelists are assigned randomly to evaluate each texture. The test results are shown below. Each cell shows the average rating by panelists who evaluated each texture. *Research question:* Is mean rating affected by age group and/or by surface type? **Texture**

Mean Ratings of Dashboard Surface Texture

Age Group	Shiny	Satin	Pebbled	Pattern
Youth (under 21)	6.7	6.6	5.5	4.3
Adult (21 to 39)	5.5	5.3	6.2	5.9
Middle-Age (40 to 61)	4.5	5.1	6.7	5.5
Senior (62 and over)	3.9	4.5	6.1	4.1

11.37 In a call center, the average waiting time for an answer (in seconds) is shown below by time of day. *Research question:* Is mean waiting time affected by time of day and/or by day of the week? **CallWait**

Average Waiting Time for Answer (seconds)

Time	Mon	Tue	Wed	Thu	Fri
06:00	34	71	33	39	39
06:30	52	70	88	53	49
07:00	36	103	47	32	91
07:30	52	97	55	101	37
08:00	46	76	67	74	66
08:30	60	96	46	51	73
09:00	83	34	42	51	79
09:30	32	117	71	57	27
10:00	88	60	54	37	61
10:30	62	152	121	59	47
11:00	45	34	37	79	33
11:30	34	42	28	38	30
12:00	91	37	62	110	51
12:30	42	37	77	63	46
13:00	71	42	49	40	33
13:30	39	125	28	99	57
14:00	132	73	108	81	40
14:30	34	35	38	43	40
15:00	36	34	34	36	36
15:30	34	61	41	46	34
16:00	25	37	52	0	30
16:30	33	26	33	9	36
17:00	27	29	34	38	35
17:30	28	31	27	22	26
18:00	35	14	115	26	22
18:30	25	34	9	5	47

11.38 Several friends go bowling several times per month. They keep track of their scores over several months. An ANOVA was performed. (a) What kind of ANOVA is this (one-factor, two-factor, etc.)? (b) How many friends were there? How many months were observed? How many observations per bowler per month? Explain how you know. (c) What are your conclusions about bowling scores? Explain, referring either to the *F* tests or *p*-values.

ANOVA

Source of Variation	SS	df	MS	F	p-value	F crit
Month	1702.389	2	851.194	11.9793	0.0002	3.4028
Bowler	4674.000	3	1558.000	21.9265	0.0000	3.0088
Interaction	937.167	6	156.194	2.1982	0.0786	2.5082
Within	1705.333	24	71.056			
Total	9018.889	35				

11.39 Air pollution (micrograms of particulate per ml of air) was measured along four freeways at each of five different times of day, with the results shown below. (a) What kind of ANOVA is this (one-factor, two-factor, etc.)? (b) What is your conclusion about air pollution? Explain, referring either to the F tests or p-values. (c) Do you think the variances can be assumed equal? Explain your reasoning. Why does it matter? *(d) Perform an F_{max} test to test for unequal variances.

SUMMARY	Count	Sum	Average	Variance
Chrysler	5	1584	316.8	14333.7
Davidson	5	1047	209.4	3908.8
Reuther	5	714	142.8	2926.7
Lodge	5	1514	302.8	11947.2
12:00A-6:00A	4	505	126.25	872.9
6:00A-10:00A	4	1065	266.25	11060.3
10:00A-3:00P	4	959	239.75	5080.3
3:00P-7:00P	4	1451	362.75	14333.6
7:00P-12:00A	4	879	219.75	7710.9

ANOVA

Source of Variation	SS	df	MS	F	p-value	F crit
Freeway	100957.4	3	33652.45	24.903	0.000	3.490
Time of Day	116249.2	4	29062.3	21.506	0.000	3.259
Error	16216.4	12	1351.367			
Total	233423	19				

11.40 A company has several suppliers of office supplies. It receives several shipments each quarter from each supplier. The time (days) between order and delivery was recorded for several randomly chosen shipments from each supplier in each quarter, and an ANOVA was performed. (a) What kind of ANOVA is this (one-factor, two-factor, etc.)? (b) How many suppliers were there? How many quarters? How many observations per supplier per quarter? Explain how you know. (c) What are your conclusions about shipment time? Explain, referring either to the F tests or p-values.

ANOVA

Source of Variation	SS	df	MS	F	p-value	F crit
Quarter	148.04	3	49.34667	6.0326	0.0009	2.7188
Supplier	410.14	4	102.535	12.5348	0.0000	2.4859
Interaction	247.06	12	20.5883	2.5169	0.0073	1.8753
Within	654.40	80	8.180			
Total	1459.64	99				

11.41 Several friends go bowling several times per month. They keep track of their scores over several months. An ANOVA was performed. (a) What kind of ANOVA is this (one-factor, two-factor, etc.)? (b) How could you tell how many friends there were in the sample just from the ANOVA table? Explain. (c) What are your conclusions about bowling scores? Explain, referring either to the F test or p-value. (d) Do you think the variances can be assumed equal? Explain your reasoning.

SUMMARY

Bowler	Count	Sum	Average	Variance
Mary	15	1856	123.733	77.067
Bill	14	1599	114.214	200.797
Sally	12	1763	146.917	160.083
Robert	15	2211	147.400	83.686
Tom	11	1267	115.182	90.164

ANOVA

Source of Variation	SS	df	MS	F	p-value	F crit
Between Groups	14465.63	4	3616.408	29.8025	0.0000	2.5201
Within Groups	7523.444	62	121.3459			
Total	21989.07	66				

11.42 Are large companies more profitable *per dollar of assets?* The largest 500 companies in the world in 2000 were ranked according to their number of employees, with groups defined as follows: Small = Under 25,000 employees, Medium = 25,000 to 49,999 employees, Large = 50,000 to 99,000 employees, Huge = 100,000 employees or more. An ANOVA was performed using the company's profit-to-assets ratio (percent) as the dependent variable. (a) What kind of ANOVA is this (one-factor, two-factor, etc.)? (b) What is your conclusion about the research question? Explain, referring either to the F test or p-value. (c) What can you learn from the plots that compare the groups? (d) Do you think the variances can be assumed equal? Explain your reasoning. *(e) Perform an F_{max} test to test for unequal variances. (f) Which groups of companies have significantly different means? Explain.

Mean	n	Std. Dev	
1.054	119	2.8475	Small
3.058	113	4.8265	Medium
3.855	147	5.8610	Large
3.843	120	4.3125	Huge
3.004	499	4.7925	Total

ANOVA table

Source	SS	df	MS	F	p-value
Treatment	643.9030	3	214.63433	9.84	2.58E-06
Error	10,794.2720	495	21.80661		
Total	11,438.1750	498			

Post hoc analysis

Tukey simultaneous comparison t-values (d.f. = 495)

		Small	Medium	Huge	Large
		1.054	3.058	3.843	3.855
Small	1.054				
Medium	3.058	3.27			
Huge	3.843	4.62	1.28		
Large	3.855	4.86	1.37	0.02	

critical values for experimentwise error rate:

0.05	2.60
0.01	3.18

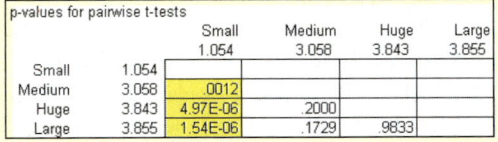

p-values for pairwise t-tests

		Small 1.054	Medium 3.058	Huge 3.843	Large 3.855
Small	1.054				
Medium	3.058	.0012			
Huge	3.843	4.97E-06	.2000		
Large	3.855	1.54E-06	.1729	.9833	

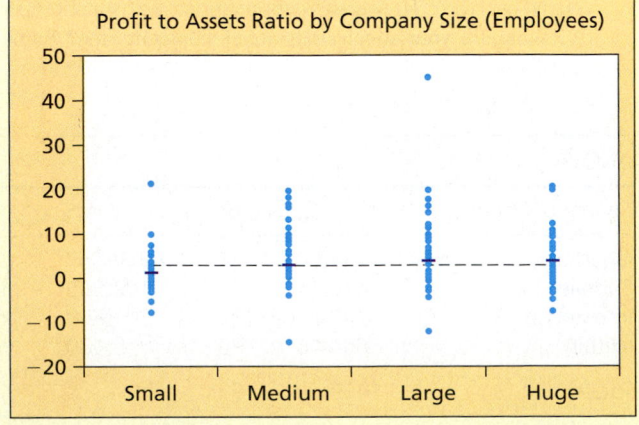

Profit to Assets Ratio by Company Size (Employees)

Box, George E.; J. Stuart Hunter; and William G. Hunter. *Statistics for Experimenters.* 2nd ed. John Wiley & Sons, 2005.

Hilbe, Joseph M. "Generalized Linear Models." *The American Statistician* 48, no. 3 (August 1994), pp. 255–65.

Miller, Rupert G. *Simultaneous Statistical Inference.* 2nd ed. Springer-Verlag, 1981.

Montgomery, Douglas C. *Design and Analysis of Experiments.* 5th ed. John Wiley & Sons, 2000.

Nachtsheim, Christopher; Michael H. Kutner; and John Neter. *Applied Linear Statistical Models.* 5th ed. McGraw-Hill, 2005.

Related Reading

LearningStats Unit 11   Analysis of Variance   LS

LearningStats Unit 11 gives examples of the three most common ANOVA tests (one-factor, two-factor, full factorial), including a simulation and tables of critical values. Your instructor may assign specific modules, or you may pursue those that sound interesting.

Topic	LearningStats Modules
Overview	Overview of ANOVA ANOVA Illustrations
Format and Excel examples	Examples: ANOVA Tests Stacked versus Unstacked Data
Simulation	One-Factor ANOVA ANOVA Data Set Generator
Case studies	One Factor: Car Braking and Noise Two Factors: Car Braking and Noise Two-Factor Replicated: ATM Data Student Project: Call Center Times One Factor: Drug Prices (details) Two Factors: Car Noise (details) Two-Factor Replicated: Braking (details)
General linear model	Insurance Claims Case Study
Tables	Appendix F—Critical Values of *F*

Key: = PowerPoint   = Word   = Excel

Visual Statistics   VS

Visual Statistics Modules on Analysis of Variance

Module	Module Name
12	VS Visualizing Analysis of Variance

Visual Statistics Module 12 (included on your CD) is designed to help you

- Become familiar with situations in which one-factor ANOVA is applicable.
- Understand how much difference must exist between groups to be detected using an *F* test.
- Appreciate the role of sample size in determining power.
- Know the ANOVA assumptions and the effects of violating them.

The worktext (included on the CD in .PDF format) contains lists of concepts covered, objectives of the modules, overviews of concepts, illustrations of concepts, orientations to module features, learning exercises (basic, intermediate, advanced), learning projects (individual, team), self-evaluation quizzes, glossaries of terms, and solutions to self-evaluation quizzes.

Bivariate Regression

Chapter Contents

Chapter Learning Objectives

When you finish this chapter you should be able to

- Calculate and test a correlation coefficient for significance.

- Explain the OLS method and use the formulas for the slope and intercept.

- Fit a simple regression on an Excel scatter plot.

- Perform regression by using Excel and another package such as MegaStat.

- Interpret confidence intervals for regression coefficients.

- Test hypotheses about the slope and intercept by using *t* tests.

- Find and interpret the coefficient of determination R^2 and standard error s_{yx}.

- Interpret the ANOVA table and use the *F* test for a regression.

- Distinguish between confidence and prediction intervals.

- Identify unusual residuals and high-leverage observations.

- Test the residuals for non-normality, heteroscedasticity, and autocorrelation.

- Explain the role of data conditioning and data transformations.

Up to this point, our study of the discipline of statistical analysis has primarily focused on learning how to describe and make inferences about single variables. It is now time to learn how to describe and summarize relationships *between* variables. Businesses of all types can be quite complex. Understanding how different variables in our business processes are related to each other helps us predict and, hopefully, improve our business performance.

Examples of quantitative variables that might be related to each other include: spending on advertising and sales revenue, produce delivery time and percentage of spoiled produce, diesel fuel prices and unleaded gas prices, preventive maintenance spending and manufacturing productivity rates. It may be that with some of these pairs there is one variable that we would like to be able to *predict* such as sales revenue, percentage of spoiled produce, and productivity rates. But first we must learn how to *visualize, describe,* and *quantify* the relationships between variables such as these.

Chapter 14

Visual Displays

Analysis of **bivariate data** (i.e., two variables) typically begins with a **scatter plot** that displays each observed data pair (x_i, y_i) as a dot on an *X-Y* grid. This diagram provides a visual indication of the strength of the relationship or association between the two variables. This simple display requires no assumptions or computation. A scatter plot is typically the precursor to more complex analytical techniques. Figure 12.1 shows a scatter plot comparing the price per gallon of diesel fuel to the price per gallon of regular unleaded gasoline.

We look at scatter plots to get an initial idea of the relationship between two variables. Is there an evident pattern to the data? Is the pattern linear or nonlinear? Are there data points that are not part of the overall pattern? We would characterize the fuel price relationship as linear (although not perfectly linear) and positive (as diesel prices increase, so do regular unleaded prices). We see one pair of values set slightly apart from the rest, above and to the right. This happens to be the state of Hawaii.

FIGURE 12.1

Fuel prices
🐝 **FuelPrices**

Source: AAA Fuel Gauge Report,
May 20, 2005,
www.fuelgaugereport.com.

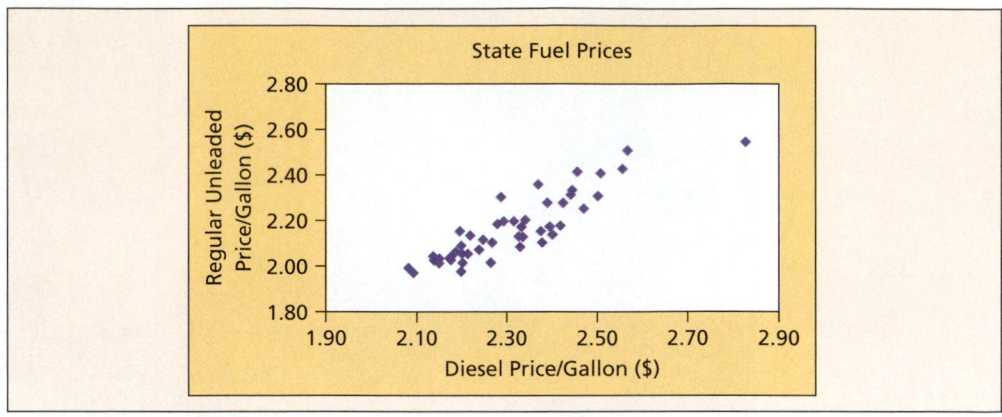

Correlation Coefficient

A visual display is a good first step in analysis but we would also like to quantify the strength of the association between two variables. Therefore, accompanying the scatter plot is the *sample correlation coefficient.* This statistic measures the degree of linearity in the relationship between X and Y and is denoted r. Its range is $-1 \leq r \leq +1$. When r is near 0 there is little or no linear relationship between X and Y. An r-value near $+1$ indicates a strong positive relationship, while an r-value near -1 indicates a strong negative relationship.

$$(12.1) \qquad r = \frac{\sum_{i=1}^{n}(x_i - \bar{x})(y_i - \bar{y})}{\sqrt{\sum_{i=1}^{n}(x_i - \bar{x})^2}\sqrt{\sum_{i=1}^{n}(y_i - \bar{y})^2}} \qquad \text{(sample correlation coefficient)}$$

To simplify the notation here and elsewhere in this chapter, we define three terms called *sums of squares:*

$$(12.2) \quad SS_{xx} = \sum_{i=1}^{n}(x_i - \bar{x})^2 \qquad SS_{yy} = \sum_{i=1}^{n}(y_i - \bar{y})^2 \qquad SS_{xy} = \sum_{i=1}^{n}(x_i - \bar{x})(y_i - \bar{y})$$

Using this notation, the formula for the sample correlation coefficient can be written

$$(12.3) \qquad r = \frac{SS_{xy}}{\sqrt{SS_{xx}}\sqrt{SS_{yy}}} \qquad \text{(sample correlation coefficient)}$$

Excel Tip

To calculate a sample correlation coefficient, use Excel's function =CORREL(array1,array2) where array1 is the range for X and array2 is the range for Y. Data may be in rows or columns. Arrays must be the same length.

The correlation coefficient for the variables shown in Figure 12.1 is $r = 0.89$, which is not surprising. We would expect to see a strong linear positive relationship between state diesel fuel prices and regular unleaded gasoline prices. Figures 12.2 through 12.7 show additional prototype scatter plots. We see that a correlation of .500 implies a great deal of random variation, and even a correlation of .900 is far from "perfect" linearity.

Tests for Significance

The sample correlation coefficient r is an estimate of the *population correlation coefficient* ρ (the Greek letter *rho*). There is no flat rule for a "high" correlation because sample size must

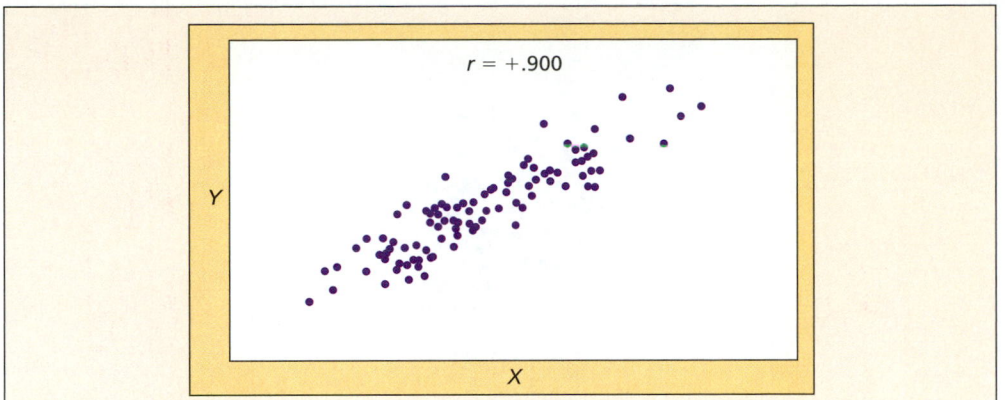

FIGURE 12.2

Strong positive correlation

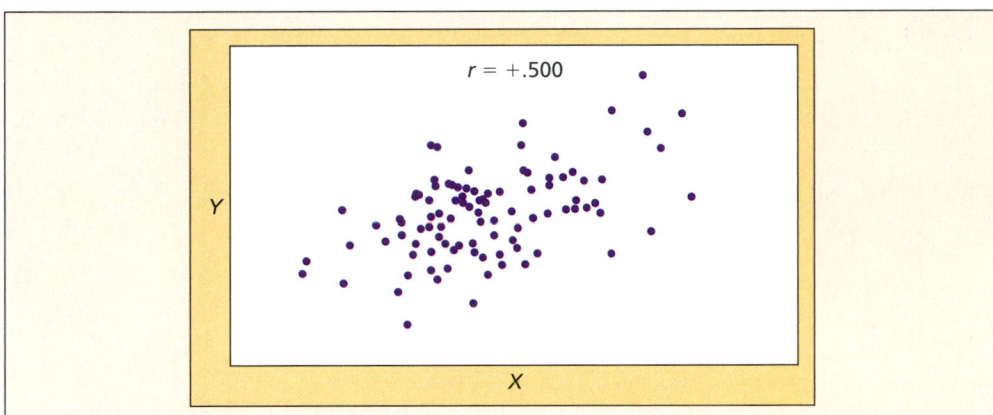

FIGURE 12.3

Weak positive correlation

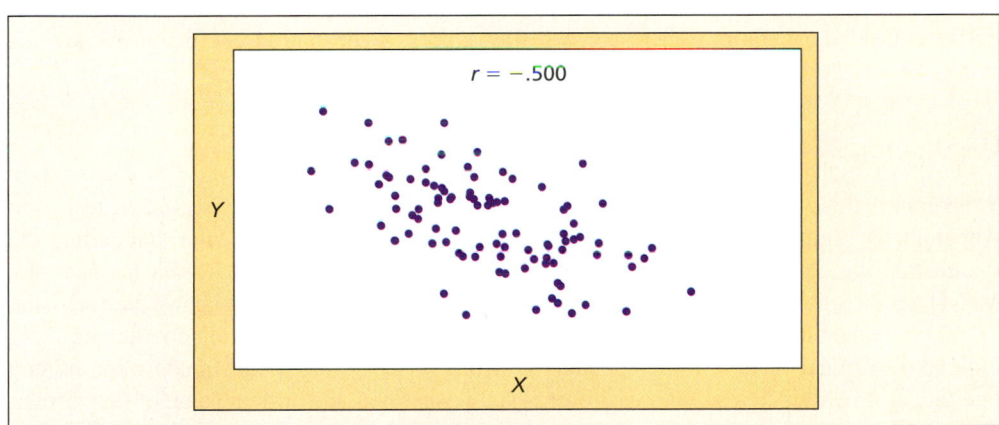

FIGURE 12.4

Weak negative correlation

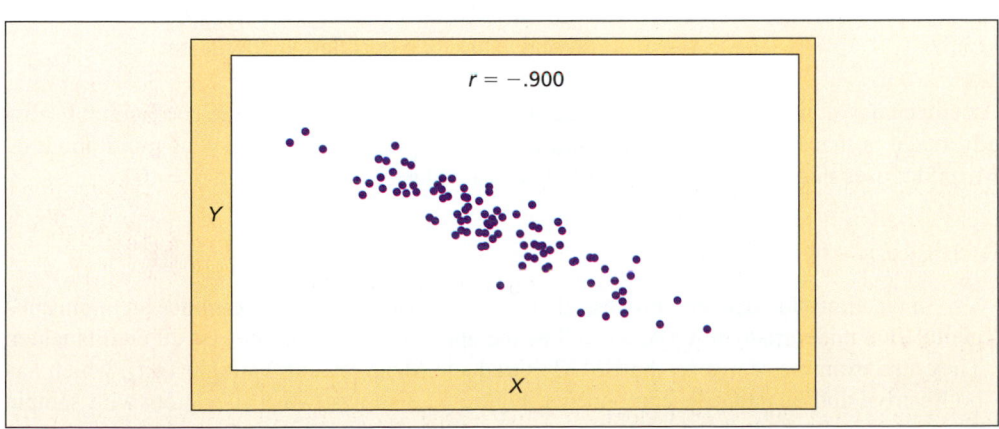

FIGURE 12.5

Strong negative correlation

FIGURE 12.6

No correlation (random)

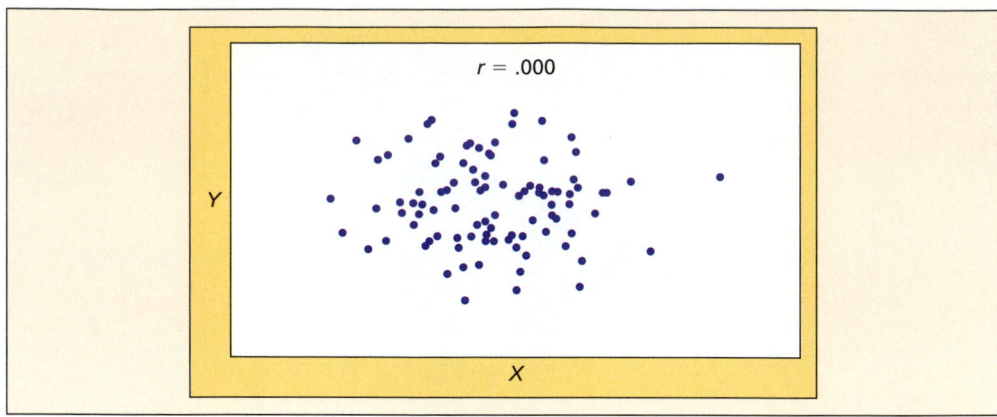

FIGURE 12.7

Nonlinear relationship

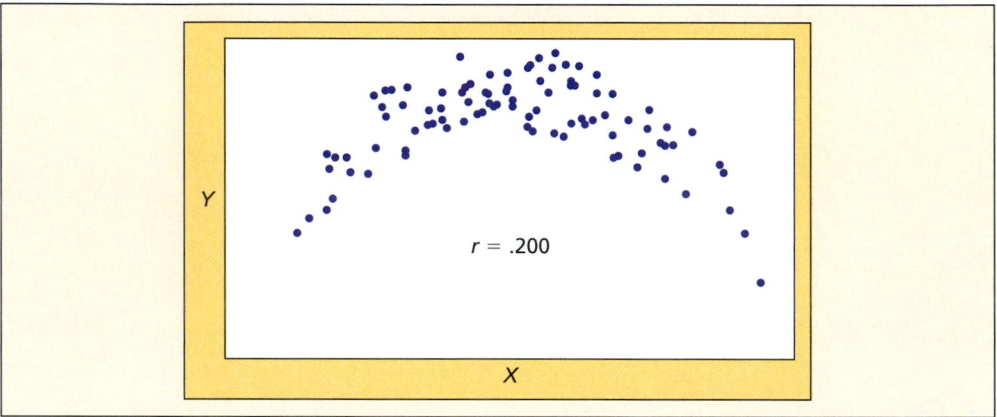

be taken into consideration. There are two ways to test a correlation coefficient for significance. To test the hypothesis H_0: $\rho = 0$, the test statistic is

$$\text{(12.4)} \qquad t = r\sqrt{\frac{n-2}{1-r^2}} \qquad \text{(test for zero correlation)}$$

We compare this t test statistic with a critical value t_α for a one-tailed or two-tailed test from Appendix D using $\nu = n - 2$ degrees of freedom and any desired α. After calculating the **t statistic,** we can find its p-value by using Excel's function =TDIST(t,deg_freedom,tails). MINITAB directly calculates the p-value for a two-tailed test without displaying the t statistic.

An equivalent approach is to calculate a critical value for the correlation coefficient. First, look up the critical value t_α from Appendix D with $\nu = n - 2$ degrees of freedom for either a one-tailed or two-tailed test, with whatever α you wish. Then, the critical value of the correlation coefficient is

$$\text{(12.5)} \qquad r_\alpha = \frac{t_\alpha}{\sqrt{t_\alpha^2 + n - 2}} \qquad \text{(critical value for a correlation coefficient)}$$

An advantage of this method is that you get a benchmark for the correlation coefficient. Its disadvantage is that there is no p-value and it is inflexible if you change your mind about α. MegaStat uses this method, giving two-tail critical values for $\alpha = .05$ and $\alpha = .01$.

EXAMPLE

MBA Applicants

MBA

In its admission decision process, a university's MBA program examines an applicant's cumulative undergraduate GPA, as well as the applicant's GPA in the last 60 credits taken. They also examine scores on the GMAT (Graduate Management Aptitude Test), which has both verbal and quantitative components. Figure 12.8 shows two scatter plots with sample correlation coefficients for 30 MBA applicants randomly chosen from 1,961 MBA applicant records at a public university in the Midwest. Is the correlation ($r = .8296$) between cumulative and last 60 credit GPA statistically significant? Is the correlation ($r = .4356$) between verbal and quantitative GMAT scores statistically significant?

FIGURE 12.8

Scatter plots for 30 MBA applicants   **MBA**

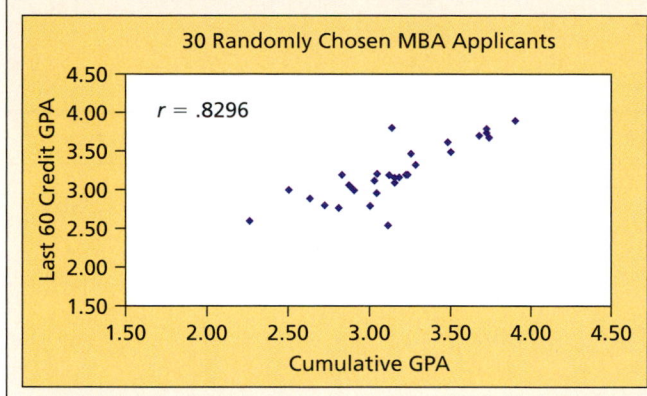
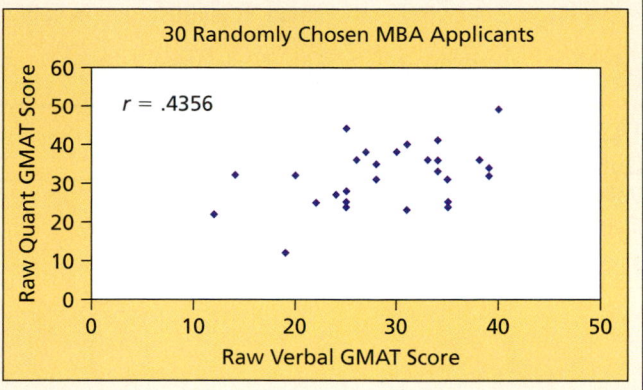

Step 1: State the Hypotheses

We will use a two-tailed test for significance at $\alpha = .05$. The hypotheses are

$H_0: \rho = 0$

$H_1: \rho \neq 0$

Step 2: Calculate the Critical Value

For a two-tailed test using $\nu = n - 2 = 30 - 2 = 28$ degrees of freedom, Appendix D gives $t_{.05} = 2.048$. The critical value of r is

$$r_{.05} = \frac{t_{.05}}{\sqrt{t_{.05}^2 + n - 2}} = \frac{2.048}{\sqrt{2.048^2 + 30 - 2}} = .3609$$

Step 3: Make the Decision

Both sample correlation coefficients ($r = .8296$ and $r = .4356$) exceed the critical value, so we reject the hypothesis of zero correlation in both cases. However, in the case of verbal and quantitative GMAT scores, the rejection is not very compelling. If we were using the t statistic method, we would calculate two test statistics. For GPA,

$$t = r\sqrt{\frac{n-2}{1-r^2}} = .8296\sqrt{\frac{30-2}{1-(.8296)^2}}$$

$$= 7.862 \qquad \text{(reject } \rho = 0 \text{ since } t = 7.862 > t_\alpha = 2.048\text{)}$$

and for GMAT score,

$$t = r\sqrt{\frac{n-2}{1-r^2}} = .4356\sqrt{\frac{30-2}{1-(.4356)^2}}$$

$$= 2.561 \qquad \text{(reject } \rho = 0 \text{ since } t = 2.561 > t_\alpha = 2.048\text{)}$$

This method has the advantage that a p-value can then be calculated by using Excel's function =TDIST(t,deg_freedom,tails). For example, for the two-tailed p-value for GPA, =TDIST(7.862,28,2) = .0000 (reject $\rho = 0$ since $p < .05$) and for the two-tailed p-value for GMAT score, =TDIST(2.561,28,2) = .0161 (reject $\rho = 0$ since $p < .05$).

Quick Rule for Significance

When the t table is unavailable, a quick test for significance of a correlation at $\alpha = .05$ is

(12.6) $|r| > 2/\sqrt{n}$ (quick 5% rule for significance)

This quick rule is derived from formula 12.5 by inserting 2 in place of t_α. It is based on the fact that two-tail t-values for $\alpha = .05$ usually are not far from 2, as you can verify from Appendix D. This quick rule is exact for $\nu = 60$ and works reasonably well as long as n is not too small. It is illustrated in Table 12.1.

TABLE 12.1

Quick 5 Percent Critical Value for Correlation Coefficients

Sample Size	Quick Rule	Quick $r_{.05}$	Actual $r_{.05}$
$n = 25$	$|r| > \dfrac{2}{\sqrt{25}}$	.400	.396
$n = 50$	$|r| > \dfrac{2}{\sqrt{50}}$	.283	.279
$n = 100$	$|r| > \dfrac{2}{\sqrt{100}}$	.200	.197
$n = 200$	$|r| > \dfrac{2}{\sqrt{200}}$	.141	.139

Role of Sample Size

Table 12.1 shows that, as sample size increases, the critical value of r becomes smaller. Thus, in very large samples, even very small correlations could be "significant." In a larger sample, smaller values of the sample correlation coefficient can be considered "significant." While a larger sample does give a better estimate of the true value of ρ, a larger sample does *not* mean that the correlation is stronger nor does its increased *significance* imply increased *importance*.

Using Excel

A correlation matrix can be created by using Excel's Tools > Data Analysis > Correlation, as illustrated in Figure 12.9. This correlation matrix is for our sample of 30 MBA students.

FIGURE 12.9

Excel's correlation matrix   **MBA**

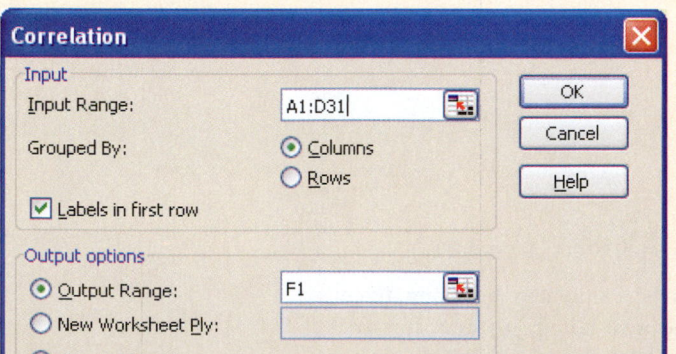

	CumGPA	60GPA	RawVerb	RawQuant
CumGPA	1.000			
60GPA	0.830	1.000		
RawVerb	0.068	0.031	1.000	
RawQuant	0.027	-0.171	0.436	1.000

Tip

In large samples, small correlations may be significant, even though the scatter plot shows little evidence of linearity. Thus, a *significant* correlation may lack practical *importance*.

EXAMPLE

Cross-Sectional State Data **States**

Eight cross-sectional variables were selected from the *LearningStats* state database (50 states):

Burglary	Burglary rate per 100,000 population
Age65%	Percent of population aged 65 and over
Income	Personal income per capita in current dollars
Unem	Unemployment rate, civilian labor force
SATQ	Average SAT quantitative test score
Cancer	Death rate per 100,000 population due to cancer
Unmar	Percent of total births by unmarried women
Urban%	Percent of population living in urban areas

For $n = 50$ states we have $v = n - 2 = 50 - 2 = 48$ degrees of freedom. From Appendix D the two-tail critical values for Student's t are $t_{.05} = 2.011$ and $t_{.01} = 2.682$ so critical values for r are as follows:

For $\alpha = .05$,

$$r_{.05} = \frac{t_{.05}}{\sqrt{t_{.05}^2 + n - 2}} = \frac{2.011}{\sqrt{(2.011)^2 + 50 - 2}} = .279$$

and for $\alpha = .01$,

$$r_{.01} = \frac{t_{.01}}{\sqrt{t_{.01}^2 + n - 2}} = \frac{2.682}{\sqrt{(2.682)^2 + 50 - 2}} = .361$$

Figure 12.10 shows a correlation matrix for these eight cross-sectional variables. The critical values are shown and significant correlations are highlighted. Four are significant at $\alpha = .01$ and seven more at $\alpha = .05$. In a two-tailed test, the sign of the correlation is of no interest, but the sign does reveal the direction of the association. For example, there is a strong positive correlation between *Cancer* and *Age65%*, and between *Urban%* and *Income*. This says that states with older populations have higher cancer rates and that states with a greater degree of urbanization tend to have higher incomes. The negative correlation between *Burglary* and *Income* says that states with higher incomes tend to have fewer burglaries. Although no cause-and-effect is posited, such correlations naturally invite speculation about causation.

	Burglary	Age65%	Income	Unem	SATQ	Cancer	Unmar	Urban%
Burglary	1.000							
Age65%	−.120	1.000						
Income	−.345	−.088	1.000					
Unem	.340	−.280	−.326	1.000				
SATQ	−.179	.105	−.273	−.138	1.000			
Cancer	−.085	.867	−.091	−.151	−.044	1.000		
Unmar	.595	.125	−.291	.420	−.207	.283	1.000	
Urban%	.210	−.030	.646	−.098	−.341	−.031	.099	1.000

50 sample size   ±.279 critical value .05 (two-tail)
±.361 critical value .01 (two-tail)

FIGURE 12.10

MegaStat's correlation matrix for state data **States**

EXAMPLE

Time-Series
Macroeconomic Data

🐾 **Economy**

Eight time-series variables were selected from the *LearningStats* database of annual macroeconomic data (42 years):

GDP	Gross domestic product (billions)
C	Personal consumption expenditures (billions)
I	Gross private domestic investment (billions)
G	Government expenditures and investment (billions)
U	Unemployment rate, civilian labor force (percent)
R-Prime	Prime rate (percent)
R-10Yr	Ten-year Treasury rate (percent)
DJIA	Dow-Jones Industrial Average

For $n = 42$ years we have $v = n - 2 = 42 - 2 = 40$ degrees of freedom. From Appendix D the two-tail critical values for Student's t are $t_{.05} = 2.021$ and $t_{.01} = 2.704$ so critical values for r are as follows:

For $\alpha = .05$,

$$r_{.05} = \frac{t_{.05}}{\sqrt{t_{.05}^2 + n - 2}} = \frac{2.021}{\sqrt{(2.021)^2 + 42 - 2}} = .304$$

and for $\alpha = .01$,

$$r_{.01} = \frac{t_{.01}}{\sqrt{t_{.01}^2 + n - 2}} = \frac{2.704}{\sqrt{(2.704)^2 + 42 - 2}} = .393$$

Figure 12.11 shows the MegaStat correlation matrix for these eight variables. There are 13 significant correlations at $\alpha = .01$, some of them extremely high. In time-series data, high correlations are common due to time trends and definition (e.g., C, I, and G are components of GDP so they are highly correlated with GDP).

FIGURE 12.11

MegaStat's correlation
matrix for time-series data
🐾 **Economy**

	GDP	C	I	G	U	R-Prime	R-10Yr	DJIA
GDP	1.000							
C	1.000	1.000						
I	.991	.990	1.000					
G	.996	.994	.979	1.000				
U	−.010	−.021	−.042	.041	1.000			
R-Prime	.270	.254	.301	.296	.419	1.000		
R-10Yr	.159	.140	.172	.208	.642	.904	1.000	
DJIA	.881	.888	.907	.838	−.299	.042	−.157	1.000

42 sample size   ±.304 critical value .05 (two-tail)
±.393 critical value .01 (two-tail)

Regression: The Next Step?

Correlation coefficients and scatter plots provide clues about relationships among variables and may suffice for some purposes. But often, the analyst would like to model the relationship for prediction purposes. This process, called *regression,* is the subject of the next section.

SECTION EXERCISES

12.1 For each sample, do a test for zero correlation. (a) Use Appendix D to find the critical value of t_α. (b) State the hypotheses about ρ. (c) Perform the t test and report your decision. (d) Find the critical value of r_α and use it to perform the same hypothesis test.

a. $r = +.45, n = 20, \alpha = .05$, two-tailed test
b. $r = −.35, n = 30, \alpha = .10$, two-tailed test

c. $r = +.60$, $n = 7$, $\alpha = .05$, one-tailed test

d. $r = -.30$, $n = 61$, $\alpha = .01$, one-tailed test

Instructions for Exercises 12.2 and 12.3: (a) Make an Excel scatter plot. What does it suggest about the population correlation between X and Y? (b) Make an Excel worksheet to calculate SS_{xx}, SS_{yy}, and SS_{xy}. Use these sums to calculate the sample correlation coefficient. Check your work by using Excel's function =CORREL(array1,array2). (c) Use Appendix D to find $t_{.05}$ for a two-tailed test for zero correlation. (d) Calculate the t test statistic. Can you reject $\rho = 0$? (e) Use Excel's function =TDIST(t,deg_freedom,tails) to calculate the two-tail p-value.

12.2 Part-Time Weekly Earnings ($) by College Students   WeekPay

Hours Worked (X)	Weekly Pay (Y)
10	93
15	171
20	204
20	156
35	261

12.3 Data Set Telephone Hold Time (min.) for Concert Tickets   CallWait

Operators (X)	Wait Time (Y)
4	385
5	335
6	383
7	344
8	288

Instructions for Exercises 12.4–12.6: (a) Make a scatter plot of the data. What does it suggest about the correlation between X and Y? (b) Use Excel, MegaStat, or MINITAB to calculate the correlation coefficient. (c) Use Excel or Appendix D to find $t_{.05}$ for a two-tailed test. (d) Calculate the t test statistic. (e) Calculate the critical value of r_α. (f) Can you reject $\rho = 0$?

12.4 Moviegoer Spending ($) on Snacks   Movies

Age (X)	Spent (Y)
30	2.85
50	6.50
34	1.50
12	6.35
37	6.20
33	6.75
36	3.60
26	6.10
18	8.35
46	4.35

12.5 Portfolio Returns on Selected Mutual Funds 🐾 Portfolio

Last Year (X)	This Year (Y)
11.9	15.4
19.5	26.7
11.2	18.2
14.1	16.7
14.2	13.2
5.2	16.4
20.7	21.1
11.3	12.0
−1.1	12.1
3.9	7.4
12.9	11.5
12.4	23.0
12.5	12.7
2.7	15.1
8.8	18.7
7.2	9.9
5.9	18.9

12.6 Number of Orders and Shipping Cost ($) 🐾 ShipCost

Orders (X)	Ship Cost (Y)
1,068	4,489
1,026	5,611
767	3,290
885	4,113
1,156	4,883
1,146	5,425
892	4,414
938	5,506
769	3,346
677	3,673
1,174	6,542
1,009	5,088

12.7 (a) Use Excel, MegaStat, or MINITAB to calculate a matrix of correlation coefficients. (b) Calculate the critical value of r_α. (c) Highlight the correlation coefficients that lead you to reject $\rho = 0$ in a two-tailed test. (d) What conclusions can you draw about rates of return?

Average Annual Returns for 12 Home Construction Companies 🐾 Construction

Company Name	1-Year	3-Year	5-Year	10-Year
Beazer Homes USA	50.3	26.1	50.1	28.9
Centex	23.4	33.3	40.8	28.6
D.R. Horton	41.4	42.4	52.9	35.8
Hovnanian Ent	13.8	67.0	73.1	33.8
KB Home	46.1	38.8	35.3	24.9
Lennar	19.4	39.3	50.9	36.0
M.D.C. Holdings	48.7	41.6	53.2	39.7
NVR	65.1	55.7	74.4	63.9
Pulte Homes	36.8	42.4	42.1	27.9
Ryland Group	30.5	46.9	59.0	33.3
Standard Pacific	33.0	39.5	44.2	27.8
Toll Brothers	72.6	46.2	49.1	29.9

Source: *The Wall Street Journal,* February 28, 2005. *Note:* Data are intended for educational purposes only.

Mini Case

12.1

Alumni Giving

Private universities (and, increasingly, public ones) rely heavily on alumni donations. Do highly selective universities have more loyal alumni? Figure 12.12 shows a scatter plot of freshman acceptance rates against percent of alumni who donate at 115 nationally ranked U.S. universities (those that offer a wide range of undergraduate, master's, and doctoral degrees). The correlation coefficient, calculated in Excel by using Tools > Data Analysis > Correlation is $r = -.6248$. This negative correlation suggests that more competitive universities (lower acceptance rate) have more loyal alumni (higher percentage contributing annually). But is the correlation statistically significant?

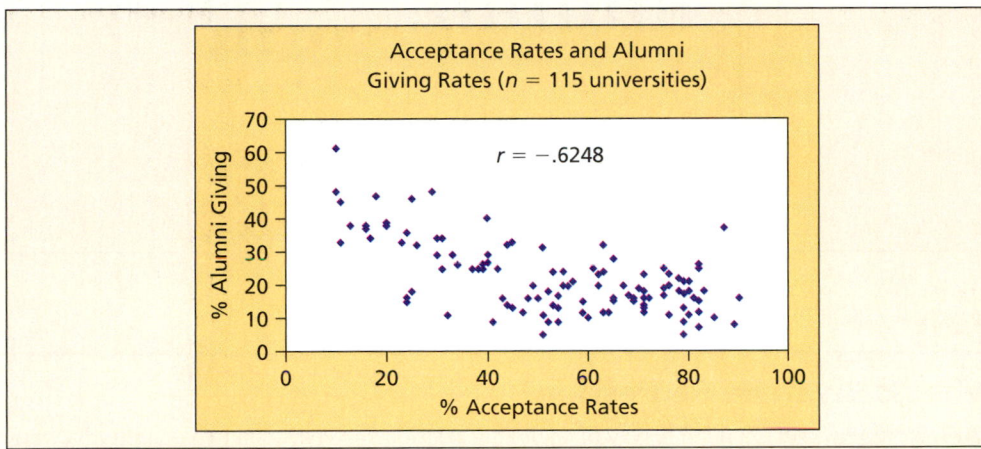

FIGURE 12.12

Scatter plot for acceptance rates and alumni giving

Since we have a prior hypothesis of an inverse relationship between X and Y, we choose a left-tailed test:

$H_0: \rho \geq 0$

$H_1: \rho < 0$

With $v = n - 2 = 115 - 2 = 113$ degrees of freedom, for $\alpha = .05$, we use Excel's *two-tailed* function =TINV(0.10,113) to obtain the *one-tail* critical value $t_{.05} = 1.65845$. Since we are doing a left-tailed test, the critical value is $t_{.05} = -1.65845$. The t test statistic is

$$t = r\sqrt{\frac{n-2}{1-r^2}} = (-.6248)\sqrt{\frac{115-2}{1-(-.6248)^2}} = -8.506$$

Since the test statistic $t = -8.506$ is less than the critical value $t_{.05} = -1.65845$, we conclude that the true correlation is negative. We can use Excel's function =TDIST(8.506,113,1) to obtain $p = .0000$. Alternatively, we could calculate the critical value of the correlation coefficient:

$$r_{.05} = \frac{t_{.05}}{\sqrt{t_{.05}^2 + n - 2}} = \frac{-1.65845}{\sqrt{(-1.65845)^2 + 115 - 2}} = -.1542$$

Since the sample correlation $r = -.6248$ is less than the critical value $r_{.05} = -.1542$, we conclude that the true correlation is negative. We can choose either the t test method or the correlation critical value method, depending on which calculation seems easier.

See *U.S. News & World Report,* August 30, 2004, pp. 94–96.

Autocorrelation  Sunoco

Autocorrelation is a special type of correlation analysis useful in business for time series data. The ***autocorrelation coefficient*** at lag k is the simple correlation between y_t and y_{t-k} where k

is any lag. Below is an autocorrelation plot up to $k = 20$ for the daily closing price of common stock of Sunoco, Inc. (an oil company). Sunoco's autocorrelations are significant for short lags (up to $k = 3$) but diminish rapidly for longer lags. In other words, today's stock price closely resembles yesterday's, but the correlation weakens as we look farther into the past. Similar patterns are often found in other financial data. You will hear more about autocorrelation later in this chapter.

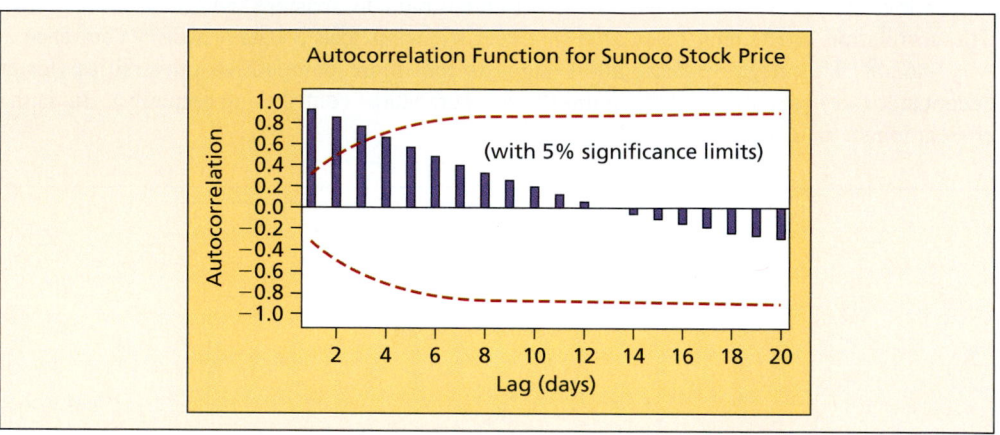

12.2

BIVARIATE REGRESSION

What Is Bivariate Regression?

Bivariate regression is a flexible way of analyzing relationships between two quantitative variables. It can help answer practical questions. For example, a business might hypothesize that

$$\text{Quarterly sales revenue} = f(\text{advertising expenditures})$$
$$\text{Prescription drug cost per employee} = f(\text{number of dependents})$$
$$\text{Monthly rent} = f(\text{apartment size})$$
$$\text{Business lunch reimbursement expense} = f(\text{number of persons in group})$$
$$\text{Number of product defects per unit} = f(\text{assembly line speed in units per hour})$$

These are *bivariate* models because they specify one *dependent* variable (sometimes called the *response*) and one *independent* variable (sometimes called the *predictor*). If the exact form of these relationships were known, the business could explore policy questions such as:

- How much extra sales will be generated, on average, by a $1 million increase in advertising expenditures? What would expected sales be with no advertising?

- How much do prescription drug costs per employee rise, on average, with each extra dependent? What would be the expected cost if the employee had no dependents?

- How much extra rent, on average, is paid per extra square foot?

- How much extra luncheon cost, on average, is generated by each additional member of the group? How much could be saved by restricting luncheon groups to three persons?

- If the assembly line speed is increased by 20 units per hour, what would happen to the mean number of product defects?

Model Form

The hypothesized bivariate relationship may be linear, quadratic, or whatever you want. The examples in Figure 12.13 illustrate situations in which it might be necessary to consider nonlinear model forms. For now we will mainly focus on the simple linear (straight-line) model. However, we will examine nonlinear relationships later in the chapter.

FIGURE 12.13

Possible model forms

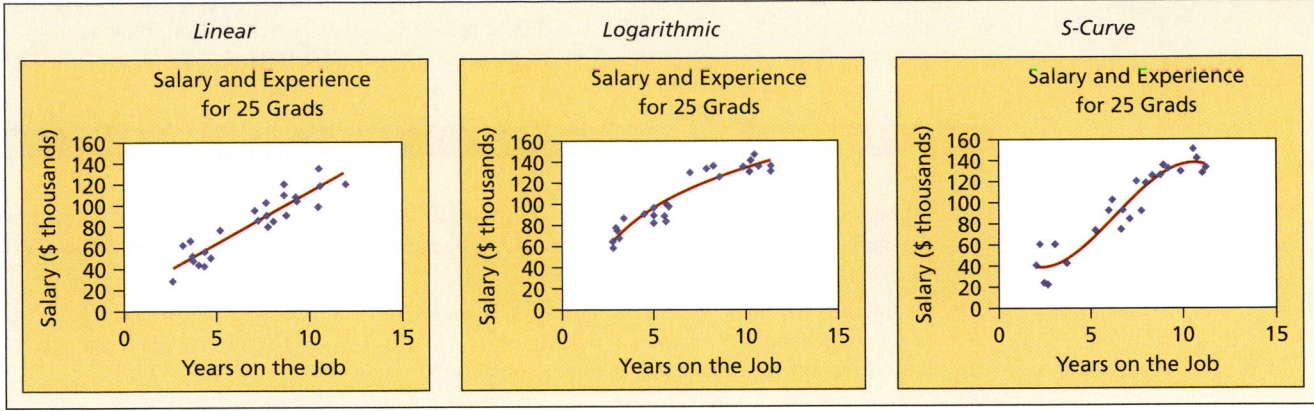

Interpreting a Fitted Regression

The intercept and slope of a *fitted regression* can provide useful information. For example:

Sales $= 268 + 7.37\ Ads$	Each extra \$1 million of advertising will generate \$7.37 million of sales on average. The firm would average \$268 million of sales with zero advertising. However, the intercept may not be meaningful because *Ads* $= 0$ may be outside the range of observed data.
DrugCost $= 410 + 550\ Dependents$	Each extra dependent raises the mean annual prescription drug cost by \$550. An employee with zero dependents averages \$410 in prescription drugs.
Rent $= 150 + 1.05\ SqFt$	Each extra square foot adds \$1.05 to monthly apartment rent. The intercept is not meaningful because no apartment can have *SqFt* $= 0$.
Cost $= 15.22 + 19.96\ Persons$	Each additional diner increases the mean dinner cost by \$19.96. The intercept is not meaningful because *Persons* $= 0$ would not be observable.
Defects $= 3.2 + 0.045\ Speed$	Each unit increase in assembly line speed adds an average of 0.045 defects per million. The intercept is not meaningful since zero assembly line speed implies no production at all.

When we propose a regression model, we have a causal mechanism in mind, but cause-and-effect is not proven by a simple regression. We should not read too much into a fitted equation.

Prediction Using Regression

One of the main uses of regression is to make predictions. Once we have a fitted regression equation that shows the estimated relationship between X and Y, we can plug in any value of X to obtain the prediction for Y. For example:

Sales $= 268 + 7.37\ Ads$	If the firm spends \$10 million on advertising, its expected sales would be \$341.7 million, that is, *Sales* $= 268 + 7.37(10) = 341.7$.
DrugCost $= 410 + 550\ Dependents$	If an employee has four dependents, the expected annual drug cost would be \$2,610, that is, *DrugCost* $= 410 + 550(4) = 2,610$.
Rent $= 150 + 1.05\ SqFt$	The expected rent on an 800 square foot apartment is \$990, that is, *Rent* $= 150 + 1.05(800) = 990$.

$$Cost = 15.22 + 19.96 \, Persons$$

The expected cost of dinner for two couples would be $95.06, that is, $Cost = 15.22 + 19.96(4) = 95.06$.

$$Defects = 3.2 + 0.045 \, Speed$$

If 100 units per hour are produced, the expected defect rate is 7.7 defects per million, that is, $Defects = 3.2 + 0.045(100) = 7.7$.

SECTION EXERCISES

12.8 (a) Interpret the slope of the fitted regression $Sales = 842 - 37.5 \, Price$. (b) If $Price = 20$, what is the prediction for $Sales$? (c) Would the intercept be meaningful if this regression represents DVD sales at Blockbuster?

12.9 (a) Interpret the slope of the fitted regression $HomePrice = 125{,}000 + 150 \, SquareFeet$. (b) What is the prediction for $HomePrice$ if $SquareFeet = 2{,}000$? (c) Would the intercept be meaningful if this regression applies to home sales in a certain subdivision?

12.3 REGRESSION TERMINOLOGY

Models and Parameters

The model's *unknown parameters* are denoted by Greek letters β_0 (the **intercept**) and β_1 (the **slope**). The *assumed model* for a linear relationship is

(12.7) $$y_i = \beta_0 + \beta_1 x_i + \varepsilon_i \qquad \text{(assumed linear relationship)}$$

This relationship is assumed to hold for all observations ($i = 1, 2, \ldots, n$). Inclusion of a random error ε_i is necessary because other unspecified variables may also affect Y and also because there may be measurement error in Y. The error is not observable. We assume that the error term ε_i is a normally distributed random variable with mean 0 and standard deviation σ. Thus, the regression model actually has three unknown parameters: β_0, β_1, and σ. From the sample, we estimate the **fitted model** and use it to predict the *expected* value of Y for a given value of X:

(12.8) $$\hat{y}_i = b_0 + b_1 x_i \qquad \text{(fitted linear regression model)}$$

Roman letters denote the *fitted coefficients* b_0 (the estimated intercept) and b_1 (the estimated slope). For a given value x_i the *fitted* value (or estimated value) of the dependent variable is $\hat{y}_i$. (You can read this as "y-hat".) The difference between the observed value y_i and the fitted value $\hat{y}_i$ is the **residual** and is denoted e_i. A residual will always be calculated as the observed value minus the estimated value.

(12.9) $$e_i = y_i - \hat{y}_i \qquad \text{(residual)}$$

The residuals may be used to estimate σ, the standard deviation of the errors.

Estimating a Regression Line by Eye

From a scatter plot, you can visually estimate the slope and intercept, as illustrated in Figure 12.14. In this graph, the approximate slope is 10 and the approximate intercept (when $X = 0$) is around 15 (i.e., $\hat{y}_i = 15 + 10x_i$). This method, of course, is inexact. However, experiments suggest that people are pretty good at "eyeball" line fitting. You intuitively try to adjust the line so as to ensure that the residuals sum to zero (i.e., the positive residuals offset the negative residuals) and to ensure that no other values for the slope or intercept would give a better "fit."

Fitting a Regression on a Scatter Plot in Excel

A more precise method is to let Excel do the estimates. We enter observations on the independent variable $x_1, x_2, \ldots, x_n$ and the dependent variable $y_1, y_2, \ldots, y_n$ into separate columns, and let Excel fit the regression equation.* The easiest way to find the equation of the

---

*Excel calls its regression equation a "trendline," although actually that would refer to a time-series trend.

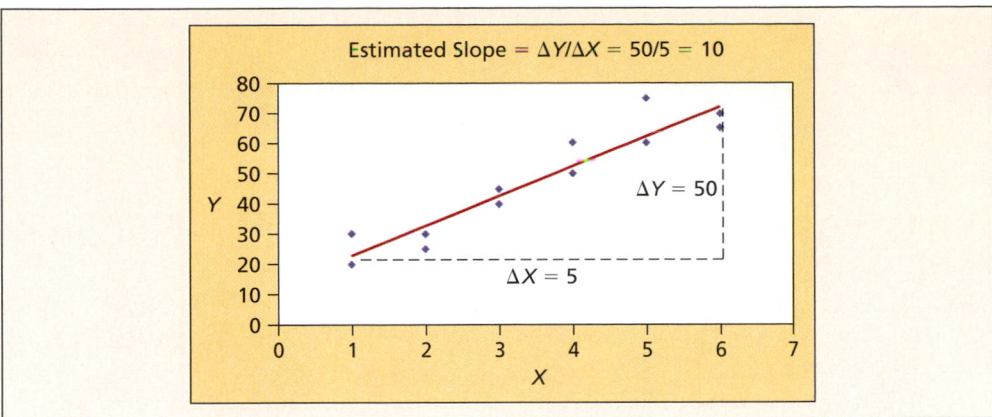

FIGURE 12.14

"Eyeball" regression line
fitting

regression line is to have Excel add the line onto a scatter plot, using the following steps:

- Step 1:   Highlight the data columns.
- Step 2:   Click on the Chart Wizard and choose XY (Scatter) to create a graph.
- Step 3:   Click on the scatter plot points to select the data.
- Step 4:   Right-click and choose Add Trendline.
- Step 5:   Choose Options and check Display equation on chart.

The menus are shown in Figure 12.15. (The R-squared statistic is actually the correlation coefficient squared. It tells us what proportion of the variation in Y is explained by X. We will more fully define R^2 in section 12.4.) Excel will choose the regression coefficients so as to produce a good fit. In this case, Excel's fitted regression $\hat{y}_i = 13 + 9.857x_i$ is close to our "eyeball" regression equation.

FIGURE 12.15

Excel's trendline menus

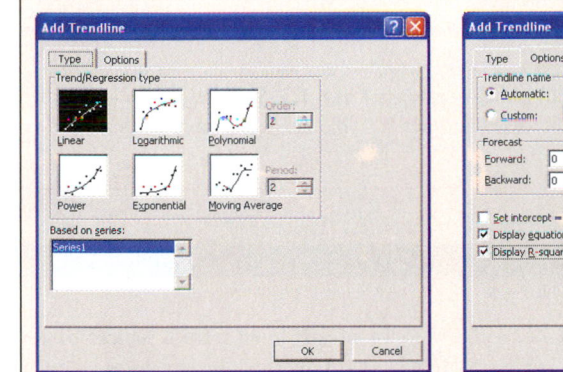 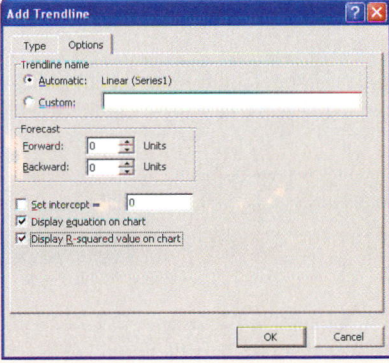 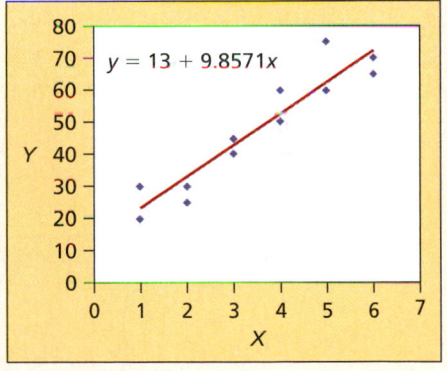

Illustration: Piper Cheyenne Fuel Consumption   Cheyenne

Table 12.2 shows a sample of fuel consumption and flight hours for five legs of a cross-country test flight in a Piper Cheyenne, a twin-engine piston business aircraft. Figure 12.16 displays the Excel graph and its fitted regression equation.

Flight Hours	Fuel Used (lbs.)
2.3	145
4.2	258
3.6	219
4.7	276
4.9	283

TABLE 12.2
Piper Cheyenne Fuel Usage

Source: *Flying* 130, no. 4 (April 2003), p. 99.

FIGURE 12.16

Fitted regression

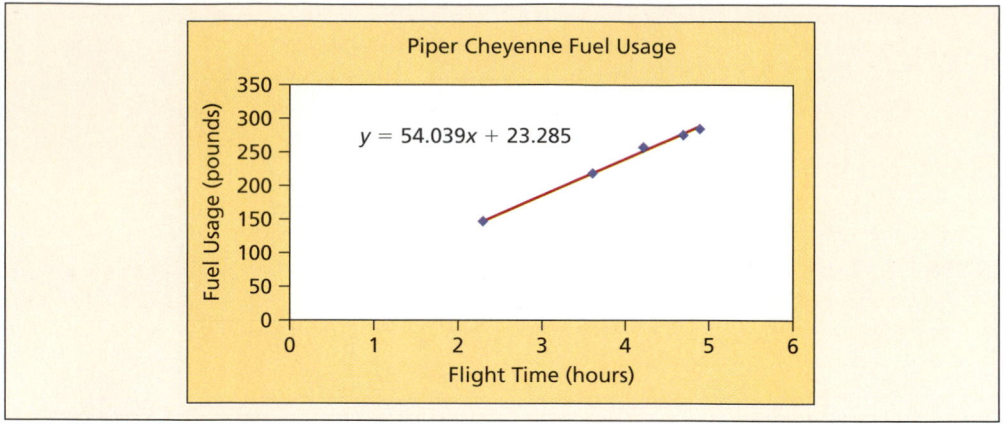

Slope Interpretation   The fitted regression is $\hat{y} = 23.295 + 54.039x$. The slope ($b_1 = 54.039$) says that for each additional hour of flight, the Piper Cheyenne consumed about 54 pounds of fuel (1 gallon $\approx$ 6 pounds). This estimated slope is a *statistic,* since a different sample might yield a different estimate of the slope. Bear in mind also that the sample size is very small.

Intercept Interpretation   The intercept ($b_0 = 23.295$) suggests that even if the plane is not flying ($X = 0$) some fuel would be consumed. However, the intercept has little meaning in this case, not only because zero flight hour makes no logical sense, but also because extrapolating to $X = 0$ is beyond the range of the observed data.

Regression Caveats

- The "fit" of the regression does *not* depend on the sign of its slope. The sign of the fitted slope merely tells whether X has a positive or negative association with Y.

- View the intercept with skepticism unless $X = 0$ is logically possible and was actually observed in the data set.

- Regression does not demonstrate cause-and-effect between X and Y. A good fit only shows that X and Y vary together. Both could be affected by another variable or by the way the data are defined.

SECTION EXERCISES

12.10 The regression equation *NetIncome* $= 2{,}277 + .0307$ *Revenue* was fitted from a sample of 100 leading world companies (variables are in millions of dollars). (a) Interpret the slope. (b) Is the intercept meaningful? Explain. (c) Make a prediction of *NetIncome* when *Revenue* $= 1{,}000$. (Data are from www.forbes.com and *Forbes* 172, no. 2 [July 21, 2003], pp. 108–110.)   **Global100**

12.11 The regression equation *HomePrice* $= 51.3 + 2.61$ *Income* was fitted from a sample of 34 cities in the eastern United States. Both variables are in thousands of dollars. *HomePrice* is the median selling price of homes in the city, and *Income* is median family income for the city. (a) Interpret the slope. (b) Is the intercept meaningful? Explain. (c) Make a prediction of *HomePrice* when *Income* $= 50$ and also when *Income* $= 100$. (Data are from *Money Magazine* 32, no. 1 [January 2004], pp. 102–103.)   **HomePrice**

12.12 The regression equation *Credits* $= 15.4 - .07$ *Work* was fitted from a sample of 21 statistics students. *Credits* is the number of college credits taken and *Work* is the number of hours worked per week at an outside job. (a) Interpret the slope. (b) Is the intercept meaningful? Explain. (c) Make a prediction of *Credits* when *Work* $= 0$ and when *Work* $= 40$. What do these predictions tell you?   **Credits**

12.13 Below are fitted regressions for $Y =$ asking price of a used vehicle and $X =$ the age of the vehicle. The observed range of X was 1 to 8 years. The sample consisted of all vehicles listed for sale in a particular week in 2005. (a) Interpret the slope of each fitted regression. (b) Interpret the intercept of each fitted regression. Does the intercept have meaning? (c) Predict the price of a 5-year-old Chevy Blazer. (d) Predict the price of a 5-year-old Chevy Silverado. (Data are from *AutoFocus* 4, Issue 38 (Sept. 17–23, 2004) and are for educational purposes only.)   **CarPrices**

> Chevy Blazer: *Price* $= 16,189 - 1,050$ *Age* ($n = 21$ vehicles, observed X range was 1 to 8 years).
>
> Chevy Silverado: *Price* $= 22,951 - 1,339$ *Age* ($n = 24$ vehicles, observed X range was 1 to 10 years).

12.14 These data are for a sample of 10 college students who work at weekend jobs in restaurants. (a) Fit an "eyeball" regression equation to this scatter plot of $Y =$ tips earned last weekend and $X =$ hours worked. (b) Interpret the slope. (c) Interpret the intercept. Would the intercept have meaning in this example?

12.15 These data are for a sample of 10 different vendors in a large airport. (a) Fit an "eyeball" regression equation to this scatter plot of $Y =$ bottles of Evian water sold and $X =$ price of the water. (b) Interpret the slope. (c) Interpret the intercept. Would the intercept have meaning in this example?

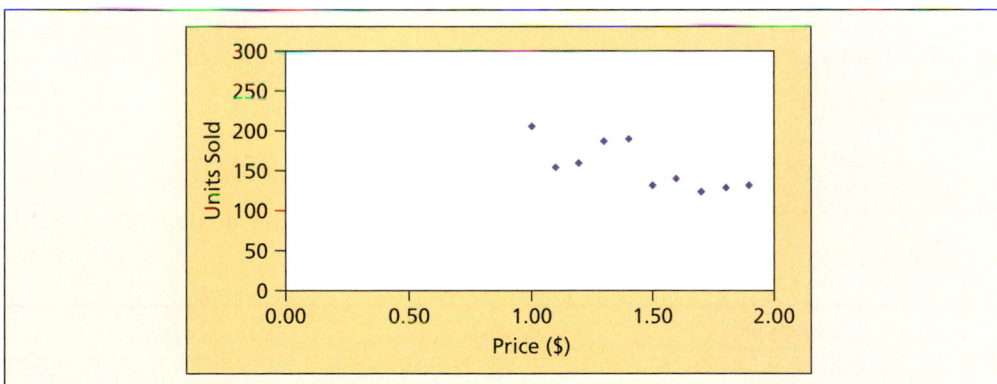

Slope and Intercept

The **ordinary least squares** method (or **OLS** method for short) is used to estimate a regression so as to ensure the best fit. "Best" fit in this case means that we have selected the slope and intercept so that our residuals are as small as possible. However, it is a characteristic of the OLS estimation method that the residuals around the regression line always sum to zero. That is, the positive residuals exactly cancel the negative ones:

$$\sum_{i=1}^{n} (y_i - \hat{y}_i) = 0 \qquad \text{(OLS residuals always sum to zero)} \qquad (12.10)$$

Therefore to work with an equation that has a nonzero sum we square the residuals, just as we squared the deviations from the mean when we developed the equation for variance back in chapter 4. The fitted coefficients b_0 and b_1 are chosen so that the fitted linear model $\hat{y}_i = b_0 + b_1 x_i$ has the smallest possible sum of squared residuals (*SSE*):

$$(12.11) \qquad SSE = \sum_{i=1}^{n} (y_i - \hat{y}_i)^2 = \sum_{i=1}^{n} (y_i - b_0 - b_1 x_i)^2 \qquad \text{(sum to be minimized)}$$

This is an optimization problem that can be solved for b_0 and b_1 by using Excel's Solver Add-In. However, we can also use calculus (see derivation in *LearningStats* Unit 12) to solve for b_0 and b_1.

$$(12.12) \qquad b_1 = \frac{\sum_{i=1}^{n} (x_i - \bar{x})(y_i - \bar{y})}{\sum_{i=1}^{n} (x_i - \bar{x})^2} \qquad \text{(OLS estimator for slope)}$$

$$(12.13) \qquad b_0 = \bar{y} - b_1 \bar{x} \qquad \text{(OLS estimator for intercept)}$$

If we use the notation for sums of squares (see formula 12.2), then the OLS formula for the slope can be written

$$(12.14) \qquad b_1 = \frac{SS_{xy}}{SS_{xx}} \qquad \text{(OLS estimator for slope)}$$

These formulas require only a few spreadsheet operations to find the means, deviations around the means, and their products and sums. They are built into Excel and many calculators. The OLS formulas give unbiased and consistent estimates* of β_0 and β_1. The OLS regression line always passes through the point $(\bar{x}, \bar{y})$.

Illustration: Exam Scores and Study Time

Table 12.3 shows study time and exam scores for 10 students. The worksheet in Table 12.4 shows the calculations of the sums needed for the slope and intercept. Figure 12.17 shows a fitted regression line. The vertical line segments in the scatter plot show the differences between the actual and fitted exam scores (i.e., residuals). The OLS residuals always sum to zero. We have:

$$b_1 = \frac{SS_{xy}}{SS_{xx}} = \frac{519.50}{264.50} = 1.9641 \qquad \text{(fitted slope)}$$

$$b_0 = \bar{y} - b_1 \bar{x} = 70.1 - (1.9641)(10.5) = 49.477 \qquad \text{(fitted intercept)}$$

TABLE 12.3

Study Time and Exam Scores 🐝 **ExamScores**

Student	Study Hours	Exam Score
Tom	1	53
Mary	5	74
Sarah	7	59
Oscar	8	43
Cullyn	10	56
Jaime	11	84
Theresa	14	96
Knut	15	69
Jin-Mae	15	84
Courtney	19	83
Sum	105	701
Mean	$\bar{x} = 10.5$	$\bar{y} = 70.1$

---

*Recall from Chapter 9 that an unbiased estimator's expected value is the true parameter and that a consistent estimator approaches ever closer to the true parameter as the sample size increases.

Student	x_i	y_i	$x_i - \bar{x}$	$y_i - \bar{y}$	$(x_i - \bar{x})(y_i - \bar{y})$	$(x_i - \bar{x})^2$
Tom	1	53	−9.5	−17.1	162.45	90.25
Mary	5	74	−5.5	3.9	−21.45	30.25
Sarah	7	59	−3.5	−11.1	38.85	12.25
Oscar	8	43	−2.5	−27.1	67.75	6.25
Cullyn	10	56	−0.5	−14.1	7.05	0.25
Jaime	11	84	0.5	13.9	6.95	0.25
Theresa	14	96	3.5	25.9	90.65	12.25
Knut	15	69	4.5	−1.1	−4.95	20.25
Jin-Mae	15	84	4.5	13.9	62.55	20.25
Courtney	19	83	8.5	12.9	109.65	72.25
Sum	105	701	0	0	$SS_{xy} = 519.50$	$SS_{xx} = 264.50$
Mean	$\bar{x} = 10.5$	$\bar{y} = 70.1$				

TABLE 12.4
Worksheet for Slope and Intercept Calculations
   ExamScores

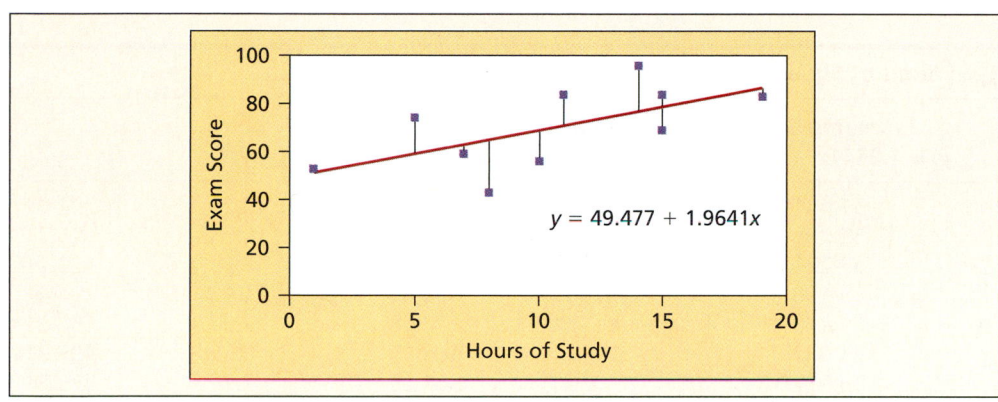

FIGURE 12.17

Scatter plot with fitted line and residuals shown as vertical line segments

Interpretation   The fitted regression *Score* = 49.477 + 1.9641 *Study* says that, on average, each additional hour of study yields a little less than 2 additional exam points (the slope). A student who did not study (*Study* = 0) would expect a score of about 49 (the intercept). In this example, the intercept is meaningful because zero study time not only is possible (though hopefully uncommon) but also was almost within the range of observed data. Excel's R^2 is fairly low, indicating that only about 39 percent of the variation in exam scores from the mean is *explained* by study time. The remaining 61 percent of *unexplained* variation in exam scores reflects other factors (e.g., previous night's sleep, class attendance, test anxiety). We can use the fitted regression equation $\hat{y}_i = 1.9641x_i + 49.477$ to find each student's *expected* exam score. Each prediction is a *conditional mean,* given the student's study hours. For example:

Student and Study Time	Expected Exam Score
Oscar, 8 hours	$\hat{y}_i = 49.48 + 1.964\,(8) = 65.19$ (65 to nearest integer)
Theresa, 14 hours	$\hat{y}_i = 49.48 + 1.964\,(14) = 76.98$ (77 to nearest integer)
Courtney, 19 hours	$\hat{y}_i = 49.48 + 1.964\,(19) = 86.79$ (87 to nearest integer)

Oscar's actual exam score was only 43, so he did worse than his predicted score of 65. Theresa scored 96, far above her predicted score of 77. Courtney, who studied the longest (19 hours), scored 83, fairly close to her predicted score of 87. These examples show that study time is not a perfect predictor of exam scores.

Assessing Fit

The *total variation* in *Y* around its mean (denoted *SST*) is what we seek to explain:

$$SST = \sum_{i=1}^{n} (y_i - \bar{y}_i)^2 \qquad \text{(total sum of squares)} \qquad \textbf{(12.15)}$$

How much of the total variation in our dependent variable *Y* can be explained by our regression? The *explained variation* in *Y* (denoted *SSR*) is the sum of the squared differences between the conditional mean $\hat{y}_i$ (conditioned on a given value x_i) and the unconditional mean $\bar{y}$ (same for all x_i):

(12.16) $$SSR = \sum_{i=1}^{n} (\hat{y}_i - \bar{y})^2 \qquad \text{(regression sum of squares, explained)}$$

The *unexplained variation* in Y (denoted *SSE*) is the sum of *squared* residuals, sometimes referred to as the **error sum of squares.***

(12.17) $$SSE = \sum_{i=1}^{n} (y_i - \hat{y}_i)^2 \qquad \text{(error sum of squares, unexplained)}$$

If the fit is good, *SSE* will be relatively small compared to *SST*. If each observed data value y_i is exactly the same as its estimate $\hat{y}_i$ (i.e., a perfect fit), then *SSE* will be zero. There is no upper limit on *SSE*. Table 12.5 shows the calculation of *SSE* for the exam scores.

TABLE 12.5   Calculations of Sums of Squares   🐝 ExamScores

Student	Hours x_i	Score y_i	Estimated Score $\hat{y}_i = 1.9641x_i + 49.477$	Residual $y_i - \hat{y}_i$	$(y_i - \hat{y}_i)^2$	$(\hat{y}_i - \bar{y})^2$	$(y_i - \bar{y})^2$
Tom	1	53	51.441	1.559	2.43	348.15	292.41
Mary	5	74	59.298	14.702	216.15	116.68	15.21
Sarah	7	59	63.226	−4.226	17.86	47.25	123.21
Oscar	8	43	65.190	−22.190	492.40	24.11	734.41
Cullyn	10	56	69.118	−13.118	172.08	0.96	198.81
Jaime	11	84	71.082	12.918	166.87	0.96	193.21
Theresa	14	96	76.974	19.026	361.99	47.25	670.81
Knut	15	69	78.939	−9.939	98.78	78.13	1.21
Jin-Mae	15	84	78.939	5.061	25.61	78.13	193.21
Courtney	19	83	86.795	−3.795	14.40	278.72	166.41
					SSE = 1,568.57	SSR = 1,020.34	SST = 2,588.90

Coefficient of Determination

Since the magnitude of *SSE* is dependent on sample size and on the units of measurement (e.g., dollars, kilograms, ounces) we need a *unit-free* benchmark. The **coefficient of determination** or R^2 is a measure of *relative fit* based on a comparison of *SSR* and *SST*. Excel calculates this statistic automatically. It may be calculated in either of two ways:

(12.18) $$R^2 = 1 - \frac{SSE}{SST} \quad \text{or} \quad R^2 = \frac{SSR}{SST}$$

The range of the coefficient of determination is $0 \leq R^2 \leq 1$. The highest possible R^2 is 1 because, if the regression gives a perfect fit, then $SSE = 0$:

$$R^2 = 1 - \frac{SSE}{SST} = 1 - \frac{0}{SST} = 1 - 0 = 1 \quad \text{if } SSE = 0 \text{ (perfect fit)}$$

The lowest possible R^2 is 0 because, if knowing the value of X does not help predict the value of Y, then $SSE = SST$:

$$R^2 = 1 - \frac{SSE}{SST} = 1 - \frac{SST}{SST} = 1 - 1 = 0 \quad \text{if } SSE = SST \text{ (worst fit)}$$

---

*But bear in mind that the residual e_i (observable) is not the same as the true error ε_i (unobservable).

For the exam scores, the coefficient of determination is

$$R^2 = 1 - \frac{SSE}{SST} = 1 - \frac{1{,}568.57}{2{,}588.90} = 1 - 0.6059 = .3941$$

Because a coefficient of determination always lies in the range $0 \leq R^2 \leq 1$, it is often expressed as a *percent of variation explained*. Since the exam score regression yields $R^2 = .3941$, we could say that X (hours of study) "explains" 39.41 percent of the variation in Y (exam scores). On the other hand, 60.59 percent of the variation in exam scores is *not* explained by study time. The *unexplained variation* reflects factors not included in our model (e.g., reading skills, hours of sleep, hours of work at a job, physical health, etc.) or just plain random variation. Although the word "explained" does not necessarily imply causation, in this case we have *a priori* reason to believe that causation exists, that is, that increased study time improves exam scores.

Tip

In a bivariate regression, R^2 is the square of the correlation coefficient r. Thus, if $r = .50$ then $R^2 = .25$. For this reason, MegaStat (and some textbooks) denotes the coefficient of determination as r^2 instead of R^2. In this textbook, the uppercase notation R^2 is used to indicate the difference in their definitions. It is tempting to think that a low R^2 indicates that the model is not useful. Yet in some applications (e.g., predicting crude oil future prices) even a slight improvement in predictive power can translate into millions of dollars.

SECTION EXERCISES

Instructions for Exercises 12.16 and 12.17: (a) Make an Excel worksheet to calculate SS_{xx}, SS_{yy}, and SS_{xy} (the same worksheet you used in Exercises 12.2 and 12.3). (b) Use the formulas to calculate the slope and intercept. (c) Use your estimated slope and intercept to make a worksheet to calculate *SSE*, *SSR*, and *SST*. (d) Use these sums to calculate the R^2. (e) To check your answers, make an Excel scatter plot of X and Y, select the data points, right-click, select Add Trendline, select the Options tab, and choose Display equation on chart and Display R-squared value on chart.

12.16 Part-Time Weekly Earnings by College Students   🖳   WeekPay

Hours Worked (X)	Weekly Pay (Y)
10	93
15	171
20	204
20	156
35	261

12.17 Seconds of Telephone Hold Time for Concert Tickets   🖳   CallWait

Operators On Duty (X)	Wait Time (Y)
4	385
5	335
6	383
7	344
8	288

Instructions for Exercises 12.18–12.20: (a) Use Excel to make a scatter plot of the data. (b) Select the data points, right-click, select Add Trendline, select the Options tab, and choose Display equation on chart and Display R-squared value on chart. (c) Interpret the fitted slope. (d) Is the intercept meaningful? Explain. (e) Interpret the R^2.

12.18   Portfolio Returns (%) on Selected Mutual Funds   Portfolio

Last Year (X)	This Year (Y)
11.9	15.4
19.5	26.7
11.2	18.2
14.1	16.7
14.2	13.2
5.2	16.4
20.7	21.1
11.3	12.0
−1.1	12.1
3.9	7.4
12.9	11.5
12.4	23.0
12.5	12.7
2.7	15.1
8.8	18.7
7.2	9.9
5.9	18.9

12.19   Number of Orders and Shipping Cost   ShipCost

Orders (X)	($) Ship Cost (Y)
1,068	4,489
1,026	5,611
767	3,290
885	4,113
1,156	4,883
1,146	5,425
892	4,414
938	5,506
769	3,346
677	3,673
1,174	6,542
1,009	5,088

12.20   Moviegoer Spending on Snacks   Movies

Age (X)	($) Spent (Y)
30	2.85
50	6.50
34	1.50
12	6.35
37	6.20
33	6.75
36	3.60
26	6.10
18	8.35
46	4.35

Standard Error of Regression

A measure of overall fit is the **standard error** of the regression, denoted s_{yx}:

$$s_{yx} = \sqrt{\frac{SSE}{n-2}} \qquad \text{(standard error)} \qquad (12.19)$$

If the fitted model's predictions are perfect ($SSE = 0$), the standard error s_{yx} will be zero. In general, a smaller value of s_{yx} indicates a better fit. For the exam scores, we can use SSE from Table 12.5 to find s_{yx}:

$$s_{yx} = \sqrt{\frac{SSE}{n-2}} = \sqrt{\frac{1,568.57}{10-2}} = \sqrt{\frac{1,568.57}{8}} = 14.002$$

The standard error s_{yx} is an estimate of σ (the standard deviation of the unobservable errors). Because it measures overall fit, the standard error s_{yx} serves somewhat the same function as the coefficient of determination. However, unlike R^2, the magnitude of s_{yx} depends on the units of measurement of the dependent variable (e.g., dollars, kilograms, ounces) and on the data magnitude. For this reason, R^2 is often the preferred measure of overall fit because its scale is always 0 to 1. The main use of the standard error s_{yx} is to construct confidence intervals.

Confidence Intervals for Slope and Intercept

Once we have the standard error s_{yx}, we construct confidence intervals for the coefficients from the formulas shown below. Excel, MegaStat, and MINITAB find them automatically.

$$s_{b_1} = \frac{s_{yx}}{\sqrt{\sum_{i=1}^{n}(x_i - \bar{x})^2}} \quad \text{or} \quad s_{b_1} = \frac{s_{yx}}{\sqrt{SS_{xx}}} \qquad \text{(standard error of slope)} \qquad (12.20)$$

$$s_{b_0} = s_{yx}\sqrt{\frac{1}{n} + \frac{\bar{x}^2}{\sum_{i=1}^{n}(x_i - \bar{x})^2}} \quad \text{or}$$

$$s_{b_0} = s_{yx}\sqrt{\frac{1}{n} + \frac{\bar{x}^2}{SS_{xx}}} \qquad \text{(standard error of intercept)} \qquad (12.21)$$

For the exam score data, plugging in the sums from Table 12.4, we get

$$s_{b_1} = \frac{s_{yx}}{\sqrt{\sum_{i=1}^{n}(x_i - \bar{x})^2}} = \frac{14.002}{\sqrt{264.50}} = 0.86095$$

$$s_{b_0} = s_{yx}\sqrt{\frac{1}{n} + \frac{\bar{x}^2}{\sum_{i=1}^{n}(x_i - \bar{x})^2}} = 14.002\sqrt{\frac{1}{10} + \frac{(10.5)^2}{264.50}} = 10.066$$

These standard errors are used to construct confidence intervals for the true slope and intercept, using Student's t with $\nu = n - 2$ degrees of freedom and any desired confidence level. Some software packages (e.g., Excel and MegaStat) provide confidence intervals automatically, while others do not (e.g., MINITAB).

$$b_1 - t_{n-2}s_{b_1} \leq \beta_1 \leq b_1 + t_{n-2}s_{b_1} \qquad \text{(CI for true slope)} \qquad (12.22)$$

$$b_0 - t_{n-2}s_{b_0} \leq \beta_0 \leq b_0 + t_{n-2}s_{b_0} \qquad \text{(CI for true intercept)} \qquad (12.23)$$

For the exam scores, degrees of freedom are $n - 2 = 10 - 2 = 8$, so from Appendix D we get $t_{n-2} = 2.306$ for 95 percent confidence. The 95 percent confidence intervals for the coefficients are

Slope

$$b_1 - t_{n-2}s_{b_1} \le \beta_1 \le b_1 + t_{n-2}s_{b_1}$$

$$1.9641 - (2.306)(0.86101) \le \beta_1 \le 1.9641 + (2.306)(0.86101)$$

$$-0.0213 \le \beta_1 \le 3.9495$$

Intercept

$$b_0 - t_{n-2}s_{b_0} \le \beta_0 \le b_0 + t_{n-2}s_{b_0}$$

$$49.477 - (2.306)(10.066) \le \beta_0 \le 49.477 + (2.306)(10.066)$$

$$26.26 \le \beta_0 \le 72.69$$

These confidence intervals are fairly wide. The width of any confidence interval can be reduced by obtaining a larger sample, partly because the *t*-value would shrink (toward the normal *z*-value) but mainly because the standard errors shrink as *n* increases. For the exam scores, the slope includes zero, suggesting that the true slope could be zero.

Hypothesis Tests

Is the true slope different from zero? This is an important question because if $\beta_1 = 0$, then X cannot influence Y and the regression model collapses to a constant β_0 plus a random error term:

Initial Model	*If $\beta_1 = 0$*	*Then*
$y_i = \beta_0 + \beta_1 x_i + \varepsilon_i$	$y_i = \beta_0 + (0)x_i + \varepsilon_i$	$y_i = \beta_0 + \varepsilon_i$

We could also test for a zero intercept. The hypotheses to be tested are

Test for Zero Slope	*Test for Zero Intercept*
$H_0: \beta_1 = 0$	$H_0: \beta_0 = 0$
$H_1: \beta_1 \ne 0$	$H_1: \beta_0 \ne 0$

For either coefficient, we use a *t* test with $v = n - 2$ degrees of freedom. The test statistics are

(12.24)
$$t = \frac{b_1 - 0}{s_{b_1}} \qquad \text{(slope)}$$

(12.25)
$$t = \frac{b_0 - 0}{s_{b_0}} \qquad \text{(intercept)}$$

Usually we are interested in testing whether the parameter is equal to zero as shown here, but you may substitute another value in place of 0 if you wish. The critical value of t_{n-2} is obtained from Appendix D or from Excel's function =TDIST(t,deg_freedom, tails) where tails is 1 (one-tailed test) or 2 (two-tailed test). Often, the researcher uses a two-tailed test as the starting point, because rejection in a two-tailed test always implies rejection in a one-tailed test (but not vice versa).

Test for Zero Slope: Exam Scores 🐝 ExamScores

For the exam scores, we would anticipate a positive slope (i.e., more study hours should improve exam scores) so we will use a right-tailed test:

Hypotheses	Test Statistic	Critical Value	Decision
$H_0: \beta_1 \le 0$ $H_1: \beta_1 > 0$	$t = \dfrac{b_1 - 0}{s_{b_1}} = \dfrac{1.9641 - 0}{0.86095} = 2.281$	$t_{.05} = 1.860$	Reject H_0 (i.e., slope is positive)

We can reject the hypothesis of a zero slope in a right-tailed test. (We would be unable to do so in a two-tailed test because the critical value of our *t* statistic would be 2.306.) Once we have the test statistic for the slope or intercept, we can find the *p*-value by using Excel's function =TDIST(t, deg_freedom, tails). The *p*-value method is preferred by researchers, because it obviates the need for prior specification of α.

Parameter	Excel Function	p-Value
Slope	=TDIST(2.281,8,1)	.025995 (right-tailed test)

Using Excel: Exam Scores ExamScores

These calculations are normally done by computer (we have demonstrated the calculations only to illustrate the formulas). The Excel menu to accomplish these tasks is shown in Figure 12.18. The resulting output, shown in Figure 12.19, can be used to verify our calculations. Excel always does two-tailed tests, so you must halve the *p*-value if you need a one-tailed test. You may specify the confidence level, but Excel's default is 95 percent confidence.

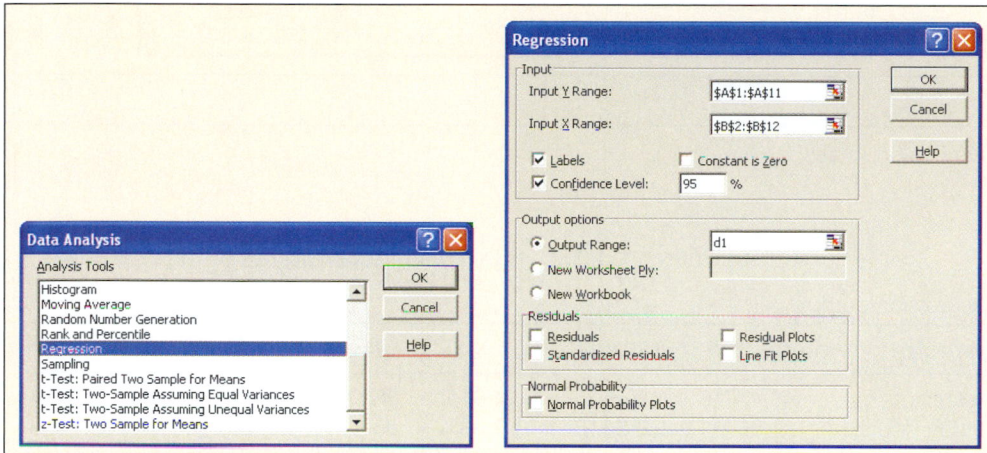

FIGURE 12.18

Excel's regression menu

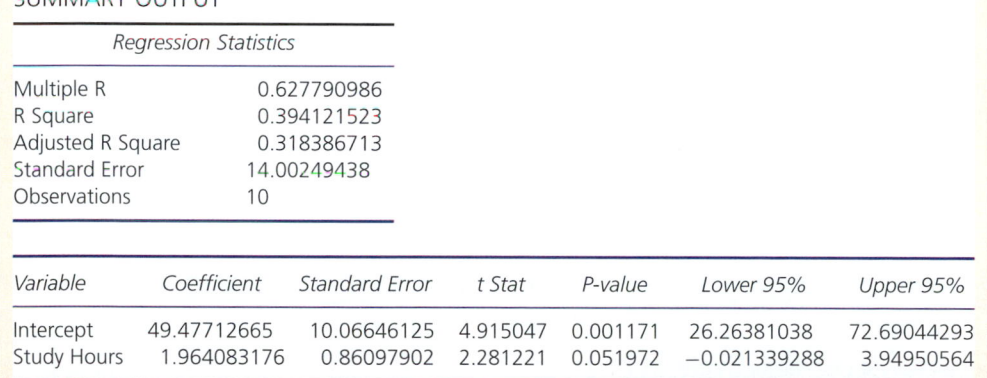

FIGURE 12.19

Excel's regression results for exam scores

SUMMARY OUTPUT

Regression Statistics

Multiple R	0.627790986
R Square	0.394121523
Adjusted R Square	0.318386713
Standard Error	14.00249438
Observations	10

Variable	Coefficient	Standard Error	t Stat	P-value	Lower 95%	Upper 95%
Intercept	49.47712665	10.06646125	4.915047	0.001171	26.26381038	72.69044293
Study Hours	1.964083176	0.86097902	2.281221	0.051972	−0.021339288	3.94950564

Tip

Avoid checking the Constant is Zero box in Excel's menu. This would force the intercept through the origin, changing the model drastically. Leave this option to the experts.

Using MegaStat: Exam Scores ExamScores

Figure 12.20 shows MegaStat's menu, and Figure 12.21 shows MegaStat's regression output for this data. The output format is similar to Excel's, except that MegaStat highlights coefficients that differ significantly from zero at $\alpha = .05$ in a two-tailed test.

FIGURE 12.20

MegaStat's regression menu

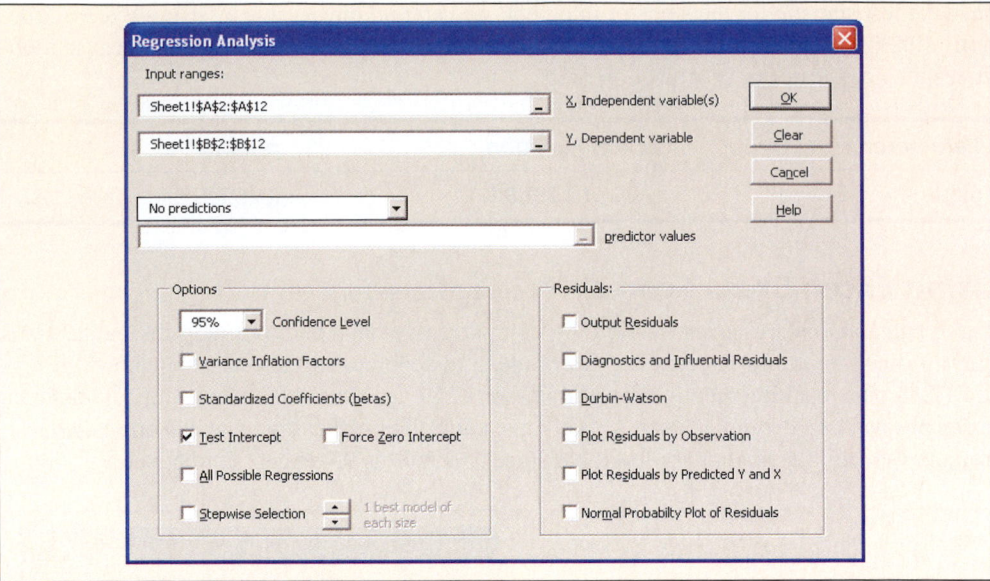

FIGURE 12.21

MegaStat's regression results for exam scores

Regression Analysis

	r^2	0.394		n	10	
	r	0.628		k	1	
	Std. Error	14.002		Dep. Var.	Exam Score	

Regression output					confidence interval	
variables	coefficients	std. error	t (df = 8)	p-value	95% lower	95% upper
Intercept	49.4771	10.0665	4.915	.0012	26.2638	72.6904
Study Hours	1.9641	0.8610	2.281	.0520	−0.0213	3.9495

Using MINITAB: Exam Scores ExamScores

Figure 12.22 shows MINITAB's regression menus, and Figure 12.23 shows MINITAB's regression output for this data. MINITAB gives you the same general output as Excel, but with strongly rounded results.*

FIGURE 12.22

MINITAB's regression menus

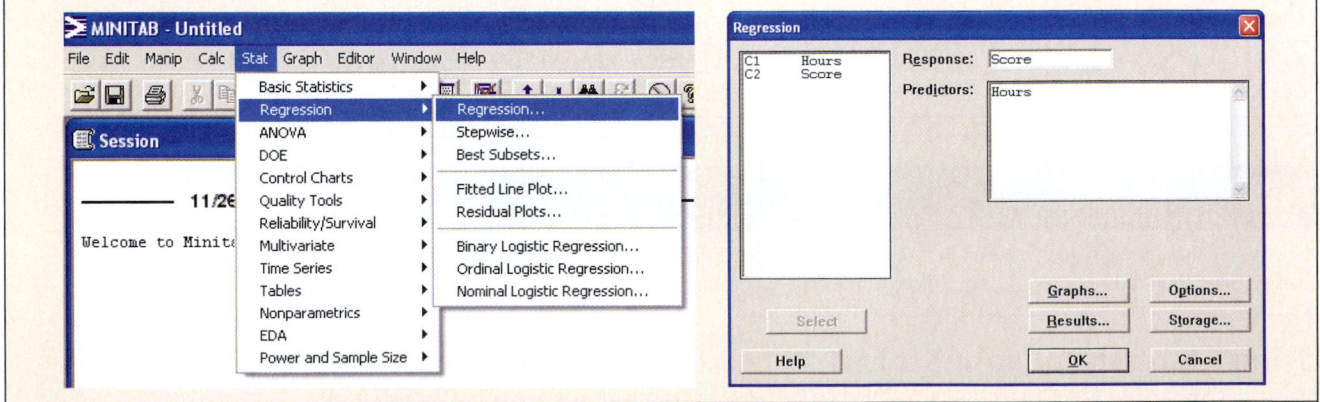

---

*You may have noticed that both Excel and MINITAB calculated something called "adjusted R-Square." For a bivariate regression, this statistic is of little interest, but in the next chapter it becomes important.

FIGURE 12.23

MINITAB's regression results
for exam scores

The regression equation is
Score = 49.5 + 1.96 Hours

Predictor	Coef	SE Coef	T	P
Constant	49.48	10.07	4.92	0.001
Hours	1.9641	0.8610	2.28	0.052

S = 14.00	R-Sq = 39.4%	R-Sq(adj) = 31.8%

Time-series data generally yield better "fit" than cross-sectional data, as we can illustrate by using a sample of the same size as the exam scores. In the United States, taxes are collected at a variety of levels: local, state, and federal. During the prosperous 1990s, personal income rose dramatically, but so did taxes, as indicated in Table 12.6.

EXAMPLE

Aggregate U.S. Tax Function   **Taxes**

TABLE 12.6   U.S. Income and Taxes, 1991–2000

Year	Personal Income ($ billions)	Personal Taxes ($ billions)
1991	5,085.4	610.5
1992	5,390.4	635.8
1993	5,610.0	674.6
1994	5,888.0	722.6
1995	6,200.9	778.3
1996	6,547.4	869.7
1997	6,937.0	968.8
1998	7,426.0	1,070.4
1999	7,777.3	1,159.2
2000	8,319.2	1,288.2

Source: *Economic Report of the President, 2002.*

We will assume a linear relationship:

$$Taxes = \beta_0 + \beta_1 Income + \varepsilon_i$$

Since taxes do not depend solely on income, the random error term will reflect all other factors that influence taxes as well as possible measurement error.

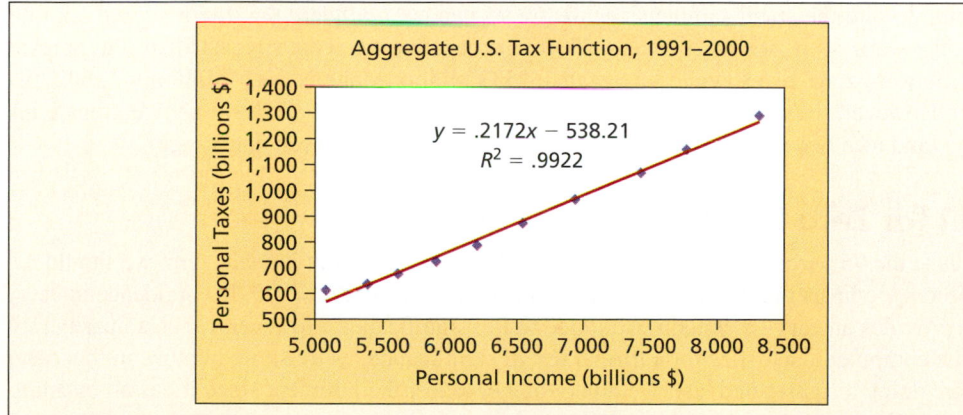

FIGURE 12.24

U.S. aggregate income
and taxes

Based on the scatter plot and Excel's fitted linear regression, displayed in Figure 12.24, the linear model seems justified. The very high R^2 says that *Income* "explains" over 99 percent of the variation in *Taxes*. Such a good fit is not surprising, since the federal government and most states (and some cities) rely on income taxes. However, many aggregate financial variables are correlated due to inflation and general economic growth. Although causation can be assumed between *Income* and *Taxes* in our model, some of the excellent "fit" is due to time trends (a common problem in time-series data).

Using MegaStat: U.S. Income and Taxes ✦ Taxes

For a more detailed look, we examine MegaStat's regression output for this data, shown in Figure 12.25. On average, each extra $100 of income yielded an extra $21.72 in taxes ($b_1 = .2172$). Both coefficients are nonzero in MegaStat's two-tailed test, as indicated by the tiny p-values (highlighting indicates that significance at $\alpha = .01$). For all practical purposes, the p-values are zero, which indicates that this sample result did not arise by chance (rarely would you see such small p-values in cross-sectional data, but they are not unusual in time-series data).

FIGURE 12.25

MegaStat's regression results for tax data

Regression output						Confidence Interval	
Variables	Coefficients	Std. Error	t (df = 8)	p-value	95% lower	95% upper
Intercept	−538.207	45.033	−11.951	2.21E-06	−642.0530	−434.3620
Income	0.2172	0.00683	31.830	1.03E-09	0.2015	0.2330

MegaStat's Confidence Intervals: U.S. Income and Taxes ✦ Taxes

Degrees of freedom are $n - 2 = 10 - 2 = 8$, so from Appendix D we obtain $t_{n-2} = 2.306$ for 95 percent confidence. Using MegaStat's estimated standard errors for the coefficients, we verify MegaStat's confidence intervals for the true coefficients:

Slope

$$b_1 - t_{n-2}s_{b_1} \leq \beta_1 \leq b_1 + t_{n-2}s_{b_1}$$

$$0.2172 - (2.306)(0.00683) \leq \beta_1 \leq 0.2172 + (2.306)(0.00683)$$

$$0.2015 \leq \beta_1 \leq 0.2330$$

Intercept

$$b_0 - t_{n-2}s_{b_0} \leq \beta_0 \leq b_0 + t_{n-2}s_{b_0}$$

$$-538.207 - (2.306)(45.0326) \leq \beta_0 \leq -538.207 + (2.306)(45.0326)$$

$$-642.05 \leq \beta_0 \leq -434.36$$

The narrow confidence interval for the slope suggests a high degree of precision in the estimate, despite the small sample size. We are 95 percent confident that the marginal tax rate (i.e., the slope) is between .2015 and .2330. The negative intercept suggests that if aggregate income were zero, taxes would be *negative* $538 billion (range is −434 billion to −642 billion). However, the intercept makes no sense, since no economy can have zero aggregate income (and also because *Income* = 0 is very far outside the observed data range).

Test for Zero Slope: Tax Data ✦ Taxes

Because the 95 percent confidence interval for the slope does not include zero, we should reject the hypothesis that the slope is zero in a two-tailed test at $\alpha = .05$. A confidence interval thus provides an easy-to-explain two-tailed test of significance. However, we customarily rely on the computed t statistics for a formal test of significance, as illustrated below. In this case, we are doing a right-tailed test. We do not bother to test the intercept since it has no meaning in this problem.

Hypotheses	Test Statistic	Critical Value	Decision
$H_0: \beta_1 \leq 0$	$t = \dfrac{b_1 - 0}{s_{b_1}} = \dfrac{0.2172 - 0}{0.00683} = 31.83$	$t_{.05} = 1.860$	Reject H_0 (i.e., slope is positive)
$H_1: \beta_1 > 0$			

Tip

The test for zero slope always yields a *t* statistic that is identical to the test for zero correlation coefficient. Therefore, it is not necessary to do both tests. Since regression output always includes a *t*-test for the slope, that is the test we usually use.

SECTION EXERCISES

12.21 A regression was performed using data on 32 NFL teams in 2003. The variables were $Y =$ current value of team (millions of dollars) and $X =$ total debt held by the team owners (millions of dollars). (a) Write the fitted regression equation. (b) Construct a 95 percent confidence interval for the slope. (c) Perform a right-tailed *t* test for zero slope at $\alpha = .05$. State the hypotheses clearly. (d) Use Excel to find the *p*-value for the *t* statistic for the slope. (Data are from *Forbes* 172, no. 5, pp. 82–83.)   **NFL**

variables	coefficients	std. error
Intercept	557.4511	25.3385
Debt	3.0047	0.8820

12.22 A regression was performed using data on 16 randomly selected charities in 2003. The variables were $Y =$ expenses (millions of dollars) and $X =$ revenue (millions of dollars). (a) Write the fitted regression equation. (b) Construct a 95 percent confidence interval for the slope. (c) Perform a right-tailed *t* test for zero slope at $\alpha = .05$. State the hypotheses clearly. (d) Use Excel to find the *p*-value for the *t* statistic for the slope. (Data are from *Forbes* 172, no. 12, p. 248, and www.forbes.com.)   **Charities**

variables	coefficients	std. error
Intercept	7.6425	10.0403
Revenue	0.9467	0.0936

Decomposition of Variance

12.6
ANALYSIS OF VARIANCE: OVERALL FIT

A regression seeks to explain variation in the dependent variable around its mean. A simple way to see this is to express the deviation of y_i from its mean $\bar{y}$ as the sum of the deviation of y_i from the regression estimate $\hat{y}_i$ plus the deviation of the regression estimate $\hat{y}_i$ from the mean $\bar{y}$:

$$y_i - \bar{y} = (y_i - \hat{y}_i) + (\hat{y}_i - \bar{y}) \qquad \text{(adding and subtracting } \hat{y}_i) \qquad \textbf{(12.26)}$$

It can be shown that this same decomposition also holds for the *sums of squares:*

$$\sum_{i=1}^{n}(y_i - \bar{y})^2 = \sum_{i=1}^{n}(y_i - \hat{y}_i)^2 + \sum_{i=1}^{n}(\hat{y}_i - \bar{y})^2 \qquad \text{(sums of squares)} \qquad \textbf{(12.27)}$$

This *decomposition of variance* may be written as

$$\begin{array}{ccccc} SST & = & SSE & + & SSR \\ \text{(\textit{total} variation} & & \text{(unexplained} & & \text{(variation explained} \\ \text{around the mean)} & & \text{or \textit{error} variation)} & & \text{by the \textit{regression})} \end{array}$$

F Statistic for Overall Fit

Regression output always includes the analysis of variance (ANOVA) table that shows the magnitudes of *SSR* and *SSE* along with their degrees of freedom and *F* statistic. For a bivariate regression, the *F* statistic is

$$(12.28) \quad F = \frac{MSR}{MSE} = \frac{SSR/1}{SSE/(n-2)} = (n-2)\frac{SSR}{SSE} \quad (F \text{ statistic for bivariate regression})$$

The *F* statistic reflects both the sample size and the ratio of *SSR* to *SSE*. For a given sample size, a larger *F* statistic indicates a better fit (larger *SSR* relative to *SSE*), while *F* close to zero indicates a poor fit (small *SSR* relative to *SSE*). The *F* statistic must be compared with a critical value $F_{1,n-2}$ from Appendix F for whatever level of significance is desired, and we can find the *p*-value by using Excel's function =FDIST(F,1,n-2). Software packages provide the *p*-value automatically.

EXAMPLE

Exam Scores:
F Statistic

ExamScores

Figure 12.26 shows MegaStat's ANOVA table for the exam scores. The *F* statistic is

$$F = \frac{MSR}{MSE} = \frac{1020.3412}{196.0698} = 5.20$$

From Appendix F the critical value of $F_{1,8}$ at the 5 percent level of significance would be 5.32, so the exam score regression is not quite significant at $\alpha = .05$. The *p*-value of .052 says a sample such as ours would be expected about 52 times in 1,000 samples if *X* and *Y* were unrelated. In other words, if we reject the hypothesis of no relationship between *X* and *Y*, we face a Type I error risk of 5.2 percent. This *p*-value might be called *marginally significant*.

FIGURE 12.26

MegaStat's ANOVA table for exam data

ANOVA table

Source	SS	df	MS	F	p-value
Regression	1,020.3412	1	1,020.3412	5.20	.0520
Residual	1,568.5588	8	196.0698		
Total	2,588.9000	9			

From the ANOVA table, we can calculate the standard error from the mean square for the residuals:

$$s_{yx} = \sqrt{MSE} = \sqrt{196.0698} = 14.002 \quad \text{(standard error for exam scores)}$$

Tip

In a bivariate regression, the *F* test always yields the same *p*-value as a two-tailed *t* test for zero slope, which in turn always gives the same *p*-value as a two-tailed test for zero correlation. The relationship between the test statistics is $F = t^2$.

SECTION EXERCISES

12.23 Below is a regression using *X* = home price (000), *Y* = annual taxes (000), *n* = 20 homes. (a) Write the fitted regression equation. (b) Write the formula for each *t* statistic and verify the *t* statistics shown below. (c) State the degrees of freedom for the *t* tests and find the two-tail critical value for *t* by using Appendix D. (d) Use Excel's function =TDIST(t, deg_freedom, tails) to verify the *p*-value shown for each *t* statistic (slope, intercept). (e) Verify that $F = t^2$ for the slope. (f) In your own words, describe the fit of this regression.

R²	0.452
Std. Error	0.454
n	12

ANOVA table

Source	SS	df	MS	F	p-value
Regression	1.6941	1	1.6941	8.23	.0167
Residual	2.0578	10	0.2058		
Total	3.7519	11			

Regression output | | | | | confidence interval | |

variables	coefficients	std. error	t (df = 10)	p-value	95% lower	95% upper
Intercept	1.8064	0.6116	2.954	.0144	0.4438	3.1691
Slope	0.0039	0.0014	2.869	.0167	0.0009	0.0070

12.24 Below is a regression using *X* average price, *Y* = units sold, *n* = 20 stores. (a) Write the fitted regression equation. (b) Write the formula for each *t* statistic and verify the *t* statistics shown below. (c) State the degrees of freedom for the *t* tests and find the two-tail critical value for *t* by using Appendix D. (d) Use Excel's function =TDIST(t, deg_freedom, tails) to verify the *p*-value shown for each *t* statistic (slope, intercept). (e) Verify that $F = t^2$ for the slope. (f) In your own words, describe the fit of this regression.

R²	0.200
Std. Error	26.128
n	20

ANOVA table

Source	SS	df	MS	F	p-value
Regression	3,080.89	1	3,080.89	4.51	.0478
Residual	12,288.31	18	682.68		
Total	15,369.20	19			

Regression output | | | | | confidence interval | |

variables	coefficients	std. error	t (df = 18)	p-value	95% lower	95% upper
Intercept	614.9300	51.2343	12.002	.0000	507.2908	722.5692
Slope	−109.1120	51.3623	−2.124	.0478	−217.0202	−1.2038

Instructions for Exercises 12.25–12.27: (a) Use Excel's Tools > Data Analysis > Regression (or MegaStat or MINITAB) to obtain regression estimates. (b) Interpret the 95 percent confidence interval for the slope. Does it contain zero? (c) Interpret the t test for the slope and its p-value. (d) Interpret the F statistic. (e) Verify that the p-value for F is the same as for the slope's t statistic, and show that $t^2 = F$. (f) Describe the fit of the regression.

12.25   Portfolio Returns (%) on Selected Mutual Funds ($n = 17$ funds)   Portfolio

Last Year (X)	This Year (Y)
11.9	15.4
19.5	26.7
11.2	18.2
14.1	16.7
14.2	13.2
5.2	16.4
20.7	21.1
11.3	12.0
−1.1	12.1
3.9	7.4
12.9	11.5
12.4	23.0
12.5	12.7
2.7	15.1
8.8	18.7
7.2	9.9
5.9	18.9

12.26   Number of Orders and Shipping Cost ($n = 12$ orders)   ShipCost

Orders (X)	($) Ship Cost (Y)
1,068	4,489
1,026	5,611
767	3,290
885	4,113
1,156	4,883
1,146	5,425
892	4,414
938	5,506
769	3,346
677	3,673
1,174	6,542
1,009	5,088

12.27   Moviegoer Spending on Snacks ($n = 10$ purchases)   Movies

Age (X)	$ Spent (Y)
30	2.85
50	6.50
34	1.50
12	6.35
37	6.20
33	6.75
36	3.60
26	6.10
18	8.35
46	4.35

Mini Case   12.2

Airplane Cockpit Noise 🦅 Cockpit

Career airline pilots face the risk of progressive hearing loss, due to the noisy cockpits of most jet aircraft. Much of the noise comes not from engines but from air roar, which increases at high speeds. To assess this workplace hazard, a pilot measured cockpit noise at randomly selected points during the flight by using a handheld meter. Noise level (in decibels) was measured in seven different aircraft at the first officer's left ear position using a handheld meter. For reference, 60 dB is a normal conversation, 75 is a typical vacuum cleaner, 85 is city traffic, 90 is a typical hair dryer, and 110 is a chain saw. Table 12.7 shows 61 observations on cockpit noise (decibels) and airspeed (knots indicated air speed, KIAS) for a Boeing 727, an older type of aircraft lacking design improvements in newer planes.

TABLE 12.7   **Cockpit Noise Level and Airspeed for B-727 (*n* = 61)** 🦅 **Cockpit**

Speed	Noise	Speed	Noise	Speed	Noise	Speed	Noise	Speed	Noise	Speed	Noise
250	83	380	93	340	90	330	91	350	90	272	84.5
340	89	380	91	340	91	360	94	380	92	310	88
320	88	390	94	380	96	370	94.5	310	88	350	90
330	89	400	95	385	96	380	95	295	87	370	91
346	92	400	96	420	97	395	96	280	86	405	93
260	85	405	97	230	82	365	91	320	88	250	82
280	84	320	89	340	91	320	88	330	90		
395	92	310	88.5	250	86	250	85	320	88		
380	92	250	82	320	89	250	82	340	89		
400	93	280	87	340	90	320	88	350	90		
335	91	320	89	320	90	305	88	270	84		

The scatter plot in Figure 12.27 suggests that a linear model provides a reasonable description of the data. The fitted regression shows that each additional knot of airspeed increases the noise level by 0.0765 dB. Thus, a 100-knot increase in airspeed would add about 7.65 dB of noise. The intercept of 64.229 suggests that if the plane were not flying (*KIAS* = 0) the noise level would be only slightly greater than a normal conversation.

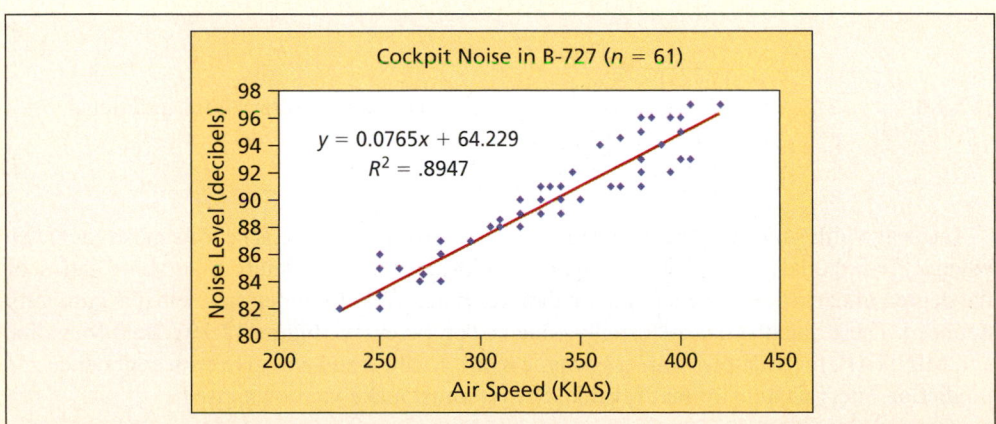

FIGURE 12.27

Scatter plot of cockpit noise
Data courtesy of
Capt. R. E. Hartl (ret) of
Delta Airlines.

The regression results in Figure 12.28 show that the fit is very good (R^2 = .895) and that the regression is highly significant (F = 501.16, $p < .001$). Both the slope and intercept have *p*-values below .001, indicating that the true parameters are nonzero. Thus, the regression is significant, as well as having practical value.

FIGURE 12.28

Regression results of cockpit noise

Regression Analysis

r²	0.895	n	61	
r	0.946	k	1	
Std. Error	1.292	Dep. Var.	**Noise**	

ANOVA table

Source	SS	df	MS	F	p-value
Regression	836.9817	1	836.9817	501.16	1.60E-30
Residual	98.5347	59	1.6701		
Total	935.5164	60			

Regression output   *confidence interval*

variables	coefficients	std. error	t (df = 59)	p-value	95% lower	95% upper
Intercept	64.2294	1.1489	55.907	8.29E-53	61.9306	66.5283
Speed	0.0765	0.0034	22.387	1.60E-30	0.0697	0.0834

12.7 CONFIDENCE AND PREDICTION INTERVALS FOR Y

How to Construct an Interval Estimate for Y

The regression line is an estimate of the *conditional mean* of Y (i.e., the expected value of Y for a given value of X). But the estimate may be too high or too low. To make this *point estimate* more useful, we need an *interval estimate* to show a range of likely values. To do this, we insert the x_i value into the fitted regression equation, calculate the estimated $\hat{y}_i$, and use the formulas shown below. The first formula gives a **confidence interval** for the conditional mean of Y, while the second is a **prediction interval** for individual values of Y. The formulas are similar, except that prediction intervals are wider because *individual Y* values vary more than the *mean* of Y.

$$(12.29) \qquad \hat{y}_i \pm t_{n-2} s_{yx} \sqrt{\frac{1}{n} + \frac{(x_i - \bar{x})^2}{\displaystyle\sum_{i=1}^{n}(x_i - \bar{x})^2}} \qquad \text{(confidence interval for mean of } Y\text{)}$$

$$(12.30) \qquad \hat{y}_i \pm t_{n-2} s_{yx} \sqrt{1 + \frac{1}{n} + \frac{(x_i - \bar{x})^2}{\displaystyle\sum_{i=1}^{n}(x_i - \bar{x})^2}} \qquad \text{(prediction interval for individual } Y\text{)}$$

Interval width varies with the value of x_i, being narrowest when x_i is near its mean (note that when $x_i = \bar{x}$ the last term under the square root disappears completely). For some data sets, the degree of narrowing near $\bar{x}$ is almost indiscernible, while for other data sets it is quite pronounced. These calculations are usually done by computer (see Figure 12.29). Both MegaStat and MINITAB, for example, will let you type in the x_i values and will give both confidence and prediction intervals *only* for that x_i value, but you must make your own graphs.

Two Illustrations: Exam Scores and Taxes 🐭 **ExamScores,** 🐭 **Taxes**

Figures 12.30 (exam scores) and 12.31 (taxes) illustrate these formulas (a complete calculation worksheet is shown in *LearningStats*). The contrast between the two graphs is striking.

FIGURE 12.29

MegaStat's confidence and prediction intervals

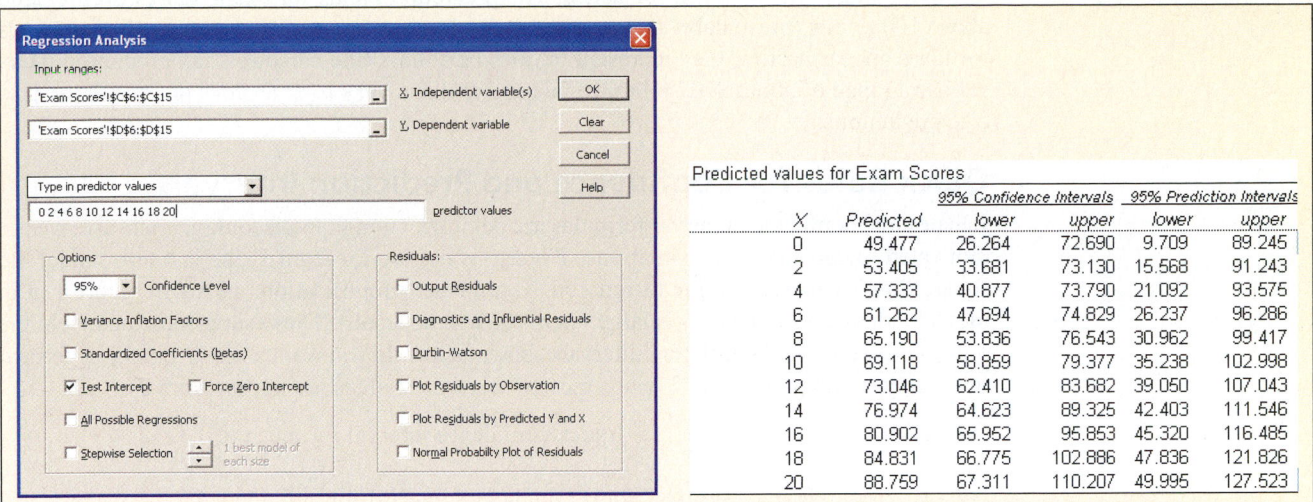

FIGURE 12.30

Intervals for exam scores

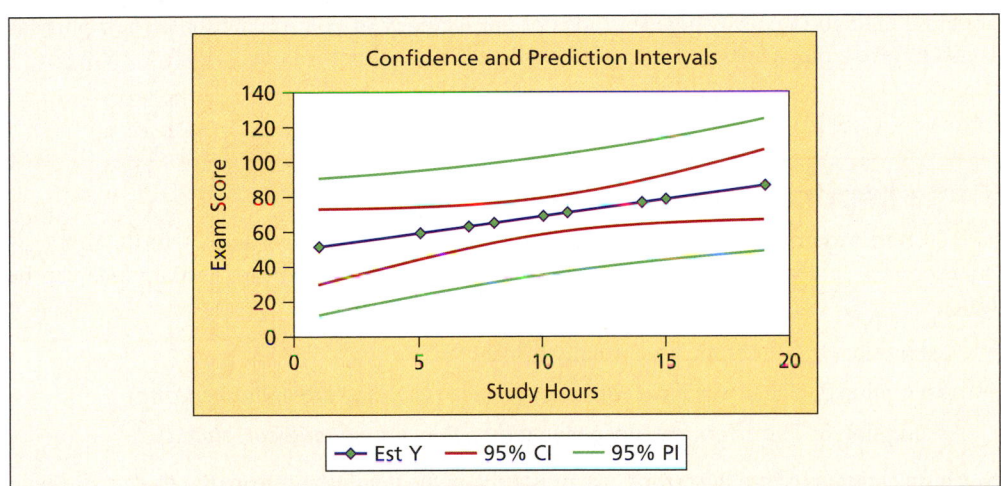

FIGURE 12.31

Intervals for taxes

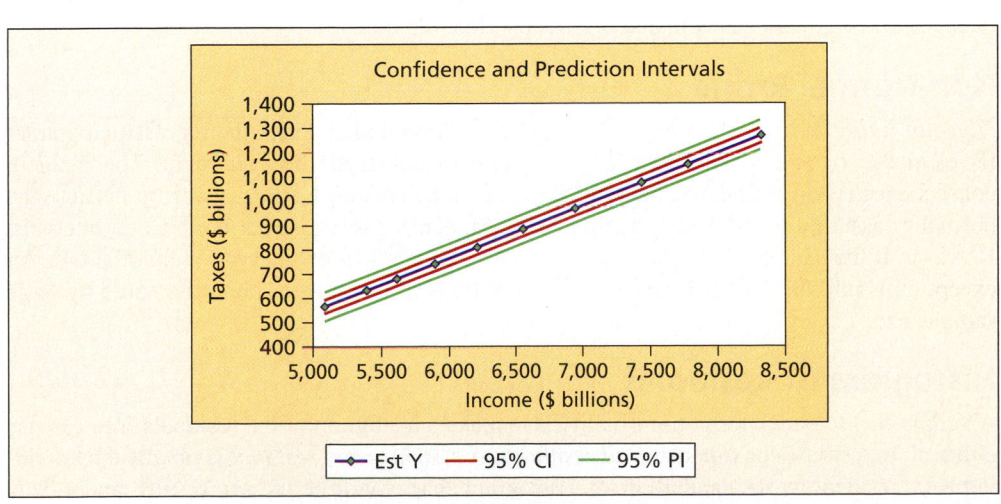

Confidence and prediction intervals for exam scores are wide and clearly curved, while for taxes they are narrow and almost straight. We would expect this from the scatter plots ($R^2 = .3941$ for exams, $R^2 = .9922$ for taxes). The prediction bands for exam scores even extend above 100 points (presumably the upper limit for an exam score). While the prediction bands for taxes appear narrow, they represent billions of dollars (the narrowest tax prediction interval has a range of about \$107 billion). This shows that a very high R^2 does not guarantee precise predictions.

Quick Rules for Confidence and Prediction Intervals

Because the confidence interval formulas are complex enough to discourage their use, we are motivated to consider approximations. When x_i is not too far from $\bar{x}$, the last term under the square root is small and might be ignored. As a further simplification, we might ignore $1/n$ in the individual Y formula (if n is large, then $1/n$ will be small). These simplifications yield the quick confidence and prediction intervals shown below. If you want a *really* quick 95 percent interval, you can plug in $t = 2$ (since most 95 percent t-values are not far from 2).

$$(12.31) \qquad \hat{y}_i \pm t_{n-2} \frac{s_{yx}}{\sqrt{n}} \qquad \text{(quick confidence interval for mean of } Y)$$

$$(12.32) \qquad \hat{y}_i \pm t_{n-2} s_{yx} \qquad \text{(quick prediction interval for individual } Y)$$

These quick rules lead to constant width intervals and are *not* conservative (i.e., the resulting intervals will be somewhat too narrow). They work best for large samples and when X is near its mean. They are questionable when X is near either extreme of its range. Yet they often are close enough to convey a general idea of the accuracy of your predictions. Their purpose is just to give a quick answer without getting lost in unwieldy formulas.

12.8 VIOLATIONS OF ASSUMPTIONS

Three Important Assumptions

The OLS method makes several assumptions about the random error term ε_i. Although ε_i is unobservable, clues may be found in the residuals e_i. Three important assumptions can be tested:

- Assumption 1: The errors are normally distributed.
- Assumption 2: The errors have constant variance (i.e., they are *homoscedastic*).
- Assumption 3: The errors are independent (i.e., they are *nonautocorrelated*).

Since we cannot observe the error ε_i we must rely on the residuals e_i from the fitted regression for clues about possible violations of these assumptions. Regression residuals often violate one or more of these assumptions. Fortunately, regression is fairly robust in the face of moderate violations of these assumptions. We will examine each violation, explain its consequences, show how to check it, and discuss possible remedies.

Non-Normal Errors

Non-normality of errors is usually considered a mild violation, since the regression parameter estimates b_0 and b_1 and their variances remain unbiased and consistent. The main ill consequence is that confidence intervals for the parameters may be untrustworthy, because the normality assumption is used to justify using Student's t to construct confidence intervals. However, if the sample size is large (say, $n > 30$), the confidence intervals should be OK. An exception would be if outliers exist, posing a serious problem that cannot be cured by large sample size.

Histogram of Residuals 🛩 Cockpit

A simple way to check for non-normality is to make a histogram of the residuals. You can use either plain residuals or **standardized residuals.** A *standardized residual* is obtained by dividing each residual by its standard error. Histogram shapes will be the same, but standardized residuals offer the advantage of a predictable scale (between −3 and +3 unless there are outliers). A simple "eyeball test" can usually reveal outliers or serious asymmetry. Figure 12.32 shows a standardized residual histogram for Mini Case 12.2. There are no outliers and the histogram is roughly symmetric, albeit possibly platykurtic (i.e., flatter than normal).

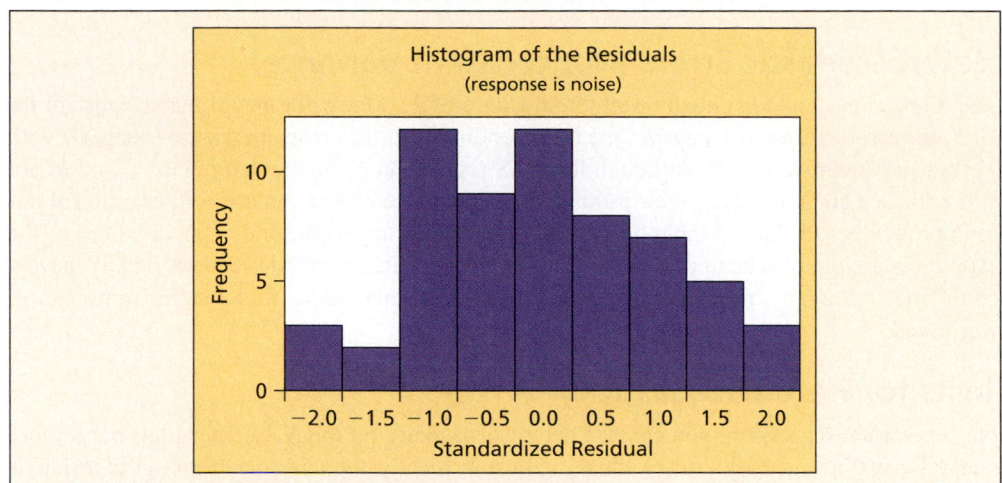

FIGURE 12.32

Cockpit noise residuals
(histogram)

Normal Probability Plot

Another visual test for normality is the probability plot. It is produced as an option by MINITAB and MegaStat. The hypotheses are

H_0: Errors are normally distributed

H_1: Errors are not normally distributed

If the null hypothesis is true, the residual probability plot should be linear. For example in Figure 12.33 we see slight deviations from linearity at the lower and upper ends of the residual probability plot for Mini Case 12.2 (cockpit noise). But overall, the residuals seem to be consistent with the hypothesis of normality. In later chapters we will examine formal tests for normality, but the histogram and probability plot suffice for most purposes.

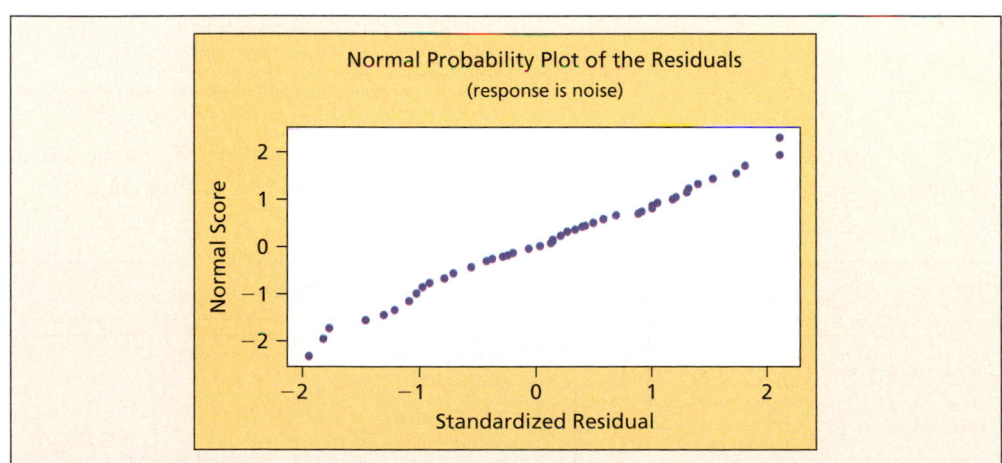

FIGURE 12.33

Cockpit noise residuals
(normal probability plot)

What to Do About Non-Normality?

First, consider trimming outliers—but only if they clearly are mistakes. Second, can you increase the sample size? If so, it will help assure asymptotic normality of the estimates. Third, you could try a logarithmic transformation of both X and Y. However, this is a new model specification which may require advice from a professional statistician. We will discuss data transformations later in this chapter. Fourth, you could do nothing—just be aware of the problem.

Tip

Non-normality is not considered a major violation, so don't worry too much about it *unless* you have major outliers.

Heteroscedastic Errors (Nonconstant Variance)

The regression should fit equally well for all values of X. If the error magnitude is constant for all X, the errors are **homoscedastic** (the ideal condition). If the errors increase or decrease with X, they are **heteroscedastic.** Although the OLS regression parameter estimates b_0 and b_1 are still unbiased and consistent, their estimated variances are biased and are neither efficient nor asymptotically efficient. In the most common form of heteroscedasticity, the variances of the estimators are likely to be understated, resulting in overstated t statistics and artificially narrow confidence intervals. Your regression estimates may thus seem more significant than is warranted.

Tests for Heteroscedasticity

For a bivariate regression, you can see heteroscedasticity on the XY scatter plot, but a more general visual test is to plot the residuals against X. Ideally, there is no pattern in the residuals as we move from left to right:

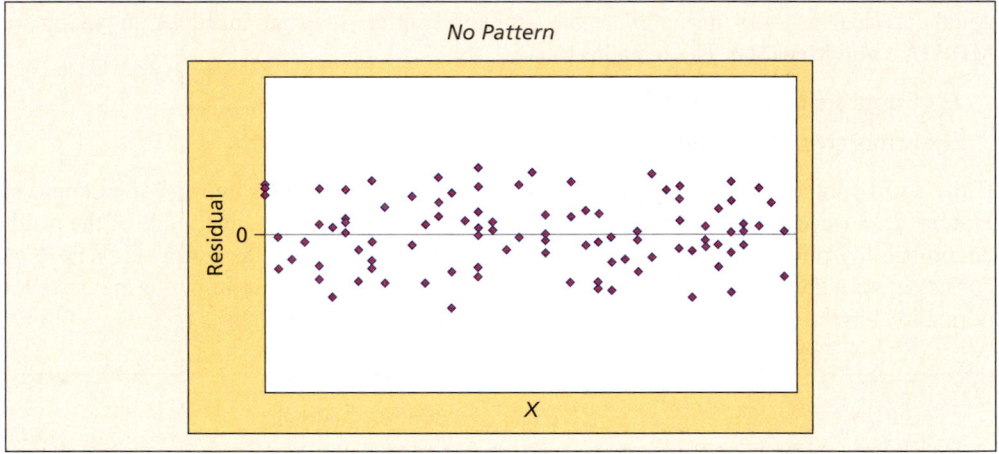

Notice that the residuals *always* have a mean of zero. Although many patterns of nonconstant variance might exist, the "fan-out" pattern (increasing residual variance) is most common:

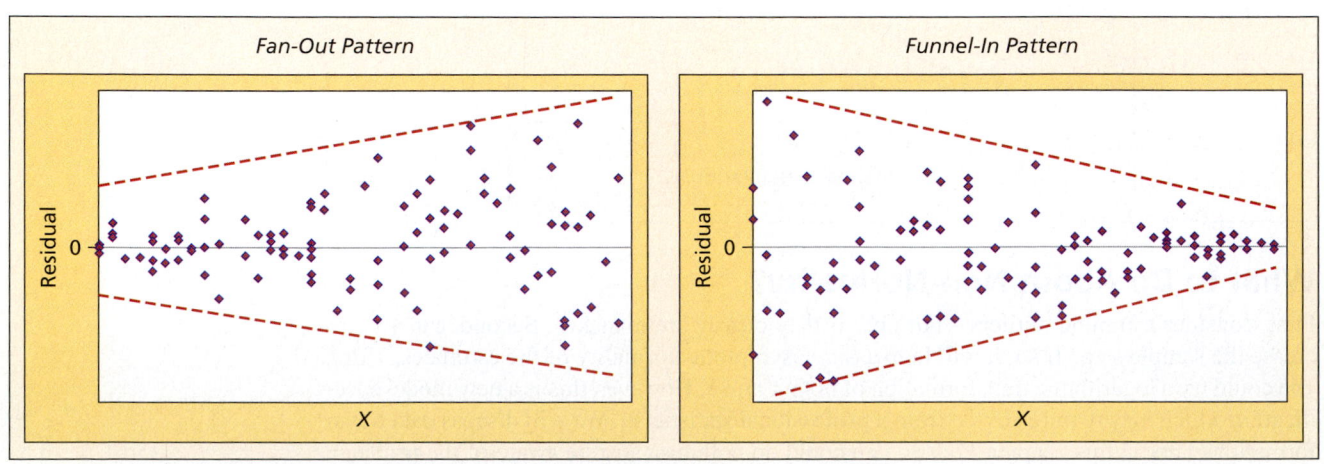

Residual plots provide a fairly sensitive "eyeball test" for heteroscedasticity. The residual plot is therefore considered an important tool in the statistician's diagnostic kit. The hypotheses are

H_0: Errors have constant variance (homoscedastic)

H_1: Errors have nonconstant variance (heteroscedastic)

Figure 12.34 shows a residual plot for Mini Case 12.2 (cockpit noise). In the residual plot, we see residuals of the same magnitude as we look from left to right. A random pattern like this is consistent with the hypothesis of homoscedasticity (constant variance), although some observers might see a hint of a "fan-out" pattern.

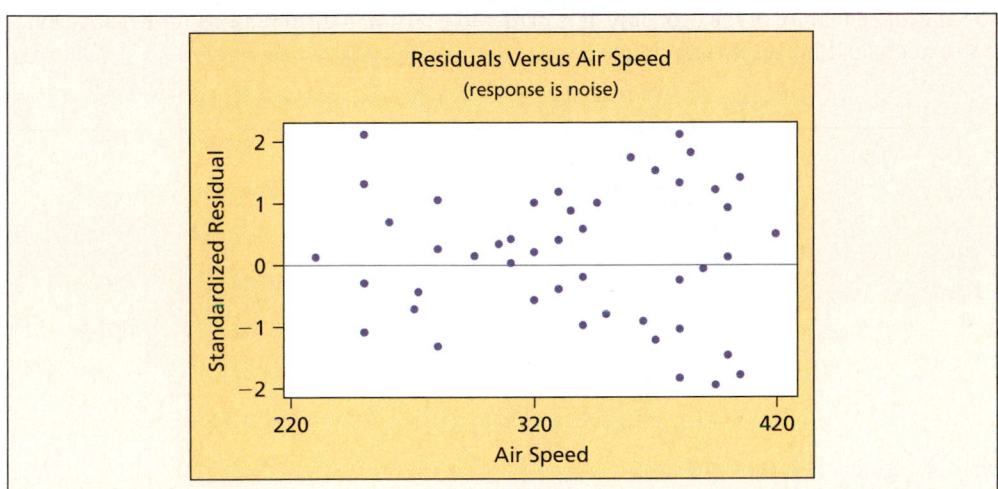

FIGURE 12.34

Cockpit noise residual plot

What to Do About Heteroscedasticity?

Heteroscedasticity may arise in economic time-series data if X and Y increase in magnitude over time, causing the errors also to increase. In financial data (e.g., GDP) heteroscedasticity can sometimes be reduced by expressing the data in constant dollars (dividing by a price index). In cross-sectional data (e.g., total crimes in a state) heteroscedasticity may be mitigated by expressing the data in relative terms (e.g., per capita crime). A more general approach to reducing heteroscedasticity is to transform both X and Y (e.g., by taking logs). However, this is a new model specification, which requires a reverse transformation when making predictions of Y. This approach will be considered later in this chapter.

Tip

Although it can widen the confidence intervals for the coefficients, heteroscedasticity does not bias the estimates. At this stage of your training, it is sufficient just to recognize its existence.

Autocorrelated Errors

Autocorrelation is a pattern of nonindependent errors, mainly found in time-series data.* In a time-series regression, each residual e_t should be independent of its predecessors $e_{t-1}, e_{t-2}, \ldots, e_{t-n}$. Violations of this assumption can show up in different ways. In the simple model of *first-order autocorrelation* we would find that e_t is correlated with e_{t-1}. The OLS estimators b_0 and b_1 are still unbiased and consistent, but their estimated variances are biased in a way that typically leads to confidence intervals that are too narrow and t statistics that are too large. Thus, the model's fit may be overstated.

---

*Cross-sectional data may exhibit autocorrelation, but typically it is an artifact of the order of data entry.

Runs Test for Autocorrelation

Positive autocorrelation is indicated by runs of residuals with the *same* sign, while *negative autocorrelation* is indicated by runs of residuals with *alternating* signs. Such patterns can sometimes be seen in a plot of the residuals against the order of data entry. In the *runs test,* we count the number of sign reversals (i.e., how often does the residual plot cross the zero centerline?). If the pattern is random, the number of sign changes should be approximately $n/2$. Fewer than $n/2$ centerline crossings would suggest positive autocorrelation, while more than $n/2$ centerline crossings would suggest negative autocorrelation. For example, if $n = 50$, we would expect about 25 centerline crossings. In the first illustration, there are only 11 crossings (positive autocorrelation) while in the second illustration there are 36 crossings (negative autocorrelation). Positive autocorrelation is common in economic time-series regressions, due to the cyclical nature of the economy. It is harder to envision logical reasons for negative autocorrelation, and in fact it is rarely observed.

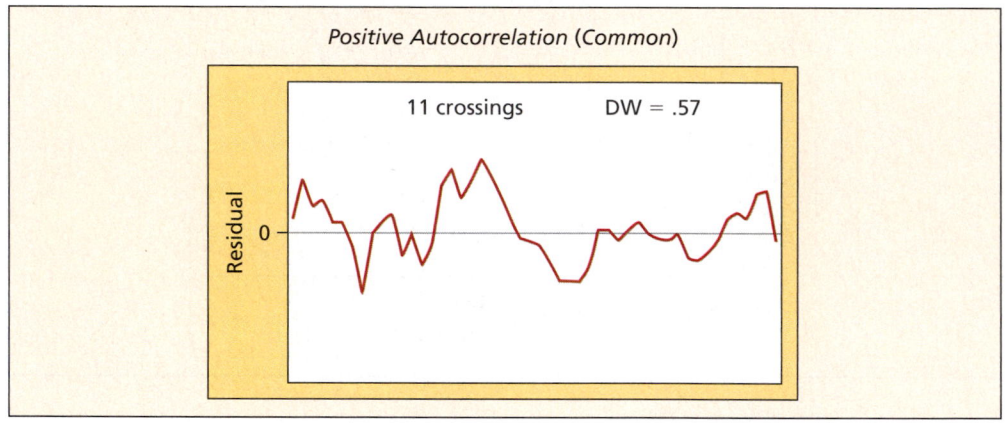

Positive Autocorrelation (Common)

11 crossings   DW = .57

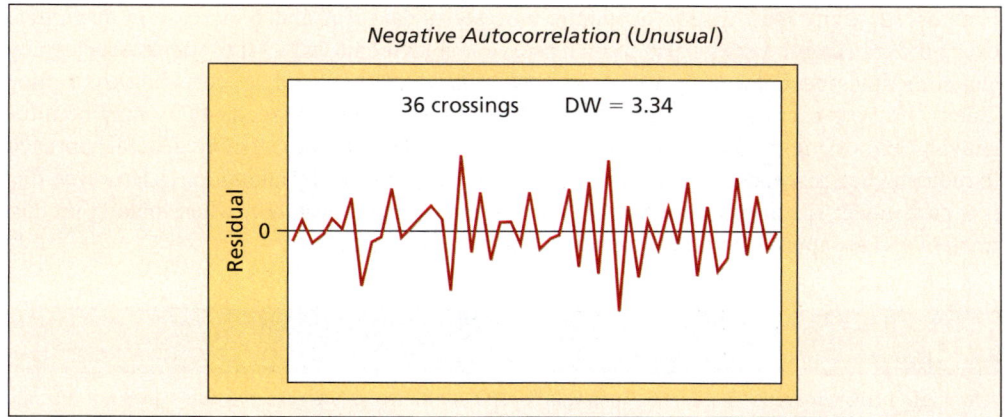

Negative Autocorrelation (Unusual)

36 crossings   DW = 3.34

Durbin-Watson Test

The most widely used test for autocorrelation is the **Durbin-Watson test.** The hypotheses are

H_0: Errors are nonautocorrelated

H_1: Errors are autocorrelated

The Durbin-Watson test statistic for autocorrelation is

$$\textbf{(12.33)} \qquad DW = \frac{\sum\limits_{t=2}^{n}(e_t - e_{t-1})^2}{\sum\limits_{t=1}^{n}e_t^2} \qquad \text{(Durbin-Watson test statistic)}$$

When there is no autocorrelation, the *DW* statistic will be near 2, though its range is from 0 to 4. For a formal hypothesis test, a special table is required. For now, we simply note that in general

> $DW < 2$ suggests positive autocorrelation (common).
>
> $DW \approx 2$ suggests no autocorrelation (ideal).
>
> $DW > 2$ suggests negative autocorrelation (rare).

What to Do About Autocorrelation?

A cure for first-order time-series autocorrelation is to transform both variables. A very simple transformation is the *method of first differences* in which both variables are redefined as *changes:*

$\Delta x_t = x_t - x_{t-1}$ (change in X from period $t - 1$ to period t)

$\Delta y_t = y_t - y_{t-1}$ (change in Y from period $t - 1$ to period t)

Then we regress ΔY against ΔX. This transformation can easily be done in a spreadsheet by subtracting each cell from its predecessor and then re-running the regression. One observation is lost, since the first observation has no predecessor. The method of first differences has logical appeal, since there is little conceptual difference between regressing taxes against income and regressing the *change in taxes* against the *change in income*. The new slope should be the same as in the original model but the new intercept should be zero. You will learn about more general transformations, favored by researchers, if you study econometrics.*

Tip

Although it can widen the confidence intervals for the coefficients, autocorrelation does not bias the estimates. At this stage of your training, it is sufficient just to recognize when you have autocorrelation.

Mini Case   12.3

Money and Inflation 🌐 Money

Does inflation mainly reflect changes in the money supply? Table 12.8 shows data for a time-series regression of the U.S. inflation rate (as measured by the change in the Consumer Price Index or CPI) against the growth of the monetary base (as measured by the change in $M1$ one year earlier). The regression covers the period 1960–2000, or 41 years.

TABLE 12.8   **Percent Change in CPI and Percent Change in M1 in Prior Year**

Year	ΔM1	ΔCPI	Year	ΔM1	ΔCPI	Year	ΔM1	ΔCPI
1960	0.5	0.7	1974	4.3	6.9	1988	4.9	4.6
1961	3.2	1.3	1975	4.7	4.9	1989	0.8	6.1
1962	1.8	1.6	1976	6.7	6.7	1990	4.0	3.1
1963	3.7	1.0	1977	8.0	9.0	1991	8.7	2.9
1964	4.6	1.9	1978	8.0	13.3	1992	14.3	2.7
1965	4.7	3.5	1979	6.9	12.5	1993	10.3	2.7
1966	2.5	3.0	1980	7.0	8.9	1994	1.8	2.5
1967	6.6	4.7	1981	6.9	3.8	1995	−2.1	3.3
1968	7.7	6.2	1982	8.7	3.8	1996	−4.1	1.7
1969	3.3	5.6	1983	9.8	3.9	1997	−0.7	1.6
1970	5.1	3.3	1984	5.8	3.8	1998	2.2	2.7
1971	6.5	3.4	1985	12.3	1.1	1999	2.5	3.4
1972	9.2	8.7	1986	16.9	4.4	2000	−3.3	1.6
1973	5.5	12.3	1987	3.5	4.4			

Source: *Economic Report of the President, 2002.*

---

*Chapter 14 discusses the use of time-series data for forecasting. Autocorrelation will be revisited and you will learn that some forecasting models actually try to take advantage of the dependency among error terms.

The fitted model is $\Delta CPI_t = 3.4368 + 0.1993 \Delta M1_{t-1} (R^2 = .075, F = 3.17)$. The overall fit is not very strong. The probability plot in Figure 12.35 suggests possible non-normality. The plot of residuals in Figure 12.36 shows no strong evidence of heteroscedasticity. In the residual plotted against time (Figure 12.37) we would expect 20 or 21 centerline crossings, but we only see 8, indicating positive autocorrelation (i.e., there are runs of the same sign). The DW statistic is $DW = .58$, also indicating strong positive autocorrelation.

FIGURE 12.35

Residual test for non-normality

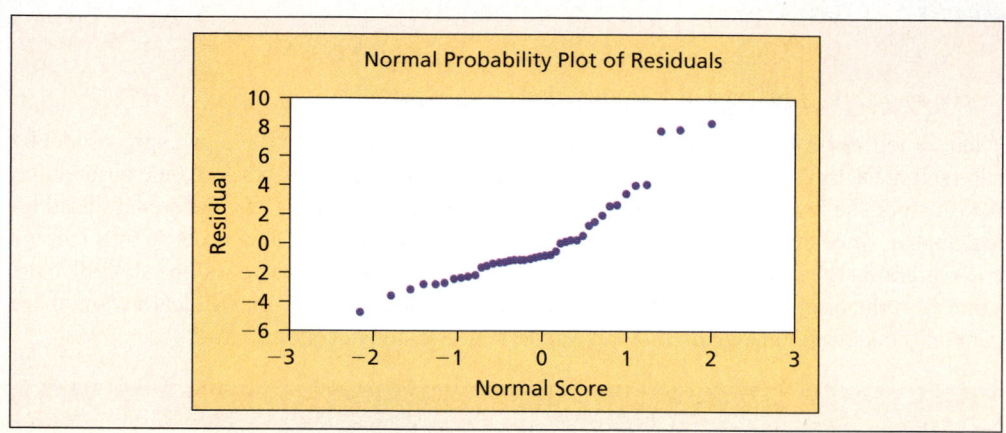

FIGURE 12.36

Residual test for heteroscedasticity

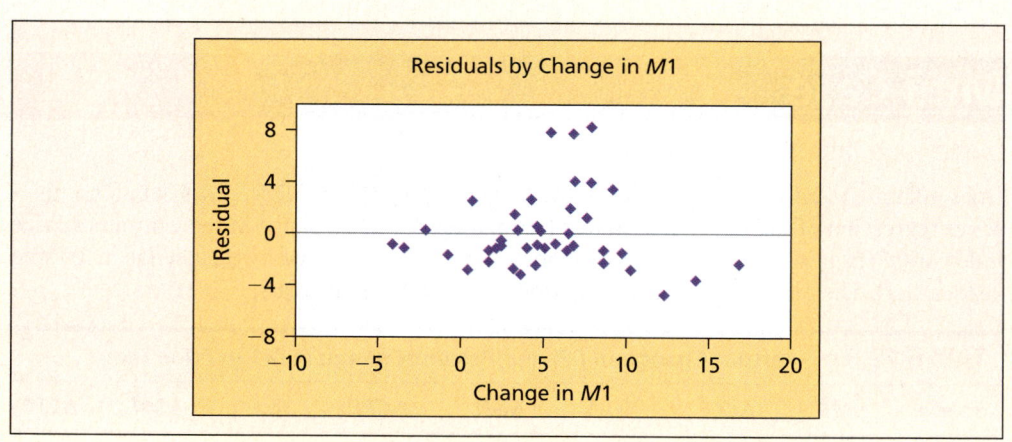

FIGURE 12.37

Residual test for autocorrelation

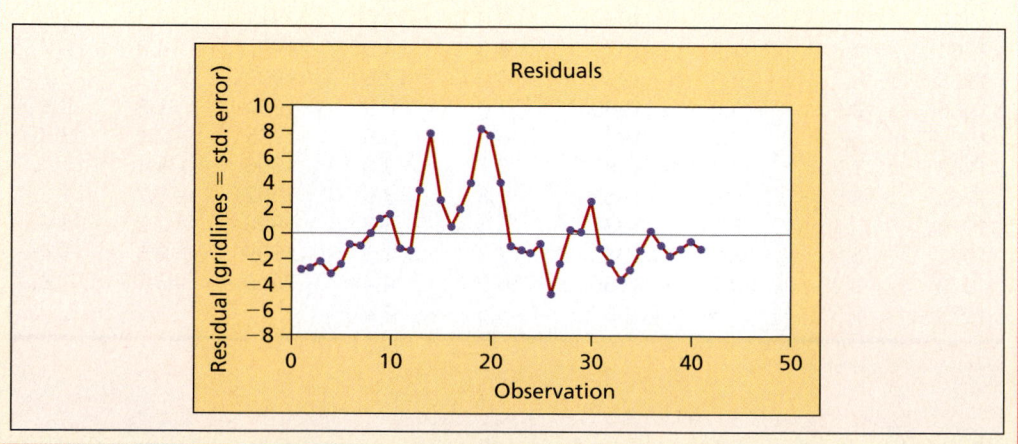

In a regression, we look for observations that are unusual. An observation could be unusual because its *Y*-value is poorly predicted by the regression model (*unusual residual*) or because its unusual *X*-value greatly affects the regression line (*high leverage*). Tests for unusual residuals and high leverage are important diagnostic tools in evaluating the fitted regression.

12.9
UNUSUAL OBSERVATIONS

Standardized Residuals: Excel

Excel's Tools > Data Analysis > Regression provides residuals as an option, as shown in Figure 12.38. Since every regression may have different *Y* units (e.g., stock price in dollars, shipping time in days) it is helpful to *standardize* the residuals by dividing each residual by its standard error. As a rule of thumb (the Empirical Rule) any *standardized residual* whose absolute value is 2 or more is unusual, and any residual whose absolute value is 3 or more would be considered an outlier. Excel obtains its "standardized residuals" by dividing each residual by the standard deviation of the column of residuals. This procedure is not quite correct, as explained below, but generally suffices to identify unusual residuals. Using the Empirical Rule, there are no unusual standardized residuals in Figure 12.38.

FIGURE 12.38

Excel's exam score regression with residuals   **ExamScores**

SUMMARY OUTPUT

Regression Statistics	
Multiple R	0.627790986
R Square	0.394121523
Adjusted R Square	0.318386713
Standard Error	14.00249438
Observations	10

ANOVA

	df	SS	MS	F	Significance F
Regression	1	1020.34121	1020.34121	5.203967954	0.051972204
Residual	8	1568.55879	196.0698488		
Total	9	2588.9			

	Coefficients	Standard Error	t Stat	P-value	Lower 95%	Upper 95%
Intercept	49.47712665	10.06646125	4.915046652	0.001171307	26.26381038	72.69044293
Study Hours	1.964083176	0.86097902	2.281220716	0.051972204	-0.021339288	3.94950564

RESIDUAL OUTPUT

Observation	Predicted Score	Residuals	Standard Residuals
1	51.44120983	1.55879017	0.118075152
2	59.29754253	14.70245747	1.113680937
3	63.22570888	-4.225708885	-0.320088764
4	65.18979206	-22.18979206	-1.680831145
5	69.11795841	-13.11795841	-0.99365839
6	71.08204159	12.91795841	0.978508801
7	76.97429112	19.02570888	1.441158347
8	78.93837429	-9.938374291	-0.752811428
9	78.93837429	5.061625709	0.383407745
10	86.79470699	-3.794706994	-0.287441256

Regression dialog box:

Input
- Input Y Range: $B$1:$B$11
- Input X Range: $C$1:$C$11
- ☑ Labels   ☐ Constant is Zero
- ☐ Confidence Level: 95 %

Output options
- ⦿ Output Range: e1
- ○ New Worksheet Ply:
- ○ New Workbook

Residuals
- ☑ Residuals   ☑ Residual Plots
- ☑ Standardized Residuals   ☐ Line Fit Plots

Normal Probability
- ☐ Normal Probability Plots

[OK] [Cancel] [Help]

Studentized Residuals: MINITAB

MINITAB gives you the same general output as Excel, but with rounded results and more detailed residual information. Its menus are shown in Figure 12.39. MINITAB uses ***studentized residuals,*** obtained by dividing each residual by its *true standard error*. This calculation requires a unique adjustment for each residual, based on the observation's distance from the mean. Studentized residuals are always less than or equal to Excel's "standardized" residuals, but the two generally are not far apart. MINITAB's results confirm that there are no unusual residuals in the exam score regression. An attractive feature of MINITAB is that actual and fitted *Y*-values are displayed (Excel shows only the fitted *Y*-values). MINITAB also gives the standard error for the mean of *Y* (the output column labeled SE Fit), which you can multiply by *t* to get the confidence interval width.

FIGURE 12.39

MINITAB's regression with residuals **ExamScores**

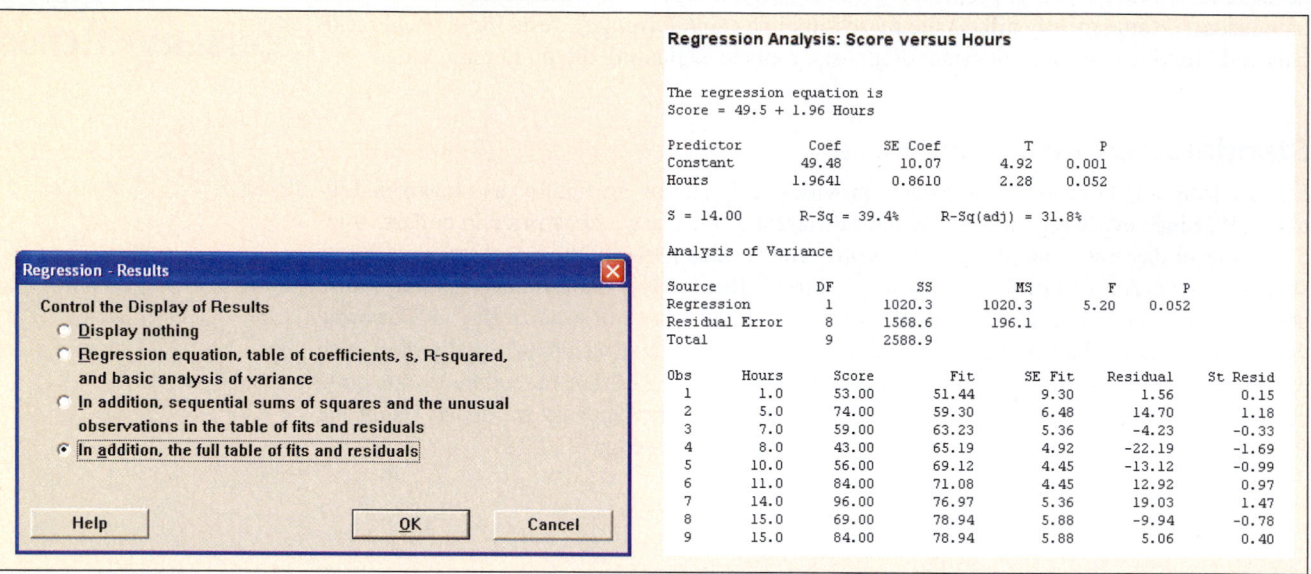

Studentized Residuals: MegaStat

MegaStat gives you the same general output as Excel and MINITAB. Its regression menu is shown in Figure 12.40. Like MINITAB, it offers studentized residuals, as well as several other residual diagnostics that we will discuss shortly. Also like MINITAB, MegaStat rounds off things to make the output more readable. It also highlights significant items.

FIGURE 12.40

MegaStat's regression with residuals **ExamScores**

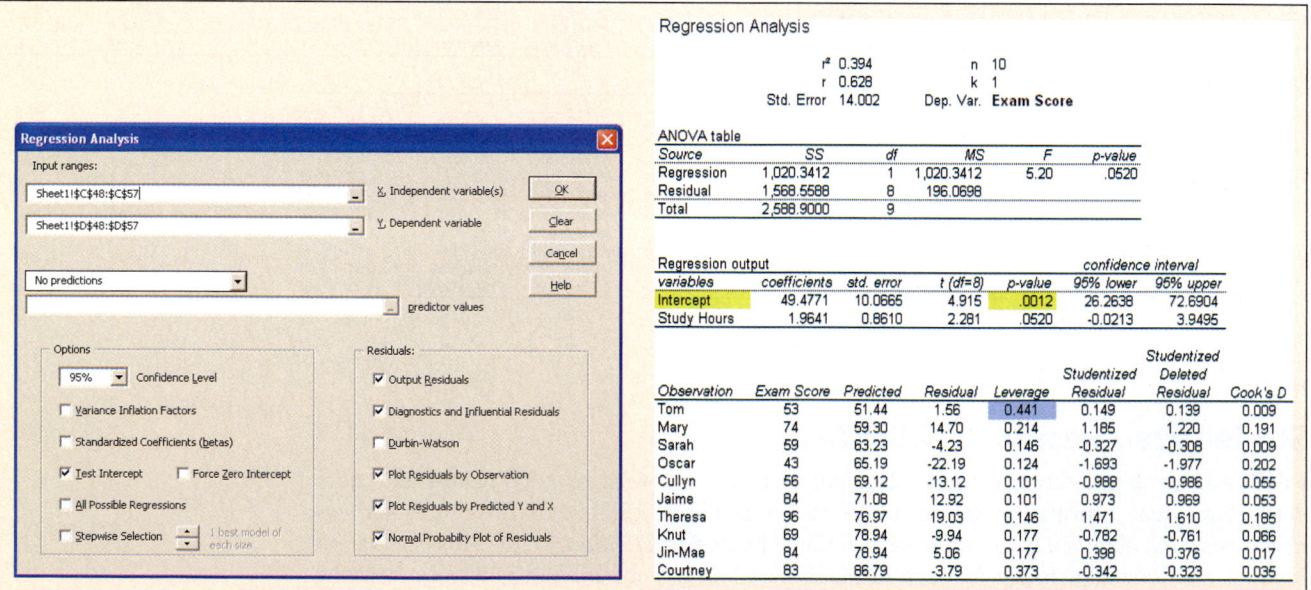

Leverage and Influence

A high *leverage* statistic indicates that the observation is far from the mean of X. Such observations have great influence on the regression estimates, because they are at the "end of the lever." Figure 12.41 illustrates this concept. One individual worked 65 hours, while the others worked between 12 and 42 hours. This individual will have a big effect on the slope estimate, because he is so far above the mean of X. Yet this highly leveraged data point is *not* an outlier (i.e., the fitted regression line comes very close to the data point, so its residual will be small).

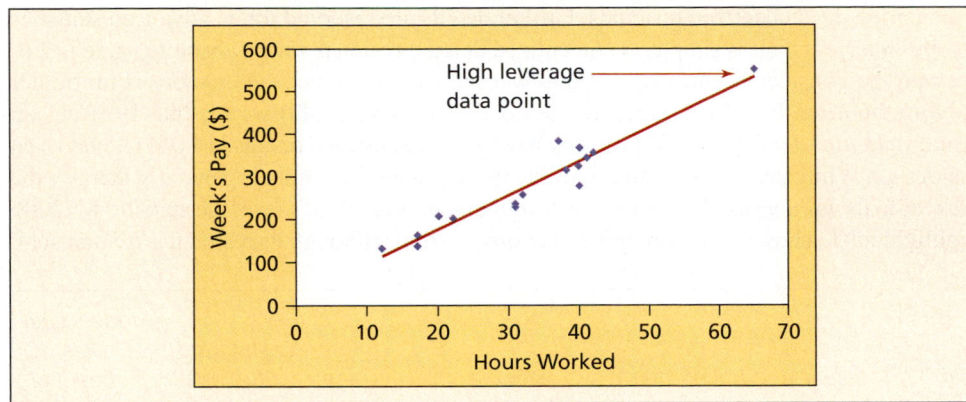

FIGURE 12.41

Illustration of high leverage
Leverage

The leverage for observation i is denoted h_i and is calculated as

$$h_i = \frac{1}{n} + \frac{(x_i - \bar{x})^2}{\sum\limits_{i=1}^{n}(x_i - \bar{x})^2}$$ **(12.34)**

As a rule of thumb, a leverage statistic that exceeds $3/n$ is unusual (note that if $x_i = \bar{x}$ the leverage statistic h_i is $1/n$ so the rule of thumb is just three times this value).

We see from Figure 12.42 that two data points (Tom and Courtney) are likely to have high leverage because Tom studied for only 1 hour (far below the mean) while Courtney studied for 19 hours (far above the mean). Using the information in Table 12.4 (p. 507) we can calculate their leverages:

$$h_{\text{Tom}} = \frac{1}{10} + \frac{(1 - 10.5)^2}{264.50} = .441 \qquad \text{(Tom's leverage)}$$

$$h_{\text{Courtney}} = \frac{1}{10} + \frac{(19 - 10.5)^2}{264.50} = .373 \qquad \text{(Courtney's leverage)}$$

EXAMPLE

Exam Scores: Leverage and Influence
ExamScores

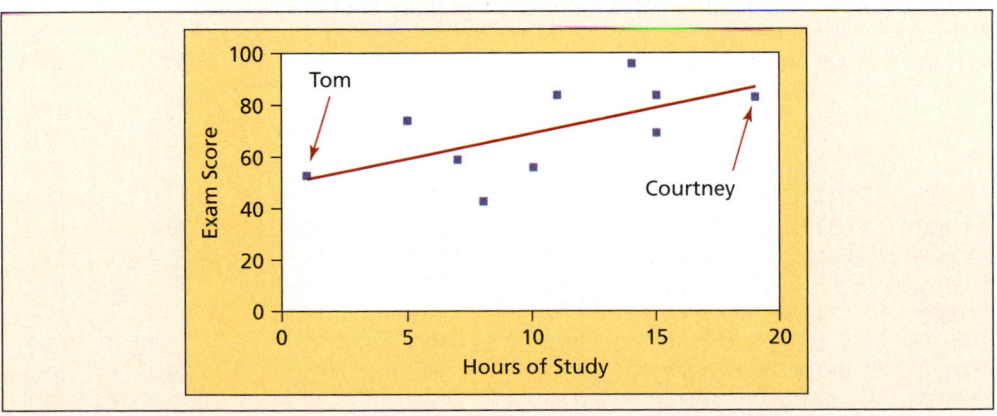

FIGURE 12.42

Scatter plot for exam data   **ExamScores**

By the quick rule, both exceed $3/n = 3/10 = .300$, so these two observations are *influential*. Yet despite their high leverages, the regression fits Tom's and Courtney's actual exam scores well, so their *residuals* are not unusual. This illustrates that *high leverage* and *unusual residuals* are two different concepts.

Studentized Deleted Residuals

Unusual residuals give important clues about the model's adequacy. MegaStat also shows *studentized deleted residuals*—yet another way to identify unusual residuals. The calculation is equivalent to re-running the regression n times, with each observation omitted in turn, and re-calculating the studentized residuals. Further details are reserved for an advanced statistics class, but interpretation is simple. A studentized deleted residual whose absolute value is 2 or more may be considered unusual, and one whose absolute value is 3 or more is an outlier (applying the usual Empirical Rule). In the tax data (Figure 12.43) we see that 1991 has an unusual *studentized* residual (2.371) and by its *studentized deleted* residual (4.066) it may even be an outlier. While the various methods of identifying unusual residuals generally identify the same residuals as "unusual," there can be disagreement. MegaStat's leverage statistic for 2000 is highlighted* to show that it is an influential observation, although its residual is *not* unusual.

FIGURE 12.43

MegaStat's residual table

🐾 **Taxes**

Year	Actual Y	Predicted Y	Residual	Leverage	Studentized Residual	Studentized Deleted Residual
1991	610.50	566.55	43.95	0.296	2.371	4.066
1992	635.80	632.81	2.99	0.221	0.153	0.144
1993	674.60	680.52	−5.92	0.179	−0.296	−0.278
1994	722.60	740.91	−18.31	0.138	−0.893	−0.880
1995	778.30	808.89	−30.59	0.110	−1.467	−1.606
1996	869.70	884.16	−14.46	0.100	−0.690	−0.666
1997	968.80	968.80	0.00	0.117	0.000	0.000
1998	1,070.40	1,075.03	−4.63	0.179	−0.231	−0.217
1999	1,159.20	1,151.35	7.85	0.251	0.411	0.388
2000	1,288.20	1,269.07	19.13	0.410	1.127	1.149

Mini Case   12.4

Body Fat   🐾   BodyFat

Is waistline a good predictor of body fat? Table 12.9 shows a random sample of 50 men's weights (pounds) and girths (centimeters). Figure 12.44 suggests that a linear regression is appropriate, and the MegaStat output in Figure 12.45 shows that the regression is highly significant ($F = 97.68$, $t = 9.883$, $p = .0000$).

TABLE 12.9   **Abdomen Measurement and Body Fat ($n = 50$ men)**

Girth	Fat%	Girth	Fat%	Girth	Fat%	Girth	Fat%
99.1	19.0	78.0	7.3	93.0	18.1	95.0	21.6
76.0	8.4	83.2	13.4	76.0	13.7	86.0	8.8
83.1	9.2	85.6	22.3	106.1	28.1	90.6	19.5
88.5	21.8	90.3	20.2	109.3	23.0	105.5	31.0
118.0	33.6	104.5	16.8	104.3	30.8	79.4	10.4
104.3	31.7	95.6	18.4	100.5	16.5	126.2	33.1
79.5	6.4	103.1	27.7	77.9	7.4	98.0	20.2
108.8	24.6	89.9	17.4	101.6	18.2	95.5	21.9
81.9	4.1	104.0	26.4	99.7	25.1	73.7	11.2
76.6	12.8	95.3	11.3	96.7	16.1	86.4	10.9
88.7	12.3	105.0	27.1	95.8	30.2	122.1	45.1
90.9	8.5	83.5	17.2	104.8	25.4		
89.0	26.0	86.7	10.7	92.4	25.9		

Data are from a larger sample of 252 men in Roger W. Johnson, *Journal of Statistics Education* 4, No. 1 (1996).

---

*MegaStat uses a more sophisticated test for leverage than the $3/n$ quick rule, but the conclusions generally agree.

FIGURE 12.44

Body fat regression

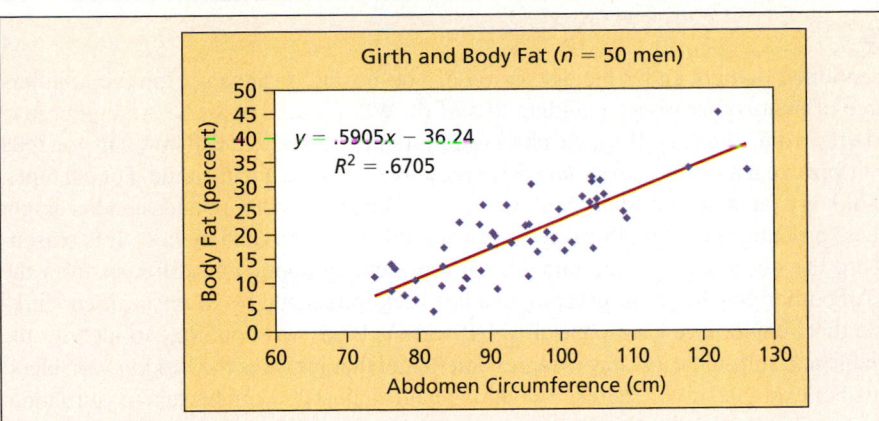

Girth and Body Fat (n = 50 men)

$y = .5905x - 36.24$
$R^2 = .6705$

FIGURE 12.45

Body fat scatter plot

Regression Analysis

r^2	0.671		n	50
r	0.819		k	1
Std. Error	5.086		Dep. Var.	Fat%1

ANOVA table

Source	SS	df	MS	F	p-value
Regression	2,527.1190	1	2,527.1190	97.68	3.71E-13
Residual	1,241.8162	48	25.8712		
Total	3,768.9352	49			

Regression output   confidence interval

variables	coefficients	std. error	t (df = 48)	p-value	95% lower	95% upper
Intercept	−36.2397	5.6690	−6.393	6.28E-08	−47.6379	−24.8415
Abdomen	0.5905	0.0597	9.883	3.71E-13	0.4704	0.7107

   MegaStat's table of residuals, shown in Figure 12.46, highlights four unusual observations. Observations 5, 45, and 50 have high leverage values (exceeding $3/n = 3/50 = .06$) because their abdomen measurements (italicized and boldfaced in Table 12.9) are far from the mean. Observation 37 has a large studentized deleted residual (actual body fat of 30.20 percent is much greater than the predicted 20.33 percent). "Well-behaved" observations are omitted because they are not unusual according to any of the diagnostic criteria (leverage, studentized residual, or studentized deleted residual).

FIGURE 12.46

Unusual body fat residuals

Observation	Fat%1	Predicted	Residual	Leverage	Studentized Residual	Studentized Deleted Residual
5	33.60	33.44	0.16	0.099	0.033	0.032
37	30.20	20.33	9.87	0.020	1.960	2.022
45	33.10	38.28	−5.18	0.162	−1.114	−1.116
50	45.10	35.86	9.24	0.128	1.945	2.005

12.10

OTHER REGRESSION PROBLEMS (OPTIONAL)

Outliers

We have mentioned outliers under the discussion of non-normal residuals. However, outliers are the source of many other woes, including loss of fit. What causes outliers? An outlier may be an error in recording the data. If so, the observation should be deleted. But how can you tell? Impossible or bizarre data values are *prima facie* reasons to discard a data value. For example, in a sample of body fat data, one adult man's weight was reported as 205 pounds and his height as 29.5 inches (probably a typographical error that should have been 69.5 inches). It is reasonable to discard the observation on grounds that it represents a population different from the other men. An outlier may be an observation that has been influenced by an unspecified "lurking" variable that should have been controlled but wasn't. If so, we should try to identify the lurking variable and formulate a *multiple* regression model that includes the lurking variable(s) as predictors. For example, if you regress $Y =$ tuition paid against $X =$ credits taken, you should at least include a binary variable for university type $Z = 0, 1$ (public, private).

Model Misspecification

If a relevant predictor has been omitted, then the model is *misspecified*. Instead of bivariate regression, you should use *multiple regression*. Such a situation is so common that it is almost a warning against relying on bivariate regression, since we usually can think of more than one explanatory variable. Even our tax function, which gave an excellent fit, might be improved if we added more predictors. As you will see in the next chapter, multiple regression is computationally easy because the computer does all the work. In fact, most computer packages just call it "regression" regardless of the number of predictors.

Ill-Conditioned Data

Variables in the regression should be of the same general order of magnitude, and most people take steps intuitively to make sure this is the case (***well-conditioned data***). Unusually large or small data (called ***ill-conditioned***) can cause loss of regression accuracy or can create awkward estimates with exponential notation. Consider the data in Table 12.10 for 30 randomly selected large companies (only a few of the 30 selected are shown in this table). The table shows two ways of displaying the same data, but with the decimal point changed. Figures 12.47 and 12.48

TABLE 12.10

Net Income and Revenue for Selected Global 100 Companies

🐝 **Global30**

Source: www.forbes.com and *Forbes* 172, no. 2 (July 21, 2003), pp. 108–110.

Company	Net Income in Thousands	Revenue in Thousands	Net Income in Millions	Revenue in Millions
Allstate	1,714,000	30,142,000	1,714	30,142
American Int'l Group	5,493,000	70,272,000	5,493	70,272
Barclays	3,348,000	26,565,000	3,348	26,565
⋮	⋮	⋮	⋮	⋮
Volkswagen Group	2,432,000	84,707,000	2,432	84,707
Wachovia	3,693,000	23,455,000	3,693	23,455
Walt Disney	1,024,000	26,255,000	1,024	26,255

FIGURE 12.47

Ill-conditioned data

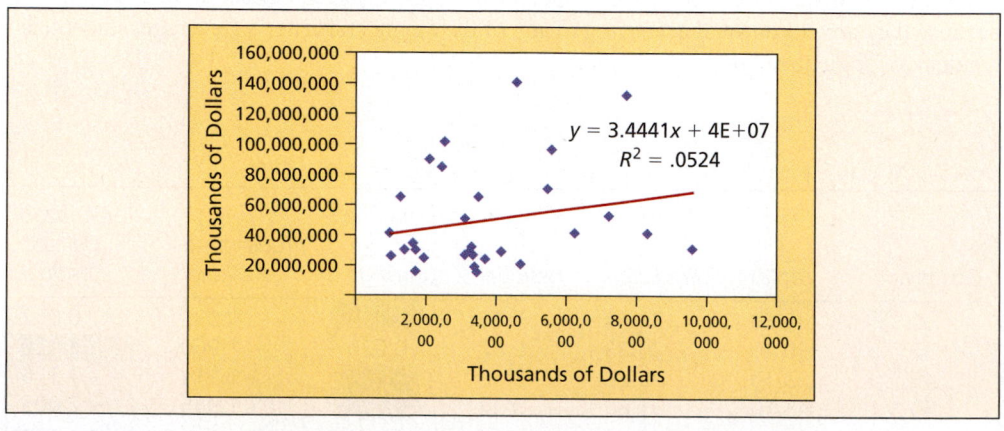

FIGURE 12.48

Well-conditioned data

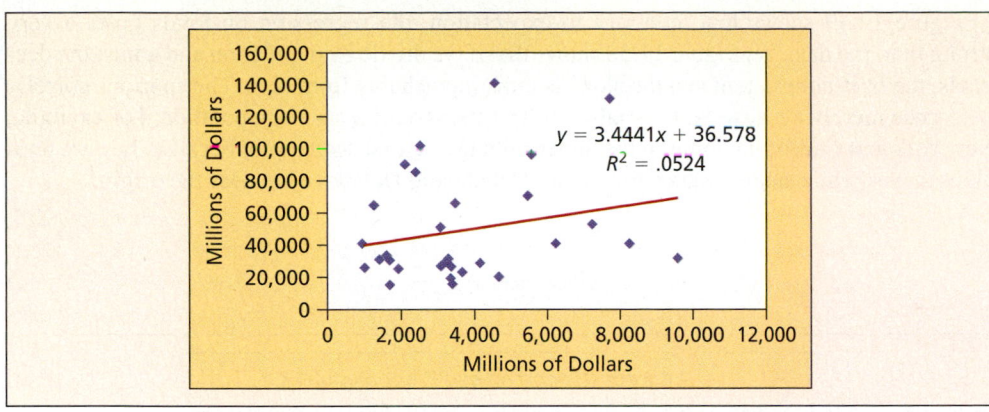

show Excel scatter plots with regression lines. Their appearance is the same, but the first graph has disastrously crowded axis labels. The graphs have the same slope and R^2, but the first regression has an unintelligible intercept (4E+07).

Awkwardly small numbers may also require adjustment. For example, the number of automobile thefts per capita in the United States in 1990 was 0.004207. However, this statistic is easier to work with if it is reported "per 100,000 population" as 420.7. Worst of all would be to mix very large data with very small data. For example, in 1999 the per capita income in New York was $27,546 and the number of active physicians per capita was 0.00395. To avoid mixing magnitudes, we can redefine the variables as per capita income in thousands of dollars (27.546) and the number of active physicians per 10,000 population (39.5).

Tip

Adjust the magnitude of your data *before* running the regression.

Spurious Correlation   Prisoners

In a *spurious correlation,* two variables appear related because of the way they are defined. For example, consider the hypothesis that a state's spending on education is a linear function of its prison population. Such a hypothesis seems absurd, and we would expect the regression to be insignificant. But if the variables are defined as *totals* without adjusting for population, we will observe significant correlation. This phenomenon is called the *size effect* or the *problem of totals.* Table 12.11 shows selected data, first with the variables as *totals* and then as adjusted for population.

		Using Totals		Using Per Capita Data	
State	**Total Population (millions)**	**K–12 Spending ($ billions)**	**No. of Prisoners (thousands)**	**K–12 Spending per Capita ($)**	**Prisoners per 1,000 Pop.**
Alabama	4.447	4.52	24.66	1,016	5.54
Alaska	0.627	1.33	3.95	2,129	6.30
⋮	⋮	⋮	⋮	⋮	⋮
Wisconsin	5.364	8.48	20.42	1,580	3.81
Wyoming	0.494	0.76	1.71	1,543	3.47

TABLE 12.11

State Spending on Education and State and Federal Prisoners
Prisoners

Source: *Statistical Abstract of the United States, 2001.*

Figure 12.49 shows that, contrary to expectation, the regression on totals gives a very strong fit to the data. Yet Figure 12.50 shows that if we divide by population and adjust the decimals, the fit is nonexistent and the slope is indistinguishable from zero. The spurious correlation arose merely because both variables reflect the size of a state's population. For example, New York and California lie far to the upper right on the first scatter plot because they are populous states, while smaller states like South Dakota and Delaware are near the origin.

FIGURE 12.49

Spurious model using totals

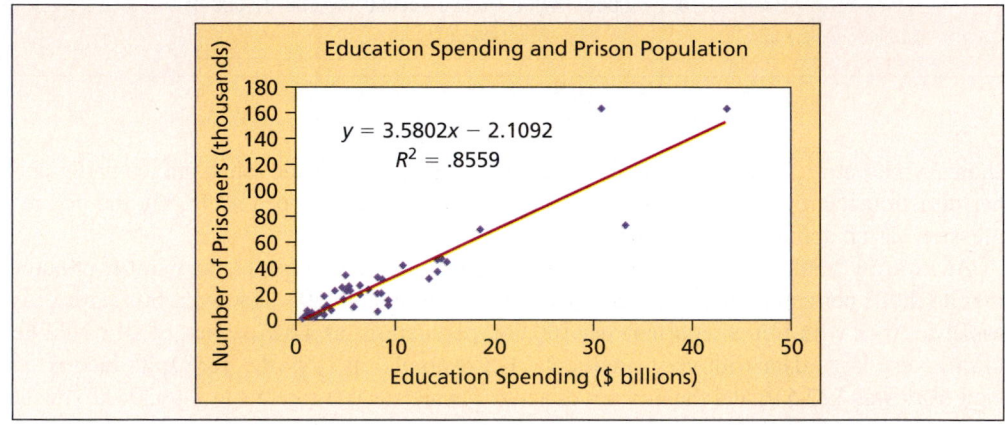

FIGURE 12.50

Better model: Per capita data

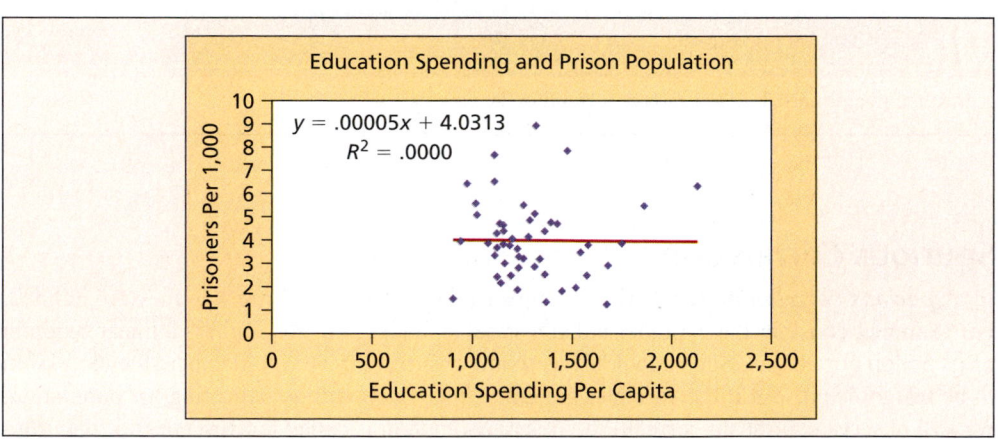

Model Form and Variable Transforms  MPG

Sometimes a relationship cannot be modeled using a linear regression. For example, Figure 12.51 shows fuel efficiency (city MPG) and engine size (horsepower) for a sample of 93 vehicles with a nonlinear model form fitted by Excel. This is one of several nonlinear forms offered by Excel (there are also logarithmic and exponential functions). Figure 12.52 shows an alternative, which is a linear regression after taking *logarithms* of each variable. These logarithms are in base 10, but any base will do (scientists prefer base *e*). This is an example of a *variable transform* to improve fit. An advantage of the *log transformation* is that it reduces heteroscedasticity and improves the normality of the residuals, especially when dealing with totals (the *size problem* mentioned earlier). But log transforms will not work if any data values are zero or negative.

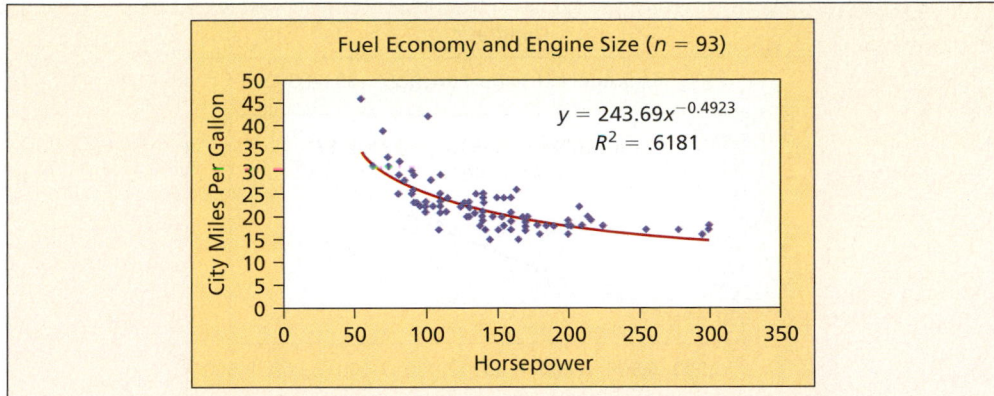

FIGURE 12.51

Nonlinear regression

Source: Robin H. Lock, *Journal of Statistics Education* 1, no. 1 (1993).

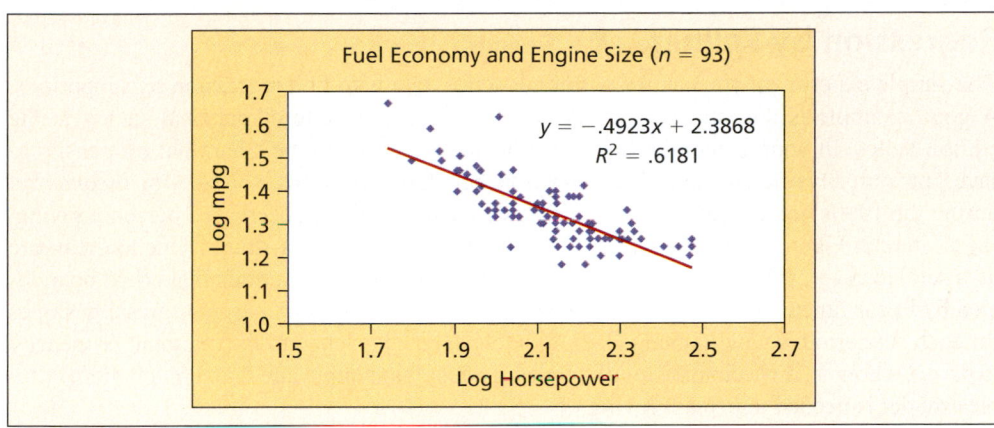

FIGURE 12.52

After log transform

For the tax data examined earlier, Figures 12.53 and 12.54 show that a quadratic model would give a slightly better fit than a linear model, as measured by R^2. But would a government fiscal analyst get better predictions for aggregate taxes for the next year by using a quadratic model? Excel makes it easy to fit all sorts of regression models. But fit is only one criterion for evaluating a regression model. There really is no logical basis for imagining that income and taxes are related by a polynomial model (a better case might be made for the exponential model). Since nonlinear models might be hard to justify or explain to others, the principle of *Occam's Razor* (choosing the simplest explanation that fits the facts) favors linear regression, unless there are other compelling factors.

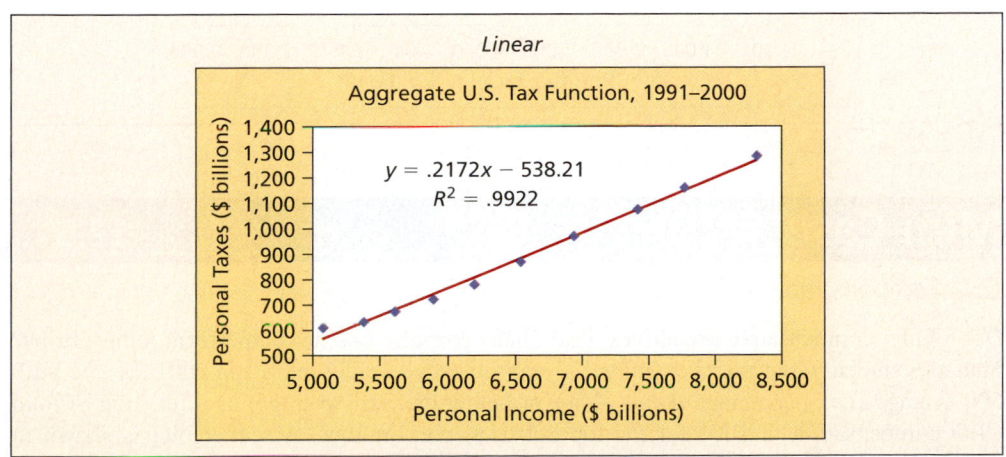

FIGURE 12.53

Linear model

FIGURE 12.54

Quadratic model

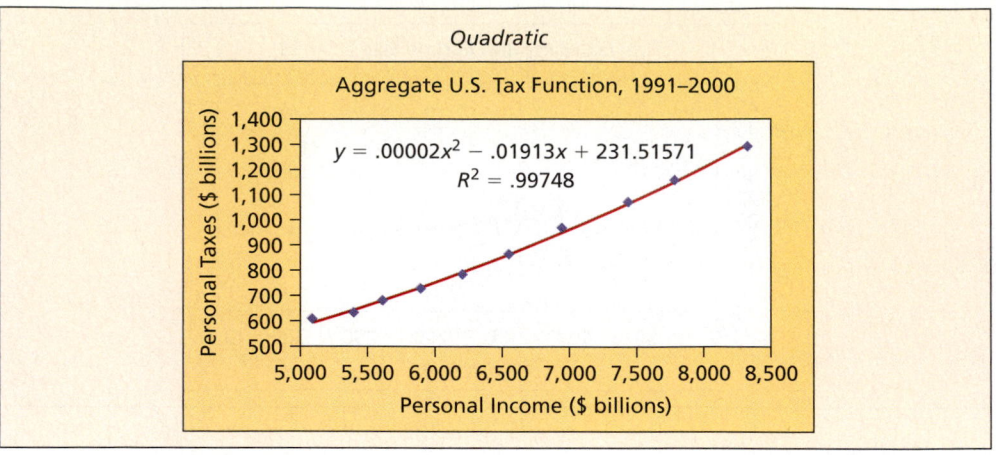

Regression by Splines 🐝 Savings

One simple experiment you can try with time-series data is to fit a regression by subperiods. A good example is the interesting problem of the declining rate of personal saving in the United States. In your economics class, you heard references to the "marginal propensity to save," presumably referring to β_1 in an equation something like $Saving = \beta_0 + \beta_1\ Income$. Yet during the 1990s, increasing personal income was associated with decreased personal saving. If you look at Figure 12.55 you will see that there is no way to fit a straight line to the entire data set. However, you might divide the data into three or four subperiods that could be modeled by linear functions. This is called *regression by splines.* By comparing regression slopes for each subperiod, you will obtain clues about what has happened to the marginal propensity to save. Of course, any economist will tell you it is not that simple and that a much more complex model is needed to explain saving.

FIGURE 12.55

Aggregate U.S. saving and income 🐝 **Saving**

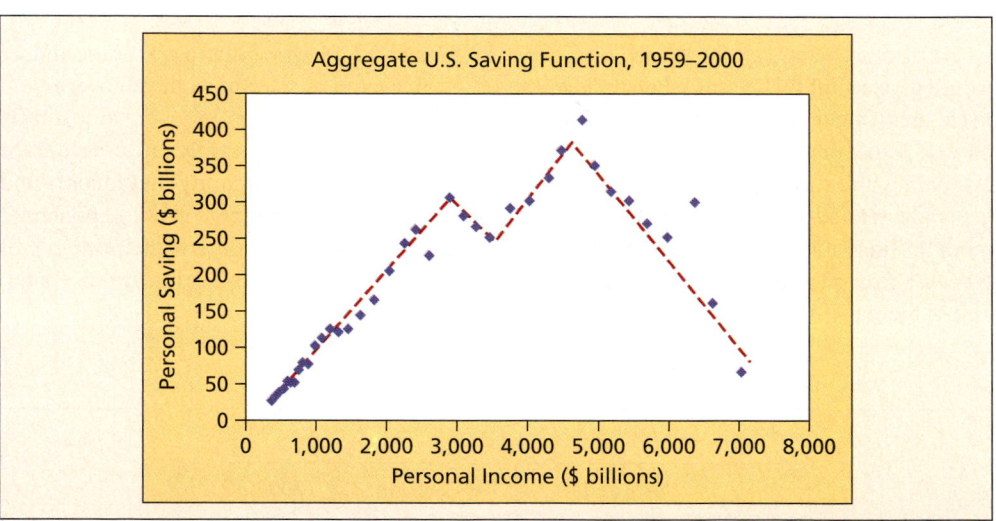

Mini Case 12.5

CEO Compensation 🐝 CEO

Do highly compensated executives lead their corporations to outperform other firms? Statistics student Greg Burks examined 1-year total shareholder returns in 2001 less the S&P 500 average (i.e., percentage points above or below the S&P average) as a function of total CEO compensation in 2001 for the top 200 U.S. corporations. A scatter plot is shown in

Figure 12.56. There appears to be little relationship, but a dozen or so hugely compensated CEOs (e.g., those earning over 50 million) stretch the X-axis scale while many others are clustered near the origin. A log transformation of X (using base 10) is shown in Figure 12.57. Neither fitted regression is significant. That is, there is little relationship between CEO compensation and stockholder returns (if anything, the slope is negative). However, the transformed data give a clearer picture. An advantage of the log transformation is that it improves the scatter of the residuals, producing a more homoscedastic distribution. In short, a log transformation with skewed data is an excellent option to consider.

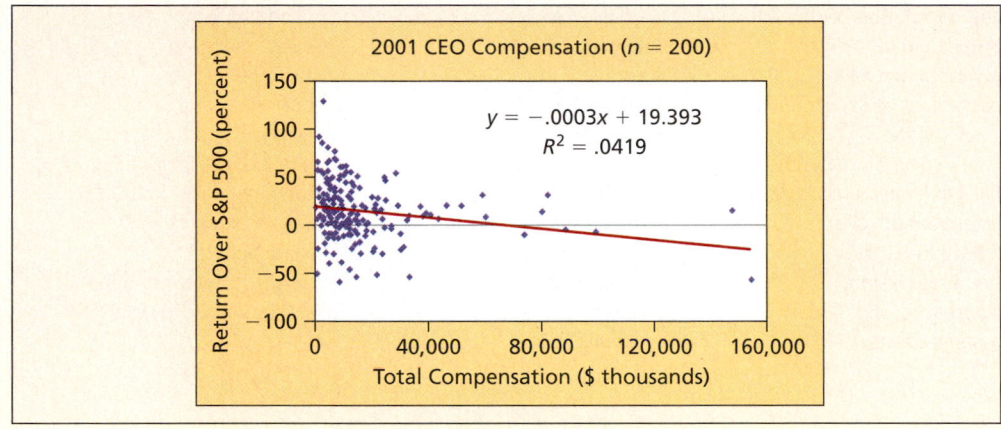

FIGURE 12.56

CEO compensation and stock returns

Source: *The New York Times,* Apr. 4, 2004, pp. 8–9.

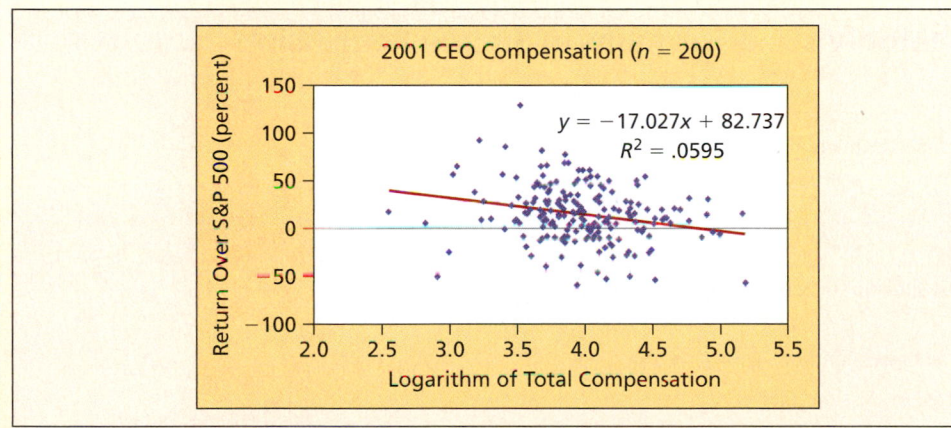

FIGURE 12.57

After log transformation

Chapter Summary

The **sample correlation coefficient** r measures linear association between X and Y, with values near 0 indicating a lack of linearity while values near -1 (negative correlation) or $+1$ (positive correlation) suggest linearity. The **t test** is used to test hypotheses about the **population correlation** ρ. In **bivariate regression** there is an assumed linear relationship between the independent variable X (the **predictor**) and the dependent variable Y (the **response**). The slope (β_1) and intercept (β_0) are unknown **parameters** that are estimated from a sample. **Residuals** are the differences between **observed** and **fitted** Y-values. The **ordinary least squares** (OLS) method yields **regression coefficients** for the slope (b_1) and intercept (b_0) that minimize the sum of squared residuals. The **coefficient of determination** (R^2) measures the overall fit of the regression, with R^2 near 1 signifying a good fit and R^2 near 0 indicating a poor fit. The **F statistic** in the **ANOVA table** is used to test for significant overall regression, while the **t statistics** (and their p-values) are used to test hypotheses about the slope and intercept. The **standard error** of the regression is used to create **confidence intervals** or **prediction intervals** for Y. Regression assumes that the errors are normally distributed, independent random variables with constant variance σ^2. **Residual tests** identify possible **violations** of assumptions (**non-normality, autocorrelation,** heteroscedasticity). Data values with high **leverage** (unusual X-values) have strong influence on the regression. Unusual **standardized residuals** indicate cases where the regression gives a poor fit. **Ill-conditioned** data may lead to **spurious** correlation or other problems. **Data transforms** may help, but they also change the **model specification.**

Key Terms

autocorrelation, *500*
autocorrelation coefficient, *500*
bivariate data, *489*
bivariate regression, *500*
coefficient of determination, *R^2, 508*
confidence interval, *522*
Durbin-Watson test, *528*
error sum of squares, *508*
fitted model, *502*
fitted regression, *501*
heteroscedastic, *526*
homoscedastic, *526*

ill-conditioned data, *536*
intercept, *502*
leverage, *532*
log transformation, *538*
non-normality, *524*
ordinary least squares (OLS), *505*
population correlation coefficient, *ρ, 490*
prediction interval, *522*
regression by splines, *540*
residual, *502*

sample correlation coefficient, *r, 490*
scatter plot, *489*
slope, *502*
spurious correlation, *537*
standard error, *511*
standardized residuals, *524*
studentized residuals, *531*
sums of squares, *490*
t statistic, *492*
variable transform, *538*
well-conditioned data, *536*

Commonly Used Formulas in Simple Regression

Sample correlation coefficient: $r = \dfrac{\sum\limits_{i=1}^{n}(x_i - \bar{x})(y_i - \bar{y})}{\sqrt{\sum\limits_{i=1}^{n}(x_i - \bar{x})^2}\sqrt{\sum\limits_{i=1}^{n}(y_i - \bar{y})^2}}$

Test statistic for zero correlation: $t = r\sqrt{\dfrac{n-2}{1-r^2}}$

True regression line: $y_i = \beta_0 + \beta_1 x_i + \varepsilon_i$

Fitted regression line: $\hat{y}_i = b_0 + b_1 x_i$

Slope of fitted regression: $b_1 = \dfrac{\sum\limits_{i=1}^{n}(x_i - \bar{x})(y_i - \bar{y})}{\sum\limits_{i=1}^{n}(x_i - \bar{x})^2}$

Intercept of fitted regression: $b_0 = \bar{y} - b_1\bar{x}$

Sum of squared residuals: $SSE = \sum\limits_{i=1}^{n}(y_i - \hat{y}_i)^2 = \sum\limits_{i=1}^{n}(y_i - b_0 - b_1 x_i)^2$

Coefficient of determination: $R^2 = 1 - \dfrac{\sum\limits_{i=1}^{n}(y_i - \hat{y}_i)^2}{\sum\limits_{i=1}^{n}(y_i - \bar{y})^2} = 1 - \dfrac{SSE}{SST}$

Standard error of the estimate: $s_{yx} = \sqrt{\dfrac{\sum\limits_{i=1}^{n}(y_i - \hat{y}_i)^2}{n-2}} = \sqrt{\dfrac{SSE}{n-2}}$

Standard error of the slope: $s_{b_1} = \dfrac{s_{yx}}{\sqrt{\sum\limits_{i=1}^{n}(x_i - \bar{x})^2}}$

t test for zero slope: $t = \dfrac{b_1 - 0}{s_{b_1}}$

Confidence interval for true slope: $b_1 - t_{n-2}s_{b_1} \leq \beta_1 \leq b_1 + t_{n-2}s_{b_1}$

Confidence interval for conditional mean of Y: $\hat{y}_i \pm t_{n-2}s_{yx}\sqrt{\dfrac{1}{n} + \dfrac{(x_i - \bar{x})^2}{\sum\limits_{i=1}^{n}(x_i - \bar{x})^2}}$

Prediction interval for Y: $\hat{y}_i \pm t_{n-2}s_{yx}\sqrt{1 + \dfrac{1}{n} + \dfrac{(x_i - \bar{x})^2}{\sum\limits_{i=1}^{n}(x_i - \bar{x})^2}}$

Note: Exercises marked * are based on optional material.

1. (a) How does correlation analysis differ from regression analysis? (b) What does a correlation coefficient reveal? (c) State the quick rule for a significant correlation and explain its limitations. (d) What sums are needed to calculate a correlation coefficient? (e) What are the two ways of testing a correlation coefficient for significance?

2. (a) What is a bivariate regression model? Must it be linear? (b) State three caveats about regression. (c) What does the random error component in a regression model represent? (d) What is the difference between a regression residual and the true random error?

3. (a) Explain how you fit a regression to an Excel scatter plot. (b) What are the limitations of Excel's scatter plot fitted regression?

4. (a) Explain the logic of the ordinary least squares (OLS) method. (b) How are the least squares formulas for the slope and intercept derived? (c) What sums are needed to calculate the least squares estimates?

5. (a) Why can't we use the sum of the residuals to assess fit? (b) What sums are needed to calculate R^2? (c) Name an advantage of using the R^2 statistic instead of the standard error s_{yx} to measure fit. (d) Why do we need the standard error s_{yx}?

6. (a) Explain why a confidence interval for the slope or intercept would be equivalent to a two-tailed hypothesis test. (b) Why is it especially important to test for a zero slope?

7. (a) What does the F statistic show? (b) What is its range? (c) What is the relationship between the F test and the t tests for the slope and correlation coefficient?

8. (a) For a given X, explain the distinction between a confidence interval for the conditional mean of Y and a prediction interval for an individual Y-value. (b) Why is the individual prediction interval wider? (c) Why are these intervals narrowest when X is near its mean? (d) When can quick rules for these intervals give acceptable results, and when not?

9. (a) What is a residual? (b) What is a standardized residual and why it is useful? (c) Name two alternative ways to identify unusual residuals.

10. (a) When does a data point have high leverage (refer to the scatter plot)? (b) Name one test for unusual leverage.

11. (a) Name three assumptions about the random error term in the regression model. (b) Why are the residuals important in testing these assumptions?

12. (a) What are the consequences of non-normal errors? (b) Explain two tests for non-normality. (c) What can we do about non-normal residuals?

Chapter Review

13. (a) What is heteroscedasticity? Identify its two common forms. (b) What are its consequences? (c) How do we test for it? (d) What can we do about it?

14. (a) What is autocorrelation? Identify two main forms of it. (b) What are its consequences? (c) Name two ways to test for it. (d) What can we do about it?

*15. (a) Why might there be outliers in the residuals? (b) What actions could be taken?

*16. (a) What is ill-conditioned data? How can it be avoided? (b) What is spurious correlation? How can it be avoided?

*17. (a) What is a log transform? (b) What are its advantages and disadvantages?

*18. (a) What is regression by splines? (b) Why might we do it?

CHAPTER EXERCISES

Instructions: Choose one or more of the data sets *A–I* below, or as assigned by your instructor. Choose the dependent variable (the *response variable* to be "explained") and the independent variable (the *predictor* or *explanatory variable*) as you judge appropriate. Use a spreadsheet or a statistical package (e.g., MegaStat or MINITAB) to obtain the bivariate regression and required graphs. Write your answers to exercises 12.28 through 12.43 (or those assigned by your instructor) in a concise report, labeling your answers to each question. Insert tables and graphs in your report as appropriate. You may work with a partner if your instructor allows it.

12.28 Are the variables cross-sectional data or time-series data?

12.29 How do you imagine the data were collected?

12.30 Is the sample size sufficient to yield a good estimate? If not, do you think more data could easily be obtained, given the nature of the problem?

12.31 State your *a priori* hypothesis about the sign of the slope. Is it reasonable to suppose a cause and effect relationship?

12.32 Make a scatter plot of Y against X. Discuss what it tells you.

12.33 Use Excel's Add Trendline feature to fit a linear regression to the scatter plot. Is a linear model credible?

12.34 Interpret the slope. Does the intercept have meaning, given the range of the data?

12.35 Use Excel, MegaStat, or MINITAB to fit the regression model, including residuals and standardized residuals.

12.36 (a) Does the 95 percent confidence interval for the slope include zero? If so, what does it mean? If not, what does it mean? (b) Do a two-tailed *t* test for zero slope at $\alpha = .05$. State the hypotheses, degrees of freedom, and critical value for your test. (c) Interpret the *p*-value for the slope. (d) Which approach do you prefer, the *t* test or the *p*-value? Why? (e) Did the sample support your hypothesis about the sign of the slope?

12.37 (a) Based on the R^2 and ANOVA table for your model, how would you assess the fit? (b) Interpret the *p*-value for the *F* statistic. (c) Would you say that your model's fit is good enough to be of practical value?

12.38 Study the table of residuals. Identify as *outliers* any standardized residuals that exceed 3 and as *unusual* any that exceed 2. Can you suggest any reasons for these unusual residuals?

*12.39 (a) Make a histogram (or normal probability plot) of the residuals and discuss its appearance. (b) Do you see evidence that your regression may violate the assumption of normal errors?

*12.40 Inspect the residual plot to check for heteroscedasticity and report your conclusions.

*12.41 Is an autocorrelation test appropriate for your data? If so, perform one or more tests of the residuals (eyeball inspection of residual plot against observation order, runs test, and/or Durbin-Watson test).

*12.42 Use MegaStat or MINITAB to generate 95 percent confidence and prediction intervals for various X-values.

*12.43 Use MegaStat or MINITAB to identify observations with high leverage.

DATA SET A   Median Income and Home Prices in Eastern Cities ($ thousands) (*n* = 34 cities)   HomePrice1

City	Income	Home	City	Income	Home
Alexandria, VA	59.976	290.000	Hunter Mill, VA	93.987	290.000
Bernards Twp., NJ	112.435	279.900	Lower Makefield Twp., PA	102.997	205.000
Brentwood, TN	107.866	338.250	Manalapan Twp., NJ	91.245	410.000
Bridgewater, NJ	93.484	316.000	Marlboro Twp., NJ	108.759	379.975
Cary, NC	77.091	207.000	Matoaca, VA	65.149	135.000
Centreville, VA	77.243	250.000	Newtown, CT	97.723	358.500
Chantilly, VA	94.864	320.000	North Andover, MA	79.169	342.500
Chesapeake, VA	53.758	150.000	Oakton, VA	90.824	341.000
Collierville, TN	85.716	230.000	Olney, MD	100.716	287.450
Columbia, MD	77.033	199.000	Peachtree City, GA	79.805	214.500
Coral Springs, FL	62.632	218.500	Ramapo, NY	64.954	330.875
Dranesville, VA	109.502	290.000	Randolph Twp., NJ	104.121	444.500
Dunwoody, GA	86.971	315.000	Reston, VA	85.264	240.000
Ellicott City, MD	83.583	248.000	Roswell, GA	76.530	226.450
Franconia, VA	84.537	290.000	Sugarland Run, VA	103.350	278.250
Gaithersburg, MD	64.944	220.000	Sully, VA	92.942	290.000
Hoover, AL	64.431	170.450	Wellington, FL	76.076	230.000

Source: *Money* 32, no. 1 (January 2004), pp. 102–103.

Note: Data are for educational purposes only.

DATA SET B   Employees and Revenue Large Automotive Companies in 1999 (*n* = 24)   CarFirms

Company	Employees	Revenue	Company	Employees	Revenue
BMW	119.9	35.9	MAN	64.1	13.8
DaimlerChrysler	441.5	154.6	Mazda Motor	31.9	16.1
Dana	86.4	12.8	Mitsubishi Motors	26.7	27.5
Denso	72.4	13.8	Nissan Motor	131.3	51.5
Fiat	220.5	51.0	Peugeot	156.5	37.5
Ford Motor	345.2	144.4	Renault	138.3	41.4
Fuji Heavy Industries	19.9	10.6	Robert Bosch	189.5	28.6
General Motors	594.0	161.3	Suzuki Motor	13.9	11.4
Honda Motor	112.2	48.7	Toyota Motor	183.9	99.7
Isuzu Motors	28.5	12.7	TRW	78.0	11.9
Johnson Controls	89.0	12.6	Volkswagen	297.9	76.3
Lear	65.5	9.1	Volvo	70.3	26.8

Source: Project by statistics students Paul Ruskin, Kristy Bielewski, and Linda Stengel.

DATA SET C   Estimated and Actual Length of Stay (months) for 16 Patients   Hospital

Patient	ELOS	ALOS	Patient	ELOS	ALOS
1	10.5	10	9	6	8
2	4.5	2	10	12	16
3	7.5	4	11	7	6.5
4	12	11	12	4.5	6
5	7.5	11	13	3.5	3.5
6	9	11	14	6	10
7	6	6.5	15	7.5	7
8	5	5	16	3	5.5

Source: Records of a hospital outpatient cognitive retraining clinic.

Notes: ELOS was estimated using a 42-item assessment instrument combined with expert judgment by teams. Patients had suffered head trauma, stroke, or other medical conditions affecting cognitive function.

DATA SET D   Single-Engine Aircraft Performance (*n = 52 airplanes*)   🛩 **Airplanes**

Manufacturer/Model	Cruise Speed	TotalHP	Manufacturer/Model	Cruise Speed	TotalHP
AMD CH 2000	100	116	Diamond C1 Eclipse	140	125
Beech Baron 58	200	600	Extra Extra 400	235	350
Beech Baron 58P	241	650	Lancair Columbia 300	191	310
Beech Baron D55	199	570	Liberty XL-2	132	125
Beech Bonanza B36 TC	174	300	Maule Comet	115	180
Beech Duchess	164	360	Mooney 231	170	210
Beech Sierra	141	360	Mooney Eagle M205	175	244
Bellanca Super Viking	161	300	Mooney M20C	156	200
Cessna 152	107	110	Mooney Ovation 2 M20R	188	280
Cessna 170B	104	145	OMF Aircraft Symphony	128	160
Cessna 172 R Skyhawk	122	160	Piper 125 Tri Pacer	107	125
Cessna 172 RG Cutlass	129	180	Piper 6X	148	300
Cessna 182Q Skylane	144	230	Piper Archer III	129	180
Cessna 310 R	194	570	Piper Aztec F	191	500
Cessna 337G Skymotor II	170	420	Piper Dakota	147	235
Cessna 414A	223	620	Piper Malibu Mirage	213	350
Cessna 421B	234	750	Piper Saratoga II TC	186	300
Cessna Cardinal	124	180	Piper Satatoga SP	148	300
Cessna P210	186	285	Piper Seneca III	180	440
Cessna T210K	190	285	Piper Seneca V	186	440
Cessna T303 Crusader	190	500	Piper Super Cab	100	150
Cessna Turbo Skylane RG	159	235	Piper Turbo Lance	176	300
Cessna Turbo Skylane T182T	160	235	Rockwell Commander 114	151	260
Cessna Turbo Stationair TU206	148	310	Sky Arrow 650 TC	98	81
Cessna U206H	143	300	Socata TB20 Trinidad	163	250
Cirrus SR20	160	200	Tiger AG-5B	143	180

Source: New and used airplane reports in *Flying*, various issues.

Note: Data are intended for educational purposes only. Cruise speed is in knots (nautical miles per hour).

DATA SET E   Ages and Weights of 31 Randomly Chosen U.S. Nickels (*n = 31 nickels*)   🪙 **Nickels**

Obs	Age (yr)	Weight (gm)	Obs	Age (yr)	Weight (gm)
1	2	5.043	17	15	4.956
2	15	4.893	18	5	5.043
3	22	4.883	19	10	5.032
4	27	4.912	20	2	5.036
5	38	4.980	21	14	4.999
6	2	5.003	22	1	5.004
7	0	5.022	23	21	4.948
8	28	4.796	24	12	5.045
9	12	4.967	25	40	4.917
10	17	4.951	26	1	5.014
11	13	4.932	27	9	5.001
12	1	4.970	28	22	4.801
13	1	5.043	29	21	4.927
14	4	5.040	30	1	5.035
15	1	4.998	31	16	4.983
16	9	4.956			

Source: Randomly chosen circulated nickels were weighed by statistics student Dorothy Duffy as an independent project. Nickels were weighed on a Mettler PE 360 Delta Range scale, accurate to 0.001 gram. The coin's age is the difference between the current year and the mint year.

DATA SET F U.S. Inflation and Changes in Money Supply (*n* = 40 years) **Inflation**

Year	%ChgCPI	%ChgM3	Year	%ChgCPI	%ChgM3
1961	1.3	5.2	1981	3.8	10.3
1962	1.6	8.1	1982	3.8	13.0
1963	1.0	8.9	1983	3.9	9.1
1964	1.9	9.3	1984	3.8	9.6
1965	3.5	9.0	1985	1.1	10.9
1966	3.0	9.0	1986	4.4	7.3
1967	4.7	4.8	1987	4.4	9.1
1968	6.2	10.4	1988	4.6	5.4
1969	5.6	8.8	1989	6.1	6.6
1970	3.3	1.4	1990	3.1	3.8
1971	3.4	9.9	1991	2.9	1.9
1972	8.7	14.6	1992	2.7	1.3
1973	12.3	14.2	1993	2.7	0.3
1974	6.9	11.2	1994	2.5	1.5
1975	4.9	8.6	1995	3.3	1.9
1976	6.7	9.4	1996	1.7	6.1
1977	9.0	11.9	1997	1.6	7.5
1978	13.3	12.2	1998	2.7	9.2
1979	12.5	11.8	1999	3.4	11.0
1980	8.9	10.0	2000	1.6	8.3

Source: *Economic Report of the President, 2002.*

Note: %ChgCPI is the percent change in the Consumer Price Index and %ChgM3 is the percent change in the M3 component of the money supply lagged 1 year.

DATA SET G Mileage and Vehicle Weight **MPG**

Vehicle	City MPG	Weight	Vehicle	City MPG	Weight
Acura CL	20	3,450	Land Rover Freelander	17	3,640
Acura TSX	23	3,320	Lexus IS300	18	3,390
BMW 3-Series	19	3,390	Lincoln Aviator	13	5,000
Buick Century	20	3,350	Mazda MPV	18	3,925
Buick Rendezvous	18	4,230	Mazda6	19	3,355
Cadillac Seville	18	4,050	Mercedes-Benz S-Class	17	4,195
Chevrolet Corvette	19	3,255	Mercury Sable	20	3,340
Chevrolet Silverado 1500	14	4,935	Mitsubishi Galant	20	3,285
Chevrolet TrailBlazer	15	4,660	Nissan 350Z	20	3,345
Chrysler Pacifica	17	4,660	Nissan Pathfinder	15	4,270
Dodge Caravan	18	4,210	Nissan Xterra	16	4,315
Dodge Ram 1500	13	5,300	Pontiac Grand Am	25	3,095
Ford Expedition	13	5,900	Pontiac Vibe	28	2,805
Ford Focus	26	2,760	Saturn Ion	24	2,855
GMC Envoy	15	4,660	Subaru Baja	21	3,575
Honda Accord	21	3,390	Suzuki Vitara/XL-7	17	3,590
Honda Odyssey	18	4,315	Toyota Celica	23	2,570
Hyundai Elantra	24	2,880	Toyota Matrix	26	2,985
Infiniti FX	16	4,295	Toyota Sienna	19	4,120
Isuzu Ascender	15	4,965	Volkswagen Jetta	34	3,045
Jaguar XJ8	18	3,805	Volvo C70	20	3,690
Kia Rio	25	2,295			

Source: © 2003 by Consumers Union of U.S., Inc., Yonkers, NY 10703–1057 from *Consumer Reports New Car Buying Guide 2003–2004.* Used with permission.

Notes: Sampling methodology was to select the vehicle on every fifth page starting at page 40. Data are intended for purposes of statistical education and should not be viewed as a guide to vehicle performance. Vehicle weights are in pounds.

DATA SET H   **Calories and Fat Calories for Selected Pasta Sauces**   🍝   **Pasta**

Product	Calories Per Gram	Fat Calories Per Gram
Barilla Roasted Garlic & Onion	0.64	0.20
Barilla Tomato & Basil	0.56	0.12
Classico Tomato & Basil	0.40	0.08
Del Monte Mushroom	0.48	0.04
Five Bros. Tomato & Basil	0.64	0.12
Healthy Choice Traditional	0.40	0.00
Master Choice Chunky Garden Veg.	0.56	0.08
Meijer All Natural Meatless	0.55	0.08
Newman's Own Traditional	0.48	0.12
Paul Newman Venetian	0.48	0.12
Prego Fresh Mushrooms	1.25	0.38
Prego Hearty Meat—Pepperoni	1.00	0.33
Prego Hearty Meat—Hamburger	1.00	0.29
Prego Traditional	1.17	0.33
Prego Roasted Red Pepper & Garlic	0.92	0.25
Ragu Old World Style w/meat	0.67	0.25
Ragu Roasted Red Pepper & Onion	0.86	0.20
Ragu Roasted Garlic	0.70	0.19
Ragu Traditional	0.56	0.20
Sutter Home Tomato & Garlic	0.64	0.16

Source: This data set was created by statistics students Donna Bennett, Nicole Cook, Latrice Haywood, and Robert Malcolm using nutrition information on the labels of sauces chosen from supermarket shelves.

Note: Data are intended for educational purposes only and should not be viewed as a nutrition guide.

DATA SET I   **Electric Bills and Consumption for a Residence** (*n* = 24 months)   ⚡   **Electric**

Month	Dollars	Usage (kWh)	Month	Dollars	Usage (kWh)
1	85.26	895	13	112.43	1,156
2	71.12	746	14	80.70	876
3	64.42	687	15	63.51	675
4	45.07	498	16	49.17	574
5	49.85	541	17	55.96	604
6	54.87	596	18	69.65	732
7	98.32	1,012	19	84.46	880
8	87.79	907	20	104.34	1,060
9	113.48	1,159	21	92.93	956
10	45.38	501	22	57.57	617
11	48.47	528	23	53.61	577
12	70.50	740	24	80.98	847

12.44 Researchers found a correlation coefficient of $r = .50$ on personality measures for identical twins. A reporter interpreted this to mean that "the environment orchestrated one-half of their personality differences." Do you agree with this interpretation? Discuss. (See *Science News* 140 [December 7, 1991], p. 377.)

12.45 A study of the role of spreadsheets in planning in 55 small firms defined Y = "satisfaction with sales growth" and X = "executive commitment to planning." Analysis yielded an overall correlation of $r = .3043$. Do a two-tailed test for zero correlation at $\alpha = .025$.

12.46 In a study of stock prices from 1970 to 1994, the correlation between Nasdaq closing prices on successive days (i.e., with a 1-day lag) was $r = .13$ with a t statistic of 5.47. Interpret this result. (See David Nawrocki, "The Problems with Monte Carlo Simulation," *Journal of Financial Planning* 14, no. 11 [November 2001], p. 96.)

12.47 Regression analysis of free throws by 29 NBA teams during the 2002–2003 season revealed the fitted regression $Y = 55.2 + .73X$ ($R^2 = .874$, $s_{yx} = 53.2$) where $Y =$ total free throws made and $X =$ total free throws attempted. The observed range of X was from 1,620 (New York Knicks) to 2,382 (Golden State Warriors). (a) Find the expected number of free throws made for a team that shoots 2,000 free throws. (b) Do you think that the intercept is meaningful? *Hint:* Make a scatter plot and let Excel fit the line. (c) Use the quick rule to make a 95 percent prediction interval for Y when $X = 2,000$.   **FreeThrows**

12.48 In the following regression, $X =$ weekly pay, $Y =$ income tax withheld, and $n = 35$ McDonald's employees. (a) Write the fitted regression equation. (b) State the degrees of freedom for a two-tailed test for zero slope, and use Appendix D to find the critical value at $\alpha = .05$. (c) What is your conclusion about the slope? (d) Interpret the 95 percent confidence limits for the slope. (e) Verify that $F = t^2$ for the slope. (f) In your own words, describe the fit of this regression.

R^2	0.202
Std. Error	6.816
n	35

ANOVA table

Source	SS	df	MS	F	p-value
Regression	387.6959	1	387.6959	8.35	.0068
Residual	1,533.0614	33	46.4564		
Total	1,920.7573	34			

Regression output — confidence interval

variables	coefficients	std. error	t (df = 33)	p-value	95% lower	95% upper
Intercept	30.7963	6.4078	4.806	.0000	17.7595	43.8331
Slope	0.0343	0.0119	2.889	.0068	0.0101	0.0584

12.49 In the following regression, $X =$ monthly maintenance spending (dollars), $Y =$ monthly machine downtime (hours), and $n = 15$ copy machines. (a) Write the fitted regression equation. (b) State the degrees of freedom for a two-tailed test for zero slope, and use Appendix D to find the critical value at $\alpha = .05$. (c) What is your conclusion about the slope? (d) Interpret the 95 percent confidence limits for the slope. (e) Verify that $F = t^2$ for the slope. (f) In your own words, describe the fit of this regression.

R^2	0.370
Std. Error	286.793
n	15

ANOVA table

Source	SS	df	MS	F	p-value
Regression	628,298.2	1	628,298.2	7.64	.0161
Residual	1,069,251.8	13	82,250.1		
Total	1,697,550.0	14			

Regression output — confidence interval

variables	coefficients	std. error	t (df = 13)	p-value	95% lower	95% upper
Intercept	1,743.57	288.82	6.037	.0000	1,119.61	2,367.53
Slope	−1.2163	0.4401	−2.764	.0161	−2.1671	−0.2656

12.50 In the following regression, $X =$ total assets ($ billions), $Y =$ total revenue ($ billions), and $n = 64$ large banks. (a) Write the fitted regression equation. (b) State the degrees of freedom for a two-tailed test for zero slope, and use Appendix D to find the critical value at $\alpha = .05$. (c) What is your conclusion about the slope? (d) Interpret the 95 percent confidence limits for the slope. (e) Verify that $F = t^2$ for the slope. (f) In your own words, describe the fit of this regression.

R^2	0.519	
Std. Error	6.977	
n	64	

ANOVA table

Source	SS	df	MS	F	p-value
Regression	3,260.0981	1	3,260.0981	66.97	1.90E-11
Residual	3,018.3339	62	48.6828		
Total	6,278.4320	63			

Regression output

					confidence interval	
variables	coefficients	std. error	t (df = 62)	p-value	95% lower	95% upper
Intercept	6.5763	1.9254	3.416	.0011	2.7275	10.4252
X1	0.0452	0.0055	8.183	1.90E-11	0.0342	0.0563

12.51 Do stock prices of competing companies move together? Below are daily closing prices of two computer services firms (IBM = International Business Machines Corporation, EDS = Electronic Data Systems Corporation). (a) Calculate the sample correlation coefficient (e.g., using Excel or MegaStat). (b) At $\alpha = .01$ can you conclude that the true correlation coefficient is greater than zero? (c) Make a scatter plot of the data. What does it say? (Data are from Center for Research and Security Prices, University of Chicago.)   **StockPrices**

Daily Closing Price ($) of Two Stocks in October and November 2004

Date	IBM	EDS	Date	IBM	EDS
9/1/04	84.22	19.31	10/1/04	86.72	20.00
9/2/04	84.57	19.63	10/4/04	87.16	20.36
9/3/04	84.39	19.19	10/5/04	87.32	20.38
9/7/04	84.97	19.35	10/6/04	88.04	20.49
9/8/04	85.86	19.47	10/7/04	87.42	20.43
9/9/04	86.44	19.51	10/8/04	86.71	20.02
9/10/04	86.76	20.10	10/11/04	86.63	20.24
9/13/04	86.49	19.81	10/12/04	86.00	20.14
9/14/04	86.72	19.79	10/13/04	84.98	19.47
9/15/04	86.37	19.83	10/14/04	84.78	19.30
9/16/04	86.12	20.10	10/15/04	84.85	19.54
9/17/04	85.74	19.90	10/18/04	85.92	19.43
9/20/04	85.70	19.82	10/19/04	89.37	19.26
9/21/04	85.72	20.16	10/20/04	88.82	19.17
9/22/04	84.31	19.89	10/21/04	88.10	19.63
9/23/04	83.88	19.70	10/22/04	87.39	19.75
9/24/04	84.43	19.22	10/25/04	88.43	20.03
9/27/04	84.16	19.16	10/26/04	89.00	20.99
9/28/04	84.48	19.30	10/27/04	90.00	21.26
9/29/04	84.98	19.10	10/28/04	89.50	21.41
9/30/04	85.74	19.39	10/29/04	89.75	21.27

12.52 Below are average gestation days and longevity data for 22 animals. (a) Make a scatter plot. (b) Find the correlation coefficient and interpret it. (c) Test the correlation coefficient for significance, clearly stating the degrees of freedom. (Data are from *The World Almanac and Book of Facts, 2005*, p. 180. Used with permission.) 🍄 **Gestation**

Gestation (days) and Longevity (Years) for Selected Animals (*n* = 22)

Animal	Gestation	Longevity	Animal	Gestation	Longevity
Ass	365	12	Horse	330	20
Baboon	187	20	Kangaroo	42	7
Beaver	122	5	Lion	100	15
Buffalo	278	15	Moose	240	12
Camel	406	12	Mouse	21	3
Cat	63	12	Possum	15	1
Dog	61	12	Rabbit	31	5
Deer	201	8	Rhino	450	15
Elephant	645	40	Sheep	154	12
Fox	52	7	Wolf	63	5
Guinea Pig	68	4	Zebra	365	15

12.53 Below are fertility rates (average children born per woman) in 15 EU nations for 2 years. (a) Make a scatter plot. (b) Find the correlation coefficient and interpret it. (c) Test the correlation coefficient for significance, clearly stating the degrees of freedom. (Data are from the World Health Organization.) 🍄 **Fertility**

Fertility Rates for 15 EU Nations

Nation	1990	2000
Austria	1.5	1.3
Belgium	1.6	1.5
Denmark	1.6	1.7
Finland	1.7	1.6
France	1.8	1.8
Germany	1.4	1.3
Greece	1.5	1.3
Ireland	2.1	2.0
Italy	1.3	1.2
Luxembourg	1.6	1.7
Netherlands	1.6	1.5
Portugal	1.6	1.5
Spain	1.4	1.1
Sweden	2.0	1.4
U.K.	1.8	1.7

12.54 Consider the following prices and accuracy ratings for 27 stereo speakers. (a) Make a scatter plot of accuracy rating as a function of price. (b) Calculate the correlation coefficient. At $\alpha = .05$, does the correlation differ from zero? (c) In your own words, describe the scatter plot. (Data are from *Consumer Reports* 68, no. 11 [November 2003], p. 31. Data are intended for statistical education and not as a guide to speaker performance.) 🍄 **Speakers**

Price and Accuracy of Selected Stereo Speakers (n = 27)

Brand and Model	Type	Price ($)	Accuracy
BIC America Venturi DV62si	Shelf	200	91
Bose 141	Shelf	100	86
Bose 201 Series V	Shelf	220	89
Bose 301 Series V	Shelf	330	86
Bose 601 Series IV	Floor	600	84
Bose 701 Series II	Floor	700	82
Bose Acoustimass 3 Series IV	Shelf 3-Pc	300	94
Bose Acoustimass 5 Series III	Shelf 3-Pc	600	94
Boston Acoustics CR75	Shelf	300	90
Boston Acoustics CR85	Shelf	400	86
Boston Acoustics VR-M50	Shelf	700	90
Cambridge Soundworks Model Six	Shelf	150	89
Cambridge Soundworks Newton Series M60	Shelf	300	90
Cambridge Soundworks Newton Series M80	Shelf	400	94
Cerwin Vega E-710	Floor	300	90
Jensen Champion Series C-5	Floor	180	86
KLH 911B	Shelf	85	82
Klipsch Synergy SB-3 Monitor	Shelf	450	79
Pioneer S-DF1-K	Shelf	200	88
Pioneer S-DF2-K	Shelf	260	88
Polk Audio R20	Shelf	150	83
Polk Audio R30	Floor	300	89
Polk Audio R50	Floor	400	84
PSB Image 2B	Shelf	370	88
Sony SS-MB350H	Shelf	100	92
Sony SS-MF750H	Floor	280	91
Sony SS-X30ED	Shelf	500	83

12.55 Choose *one* of these three data sets. (a) Make a scatter plot. (b) Let Excel estimate the regression line, with fitted equation and R^2. (c) Describe the fit of the regression. (d) Write the fitted regression equation and interpret the slope. (e) Do you think that the estimated intercept is meaningful? Explain.

Commercial Real Estate (X = assessed value, $000; Y = floor space, sq. ft.)
Assessed

Assessed	Size
1,796	4,790
1,544	4,720
2,094	5,940
1,968	5,720
1,567	3,660
1,878	5,000
949	2,990
910	2,610
1,774	5,650
1,187	3,570
1,113	2,930
671	1,280
1,678	4,880
710	1,620
678	1,820

Sasnak Co. Salaries (*X* = employee age; *Y* = employee salary, $000)   **Salaries**

Employee	Age	Salary
Mary	23	28.6
Frieda	31	53.3
Alicia	44	73.8
Tom	22	26.0
Gillian	25	34.3
Bob	54	63.5
Vivian	51	96.4
Cecil	60	122.9
Barry	40	63.8
Jaime	64	111.1
Wanda	34	82.5
Sam	63	80.4
Saundra	40	69.3
Pete	31	52.8
Steve	28	54.0
Juan	36	58.7
Dick	58	72.3
Lee	52	88.6
Judd	43	60.2
Sunil	28	61.0
Marcia	54	75.8
Ellen	44	79.8
Iggy	36	70.2

Poway Big Homes, Ltd. (*X* = home size, sq. ft.; *Y* = selling price, $000)
HomePrice2

SqFt	Price
3,570	861
3,410	740
2,690	563
3,260	698
3,130	624
3,460	737
3,340	806
3,240	809
2,660	639
3,160	778
3,340	809
2,780	621
2,790	687
3,740	840
3,260	789
3,310	760
2,930	729
3,020	720
2,320	575
3,130	785

12.56 Bivariate regression was employed to establish the effects of childhood exposure to lead. The effective sample size was about 122 subjects. The independent variable was the level of dentin lead (parts per million). Below are regressions using various dependent variables. (a) Calculate the t statistic for each slope. (b) From the p-values, which slopes differ from zero at $\alpha = .01$? (c) Do you feel that cause and effect can be assumed? *Hint:* Do a Web search for information about effects of childhood lead exposure. (Data are from H. L. Needleman et al., *The New England Journal of Medicine* 322, no. 2 [January 1990], p. 86.)

Dependent Variable	R^2	Estimated Slope	Std Error	p-value
Highest grade achieved	.061	−0.027	0.009	.008
Reading grade equivalent	.121	−0.070	0.018	.000
Class standing	.039	−0.006	0.003	.048
Absence from school	.071	4.8	1.7	.006
Grammatical reasoning	.051	0.159	0.062	.012
Vocabulary	.108	−0.124	0.032	.000
Hand-eye coordination	.043	0.041	0.018	.020
Reaction time	.025	11.8	6.66	.080
Minor antisocial behavior	.025	−0.639	0.36	.082

12.57 Below are recent financial ratios for a random sample of 20 integrated health care systems. *Operating Margin* is total revenue minus total expenses divided by total revenue plus net operating profits. *Equity Financing* is fund balance divided by total assets. (a) Make a scatter plot of $Y =$ operating margin and $X =$ equity financing (both variables are in percent). (b) Use Excel to fit the regression, with fitted equation and R^2. (c) In your own words, describe the fit. (Data are from *Hospitals & Health Networks* 71, no. 6 [March 20, 1997], pp. 48–49. Copyright © 1997 by Health Forum, Inc. Used with permission. Data are intended for statistical education and not as a guide to financial performance.)   **HealthCare**

Financial Ratios for Selected Health Care Systems ($n = 20$)

Name of Health Care System	Operating Margin	Equity Financing
Albert Einstein Healthcare Network	3.89	35.58
Alliant Health Systems	8.23	59.68
Baptist Memorial Health Care System	2.56	40.48
Camcare Health System	4.45	45.63
Camino Health System	−4.46	64.45
Carondelet Health System	3.54	42.30
Dimensions Healthcare System	1.77	26.65
Greenville Hospital System	4.98	37.74
Group Health Co-op of Puget Sound	−2.36	32.75
Health Management Associates	11.92	68.08
Kaiser Permanente Health Plan of Texas	−5.07	15.92
Kettering Healthcare System	10.28	62.81
Lake Hospital System	6.83	53.77
Legacy Health System	4.35	43.12
MeritCare Health System	5.89	55.07
MetroHealth System	1.02	52.34
Oakwood Healthcare System	0.00	34.28
OSF Healthcare Network	4.75	54.21
Samaritan Health System	0.00	59.73
Scottsdale Memorial Health System	10.79	46.21

12.58 Consider the following data on 20 chemical reactions, with $Y =$ chromatographic retention time (seconds) and $X =$ molecular weight (gm/mole). (a) Make a scatter plot. (b) Use Excel to fit the regression, with fitted equation and R^2. (c) In your own words, describe the fit. (Data provided by John Seeley of Oakland University.)   **Chemicals**

Retention Time and Molecular Weight

Name	Retention Time	Molecular Weight
alpha-pinene	234.50	136.24
cyclopentene	95.27	68.12
p-diethylbenzene	284.00	134.22
decane	250.60	142.29
toluene	174.00	92.14
benzene	135.70	78.11
2-methylpentane	97.24	86.18
2,3 dimethylbutane	100.70	86.18
1,7-octadiene	172.20	110.20
1,2,4-trimethylbenzene	262.70	120.19
2,3,4-trimethylpentane	160.98	114.23
ethylcyclohexane	195.07	112.22
limonene	271.50	136.24
methylcyclohexane	153.57	98.19
m-diethylbenzene	281.50	134.22
2,3-dimethylpentane	131.83	100.20
2,2-dimethylbutane	89.34	86.18
pentane	78.00	72.15
isooctane	136.90	114.23
hexane	106.00	86.18

12.59 A common belief among faculty is that teaching ratings are lower in large classes. Below are MINITAB results from a regression using $Y =$ mean student evaluation of the professor and $X =$ class size for 364 business school classes taught during the 2002–2003 academic year. Ratings are on a scale of 1 (lowest) to 5 (highest). (a) What do these regression results tell you about the relationship between class size and faculty ratings? (b) Is a bivariate model adequate? If not, suggest additional predictors to be considered.

Predictor	Coef	SE Coef	T	P
Constant	4.18378	0.07226	57.90	0.000
Enroll	0.000578	0.002014	0.29	0.774

$S = 0.5688$ R-Sq $= 0.0\%$ R-Sq(adj) $= 0.0\%$

12.60 Below are revenue and profit (both in $ billions) for nine large entertainment companies. (a) Make a scatter plot of profit as a function of revenue. (b) Use Excel to fit the regression, with fitted equation and R^2. (c) In your own words, describe the fit. (Data are from *Fortune* 149, no. 7 [April 5, 2005], p. F-50.)   **Entertainment**

Revenue and Profit of Nine Entertainment Companies

Company	Revenue	Profit
AMC Entertainment	1.792	−0.020
Clear Channel Communication	8.931	1.146
Liberty Media	2.446	−0.978
Metro-Goldwyn-Mayer	1.883	−0.162
Regal Entertainment Group	2.490	0.185
Time Warner	43.877	2.639
Univision Communications	1.311	0.155
Viacom	26.585	1.417
Walt Disney	27.061	1.267

12.61 Below are fitted regressions based on used vehicle ads. Observed ranges of X are shown. The assumed regression model is *AskingPrice* $= f(VehicleAge)$. (a) Interpret the slopes. (b) Are the intercepts meaningful? Explain. (c) Assess the fit of each model. (d) Is a bivariate model adequate to explain vehicle prices? If not, what other predictors might be considered? (Data are from *Detroit's AutoFocus* 4, Issue 38 [September 17–23, 2004]. Data are for educational purposes only and should not be viewed as a guide to vehicle prices.)

Vehicle	n	Intercept	Slope	R^2	Min Age	Max Age
Ford Explorer	31	22,252	−2,452	.643	2	6
Ford F-150 Pickup	43	26,164	−2,239	.713	1	37
Ford Mustang	33	21,308	−1,691	.328	1	10
Ford Taurus	32	13,160	−906	.679	1	14

12.62 Below are results of a regression of Y = average stock returns (in percent) as a function of X = average price/earnings ratios for the period 1949–1997 (49 years). Separate regressions were done for various holding periods (sample sizes are therefore variable). (a) Summarize what the regression results tell you. (b) Would you anticipate autocorrelation in this type of data? Explain. (Data are from Ruben Trevino and Fiona Robertson, "P/E Ratios and Stock Market Returns," *Journal of Financial Planning* 15, no. 2 [February 2002], p. 78.)

Holding Period	Intercept	Slope	t	R^2	p
1-Year	28.10	−0.92	1.86	.0688	.0686
2-Year	26.11	−0.86	2.57	.1252	.0136
5-Year	20.67	−0.57	2.99	.1720	.0046
8-Year	24.73	−0.94	6.93	.5459	.0000
10-Year	24.51	−0.95	8.43	.6516	.0000

12.63 Adult height is somewhat predictable from average height of both parents. For females, a commonly used equation is *YourHeight* = *ParentHeight* − 2.5 while for males the equation is *YourHeight* = *ParentHeight* + 2.5. (a) Test these equations on yourself (or on somebody else). (b) How well did the equations predict your height? (c) How do you suppose these equations were derived?

LearningStats Unit 12   Regression I

LS

LearningStats Unit 12 covers correlation and simple bivariate regression. It includes demonstrations of the least squares method, regression formulas, effects of model form and range of *X*, confidence and prediction intervals, violations of assumptions, and examples of student projects. Your instructor may assign specific modules, or you may decide to check them out because the topic sounds interesting

Topic	LearningStats Modules
Correlation	Overview of Correlation Correlation Analysis
Regression	Overview of Simple Regression Using Excel for Regression
Ordinary least squares estimators	Least Squares Method Demonstration Doing Regression Calculations Effect of Model Form Effect of *X* Range
Confidence and prediction intervals	Confidence and Prediction Intervals Calculations for Confidence Intervals Superimposing Many Fitted Regressions
Violations of assumptions	Non-Normal Errors Heteroscedastic Errors Autocorrelated Errors Cochrane-Orcutt Transform
Formulas	Derivation of OLS Estimators Formulas for OLS Estimates Formulas for Significance Tests
Student presentations	Birth Rates Life Expectancy and Literacy Effects of Urbanization
Tables of critical values	Appendix D—Student's *t* Appendix F—*F* Distribution

Key: = PowerPoint = Word = Excel

Visual Statistics

Visual Statistics Modules on Describing Data

Module	Module Name
14	Bivariate Data Analysis
15	Simple Regression
16	Regression Assumptions
18	Regression Models

Visual Statistics modules 14, 15, 16, and 18 (included on your CD) are designed with the following objectives:

Module 14

- Become familiar with ways to display bivariate data.
- Understand measures of association in bivariate data.
- Be able to interpret bivariate regression statistics and assess their significance.

Module 15

- Understand OLS terminology.
- Understand how sample size, standard error, and range of X affect estimation accuracy.
- Understand confidence intervals for $E(y|x)$ and prediction intervals for $y|x$.

Module 16

- Learn the regression assumptions required to ensure desirable properties for OLS estimators.
- Learn to recognize violations of the regression assumptions.
- Be able to identify the effects of assumption violations.

Module 18

- Know the common variable transformations and their purposes.
- Learn the effects of variable transformations on the fitted regression and statistics of fit.
- Understand polynomial models.

The worktext chapter (included on the CD in .PDF format) contains a list of concepts covered, objectives of the module, overview of concepts, illustration of concepts, orientation to module features, learning exercises (basic, intermediate, advanced), learning projects (individual, team), self-evaluation quiz, glossary of terms, and solutions to self-evaluation quiz.

Multiple Regression

Chapter Learning Objectives

When you finish this chapter you should be able to

- Use a fitted multiple regression equation to make predictions.

- Interpret the R^2 and perform an F test for overall significance.

- Test individual predictors for significance.

- Interpret confidence intervals for regression coefficients.

- Distinguish between confidence and prediction intervals.

- Identify unusual residuals and outliers by using standardized residuals.

- Interpret residual tests for leverage.

- Analyze the residuals to check for violations of regression assumptions.

- Explain the role of data conditioning and data transformations.

Bivariate or Multivariate?

Multiple regression extends bivariate regression to include several independent variables (or *predictors*). Everything you learned about *bivariate regression* is a special case of multiple regression. The interpretation of multiple regression is similar, except that two-dimensional *X-Y* scatter plots are of limited value in higher-dimensional models. Since all calculations are done by computer, there is no extra computational burden. In fact, statisticians make no distinction between bivariate and multivariate regression—they just call it *regression*.

Multiple regression is required when a single-predictor model is inadequate to describe the true relationship between the dependent variable Y (the response variable) and its potential predictors ($X_1, X_2, X_3, \ldots$). Adding predictors is more than a matter of "improving the fit." Rather, it is a question of specifying a correct model. Omission of relevant predictors (*model misspecification*) can cause biased estimates and misleading results. A low R^2 in a bivariate regression model does not necessarily mean that X and Y are unrelated, but may simply indicate that the model is incorrectly specified.

Chapter 17

Limitations of Bivariate Regression

- Often simplistic (multiple relationships usually exist).
- Biased estimates if relevant predictors are omitted.
- Lack of fit does not show that X is unrelated to Y if the true model is multivariate.

Since multiple predictors usually are relevant, bivariate regression is only used when there is a compelling need for a simple model, or when other predictors have only modest effects and a single logical predictor "stands out" as doing a very good job all by itself.

Regression Terminology

The *response variable* (Y) is assumed to be related to the k *predictors* ($X_1, X_2, \ldots, X_k$) by a linear equation called the *population regression model:*

(13.1)
$$Y = \beta_0 + \beta_1 X_1 + \beta_2 X_2 + \cdots + \beta_k X_k + \varepsilon$$

Each value of Y is assumed to differ from the *conditional mean* $E(Y) = \beta_0 + \beta_1 X_1 + \beta_2 X_2 + \cdots + \beta_k X_k$ by a *random error* ε representing everything that is not part of the model. The unknown regression coefficients $\beta_0, \beta_1, \beta_2, \ldots, \beta_k$ are *parameters* and are denoted by Greek letters. Each coefficient β_j shows the change in the expected value of Y for a unit change in X_j while holding everything else constant (*ceteris paribus*). The errors are assumed to be unobservable, independent random disturbances that are normally distributed with zero mean and constant variance, that is, $\varepsilon \sim N(0, \sigma^2)$. Under these assumptions, the ordinary least squares (OLS) estimation method yields unbiased, consistent, efficient estimates of the unknown parameters. The *sample estimates* of the regression coefficients are denoted by Roman letters $b_0, b_1, b_2, \ldots, b_k$. The *predicted* value of the response variable is denoted $\hat{Y}$ and is calculated by inserting the values of the predictors into the *fitted regression equation:*

(13.2) $\qquad \hat{Y} = b_0 + b_1 X_1 + b_2 X_2 + \cdots + b_k X_k \qquad$ (predicted value of Y)

In this chapter, we will not show formulas for the estimated coefficients $b_0, b_1, b_2, \ldots, b_k$ because they entail matrix algebra. All regressions are fitted by computer software (Excel, MegaStat, MINITAB, etc.) utilizing the appropriate formulas.

Data Format

To obtain a fitted regression we need n observed values of the response variable Y and its proposed predictors $X_1, X_2, \ldots, X_k$. A multivariate data set is a single column of Y-values and k columns of X-values. The form of this $n \times k$ matrix of observations is shown in Figure 13.1.

FIGURE 13.1

Data for a multiple regression

Response		Predictors		
Y	X_1	X_2	$\ldots$	X_k
y_1	x_{11}	x_{12}	$\ldots$	x_{1k}
y_2	x_{21}	x_{22}	$\ldots$	x_{2k}
$\vdots$	$\vdots$	$\vdots$	$\vdots$	$\vdots$
y_n	x_{n1}	x_{n2}	$\ldots$	x_{nk}

In Excel's Tools > Data Analysis > Regression you are required to have the X data in contiguous columns. However, MegaStat and MINITAB permit nonadjacent columns of X data. Flexibility in choosing data columns is useful if you decide to omit one or more X data columns and re-run the regression (e.g., to seek parsimony).

Illustration: Home Prices

Table 13.1 shows sales of 30 new homes in an upscale development. Although the selling price of a home (the *response variable*) may depend on many factors, we will examine three potential *explanatory variables.*

Definition of Variable	Short Name
$Y =$ selling price of a home (thousands of dollars)	*Price*
$X_1 =$ home size (square feet)	*SqFt*
$X_2 =$ lot size (thousand square feet)	*LotSize*
$X_3 =$ number of bathrooms	*Baths*

TABLE 13.1   **Characteristics of 30 New Homes**   🐿   **NewHomes**

Home	Price	SqFt	LotSize	Baths	Home	Price	SqFt	LotSize	Baths
1	505.5	2,192	16.4	2.5	16	675.1	3,076	19.8	3.0
2	784.1	3,429	24.7	3.5	17	710.4	3,259	20.8	3.5
3	649.0	2,842	17.7	3.5	18	674.7	3,162	19.4	4.0
4	689.8	2,987	20.3	3.5	19	663.6	2,885	23.2	3.0
5	709.8	3,029	22.2	3.0	20	606.6	2,550	20.2	3.0
6	590.2	2,616	20.8	2.5	21	758.9	3,380	19.6	4.5
7	643.3	2,978	17.3	3.0	22	723.7	3,131	22.5	3.5
8	789.7	3,595	22.4	3.5	23	621.8	2,754	19.2	2.5
9	683.0	2,838	27.4	3.0	24	622.4	2,710	21.6	3.0
10	544.3	2,591	19.2	2.0	25	631.3	2,616	20.8	2.5
11	822.8	3,633	26.9	4.0	26	574.0	2,608	17.3	3.5
12	637.7	2,822	23.1	3.0	27	863.8	3,572	29.0	4.0
13	618.7	2,994	20.4	3.0	28	652.7	2,924	21.8	2.5
14	619.3	2,696	22.7	3.5	29	844.2	3,614	25.5	3.5
15	490.5	2,134	13.4	2.5	30	629.9	2,600	24.1	3.5

Using short variable names instead of Y and X we may write the regression model in an intuitive form:

$$Price = \beta_0 + \beta_1\, SqFt + \beta_2\, LotSize + \beta_3\, Baths + \varepsilon$$

Logic of Variable Selection

Before doing the estimation, it is desirable to state our hypotheses about the sign of the coefficients in the model. In so doing, we force ourselves to think about our motives for including each predictor, instead of just throwing predictors into the model willy-nilly. Sometimes, of course, we may include a predictor as a "wild card" without any clear expectation about its sign. In the home price example, each predictor is expected to contribute positively to the selling price.

Predictor	Anticipated Sign	Reasoning
SqFt	>0	Larger homes cost more to build and give greater utility to the buyer.
LotSize	>0	Larger lots are desirable for privacy, gardening, and play.
Baths	>0	Additional baths give more utility to the purchaser with a family.

Explicit *a priori* reasoning about cause-and-effect permits us to compare the regression estimates with our expectation and to recognize any surprising results that may occur. However, we would not abandon a predictor whose relevance is grounded solidly in existing theory or common sense simply because it was not a "significant" predictor of Y.

Fitted Regression

A regression can be fitted by using Excel, MegaStat, MINITAB, or any other statistical package. Using the sample of $n = 30$ home sales, we obtain the fitted regression and its statistics of fit (R^2 is the coefficient of determination, SE is the standard error):

$$Price = -28.85 + 0.171\, SqFt + 6.78\, LotSize + 15.54\, Baths \quad (R^2 = .956,\ SE = 20.31)$$

The intercept is not meaningful, since there can be no home with $SqFt = 0$, $LotSize = 0$, and $Baths = 0$. Each additional square foot seems to add about 0.171 (i.e., $171, since *Price* is measured in thousands of dollars) to the average selling price, *ceteris paribus*. The coefficient of *LotSize* implies that, on average, each additional thousand square feet of lot size adds 6.78 (i.e., $6,780) to the selling price. The coefficient of *Baths* says that, on average, each additional bathroom adds 15.54 (i.e., $15,540) to the selling price. Although the three-predictor model's fit ($R^2 = .956$) is good, its standard error (20.31 or $20,310) suggests that prediction intervals will be rather wide.

Two-Predictor Model

In the quest for a more parsimonious model, suppose that we drop the predictor *Baths*. The new fitted regression is:

$$Price = -23.21 + 0.187\ SqFt + 6.60\ LotSize\ (R^2 = .951,\ SE = 20.99)$$

The intercept is not meaningful, since there can be no home with $SqFt = 0$ and $LotSize = 0$. The coefficient of *SqFt* is larger than in the three-predictor model. Each additional square foot seems to add only 0.187 (i.e., $187, since *Price* is measured in thousands of dollars) to the mean selling price, *ceteris paribus*. The coefficient of *LotSize* implies that, on average, each additional thousand square feet of lot size adds 6.60 (i.e., $6,600) to the selling price. Dropping the predictor *Baths* reduces the R^2 only slightly to 95.1 percent and increases the standard error only slightly to 20.99 (i.e., $20,990).

One-Predictor Model

Seeking an even simpler model, we could drop the predictor *LotSize*. The new fitted regression is:

$$Price = 15.47 + 0.222\ SqFt\ (R^2 = .914,\ SE = 27.28)$$

The coefficient of *SqFt* says that each additional square foot adds about 0.222 (i.e., $222, since *Price* is in thousands of dollars) to the average selling price. The intercept suggests that a "home" with $SqFt = 0$ would still sell for a positive price (the price of a vacant lot?), but such a situation is far outside the range of observed data and so the intercept is not meaningful. The model still shows a reasonable fit, with *SqFt* explaining 91.4 percent of the variation in *Price*. However, the standard error 27.28 (i.e., $27,280) is noticeably worse than in the two- or three-predictor models. These experiments show that varying the predictors will affect the estimated coefficients, as well as the statistics of "fit."

Common Misconceptions about Fit

A common mistake is to assume that the model with the best fit is preferred. Sometimes a model with a low R^2 may give useful predictions, while a model with a high R^2 may conceal problems. Fit is only one criterion for assessing a regression. For example, although the multivariate models of *Price* give a better fit, the bivariate model does a pretty good job of predicting *Price* and has an attractive simplicity. Should we perhaps prefer the simpler model? The principle of **Occam's Razor** says that a complex model that is only slightly better may not be preferred if a simpler model will do the job.

Principle of Occam's Razor

When two explanations are otherwise equivalent, we prefer the simpler, more parsimonious one.

Further, we have an unanswered question regarding the predictors. What is the "best" estimate of the coefficient of *SqFt*? Is it 0.222 (one-predictor model)? Is it 0.187 (two-predictor model)? Is it 0.171 (three-predictor model)? Or is it something else (if we were to add more predictors)? How can we choose among several potential models that give a similar degree of "fit"?

Also, a high R^2 only indicates a good fit for the observed data set ($i = 1, 2, \ldots, n$). If we wanted to use the fitted regression equation to predict Y from a different set of X's, the fit might not be the same. For this reason, if the sample is large enough, a statistician likes to use half the data to *estimate* the model and the other half to *test* the model's predictions.

Regression Modeling

The choice of predictors and model form (e.g., linear or nonlinear) are tasks of *regression modeling*. To begin with, we restrict our attention to predictors that meet the test of *a priori* logic, to avoid endless "data shopping." Naturally, we want predictors that are significant in "explaining" the variation in Y (i.e., predictors that improve the "fit"). But we also prefer predictors that add new information, rather than mirroring one another.

For example, we would expect that *LotSize* and *SqFt* are related (a bigger house may require a bigger lot) and likewise *SqFt* and *Baths* (a bigger house is likely to require more baths). If so, there may be overlap in their contributions to explaining *Price*. Closely related predictors can introduce instability in the regression estimates. If we include too many predictors, we violate the principle of Occam's Razor, which favors simple models, *ceteris paribus*. In this chapter, you will see how these criteria can be used to develop and assess regression models.

Four Criteria for Regression Assessment

- **Logic**   Is there an *a priori* reason to expect a causal relationship between the predictors and the response variable?

- **Fit**   Does the *overall* regression show a significant relationship between the predictors and the response variable?

- **Parsimony**   Does *each predictor* contribute significantly to the explanation? Are some predictors not worth the trouble?

- **Stability**   Are the predictors related to one another so strongly that regression estimates become erratic?

SECTION EXERCISES

13.1   Observations are taken on net revenue from sales of a certain plasma TV at 50 retail outlets. The regression model was Y = net revenue (thousands of dollars), X_1 = shipping cost (dollars per unit), X_2 = expenditures on print advertising (thousands of dollars), X_3 = expenditure on electronic media ads (thousands), X_4 = rebate rate (percent of retail price). (a) Write the fitted regression equation. (b) Interpret each coefficient. (c) Would the intercept be likely to have meaning in this regression? (d) Use the fitted equation to make a prediction for *NetRevenue* when *ShipCost* = 10, *PrintAds* = 50, *WebAds* = 40, and *Rebate%* = 15.   🐱 **PlasmaTV**

Predictor	Coefficient
Intercept	4.310
ShipCost	−0.082
PrintAds	2.265
WebAds	2.498
Rebate%	16.70

13.2   Observations are taken on sales of a certain mountain bike in 30 sporting goods stores. The regression model was Y = total sales (thousands of dollars), X_1 = display floor space (square meters), X_2 = competitors' advertising expenditures (thousands of dollars), X_3 = advertised price (dollars per unit). (a) Write the fitted regression equation. (b) Interpret each coefficient. (c) Would the intercept seem to have meaning in this regression? (d) Make a prediction for *Sales* when *FloorSpace* = 80, *CompetingAds* = 100, and *Price* = 1,200.   🐱 **Bikes**

Predictor	Coefficient
Intercept	1225
FloorSpace	11.52
CompetingAds	−6.935
Price	−0.1496

13.2 ASSESSING OVERALL FIT

F Test for Significance

Overall fit of a regression is assessed using the **F test.** For a regression with k predictors, the hypotheses to be tested are

H_0: All the true coefficients are zero ($\beta_1 = \beta_2 = \cdots = \beta_k = 0$)

H_1: At least one of the coefficients is nonzero

The basis for the F test is the **ANOVA table,** which decomposes variation of the response variable around its mean into two parts:

$$SST \quad = \quad SSR \quad + \quad SSE$$

Total variation	Explained by regression	Unexplained error

(13.3)
$$\sum_{i=1}^{n}(y_i - \bar{y})^2 = \sum_{i=1}^{n}(\hat{y}_i - \bar{y})^2 + \sum_{i=1}^{n}(y_i - \hat{y}_i)^2$$

SSE is the sum of the squared residuals, just as it was in a simple regression (Chapter 12) except now each predicted value $\hat{y}_i$ is based on a fitted regression equation with k predictors. The ANOVA calculations for a k-predictor model can be summarized in a table like Table 13.2.

TABLE 13.2
ANOVA Table Format

Source	Sum of Squares	d.f.	Mean Square	F
Regression	SSR	k	$MSR = SSR/k$	$F = MSR/MSE$
Error	SSE	$n - k - 1$	$MSE = SSE/(n - k - 1)$	
Total	SST	$n - 1$		

MINITAB and MegaStat will do all the calculations and print the ANOVA table. Table 13.3 shows the ANOVA table for the home price regression with $n = 30$ observations and $k = 3$ predictors.

TABLE 13.3
ANOVA Results for Three-Predictor Home Price Regression

Source	Sum of Squares	d.f.	Mean Square	F
Regression	232,450	3	77,483	187.92
Error	10,720	26	412.32	
Total	243,170	29		

The hypotheses to be tested are

H_0: All the coefficients are zero ($\beta_1 = \beta_2 = \beta_3 = 0$)

H_1: At least one coefficient is nonzero

Calculation of the sums SSR, SSE, and SST would be tedious without the computer. The F test statistic is $F = MSR/MSE = 77,483/412.32 = 187.92$. Degrees of freedom are $k = 3$ for the numerator and $n - k - 1 = 30 - 3 - 1 = 26$ for the denominator. For $\alpha = .05$, Appendix F gives a critical value of $F_{3,26} = 2.98$, so the regression clearly is significant overall. MINITAB and MegaStat calculate the p-value ($p = .000$) for the F statistic. Alternatively, we can also use Excel's function =FDIST(187.92,3,26) to verify the p-value ($p = .000$).

Coefficient of Determination (R^2)

The most common measure of overall fit is the ***coefficient of determination*** or R^2, which is based on the ANOVA table's sums of squares. It can be calculated in two ways by using the error sum of squares (*SSE*), regression sum of squares (*SSR*), and total sum of squares (*SST*). The formulas are illustrated using the three-predictor regression of home prices.

$$R^2 = 1 - \frac{SSE}{SST} = 1 - \frac{\sum_{i=1}^{n}(y_i - \hat{y}_i)^2}{\sum_{i=1}^{n}(y_i - \bar{y}_i)^2} = 1 - \frac{10,720}{243,170} = 1 - .044 = .956 \qquad (13.4)$$

or equivalently

$$R^2 = \frac{SSR}{SST} = 1 - \frac{\sum_{i=1}^{n}(\hat{y}_i - \bar{y}_i)^2}{\sum_{i=1}^{n}(y_i - \bar{y}_i)^2} = \frac{232,450}{243,170} = .956 \qquad (13.5)$$

For the home price data, the R^2 statistic indicates that 95.6 percent of the variation in selling price is "explained" by our three predictors. While this indicates a very good fit, there is still some unexplained variation. Adding more predictors can *never* decrease the R^2, and generally will raise R^2. However, when R^2 already is high, there is not a lot of room for improvement.

Adjusted R^2

In multiple regression, it is generally possible to raise the coefficient of determination R^2 by including additional predictors. This may tempt you to imagine that we should always include many predictors to get a "better fit." To discourage this tactic (called *overfitting* the model) an adjustment can be made in the R^2 statistic to penalize the inclusion of useless predictors. The ***adjusted coefficient of determination*** using n observations and k predictors is

$$R^2_{adj} = 1 - (1 - R^2)\left(\frac{n-1}{n-k-1}\right) \qquad \text{(adjusted } R^2) \qquad (13.6)$$

R^2_{adj} is always less than or equal to R^2. As you add predictors, R^2 cannot decline, and generally will rise. But R^2_{adj} may rise, remain the same, or fall, depending on whether the added predictors increase R^2 sufficiently to offset the penalty. If R^2_{adj} is substantially smaller than R^2, it suggests that the model contains useless predictors. For the home price data with three predictors, both statistics are similar ($R^2 = .956$ and $R^2_{adj} = .951$), which suggests that the model does not contain useless predictors.

$$R^2_{adj} = 1 - (1 - .956)\left(\frac{30-1}{30-3-1}\right) = .951$$

How Many Predictors?

One way to prevent overfitting the model is to limit the number of predictors based on the sample size. A conservative rule (***Evans's Rule***) suggests that n/k should be at least 10 (i.e., at least 10 observations per predictor). A more relaxed rule (***Doane's Rule***) suggests that n/k be only at least 5 (i.e., at least 5 observations per predictor). For the home price regression with $n = 30$ and $k = 3$ example, $n/k = 30/3 = 10$ so either guideline is met.

Evans's Rule (conservative): $n/k \geq 10$ (at least 10 observations per predictor)

Doane's Rule (relaxed): $n/k \geq 5$ (at least 5 observations per predictor)

These rules are merely suggestions. Technically, a regression is possible as long as the sample size exceeds the number of predictors. But when n/k is small, the R^2 no longer gives a reliable indication of fit. Sometimes, researchers must work with small samples that cannot be enlarged. For example, a start-up business selling health food might have only 12 observations on quarterly sales. Should they attempt a regression model to predict sales using four predictors (advertising, product price, competitor prices, and population density)? Although $n = 12$ and $k = 3$ would violate even the lax guideline ($n/k = 12/4 = 3$), the firm might feel that an imperfect analysis is better than none at all.

SECTION EXERCISES

13.3   Refer to the ANOVA table for this regression. (a) State the degrees of freedom for the F test for overall significance. (b) Use Appendix F to look up the critical value of F for $\alpha = .05$. (c) Calculate the F statistic. Is the regression significant overall? (d) Calculate R^2 and R^2_{adj}, showing your formulas clearly.   **PlasmaTV**

Source	d.f.	SS	MS
Regression	4	259,412	64,853
Error	45	224,539	4,990
Total	49	483,951	

13.4   Refer to the ANOVA table for this regression. (a) State the degrees of freedom for the F test for overall significance. (b) Use Appendix F to look up the critical value of F for $\alpha = .05$. (c) Calculate the F statistic. Is the regression significant overall? (d) Calculate R^2 and R^2_{adj}, showing your formulas clearly.   **Bikes**

Source	d.f.	SS	MS
Regression	3	1,196,410	398,803
Error	26	379,332	14,590
Total	29	1,575,742	

13.3
PREDICTOR SIGNIFICANCE

Chapter 17

Hypothesis Tests

Each estimated coefficient shows the change in the conditional mean of Y associated with a one-unit change in an explanatory variable, holding the other explanatory variables constant. We are usually interested in testing each fitted coefficient to see whether it is significantly different from zero. If there is an *a priori* reason to anticipate a particular direction of association, we could choose a right-tailed or left-tailed test. For example, we would expect *SqFt* to have a positive effect on *Price*, so a right-tailed test might be used. However, the default choice is a two-tailed test because, if the null hypothesis can be rejected in a two-tailed test, it can also be rejected in a one-tailed test at the same level of significance.

Hypothesis Tests for Predictor X_j

Two-Tailed Test	Right-Tailed Test	Left-Tailed Test
$H_0: \beta_j = 0$	$H_0: \beta_j = 0$	$H_0: \beta_j = 0$
$H_1: \beta_j \neq 0$	$H_1: \beta_j > 0$	$H_1: \beta_j < 0$

Tip

Software packages like Excel, MegaStat, or MINITAB report only two-tail *p*-values because, if you can reject H_0 in a two-tailed test, you can also reject H_0 in a one-tailed test at the same α.

If we cannot reject the hypothesis that a coefficient is zero, then the corresponding predictor does not contribute to the prediction of Y. For example, consider a three-predictor model:

$$Y = \beta_0 + \beta_1 X_1 + \beta_2 X_2 + \beta_3 X_3 + \varepsilon$$

Does X_2 help us to predict Y? To find out, we might choose a two-tailed test:

H_0: $\beta_2 = 0$ (X_2 is *not* related to Y)

H_1: $\beta_2 \neq 0$ (X_2 *is* related to Y)

If we are unable to reject H_0, the term involving X_2 will drop out:

$$Y = \beta_0 + \beta_1 X_1 + \boxed{0X_2} + \beta_3 X_3 + \varepsilon \qquad (X_2 \text{ term drops out if } \beta_2 = 0)$$

and the regression will collapse to a *two-variable* model:

$$Y = \beta_0 + \beta_1 X_1 + \beta_3 X_3 + \varepsilon$$

Test Statistic

Rarely would a fitted coefficient be *exactly* zero, so we use a t test to test whether the difference from zero* is *significant*. For predictor X_j the test statistic for k predictors is Student's t with $n - k - 1$ degrees of freedom. To test for a zero coefficient, we take the ratio of the fitted coefficient b_j to its standard error s_j:

$$t_j = \frac{b_j - 0}{s_j} \qquad \text{(test statistic for coefficient of predictor } X_j) \qquad \textbf{(13.7)}$$

We can use Appendix D to find a critical value of t_α for a chosen level of significance α, or we could find the p-value for the t statistic using Excel's function =TDIST(t, deg_freedom, tails). All computer packages report the t statistic and the p-value for each predictor, so we actually do not need tables. To test for a zero coefficient, we could alternatively construct a confidence interval for the true coefficient β_j, and see whether the interval includes zero. Excel and MegaStat show a confidence interval for each estimated coefficient, using this form:

$$b_j - t_{n-k-1} s_j \leq \beta_j \leq b_j + t_{n-k-1} s_j \qquad \text{(95\% confidence interval for coefficient } \beta_j) \qquad \textbf{(13.8)}$$

MegaStat allows 99, 95, or 90 percent confidence intervals, while in Excel you can enter any confidence level you wish. All calculations are provided by Excel, so you only have to know how to interpret the results.

Tip

Checking to see whether the confidence interval includes zero is equivalent to a two-tailed test of H_0: $\beta_j = 0$.

EXAMPLE

Home Prices

Figure 13.2 shows MegaStat's fitted regression for the three-predictor model, including a table of estimated coefficients, standard errors, t statistics, and p-values. MegaStat computes two-tail p-values, as do most statistical packages. Notice that 0 is within the 95 percent confidence interval for *Baths,* while the confidence intervals for *SqFt* and *LotSize* do not include 0. This suggests that the hypothesis of a zero coefficient can be rejected for *SqFt* and *LotSize* but not for *Baths.*

---

*You needn't use 0 in the t test. For example, if you want to know whether an extra square foot adds at least \$200 to a home's selling price, you would use 200 instead of 0 in the formula for the test statistic. However, $\beta = 0$ is the default hypothesis in Excel and other statistical packages.

FIGURE 13.2

MegaStat's regression for
home prices (three
predictors)

| Regression output | | | | | | confidence interval |
variables	coefficients	std. error	t(df = 26)	p-value	95% lower	95% upper
Intercept	−28.8477	29.7115	−0.971	0.3405	−89.9206	32.2251
SqFt	0.1709	0.0154	11.064	0.0000	0.1392	0.2027
LotSize	6.7777	1.4213	4.769	0.0001	3.8562	9.6992
Baths	15.5347	9.2083	1.687	0.1036	−3.3932	34.4626

There are four estimated coefficients (counting the intercept). For reasons stated previously, the intercept is of no interest. For the three predictors, each t test uses $n - k - 1$ degrees of freedom. Since we have $n = 30$ observations and $k = 3$ predictors, we have $n - k - 1 = 30 - 3 - 1 = 26$ degrees of freedom. From Appendix D we can obtain two-tail critical values of $t_{.10} = 1.706$, $t_{.05} = 2.056$, and $t_{.01} = 2.779$. However, since p-values are provided, we do not really need these critical values.

$SqFt$: $t = 0.1709/0.01545 = 11.06$ $(p = .0000)$

$LotSize$: $t = 6.778/1.421 = 4.77$ $(p = .0001)$

$Baths$: $t = 15.535/9.208 = 1.69$ $(p = .1036)$

The coefficients of $SqFt$ and $LotSize$ differ significantly from zero at any common α because their p-values are practically zero. The coefficient of $Baths$ is not quite significant at $\alpha = .10$. Based on the t-values, we conclude that $SqFt$ is a very strong predictor of $Price$, followed closely by $LotSize$, while $Baths$ is of marginal significance.

SECTION EXERCISES

13.5 Observations are taken on net revenue from sales of a certain plasma TV at 50 retail outlets. The regression model was Y = net revenue (thousands of dollars), X_1 = shipping cost (dollars per unit), X_2 = expenditures on print advertising (thousands of dollars), X_3 = expenditure on electronic media ads (thousands), X_4 = rebate rate (percent of retail price). (a) Calculate the t statistic for each coefficient to test for $\beta = 0$. (b) Look up the critical value of Student's t in Appendix D for a two-tailed test at $\alpha = .01$. Which coefficients differ significantly from zero? (c) Use Excel to find the p-value for each coefficient.   **PlasmaTV**

Predictor	Coefficient	SE
Intercept	4.310	70.82
ShipCost	−0.0820	4.678
PrintAds	2.265	1.050
WebAds	2.498	0.8457
Rebate%	16.697	3.570

13.6 Observations are taken on sales of a certain mountain bike in 30 sporting goods stores. The regression model was Y = total sales (thousands of dollars), X_1 = display floor space (square meters), X_2 = competitors' advertising expenditures (thousands of dollars), X_3 = advertised price (dollars per unit), X_4 = rebate rate (percent of retail price). (a) Calculate the t statistic for each coefficient to test for $\beta = 0$. (b) Look up the critical value of Student's t in Appendix D for a two-tailed test at $\alpha = .01$. Which coefficients differ significantly from zero? (c) Use Excel to find the p-value for each coefficient.   **Bikes**

Predictor	Coefficient	SE
Intercept	1225.4	397.3
FloorSpace	11.522	1.330
CompetingAds	−6.935	3.905
Price	−0.14955	0.08927

13.4
CONFIDENCE INTERVALS FOR Y

Standard Error

Another important measure of fit is the ***standard error (SE) of the regression,*** derived from the sum of squared residuals (*SSE*) for *n* observations and *k* predictors:

$$SE = \sqrt{\frac{\sum_{i=1}^{n}(y_i - \hat{y}_i)^2}{n-k-1}} = \sqrt{\frac{SSE}{n-k-1}} \qquad \text{(standard error of the regression)} \qquad (13.9)$$

The standard error is measured in the same units as the response variable *Y* (dollars, square feet, etc). A smaller *SE* indicates a better fit. If all predictions were perfect (i.e., if $y_i = \hat{y}_i$ for all observations), then *SE* would be zero. However, perfect predictions are unlikely.

EXAMPLE

Home Prices II

From the ANOVA table for the three-predictor home price model we obtain $SSE = 10{,}720$, so

$$SE = \sqrt{\frac{SSE}{n-k-1}} = \sqrt{\frac{10{,}720}{30-3-1}} = 20.31$$

$SE = 20.31$ (i.e., \$20,310 since *Y* is measured in thousands of dollars) suggests that the model has room for improvement, despite its good fit ($R^2 = .956$). Forecasters find the standard error more useful than R^2 because *SE* tells more about the *practical utility* of the forecasts, especially when it is used to make confidence or prediction intervals.

Approximate Confidence and Prediction Intervals for Y

We can use the standard error to create approximate confidence or prediction intervals for values of $X_1, X_2, \ldots, X_k$ that are not far from their respective means.* Although these approximate intervals somewhat understate the interval widths, they are helpful when you only need a general idea of the accuracy of your model's predictions.

$$\hat{y}_i \pm t_{n-k-1}\frac{SE}{\sqrt{n}} \qquad \text{(approximate 95\% confidence interval for conditional mean of } Y) \qquad (13.10)$$

$$\hat{y}_i \pm t_{n-k-1}SE \qquad \text{(approximate 95\% prediction interval for individual } Y\text{-value)} \qquad (13.11)$$

EXAMPLE

Home Prices III

For home prices using the three-predictor model ($SE = 20.31$) the 95 percent confidence interval would require $n - k - 1 = 30 - 3 - 1 = 26$ degrees of freedom. From Appendix D we obtain $t = 2.056$ so the *approximate* intervals are

---

*The exact formulas for a confidence or prediction interval for $\mu_{Y|X}$ or *Y* require matrix algebra. If you need exact intervals, you should use MINITAB or a similar computer package. You must specify the value of *each predictor* for which the confidence interval or prediction is desired.

$$\hat{y}_i \pm (2.056)\frac{20.31}{\sqrt{30}} = \hat{y}_i \pm 7.62 \qquad \text{(quick confidence interval for conditional mean)}$$

$$\hat{y}_i \pm (2.056)(20.31) = \hat{y}_i \pm 41.76 \qquad \text{(quick prediction interval for individual home price)}$$

Exact 95 percent confidence and prediction intervals for a home with $SqFt = 2,950$, $LotSize = 21$, and $Baths = 3$ (these values are very near the predictor means for our sample) are $\hat{y}_i \pm 8.55$ and $\hat{y}_i \pm 42.61$, respectively. Thus, our *approximate* intervals are not conservative (i.e., slightly too narrow). Nonetheless, the approximate intervals provide a ballpark idea of the accuracy of the model's predictions. Despite its good fit ($R^2 = .956$) we see that the three-predictor model's predictions are far from perfect. For example, the 95 percent prediction interval for an individual home price is $\pm \$41,760$.

Quick 95 Percent Prediction Interval for Y

The *t*-values for 95 percent confidence are typically near 2 (as long as n is not too small). This suggests a quick prediction interval without using a *t* table:

(13.12) $\qquad \hat{y}_i \pm 2\dfrac{SE}{\sqrt{n}} \qquad$ (quick 95% confidence interval for conditional mean of Y)

(13.13) $\qquad \hat{y}_i \pm 2SE \qquad$ (quick 95% prediction interval for individual Y-value)

These quick formulas are suitable only for rough calculations when you lack access to regression software or *t* tables (e.g., when taking a statistics exam).

SECTION EXERCISES

13.7 A regression of accountants' starting salaries in a large firm was estimated using 40 new hires and five predictors (college GPA, gender, score on CPA exam, years' prior experience, size of graduating class). The standard error was $3,620. Find the approximate width of a 95 percent prediction interval for an employee's salary, assuming that the predictor values for the individual are near the means of the sample predictors. Would the quick rule give similar results?

13.8 An agribusiness performed a regression of wheat yield (bushels per acre) using observations on 25 test plots with four predictors (rainfall, fertilizer, soil acidity, hours of sun). The standard error was 1.17 bushels. Find the approximate width of a 95 percent prediction interval for wheat yield, assuming that the predictor values for a test plot are near the means of the sample predictors. Would the quick rule give similar results?

Mini Case   13.1

Birth Rates and Life Expectancy   BirthRates1

Table 13.4 shows the birth rate ($Y =$ births per 1,000 population), life expectancy ($X_1 =$ life expectancy at birth), and literacy ($X_2 =$ percent of population that can read and write) for a random sample of 49 world nations.

From Figure 13.3, the fitted regression equation is *BirthRate* $= 65.9 - 0.362$ *LifeExp* $- 0.233$ *Literate,* which says, *ceteris paribus,* that one year's increase in *LifeExp* is associated with 0.362 fewer babies per 1,000 persons, while one extra percent of *Literate* is associated with 0.233 fewer babies per 1,000 persons. The coefficient of determination is fairly high ($R^2 = .743$) and the overall regression is significant ($F = 66.42$, $p = .000$). Since both

TABLE 13.4 Birth Rates, Life Expectancy, and Literacy in Selected World Nations

Nation	BirthRate	LifeExp	Literate	Nation	BirthRate	LifeExp	Literate
Albania	18.59	72.1	93	Mauritius	16.34	71.5	83
Algeria	22.34	70.2	62	Mozambique	36.41	35.5	42
Australia	12.71	80.0	100	Nepal	32.94	58.6	28
Bangladesh	25.12	60.9	56	Nicaragua	26.98	69.4	68
Belgium	10.58	78.1	98	Pakistan	30.40	62.7	43
Botswana	28.04	35.9	70	Panama	18.60	75.9	91
Burundi	39.87	45.9	36	Peru	23.36	70.6	88
Cambodia	32.93	57.1	35	Puerto Rico	15.04	76.0	89
Chile	16.46	76.1	95	Senegal	36.99	62.9	39
Costa Rica	19.83	76.2	96	Serbia/Montenegro	12.80	73.7	93
Croatia	12.80	74.1	97	Sri Lanka	16.36	72.4	90
Denmark	11.74	76.9	100	Swaziland	39.59	37.0	78
Dom. Republic	24.40	73.7	82	Switzerland	9.84	79.9	99
Ecuador	25.47	71.6	90	Taiwan	14.21	76.7	94
Gabon	27.24	49.1	63	Tanzania	39.12	51.7	68
Iran	17.54	70.3	72	Thailand	16.39	69.2	94
Iraq	34.20	67.4	58	Turkey	17.95	71.5	85
Japan	10.03	80.9	99	United Kingdom	11.34	78.0	99
Korea N	17.95	71.3	99	Uruguay	17.28	75.7	97
Korea S	14.55	74.9	98	Uzbekistan	26.09	63.9	99
Kuwait	21.84	79.5	79	Venezuela	20.22	73.6	91
Lesotho	30.72	47.0	83	Yemen	43.30	60.6	38
Libya	27.59	75.9	76	Zambia	41.01	37.4	79
Madagascar	42.41	55.7	80	Zimbabwe	24.59	36.5	85
Mauritania	42.54	54.5	41				

FIGURE 13.3

MegaStat's output for birth rate data

Regression Analysis: Birth Rates

R^2	0.743	n	49
Adjusted R^2	0.732	k	2
Std. Error	5.190	Dep. Var.	**BirthRate**

ANOVA table

Source	SS	df	MS	F	p-value
Regression	3,578.2364	2	1,789.1182	66.42	0.0000
Residual	1,239.1479	46	26.9380		
Total	4,817.3843	48			

Regression output — confidence interval

variables	coefficients	std. error	t(df = 46)	p-value	95% lower	95% upper
Intercept	65.8790	3.8513	17.106	0.0000	58.1268	73.6312
LifeExp	−0.3618	0.0666	−5.431	0.0000	−0.4960	−0.2277
Literate	−0.2330	0.0415	−5.610	0.0000	−0.3166	−0.1494

predictors are significant ($t = -5.431$ and $t = -5.610$, p-values near .000) the evidence favors the hypothesis that birth rates tend to fall as nations achieve higher life expectancy and greater literacy. Although cause-and-effect is unproven, the conclusions are consistent with what we know about nutrition, health, and education.

Source: Central Intelligence Agency, *The World Factbook, 2003.*

13.5
BINARY PREDICTORS

VS

Chapter 19

What Is a Binary Predictor?

A binary predictor has two values, denoting the presence or absence of a condition (usually coded 0 and 1). Statisticians like to use intuitive names for the binary variable. For example:

For *n* Graduates from an MBA Program

Employed $= 1$ (if the individual is currently employed)

Employed $= 0$ (otherwise)

For *n* Quarters of Sales Data

Recession $= 1$ (if the sales data is for a recession year)

Recession $= 0$ (otherwise)

For *n* Business Schools

AACSB $= 1$ (if the school is accredited by the AACSB)

AACSB $= 0$ (otherwise)

For *n* States

West $= 1$ (if the state is west of the Mississippi)

West $= 0$ (otherwise)

Binary predictors are easy to create and are extremely important, because they allow us to capture the effects of nonquantitative (categorical) variables such as gender (female, male) or stock fund type (load, no-load). Such variables are also called ***dummy*** or ***indicator variables.***

Tip

Name the binary variable for the characteristic that is present when the variable is 1 (e.g., *Male*) so that others can immediately see what the "1" stands for.

Effects of a Binary Predictor

A binary predictor is sometimes called a ***shift variable*** because it shifts the regression plane up or down. Suppose that we have a two-predictor fitted regression $Y = b_0 + b_1 X_1 + b_2 X_2$ where X_1 is a binary predictor. Since the only values that X_1 can take on are either 0 or 1, its contribution to the regression is either b_1 or nothing, as seen in this example:

If $X_1 = 0$, then $Y = b_0 + b_1(0) + b_2 X_2$, so $Y = b_0 + b_2 X_2$.

If $X_1 = 1$, then $Y = b_0 + b_1(1) + b_2 X_2$, so $Y = (b_0 + b_1) + b_2 X_2$.

The slope of the regression plane on the X_2-axis (b_2) is the same, regardless of the value of X_1, but the intercept either is b_0 (when $X_1 = 0$) or $b_0 + b_1$ (when $X_1 = 1$).

For example, suppose we have a fitted regression of fuel economy based on a sample of 43 cars:

$$MPG = 39.5 - 0.00463 \, Weight + 1.51 \, Manual$$

where

Weight $=$ vehicle curb weight as tested (pounds)

Manual $= 1$ if manual transmission, 0 if automatic

If *Manual* = 0, then

$$MPG = 39.5 - 0.00463 \ Weight + 1.51(0)$$

$$= 39.5 - 0.00463 \ Weight$$

If *Manual* = 1, then

$$MPG = 39.5 - 0.00463 \ Weight + 1.51(1)$$

$$= 41.01 - 0.00463 \ Weight$$

Thus, the binary variable shifts the intercept, leaving the slope unchanged. The situation is illustrated in Figure 13.4. In this case, we see that, although a manual transmission raises *MPG* slightly (by 1.51 miles per gallon, on average) the change in the intercept is rather small (i.e., manual transmission did not have a very large effect). A different sample could, of course, yield a different result. Many experts feel that the choice of automatic versus manual transmission makes very little difference in fuel economy today.

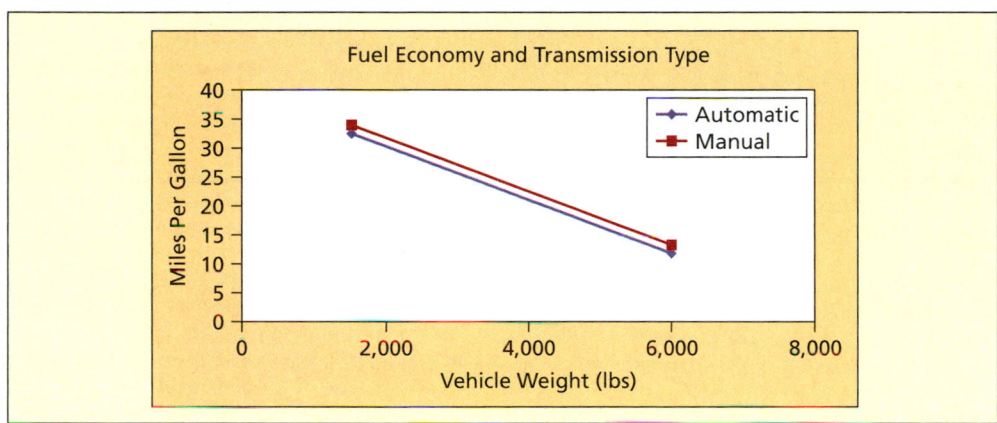

FIGURE 13.4

Binary shift variable
illustrated

Testing a Binary for Significance

We test the degree of significance of the binary predictor just as we would test any other predictor, using a *t* test. In multiple regression, binary predictors require no special treatment.

EXAMPLE

*Subdivision
Home Prices*

OakKnoll

We know that location is an important determinant of home price. But how can we include "location" in a regression? The answer is to code it as a binary predictor. Table 13.5 shows 20 home sales in two different subdivisions, Oak Knoll and Hidden Hills. We create a binary predictor, arbitrarily designating *OakKnoll* = 1 if the home is in the Oak Knoll subdivision, and *OakKnoll* = 0 otherwise. We then do an ordinary regression, shown in Figure 13.5.

The model has a rather good fit (R^2 = .922) and is significant overall (F = 100.94, p = .0000). Both predictors have a significant effect on *Price* at α = .05, although *SqFt* (t = 14.008, p = .0000) is a much stronger predictor than *OakKnoll* (t = 2.340, p = .0317). The fitted coefficient of *OakKnoll* tells us that, on average, a home in the Oak Knoll subdivision sells for 33.538 more than a home in Hidden Hills (i.e., $33,538 since *Price* is in thousands of dollars). Rounded off a bit, the fitted regression equation is *Price* = 10.6 + 0.199 *SqFt* + 33.5 *OakKnoll*. The intercept (t = 0.237, p = .8154) does not differ significantly from zero, as can also be seen from the 95 percent confidence interval for the intercept (which includes zero).

TABLE 13.5   **Home Prices with Binary Predictor**   🏠   **OakKnoll**

Obs	Price ($000)	SqFt	OakKnoll	Subdivision
1	615.6	3,055	0	Hidden Hills
2	557.4	2,731	0	Hidden Hills
3	472.6	2,515	0	Hidden Hills
4	595.3	3,011	0	Hidden Hills
5	696.9	3,267	1	Oak Knoll
6	409.2	2,061	1	Oak Knoll
7	814.2	3,842	1	Oak Knoll
8	592.4	2,777	1	Oak Knoll
9	695.5	3,514	0	Hidden Hills
10	495.3	2,145	1	Oak Knoll
11	488.4	2,277	1	Oak Knoll
12	605.4	3,200	0	Hidden Hills
13	635.7	3,065	0	Hidden Hills
14	654.8	2,998	0	Hidden Hills
15	565.6	2,875	0	Hidden Hills
16	642.2	3,000	0	Hidden Hills
17	568.9	2,374	1	Oak Knoll
18	686.5	3,393	1	Oak Knoll
19	724.5	3,457	0	Hidden Hills
20	749.7	3,754	0	Hidden Hills

FIGURE 13.5

OakKnoll regression for 20 home sales

Regression Analysis: Subdivision Binary (n = 20)

R^2	0.922			
Adjusted R^2	0.913		n	20
R	0.960		k	2
Std. Error	29.670		Dep. Var.	**Price (000)**

ANOVA table

Source	SS	df	MS	F	p-value
Regression	177,706.7957	2	88,853.3979	100.94	.0000
Residual	14,964.9538	17	880.2914		
Total	192,671.7495	19			

Regression output   confidence interval

variables	coefficients	std. error	t (df = 17)	p-value	95% lower	95% upper
Intercept	10.6185	44.7725	0.237	.8154	−83.8433	105.0803
SqFt	0.1987	0.0142	14.008	0.0000	0.1688	0.2286
OakKnoll	33.5383	14.3328	2.340	.0317	3.2986	63.7780

More Than One Binary

A variable like gender (male, female) requires only one binary predictor (e.g., *Male*) because *Male* = 0 would indicate a female. But what if we need several binary predictors to code the data? This occurs when the number of categories to be coded exceeds two. For example, we might have home sales in five subdivisions, or quarterly Wal-Mart profits, or student GPA by class level:

    Home sales by subdivision: *OakKnoll, HiddenHills, RockDale, Lochmoor, KingsRidge*

    Wal-Mart profit by quarter: *Qtr1, Qtr2, Qtr3, Qtr4*

    GPA by class level: *Freshman, Sophomore, Junior, Senior, Master's, Doctoral*

Each category is a binary variable denoting the presence (1) or absence (0) of the characteristic of interest. For example:

Freshman = 1 if the student is a freshman, 0 otherwise

Sophomore = 1 if the student is a sophomore, 0 otherwise

Junior = 1 if the student is a junior, 0 otherwise

Senior = 1 if the student is a senior, 0 otherwise

Master's = 1 if the student is a master's candidate, 0 otherwise

Doctoral = 1 if the student is a PhD candidate, 0 otherwise

But if there are c categories (assuming they are mutually exclusive and collectively exhaustive), we need only $c - 1$ binaries to code each observation. This is equivalent to omitting any *one* of the categories. This is possible because the $c - 1$ remaining binary values uniquely determine the remaining binary. For example, Table 13.6 shows that we could omit the last binary column without losing any information. Since only one column can be 1 and the other columns must be 0, the following relation holds:

$$Freshman + Sophomore + Junior + Senior + Master's + Doctoral = 1$$

that is,

$$Doctoral = 1 - Freshman - Sophomore - Junior - Senior - Master's$$

Name	Freshman	Sophomore	Junior	Senior	Master's	Doctoral
Jaime	0	0	1	0	0	0
Fritz	0	1	0	0	0	0
Mary	0	0	0	0	0	1
Jean	0	0	0	1	0	0
Otto	0	0	0	0	1	0
Gail	1	0	0	0	0	0
etc.	...	...	...	...	...	...

TABLE 13.6
Why We Need Only $c - 1$ Binaries to Code c Categories

That Mary is a doctoral student can be inferred from the fact that 0 appears in all the other columns. Since Mary is *not* in any of the other five categories, she must be in the sixth category:

$$Doctoral = 1 - 0 - 0 - 0 - 0 - 0 = 1$$

There is nothing special about the last column; we could have omitted any other column instead. Similarly, we might omit the *KingsRidge* data column from home sales data, since a home that is not in one of the first four subdivisions must be *KingsRidge*. We could omit the *Qtr4* column from the Wal-Mart time series, since if an observation is not from the first, second, or third quarter, it must be from *Qtr4*:

Home sales: *OakKnoll, HiddenHills, RockDale, Lochmoor, KingsRidge*

Wal-Mart profit: *Qtr1, Qtr2, Qtr3, Qtr4*

Again, there is nothing special about omitting the last category. We can omit any single binary instead. The omitted binary becomes the base reference point for the regression; that is, it is part of the intercept. No information is lost.

What If I Forget to Exclude One Binary?

If you include all c binaries for c categories, you will introduce a serious problem for the regression estimation, because one column in the X data matrix will then be a perfect linear combination of the other column(s). The least squares estimation would then fail because the data matrix would be singular (i.e., would have no inverse). MINITAB automatically checks for such a situation and omits one of the offending predictors, but it is safer to decide for yourself which binary to exclude. Excel merely gives an error.

Mini Case

13.2

Age or Gender Bias? 🐾 Oxnard

We can't use simple t tests to compare employee groups based on gender or age or job classification because they fail to take into account relevant factors such as education and experience. A simplistic equity study that fails to account for such control variables would be subject to criticism. Instead, we can use binary variables to study the effects of age, experience, gender, and education on salaries within a corporation. Gender and education can be coded as binary variables, and age can be forced into a binary variable that defines older employees explicitly, rather than assuming that age has a linear effect on salary.

Table 13.7 shows salaries for 25 employees in the advertising department at Oxnard Petro, Ltd. As an initial step in a salary equity study, the human resources consultant performed a linear regression using the proposed model $Salary = \beta_0 + \beta_1\ Male + \beta_2\ Exper + \beta_3\ Ovr50 + \beta_4\ MBA$. *Exper* is the employee's experience in years; *Salary* is in thousands of dollars. Binaries are used for gender ($Male = 0, 1$), age ($Ovr50 = 0, 1$), and MBA degree ($MBA = 0, 1$). Can we reject the hypothesis that the coefficients of *Male* and *Ovr50* are zero? If so, it would suggest salary inequity based on gender and/or age.

TABLE 13.7   Salaries of Advertising Staff of Oxnard Petro, Ltd.

Obs	Employee	Salary	Male	Exper	Ovr50	MBA
1	Mary	28.6	0	0	0	1
2	Frieda	53.3	0	4	0	1
3	Alicia	73.8	0	12	0	0
4	Tom	26.0	1	0	0	0
5	Nicole	77.5	0	19	0	0
6	Xihong	95.1	1	17	0	0
7	Ellen	34.3	0	1	0	1
8	Bob	63.5	1	9	0	0
9	Vivian	96.4	0	19	0	0
10	Cecil	122.9	1	31	0	0
11	Barry	63.8	1	12	0	0
12	Jaime	111.1	1	29	1	0
13	Wanda	82.5	0	12	0	1
14	Sam	80.4	1	19	1	0
15	Saundra	69.3	0	10	0	0
16	Pete	52.8	1	8	0	0
17	Steve	54.0	1	2	0	1
18	Juan	58.7	1	11	0	0
19	Dick	72.3	1	14	0	0
20	Lee	88.6	1	21	0	0
21	Judd	60.2	1	10	0	0
22	Sunil	61.0	1	7	0	0
23	Marcia	75.8	0	18	0	0
24	Vivian	79.8	0	19	0	0
25	Igor	70.2	1	12	0	0

The coefficients in Figure 13.6 suggest that, *ceteris paribus,* a male ($Male = 1$) makes $3,013 more on average than a female. However, the coefficient of *Male* does not differ significantly from zero even at $\alpha = .10$ ($t = 0.86, p = .399$). The evidence for age discrimination is a little stronger. Although an older employee ($Ovr50 = 1$) makes $8,598 less than others, on average, the p-value for *Ovr50* ($t = -1.36, p = .189$) is not convincing at $\alpha = .10$. The coefficient of MBA indicates that, *ceteris paribus,* MBA degree holders earn $9,587 more than

The regression equation is
Salary = 28.9 + 3.01 Male − 8.60 Ovr50 + 3.02 Exper + 9.59 MBA

Predictor	Coef	SE Coef	T	P
Constant	28.878	4.925	5.86	0.000
Male	3.013	3.496	0.86	0.399
Ovr50	−8.598	6.324	−1.36	0.189
Exper	3.0190	0.2499	12.08	0.000
MBA	9.587	5.003	1.92	0.070

S = 7.44388   R-Sq = 91.3%   R-Sq(adj) = 89.6%

FIGURE 13.6

MINITAB results for Oxnard salary equity study

others, and the coefficient differs from zero at $\alpha = .10$ ($t = 1.92, p = .070$). Salaries at Oxnard Petro are dominated by *Exper* ($t = 12.08, p = .000$). Each additional year of experience adds \$3,019, on average, to an employee's salary. The regression is significant overall ($F = 52.62, p = .000$) and has a good fit ($R^2 = .913$). Although the sample fails Evans's 10:1 ratio test for n/k, it passes Doane's 5:1 ratio test. A more complete equity study might consider additional predictors.

Regional Binaries

One very common use of binaries is to code regions. Figure 13.7 shows how the 50 states of the United States could be divided into four regions by using these binaries:

Midwest = 1 if state is in the Midwest, 0 otherwise

Neast = 1 if state is in the Northeast, 0 otherwise

Seast = 1 if state is in the Southeast, 0 otherwise

West = 1 if state is in the West, 0 otherwise

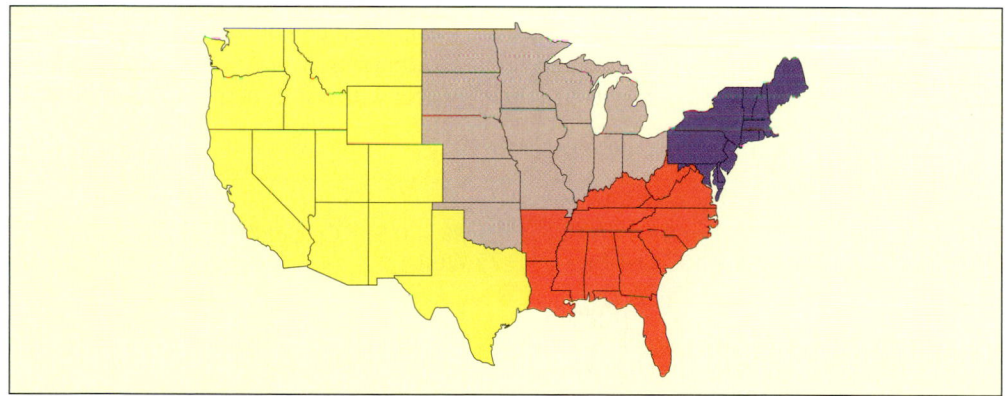

FIGURE 13.7

Four regional binaries

These are the same regional binaries that are used in the *LearningStats* state databases (cross-sectional data). For example, we can use regression to analyze the U.S. voting patterns in the 2000 U.S. presidential election. Binary predictors could permit us to analyze the effects of region (a qualitative variable) on voting patterns.

Mini Case   13.3

Regional Voting Patterns   **Election2000**

Table 13.8 shows abbreviated data for the 50 U.S. states from the *LearningStats* 2000 database. There are four regional binaries. Arbitrarily, we omit the *Seast* column, which becomes the baseline for the regression to examine a hypothesis about the effects of population age, urbanization, college graduation rates, unionization, and region on voting patterns in the 2000

U.S. presidential election. The dependent variable (*Bush%*) is the percentage vote for George W. Bush, and the proffered hypothesis to be investigated is

$$Bush\% = \beta_0 + \beta_1 \, Age65\% + \beta_2 \, Urban\% + \beta_3 \, ColGrad\% + \beta_4 \, Union\%$$
$$+ \beta_5 \, Midwest + \beta_6 \, Neast + \beta_7 \, West$$

TABLE 13.8   Characteristics of U.S. States in 2000 Election

State	Bush%	Age65%	Urban%	ColGrad%	Union%	Midwest	Neast	Omitted Seast	West
AL	56.5	13.0	69.9	20.4	9.6	0	0	1	0
AK	58.6	5.7	41.5	28.1	21.9	0	0	0	1
AZ	51.0	13.0	88.2	24.6	6.4	0	0	0	1
AR	51.3	14.0	49.9	18.4	5.8	0	0	1	0
CA	41.7	10.6	96.7	27.5	16.0	0	0	0	1
CO	50.8	9.7	83.9	34.6	9.0	0	0	0	1
CT	38.4	13.8	95.6	31.6	16.3	0	1	0	0
⋮	⋮	⋮	⋮	⋮	⋮	⋮	⋮	⋮	⋮
etc.	etc.	etc.	etc.	etc.	etc.	etc.	etc.	etc.	etc.

The fitted regression shown in Figure 13.8 has four quantitative predictors and three binaries. The regression is significant overall ($F = 22.92$, $p = .000$). It suggests that, *ceteris paribus,* the percent of voters choosing Bush was lower in states with older citizens, greater urbanization, higher percentage of college graduates, and more unionization. The Bush vote was, *ceteris paribus,* significantly higher in the Midwest ($t = 2.79$, $p = .008$) and, to a lesser extent, in the West ($t = 1.87$, $p = .069$). The coefficient of *Neast* suggests less Bush support in the Northeast ($t = -0.65$, $p = .522$) but the coefficient of *Neast* is not statistically significant (perhaps masked by quantitative variables such as *Urban%* and *Union%*, which tend to distinguish the northeastern states). Using regional binaries allows us to analyze the effects of these *qualitative* factors. Those who say statistics can only deal with numbers must think again.

FIGURE 13.8

MINITAB output for voting patterns

```
The regression equation is
Bush% = 94.6 − 1.29 Age65% − 0.0983 Urban% − 0.582 ColGrad% − 0.728 Union%
        + 5.67 Midwest − 1.61 Neast + 3.75 West

Predictor          Coef      SE Coef         T        P      VIF
Constant         94.550        7.525     12.56    0.000
Age65%          −1.2869        0.4010     −3.21    0.003      1.6
Urban%         −0.09827       0.03476     −2.83    0.007      1.4
ColGrad%        −0.5815        0.1933     −3.01    0.004      1.9
Union%          −0.7281        0.1327     −5.49    0.000      1.5
Midwest          5.671         2.034       2.79    0.008      2.2
Neast           −1.606         2.490      −0.65    0.522      2.9
West             3.748         2.007       1.87    0.069      2.2

S = 4.28656      R-Sq = 79.3%       R-Sq(adj) = 75.8%

Analysis of Variance

Source            DF          SS         MS        F        P
Regression         7     2948.11     421.16    22.92    0.000
Residual Error    42      771.73      18.37
Total             49     3719.84
```

Tests for Nonlinearity

Sometimes the effect of a predictor is nonlinear. A simple example would be estimating the volume of lumber to be obtained from a tree. This is a practical problem facing a timber farm, since the manager can inventory the trees and measure their heights and diameters without cutting any trees. In addition to improving the accuracy of asset valuation on the balance sheet, the manager can decide the best time to cut the trees, based on their expected growth rates.

The volume of lumber that can be milled from a tree depends on the height of the tree and its radius, that is, *Volume* = $f(Height, Radius)$. But what is the appropriate model form? Figure 13.9 shows the MINITAB regression output for two regressions of *Volume* on *Height* and *Radius*:

Model 1: Volume = $-58.0 + 0.3393\ Height + 9.4163\ Radius\ (R^2 = .948,\ SE = 3.88)$

Model 2: Volume = $-27.5 + 0.3488\ Height + 0.6738\ Radius^2\ (R^2 = .973,\ SE = 2.78)$

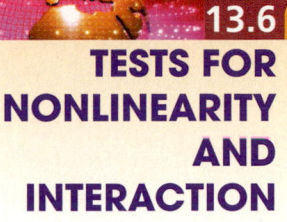

13.6

TESTS FOR NONLINEARITY AND INTERACTION

Chapter 18

FIGURE 13.9

Regression results for tree data

```
Model 1: The regression equation is
Volume = −58.0 + 0.339 Height + 9.42 Radius

Predictor        Coef      SE Coef        T         P
Constant      −57.988        8.638     −6.71     0.000
Height         0.3393       0.1302      2.61     0.014
Radius         9.4163       0.5285     17.82     0.000

S = 3.88183      R-Sq = 94.8%      R-Sq(adj) = 94.4%
```

```
Model 2: The regression equation is
Volume = −27.5 + 0.349 Height + 0.674 Radius2

Predictor        Coef      SE Coef        T         P
Constant      −27.512        6.558     −4.20     0.000
Height        0.34881      0.09315      3.74     0.001
Radius2       0.67383      0.02672     25.22     0.000

S = 2.79946      R-Sq = 97.3%      R-Sq(adj) = 97.1%
```

If we regard a log as a cylinder, we would prefer the second regression since the usable volume of a cylinder is proportional to the square of its radius.* The *t* statistics for both *Height* and *Radius* are improved in model 2, and the higher R^2 and reduced standard errors indicate a better fit. Note that this is still a linear regression, except that one of the predictors happens to be the square of another predictor. No special estimation is needed to introduce "nonlinearity" into the model. This example illustrates the importance of model specification.

To test for suspected nonlinearity of any predictor, we can include its square in the regression. For example, instead of

$$Y = \beta_0 + \beta_1 X_1 + \beta_2 X_2 + \varepsilon \tag{13.14}$$

we would estimate

$$Y = \beta_0 + \beta_1 X_1 + \beta_2 X_1^2 + \beta_3 X_2 + \beta_4 X_2^2 + \varepsilon \tag{13.15}$$

If the linear model is the correct one, the coefficients of the squared predictors (β_2 and β_4) would not be expected to differ significantly from zero, that is, the model will collapse to a

---

*$V = \pi h r^2$ would describe the relationship between the tree's radius (r), height (h), and volume (V). A logarithmic model $ln(Volume) = \beta_0 + \beta_1\ ln(Height) + \beta_2\ ln(Radius)$ might be even more appropriate, although the resulting R^2 and *SE* would not be comparable to the models shown above because the dependent variable would be in different units.

linear model. On the other hand, rejection of the hypothesis $H_0: \beta_2 = 0$ would suggest a quadratic relationship between Y and X_1, and similarly for Y and X_2. Inclusion of squared predictors merely gives the regression a chance to be nonlinear. Some researchers include squared predictors as a matter of course in large studies where there is no *a priori* reason to assume linearity. Squared predictors add model complexity and impose a cost of reduced degrees of freedom for significance tests (we lose 1 degree of freedom for each squared predictor), but the potential reward is a more appropriate model specification.

Tests for Interaction

We can test for *interaction* between two predictors by including their product in the regression. For example, we might hypothesize that Y depends on X_1 and X_2, and X_1X_2. To test for interaction, we estimate the model:

(13.16)
$$Y = \beta_0 + \beta_1 X_1 + \beta_2 X_2 + \beta_3 X_1 X_2 + \varepsilon$$

If the t test for β_3 allows us to reject the hypothesis $H_0: \beta_3 = 0$, then we conclude that there is a significant interaction effect that transcends the roles of X_1 and X_2 separately (similar to the two-factor ANOVA tests for interaction in Chapter 11). Interaction effects require careful interpretation and cost 1 degree of freedom per interaction. However, if the interaction term improves the model specification, it is well worth the cost. For example, a bank's lost revenue (*Loss*) due to loan defaults depends on the loan size (*Size*) and the degree of risk (*Risk*). Small loans may be risky but may not contribute much to the total losses. Large loans may be less risky but potentially represent a large loss. An interaction term (*Size* × *Risk*) would be large if either predictor is large, thereby capturing the effect of both predictors. Thus, the interaction term might be a significant predictor in the model:

$$Loss = b_0 + b_1 \, Size + b_2 \, Risk + b_3 \, Size \times Risk$$

Mini Case 13.4

Cockpit Noise 🐦 CockpitNoise

Cockpit sound level was measured 61 times at various flight phases for seven different B-727 aircraft (an older model) at the first officer's left ear position using a handheld meter. Sound level was measured in decibels. For reference, 60 dB is a normal conversation, 75 is a typical vacuum cleaner, 85 is city traffic, 90 is a typical hair dryer, and 110 is a chain saw. The proposed regression model is $Noise = \beta_0 + \beta_1 \, Climb + \beta_2 \, Descent + \beta_3 \, Speed + \beta_4 \, Speed^2 + \beta_5 \, Alt + \beta_6 \, Alt^2$. The airspeed (*Speed*) is in KIAS (knots indicated air speed) or nautical miles per hour. Altitude (*Alt*) is in thousands of feet above MSL (mean sea level). Squared predictors (*SpeedSqr* and *AltSqr*) are included for tests of nonlinearity (*SpeedSqr* is divided by 1,000 to improve data conditioning). There are three flight phases, represented by binaries (*Climb, Cruise, Descent*) but *Cruise* is omitted from the regression since it is implied by the other two binaries (i.e., if *Climb* = 0 and *Descent* = 0 then necessarily *Cruise* = 1). Table 13.9 shows a partial data list.

TABLE 13.9   **Cockpit Noise in B-727 Aircraft** 🐦 **CockpitNoise**

Obs	Noise	Climb	Cruise	Descent	Speed	Alt	SpeedSqr	AltSqr
1	83	1	0	0	250	10	62.50	100
2	89	1	0	0	340	15	115.60	225
3	88	1	0	0	320	18	102.40	324
4	89	0	1	0	330	24	108.90	576
5	92	0	1	0	346	27	119.72	729
...	...	...	...	...	...	...	...	...
61	82	0	0	1	250	4.5	62.50	20.25

Regression Analysis: Cockpit Noise ($n = 61$ flights)

R^2	0.920		
Adjusted R^2	0.911	n	61
R	0.959	k	6
Std. Error	1.179	Dep. Var.	**Noise**

ANOVA table

Source	SS	df	MS	F	p-value
Regression	860.4680	6	143.4113	103.19	0.0000
Residual	75.0484	54	1.3898		
Total	935.5164	60			

Regression output | | | | | confidence interval | |

variables	coefficients	std. error	t (df = 54)	p-value	95% lower	95% upper
Intercept	83.0833	8.0747	10.289	0.0000	66.8946	99.2721
Climb	−0.8140	0.5649	−1.441	0.1553	−1.9465	0.3185
Descent	−1.6612	0.5557	−2.989	0.0042	−2.7754	−0.5471
Speed	−0.0492	0.0525	−0.936	0.3533	−0.1545	0.0561
Alt	0.3134	0.1328	2.361	0.0219	0.0472	0.5796
SpeedSqr	0.1867	0.0799	2.336	0.0232	0.0265	0.3470
AltSqr	−0.0074	0.0031	−2.348	0.0226	−0.0137	−0.0011

Regression results are shown in Figure 13.10. The coefficient of *Climb* indicates a slight average reduction in *Noise* of 0.814 decibels during the climb flight phase (relative to the baseline of *Cruise*). The coefficient of *Descent* indicates a significant reduction of 1.66 decibels during the descent flight phase. *Speed* and *Alt* have nonlinear effects, as indicated by the significance of *SpeedSqr* ($t = 2.336$, $p = .0232$) and *AltSqr* ($t = −2.348$, $p = .0226$).

What Is Multicollinearity?

13.7
MULTICOL-LINEARITY

When the independent variables $X_1, X_2, \ldots, X_m$ are intercorrelated instead of being independent, we have a condition known as ***multicollinearity.*** If only two predictors are correlated, we have ***collinearity.*** Almost any data set will have some degree of correlation among the predictors. The depth of our concern would depend on the *degree* of multicollinearity.

Variance Inflation

Chapter 17

Multicollinearity does not bias the least squares estimates, but it does induce *variance inflation.* When predictors are strongly intercorrelated, the variances of their estimated coefficients tend to become inflated, widening the confidence intervals for the true coefficients $\beta_1, \beta_2, \ldots, \beta_k$ and making the *t* statistics less reliable. It can thus be difficult to identify the separate contribution of each predictor to "explaining" the response variable, due to the entanglement of their roles. Consequences of variance inflation can range from trivial to severe. In the most extreme case, when one *X* data column is an exact linear function of one or more other *X* data columns, the least squares estimation will fail.* That could happen, for example, if you inadvertently included the same predictor twice, or if you forgot to omit one of the *c* binaries used to code *c* attribute categories. Some software packages (e.g., MINITAB) will

*If the *X* data matrix has no inverse, we cannot solve for the OLS estimates.

check for perfect multicollinearity and will remove one of the offending predictors, but don't count on it.

Variance inflation generally does not cause major problems, and some researchers suggest that it is best ignored except in extreme cases. However, it is a good idea to investigate the degree of multicollinearity in the regression model. There are several ways to do this.

Correlation Matrix

To check whether two predictors are correlated (*collinearity*) we can inspect the **correlation matrix** for the predictors using Excel's function =CORREL(Data) or MegaStat's Correlation Matrix or MINITAB's Stat > Basic Statistics > Correlation. The correlation matrix for Mini Case 13.4 (cockpit noise) is shown in Table 13.10. The response variable (*Noise*) is not included, since collinearity *among the predictors* is the condition we are investigating. Cells above the diagonal are redundant and hence are not shown. Correlations that differ from zero at $\alpha = .05$ in a two-tailed test are highlighted in blue in Table 13.10. In this example, a majority of the predictors are significantly correlated, which is not an unusual situation in regression modeling. The very high correlations between *Speed* and *SpeedSqr* and between *Alt* and *AltSqr* are highlighted in yellow. These are an artifact of the model specification (i.e., using squared predictors as tests for nonlinearity) and are not necessarily a cause for removal of either predictor.*

TABLE 13.10

Correlation Matrix for Cockpit Noise Data

🦅 **CockpitNoise**

	Climb	Cruise	Descent	Speed	Alt	SpeedSqr
Cruise	−0.391					
Descent	−0.694	−0.391				
Speed	−0.319	−0.044	0.353			
Alt	−0.175	0.584	−0.282	0.063		
SpeedSqr	−0.351	−0.055	0.393	0.997	0.040	
AltSqr	−0.214	0.624	−0.274	−0.087	0.972	−0.103

Quick Rule

A sample correlation whose absolute value exceeds $2/\sqrt{n}$ probably differs significantly from zero in a two-tailed test at $\alpha = .05$. This quick rule applies to samples that are not too small (say, 20 or more).

Significant predictor correlations do not *per se* indicate a serious problem. **Klein's Rule** (see Related Reading) suggests that we should worry about the stability of the regression coefficient estimates only when a pairwise predictor correlation exceeds the multiple correlation coefficient R (i.e., the square root of R^2). In Mini Case 13.4 (cockpit noise) the correlations between *Speed* and *SpeedSqr* ($r = .997$) and between *Alt* and *AltSqr* ($r = .972$) do exceed the multiple correlation coefficient ($R = .959$), which suggests that the confidence intervals and t tests may be affected.

Predictor Matrix Plots

MINITAB and some other statistical packages produce scatter plots of all variables. Figure 13.11 shows scatter plots for the four numerical predictors in the cockpit noise data. No scatter plots were requested for the binary predictors (*Climb, Cruise, Descent*) because scatter plots for 0s and 1s would not be instructive. The collinearity for the squared predictors is easily seen. These visual displays are attractive and can reveal data characteristics that are not apparent from the correlation matrix, although they don't provide a precise statistical test.

---

*See *LearningStats* Unit 13 for more examples and a discussion of squared predictors.

FIGURE 13.11

MINITAB's matrix scatter
plot for cockpit noise
predictors

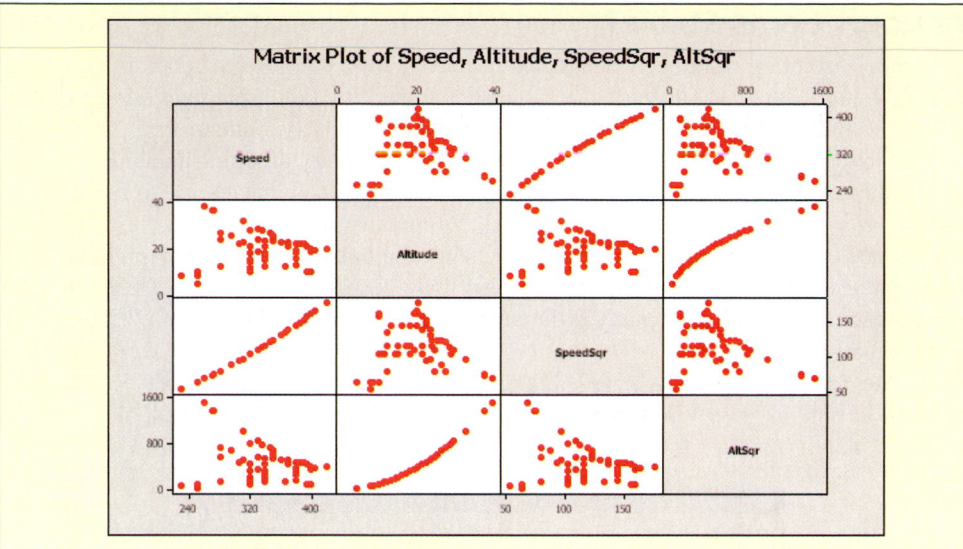

Variance Inflation Factor (VIF)

Although the matrix scatter plots and correlation matrix are easy to understand, they only show correlations between *pairs* of predictors (e.g., X_1 and X_2). A general test for multicollinearity should reveal more complex relationships *among* predictors. For example, X_2 might be a linear function of X_1, X_3, and X_4 even though its pairwise correlation with each is not very large. The ***variance inflation factor (VIF)*** for each predictor provides a more comprehensive test. For a given predictor j the VIF is defined as

$$VIF_j = \frac{1}{1 - R_j^2} \tag{13.17}$$

where R_j^2 is the coefficient of determination when predictor j is regressed against *all* the other predictors (excluding Y). If predictor j is unrelated to the other predictors, its R_j^2 will be 0 and its VIF will be 1 (an ideal situation that will rarely be seen with actual data). Some possible situations are:

R_j^2	VIF_j	Interpretation
0.00	$\dfrac{1}{1 - R_j^2} = \dfrac{1}{1 - 0.00} = 1.0$	No variance inflation
0.50	$\dfrac{1}{1 - R_j^2} = \dfrac{1}{1 - 0.50} = 2.0$	Mild variance inflation
0.90	$\dfrac{1}{1 - R_j^2} = \dfrac{1}{1 - 0.90} = 10.0$	Strong variance inflation
0.99	$\dfrac{1}{1 - R_j^2} = \dfrac{1}{1 - 0.99} = 100.0$	Severe variance inflation

Rules of Thumb

There is no limit on the magnitude of a VIF. Some researchers suggest that when a VIF exceeds 10, there is cause for concern, or even removal of predictor j from the model. But that rule of thumb is perhaps too conservative. A VIF of 10 says that the other predictors "explain" 90 percent of the variation in predictor j. While a VIF of 10 shows that predictor j is strongly related to the other predictors, it is not necessarily indicative of instability in the least squares estimates. Removing a relevant predictor is a step that should not be taken lightly, for it could result in misspecification of the model. A better way to think of it is that a large VIF is a warning to consider whether predictor j really belongs in the model.

Are Coefficients Stable?

Evidence of instability would be when X_1 and X_2 have a high pairwise correlation with Y, yet one or both predictors have insignificant t statistics in the fitted multiple regression. Another symptom would be if X_1 and X_2 are positively correlated with Y, yet one of them has a negative slope in the multiple regression. As a general test, you can try dropping a collinear predictor from the regression and watch what happens to the fitted coefficients in the re-estimated model. If they do not change very much, multicollinearity was probably not a concern. If dropping one collinear predictor causes sharp changes in one or more of the remaining coefficients in the model, then your multicollinearity may be causing instability. Keep in mind that a predictor must be significantly different from zero in order to say that it "changed" in the re-estimation.

Both MegaStat and MINITAB will calculate variance inflation factors, but you must request it as an option. Their VIF menu options are shown in Figures 13.12 and 13.13.

FIGURE 13.12

MegaStat's VIF menu option

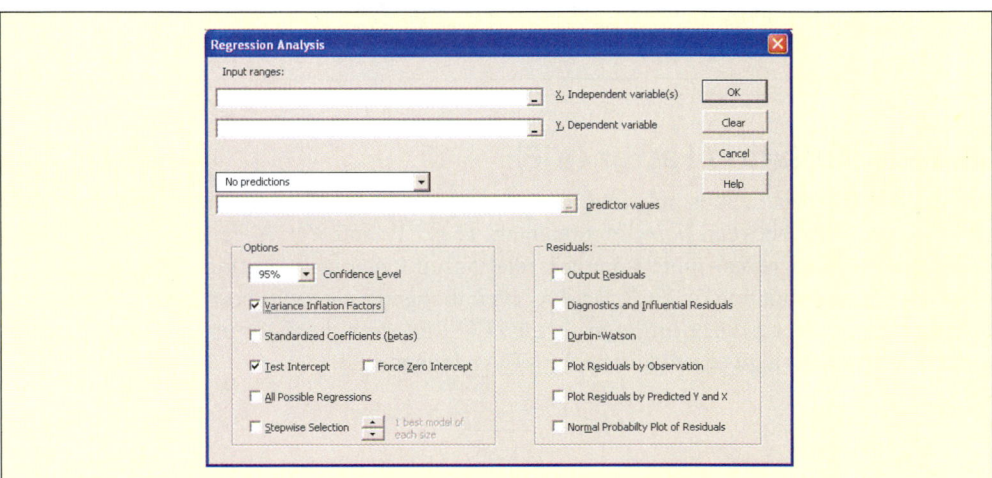

FIGURE 13.13

MINITAB's VIF menu option

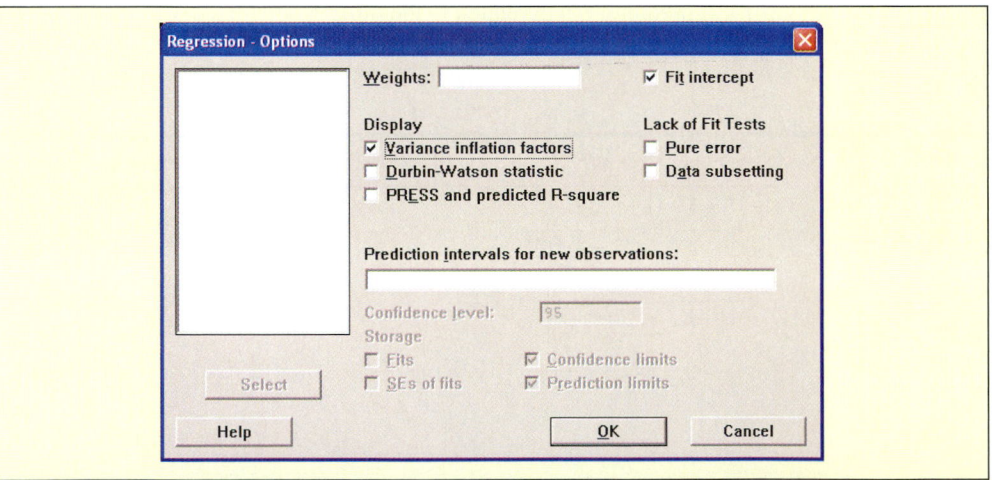

Mini Case   13.5

Regional Voting Patterns   Election2000

Mini Case 13.3 investigated a hypothesis about predictors for the percentage vote for George W. Bush in each of the 50 states. The proffered model was *Bush%* = β_0 + β_1 *Age65%* + β_2 *Urban%* + β_3 *ColGrad%* + β_4 *Union%* + β_5 *Midwest* + β_6 *Neast* + β_7 *West*. Table 13.11 and Figure 13.14 show the correlation matrix and matrix plot for the predictors (binary predictors omitted from the scatter plots). The quick rule for $n = 50$ says that a correlation is significant if it exceeds $2/\sqrt{n} = 2/\sqrt{50} = 0.28$. By this rule, a majority of the predictor correlations are significant at $\alpha = .05$ (shaded cells in table). However, none is close to the multiple correlation coefficient ($R = .890$) so by Klein's Rule we should not worry.

TABLE 13.11 Correlation Matrix for 2000 Election Predictors   Election2000

	Age65%	Urban%	ColGrad%	Union%	Midwest	Neast	Seast
Urban%	−0.030						
ColGrad%	−0.204	0.406					
Union%	0.006	0.342	0.308				
Midwest	0.237	−0.140	−0.031	0.088			
Neast	0.230	0.266	0.439	0.335	−0.315		
Seast	0.073	−0.109	−0.454	−0.482	−0.333	−0.298	
West	−0.513	−0.006	0.057	0.063	−0.370	−0.331	−0.350

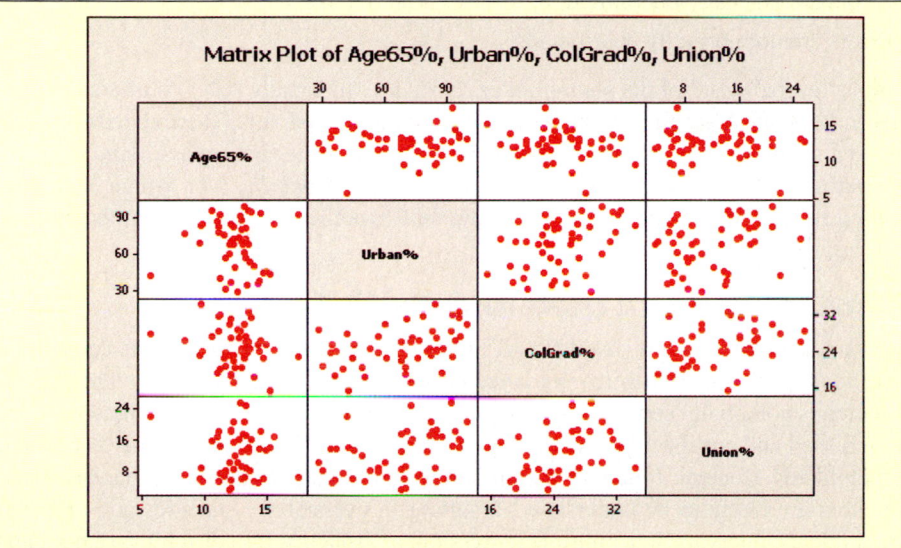

FIGURE 13.14

MINITAB's matrix scatter plot for 2000 election predictors

Despite the significant correlations between certain predictors, Figure 13.15 shows that for the election data no VIF exceeds 10 and the overall mean VIF is small. Thus, the confidence intervals should be reliable.

Regression output						confidence interval		
variables	coefficients	std. error	t (df = 42)	p-value	95% lower	95% upper	VIF
Intercept	94.5502	7.5254	12.564	0.0000	79.3633	109.7370	
Age65%	−1.2869	0.4010	−3.210	0.0025	−2.0961	−0.4777	1.555
Urban%	−0.0983	0.0348	−2.827	0.0072	−0.1684	−0.0281	1.361
ColGrad%	−0.5815	0.1933	−3.008	0.0044	−0.9716	−0.1914	1.853
Union%	−0.7281	0.1327	−5.485	0.0000	−0.9960	−0.4602	1.517
Midwest	5.6715	2.0340	2.788	0.0079	1.5666	9.7763	2.166
Neast	−1.6063	2.4902	−0.645	0.5224	−6.6318	3.4191	2.896
West	3.7483	2.0071	1.868	0.0688	−0.3022	7.7988	2.210

FIGURE 13.15

MegaStat's VIFs for election study   **Election2000**

13.8
VIOLATIONS OF ASSUMPTIONS

Chapter 16

Recall that the least squares method makes several assumptions about random errors ε_i. Although ε_i is unobservable, clues may be found in the residuals e_i. We routinely test three important assumptions:

- *Assumption* 1: The errors are normally distributed.
- *Assumption* 2: The errors have constant variance (i.e., they are homoscedastic).
- *Assumption* 3: The errors are independent (i.e., they are nonautocorrelated).

Regression residuals often violate one or more of these assumptions. The consequences may be mild, moderate, or severe, depending on various factors. ***Residual tests*** for violations of regression assumptions are routinely provided by regression software. These tests were discussed in detail in sections 12.8 and 12.9. We briefly review each assumption.

Non-Normal Errors

Except when there are major outliers, non-normal residuals are usually considered a mild violation. The regression coefficients and their variances remain unbiased and consistent. The main ill consequence is that confidence intervals for the parameters may be unreliable because the normality assumption is used to construct them. However, if the sample size is large (say, $n > 30$) the confidence intervals generally are OK unless serious outliers exist. The hypotheses are:

H_0: Errors are normally distributed

H_1: Errors are not normally distributed

A simple "eyeball test" of the *histogram of residuals* can usually reveal outliers or serious asymmetry. You can use either plain residuals or standardized (i.e., studentized) residuals. Standardized residuals offer the advantage of a predictable scale (between -3 and $+3$ unless there are outliers). Another visual test for normality is the *probability plot,* which is produced as an option by MINITAB and MegaStat. If the null hypothesis is true, the probability plot should be approximately linear.

Nonconstant Variance (Heteroscedasticity)

The regression should fit equally well for all values of X. If the error variance is constant, the errors are *homoscedastic*. If the error variance is nonconstant, the errors are *heteroscedastic*. This violation is potentially serious. Although the least squares regression parameter estimates are still unbiased and consistent, their estimated variances are biased and are neither efficient nor asymptotically efficient. In the most common form of heteroscedasticity, the variances of the estimators are likely to be understated, resulting in overstated t statistics and artificially narrow confidence intervals. In a multiple regression, a visual test for constant variance can be

FIGURE 13.16

Heteroscedastic residual plots

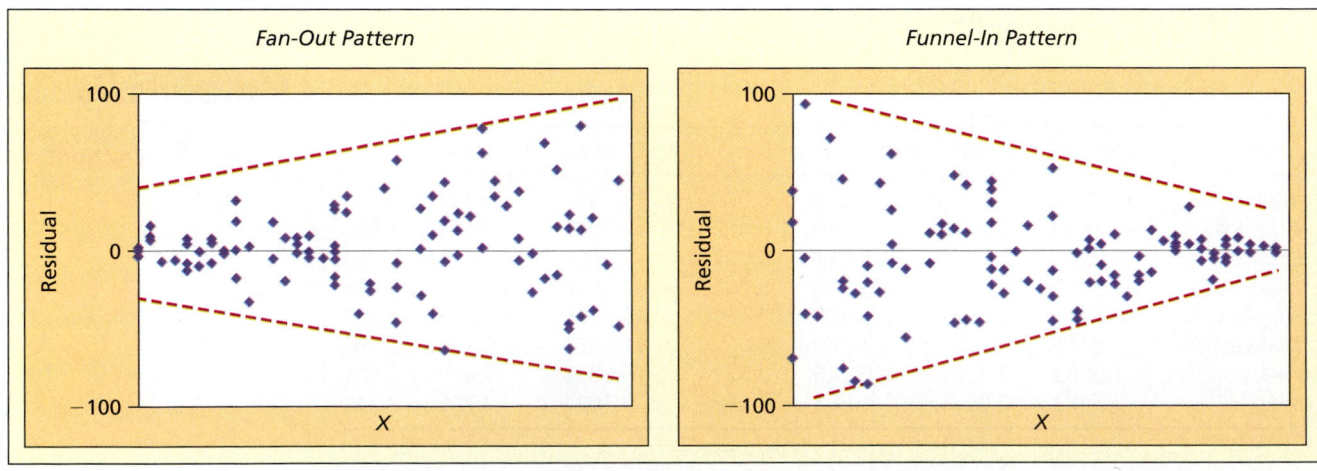

performed by examining scatter plots of the residuals against each predictor or against the fitted Y-values. Ideally, there will be no pattern and the vertical spread (residual variance) will be similar regardless of the X-values. The hypotheses are:

H_0: Errors have constant variance (homoscedastic)

H_1: Errors have nonconstant variance (heteroscedastic)

Although many patterns of nonconstant variance might exist, the "fan-out" pattern of increasing variance is most common (see Figure 13.16). The zero line appears more or less in the center of the residual plot, since the residuals always sum to zero (see *LearningStats* Unit 13 for details).

Mini Case
13.6

Non-Normality and Heteroscedasticity   HeartDeaths

Figure 13.17 shows MINITAB regression diagnostics for a regression model of heart deaths in all 50 U.S. states for the year 2000. The dependent variable is *Heart* = heart deaths per 100,000 population and the three predictors are *Age65%* = percent of population age 65 and over, *Income* = per capita income in thousands of dollars, and *Black%* = percent of population that is African American.

FIGURE 13.17

MINITAB diagnostics for heart death regression

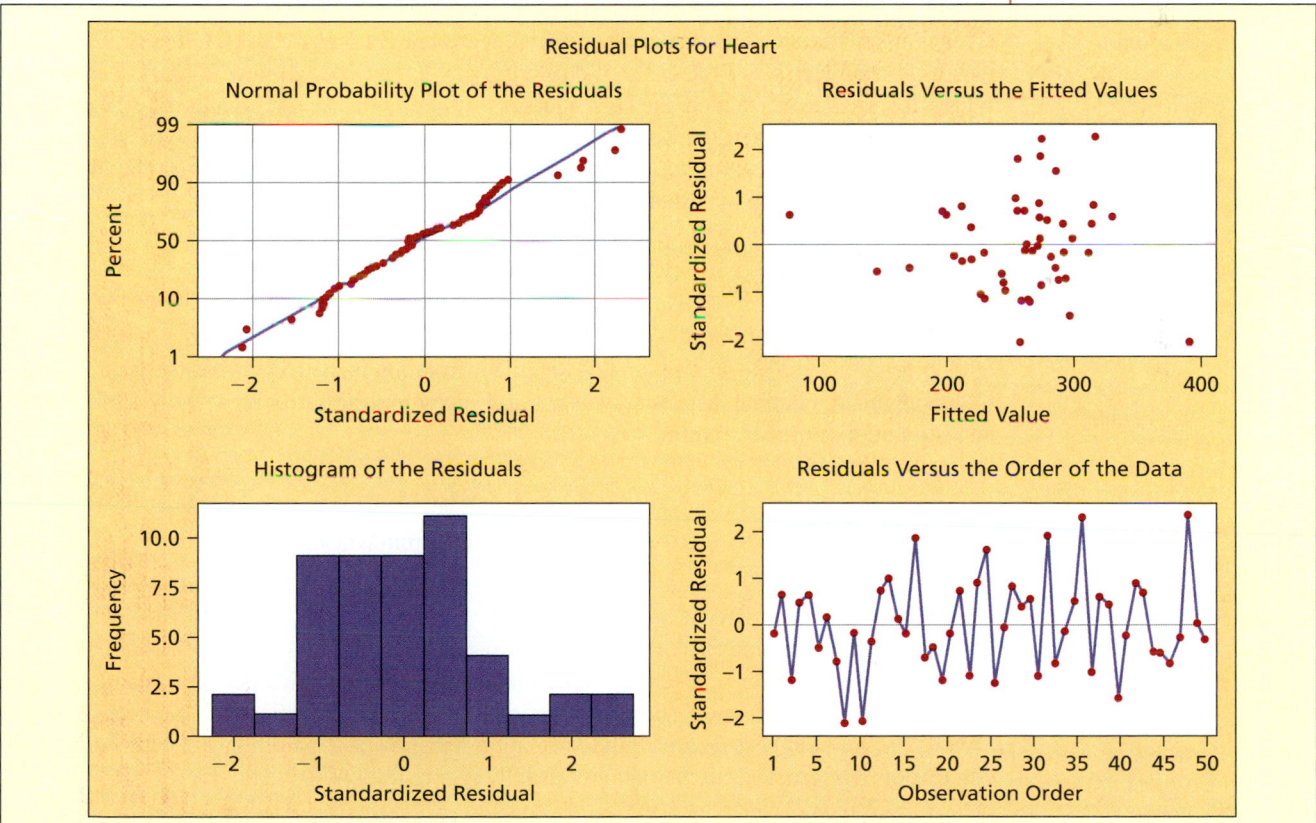

The histogram is arguably bell-shaped. Since the residuals have been standardized, we can see that there are no outliers (more than 3 standard errors from zero). The probability plot reveals slight deviations from linearity at the lower and upper ends, but overall the plot is consistent with the hypothesis of normality. For an overall test for heteroscedasticity, we can look at the plot of residuals against the fitted Y-values in Figure 13.17. It shows no clear pattern, so we are disinclined to suspect heteroscedasticity. But we should also examine residual plots against each predictor. The residual plots for the three predictors (Figure 13.18) show no pronounced consistent "fan-out" or "funnel-in" pattern, thereby favoring the hypothesis of homoscedasticity (constant variance).

FIGURE 13.18

MINITAB residual plots for heart death regression

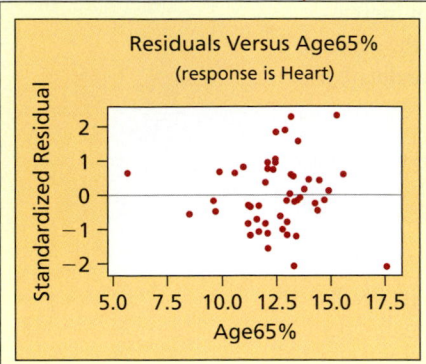
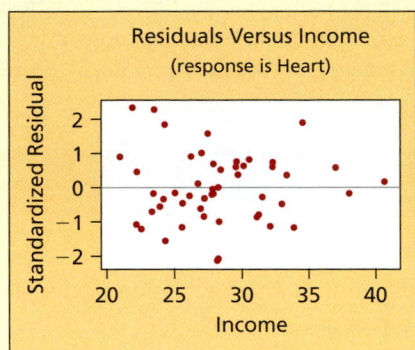
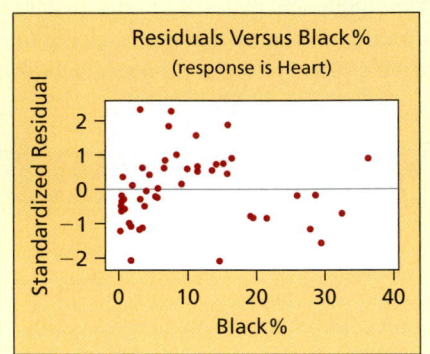

Autocorrelation (Optional)

If you are working with time-series data, you need to be aware of the possibility of *autocorrelation,* a pattern of nonindependent errors that violates the regression assumption that each error is independent of its predecessor. Cross-sectional data may exhibit autocorrelation, but usually it is an artifact of the order of data entry and so may be ignored. When the errors in a regression are autocorrelated, the least squares estimators of the coefficients are still unbiased and consistent. However, their estimated variances are biased in a way that typically leads to confidence intervals that are too narrow and t statistics that are too large. Thus, the model's fit may be overstated. The hypotheses are:

H_0: Errors are nonautocorrelated

H_1: Errors are autocorrelated

Since the true errors are unobservable, we rely on the residuals $e_1, e_2, \ldots, e_n$ for evidence of autocorrelation. The most common test for autocorrelation is the Durbin-Watson test. Using e_t to denote the tth residual (assuming you are working with time-series data) the Durbin-Watson test statistic for autocorrelation is

(13.18)
$$DW = \frac{\sum_{t=2}^{n}(e_t - e_{t-1})^2}{\sum_{t=1}^{n}e_t^2}$$
(Durbin-Watson test statistic)

If you study econometrics or forecasting, you will use a special table to test the DW statistic for significance. For now, simply note that the DW statistic lies between 0 and 4. When the null hypothesis is true (no autocorrelation) the DW statistic will be near 2, while DW < 2 would suggest *positive* autocorrelation and DW > 2 would suggest *negative* autocorrelation. For cross-sectional data, we usually ignore the DW statistic.

Unusual Observations

Several tests for unusual observations are routinely provided by regression software. An observation may be unusual for two reasons: (1) because the fitted model's prediction is poor (*unusual residuals*), or (2) because one or more predictors may be having a large influence on the regression estimates (*unusual leverage*). Unusual observations may be highlighted (MegaStat), displayed separately and marked (MINITAB), or not indicated at all (Excel).

To check for unusual residuals, we can simply inspect the residuals to find instances where the model does not predict well. For example, the model might fit well in Alabama but not in

Alaska. We apply the Empirical Rule (standardized residuals more than 2 SE from zero are *unusual,* while residuals more than 3 SE from zero are outliers). MegaStat highlights unusual residuals in blue, while MINITAB marks them with an "R."

To check for unusual leverage, we look at the *leverage statistic* for each observation. It shows how far the predictors are from their means. As you saw in Chapter 12 (section 12.8) such observations potentially have great influence on the regression estimates, because they are at the "end of the lever." For *n* observations and *k* predictors, any observation whose leverage statistic exceeds $2(k + 1)/n$ is highlighted in green by MegaStat, while MINITAB marks it with an "X."

Mini Case   13.7

Unusual Observations   HeartDeaths

Figure 13.19 shows MegaStat's regression results for a regression model of heart deaths in the 50 U.S. states for the year 2000 (variables are drawn from the *LearningStats* state database). The response variable is *Heart* = heart deaths per 100,000 population, with predictors

FIGURE 13.19

MegaStat output for heart death regression

Regression Analysis: Heart Deaths per 100,000

R^2	0.779		
Adjusted R^2	0.764	n	50
R	0.883	k	3
Std. Error	27.422	Dep. Var.	**Heart**

ANOVA table

Source	SS	df	MS	F	p-value
Regression	121,809.5684	3	40,603.1895	54.00	0.0000
Residual	34,590.3558	46	751.9643		
Total	156,399.9242	49			

Regression output

variables	coefficients	std. error	t (df = 46)	p-value	95% lower	95% upper	VIF
Intercept	−37.0813	39.2007	−0.946	0.3491	−115.9882	41.8256	
Age65%	24.2509	2.0753	11.686	0.0000	20.0736	28.4282	1.018
Income	−1.0800	0.9151	−1.180	0.2440	−2.9220	0.7620	1.012
Black%	2.2682	0.4116	5.511	0.0000	1.4398	3.0967	1.013

confidence interval

Unusual Observations

Observation	Heart	Predicted	Residual	Leverage	Studentized Residual	Studentized Deleted Residual
AK	90.90	76.62	14.28	0.304	0.624	0.620
CT	278.10	274.33	3.77	0.208	0.154	0.153
FL	340.40	392.45	−52.05	0.177	−2.092	−2.176
GA	225.90	230.65	−4.75	0.137	−0.186	−0.184
HI	203.30	259.06	−55.76	0.037	−2.072	−2.152
MS	337.20	316.02	21.18	0.223	0.876	0.874
OK	335.40	274.87	60.53	0.047	2.261	2.372
UT	130.80	145.05	−14.25	0.172	−0.571	−0.567
WV	377.50	317.55	59.95	0.108	2.315	2.436

Age65% = percent of population age 65 and over, *Income* = per capita income in thousands of dollars, and *Black%* = percent of population classified as African American. The fitted regression is

$$Heart = -37.1 + 24.3\, Age65\% - 1.08\, Income + 2.27\, Black\%$$

Age65% has the anticipated positive sign and is highly significant, and similarly for *Black%*. Income has a negative sign but is not significant even at $\alpha = .10$. The regression overall is significant ($F = 54.00$, $p = .0000$). The R^2 shows that the predictors explain 77.9 percent of the variation in *Heart* among the states. The adjusted R^2 is 76.4 percent, indicating that no unhelpful predictors are present. Since this is cross-sectional data, the DW statistic was not requested.

MegaStat's table of residuals, shown in Figure 13.19, highlights five states with high leverage (AK, CT, FL, MS, UT), indicating that these states differ noticeably from the means of one or more *X* predictors (*Age65%, Income,* or *Black%*. The rule of thumb for a leverage statistic states that if the leverage exceeds $2(k + 1)/n = (2)(3 + 1)/50 = 0.16$, then that observation is an influential observation. Only by inspecting the data columns could we identify the nature of their unusual *X*-values. The studentized residuals reveal that FL and HI have *Heart* values at least 2 standard deviations below the predicted values, while OK and WV are higher than predicted. The other residuals are not displayed because they are not unusual.

13.9 OTHER REGRESSION TOPICS

Outliers: Causes and Cures

An outlier may be due to an error in recording the data. If so, the observation should be deleted. But how can you tell? Impossible or truly bizarre data values are apparent reasons to discard an observation. For example, a realtor's database of recent home sales in a million-dollar neighborhood contained this observation:

Price	BR	Bath	Basement	Built	SqFeet	Garage
95,000	4	3	Y	2001	4,335	Y

This must be a typographical error (most likely, the selling price was $950,000). Even if the price were correct, it would be reasonable to discard the observation on grounds that is represents a different population than the other homes (e.g., a "gift" sale by a wealthy parent to a newlywed child).

Missing Predictors

An outlier may also be an observation that has been influenced by an unspecified "lurking" variable that should have been controlled but wasn't. In this case, we should try to identify the lurking variable and formulate a multiple regression model that includes both predictors. For example, a reasonable model such as Y = home price, X_1 = square feet, and X_2 = lot size might give poor predictions unless we add a neighborhood binary predictor (you can probably think of areas where a large house on a large lot might still command a poor price). If there are unspecified "lurking" variables, our fitted regression model will not give accurate predictions.

Ill-Conditioned Data

All variables in the regression should be of the same general order of magnitude (not too small, not too large). If your coefficients come out in exponential notation (e.g., 7.3154 E+06), you probably should adjust the decimal point in one or more variables. For example, the number of automobile thefts per capita in the United States in 1990 was 0.004207. However, this statistic is easier to work with if it is reported as 420.7 thefts *per 100,000 persons*. Worst of all would be to mix very large data with very small data. For example, in 1999 the per capita income in New York was $27,546 and the number of active physicians per capita was 0.00395. To avoid mixing magnitudes, we can merely adjust the decimal point in both variables, e.g., 27.546 *thousand dollars,* and 395 physicians *per 100,000 persons.* You can always shift the decimal point left or right to a convenient magnitude, as long as you treat all the values in the same data column consistently. The decimal adjustments for each data column need not be the same.

Significance in Large Samples

Statistical significance may not imply *practical importance*. In a large sample, we can obtain very large t statistics with low p-values for our predictors when, in fact, their effect on Y is very slight. Pilots like to say that even a barn door will fly if you can make it move fast enough. Similarly, there is an old saying in statistics that you can make anything significant if you get a large enough sample. In medical research, where thousands of patients are enrolled in clinical trials, this is a familiar problem. It can become difficult in such models to figure out which variables are really important.

Model Specification Errors

If you estimate a linear model when actually a nonlinear model is required, or when you omit a relevant predictor, then you have a *misspecified model*. How can you detect misspecification? You can:

- Plot the residuals against estimated Y (should be no discernable pattern).
- Plot the residuals against actual Y (should be no discernable pattern).
- Plot the fitted Y against the actual Y (should be a 45-degree line).

What are the cures for misspecification? Start by looking for a missing relevant predictor, seek a model with a better theoretical basis, or redefine your variables (e.g., assume a multiplicative model of the form $Y = \beta_0 X_1^{\beta 1} X_2^{\beta 2} \cdots X_m^{\beta m}$ for a production function, which becomes linear if you take logarithms). Model specification is a topic that will be covered in considerable depth if you study econometrics. For now, just remember that *residual patterns* are clues that the model may be incorrectly specified.

Missing Data

If many values in a data column are missing, we might want to discard that variable. If a Y data value is missing, we must discard the entire observation. If any X data values are missing, the conservative action is to discard the entire observation. However, since discarding an entire observation would mean losing other good information, statisticians have developed procedures for imputing missing values, such as using the mean of the X data column or by a regression procedure to "fit" the missing X-value from the complete observations. Imputing missing values requires specialized software and expert statistical advice.

Binary Dependent Variable

We have seen that binary predictors pose no special problem. However, when the response variable Y is binary (0, 1) the least squares estimation method no longer is appropriate. Specialized regression methods such as logit and probit are called for. MINITAB and other software packages handle this situation easily, but a different interpretation is required. See *LearningStats* Unit 20 for a case study with binary Y.

Stepwise and Best Subsets Regression

It may have occurred to you that there ought to be a way to automate the task of fitting the "best" regression using k predictors. The *stepwise regression* procedure uses the power of the computer to fit the best model using 1, 2, 3, . . . , k predictors. For example, aerospace engineers had a large data set of 469 observations on *Thrust* (takeoff thrust of a jet turbine) along with seven potential predictors (*TurbTemp, AirFlow, TurbSpeed, OilTemp, OilPres, RunTime, ThermCyc*). In the absence of a theoretical model, a stepwise regression was run, with the results shown in Figure 13.20. Only p-values are shown for each predictor, along with R^2, R^2_{adj}, and standard error. You can easily assess the effect of adding more predictors. In this example, most p-values are tiny due to the large n. While stepwise regression is an efficient way to identify the "best" model for each number of predictors (1, 2, . . . , k), it is appropriate only when there is no theoretical model that specifies which predictors *should* be used. A further degree of automation of the regression task is to perform *best subsets* regression using all possible combinations of predictors. This option is offered by many computer packages, but is not recommended because it yields too much output and too little additional insight.

FIGURE 13.20

MegaStat's stepwise regression of turbine data

🔍 **Turbines**

Regression Analysis—Stepwise Selection displaying the best model of each size

469 observations
Thrust is the dependent variable

p-values for the coefficients

Nvar	TurbTemp	Airflow	TurbSpeed	OilTemp	OilPres	RunTime	ThermCyc	s	Adj R²	R²
1		.0000						12.370	.252	.254
2		.0000			.0004			12.219	.270	.273
3	.0003	.0000					.0005	12.113	.283	.287
4		.0000		.0081	.0000		.0039	12.041	.291	.297
5	.0010	.0000		.0009	.0003		.0006	11.914	.306	.314
6	.0010	.0000	.1440	.0037	.0005		.0010	11.899	.308	.317
7	.0008	.0000	.1624	.0031	.0007	.2049	.0006	11.891	.309	.319

Chapter Summary

Multivariate regression extends bivariate regression to include multiple **predictors** of the **response variable**. Criteria to judge a fitted regression model include **logic, fit, parsimony,** and **stability**. Using too many predictors violates the principle of **Occam's Razor**, which favors a simpler model if it is adequate. If the R^2 differs greatly from R^2_{adj}, the model may contain unhelpful predictors. The ANOVA table and **F test** measure overall significance, while the **t test** is used to test hypotheses about individual predictors. A **confidence interval** for each unknown **parameter** is equivalent to a two-tailed hypothesis test for $\beta = 0$. The **standard error** of the regression is used to create **confidence intervals** or **prediction intervals** for Y. A **binary predictor** (also called a **dummy variable** or an **indicator**) has value 1 if the condition of interest is present, 0 otherwise. For c categories, we only include $c - 1$ binaries or the regression will fail. Including a squared predictor provides a test for **nonlinearity**. Including the product of two predictors is a test for **interaction**. Collinearity (correlation between *two* predictors) is detected in the **correlation matrix**, while **multicollinearity** (when a predictor depends on *several* other predictors) is identified from the **variance inflation factor** (VIF) for each predictor. Regression assumes that the errors are normally distributed, independent random variables with constant variance. **Residual tests** identify possible **non-normality, autocorrelation,** or **heteroscedasticity.**

Key Terms

adjusted coefficient of
    determination R^2, 565
ANOVA table, 564
coefficient of determination
    (R^2), 565
collinearity, 581
correlation matrix, 582
Doane's Rule, 565
dummy variable, 572
Evans's Rule, 565

fit, 563
F test, 564
indicator variable, 572
interaction, 580
Klein's Rule, 582
logic, 563
multicollinearity, 581
multiple regression, 559
Occam's Razor, 562
parsimony, 563

predictors, 560
residual tests, 586
response variable, 560
shift variable, 572
stability, 563
standard error (SE) of the
    regression, 569
variance inflation factor
    (VIF), 583

Commonly Used Formulas

Population regression model for k predictors: $Y = \beta_0 + \beta_1 X_1 + \beta_2 X_2 + \cdots + \beta_k X_k + \varepsilon$

Fitted regression equation for k predictors: $\hat{Y} = b_0 + b_1 X_1 + b_2 X_2 + \cdots + b_k X_k$

Residual for ith observation: $e_i = y_i - \hat{y}_i$ (for $i = 1, 2, \ldots, n$)

ANOVA sums: $SST = SSR + SSE$

SST (total sum of squares): $\sum_{i=1}^{n} (y_i - \bar{y})^2$

SSR (regression sum of squares): $\sum_{i=1}^{n}(\hat{y}_i - \bar{y})^2$

SSE (error sum of squares): $\sum_{i=1}^{n}(y_i - \hat{y}_i)^2$

MSR (regression mean square): $MSR = SSR/k$

MSE (error mean square): $MSE = SSE/(n - k - 1)$

F test statistic for overall significance: $F = MSR/MSE$

Coefficient of determination: $R^2 = 1 - \dfrac{SSE}{SST}$ or $R^2 = \dfrac{SSR}{SST}$

Adjusted R^2: $R^2_{adj} = 1 - (1 - R^2)\left(\dfrac{n-1}{n-k-1}\right)$

Test statistic for coefficient of predictor X_j: $t_j = \dfrac{b_j - 0}{s_j}$ where s_j is the standard error of b_j

Confidence interval for coefficient β_j: $b_j - t_{n-k-1}s_j \le \beta_j \le b_j + t_{n-k-1}s_j$

Estimated standard error of the regression: $SE = \sqrt{\dfrac{\sum_{i=1}^{n}(y_i - \hat{y}_i)^2}{n-k-1}} = \sqrt{\dfrac{SSE}{n-k-1}}$

Approximate confidence interval for $E(Y/X)$: $\hat{y}_i \pm t_{n-k-1}\dfrac{SE}{\sqrt{n}}$

Approximate prediction interval for Y: $\hat{y}_i \pm t_{n-k-1}SE$

Variance inflation factor for predictor j: $VIF_j = \dfrac{1}{1 - R_j^2}$

Evans's Rule (conservative): $n/k \ge 10$ (10 observations per predictor)

Doane's Rule (relaxed): $n/k \ge 5$ (5 observations per predictor)

Chapter Review

1. (a) List two limitations of bivariate regression. (b) Why is estimating a multiple regression model just as easy as bivariate regression?

2. (a) What does ε represent in the regression model? (b) What assumptions do we make about ε? What is the distinction between Greek letters (β) and Roman letters (b) in representing a regression equation?

3. (a) Describe the format of a multiple regression data set. (b) Why is it a good idea to write down our *a priori* reasoning about a proposed regression?

4. (a) Why does a higher R^2 not always indicate a good model? (b) State the principle of Occam's Razor. (c) List four criteria for assessing a regression model.

5. (a) What is the role of the F test in multiple regression? (b) How is the F statistic calculated from the ANOVA table? (c) Why are tables rarely needed for the F test?

6. (a) Why is testing $H_0: \beta = 0$ a very common test for a predictor? (b) How many degrees of freedom do we use in a t test for an individual predictor's significance?

7. (a) Explain why a confidence interval for a predictor coefficient is equivalent to a two-tailed test of significance. (b) Why are t tables rarely needed in performing significance tests?

8. (a) What does a coefficient of determination (R^2) measure? (b) When R^2 and R^2_{adj} differ considerably, what does it indicate?

9. State some guidelines to prevent inclusion of too many predictors in a regression.

10. (a) State the formula for the standard error of the regression. (b) Why is it sometimes preferred to R^2 as a measure of "fit"? (c) What is the formula for a quick prediction interval for individual Y-values? (d) When you need an exact prediction, what must you do?

11. (a) What is a binary predictor? (b) Why is a binary predictor sometimes called a "shift variable"? (c) How do we test a binary predictor for significance?

12. If we have c categories for an attribute, why do we only use $c - 1$ binaries to represent them in a fitted regression?

13. (a) Explain why it might be useful to include a quadratic term in a regression. (b) Explain why it might be useful to include an interaction term between two predictors in a regression. (c) Name a drawback to including quadratic or interaction terms in a regression.

14. (a) What is multicollinearity? (b) What are its potential consequences? (c) Why is it a matter of degree? (d) Why might it be ignored?

15. (a) How does multicollinearity differ from collinearity? (b) Explain how we can use the correlation matrix to test for collinearity. (c) State a quick rule to test for significant collinearity in a correlation matrix. (d) What is Klein's Rule?

16. (a) State the formula for a variance inflation factor (VIF) for a predictor. (b) Why does the VIF provide a more general test for multicollinearity than a correlation matrix or a matrix plot? (c) State a rule of thumb for detecting strong variance inflation.

17. If multicollinearity is severe, what might its symptoms be?

18. (a) How can we detect an unusual residual? An outlier? (b) How can we identify an influential observation?

19. (a) Name two ways to detect non-normality of the residuals. (b) What are the potential consequences of this violation? (c) What remedies might be appropriate?

20. (a) Name two ways to detect heteroscedastic residuals. (b) What are the potential consequences of this violation? (c) What remedies might be appropriate?

21. (a) Name two ways to detect autocorrelated residuals. (b) What are the potential consequences of this violation? (c) What remedies might be appropriate?

22. (a) What is a lurking variable? How might it be inferred? (b) What are ill-conditioned data?

CHAPTER EXERCISES

Instructions for Data Sets: Choose one of the data sets $A - J$ below or as assigned by your instructor. Only the first 10 observations are shown for each data set (files are on the CD). In each data set, the dependent variable (*response*) is the first variable. Choose the independent variables (*predictors*) as you judge appropriate. Use a spreadsheet or a statistical package (e.g., MegaStat or MINITAB) to perform the necessary regression calculations and to obtain the required graphs. Write a concise report answering questions 13.9 through 13.25 (or a subset of these questions assigned by your instructor). Label sections of your report to correspond to the questions. Insert tables and graphs in your report as appropriate. You may work with a partner if your instructor allows it.

13.9 Is this cross-sectional data or time-series data? What is the unit of observation (e.g., firm, individual, year)?

13.10 Are the X and Y data well-conditioned? If not, make any transformations that may be necessary and explain.

13.11 State your *a priori* hypotheses about the sign (+ or −) of each predictor and your reasoning about cause and effect. Would the intercept have meaning in this problem? Explain.

13.12 Does your sample size fulfill Evans's Rule ($n/k \geq 10$) or at least Doane's Rule ($n/k \geq 5$)?

13.13 Perform the regression and write the estimated regression equation (round off to 3 or 4 significant digits for clarity). Do the coefficient signs agree with your *a priori* expectations?

13.14 Does the 95 percent confidence interval for each predictor coefficient include zero? What conclusion can you draw? *Note:* Skip this question if you are using MINITAB, since predictor confidence intervals are not shown.

13.15 Do a two-tailed t test for zero slope for each predictor coefficient at $\alpha = .05$. State the degrees of freedom and look up the critical value in Appendix D (or from Excel).

13.16 (a) Which p-values indicate predictor significance at $\alpha = .05$? (b) Do the p-values support the conclusions you reached from the t tests? (c) Do you prefer the t test or the p-value approach? Why?

13.17 Based on the R^2 and ANOVA table for your model, how would you describe the fit?

13.18 Use the standard error to construct an *approximate* prediction interval for Y. Based on the width of this prediction interval, would you say the predictions are good enough to have practical value?

13.19 (a) Generate a correlation matrix for your predictors. Round the results to three decimal places. (b) Based on the correlation matrix, is collinearity a problem? What rules of thumb (if any) are you using?

13.20 (a) If you did not already do so, re-run the regression requesting variance inflation factors (VIFs) for your predictors. (b) Do the VIFs suggest that multicollinearity is a problem? Explain.

13.21 (a) If you did not already do so, request a table of standardized residuals. (b) Are any residuals *outliers* (three standard errors) or *unusual* (two standard errors)?

13.22 If you did not already do so, request leverage statistics. Are any observations influential? Explain.

13.23 If you did not already do so, request a histogram of standardized residuals and/or a normal probability plot. Do the residuals suggest non-normal errors? Explain.

13.24 If you did not already do so, request a plot of residuals versus the fitted Y. Is heteroscedasticity a concern?

13.25 If you are using time-series data, perform one or more tests for autocorrelation (visual inspection of residuals plotted against observation order, runs test, Durbin-Watson test). Is autocorrelation a concern?

DATA SET A   **Mileage and Other Characteristics of Randomly Selected Vehicles**
($n = 43$, $k = 4$)   **Mileage**

Obs	Vehicle	City	Length	Width	Weight	Japan
1	Acura CL	20	192	69	3,450	1
2	Acura TSX	23	183	59	3,320	1
3	BMW 3-Series	19	176	69	3,390	0
4	Buick Century	20	195	73	3,350	0
5	Buick Rendezvous	18	187	74	4,230	0
6	Cadillac Seville	18	201	75	4,050	0
7	Chevrolet Corvette	19	180	74	3,255	0
8	Chevrolet Silverado 1500	14	228	79	4,935	0
9	Chevrolet TrailBlazer	15	192	75	4,660	0
10	Chrysler Pacifica	17	199	79	4,660	0
⋮	⋮	⋮	⋮	⋮	⋮	⋮

City = EPA miles per gallon in city driving, *Length* = vehicle length (inches), *Width* = vehicle width (inches), *Weight* = weight (pounds), *Japan* = 1 if carmaker is Japanese, 0 otherwise.

Source: *Consumer Reports New Car Buying Guide 2003–2004* (Consumers Union, 2003). Sampling methodology was to select the vehicle on every fifth page starting at page 40. Data are intended for purposes of statistical education and should not be viewed as a guide to vehicle performance.

DATA SET B   **Loudspeaker Accuracy, Price, and Type ($n = 27$, $k = 2$)**
Speakers

Obs	Brand and Model	Accuracy	Price	Shelf
1	BIC America Venturi DV62si	91	200	1
2	Bose 141	86	100	1
3	Bose 201 Series V	89	220	1
4	Bose 301 Series V	86	330	1
5	Bose 601 Series IV	84	600	0
6	Bose 701 Series II	82	700	0
7	Bose Acoustimass 3 Series IV	94	300	1
8	Bose Acoustimass 5 Series III	94	600	1
9	Boston Acoustics CR75	90	300	1
10	Boston Acoustics CR85	86	400	1
⋮	⋮	⋮	⋮	⋮

Accuracy = accuracy as measured by test panel, *Price* = price of speaker set in dollars, *Shelf* = 1 if shelf speaker, 0 if floor speaker.

Source: *Consumer Reports* 68, no. 11 (November 2003), p. 31. Data are intended for purposes of statistical education and should not be viewed as a guide to speaker performance.

DATA SET C   Assessed Value of Small Medical Office Buildings ($n = 32$, $k = 5$)
Assessed

Obs	Assessed	Floor	Offices	Entrances	Age	Freeway
1	1,796	4,790	4	2	8	0
2	1,544	4,720	3	2	12	0
3	2,094	5,940	4	2	2	0
4	1,968	5,720	4	2	34	1
5	1,567	3,660	3	2	38	1
6	1,878	5,000	4	2	31	1
7	949	2,990	2	1	19	0
8	910	2,610	2	1	48	0
9	1,774	5,650	4	2	42	0
10	1,187	3,570	2	1	4	1
⋮	⋮	⋮	⋮	⋮	⋮	⋮

Assessed = assessed value (thousands of dollars), *Floor* = square feet of floor space, *Offices* = number of offices in the building, *Entrances* = number of customer entrances (excluding service doors), *Age* = age of the building (years), *Freeway* = 1 if within one mile of freeway, 0 otherwise.

DATA SET D   Changes in Consumer Price Index and Money Supply Components ($n = 41$, $k = 4$)   Money

Year	ChgCPI	CapUtil	ChgM1	ChgM2	ChgM3
1960	0.7	80.1	0.5	4.9	5.2
1961	1.3	77.3	3.2	7.4	8.1
1962	1.6	81.4	1.8	8.1	8.9
1963	1	83.5	3.7	8.4	9.3
1964	1.9	85.6	4.6	8.0	9.0
1965	3.5	89.5	4.7	8.1	9.0
1966	3	91.1	2.5	4.6	4.8
1967	4.7	87.2	6.6	9.3	10.4
1968	6.2	87.1	7.7	8.0	8.8
1969	5.6	86.6	3.3	3.7	1.4
1978	13.3	85.2	8.0	7.5	11.8
1979	12.5	85.3	6.9	7.9	10.0
⋮	⋮	⋮	⋮	⋮	⋮

ChCPI = percent change in the Consumer Price Index (CPI) over previous year, *CapUtil* = percent utilization of manufacturing capacity in current year, *ChgM1* = percent change in currency and demand deposits (M1) over previous year, *ChgM2* = percent change in small time deposits and other near-money (M2) over previous year, *ChgM3* = percent change in large time deposits, Eurodollars, and other institutional balances (M3) over previous year.

Source: *Economic Report of the President, 2003*. These variables are selected from *LearningStats* (Time-Series Data).

DATA SET E College Graduation Rate and Selected Characteristics of U.S. States in 1990 (*n* = 50, *k* = 8)
ColGrads

State	ColGrad%	Dropout	EdSpend	Urban	Age	Femlab	Neast	Seast	West
AL	15.6	35.3	3627	60.4	33.0	51.8	0	1	0
AK	23.0	31.6	8330	67.5	29.4	64.9	0	0	1
AZ	20.3	27.5	4309	87.5	32.2	55.6	0	0	1
AR	13.4	23.3	3700	53.5	33.8	53.6	0	1	0
CA	23.4	32.2	4491	92.6	31.5	56.0	0	0	1
CO	27.0	25.9	5064	82.4	32.5	63.3	0	0	1
CT	27.2	25.1	7602	79.1	34.4	63.9	1	0	0
DE	21.4	31.5	5865	73.0	32.9	60.7	1	0	0
FL	18.3	38.9	5276	84.8	36.4	54.6	0	1	0
GA	19.3	37.3	4466	63.2	31.6	57.4	0	1	0
⋮	⋮	⋮	⋮	⋮	⋮	⋮	⋮	⋮	⋮

ColGrad% = percent of state population with a college degree, *Dropout* = percent of high school students who do not graduate, *EdSpend* = per capita spending on K–12 education, *Urban* = percent of state population living in urban areas, *Age* = median age of state's population, *FemLab* = percent of adult females who are in the labor force, *Neast* = 1 if state is in the Northeast, 0 otherwise, *Seast* = 1 if state is in the Southeast, 0 otherwise, *West* = 1 if state is in the West, 0 otherwise.

Source: *Statistical Abstract of the United States.* These variables are selected from *LearningStats* (States).

DATA SET F Characteristics of Selected Piston Aircraft (*n* = 55, *k* = 4)
CruiseSpeed

Obs	Manufacturer/Model	Cruise	Year	TotalHP	NumBlades	Turbo
1	Cessna Turbo Stationair TU206	148	1981	310	3	1
2	Cessna 310 R	194	1975	570	3	0
3	Piper 125 Tri Pacer	107	1951	125	2	0
4	Maule Comet	115	1996	180	2	0
5	Cessna P210	186	1982	285	3	0
6	Piper Dakota	147	1979	235	2	0
7	Cessna 1825 Skylane	140	1997	230	3	0
8	Cessna 421B	234	1974	750	3	0
9	Cessna T210K	190	1970	285	3	1
10	Piper Super Cab	100	1975	150	2	0
⋮	⋮	⋮	⋮	⋮	⋮	⋮

Cruise = best cruise speed (knots indicated air speed) at 65–75 percent power, *Year* = year of manufacture, *TotalHP* = total horsepower (both engines if twin), *NumBlades* = number of propeller blades, *Turbo* = 1 if turbocharged, 0 otherwise.

Source: *Flying Magazine* (various issues). Data are for educational purposes only and not as a guide to performance. These variables are selected from *LearningStats* (Technology Data).

DATA SET G   Characteristics of Randomly Chosen Hydrocarbons ($n = 35$, $k = 7$)   Retention

Obs	Name	Ret	MW	BP	RI	H1	H2	H3	H4	H5
1	2,4,4-trimethyl-2-pentene	153.57	112.215	105.06	1.4135	0	1	0	0	0
2	1,5-cyclooctadiene	237.56	108.183	150.27	1.4905	0	0	0	1	0
3	methylcyclohexane	153.57	98.188	101.08	1.4206	0	0	1	0	0
4	m-diethylbenzene	281.50	134.221	181.29	1.4931	0	0	0	0	1
5	2,2,4-trimethylpentane	139.24	114.231	99.39	1.3890	1	0	0	0	0
6	undecane	288.50	156.310	196.00	1.4170	1	0	0	0	0
7	toluene	174.00	92.140	110.60	1.4970	0	0	0	0	1
8	1,7-octadiene	172.20	110.200	117.00	1.4220	0	1	0	0	0
9	beta-pinene	254.00	136.240	165.00	1.4780	0	0	0	1	0
10	methylcyclohexane	152.40	98.190	101.00	1.4220	0	0	1	0	0
⋮	⋮	⋮	⋮	⋮	⋮	⋮	⋮	⋮	⋮	⋮

Ret = Chromatographic retention time (seconds), *MW* = molecular weight (gm/mole), *BP* = boiling point in °C, *RI* = refractive index (dimensionless), *Class* = hydrocarbon class (*H1* = acyclic saturated, *H2* = acyclic unsaturated, *H3* = cyclic saturated, *H4* = cyclic unsaturated, *H5* = aromatic).

Source: Data are courtesy of John Seeley of Oakland University. This is a 50 percent sample of the full data set found in *LearningStats* (Technology Data).

DATA SET H   Michigan High School Top 50 Football Players in 2003 ($n = 50$, $k = 5$)   Football50

Obs	Position	Weight	Height	Line	LB	DB	RB
1	OT	317	77	1	0	0	0
2	LB/FB	235	74	0	1	0	0
3	LB	220	73	0	1	0	0
4	RB	190	70	0	0	0	1
5	DT	285	76	1	0	0	0
6	OL	315	75	1	0	0	0
7	DE	245	76	1	0	0	0
8	DL	255	77	1	0	0	0
9	WR	180	69	0	0	0	1
10	LB	212	75	0	1	0	0
⋮	⋮	⋮	⋮	⋮	⋮	⋮	⋮

Weight = weight in pounds, *Height* = height in inches, *Line* = lineman (0, 1) , *LB* = linebacker (0, 1), *DB* = defensive back (0, 1), *RB* = running back (0,1). Source: *Detroit Free Press,* February 5, 2004, p. 9-D.

DATA SET I Body Fat and Personal Measurements for Males ($n = 50$, $k = 8$) 🐞 **BodyFat2**

Obs	Fat%	Age	Weight	Height	Neck	Chest	Abdomen	Hip	Thigh
1	12.6	23	154.25	67.75	36.2	93.1	85.2	94.5	59.0
2	6.9	22	173.25	72.25	38.5	93.6	83.0	98.7	58.7
3	24.6	22	154.00	66.25	34.0	95.8	87.9	99.2	59.6
4	10.9	26	184.75	72.25	37.4	101.8	86.4	101.2	60.1
5	27.8	24	184.25	71.25	34.4	97.3	100.0	101.9	63.2
6	20.6	24	210.25	74.75	39.0	104.5	94.4	107.8	66.0
7	19.0	26	181.00	69.75	36.4	105.1	90.7	100.3	58.4
8	12.8	25	176.00	72.50	37.8	99.6	88.5	97.1	60.0
9	5.1	25	191.00	74.00	38.1	100.9	82.5	99.9	62.9
10	12.0	23	198.25	73.50	42.1	99.6	88.6	104.1	63.1
⋮	⋮	⋮	⋮	⋮	⋮	⋮	⋮	⋮	⋮

Fat% = percent body fat, *Age* = age (yrs.), *Weight* = weight (lbs.), *Height* = height (in.), *Neck* = neck circumference (cm), *Chest* = chest circumference (cm), *Abdomen* = abdomen circumference (cm), *Hip* = hip circumference (cm), *Thigh* = thigh circumference (cm).

Data are a subsample of 252 males analyzed in Roger W. Johnson (1996), "Fitting Percentage of Body Fat to Simple Body Measurements," *Journal of Statistics Education* 4, no. 1.

DATA SET J Used Vehicle Prices ($n = 637$ observations, $k = 4$ predictors)
🐞 **Vehicles**

Obs	Model	Price	Age	Car	Truck	SUV
1	Astro GulfStream Conversion	12,988	3	0	0	0
2	Astro LS 4.3L V6	5,950	9	0	0	0
3	Astro LS V6	19,995	4	0	0	0
4	Astro V6 7 Passenger	5,763	6	0	0	0
5	Avalanche 4×4	20,988	3	0	1	0
6	Avalanche 5.3L V8 4×4	22,700	3	0	1	0
7	Avalanche V8 4 DR	23,671	2	0	1	0
8	Avalanche V8 4×4	24,995	2	0	1	0
9	Avalanche V8 4×4 & 2×2	19,990	3	0	1	0
10	Avalanche Z71	20,995	3	0	1	0
⋮	⋮	⋮	⋮	⋮	⋮	⋮

Price = asking price ($), *Age* = vehicle age (yrs), *Car* = 1 if passenger car, 0 otherwise, *Truck* = 1 if truck, 0 otherwise, *SUV* = 1 if sport utility vehicle, 0 otherwise. (*Van* is the omitted fourth binary).

Source: *Detroit AutoFocus* 4, Issue 38 (Sept. 17–23, 2004). Data are for educational purposes only and should not be used as a guide to depreciation.

GENERAL EXERCISES

13.26 In a model of Ford's quarterly revenue *TotalRevenue* $= \beta_0 + \beta_1$ *CarSales* $+ \beta_2$ *TruckSales* $+ \beta_3$ *SUVSales* $+ \varepsilon$, the three predictors are measured in number of units sold (not dollars). (a) Interpret each slope. (b) Would the intercept be meaningful? (c) What factors might be reflected in the error term? Explain.

13.27 In a study of paint peel problems, a regression was suggested to predict defects per million (the response variable). The intended predictors were supplier (four suppliers, coded as binaries) and substrate (four materials, coded as binaries). There were 11 observations. Explain why regression is impractical in this case, and suggest a remedy.

13.28 A hospital emergency room analyzed $n = 17,664$ hourly observations on its average occupancy rates using six binary predictors representing days of the week and two binary predictors representing the 8-hour work shift (12 A.M.–8 A.M., 8 A.M.–4 P.M., 4 P.M.–12 A.M.) when the ER census was taken. The fitted regression equation was $AvgOccupancy = 11.2 + 1.19\ Mon - 0.187\ Tue - 0.785\ Wed - 0.580$ $Thu - 0.451\ Fri - 0.267\ Sat - 4.58\ Shift1 - 1.65\ Shift2$ ($SE = 6.18$, $R^2 = .094$, $R^2_{adj} = .093$). (a) Why did the analyst use only six binaries for days when there are 7 days in a week? (b) Why did the analyst use only two work shift binaries when there are three work shifts? (c) Which is the busiest day? (d) Which is the busiest shift? (e) Interpret the intercept. (f) Assess the regression's fit.

13.29 Using test data on 20 types of laundry detergent, an analyst fitted a regression to predict *CostPerLoad* (average cost per load in cents per load) using binary predictors *TopLoad* (1 if washer is a top-loading model, 0 otherwise) and *Powder* (if detergent was in powder form, 0 otherwise). Interpret the results. (Data are from *Consumer Reports* 68, no. 8 [November 2003], p. 42.) 🐞 **Laundry**

R^2	0.117		
Adjusted R^2	0.006	n	19
R	0.341	k	2
Std. Error	5.915	Dep. Var.	**Cost Per Load**

ANOVA table

Source	SS	df	MS	F	p-value
Regression	73.8699	2	36.9350	1.06	.3710
Residual	559.8143	16	34.9884		
Total	633.6842	18			

Regression output — confidence interval

variables	coefficients	std. error	t(df = 16)	p-value	95% lower	95% upper
Intercept	26.0000	4.1826	6.216	1.23E-05	17.1333	34.8667
Top-Load	−6.3000	4.5818	−1.375	.1881	−16.0130	3.4130
Powder	−0.2714	2.9150	−0.093	.9270	−6.4509	5.9081

13.30 A researcher used stepwise regression to create regression models to predict *BirthRate* (births per 1,000) using five predictors: *LifeExp* (life expectancy in years), *InfMort* (infant mortality rate), *Density* (population density per square kilometer), *GDPCap* (Gross Domestic Product per capita), and *Literate* (literacy percent). Interpret these results. 🐞 **BirthRates2**

Regression Analysis—Stepwise Selection (best model of each size)

153 observations
BirthRate is the dependent variable

Nvar	LifeExp	InfMort	Density	GDPCap	Literate	s	Adj R^2	R^2
1		.0000				6.318	.722	.724
2		.0000			.0000	5.334	.802	.805
3		.0000		.0242	.0000	5.261	.807	.811
4	.5764	.0000		.0311	.0000	5.273	.806	.812
5	.5937	.0000	.6289	.0440	.0000	5.287	.805	.812

p-values for the coefficients

13.31 A sports enthusiast created an equation to predict *Victories* (the team's number of victories in the National Basketball Association regular season play) using predictors *FGP* (team field goal percentage), *FTP* (team free throw percentage), *Points =* (team average points per game), *Fouls* (team average number of fouls per game), *TrnOvr* (team average number of turnovers per game), and *Rbnds* (team average number of rebounds per game). The fitted regression was $Victories = -281 + 523\ FGP + 3.12\ FTP + 0.781\ Points - 2.90\ Fouls + 1.60\ TrnOvr + 0.649\ Rbnds$ ($R^2 = .802$, $F = 10.80$, $SE = 6.87$). The strongest predictors were *FGP* ($t = 4.35$) and *Fouls* ($t = -2.146$). The other predictors were only marginally significant and *FTP* and *Rbnds* were not significant. The matrix of correlations is shown below. At the time of this analysis, there were 23 NBA teams. (a) Do the regression coefficients make sense? (b) Is the intercept meaningful? Explain. (c) Is the sample size a problem (using Evans's Rule or Doane's Rule)? (c) Why might collinearity account for the lack of significance of some predictors? (Data are from a research project by MBA student Michael S. Malloy.)

	FGP	FTP	Points	Fouls	TrnOvr	Rbnds
FGP	1.000					
FTP	−0.039	1.000				
Points	0.475	0.242	1.000			
Fouls	−0.014	0.211	0.054	1.000		
TrnOvr	0.276	0.028	0.033	0.340	1.000	
Rbnds	0.436	0.137	0.767	−0.032	0.202	1.000

13.32 An expert witness in a case of alleged racial discrimination in a state university school of nursing introduced a regression of the determinants of *Salary* of each professor for each year during an 8-year period ($n = 423$) with the following results, with dependent variable *Year* (year in which the salary was observed) and predictors *YearHire* (year when the individual was hired), *Race* (1 if individual is black, 0 otherwise), and *Rank* (1 if individual is an assistant professor, 0 otherwise). Interpret these results.

Variable	Coefficient	t	p
Intercept	−3,816,521	−29.4	.000
Year	1,948	29.8	.000
YearHire	−826	−5.5	.000
Race	−2,093	−4.3	.000
Rank	−6,438	−22.3	.000

$R^2 = 0.811$ $R_{adj}^2 = 0.809$ $s = 3,318$

13.33 Analysis of a Detroit Marathon ($n = 1,015$ men, $n = 150$ women) produced the regression results shown below, with dependent variable *Time* (the marathon time in minutes) and predictors *Age* (runner's age), *Weight* (runner's weight in pounds), *Height* (runner's height in inches), and *Exp* (1 if runner had prior marathon experience, 0 otherwise). (a) Interpret the coefficient of *Exp*. (b) Does the intercept have any meaning? (c) Why do you suppose squared predictors were included? (d) Plug in your own *Age, Height, Weight,* and *Exp* to predict your own running time. Do you believe it? (Data courtesy of Detroit Striders.)

Variable	Men ($n = 1,015$)		Women ($n = 150$)	
	Coefficient	t	Coefficient	t
Intercept	−366		−2,820	
Age	−4.827	−6.1	−3.593	−2.5
Age^2	0.07671	7.1	0.05240	2.6
Weight	−1.598	−1.9	3.000	0.7
Weight^2	0.008961	3.4	−0.004041	−2.0
Height	24.65	1.5	96.13	1.6
Height^2	−0.2074	−1.7	−0.8040	−1.8
Exp	−41.74	−17.0	−28.65	−4.3

$R^2 = 0.423$ $R^2 = 0.334$

Related Readings

Evans, Martin G. "The Problem of Analyzing Multiplicative Composites." *American Psychologist,* January 1991, p. 675 (Evans's Rule).

Kennedy, Peter. *A Guide to Econometrics.* 5th ed. MIT Press, 2003, p. 132 (Klein's Rule).

Kutner, Michael H.; Christopher J. Nachtsheim; and John Neter. *Applied Linear Regression Models.* 4th ed. McGraw-Hill/Irwin, 2004.

Ryan, Thomas P. *Modern Regression Methods.* Wiley, 1996.

LearningStats Unit 13   Multiple Regression

LS

LearningStats Unit 13 illustrates uses of multiple regression, assessing fit (e.g., R^2 and R^2_{adj}), tests for significance (e.g., ANOVA, t tests), and model adequacy (e.g., residual tests). Binary predictors and tests for nonlinearity are illustrated. Special attention is given to the issue of multicollinearity and its effects on tests for significance of individual predictors. Your instructor may assign specific modules, or you may pursue those that sound interesting.

Topic	*LearningStats Modules*
Multiple regression overview	Multiple Regression Overview
	Violations of Assumptions
Using Excel and MINITAB	Regression Using Excel
	Regression Using MINITAB
Simulation	Effects of Collinearity
	Effects of Multicollinearity
	Salary Data Modeling
Case studies	Binary Predictors
	Variance Inflation
	Stepwise Regression
	Squared Predictors
Student presentations	Murder Rates
	Birth Weight
	Cancer Deaths
	Birth Rates
	Car Theft
Student reports	Income Per Capita
	Student Worksheets
Formulas	Useful Regression Formulas
Tables	Appendix D—Student's t
	Appendix F—Critical Values of F

Key: = PowerPoint   = Word   = Excel

Visual Statistics

Visual Statistics Modules on Multiple Regression

Module	Module Name
17	**VS** Visualizing Multiple Regression Analysis
18	**VS** Visualizing Regression Models
19	**VS** Visualizing Binary Predictors in Regression

Visual Statistics Modules 17, 18, and 19 (included on your CD) are designed to help you:

- Recognize and use the terminology of multiple regression.
- Be able to perform significance tests and interpret confidence intervals for model parameters.
- Understand the importance of data conditioning and the potential effects of ill-conditioned data.
- Detect multicollinearity and recognize its common symptoms.
- Learn when a model may be overfitted and why that can be a problem.
- Use visual displays to check residuals for non-normality, autocorrelation, and heteroscedasticity.
- Know the commonly used variable transformations and their purposes.
- Understand how to use polynomial models and interaction tests.
- Be able to interpret regressions with intercept binaries or slope binaries.

The worktext (included on the CD in .PDF format) contains lists of concepts covered, objectives of the modules, overviews of concepts, illustrations of concepts, orientations to module features, learning exercises (basic, intermediate, advanced), learning projects (individual, team), self-evaluation quizzes, glossaries of terms, and solutions to self-evaluation quizzes.

Time-Series Analysis

Chapter Learning Objectives

When you finish this chapter you should be able to

- Define time-series data and its components.

- Interpret a linear, exponential, or quadratic trend model.

- Fit any common trend model and use it to make forecasts.

- Know the definitions of common fit measures (R^2, *MAPE, MAD, MSD*).

- Interpret a moving average and use Excel to create it.

- Use exponential smoothing to forecast trendless data.

- Use software to deseasonalize a time-series.

- Use regression with seasonal binaries to make forecasts.

Time-Series Data

Businesses must track their performance. By looking at their output over time businesses can tell where they've been, whether they are performing poorly or satisfactorily, and how much improvement is needed, both in the short term and the long term. A *time-series variable* (denoted Y) consists of data observed over n periods of time. Consider a clothing retailer that specializes in blue jeans. Examples of time-series data this company might be interested in tracking would be the number of jeans sold and the company's market share. Or, from the manufacturing perspective, the company might track cost of raw materials over time.

Businesses also use time-series data to monitor whether a particular process is stable or unstable. And they use time-series data to help predict the future, a process we call *forecasting*. In addition to business time-series data we see economic time-series data in *The Wall Street Journal* or *BusinessWeek,* and also in *USA Today* or *Time,* or even when we browse the Web. Although business and economic time-series data are most common, we can see time-series data for population, health, crime, sports, and social problems. Usually, time-series data are presented in a graph, like Figures 14.1 and 14.2.

It is customary to plot time-series data either as a line graph or a bar graph, with time on the horizontal axis to reveal how a variable of interest changes over time. In a line graph, the X-Y data points are connected with line segments to make it easier to see fluctuations. While anyone can understand time-series graphs in a general way, this chapter explains how to interpret time-series data *statistically* and to make defensible forecasts. Our analysis begins with sample observations $y_1, y_2, \ldots, y_n$ covering n time periods. The following notation is used:

- y_t is the value of the time-series in period t.
- t is an index denoting the time period ($t = 1, 2, \ldots, n$).
- n is the number of time periods.
- $y_1, y_2, \ldots, y_n$ is the data set for analysis.

Chapter 20

FIGURE 14.1

U.S. employment (monthly)

Source: www.clevelandfed.org.

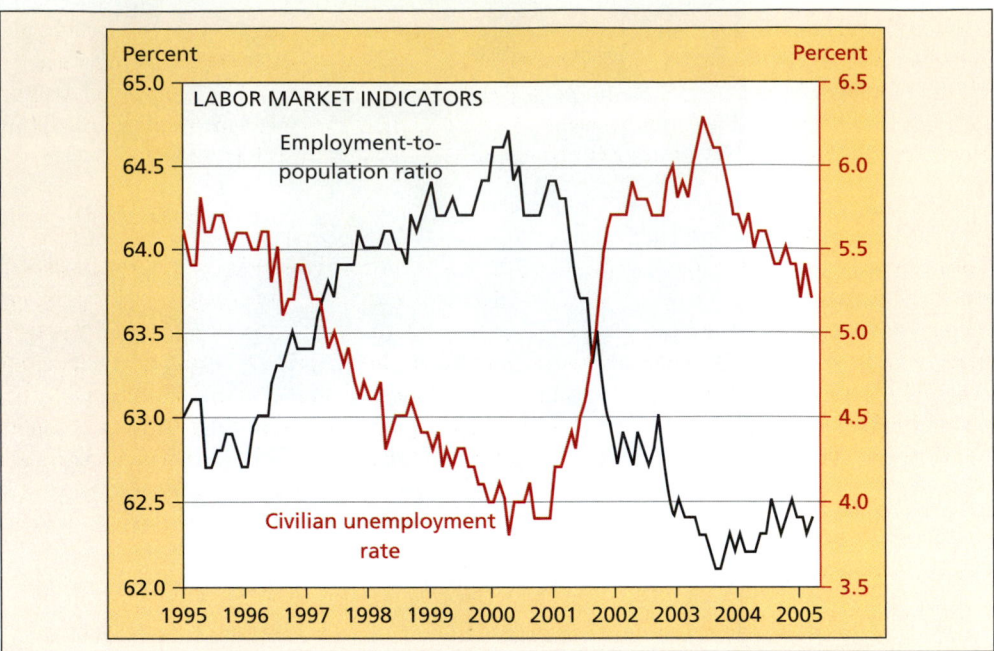

FIGURE 14.2

Exchange rates (daily)

Source: www.clevelandfed.org.

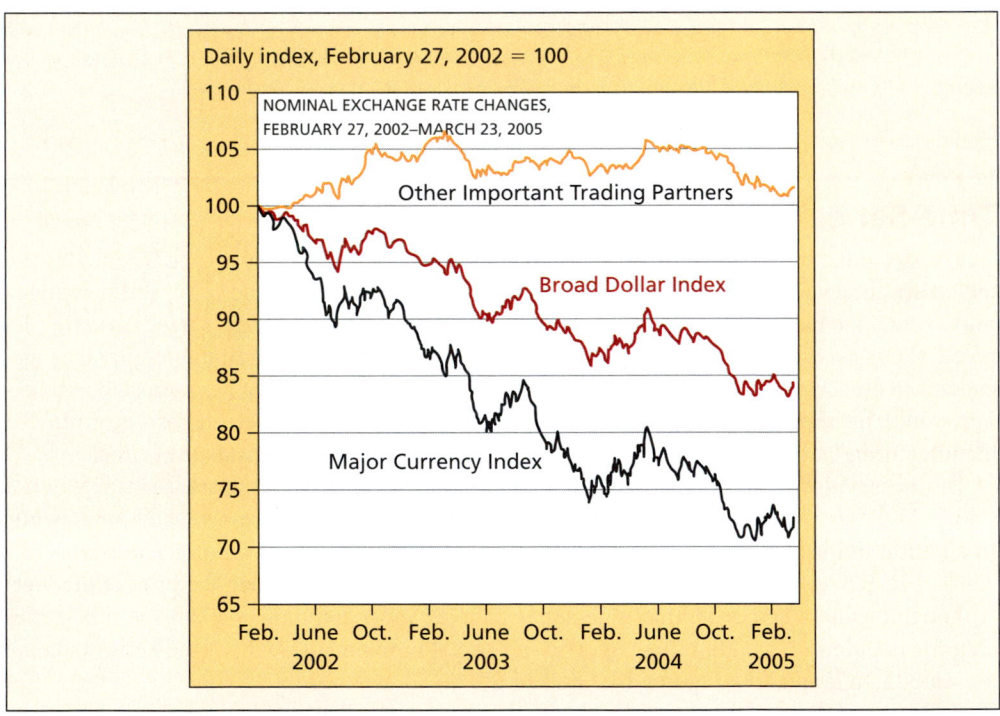

To distinguish time-series data from cross-sectional data, we use y_t instead of x_i for an individual observation, and a subscript t instead of i.

Stocks and Flows

Time-series data may be measured *at a point in time* (a **stock**) or *over an interval of time* (a **flow**). For example, in accounting, balance sheet data are stocks (e.g., measured at the end of the fiscal year) while income statement data are flows (e.g., measured over an entire fiscal year). The concept is quite general. For example, the Gross Domestic Product (GDP) is a flow of goods and services measured *over an interval of time,* while the prime rate of interest is measured *at a point in time*. Your GPA is measured *at a point in time* while your weekly pay is measured *over an interval of time*. The distinction is sometimes vague in reported data, but a little thought will usually clarify matters. For example, Canada's 2002 unemployment rate (7.6 percent) would be measured at a point in time (e.g., at year's end) while Canada's 2001 electricity production (566.3 billion kWh) would be measured over the entire year.

Periodicity

The *periodicity* is the time interval over which data are collected (decade, year, quarter, month, week, day, hour). For example, the U.S. population is measured each *decade,* your personal income tax is calculated *annually,* GDP is reported *quarterly,* the unemployment rate is estimated *monthly,* and *The Wall Street Journal* reports the closing price of General Motors stock *daily* (although stock prices are also monitored continuously on the Web). Firms typically report profits by quarter, but pension liabilities only at year's end. Any periodicity is possible, but the principles of time-series modeling can be understood with these three common data types:

- Annual data (1 observation per year)
- Quarterly data (4 observations per year)
- Monthly data (12 observations per year)

Additive versus Multiplicative Models

Time-series *decomposition* seeks to separate a time-series Y into four components: trend (T), cycle (C), seasonal (S), and irregular (I). These components are assumed to follow either an additive or a multiplicative model, as shown in Table 14.1.

Model	Components	Used For
Additive	$Y = T + C + S + I$	Data of similar magnitude (short-run or trend-free data) with constant *absolute* growth or decline.
Multiplicative	$Y = T \times C \times S \times I$	Data of increasing or decreasing magnitude (long-run or trended data) with constant *percent* growth or decline.

TABLE 14.1
Components of a Time-Series

The additive form is attractive for its simplicity, but the multiplicative model is often more useful for forecasting financial data, particularly when the data vary over a range of magnitudes. Especially in the short run, it may not matter greatly which form is assumed. In fact, the model forms are fundamentally equivalent since the multiplicative model becomes additive if logarithms are taken (as long as the data are nonnegative):

$$\log(Y) = \log(T \times C \times S \times I) = \log(T) + \log(C) + \log(S) + \log(I)$$

A Graphical View

Figure 14.3 illustrates these four components in a hypothetical time series. The four components may be thought of as layering atop one another to produce the actual time series. In this example, the irregular component (I) is large enough to obscure the cycle (C) and seasonal (S) components, but not the trend (T). However, we can usually extract the original components from the time series by using statistical methods.

Trend

Trend (T) is a general movement over all years ($t = 1, 2, \ldots, n$). Change over a few years is not a trend. Some trends are steady and predictable. For example, the data may be steadily growing (e.g., total U.S. population), neither growing nor declining (e.g., your current car's mpg), or steadily declining (infant mortality rates in a developing nation). Most of us think of three general patterns: growth, stability, or decline. But there are subtler trends within each

FIGURE 14.3

Four components of a time series

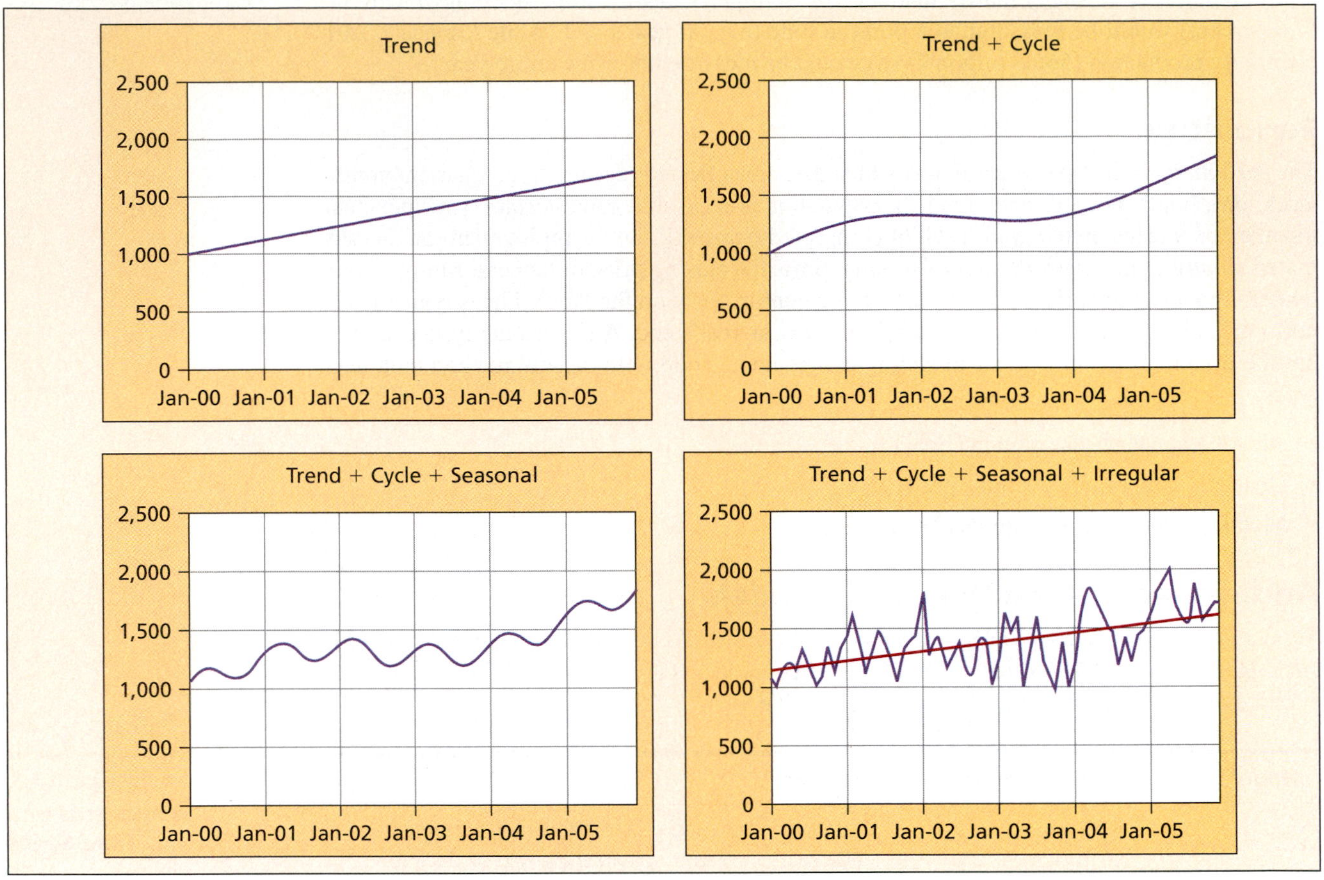

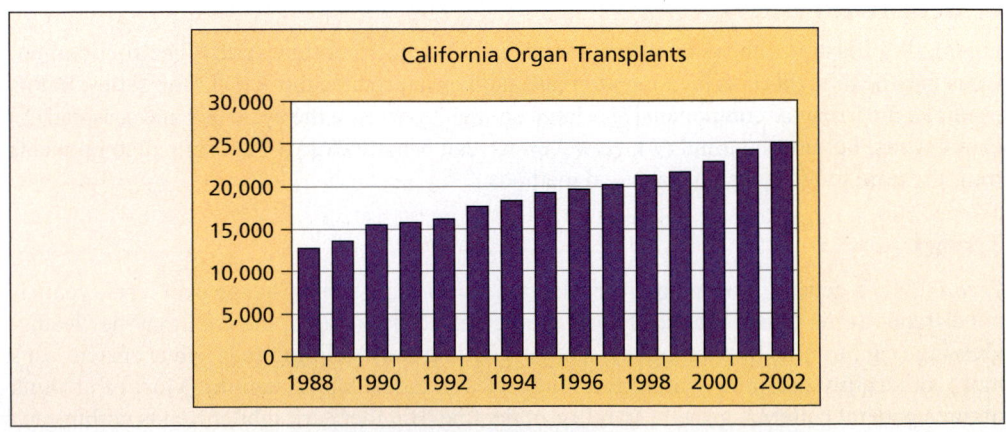

category. A time series can increase at a steady *linear* rate (e.g., the number of books you have read in your lifetime), at an *increasing* rate (e.g., Medicare costs for an aging population), or at a *decreasing* rate (e.g., live attendance at NFL football games). It can grow for awhile and then level off (e.g., sales of HDTV) or grow toward an asymptote (e.g., percent of adults owning a camera phone). A mathematical trend can be fitted to any data, but its predictive value depends on the situation. For example, to predict future organ transplants (Figure 14.4) a mathematical trend might be useful, but a mathematical model might not be very helpful for predicting space launches (Figure 14.5).

FIGURE 14.4

Steady trend

Transplants

Source: www.gsds.org.
© Golden State Donor Services

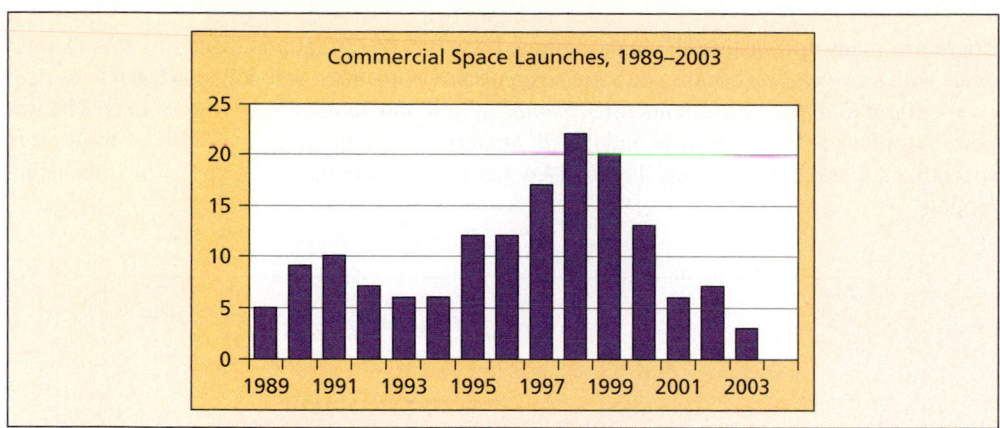

FIGURE 14.5

Erratic pattern
SpaceLaunch

Source: http://ast.faa.gov.

Cycle

Cycle (*C*) is a repetitive up-and-down movement around the trend that covers *several years*. For example, industry analysts have studied cycles for sales of new automobiles, new home construction, inventories, and business investment. These cycles are based primarily on product life and replacement cycles. In any market economy there are broad business cycles that affect employment and production. But there is no general theory of cycles, and even those cycles that have been identified in specific industries have erratic timing and complex causes that defy generalization. Over a small number of time periods (a typical forecasting situation) cycles are undetectable or may resemble a trend. For this reason cycles are not discussed further in this chapter.

Seasonal

Seasonal (*S*) is a repetitive cyclical pattern *within a year.** For example, many retail businesses experience strong sales during the fourth quarter because of Christmas. Automobile sales rise when new models are released. Peak demand for airline flights to Europe occurs during summer vacation travel. Although often imagined as sine waves, seasonal patterns may not be smooth. Peaks and valleys can occur in any month or quarter, and each industry may face its own unique seasonal pattern. For example, June weddings tend to create a "spike" in bridal sales, but there is no "sine wave" pattern in bridal sales. By definition, annual data have no seasonality.

Irregular

Irregular (*I*) is a random disturbance that follows no apparent pattern. It is also called the *error* component or *random noise* reflecting all factors other than trend, cycle, and seasonality. Large error components are not unusual. For example, daily prices of many common stocks fluctuate greatly. When the irregular component is large, it may be difficult to isolate other individual model components. Some data are pure *I* (lacking meaningful *T* or *S* or *C* components). In such cases, we use special techniques (e.g., **moving average** or **exponential smoothing**) to make short-run forecasts. Faced with erratic data, experts may use their own knowledge of a particular industry to make *judgment forecasts*. For example, monthly sales forecasts of a particular automobile may combine judgment forecasts from dealers, financial staff, and economists.

---

*Repetitive patterns within a week, day, or other time period may also be considered seasonal. For example, mail volume in the U.S. Post Service is higher on Monday. Emergency arrivals at hospitals are lower during the first shift (midnight and 6:00 A.M.). In this chapter, we will discuss only *monthly* and *quarterly* seasonal patterns, because these are most typical of business data.

14.2
TREND FORECASTING

There are many forecasting methods designed for specific situations. Much of this chapter deals with *trend models* because they are so common in business. You will also learn to use *decomposition* to make adjustments for *seasonality*, and how to use *smoothing models*. The important topics of *ARIMA models* and *causal models* using regression are reserved for a more specialized class in forecasting. Figure 14.6 summarizes the main categories of forecasting models.

FIGURE 14.6

Overview of forecasting

Chapter 20

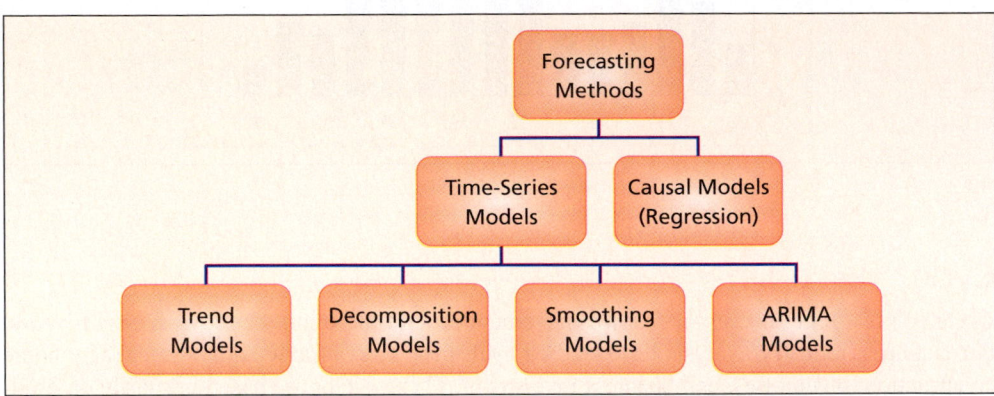

Three Trend Models

There are many possible trend models, but three of them are especially useful in business:

$$(14.1) \qquad y_t = a + bt \qquad \text{for } t = 1, 2, \ldots, n \text{ (linear trend)}$$

$$(14.2) \qquad y_t = ae^{bt} \qquad \text{for } t = 1, 2, \ldots, n \text{ (exponential trend)}$$

$$(14.3) \qquad y_t = a + bt + ct^2 \quad \text{for } t = 1, 2, \ldots, n \text{ (quadratic trend)}$$

The linear and exponential models are widely used because they have only two parameters and are familiar to most business audiences. The quadratic model may be useful when the data have a turning point. All three can be fitted by Excel, MegaStat, or MINITAB. Each model will be examined in turn.

Linear Trend Model

The ***linear trend*** model has the form $y_t = a + bt$. It is useful for a time-series that grows or declines by the same amount (b) in each period, as shown in Figure 14.7. It is the simplest model and may suffice for short-run forecasting. It is generally preferred in business as a baseline forecasting model unless there are compelling reasons to consider a more complex model.

FIGURE 14.7

Linear trend models

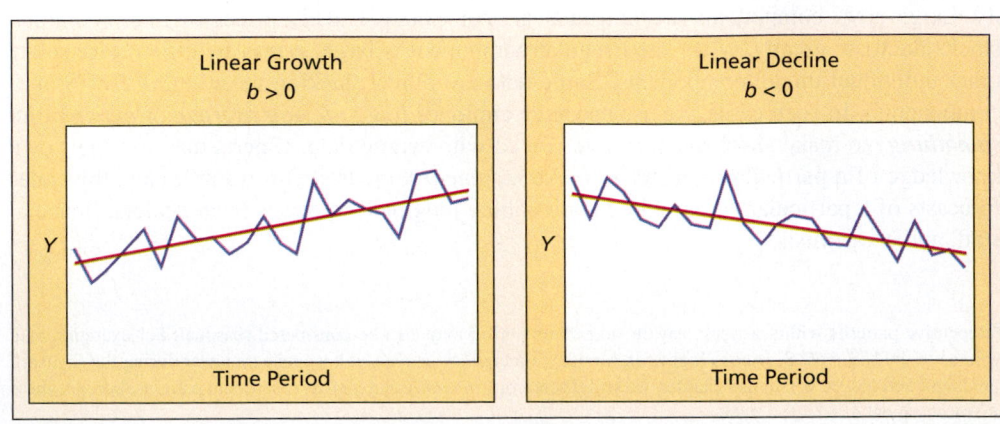

Illustration: Linear Trend

In recent years, the number of U.S. franchised new car dealerships has been declining, due to phasing out of low-volume dealerships and consolidation of market areas. What has been the average annual decline? Based on the line graph in Figure 14.8, the linear model seems appropriate to describe this trend. The slope of Excel's fitted trend indicates that, on average, 235 dealerships are being lost annually.

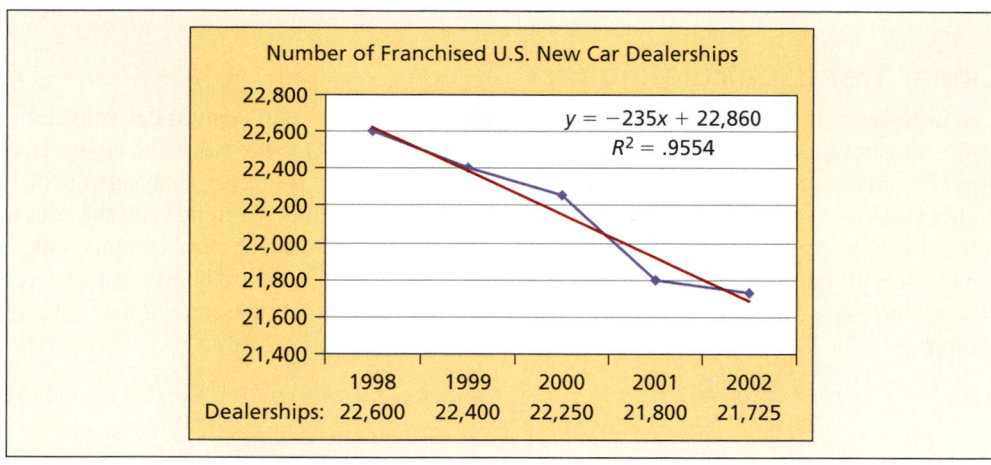

FIGURE 14.8

Excel's Linear trend

CarDealers

Source: *Statistical Abstract of the United States, 2003.*

Linear Trend Calculations

The linear trend is fitted in the usual way by using the ordinary least squares formulas, as illustrated in Table 14.2. Since you are already familiar with regression, we will only point out the use of the index $x_t = 1, 2, 3, 4, 5$ for the calculations (instead of using the years 1998, 1999, 2000, 2001, 2002). We use this time index to simplify the calculations and keep the data magnitudes under control (Excel uses this method too).

$$\text{Slope:} \quad b = \frac{\sum_{t=1}^{n} (x_t - \bar{x})(y_t - \bar{y})}{\sum_{t=1}^{n} (x_t - \bar{x})^2} = \frac{-2,350}{10} = -235$$

$$\text{Intercept:} \quad a = \bar{y} - b\bar{x} = 22,155 - (-235)(3) = 22,860$$

Year	x_t	y_t	$x_t - \bar{x}$	$y_t - \bar{y}$	$(x_t - \bar{x})^2$	$(x_t - \bar{x})(y_t - \bar{y})$
1998	1	22,600	−2	445	4	−890
1999	2	22,400	−1	245	1	−245
2000	3	22,250	0	95	0	0
2001	4	21,800	1	−355	1	−355
2002	5	21,725	2	−430	4	−860
Sum	15	110,775	0	0	10	−2,350
Mean	3	22,155	0	0	2	−470

TABLE 14.2

Sums for Least Squares Calculations

Interpreting a Linear Trend

The *slope* of the fitted trend $y_t = 22,860 - 235t$ says that we expect to lose 235 dealerships each year ($dy_t/dt = -235$). The *intercept* is the "starting point" for the time-series in period $t = 0$; that is, $y_0 = 22,860 - 235(0) = 22,860$.

Forecasting a Linear Trend

We can make a forecast for any future year by using the fitted model. In the car dealer example, the fitted trend equation is based on only 5 years' data, so we should be wary of extrapolating very far ahead:

For 2003 ($t = 6$): $y_6 = 22{,}860 - 235(6) = 21{,}450$

For 2004 ($t = 7$): $y_7 = 22{,}860 - 235(7) = 21{,}215$

For 2005 ($t = 8$): $y_8 = 22{,}860 - 235(8) = 20{,}980$

Linear Trend: Calculating R^2

The worksheet shown in Table 14.3 shows the calculation of the coefficient of determination. In this illustration, the linear model gives a good fit ($R^2 = .9554$) to the *past* data. However, a good fit to the past data does not guarantee good *future* forecasts. A deeper analysis of underlying causes of dealership consolidation is needed. What is causing the trend? Are the causal forces likely to remain the same in subsequent years? Could the current trend continue indefinitely, or will it approach an asymptote or limit of some kind? These are questions that forecasters must ask. The forecast is simply a projection of current trend assuming that nothing changes.

$$\text{Coefficient of determination:} \quad R^2 = 1 - \frac{\sum_{t=1}^{n}(y_t - \hat{y}_t)^2}{\sum_{t=1}^{n}(y_t - \bar{y})^2} = 1 - \frac{25{,}750}{578{,}000} = .9554$$

TABLE 14.3
Sums for R^2 Calculations

Year	t	y_t	$\hat{y}_t = 22{,}860 - 235t$	$y_t - \hat{y}_t$	$(y_t - \hat{y}_t)^2$	$(y_t - \bar{y})^2$
1998	1	22,600	22,625	−25	625	198,025
1999	2	22,400	22,390	10	100	60,025
2000	3	22,250	22,155	95	9,025	9,025
2001	4	21,800	21,920	−120	14,400	126,025
2002	5	21,725	21,685	40	1,600	184,900
Sum	15		110,775	0	25,750	578,000

Exponential Trend Model

The *exponential trend* model has the form $y_t = ae^{bt}$. It is useful for a time-series that grows or declines at the same *rate* (b) in each period, as shown in Figure 14.9. When the growth rate is positive ($b > 0$), then Y grows by an *increasing* amount each period (unlike the linear model, which assumes a *constant* increment each period). If the growth rate is negative ($b < 0$), then Y declines by a *decreasing* amount each period (unlike the linear model, which assumes a *constant* decrement each period).

FIGURE 14.9

Exponential trend models

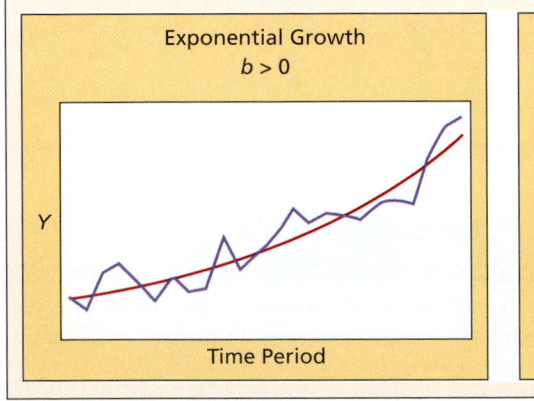 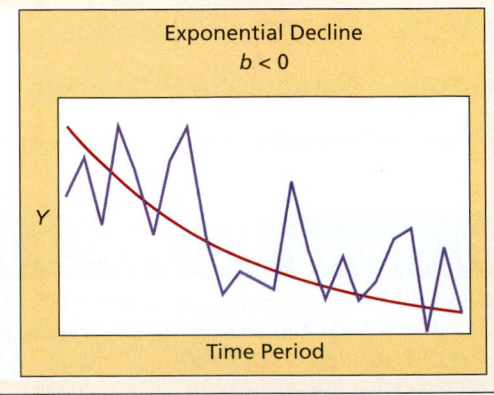

When to Use the Exponential Model

The exponential model is often preferred for financial data or data that covers a longer period of time. When you invest money in a commercial bank savings account, interest accrues at a given percent. Your savings grow faster than a linear rate because you earn interest on the accumulated interest. Banks use the exponential formula to calculate interest on CDs. Financial analysts often find the exponential model attractive because costs, revenue, and salaries are best projected under assumed *percent* growth rates.

Another nice feature of the exponential model is that you can compare two growth rates in two time-series variables with dissimilar data units (i.e., a percent growth rate is *unit-free*). For example, between 1990 and 2000 the number of Medicare enrollees grew from 34.3 million persons to 39.6 million persons (1.45 percent growth per annum), while Medicare payments to hospitals grew from $65.7 billion to $126.0 billion (6.73 percent growth per annum). Comparing the percents, we see that Medicare insurance payments have been growing more than four times as fast as the Medicare head count. These facts underlie the ongoing debate about Medicare spending in the United States.

There may not be much difference between a linear and exponential model when the growth rate is small and the data set covers only a few time periods. For example, suppose your starting salary is $50,000. Table 14.4 compares salary increases of $2,500 each year ($y_t = 50,000 + 2,500t$) with a continuously compounded 4.879 percent salary growth ($y_t = 50,000e^{.04879t}$). Over the first few years, there is little difference. But after 20 years, the difference is obvious, as shown in Figure 14.10. Despite its attractive simplicity* the linear model's assumptions may be inappropriate for some financial variables.

t	$y_t = 50,000 + 2,500t$ *Linear*	$y_t = 50,000\ e^{.04879t}$ *Exponential*
0	50,000	50,000
5	62,500	63,814
10	75,000	81,445
15	87,500	103,946
20	100,000	132,665

TABLE 14.4

Two Models of Salary Growth

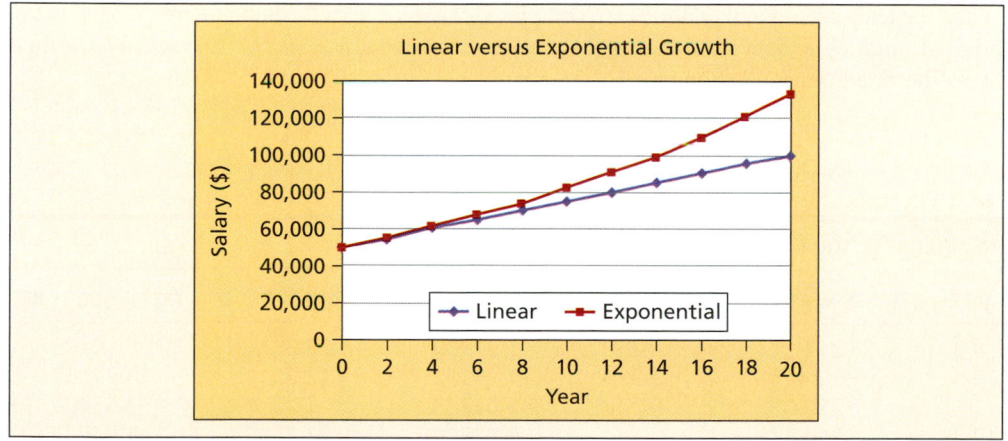

FIGURE 14.10

Linear and exponential growth compared

Illustration: Exponential Trend

Debit card usage in the United States has shown explosive growth, as indicated in Figure 14.11. Clearly, a linear trend (constant *dollar* growth) would be inadequate. It is more reasonable to assume a constant *percent* rate of growth and fit an exponential model. For the debit

---

*In a sense, the linear model ($y_t = a + bt$) and the exponential model ($y_t = ae^{bt}$) are equally simple because they are two-parameter models, and a log-transformed exponential model $\ln(y_t) = \ln(a) + bt$ is actually linear.

FIGURE 14.11

Excel's exponential trend
DebitCards

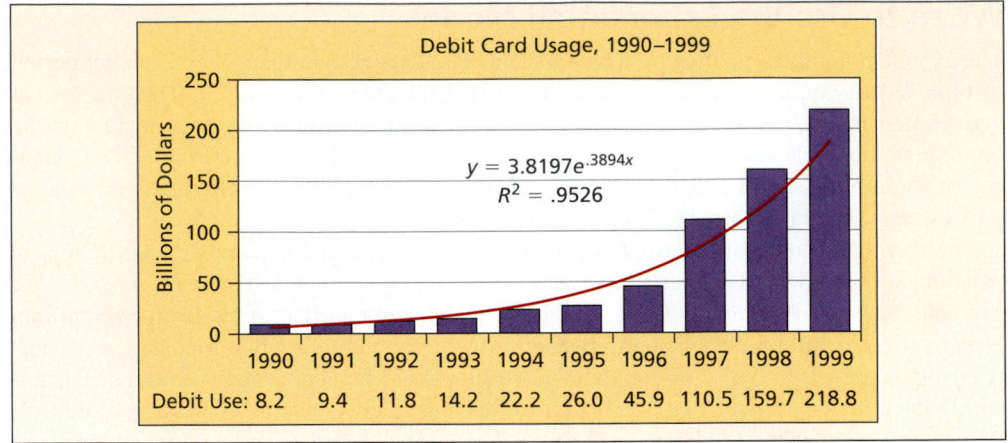

Debit Use: 8.2   9.4   11.8   14.2   22.2   26.0   45.9   110.5   159.7   218.8

card data, the fitted exponential trend is $y_t = 3.8197e^{.3894t}$. The value of b in the exponential model $y_t = ae^{bt}$ is the continuously compounded growth rate, so we can say that debit card usage is growing at an astonishing rate of 38.94 percent per year. A negative value of b in the equation $y_t = ae^{bt}$ would indicate *decline* instead of growth. The intercept a is the "starting point" in period $t = 0$. For example, $y_0 = 3.8197e^{.3894(0)} = 3.8197$.

Exponential Trend Calculations

Table 14.5 shows the worksheet for the required sums. Calculations of the exponential trend are done by using a transformed variable $z_t = \ln(y_t)$ instead of y_t, to produce a linear equation so that we can use the least squares formulas.

$$\text{Slope:} \quad b = \frac{\sum_{t=1}^{n} (x_t - \bar{x})(z_t - \bar{z})}{\sum_{t=1}^{n} (x_t - \bar{x})^2} = \frac{32.12329}{82.5} = .3893732$$

$$\text{Intercept:} \quad a = \bar{z} - b\bar{x} = 3.481731 - (.3893732)(5.5) = 1.340178$$

When the least squares calculations are completed, we must transform the intercept back to the original units by exponentiation to get the correct intercept $a = e^{1.340178} = 3.8197$. In final form, the fitted trend equation is

$$y_t = ae^{bt} = 3.8197e^{.38937t}$$

TABLE 14.5   Least Squares Sums for the Exponential Model

Year	x_t	y_t	$z_t = \ln(y_t)$	$x_t - \bar{x}$	$z_t - \bar{z}$	$(x_t - \bar{x})^2$	$(x_t - \bar{x})(z_t - \bar{z})$
1990	1	8.2	2.10413	−4.5	−1.37760	20.25	6.19919
1991	2	9.4	2.24071	−3.5	−1.24102	12.25	4.34357
1992	3	11.8	2.46810	−2.5	−1.01363	6.25	2.53408
1993	4	14.2	2.65324	−1.5	−0.82849	2.25	1.24273
1994	5	22.2	3.10009	−0.5	−0.38164	0.25	0.19082
1995	6	26.0	3.25810	0.5	−0.22363	0.25	−0.11182
1996	7	45.9	3.82647	1.5	0.34473	2.25	0.51710
1997	8	110.5	4.70502	2.5	1.22328	6.25	3.05821
1998	9	159.7	5.07330	3.5	1.59157	12.25	5.57048
1999	10	218.8	5.38816	4.5	1.90643	20.25	8.57892
Sum	55	626.7	34.81731	0.0	0.00000	82.5	32.12329
Mean	5.5	62.67	3.481731				

Forecasting an Exponential Trend

We can make a forecast of debit card usage for any future year by using the fitted model*:

> For 2001 ($t = 11$): $y_{11} = 3.8197e^{.38937(11)} = 276.8$
>
> For 2002 ($t = 12$): $y_{12} = 3.8197e^{.38937(12)} = 408.5$
>
> For 2003 ($t = 13$): $y_{13} = 3.8197e^{.38937(13)} = 603.0$

Can debit card usage actually continue to grow at a rate of 38.937 percent? It seems unlikely. Typically, when a new product is introduced, its growth rate at first is very strong, but eventually slows down.

Exponential Trend: Calculating R^2

We can calculate R^2 using a worksheet like Table 14.6. Note that all calculations of R^2 are done in terms of $\ln(y_t)$. In this example, the exponential trend gives a very good fit ($R^2 = .9526$) to the past data. Although a high R^2 does not guarantee good forecasts, in the case of debit card usage we might expect the near future to resemble the recent past. Debit cards appear poised to reach a much wider audience of consumers who have traditionally relied on checks or credit cards.

$$\text{Coefficient of determination:} \quad R^2 = 1 - \frac{\sum_{t=1}^{n}(z_t - \hat{z}_t)^2}{\sum_{t=1}^{n}(z_t - \bar{z})^2} = 1 - \frac{0.622275}{13.130224} = .9526$$

TABLE 14.6   **Sums for R^2 Calculations (Exponential Model)**

x_t	$z_t = \ln(y_t)$	$\hat{z}_t = 1.340178 + .389373\, x_t$	$z_t - \hat{z}_t$	$(z_t - \hat{z}_t)^2$	$(z_t - \bar{z})^2$
1	2.10413	1.72955	0.37458	0.14031	1.89777
2	2.24071	2.11892	0.12178	0.01483	1.54013
3	2.46810	2.50830	−0.04020	0.00162	1.02745
4	2.65324	2.89767	−0.24443	0.05975	0.68639
5	3.10009	3.28704	−0.18695	0.03495	0.14565
6	3.25810	3.67642	−0.41832	0.17499	0.05001
7	3.82647	4.06579	−0.23933	0.05728	0.11884
8	4.70502	4.45516	0.24985	0.06243	1.49643
9	5.07330	4.84454	0.22876	0.05233	2.53308
10	5.38816	5.23391	0.15425	0.02379	3.63446
Sum	34.81731	34.81731	0	0.622275	13.130224
Mean	3.48173				

Quadratic Trend Model

The *quadratic trend* model has the form $y_t = a + bt + ct^2$. It is useful for a time series that has a turning point or that is not captured by the exponential model. If $c = 0$, the quadratic model $y_t = a + bt + ct^2$ becomes a linear model because the term ct^2 drops out of the

---

*Excel uses the exponential formula $y_t = ae^{bt}$ in which the coefficient b is the *continuously compounded* growth rate. But MINITAB uses an equivalent formula $y_t = y_0(1 + r)^t$, which you may recognize as the formula for compound interest. Although the formulas appear different, they give identical forecasts. For example, for the debit card data, MINITAB's fitted trend is $y_t = 3.81972(1.47606)^t$ so the forecasts are

> For 2001 ($t = 11$): $y_{11} = 3.81972(1.47606)^{11} = 276.8$
>
> For 2002 ($t = 12$): $y_{12} = 3.81972(1.47606)^{12} = 408.5$
>
> For 2003 ($t = 13$): $y_{13} = 3.81972(1.47606)^{13} = 603.0$

To convert MINITAB's fitted equation to Excel's, set $a = y_0$ and $b = \ln(1 + r)$. To convert Excel's fitted equation to MINITAB's, set $y_0 = a$ and $r = e^b - 1$.

FIGURE 14.12

Four quadratic trend models

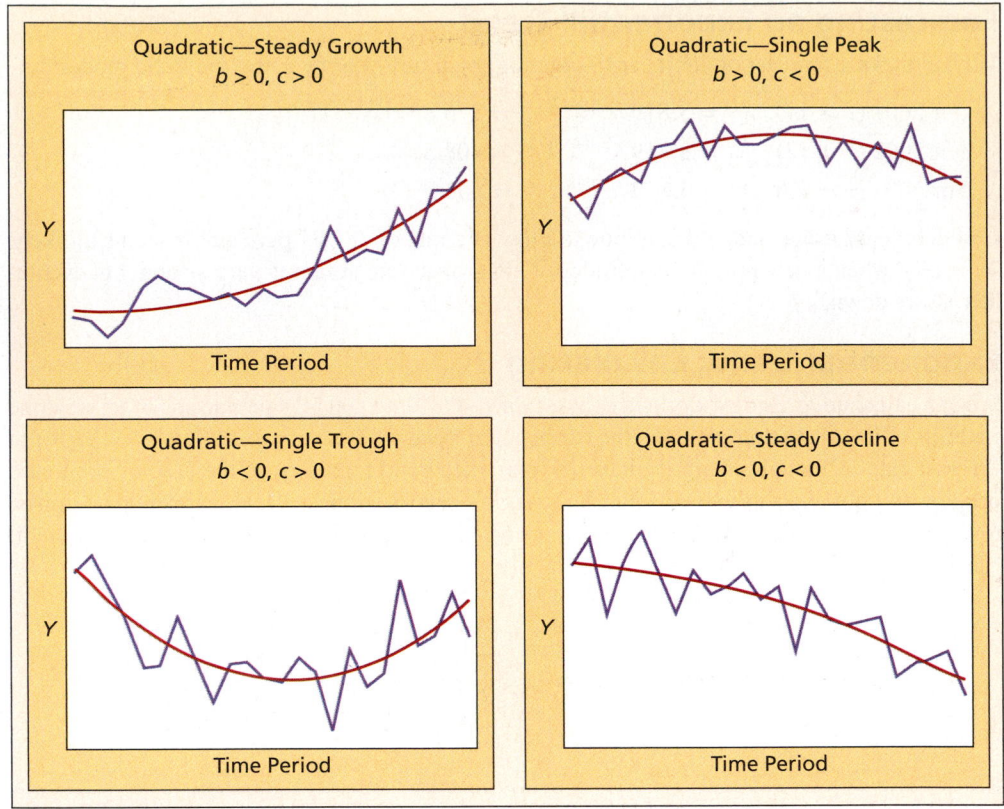

equation (i.e., the linear model is a special case of the quadratic model). Some forecasters fit a quadratic model as a way of checking for nonlinearity. If the coefficient c does not differ significantly from zero, then the linear model would suffice. Depending on the values of b and c, the quadratic model can assume any of four shapes, as shown in Figure 14.12.

Illustration: Quadratic Trend

The number of hospital beds (Table 14.7) in the United States declined during the late 1990s, but then showed signs of leveling out or even increasing again. What trend would we choose if the objective is to make a realistic 1-year forecast?

TABLE 14.7

U.S. Hospital Beds, 1995–2001

🐝 **HospitalBeds**

Source: *Statistical Abstract of the United States, 2003*

Year	1995	1996	1997	1998	1999	2000	2001
Beds (000)	1,081	1,062	1,035	1,013	994	984	987

Figures 14.13 and 14.14 show 1-year projections using the linear and quadratic models. Many observers would think that the quadratic model offers a more believable prediction, because the quadratic model is able to capture the slight curvature in the data pattern. But this gain in forecast credibility must be weighed against the added complexity of the quadratic model. It appears that the forecasts would turn upward if projected more than 1 year ahead. We should be especially skeptical of any polynomial model that is projected more than one or two periods into the future.

Because the quadratic trend model $y_t = a + bt + ct^2$ is a multiple regression with two predictors (t and t^2), the least squares calculations are not shown. However, Figure 14.15 shows the MINITAB fitted regression. Note that both t and t^2 are significant predictors (large t, small p).

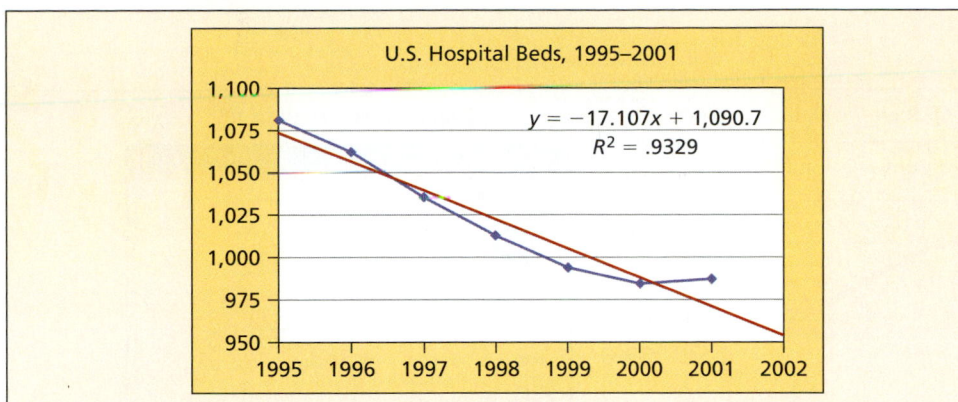

FIGURE 14.13

Linear trend

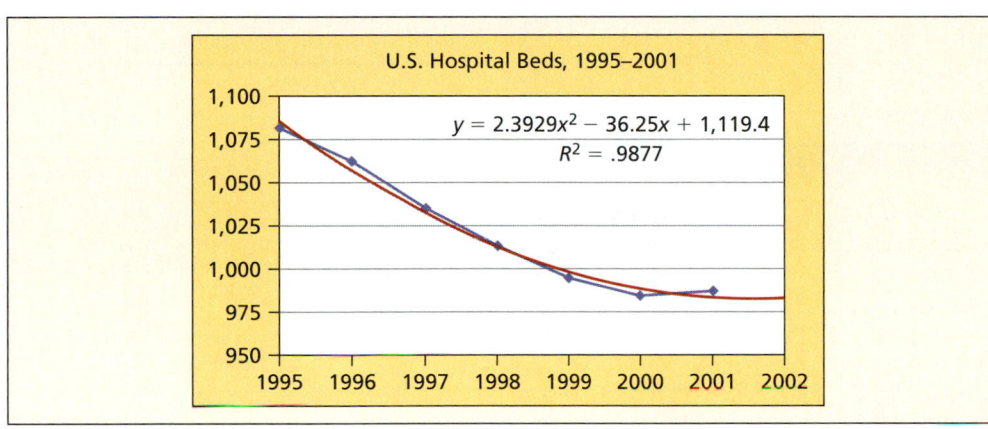

FIGURE 14.14

Quadratic trend

```
The regression equation is
Beds = 1119 − 36.2 Time + 2.39 Time2

Predictor        Coef      SE Coef         T          P
Constant      1119.43         8.10    138.15      0.000
Time          −36.250        4.644     −7.81      0.001
Time2          2.3929       0.5673      4.22      0.014

S = 5.19959        R-Sq = 98.8%         R-Sq(adj) = 98.2%
```

FIGURE 14.15

MINITAB's quadratic regression

Using Excel for Trend Fitting

Plot the data, right-click on the data, and choose a trend. Figure 14.16 shows Excel's menu of six trend options. The menu includes a sketch of each trend type. Click the Options tab if you want to display the R^2 and fitted equation on the graph, or if you want to plot forecasts (trend extrapolations) on the graph. The quadratic model is a ***polynomial model*** of order 2. Despite the many choices, some patterns cannot be captured by any of the common trend models. By default, Excel only reports four decimal accuracy. However, you can click on Excel's fitted trend equation, choose Format Data Labels, choose Number, and set the number of decimal places you want to see.

Trend-Fitting Criteria

It is so easy to fit a trend in Excel that it is tempting to "shop around" for the best fit. But forecasters prefer the simplest trend model that adequately matches the trend (the principle of

FIGURE 14.16

Excel's trend-fitting menus

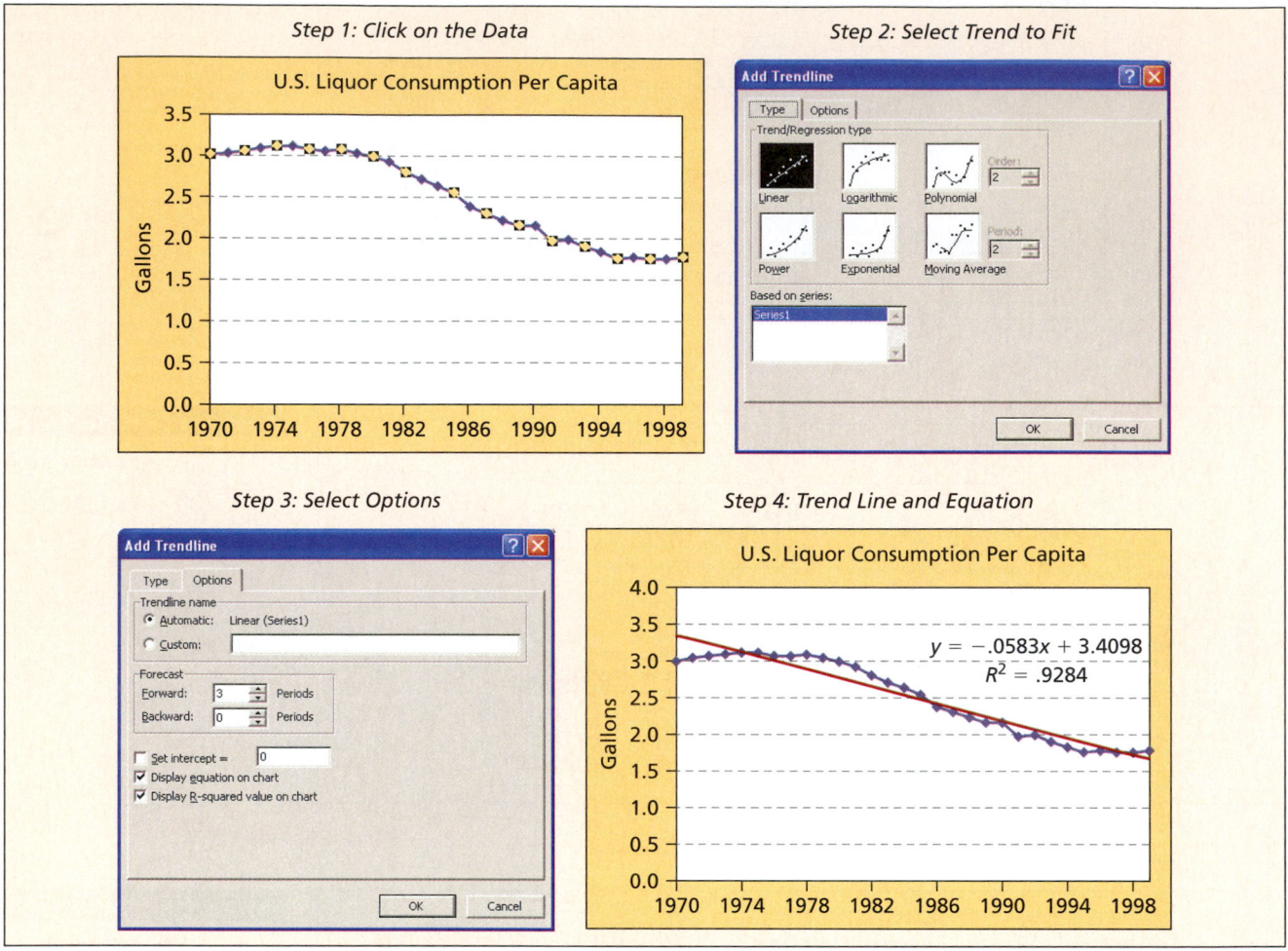

Occam's Razor). Simple models are easier to interpret and explain to others. Criteria for selecting a trend model for forecasting include:

Criterion	*Ask Yourself*
• Occam's Razor	Would a simpler model suffice?
• Overall fit	How does the trend fit the past data?
• Believability	Does the extrapolated trend "look right"?
• Fit to recent data	Does the fitted trend match the last few data points?

EXAMPLE

Comparing Trends

You can usually increase the R^2 by choosing a more complex model. But if you are making a *forecast,* this is not the only relevant issue, because R^2 measures the fit to the *past* data. Figure 14.17 shows four fitted trends using the same data, with three-period forecasts. For this data set, the linear model may be inadequate because its fit to recent periods is marginal (we prefer the simplest model *only if* it "does the job"). Here, the cubic trend yields the highest R^2, but the fitted equation is nonintuitive and would be hard to explain or defend. Also, its forecasts appear to be increasing too rapidly. In this example, the exponential model has the lowest R^2, yet matches the recent data fairly well and its forecasts appear credible when projected a few periods ahead.

FIGURE 14.17

Four fitted trends using the same data

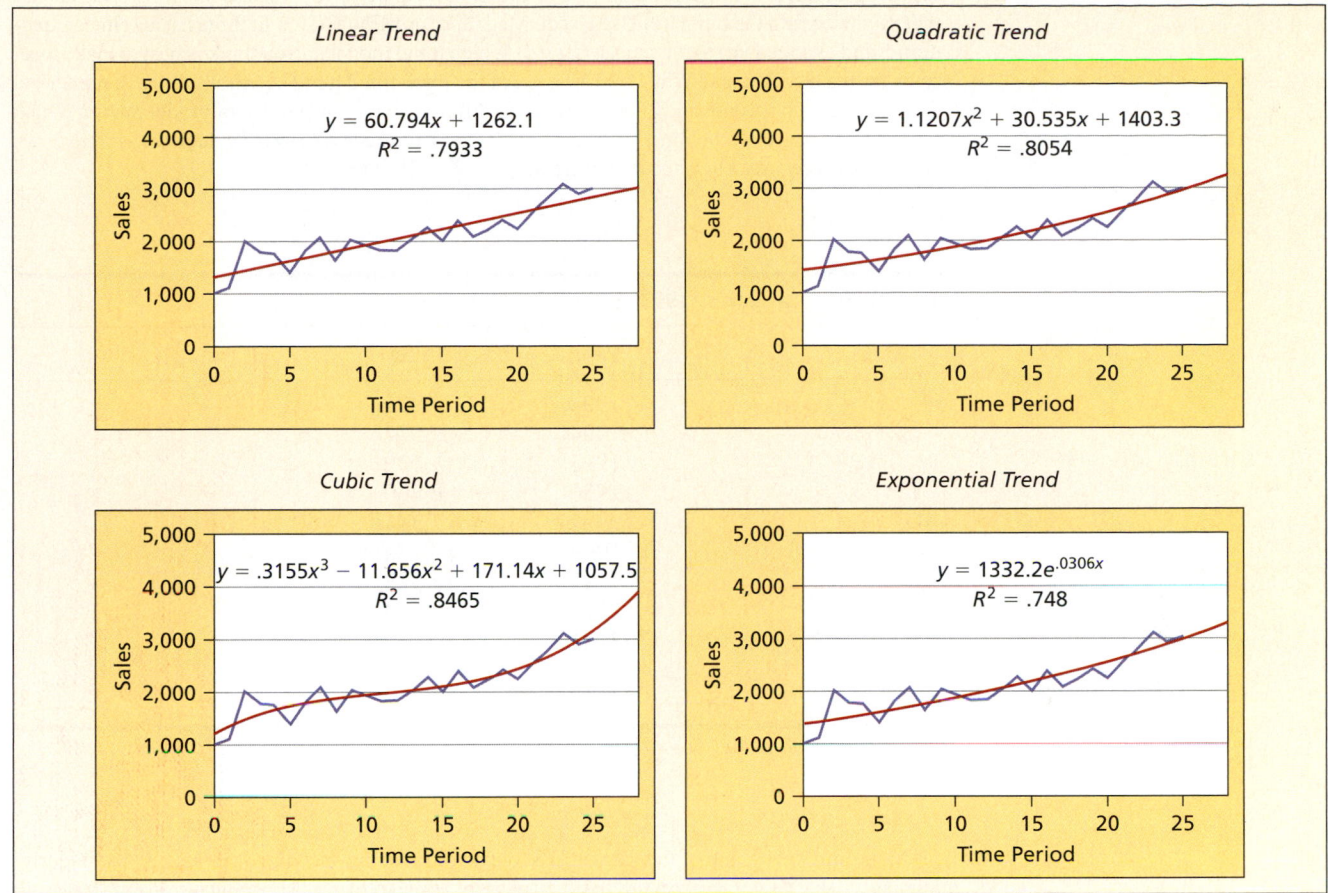

Any trend model's forecasts become less reliable as they are extrapolated farther into the future. The quadratic trend, the simplest of Excel's polynomial models, is sometimes acceptable for short-term forecasting. However, forecasters avoid higher-order polynomial models (cubic and higher) not only because they are complex, but also because they can give bizarre forecasts when extrapolated more than one period ahead. Table 14.8 compares the features of the three most common trend models.

TABLE 14.8   **Comparison of Three Trend Models**

Model	Pro	Con
Linear	1. Simple, familiar to everyone. 2. May suffice for short-run data.	1. Assumes constant slope. 2. Cannot capture nonlinear change.
Exponential	1. Familiar to financial analysts. 2. Shows compound percent growth rate.	1. Some managers are unfamiliar with e^x. 2. Data values must be positive.
Quadratic	1. Useful for data with a turning point. 2. Useful test for nonlinearity.	1. Complex and no intuitive interpretation. 2. Can give untrustworthy forecasts if extrapolated too far.

SECTION EXERCISES

14.1 (a) Make an Excel graph of the data on U.S. diesel new car sales. (b) Discuss the underlying causes that might explain the trend. (c) Use Excel, MegaStat, or MINITAB to fit three trends (linear, quadratic, and exponential) to the time series. (d) Which trend model do you think is best to make forecasts for the next 3 years? Why? (e) Use *each* of the three fitted trend equations to make numerical forecasts for 2004, 2005, and 2006. How much difference does the choice of model make? Which forecasts do you trust the most, and why? (f) If you have access to *Ward's Automotive Yearbook,* check your forecasts. How accurate were they? 🐾 **Diesel**

U.S. Diesel New Car Sales, 1993–2003

Year	Sales
1993	2,800
1994	3,577
1995	3,139
1996	8,469
1997	7,331
1998	10,972
1999	13,573
2000	22,634
2001	15,077
2002	31,430
2003	38,524

Source: *Ward's Automotive Yearbook, 2004,* 66th ed., p. 40.

14.2 (a) Make an Excel graph of the data on U.S. online advertising spending. (b) Discuss the underlying causes that might explain the trend or pattern. (c) Use Excel, MegaStat, or MINITAB to fit three trends (linear, quadratic, exponential) to the time-series. (d) Which trend model do you think is best to make forecasts for the next 3 years? Why? (e) Use *each* of the three fitted trend equations to make a numerical forecast for 2007. How similar are the three models' forecasts? 🐾 **Online**

U.S. Online Advertising, 2000–2006 (billions)

Year	Spending
2000	8.1
2001	7.1
2002	6.0
2003	6.3
2004	6.8
2005	7.2
2006	8.1

Source: William F. Arens, *Contemporary Advertising,* 9th ed. (McGraw-Hill, 2004), p. 549.

14.3 (a) Make an Excel line graph of the data on computer viruses. (b) Discuss the underlying causes that might explain the trend or pattern. (c) Fit three trends (linear, exponential, quadratic). (d) Which trend model is best, and why? If none is satisfactory, explain. (e) Make a forecast for 2003, using a trend model of your choice or a judgment forecast. 🐾 **PCViruses**

Virus Infections Per Month Per 1,000 PCs

Year	Viruses
1996	10
1997	21
1998	32
1999	80
2000	91
2001	103
2002	105

Source: *PC Magazine* 22 no. 9 (May 27, 2003), p. 23.

14.4 (a) Make an Excel line graph of the work hours data. (b) Discuss the underlying causes that might explain the trend or pattern. (c) Fit three trends (linear, exponential, quadratic). (d) Which trend model is best, and why? If none is satisfactory, explain. (e) Make a forecast for 2000, using a trend model of your choice or a judgment forecast.   **WorkHours**

Average Annual Hours of Work, Married Couple with Children

Year	Hours	Year	Hours
1982	3,160	1991	3,515
1983	3,194	1992	3,491
1984	3,289	1993	3,536
1985	3,309	1994	3,589
1986	3,391	1995	3,616
1987	3,451	1996	3,638
1988	3,460	1997	3,679
1989	3,534	1998	3,685
1990	3,536	1999	3,714

Source: *Statistical Abstract of the United States, 2002.*

14.5 (a) Plot the data on fruit and vegetable consumption. (b) Discuss the underlying causes that might explain the trend or pattern. (c) Fit a linear trend to the data. (d) Interpret the trend equation. What are its implications for producers? (e) Make a forecast for 2005. *Note:* Time increments are 5 years, so use $t = 6$ for your 2005 forecast.   **Fruits**

U.S. Per Capita Consumption of Commercially Produced Fruits and Vegetables (pounds)

Year	Total
1980	608.0
1985	629.3
1990	659.2
1995	690.0
2000	705.4

Source: *Statistical Abstract of the United States, 2003.*

Mini Case   14.1

U.S. Trade Deficit

The imbalance between imports and exports (Table 14.9) has been a vexing policy problem for U.S. policymakers for decades. The last time the United States had a trade surplus was in 1975, partly due to reduced dependency on foreign oil through conservation measures enacted after the oil crisis (shortages and gas lines) in the early 1970s. However, the trade deficit has become more acute over time, due partly to continued oil imports, and, more recently, to availability of cheaper goods from China and other emerging economies.

TABLE 14.9	U.S. International Trade, 1990–2002	🎯 TradeDeficit	
Period	**Year**	**Exports**	**Imports**
1	1990	387.4	498.4
2	1991	414.1	491.0
3	1992	439.6	536.5
4	1993	456.9	589.4
5	1994	502.9	668.7
6	1995	575.2	749.4
7	1996	612.1	803.1
8	1997	678.4	876.5
9	1998	670.4	917.1
10	1999	684.0	1,030.0
11	2000	772.0	1,224.4
12	2001	718.7	1,145.9
13	2002	681.9	1,164.7

Source: *Statistical Abstract of the United States, 2003.* Figures are in billions of current dollars.

Figure 14.18 shows the data graphically, with fitted exponential trends. The trends fit well except for 2001–2002. Imports fell in the recession that began in 2000, but then began to pick up, while exports remained weak. The fitted trend equations reveal that imports have been growing at a compound annual rate of 8.29 percent, while exports have only grown at a compound annual rate of 5.69 percent.

FIGURE 14.18

U.S. trade, 1990–2002

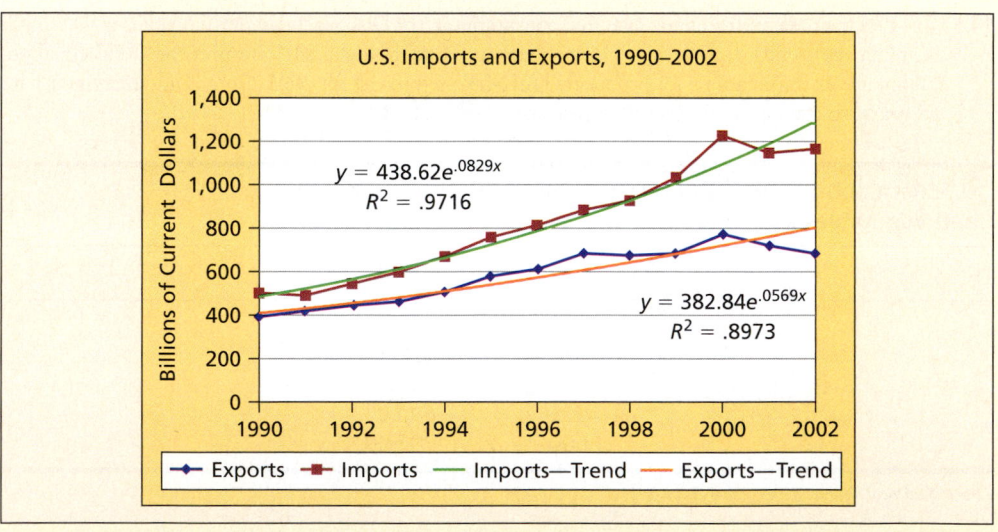

If we project these disparate growth rates, we would predict a widening trade deficit (calculations shown below). Of course, the assumption of *ceteris paribus* may not hold. Policymakers may seek to weaken the dollar or to change fuel efficiency of U.S. vehicles, or there could be changes in foreign economies (e.g., China). Forecasts are less a way of predicting the future than of showing where we are heading *if* nothing changes. A paradox of forecasting is that, as soon as decision makers see the implications of the forecast, they take steps to make sure the forecast is wrong!

Year (Period)	Imports Trend Projection	Exports Trend Projection
2004 (15)	$y_t = 438.62e^{.0829(15)} = 1{,}521$	$y_t = 382.84e^{.0569(15)} = 899$
2006 (17)	$y_t = 438.62e^{.0829(17)} = 1{,}795$	$y_t = 382.84e^{.0569(17)} = 1{,}007$
2008 (19)	$y_t = 438.62e^{.0829(19)} = 2{,}119$	$y_t = 382.84e^{.0569(19)} = 1{,}129$
2010 (21)	$y_t = 438.62e^{.0829(21)} = 2{,}501$	$y_t = 382.84e^{.0569(21)} = 1{,}265$

Five Measures of Fit

14.3
ASSESSING FIT

In time-series analysis, you are likely to encounter several different measures of "fit" that show how well the estimated trend model matches the observed time series. "Fit" refers to historical data, and you should bear in mind that a good fit is no guarantee of good forecasts—the usual goal. Five common measures of fit are shown in Table 14.10.

TABLE 14.10 Five Measures of Fit

Statistic	Description	Pro	Con
(14.4) $R^2 = 1 - \dfrac{\sum\limits_{t=1}^{n}(y_t - \hat{y}_t)^2}{\sum\limits_{t=1}^{n}(y_t - \bar{y}_t)^2}$	Coefficient of determination	1. Unit-free measure. 2. Very common.	1. Often interpreted incorrectly (e.g., "percent of correct predictions").
(14.5) $MAPE = \dfrac{100}{n}\sum\limits_{t=1}^{n}\dfrac{\|y_t - \hat{y}_t\|}{y_t}$	Mean Absolute Percent Error (MAPE)	1. Unit-free measure (%). 2. Intuitive meaning.	1. Requires $y_t > 0$. 2. Lacks nice math properties.
(14.6) $MAD = \dfrac{1}{n}\sum\limits_{t=1}^{n}\|y_t - \hat{y}_t\|$	Mean Absolute Deviation (MAD)	1. Intuitive meaning. 2. Same units as y_t.	1. Not unit-free. 2. Lacks nice math properties.
(14.7) $MSD = \dfrac{1}{n}\sum\limits_{t=1}^{n}(y_t - \hat{y}_t)^2$	Mean Squared Deviation (MSD)	1. Nice math properties. 2. Penalizes big errors more.	1. Nonintuitive meaning. 2. Rarely reported.
(14.8) $SE = \sqrt{\sum\limits_{t=1}^{n}\dfrac{(y_t - \hat{y}_t)^2}{n-2}}$	Standard error	1. Same units as y_t. 2. For confidence intervals.	1. Nonintuitive meaning.

Figure 14.19 shows a MINITAB graph with fitted linear trend and 3-year forecasts for aggregate U.S. fire losses between 1980 and 2000. Notice that, instead of R^2, MINITAB displays *MAPE*, *MAD*, and *MSD* statistics. Table 14.11 shows the calculations for these statistics

EXAMPLE

Fire Losses

FIGURE 14.19

MINITAB's time-series trend—linear model   **FireLosses**

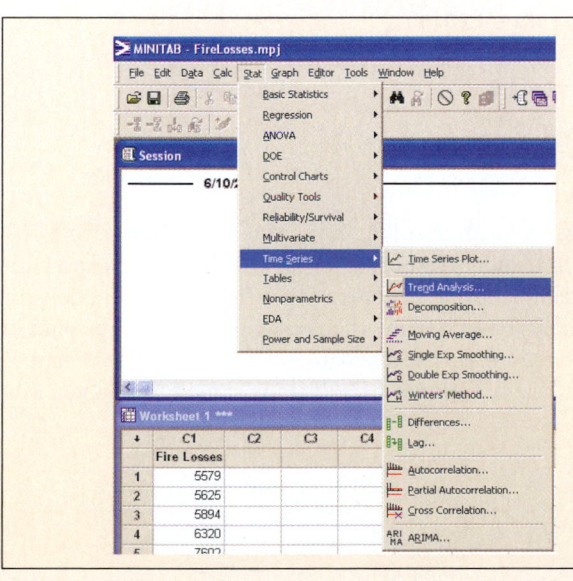
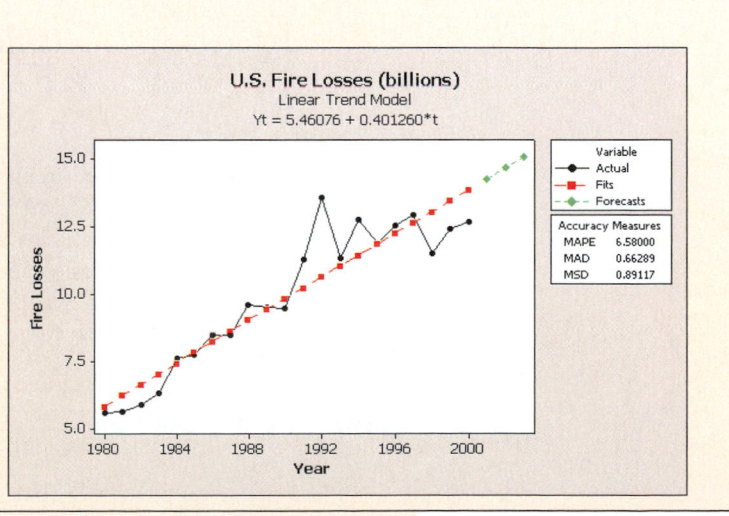

TABLE 14.11   Sums for *MAD, MAPE, MSD,* and Standard Error   **FireLosses**

Period	Year	Losses	$\hat{y}_t = 5.46076 + .401260t$	$y_t - \hat{y}_t$	$|y_t - \hat{y}_t|$	$|y_t - \hat{y}_t|/y_t$	$(y_t - \hat{y}_t)^2$
1	1980	5.579	5.8620	−0.2830	0.2830	0.0507	0.0801
2	1981	5.625	6.2633	−0.6383	0.6383	0.1135	0.4074
3	1982	5.894	6.6645	−0.7705	0.7705	0.1307	0.5937
4	1983	6.320	7.0658	−0.7458	0.7458	0.1180	0.5562
5	1984	7.602	7.4671	0.1349	0.1349	0.0178	0.0182
6	1985	7.753	7.8683	−0.1153	0.1153	0.0149	0.0133
7	1986	8.488	8.2696	0.2184	0.2184	0.0257	0.0477
8	1987	8.504	8.6708	−0.1668	0.1668	0.0196	0.0278
9	1988	9.626	9.0721	0.5539	0.5539	0.0575	0.3068
10	1989	9.514	9.4734	0.0406	0.0406	0.0043	0.0017
11	1990	9.495	9.8746	−0.3796	0.3796	0.0400	0.1441
12	1991	11.302	10.2759	1.0261	1.0261	0.0908	1.0529
13	1992	13.588	10.6771	2.9109	2.9109	0.2142	8.4731
14	1993	11.331	11.0784	0.2526	0.2526	0.0223	0.0638
15	1994	12.778	11.4797	1.2983	1.2983	0.1016	1.6857
16	1995	11.887	11.8809	0.0061	0.0061	0.0005	0.0000
17	1996	12.544	12.2822	0.2618	0.2618	0.0209	0.0686
18	1997	12.940	12.6834	0.2566	0.2566	0.0198	0.0658
19	1998	11.510	13.0847	−1.5747	1.5747	0.1368	2.4797
20	1999	12.428	13.4860	−1.0580	1.0580	0.0851	1.1193
21	2000	12.659	13.8872	−1.2282	1.2282	0.0970	1.5085
			Sum	0.00	13.9206	1.3818	18.7145
			Mean	0.00	0.66289	0.0658	0.89117

of fit. Since the residuals $y_t - \hat{y}_t$ sum to zero, we see why it's necessary to sum either their absolute values or their squares to obtain a measure of fit. *MAPE, MAD, MSD* and SE would be zero if the trend provided a perfect fit to the time series.

Calculations

Using the sums in Table 14.11, we can apply the formulas for each fit statistic:

$$MAPE = \frac{100}{n} \sum_{t=1}^{n} \frac{|y_t - \hat{y}_t|}{y_t} = \frac{100}{21}(1.3818) = 6.58\%$$

$$MAD = \frac{1}{n} \sum_{t=1}^{n} |y_t - \hat{y}_t| = \frac{1}{21}(13.9206) = .66289$$

$$MSD = \frac{1}{n} \sum_{t=1}^{n} (y_t - \hat{y}_t)^2 = \frac{1}{21}(18.7145) = .89117$$

$$SE = \sqrt{\sum_{t=1}^{n} \frac{(y_t - \hat{y}_t)^2}{n-2}} = \sqrt{\frac{18.7145}{21-2}} = .99246$$

Interpretation

The *MAPE* says that our fitted trend has a mean absolute error of 6.58 percent. The *MAD* says that the average error is .66289 billion dollars (ignoring the sign). The *MSD* lacks a simple interpretation. These fit statistics are most useful in comparing different trend models for the same data. All the statistics (especially the *MSD*) are affected by the unusual residual in 1992, when fire losses greatly exceeded the trend. The standard error is useful if we want to make a prediction interval for a forecast, using formula 14.9. It is the same formula you saw in Chapter 12.

$$\textbf{(14.9)} \qquad \hat{y}_t \pm t_{n-2}SE \sqrt{1 + \frac{1}{n} + \frac{(x_t - \bar{x})^2}{\sum_{t=1}^{n}(x_t - \bar{x})^2}} \qquad \text{(prediction interval for future } y_t\text{)}$$

You may recall from Chapter 12 that you can get a "quick" approximate 95 percent prediction interval by using $\hat{y}_t \pm 2\,SE$. However, for forecasts beyond the range of the observed data, you should use formula 14.9, which widens the confidence intervals when the time index is far from its historic mean.

Trendless or Erratic Data

What if the time series $y_1, y_2, \ldots, y_n$ is erratic or has no consistent trend? In such cases, there may be little point in fitting a trend. A conservative approach is to calculate a *moving average*. There are two main types of moving averages: trailing or centered. We will illustrate each.

Trailing Moving Average (*TMA*)

The simplest kind of moving average is the **trailing moving average** (**TMA**) over the last m periods.

$$\hat{y}_t = \frac{y_t + y_{t-1} + \cdots + y_{t-m+1}}{m} \qquad \text{(trailing moving average over } m \text{ periods)} \qquad \textbf{(14.10)}$$

The *TMA* smoothes the past fluctuations in the time-series, helping us see the pattern more clearly. The choice of m depends on the situation. A larger m yields a "smoother" *TMA*, but requires more data. The value of $\hat{y}_t$ may also be used as a forecast for period $t + 1$. Beyond the range of the observed data $y_1, y_2, \ldots, y_n$ there is no way to update the moving average, so it is best regarded as a *one-period-ahead forecast*.

Many drivers keep track of their fuel economy. For a given vehicle, there is likely to be little trend over time, but there is always random fluctuation. Also, current driving conditions (e.g., snow, hot weather, road trips) could temporarily affect mileage over several consecutive time periods. In this situation, a moving average might be considered. Table 14.12 shows

EXAMPLE

Fuel Economy

TABLE 14.12   Andrew's Miles Per Gallon ($n = 20$)   AndrewsMPG

Obs	Date	Miles Driven	Gallons	MPG	TMA	CMA
1	5-Jan	285	11.324	25.168		
2	7-Jan	185	8.731	21.189		23.074
3	11-Jan	250	10.934	22.864	23.074	22.815
4	15-Jan	296	12.135	24.392	22.815	22.905
5	19-Jan	232	10.812	21.458	22.905	23.326
6	25-Jan	301	12.475	24.128	23.326	22.158
7	30-Jan	285	13.645	20.887	22.158	22.581
8	3-Feb	263	11.572	22.727	22.581	22.747
9	7-Feb	250	10.152	24.626	22.747	23.856
10	14-Feb	307	12.678	24.215	23.856	23.283
11	22-Feb	242	11.520	21.007	23.283	22.942
12	29-Feb	288	12.201	23.605	22.942	22.937
13	5-Mar	285	11.778	24.198	22.937	24.103
14	8-Mar	313	12.773	24.505	24.103	22.638
15	13-Mar	283	14.732	19.210	22.638	23.330
16	18-Mar	318	12.103	26.274	23.330	21.620
17	22-Mar	195	10.064	19.376	21.620	23.746
18	28-Mar	320	12.506	25.588	23.746	22.904
19	2-Apr	270	11.369	23.749	22.904	23.910
20	12-Apr	259	11.566	22.393	23.910	

Source: Data were collected by statistics student Andrew Fincher for his 11-year-old Pontiac Bonneville 3.8L V6.

Andrew's fuel economy data set. Column six shows a three-period *TMA*. For example, for period 6 (yellow-shaded cells) the *TMA* is

$$\hat{y}_6 = \frac{24.392 + 21.458 + 24.128}{3} = 23.326$$

It is easiest to appreciate the moving average's "smoothing" of the data when it is displayed on a graph, as in Figure 14.20. It is clear that Andrew's mean is around 23 mpg, though the moving average fluctuates over a range of approximately ±2 mpg.

FIGURE 14.20

Three-period moving average of MPG

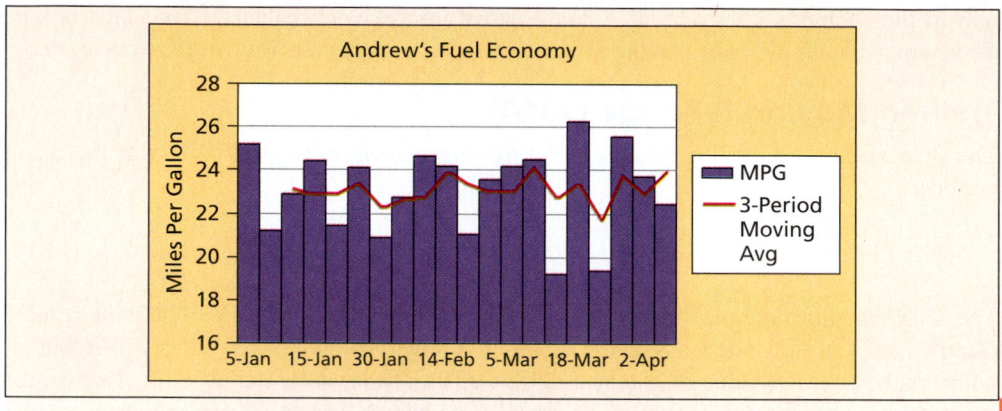

Centered Moving Average (*CMA*)

Another moving average is the ***centered moving average* (*CMA*)**. Formula 14.11 shows a *CMA* for $m = 3$ periods. The formula looks both forward *and* backward in time, to express the current "forecast" as the mean of the current observation *and* observations on either side of the current data.

(14.11) $$\hat{y}_t = \frac{y_{t-1} + y_t + y_{t+1}}{3}$$ (centered moving average over *m* periods)

This is not really a forecast at all, but merely a way of smoothing the data. In Table 14.12, column seven shows the *CMA* for Andrew's MPG data. For example, for period 14 (blue-shaded cells) the *CMA* is

$$\hat{y}_t = \frac{24.198 + 24.505 + 19.210}{3} = 22.638$$

When *n* is odd ($m = 3$, 5, etc.) the *CMA* is easy to calculate. When *m* is even, the formula is more complex, because the mean of an even number of data points would lie *between* two data points and would not be correctly centered. Instead, we take a double moving average (yipe!) to get the resulting *CMA* centered properly. For example, for $m = 4$, we would average y_{t-1} through y_{t+1}, then average y_{t-1} through y_{t+2}, and finally average the two averages! You need not worry about this formula for now. It will be illustrated shortly in the context of seasonal data.

Using Excel for a TMA

Excel offers a *TMA* in its Add Trendline option when you click on a time-series line graph or bar chart. Its menus are displayed in Figure 14.21. The *TMA* is a conservative choice whenever you doubt that one of Excel's five other trend models (linear, logarithmic, polynomial, power, exponential) would be appropriate. However, Excel does *not* give you the option of making any forecasts with its moving average model.

FIGURE 14.21

Excel's moving average menus

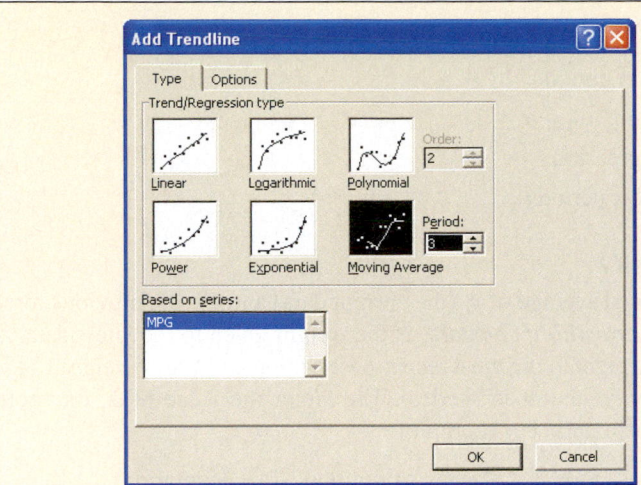
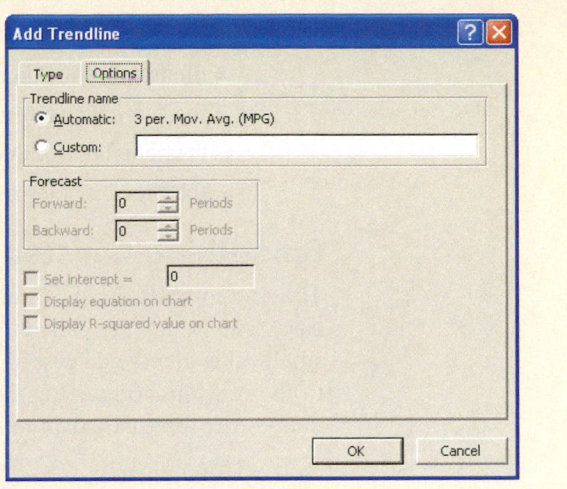

SECTION EXERCISES

14.6   (a) Make an Excel line graph of the exchange rate data. Describe the pattern. (b) Click on the data and choose Add Trendline > Moving Average. Describe the effect of increasing m (e.g., $m = 2, 4, 6$, etc.). Include a copy of each graph with your answer. (c) Discuss how this moving average might help a currency speculator.   **DollarEuro**

Daily Dollar/Euro Exchange Rate for First 3 Months of 2005 ($n = 64$ days)

Date	Rate	Date	Rate	Date	Rate	Date	Rate
3-Jan	1.3476	25-Jan	1.2954	16-Feb	1.2994	10-Mar	1.3409
4-Jan	1.3295	26-Jan	1.3081	17-Feb	1.3083	11-Mar	1.3465
5-Jan	1.3292	27-Jan	1.3032	18-Feb	1.3075	14-Mar	1.3346
6-Jan	1.3187	28-Jan	1.3033	21-Feb	1.3153	15-Mar	1.3315
7-Jan	1.3062	31-Jan	1.3049	22-Feb	1.3230	16-Mar	1.3423
10-Jan	1.3109	1-Feb	1.3017	23-Feb	1.3208	17-Mar	1.3373
11-Jan	1.3161	2-Feb	1.3015	24-Feb	1.3205	18-Mar	1.3311
12-Jan	1.3281	3-Feb	1.2959	25-Feb	1.3195	21-Mar	1.3165
13-Jan	1.3207	4-Feb	1.2927	28-Feb	1.3274	22-Mar	1.3210
14-Jan	1.3106	7-Feb	1.2773	1-Mar	1.3189	23-Mar	1.3005
17-Jan	1.3075	8-Feb	1.2783	2-Mar	1.3127	24-Mar	1.2957
18-Jan	1.3043	9-Feb	1.2797	3-Mar	1.3130	25-Mar	1.2954
19-Jan	1.3036	10-Feb	1.2882	4-Mar	1.3244	28-Mar	1.2877
20-Jan	1.2959	11-Feb	1.2864	7-Mar	1.3203	29-Mar	1.2913
21-Jan	1.3049	14-Feb	1.2981	8-Mar	1.3342	30-Mar	1.2944
24-Jan	1.3041	15-Feb	1.2986	9-Mar	1.3384	31-Mar	1.2969

Source: www.federalreserve.gov.

Forecast Updating

14.5

EXPONENTIAL SMOOTHING

The *exponential smoothing* model is a special kind of moving average. It is used for ongoing one-period-ahead forecasting for data that has up-and-down movements but no consistent trend. For example, a retail outlet may place orders for thousands of different stock-keeping units (SKUs) each week, so as to maintain its inventory of each item at the desired level (to avoid emergency calls to warehouses or suppliers). For such forecasts, many firms choose exponential smoothing, a simple forecasting model with only two inputs and one constant. The updating formula for the forecasts is

(14.12) $F_{t+1} = \alpha y_t + (1 - \alpha)F_t$ (smoothing update)

where

F_{t+1} = the forecast for the next period

α = the "smoothing constant" $(0 \leq \alpha \leq 1)$

y_t = the actual data value in period t

F_t = the previous forecast for period t

Smoothing Constant (α)

The next forecast F_{t+1} is a weighted average of y_t (the current data) and F_t (the previous forecast). The value of α, called the *smoothing constant,* is the weight given to the latest data. A small value of α would give low weight to the most recent observation and heavy weight $1 - \alpha$ to the previous forecast (a "heavily smoothed" series). The larger the value of α, the more quickly the forecasts adapt to recent data. For example,

If $\alpha = .05$, then $F_{t+1} = .05y_t + .95F_t$ (heavy smoothing, slow adaptation)

If $\alpha = .20$, then $F_{t+1} = .20y_t + .80F_t$ (moderate smoothing, moderate adaptation)

If $\alpha = .50$, then $F_{t+1} = .50y_t + .50F_t$ (little smoothing, quick adaptation)

Choosing the Value of α

If $\alpha = 1$, there is no smoothing at all, and the forecast for next period is the same as the latest data point, which basically defeats the purpose of exponential smoothing. MINITAB uses $\alpha = .20$ (i.e., moderate smoothing) as its default, which is a fairly common choice of α. The fit of the forecasts to the data will change as you try different values of α. Most computer packages can, as an option, solve for the "best" α using a criterion such as minimum *SSE*.

Over time, earlier data values have less effect on the exponential smoothing forecasts than more recent y-values. To see this, we can replace F_t in equation 14.12 with the prior forecast F_{t-1}, and repeat this type of substitution indefinitely to obtain this result:

(14.13) $F_{t+1} = \alpha y_t + \alpha(1 - \alpha)y_{t-1} + \alpha(1 - \alpha)^2 y_{t-2} + \alpha(1 - \alpha)^3 y_{t-3} + \cdots$

We see that the next forecast F_{t+1} depends on *all* the prior data (y_{t-1}, y_{t-2}, etc). As long as $\alpha < 1$, as we go farther into the past, each prior data value has less and less impact on the current forecast.

Initializing the Process

From equation 14.12, we see that F_{t+1} depends on F_t, which in turn depends on F_{t-1}, and so on, all the way back to F_1. But where do we get F_1 (the initial forecast)? There are many ways to initialize the forecasting process. For example, Excel simply sets the initial forecast equal to the first actual data value:

Method A

Set $F_1 = y_1$ (use the first data value)

This method has the advantage of simplicity, but if y_1 happens to be unusual, it could take a few iterations for the forecasts to stabilize. Another approach is to set the initial forecast equal to the average of the first several observed data values. For example, MINITAB uses the first six data values:

Method B

Set $F_1 = \dfrac{y_1 + y_2 + y_3 + y_4 + y_5 + y_6}{n}$ (average of first 6 data values)

This method tends to iron out the effects of unusual y-values, but it consumes more data and is still vulnerable to unusual y-values.

Method C

Set $F_1 = $ prediction from *backcasting* (backward extrapolation)

You may think of this method as fitting a trend to the data *in reverse time order* and extrapolating the trend to "predict" the initial value in the series. This method is common because it tends to generate a more appropriate initial forecast F_1. However, backcasting requires special software, so it will not be discussed here.

↘   Table 14.13 shows weekly sales of deck sealer (a paint product sold in gallon containers) at a large do-it-yourself warehouse-style retailer. For exponential smoothing forecasts, the company uses $\alpha = .10$. Its choice of α is based on experience. Since α is fairly small, it will provide strong smoothing. The last two columns compare the two methods of initializing the forecasts. Unusually high sales in week 5 have a strong effect on method *B*'s starting point. At first, the difference in forecasts is striking, but over time the methods converge.

EXAMPLE

Weekly Sales Data

TABLE 14.13   **Deck Sealer Sales: Exponential Smoothing ($n = 18$ weeks)**
🔖 **DeckSealer**

Week	Sales in Gallons	Method A: $F_1 = y_1$	Method B: $F_1 = $ Average (1st 6)
1	106	106.000	127.833
2	110	106.000	125.650
3	108	106.400	124.085
4	97	106.560	122.477
5	210	105.604	119.929
6	136	116.044	128.936
7	128	118.039	129.642
8	134	119.035	129.478
9	107	120.532	129.930
10	123	119.179	127.637
11	139	119.561	127.174
12	140	121.505	128.356
13	144	123.354	129.521
14	94	125.419	130.969
15	108	122.277	127.272
16	168	120.849	125.344
17	179	125.564	129.610
18	120	130.908	134.549

Smoothed forecasts using $\alpha = .10$.

Using Method A:

$$F_2 = \alpha y_1 + (1 - \alpha)F_1 = (.10)(106) + (.90)(106) = 106$$
$$F_3 = \alpha y_2 + (1 - \alpha)F_2 = (.10)(110) + (.90)(106) = 106.4$$
$$F_4 = \alpha y_3 + (1 - \alpha)F_3 = (.10)(108) + (.90)(106.4) = 106.56$$
$$\vdots$$
$$F_{19} = \alpha y_{18} + (1 - \alpha)F_{18} = (.10)(120) + (.90)(130.908) = 129.82$$

Using Method B:

$$F_2 = \alpha y_1 + (1 - \alpha)F_1 = (.10)(106) + (.90)(127.833) = 125.650$$
$$F_3 = \alpha y_2 + (1 - \alpha)F_2 = (.10)(110) + (.90)(125.650) = 124.085$$
$$F_4 = \alpha y_3 + (1 - \alpha)F_3 = (.10)(108) + (.90)(124.085) = 122.477$$
$$\vdots$$
$$F_{19} = \alpha y_{18} + (1 - \alpha)F_{18} = (.10)(120) + (.90)(134.549) = 133.094$$

Despite their different starting points, the forecasts for period 19 do not differ greatly. Rounding to the next higher integer, for week 19, the firm would order 130 gallons (using method *A*) or 134 gallons (using method *B*). Figures 14.22 and 14.23 show the similarity in *patterns* of the forecasts, although the *level* of forecasts is always higher in method *B* because of its higher initial value. This demonstrates that the choice of starting values *does* affect the forecasts.

FIGURE 14.22

Using the first *y*-value

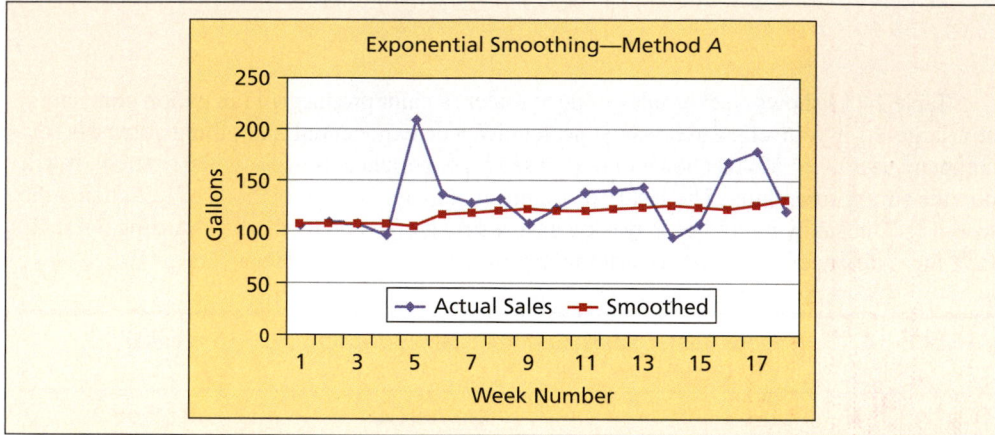

FIGURE 14.23

Averaging the first six *y*-values

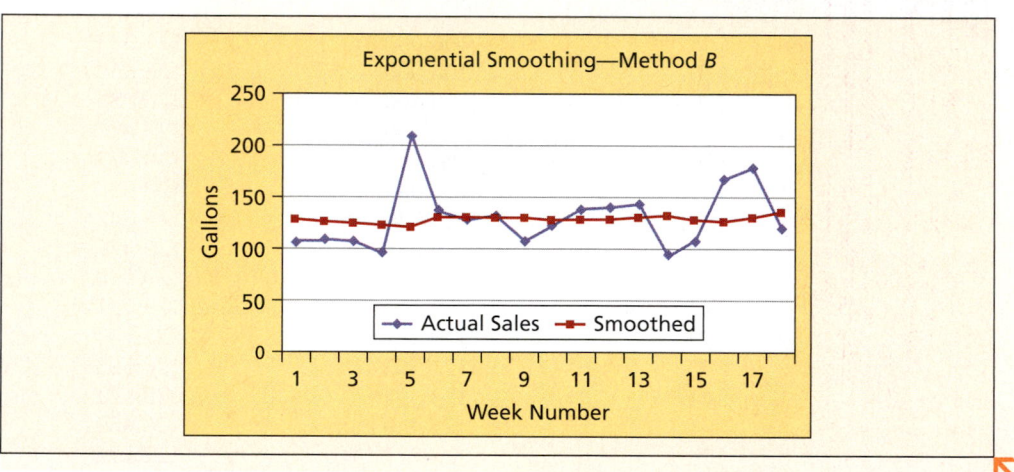

Using MINITAB

Figure 14.24 shows MINITAB's single exponential smoothing and 4 weeks' forecasts. After week 18, the exponential smoothing method cannot be updated with actual data, so the forecasts are constant. The wide 95 percent confidence intervals reflect the rather erratic past sales pattern.

FIGURE 14.24

MINITAB's exponential smoothing

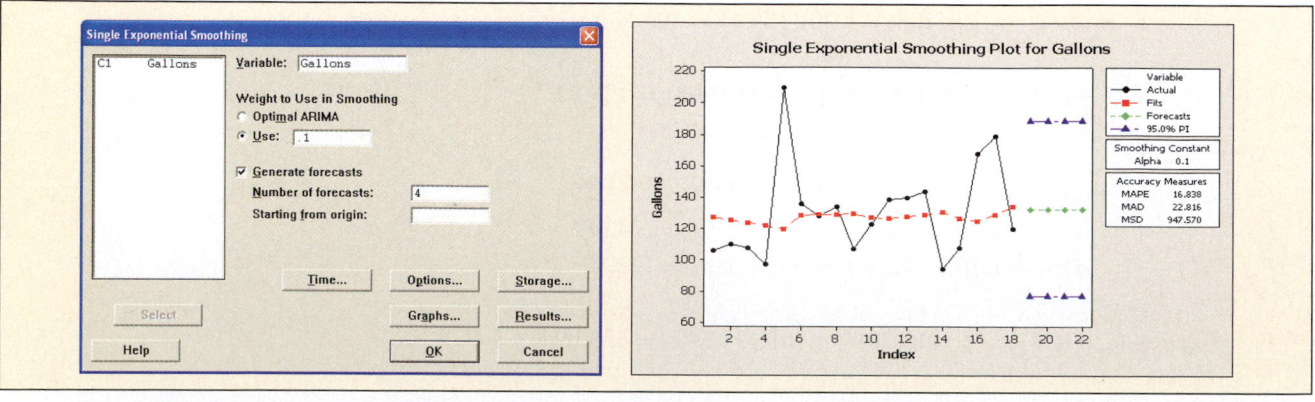

Using Excel

Excel also has an exponential smoothing option. It is found in Data Analysis under the Tools menu. One difference to be noted is that Excel asks for a *damping factor,* which is equal to $1 - \alpha$. Excel uses method A to initialize the exponential smoothing forecasts. Figure 14.25 shows Excel's exponential smoothing dialogue box and a line chart of the actual values and forecast values. Notice that there are no forecast values beyond period 18 and that there are no confidence intervals as with MINITAB.

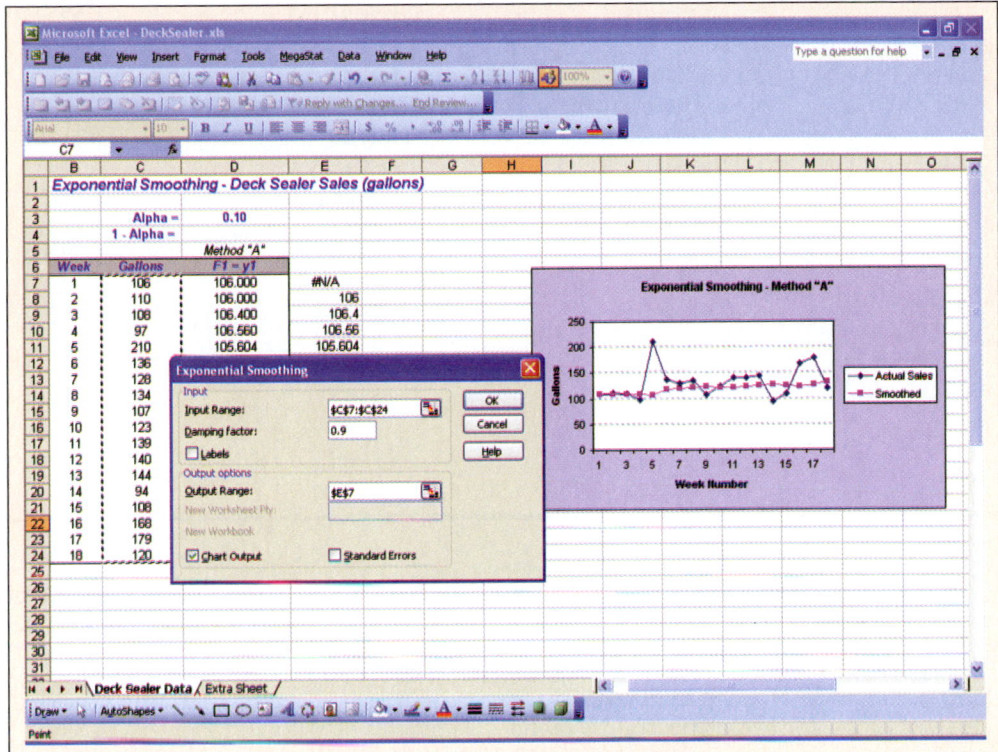

FIGURE 14.25

Excel's exponential smoothing

Smoothing with Trend and Seasonality

Single exponential smoothing is intended for *trendless* data. If your data have a trend, you can try *Holt's method* with *two* smoothing constants (one for *trend,* one for *level*). If you have both trend and seasonality, you can try *Winters's method* with *three* smoothing constants (one for *trend,* one for *level,* one for *seasonality*). These advanced methods are similar to single smoothing in that they use simple formulas to update the forecasts, and you may use them without special caution. *LearningStats* contains examples, explanations, and applications of these methods. Since these topics are usually reserved for a class in forecasting, they will not be explained here.

Mini Case   14.2

Exchange Rates

We have data for March 1 to March 30 and want to forecast 1 day ahead to March 31 by using exponential smoothing. We choose a smoothing constant value of $\alpha = .20$ and set the initial forecast F_1 to the average of the first six data values. Table 14.14 shows the actual data (y_t) and MINITAB's forecasts (F_t) for each date. The March 31 forecast is $F_{23} = \alpha y_{22} + (1 - \alpha) F_{22} = (.20)(1.2164) + (.80)(1.21395) = 1.2144$.

t	Date	y_t	F_t
1	1-Mar-05	1.2425	1.23450
2	2-Mar-05	1.2395	1.23610
3	3-Mar-05	1.2463	1.23678
4	4-Mar-05	1.2324	1.23868
5	7-Mar-05	1.2300	1.23743
6	8-Mar-05	1.2163	1.23594
7	9-Mar-05	1.2064	1.23201
8	10-Mar-05	1.2050	1.22689
9	11-Mar-05	1.2041	1.22251
10	14-Mar-05	1.2087	1.21883
11	15-Mar-05	1.2064	1.21680
12	16-Mar-05	1.2038	1.21472
13	17-Mar-05	1.2028	1.21254
14	18-Mar-05	1.2027	1.21059
15	21-Mar-05	1.2110	1.20901
16	22-Mar-05	1.2017	1.20941
17	23-Mar-05	1.2133	1.20787
18	24-Mar-05	1.2150	1.20895
19	25-Mar-05	1.2180	1.21016
20	28-Mar-05	1.2234	1.21173
21	29-Mar-05	1.2135	1.21406
22	30-Mar-05	1.2164	1.21395
23	31-Mar-05		1.21444

TABLE 14.14   Exchange Rate Canada/U.S. Dollar    Canada

Source: www.federalreserve.gov.

Figure 14.26 shows MINITAB's plot of the data and forecasts. The forecasts adapt, but always with a lag. The actual exchange rate on March 31 was 1.2094, slightly lower than the forecast, but well within the 95 percent prediction limits.

FIGURE 14.26

MINITAB's exponential smoothing ($\alpha = .20$)

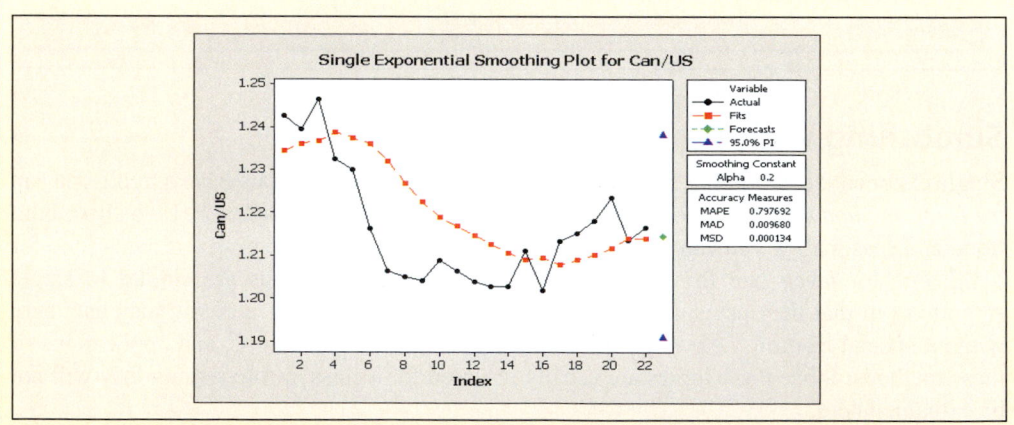

SECTION EXERCISES

14.7 (a) Make an Excel line graph of the following bond yield data. Describe the pattern. Is there a consistent trend? (b) Use exponential smoothing (MegaStat, MINITAB, or Excel) with $\alpha = .20$. Use both methods *A* and *B* to initialize the forecast (the default in both MegaStat and MINITAB). (c) Record the statistics of fit (MegaStat uses *MSE* and *MSD,* MINITAB uses *MSD* and *MAPE*). With Excel you will have to calculate these by creating cell formulas). (d) Do the smoothing again with $\alpha = .10$ and then with $\alpha = .30$, recording the statistics of fit. (e) Compare the statistics of fit for the three values of α. (f) Make a one-period forecast (i.e., $t = 53$) using each of the three α values. How did α affect your forecasts?   **BondYield**

U.S. Treasury 10-Year Bond Yields at Week's End (*n* = 52 weeks)

Week	Yield	Week	Yield	Week	Yield	Week	Yield
4/2/04	3.95	7/2/04	4.63	10/1/04	4.10	12/31/04	4.29
4/9/04	4.21	7/9/04	4.49	10/8/04	4.20	1/7/05	4.28
4/16/04	4.36	7/16/04	4.47	10/15/04	4.08	1/14/05	4.25
4/23/04	4.43	7/23/04	4.46	10/22/04	4.03	1/21/05	4.19
4/30/04	4.49	7/30/04	4.56	10/29/04	4.05	1/28/05	4.19
5/7/04	4.62	8/6/04	4.41	11/5/04	4.12	2/4/05	4.14
5/14/04	4.81	8/13/04	4.28	11/12/04	4.22	2/11/05	4.06
5/21/04	4.74	8/20/04	4.23	11/19/04	4.17	2/18/05	4.16
5/28/04	4.68	8/27/04	4.25	11/26/04	4.20	2/25/05	4.28
6/4/04	4.74	9/3/04	4.19	12/3/04	4.35	3/4/05	4.37
6/11/04	4.80	9/10/04	4.21	12/10/04	4.19	3/11/05	4.45
6/18/04	4.75	9/17/04	4.14	12/17/04	4.16	3/18/05	4.51
6/25/04	4.69	9/24/04	4.04	12/24/04	4.21	3/25/05	4.59

Source: www.federalreserve.gov.

When and How to Deseasonalize

When the data periodicity is monthly or quarterly we should calculate a seasonal index and use it to *deseasonalize* the data (annual data have no seasonality). For a multiplicative model (the usual assumption) a seasonal index is a *ratio*. For example, if the seasonal index for July is 1.25, it means that July is 125 percent of the monthly average. If the seasonal index for January is 0.84, it means that January is 84 percent of the monthly average. If the seasonal index for October is 1.00, it means that October is an average month. The seasonal indexes must sum to 12 for monthly data or 4 for quarterly data. The following steps are used to deseasonalize data for time-series observations:

- Step 1   Calculate a centered moving average (*CMA*) for each month (quarter).
- Step 2   Divide each observed y_t value by the *CMA* to obtain seasonal ratios.
- Step 3   Average the seasonal ratios by month (quarter) to get raw seasonal indexes.
- Step 4   Adjust the raw seasonal indexes so they sum to 12 (monthly) or 4 (quarterly).
- Step 5   Divide each y_t by its seasonal index to get deseasonalized data.

In step 1, we lose 12 observations (monthly data) or 4 observations (quarterly data) because of the centering process. We will illustrate this technique for quarterly data.

Illustration of Calculations

Table 14.15 shows 6 years' data on quarterly revenue from sales of carpeting, tile, wood, and vinyl flooring by a floor-covering retailer. The data have an upward trend (see Figure 14.27), perhaps due to a boom in consumer spending on home improvement and new homes. There also appears to be seasonality, with lower sales in the third quarter (summer) and higher sales in the first quarter (winter).

Quarter	2000	2001	2002	2003	2004	2005
1	259	306	379	369	515	626
2	236	300	262	373	373	535
3	164	189	242	255	339	397
4	222	275	296	374	519	488

TABLE 14.15
Sales of Floor Covering Materials ($ thousands)
FloorSales

The seasonal decomposition of this data is shown in Table 14.16 and Figure 14.27. Calculations are handled automatically by *MegaStat* so it's actually easy to perform the decomposition. Since the number of subperiods (quarters) is even ($m = 4$) each value of the *CMA* is the average of two averages. For example, the first *CMA* value 226.125 is the average of $(259 + 236 + 164 + 222)/4$ and $(236 + 164 + 222 + 306)/4$. Table 14.17 shows how the indexes are averaged. The *CMA* loses two quarters at the beginning and two quarters at the end, so each seasonal index is an average of only five quarters (instead of six). Each mean is then adjusted to force the sum to be 4.000, and these become the seasonal indexes. If we had monthly data, the indexes would be adjusted so that their sum would be 12.000.

TABLE 14.16

Calculation of
Deseasonalized Sales
(n = 24 quarters)
🦅 **FloorSales**

Obs	Year	Quarter	Sales	CMA	Sales/CMA	Seasonal Index	Deseasonalized
1	2000	1	259			1.252	206.9
2		2	236			1.021	231.1
3		3	164	*226.125*	0.725	0.740	221.7
4		4	222	240.000	0.925	0.987	224.9
5	2001	1	306	251.125	1.219	1.252	244.4
6		2	300	260.875	1.150	1.021	293.8
7		3	189	276.625	0.683	0.740	255.5
8		4	275	281.000	0.979	0.987	278.6
9	2002	1	379	282.875	1.340	1.252	302.7
10		2	262	292.125	0.897	1.021	256.6
11		3	242	293.500	0.825	0.740	327.2
12		4	296	306.125	0.967	0.987	299.8
13	2003	1	369	321.625	1.147	1.252	294.7
14		2	373	333.000	1.120	1.021	365.3
15		3	255	361.000	0.706	0.740	344.7
16		4	374	379.250	0.986	0.987	378.8
17	2004	1	515	389.750	1.321	1.252	411.3
18		2	373	418.375	0.892	1.021	365.3
19		3	339	450.375	0.753	0.740	458.3
20		4	519	484.500	1.071	0.987	525.7
21	2005	1	626	512.000	1.223	1.252	500.0
22		2	535	515.375	1.038	1.021	524.0
23		3	397			0.740	536.7
24		4	488			0.987	494.3

FIGURE 14.27

MegaStat's
deseasonalized trend

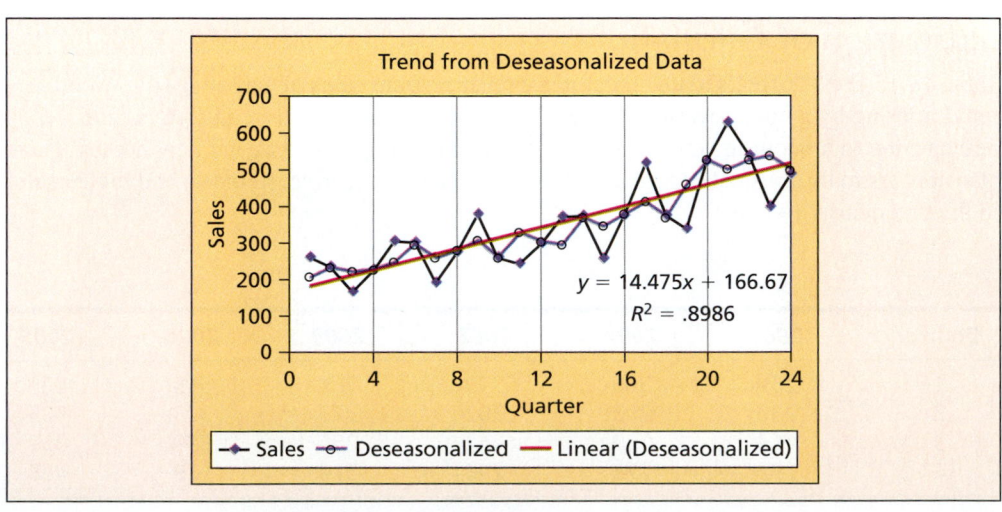

Trend from Deseasonalized Data

$y = 14.475x + 166.67$
$R^2 = .8986$

Quarter	2000	2001	2002	2003	2004	2005	Mean	Adjusted
1		1.219	1.340	1.147	1.321	1.223	1.250	1.252
2		1.150	0.897	1.120	0.892	1.038	1.019	1.021
3	0.725	0.683	0.825	0.706	0.753		0.738	0.740
4	0.925	0.979	0.967	0.986	1.071		0.986	0.987
							3.993	4.000

TABLE 14.17
Calculation of
Seasonal Indexes
FloorSales

Due to rounding, details may not yield the result shown.

After the data have been deseasonalized, the trend is fitted. Figure 14.27 shows the fitted trend from MegaStat, based on the deseasonalized data. The sharper peaks and valleys in the original time-series (Y) have been smoothed by removing the seasonality (S). Any remaining variation about the trend (T) is irregular (I) or "random noise."

Using MINITAB to Deseasonalize

MINITAB performs its deseasonalization in a similar way, although it averages the seasonal factors using *medians* instead of *means,* so the results are not exactly the same as MegaStat's. For example, using the same floor covering sales data:

Quarter	MegaStat's Seasonal Index	MINITAB's Seasonal Index
1	1.252	1.234
2	1.021	1.047
3	0.740	0.732
4	0.987	0.987
Sum	4.000	4.000
Fitted trend	$y_t = 166.67 + 14.475t$	$y_t = 166.62 + 14.483t$

MINITAB offers nice graphical displays for decomposition, as well as forecasts, as shown in Figure 14.28. MINITAB also offers additive as well as multiplicative seasonality. In an additive model, the *CMA* is calculated in the same way, but the raw seasonals are *differences* (instead of ratios) and the seasonal indexes are forced to sum to *zero* (e.g., months with higher sales must exactly balance months with lower sales). Since most analysts prefer multiplicative models (assuming trended data) the additive model is not discussed in detail here.

FIGURE 14.28

MINITAB's graphs for floor covering sales

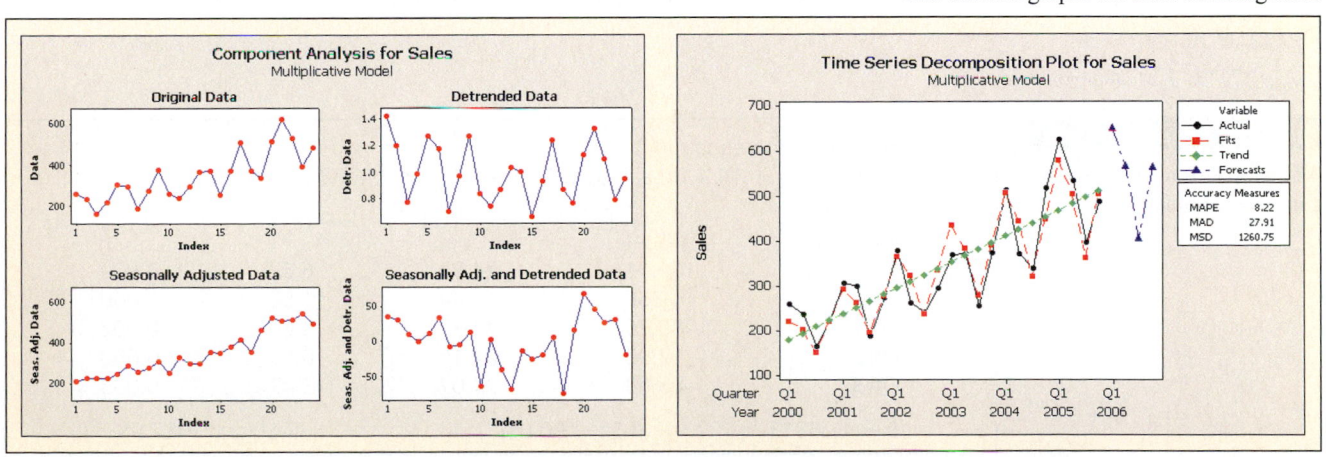

Chapter 19

Seasonal Forecasts Using Binary Predictors

Another way to address seasonality is to estimate a regression model using *seasonal binaries* as predictors. For quarterly data, for example, the data set would look as shown in Table 14.18. When we have four binaries (i.e., four quarters) we must exclude one binary to prevent perfect multicollinearity (see Chapter 13, Section 13.5). Arbitrarily, we exclude the fourth quarter binary $Qtr4$ (it will be a portion of the intercept when $Qtr1 = 0$ and $Qtr2 = 0$ and $Qtr3 = 0$).

TABLE 14.18

Sales Data with Seasonal Binaries

FloorSales

Year	Quarter	Sales	Time	Qtr1	Qtr2	Qtr3
2000	1	259	1	1	0	0
	2	236	2	0	1	0
	3	164	3	0	0	1
	4	222	4	0	0	0
2001	1	306	5	1	0	0
	2	300	6	0	1	0
	3	189	7	0	0	1
	4	275	8	0	0	0
2002	1	379	9	1	0	0
	2	262	10	0	1	0
	3	242	11	0	0	1
	4	296	12	0	0	0
2003	1	369	13	1	0	0
	2	373	14	0	1	0
	3	255	15	0	0	1
	4	374	16	0	0	0
2004	1	515	17	1	0	0
	2	373	18	0	1	0
	3	339	19	0	0	1
	4	519	20	0	0	0
2005	1	626	21	1	0	0
	2	535	22	0	1	0
	3	397	23	0	0	1
	4	488	24	0	0	0

We assume a linear trend, and specify the regression model *Sales* = f(*Time, Qtr1, Qtr2, Qtr3*). MINITAB's estimated regression is shown in Figure 14.29. This is an additive model of the form $Y = T + S + I$ (recall that we omit the cycle C in practice). The fitted equation is

$$Sales = 161 + 14.4 \ Time + 89.8 \ Qtr1 + 12.9 \ Qtr2 - 83.6 \ Qtr3$$

FIGURE 14.29

MINITAB's fitted regression for seasonal binaries

```
The regression equation is
Sales = 161 + 14.4 Time + 89.8 Qtr1 + 12.9 Qtr2 - 83.6 Qtr3

Predictor          Coef        SE Coef          T          P
Constant         161.21          24.33       6.62      0.000
Time             14.366           1.244      11.55      0.000
Qtr1             89.76           24.32        3.69      0.002
Qtr2             12.90           24.16        0.53      0.600
Qtr3            -83.63           24.07       -3.47      0.003

S = 41.6313          R-Sq = 90.0%           R-Sq(adj) = 87.9%
```

Time is a significant predictor ($p = .000$) indicating significant linear trend. Two of the binaries are significant: *Qtr1* ($p = .002$) and *Qtr3* ($p = .003$). The second quarter binary *Qtr2* ($p = .600$) is not significant. The model gives a good overall fit ($R^2 = .90$). The main virtue of the seasonal regression model is its versatility. We can plug in future values of *Time* and the seasonal binaries to create forecasts as far ahead as we wish. For example, the forecasts for 2006 are

Period 25: Sales $= 161 + 14.4(25) + 89.8(1) + 12.9(0) - 83.6(0) = 610.8$

Period 26: Sales $= 161 + 14.4(26) + 89.8(0) + 12.9(1) - 83.6(0) = 548.3$

Period 27: Sales $= 161 + 14.4(27) + 89.8(0) + 12.9(0) - 83.6(1) = 466.2$

Period 28: Sales $= 161 + 14.4(28) + 89.8(0) + 12.9(0) - 83.6(0) = 564.2$

SECTION EXERCISES

14.8   (a) Use MegaStat or MINITAB to deseasonalize the quarterly data on PepsiCo's revenues and fit a trend. Interpret the results. (b) Use MegaStat or MINITAB to perform a regression using seasonal binaries. Interpret the results. (c) Use the regression equation to make a prediction for each quarter in 2005. (d) If you have access to *Standard & Poor's Stock Reports, 2006,* check your forecasts. How accurate were they?   **PepsiCo**

PepsiCo Revenues ($ millions), 1998–2003

Quarter	1999	2000	2001	2002	2003	2004
1	5,114	4,191	5,330	5,101	5,530	6,131
2	4,982	4,928	6,713	6,178	6,538	7,070
3	4,591	4,909	6,906	6,376	6,830	7,257
4	5,680	6,410	7,986	7,457	8,073	8,803
Year	20,367	20,438	26,935	25,112	26,971	29,261

Source: *Standard & Poor's Stock Reports,* March 2005.

14.9   (a) Use MegaStat or MINITAB to deseasonalize the monthly Corvette sales data and fit a trend. Interpret the results. (b) Use MegaStat or MINITAB to perform a regression using seasonal binaries. Interpret the results. (c) Use the regression equation to make a prediction for each month in 2004. (d) If you have access to *Ward's Automotive Yearbook, 2005* (67th edition), check your forecasts. How accurate were they?   **Corvette**

U.S. Corvette Sales, 2000–2004 (number of cars sold)

Month	2000	2001	2002	2003
Jan	1,863	2,252	2,443	1,468
Feb	2,765	2,766	3,354	1,724
Mar	3,440	2,923	1,877	2,792
Apr	3,018	2,713	2,176	6,249
May	2,725	2,847	3,049	2,441
Jun	2,538	2,521	2,708	2,272
Jul	1,598	2,000	2,960	2,007
Aug	2,861	2,789	2,912	2,107
Sep	2,942	3,639	2,960	1,615
Oct	2,748	4,647	3,094	1,878
Nov	2,376	2,910	2,163	1,596
Dec	2,334	1,648	2,859	1,825
Total	31,208	33,655	32,555	27,974

Source: *Ward's Automotive Yearbook, 2001–2004.*

Mini Case   14.3

Beer Shipments 🍺 Beer

Table 14.19 shows U.S. beer shipments by month for 1995–2000. To analyze trend and seasonality, we create a regression data set with linear trend (*Time* = 1, 2, . . . , 72) and 11 seasonal binaries (e.g., *Jan* = 1 if it's January, 0 otherwise). The December binary is omitted to prevent perfect multicollinearity.

TABLE 14.19   U.S. Beer Shipments, 1995–2000 (thousands of gross) 🍺 Beer

Month	1995	1996	1997	1998	1999	2000
Jan	8,635	8,606	9,161	9,574	9,673	9,827
Feb	8,179	8,577	8,774	9,098	9,757	9,907
Mar	9,820	9,830	10,198	10,263	11,647	11,067
Apr	8,735	10,188	10,499	10,160	10,834	10,599
May	10,332	11,289	11,022	10,871	11,337	11,710
Jun	10,336	9,933	11,034	11,812	12,034	11,799
Jul	9,864	11,233	11,169	11,679	10,958	11,279
Aug	10,182	10,258	10,373	10,692	10,717	11,537
Sep	9,422	9,249	10,143	10,165	10,406	10,412
Oct	9,671	9,913	9,822	9,917	9,755	10,512
Nov	8,469	8,742	8,895	9,528	10,204	9,874
Dec	7,385	8,077	9,091	8,963	9,373	9,007
Total	111,030	115,895	120,181	122,722	126,695	127,530

Note: One gross equals 144 bottles.

Source: An independent project by statistics student Mai Lee using data from The U.S. Dept. of Commerce.

The regression results, shown in Figure 14.30, indicate a good fit ($R^2 = .892$), significant upward trend ($p = .000$ for *Time*), and significant seasonal binaries (all have very small p-values). The coefficients of the monthly binaries indicate high beer sales in May, June, and July, presumably because people drink more beer in hot weather.

FIGURE 14.30

MINITAB's fitted regression for seasonal binaries

The regression equation is
Beer = 7671 + 23.3 Time + 853 Jan + 632 Feb + 2031 Mar + 1706 Apr
    + 2607 May + 2648 Jun + 2498 Jul + 2070 Aug + 1387 Sep
    + 1329 Oct + 659 Nov

Predictor	Coef	SE Coef	T	P
Constant	7670.7	172.4	44.50	0.000
Time	23.302	2.090	11.15	0.000
Jan	853.0	211.1	4.04	0.000
Feb	632.4	210.8	3.00	0.004
Mar	2031.2	210.6	9.64	0.000
Apr	1706.2	210.5	8.11	0.000
May	2607.3	210.3	12.40	0.000
Jun	2648.5	210.2	12.60	0.000
Jul	2497.5	210.1	11.89	0.000
Aug	2070.4	210.0	9.86	0.000
Sep	1386.7	209.9	6.61	0.000
Oct	1328.9	209.8	6.33	0.000
Nov	659.3	209.8	3.14	0.003

S = 363.379   R-Sq = 89.2%   R-Sq (adj) = 87.0%

Role of Forecasting

In many ways, forecasting resembles planning. *Forecasting* is an analytical way to describe a "what-if" future that might confront the organization. *Planning* is the organization's attempt to determine a set of actions it will take under each foreseeable contingency. Forecasts help decision makers become aware of trends or patterns that will require a response. Actions taken by the decision makers may actually head off the contingency envisioned in the forecast. Thus, forecasts tend to be self-defeating because they trigger homeostatic organizational responses.

Behavioral Aspects of Forecasting

Forecasts can facilitate organizational communication. The forecast (or even just a nicely prepared time-series chart) lets everyone examine the same facts concurrently, and perhaps argue with the data or the assumptions that underlie the forecast or its relevance to the organization. A quantitative forecast helps *make assumptions explicit*. Those who prepare the forecast must explain and defend their assumptions, while others must challenge them. In the process, everyone gains understanding of the data, the underlying realities, and the imperfections in the data. Forecasts *focus the dialogue* and can make it more productive.

Of course, this assumes a certain maturity among the individuals around the table. Strong leaders (or possibly meeting facilitators) can play a role in guiding the discourse to produce a positive result. The danger is that people may try to find scapegoats (yes, they do tend to blame the forecaster), deny facts, or avoid responsibility for tough decisions. But one premise of this book is that statistics, when done well, can strengthen any dialogue and lead to better decisions.

Forecasts Are Always Wrong

We discussed several measures to use to determine if a forecast model fits the time series. Successful forecasters understand that a forecast is never precise. There is always some error, but we can *use* the error measures to track forecast error. Many companies use several different forecasting models and rely on the model that has had the least error over some time period. We have described simple models in this chapter. You may take a class specifically focusing on forecasting in which you will learn about other time-series models including AR (autoregressive) models. AR models take advantage of the dependency that might exist between values in the time series, and belong to a class of models called ARIMA (autoregressive integrated moving average) models.

To ensure good forecast outcomes

- Maintain up-to-date databases of *relevant* data.
- Allow sufficient lead time to analyze the data.
- State several alternative forecasts or scenarios.
- Track forecast errors over time.
- State your assumptions and qualifications.
- Bear in mind the purpose of the forecasts.
- Consider the time horizon for the decision.
- Don't underestimate the power of a good graph.

There is always a role for "judgment" forecasts when time is short, patterns are unclear, or you have erratic or low-quality data. Watch out for unbelievable forecasts—they may be telling you that something is wrong somewhere. Don't try to dazzle people with equations that are not helpful. Consider ignoring the earlier part of the time-series if the series is long. And remember the principle of Occam's Razor.

Principle of Occam's Razor

Given two *sufficient* explanations, we prefer the simpler one.
    William of Occam (1285–1347)

Chapter Summary

A **time series** is assumed to have four components. For most business data, **trend** is the general pattern of change over all years observed while **cycle** is a repetitive pattern of change around the trend over several years and **seasonality** is a repetitive pattern within a year. The **irregular** component is a random disturbance that follows no pattern. The **additive model** is adequate in the short run because the four components' magnitude does not change much, but for observations over longer periods of time, the **multiplicative model** is preferred. Common trend models include **linear** (constant slope and no turning point), **quadratic** (one turning point), and **exponential** (constant percent growth or decline). Higher polynomial models are untrustworthy and liable to give strange forecasts, though any trend model is less reliable the farther out it is projected. In forecasting, forecasters use fit measures besides R^2, such as mean absolute percent error (**MAPE**), mean absolute deviation (**MAD**), and mean squared deviation (**MSD**). For trendless or erratic data, we use a **moving average** over m periods or **exponential smoothing.** Forecasts adapt rapidly to changing data when the **smoothing constant** α is large (near 1) and conversely for a small α (near 0). For monthly or quarterly data, a **seasonal adjustment** is required before extracting the trend. Alternatively, regression with **seasonal binaries** can be used to capture seasonality and make forecasts.

Key Terms

centered moving average (CMA), *626*
coefficient of determination, *623*
cycle, *609*
deseasonalize, *633*
exponential smoothing, *609*
exponential trend, *612*
flow, *606*
irregular, *609*

linear trend, *610*
MAD, *623*
MAPE, *623*
moving average, *609*
MSD, *623*
Occam's Razor, *618*
periodicity, *607*
polynomial model, *617*
quadratic trend, *615*

seasonal, *609*
seasonal binaries, *636*
smoothing constant, *628*
standard error (SE), *623*
stock, *606*
time-series variable, *605*
trailing moving average (TMA), *625*
trend, *607*

Commonly Used Formulas

Additive time-series model: $Y = T + C + S + I$

Multiplicative time-series model: $Y = T \times C \times S \times I$

Linear trend model: $y_t = a + bt$

Exponential trend model: $y_t = ae^{bt}$

Quadratic trend model: $y_t = a + bt + ct^2$

Coefficient of determination: $R^2 = 1 - \dfrac{\sum\limits_{t=1}^{n}(y_t - \hat{y}_t)^2}{\sum\limits_{t=1}^{n}(y_t - \bar{y})^2}$

Mean absolute percent error: $MAPE = \dfrac{100}{n}\sum\limits_{t=1}^{n}\dfrac{|y_t - \hat{y}_t|}{y_t}$

Mean absolute deviation: $MAD = \dfrac{1}{n}\sum\limits_{t=1}^{n}|y_t - \hat{y}_t|$

Mean squared deviation: $MSD = \dfrac{1}{n}\sum\limits_{t=1}^{n}(y_t - \hat{y}_t)^2$

Standard error: $SE = \sqrt{\sum\limits_{t=1}^{n}\dfrac{(y_t - \hat{y}_t)^2}{n-2}}$

Forecast updating equation for exponential smoothing: $F_{t+1} = \alpha y_t + (1 - \alpha)F_t$

Note: Questions marked with an asterisk * refer to optional material.

1. Explain the difference between (a) stocks and flows; (b) cross-sectional and time-series data; (c) additive and multiplicative models.

2. (a) What is periodicity? (b) Give original examples of data with different periodicity.

3. (a) What are the distinguishing features of each component of a time series (trend, cycle, seasonal, irregular)? (b) Why is cycle usually ignored in time-series modeling?

4. Name four criteria for assessing a trend forecast.

5. Name two advantages and two disadvantages of each of the common trend models (linear, exponential, quadratic).

6. When would the exponential trend model be preferred to a linear trend model?

7. Explain how to obtain the compound percent growth rate from a fitted exponential model.

8. (a) When might a quadratic model be useful? (b) What precautions must be taken when forecasting with a quadratic model? (c) Why are higher-order polynomial models dangerous?

9. Name five measures of fit for a trend, and state their advantages and disadvantages.

10. (a) When do we use a moving average? (b) Name two types of moving averages. (c) When is a centered moving average harder to calculate?

11. (a) When is exponential smoothing most useful? (b) Interpret the smoothing constant α. What is its range? (c) What does a small α say about the degree of smoothing? A large α?

12. (a) Explain two ways to initialize the forecasts in an exponential smoothing process. (b) Name an advantage and a disadvantage of each method.

13. (a) Why is seasonality irrelevant for annual data? (b) List the steps in deseasonalizing a monthly time series. (c) What is the sum of a monthly seasonal index? A quarterly index?

14. (a) How can forecasting improve communication within an organization? (b) List five tips for ensuring effective forecasting outcomes.

*15. (a) Explain how seasonal binaries can be used to model seasonal data. (b) What is the advantage of using seasonal binaries?

*16. Explain the equivalency between the two forms of an exponential trend model.

CHAPTER EXERCISES

Instructions: For each exercise, use Excel, MegaStat, or MINITAB to make an attractive, well-labeled time-series line chart. Adjust the *Y*-axis scale if necessary to show more detail (since Excel usually starts the scale at zero). If a fitted trend is called for, use Excel's option to display the equation and R^2 statistic (or *MAPE, MAD,* and *MSD* in MINITAB). Include printed copies of all relevant graphs with your answers to each exercise.

14.10 (a) Choose *one* time-series describing Spirit Airlines and make a line chart. (b) Describe the trend (if any) and discuss possible causes. (c) Fit both a linear and an exponential trend to the data. (d) Which model is preferred? Why? (e) Make a forecast for 2003, using a trend model of your choice (or a judgment forecast). 🐦 **Spirit**

Growth of Spirit Airlines, 1998–2002

Year	Revenue ($ mil)	Aircraft	FT Employees
1998	131	14	860
1999	227	20	1,440
2000	311	24	1,729
2001	354	27	2,094
2002	403	28	2,345

Source: *Detroit Free Press,* August 21, 2003, p. F1.

14.11 (a) Plot both Swiss watch time series on the same graph. (b) Describe the trend (if any) and discuss possible causes. (c) Fit an exponential trend to each time series. (d) Interpret each fitted trend carefully. What conclusion do you draw? (e) Make forecasts for 2003, using the linear trend model. Do you feel confident in your forecasts? Explain. 🌐 **Swiss**

Swiss Watch Exports (thousands of units), 1998–2003

Year	Mechanical	Electronic
1998	2,558	29,678
1999	2,526	28,766
2000	2,549	27,313
2001	2,580	23,811
2002	2,722	24,107
2003	2,718	21,864

Source: Fédération de L'Industrie Horlogère Suisse, Swiss Watch Exports, www.fhs.ch.

14.12 (a) Plot the total minutes of TV viewing time per household. (b) Describe the trend (if any) and discuss possible causes. (c) Fit a linear trend to the data. (d) Would this model give reasonable forecasts? Would another trend model be better? Explain. (e) Make a forecast for 2005. Check the forecast if you have access to the Web. Show the forecast calculations. (f) Would this data ever approach an asymptote? Explain. *Note:* Time is in 5-year increments, so use $t = 12$ for the 2005 forecast. 🌐 **Television**

Average Daily TV Viewing Time Per U.S. Household

Year	Hours	Min	Total Min
1950	4	35	275
1955	4	51	291
1960	5	6	306
1965	5	29	329
1970	5	56	356
1975	6	7	367
1980	6	36	396
1985	7	10	430
1990	6	53	413
1995	7	17	437
2000	7	35	455

Source: As published by the TVB based on Nielsen Media Research data. Used with permission.

14.13 (a) Plot the voter participation rate. (b) Describe the trend (if any) and discuss possible causes. (c) Fit both a linear and an exponential trend to the data. (d) Which model is preferred? Why? (e) Make a forecast for 2004, using a trend model of your choice (or a judgment forecast). (f) Check the Web for the actual 2004 voter participation rate. How close was your forecast? *Note:* Time is in 4-year increments, so use $t = 19$ for the 2004 forecast. 🌐 **Voters**

U.S. Presidential Election Voter Participation, 1932–2000

Year	Voting Age Population	Voted for President	% Voting Pres
1932	75,768	39,758	52.5
1936	80,174	45,654	56.9
1940	84,728	49,900	58.9
1944	85,654	47,977	56.0
1948	95,573	48,794	51.1
1952	99,929	61,551	61.6
1956	104,515	62,027	59.3
1960	109,672	68,838	62.8
1964	114,090	70,645	61.9
1968	120,285	73,212	60.9
1972	140,777	77,719	55.2
1976	152,308	81,556	53.5
1980	163,945	86,515	52.8
1984	173,995	92,653	53.3
1988	181,956	91,595	50.3
1992	189,524	104,425	55.1
1996	196,928	96,278	49.0
2000	207,884	105,397	50.7

Source: *Statistical Abstract of the United States, 2001,* www.census.gov.

14.14 (a) Plot the market-share data. (b) Describe the trend (if any) and discuss possible causes. (c) Fit three trends (linear, exponential, quadratic). (d) Which trend model is best, and why? If none is satisfactory, explain. (e) Make a forecast for 2004 by using a trend model of your choice or a judgment forecast.   **Trucks**

Asian and European Share of U.S. Light Truck Sales, 1990–2003

Year	Percent	Year	Percent
1990	16.4	1997	15.4
1991	17.1	1998	16.2
1992	14.3	1999	18.4
1993	13.7	2000	21.2
1994	14.2	2001	23.1
1995	13.6	2002	23.9
1996	13.6	2003	26.6

Source: *Detroit Free Press,* November 19, 2003, p. 1A.

14.15 (a) Choose *one* category of consumer credit and plot it. (b) Describe the trend (if any) and discuss possible causes. (c) Fit a trend model of your choice. (d) Make a forecast for 2004, using a trend model of your choice. *Note:* Revolving credit is mostly credit card and home equity loans, while nonrevolving credit is for a specific purchase such as a car.   **Consumer**

Consumer Credit Outstanding, 1994–2003 ($ billions)

Year	Total	Revolving	Nonrevolving
1995	1,141	443	698
1996	1,242	499	743
1997	1,305	522	783
1998	1,400	563	837
1999	1,513	590	922
2000	1,686	659	1,027
2001	1,822	704	1,118
2002	1,903	717	1,186
2003	2,002	745	1,257

Source: *Statistical Abstract of the United States, 2004.*

14.16 (a) Plot the data on U.S. general aviation shipments. (b) Describe the pattern and discuss possible causes. (c) Would a fitted trend be helpful? Explain. (d) Make a similar graph for 1992–2003 only. Would a fitted trend be helpful in making a prediction for 2004? (e) Fit a trend model of your choice to the 1992–2003 data. (f) Make a forecast for 2004, using either the fitted trend model or a judgment forecast. Why is it best to ignore earlier years in this data set? 🐦 **Airplanes**

U.S. Manufactured General Aviation Shipments, 1966–2003

Year	Planes	Year	Planes	Year	Planes	Year	Planes
1966	15,587	1976	15,451	1986	1,495	1996	1,053
1967	13,484	1977	16,904	1987	1,085	1997	1,482
1968	13,556	1978	17,811	1988	1,143	1998	2,115
1969	12,407	1979	17,048	1989	1,535	1999	2,421
1970	7,277	1980	11,877	1990	1,134	2000	2,714
1971	7,346	1981	9,457	1991	1,021	2001	2,538
1972	9,774	1982	4,266	1992	856	2002	2,169
1973	13,646	1983	2,691	1993	870	2003	2,090
1974	14,166	1984	2,431	1994	881		
1975	14,056	1985	2,029	1995	1,028		

Source: U.S. Manufactured General Aviation Shipments, *Statistical Databook 2003*, General Aviation Manufacturers Association, used with permission.

14.17 (a) Choose *one* beverage category and plot the data. (b) Describe the trend (if any) and discuss possible causes. (c) Would a fitted trend be helpful? Explain. (d) Fit several trend models. Which is best, and why? If none is satisfactory, explain. (e) Make a forecast for 2005, using a trend model of your choice or a judgment forecast. Discuss. *Note:* Time increments are 5 years, so use $t = 6$ for your 2005 forecast. 🐦 **Beverages**

U.S. Per Capita Annual Consumption of Selected Beverages (gallons)

Beverage	1980	1985	1990	1995	2000
Milk	27.6	26.7	25.7	23.9	22.5
Whole	17.0	14.3	10.5	8.6	8.1
Reduced-fat	10.5	12.3	15.2	15.3	14.4
Carbonated soft drinks	35.1	35.7	46.2	47.4	49.3
Diet	5.1	7.1	10.7	10.9	11.6
Regular	29.9	28.7	35.6	36.5	37.7
Fruit juices	7.4	7.8	7.8	8.3	8.7
Alcoholic	28.3	28.0	27.5	24.7	24.9
Beer	24.3	23.8	23.9	21.8	21.7
Wine	2.1	2.4	2.0	1.7	2.0
Distilled spirits	2.0	1.8	1.5	1.2	1.3

Source: *Statistical Abstract of the United States, 2003.*

14.18 (a) Plot *either* receipts and outlays *or* federal debt and GDP (plot both time series on the same graph). (b) Describe the trend (if any) and discuss possible causes. (c) Fit an exponential trend to each. (d) Interpret each fitted trend equation, explaining its implications. (e) To whom is this issue relevant? 🐦 **FedBudget**

U.S. Federal Finances, 1990–2004 ($ billions current)

Year	Receipts	Outlays	Federal Debt	GDP
1990	1,032	1,253	3,206	5,803
1991	1,055	1,324	3,598	5,996
1992	1,091	1,382	4,002	6,338
1993	1,154	1,410	4,351	6,657
1994	1,259	1,462	4,643	7,072
1995	1,352	1,516	4,921	7,398
1996	1,453	1,561	5,182	7,817
1997	1,579	1,601	5,369	8,304
1998	1,722	1,653	5,478	8,747
1999	1,828	1,702	5,606	9,268
2000	2,025	1,789	5,629	9,817
2001	1,991	1,863	5,770	10,128
2002	1,853	2,011	6,198	10,487
2003	1,782	2,160	6,760	11,004
2004	1,880	2,292	7,355	11,728

Source: *Economic Report of the President, 2004.*

14.19 (a) Plot both men's and women's winning times on the same graph. (b) Fit a linear trend model to each series. From the fitted trends, will the times eventually converge? *Hint:* Ask Excel for forecasts (e.g., 20 years ahead). (c) Make a copy of your graph, and click each fitted trend and change it to a moving average trend type. (d) Would a moving average be a reasonable approach to modeling these data sets? *Note:* The data file **Boston** has the data converted to decimal minutes.

Boston Marathon Champions, 1980–2005

Year	Men — Name of Winner	Time	Women — Name of Winner	Time
1980	Bill Rodgers	2:12:11	Jacqueline Gareau	2:34:28
1981	Toshihiko Seko	2:09:26	Allison Roe	2:26:46
1982	Alberto Salazar	2:08:52	Charlotte Teske	2:29:33
1983	Greg Meyer	2:09:00	Joan Benoit	2:22:43
1984	Geoff Smith	2:10:34	Lorraine Moller	2:29:30
1985	Geoff Smith	2:14:05	Lisa Larsen Weidenbach	2:34:10
1986	Robert de Castella	2:07:51	Ingrid Kristiansen	2:24:55
1987	Toshihiko Seko	2:11:50	Rosa Mota	2:25:21
1988	Ibrahim Hussein	2:08:43	Rosa Mota	2:24:30
1989	Abebe Mekonnen	2:09:06	Ingrid Kristiansen	2:24:33
1990	Gelindo Bordin	2:08:19	Rosa Mota	2:25:24
1991	Ibrahim Hussein	2:11:06	Wanda Panfil	2:24:18
1992	Ibrahim Hussein	2:08:14	Olga Markova	2:23:43
1993	Cosmas Ndeti	2:09:33	Olga Markova	2:25:27
1994	Cosmas Ndeti	2:07:15	Uta Pippig	2:21:45
1995	Cosmas Ndeti	2:09:22	Uta Pippig	2:25:11
1996	Moses Tanui	2:09:15	Uta Pippig	2:27:12
1997	Lameck Aguta	2:10:34	Fatuma Roba	2:26:23
1998	Moses Tanui	2:07:34	Fatuma Roba	2:23:21
1999	Joseph Chebet	2:09:52	Fatuma Roba	2:23:25
2000	Elijah Lagat	2:09:47	Catherine Ndereba	2:26:11
2001	Lee Bong-Ju	2:09:43	Catherine Ndereba	2:23:53
2002	Rodgers Rop	2:09:02	Margaret Okayo	2:20:43
2003	Robert Kipkoech Cheruiyot	2:10:11	Svetlana Zakharova	2:25:20
2004	Timothy Cherigat	2:10:37	Catherine Ndereba	2:24:27
2005	Hailu Negussie	2:11:45	Catherine Ndereba	2:25:13

Source: www.boston.com/marathon/history.

14.20 (a) Choose *either* commercial banks *or* savings institutions. On the same graph, plot both the main and branch data. (b) Fit a linear trend to each. (c) Interpret each fitted linear trend equation, explaining its implications for bank customers. (d) Make a copy of your graph, click each trend line, and change the trend type to exponential. (e) Interpret each fitted exponential trend. (f) Which is preferable, the linear or exponential trend model? 🐝 **FDIC**

Number of FDIC-Insured Financial Institutions, 1995–2003

Year	Commercial Banks			Savings Institutions		
	Banks	Main	Branches	Institutions	Main	Branches
1995	65,888	9,971	55,917	15,462	2,030	13,432
1996	66,810	9,553	57,258	15,767	1,926	13,841
1997	68,810	9,165	59,645	14,831	1,780	13,051
1998	70,052	8,793	61,259	14,535	1,690	12,845
1999	71,534	8,597	62,937	14,506	1,642	12,864
2000	71,911	8,331	63,580	14,041	1,589	12,452
2001	72,458	8,095	64,363	14,048	1,534	12,514
2002	74,072	7,887	66,185	13,765	1,467	12,298
2003	75,159	7,769	67,390	13,937	1,413	12,524

Source: *Statistical Abstract of the United States, 2004.*

14.21 (a) Plot the data on fractional ownership of aircraft (i.e., shared ownership of available flight time). (b) Describe the trend (if any) and discuss possible causes. *Hint:* If you do not know what fractional ownership of aircraft is, use Google. (c) Fit the exponential trend to the data. Would this model give reasonable forecasts? Explain. (d) Make a forecast for 2003, using a trend model of your choice, or a judgment forecast. 🐝 **Fractional**

Fractional Shares of Aircraft Ownership, 1986–2002

Year	Shares
1986	3
1987	5
1988	26
1989	51
1990	57
1991	71
1992	84
1993	110
1994	158
1995	285
1996	548
1997	957
1998	1551
1999	2607
2000	3834
2001	4871
2002	5827

Source: Chris Martin, David Jones, and Pinar Keskinocak, "Optimizing On-Demand Aircraft Schedules for Fractional Aircraft Operators," *Interfaces* 33, no. 5 (Sept.–Oct. 2003), p. 23.

14.22 (a) Plot all four time series on fuel efficiency on the same graph. (b) Fit a linear trend to each. (c) Interpret each fitted trend equation, explaining its implications. (d) To whom is this issue relevant? *Note:* If you think your graph is too cluttered, break it into two graphs (existing vehicles, new vehicles) with two time series on each graph. 🐝 **FuelMPG**

Average Fuel Efficiency of U.S. Passenger Cars and Light Trucks (miles per gallon)

| Year | Existing Vehicles | | New Vehicles | |
	Passenger Car	Other Vehicles	Car	Light Truck
1990	20.3	16.1	28.0	20.8
1991	21.2	17.0	28.4	21.3
1992	21.0	17.3	27.9	20.8
1993	20.6	17.4	28.4	21.0
1994	20.8	17.3	28.3	20.8
1995	21.1	17.3	28.6	20.5
1996	21.2	17.2	28.5	20.8
1997	21.5	17.2	28.7	20.6
1998	21.6	17.2	28.8	21.1
1999	21.4	17.0	28.3	20.9
2000	21.9	17.4	28.5	21.3
2001	22.1	17.6	28.6	20.9

Source: U.S. Dept. of Transportation, www.bts.gov.

14.23 (a) Plot the data on law enforcement officers killed. (b) Describe the trend (if any) and discuss possible causes. (c) Would a fitted trend be helpful? Explain. (c) Make a forecast for 2002 using any method you like (including judgment).   🔫 **LawOfficers**

U.S. Law Enforcement Officers Killed, 1994–2002

Year	Officers Killed
1994	141
1995	133
1996	113
1997	133
1998	142
1999	107
2000	134
2001	218
2002	132

Source: *Statistical Abstract of the United States, 2004.*

14.24 (a) Plot the data on lightning deaths. (b) Describe the trend (if any) and discuss possible causes. (c) Fit an exponential trend to the data. Interpret the fitted equation. (d) Make a forecast for 2005, using a trend model of your choice (or a judgment forecast). Explain the basis for your forecast. *Note:* Time is in 5-year increments, so use $t = 14$ for your 2005 forecast.   🔫 **Lightning**

U.S. Lightning Deaths, 1940–2000

Year	Deaths
1940	340
1945	268
1950	219
1955	181
1960	129
1965	149
1970	122
1975	91
1980	74
1985	74
1990	74
1995	85
2000	51

Source: *Statistical Abstract of the United States, 2003,* and *U.S. News & World Report* 108, no. 22 (June 4, 1990), p. 78.

14.25 (a) Plot the data on full-time mathematics graduate students. (b) Would a fitted trend be helpful? Explain. (c) Make a forecast for 2003, using a trend model of your choice (or a judgment forecast).   🐝 **MathGrads**

Full-Time Mathematics Graduate Students, 1993–2002

Year	Total
1993	10,525
1994	10,185
1995	9,761
1996	9,476
1997	9,003
1998	8,791
1999	8,838
2000	9,637
2001	9,361
2002	9,972

Source: American Mathematical Association.

14.26 (a) Plot both men's and women's winning times on the same graph. (b) Fit a linear trend model to each series (men, women). (c) Use Excel's option to forecast each trend graphically to 2040 (i.e., to period $t = 27$ periods, since observations are in 4-year increments). From these projections, does it appear that the times will eventually converge? *(d) Set the fitted trends equal, solve for x (the time period when the trends will cross), and convert x to a year. Is the result plausible? Explain. (e) Use the Web to check your 2004 forecasts.   🐝 **Olympic**

Summer Olympics 100-Meter Winning Times

Year	Men's 100-Meter Winner	Seconds	Women's 100-Meter Winner	Seconds
1928	Percy Williams, Canada	10.80	Elizabeth Robinson, United States	12.20
1932	Eddie Tolan, United States	10.30	Stella Walsh, Poland	11.90
1936	Jesse Owens, United States	10.30	Helen Stephens, United States	11.50
1948	Harrison Dillard, United States	10.30	Fanny Blankers-Koen, Netherlands	11.90
1952	Lindy Remigino, United States	10.40	Marjorie Jackson, United States	11.50
1956	Bobby Morrow, United States	10.50	Betty Cuthbert, Australia	11.50
1960	Armin Hary, West Germany	10.20	Wilma Rudolph, United States	11.00
1964	Bob Hayes, United States	10.00	Wyomia Tyus, United States	11.40
1968	Jim Hines, United States	9.95	Wyomia Tyus, United States	11.00
1972	Valery Borzov, USSR	10.14	Renate Stecher, East Germany	11.07
1976	Hasely Crawford, Trinidad	10.06	Annegret Richter, West Germany	11.08
1980	Allan Wells, Great Britain	10.25	Lyudmila Kondratyeva, USSR	11.06
1984	Carl Lewis, United States	9.99	Evelyn Ashford, United States	10.97
1988	Carl Lewis, United States	9.92	Florence Griffith-Joyner, United States	10.54
1992	Linford Christie, Great Britain	9.96	Gail Devers, United States	10.82
1996	Donovan Bailey, Canada	9.84	Gail Devers, United States	10.94
2000	Maurice Greene, United States	9.87	Marion Jones, United States	10.75

Source: Summer Olympics 100-meter times, *The World Almanac, 2002*, pp. 900–904.

14.27 (a) Choose *one* time series on U.S. petroleum use, and plot it on a graph. (b) Describe the trend (if any) and discuss possible causes. (c) Fit both a linear and an exponential trend. (c) Interpret each fitted trend equation, explaining the implications. (d) Make a projection for 2005. Do you believe it? (e) To whom is this issue relevant? *Note:* Time increments are 5 years, so use $t = 10$ for the 2005 forecast.   🐝 **Petroleum**

U.S. Petroleum Imports, Exports, and Consumption (million barrels per day)

Year	Imports	Exports	Net Imports	Total	% of World
1960	1.810	0.200	1.610	9.800	45.9
1965	2.470	0.190	2.280	11.510	37.0
1970	3.420	0.260	3.160	14.700	31.4
1975	6.056	0.209	5.846	16.322	29.0
1980	6.909	0.544	6.365	17.056	27.0
1985	5.067	0.781	4.286	15.726	26.2
1990	8.018	0.857	7.161	16.988	25.7
1995	8.840	0.949	7.886	17.720	25.3
2000	11.460	1.040	10.419	19.701	25.6

Source: U.S. Dept. of Transportation, www.bts.gov.

14.28 (a) Choose *one* prison time series and plot it on a graph. (b) Describe the trend (if any) and discuss possible causes. (c) Fit both a linear and an exponential trend. (d) Interpret each fitted trend equation, explaining its implications. (e) Using both models, make a projection for 2010. Do you believe it? Explain.   **Prisoners**

U.S. Adults on Probation, in Jail or Prison, or on Parole: 1986–2002 (thousands)

Year	Total	% of Adult Pop	Probation	Jail	Prison	Parole
1986	3,239	1.8	2,115	273	526	326
1987	3,460	1.9	2,247	294	563	356
1988	3,714	2.0	2,356	342	608	408
1989	4,056	2.2	2,522	393	683	457
1990	4,348	2.3	2,670	403	743	531
1991	4,536	2.4	2,728	424	793	590
1992	4,763	2.5	2,812	442	851	659
1993	4,944	2.6	2,903	456	909	676
1994	5,141	2.7	2,981	480	990	690
1995	5,335	2.8	3,078	499	1,079	679
1996	5,483	2.8	3,165	510	1,128	680
1997	5,726	2.9	3,297	558	1,177	695
1998	6,126	3.1	3,670	584	1,224	696
1999	6,331	3.1	3,780	596	1,287	714
2000	6,437	3.1	3,826	614	1,316	724
2001	6,574	3.1	3,932	624	1,330	732
2002	6,684	3.1	3,955	658	1,368	753

Source: *Statistical Abstract of the United States, 2004.*

14.29 (a) Choose *two* time series on SAT scores that you would like to compare. Plot both series on the same graph. (b) Fit a linear trend to each series. (c) Interpret each fitted trend equation. (d) What are the implications (if any) of your analysis, and for whom?   **SAT**

SAT Averages for College-Bound H.S. Seniors, 1990–2001

Year	Verbal Score			Mathematical Score		
	Total	Male	Female	Total	Male	Female
1990–91	499	503	495	500	520	482
1991–92	500	504	496	501	521	484
1992–93	500	504	497	503	524	484
1993–94	499	501	497	504	523	487
1994–95	504	505	502	506	525	490
1995–96	505	507	503	508	527	492
1996–97	505	507	503	511	530	494
1997–98	505	509	502	512	531	496
1998–99	505	509	502	511	531	495
1999–00	505	507	504	514	533	498
2000–01	506	509	502	514	533	498

Source: College Entrance Examination Board, National Report on College-Bound Seniors, various years. Copyright © 2001, collegeboard.com. Reproduced with permission. All rights reserved. www.collegeboard.com.

14.30 (a) Use Excel, MegaStat, or MINITAB to fit an m-period moving average to the exchange rate data shown below with $m = 2, 3, 4$, and 5 periods. Make a line chart. (b) Which value of m do you prefer? Why? (c) Is a moving average appropriate for this kind of data? Include a chart for each value of m. **Sterling**

Daily Spot Exchange Rate, U.S. Dollars per Pound Sterling

Date	Rate	Date	Rate	Date	Rate	Date	Rate
1-Apr-04	1.8564	16-Apr-04	1.8004	3-May-04	1.7720	18-May-04	1.7695
2-Apr-04	1.8293	19-Apr-04	1.8055	4-May-04	1.7907	19-May-04	1.7827
5-Apr-04	1.8140	20-Apr-04	1.7914	5-May-04	1.7932	20-May-04	1.7710
6-Apr-04	1.8374	21-Apr-04	1.7720	6-May-04	1.7941	21-May-04	1.7880
7-Apr-04	1.8410	22-Apr-04	1.7684	7-May-04	1.7842	24-May-04	1.7908
8-Apr-04	1.8325	23-Apr-04	1.7674	10-May-04	1.7723	25-May-04	1.8135
9-Apr-04	1.8322	26-Apr-04	1.7857	11-May-04	1.7544	26-May-04	1.8142
12-Apr-04	1.8358	27-Apr-04	1.7925	12-May-04	1.7743	27-May-04	1.8369
13-Apr-04	1.8160	28-Apr-04	1.7720	13-May-04	1.7584	28-May-04	1.8330
14-Apr-04	1.7902	29-Apr-04	1.7751	14-May-04	1.7572		
15-Apr-04	1.7785	30-Apr-04	1.7744	17-May-04	1.7695		

Source: Federal Reserve Board of Governors.

14.31 Refer to exercise 14.30. (a) Plot the dollar/pound exchange rate data. Make the graph nice, then copy and paste it so you have four copies. (b) Use MegaStat or MINITAB to perform a simple exponential smoothing using $\alpha = .05, .10, .20$, and $.50$, using a different line chart for each. (c) Which value of α do you prefer? Why? (d) Is an exponential smoothing process appropriate for this kind of data? **Sterling**

14.32 (a) Plot the data on gas bills. (b) Can you see seasonal patterns? Explain. (c) Use MegaStat or MINITAB to calculate estimated seasonal indexes and trend. (d) Which months are the most expensive? The least expensive? Can you explain this pattern? (e) Is there a trend in the deseasonalized data? *(f) Use MegaStat or MINITAB to perform a regression using seasonal binaries. Interpret the results. **GasBills**

Natural Gas Bills for a Residence, 2000–2003

Month	2000	2001	2002	2003
Jan	78.98	118.86	101.44	155.37
Feb	84.44	111.31	122.20	148.77
Mar	65.54	75.62	99.49	115.12
Apr	62.60	77.47	55.85	85.89
May	29.24	29.23	44.94	46.84
Jun	18.10	17.10	19.57	24.93
Jul	91.57	16.59	15.98	20.84
Aug	6.48	27.64	14.97	26.94
Sep	19.35	28.86	18.03	34.17
Oct	29.02	48.21	56.98	88.58
Nov	94.09	67.15	115.27	100.63
Dec	101.65	125.18	130.95	174.63

Source: Homeowner's records.

14.33 (a) Plot the data on building permits. (b) Can you see seasonal patterns? Explain. (c) Use MegaStat or MINITAB to calculate estimated seasonal indexes and trend. (d) Which months have the most permits? The fewest? Is this logical? (e) Is there a trend in the deseasonalized data? **Permits**

Single Family Home Building Permits in Southeastern Michigan

Month	1995	1996	1997	1998	1999	2000
Jan	763	981	986	999	830	1,155
Feb	877	1,058	1,146	1,129	1,029	1,138
Mar	1,330	1,448	1,384	1,705	1,716	1,779
Apr	1,530	2,080	2,100	1,817	1,845	1,670
May	1,719	2,036	1,699	1,762	1,909	1,692
Jun	1,787	1,723	1,643	1,955	2,037	1,634
Jul	1,440	1,869	1,605	1,746	1,841	1,414
Aug	1,790	1,737	1,635	1,476	1,885	1,614
Sep	1,529	1,502	1,593	1,625	1,584	1,418
Oct	1,536	1,767	1,672	1,720	1,643	1,618
Nov	1,346	1,217	1,059	1,530	1,296	1,173
Dec	938	1,050	1,111	1,367	1,158	693

Source: www.semcog.org.

14.34 (a) Plot the data on airplane shipments. (b) Can you see seasonal patterns? Explain. (c) Use MegaStat or MINITAB to calculate estimated seasonal indexes and trend. Is there a trend in the deseasonalized data? **AirplanesQtr**

U.S. Manufactured General Aviation Shipments, 1986–2003

Year	Qtr 1	Qtr 2	Qtr 3	Qtr 4	Total
1986	285	364	393	453	1,495
1987	227	330	239	289	1,085
1988	260	291	252	340	1,143
1989	304	361	425	445	1,535
1990	269	294	274	297	1,144
1991	250	262	237	272	1,021
1992	193	200	238	225	941
1993	170	194	246	260	964
1994	181	225	209	266	928
1995	208	248	257	315	1,077
1996	229	284	230	310	1,115
1997	253	337	367	525	1,549
1998	481	486	546	602	2,200
1999	502	611	606	702	2,504
2000	613	704	685	712	2,816
2001	568	711	586	673	2,632
2002	442	576	510	641	2,207
2003	393	526	492	679	2,137

Note: Quarterly shipments may not add to annual total because some manufacturers report only annual totals.

Source: U.S. Manufactured General Aviation Shipments, *Statistical Databook 2003,* General Aviation Manufacturers Association, used with permission.

14.35 (a) Plot the data on revolving credit (credit cards and home equity lines of credit are the two major types of revolving credit). (b) Use MegaStat or MINITAB to calculate estimated seasonal indexes and trend. Is there a trend in the deseasonalized data? (c) Which months have the most borrowing? The least? Is this logical? **Revolving**

U.S. Consumers Revolving Credit (billions)

Month	2001	2002	2003	2004
Jan	223.2	232.5	240.6	276.7
Feb	221.5	229.7	239.7	272.8
Mar	220.1	230.2	234.0	268.3
Apr	227.7	235.6	235.4	270.6
May	229.1	233.1	240.4	278.0
Jun	225.7	231.0	240.7	275.6
Jul	222.1	229.9	238.6	278.7
Aug	219.6	241.1	240.7	286.4
Sep	216.3	243.1	239.9	286.7
Oct	223.3	242.4	235.8	286.1
Nov	233.2	244.2	269.5	285.8
Dec	238.3	250.2	284.7	315.8

Source: www.federalreserve.gov.

14.36 (a) Plot the data on jewelry sales. (b) Use MegaStat or MINITAB to calculate estimated seasonal indexes and trend. Is there a trend in the deseasonalized data? (c) Which months have the most sales? The least? Is this logical? *(d) Use MegaStat or MINITAB to perform a regression using seasonal binaries. Interpret the results. **Jewelry**

U.S. Jewelry Sales, 1990–1995 ($ millions)

Month	1990	1991	1992	1993	1994	1995
Jan	846	821	813	801	897	921
Feb	1,025	998	1,042	1,001	1,181	1,230
Mar	984	967	930	901	1,048	1,145
Apr	1,004	1,012	985	1,005	1,159	1,213
May	1,263	1,313	1,190	1,244	1,354	1,616
Jun	1,134	1,099	1,111	1,268	1,244	1,402
Jul	1,075	1,021	1,051	1,277	1,213	1,272
Aug	1,132	1,058	1,103	1,268	1,308	1,408
Sep	996	963	1,046	1,188	1,234	1,340
Oct	1,084	1,080	1,135	1,210	1,313	1,387
Nov	1,400	1,329	1,378	1,557	1,717	1,891
Dec	3,238	3,071	3,475	3,822	4,171	4,526

Source: **www.census.gov,** project by statistics student Devora Davis.

14.37 (a) Plot the data on M1 money stock. (b) Use MegaStat or MINITAB to calculate estimated seasonal indexes and trend. Is there a trend in the deseasonalized data? (c) Make monthly forecasts for 2002. *Note:* M1 includes currency, travelers checks, demand deposits, and other checkable deposits. **MoneyStock**

U.S. Money Stock M1 Component, 1995–2001 ($ billions)

Month	1995	1996	1997	1998	1999	2000	2001
Jan	1,159.0	1,129.4	1,086.3	1,079.4	1,103.0	1,126.4	1,099.6
Feb	1,134.9	1,105.1	1,065.2	1,065.5	1,084.3	1,096.8	1,087.5
Mar	1,138.9	1,117.3	1,067.5	1,075.2	1,096.6	1,108.1	1,107.4
Apr	1,159.9	1,131.1	1,073.1	1,086.9	1,112.6	1,124.9	1,122.7
May	1,133.5	1,105.1	1,053.6	1,070.0	1,095.4	1,100.4	1,111.0
Jun	1,140.4	1,114.2	1,064.1	1,074.3	1,097.2	1,102.6	1,122.6
Jul	1,145.2	1,110.0	1,065.3	1,073.5	1,096.7	1,104.0	1,135.9
Aug	1,138.9	1,097.0	1,068.7	1,068.6	1,092.7	1,095.9	1,141.3
Sep	1,138.0	1,091.2	1,059.1	1,070.0	1,086.3	1,090.5	1,194.3
Oct	1,132.4	1,077.6	1,057.1	1,076.8	1,095.3	1,093.6	1,155.5
Nov	1,138.0	1,086.4	1,073.6	1,097.3	1,113.3	1,093.3	1,164.8
Dec	1,152.1	1,104.7	1,096.9	1,120.4	1,148.3	1,112.3	1,202.2

Source: Federal Reserve Board of Governors, **www.federalreserve.gov.** Data not seasonally adjusted.

14.38 (a) Use MegaStat or MINITAB to deseasonalize the quarterly data on Coca-Cola's revenues and fit a trend. Interpret the results. (b) Use MegaStat or MINITAB to perform a regression using seasonal binaries. Interpret the results. (c) Use the regression equation to make a prediction for each quarter in 2005. *(d) If you have access to *Standard & Poor's Stock Reports, 2006,* check your forecasts. How accurate were they? **CocaCola**

Coca-Cola Revenues ($ millions), 1999–2004

Quarter	1999	2000	2001	2002	2003	2004
1	4,428	4,391	4,479	4,079	4,502	5,078
2	5,379	5,621	5,293	5,368	5,695	5,965
3	5,195	5,543	5,397	5,322	5,671	5,662
4	4,931	4,903	4,923	4,795	5,176	5,257
Year	19,933	20,458	20,092	19,564	21,044	21,962

Source: *Standard & Poor's Stock Reports,* March 2005.

14.39 (a) Use MegaStat or MINITAB to perform a regression using seasonal binaries. Interpret the results. (b) Make monthly forecasts for 1997. If you can find data on the Web, check your forecasts.
StudentPilots

Student Pilot Certificates Issued By Month, 1991–1996

Month	1991	1992	1993	1994	1995	1996
Jan	5,704	6,104	4,802	4,394	4,505	4,067
Feb	5,541	5,773	5,144	4,562	4,307	4,057
Mar	5,950	6,773	5,835	5,696	5,189	4,301
Apr	6,513	6,703	5,507	5,308	4,744	4,758
May	6,622	6,299	5,597	5,788	5,396	5,065
Jun	7,932	7,819	6,683	6,837	5,878	5,031
Jul	8,442	8,074	6,758	6,011	5,708	5,807
Aug	8,580	7,210	7,191	7,054	6,590	5,564
Sep	7,630	7,251	6,343	6,274	6,001	5,192
Oct	7,956	6,760	5,797	5,790	4,000	5,310
Nov	7,661	5,240	5,117	4,785	4,179	4,240
Dec	3,674	4,371	4,404	4,002	4,000	3,261

Source: Federal Aviation Administration, http://api.hq.faa.gov/handbook/1996.

*14.40 Translate each of the following fitted exponential trend models into a compound interest model of the form $y_t = y_0(1 + r)^t$. *Hint:* See *LearningStats* Unit 14 or footnote on p. 615.

a. $y_t = 456e^{.123t}$ b. $y_t = 228e^{.075t}$ c. $y_t = 456e^{-.038t}$

*14.41 Translate each of the following fitted compound interest trend models into an exponential model of the form $y_t = ae^{bt}$. *Hint:* See *LearningStats* Unit 14 or footnote on p. 615.

a. $y_t = 123(1.089)^t$ b. $y_t = 654(1.217)^t$ c. $y_t = 308(.942)^t$

Related Reading

Brocklebank, John C.; and David A. Dickey. *SAS for Forecasting Time-Series*. Wiley, 2003.

DeLurgio, Stephen A. *Forecasting Principles and Applications*. Irwin/McGraw-Hill, 1998.

Diebold, Francis X. *Elements of Forecasting*. 3rd ed. South-Western, 2004.

Gaynor, Patricia E.; and Rickey C. Kirkpatrick. *Introduction to Time-Series Modeling and Forecasting in Business and Economics*. McGraw-Hill, 1994.

Granger, C. W. J. *Forecasting in Business and Economics*. 2nd ed. Academic Press, 1989.

Hanke, John E.; and Dean W. Wichern. *Business Forecasting*. 8th ed. Prentice-Hall, 2005.

Pindyck, Robert S.; and Daniel L. Rubinfeld. *Econometric Models and Economic Forecasts*. 4th ed. Irwin/McGraw-Hill, 1998.

Wilson, J. Holton; and Barry Keating. *Business Forecasting*. 4th ed. Irwin, 2002.

Makridakis, Spyros; Steven C. Wheelwright; and Rob J. Hyndman. *Forecasting: Methods and Applications*. 4th ed. Wiley, 2006.

LearningStats Unit 14   Time-Series Analysis

LearningStats Unit 14 contains simulations to generate quarterly and monthly data, case studies of various kinds of fitted trends, illustrations of the components of a time series, and examples of student projects using fitted trends. Modules are designed for self-study, so you can concentrate on material that is new, and pass quickly over things that you already know or do not find interesting. Your instructor may assign specific modules, or you may decide to check them out because the topic sounds interesting. In addition to helping you learn about statistics, they may be useful as references later on.

Topic	*LearningStats Modules*
Trends and forecasting	Time-Series Components Trend Fitting Trend Forecasting
Using Excel	Excel Trends—1 Excel Trends—2 Exponential Trend Dissimilar Magnitudes Exponential Smoothing
Simulations	Time-Series Components Trend Simulator Seasonal Time-Series Generator
Fit and seasonality	Trend Fit Measures Seasonal Factors
Case studies	Health Trends Olympic Times Federal Budget Male/Female Income Brad's Bowling Scores
Student projects	Gas Prices Investing Olympic Times

Key: = PowerPoint   = Word   = Excel

Visual Statistics

Visual Statistics Modules on Time-Series

Module	*Module Name*
20	Visualizing Time-Series Data

Visual Statistics Module 20 is designed to help you

- Understand the importance of the data collection period.
- Recognize the difficulty in separating trend, seasonality.
- See why sample size is important.
- Understand the difference between additive and multiplicative seasonality.
- Understand common statistics of fit (*MAPE, R^2*, standard error).

The worktext (included on the CD in .PDF format) contains lists of concepts covered, objectives of the modules, overviews of concepts, illustrations of concepts, orientations to module features, learning exercises (basic, intermediate, advanced), learning projects (individual, team), self-evaluation quizzes, glossaries of terms, and solutions to self-evaluation quizzes.

CHAPTER 15

Chi-Square Tests

Chapter Learning Objectives

When you finish this chapter you should be able to

- Recognize a contingency table (cross-tabulation of frequencies).

- Find degrees of freedom and use the chi-square table of critical values.

- Perform a chi-square test for independence on a contingency table.

- Perform a goodness-of-fit (GOF) test for a uniform distribution.

- Explain the GOF test for a Poisson distribution.

- Use computer software to perform a chi-square GOF test for normality.

- State advantages of ECDF tests as compared to chi-square GOF tests.

Not all information pertaining to business can be summarized numerically. We are often interested in answers to questions such as: Do employees in different age groups choose different types of health plans? Do consumers prefer red, yellow, or blue package lettering on our bread bags? Does the name of our new lawn mower influence how we perceive the quality? Answers to questions such as these are not measurements on a numerical scale. The variables that we are interested in learning about are not quantifiable. Health plans are categorized by the way services are paid, so the variable *health plan* might have four different categories: Catastrophic, HMO (health maintenance organization), POS (point of service), and CDHP (consumer-driven health plan). The variable *package lettering color* would have categories red, yellow, and blue, and the variable *perceived quality* might have categories excellent, satisfactory, and poor.

We can collect observations on these variables to answer the types of questions posed either by surveying our customers and employees or by conducting carefully designed experiments. Once our data has been collected we summarize by tallying response frequencies on a table that we call a *contingency table*.

Contingency Tables

A **contingency table** is a cross-tabulation of n paired observations into categories. Each cell shows the count of observations that fall into the category defined by its row and column heading, as shown in Table 15.1. Variable A has c levels (columns) and variable B has r levels (rows) so we call this an $r \times c$ contingency table.

Variable B	Variable A				Row Total
	1	2		c	
1	f_{11}	f_{12}	$\cdots$	f_{1c}	R_1
2	f_{21}	f_{22}	$\cdots$	f_{2c}	R_2
$\vdots$	$\vdots$	$\vdots$	$\vdots$	$\vdots$	$\vdots$
r	f_{r1}	f_{r2}	$\cdots$	f_{rc}	R_r
Col Total	C_1	C_2	$\cdots$	C_c	n

TABLE 15.1
Table of Observed Frequencies

EXAMPLE

Web Pages (4 × 3 Table)

As online shopping has grown, opportunity has also grown for personal data collection and invasion of privacy. Mainstream online retailers have policies known as "privacy disclaimers" that define the rules regarding their uses of information collected, the customer's right to refuse third-party promotional offers, and so on. You can access these policies through a Web link, found either on the Web site's home page, on the order page (i.e., as you enter your credit card information), on a client Web page, or on some other Web page. In the United States, such links are voluntary, while in the European Union (EU) they are mandated by law. Location of the privacy disclaimer is considered to be a measure of the degree of consumer protection (the farther the link is from the home page, the less likely it is to be noticed). Marketing researchers did a survey of 291 Web sites in three nations (France, U.K., U.S.) and obtained the *contingency table* shown here as Table 15.2. Is location of the privacy disclaimer *independent* of the Web site's nationality? This question can be answered by using a test based on the frequencies in this contingency table.

TABLE 15.2   **Privacy Disclaimer Location and Web Site Nationality**    **WebSites**

Location of Disclaimer	Nationality of Web Site			Row Total
	France	*U.K.*	*U.S.*	
Home page	56	68	35	159
Order page	19	19	28	66
Client page	6	10	16	32
Other page	12	9	13	34
Col Total	93	106	92	291

Source: Calin Gurau, Ashok Ranchhod, and Claire Gauzente, "To Legislate or Not to Legislate: A Comparative Exploratory Study of Privacy/Personalisation Factors Affecting French, UK, and US Web Sites," *Journal of Consumer Marketing* 20, no. 7 (2003), p. 659. Used with permission, Emerald Group Publishing Limited.

Chi-Square Test

In a test of independence for an $r \times c$ contingency table, the hypotheses are:

H_0: Variable A is independent of variable B

H_1: Variable A is not independent of variable B

To test these hypotheses, we use the **chi-square test** *for independence,* developed by Karl Pearson (1857–1936). It is a test based on *frequencies.* It measures the association between the two variables A and B in the contingency table. The chi-square test is a *nonparametric* test because no parameters are estimated. The only operation performed is classifying the n data pairs into c columns (variable A) and r rows (variable B), and then comparing the **observed frequency** f_{jk} in each cell of the contingency table with the **expected frequency** e_{jk} under the assumption of independence. The chi-square test statistic measures the *relative* difference between expected and observed frequencies:

(15.1)
$$\chi^2 = \sum_{j=1}^{r} \sum_{k=1}^{c} \frac{[f_{jk} - e_{jk}]^2}{e_{jk}}$$

If the two variables are **independent,** then f_{jk} should be close to e_{jk}, leading to a chi-square test statistic near zero. Conversely, large differences between f_{jk} and e_{jk} will lead to a large chi-square test statistic. The chi-square test statistic cannot be negative (due to squaring) so it is always a right-tailed test. If the test statistic is far enough in the right tail, we will reject the hypothesis of independence. Squaring each difference removes the sign, so it doesn't matter whether e_{jk} is above or below f_{jk}. Each squared difference is expressed *relative* to e_{jk}.

Chi-Square Distribution

The test statistic is compared with a critical value from the **chi-square probability distribution.** It has one parameter ν called **degrees of freedom.** For the $r \times c$ contingency table, the degrees of freedom are:

$$\nu = \text{degrees of freedom} = (r - 1)(c - 1) \qquad \textbf{(15.2)}$$

where

$r = $ the number of rows in the contingency table

$c = $ the number of columns in the contingency table

There is a different chi-square distribution for each value of ν. Appendix E contains critical values for right-tail areas of the chi-square distribution. Its mean is ν and its variance is 2ν. As illustrated in Figure 15.1, all chi-square distributions are skewed to the right, but become more symmetric as ν increases. For $\nu = 1$ the distribution is discontinuous near the origin. As ν increases the shape begins to resemble a normal, bell-shaped curve. However, for the contingency tables you are likely to encounter, degrees of freedom will not be large enough to assume normality.

FIGURE 15.1

Various chi-square distributions

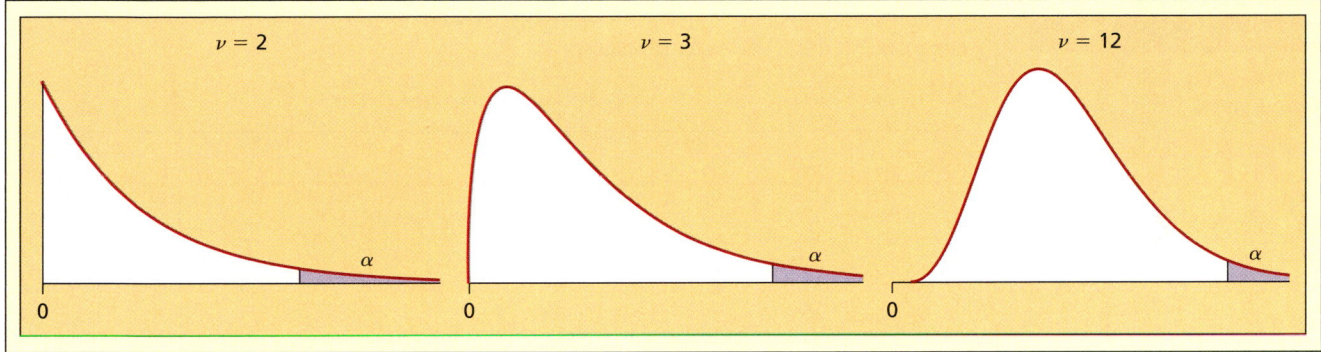

Expected Frequencies

Assuming that H_0 is true, the expected frequency of row j and column k is

$$e_{jk} = R_j C_k / n \qquad \text{(expected frequency in row } j \text{ and column } k) \qquad \textbf{(15.3)}$$

where

$R_j = $ total for row j $(j = 1, 2, \ldots, r)$

$C_k = $ total for column k $(k = 1, 2, \ldots, c)$

$n = $ sample size (or number of responses)

This formula for expected frequencies stems from the definition of independent events (see Chapter 5). When two events are independent, their *joint* probability is the product of their marginal probabilities, so for a cell in row j and column k the joint probability would be $(R_j/n)(C_k/n)$. To get the expected cell frequency, we multiply this joint probability by the sample size n to obtain $e_{jk} = R_j C_k / n$. The expected frequencies may be presented in a table, like Table 15.3. The e_{jk} always sums to the same row and column frequencies as the observed frequencies. Expected frequencies will not, in general, be integers.

TABLE 15.3

Table of Expected Frequencies

Variable B	Variable A				Row Total
	1	2	. . .	c	
1	e_{11}	e_{12}	. . .	e_{1c}	R_1
2	e_{21}	e_{22}	. . .	e_{2c}	R_2
:	:	:	:	:	:
r	e_{r1}	e_{r2}	. . .	e_{rc}	R_r
Col Total	C_1	C_2	. . .	C_c	n

Illustration of the Chi-Square Calculations

We will illustrate the chi-square test by using the Web page frequencies from the contingency table (Table 15.2). We follow the usual five-step hypothesis testing procedure:

Step 1: State the Hypotheses For the Web page example, the hypotheses are:

H_0: Privacy disclaimer location is independent of Web site nationality

H_1: Privacy disclaimer location is dependent on Web site nationality

Step 2: State the Decision Rule For the Web page contingency table, we have $r = 4$ rows and $c = 3$ columns, so degrees of freedom are $v = (r - 1)(c - 1) = (4 - 1)(3 - 1) = 6$. We will choose $\alpha = .05$ for the test. Figure 15.2 shows that the right-tail critical value from Appendix E with $v = 6$ is $\chi^2_{.05} = 12.59$. This critical value could also be obtained from Excel using =CHIINV(.05,6).

FIGURE 15.2

Critical value of chi-square from Appendix E

Appendix E: Critical Values for Chi-Square

This table shows the critical value that defines the specified area for the stated degrees of freedom (v).

	Left Tail Area					Right Tail Area				
v	0.005	0.01	0.025	0.05	0.10	0.10	0.05	0.025	0.01	0.005
1	0.000	0.000	0.001	0.004	0.016	2.706	3.841	5.024	6.635	7.879
2	0.010	0.020	0.051	0.103	0.211	4.605	5.991	7.378	9.210	10.60
3	0.072	0.115	0.216	0.352	0.584	6.251	7.815	9.348	11.34	12.84
4	0.207	0.297	0.484	0.711	1.064	7.779	9.488	11.14	13.28	14.86
5	0.412	0.554	0.831	1.145	1.610	9.236	11.07	12.83	15.09	16.75
6	0.676	0.872	1.237	1.635	2.204	10.64	12.59	14.45	16.81	18.55
7	0.989	1.239	1.690	2.167	2.833	12.02	14.07	16.01	18.48	20.28
8	1.344	1.646	2.180	2.733	3.490	13.36	15.51	17.53	20.09	21.95
9	1.735	2.088	2.700	3.325	4.168	14.68	16.92	19.02	21.67	23.59
10	2.156	2.558	3.247	3.940	4.865	15.99	18.31	20.48	23.21	25.19

For $\alpha = .05$ in a right-tailed test, the decision rule is:

Reject H_0 if $\chi^2 > 12.59$

Otherwise do no reject H_0

The decision rule is illustrated in Figure 15.3.

FIGURE 15.3

Right-tailed chi-square test for $v = 6$

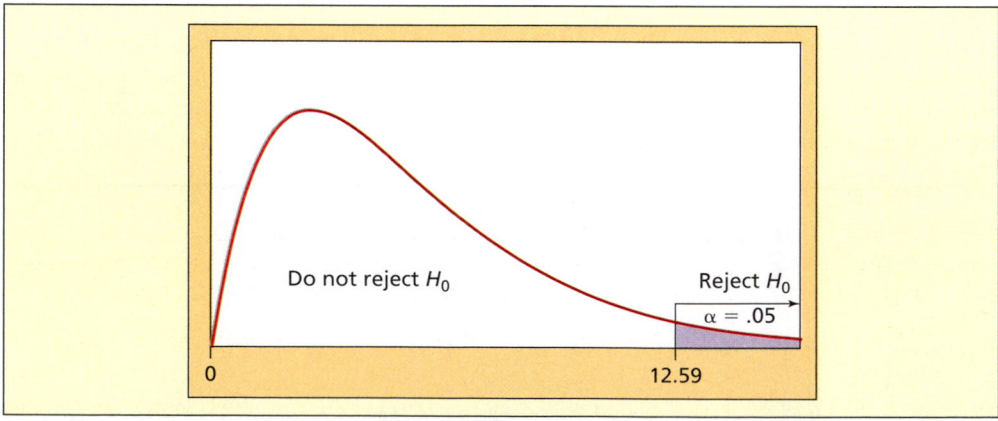

Do not reject H_0

Reject H_0

$\alpha = .05$

0

12.59

Step 3: Calculate the Expected Frequencies The expected frequency in row j and column k is $e_{jk} = R_j C_k / n$. It is easiest to organize the calculations in a table:

Expected Frequencies

Location	France	U.K.	U.S.	Row Total
Home	(159 × 93)/291 = 50.81	(159 × 106)/291 = 57.92	(159 × 92)/291 = 50.27	159
Order	(66 × 93)/291 = 21.09	(66 × 106)/291 = 24.04	(66 × 92)/291 = 20.87	66
Client	(32 × 93)/291 = 10.23	(32 × 106)/291 = 11.66	(32 × 92)/291 = 10.12	32
Other	(34 × 93)/291 = 10.87	(34 × 106)/291 = 12.38	(34 × 92)/291 = 10.75	34
Col Total	93	106	92	291

Step 4: Calculate the Test Statistic   The chi-square test statistic is

$$\chi^2 = \sum_{j=1}^{r} \sum_{k=1}^{c} \frac{[f_{jk} - e_{jk}]^2}{e_{jk}} = \frac{(56 - 50.81)^2}{50.81} + \cdots + \frac{(13 - 10.75)^2}{10.75}$$

$$= 0.53 + \cdots + 0.47 = 17.54$$

Even for this simple problem, the calculations are too lengthy to show in full. In fact, few would choose to do the calculations of the expected frequencies and chi-square test statistic without a spreadsheet. Fortunately, any statistical package will do a chi-square test. MegaStat's setup and output are shown in Figure 15.4. As you can see, MegaStat's calculations are arranged in a tabular form.

FIGURE 15.4

MegaStat's chi-square test for Web page data

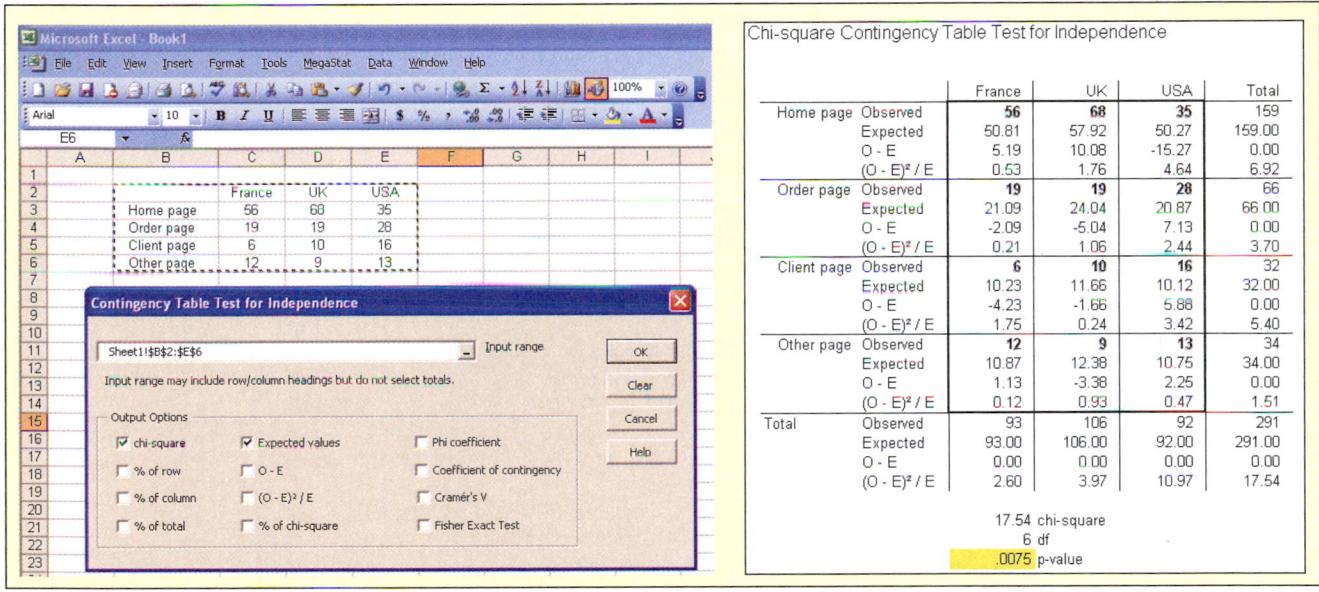

Step 5: Make the Decision   Since the test statistic $\chi^2 = 17.54$ exceeds 12.59, we conclude that the observed differences between expected and observed frequencies are significant at $\alpha = .05$. The *p*-value (.0075) indicates that H_0 should be rejected at $\alpha = .05$. You can obtain this same *p*-value using Excel's function =CHIDIST(χ^2, ν) or in this case =CHIDIST(17.54,6), which gives a right-tail area of .0075. This *p*-value indicates that privacy disclaimer location is *not* independent of nationality at $\alpha = .05$, based on this sample of 291 Web sites.

Discussion   MegaStat rounds things off for display purposes, though it maintains full internal accuracy in the calculations (as you must, if you do these calculations by hand). Differences between observed and expected frequencies O–E must sum to zero across each row and down each column. If you are doing these calculations by hand, check these sums (if they are not zero, you have made an error). From Figure 15.4 we see that only three cells (column 3, rows 1, 2, and 3) contribute a majority (4.64, 2.44, 3.42) of the chi-square sum (17.54). The hypothesis of independence fails largely because of these three cells.

EXAMPLE

*Night Flying
(2 × 2 Table)*

After the accident in which U.S. Senator John F. Kennedy, Jr., died while piloting his airplane at night from New York to Cape Cod, a random telephone poll was taken in which 409 New Yorkers were asked, "Should private pilots be allowed to fly at night without an instrument rating?" The same question was posed to 70 aviation experts. Results are shown in Table 15.4. The totals exclude those who had "No Opinion" (1 expert and 25 general public).

TABLE 15.4 **Should Noninstrument Rated Pilots Fly at Night?** 🐦 **Pilots**

Opinion	Experienced Pilots	General Public	Row Total
Yes	40	61	101
No	29	323	352
Col Total	69	384	453

Source: Siena College Research Institute.

The hypotheses are:

H_0: Opinion is independent of aviation expertise

H_1: Opinion is not independent of aviation expertise

The test results from MegaStat are shown in Figure 15.5. Degrees of freedom are $v = (r - 1)(c - 1) = (2 - 1)(2 - 1) = 1$. Appendix E shows that the critical value of chi-square for $\alpha = .005$ is 7.879. Since the test statistic $\chi^2 = 59.80$ greatly exceeds 7.879, we firmly reject the hypothesis. The p-value (.0000) confirms that opinion is *not* independent of aviation experience.

FIGURE 15.5

MegaStat chi-square test with $v = 1$

Chi-square Contingency Table Test for Independence

	Col 1	Col 2	Total
Row 1 Observed	**40**	**61**	101
Expected	15.38	85.62	101.00
O − E	24.62	−24.62	0.00
$(O − E)^2/E$	39.39	7.08	46.47
Row 2 Observed	**29**	**323**	352
Expected	53.62	298.38	352.00
O − E	−24.62	24.62	0.00
$(O − E)^2/E$	11.30	2.03	13.33
Total Observed	69	384	453
Expected	69.00	384.00	453.00
O − E	0.00	0.00	0.00
$(O − E)^2/E$	50.69	9.11	59.80

59.80	chi-square
1	df
1.05E-14	p-value
1.38E-12	Fisher Exact Probability

Test of Two Proportions

For a 2 × 2 contingency table, the chi-square test is equivalent to a two-tailed z test for two proportions, if the samples are large enough to ensure normality. The hypotheses are:

H_0: $\pi_1 = \pi_2$

H_1: $\pi_1 \neq \pi_2$

In the aviation survey example, the proportion of aviation experts who said yes on the survey is $p_1 = x_1/n_1 = 40/69 = .57971$, or 58.0 percent, compared to the proportion of the general public $p_2 = x_2/n_2 = 61/384 = .15885$, or 15.9 percent. The pooled proportion is $\bar{p} = (x_1 + x_2)/(n_1 + n_2) = 101/453 = .22295$. The z test statistic is then:

$$z = \frac{p_1 - p_2}{\sqrt{\bar{p}(1 - \bar{p})\left[\dfrac{1}{n_1} + \dfrac{1}{n_2}\right]}} = \frac{.57971 - .15885}{\sqrt{.22295(1 - .22295)\left[\dfrac{1}{69} + \dfrac{1}{384}\right]}} = 7.7329$$

The z test statistic of the two-tailed test of two proportions is the same as the chi-square test statistic for the corresponding 2×2 table (in the aviation example, $z^2 = 7.7329^2 = 59.80 = \chi^2$). Because such tables are so common, the 2×2 contingency table has been extensively studied by statisticians, and many alternative tests for significance are available.*

Small Expected Frequencies

The chi-square test is unreliable if the *expected* frequencies are too small. As you can see from the formula for the test statistic, when e_{jk} in the denominator is small, the chi-square statistic may be inflated. A commonly used rule of thumb known as **Cochran's Rule** requires that $e_{jk} > 5$ for all cells. Another rule of thumb says that up to 20 percent of the cells may have $e_{jk} < 5$. Statisticians generally become quite nervous when $e_{jk} < 2$, and there is agreement that a chi-square test is infeasible if $e_{jk} < 1$ in any cell. Computer packages may offer warnings or refuse to proceed when expected frequencies are too small. When this happens, it may be possible to salvage the test by combining adjacent rows or columns to enlarge the expected frequencies. In the Web page example, all the expected frequencies are safely greater than 5.

Cross-Tabulating Raw Data

Chi-square tests for independence are quite flexible. Although most often used with nominal data such as gender (male, female), we can also analyze quantitative variables (such as salary) by coding them into categories (e.g., under \$25,000; \$25,000 to \$50,000; \$50,000 and over). Open-ended classes are acceptable. We can mix data types as required (nominal, ordinal, interval, ratio) by defining the bins appropriately. Few statistical tests are so versatile. Continuous data may be classified into any categories that make sense. To tabulate a continuous variable into two classes, we would make the cut at the median. For three bins, we would use the 33rd and 67th percentiles as cutpoints. For four bins, we would use the 25th, 50th, and 75th percentiles as cutpoints. We prefer classes that yield approximately equal frequencies for each cell to help protect against small expected frequencies (recall that Cochran's Rule requires expected frequencies be at least 5). Our bin choices are limited when we have integer data with a small range (e.g., a Likert scale with responses 1, 2, 3, 4, 5), but we can still define classes however we wish (e.g., 1 or 2, 3, 4 or 5).

EXAMPLE

Doctors and Infant Mortality

Let $X =$ doctors per 100,000 residents of a state, and $Y =$ infant deaths per 1,000 births in the state. We might reasonably hypothesize that states with more doctors relative to population would have lower infant mortality, but do they? We are reluctant to assume normality and equal variances, so we prefer to avoid a t test. Instead, we hypothesize:

H_0: Infant mortality rate is independent of doctors per 100,000 population

H_1: Infant mortality rate is not independent of doctors per 100,000 population

Depending on how we form the contingency table, we could get different results. Figure 15.6 shows 2×2 and 3×3 tables created using Visual Statistics. Each table shows both actual and expected frequencies assuming the null hypothesis. Neither p-value indicates a very strong relationship. Since we cannot reject H_0 at any customary level of significance, we conclude that doctors and infant mortality are not strongly related. A *multivariate* regression model might be

---

*One alternative is the *Fisher exact test* whose p-value is based on hypergeometric probabilities (MegaStat provides the Fisher exact probability for the 2×2 contingency table). For a 2×2 contingency table with $v = (r - 1)(c - 1) = 1$ the chi-square test may sometimes be improved by using *Yates's correction for continuity* (named for Frank Yates, 1902–1994). The correction subtracts $\frac{1}{2}$ from each absolute difference before squaring. However, research shows that it is often inadvisable to use Yates's correction, and most software packages ignore it.

the next step, to explore other predictors (e.g., per capita income, per capita Medicaid spending, percent of college graduates) that might be related to infant mortality in a state.

FIGURE 15.6

Visual Statistics contingency tables

2 × 2 Table Doctors Per 100,000			
Infant Deaths Per 1,000	Low	High	Total
High	15/13.0	11/13.0	26
Low	10/12.0	14/12.0	24
Total	25	25	50

Chi-square test statistic = 1.282 (p = .258)

3 × 3 Table Doctors Per 100,000				
Infant Deaths Per 1,000	Low	Med	High	Total
High	8/5.4	4/5.4	4/5.1	16
Med	4/5.4	6/5.4	6/5.1	16
Low	5/6.1	7/6.1	6/5.8	18
Total	17	17	16	50

Chi-square test statistic = 2.762 (p = .598)

3-Way Tables and Higher

There is no conceptual reason to limit ourselves to two-way contingency tables comparing two variables. However, such tables become rather hard to visualize, even when they are "sliced" into a series of 2-way tables. A table comparing three variables can be visualized as a *cube* or as a stack of tiled 2-way contingency tables. Major computer packages (SAS, SPSS, and others) permit 3-way contingency tables. For four or more variables, there is no physical analog to aid us, and their cumbersome nature would suggest analytical methods other than chi-square tests.

SECTION EXERCISES

Instructions: For each exercise, include MegaStat or Excel exhibits to support your chi-square calculations. (a) State the hypotheses. (b) Show how the degrees of freedom are calculated for the contingency table. (c) Using the level of significance specified in the exercise, find the critical value of chi-square from Appendix E or from Excel's function =CHIINV(alpha, deg_freedom). (d) Carry out the calculations for a chi-square test for independence and draw a conclusion. (e) Which cells of the contingency table contribute the most to the chi-square test statistic? (f) Are any of the expected frequencies too small? (g) Interpret the *p*-value. If necessary, you can calculate the *p*-value using Excel's function =CHIDIST(test statistic, deg_freedom). *(h) If it is a 2 × 2 table, perform a two-tailed two-sample z test for $\pi_1 = \pi_2$ and verify that z^2 is the same as your chi-square statistic. *Note:* Exercises marked with an asterisk (*) are more difficult.

15.1 In a study of how managers attempt to manage earnings, researchers analyzed a sample of 515 earnings-management attempts from a survey of experienced auditors. The frequency of effects is summarized in the table shown. *Research question:* At $\alpha = .01$, is the effect on earnings independent of the approach used? (Data are from Mark W. Nelson, John A. Elliott, and Robin L. Tarpley, "How Are Earnings Managed? Examples from Auditors," *Accounting Horizons,* Supplement, 2003, pp. 17–35.) **Earnings**

Current-Period Income Effect of Four Earnings Management Approaches

Approach Used	Increase	Decrease	No Clear Effect	Row Total
Expenses and Other Losses	133	113	23	269
Revenue and Other Gains	86	20	8	114
Business Combinations	12	22	33	67
Other Approaches	41	4	20	65
Col Total	272	159	84	515

15.2   Teenagers make up a large percentage of the market for clothing. Below are data on running shoe ownership in four world regions (excluding China). *Research question:* At $\alpha = .01$, does this sample show that teenage running shoe ownership depends on world region? (See J. Paul Peter and Jerry C. Olson, *Consumer Behavior and Marketing Strategy,* 9th ed. [McGraw-Hill, 2004], p. 64.)   **Running**

Running Shoe Ownership in World Regions

Owned By	U.S.	Europe	Asia	Latin America	Row Total
Teens	80	89	69	65	303
Adults	20	11	31	35	97
Col Total	100	100	100	100	400

15.3   Students applying for admission to an MBA program must submit scores from the GMAT test, which includes a verbal and a quantitative component. Shown here are raw scores for 100 randomly chosen MBA applicants at a Midwestern, public, AACSB-accredited business school. *Research question:* At $\alpha = .005$, is the quantitative score independent of the verbal score?   **GMAT**

	Quantitative			
Verbal	Under 25	25 to 35	35 or More	Row Total
Under 25	25	9	1	35
25 to 35	4	28	18	50
35 or More	1	3	11	15
Col Total	30	40	30	100

15.4   Computer abuse by employees is an ongoing worry to businesses. A study revealed the data shown below. *Research question:* At $\alpha = .01$, is the frequency of disciplinary action independent of the abuser's level of privilege? (Data are from Detmar W. Straub and William D. Nance, "Discovering and Disciplining Computer Abuse in Organizations," *MIS Quarterly* 14, no. 1 [March 1990], pp. 45–60.)   **Abuse**

Computer Abuse Incidents Cross-Tabulated by Punishment and Privilege

Level of Privilege	Disciplined	Not Disciplined	Row Total
Low	20	11	31
Medium	42	3	45
High	33	3	36
Col Total	95	17	112

15.5   Marketing researchers prepared an advance notification card announcing an upcoming mail survey and describing the purpose of their research. Half the target customers received the prenotification, followed by the survey. The other half received only the survey. The survey return rates are shown below. *Research question:* At $\alpha = .025$, is return rate independent of prenotification? (Data are from Paul R. Murphy, Douglas R. Dalenberg, and James M. Daley, "Improving Survey Responses with Postcards," *Industrial Marketing Management* 19, no. 4 [November 1990], pp. 349–355.)   **Advance**

Cross-Tabulation of Returns by Notification

Pre-Notified?	Returned	Not Returned	Row Total
Yes	39	155	194
No	22	170	192
Col Total	61	325	386

Mini Case   15.1

Student Work and Car Age

Do students work longer hours to pay for newer cars? This hypothesis was tested using data from a 2001 survey of introductory business statistics students at a large commuter university campus. The survey contained these two fill-in-the-blank questions:

> About how many hours per week do you expect to work at an outside job this semester?
>
> What is the age (in years) of the car you usually drive?

The contingency table shown in Table 15.5 summarizes the responses of 162 students. Very few students worked less than 15 hours, and a majority worked 25 hours or more. Most drove cars less than 3 years old, although a few drove cars 10 years old or more. Neither variable was normally distributed (and there were outliers) so a chi-square test was preferable to a correlation or regression model. The hypotheses to be tested are:

H_0: Car age is independent of work hours

H_1: Car age is not independent of work hours

TABLE 15.5   **Frequency Classification for Work Hours and Car Age**   **CarAge**

Hours of Outside Work Per Week	Age of Car Usually Driven				Row Total
	Less than 3	3 to 6	6 to 10	10 or More	
Under 15	9	8	8	4	29
15 to 25	34	17	11	9	71
25 or More	28	20	8	6	62
Col Total	71	45	27	19	162

Figure 15.7 shows MegaStat's analysis of the 3 × 4 contingency table. Two expected frequencies (upper right) are below 5, so Cochran's Rule is not quite met. MegaStat has highlighted these cells to call attention to this concern. But the most striking feature of this table is that almost all of the actual frequencies are very close to the frequencies expected under the hypothesis of independence, leading to a very small chi-square test statistic (5.24). The test requires six degrees of freedom, i.e. $v = (r - 1)(c - 1) = (3 - 1)(4 - 1) = 6$. From Appendix E we obtain the right-tail critical value $\chi^2_{.10} = 10.64$ at $\alpha = .10$. Even at this rather weak level of significance, we cannot reject H_0. MegaStat's p-value (.5132) says that a test statistic of this magnitude could arise by chance more than half the time in samples from a population in which the two variables really were independent. Hence, the data lend no support to the hypothesis that students work longer hours to support newer cars.

Chi-square Contingency Table Test for Independence

		Less than 3	3 to 6	6 to 10	10 or More	Total
Under 15	Observed	**9**	**8**	**8**	**4**	29
	Expected	12.71	8.06	4.83	3.40	29.00
	O − E	−3.71	−0.06	3.17	0.60	0.00
	(O − E)²/E	1.08	0.00	2.07	0.11	3.26
15 to 25	Observed	**34**	**17**	**11**	**9**	71
	Expected	31.12	19.72	11.83	8.33	71.00
	O − E	2.88	−2.72	−0.83	0.67	0.00
	(O − E)²/E	0.27	0.38	0.06	0.05	0.76
25 or More	Observed	**28**	**20**	**8**	**6**	62
	Expected	27.17	17.22	10.33	7.27	62.00
	O − E	0.83	2.78	−2.33	−1.27	0.00
	(O − E)²/E	0.03	0.45	0.53	0.22	1.22
Total	Observed	71	45	27	19	162
	Expected	71.00	45.00	27.00	19.00	162.00
	O − E	0.00	0.00	0.00	0.00	0.00
	(O − E)²/E	1.38	0.82	2.66	0.38	5.24

5.24	chi-square
6	df
.5132	p-value

FIGURE 15.7

MegaStat's analysis of car age data

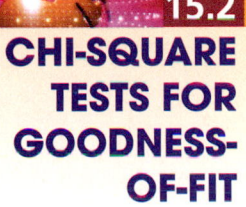

15.2
CHI-SQUARE TESTS FOR GOODNESS-OF-FIT

Chapter 13

Purpose of the Test

A *goodness-of-fit test* (or GOF test) is intended to help you decide whether your sample re-sembles a particular kind of population. Tests for goodness-of-fit are easy to understand, but until spreadsheets came along, the calculations were tedious. Today, computers make it easy, and tests for departure from normality or any other distribution are routine. We will illustrate GOF tests for three familiar distributions (uniform, Poisson, and normal). Although there are many tests for goodness-of-fit, the *chi-square test* is attractive because it is versatile and easy to understand.

Hypotheses for GOF

The hypotheses are of the form:

H_0: The population follows a _____ distribution

H_1: The population doesn't follow a _____ distribution

Test Statistic and Degrees of Freedom for GOF

The blank may contain the name of any theoretical distribution (e.g., uniform, Poisson, nor-mal). Assuming that we have n observations, we group the observations into c classes and then find the *chi-square test statistic:*

$$\chi^2 = \sum_{j=1}^{c} \frac{[f_j - e_j]^2}{e_j} \qquad (15.4)$$

where

f_j = the observed frequency of observations in class j

e_j = the expected frequency in class j if H_0 were true

If the proposed distribution gives a good fit to the sample, the test statistic will be near zero because f_j and e_j will be approximately equal. Conversely, if f_j and e_j differ greatly, the test sta-tistic will be large. The test statistic follows the chi-square distribution. It is always a right-tailed test. We will reject H_0 if the test statistic exceeds the chi-square critical value chosen from Appendix E. The rule for degrees of freedom is

$$(15.5) \qquad\qquad v = c - m - 1$$

where c is the number of classes used in the test and m is the number of parameters estimated. If we are using sample data to *estimate* the distribution's parameters:

(15.6)	**Uniform:**	$v = c - m - 1 = v = c - 0 - 1 = c - 1$	(since no parameters are estimated)
(15.7)	**Poisson:**	$v = c - m - 1 = v = c - 1 - 1 = c - 2$	(since λ is estimated)
(15.8)	**Normal:**	$v = c - m - 1 = v = c - 2 - 1 = c - 3$	(since μ and σ are estimated)

Data-Generating Situations

"Fishing" for a good-fitting model is inappropriate. Instead, we visualize *a priori* the characteristics of the underlying *data-generating process.* It is undoubtedly true that the most common GOF test is for the normal distribution, simply because so many parametric tests assume normality, and that assumption must be tested. Also, the normal distribution may be used as a default benchmark for any mound-shaped data that has centrality and tapering tails, as long as you have reason to believe that a constant mean and variance would be reasonable (e.g., weights of circulated dimes). However, you would not consider a Poisson distribution for continuous data (e.g., gasoline price per liter) or certain integer variables (e.g., exam scores) because a Poisson model only applies to integer data on arrivals or rare, independent events (e.g., number of paint defects per square meter). We remind you of this because software makes it possible to fit inappropriate distributions all too easily.

Mixtures: A Problem

Your sample may not resemble any known distribution. One common problem is *mixtures.* A sample may have been created by more than one data-generating process superimposed on top of one another. For example, adult heights of either sex would follow a normal distribution, but a combined sample of both genders will be bimodal, and its mean and standard deviation may be unrepresentative of either sex. Obtaining a good fit is not *per se* sufficient justification for assuming a particular model. Each probability distribution has its own logic about the nature of the underlying process, so we must also examine the data-generating situation and be convinced that the proposed model is both logical *and* empirically apt.

Eyeball Tests

A simple "eyeball" inspection of the histogram or dot plot may suffice to rule out a hypothesized population. For example, if the sample is strongly bimodal or skewed, or if outliers are present, we would anticipate a poor fit to a normal distribution. The shape of the histogram can give you a rough idea whether a normal distribution is a likely candidate for a good fit. You can be fairly sure that a formal test will agree with what your common sense tells you, as long as the sample size is not too small.

Yet a limitation of eyeball tests is that we may be unsure just how much variation is expected for a given sample size. If anything, the human eye is overly sensitive, causing us to commit α error (rejecting a true null hypothesis) too often. People are sometimes unduly impressed by a small departure from the hypothesized distribution, when actually it is within chance. We will see examples of this.

Small Expected Frequencies

Goodness-of-fit tests may lack power in small samples. The minimum necessary sample size depends on the type of test being employed. As a guideline, a chi-square goodness-of-fit test should be avoided if $n < 25$ (some experts would suggest a higher number). *Cochran's Rule* that expected frequencies should be at least 5 (i.e., all $e_j \geq 5$) also provides a guideline, although some experts would weaken the rule to require only $e_j \geq 2$.

Multinomial Distribution

The chi-square test can be used to compare sample frequencies with any probability distribution. A **multinomial distribution** is defined by any k probabilities $\pi_1, \pi_2, \ldots, \pi_k$ that sum to 1. For example, the "official" proportions of M&M colors are shown in Table 15.6. In a statistics class, students opened four bags of M&Ms and counted those of each color. Observed frequencies (f_j) are to be compared with expected frequencies (e_j) using a chi-square GOF test. Each expected frequency (e_j) is calculated by multiplying the sample size (n) by the hypothesized proportion (π_j). That is, $e_j = n \times \pi_j$.

TABLE 15.6
Hypothesis Test of M&M Proportions
🍫 MM

Color	Official π_j	Observed f_j	Expected e_j	$f_j - e_j$	$(f_j - e_j)^2/e_j$
Brown	0.30	58	66	−8	0.9697
Red	0.20	40	44	−4	0.3636
Blue	0.10	34	22	12	6.5455
Orange	0.10	22	22	0	0.0000
Green	0.10	30	22	8	2.9091
Yellow	0.20	36	44	−8	1.4545
Sum	1.00	220	220	0	$\chi^2 = 12.2424$

The hypotheses are:

H_0: $\pi_1 = .30, \pi_2 = .20, \pi_3 = .10, \pi_4 = .10, \pi_5 = .10, \pi_6 = .20$

H_1: At least one of the π_j differs from the hypothesized value

No parameters are estimated ($m = 0$) and we have six classes ($c = 6$), so degrees of freedom are $v = c - m - 1 = v = 6 - 0 - 1 = 5$. From Appendix E, the critical value of chi-square for $\alpha = .01$ is $\chi^2_{.01} = 15.09$, so we cannot reject the hypothesis that the M&Ms came from a population with the stated proportions. All expected frequencies are at least 5, so Cochran's Rule is satisfied.

Uniform Distribution

The uniform goodness-of-fit test is a special case of the multinomial in which every value has the same chance of occurrence. Uniform data-generating situations are rare, but some data *must* be from a **uniform distribution,** such as winning lottery numbers or random digits generated by a computer for random sampling. Another use of the uniform distribution is as a worst case scenario for an unknown distribution whose range is specified in a what-if analysis.

The chi-square test for a uniform distribution is a generalization of the test for equality of two proportions. The hypotheses are:

H_0: $\pi_1 = \pi_2 = \cdots = \pi_c = 1/c$

H_1: Not all the π_j are equal

The chi-square test compares all c groups *simultaneously*. Each discrete outcome should have probability $1/c$, so the test is very easy to perform. Evidence against H_0 would consist of sample frequencies that were not the same for all categories.

Classes need not represent numerical values. For example, we might compare the total number of items scanned per hour by four supermarket checkers (Bob, Frieda, Sam, and Wanda). The uniform test is quite versatile. For numerical variables, bins do not have to be of equal width and can be open-ended. For example, we might be interested in the ages of X-ray machines in a hospital (under 2 years, 2 to 5 years, 5 to 10 years, 10 years and over). In a uniform population, each category would be expected to have $e_j = n/c$ observations, so the calculation of expected frequencies is simple.

Uniform GOF Test: Grouped Data

The test is easiest if data are already tabulated into groups, which saves us the effort of defining the groups. For example, one year, a certain state had 756 traffic fatalities. Table 15.7 suggests

TABLE 15.7

Traffic Fatalities by Day of Week 🐾 **Traffic**

Day	f_j	e_j	$f_j - e_j$	$(f_j - e_j)^2$	$(f_j - e_j)^2/e_j$
Sun	121	108	13	169	1.565
Mon	96	108	−12	144	1.333
Tue	91	108	−17	289	2.676
Wed	92	108	−16	256	2.370
Thu	96	108	−12	144	1.333
Fri	122	108	14	196	1.815
Sat	138	108	30	900	8.333
Total	756	756	0		$\chi^2 = 19.426$

Source: Based on www-nrd.nhtsa.dot.gov.

that fatalities are not uniformly distributed by day of week, being higher on weekends. Can we reject the hypothesis of a uniform distribution, say, at $\alpha = .005$? The hypotheses are:

H_0: Traffic fatalities are uniformly distributed by day of the week

H_1: Traffic fatalities are not uniformly distributed by day of the week

Under H_0 the expected frequency for each weekday is $e_j = n/c = 756/7 = 108$. The expected frequencies happen to be integers, although this is not true in general. Since no parameters were estimated ($m = 0$) to form the seven classes ($c = 7$) the chi-square test will have $v = c - m - 1 = 7 - 0 - 1 = 6$ degrees of freedom. From Appendix E the critical value of chi-square for the 1 percent level of significance is $\chi^2_{.01} = 18.55$, so the hypothesis of a rectangular or uniform population can be rejected. The p-value (.0035) can be obtained from the Excel function =CHIDIST(19.426,6). The p-value tells us that such a sample result would occur by chance only about 35 times in 10,000 samples. There is a believable underlying causal mechanism at work (e.g., people may drink and drive more often on weekends).

Uniform GOF Test: Raw Data

When we are using raw data, we must form c bins of equal width and create our own frequency distribution. For example, suppose an auditor is checking the fairness of a state's "Daily 3" lottery. Table 15.8 shows winning three-digit lottery numbers for 100 consecutive days. All numbers from 000 to 999 are supposed to be equally likely, so the auditor is testing these hypotheses:

H_0: Lottery numbers are uniformly distributed

H_1: Lottery numbers are not uniformly distributed

TABLE 15.8

100 Consecutive Winning Three-Digit Lottery Numbers 🐾 **Lottery-A**

367	865	438	437	596	567	121	244	036	337
152	260	470	821	452	606	417	674	786	311
739	611	359	739	184	229	418	565	547	403
103	344	303	531	054	496	167	550	403	785
341	237	913	991	656	661	178	983	431	472
315	792	676	299	738	080	450	991	673	846
500	001	016	581	154	677	457	617	261	807
452	048	052	018	037	517	760	522	711	898
294	605	135	333	886	257	533	119	882	899
814	490	490	885	329	033	033	707	551	651

We know that three-digit lottery numbers must lie in the range 000 to 999, so there are many ways we could define our classes (e.g., 5 bins of width 200, 10 bins of width 100, 20 bins of width 50). We will use 10 bins, with the realization that we might get a different result if we chose different bins. The steps are:

- Step 1   Divide the range into 10 bins of equal width.
- Step 2   Calculate the observed frequency f_j for each bin.
- Step 3   Define $e_j = n/c = 100/10 = 10$.
- Step 4   Perform the chi-square calculations (see Table 15.9).
- Step 5   Make the decision.

Bin	f_j	e_j	$f_j - e_j$	$(f_j - e_j)^2$	$(f_j - e_j)^2/e_j$
$0 < 100$	11	10	1	1	0.100
$100 < 200$	9	10	−1	1	0.100
$200 < 300$	8	10	−2	4	0.400
$300 < 400$	10	10	0	0	0.000
$400 < 500$	16	10	6	36	3.600
$500 < 600$	12	10	2	4	0.400
$600 < 700$	11	10	1	1	0.100
$700 < 800$	9	10	−1	1	0.100
$800 < 900$	10	10	0	0	0.000
$900 < 1,000$	4	10	−6	36	3.600
Total	100	100	0		$\chi^2 = 8.400$

TABLE 15.9

Uniform GOF Test for Lottery Numbers

Since no parameters were estimated ($m = 0$) to form the 10 classes ($c = 10$) we have $v = c - m - 1 = 10 - 0 - 1 = 9$ degrees of freedom. From Appendix E the critical value of chi-square for the 10 percent level of significance is $\chi^2_{.10} = 14.684$. Since the test statistic is 8.400, the hypothesis of a uniform distribution cannot be rejected.

If the bin limits cannot be set using *a priori* knowledge (as was possible in the lottery example), we maximize the test's power by defining bin width as the range divided by the number of classes:

$$\text{Bin width} = \frac{x_{\max} - x_{\min}}{c} \qquad \text{(setting bin width from sample data)} \qquad \textbf{(15.9)}$$

The resulting bin limits may not be aesthetically pleasing, but the expected frequencies will be as large as possible (you might be able to round the bin limits to a "nice" number without affecting the calculations very much). If the sample size is small, small expected frequencies could be a problem. Since all expected frequencies are the same in a uniform model, this problem will exist in all classes simultaneously. For example, we could not classify 25 observations into 10 classes without violating Cochran's Rule (although the more relaxed rule $ej \geq 2$ would be satisfied).

The histograms in Figures 15.8 and 15.9 suggest too many winning lottery numbers in the middle and too few at the top. But histogram appearance is affected by the way we define our bins and the number of classes, so the chi-square test is a more reliable guide. Humans are adept at finding patterns in sample distributions that actually are within the realm of chance.

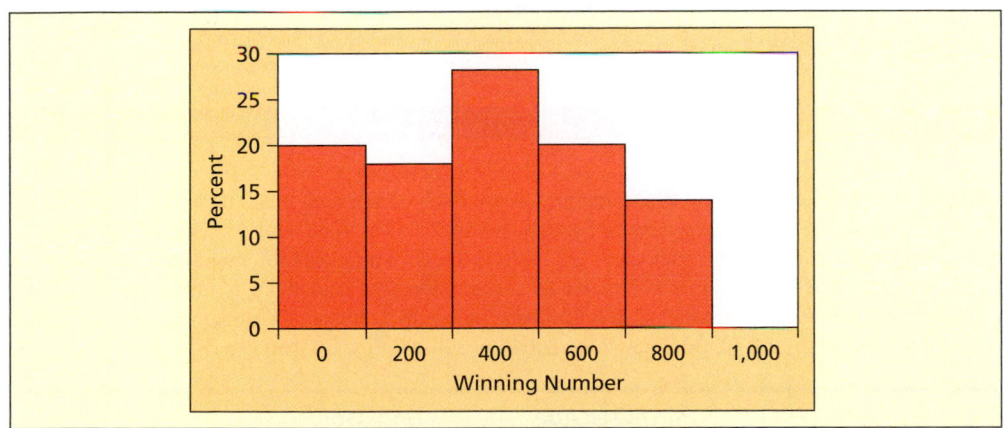

FIGURE 15.8

Five-bin histogram

As you learned in Chapter 6, a discrete uniform distribution with range a to b is symmetric with mean $\mu = (a + b)/2$ and $\sigma = \sqrt{[(b - a + 1)^2 - 1]/12}$. For the lottery, we have $a = 000$ and $b = 999$, so we expect the mean to be $\mu = (0 + 999)/2 = 499.5$ and $\sigma = \sqrt{[(999 - 0 + 1)^2 - 1]/12} = 288.7$. For the sample, Table 15.10 shows that the low (001) and high (991) are near their theoretical values, as are the sample mean (472.2), standard deviation (271.0), and skewness coefficient (.01). The first quartile (260.5) is close to its expected value (.25 × 999 = 249.8), while the third quartile (675.5) is smaller than expected (.75 × 999 = 749.3).

FIGURE 15.9

Ten-bin histogram

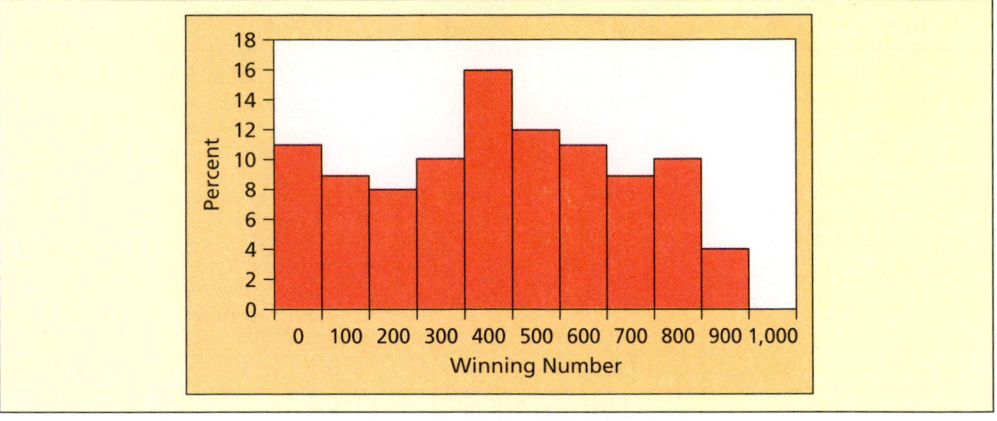

TABLE 15.10

Descriptive Statistics

Statistic	Sample	If Uniform
Minimum	001	000
Maximum	991	999
Mean	472.2	499.5
Median	471.0	499.5
Standard Deviation	271.0	288.7
Quartile 1	260.5	249.8
Quartile 3	675.5	749.3
Skewness	0.01	0.00

Since the data are not skewed (mean ≈ median) and the sample size is large ($n \geq 30$), the mean is approximately normally distributed, so we can use the normal distribution to test the sample mean for a significant difference from the hypothesized uniform mean, assuming that $\sigma = 288.7$ as would be true if the data were uniform:

$$z = \frac{\bar{X} - \mu}{\frac{\sigma}{\sqrt{n}}} = \frac{472.2 - 499.5}{\frac{288.7}{\sqrt{100}}} = -0.95 \qquad \text{(two-tail } p\text{-value} = .34)$$

The difference is not significant at any common level of α. Overall, these statistics show no convincing evidence of departure from a uniform distribution, thereby confirming the chi-square test's conclusion.

SECTION EXERCISES

15.6 Advertisers need to know which age groups are likely to see their ads. Purchasers of 120 copies of *Cosmopolitan* are shown by age group. (a) Make a bar chart and describe it. (b) Calculate expected frequencies for each class. (c) Perform the chi-square test for a uniform distribution. At $\alpha = .01$, does this sample contradict the assumption that readership is uniformly distributed among these six age groups? (See J. Paul Peter and Jerry C. Olson, *Consumer Behavior and Marketing Strategy,* 9th ed. [McGraw-Hill, 2004], p. 300.) 🏵 **Cosmo**

Purchaser Age	Units Sold
18–24	38
25–34	28
35–44	19
45–54	16
55–64	10
65+	9
Total	120

15.7   One-year sales volume of four similar 20-oz. beverages on a college campus is shown. (a) Make a bar chart and describe it. (b) Calculate expected frequencies for each class. (c) Perform the chi-square test for a uniform distribution. At $\alpha = .05$, does this sample contradict the assumption that sales are the same for each beverage?   **Frapp**

Beverage	Sales (Cases)
Frappuccino Coffee	18
Frappuccino Mocha	23
Frappuccino Vanilla	23
Frappuccino Caramel	20
Total	84

15.8   In a three-digit lottery, each of the three digits is supposed to have the same probability of occurrence (counting initial blanks as zeros, e.g., 32 is treated as 032). The table shows the frequency of occurrence of each digit for 90 consecutive daily three-digit drawings. (a) Make a bar chart and describe it. (b) Calculate expected frequencies for each class. (c) Perform the chi-square test for a uniform distribution. At $\alpha = .05$, can you reject the hypothesis that the digits are from a uniform population?   **Lottery3**

Digit	Frequency
0	33
1	17
2	25
3	30
4	31
5	28
6	24
7	25
8	32
9	25
Total	270

15.9   Ages of 56 attendees of a Harry Potter movie are shown. (a) Form seven age classes (10 to 20, 20 to 30, etc.). Tabulate the frequency of attendees in each class. (b) Calculate expected frequencies for each class. (c) Perform a chi-square GOF test for a uniform distribution, using the 5 percent level of significance.   **Harry**

10	22	58	11	73	22	57
35	33	33	59	54	55	75
79	24	13	73	52	69	30
71	64	17	50	72	67	50
72	35	26	59	47	65	35
64	34	39	66	37	41	58
51	43	29	74	73	50	62
58	34	50	27	13	67	67

Poisson Data-Generating Situations

15.4 POISSON GOODNESS-OF-FIT TEST

In a *Poisson distribution* model, X represents the number of events per unit of time or space. By definition, X is a discrete nonnegative integer ($X = 0, 1, 2, \ldots$). Event arrivals must be independent of one another. Events that tend to fit this definition might include customer arrivals per minute at an ATM, calls per minute at Ticketmaster, or alarms per hour at a fire station. In such cases, the mean arrival rate would vary by time of day, day of the week, and so on. The Poisson has been demonstrated to apply to scores in some sports events (goals scored per soccer game, goals in hockey games) and to defects in manufactured components such as LCDs, printed circuits, and automobile paint jobs. Typically X has a fairly small mean, which is why the Poisson is sometimes called a model of *rare events*. If the mean is large, we might fit a normal distribution instead. Poisson random number generators are used by researchers who model queues, an important application in dense urban cultures. The Poisson distribution is inappropriate for noninteger data or financial data such as you would find in company annual reports. Remembering these facts can spare you from wasted time trying to fit a Poisson model when it is inappropriate.

Poisson Goodness-of-Fit Test

A Poisson model is completely described by its one parameter, the mean λ. Assuming that λ is unknown and must be estimated from the sample, the initial steps are:

- Step 1   Tally the observed frequency f_j of each X-value.
- Step 2   Estimate the mean λ from the sample.
- Step 3   Use the estimated λ to find the Poisson probability $P(X)$ for each value of X.
- Step 4   Multiply $P(X)$ by the sample size n to get expected Poisson frequencies e_j.
- Step 5   Perform the chi-square calculations.
- Step 6   Make the decision.

If the data are already tabulated, we can skip the first step. A Poisson test always has an open-ended class on the high end, since technically X has no upper limit. Unfortunately, Poisson tail probabilities are very small, and so will be the corresponding expected frequencies. But classes can be combined from each end inward until expected frequencies become large enough for the test (at least until $e_j \geq 2$). Combining classes implies using fewer classes than you would wish, but a more detailed breakdown isn't justified unless the sample is very large.

Poisson GOF Test: Tabulated Data

The number of U.S. Supreme Court appointments in a given year might be hypothesized to be a Poisson variable, since rare events that occur independently over time are often well approximated by the Poisson model. We formulate these hypotheses:

H_0: Supreme Court appointments follow a Poisson distribution

H_1: Supreme Court appointments do not follow a Poisson distribution

The frequency of U.S. Supreme Court appointments for the period 1900 through 1999 is summarized in Table 15.11. This sample of 100 years should be large enough to obtain a valid hypothesis test. In a typical year, there are no appointments, and only twice have there been three or four appointments (1910 and 1941).

TABLE 15.11

Number of Annual U.S. Supreme Court Appointments, 1900–1999

🦅 **Supreme**

Source: *The World Almanac and Book of Facts,* 2002, p. 94. Copyright © 2002 World Almanac Education Group, Inc.

X	f_j	$X_j f_j$
0	59	0
1	31	31
2	8	16
3	1	3
4	1	4
Total	100	54

The total number of appointments is

$$\sum_{j=1}^{c} x_j f_j = (0)(59) + (1)(31) + (2)(8) + (3)(1) + (4)(1) = 54$$

so the sample mean is

$$\hat{\lambda} = \frac{54}{100} = 0.54 \text{ appointments per year}$$

Using the estimated mean $\hat{\lambda} = 0.54$ we can calculate the Poisson probabilities, either by using the Poisson formula $P(x) = (\lambda^x e^{-\lambda})/x!$ or Excel's function =POISSON(x,mean,0). We multiply $P(X)$ by n to get the expected frequencies, with $n = 100$ years, as shown in Table 15.12.

TABLE 15.12
Fitted Poisson Probabilities

X	P(X)	$e_j = nP(X)$
0	0.58275	100 × 0.58275 = 58.275
1	0.31468	100 × 0.31468 = 31.468
2	0.08496	100 × 0.08496 = 8.496
3	0.01529	100 × 0.01529 = 1.529
4	0.00206	100 × 0.00206 = 0.206
5	0.00022	100 × 0.00022 = 0.022
6 or more	0.00004	100 × 0.00004 = 0.004
Sum	1.00000	100.00

The probabilities rapidly become small as X increases. To ensure that $e_j \geq 2$ it is necessary to combine the top classes to end up with only three classes, the top class being "2 or more" before doing the chi-square calculations shown in Table 15.13. Since f_j and e_j are almost identical, the Poisson distribution obviously gives an excellent fit, so we are not surprised that the test statistic (0.022) is very near zero.

TABLE 15.13
Chi-Square Test for Supreme Court Data

X	f_j	e_j	$f_j - e_j$	$(f_j - e_j)^2$	$(f_j - e_j)^2/e_j$
0	59	58.275	0.725	0.525625	0.009
1	31	31.468	−0.468	0.219024	0.007
2 or more	10	10.257	−0.257	0.066049	0.006
Total	100	100			$\chi^2 = 0.022$

Using $c = 3$ classes in the test and with $m = 1$ parameter estimated, the degrees of freedom are $\nu = c - m - 1 = 3 - 1 - 1 = 1$. From Appendix E, we see that the critical value for $\alpha = .10$ is $\chi^2_{.10} = 2.706$, so we clearly cannot reject the hypothesis of a Poisson distribution, even at a modest level of significance. Excel's function =CHIDIST(.022,1) gives the *p*-value .882, which indicates an excellent fit. Although we can never *prove* that the annual U.S. Supreme Court appointments follow a Poisson distribution, we can see that the Poisson distribution fits the sample well, as in the Visual Statistics graph in Figure 15.10 (orange bar is actual, green line is fitted Poisson).

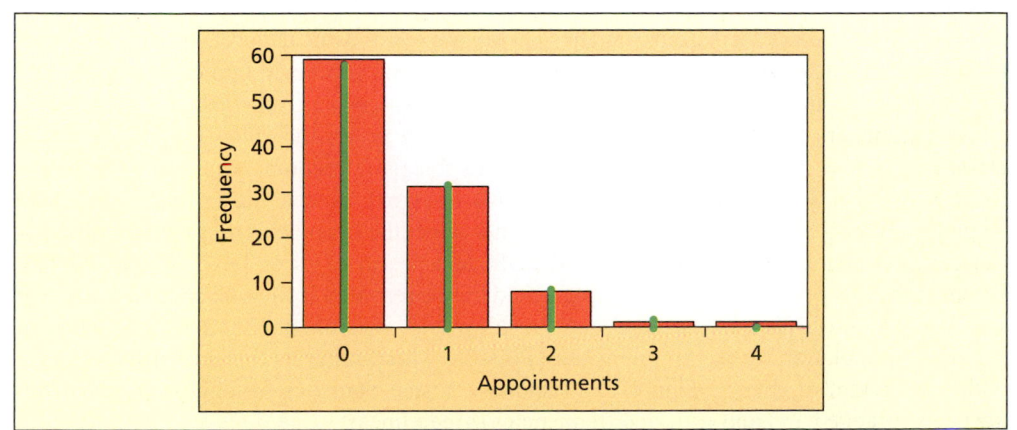

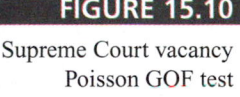

FIGURE 15.10

Supreme Court vacancy Poisson GOF test

Poisson GOF Test: Raw Data

Figure 15.11 shows the menu from Excel's Tools > Data Analysis > Random Number Generation, which was used to create 100 Poisson random numbers with a mean of $\lambda = 4.0$. We would like to test this generator's accuracy.

FIGURE 15.11

Excel's Poisson random number generator

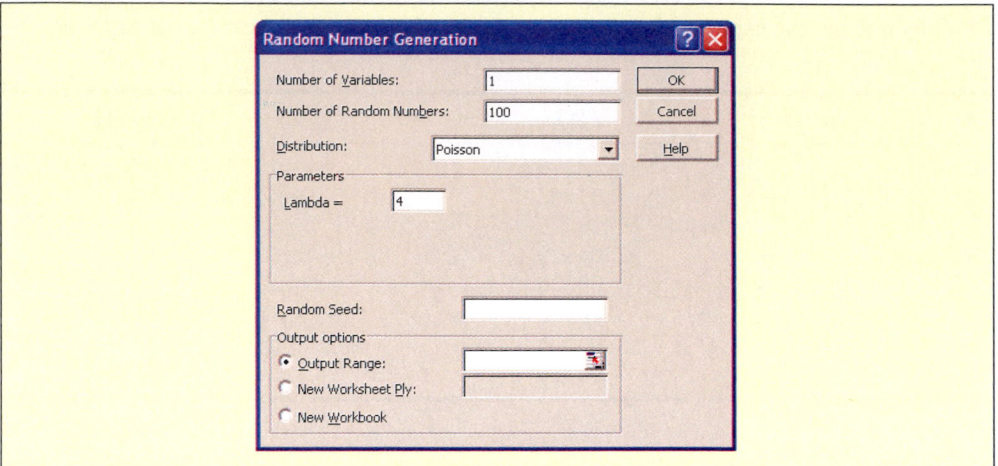

Table 15.14 shows 100 Excel-generated Poisson arrivals whose mean is supposed to be $\lambda = 4.0$ arrivals per minute. Is Excel's simulation algorithm working properly? A visual inspection shows two possibly unusual observations (two 11s) but beyond that it is hard to tell.

TABLE 15.14

100 Random Poisson Arrivals with $\lambda = 4$

RandPoisson

5	3	11	4	5	1	7	4	4	5
3	2	5	7	4	4	6	5	5	7
2	4	9	7	5	5	4	5	4	3
4	6	3	3	3	4	6	2	6	7
6	2	7	3	6	6	4	4	2	0
4	8	4	4	4	2	5	2	5	4
3	6	7	8	4	5	4	3	7	5
2	3	2	4	3	5	2	6	5	7
2	3	7	2	1	4	2	3	4	5
0	3	3	7	3	8	5	5	6	11

The hypotheses are:

H_0: Excel's random data are from a Poisson distribution

H_1: Excel's random data are not from a Poisson distribution

Figure 15.12 shows the Visual Statistics chi-square test for this data set. To ensure that all expected frequencies are at least 2, the 0s and 1s have been combined into one category, and all values of 9 or more have been combined.

No parameters were estimated, since we specified *a priori* the value $\lambda = 4$. For $c = 9$ classes and $m = 0$ parameters estimated, the degrees of freedom are $v = c - m - 1 = c - 1 = 8$. At $\alpha = .10$, the test statistic (9.046) does not exceed the critical value from Appendix E for $v = 8$ ($\chi^2_{.10} = 6.251$) so we do not reject the hypothesis of a Poisson distribution despite the surfeit of 7s ($f = 11$, $e = 5.95$) and dearth of 0s or 1s ($f = 4$, $e = 9.16$). Presumably, this peculiarity of our sample would not be repeated if we took another sample of 100. The *p*-value (.338) suggests that such a result would occur about 338 times in 1,000 samples if the population we are sampling were Poisson, which suggests that any differences are within the realm of chance. Figure 15.13 shows a Visual Statistics histogram of actual frequencies (orange bars) and expected frequencies (green lines).

FIGURE 15.12

Visual Statistics
chi-square test

Arrivals	Obs	Exp	Obs-Exp	Chi-Square
1 or less	4	9.16	−5.16	2.905
2	13	14.65	−1.65	0.186
3	16	19.54	−3.54	0.640
4	22	19.54	2.46	0.311
5	18	15.63	2.37	0.360
6	10	10.42	−0.42	0.017
7	11	5.95	5.05	4.276
8	3	2.98	0.02	0.000
9 or more	3	2.13	0.87	0.351
Total	100	100	0	9.046
Parameters from user			d.f. = 8	$p < 0.338$

FIGURE 15.13

Visual Statistics
histogram

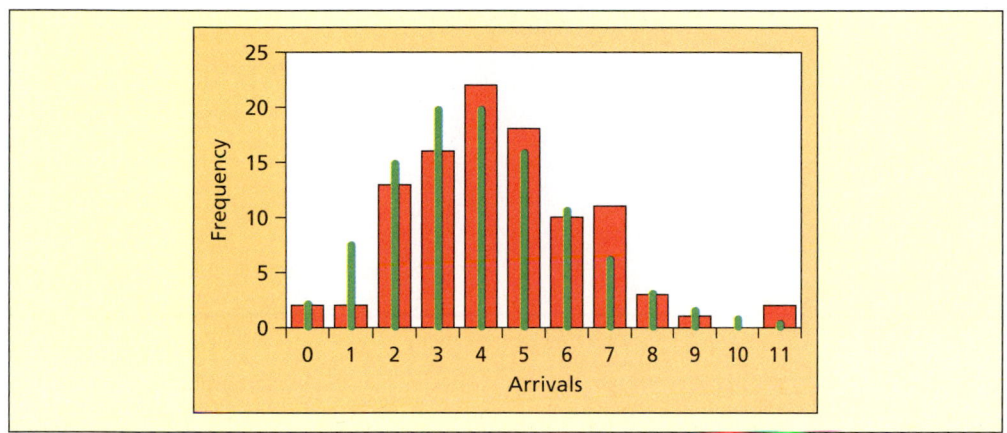

In addition to a chi-square GOF test, we can examine the sample statistics to see if they resemble what would be expected for a Poisson distribution. In a Poisson distribution, the mean is λ, the standard deviation is $\sqrt{\lambda}$, and the skewness is $1/\sqrt{\lambda}$. Table 15.15 shows that the sample mean (4.46) is a little larger than expected ($\mu = \lambda = 4.0$), but the sample standard deviation (2.072) is very close to the expected Poisson standard deviation ($\sigma = \sqrt{\lambda} = \sqrt{4} = 2$). The sample skewness (0.57) is close to the expected skewness ($1/\sqrt{4} = 0.50$). All in all, the evidence is compatible with the hypothesis that Excel's data follow a Poisson distribution.

Statistic	Sample	If Poisson
Mean	4.460	4.000
Standard Deviation	2.072	2.000
Skewness	0.57	0.50

TABLE 15.15
Statistics for Excel Sample

As a last check, since the sample is large enough ($n \geq 30$) to assume normality of the mean, we can do a z test to see whether the sample mean equals the theoretical mean $\lambda = 4.0$. Interestingly, the z test does indicate a potentially significant difference in the sample mean from the intended mean:

$$z = \frac{\bar{X} - \mu}{\frac{\sigma}{\sqrt{n}}} = \frac{4.460 - 4.000}{\frac{2}{\sqrt{100}}} = 2.300 \qquad (p = .021 \text{ in a two-tailed test})$$

The p-value says that such a difference could occur about 21 times in 1,000 samples if the null hypothesis is true. Depending on our α, this could be a significant difference. This difference between the sample mean and the theoretical mean arises from the two outliers (at $X = 11$), which did not have much effect on the chi-square test.

15.10 Excel was asked to generate 50 Poisson random numbers with mean $\lambda = 5$. (a) Calculate the sample mean. How close is it to the desired value? (b) Calculate the expected frequencies assuming a Poisson distribution with $\lambda = 5$. Show your calculations in a spreadsheet format. (c) Carry out the chi-square test at $\alpha = .05$, combining end categories as needed to ensure that all expected frequencies are at least five. Show your degrees of freedom calculation. (d) Do you think your calculations would have been materially different if you had used the sample mean instead of $\lambda = 5.0$? Explain.   **RandPoisB**

X	Frequency
0	1
1	1
2	4
3	7
4	7
5	8
6	10
7	3
8	3
9	4
10	1
11	1

15.11 During the 1973–74 hockey season, the Boston Bruins played 39 home games and scored 193 points, as shown below. (a) Estimate the mean from the sample. (b) Calculate the expected frequencies assuming a Poisson distribution. Show your calculations in a spreadsheet format. (c) Carry out the chi-square test, combining end categories as needed to ensure that all expected frequencies are at least five. Show your degrees of freedom calculation. (d) At $\alpha = .05$, can you reject the hypothesis that goals per game follow a Poisson process? (Data are from Gary M. Mullett, "Simeon Poisson and the National Hockey League," *The American Statistician* 31, no. 1 [1977], p. 9.)   **Boston**

Number of Goals Scored (per game) by Boston Bruins, 1973–74

	0	1	2	3	4	5	6	7	8	9	10	Total
						Number of Goals						
Frequency	0	1	2	5	9	10	5	2	3	1	1	39

15.12 At a local supermarket receiving dock, the number of truck arrivals per day is recorded for 100 days. (a) Estimate the mean from the sample. (b) Calculate the expected frequencies assuming a Poisson distribution. Show your calculations in a spreadsheet format. (c) Carry out the chi-square test, combining end categories as needed to ensure that all expected frequencies are at least five. Show your degrees of freedom calculation. (d) At $\alpha = .05$, can you reject the hypothesis that arrivals per day follow a Poisson process?   **Trucks**

Arrivals per Day at a Loading Dock

	0	1	2	3	4	5	6	7	Total
				Number of Arrivals					
Frequency	4	23	28	22	8	9	4	2	100

Normal Data-Generating Situations

Any normal population is fully described by the two parameters μ and σ. Many data-generating situations could be compatible with a ***normal distribution,*** if the data possess a reasonable degree of central tendency and are not badly skewed. Measurements of continuous variables such as physical attributes (e.g., weight, size, travel time) may have a constant mean and variance if the underlying process is stable and the population is homogeneous. The normal model might apply to discrete or integer data if the range is relatively large, such as the number of successes in a large binomial sample or Poisson occurrences if the mean is large. Unless μ and σ parameters are known *a priori* (a rare circumstance) they must be estimated from a sample by using $\bar{x}$ and s. Using these statistics, we can set up the chi-square goodness-of-fit test. There are several ways this could be done.

Method 1: Standardizing the Data

There are various ways to calculate the frequencies for a chi-square test. One way is to transform the sample observations $x_1, x_2, \ldots, x_n$ into standardized values:

$$z = \frac{x_i - \bar{x}}{s} \qquad \text{(standardized data transformation)} \qquad \textbf{(15.10)}$$

We could count the sample observations f_j within intervals of the form $\bar{x} \pm ks$ and compare them with the known frequencies e_j based on the normal distribution, as illustrated in Figure 15.14. We could break the intervals down into more classes if we wish. This method has the advantage of using a standardized scale, but the disadvantage that data no longer are in the original units of measurement (e.g., kilograms) plus the effort required to standardize the data.

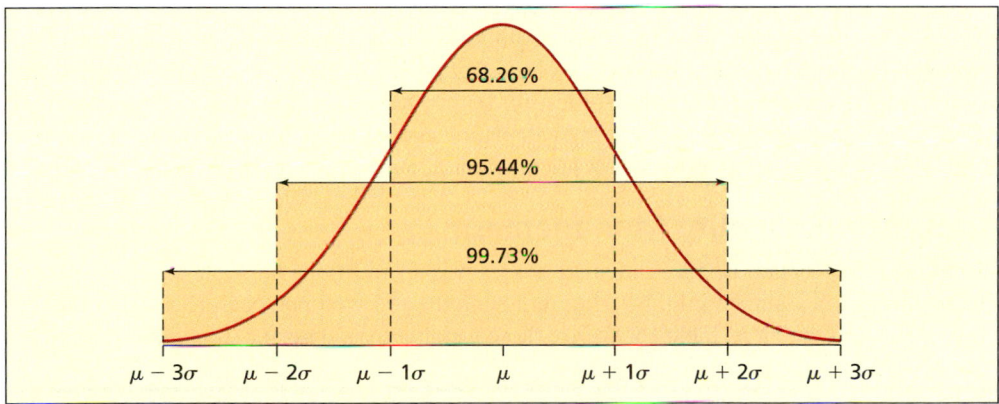

FIGURE 15.14

Normal areas

Method 2: Equal Bin Widths

An alternative approach is to create a histogram for the original data with equal-width bins. Rather than using "nice" bin limits (as we often do for histograms) we divide the *exact data range* into c groups of equal width.

$$\text{Bin width} = \frac{x_{\max} - x_{\min}}{c} \qquad \text{(setting bin width from sample data)} \qquad \textbf{(15.11)}$$

This avoids "empty" space within histogram intervals. We then proceed as follows:

- Step 1   Count the sample observations in each bin to get observed frequencies f_j.
- Step 2   Convert the bin limits into standardized z-values by using formula 15.10.
- Step 3   Find the area within each bin assuming a normal distribution.
- Step 4   Find expected frequencies e_j by multiplying each normal area by the sample size n.

An advantage of this test is that it corresponds directly to the histogram. Its disadvantage is that, in the end classes, very few observations would be expected. Since small expected frequencies can cause trouble for a chi-square test, classes may need to be collapsed from the ends inward, to enlarge the expected frequencies.

Method 3: Equal Expected Frequencies

A third method is to define histogram bins in such a way that an equal number of observations would be *expected* within each bin under the null hypothesis. That is, define bin limits so that

(15.12) $e_j = n/c$ (define bins to get equal expected frequencies)

We want a normal area of $1/c$ in each of the c bins. The first and last classes must be open-ended for a normal distribution, so to define c bins we need $c - 1$ cutpoints. The upper limit of bin j can be found directly by using Excel's function =NORMINV($j/c, \bar{x}, s$). Alternatively, we can find z_j for bin j with Excel's standard normal function =NORMSINV($j/c,0,1$) and then calculate the upper limit for bin j as $\bar{x} + z_j s$. Table 15.16 shows some typical z-values to put an area of $1/c$ in each bin.

TABLE 15.16
Standard Normal Cutpoints for Equal Area Bins

Bin	3 Bins	4 Bins	5 Bins	6 Bins	7 Bins	8 Bins
1	−0.431	−0.675	−0.842	−0.967	−1.068	−1.150
2	0.431	0.000	−0.253	−0.431	−0.566	−0.675
3		0.675	0.253	0.000	−0.180	−0.319
4			0.842	0.431	0.180	0.000
5				0.967	0.566	0.319
6					1.068	0.675
						1.150

Once the bins are defined, we count the observations f_j within each bin and compare them with the expected frequencies $e_j = n/c$. Although the bin limits will not be "nice," the compelling advantage of this method is that it guarantees the largest possible expected frequencies, and hence the most powerful test for c bins. MegaStat uses this method (Descriptive Statistics > Normal Curve Goodness of Fit) and calculations are automatic, but you cannot vary the number of bins (MegaStat always uses the maximum number of bins while keeping $e_j \geq 5$).

Application: Quality Management

A sample of 35 Hershey's Milk Chocolate Kisses was taken from a bag containing 84 Kisses. The population is assumed infinite. After removing the foil wrapper, each Kiss was weighed. The weights are shown in Table 15.17. Are these weights from a normal population?

TABLE 15.17
Weights of 35 Hershey's Milk Chocolate Kisses (in grams) 🍫 **Kisses**

4.666	4.854	4.868	4.849	4.700	4.683	5.064
4.800	4.694	4.760	5.075	4.780	4.781	5.103
4.568	4.983	5.076	4.808	5.084	4.749	5.092
4.783	4.520	4.698	5.084	4.880	4.883	4.880
4.928	4.651	4.797	4.682	4.756	5.041	4.906

Source: An independent project by MBA student Frances Williams. Kisses were weighed on an American Scientific Model S/P 120 analytical balance accurate to 0.0001 gm.

It might be supposed *a priori* that Kiss weights would be normally distributed, since the manufacturing process should have a single, constant mean and standard deviation. Variation is inevitable in any manufacturing process. Chocolate is especially difficult to handle, because liquid chocolate must be dropped in precisely measured amounts, solidified, wrapped, and bagged. Since chocolate is soft and crumbles easily, even the process of weighing the Kisses may abrade some chocolate and introduce measurement error. We will test the following hypotheses:

H_0: Kisses' weights are from a normal distribution

H_1: Kisses' weights aren't from a normal distribution

Before undertaking a GOF test, consider the histograms in Figure 15.15. Visual Statistics has fitted a normal distribution to the data, based on the estimated mean and standard deviation. Although it is only a visual aid, the fitted normal gives you a clue as to the likely outcome of the test. The histograms reveal no apparent outliers, and nothing in conflict with the idea of a normal population except a second mode toward the high end of the scale and perhaps a flatter appearance than normal. Since histogram appearance can vary, depending on the number of classes and the way the bin limits are specified, further tests are needed.

FIGURE 15.15

Visual Statistics histograms of 35 Hershey's Kiss weights

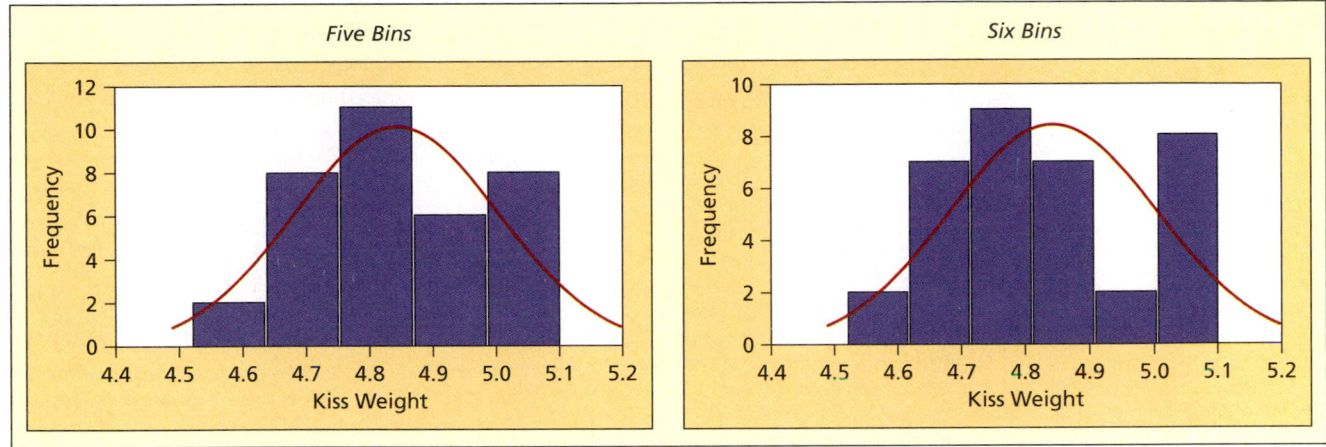

Table 15.18 compares the sample statistics with parameters expected for a normal distribution. Since the mean and standard deviation were fitted from the data, they tell us nothing. The median (4.808) is slightly less than the mean (4.844), but the skewness coefficient (0.14) is fairly close to the value (0.00) that would be expected in a symmetric normal distribution. The sample quartiles (4.700 and 4.983) are nearly what we expect for a normal distribution using the 25th and 75th percentiles ($\bar{x} \pm 0.675s$). There are no outliers, as the smallest Kiss (4.520 grams) is 2.01 standard deviations below the mean, while the largest Kiss (5.103 grams) is 1.61 standard deviations above the mean.

TABLE 15.18

Sample vs. Normal

Statistic	Kiss Weight	If Normal
Mean	4.844	4.844
Standard Deviation	0.161	0.161
Quartile 1	4.700	4.735
Median	4.808	4.844
Quartile 3	4.983	4.952
Skewness	0.14	0.00

For a chi-square GOF test, degrees of freedom are $v = c - m - 1$, where c is the number of classes used in the test and m is the number of parameters estimated. Since two parameters, μ and σ, are estimated from the sample, $m = 2$. The degrees of freedom and critical values for various numbers of bins are shown in Table 15.19. We need at least four bins to ensure at least

TABLE 15.19

Critical Values for Normal GOF Test

Number of Bins	Degrees of Freedom	$\chi^2_{.10}$	$\chi^2_{.05}$
4	$v = c - m - 1 = c - 2 - 1 = 4 - 3 = 1$	2.706	3.841
5	$v = c - m - 1 = c - 2 - 1 = 5 - 3 = 2$	4.605	5.991
6	$v = c - m - 1 = c - 2 - 1 = 6 - 3 = 3$	6.251	7.815
7	$v = c - m - 1 = c - 2 - 1 = 7 - 3 = 4$	7.779	9.488

1 degree of freedom, while Cochran's Rule (at least 5 *expected* observations per bin) suggests a maximum of 7 bins for $n = 35$ data points (since $35/7 = 5$).

Because we anticipate that the number of bins may affect the results, we will vary the number of bins from 4 to 7. We will concentrate on seeing whether the result is affected by the number of bins, and whether certain bins have a disproportionate effect on the chi-square test statistic. We will use method 3 (equal expected frequencies) because it is the most powerful, and will rely on Visual Statistics to handle the calculations (MegaStat would give the same result except that it insists on using 7 bins, the maximum allowable under Cochran's Rule).

Using four bins (Figure 15.16) the chi-square test statistic (0.086) is not significant at $\alpha = .10$ ($\chi^2_{.10} = 2.706$) and its *p*-value (.770) indicates that such a result would be expected about 770 times in 1,000 samples if the population were normal. Using five bins (Figure 15.17) the chi-square test statistic (4.857) is barely significant at $\alpha = .10$ ($\chi^2_{.10} = 4.605$) and its *p*-value (.088) indicates that such a result would be expected about 88 times in 1,000 samples if the population were normal. Bin four (highlighted) contributes heavily to the chi-square statistic.

FIGURE 15.16

Four bins ($c = 4$)

Kiss Weight	Obs	Exp	Obs-Exp	Chi-Square
Under 4.735	9	8.75	0.25	0.007
4.735 < 4.844	9	8.75	0.25	0.007
4.844 < 4.952	8	8.75	−0.75	0.064
4.952 or more	9	8.75	0.25	0.007
Total	35	35	0	0.086
Parameters from sample			d.f. = 1	p < 0.770

FIGURE 15.17

Five bins ($c = 5$)

Kiss Weight	Obs	Exp	Obs-Exp	Chi-Square
Under 4.708	9	7.00	2.00	0.571
4.708 < 4.803	8	7.00	1.00	0.143
4.803 < 4.884	7	7.00	0.00	0.000
4.884 < 4.979	2	7.00	−5.00	3.571
4.979 or more	9	7.00	2.00	0.571
Total	35	35	0	4.857
Parameters from sample			d.f. = 2	p < 0.088

Using six bins (Figure 15.18), the chi-square test statistic (3.571) is not significant at $\alpha = .10$ ($\chi^2_{.10} = 6.251$) and its *p*-value (.312) indicates that such a result would be expected about 312 times in 1,000 samples if the population were normal. Bin five (highlighted)

FIGURE 15.18

Six bins ($c = 6$)

Kiss Weight	Obs	Exp	Obs-Exp	Chi-Square
Under 4.688	6	5.83	0.17	0.005
4.688 < 4.774	6	5.83	0.17	0.005
4.774 < 4.844	6	5.83	0.17	0.005
4.844 < 4.913	7	5.83	1.17	0.233
4.913 < 4.999	2	5.83	−3.83	2.519
4.999 or more	8	5.83	2.17	0.805
Total	35	35	0	3.571
Parameters from sample			d.f. = 3	p < 0.312

contributes heavily to the chi-square statistic. Using seven bins (Figure 15.19), the chi-square test statistic (8.000) is not quite significant at $\alpha = .10$ ($\chi^2_{.10} = 7.779$) and its *p*-value (.092) indicates that such a result would be expected about 92 times in 1,000 samples if the population were normal. Bin six (highlighted) contributes heavily to the chi-square statistic.

Kiss Weight	Obs	Exp	Obs-Exp	Chi-Square
Under 4.672	4	5.00	−1.00	0.200
4.672 < 4.752	6	5.00	1.00	0.200
4.752 < 4.815	8	5.00	3.00	1.800
4.815 < 4.873	3	5.00	−2.00	0.800
4.873 < 4.935	5	5.00	0.00	0.000
4.935 < 5.015	1	5.00	−4.00	3.200
5.015 or more	8	5.00	3.00	1.800
Total	35	35	0	8.000
Parameters from sample			d.f. = 4	$p < 0.092$

FIGURE 15.19

Seven bins ($c = 7$)

Interpretation   Depending on the number of bins, the chi-square tests either fail to reject the hypothesis of normality or reject it at a weak level of significance. These results fail to *disprove* normality convincingly. However, the histograms do suggest a bimodal shape. This could occur if the Kisses were molded by two or more different machines. If each machine has a different μ and σ, this could lead to the "mixture of distributions" problem mentioned earlier. If so, a platykurtic distribution (flatter than normal) would be likely. This issue bears further investigation. A quality control analyst would probably take a larger sample and study the manufacturing methods to see what could be learned.

SECTION EXERCISES

Note: Exercises marked with an asterisk (*) are more difficult.

15.13 Exam scores of 40 students in a statistics class are shown. (a) Estimate the mean and standard deviation from the sample. (b) Assuming that the data are from a normal distribution, define bins by using method 3 (equal expected frequencies). Use 8 bins. (c) Set up an Excel worksheet for your chi-square calculations, with a column showing the expected frequency for each bin (they must add to 40). (d) Tabulate the observed frequency for each bin and record it in the next column. (e) Carry out the chi-square test, using $\alpha = .05$. Can you reject the hypothesis that the exam scores came from a normal population? *(f) Enter the data into the Visual Statistics data editor in Module 13 (Goodness-of-Fit Tests) and do chi-square tests with varying options. Was Visual Statistics helpful?   **ExamScores**

79	75	77	57	81	70	83	66
81	89	59	83	75	60	96	86
78	76	71	78	78	70	54	60
71	81	79	88	77	82	75	68
77	69	83	79	79	76	78	71

15.14 One Friday night, there were 42 carry-out orders at Ashoka Curry Express. (a) Estimate the mean and standard deviation from the sample. (b) Assuming that the data are from a normal distribution, define bins by using method 3 (equal expected frequencies). Use 8 bins. (c) Set up an Excel worksheet for your chi-square calculations, with a column showing the expected frequency for each bin (they must add to 42). (d) Tabulate the observed frequency for each bin and record it in the next column. (e) Do the chi-square test at $\alpha = .025$. Can you reject the hypothesis that carry-out orders follow a normal population? *(f) Enter the data into the Visual Statistics data editor in

Module 13 (Goodness-of-Fit Tests) and do chi-square tests with varying options. Was Visual Statistics helpful? **TakeOut**

18.74	21.05	31.19	23.06	20.17	25.12	24.30
46.04	33.96	45.04	34.63	35.24	30.13	29.93
52.33	26.52	19.68	19.62	32.96	42.07	47.82
38.62	31.88	44.97	36.35	21.50	41.42	33.87
26.43	35.28	21.88	24.80	27.49	18.30	44.47
28.40	36.72	26.30	47.08	34.33	13.15	15.51

15.6
ECDF TESTS (OPTIONAL)

Kolmogorov-Smirnov and Lilliefors Tests

There are many alternatives to the chi-square test, based on the *empirical cumulative distribution function (ECDF)*. One such test is the *Kolmogorov-Smirnov test*. The K-S test statistic D is the largest absolute difference between the actual and expected cumulative relative frequency of the n data values:

$$(15.13) \qquad\qquad D = \mathrm{Max}\ |F_a - F_e|$$

The K-S test is not recommended for grouped data, as it may be less powerful than the chi-square test.

F_a is the actual cumulative frequency at observation i, and F_e is the expected cumulative frequency at observation i under the assumption that the data came from the hypothesized distribution. The K-S test assumes that no parameters are estimated. If they are (e.g., the mean and variance may be estimated) we use a *Lilliefors test,* whose test statistic is the same, but with a different table of critical values. Since these tests are always done by computer (F_e requires the inverse CDF for the hypothesized distribution), we will omit further details and merely illustrate the test visually. Because observations are treated individually, information is not lost by combining categories, as in a chi-square test. Thus, ECDF tests may surpass the chi-square test in their ability to detect departures from the distribution specified in the null hypothesis, if raw data are available.

Illustrations: Lottery Numbers and Kiss Weights

Figure 15.20 shows a Visual Statistics screen displaying the Kolmogorov-Smirnov test for *uniformity* in the 100 lottery numbers tested earlier in a chi-square test. The largest difference (.087) occurs at observation 77, but the large *p*-value does not warrant rejection of the hypothesis of a uniform distribution. The CDF under the hypothesis of uniformity is a straight

FIGURE 15.20

K-S test for uniformity

Chapter 13

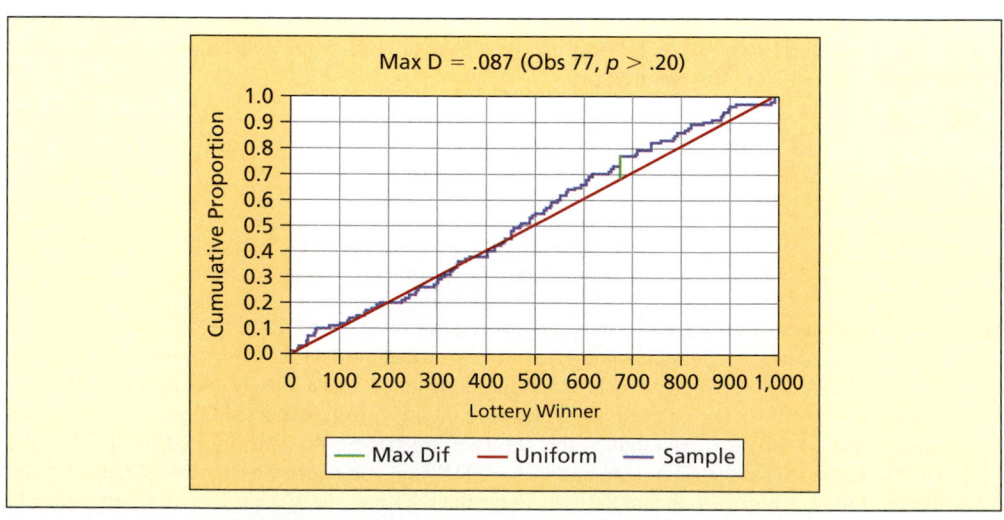

line, while for a normal distribution, the CDF would be *S*-shaped. Figure 15.21 shows a *normality* test for weights of Hershey's Kisses. The largest difference occurs at observation 28, but the *p*-value does not warrant rejection of the hypothesis of normality. For this data set, the K-S test lacks sufficient power to reject *either* a uniform *or* a normal distribution.

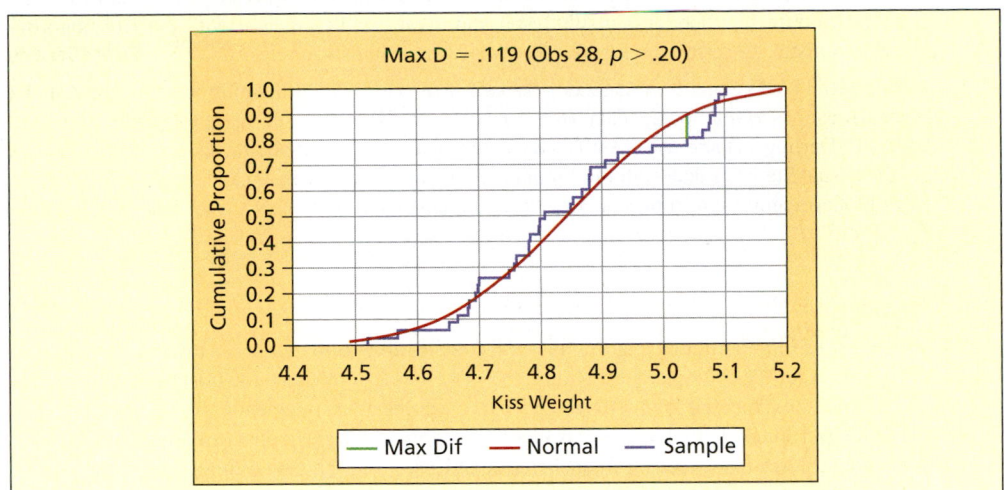

FIGURE 15.21

K-S test for normality

Anderson-Darling Test

The **Anderson-Darling test,** another ECDF test, is perhaps the most widely used test for non-normality because of its power. It is always done on a computer since it requires the inverse CDF for the hypothesized distribution. The A-D test is based on a **probability plot.** When the data fit the hypothesized distribution closely, the probability plot will be close to a straight line. The A-D test statistic measures the overall distance between the actual and the hypothesized distributions, using a weighted squared distance. It provides a *p*-value to complement the visual plot. The A-D statistic is not difficult to calculate, but its formula is rather complex, so it is omitted. Figure 15.22 shows a graph displaying the probability plot and A-D statistic for the Hershey's Kiss data using MINITAB's Stats > Basic Statistics > Normality Test. The *p*-value (.091) suggests a departure from normality at the 10 percent level of significance, but not at the 5 percent level. This result is consistent with our previous findings. The A-D test is more powerful than a chi-square test if raw data are available, because it treats the observations individually. Also, the probability plot has the attraction of revealing discrepancies between the sample and the hypothesized distribution, and it is usually easy to spot outliers.

FIGURE 15.22

MINITAB's probability plot and Anderson-Darling test for Kiss weights

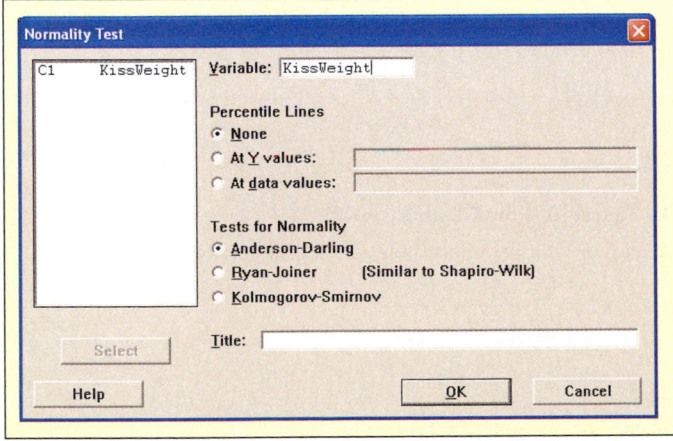

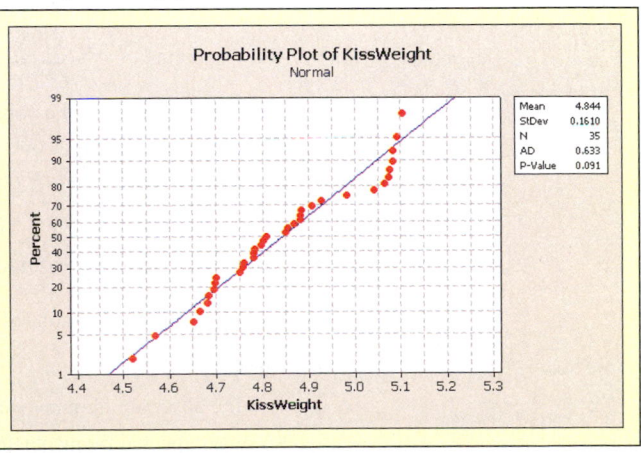

*15.15 (a) Use MINITAB's Stat > Basic Statistics > Normality Test to obtain a probability plot for the exam score data (see Exercise 15.13). Interpret the probability plot and Anderson-Darling statistic. Was MINITAB easier to use than the chi-square test? (b) Enter the data into the Visual Statistics data editor in Module 13 (Goodness-of-Fit Tests) and create an ECDF plot with the Kormogorov-Smirnov statistic. Describe the ECDF plot. Was Visual Statistics helpful?   🐝 **ExamScores**

*15.16 (a) Use MINITAB's Stat > Basic Statistics > Normality Test to obtain a probability plot for the Ashoka Curry House carry-out order data (see Exercise 15.14). Interpret the probability plot and Anderson-Darling statistic. Was MINITAB easier to use than the chi-square test? (b) Enter the data into the Visual Statistics data editor in Module 13 (Goodness-of-Fit Tests) and create an ECDF plot with the Kormogorov-Smirnov statistic. Describe the ECDF plot. Was Visual Statistics helpful?   🐝 **TakeOut**

Chapter Summary

A **chi-square test of independence** requires an $r \times c$ **contingency table** that has r rows and c columns. Degrees of freedom for the chi-square test will be $(r-1)(c-1)$. In this test, the **observed frequencies** are compared with the **expected frequencies** under the hypothesis of independence. The test assumes categorical data (attribute data) but can also be used with numerical data grouped into classes. **Cochran's Rule** requires that expected frequencies be at least 5 in each cell, although this rule is often relaxed. A test for **goodness-of-fit (GOF)** uses the chi-square statistic to decide whether a sample is from a specified distribution (e.g., multinomial, uniform, Poisson, normal). The **parameters** of the fitted distribution (e.g., the mean) may be specified *a priori,* but more often are estimated from the sample. Degrees of freedom for the GOF test are $c - m - 1$ where c is the number of categories and m is the number of parameters estimated. The **Kolmogorov-Smirnov** and **Lilliefors** tests are **ECDF-based tests** that look at differences between the sample's empirical cumulative distribution function (ECDF) and the hypothesized distribution. They are best used with n individual observations. The **Anderson-Darling** test and the **probability plot** are the most common ECDF tests, most often used to test for normality.

Key Terms

Anderson-Darling test, *685*
chi-square probability
    distribution, *658*
chi-square test, *658*
Cochran's Rule, *663*
contingency table, *657*
degrees of freedom, *658*

empirical cumulative
    distribution function
    (ECDF), *684*
expected frequency, *658*
goodness-of-fit test, *667*
independent, *658*
Kolmogorov-Smirnov test, *684*

Lilliefors test, *684*
multinomial distribution, *669*
normal distribution, *679*
observed frequency, *658*
Poisson distribution, *673*
probability plot, *685*
uniform distribution, *669*

Commonly Used Formulas

Chi-Square Test for Independence

Test statistic for independence in a contingency table with r rows and c columns: $\chi^2 = \sum_{j=1}^{r} \sum_{k=1}^{c} \frac{[f_{jk} - e_{jk}]^2}{e_{jk}}$

Degrees of freedom for a contingency table with r rows and c columns: $\nu = (r-1)(c-1)$

Expected frequency in row j and column k: $e_{jk} = R_j C_k / n$

Chi-Square Test for Goodness-of-Fit

Test statistic for observed frequencies in c classes under an hypothesized distribution H_0 (e.g., uniform, Poisson, normal): $\chi^2 = \sum_{j=1}^{c} \frac{[f_j - e_j]^2}{e_j}$

where

f_j = the observed frequency in class j

e_j = the expected frequency in class j

Degrees of freedom for the chi-square GOF test: $v = c - m - 1$

where

c = the number of classes used in the test
m = the number of parameters estimated

Estimated mean of Poisson distribution with c classes: $\lambda = \sum_{j=1}^{c} x_j f_j$

where

x_j = the value of X in class j
f_j = the observed frequency in class j

Expected frequency in class j assuming a uniform distribution with c classes: $e_j = n/c$

Chapter Review

Note: Questions labeled * are based on optional material from this chapter.

1. (a) What are the hypotheses in a chi-square test for independence? (b) Why do we call it a test of frequencies? (c) What distribution is used in this test? (d) How do we calculate the degrees of freedom for an $r \times c$ contingency table?

2. How do we calculate the expected frequencies for each cell of the contingency table?

3. (a) What is Cochran's Rule, and why is it needed? Why do we call it a "rule of thumb"?

4. (a) Explain why the 2×2 table is analogous to a z test for two proportions. (b) What is the relationship between z and χ^2 in the 2×2 table?

5. (a) What are the hypotheses for a GOF test? (b) Explain how a chi-square GOF test is carried out in general.

6. What is the general formula for degrees of freedom in a chi-square GOF test?

7. (a) In a uniform GOF test, how do we calculate the expected frequencies? (b) Why is the test easier if the data are already grouped?

8. (a) In a Poisson GOF test, how do we calculate the expected frequencies? (b) Why do we need the mean λ before carrying out the chi-square test?

9. (a) Very briefly describe three ways of calculating expected frequencies for a normal GOF test. (b) Name advantages and disadvantages of each way. (c) Why is a normal GOF test almost always done on a computer?

*10. What is an ECDF test? Give an example.

*11. (a) Name potential advantages of the Kolmogorov-Smirnov or Lilliefors tests. (b) Why would this type of test almost always be done on a computer?

*12. (a) What does a probability plot show? (b) If the hypothesized distribution is a good fit to the data, what would be the appearance of the probability plot? (c) What are the advantages and disadvantages of a probability plot?

*13. (a) Name two advantages of the Anderson-Darling test. (b) Why is it almost always done on a computer?

CHAPTER EXERCISES

Instructions: In all exercises, include MegaStat, Excel, or MINITAB exhibits to support your calculations. State the hypotheses, show how the degrees of freedom are calculated, find the critical value of chi-square from Appendix E or from Excel's function =CHIINV(alpha, deg_freedom), and interpret the p-value. Tell whether the conclusion is sensitive to the level of significance chosen, identify cells that contribute the most to the chi-square test statistic, and check for small expected frequencies. If necessary, you can calculate the p-value by using Excel's function =CHIDIST(test statistic,deg_freedom). *Note:* Exercises marked * are harder or require optional material.

15.17 Employees of Axolotl Corporation were sampled at random from pay records and asked to complete an anonymous job satisfaction survey, yielding the tabulation shown. *Research question:* At $\alpha = .05$, is job satisfaction independent of pay category? **Employees**

Pay Type	Satisfied	Neutral	Dissatisfied	Total
Salaried	20	13	2	35
Hourly	135	127	58	320
Total	155	140	60	355

15.18 Sixty-four students in an introductory college economics class were asked how many credits they had earned in college, and how certain they were about their choice of major. *Research question:* At $\alpha = .01$, is the degree of certainty independent of credits earned? **Certainty**

Credits Earned	Very Uncertain	Somewhat Certain	Very Certain	Row Total
0–9	12	8	3	23
10–59	8	4	10	22
60 or more	1	7	11	19
Col Total	21	19	24	64

15.19 To see whether students who finish an exam first get the same grades as those who finish later, a professor kept track of the order in which papers were handed in. Of the first 25 papers, 10 received a "B" or better compared with 8 of the last 24 papers handed in. *Research question:* At $\alpha = .10$, is the grade independent of the order handed in? Since it is a 2×2 table, try also a two-tailed two-sample z test for $\pi_1 = \pi_2$ (see Chapter 10) and verify that z^2 is the same as your chi-square statistic. Which test do you prefer? Why? **Grades**

Grade	Earlier Hand-In	Later Hand-In	Row Total
"B" or better	10	8	18
"C" or worse	15	16	31
Col Total	25	24	49

15.20 A study of health care planning undertook a mail survey of hospital administrators in Arkansas, Louisiana, and east Texas. *Research question:* At $\alpha = .05$, is the type of planning independent of the intensity of competition? (Data are from D. O. McKee, P. R. Varadarajan, and J. Vassar, "A Taxonomy of Marketing Planning Styles," *Journal of the Academy of Marketing Science* 18, no. 2 [Spring 1990], pp. 131–41.) **Planning**

Degree of Competition	Limited Planning	Constituency Planning	Comprehensive Planning	Row Total
Low	11	25	33	69
Moderate	19	23	15	57
High	43	25	17	85
Col Total	73	73	65	211

15.21 Results of a study of male freshman athletes in the Big Ten Conference are shown. Before doing any formal tests, examine the contingency table and discuss any obvious patterns. Is a statistical test needed? *Research question:* At $\alpha = .01$, is graduation independent of sport? (Data are from *The Detroit News,* May 6, 1990, p. 10E. Big Ten athlete graduation rates have improved since this study, but see *U.S. News and World Report,* 135, no. 9 [September 22, 2003], p. 27.) **BigTen**

Sport	Graduate in 6 Years	Not Graduate in 6 Years	Row Total
Tennis	42	16	58
Swimming	116	51	167
Soccer	35	17	52
Gymnastics	40	23	63
Golf	30	21	51
Track	97	69	166
Football	267	317	584
Wrestling	70	87	157
Baseball	77	98	175
Hockey	39	66	105
Basketball	36	61	97
Other	18	5	23
Col Total	867	831	1,698

15.22 A student team examined parked cars in four different suburban shopping malls. One hundred vehicles were examined in each location. *Research question:* At $\alpha = .05$, does vehicle type vary by mall location? (Data are from a project by MBA students Steve Bennett, Alicia Morais, Steve Olson, and Greg Corda.) **Vehicles**

Vehicle Type	Somerset	Oakland	Great Lakes	Jamestown	Row Total
Car	44	49	36	64	193
Minivan	21	15	18	13	67
Full-sized Van	2	3	3	2	10
SUV	19	27	26	12	84
Truck	14	6	17	9	46
Col Total	100	100	100	100	400

15.23 Choose either 2×2 contingency table shown below (males *or* females). *Research question:* At $\alpha = .005$, is smoking independent of race? (Smoking rates are from *Statistical Abstract of the United States, 2001,* pp. 16 and 12, applied to hypothetical samples of 500.) **Smoking**

Smoking by Race for Males Aged 18–24

Race	Smoker	Nonsmoker	Row Total
White	145	280	425
Black	15	60	75
Col Total	160	340	500

Smoking by Race for Females Aged 18–24

Race	Smoker	Nonsmoker	Row Total
White	116	299	415
Black	7	78	85
Col Total	123	377	500

15.24 High levels of cockpit noise in an aircraft can damage the hearing of pilots who are exposed to this hazard for many hours. A Boeing 727 co-pilot collected 61 noise observations using a handheld sound meter. Noise level is defined as "Low" (under 88 decibels), "Medium" (88 to 91 decibels), or "High" (92 decibels or more). There are three flight phases (Climb, Cruise, Descent). *Research question:* At $\alpha = .05$, is the cockpit noise level independent of flight phase? (Data are from Capt. Robert E. Hartl, retired.) 🔨 **Noise**

Noise Level	Climb	Cruise	Descent	Row Total
Low	6	2	6	14
Medium	18	3	8	29
High	1	3	14	18
Col Total	25	8	28	61

15.25 Forecasters' interest rate predictions over the period 1982–1990 were studied to see whether the predictions corresponded to what actually happened. The 2×2 contingency table below shows the frequencies of actual and predicted interest rate movements. *Research question:* At $\alpha = .10$, is the actual change independent of the predicted change? (Data are from R. A. Kolb and H. O. Steckler, "How Well Do Analysts Forecast Interest Rates?" *Journal of Forecasting* 15, no. 15 [1996], pp. 385–394.) 🔨 **Forecasts**

Forecasted Change	Rates Fell	Rates Rose	Row Total
Rates would fall	7	12	19
Rates would rise	9	6	15
Col Total	16	18	34

15.26 In a study of childhood asthma, 4,317 observations were collected on education and smoking during pregnancy, shown in the 4×3 contingency table below. *Research question:* At $\alpha = .005$, is smoking during pregnancy independent of education level? (Data are from Michael Weitzman and Deborah Klein Walker, "Maternal Smoking and Asthma," *Pediatrics* 85, no. 4 [April 1990], p. 507.) 🔨 **Pregnancy**

Education	No Smoking	$<\frac{1}{2}$ Pack	$\geq\frac{1}{2}$ Pack	Row Total
<High School	641	196	196	1,033
High School	1,370	290	270	1,930
Some College	635	68	53	756
College	550	30	18	598
Col Total	3,196	584	537	4,317

15.27 Two contingency tables below show return on investment (ROI) and percent of sales growth over the previous 5 years for 85 U.S. firms. ROI is defined as percentage of return on a combination of stockholders' equity (both common and preferred) plus capital from long-term debt including current maturities, minority stockholders' equity in consolidated subsidiaries, and accumulated deferred taxes and investment tax credits. *Research question:* At $\alpha = .05$, is ROI independent of sales growth? Would you expect it to be? Do the two tables (2×2 and 3×3) agree? Are small expected frequencies a problem? (Data are adapted from a research project by MBA student B. J. Oline.) 🔨 **ROI**

2 × 2 Cross-Tabulation of Companies

ROI	Low Growth	High Growth	Row Total
Low ROI	24	16	40
High ROI	14	31	45
Col Total	38	47	85

3 × 3 Cross-Tabulation of Companies

ROI	Low Growth	Medium Growth	High Growth	Row Total
Low ROI	9	12	7	28
Medium ROI	6	14	7	27
High ROI	1	12	17	30
Col Total	16	38	31	85

15.28 Can people really identify their favorite brand of cola? Volunteers tasted Coca-Cola Classic, Pepsi, Diet Coke, and Diet Pepsi, with the results shown below. *Research question:* At $\alpha = .05$, is the correctness of the prediction different for the two types of cola drinkers? Could *you* identify your favorite brand in this kind of test? Since it is a 2 × 2 table, try also a two-tailed two-sample z test for $\pi_1 = \pi_2$ (see Chapter 10) and verify that z^2 is the same as your chi-square statistic. Which test do you prefer? Why? (Data are from *Consumer Reports* 56, no. 8 [August 1991], p. 519.)   **Cola**

Correct?	Regular Cola	Diet Cola	Row Total
Yes, got it right	7	7	14
No, got it wrong	12	20	32
Col Total	19	27	46

15.29 A survey of randomly chosen new students at a certain university revealed the data below concerning the main reason for choosing this university instead of another. *Research question:* At $\alpha = .01$, is the main reason for choosing the university independent of student type?   **Students**

New Student	Tuition	Location	Reputation	Row Total
Freshmen	50	30	35	115
Transfers	15	29	20	64
MBAs	5	20	60	85
Col Total	70	79	115	264

15.30 In the 1970s, there was discussion of legalizing marijuana. A 1979 survey was given to a sample of 50 college students, asking which parent was dominant, and whether the respondent favored legalizing marijuana. *Research question:* At $\alpha = .10$, is opinion independent of which parent is dominant? Do you think opinions now are different? (Data are from a survey of introductory statistics students; see *LearningStats* for details.)   **Parent**

Legalize?	Mother Dominant	Neither Dominant	Father Dominant	Row Total
No	9	13	12	34
Yes	9	4	3	16
Col Total	18	17	15	50

15.31 Here is a table showing the season in which the first 36 U.S. presidents died. *Research question:* At $\alpha = .10$, can you reject the hypothesis that presidents' deaths are uniformly distributed by season? (Data are from *The World Almanac and Book of Facts, 2002*, pp. 545–556.)   **Presidents-A**

Month of Demise	Deaths
January–March	11
April–June	9
July–September	10
October–December	6
Total	36

15.32 Prof. Green's multiple-choice exam had 50 questions with the distribution of correct answers shown below. *Research question:* At $\alpha = .05$, can you reject the hypothesis that Green's exam answers came from a uniform population?   **Correct**

Correct Answer	Frequency
A	8
B	8
C	9
D	11
E	14
Total	50

15.33 Oxnard Kortholt, Ltd., employs 50 workers. During the last year, the company noted the number of visits with health care professionals (doctor, emergency, home) for each of its employees. U.S. national averages are shown. *Research question:* At $\alpha = .05$, do Oxnard employees differ significantly from the national percent distribution? (National averages are from *The World Almanac and Book of Facts, 2005* [World Almanac Education Group, Inc., 2005], p. 180.)   **Oxnard**

Health Care Visits	National Average (%)	Oxnard Employees (%)
No visits	16.5	4
1–3 visits	45.8	20
4–9 visits	24.4	15
10 or more visits	13.3	11
Total	100.0	50

15.34 In a four-digit lottery, each of the four digits is supposed to have the same probability of occurrence. The table shows the frequency of occurrence of each digit for 89 consecutive daily four-digit drawings. *Research question:* At $\alpha = .01$, can you reject the hypothesis that the digits are from a uniform population? Why do the frequencies add to 356?   **Lottery4**

Digit	Frequency
0	39
1	27
2	35
3	39
4	35
5	35
6	27
7	42
8	36
9	41
Total	356

15.35 A student rolled a supposedly fair die 60 times, resulting in the distribution of dots shown. *Research question:* At $\alpha = .10$, can you reject the hypothesis that the die is fair?   **Dice**

			Number of Dots				
	1	2	3	4	5	6	Total
Frequency	7	14	9	13	7	10	60

15.36 The World Cup soccer tournament is held every 4 years, with 32 teams from various nations competing. In the World Cup tournaments between 1990 and 2002, there were 232 games with the distribution of goals shown in this worksheet. *Research question:* At $\alpha = .025$, can you reject the hypothesis that goals per game follow a Poisson process? *Hint:* You must calculate the mean and look up the Poisson probabilities in Appendix B or Excel. (Data are from Singfat Chu, "Using Soccer Goals to Motivate the Poisson Process," *INFORMS Transactions on Education* 3, no. 2, pp. 62–68.)   **WorldCup**

Goals	f_j	$P(X)$	e_j	$f_j - e_j$	$(f_j - e_j)^2$	$(f_j - e_j)^2/e_j$
0	19					
1	49					
2	60					
3	47					
4	32					
5	18					
6 or more	7					
Total games	232					
Total goals	575					
Mean goals/game						

*15.37 The table below shows the number of ATM customer arrivals per minute in 60 randomly chosen minutes. *Research question:* At $\alpha = .025$, can you reject the hypothesis that the number of arrivals per minute follows a Poisson process?   **ATM**

0	0	0	1	3	0	0	0	2	5	2	0	1	1	1	2	1	1	0	2
3	0	0	3	0	1	0	1	1	1	1	2	0	2	0	3	0	2	0	1
1	0	0	0	0	1	3	2	1	0	0	0	4	1	0	1	0	3	3	1

15.38 Pick *one* Excel data set (A through F) and investigate whether the data could have come from a normal population using $\alpha = .01$. Use any test you wish, including a chi-square test in MegaStat, the various GOF tests offered by Visual Statistics (using the data editor to paste the data from Excel), or MINITAB's Stats > Basic Statistics > Normality Test to obtain a probability plot with the Anderson-Darling statistic. Interpret the *p*-value from your tests. For larger data sets, only the first five and last five observations are shown.

DATA SET A   Kentucky Derby Winning Time (Seconds), 1950–2005 ($n = 56$)
  Derby

Year	Derby Winner	Time
1950	Middleground	121.6
1951	Count Turf	122.6
1952	Hill Gail	121.6
1953	Dark Star	122.0
1954	Determine	123.0
⋮	⋮	⋮
2001	Monarchos	120.0
2002	War Emblem	121.1
2003	Funny Cide	121.2
2004	Smarty Jones	124.1
2005	Giacomo	122.8

Source: *Information Please Sports Almanac* (ESPN Books, 1998), *Facts on File, Detroit Free Press,* and *The New York Times,* selected issues.

DATA SET B   National League Runs Scored Leader, 1900–2004 ($n = 105$)   🐝 **Runs**

Year	Player	Runs
1900	Roy Thomas, Phil	131
1901	Jesse Burkett, StL	139
1902	Honus Wagner, Pitt	105
1903	Ginger Beaumont, Pitt	137
1904	George Browne, NY	99
⋮	⋮	⋮
2000	Jeff Bagwell, Hou	152
2001	Sammy Sosa, Chi	146
2002	Sammy Sosa, Chi	122
2003	Albert Pujols, StL	137
2004	Albert Pujols, StL	133

Source: *Sports Illustrated 2003 Almanac*, pp. 100–113, www.baseball-almanac.com, and www.hickoksports.com.

DATA SET C   Weight (in grams) of Pieces of Halloween Candy ($n = 78$)   🐝 **Candy**

1.6931	1.8320	1.3167	0.5031	0.7097	1.4358
1.8851	1.6695	1.6101	1.6506	1.2105	1.4074
1.5836	1.1164	1.2953	1.4107	1.3212	1.6353
1.5435	1.7175	1.3489	1.1688	1.5543	1.3566
1.4844	1.4636	1.1701	1.5238	1.7346	1.1981
1.6601	1.8359	1.1334	1.7030	1.2481	1.4356
1.3756	1.3172	1.3700	1.0145	1.0062	0.9409
1.4942	1.2316	1.6505	1.7088	1.1850	1.3583
1.5188	1.3460	1.3928	1.6522	0.5303	1.6301
1.0474	1.4664	1.2902	1.9638	1.9687	1.2406
1.6759	1.6989	1.4959	1.4180	1.5218	2.1064
1.3213	1.1116	1.4535	1.4289	1.9156	1.8142
1.3676	1.7157	1.4493	1.4303	1.2912	1.7137

Source: Independent project by statistics student Frances Williams. Weighed on an American Scientific Model S/P 120 analytical balance accurate to 0.0001 gram.

DATA SET D   Price/Earnings Ratios for Specialty Retailers ($n = 58$)   🐝 **PERatios**

Company	PE Ratio
Abercrombie and Fitch	19
Advance AutoParts	16
American Eagle Outfitters	30
Ann Taylor Stores	14
Asbury Automotive Group	24
⋮	⋮
Toys "R" Us	30
Tractor Supply	30
United Auto Group	12
Williams-Sonoma	28
Zale	15

Source: *BusinessWeek*, November 22, 2004, pp. 95–98.

DATA SET E   U.S. Presidents' Ages at Inauguration ($n = 43$)   🐝 **Presidents-B**

President	Age
Washington	57
J. Adams	61
Jefferson	57
Madison	57
Monroe	58
⋮	⋮
Carter	52
Reagan	69
G. H. W. Bush	64
Clinton	46
G. W. Bush	54

Source: *The World Almanac and Book of Facts*, 2002, p. 545.

DATA SET F	**Weights of 31 Randomly Chosen Circulated Nickels ($n = 31$)**							
	🐦 **Nickels**							
5.043	4.980	4.967	5.043	4.956	4.999	4.917	4.927
4.893	5.003	4.951	5.040	5.043	5.004	5.014	5.035
4.883	5.022	4.932	4.998	5.032	4.948	5.001	4.983
4.912	4.796	4.970	4.956	5.036	5.045	4.801	

Note: Weighed by statistics student Dorothy Duffy as an independent project. Nickels were weighed on a Mettler PE 360 Delta Range scale, accurate to 0.001 gram.

INTEGRATIVE PROJECTS

*15.39 In 2002, the Anaheim Angels defeated the San Francisco Giants in the World Series 4 games to 3. The table below shows the inning-by-inning breakdown of runs by each team ($\times$ indicates unnecessary last half of inning). (a) Estimate λ (the mean runs per game). (b) Use Excel's function =POISSON(x,mean,0) to fill in the $P(X)$ column. (c) Multiply $P(X)$ by 121 to obtain the expected frequencies. (d) Carry out the chi-square test at $d = .05$, combining classes as needed to enlarge expected frequencies. (e) Explain how you obtained the degrees of freedom. (f) Which cells show the largest contribution to the chi-square test statistic? (g) Obtain the p-value using Excel's function =CHIDIST(test statistic,deg_freedom). (h) Why is the Poisson distribution a poor fit for baseball runs, even though it fits hockey goals pretty well?   🐦 **WorldSeries**

2002 World Series Runs by Inning

					Inning						
		1	*2*	*3*	*4*	*5*	*6*	*7*	*8*	*9*	*Score*
1	San Fran	0	2	0	0	0	2	0	0	0	4
	Anaheim	0	1	0	0	0	2	0	0	0	3
2	San Fran	0	4	1	0	4	0	0	0	1	10
	Anaheim	5	2	0	0	1	1	0	2	$\times$	11
3	Anaheim	0	0	4	4	0	1	0	1	0	10
	San Fran	1	0	0	0	3	0	0	0	0	4
4	Anaheim	0	1	2	0	0	0	0	0	0	3
	San Fran	0	0	0	0	3	0	0	1	$\times$	4
5	Anaheim	0	0	0	0	3	1	0	0	0	4
	San Fran	3	3	0	0	0	2	4	4	$\times$	16
6	San Fran	0	0	0	0	3	1	1	0	0	5
	Anaheim	0	0	0	0	0	0	3	3	$\times$	6
7	San Fran	0	1	0	0	0	0	0	0	0	1
	Anaheim	0	1	3	0	0	0	0	0	$\times$	4

Source: The Baseball Encyclopedia, 10th ed. (Macmillan, 1996), and *Baseball Almanac* at www.cnnsi.com.

Runs	f_j	$P(X)$	e_j	$f_j - e_j$	$(f_j - e_j)^2$	$(f_j - e_j)^2/e_j$
0	83					
1	15					
2	7					
3	9					
4	6					
5 or more	1					
Total ½ innings	121					
Total runs	85					
Mean runs/inning						

*15.40 Refer to the previous problem. In the 2002 World Series, a total of 85 runs were scored. (a) Before doing any calculations, based on your understanding of baseball, why might runs per inning *not* be uniform? (b) Complete the tabulation below, by counting the frequency of runs in each of the nine innings with all games combined. (c) Calculate the frequency of runs per inning by dividing the total number of runs by 9. (d) Perform the chi-square goodness-of-fit test and obtain a p-value using Excel's function =CHIDIST(test statistic,deg_freedom). (e) State your conclusions plainly.   🐦 **WorldSeries**

Inning	f_j	e_j	$f_j - e_j$	$(f_j - e_j)^2$	$(f_j - e_j)^2/e_j$
1					
2					
3					
4					
5					
6					
7					
8					
9					
Total					

*15.41 (a) Use either MINITAB or MegaStat or Excel's function =NORMINV(RAND(),0,1) or Excel's Tools > Data Analysis > Random Numbers to generate 100 normally distributed random numbers with a mean of 0 and a standard deviation of 1. (b) Make a histogram of your sample and assess its shape. Are there outliers? (c) Calculate descriptive statistics. Are the sample mean and standard deviation close to their intended values? (d) See if the first and third quartiles are approximately -0.675 and $+0.675$, as they should be. (e) Use a z test

$$z = \frac{\bar{x} - \mu}{\sigma/\sqrt{n}} = \frac{\bar{x} - 0}{1/\sqrt{100}} = 10\bar{x}$$

to compare the sample mean to the desired mean. *Note:* Use z instead of t because the hypothesized mean $\mu = 0$ and standard deviation $\sigma = 1$ are known. (f) Use the data editor option of Visual Statistics to perform a chi-square test for normality with known parameters $\mu = 0$ and standard deviation $\sigma = 1$. Interpret the results. (g) What would happen if 100 statistics students performed similar experiments, assuming that the random number generator is working correctly?

*15.42 (a) Use either MegaStat or Excel's function =RAND() or Excel's Tools > Data Analysis > Random Numbers to generate 100 uniformly distributed random numbers between 0 and 1. (b) Make a histogram of your sample and assess its shape. (c) Calculate descriptive statistics. Are the sample mean and standard deviation close to their intended values $\mu = (0 + 1)/2 = 0.5000$ and $\sigma = \sqrt{1/12} = 0.288675$? (d) See if the first and third quartiles are approximately 0.25 and 0.75, as they should be. (e) Use a z test

$$z = \frac{\bar{x} - \mu}{\sigma/\sqrt{n}} = \frac{\bar{x} - 0.5000}{(0.288675)/\sqrt{100}}$$

to compare the sample mean to the desired mean. *Note:* Use z instead of t because the hypothesized mean $\mu = 0.5000$ and standard deviation $\sigma = 0.288675$ are known. (f) Use the data editor option of Visual Statistics to perform a chi-square test for uniformity with known parameters $a = 0$ and $b = 1$. Interpret the results. (g) What would happen if 100 statistics students performed similar experiments, assuming that the random number generator is working correctly?

*15.43 (a) Use Excel's Tools > Data Analysis > Random Numbers to generate 100 Poisson-distributed random numbers with a mean of $\lambda = 4$. (b) Make a histogram of your sample and assess its shape. (c) Calculate descriptive statistics. Are the sample mean and standard deviation close to their intended values $\lambda = 4$ and $\sigma = \sqrt{\lambda} = \sqrt{4} = 2$? (d) Use a z test

$$z = \frac{\bar{x} - \mu}{\sigma/\sqrt{n}} = \frac{\bar{x} - 4}{2/\sqrt{100}} = 5\bar{x} - 20$$

to compare the sample mean to the desired mean. *Note:* Use z instead of t because the hypothesized mean $\mu = 0.5000$ and standard deviation $\sigma = 0.2887$ are known. (f) Use the data editor option of Visual Statistics to perform a chi-square test for uniformity with known parameters $a = 0$ and $b = 1$. Interpret the results. (g) What would happen if 100 statistics students performed similar experiments, assuming that Excel's random number generator is working correctly?

Related Reading

Bowman, K. O.; and L. R. Shenton. "Omnibus Test Contours for Departures from Normality Based on β_1 and β_2." *Biometrika* 62, no. 2 (1975), pp. 243–50.

Conover, William J. "Some Reasons for Not Using the Yates Continuity Correction on 2×2 Contingency Tables." *Journal of the American Statistical Association* 69 (1974), pp. 374–76.

D'Agostino, Ralph B.; and Michael A. Stephens. *Goodness-of-Fit Techniques.* Marcel Dekker, 1986.

Haber, Michael. "A Comparison of Some Continuity Corrections for the Chi-Squared Test on 2 × 2 Tables." *Journal of the American Statistical Association* 75, no. 371 (1980), pp. 510–15.

Mantel, Nathan. "The Continuity Correction." *The American Statistician* 30, no. 2 (May 1976), pp. 103–104.

Thode, Henry C., Jr. *Testing for Normality.* Marcel Dekker, 2002.

LearningStats Unit 15   Chi-Square Tests

LearningStats Unit 15 explains the chi-square test for independence in contingency tables and illustrates goodness-of-fit tests for uniform, Poisson, and normal distributions. Attention is also given to other tests for normality based on ECDF plots. Your instructor may assign a specific module, but you can work on the others if they sound interesting.

Topic	LearningStats Modules
Overview	▣ Chi-Square Test for Independence ▣ Goodness-of-Fit Tests
Chi-square tests on contingency tables	▣ Effects of Table Size ▣ Simulation and Type I Error ▣ Using Raw Data
Goodness-of-fit tests	▣ Normal and Uniform Tests ▣ Uniform Tests: Choosing Letters ▣ Uniform Tests: World Series Runs ▣ ECDF Plots Illustrated ▣ Probability Plots: A Simulation ▣ CDF Normality Test
@Risk Projects	▣ Table of Chi-Square Critical Values

Key: ▣ = PowerPoint   ▣ = Excel

Visual Statistics

Visual Statistics Goodness-of-Fit and Independence Tests

Module	Module Name
13	**VS** Visualizing Goodness-of-Fit Tests
14	**VS** Visualizing Bivariate Data Analysis

Visual Statistics Modules 13 and 14 (included on your CD) are designed to help you

- Know how to use and interpret a chi-square test for independence in cross-tabulated data.
- Recognize characteristics of data-generating situations that suggest appropriate distributions to fit.
- Interpret common data displays that may reveal whether a specified distribution is appropriate.
- Learn how the chi-square goodness-of-fit test works and how class formation affects it.
- Recognize limitations of the chi-square goodness-of-fit test and alternatives that are available.
- Use visual and analytical ECDF-based tests for goodness-of-fit and compare them with chi-square.

The worktext (included on the CD in .PDF format) contains a list of concepts covered, objectives of the module, overview of concepts, illustration of concepts, orientation to module features, learning exercises (basic, intermediate, advanced), learning projects (individual, team), self-evaluation quiz, glossary of terms, and solutions to self-evaluation quiz.

Nonparametric Tests

Chapter Learning Objectives

When you finish this chapter you should be able to

- Explain what a nonparametric test is and when it may have advantages over a parametric test.

- Know and use several common nonparametric tests.

- Use computer software to perform the tests and obtain *p*-values.

The hypothesis tests in previous chapters require the estimation of one or more unknown parameters (for example, the population mean or variance). These tests often make unrealistic assumptions about the normality of the underlying population or require large samples to invoke the Central Limit Theorem. In contrast, *nonparametric tests* or distribution-free tests usually focus on the sign or rank of the data rather than the exact numerical value of the variable, do not specify the shape of the parent population, can often be used in smaller samples, and can be used for ordinal data (when the measurement scale is not interval or ratio). Table 16.1 highlights the advantages and disadvantages of nonparametric tests.

Advantages	Disadvantages
1. Can often be used in small samples.	1. Require special tables for small samples.
2. Generally more powerful than parametric tests when normality cannot be assumed.	2. If normality *can* be assumed, parametric tests are generally more powerful.
3. Can be used for ordinal data.	

TABLE 16.1
Advantages and Disadvantages of Nonparametric Tests

Rejection of a hypothesis using a nonparametric test is especially convincing, since nonparametric tests generally make fewer assumptions about the population. If two methods are justified and have similar *power,* the principle of Occam's Razor favors the simpler method. For this reason, statisticians have long been attracted to nonparametric tests, particularly in applications where data are likely to be ill-behaved and when samples are small.

You might expect that nonparametric tests would primarily be used in areas of business where nominal or ordinal data are common (e.g., human resources, marketing). Yet business analysts who mostly use ratio data (e.g., accounting, finance) may encounter skewed populations that render parametric tests unreliable. These analysts might use nonparametric tests as a *complement* to their customary *parametric tests.* Figure 16.1 shows common nonparametric tests and their parametric counterparts, which you have seen in earlier chapters.

FIGURE 16.1

Some common nonparametric tests

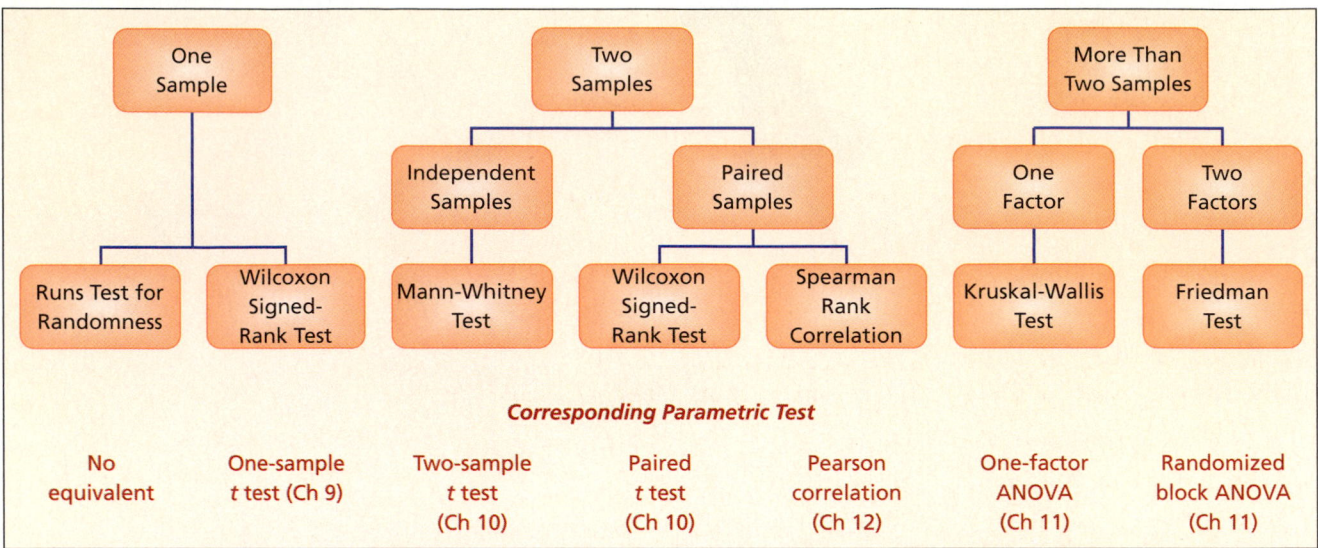

| No equivalent | One-sample *t* test (Ch 9) | Two-sample *t* test (Ch 10) | Paired *t* test (Ch 10) | Pearson correlation (Ch 12) | One-factor ANOVA (Ch 11) | Randomized block ANOVA (Ch 11) |

This chapter illustrates only a few of the many nonparametric techniques that are available. The selections are those you are most likely to encounter. Small-sample nonparametric tests are omitted, but references are shown at the end of the chapter for those who need them.

16.2
ONE-SAMPLE RUNS TEST

The one-sample ***runs test*** is also called the ***Wald-Wolfowitz test*** after its inventor Abraham Wald (1902–1950) and his student Jacob Wolfowitz. Its purpose is to detect nonrandomness. A nonrandom pattern suggests that the observations are not *independent*—a fundamental assumption of many statistical tests. We are asking whether each observation in a sequence is independent of its predecessor. In a time series, a nonrandom pattern of residuals indicates *autocorrelation* (as in Chapters 12 and 13). In quality control, a nonrandom pattern of deviations from the design specification may indicate an *out-of-control* process. We will illustrate only the large sample version of this test (defined as samples of 10 or more).

Runs Test

This test is to determine whether a sequence of binary events follows a random pattern. A nonrandom sequence suggests nonindependent observations.

The hypotheses are:

H_0: Events follow a random pattern

H_1: Events do not follow a random pattern

To test the hypothesis of randomness we first count the number of outcomes of each type:

n_1 = number of outcomes of the first type

n_2 = number of outcomes of the second type

n = total sample size = $n_1 + n_2$

Application: Quality Inspection   Defects

Inspection of 44 computer chips reveals the following sequence of defective (*D*) or acceptable (*A*) chips:

DAAAAAAADDDDDAAAAAAAADDAAAAAAAADDDDDAAAAAAAAA

Do defective chips appear at random? A pattern could indicate that the assembly process has a cyclic problem due to unknown causes. The hypotheses are:

H_0: Defects follow a random sequence

H_1: Defects follow a nonrandom sequence

A *run* is a series of consecutive outcomes of the same type, surrounded by a sequence of outcomes of the other type. We group sequences of similar outcomes and count the runs:

D	AAAAAAA	DDDD	AAAAAAAA	DD	AAAAAAAA	DDDD	AAAAAAAAAA
1	2	3	4	5	6	7	8

A run can be a single outcome if it is preceded and followed by outcomes of the other type. There are 8 runs in our sample ($R = 8$). The number of outcomes of each type is:

n_1 = number of defective chips $(D) = 11$

n_2 = number of acceptable chips $(A) = 33$

n = total sample size = $n_1 + n_2 = 11 + 33 = 44$

In a large-sample situation (when $n_1 \geq 10$ and $n_2 \geq 10$), the number of runs R may be assumed to be normally distributed with mean μ_R and standard deviation σ_R.

$$z = \frac{R - \mu_R}{\sigma_R} \qquad \text{(test statistic comparing R with its expected value μ_R)} \qquad \textbf{(16.1)}$$

$$\mu_R = \frac{2n_1 n_2}{n} + 1 \qquad \text{(expected value of R if H_0 is true)} \qquad \textbf{(16.2)}$$

$$\sigma_R = \sqrt{\frac{2n_1 n_2(2n_1 n_2 - n)}{n^2(n - 1)}} \qquad \text{(standard error of R if H_0 is true)} \qquad \textbf{(16.3)}$$

For our data, the expected number of runs would be

$$\mu_R = \frac{2n_1 n_2}{n} + 1 = \frac{2(11)(33)}{44} + 1 = 17.5$$

Since the actual number of runs ($R = 8$) is less than expected ($\mu_R = 17.5$) our sample suggests that the null hypothesis may be false, depending on the standard deviation. For our data, the standard deviation is

$$\sigma_R = \sqrt{\frac{2n_1 n_2(2n_1 n_2 - n)}{n^2(n - 1)}} = \sqrt{\frac{2(11)(33)[2(11)(33) - 44]}{44^2(44 - 1)}} = 2.438785$$

Since the actual number of runs is $R = 8$, the test statistic is

$$z = \frac{R - \mu_R}{\sigma_R} = \frac{8 - 17.5}{2.438785} = -3.90$$

If we choose the .01 level of significance, the critical value $z_{.01}$ for a two-tailed test would be ± 2.326 so the decision rule would be:

Reject the hypothesis of a random pattern if $z < -2.326$ or $z > +2.326$

Otherwise the observed difference is attributable to chance

Since the test statistic $z = -3.90$ is well below the lower critical limit, as shown in Figure 16.2, we can easily reject the hypothesis of randomness. The difference between the observed number of runs and the expected number of runs is too great to be due to chance ($p = .0001$).

Figure 16.3 shows the MegaStat output for this problem, which also includes the *p*-value and the entire distribution for various values of R (not shown because it is lengthy). As with any

FIGURE 16.2

Decision rule for large-sample runs test

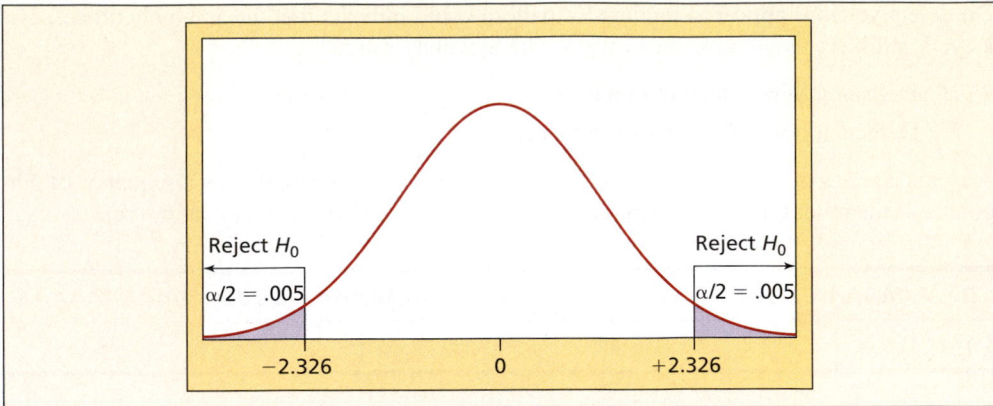

FIGURE 16.3

MegaStat's runs test

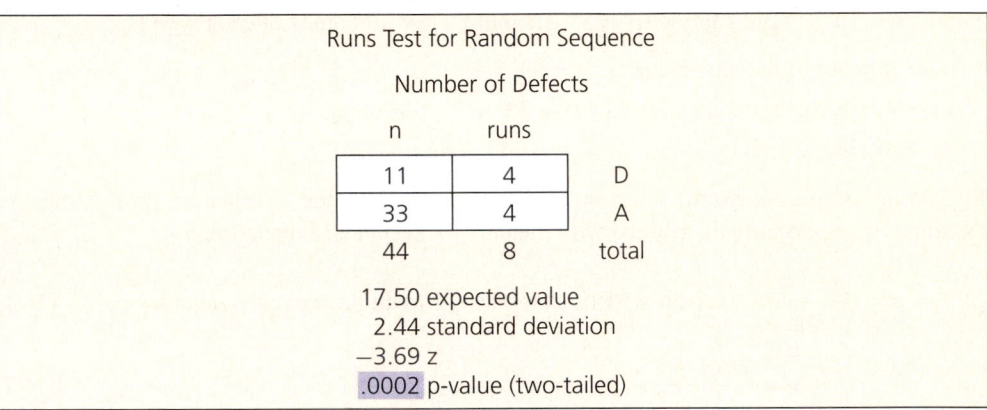

Runs Test for Random Sequence

Number of Defects

n	runs	
11	4	D
33	4	A
44	8	total

17.50 expected value
2.44 standard deviation
−3.69 z
.0002 p-value (two-tailed)

hypothesis test, the smaller the p-value, the stronger the evidence against H_0. Here, the small p-value provides very strong evidence that H_0 is false (i.e., that the sequence is not random).

Small Samples

There are tables of critical values that extend the test to small samples ($n < 10$). The problem with small samples is that they lack power. That is, in a small sample, it would take an extremely small or large number of runs to convince us that the sequence is nonrandom. While some researchers must deal with small samples, business analysts (e.g., quality control) often have hundreds of observations, so small samples rarely pose a problem.

SECTION EXERCISES

16.1 Using $\alpha = .05$, perform a runs test for randomness on the sample data ($n = 27$).

A A B B A A B B A B A A B B B A A B B B B A A B A B B

16.2 Using $\alpha = .10$, perform a runs test for randomness on the sample data ($n = 24$).

F T F F F F T T T T F T T T F T T T F T T F F T

16.3
WILCOXON SIGNED-RANK TEST

The **Wilcoxon signed-rank test** was developed by Frank Wilcoxon (1892–1965) to compare a single sample with a benchmark using only **ranks** of the data instead of the original observations, as in a one-sample t test. It is more often used to compare *paired* observations, as an alternative to the paired-sample t test, which is a special case of the one-sample t test. The advantages of the Wilcoxon test are its freedom from the normality assumption, its robustness to outliers, and its applicability to ordinal data. Although the test does require the population to be roughly symmetric, it has fairly good power over a range of possible non-normal population shapes. It is slightly less powerful than the one-sample t test when the population is normal.

Wilcoxon Signed-Rank Test

The Wilcoxon signed-rank test is a nonparametric test to compare a sample median with a benchmark or to test differences in paired samples. It does not require normality but does assume symmetric populations.

When we use the test to compare the sample *median M* with a benchmark *median M_0*, the hypotheses are:

Left-Tailed Test	*Two-Tailed Test*	*Right-Tailed Test*
$H_0: M \geq M_0$	$H_0: M = M_0$	$H_0: M \leq M_0$
$H_1: M < M_0$	$H_1: M \neq M_0$	$H_1: M > M_0$

When the variable of interest is the difference between paired observations, the test is the same, but we use the symbol M_d for the median *difference* and (generally) use zero as the benchmark:

Left-Tailed Test	*Two-Tailed Test*	*Right-Tailed Test*
$H_0: M_d \geq 0$	$H_0: M_d = 0$	$H_0: M_d \leq 0$
$H_1: M_d < 0$	$H_1: M_d \neq 0$	$H_1: M_d > 0$

We calculate the difference between each observation and the median (or the differences between the paired observations), rank them from smallest to largest by absolute value, and add the ranks of the *positive* differences to obtain the rank sum W. Its expected value and variance depend only on the sample size n.

$$W = \sum_{i=1}^{n} R^+ \qquad \text{(the sum of all positive ranks)} \qquad \textbf{(16.4)}$$

$$\mu_W = \frac{n(n+1)}{4} \qquad \text{(expected value of the } W \text{ statistic)} \qquad \textbf{(16.5)}$$

$$\sigma_W = \sqrt{\frac{n(n+1)(2n+1)}{24}} \qquad \text{(standard deviation of the } W \text{ statistic)} \qquad \textbf{(16.6)}$$

For small samples, a special table is required to obtain critical values. For large samples ($n \geq 20$) the test statistic is approximately normal.

$$z = \frac{W - \dfrac{n(n+1)}{4}}{\sqrt{\dfrac{n(n+1)(2n+1)}{24}}} \qquad \text{(Wilcoxon test statistic for large } n) \qquad \textbf{(16.7)}$$

Application: Median versus Benchmark

Do price/earnings ratios of stocks in specialty retail stores (e.g., Abercrombie & Fitch) differ from those of multiline retail stores (e.g., J. C. Penney)? In the third quarter of 2004, the median P/E ratio of all large specialty retail stores was 19 (it is customary to round P/E ratios to the nearest integer, despite some loss of accuracy). Table 16.2 shows P/E ratios for a sample of 18 multiline stores for the corresponding time period. We will test these hypotheses:

$H_0: M = 19$ (the median P/E ratio for multiline stores is 19)

$H_1: M \neq 19$ (the median P/E ratio for multiline stores is not 19)

To perform the test, we subtract 19 from each multiline store's P/E ratio, take absolute values, convert to ranks, and sum the *positive* ranks. Since Dollar Tree is exactly at the benchmark, its difference is zero (neither positive nor negative) so it is excluded from the analysis (i.e., the sample size is reduced to $n = 17$). Tie ranks are assigned so that the sum of tied values is the same as if they were not tied. For example, the value "1" occurs four times. If not tied, these four occurrences would have positions 2, 3, 4, 5 so we assign rank 3.5 to each value "1."

TABLE 16.2

Wilcoxon Signed-Rank Test of P/E Ratios (n = 18 firms)

🐾 **MultiLinePE**

Source: *BusinessWeek,* November 22, 2004, pp. 95–98.

Company	x_i	$x_i - 19$	$\lvert x_i - 19 \rvert$	Rank	R^+	R^-
Big Lots	16	−3	3	8.5		8.5
Dillard's	29	10	10	17	17	
Dollar General	22	3	3	8.5	8.5	
Dollar Tree Stores	19	0	0	1		
Family Dollar Stores	20	1	1	3.5	3.5	
Federated Dept. Stores	14	−5	5	12.5		12.5
Fred's	22	3	3	8.5	8.5	
Kmart Holding Corp.	18	−1	1	3.5		3.5
Kohl's	28	9	9	16	16	
May Dept. Stores	13	−6	6	14		14
Neiman Marcus Stores	16	−3	3	8.5		8.5
Nordstrom	20	1	1	3.5	3.5	
Penney (J. C.)	21	2	2	6	6	
Retail Ventures	23	4	4	11	11	
Saks	20	1	1	3.5	3.5	
Sears, Roebuck	3	−16	16	18		18
ShopKo Stores	14	−5	5	12.5		12.5
Target	27	8	8	15	15	
				171	92.5	77.5

Although the sample size is under 20, we will illustrate the test using the large-sample formula. The large-sample test statistic is

$$z = \frac{W - \dfrac{n(n+1)}{4}}{\sqrt{\dfrac{n(n+1)(2n+1)}{24}}} = \frac{92.5 - \dfrac{17(17+1)}{4}}{\sqrt{\dfrac{17(17+1)(34+1)}{24}}} = \frac{92.5 - 76.5}{21.1246} = 0.76$$

Using Excel or Appendix C, we get a two-tail *p*-value of .4492, so at any customary level of significance, we cannot reject the hypothesis that multiline retail P/E ratios have the same median as specialty stores. For a more accurate test, we could consult a special small-sample table of critical values of the Wilcoxon signed-rank test.

Application: Paired Data

In the petroleum refining industry, employment depends on the overall economy, the price of crude oil, and other factors. Between 2004 and 2005, many petroleum refiners reduced their employee headcount, while others did not. Table 16.3 shows employment in 13 refiners. Has there been a significant change? We cannot assume normality because the data are skewed, so the Wilcoxon test is attractive. We will use a two-tailed test at $\alpha = .05$ with the hypotheses

H_0: $M_d = 0$ (the median difference in employment is zero)

H_1: $M_d \neq 0$ (the median difference in employment is not zero)

Table 16.3 shows the calculations for the Wilcoxon signed-rank statistic.

Although the sample size is small (under 20) we will illustrate the test using the large-sample test statistic:

$$z = \frac{W - \dfrac{n(n+1)}{4}}{\sqrt{\dfrac{n(n+1)(2n+1)}{24}}} = \frac{73 - \dfrac{13(13+1)}{4}}{\sqrt{\dfrac{13(13+1)(26+1)}{24}}} = \frac{73 - 45.5}{14.309} = 1.92$$

Using Excel or Appendix C, we find that the two-tail *p*-value is .0546, so we reject the hypothesis that there is no change in employment (for greater precision, we would need a small-sample table). Figure 16.4 shows that MegaStat confirms our calculations.

Company	2004	2005	d	|d|	Rank	R⁺	R⁻
AmeradaHess	11,481	11,119	362	362	6	6	
ChevronTexaco	61,533	56,000	5,533	5,533	13	13	
ConocoPhillips	39,000	35,800	3,200	3,200	12	12	
ExxonMobil	88,300	85,900	2,400	2,400	11	11	
Frontier Oil	748	731	17	17	1	1	
Giant Industries	2,335	2,235	100	100	3	3	
Holly	560	845	−285	285	5		5
Marathon Oil	27,007	25,804	1,203	1,203	10	10	
Murphy Oil	4,789	3,982	807	807	9	9	
Premcor	1,770	2,300	−530	530	7		7
Sunoco	14,900	14,200	700	700	8	8	
Tesoro Petroleum	3,570	3,640	−70	70	2		2
Valero Energy	19,621	19,797	−176	176	4		4
					91	73	18

TABLE 16.3

Wilcoxon Signed-Rank Test for Employment (n = 13 firms)

🐁 **Employed**

Source: *Fortune* 149, no. 7 (April 5, 2004), p. F-51, and 151, no. 8 (April 18, 2005), p. F53.

```
           Wilcoxon Signed-Rank Test

              73 sum of positive ranks
              18 sum of negative ranks

              13 n
           45.50 expected value
           14.31 standard deviation
            1.92 z
           .0273 p-value (one-tailed, upper)
```

FIGURE 16.4

MegaStat's signed-rank test for paired data

SECTION EXERCISES

16.3 A sample of 28 student scores on the chemistry midterm exam is shown. (a) At $\alpha = .10$, does the population median differ from 50? Make a worksheet in Excel for your calculations. (b) Make a histogram of the data. Would you be justified in using a parametric t test that assumes normality? Explain.   🐁 **Chemistry**

74	60	7	97	62	2	100
5	99	78	93	32	43	64
87	37	70	54	60	62	17
26	45	84	24	66	7	48

16.4 Final exam scores for a sample of 20 students in a managerial accounting class are shown. (a) At $\alpha = .05$, is there a difference in the population median scores on the two exams? Make an Excel worksheet for your Wilcoxon signed-rank test calculations and check your work by using MegaStat or a similar computer package. (b) Perform a two-tailed parametric t test for paired two-sample means by using Excel or MegaStat. Do you get the same decision?   🐁 **Accounting**

Student	Exam 1	Exam 2	Student	Exam 1	Exam 2
1	70	81	11	84	96
2	74	89	12	95	96
3	65	59	13	83	99
4	60	68	14	81	76
5	63	75	15	59	68
6	58	77	16	54	47
7	72	82	17	75	84
8	71	69	18	92	100
9	52	53	19	70	81
10	79	84	20	54	58

16.4
MANN-WHITNEY TEST

The *Mann-Whitney test,* named after Henry B. Mann (1905–2000) and D. R. Whitney, is a nonparametric test that compares two populations. The Mann-Whitney test does not assume normality. Assuming that the populations differ only in centrality (i.e., location) it is a test for equality of *medians*. It is analogous to the *t* test for two independent sample means.

Mann-Whitney Test

The Mann-Whitney test is a nonparametric test to compare two populations, utilizing only the ranks of the data from two independent samples. It does not require normality, but does assume equal variances.

Studies suggest that the Mann-Whitney test has only slightly less power in distinguishing between centrality of two populations than the *t* test for two independent sample means, which you studied in Chapter 10. The Mann-Whitney test requires independent samples from populations with equal variances,* but the populations need not be normal. To avoid the use of special tables, we will illustrate only a large-sample version of this test (defined as samples of 10 or more).

Assuming that the only difference in the populations is in location, the hypotheses for a two-tailed test of the population medians would be:

H_0: $M_1 = M_2$ (no difference in satisfaction)

H_1: $M_1 \neq M_2$ (satisfaction differs for the two groups)

Application: Restaurant Quality   🐾   Restaurants

Does spending more at a restaurant lead to greater customer satisfaction? Readers of *Consumer Reports* rated 29 American, Italian, and Mexican chain restaurants on a scale of 0 to 100, based mainly on the taste of the food. Results are shown in Table 16.4, sorted by satisfaction rating (note that, in this test, the lowest data value is assigned a rank of 1, which is rather counterintuitive for restaurant ratings). Each restaurant is assigned to one of two price groups: *Low* (under $15 per person) and *High* ($15 or more per person). Is there a significant difference in satisfaction between the higher-priced restaurants and the lower-priced ones? The parametric *t* test for two means would require that the variable be measured on a ratio or interval level. Because the satisfaction ratings are solely based on human perception, we are unwilling to assume the strong measurement properties associated with ratio or interval data. Instead, we treat these measurements as ordinal data (i.e., ranked data).

In Table 16.4, we convert the customer satisfaction ratings into ranks by sorting the *combined* samples from lowest to highest satisfaction, and then assigning a rank to each satisfaction score. If values are tied, the average of the ranks is assigned to each. Restaurants are then separated into two groups based on the price category (*Low, High*) as displayed in Table 16.5.

The ranks are summed for each column to get $T_1 = 164$ and $T_2 = 271$. The sum $T_1 + T_2$ must be $n(n + 1)/2$ where $n = n_1 + n_2 = 15 + 14 = 29$. Since $n(n + 1)/2 = (29)(30)/2 = 435$ and the sample sums are $T_1 + T_2 = 164 + 271 = 435$, our calculations check.** Next, we calculate the mean rank sums $\bar{T}_1$ and $\bar{T}_2$. If there is no difference between groups, we would expect $\bar{T}_1 - \bar{T}_2$ to be near zero. For large samples ($n_1 \geq 10$, $n_2 \geq 10$) we can use a *z* test. The test statistic is

(16.8)
$$z = \frac{\bar{T}_1 - \bar{T}_2}{(n_1 + n_2)\sqrt{\dfrac{n_1 + n_2 + 1}{12 n_1 n_2}}}$$

---

*If populations are normal but have unequal variances, the unpooled two-sample *t*-test with Welch's correction is preferred to the Mann-Whitney test. You can test for equal variances by using the *F* test discussed in Chapter 10.

**If the sum $T_1 + T_2$ does not check, you have made an error in calculating the ranks. It is more reliable to use MINITAB's Calc function RANK() to convert a column of data into ranks. Avoid Excel's =RANK() function, because it does not adjust for ties.

Obs	Price	Satisfaction	Rank
1	Low	73	1
2	Low	76	2.5
3	High	76	2.5
4	Low	77	4.5
5	Low	77	4.5
6	Low	78	7
7	High	78	7
8	High	78	7
9	Low	79	10
10	Low	79	10
11	Low	79	10
12	Low	80	13.5
13	Low	80	13.5
14	Low	80	13.5
15	High	80	13.5
16	Low	81	16.5
17	Low	81	16.5
18	High	82	18.5
19	High	82	18.5
20	Low	83	20.5
21	Low	83	20.5
22	High	84	22.5
23	High	84	22.5
24	High	85	25
25	High	85	25
26	High	85	25
27	High	86	28
28	High	86	28
29	High	86	28

TABLE 16.4
Satisfaction and Ranks for 29 Chain Restaurants
🦞 **Restaurants**

Source: © 2003 by Consumers Union of U.S., Inc., Yonkers, NY 10703-1057, excerpted or adapted with permission from the July 2003 issue of *Consumer Reports* for educational purposes only.

Low-Priced Restaurants ($n_1 = 15$)		High-Priced Restaurants ($n_2 = 14$)	
Satisfaction	Rank	Satisfaction	Rank
73	1	76	2.5
76	2.5	78	7
77	4.5	78	7
77	4.5	80	13.5
78	7	82	18.5
79	10	82	18.5
79	10	84	22.5
79	10	84	22.5
80	13.5	85	25
80	13.5	85	25
80	13.5	85	25
81	16.5	86	28
81	16.5	86	28
83	20.5	86	28
83	20.5		
Rank sum: $T_1 = 164$		Rank sum: $T_2 = 271$	
Sample size $n_1 = 15$		Sample size $n_2 = 14$	
Mean rank: $\bar{T}_1 = 164/15 = 10.93333$		Mean rank: $\bar{T}_2 = 271/14 = 19.35714$	

TABLE 16.5
Chain Restaurant Customer Satisfaction Score

For our data:

$$z = \frac{10.93333 - 19.35714}{(15 + 14)\sqrt{\dfrac{15 + 14 + 1}{(12)(15)(14)}}} = -2.662$$

FIGURE 16.5

MegaStat's Mann-Whitney
test

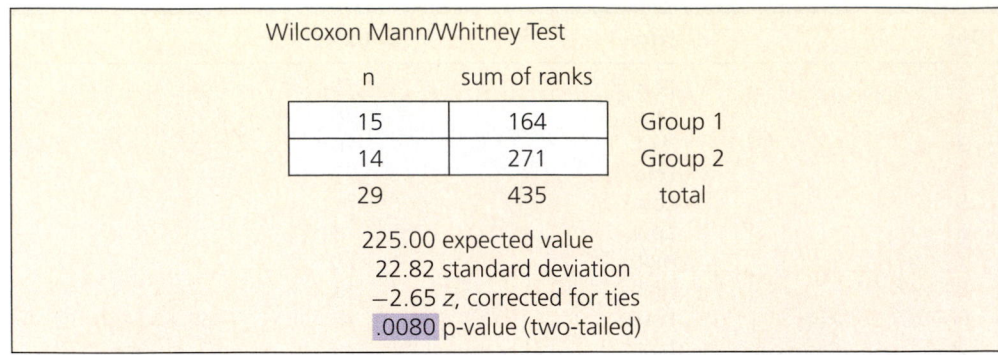

At $\alpha = .01$, rejection in a two-tailed test requires $z > +2.326$ or $z < -2.326$, so we would reject the hypothesis that the population medians are the same. From Appendix C the two-tail *p*-value is .0078, which says that a sample difference of this magnitude would be expected only about 8 times in 1,000 samples if the populations were the same. MegaStat uses a different version of this test,* but obtains a similar result, as shown in Figure 16.5.

SECTION EXERCISES

16.5   Bob and Tom are "paper investors." They each "buy" stocks they think will rise in value and "hold" them for a year. At the end of the year, they compare their stocks' appreciation (percent). (a) At $\alpha = .05$, is there a difference in the medians (assume these are samples of Bob's and Tom's stock-picking skills). Use MegaStat or a similar computer package for the Mann-Whitney (Wilcoxon rank-sum test) calculations. (b) Perform a right-tailed parametric *t* test for two independent sample means by using Excel or MegaStat. Do you get the same decision?
  Investors

Bob's Portfolio (n = 10 stocks)	Tom's Portfolio (n = 12 stocks)
7.0	5.2
2.5	0.4
6.2	2.6
4.4	−0.2
4.2	4.0
8.5	5.2
10.0	8.6
6.4	4.3
3.6	3.0
7.6	0.0
	8.6
	7.5

16.6   An experimental bumper was designed to reduce damage in low-speed collisions. This bumper was installed on an experimental group of vans in a large fleet, but not on a control group. At the end of a trial period, there were 12 repair incidents (a "repair incident" is an accident that resulted in a repair invoice) for the experimental group and 9 repair incidents for the control group. The dollar cost per repair incident is shown below. (a) Use MegaStat or MINITAB to perform a two-tailed Mann-Whitney test at $\alpha = .05$. (b) Perform a one-tailed parametric *t* test for two independent sample means by using Excel or MegaStat. Do you get the same

---

*The *Mann-Whitney test* is also called the *Wilcoxon rank-sum test,* hence MegaStat's heading. When statistical tests were developed or popularized independently by more than one statistician, the names may vary.

decision? (Data are from Floyd G. Willoughby and Thomas W. Lauer, confidential case study.)

🐝 **Damage**

> *Old bumper:* 1,185, 885, 2,955, 815, 2,852, 1,217, 1,762, 2,592, 1,632
> *New bumper:* 1,973, 403, 509, 2,103, 1,153, 292, 1,916, 1,602, 1,559, 547, 801, 359

16.5 KRUSKAL-WALLIS TEST FOR INDEPENDENT SAMPLES

William H. Kruskal and W. Allen Wallis proposed a test to compare c independent samples. It may be viewed as a generalization of the Mann-Whitney test, which compares two independent samples. Groups can be of different sizes if each has five or more observations. If we assume that the populations differ only in centrality (i.e., location), the ***Kruskal-Wallis test*** (K-W test) compares the medians of c independent samples. It is analogous to one-factor ANOVA (completely randomized model). The K-W test requires that the populations be of similar shape, but does not require normal populations as in ANOVA, making it an attractive alternative for applications in finance, engineering, and marketing.

Kruskal-Wallis Test

The K-W test compares the medians of c independent samples. It may be viewed as a generalization of the Mann-Whitney test and is a nonparametric alternative to one-factor ANOVA.

Assuming that the populations are otherwise similar, the hypotheses to be tested are:

H_0: All c population medians are the same

H_1: Not all the population medians are the same

In testing for equality of location, the K-W test may be almost as powerful as one-factor ANOVA. It can even be useful for ratio or interval data when there are outliers or unequal group variances, or if the population is thought to be non-normal. For a completely randomized design with c groups the test statistic is

$$H = \frac{12}{n(n+1)} \sum_{j=1}^{c} \frac{T_j^2}{n_j} - 3(n+1) \qquad \text{(Kruskal-Wallis test statistic)} \qquad \textbf{(16.9)}$$

where

$n = n_1 + n_2 + \cdots + n_c$

n_j = number of observations in group j

T_j = sum of ranks for group j

Application: Employee Absenteeism

The *XYZ* Corporation is interested in possible differences in days worked by salaried employees in three departments in the financial area. Table 16.6 shows annual days worked by 23 randomly chosen employees from these departments. Because the sampling methodology reflects the department sizes, the sample sizes are unequal.

Department	Days Worked									
Budgets	278	260	265	245	258					
Payables	205	270	220	240	255	217	266	239	240	228
Pricing	240	258	233	256	233	242	244	249		

TABLE 16.6
Annual Days Worked by Department
🐝 **Days**

To get the test statistic, we combine the samples and assign a rank to each observation in each group, as shown in Table 16.7. We use a column worksheet so the calculations are easier to follow. When a tie occurs, each observation is assigned the average of the ranks.

TABLE 16.7

Merged Data Converted to Ranks

Obs	Rank	Days	Dept
1	1	205	Payables
2	2	217	Payables
3	3	220	Payables
4	4	228	Payables
5	5.5	233	Pricing
6	5.5	233	Pricing
7	7	239	Payables
8	9	240	Payables
9	9	240	Payables
10	9	240	Pricing
11	11	242	Pricing
12	12	244	Pricing
13	13	245	Budgets
14	14	249	Pricing
15	15	255	Payables
16	16	256	Pricing
17	17.5	258	Budgets
18	17.5	258	Pricing
19	19	260	Budgets
20	20	265	Budgets
21	21	266	Payables
22	22	270	Payables
23	23	278	Budgets

Next, the data are arranged by groups, as shown in Table 16.8, and the ranks are summed to give T_1, T_2, and T_3. As a check on our work, the sum of the ranks must be $n(n + 1)/2 = (23)(23 + 1)/2 = 276$. This is easily verified since $T_1 + T_2 + T_3 = 92.5 + 93.0 + 90.5 = 276$.

TABLE 16.8

Worksheet for Rank Sums

Budgets	Rank	Payables	Rank	Pricing	Rank
245	13	205	1	233	5.5
258	17.5	217	2	233	5.5
260	19	220	3	240	9
265	20	228	4	242	11
278	23	239	7	244	12
		240	9	249	14
		240	9	256	16
		255	15	258	17.5
		266	21		
		270	22		
Sum of ranks	92.5	Sum of ranks	93	Sum of ranks	90.5
Sample size	$n_1 = 5$	Sample size	$n_2 = 10$	Sample size	$n_3 = 8$

The value of the test statistic is

$$H = \frac{12}{n(n + 1)} \sum_{j=1}^{c} \frac{T_j^2}{n_j} - 3(n + 1)$$

$$= \frac{12}{(23)(23 + 1)} \left[\frac{92.5^2}{5} + \frac{93^2}{10} + \frac{90.5^2}{8} \right] - 3(23 + 1) = 6.259$$

The H test statistic follows a chi-square distribution with degrees of freedom $v = c - 1 = 3 - 1 = 2$. This is a right-tailed test (i.e., we will reject the null hypothesis of equal medians if H exceeds its critical value). Using $v = 2$, from Appendix E we obtain critical values for various levels of significance:

α	χ^2_α	Interpretation
.10	4.605	Reject H_0—conclude that the means differ
.05	5.991	Reject H_0—conclude that the means differ
.025	7.378	Do not reject H_0—conclude that the means are not different

In this instance, our decision is sensitive to the level of significance chosen. The *p*-value is between .05 and .025, so it seems appropriate to conclude that the difference among the three groups is not overwhelming. MegaStat gives the exact *p*-value (.0437) as shown in Figure 16.6. We could also obtain this *p*-value from Excel's function =CHIDIST(6.259,2). The stacked dot plots in Figure 16.7 reveal that the three distributions overlap quite a bit, so there may be little practical difference in the distributions. The MINITAB K-W test is similar, but requires unstacked data (one column for the data, one column for the group name). MINITAB warns you if the sample size is too small.

Kruskal-Wallis Test

Median	n	Avg. Rank	
260.00	5	18.50	Budgets
239.50	10	9.30	Payables
243.00	8	11.31	Pricing
244.00	23		Total
		6.259	H
		2	d.f.
		.0437	p-value

FIGURE 16.6

MegaStat's Kruskal-Wallis test

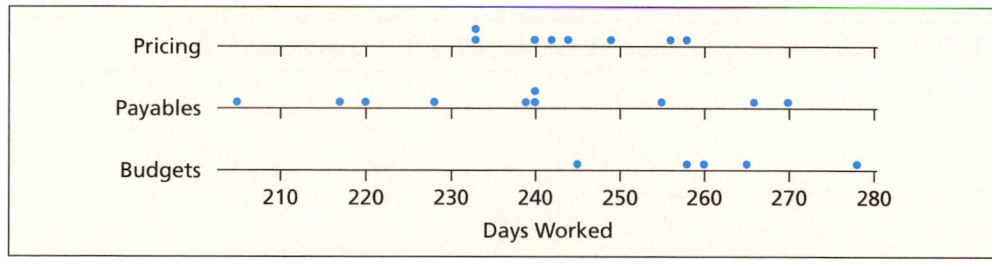

FIGURE 16.7

MINITAB's stacked dot plots for days worked

SECTION EXERCISES

16.7 Samples are shown of volatility (coefficient of variation) for sector stocks over a certain period of time. (a) At $\alpha = .05$, is there a difference in median volatility in these four portfolios? Use Mega-Stat, MINITAB, or a similar computer package for the calculations. (b) Use one-factor ANOVA to compare the means. Do you reach the same conclusion? (c) Make a histogram or other display of each sample. Would you be willing to assume normality? **Volatile**

Health	Energy	Retail	Leisure
14.5	23.0	19.4	17.6
18.4	19.9	20.7	18.1
13.7	24.5	18.5	16.1
16.9	24.2	15.5	23.2
16.2	19.4	17.7	17.6
21.6	22.1	21.4	25.5
25.6	31.6	26.5	24.1
21.4	22.4	21.5	25.9
26.6	31.3	22.8	25.5
19.0	32.5	27.4	26.3
12.6	12.8	22.0	12.9
13.5	14.4	17.1	11.1
13.5		24.8	4.9
13.0		13.4	
13.6			

16.8 The results shown below are mean productivity measurements (average number of assemblies completed per hour) for a random sample of workers at each of three work stations. (a) At $\alpha = .05$, is there a difference in median productivity? Use MegaStat, MINITAB, or a similar computer package for the calculations. (b) Use one-factor ANOVA to compare the means. Do you reach the same conclusion? (c) Make a histogram or other display of the pooled data. Does the assumption of normality seem justified? 🐝 **Workers**

Hourly Productivity of Assemblers in Plants

Work Station	Finished Units Produced Per Hour								
A (9 workers)	3.6	5.1	2.8	4.6	4.7	4.1	3.4	2.9	4.5
B (6 workers)	2.7	3.1	5.0	1.9	2.2	3.2			
C (10 workers)	6.8	2.5	5.4	6.7	4.6	3.9	5.4	4.9	7.1	8.4

Mini Case 16.1

Price/Earnings Ratios

Are price/earnings ratios different for firms in the five sectors shown in Table 16.9? Since the data are interval, we could try either one-factor ANOVA or a Kruskal-Wallis test. How can we decide?

TABLE 16.9 **Common Stock P/E Ratios of Selected Companies** 🐝 **PERatios**

Automotive and Components (n = 17)

9	13	14	29	10	32	16	14	9
21	17	21	10	7	20	13	17	

Energy Equipment and Services (n = 12)

31	22	39	25	46	7	29	36	42
36	49	35						

Food and Staples Retailing (n = 22)

25	22	18	24	27	21	66	30	24
22	21	9	11	16	13	32	15	25
36	29	25	18					

Hotels, Restaurants, and Leisure (n = 18)

34	26	74	24	17	19	22	34	30
22	24	19	23	19	21	31	16	19

Multiline Retail Firms (n = 18)

16	29	22	19	20	14	22	18	28
13	16	20	21	23	20	3	14	27

Source: *BusinessWeek*, November 22, 2004.

Combining the samples, the histogram in Figure 16.8 and the probability plot in Figure 16.9 suggest non-normality, so instead of one-factor ANOVA we would prefer the nonparametric Kruskal-Wallis test with $v = c - 1 = 5 - 1 = 4$ degrees of freedom. MINITAB's output in Figure 16.10 shows that the medians differ ($p = .000$). The test statistic ($H = 25.32$) exceeds the chi-square critical value for $\alpha = .01$ (13.28).

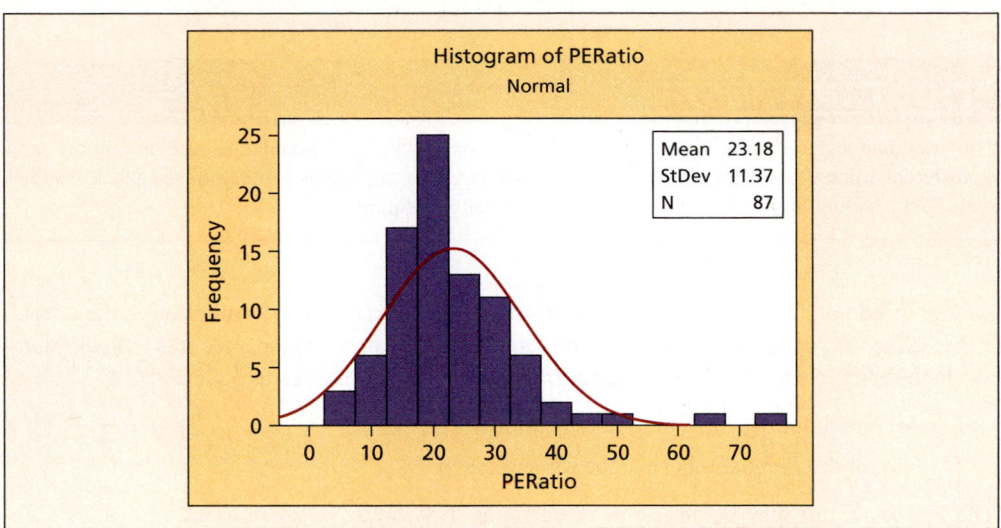

FIGURE 16.8

Histogram of combined samples ($n = 87$)

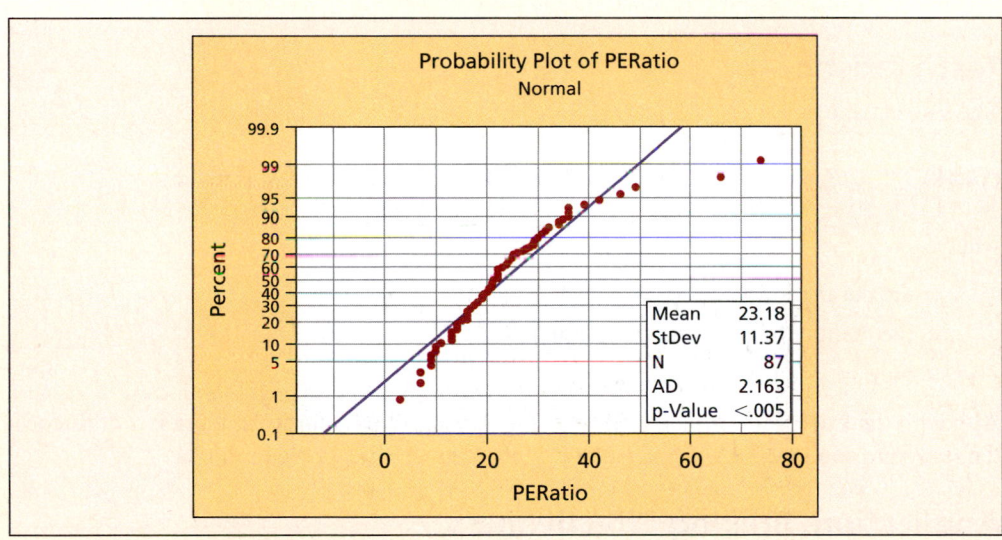

FIGURE 16.9

Probability plot of combined samples ($n = 87$)

FIGURE 16.10

MINITAB's Kruskal-Wallis test

Kruskal-Wallis Test: PERatio versus Sector

Sector	N	Median	Ave Rank	z
Auto	17	14.00	24.4	−3.58
EnergyEq	12	35.50	68.5	3.62
FoodDrug	22	23.00	46.9	0.62
Leisure	18	22.50	51.1	1.34
Retail	18	20.00	35.6	−1.58
Overall	87		44.0	

$H = 25.27$ $DF = 4$ $P = 0.000$
$H = 25.32$ $DF = 4$ $P = 0.000$ (adjusted for ties)

16.6
FRIEDMAN TEST FOR RELATED SAMPLES

The *Friedman test* is a nonparametric test that will reveal whether c treatments have the same central tendency when there is a second factor with r levels. If the populations are assumed the same except for centrality (location), the test is a comparison of medians. The test is analogous to two-factor ANOVA without replication (or randomized block design) with one observation for each cell. The groups must be of the same size, treatments should be randomly assigned within the blocks, and data should be at least interval scale.

Friedman Test

The Friedman test is a nonparametric procedure to discover whether c population medians are the same or different when classification is based on two factors. It is analogous to randomized block ANOVA (two-factor without replication) but without the normality assumption.

The Friedman test resembles the Kruskal-Wallis test except that, in addition to the c treatment levels that define the columns of the observation matrix, it also specifies r block factor levels to define each row of the observation matrix. The hypotheses to be tested are:

H_0: All c populations have the same median

H_1: Not all the populations have the same median

The Friedman test may be almost as powerful as two-way ANOVA without replication (randomized block design) and may be used with ratio or interval data when there is concern for outliers or non-normality of the underlying populations. It is a rare population that meets the normality requirement, so Friedman's test is quite useful.

Test Statistic

The test statistic is

$$(16.10) \qquad F = \frac{12}{rc(c+1)} \sum_{j=1}^{c} T_j^2 - 3r(c+1) \qquad \text{(Friedman test statistic)}$$

where

$r =$ the number of blocks (rows)

$c =$ the number of treatments (columns)

$T_j =$ the sum of ranks for treatment j

Although the Friedman formula resembles the Kruskal-Wallis formula, there is a difference: the ranks are computed *within each block* rather than within a pooled sample.

Application: Braking Effectiveness

Experiments are being conducted to test the effect of brake pad composition on stopping distance. Five prototype brake pads are prepared. Each pad is installed on the same automobile, which is accelerated to 100 kph and then braked to the shortest possible stop without loss of control. This test is repeated four times in rapid succession to reveal brake fade due to heating and lining abrasion. Car weight and balance are identical in all tests, and the same expert driver performs all tests. The pavement is dry and the outside air temperature is the same for all tests. To eliminate potential bias, the driver has no information about which pad is installed for a given test. The results are shown in Table 16.10.

The Friedman test requires that either the number of blocks or the number of treatments be at least 5. Our matrix meets this requirement since $r = 4$ and $c = 5$. Ranks are computed *within each row*. As a check on our arithmetic, we may utilize the fact that the ranks must sum to $rc(c+1)/2 = (4)(5)(5+1)/2 = 60$. We see that our sums are correct because $T_1 + T_2 + T_3 + T_4 + T_5 = 15 + 14 + 5 + 19 + 7 = 60$.

	Pad 1		Pad 2		Pad 3		Pad 4		Pad 5	
	Feet	*Rank*	*Feet*	*Rank*	*Feet*	*Rank*	*Feet*	*Rank*	*Feet*	*Rank*
Trial 1	166	3	176	4	152	2	198	5	148	1
Trial 2	174	4	170	3	148	1	206	5	152	2
Trial 3	184	3	186	4	160	1	212	5	168	2
Trial 4	220	5	204	3	184	1	216	4	196	2
Rank sum	$T_1 = 15$		$T_2 = 14$		$T_3 = 5$		$T_4 = 19$		$T_5 = 7$	

TABLE 16.10

Stopping Distance from 100 kph 🔖 **Braking**

We now compute the test statistic:

$$F = \frac{12}{rc(c+1)} \sum_{j=1}^{c} T_j^2 - 3r(c+1)$$

$$= \frac{12}{(4)(5)(5+1)} [15^2 + 14^2 + 5^2 + 19^2 + 7^2] - 3(4)(5+1) = 13.6$$

The Friedman test statistic follows a chi-square distribution with degrees of freedom $v = c - 1 = 5 - 1 = 4$. Using $v = 4$, from Appendix E we obtain the critical values for various α levels:

α	χ_α^2	*Interpretation*
.025	11.143	Reject H_0—conclude that the medians differ
.01	13.277	Reject H_0—conclude that the medians differ
.005	14.861	Do not reject H_0—the medians do not differ

The p-value is between .01 and .005, so we conclude that there is a significant difference in brake pads except at very strict Type I error levels. The results from MegaStat shown in Figure 16.11 show the exact p-value (.0087). We could also obtain this p-value by using Excel's function =CHIDIST(13.6,4).

Friedman Test

Sum of Ranks	*Avg. Rank*	
15.00	3.75	
14.00	3.50	
5.00	1.25	
19.00	4.75	
7.00	1.75	
60.00	3.00	Total
	4	n
	13.600	chi-square
	4	d.f.
	.0087	p-value

FIGURE 16.11

MegaStat's Friedman test for brake pads

SECTION EXERCISES

16.9 Consumers are asked to rate the attractiveness of four potential dashboard surface textures on an interval scale (1 = least attractive, 10 = most attractive). Use MegaStat or another software package to perform a Friedman test to see whether the median ratings of surfaces differ at $\alpha = .05$, using age as the blocking factor. 🔖 **Texture**

	Shiny	Satin	Pebbled	Pattern	Embossed
Youth (Under 21)	6.7	6.6	5.5	4.3	4.4
Adult (21 to 39)	5.5	5.3	6.2	5.9	6.2
Middle-Age (40 to 61)	4.5	5.1	6.7	5.5	5.4
Senior (62 and over)	3.9	4.5	6.1	4.1	4.9

16.10 JavaMax is a neighborhood take-out coffee shop that offers three sizes. Yesterday's sales are shown. Use MegaStat or another software package to perform a Friedman test to see whether the median sales of coffee sizes differ at $\alpha = .05$, using time of day as the blocking factor. **Coffee**

	Small	Medium	Large
6 A.M. to 8 A.M.	60	77	85
8 A.M. to 11 A.M.	65	74	76
11 A.M. to 3 P.M.	70	70	70
3 P.M. to 7 P.M.	61	60	55
7 P.M. to 11 P.M.	55	50	48

16.7 SPEARMAN RANK CORRELATION TEST

An overall nonparametric test of association between two variables can be performed by using *Spearman's rank correlation* coefficient (sometimes called *Spearman's rho*). This statistic is useful when it is inappropriate to assume an interval scale (a requirement of the Pearson correlation coefficient you learned in Chapter 12). The statistic is named for Charles E. Spearman (1863–1945), a British behavioral psychologist who was interested in assessment of human intelligence. The research question was the extent of agreement between different I.Q. tests (e.g., Stanford-Binet and Wechsler's WAIS). However, ordinal data are also common in business. For example, Moody's bond ratings (e.g., Aaa, Aa, A, Baa, Ba, B, etc.), bank safety ratings (e.g., by Veribanc or BankRate.com), or Morningstar's mutual fund ratings (e.g., 5/5, 5/4, 4/4, etc.) are ordinal (not interval) measurements. We could use Spearman's rank correlation to answer questions like these:

- When *n* corporate bonds are assigned a quality rating by two different agencies (e.g., Moody and Dominion), to what extent do the ratings agree?
- When creditworthiness scores are assigned to *n* individuals by different credit-rating agencies (e.g., Equifax and TransUnion), to what extent do the scores agree?

In cases like these, we would expect strong agreement, since presumably the rating agencies are trying to measure the same thing. In other cases, we may have ratio or interval data, but prefer to rely on rank-based tests because of serious non-normality or outliers. For example:

- To what extent do rankings of *n* companies based on revenues agree with their rankings based on profits?
- To what extent do rankings of *n* mutual funds based on 1-year rates of return agree with their rankings based on 5-year rates of return?

Spearman Rank Correlation

Spearman rank correlation is a nonparametric test that measures the strength of the association, if any, between two variables using only ranks. It does not assume interval measurement.

The formula for Spearman's rank correlation coefficient for a sample is

$$r_s = 1 - \frac{6 \sum_{i=1}^{n} d_i^2}{n(n^2 - 1)} \qquad \text{(Spearman rank correlation)} \qquad \textbf{(16.11)}$$

where

d_i = difference in ranks for case i

n = sample size

The sample rank correlation coefficient r_s must fall in the range $-1 \leq r_s \leq +1$. Its sign tells whether the relationship is direct (ranks tend to vary in the same direction) or inverse (ranks tend to vary in opposite directions). If r_s is near zero, there is little or no agreement between the rankings. If r_s is near $+1$, there is strong agreement between the ranks, while if r_s is near -1, there is strong *inverse* agreement between the ranks.

Application: Calories and Fat

Calories come from fat, but also from carbohydrates. How closely related are fat calories and total calories? As an experiment, a student team examined a sample of 20 brands of pasta sauce, obtaining the data shown in Table 16.11. Since the serving sizes (in grams) varied, each product's total calories and fat calories were divided by serving size to obtain a per-gram measurement. Ranks were then calculated for each measure of calories. If more than one value was the same, they were assigned the average of the ranks. As a check, the sums of ranks within each column must always be $n(n + 1)/2$, which in our case is $(20)(20 + 1)/2 = 210$. After checking the ranks, the difference in ranks d_i is computed for each observation. As a further check on our calculations, we verify that the rank differences sum to zero (if not, we have made an error somewhere). The sample rank correlation coefficient $r_s = .9109$ indicates positive agreement:

$$r_s = 1 - \frac{6 \sum_{i=1}^{n} d_i^2}{n(n^2 - 1)} = 1 - \frac{(6)(118.5)}{(20)(20^2 - 1)} = .9109$$

Product	Total Calories		Fat Calories		d_i	d_i^2
	Per Gram	Rank	Per Gram	Rank		
Barilla Roasted Garlic & Onion	0.64	10	0.20	8	2	4
Barilla Tomato & Basil	0.56	13	0.12	13.5	−0.5	0.25
Classico Tomato & Basil	0.40	19.5	0.08	17	2.5	6.25
Del Monte Mushroom	0.48	17	0.04	19	−2	4
Five Bros. Tomato & Basil	0.64	10	0.12	13.5	−3.5	12.25
Healthy Choice Traditional	0.40	19.5	0.00	20	−0.5	0.25
Master Choice Chunky Garden Veg.	0.56	13	0.08	17	−4	16
Meijer All Natural Meatless	0.55	15	0.08	17	−2	4
Newman's Own Traditional	0.48	17	0.12	13.5	3.5	12.25
Paul Newman Venetian	0.48	17	0.12	13.5	3.5	12.25
Prego Fresh Mushrooms	1.25	1	0.38	1	0	0
Prego Hearty Meat—Pepperoni	1.00	3.5	0.33	2.5	1	1
Prego Hearty Meat—Hamburger	1.00	3.5	0.29	4	−0.5	0.25
Prego Traditional	1.17	2	0.33	2.5	−0.5	0.25
Prego Roasted Red Pepper & Garlic	0.92	5	0.25	5.5	−0.5	0.25
Ragu Old World Style w/meat	0.67	8	0.25	5.5	2.5	6.25
Ragu Roasted Red Pepper & Onion	0.86	6	0.20	8	−2	4
Ragu Roasted Garlic	0.70	7	0.19	10	−3	9
Ragu Traditional	0.56	13	0.20	8	5	25
Sutter Home Tomato & Garlic	0.64	10	0.16	11	−1	1
Column Sum		210		210	0	118.5

TABLE 16.11

Calories Per Gram for 20 Pasta Sauces

🍝 **Pasta**

Source: This data set was created by statistics students Donna Bennett, Nicole Cook, Latrice Haywood, and Robert Malcolm. It is intended for training purposes only and should not be viewed as a nutrition guide.

Our sample correlation r_s is 0.9109. For a right-tailed test the hypotheses are:

H_0: True rank correlation is zero ($\rho_s \le 0$)

H_1: True rank correlation is positive ($\rho_s > 0$)

In this case we choose a right-tailed test because *a priori* we would expect positive agreement. That is, a pasta sauce that ranks high in fat calories would be expected also to rank high in total calories. If the sample size is small, a special table is required. If n is large (usually defined as at least 20 observations), then r_s may be assumed to follow the Student's t distribution with degrees of freedom $v = n - 1$ using the test statistic

(16.12)
$$t = \frac{r_s}{\sqrt{\dfrac{1 - r_s^2}{n - 2}}}$$

To illustrate this formula, we will plug in our previous sample result:

$$t = \frac{r_s}{\sqrt{\dfrac{1 - r_s^2}{n - 2}}} = \frac{0.9109}{\sqrt{\dfrac{1 - 0.9109^2}{20 - 2}}} = 9.36$$

Using Appendix D we obtain one-tail critical values of Student's t for 19 degrees of freedom for various levels of significance:

α	t_α	*Interpretation*
.025	2.093	Reject H_0
.01	2.539	Reject H_0
.005	2.861	Reject H_0

Clearly, we can reject the hypothesis of no correlation at any of the customary α levels. Using MegaStat, we can obtain equivalent results, as shown in Figure 16.12, except that the critical value of r_s is shown instead of the t statistic.

FIGURE 16.12

MegaStat's rank correlation test

Spearman Coefficient of Rank Correlation

	Total Calories/gram	Fat Calories/gram
Total Calories/gram	1.000	
Fat Calories/gram	.911	1.000

20 sample size

±.444 critical value .05 (two-tail)
±.561 critical value .01 (two-tail)

Correlation versus Causation

One final word of caution: you should remember that correlation does not prove causation. Countless examples can be found of correlations that are "significant" even when there is no causal relation between the two variables. On the other hand, causation is not ruled out. More than one scientific discovery has occurred because of an unexpected correlation. Just bear in mind that if you look at 1,000 correlation coefficients in samples drawn from uncorrelated populations, approximately 50 will be "significant" at $\alpha = .05$, approximately 10 will be "significant" at $\alpha = .01$, and so on. Testing for significance is just one step in the scientific process.

Bear in mind also that multiple causes may be present. Correlation between X and Y could be caused by an unspecified third variable Z. Even more complex systems of causation may exist. Bivariate correlations of any kind must be regarded as potentially out of context if the true relationship is *multivariate* rather than *bivariate*.

16.11 Profits of 20 consumer food companies are shown. (a) Convert the data to ranks. Check the column sums. (b) Calculate Spearman's rank correlation coefficient. Show your calculations. (c) At $\alpha = .01$ can you reject the hypothesis of zero rank correlation? (d) Check your work by using MegaStat. (e) Calculate the Pearson correlation coefficient (using Excel). (f) Why might the rank correlation be preferred?   **Food-B**

Profit of 20 Food Consumer Products Firms ($ millions)

Company	2004	2005
Campbell Soup	595	647
ConAgra Foods	775	880
Dean Foods	356	285
Del Monte Foods	134	165
Dole Food	105	134
Flowers Foods	15	51
General Mills	917	1,055
H. J. Heinz	566	804
Hershey Foods	458	591
Hormel Foods	186	232
Interstate Bakeries	27	−26
J. M. Smucker	96	111
Kellogg	787	891
Land O'Lakes	107	21
McCormick	211	215
PepsiCo	3,568	4,212
Ralcorp Holdings	7	65
Sara Lee	1,221	1,272
Smithfield Foods	26	227
Wm. Wrigley, Jr.	446	493

Source: *Fortune* 151, no. 8 (April 18, 2005), p. F-52.

16.12 Rates of return on 24 mutual funds are shown. (a) Convert the data to ranks. Check the column sums. (b) Calculate Spearman's rank correlation coefficient. Show your calculations. (c) At $\alpha = .01$ can you reject the hypothesis of zero rank correlation? (d) Check your work by using MegaStat. (e) Calculate the Pearson correlation coefficient (using Excel). (f) In this case, why might either test be used?   **Funds**

Rates of Return on 24 Selected Mutual Funds (percent)

Fund	12-Mo.	5-Year	Fund	12-Mo.	5-Year
1	11.2	10.5	13	8.0	7.3
2	−2.4	5.0	14	11.2	14.2
3	8.6	8.6	15	14.0	9.7
4	3.4	3.7	16	11.6	14.7
5	3.9	−2.9	17	13.2	11.8
6	10.3	9.6	18	−1.0	2.3
7	16.1	14.1	19	6.2	10.5
8	6.7	6.2	20	21.1	9.0
9	6.5	7.4	21	−1.2	3.0
10	11.1	14.0	22	8.7	7.1
11	9.7	10.2	23	0.9	6.0
12	0.4	9.3	24	12.7	10.0

Chapter Summary

Statisticians are attracted to **nonparametric tests** because they avoid the restrictive assumption of normality, although often there are still assumptions to be met (e.g., similar population shape). Many nonparametric tests have **similar power** to their **parametric** counterparts (and superior power when samples are small). The **runs test** (or **Wald-Wolfowitz** test) checks for random order in binary data. The **Wilcoxon signed-rank test** resembles a parametric one-sample t test, most often being used as a substitute for the parametric paired-difference t test. The **Mann-Whitney test** (also called the **Wilcoxon rank-sum test**) compares medians in independent samples, resembling a parametric two-sample t test. The **Kruskal-Wallis test** is a c-sample comparison of medians (similar to one-factor ANOVA). The **Friedman test** resembles a randomized block ANOVA except that it compares medians instead of means. **Spearman's rank correlation** is like the usual Pearson correlation except the data are ranks. Calculations of these tests are usually done by computer. Special tables are required when samples are small.

Key Terms

Friedman test, *714*

Kruskal-Wallis test, *709*

Mann-Whitney test, *706*

nonparametric tests, *699*

parametric tests, *699*

power, *699*

ranks, *702*

runs test, *700*

Spearman's rank
correlation, *716*

Spearman's rho, *716*

Wald-Wolfowitz test, *700*

Wilcoxon signed-rank
test, *702*

Commonly Used Formulas

Wald-Wolfowitz one-sample runs test for randomness (for $n_1 \geq 10$, $n_2 \geq 10$):

$$z = \frac{R - \dfrac{2n_1 n_2}{n} + 1}{\sqrt{\dfrac{2n_1 n_2 (2n_1 n_2 - n)}{n^2 (n - 1)}}}$$

where

R = number of runs
n = total sample size = $n_1 + n_2$

Wilcoxon signed-rank test for one sample median (for $n \geq 20$):

$$z = \frac{W - \dfrac{n(n + 1)}{4}}{\sqrt{\dfrac{n(n + 1)(2n + 1)}{24}}}$$

where

W = sum of positive ranks

Mann-Whitney test for equality of two medians (for $n_1 \geq 10$, $n_2 \geq 10$):

$$z = \frac{\bar{T}_1 - \bar{T}_2}{(n_1 + n_2)\sqrt{\dfrac{n_1 + n_2 + 1}{12 n_1 n_2}}}$$

where

T_1 = mean rank for sample 1
T_2 = mean rank for sample 2

Kruskal-Wallis test for equality of c medians: $H = \dfrac{12}{n(n+1)} \sum\limits_{j=1}^{c} \dfrac{T_j^2}{n_j} - 3(n+1)$

where

n_j = number of observations in group j
T_j = sum of ranks for group j
$n = n_1 + n_2 + \cdots + n_c$

Friedman test for equality of medians in an array with r rows and c columns:

$$F = \dfrac{12}{rc(c+1)} \sum\limits_{j=1}^{c} T_j^2 - 3r(c+1)$$

where

r = the number of blocks (rows)
c = the number of treatments (columns)
T_j = the sum of ranks for treatment j

Spearman's rank correlation coefficient for n paired observations:

$$r_s = 1 - \dfrac{6 \sum\limits_{i=1}^{n} d_i^2}{n(n^2 - 1)}$$

1. (a) Name three advantages of nonparametric tests. (b) Name two deficiencies in data that might cause us to prefer a nonparametric test. (c) Why is significance in a nonparametric test especially convincing?

2. (a) What is the purpose of a runs test? (b) How many runs of each type are needed for a large-sample runs test? (c) Give an example of a sequence containing runs and count the runs. (d) What distribution do we use for the large-sample runs test?

3. (a) What is the purpose of a Wilcoxon signed-rank test? (b) How large a sample is needed to use a normal table for the test statistic? (c) The Wilcoxon signed-rank test resembles which parametric test(s)?

4. (a) What is the purpose of a Mann-Whitney test? (b) The M-W test is a test of two medians under what assumption? (c) What sample sizes are needed for the large-sample M-W test? (d) The M-W test is analogous to which parametric test?

5. (a) In the Mann-Whitney test, how are ranks assigned when there is a tie? (b) What distribution do we use for the large-sample M-W test?

6. (a) What is the purpose of a Kruskal-Wallis test? (b) The K-W test is a test of c medians under what assumption? (c) The K-W test is analogous to which parametric test?

7. (a) In the Kruskal-Wallis test, what is the procedure for assigning ranks to observations in each group? (b) What distribution do we use for the K-W test? (c) What are the degrees of freedom for the K-W test?

8. (a) What is the purpose of a Friedman test? (b) The Friedman test is analogous to what parametric test? (c) How does the Friedman test differ from the ANOVA test in the way it handles the blocking factor?

9. (a) Describe the assignment of ranks in the Friedman test. (b) What distribution do we use for the Friedman test? (c) What are the degrees of freedom for the Friedman test?

10. (a) What is the purpose of the Spearman rank correlation? (b) Describe the way in which ranks are assigned in calculating the Spearman rank correlation.

11. (a) Why is a significant correlation not proof of causation? (b) When would a bivariate correlation be misleading?

Chapter Review

CHAPTER EXERCISES

Instructions: In all exercises, use a computer package (e.g., MegaStat, MINITAB) or show the calculations in a worksheet, depending on your instructor's wishes. If you use the computer, include relevant output or screen shots. If you do the calculations manually, show your work. State the hypotheses and give the test statistic and its two-tailed *p*-value. Make the decision. If the decision is close, say so. Are there issues of sample size? Is non-normality a concern?

16.13 A supplier of laptop PC power supplies uses a control chart to track the output (in watts) of each unit produced. The pattern below shows whether each unit's output was above (*A*) or below (*B*) the desired specification. *Research question:* At $\alpha = .05$, do the deviations follow a random pattern? **Watts**

$$B\,A\,A\,B\,B\,B\,A\,B\,A\,B\,A\,B\,A\,A\,B\,A\,A\,B\,B\,B\,A\,B\,B\,A\,A\,B\,A\,B\,A$$
$$A\,A\,B\,B\,A\,A\,A\,A\,B\,B\,A\,A\,B\,A\,A\,A\,A\,B\,B\,A\,A\,B\,A\,A$$

16.14 A basketball player took 35 free throws during the season. Her sequence of hits (*H*) and misses (*M*) is shown. *Research question:* At $\alpha = .01$, is her hit/miss sequence random? **FreeThrows**

$$H\,M\,M\,H\,H\,M\,H\,M\,M\,H\,H\,H\,H\,H\,M\,M\,H\,H\,M\,M\,M\,H\,M\,H\,H\,H\,H\,M\,H\,H\,H\,H\,H\,M\,M\,M\,H\,H$$

16.15 On a professional certifying exam there are 25 true-false questions. The correct answers are $T\,F\,T$ $T\,F\,F\,F\,T\,T\,F\,T\,F\,T\,T\,T\,F\,F\,T\,T\,F\,F\,T\,T\,F\,T$. *Research question:* At $\alpha = .05$, is the *T/F* pattern random? **TrueFalse**

16.16 A baseball player was at bat 33 times during preseason exhibition games. His pattern of hits (*H*) and nonhits (*N*) is shown (a nonhit is a walk or a strikeout). *Research question:* At $\alpha = .01$, is the pattern of hits random? **Hits**

$$N\,N\,N\,H\,N\,H\,N\,N\,H\,N\,N\,H\,H\,N\,N\,N\,N\,H\,N\,H\,N\,N\,N\,H\,N\,N\,H\,N\,H\,N\,N\,H\,H$$

16.17 Thirty four customers at Starbucks either ordered coffee (*C*) or did not order coffee (*X*). *Research question:* At $\alpha = .05$, is the sequence random? **Starbucks**

$$C\,X\,C\,X\,C\,C\,C\,C\,X\,X\,X\,X\,C\,X\,C\,X\,C\,X\,C\,C\,C\,X\,C\,X\,C\,C\,X\,C\,X\,X\,X\,C\,C\,X$$

16.18 The price of a particular stock over a period of 60 days rises (+) or declines (−) in the following pattern: *Research question:* At $\alpha = .05$, is the pattern random? **Stock**

$$+\,+\,-\,-\,-\,+\,+\,+\,+\,+\,+\,+\,-\,-\,-\,-\,+\,+\,-\,+\,-\,+\,-\,+\,-\,-\,-\,-\,+\,+\,+\,+$$
$$-\,+\,+\,+\,+\,-\,+\,+\,+\,-\,+\,-\,+\,-\,+\,+\,+\,-\,-\,-\,-\,-\,-\,+\,+\,+\,+\,-\,-$$

16.19 A forecasting model is fitted to sales data over 24 months. Forecasting errors are tabulated to reveal whether the model provides an overestimate (+) or an underestimate (−) for each month's sales. The results are $-\,-\,+\,+\,+\,-\,+\,-\,-\,+\,+\,-\,-\,-\,-\,-\,+\,+\,+\,+\,+\,-\,-$. *Research question:* At $\alpha = .05$, is the pattern random? **Forecast**

16.20 A cognitive retraining clinic assists outpatient victims of head injury, anoxia, or other conditions that result in cognitive impairment. Each incoming patient is evaluated to establish an appropriate treatment program and estimated length of stay (ELOS is always a multiple of 4 weeks because treatment sessions are scheduled on a monthly basis). To see if there is any difference in ELOS between the two clinics, a sample is taken, consisting of all patients evaluated at each clinic during October, with the results shown. *Research question:* At $\alpha = .10$, do the medians differ? **Cognitive**

Clinic A (10 patients): 24, 24, 52, 30, 40, 40, 18, 30, 18, 40
Clinic B (12 patients): 20, 20, 52, 36, 36, 36, 24, 32, 16, 40, 24, 16

16.21 Two manufacturing facilities produce 1280 × 1024 LED (light-emitting diode) displays. Twelve displays are chosen at random from each lab, and the number of bad pixels is noted for each display. *Research question:* At $\alpha = .05$, do the medians differ? **LED**

Defects in Randomly Inspected LED Displays

Facility	Number of Bad Pixels											
Lab *A*	2	0	5	0	1	2	0	5	0	4	1	2
Lab *B*	0	1	2	3	1	0	0	1	2	2	1	0

16.22 In the 1996 Super Bowl, Dallas beat Pittsburgh 27-17. The weights of the linemen on each team are shown below. *Research question:* At $\alpha = .01$, do the medians differ? 🏈 **Linemen**

Weights of Linemen in 1996 Super Bowl

Dallas Cowboys		Pittsburgh Steelers	
Player	Weight	Player	Weight
Derek Kennard	300	Kendall Gammon	288
Nate Newton	320	Dermontti Dawson	288
Ron Stone	309	John Jackson	297
Russell Maryland	279	Thomas Newberry	285
Michael Batiste	305	Brenden Stai	297
George Hegamin	338	Ariel Solomon	290
Dale Hellestrae	286	Leon Searcy	304
Mark Tuinei	305	Justin Strzelczyk	302
Larry Allen	326	Taase Faumui	278
Leon Lett	288	James Parrish	310
Erik Williams	322	Bill Johnson	300
Darren Benson	308	Joel Steed	300
Chad Hennings	288	Oliver Gibson	283
Hurvin McCormack	274		

Source: *Detroit Free Press*, January 28, 1996, pp. 6D–7D.

16.23 Does a class break stimulate the pulse? Here are heart rates for a sample of 30 students before and after a class break. *Research question:* At $\alpha = .05$, do the medians differ? 🏈 **HeartRate**

Heart Rate Before and After Class Break

Student	Before	After	Student	Before	After
1	60	62	16	70	64
2	70	76	17	69	66
3	77	78	18	64	69
4	80	83	19	70	73
5	82	82	20	59	58
6	82	83	21	62	65
7	41	66	22	66	68
8	65	63	23	81	77
9	58	60	24	56	57
10	50	54	25	64	62
11	82	93	26	78	79
12	56	55	27	75	74
13	71	67	28	66	67
14	67	68	29	59	63
15	66	75	30	98	82

Thanks to colleague Gene Fliedner for having his evening students take their own pulses before and after the 10-minute class break.

16.24 An experimental bumper was designed to reduce damage in low-speed collisions. This bumper was installed on an experimental group of vans in a large fleet, but not on a control group. At the end of a trial period, accident data showed 12 repair incidents for the experimental group and 9 repair incidents for the control group. The vehicle downtime (in days) per repair incident is shown. *Research question:* At $\alpha = .05$, do the medians differ? (Data are from Floyd G. Willoughby and Thomas W. Lauer, confidential case study.) **Downtime**

New bumper: 9, 2, 5, 12, 5, 4, 7, 5, 11, 3, 7, 1

Old bumper: 7, 5, 7, 4, 18, 4, 8, 14, 13

16.25 The square footage of each of the last 11 homes sold in each of two suburban neighborhoods is noted. *Research question:* At $\alpha = .01$, do the medians differ? **SqFt**

Square Footage of Homes Sold

Grosse Hills (Built in 1985)	Haut Nez Estates (Built in 2003)
3,220	3,850
3,450	3,560
3,270	4,300
3,200	4,100
4,850	3,750
3,150	3,450
2,800	3,400
3,050	3,550
2,950	3,750
3,430	4,150
3,220	3,850

16.26 Below are grade point averages for 25 randomly chosen university business students during a recent semester. *Research question:* At $\alpha = .01$, are the median grade point averages the same for students in these four class levels? **GPA**

Grade Point Averages of 25 Business Students

Freshman (5 students)	Sophomore (7 students)	Junior (7 students)	Senior (6 students)
1.91	3.89	3.01	3.32
2.14	2.02	2.89	2.45
3.47	2.96	3.45	3.81
2.19	3.32	3.67	3.02
2.71	2.29	3.33	3.01
	2.82	2.98	3.17
	3.11	3.26	

16.27 In a bumper test, three types of autos were deliberately crashed into a barrier at 5 mph, and the resulting damage (in dollars) was estimated. Five test vehicles of each type were crashed, with the results shown below. *Research question:* At $\alpha = .01$, are the median crash damages the same for these three vehicles? **Crash**

Crash Damage in Dollars

Goliath	Varmint	Weasel
1,600	1,290	1,090
760	1,400	2,100
880	1,390	1,830
1,950	1,850	1,250
1,220	950	1,920

16.28 The waiting time (in minutes) for emergency room patients with non-life-threatening injuries was measured at four hospitals for all patients who arrived between 6:00 and 6:30 P.M. on a certain Wednesday. The results are shown below. *Research question:* At $\alpha = .05$, are the median waiting times the same for emergency patients in these four hospitals?   **Emergency**

Emergency Room Waiting Time (minutes)

Hospital A (5 patients)	Hospital B (4 patients)	Hospital C (7 patients)	Hospital D (6 patients)
10	8	5	0
19	25	11	20
5	17	24	9
26	36	16	5
11		18	10
		29	12
		15	

16.29 Mean output of arrays of solar cells of three types are measured four times under random light intensity over a period of 5 minutes, yielding the results shown below. *Research question:* At $\alpha = .05$, is the median solar cell output the same for all three types?   **Solar**

Solar Cell Output (Watts)

Cell Type	Output (Watts)					
A	123	121	123	124	125	127
B	125	122	122	121	122	126
C	126	128	125	129	131	128

16.30 Below are results of braking tests of the Ford Explorer on glare ice, packed snow, and split traction (one set of wheels on ice, the other on dry pavement), using three braking methods. *Research question:* At $\alpha = .01$, is braking method related to stopping distance?   **Stopping**

Stopping Distance from 40 mph to Zero

Road Condition	Pumping	Locked	ABS
Glare Ice	441	455	460
Split Traction	223	148	183
Packed Snow	149	146	167

Source: *Popular Science* 252, no. 6 (June 1998), p. 78.

16.31 In a call center, the average waiting time for an answer (in seconds) is shown below by time of day. *Research question:* At $\alpha = .01$, does the waiting time differ by day of the week? *Note:* Only the first 5 and last 5 observations are shown.   **Wait**

Average Waiting Time (in Seconds) for Answer (n = 26)

Time	Mon	Tue	Wed	Thu	Fri
06:00	34	71	33	39	39
06:30	52	70	88	53	49
07:00	36	103	47	32	91
07:30	52	97	55	101	37
08:00	46	76	67	74	66
⋮	⋮	⋮	⋮	⋮	⋮
16:30	33	26	33	9	36
17:00	27	29	34	38	35
17:30	28	31	27	22	26
18:00	35	14	115	26	22
18:30	25	34	9	5	47

16.32 Below is the average gestation (in days) and average longevity (in years) for selected animals. *Research question:* At $\alpha = .05$, is there a significant rank correlation between gestation and longevity? Would human beings follow this pattern? *Note:* Only the first 5 and last 5 observations are shown. 🐾 **Gestation**

Gestation and Longevity for Various Animals (n = 22)

Animal	Gestation	Longevity
Ass	365	12
Baboon	187	20
Beaver	105	5
Bison	285	15
Camel	406	12
⋮	⋮	⋮
Rabbit	31	5
Rhino	480	20
Sheep	154	12
Wolf	63	5
Zebra	365	15

Source: *The World Almanac and Book of Facts, 2005*, p. 180.

16.33 Fertility rates (children born per woman) are shown for 15 EU nations in 2 years a decade apart. *Research question:* At $\alpha = .05$, is there a significant rank correlation? *Note:* Only the first 5 and last 5 nations are shown. 🐾 **Fertility**

Fertility Rates in EU Nations (n = 15)

Nation	1990	2000
Austria	1.5	1.3
Belgium	1.6	1.5
Denmark	1.6	1.7
Finland	1.7	1.6
France	1.8	1.8
⋮	⋮	⋮
Netherlands	1.6	1.5
Portugal	1.6	1.5
Spain	1.4	1.1
Sweden	2.0	1.4
United Kingdom	1.8	1.7

Source: World Health Organization.

16.34 A newspaper article listed nutritional facts for 56 frozen dinners. From that list, 16 frozen dinners were randomly selected by using the random number method. *Research question:* Choose any two variables. At $\alpha = .01$, based on this sample, is there a significant rank correlation between the two variables? *Note:* Only the first 5 and last 5 observations are shown. 🐝 **Dinners**

Frozen Dinner Nutritional Information (*n* = 16)

Company	Dinner/Entree	Fat (g)	Calories	Sodium (mg)
Budget Gourmet	French Recipe Chicken	9	240	1,000
Budget Gourmet	Chicken au Gratin	11	250	870
Budget Gourmet Light	Stuffed Turkey Breast	6	230	520
Budget Gourmet Light	Teriyaki Chicken Breast	6	270	460
Budget Gourmet Light	Chicken Breast Parmigiana	8	260	420
⋮	⋮	⋮	⋮	⋮
Tyson	Chicken Français	14	280	1,130
Weight Watchers	Chicken Fajitas	1	230	590
Weight Watchers	Filet of Fish au Gratin	6	200	700
Weight Watchers	Beef Sirloin Tips	7	220	540
Weight Watchers	Lasagna with Meat Sauce	10	320	630

Source: *Detroit Free Press,* April 10, 1991, p. 2F. This information is intended solely to illustrate statistical concepts, and should not be used as a guide to nutrition. Nutritional content of frozen dinners may have changed since the newspaper article was written.

16.35 The table below shows annual incidence of cancer of the colon in women of different nations (cases per 100,000) and average meat consumption (grams per person per day). *Research question:* At $\alpha = .05$, based on this data, is there a significant rank correlation between colon cancer and meat consumption? *Note:* Only the first 5 and last 5 nations are shown. 🐝 **Cancer**

Women's Colon Cancer Rates and Meat Consumption in Various Nations (*n* = 23)

Nation	Colon Cancer Rate	Per Capita Meat (gm)
Canada	29.5	229
Chile	7.1	81
Colombia	3.9	80
Denmark	23.4	169
E. Germany	12.5	167
⋮	⋮	⋮
Sweden	19.3	137
United Kingdom	22.1	199
USA	33.2	274
W. Germany	15.5	177
Yugoslavia	8.6	71

Source: Ian Spratley, *Living With Technology and Numeracy,* p. 7, copyright © 1982 The Open University, used with permission.

16.36 Are gasoline prices a potential policy tool in controlling carbon emissions? The table below shows 2001 gasoline prices (dollars per liter) and carbon dioxide emissions per dollar of GDP. *Research question:* At $\alpha = .05$, based on this data, is there a significant rank correlation between these two variables? *Note:* Only the first 5 and last 5 observations are shown. 🐝 **Emissions**

Gasoline Prices and Carbon Emissions for Selected Nations ($n = 31$)

Nation	Gas Price ($/L)	CO_2/GDP (kg/$)
Australia	0.489	0.79
Austria	0.888	0.25
Belgium	0.984	0.37
Canada	0.468	0.72
Chinese Taipei	0.569	0.66
⋮	⋮	⋮
Sweden	1.020	0.16
Switzerland	0.892	0.13
Turkey	1.003	0.99
United Kingdom	1.165	0.41
United States	0.381	0.63

Source: International Energy Agency, www.iea.org.

16.37 Below are the top 20 U.S. football teams in the seventh and eighth weeks of the 2003 season, along with the points awarded to each team by the *ESPN/USA Today* coaches poll. *Research question:* At $\alpha = .01$, based on this data, is there a significant rank correlation between these two variables?
 Teams

Football Ratings in *ESPN/USA Today* Coaches Poll

Team	This Week	Last Week
Oklahoma	1575	1622
Southern Cal	1502	1470
Florida State	1412	1320
LSU	1337	1241
Virginia Tech	1281	1026
Miami	1263	1563
Ohio State	1208	1226
Michigan	1135	938
Georgia	951	1378
Iowa	932	762
Texas	881	605
TCU	875	727
Wash State	827	1260
Purdue	667	487
Michigan State	645	1041
Nebraska	558	924
Tennessee	544	449
Minnesota	490	149
Florida	480	246
Bowling Green	369	577

Source: *Detroit Free Press*.

Related Reading

Agresti, Alan. *Categorical Data Analysis* (Wiley, 2002).

Conover, William J. *Practical Nonparametric Statistics*. 3rd ed. (Wiley, 1999).

Gibbons, Jean D. *Nonparametric Statistics: An Introduction* (Sage, 1999).

Huber, Peter J. *Robust Statistics* (Wiley, 2003).

Le, Chap T. *Applied Categorical Data Analysis* (Wiley, 1998).

Lehmann, Erich L. *Nonparametrics: Statistical Methods Based on Ranks*. Rev. ed. (Prentice-Hall, 1998).

LearningStats Unit 16   Nonparametric Tests

LearningStats Unit 16 shows examples of several common nonparametric tests and their parametric counterparts (if any). Your instructor may assign specific modules, but you can try the others if they sound interesting.

Topic	LearningStats Modules
Overview	What Are Nonparametric Tests?
Case studies	Runs Test: Baseball Streaks
	Wilcoxon Signed-Rank: Exam Scores
	Mann-Whitney: ATM Withdrawals
	Kruskal-Wallis: DVD Prices
	Friedman Test: Freeway Pollution
	Spearman's Rho: EU Nations Fertility
Tables	Chi-Square Critical Values

Key: = PowerPoint   = Excel

Quality Management

Chapter Learning Objectives

When you finish this chapter you should be able to

- Define quality and explain how it may be measured.
- Distinguish between common cause variation and special cause variation.
- List steps toward continuous quality improvement and variance reduction.
- Name key individuals and their contributions to the quality movement.
- List common statistical tools used in quality improvement.
- State the purposes of common control charts ($\overline{x}$, R, and p) and how to use them.
- Recognize abnormal patterns in control charts and their potential causes.
- Assess the capability of a process.

What Is Quality?

Quality can be measured in many ways. Quality may be a *physical* metric, such as the number of bad sectors on a computer hard disk or the quietness of an air conditioning fan. Quality may be an *aesthetic* attribute such as the ripeness of a banana or cleanliness of a clinic waiting room. (Does the fig bar turned in the wrong direction in Figure 17.1 affect the aesthetic quality of the product?) Quality may be a *functional* characteristic such as ergonomic accessibility of car radio controls or convenience of hours that a bank is open. It may be a *personal* attribute such as friendliness of service at a restaurant or diligence of follow-up by a veterinary clinic. It may be an *efficiency* attribute such as promptness in delivery of an order or the waiting time at a dentist's. Quality is generally understood to include these attributes:

- Conformance to specifications.
- Performance in the intended use.
- As near to zero defects as possible.

- Reliability and durability.
- Serviceability when needed.
- Favorable customer perceptions.

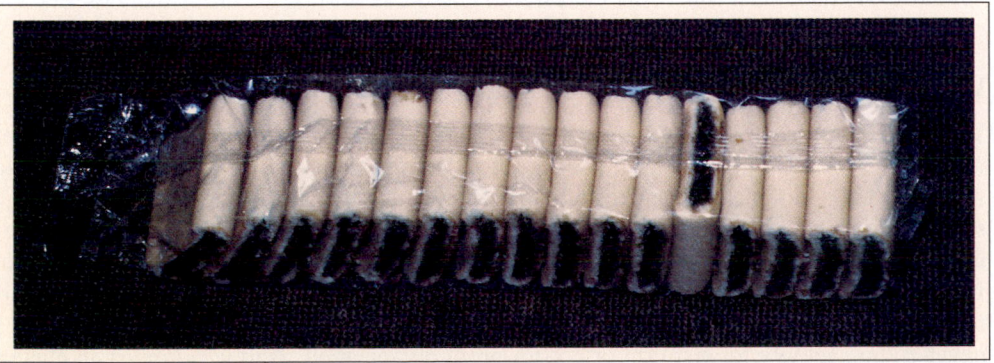

FIGURE 17.1

Unopened fig bars: Quality as an aesthetic attribute

Measurement of quality is specific to the organization and its products. In manufacturing, the focus is likely to be on physical characteristics (e.g., defects, reliability, consistency), while in services, the focus is likely to be on customer perceptions (e.g., courtesy, responsiveness, competence). Table 17.1 lists some typical quality indicators that might be important to firms engaged in manufacturing as compared to firms that deliver services.

TABLE 17.1 Typical Quality Indicators	*Manufacturing*	*Services*
	Proportion of nonconforming output	Proportion of satisfied customers
	Warranty claim costs	Average customer waiting time
	Repeat purchase rate (loyalty)	Repeat client base (loyalty)

Productivity and Quality

Productivity refers to the physical output per employee per unit of time. It is a measure of efficiency. High productivity lowers cost per unit, increases profit, and supports higher wages and salaries. Productivity, like quality, can be measured in various ways. In service industries, productivity is difficult to define. What is the productivity of an investment banker, a CEO, a kindergarten teacher, a college professor, a tax analyst, or a design engineer? Service organizations often rely on quasi-financial measurements, such as average daily sales per field representative, hours billed per attorney, or patients seen by a physician. These are imperfect proxies for productivity, but may be the best that can be devised.

In the past, manufacturing companies assumed an inverse relationship between quality and productivity. This view was based on a short-term perspective. The belief was that the only way to truly improve quality was to slow down and put more time into each product. While stopping an assembly line does imply less output today, continuing to run an ineffective production line leads to defective products, which lead to waste, rework, and lost customers. In the modern view, quality and productivity move in the same direction, because by doing it right the first time, more effort can go into producing the right output. Our focus in the 21st century is on designing and operating effective business processes to consistently meet customer requirements.

Processes and Quality Metrics

A *process* is a sequence of interconnected tasks that result in the creation of a product or in the delivery of a service. Manufacturing, assembly, or packaging operations usually come to mind when we hear the term "process." Yet service operations such as filling mail orders, providing customer support, handling loan applications, delivering health services, and meeting payrolls are also processes. Since a majority of workers are in the service sector, it is reasonable to say that nonmanufacturing processes are predominant in today's economy. *Quality control* refers to methods used by organizations to ensure that their products and services meet customer expectations and to ensure that there is improvement over time. To improve quality, we must undertake systematic data collection and careful measurement of key metrics that describe the product or service that is valued by customers.

Variance Reduction

Where does statistics enter the quality picture? Statistics focuses on the phenomenon of *variation*. Processes that produce, package, and deliver supposedly identical products and services cannot eliminate all sources of variation around the target specification(s). Although some degree of variation is normal and expected, firms do try to attain consistency in their products and services, because excessive variation is often a sign of poor quality. Although slight variation may not affect customer satisfaction, variation that affects real or perceived performance of the product or service clearly requires attention. The quest for *reduced variation* is a never-ending activity for any firm or not-for-profit organization. *Zero variation* is an elusive goal that can be approached only asymptotically, since each successive improvement usually comes at an increasing cost.

Common Cause versus Special Cause

Statisticians define two categories of variation. ***Common cause variation*** (random "noise") is normal and expected, and is present in any stable, in-control process. ***Special cause variation*** is due to factors that are abnormal and require investigation. Special cause variation will produce observations that are not from the same population as the majority of observations. Until special cause variation is eliminated, a process is not in control.

Sources of variation in processes include human abilities, training, motivation, technology, materials, management, and organization. Some of these factors are under the control of the organization, while others are fixed and cannot be changed. Most factors are fixed in the short run but may be changed in the long run. For example, technology can be changed through research and development and capital spending on new equipment, but such changes may take years. Human performance can change over time through education and training, but usually not in hours or days.

Role of Management

Management is expected to find ways to maintain process control in the short run and to reduce variation in the long run. The degree to which variance can be reduced depends on equipment, technology, and worker training. Managers may call upon statistical specialists for advice and to train nonstatisticians who comprise the majority of the workforce. Training requirements depend on the type of organization. A manufacturing firm may require broad-based statistical training for engineers, plant managers, supervisors, and even assembly workers. But financial, purchasing, marketing, and sales managers must also understand statistics, because they interact with technical experts on cost control, waste management, and quality improvement. Even in banks or health care, broad-based training in statistical methods can be helpful in increasing efficiency and improving quality.

Role of Statisticians

We use statistics to measure variation, set attainable limits for variation, and establish rules to decide whether processes are in control. Trained statisticians may perceive problems that are not immediately apparent to those who are involved in day-to-day business activities. Quality problems are a challenging domain for statisticians, requiring at times the full arsenal of statistical theory. Statisticians have made many contributions to quality management and play an active role as quality consultants.

SECTION EXERCISES

17.1   Define (a) process, (b) quality, and (c) variation.

17.2   Distinguish between common cause variation and special cause variation.

17.3   Can zero variation be achieved? Explain.

Who Is a Customer?

17.2
CUSTOMER ORIENTATION

One initial step in setting up a quality management system is defining the clients or customers who are being served. A ***customer*** is whoever consumes what you produce. *Internal customers* are employees of another branch of your organization. For example, the Accounts Payable Department provides services consumed by the Cost Department and the Purchasing Department. *External customers* are outside the organization. Vendors get paid, thereby consuming services provided by the Accounts Payable Department. Employees may be less aware of external customers because most of their dealings are with other employees of the company, but it is the external customers who provide the revenue that supports the organization.

Measuring Quality

Each customer category has its own viewpoint, so we may have to measure several aspects of the product or service to assess quality. Different customer groups may require unique quality measurements, while sometimes a single quality measurement may apply to several customer groups. Observers may not agree on the interpretation of quality measures, so planning and training are essential to ensure that employees collect meaningful data. Table 17.2 gives examples of customers and measurable aspects of quality.

TABLE 17.2   Examples of Customers and Measurable Aspects of Quality

Department or Process	Possible Customers (Type)	Measurable Aspects
Payroll department in a large hospital	Hourly and salaried employees who are to be paid on time (internal).	Percent of employees paid incorrectly or late each month.
	Federal and state tax agencies that withhold taxes (external).	Percent of employees with insufficient taxes withheld each year.
	Creditors and courts seeking to garnish employee wages for child support (external).	Number of weekly creditor telephone complaints.
Aluminum beverage container manufacturing plant	Bottling plant awaiting shipments of containers (internal).	Monthly hours of downtime due to delayed shipments.
	Staff design engineers seeking to reduce can weight while maintaining strength (internal).	Thickness and weight of alloy or number of structurally defective cans per 100,000.
	State and federal health and safety agencies such as OSHA (external).	Number of worker injuries per month.
Retail pharmacy	Individuals needing prescription filled (external).	Percent of prescriptions filled within 15 minutes.
	Doctors, HMOs, and customers phoning in prescriptions (external).	Average wait for phone to be answered or percent of callers getting a busy signal.
	Cashier waiting for pharmacist to fill prescription (internal).	Time (in minutes) a cashier must wait for pharmacist.

SECTION EXERCISES

17.4 Distinguish between internal and external customers, giving an example of each within an organization with which you are familiar.

17.5 Define a measurable aspect of quality for (a) the car dealership where you bought your car; (b) the bank or credit union where you usually make personal transactions; and (c) the movie theater where you usually go.

17.3 BEHAVIORAL ASPECTS OF QUALITY

Blame versus Solutions

Employees tend to think about their own job performance problems or the immediate demands of co-workers and internal customers, losing sight of the fact that their jobs and department budget ultimately depend on serving customers well. To succeed, management must create an atmosphere and incentives that support and reward customer orientation. Employees must take seriously quality indicators that tell whether they are doing a good job. Sometimes this is painful, since it means acknowledging bad outcomes and signs of weakening quality.

In a quality-driven organization, problems do not lead to *blame*, but to a search for *solutions*. What happens if a manager blames an employee for a quality problem? That employee is likely to quit reporting quality problems. Other employees will hear about it and adopt a negative attitude toward quality tracking. If quality problems are covered up, matters can only get worse.

W. Edwards Deming, a famous quality expert, believed that most employees want to do a good job. He found that most of quality problems do not stem from willful disregard of quality, but from flaws in the process or system, such as

- Inadequate equipment
- Inadequate maintenance
- Inadequate training
- Inadequate supervision
- Inadequate support systems
- Inadequate task design

Employee Involvement

Good solutions to quality problems will be more likely if employee representatives from each area are brought together as a *team* to address the quality problem. Team-building activities can help establish group goals, values, and communication. The team then begins the process of problem solving as a group. Teamwork is an important part of the strategy of the quality-driven organization. This goes far beyond statistics.

But organizations have finite resources. Not all problems can be solved. Which problems are most urgent? Which ones can we live with for awhile? Which solutions would have the greatest impact on improving customer satisfaction? Trade-offs must be made. This is an economic problem. There is also a behavioral aspect of resource constraints. Research shows that employee involvement is necessary to create changes that will be accepted, to ensure "buy-in" to change, and to ensure that viable options are not overlooked. Top-down decisions without employee input can create new problems, such as resentment or unworkable processes. That is why we must study organizational behavior, as well as statistics.

SECTION EXERCISES

17.6 Name five barriers to quality improvement.

17.7 What did Deming say about blaming employees for poor quality?

Brief History of Quality Control

17.4
PIONEERS IN QUALITY MANAGEMENT

During the early 1900s, quality control took the form of improved inspection and improvement in the methods of mass production, under the leadership of American experts. From about 1920 to just after World War II, techniques such as process control charts (Walter A. Shewhart) and acceptance sampling from lots (Harold F. Dodge and Harry G. Romig) were perfected and were widely applied in North America. But during the 1950s and 1960s, Japanese manufacturers (particularly automotive) shed their previous image as low-quality producers and began to apply American quality control techniques. The Japanese based their efforts largely on ideas and training from American statisticians W. Edwards Deming and Joseph M. Juran, as well as Japanese statisticians Genichi Taguchi and Kaoru Ishikawa. They developed new approaches that focused on customer satisfaction and costs of quality. By the 1970s, despite exhortation by Deming and others, North American firms had lost their initial leadership in quality control, while the Japanese devised and perfected new quality improvement methods, soon adopted by the Europeans.

During the 1980s, North American firms began a process of recommitment to quality improvement and Japanese lean production methods. In their quest for quality improvement, these firms sought training and advice by experts such as Deming, Juran, and Armand Feigenbaum. The Japanese, however, continued to push the quality frontier forward, under the teachings of Taguchi and the perfection of the Kaizen philosophy of continuous improvement. The Europeans articulated the ISO 9000 standards, now adopted by most world-class firms.

North American firms have implemented their own style of total quality management. Manufacturers now seek to build *quality* into their products and services, all the way down the supply chain. Quality is best viewed as a *management system* rather than purely as an application of statistics.

W. Edwards Deming

The late *W. Edwards Deming* (1900–1993) deserves special mention as an influential thinker. He was widely honored in his lifetime. Many know him primarily for his contributions to improving productivity and quality in Japan. In 1950, at the invitation of the Union of Japanese Scientists and Engineers, Deming gave a series of lectures to 230 leading Japanese industrialists who together controlled 80 percent of Japan's capital. His message was the same as to Americans he had taught during the previous decades. The Japanese listened carefully to his message, and their success in implementing Deming's ideas is a matter of historical record.

Deming said that *profound knowledge* of a system is needed for an individual to become a good listener who can teach others. He emphasized that all people are different, that management is not about ranking people, and that anyone's performance is governed largely by the system that he/she works in. He said that fear invites presentation of bad data. If bearers of bad news fare badly, the boss will hear only good news—guaranteeing bad management decisions.

It is difficult to encapsulate Deming's many ideas succinctly, but most observers would agree that his philosophy is reflected in his widely reproduced *14 Points,* which can be found in full on the Web or in abbreviated form here. The 14 Points are primarily statements about management, not statistics. They ask that management take responsibility for improving quality and avoid blaming workers. The 14 Points require interpretation. Deming spent much of his long life explaining these and other of his ideas, through a series of seminars aimed initially at management, an activity that continues today through the work of his followers at The W. Edwards Deming Institute (www.deming.org). Deming's impact was a function of his philosophy, his stature as a statistician, and his absorbing personal presence, not his list of 14 points.

Deming's 14 Points (abbreviated)

1. Maintain constancy of purpose.
2. Adopt a new philosophy.
3. Don't rely on inspection—design quality in.
4. Don't award contracts just on the basis of price.
5. Continuous improvement.
6. Institute training on the job.
7. Supervision should help people do a better job.
8. Drive out fear and create trust.
9. Break down barriers between departments.
10. Eliminate slogans, exhortations, and targets.
11. Eliminate numerical goals.
12. Remove barriers to pride in work.
13. Continuing education for all.
14. Act to accomplish the transformation.

Source: W. Edwards Deming, *Out of the Crisis,* copyright © 1986 W. Edwards Deming. Reprinted by permission of MIT Press.

Modern business students may find some of his recommendations simplistic. For example, "drive out fear" is an elusive goal in a large, complex organization. Deming was not unaware of the behavioral difficulty of achieving his goals. He believed that one major difficulty lay in obtaining commitment from the top leadership and was impatient when organizations did not demonstrate sufficient resolve to implement his ideas. Perhaps the best summary is to say that Deming's ideas have become a required subset of the broader principles of quality management.

Other Influential Thinkers

Walter A. Shewhart (1891–1967) invented the control chart and the concepts of special cause and common cause (assignable cause). Shewhart's charts were adopted by the American Society for Testing Materials (ASTM) in 1933 and were used to improve production during World War II. *Joseph M. Juran* (1904–) also taught quality education in Japan, contemporaneously with Deming. Like Deming, he became more influential with North American management in the 1980s. He felt that 80 percent of quality defects arise from management actions, and therefore that quality control was management's responsibility. This may seem obvious today, but before the 1980s there was a tendency to blame labor for quality problems and to assume that not much could be done about it. Juran articulated the idea of the *vital few*—a handful of causes that account for a vast majority of quality problems (the principle behind the **Pareto chart**). Effort, he said, should be concentrated on key problems, rather than diffused over many less-important problems.

Kaoru Ishikawa is a Japanese quality expert who is associated with the idea of *quality circles,* which characterize the Japanese approach. He also pioneered the idea of company-wide quality control and was influential in popularizing statistical tools for quality control. His textbook on statistical methods still is used in training, though many competitors now exist. He taught that elementary statistical tools (Pareto charts, histograms, scatter diagrams, and control charts) should be understood by everyone, while advanced tools (experimental design, regression) might best be left to specialists.

Armand V. Feigenbaum first used the term *total quality control* in 1951. He favored broad sharing of responsibility for quality assurance. This was at a time when many companies assumed that quality was the responsibility of the Quality Assurance Department alone. He felt that quality is an essential element of modern management, like marketing or finance. *Philip B. Crosby* is the author of an important book that argues that efforts at improving quality pay for themselves, and was among the first to popularize the catch-phrase "zero defects." *Genichi Taguchi* is a pioneer whose contributions are discussed further at the end of this chapter.

Other quality gurus include *Claus Moller,* whose European company specializes in management training. Moller believes that people can be inspired to do their best through development of the individual's self-esteem. Moller is known for his 12 Golden Rules and 17 hallmarks of a quality company. *Shigeo Shingo* has had great impact on Japanese industry. His basic idea (the "poka-yoke" system) is to stop a process whenever a defect occurs, define the cause, and prevent future occurrences. If source inspections are used, statistical sampling becomes unnecessary, because the worker is prevented from making errors in the first place. *Tom Peters* is an American who studied successful American companies to define a philosophy of quality improvement that discards "management" in favor of "leadership." He emphasizes customer orientation and his 12 keys to a quality revolution.

SECTION EXERCISES

17.8   Name five influential thinkers in quality control and briefly state their contributions.

17.9   List five of Deming's 14 points. Look them up on the Internet and explain their meaning.

Acronyms abound in quality management (TQM, BPR, SQC, SPC, etc.). The following are only a few that you should know before you enter the workplace.

17.5 QUALITY IMPROVEMENT

Total Quality Management (TQM)

Total quality management or *TQM* requires that all business activities should be oriented toward meeting and exceeding customer needs, empowering employees, eliminating waste or rework, and ensuring the long-run viability of the enterprise through continuous quality improvement. TQM encompasses a broad spectrum of behavioral, managerial, and technical approaches. It includes diverse but complementary elements such as statistics, benchmarking, process redesign, team building, group communications, quality function deployment, and cross-functional management.

Business Process Redesign (BPR)

Like TQM, *business process redesign* or *BPR* has a cross-functional orientation. But instead of focusing on incremental change and gradual improvement of processes, BPR seeks radical redesign of processes to achieve breakthrough improvement in performance measures—a lofty goal that is easier to state than to achieve. Business schools typically incorporate TQM and/or BPR concepts into a variety of nonstatistics core classes.

Statistical Quality Control (SQC)

Statistical quality control or *SQC* refers to a subset of quality improvement techniques that rely on statistics. A few of the descriptive tools (see Figure 17.2) have been covered in earlier chapters, while others (e.g., control charts) are discussed in this chapter.

Descriptive Tools	*Analytic Methods*
• Pareto diagrams	• Control charts
• Scatter plots	• Lot and batch inspection plans
• Box plots	• Acceptance sampling
• Fishbone diagrams	• Experimental design
• Check sheets	• Taguchi robust design

FIGURE 17.2

Three descriptive SQC tools

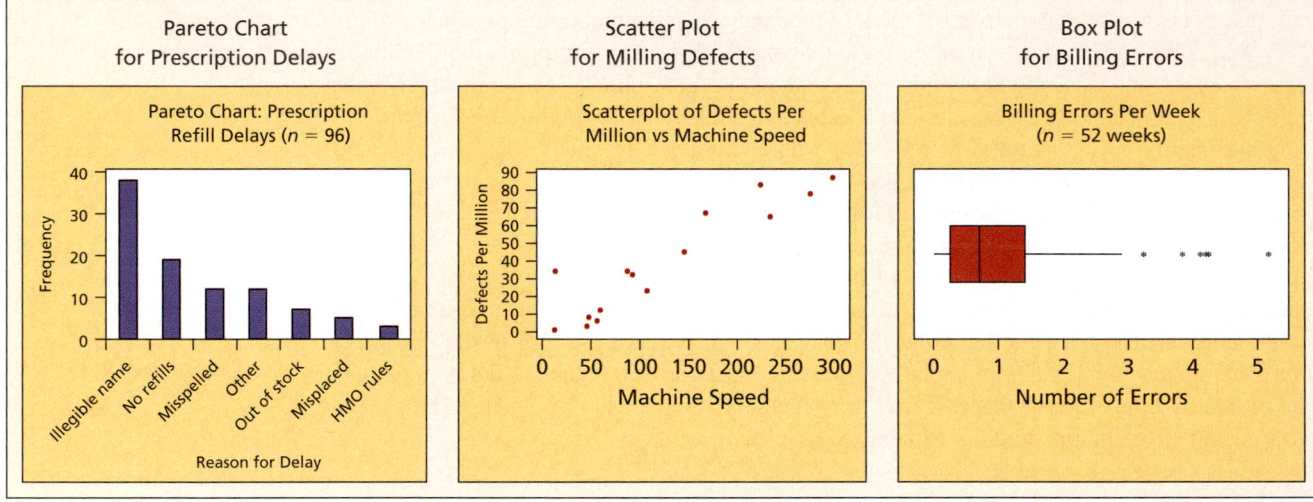

A *check sheet* is a form for counting the frequency of sources of nonconformance. The *fishbone chart* (also called a *cause-and-effect diagram*) is a visual display that summarizes the factors that increase process variation or adversely affect achievement of the target. For example, Figure 17.3 shows a fishbone chart for factors affecting patient length of stay in a hospital. The six main categories (materials, methods, people, management, measurement, technology) are general and may apply to almost any process. You can insert as many verbal descriptions ("fishbones") as you need to identify the causes of variation. The fishbone chart is not, strictly speaking, a statistical tool, but is helpful in thinking about root causes.

Statistical Process Control (SPC)

Statistical process control or *SPC* refers specifically to the monitoring of ongoing repetitive processes to ensure conformance to standards by using methods of statistics. Its main tools are *capability analysis* and *control charts*. Because this is a statistics textbook, we will focus on SPC tools, leaving SQC and TQM to other courses that you may take.

FIGURE 17.3

Fishbone (cause-and-effect) chart for patient length of stay

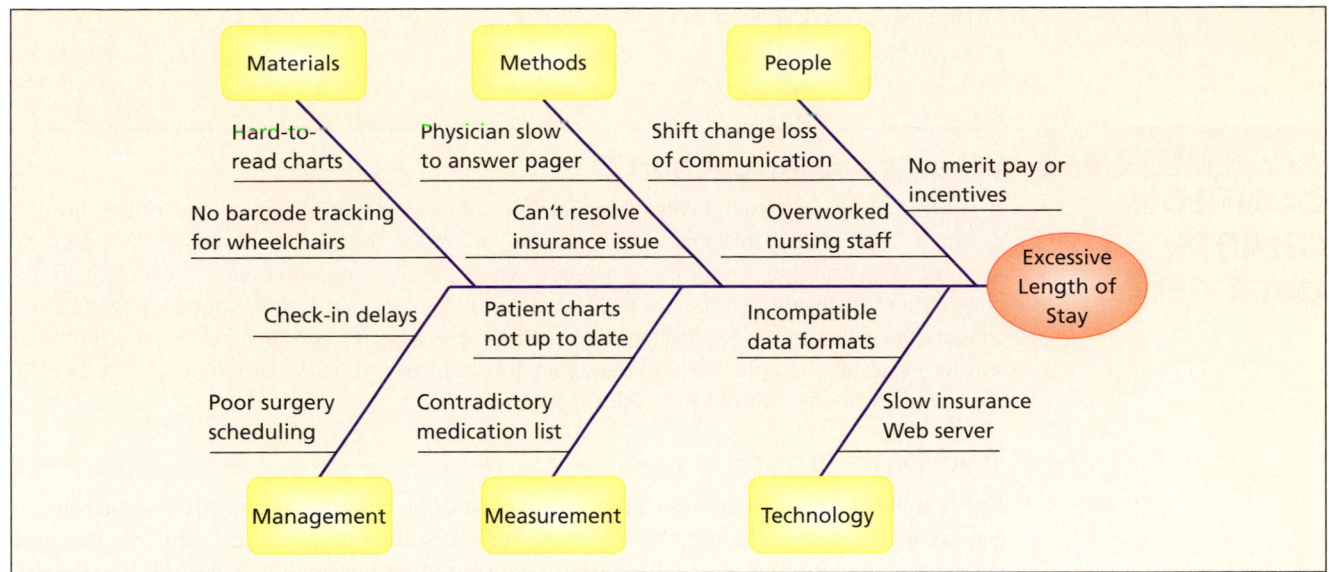

Continuous Quality Improvement (CQI)

Quality improvement begins with measurement of a *variable* (e.g., dimensions of an automobile door panel) or an *attribute* (e.g., number of emergency patients who wait more than 30 minutes). For a variable, quality improvement means reducing variation from the target specification. For an attribute, quality improvement means decreasing the rate of nonconformance. Statistical methods are used to ensure that the process is stable and in control by eliminating sources of *special cause* (nonrandom) variation, as opposed to *common cause* (random) variation that is normal and inherent in the process. We change the process whenever a way is discovered to reduce variation or to decrease nonconformance (especially if the process is incapable of meeting the target specifications). We continue to seek ways to reduce variation and/or nonconformance to even lower levels. The never-ending cycle is repeated indefinitely, giving rise to the concept of *CQI.* In the **Six Sigma** school of thought, the steps to quality improvement are abbreviated as **DMAIC** (define, measure, analyze, improve, control).

Steps to Continuous Quality Improvement

- Step 1:   Define a relevant, measurable parameter of the product or service.
- Step 2:   Establish targets or desired specifications for the product or service.
- Step 3:   Monitor the process to be sure it is stable and in control.
- Step 4:   Is the process capable of meeting the desired specifications?
- Step 5:   Identify sources of variation or nonconformance.
- Step 6:   Change the process (technology, training, management, materials).
- Step 7:   Repeat steps 3–6 indefinitely.

The Japanese are credited with perfecting and implementing the philosophy of continuous improvement, along with the related concepts of quality circles, just-in-time inventory, and robust design of products and processes (the **Taguchi method**). Different social, economic, and geographic factors prevent adoption of some Japanese approaches by North American firms, but there is general agreement on their main points. Continuous improvement now is a guiding principle for automobile manufacturers, health care providers, insurance companies, computer software designers, fast-food restaurants, and even universities, churches, entertainment, and sports teams. Permanent change and a continuous search for better ways of doing things cascade down the organizational chart and across departmental lines.

17.10 How does SPC differ from TQM and CQI?

17.11 List the steps in CQI.

17.6
CONTROL CHARTS: OVERVIEW

What Is a Control Chart?

A *control chart* is a visual display that plots the values of a sample statistic over time through repeated observation. In some manufacturing processes, inspection of every item may be possible. But random sampling is needed when process measurements are costly, time-consuming, or destructive. For example, we can't test every cell phone battery's useful life, trigger every air bag to see whether it will deploy correctly, or cut open every watermelon to test for pesticide. Sample size and frequency of sampling will vary with the problem. In SPC the sample size n is referred to as the *subgroup size*.

Two Data Types

For *numerical* data (sometimes called *variable* data) the control chart displays a measure of central tendency (e.g., the sample mean) and/or a measure of variation (e.g., the sample range or standard deviation). A *variable control chart* is used for measurable quantities like weight, diameter, or time. Typically, such data are found in manufacturing (e.g., dimensions of a metal fastener) but sometimes also in services (e.g., client waiting time). The subgroup size for numerical data may be quite small (e.g., under 10) or even a single item.

For *attribute* data (sometimes called *qualitative* data), the focus is on counting nonconforming items (those that do not meet the target specification). An *attribute control chart* may show the proportion nonconforming (assumed binomial process) or the total number nonconforming (assumed binomial or Poisson process). Attribute control charts are important in service or manufacturing environments when physical measurements are not appropriate. Subgroup size for attribute data may be large (e.g., over 100) depending on the rate of nonconformance. Since modern manufacturing processes may have very low nonconformance rates (e.g., .00001 or .0000001) even larger samples are needed.

Three Common Control Charts

For a sample mean, the control chart is called an $\bar{x}$ *chart.* For a sample range, it is called an **R** *chart.* For a sample proportion, it is called a **p** *chart.* These three charts are illustrated in Figure 17.4. Each chart plots a sample statistic over time, as well as upper and lower *control limits* that define the expected range of the sample statistic. In these illustrations, all samples fall within the control limits. Control limits are based on the sampling distribution of the statistic. This chapter will discuss each of these three types of charts in detail. While there are many others, the basic concepts of SPC and setting control limits can be illustrated with these three chart types.

FIGURE 17.4

Three common control charts (from MINITAB)

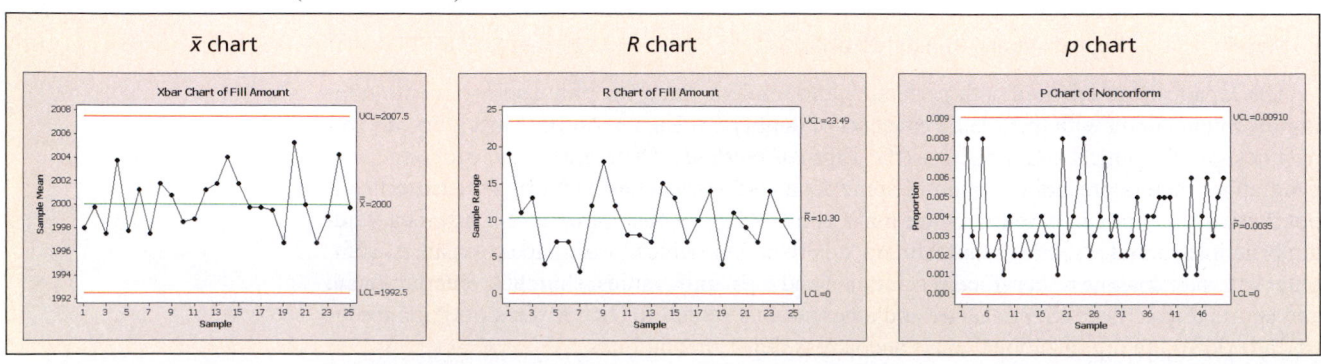

17.12 What is the difference between an attribute control chart and a variable control chart?

17.13 (a) What determines sampling frequency? (b) Why are variable samples often small? (c) Why are attribute samples often large?

x̄ Charts: Bottle-Filling Example

A bottling plant is filling 2-liter (2000 ml) soft drink bottles. It is important that the equipment neither overfill nor underfill the bottle. The filling process is stable and in control with mean fill μ and standard deviation σ. The degree of variation depends on the process technology used in the plant. Every 10 minutes, n bottles are chosen at random and their fill is measured. The unit of measurement is milliliters. For a subgroup of size $n = 5$ the sample might look like this:

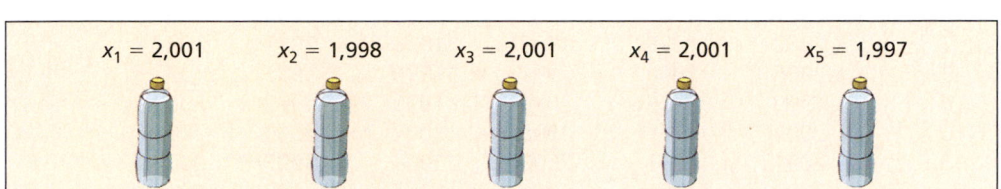

$x_1 = 2{,}001$ $x_2 = 1{,}998$ $x_3 = 2{,}001$ $x_4 = 2{,}001$ $x_5 = 1{,}997$

17.7
CONTROL CHARTS FOR A MEAN

Chapter 21

The mean fill for these five bottles is $\bar{x} = 1999.6$. Each time we take a sample of five bottles we expect a different value of the sample mean due to random variation inherent in the process. From previous chapters, we know that the sample mean is an unbiased estimator of the true process mean (i.e., its expected value is μ):

$$E(\bar{X}) = \mu \qquad (\bar{X} \text{ tends toward the true process mean}) \qquad (17.1)$$

The Central Limit Theorem says that the standard error of the sample mean is

$$\sigma_{\bar{X}} = \frac{\sigma}{\sqrt{n}} \qquad (\text{larger } n \text{ implies smaller variance of } \bar{X}) \qquad (17.2)$$

The sample mean follows a normal distribution if the population is normal, or if the sample is large enough to assure normality by the Central Limit Theorem.

Control Limits: Known μ and σ

Sample means from a process that is in control should be near the process mean μ, which is the *centerline* of the control chart. The **upper control limit (UCL)** and **lower control limit (LCL)** are set at ± 3 standard errors from the centerline, using the Empirical Rule, which says that almost all the sample means (actually 99.73 percent) will fall within "3-sigma" limits:

$$UCL = \mu + 3\frac{\sigma}{\sqrt{n}} \qquad (\text{upper control limit for } \bar{X}, \text{ known } \mu \text{ and } \sigma) \qquad (17.3)$$

$$LCL = \mu - 3\frac{\sigma}{\sqrt{n}} \qquad (\text{lower control limit for } \bar{X}, \text{ known } \mu \text{ and } \sigma) \qquad (17.4)$$

The $\bar{x}$ chart provides a kind of visual hypothesis test. Sample means will vary, sometimes above the centerline and sometimes below the centerline, but they should stay within the control limits and be symmetrically distributed on either side of the centerline. You will recognize the similarity between *control limits* and *confidence limits* covered in previous chapters. The idea is that if a sample mean falls outside these limits, we suspect that the sample may be from a different population from the one we have specified.

EXAMPLE

Bottle Filling

Table 17.3 shows 25 samples from a bottling process with $\mu = 2000$ and $\sigma = 4$. For each sample, the mean and range are calculated. The control limits are:

$$\text{UCL} = \mu + 3\frac{\sigma}{\sqrt{n}} = 2000 + 3\frac{4}{\sqrt{5}} = 2000 + 5.367 = 2005.37$$

$$\text{LCL} = \mu - 3\frac{\sigma}{\sqrt{n}} = 2000 - 3\frac{4}{\sqrt{5}} = 2000 - 5.367 = 1994.63$$

TABLE 17.3 Twenty-Five Samples of Bottle Fill with $n = 5$ **BottleFill**

Sample	Bottle 1	Bottle 2	Bottle 3	Bottle 4	Bottle 5	Mean	Range
1	2001	1998	2001	2001	1997	1999.6	4
2	1997	2004	2001	2000	2002	2000.8	7
3	2001	2000	2003	1995	1994	1998.6	9
4	2007	2007	2001	2000	1997	2002.4	10
5	1999	2001	1998	2001	1996	1999.0	5
6	2002	2002	1988	1995	2004	1998.2	16
7	2003	1998	1998	1996	2001	1999.2	7
8	2005	2000	1991	1996	1996	1997.6	14
9	1999	1997	2006	1999	1999	2000.0	9
10	2005	1999	1998	2002	2000	2000.8	7
11	2001	1997	2002	2004	2007	2002.2	10
12	2002	1995	1995	1997	2000	1997.8	7
13	2006	2006	1997	1998	1994	2000.2	12
14	2003	1997	2000	2003	2004	2001.4	7
15	2003	2008	1994	1998	1999	2000.4	14
16	1998	1997	1999	2001	1994	1997.8	7
17	1988	1996	2001	2002	2002	1997.8	14
18	2003	2003	1997	1995	2001	1999.8	8
19	2003	2004	1998	1998	2006	2001.8	8
20	2005	2001	2005	2000	2004	2003.0	5
21	2004	1996	2003	2002	1993	1999.6	11
22	1998	1996	2005	1997	1999	1999.0	9
23	2002	2001	1995	2004	2007	2001.8	12
24	2002	2002	1997	1995	2002	1999.6	7
25	2002	1999	2001	1992	1993	1997.4	10

Average over 25 samples of 5 bottles: 1999.832   9.160

FIGURE 17.5

MINITAB's $\bar{x}$ chart with known control limits

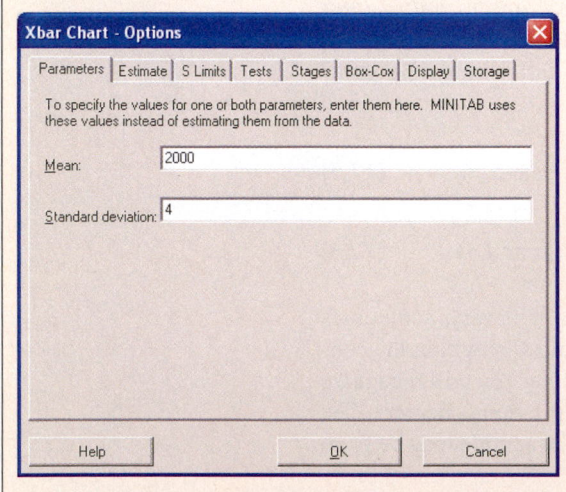
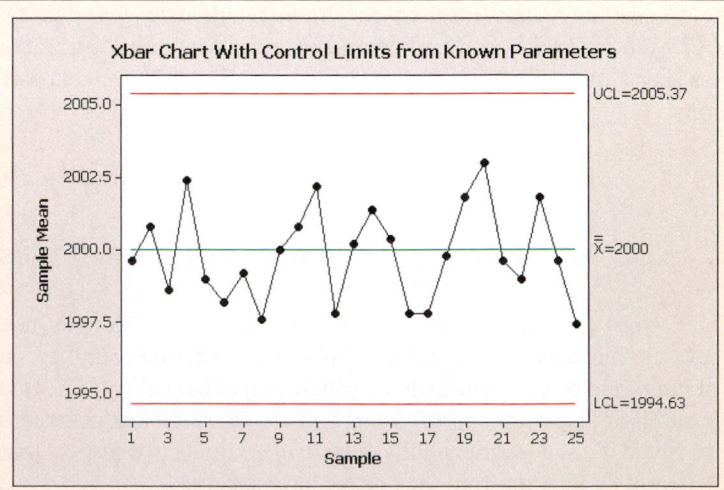

Figure 17.5 shows a MINITAB $\bar{x}$ chart for these 25 samples, with MINITAB's option to specify μ and σ instead of estimating them from the data. This chart shows a process that is *in control*. If a sample mean exceeds UCL or is below LCL, we suspect that the process may be *out of control*. More complex rules for detecting an out-of-control process will be explained shortly.

Empirical Control Limits

When the process mean μ and standard deviation are unknown (as they often are) we can estimate them from sample data, replacing μ with $\bar{\bar{x}}$ (the average of the means of many samples) and replacing σ with the standard deviation s from a pooled sample of individual X-values. It is desirable to set the control limits from samples taken independently, rather than using the same data to create the control limits and to plot the control chart. However, this is not always possible.

$$UCL = \bar{\bar{x}} + 3\frac{s}{\sqrt{n}} \qquad \text{(upper control limit for } \bar{X}, \text{ unknown } \mu \text{ and } \sigma) \qquad \textbf{(17.5)}$$

$$LCL = \bar{\bar{x}} - 3\frac{s}{\sqrt{n}} \qquad \text{(lower control limit for } \bar{X}, \text{ unknown } \mu \text{ and } \sigma) \qquad \textbf{(17.6)}$$

There are other ways to estimate the process standard deviation σ. For example, we could use $\bar{s}$, the mean of the standard deviations over many subgroups of size n, with an adjustment for bias. Or we could replace σ with an estimate $\bar{R}/d_2$ where $\bar{R}$ is the average range for many samples and d_2 is a control chart factor that depends on the subgroup size (see Table 17.4). If the number of samples is large enough, any of these methods should give reliable control limits. The $\bar{R}$ method is still common for historical reasons (easier to use prior to the advent of computers). If the $\bar{R}$ method is used, the formulas become:

$$UCL = \bar{\bar{x}} + 3\frac{\bar{R}}{d_2\sqrt{n}} \qquad \text{(upper control limit for } \bar{X}, \text{ unknown } \mu \text{ and } \sigma) \qquad \textbf{(17.7)}$$

$$LCL = \bar{\bar{x}} - 3\frac{\bar{R}}{d_2\sqrt{n}} \qquad \text{(lower control limit for } \bar{X}, \text{ unknown } \mu \text{ and } \sigma) \qquad \textbf{(17.8)}$$

Figure 17.6 shows MINITAB's menu options for estimating control limits from a sample. By default, MINITAB uses the pooled standard deviation, an attractive choice because it directly estimates σ. In Figure 17.6, using the $\bar{R}$ method, the $\bar{x}$ chart is similar to the chart in Figure 17.5, where σ was known, except that the LCL and UCL values are slightly different.

Control Chart Factors

Table 17.4 can be used to set up the control limits from sample data. We only need the first factor (d_2) for the $\bar{x}$ chart (the table also shows D_3 and D_4, which are used to construct control limits for an R chart, to be discussed shortly). The table only goes to $n = 9$ for purposes of illustration (larger tables are available in more specialized textbooks). These factors are built into MINITAB, MegaStat, Visual Statistics, and other computer packages.

Subgroup Size	d_2	D_3	D_4
2	1.128	0	3.267
3	1.693	0	2.574
4	2.059	0	2.282
5	2.326	0	2.114
6	2.534	0	2.004
7	2.704	0.076	1.924
8	2.847	0.136	1.864
9	2.970	0.184	1.816

TABLE 17.4
Control Chart Factors

Source: See Laythe C. Alwan, *Statistical Process Analysis* (Irwin/McGraw-Hill, 2000), p. 740.

FIGURE 17.6

MINITAB's $\bar{x}$ chart with estimated control limits

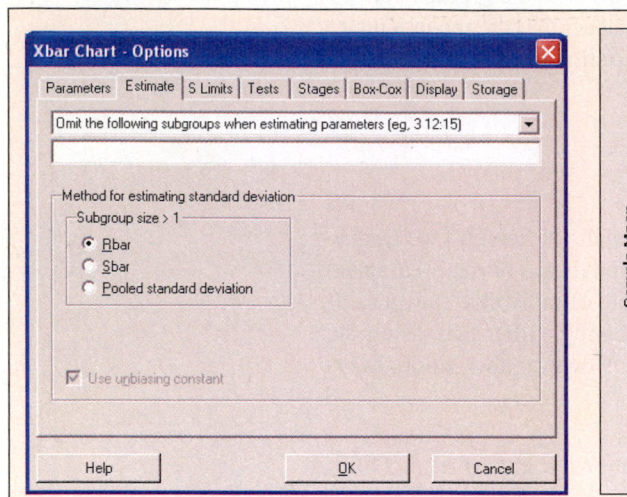
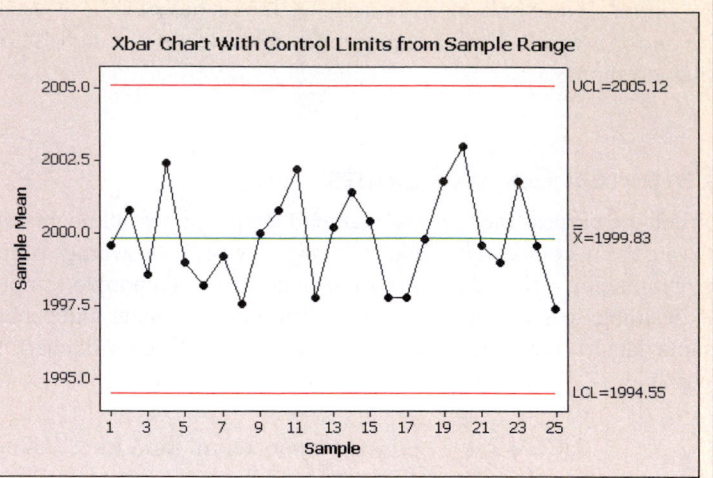

To calculate $\bar{\bar{x}}$ and $\bar{R}$ we use averages over 25 samples (see Table 17.3):

$$(17.9) \quad \bar{\bar{x}} = \frac{\bar{x}_1 + \bar{x}_2 + \cdots + \bar{x}_{25}}{25} = \frac{1999.6 + 2000.8 + \cdots + 1997.4}{25} = 1999.832$$

$$(17.10) \quad \bar{R} = \frac{R_1 + R_2 + \cdots + R_{25}}{25} = \frac{4 + 7 + \cdots + 10}{25} = 9.160$$

Using the sample estimates $\bar{\bar{x}} = 1999.832$ and $\bar{R} = 9.160$, along with $d_2 = 2.326$ for $n = 5$ from Table 17.4, the estimated empirical control limits are

$$\text{UCL} = \bar{\bar{x}} + 3\frac{\bar{R}}{d_2\sqrt{n}} = 1999.832 + 3\frac{9.160}{2.326\sqrt{5}} = 2005.12$$

$$\text{LCL} = \bar{\bar{x}} - 3\frac{\bar{R}}{d_2\sqrt{n}} = 1999.832 - 3\frac{9.160}{2.326\sqrt{5}} = 1994.55$$

Note that these *empirical* control limits (2005.12 and 1994.55) differ somewhat from the *theoretical* control limits (2005.37 and 1994.63) that we obtained using $\mu = 2000$ and $\sigma = 4$, and the *empirical* centerline (1999.83) differs from $\mu = 2000$. In practice, it would be necessary to take more than 25 samples to ensure a good estimate of the true process mean and standard deviation. Indeed, engineers may run a manufacturing process for days or weeks before its characteristics are well understood. Figure 17.7 shows MegaStat's $\bar{x}$ chart using the sample data to estimate the control limits. MegaStat *always* uses estimated control limits by the $\bar{R}$ method, and does not permit you to specify known parameters. Also, MegaStat expects the observed data to be arranged as a rectangle, with each subgroup's observations comprising a *row* (like Table 17.3). MegaStat's $\bar{x}$ chart is similar to MINITAB's except for details of scaling.

Detecting Abnormal Patterns

Sample means beyond the control limits are strong indicators of an out-of-control process. However, more subtle patterns can also indicate problems. Experts have developed "rules of thumb" to check for patterns that might indicate an out-of-control process. Here are four of them (the "sigma" refers to the *standard error of the mean*):

- *Rule 1.* Single point outside 3 sigma.
- *Rule 2.* Two of three successive points outside 2 sigma on same side of centerline.
- *Rule 3.* Four of five successive points outside 1 sigma on same side of centerline.
- *Rule 4.* Nine successive points on same side of centerline.

FIGURE 17.7

MegaStat's $\bar{x}$ chart with estimated control limits

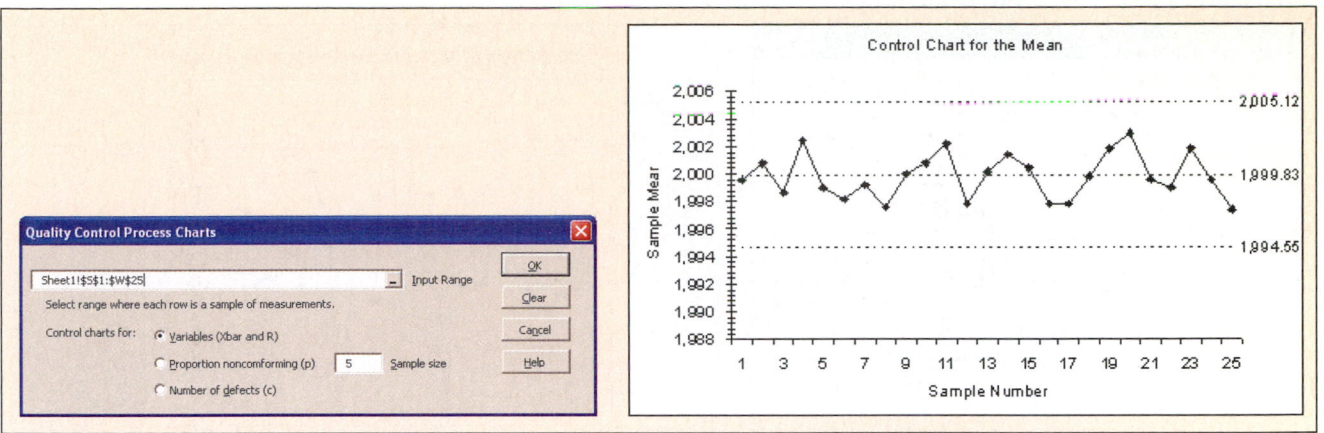

Violations of Rules 1 and 2 can usually be seen from "eyeball inspection" of control charts. Violations of the other rules are more subtle. A computer may be required to monitor a process to be sure that control chart violations are detected. Figure 17.8 illustrates these four rules, applied to a service organization (an HMO clinic conducting physical exams for babies).

Multiple rule violations are possible. Figure 17.9 shows a MINITAB $\bar{x}$ chart with these four rules applied (note that MINITAB includes many other tests and uses a different numbering

FIGURE 17.8

Red dots indicate rule violations (from Visual Statistics)

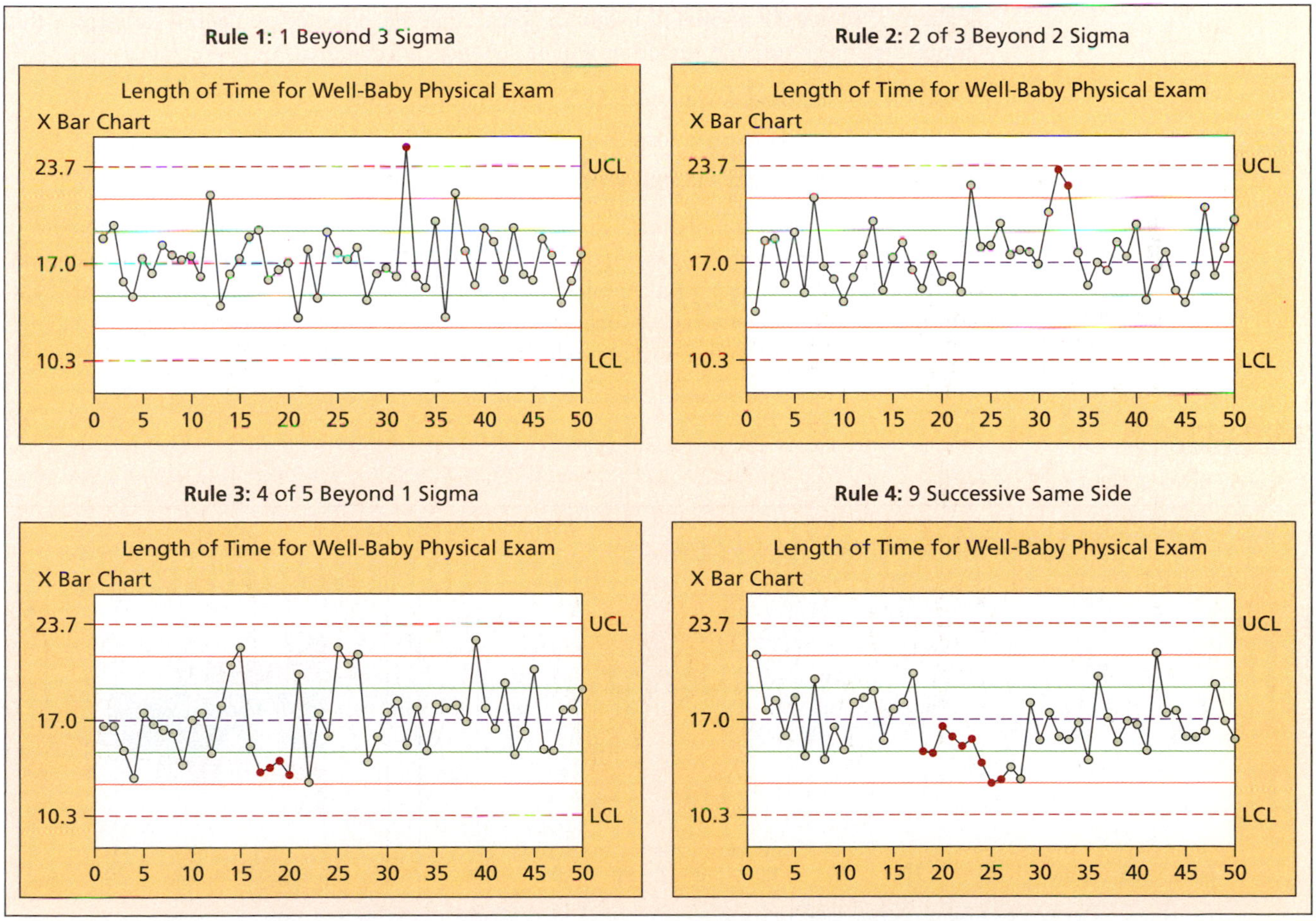

Rule 1: 1 Beyond 3 Sigma

Length of Time for Well-Baby Physical Exam
X Bar Chart

Rule 2: 2 of 3 Beyond 2 Sigma

Length of Time for Well-Baby Physical Exam
X Bar Chart

Rule 3: 4 of 5 Beyond 1 Sigma

Length of Time for Well-Baby Physical Exam
X Bar Chart

Rule 4: 9 Successive Same Side

Length of Time for Well-Baby Physical Exam
X Bar Chart

FIGURE 17.9

Violations of rules of thumb (from MINITAB)

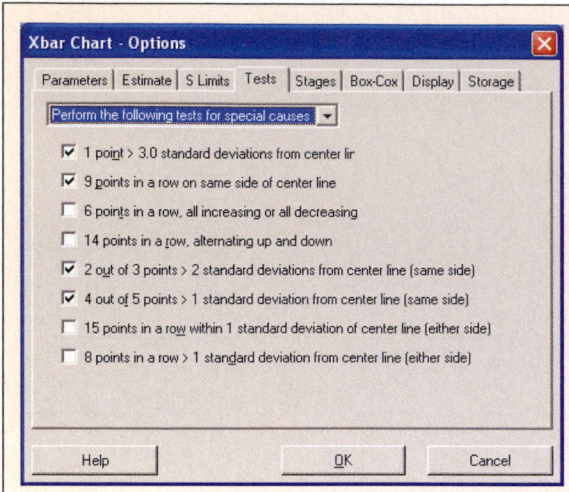
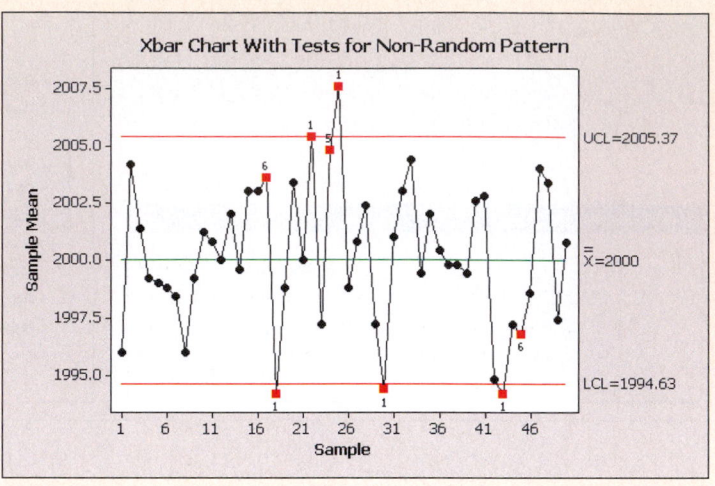

system for its rules). In this illustration, an out-of-control process is shown, with eight rule violations (each violation is numbered and highlighted in red).

Histograms

The normal curve is the reference point for variation inherent in the process or due to random sampling. UCL and LCL are set at ±3 standard errors from the mean, but we could (and should) also examine ±2 and ±1 standard error ranges to see whether the percentage of sample means follows the normal distribution. Recall that the expected percent of samples within various distances from the centerline can be stated as normal areas or percentages:

- Within ±1 standard deviation or 68.26 percent of the time.
- Within ±2 standard deviations or 95.44 percent of the time.
- Within ±3 standard deviations or 99.73 percent of the time.

The distribution of sample means can be scrutinized for symmetry and/or deviations from the expected normal percentages. Figure 17.10 shows a Visual Statistics $\bar{x}$ chart and histogram for 100 samples of acidity for a commercial cleaning product. The histogram is roughly symmetric, with 60 sample means between −1 and +1 and 97 sample means between −2 and +2, while the normal distribution would predict 68 and 95, respectively.

FIGURE 17.10

Visual Statistics $\bar{x}$ chart and histogram

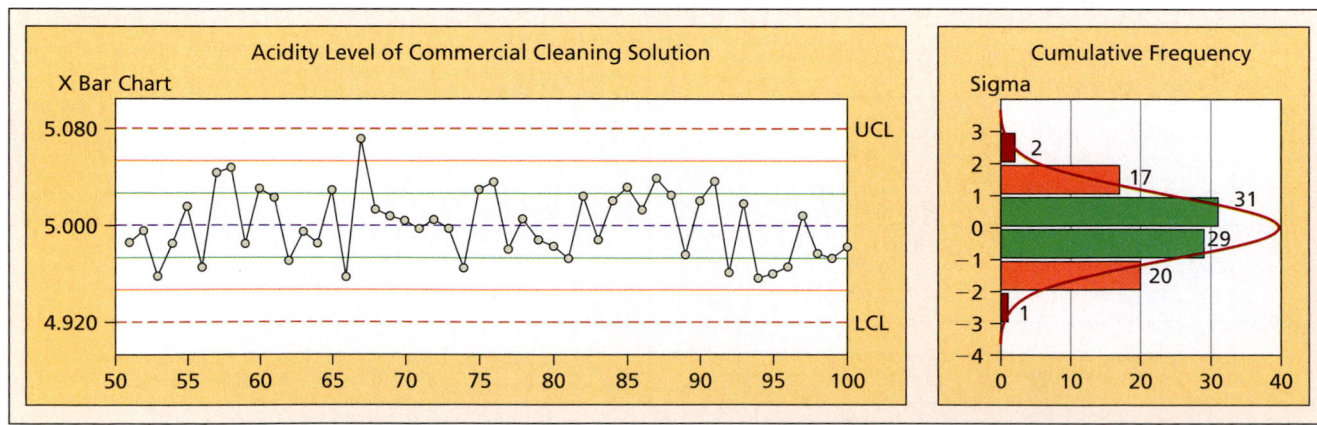

SECTION EXERCISES

17.14 To construct control limits for an $\bar{x}$ chart, name three ways to estimate σ empirically. Why is the $\bar{R}$ method often used? Why is the s method the default in MINITAB?

17.15 For an $\bar{x}$ chart, what percent of sample means should be (a) within 1 sigma of the centerline; (b) within 2 sigmas of the centerline; (c) within 3 sigmas of the centerline; (d) outside 2 sigmas of the centerline; (e) outside 3 sigmas of the centerline? *Note:* "sigma" denotes the standard error of the mean.

17.16 List four rules for detecting abnormal (special cause) observations in a control chart.

17.17 Set up control limits for an $\bar{x}$ chart, given $\bar{\bar{x}} = 12.50$, $\bar{R} = .42$, and $n = 5$.

17.18 Set up control limits for an $\bar{x}$ chart, given $\bar{\bar{x}} = 400$, $\bar{R} = 5$, and $n = 4$.

17.19 Time (in seconds) to serve an early-morning customer at a fast-food restaurant is normally distributed. Set up a control chart for the mean serving time, assuming that serving times were sampled in random subgroups of 4 customers. *Note:* Use this sample of 36 observations to estimate μ and σ.   **ServeTime**

Sample 1	Sample 2	Sample 3	Sample 4	Sample 5	Sample 6	Sample 7	Sample 8	Sample 9
65	56	84	69	75	87	87	99	102
51	87	67	81	80	84	90	61	61
94	84	71	59	76	80	65	84	88
79	70	85	75	88	52	61	79	78

17.20 To print 8.5 × 5.5 note pads, a copy shop uses standard 8.5 × 11 paper, glues the long edge, then cuts the pads in half so that the pad width is 5.5 inches. However, there is variation in the cutting process. Set up a control chart for the mean width of a note pad, assuming that, in the future, pads will be sampled in random subgroups of 5 pads. Use this sample of 40 observations (widths in inches) to estimate μ and σ.   **NotePads**

5.52	5.57	5.44	5.47	5.52	5.46	5.43	5.45
5.49	5.47	5.48	5.51	5.53	5.53	5.48	5.47
5.59	5.51	5.43	5.48	5.53	5.50	5.49	5.52
5.46	5.46	5.56	5.54	5.47	5.44	5.53	5.58
5.55	5.56	5.47	5.44	5.55	5.42	5.45	5.54

Mini Case   17.1

Control Limits for Jelly Beans   **JellyBeans**

The manufacture of jelly beans is a high-volume operation that is tricky to manage, with strict standards for food purity, worker safety, and environmental controls. Each bean's jelly core is soft and sticky, and must be coated with a harder sugar shell of the appropriate color. Hundreds of thousands of beans must be cooled and bagged, with approximately the desired color proportions. To meet consumer expectations, the surface finish of each bean and its weight must be as uniform as possible. Since jelly beans are a low-priced item, and since the market is highly competitive (i.e., there are many substitutes and many producers) it is not cost-effective to spend millions to achieve the same level of precision that might be used, say, in manufacturing a prescription drug.

So, how do we measure jelly bean quality? One obvious metric is weight. To set control limits, we need estimates of μ and σ. From a local grocery, a bag of Brach's Jelly Beans was purchased (see Figure 17.11). Each bean was weighed on a precise scale (the full data set is in *LearningStats*). The resulting sample of 182 jelly beans weights showed a bell-shaped

FIGURE 17.11

The data set ($n = 182$)

FIGURE 17.12

Dot plot for all data
($n = 182$)

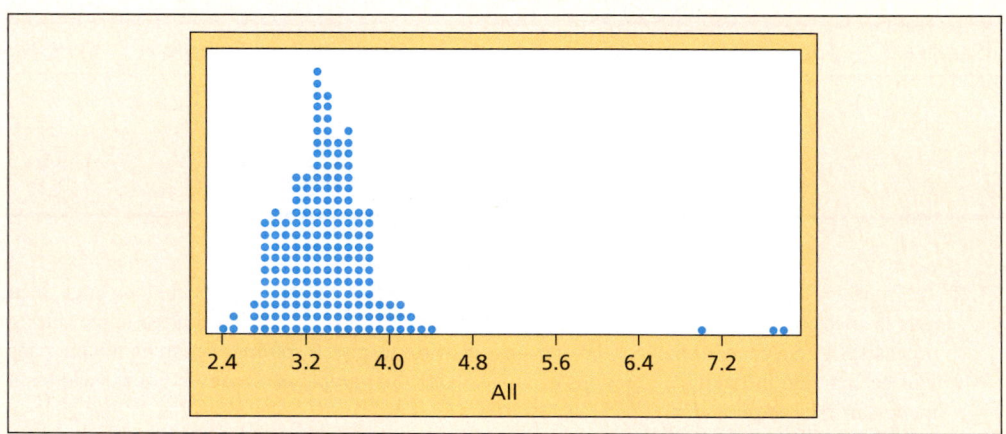

FIGURE 17.13

Normal plot for trimmed
data ($n = 179$)

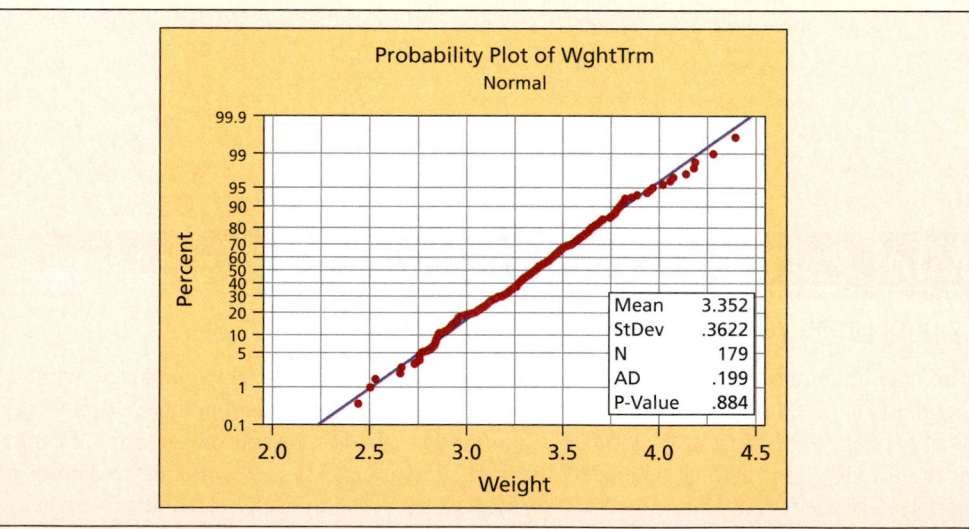

distribution, except for three high outliers, easily visible in Figure 17.12. Once the outliers are removed, the sample presents a satisfactory normal probability plot, shown in Figure 17.13. The sample mean and standard deviation ($\bar{x} = 3.352$ grams and $s = .3622$ grams) can now be used to set control limits. Referring back to Figure 17.11, some differences in size are visible. Can you spot the three oversized beans? Some consumers may regard "double" beans as a treat, rather than as a product defect. But manufacturers always strive for the most consistent product possible, subject to constraints of time, technology, and budget.

The $\bar{x}$ chart of sample means by itself is insufficient to tell whether a process is in control, because it reveals only *centrality*. We also should examine a chart showing *variation* around the mean. We could track the sample standard deviations (using an *s chart*), but it is more traditional to track the *sample range* (the difference between the largest and smallest item in each sample) using the *R chart*. The sample range is sensitive to extreme values. Nonetheless, its behavior can be predicted statistically, and control limits can be established. The *R* chart has asymmetric control limits, since the sample range is not a normally distributed statistic.

17.8
CONTROL CHARTS FOR A RANGE

Chapter 21

Control Limits for the Range

The centerline is obtained by calculating the average range $\bar{R}$ over many samples taken from the process. Estimation of $\bar{R}$ ideally would precede construction of the control chart, using a large number of independent samples, though this is not always possible in practice. Control limits based on samples may not be a good representation of the true process. It depends on the number of samples and the "luck of the draw." The control limits for the *R* chart can be set using either the average sample range $\bar{R}$ or an estimate $\hat{\sigma}$ of the process standard deviation:

$$UCL = D_4\bar{R} \quad \text{or} \quad UCL = D_4 d_2 \hat{\sigma} \qquad \text{(upper control limit of sample range)} \qquad \textbf{(17.11)}$$

$$LCL = D_3\bar{R} \quad \text{or} \quad LCL = D_3 d_2 \hat{\sigma} \qquad \text{(lower control limit of sample range)} \qquad \textbf{(17.12)}$$

EXAMPLE

Bottle Filling: R Chart

The control limits depend upon factors which must be obtained from a table. For the bottle fill data with $n = 5$, we have $D_4 = 2.114$ and $D_3 = 0$ (from Table 17.4). Using $\bar{R} = 9.16$ from the 25 samples (from Table 17.3) the control limits are:

$$\bar{R} = 9.16 \qquad \text{(centerline for R chart)}$$
$$UCL = D_4\bar{R} = (2.114)(9.160) = 19.37 \qquad \text{(upper control limit)}$$
$$LCL = D_3\bar{R} = (0)(9.160) = 0 \qquad \text{(lower control limit)}$$

Figure 17.14 shows MINITAB's *R* chart for the data in Table 17.3. Note that the *R* chart control limits could also be based on a pooled standard deviation. Using the Parameters tab, MINITAB also offers an option (not shown) to specify σ yourself (e.g., from historical experience). In this illustration, the process variation remains within the control limits.

FIGURE 17.14

MINITAB's *R* chart with control limits from sample data

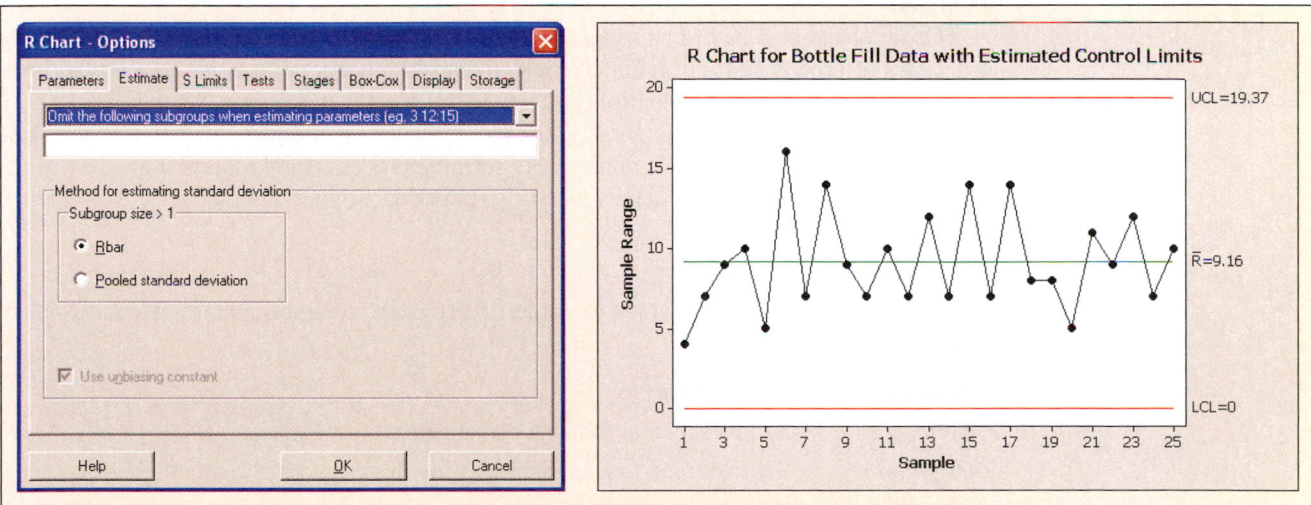

Figure 17.15 shows MegaStat's *R* chart using the same data to estimate the control limits. The MINITAB and MegaStat charts are similar except for scaling. However, MegaStat always uses estimated control limits (whereas MINITAB gives you the option).

FIGURE 17.15

MegaStat's R chart with control limits from sample data

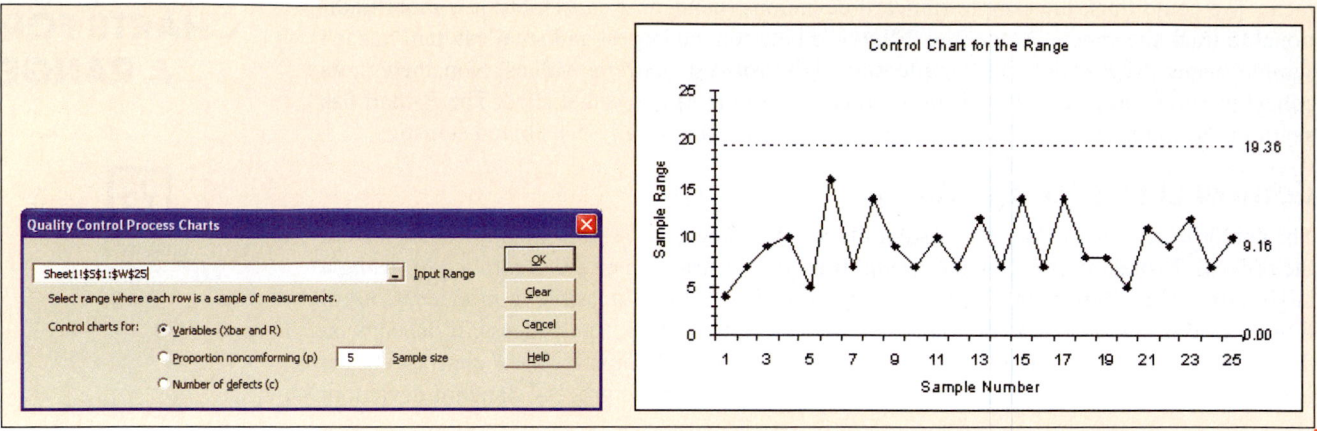

17.21 Set up limits for the R chart, given $\bar{R} = 0.82$ and $n = 6$.

17.22 Set up limits for the R chart, given $\bar{R} = 12$ and $n = 3$.

17.9

PATTERNS IN CONTROL CHARTS

Chapter 21

The Overadjustment Problem

In manufacturing, a control chart is used to guide decisions to continue the process or halt the process to make adjustments. *Overadjustment* or stopping to make unnecessary process corrections (Type I error) can lead to loss of production, downtime, unnecessary expense, foregone profit, delayed deliveries, stockout, or employee frustration. On the other hand, failing to make timely process corrections (Type II Error) can lead to poor quality, excess scrap, rework, customer dissatisfaction, adverse publicity or litigation, and employee cynicism.

Statistics allows managers to balance these Type I and II errors. It has been shown that, in the absence of statistical decision rules, manufacturing process operators tend toward overadjustment, which will actually *increase* variation above the level the process is capable of attaining.

The actions to be taken when a control chart violation is detected will depend on the consequences of Type I and II error. For example, if a health insurer notices that processing times for claim payments are out of control (i.e., relative to target benchmarks), the only action may be an investigation into the problem, because the immediate consequences are not severe. But in car manufacturing, an out-of-control metal forming process could require immediate shutdown of the assembly process to prevent costly rework or product liability.

Abnormal Patterns

Quality experts have given names to some of the more common abnormal control chart patterns:

Abnormal Control Chart Patterns

• **Cycle**	Samples tend to follow a cyclic pattern.
• **Oscillation**	Samples tend to alternate (high-low-high-low) in "sawtooth" fashion.
• **Instability**	Samples vary more than expected.
• **Level shift**	Samples shift abruptly either above or below centerline.
• **Trend**	Samples drift slowly either upward or downward.
• **Mixture**	Samples come from two different populations (increased variation).

These names are intended to help you recognize symptoms that may be associated with known causes. These concepts extend to any time-series pattern (not just control charts).

Symptoms and Assignable Causes

Each $\bar{x}$ chart in Figure 17.16 displays 100 samples, which is a long enough run to show the patterns clearly. However, the $\bar{x}$ charts shown are exaggerated to emphasize the essential features of each pattern. Abnormal patterns like these would generate violations of Rules 1, 2, 3, or 4 (or multiple rule violations) so the process would actually have been stopped *before* the pattern developed to the degree shown in Figure 17.16. Although many patterns are discussed in terms of the $\bar{x}$ chart, the R chart and histogram of sample means may also reveal abnormal patterns. It may be impossible to identify a pattern or its assignable cause(s) if the period of observation is short. Table 17.5 summarizes the symptoms and likely underlying causes of abnormal patterns.

FIGURE 17.16

Common abnormal patterns

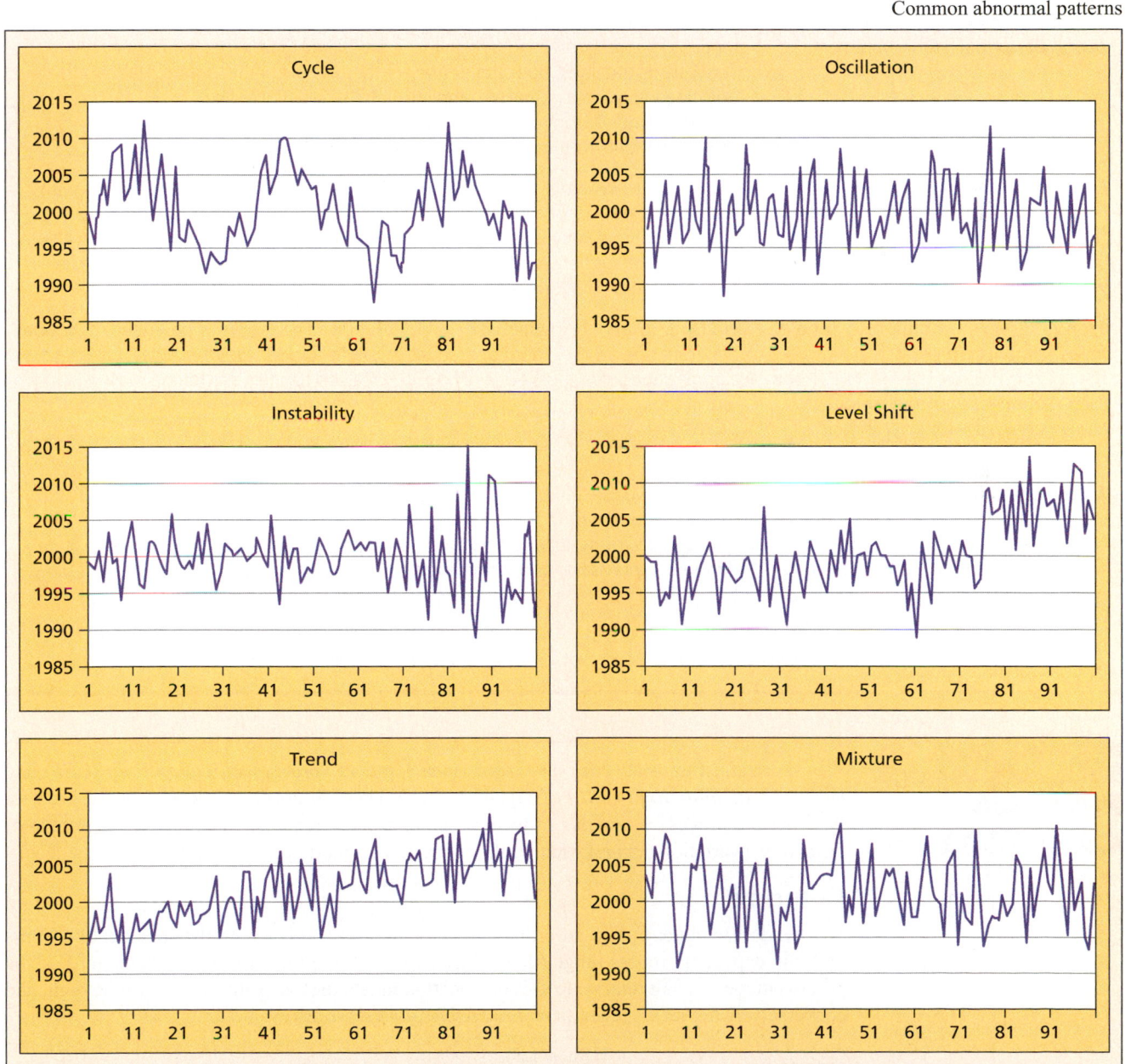

TABLE 17.5   **Pattern Descriptions and Assignable Causes**

Pattern Description	Likely Assignable Causes	Detected How?
Cycle is a repeated series of high measurements followed by a series of low measurements (+ + + + − − − + + + − − − − + + + +, etc.) relative to the centerline. Equivalent to positive autocorrelation in regression residuals.	*Industry:* worn threads or gears, humidity or temperature fluctuations, operator fatigue, voltage changes, overadjustment. *Services:* duty rotations, employee fatigue, poor scheduling, periodic distractions.	May be detected visually (fewer than $m/2$ centerline crossings in m samples) or by a runs test (see Chapter 16) or higher-than-expected tail frequencies in a histogram. Look for violations of Rule 4.
Oscillation is a pattern of alternating high and low measurements (+ − +− + − + − +, etc.) relative to the centerline (a zigzag or sawtooth pattern). Equivalent to negative autocorrelation in regression residuals.	*Industry:* alternating sampling of two machines, two settings, two inspectors, or two gauges. *Services:* attempts to compensate for performance variation on the last task, alternating task between two workers.	May be detected visually (more than $m/2$ centerline crossings in m samples) or by a runs test (see Chapter 16). Process mean stays near the centerline, though process variance may increase. May not violate any rules.
Instability is a larger than normal amount of variation preceded by a period of normal, stable variation.	*Industry:* untrained operators, overadjustment, equipment in need of repair, tool wear, defective material. *Services:* distractions, poor job design, untrained employees, flawed sampling process, samples from only one source, forms filled out from memory.	May be detectable on the $\bar{x}$ chart, but shows up most clearly on the R chart and in higher-than-expected frequencies in the tails of the histogram. Violations of Rules 1, 2, 3 are likely.
Level shift is a sudden change in measurements either above or below the centerline. It is a change in the actual process mean. Easily confused with trend.	*Industry:* new workers, change in equipment, new inspector, new machine setting, new lot of material. *Services:* changed environment, new supervisor, new work rules.	Center of the histogram shifts but with no change in variation. Violation of Rule 4 is likely, and perhaps others. May be too few centerline crossings (fewer than $m/2$).
Trend is a slow, continuous drifting of measurements either up or down from the chart centerline. Detectable visually if enough measurements are taken. Easily confused with level shift.	*Industry:* tool wear, inadequate maintenance, worker fatigue, gradual clogging (dirt, shavings, etc.), drying out of lubricant. *Services:* slow relaxing of attention, increasing task flow, bottlenecks.	Process variance may be unchanged, but the histogram grows skewed in one tail. May be too few centerline crossings (fewer than $m/2$). Violation of Rule 4 is likely, and perhaps others.
Mixture is sampling from two or more separate processes. Both may be in control, but with different means, resulting in a bimodal histogram (if the means differ) or no detectable difference (if the means are similar). With merged output from many machines, the overall process variance is increased.	*Industry:* two machines, two gauges, two shifts (day, night), two inspectors, different lots of material. *Services:* different supervisors, two work teams, two shifts.	Difficult to detect, either visually or statistically, especially if more than two processes are mixed. Histogram may be bimodal. Use same tests as for instability.

17.10

PROCESS CAPABILITY

A business must translate *customer requirements* into an **upper specification limit (USL)** and **lower specification limit (LSL)** of a quality metric. These limits do *not* depend on the process. Whether the process is *capable* of meeting these requirements depends on the magnitude of the process variation (σ) and whether the process is correctly centered (μ).

C_p Index

The *capability index C_p* is a ratio that compares the interval between the specification limits with the expected process range (defined as six times the process standard deviation). If the process range is small relative to the specification range, the capability index will be high, and conversely. A higher C_p index (a *more capable* process) is always better.

$$(17.13) \qquad C_p = \frac{\text{USL} - \text{LSL}}{6\sigma} \qquad \text{(process capability index } C_p \text{)}$$

A C_p value of 1.00 would indicate that the process is just barely capable of staying within the specifications *if* precisely centered. But managers typically require $C_p > 1.33$ (i.e., "leeway" of 2σ) to allow flexibility in case the process drifts off center. In manufacturing, a higher capability index may be required (in some applications even $C_p > 2.67$ might not be good enough, that is, leeway of 10σ).

C_{pk} Index

The index C_p is easy to understand, but fails to show whether the process is well-centered. A process with acceptable variation could be off-centerline and yet have a high C_p. To remedy this weakness, we can define another process capability index called $\boldsymbol{C_{pk}}$ that considers the relationship between USL and LSL *and* the process centerline μ:

$$z_{\text{USL}} = \frac{\text{USL} - \mu}{\sigma} \quad \text{and} \quad z_{\text{LSL}} = \frac{\mu - \text{LSL}}{\sigma} \tag{17.14}$$

These z-values measure the distance from the centerline to the specification limits in standard deviations. They would be expected to lie between 0 and 3 (assuming that USL lies above the centerline and that LSL lies below the centerline, so that both z-values are positive). The smaller of these two z-values is denoted z_{min}:

$$z_{\text{min}} = \min(z_{\text{USL}}, z_{\text{LSL}}) \tag{17.15}$$

We select the z-value that represents the shortest distance between the specification limits and the centerline. The process capability index C_{pk} is then defined as

$$C_{pk} = \frac{z_{\text{min}}}{3} \quad \text{(process capability index } C_{pk}) \tag{17.16}$$

In contrast to the C_p index, the C_{pk} index imposes a penalty when the process is off-center. A C_{pk} index of 1.00 is the minimum capability, but much higher values are preferred.

EXAMPLE

Cookie Baking

A bakery is supposed to produce cookies whose average weight after baking is 31 grams. To meet quality requirements, it has been decided that USL = 35.0 grams and LSL = 28.0 grams. The process standard deviation is 0.8 grams and the process centerline is set at 31 grams. The company requires a capability index of at least 1.33.

C_p *index:*

$$C_p = \frac{\text{USL} - \text{LSL}}{6\sigma} = \frac{35.0 - 28.0}{6(0.8)} = 1.46$$

C_{pk} *index:*

$$z_{\text{USL}} = \frac{\text{USL} - \mu}{\sigma} = \frac{35.0 - 31.0}{0.8} = 5.00$$

$$z_{\text{LSL}} = \frac{\mu - \text{LSL}}{\sigma} = \frac{31.0 - 28.0}{0.8} = 3.75$$

$$z_{\text{min}} = \min(z_{\text{USL}}, z_{\text{LSL}}) = \min\{5.00, 3.75\} = 3.75$$

$$C_{pk} = \frac{z_{\text{min}}}{3} = \frac{3.75}{3} = 1.25$$

According to the C_p index the process capability is just barely acceptable ($C_p = 1.46$), while using the C_{pk} index ($C_{pk} = 1.25$) the process capability is unacceptable. In this instance, the two indexes do not disagree dramatically. Actually, the process capability is doubtful regardless of which index is used, since both indexes are uncomfortably close to the minimum (1.33). The situation is illustrated in Figure 17.17.

FIGURE 17.17

Process capability for cookie making

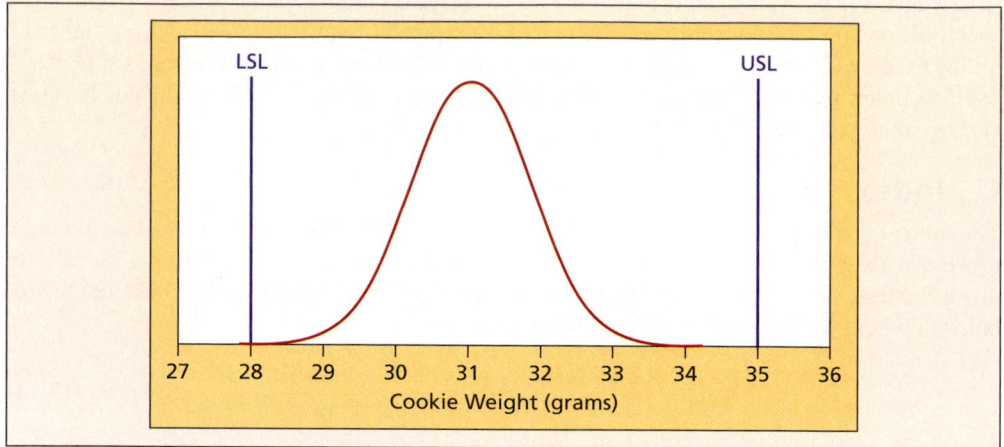

Cookie Weight (grams)

Although LSL and USL may be symmetric about the process mean, this is *not* required. In cookie-making, management is less concerned about oversized cookies than undersized ones (customers will not complain if a cookie is too big) so the limits are not symmetric, as can be seen in Figure 17.17. Note that this process is *not* incorrectly centered. It is just that the specification limits are asymmetric about the mean ($\mu = 31.0$).

FIGURE 17.18

Process variation versus specification limits

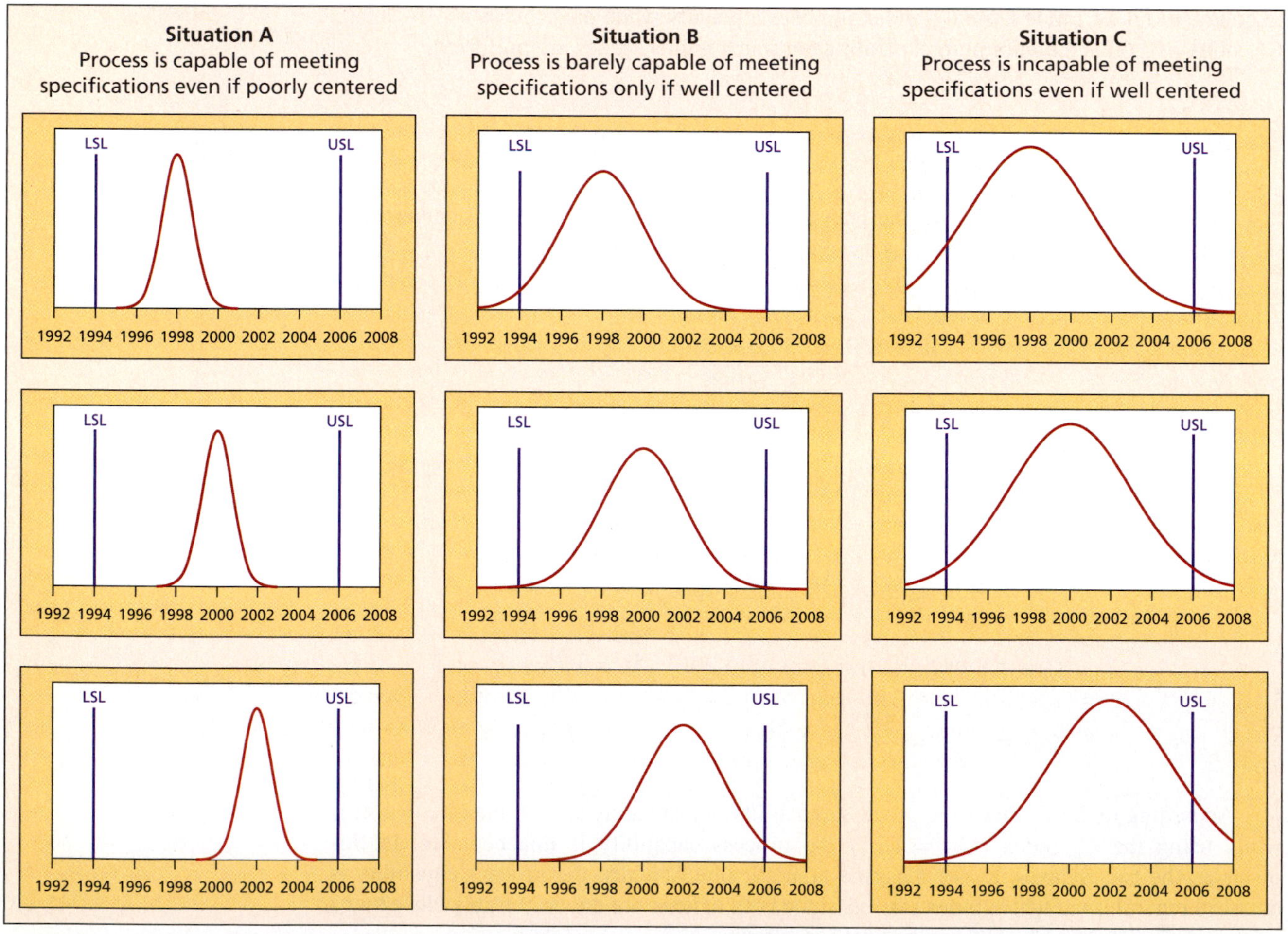

Situation A	Situation B	Situation C
Process is capable of meeting specifications even if poorly centered	Process is barely capable of meeting specifications only if well centered	Process is incapable of meeting specifications even if well centered

Bottle Filling Revisited

Figure 17.18 illustrates several possible situations, using the bottle filling scenario with symmetric specification limits LSL = 1994 and USL = 2006 and a target $\mu = 2000$. Remember that specification limits are based on customer demands (or engineering requirements) and not on the process itself. *There is no guarantee that the extant process is capable of meeting the requirements.* If it is not, there is no choice but to find ways to improve the process (i.e., by reducing σ) through improved technology, worker training, or capital investment.

SECTION EXERCISES

17.23 Find the C_p and C_{pk} indexes for a process with $\mu = 720$, $\sigma = 1.0$, LSL = 715, USL = 725. How would you rate the capability of this process? Explain.

17.24 Find the C_p and C_{pk} indexes for a process with $\mu = 0.426$, $\sigma = 0.001$, LSL = 0.423, USL = 0.432. How would you rate the capability of this process? Explain.

17.25 Find the C_p and C_{pk} indexes for a process with $\mu = 55.4$, $\sigma = 0.1$, LSL = 55.2, USL = 55.9. How would you rate the capability of this process? Explain.

Attribute Data: *p* Charts

17.11 OTHER CONTROL CHARTS

The *p chart* for attribute data plots the *proportion* of nonconforming items using the familiar sample proportion p:

$$p = \frac{\text{number of nonconforming items}}{\text{sample size}} = \frac{x}{n} \tag{17.17}$$

In manufacturing, p used to be referred to as a "defect rate," but the term "nonconforming items" is preferred because it is more neutral and better adapted to applications outside manufacturing, such as service environments. For example, for a retailer, p might refer to the proportion of customers who return their purchases for a refund. For a bank, p might refer to the proportion of checking account customers who have insufficient funds to cover one or more checks. For Ticketmaster, p might refer to the proportion of customers who have to wait "on hold" more than 5 minutes to obtain concert tickets.

The number of nonconforming items in a sample of n items is a binomial random variable, so the control limits are constructed as a confidence interval for a population proportion using one of several methods to state the *population* nonconformance rate π:

- An assumed value of π (e.g., a target rate of nonconformance).
- An empirical estimate of π based on a large number of trials.
- An estimate p from the samples being tested (if no other choice).

If n is large enough to assume normality,* the control limits would be

$$\text{UCL} = \pi + 3\sqrt{\frac{\pi(1-\pi)}{n}} \qquad (\pi \text{ is the process centerline}) \tag{17.18}$$

$$\text{LCL} = \pi - 3\sqrt{\frac{\pi(1-\pi)}{n}} \qquad (\pi \text{ is the process centerline}) \tag{17.19}$$

The logic is similar to a two-tailed hypothesis test of a proportion. The choice of 3 standard deviations is conventional, though there are applications where a different choice would be appropriate. If the LCL is negative, it is assumed to be zero. In manufacturing, the rate of nonconformance is likely to be a very small fraction (e.g., .02 or even smaller) so it is quite likely that LCL will be zero.

---

*If n is not large enough to assume normality, the binomial distribution may be used to set up control limits. MINITAB will handle this situation, although the resulting control limits may be quite wide.

EXAMPLE

Cell Phone Manufacture

A manufacturer of cell phones has a .002 historical rate of nonconformance to specifications (i.e., 2 nonconforming phones per 1,000). All phones are tested, and the nonconformance rates are plotted on a p chart, using an assumed value $\pi = .002$. Thus, the control limits are

$$UCL = .002 + 3\sqrt{\frac{(.002)(.998)}{n}} \quad \text{and} \quad LCL = .002 - 3\sqrt{\frac{(.002)(.998)}{n}}$$

Table 17.6 shows inspection data for 100 days of production (this table is abbreviated, but *LearningStats* has the full data set). Each production run (n) is around 2,000 phones per day, but does vary. Hence, the control limits are not constant, as shown in the p chart in Figure 17.19.

TABLE 17.6   Nonconforming Cell Phones   🔊 **CellPhones**

Day	Nonconforming (x)	Production (n)	x/n
1	3	2,056	0.00146
2	1	1,939	0.00052
3	4	2,079	0.00192
4	5	2,079	0.00241
5	4	1,955	0.00205
⋮	⋮	⋮	⋮
96	4	1,967	0.00203
97	6	2,077	0.00289
98	3	2,075	0.00145
99	5	1,908	0.00262
100	2	2,045	0.00098

FIGURE 17.19

MINITAB p chart for cell phones

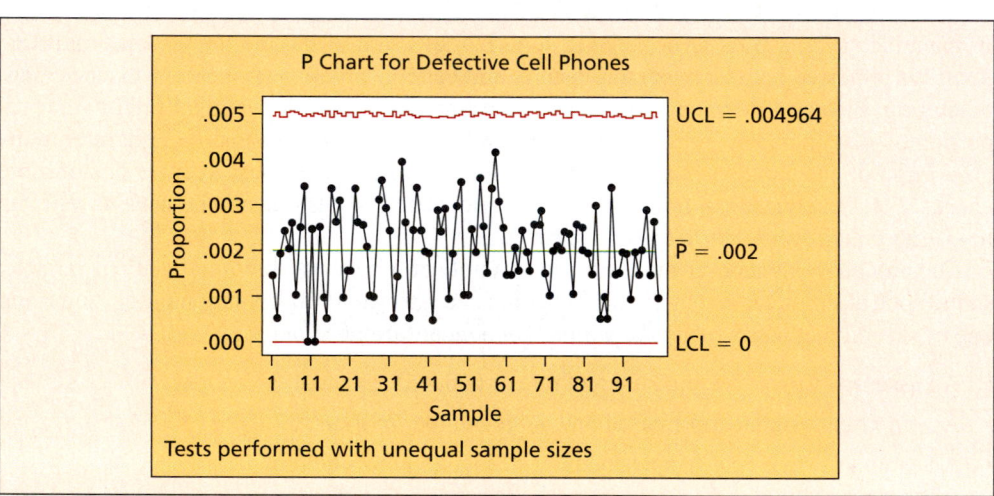

Notice that, p stays within the control limits, although it touches the LCL twice (not a problem since zero defects is ideal). Although n varies, we can illustrate the control limit calculation by using $\pi = .002$ and $n = 2,000$:

$$UCL = .002 + 3\sqrt{\frac{(.002)(.998)}{2,000}} = .004997$$

$$LCL = .002 - 3\sqrt{\frac{(.002)(.998)}{2,000}} = -.000997$$

Since a negative proportion is impossible, we just set LCL = 0. You will notice that MINITAB's UCL is not quite the same as the calculation above, because MINITAB uses a binomial calculation rather than the normal approximation. The difference may be noticeable when $n\pi < 10$ (the criterion for a normal approximation to the binomial). In this example $n\pi = (.002)(2,000) = 4$, so the binomial method is preferred (but is too complex to be explained here).

Application: Emergency Patients

Instead of being a rate of *nonconformance* to specifications, p could be a rate of *conformance* to specifications. Then

$$p = \frac{\text{number of conforming items}}{\text{sample size}} = \frac{x}{n} \qquad (17.20)$$

Ardmore Hospital's emergency facility advertises that its goal is to ensure that, on average, 90 percent of patients receive treatment within 30 minutes of arrival. Table 17.7 shows data from 100 days of emergency department records (this table is abbreviated, but *LearningStats* has the full data set).

Day	Seen In 30 Minutes (x)	Patient Volume (n)	x/n
1	87	97	0.900
2	113	122	0.924
3	106	115	0.920
4	84	90	0.928
5	82	92	0.896
⋮	⋮	⋮	⋮
96	128	142	0.900
97	101	112	0.900
98	123	135	0.908
99	128	141	0.908
100	141	149	0.944

TABLE 17.7
Emergency Patients Seen within 30 Minutes
ERPatients

The average number of patient arrivals per day is around 120, but there is considerable variation. Hence, the control limits are not constant, as shown in the p chart in Figure 17.20. Because the sample sizes are smaller than in the cell phone example, the LCL and UCL are more sensitive to the varying sample size, and hence appear more jagged. This process is in control.

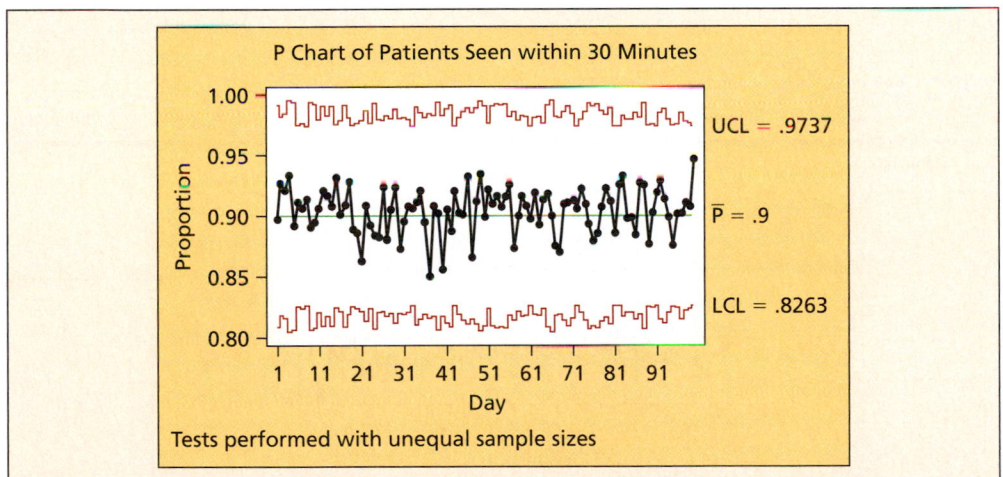

FIGURE 17.20

p Chart for ER patients

P charts are likely to be used in service operations (e.g., for benchmarking in health care delivery). Rules of thumb for detecting outliers, runs, and patterns apply to the p chart, just as for the $\bar{x}$ chart. However, tests for patterns are rarely seen outside manufacturing, except when service sector tasks are ongoing, repeatable, and easily sampled.

Other Control Charts (*s, c, np, I, MR*)

Other common types of control charts include:

- *I charts* (for individual numerical observations).
- *MR charts* (moving range for individual observations).
- *s charts* (for standard deviations).

- *c* charts (for Poisson events).
- *np* charts (for binomial totals).
- zone charts (using six regions based on σ).

The first two are used when *continuous inspection* is possible. When $n = 1$, there is no range, so a *moving range* is used. *I* chart control limits simply are $\mu \pm 3\sigma$ when $n = 1$. Mini Case 17.2 gives an illustration. Interpretation is the same as for any other control chart.

Mini Case   17.2

I-MR Charts for Jelly Beans   🐷 JellyBeans2

Table 17.8 shows a sample of weights for 44 Brach's jelly beans (all black) from a randomly chosen bag of jelly beans. Is the weight of the jelly beans in control? To construct the control limits, we use the sample mean and standard deviation from the large trimmed sample in Mini Case 17.1 ($\bar{x} = 3.352$ grams and $s = .3622$ grams) with MINITAB's *I-MR* chart option with assumed parameters $\mu = 3.352$ and $\sigma = .3622$.

In Figure 17.21 the *I* chart (upper one) reveals that two jelly beans (the 4th and 43rd observations) are not within the control limits. There is also evidence of a problem in

TABLE 17.8   Weights of 44 Black Brach's Jelly Beans

Obs	Weight	Obs	Weight	Obs	Weight	Obs	Weight
1	3.498	12	3.181	23	3.976	34	3.168
2	3.603	13	3.545	24	3.321	35	2.656
3	4.223	14	3.925	25	3.609	36	2.624
4	7.250	15	3.686	26	3.604	37	3.254
5	3.830	16	3.938	27	3.668	38	3.411
6	3.563	17	3.667	28	3.433	39	2.553
7	2.505	18	3.152	29	3.678	40	4.217
8	3.034	19	3.325	30	3.264	41	3.417
9	3.408	20	3.905	31	3.743	42	3.615
10	3.564	21	3.714	32	3.446	43	1.218
11	3.042	22	3.359	33	3.036	44	3.612

Note: Measurements taken using a Mettler DF360 Delta Range Scale.

FIGURE 17.21

Before outliers removed

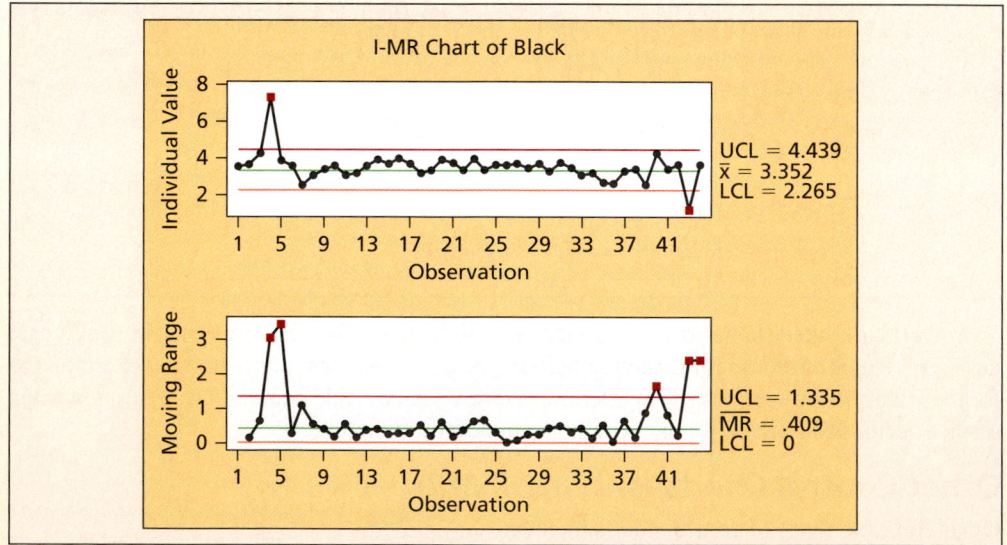

sample-to-sample variation in the *MR* chart (lower one). The explanation turned out to be rather clear. The 4th jelly bean was a "double-bean" (where two jelly beans got stuck together) and the 43rd jelly bean was a "mini-bean" (where the jelly bean was only partially formed). Figure 17.22 shows that, if we remove these outliers, the trimmed sample means stay within

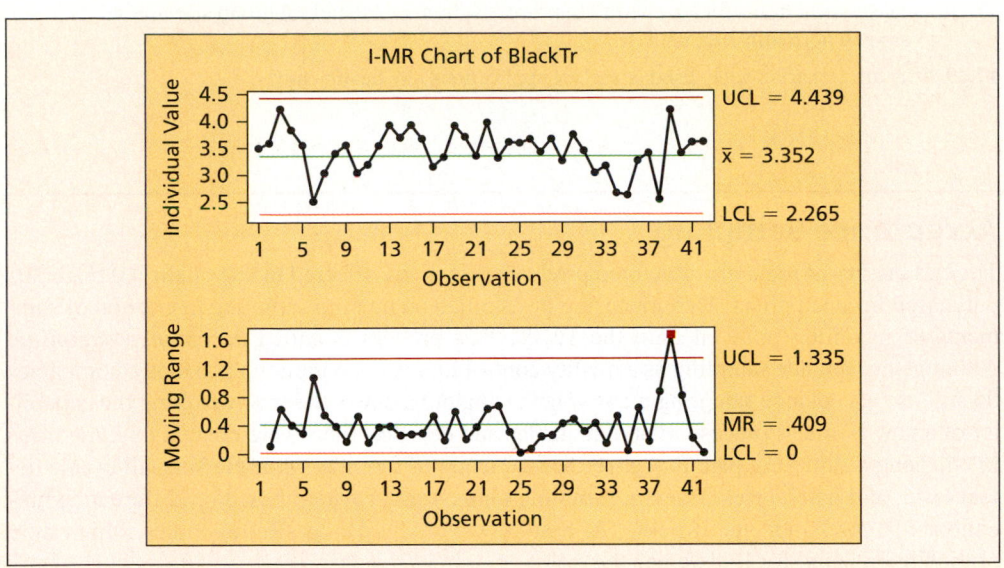

FIGURE 17.22

After outliers removal

the control limits on the *I* chart (upper one), although the *MR* chart (lower one) still has one odd point. Improved quality control for a high-volume, low-cost item like jelly beans is cost-effective only up to a point. A business case would have to be made before spending money on better technology, taking into account consumer preferences and competitors' quality levels.

Ad Hoc Charts

We said earlier that any display of a quality metric over time is a kind of control chart. If we set aside the formalities of control chart theory, anyone can create a "control chart" to monitor something of importance. For example, Figure 17.23 is not a "classic" control chart, but it shows a quality metric (patient waiting time in an emergency department) plotted over time. A box plot showing the range and quartiles over time is an *ad hoc* chart, yet it's a useful one. Organizations must develop their own approaches to quality improvement. As long as they begin with measurement, charting, and analysis, they are heading in the right direction.

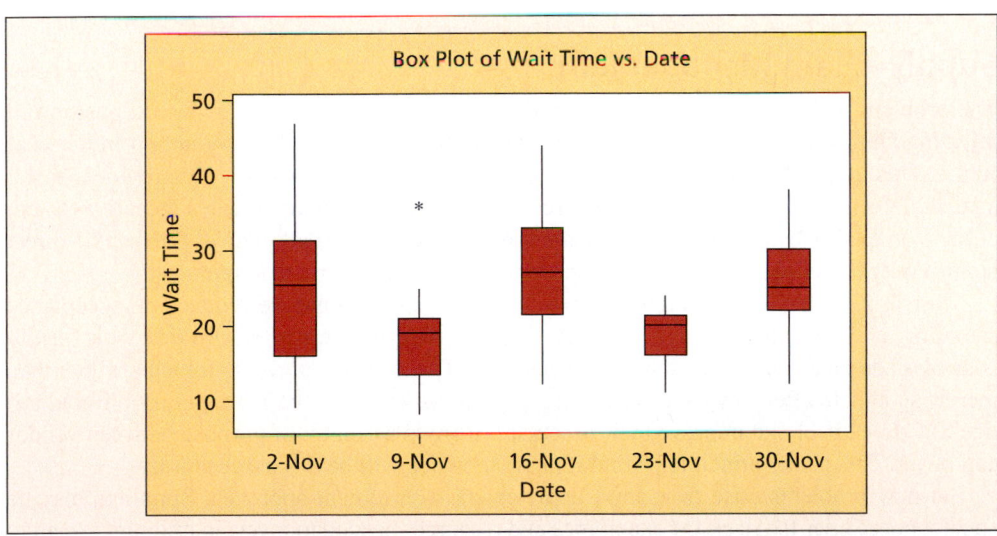

FIGURE 17.23

Box plots over time
AdHoc

17.26 Create control limits for a *p* chart for a process with $\pi = .02$ and subgroup size $n = 500$. Is it safe to assume normality? Explain.

17.27 Create control limits for a *p* chart for a process with $\pi = .50$ and subgroup size $n = 20$. Is it safe to assume normality? Explain.

17.28 Create control limits for a p chart for a process with $\pi = .90$ and subgroup size $n = 40$. Is it safe to assume normality? Explain.

17.29 Why are p charts widely used in service applications like health care?

17.12
ADDITIONAL QUALITY TOPICS (OPTIONAL)

Acceptance Sampling

The end quality of most manufactured products is strongly affected by the quality of materials purchased from suppliers. Manufacturing firms relied on random sampling inspection of shipments of incoming material until the 1970s. This process is called *acceptance sampling.* Although acceptance sampling as a quality control tool is not commonplace today, companies do still use acceptance sampling plans when trying out a new vendor or verifying the capability of a new business process. Elaborate tables and decision rules were created to guide firms in choosing a sampling plan that gave the frequency of sampling, sample size, allowable defect level, and batch size. Different sampling plans were provided based on different combinations of Type I and Type II risks. The best-known are the Dodge-Romig tables, which were originally prepared for Bell Telephone.

In acceptance sampling, *the producer's risk* (α error) is the probability of rejecting material of some stated desirable quality level, while the *consumer's risk* (β error) is the probability of accepting material of some stated undesirable quality level. These two risks must be balanced, since there is a trade-off between α and β for a given sample size. In its simplest form, lot sampling is based on the hypergeometric distribution, in which samples of n items are taken from a lot of size N containing s nonconforming items. Power curves and operating characteristic curves can be developed to guide decisions about acceptance or rejection of shipments, based on the attribute of interest (usually the proportion of nonconforming items).

Single sampling means that the decision is based on only one random sample taken from a shipment. *Double sampling* means that a decision is postponed until a second sample has been taken, unless the results from the first sample are unambiguous. A second sample may not be needed if the first sample result is extremely clear-cut. The concept can be generalized to multiple sampling or sequential sampling using any number of samples. The techniques can also be generalized to include multiple attributes as well as more complex sampling methods such as stratified or cluster sampling.

Supply-Chain Management

The problem with acceptance sampling is that it places the firm in the awkward position of rejecting shipments of purchased material, which may be needed for production in the near future. This forces the firm to increase lead times and hold larger inventory to provide a buffer against defective material. It also strains relations with suppliers and creates incentives to cut corners on quality by accepting questionable shipments. Worst of all, it gives the firm no direct control over its suppliers, except the negative control of saying no to shipments.

Most firms believe that a more constructive approach is to reduce reliance on acceptance sampling, and instead to engage in direct dialogue with suppliers to ensure that their quality control is adequate to meet the buyer's expectations. The idea is to prevent problems, rather than merely spot them after they have occurred. If suppliers implement the TQM philosophy and utilize SPC to control and improve their processes, there is harmony of purpose between vendor and buyer. This is one principle behind ISO 9000, which will be discussed shortly.

But new problems arise from this supply-chain management approach. Suppliers may be smaller companies that lack the experience and resources needed to invest in training, research, and development, and there may be coordination problems between seller and buyer. Buyers may have to subsidize the process of implementing quality control at the supplier level, for example, by sponsoring training seminars, sharing their managerial experience, and working toward common database and decision support systems. Deming felt that suppliers should not be chosen solely on the basis of lowest cost. Rather, he thought buyers should develop long-term relationships with a small group of suppliers, and then nurture the links with those suppliers. Many firms have done this. But changing the supply-chain relationships can be difficult. Overseas outsourcing makes quality control even more complex. What does a U.S., Canadian, or European original equipment manufacturer do if its low-cost Chinese supplier delivers nonconforming or defective raw materials or parts? How do they work with a Chinese supplier to resolve the problem across thousands of miles and language and cultural barriers?

These nonstatistical problems illustrate why quality management in a global environment requires understanding of international business, as well as behavioral, financial, and supply-chain management. Engineers and technical specialists often find it helpful to study business management (and maybe Chinese). If you require a more detailed understanding of quality management, you will need further training (you can start with the Related Reading list).

Quality and Design

Quality is closely tied to design. A well-designed process, product, or service is more likely to yield better quality and more customer satisfaction, with less effort and for a longer time. A poorly designed process, product, or service is more likely to yield undesired outcomes, awkward or inconvenient working arrangements, employee frustration in trying to maintain quality, and more frequent problems, breakdowns, and dissatisfied customers.

Firms may know that their products and services could be designed in a better way, but it would take time and cost money. Since customer needs must be met today, they say, "We will nurse along the old design and do the best we can with it." The problem is that, in the longer run, the customers may not be there, if more dynamic competitors capture the market. One lesson of our time is that there is no such thing as a "safe job," even in a large organization. When we can see a better way to do it, change becomes an ally and inertia an enemy. The search for design improvement is an ongoing process, not something done once. If we improve the design tomorrow, even better solutions are likely to be found later on. Successful organizations try to create a climate in which employees are encouraged to suggest new ways of doing things.

Taguchi's Robust Design

The prominence of Japanese quality expert Genichi Taguchi is mainly due to his contributions in the field of *robust design,* which uses statistically planned experiments to identify process control parameter settings that reduce a process's sensitivity to manufacturing variation. In Taguchi's taxonomy, we identify the functional characteristics that measure the final product's performance, the control parameters that can be specified by process engineers, and the sources of noise that are expensive or impossible to control. By varying control parameters in a planned experiment, we can use the results to predict control parameter settings that would make the process insensitive to noise. Parameter settings are first varied simultaneously in a few experimental runs. Then, a fractional factorial experimental design is selected (see Chapter 11), using a balancing property to choose pairs of parameter settings. Finally, predictions of improved parameter settings are made and verified through a confirming experiment.

Taguchi's methods are especially useful in manufacturing situations with many process control parameters which imply complex experimental designs. Once the problem is defined, we rely on well-known experimental design methods. In addition, Taguchi is known for explicitly including in quality measures the total loss incurred by society from the time the product is shipped, using a quadratic loss function that penalizes according to the squared difference between actual and target quality. The inclusion of customers in the model is considered a major innovation.

Six Sigma and Lean Six Sigma

Six Sigma is a broad philosophy to reduce cost, eliminate variability, and improve customer satisfaction through improved design and better management strategy. *Lean Six Sigma* integrates Six Sigma with supply-chain management to optimize resource flows, while also lowering cost and raising quality. Most of us have heard of the Six Sigma goal of 3.4 defects per million through reduced process variation (i.e., extremely high C_p and C_{pk} indexes) essentially using the tools outlined in this chapter and the DMAIC steps for process improvement. However, there is more to it than statistics, and Six Sigma experts must be certified (Green Belts, Black Belts,

Master Black Belts) through advanced training. Six Sigma implementation varies according to the organization, with health care being perhaps the latest major application.

ISO 9000

Since 1992, firms wishing to sell their products globally have had to comply with a series of ISO standards, first articulated in 1987 in Europe. These standards have continued to evolve. Now, *ISO 9000* and ISO audits (both internal and of suppliers) have become a de facto quality system standard for any company wanting to be a world-class competitor. ISO 9001 includes customer service as well as design of products and services (not just manufacturing). The broad scope of ISO 9000, ISO 14000, and QS 9000 requires special training that is not normally part of an introductory statistics class.

Malcolm Baldrige Award

To recognize the importance of achievement in attaining superior quality, in 1988 the U.S. initiated the *Malcolm Baldrige National Quality Award,* based on seven categories of quality: leadership, information/analysis, strategic planning, human resource development, process management, operational results, and customer satisfaction. The *Baldrige Award* is given by the president of the United States to firms (large or small, manufacturing or services) that have made notable achievements in design, manufacture, installation, sales, and service.

Advanced MINITAB Features

A glance at MINITAB's extensive menus (see Figure 17.24) will tell you that quality tools are one of its strengths. In addition to all types of control charts and cause-and-effect diagrams (fishbone or Ishikawa diagrams), MINITAB offers capability analysis, variable transformations to achieve normality, alternative distributions where the assumption of normality is inappropriate, and gage study for variables and attributes. If you want further study of statistical quality tools, you could do worse than to explore MINITAB's menus, help system, and data sets. Many other general-purpose software packages (e.g., SAS, SPSS) offer similar capabilities.

FIGURE 17.24

Some more MINITAB menus

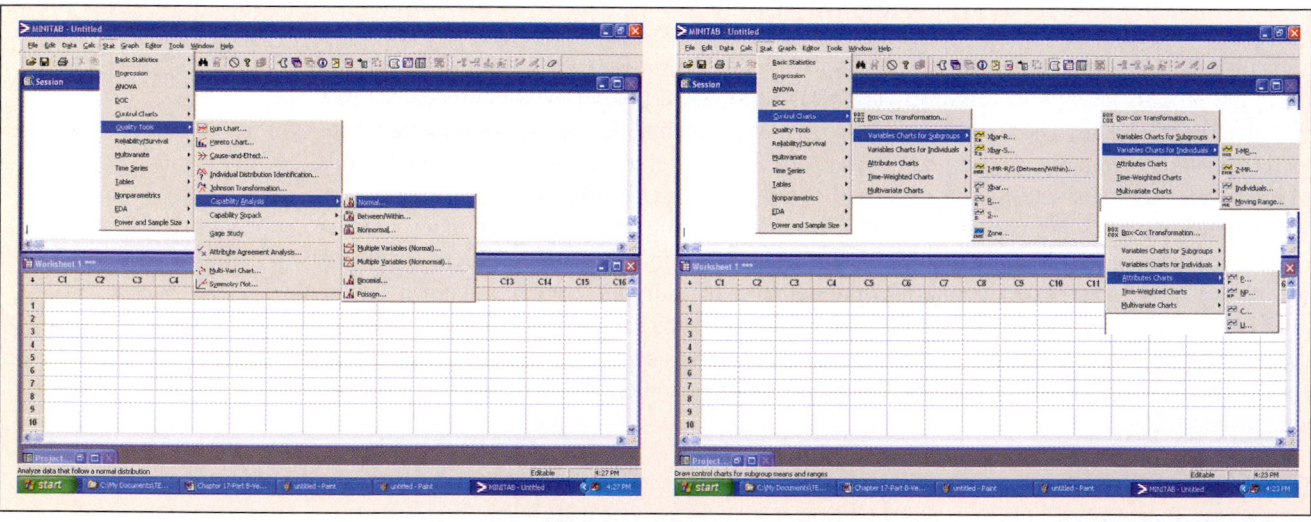

Future of Statistical Process Control

Automation, numerical control, and continuous process monitoring have changed the meaning of SPC in manufacturing. The integration of manufacturing and factory floor quality monitoring systems in manufacturing planning and control, materials requirements planning (MRP), computer-aided design and manufacturing (CAD/CAM), order entry, and financial, customer service, and support systems have continued to redefine the role of SPC. Automation has made 100 percent testing and inspection attainable in some applications where it was previously thought to be either impossible or uneconomical.

As this story unfolds, it may be that SPC itself will become part of the background that is built in to every manufacturing organization, allowing managers to focus on higher-level issues, even at the global level. As an analogy, consider that only a few decades ago chart-making required specialists who were skilled in drafting. Now, anyone with access to a computer can make excellent charts. In the service sector of the economy, quality improvement is still at an early level of implementation. In health care, financial services, and retailing, processes are harder to define and tasks are often not as repetitive or as standardized as in manufacturing. Thus, the role of SPC is still unfolding, and every business student needs to know its basic principles.

Chapter Summary

Quality is measured by a set of attributes that affect **customer satisfaction. Quality improvement** is aimed at **variance reduction. Common cause** variation is normal and expected, while **special cause** variation is abnormal and requires action, such as adjusting the **process** for producing a good or service. Quality is affected by management, resources, technology, and human factors (e.g., training, employee involvement). **Statistical process control** (SPC) involves using **control charts** of key quality metrics to make sure that the processes are **in control. The upper control limit** (UCL) and **lower control limit** (LCL) define the range of allowable variation. These limits are usually set **empirically** by observing a process over time. Control charts are used to track the **mean** ($\bar{x}$ chart), **range** (R chart), **proportion** (p chart), and other statistics. Samples may be taken by **subgroups** of n items, or by continuous monitoring with **individual charts** (I charts) and **moving range** (MR charts). There are **rules of thumb** to identify out-of-control patterns (instability, trend, level shift, cycle, oscillation) and their likely causes. A **capable** process is one whose variability (σ) is small in relation to the **upper and lower specification limits** (USL and LSL). SPC concepts were first applied to manufacturing, but can be adapted to service environments such as finance, health care, and retailing. International **ISO standards** now guide companies selling in world markets, and Six Sigma techniques are widely used to improve quality in service organizations, as well as in manufacturing.

Key Terms

acceptance sampling, *760*
Baldrige Award, *762*
business process redesign
  (BPR), *738*
C_p, *752*
C_{pk}, *753*
common cause variation, *733*
control chart, *740*
CQI, *739*
customer, *733*
cycle, *750*
Deming, W. Edwards, *736*
DMAIC, *739*
fishbone chart, *738*
I charts, *757*
instability, *750*

ISO 9000, *762*
level shift, *750*
lower control limit (LCL), *741*
lower specification limit
  (LSL), *752*
mixture, *750*
MR charts, *757*
oscillation, *750*
p chart, *740*
pareto chart, *737*
process, *732*
productivity, *732*
quality, *731*
quality control, *732*
R chart, *740*

reduced variation, *732*
Six Sigma, *739*
special cause variation, *733*
statistical process control
  (SPC), *738*
statistical quality control
  (SQC), *738*
Taguchi method, *739*
total quality management
  (TQM), *737*
trend, *750*
upper control limit (UCL), *741*
upper specification limit
  (USL), *752*
$\bar{x}$ chart, *740*

Commonly Used Formulas

Control limits for $\bar{x}$ chart (known or historical σ): $\mu \pm 3 \dfrac{\sigma}{\sqrt{n}}$

Control limits for $\bar{x}$ chart (sample estimate of σ): $\bar{\bar{x}} \pm 3 \dfrac{s}{\sqrt{n}}$

Control limits for $\bar{x}$ chart (using average range): $\bar{\bar{x}} \pm 3 \dfrac{\bar{R}}{d_2 \sqrt{n}}$

Control limits for R chart (using average range or sample standard deviation with control chart factors from a table):

$$\text{UCL} = D_4 \bar{R} \quad \text{or} \quad \text{UCL} = D_4 d_2 s$$
$$\text{LCL} = D_3 \bar{R} \quad \text{or} \quad \text{LCL} = D_3 d_2 s$$

Capability index (without centering): $C_p = \dfrac{\text{USL} - \text{LSL}}{6\sigma}$

Capability index (with centering): $C_{pk} = \dfrac{z_{min}}{3}$

where

$z_{min} = \min(z_{USL}, z_{LSL})$

$z_{USL} = \dfrac{\text{USL} - \mu}{\sigma}$

$z_{LSL} = \dfrac{\mu - \text{LSL}}{\sigma}$

Control limits for p chart: $\pi \pm 3 \sqrt{\dfrac{\pi(1 - \pi)}{n}}$

Chapter Review

Note: Questions with * are based on optional material.

1. Define (a) quality, (b) process, and (c) productivity. Why are they hard to define?

2. List six general attributes of quality.

3. Distinguish between common cause and special cause variation.

4. In quality improvement, list three roles played by (a) statisticians and (b) managers.

5. Distinguish between (a) internal versus external customers, (b) assigning blame versus seeking solutions, and (c) employee involvement versus top-down decisions.

6. In chronological order, list important phases in the evolution of the quality movement in North America. What is the main change in emphasis over the last 100 years?

7. (a) Who was W. Edwards Deming and why is he remembered? (b) List three of Deming's major ideas and explain them in your own terms.

8. List three influential thinkers other than Deming who made contributions to the quality movement and state their contributions.

9. (a) Briefly explain each acronym: TQM, BPR, SQC, SPC, CQI, DMAIC. (b) List the steps in the continuous quality improvement model.

10. (a) What is shown on the $\bar{x}$ chart? (b) Name three ways to set the control limits on the $\bar{x}$ chart. (c) How can we obtain good empirical control limits for the $\bar{x}$ chart? (d) Why are quality control samples sometimes small?

11. Explain the four rules of thumb for identifying an out-of-control process.

12. (a) What is shown on the R chart? (b) How do we set control limits for the R chart?

13. Name the six abnormal control chart patterns and tell (a) how they may be recognized, and (b) what their likely causes might be.

14. (a) State the formulas for the two capability indexes C_p and C_{pk}. (b) Why isn't C_p alone sufficient? (c) What is considered an acceptable value for these indexes? (d) Why is an *in-control* process not necessarily *capable?*

15. (a) What is shown on the p chart? (b) How do we set control limits for the p chart? (c) Why might the p chart control limits vary from sample to sample?

*16. Briefly explain (a) the overadjustment problem, (b) *ad hoc* control charts, (c) acceptance sampling, (d) supply-chain management, (e) Taguchi's robust design, (f) the Six Sigma philosophy, (g) ISO 9000, and (h) the Malcolm Baldrige Award.

CHAPTER EXERCISES

Instructions: You may use MINITAB, MegaStat, or similar software to assist you in the control chart questions. Data sets for the exercises are on the CD.

17.30 Explain each chart's purpose and the parameters that must be known or estimated to establish its control limits.
   a. $\bar{x}$ chart
   b. R chart
   c. p chart
   d. I chart

17.31 Define three possible quality metrics (not necessarily the ones actually used) to describe and monitor: (a) your performance in your college classes; (b) effectiveness of the professors in your college classes; (c) your effectiveness in managing your personal finances; (d) your textbook's effectiveness in helping you learn in a college statistics class.

17.32 Define three quality metrics that might be used to describe quality and performance for the following services: (a) your cellular phone service (e.g., Verizon); (b) your Internet service provider (e.g., AOL); (c) your dry cleaning and laundry service; (d) your physician's office; (e) your hairdresser; (f) your favorite fast-food restaurant. Do you think these data are actually collected or used? Why, or why not?

17.33 Define three quality metrics that might be used to describe quality and performance in the following consumer products: (a) your personal vehicle (e.g., car, SUV, truck, bicycle, motorcycle); (b) the printer on your computer; (c) the toilet in your bathroom; (d) a PDA (e.g., Palm Pilot); (e) an HDTV display screen; (f) a light bulb. Do you think these data are actually collected or used? Why, or why not?

17.34 Based on the cost of sampling and the presumed accuracy required, would sampling or 100 percent inspection be used to collect data on (a) the horsepower of each engine being installed in new cars; (b) the fuel consumption per seat mile of each Northwest Airlines flight; (c) the daily percent of customers who order low-carb menu items for each McDonald's restaurant; (d) the life in hours of each lithium ion battery installed in new laptop computers; (e) the number of medication errors per month in a large hospital.

17.35 Why are the control limits for an R chart asymmetric, while those of an $\bar{x}$ chart are symmetric?

17.36 Bob said, "We use the normal distribution to set the control limits for the $\bar{x}$ chart because samples from processes follow a normal distribution." Is Bob right? Explain.

17.37 Bob said, "They must not be using quality control in automobile manufacturing. Just look at the J.D. Power data showing that new cars all seem to have defects." (a) Discuss Bob's assertion, focusing on the concept of variation. (b) Can you think of processes where zero defects *could* be attained on a regular basis? Explain. (c) Can you think of processes where zero defects *cannot* be attained on a regular basis? *Hint:* Consider activities like pass completion by a football quarterback, 3-point shots by a college basketball player, or multiple-choice exams taken by a college student.

17.38 Use your favorite Internet search engine to look up any four of the following quality experts. Write a one-paragraph biographical sketch *in your own words* that lists his contributions to quality improvement.
   a. Walter A. Shewhart
   b. Harold F. Dodge
   c. Harry G. Romig
   d. Joseph M. Juran
   e. Genichi Taguchi
   f. Kaoru Ishikawa
   g. Armand V. Feigenbaum

17.39 Make a fishbone chart (cause-and-effect diagram) like the following for the reasons you have ever been (or could be) late to class. Use as many branches as necessary. Which factors are most important? Which are most easily controlled?

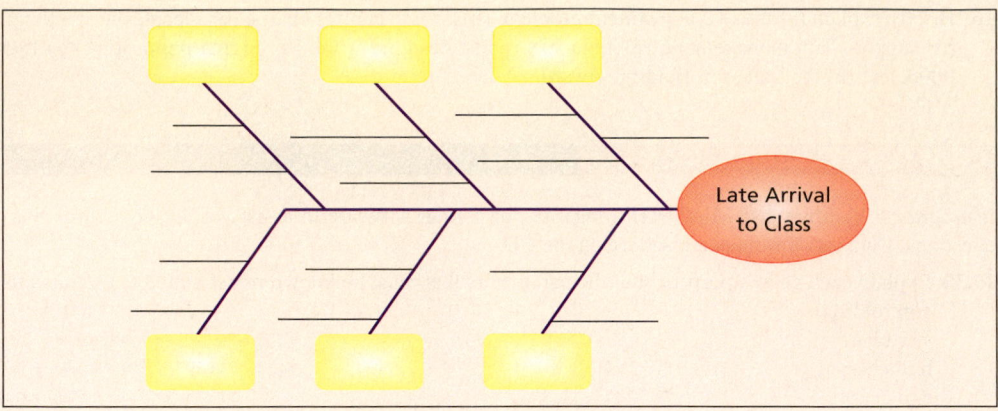

17.40 Make a fishbone chart (cause-and-effect diagram) for the reasons your end-of-month checkbook balance may not match your bank statement. Use as many branches as necessary. Which factors are most important? Which are most easily controlled?

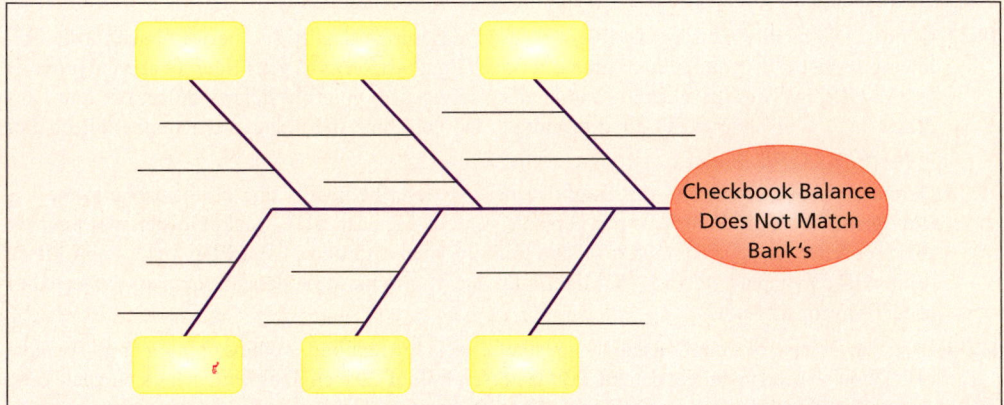

17.41 Make a fishbone chart (cause-and-effect diagram) for the reasons an airline flight might be late to arrive. Use as many branches as necessary. Which factors are most important? Which are most easily controlled?

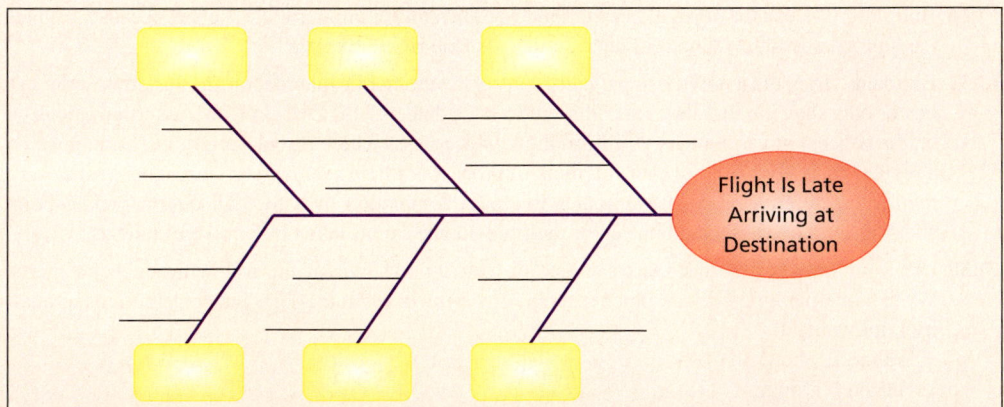

CAPABILITY

17.42 In painting an automobile, the thickness of the color coat has a lower specification limit of 0.80 mils and an upper specification limit of 1.20 mils. Find the C_p and C_{pk} capability indexes if (a) the process mean is 1.00 mils and the process standard deviation is .07 mils; and (b) the process mean is 1.00 mils and the process standard deviation is .05 mils. (c) What was the point of this exercise?

17.43 In painting an automobile, the thickness of the color coat has a lower specification limit of 0.80 mils and an upper specification limit of 1.20 mils. Find the C_p and C_{pk} capability indexes if

(a) the process mean is 1.00 mils and the process standard deviation is .05 mils; and (b) the process mean is .90 mils and the process standard deviation is .05 mils. (c) What was the point of this exercise?

17.44 Moisture content per gram of a certain baked product has specification limits of 120 mg and 160 mg. Find the C_p and C_{pk} capability indexes if (a) the process mean is 140 mg and the process standard deviation is 5 mg; and (b) the process mean is 140 mg and the process standard deviation is 3 mg. (c) What was the point of this exercise?

$\bar{x}$ CHARTS

17.45 The yield strength of a metal bolt has a mean of 6,050 pounds with a standard deviation of 100 pounds. Twenty samples of three bolts were tested, resulting in the means shown below. (a) Construct upper and lower control limits for the $\bar{x}$ chart, using the given product parameters. (b) Plot the data on the control chart. (c) Is this process in control? Explain your reasoning. 🐢 **Bolts-M**

6,107	6,031	6,075	6,115	6,039	6,079	5,995	6,097	6,114	6,039
6,154	6,054	6,028	6,002	6,062	6,094	6,051	6,031	5,965	6,082

17.46 Refer to the bolt strength problem 17.45. Assume $\mu = 6,050$ and $\sigma = 100$. Use the following 32 *individual* bolt strength observations to answer the questions posed. (a) Prepare a histogram and/or normal probability plot for the sample. (b) Does the sample support the view that yield strength is a normally distributed random variable? (c) Are the sample mean and standard deviation about where they are expected to be? 🐢 **Bolts-I**

6,121	6,100	6,007	6,166	6,164	6,032	6,276	6,151
6,054	5,836	6,024	6,105	6,033	6,066	6,079	6,192
6,028	6,087	5,983	6,040	6,062	6,054	6,100	5,983

17.47 In painting an automobile at the factory, the thickness of the color coat has a process mean of 1.00 mils and a process standard deviation of .07 mils. Twenty samples of five cars were tested, resulting in the mean paint thicknesses shown below. (a) Construct upper and lower control limits for the $\bar{x}$ chart, using the given process parameters. (b) Plot the data on the control chart. (c) Is this process in control? Explain your reasoning. 🐢 **Paint-M**

0.996	0.960	1.016	1.017	1.001	0.988	1.006	1.073	1.032	1.021
0.984	1.019	0.997	1.024	1.033	1.030	0.994	0.980	0.977	1.037

17.48 Refer to the paint thickness problem 17.47. Assume $\mu = 1.00$ and $\sigma = 0.07$. Use the following 35 *individual* observations on paint thickness to answer the questions posed. (a) Prepare a histogram and/or normal probability plot for the sample. (b) Does the sample support the view that paint thickness is a normally distributed random variable? (c) Are the mean and standard deviation about as expected? 🐢 **Paint-I**

1.026	0.949	1.069	1.105	0.995	0.955	1.080
0.932	1.014	0.899	1.031	1.042	1.022	1.082
1.111	0.995	1.005	1.004	0.964	1.065	0.909
0.912	0.978	1.037	0.992	1.010	0.974	0.977
0.905	1.008	0.971	0.951	1.200	1.065	0.972

17.49 The temperature control unit on a commercial freezer in a 24-hour grocery store is set to maintain a mean temperature of 23 degrees Fahrenheit. The temperature varies, because people are constantly opening the freezer door to remove items, but the thermostat is capable of maintaining temperature with a standard deviation of 2 degrees Fahrenheit. The desired range is 18 to 30 degrees Fahrenheit. (a) Find the C_p and C_{pk} capability indexes. (b) In words, how would you describe the process capability? (c) If improvement is desired, what might be some obstacles to increasing the capability?

17.50 Refer to the freezer problem 17.49 with $\mu = 23$ and $\sigma = 2$. Temperature measurements are recorded four times a day (at midnight, 0600, 1200, and 1800). Twenty samples of four observations are shown below. (a) Construct upper and lower control limits for the $\bar{x}$ chart, using the given process parameters. (b) Plot the data on the control chart. (c) Is this process in control? Explain your reasoning. 🐢 **Freezer**

Sample	Midnight	At 0600	At 1200	At 1800	Mean
1	25	26	23	23	24.25
2	22	23	28	22	23.75
3	20	24	25	21	22.50
4	21	25	22	23	22.75
5	21	23	21	23	22.00
6	26	25	27	26	26.00
7	21	23	25	20	22.25
8	25	23	22	25	23.75
9	22	24	24	22	23.00
10	27	23	26	25	25.25
11	24	23	20	21	22.00
12	25	21	23	20	22.25
13	26	21	21	23	22.75
14	26	22	26	22	24.00
15	21	24	20	19	21.00
16	23	26	23	23	23.75
17	23	21	24	21	22.25
18	25	22	22	23	23.00
19	24	20	21	22	21.75
20	24	21	23	21	22.25

17.51 Refer to the freezer data's 80 *individual* temperature observations in problem 17.50. (a) Prepare a histogram and/or normal probability plot for the sample. (b) Does the sample support the view that freezer temperature is a normally distributed random variable? (c) Are the sample mean and standard deviation about where they are expected to be? **Freezer**

17.52 A Nabisco Fig Newton has a mean weight of 14.00 g with a standard deviation of 0.10 g. The lower specification limit is 13.40 g and the upper specification limit is 14.60 g. (a) Describe the capability of this process, using the techniques you have learned. (b) Would you think that further variance reduction efforts would be a good idea? Explain the pros and cons of such an effort. *Hint:* Use the economic concept of opportunity cost.

17.53 A new type of smoke detector battery is developed. From laboratory tests under standard conditions, the half-life (defined as less than 50 percent of full charge) of 20 batteries are shown below. (a) Make a histogram of the data and/or a probability plot. Do you think that battery half-life can be assumed normal? (b) The engineers say that the mean battery half-life will be 8,760 hours with a standard deviation of 200 hours. Using these parameters (not the sample), set up the centerline and control limits for the $\bar{x}$ chart for a subgroup size of $n = 5$ batteries to be sampled in future production runs. (c) Repeat the previous exercise, but this time, use the sample mean and standard deviation. (d) Do you think that the control limits from this sample would be reliable? Explain, and suggest alternatives. **Battery**

8,502	8,660	8,785	8,778	8,804	9,069	8,516	9,048	8,628	9,213
8,511	8,965	8,688	8,892	8,638	8,440	8,900	8,993	8,958	8,707

17.54 A box of Wheat Chex cereal is to be filled to a mean weight of 466 grams. The lower specification limit is 453 grams (the labeled weight is 453 grams) and the upper specification limit is 477 grams (so as not to overfill the box). The process standard deviation is 2 grams. (a) Find the C_p and C_{pk} capability indexes. (b) Assess the process capability. (c) Why might it be difficult to reduce the variance in this process to raise the capability indices? *Hint:* A single Wheat Chex weighs .3 g (30 mg).

17.55 Refer to the Wheat Chex problem 17.54 with $\mu = 465$ and $\sigma = 3$. During production, samples of three boxes are weighed every 5 minutes. (a) Find the upper and lower control limit for the $\bar{x}$ chart. (b) Plot the following 20 sample means on the chart. Is the process in control? **Chex-M**

465.7	463.7	466.0	466.3	463.0	468.3	465.0	463.3	462.0	463.0
465.7	467.0	463.3	466.0	465.3	465.3	463.0	466.7	466.3	466.3

17.56 Refer to the Wheat Chex box fill problem 17.54 with $\mu = 465$ and $\sigma = 3$. Below are 30 *individual* observations on box fill. (a) Prepare a histogram and/or normal probability plot for the sample.

Does the sample support the view that box fill is a normally distributed random variable? Explain.
(b) Is the mean of these 20 same means where it should be?   🌰 **Chex-I**

461	465	462	469	463	465	462	465	467	467
460	467	466	466	465	465	462	458	470	460
465	466	464	460	465	465	466	464	465	461

17.57 Each gum drop in two bags of Sathers Gum Drops was weighed (to the nearest .001 g) on a sensitive Mettler PE 360 Delta Range scale. After removing one outlier (to improve normality) there were 84 gum drops in the sample, yielding an overall mean $\bar{x} = 11.988$ g and a pooled standard deviation $s = .2208$ g. (a) Use these sample statistics to construct control limits for an $\bar{x}$ chart, using a subgroup size $n = 6$. (b) Plot the means shown below on your control chart. Is the process in control? (c) Prepare a histogram and/or normal probability plot for the pooled sample. Does the sample support the view that gum drop weight is a normally distributed random variable? Explain.

🌰 **GumDrops**

Sample	x_1	x_2	x_3	x_4	x_5	x_6	Mean
1	11.741	11.975	11.985	12.163	12.317	12.032	12.036
2	12.206	11.970	12.179	12.182	11.756	11.975	12.045
3	12.041	12.120	11.855	12.036	11.750	11.870	11.945
4	12.002	11.800	12.092	12.017	12.340	12.488	12.123
5	12.305	12.134	11.949	12.050	12.246	11.839	12.087
6	11.862	12.049	12.105	11.894	11.995	11.722	11.938
7	11.979	12.124	12.171	12.093	12.224	11.965	12.093
8	11.941	11.855	11.587	11.574	11.752	12.345	11.842
9	12.297	12.078	12.137	11.869	11.609	11.732	11.954
10	11.677	11.879	11.926	11.852	11.781	11.932	11.841
11	12.113	12.129	12.156	12.284	12.207	12.247	12.189
12	12.510	11.904	11.675	11.880	12.086	12.458	12.086
13	12.193	11.975	12.173	11.635	11.549	11.744	11.878
14	11.880	11.784	11.696	11.804	11.823	11.693	11.780

p CHARTS

17.58 Past experience indicates that the probability of a post-surgical complication in a certain procedure is 6 percent. A hospital typically performs 200 such surgeries per month. (a) Find the control limits for the monthly p chart. (b) Would it be reasonably safe to assume that the sample proportion X/n is normally distributed? Explain.

17.59 A large retail toy store finds that, on average, a certain cheap (under $20) electronic toy has a 5 percent damage rate during shipping. From each incoming shipment, a sample of 100 is inspected. (a) Find the control limits for a p chart. (b) Plot the 10 samples below on the p chart. Is the process in control? (c) Is the sample size large enough to assume normality of the sample proportion? Explain.

🌰 **Toys**

Sample	X	n	X/n
1	3	100	0.03
2	5	100	0.05
3	4	100	0.04
4	7	100	0.07
5	2	100	0.02
6	2	100	0.02
7	0	100	0.00
8	2	100	0.02
9	7	100	0.07
10	6	100	0.06

PATTERNS IN CONTROL CHARTS

17.60 Which abnormal pattern (cycle, instability, level shift, oscillation, trend, mixture), if any, exists in each of the following $\bar{x}$ charts? If you see none, say so. If you see more than one possibility, say so. Explain your reasoning.

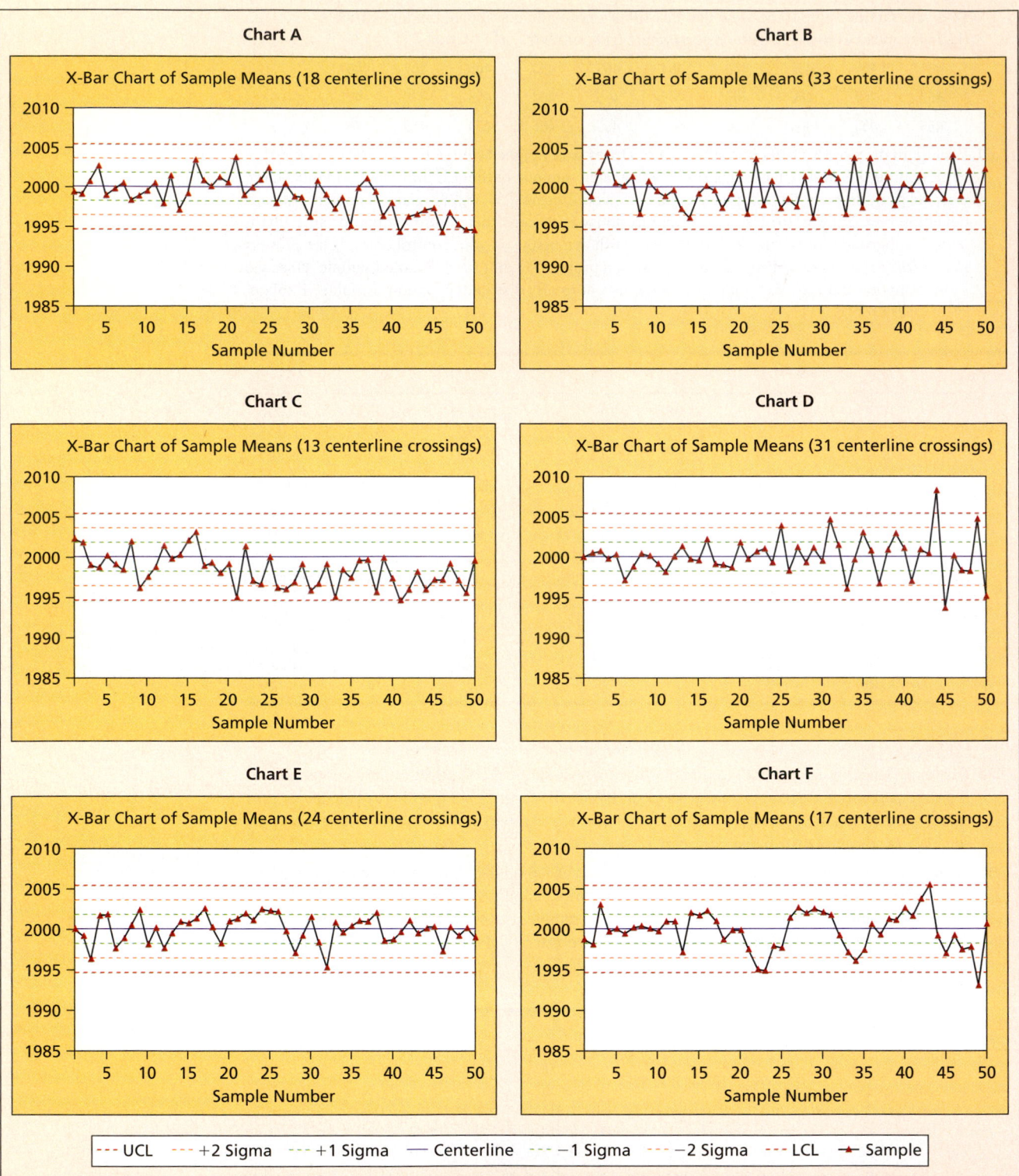

17.61 Referring to Charts *A–F*, which Rules (1, 2, 3, 4) are violated in each chart? Make a photocopy and circle the points that violate each rule.

17.62 Refer to the bolt strength problem 17.45. Assuming $\mu = 6{,}050$ and $\sigma = 100$ with $n = 3$, then LCL $= 5{,}876.8$ and UCL $= 6{,}223.2$. Below are five sets of 20 sample means using $n = 3$. Test each set of means for the pattern suggested in the column heading. This is a visual judgment question, though you can apply Rules 1–4 if you wish. **Bolts-P**

Up Trend?	Down Trend?	Unstable?	Cycle?	Oscillate?
5,907	6,100	6,048	6,079	6,122
6,060	6,009	5,975	6,029	5,983
5,987	6,145	6,092	6,006	6,105
5,919	6,049	5,894	6,012	6,024
6,029	6,039	6,083	6,098	6,123
6,114	5,956	6,069	6,124	6,022
6,063	6,103	6,073	6,092	6,082
6,084	6,140	5,972	6,114	6,018
5,980	6,054	6,112	6,071	6,031
6,056	6,062	5,988	6,097	6,107
6,078	6,042	6,006	6,038	6,031
6,118	6,152	6,226	6,099	6,047
6,051	5,961	5,989	6,000	6,055
6,021	5,926	6,111	6,004	6,041
6,068	6,109	6,026	6,054	5,972
6,157	5,904	6,057	6,083	5,987
6,041	6,049	6,098	6,148	6,043
6,129	6,042	6,082	6,071	6,137
6,026	5,847	6,050	6,095	5,930
6,174	6,033	6,084	6,092	6,057

17.63 Refer to the paint problem 17.47 with $\mu = 1.00$ and $\sigma = .07$. With $n = 5$, LCL $= .906$ and UCL $= 1.094$. Below are five sets of 20 sample means using $n = 5$. Test each set of means for the pattern suggested in the column heading. This is a visual judgment question, though you can apply Rules 1–4 if you wish. 🎨 **Paint-P**

No Pattern?	Up Trend?	Down Trend?	Unstable?	Cycle?
0.996	0.995	1.007	0.999	0.964
0.960	0.942	1.000	0.986	1.025
1.016	0.947	1.011	0.950	0.988
1.017	1.011	0.989	0.982	1.000
1.001	0.983	0.999	0.967	1.023
0.988	0.989	1.000	0.972	1.019
1.006	0.978	1.025	0.977	1.035
1.073	0.958	0.963	1.015	1.043
1.032	1.034	1.060	0.970	1.044
1.021	1.058	1.020	1.016	0.993
0.984	1.058	0.977	0.979	0.994
1.019	0.958	0.985	0.934	0.988
0.997	1.030	1.033	0.975	0.991
1.024	1.022	0.975	1.100	1.001
1.033	0.976	0.939	0.976	1.011
1.030	1.024	1.007	0.976	1.015
0.994	1.032	0.994	1.029	1.000
0.980	0.994	0.990	0.987	1.010
0.977	1.016	0.925	0.954	1.061
1.037	1.039	0.907	1.011	1.001

ESSAY QUESTIONS

17.64 Under the Hospital Quality Initiative (HQI), acute-care hospitals that want to receive full reimbursement from Medicare must report quality data on treatment of three medical conditions: heart attack, heart failures, and pneumonia. Quality is measured by 10 industry standards that define "best practice." For example, did heart attack patients receive aspirin upon arrival? Did pneumonia patients receive antibiotics in a timely manner? Did heart failure patients receive a left ventricular function assessment? (a) What kind of control chart might be employed to track these quality measures? (b) Although 100 percent compliance with the HQI standards is a desirable goal, why might it be unrealistic in practice? (c) How does cost enter into a hospital's desire to improve its compliance with HQI and similar standards? For more information, see the Centers for Medicare and Medicaid Services (CMS) Web site: www.cms.hhs.gov.

17.65 In 2002, Wampler Foods recalled 27.4 million pounds of cooked meat products, the largest recall in the history of the U.S. Department of Agriculture. This voluntary recall was due to possible contamination with *listeria* (a disease-causing bacterium). The fear was due to samples taken from floor drains. (a) Use this example to illustrate Type I and Type II error in quality control. (b) How might you estimate the cost of disposing of it? *Hint:* Start with the capacity of a 2-ton truck to take contaminated meat to a landfill. (c) How does this illustrate also the NIMBY principle of economics (look up NIMBY on the Internet if it is an unfamiliar term). (Data are from *Detroit Free Press,* October 14, 2002, p. 3A.)

17.66 In 2001, a federal court struck down U.S. Department of Agriculture rules that would have allowed the USDA to withdraw its inspectors from beef processing plants that were contaminated with the disease-causing bacterium *salmonella.* Under USDA rules, a maximum 7.5 percent rate of salmonella contamination was allowed in ground beef. The National Food Processors Association had challenged the rule, arguing that salmonella tests are an unfair way to measure the cleanliness of meat processing plants. (a) Use this example to illustrate Type I and Type II error in quality control. (b) What is the public interest in meat inspection? (Data are from *Detroit Free Press,* December 13, 2001, p. 20A.)

17.67 In 1994, General Mills threw away 50 million boxes of Cheerios and other cereals treated with a pesticide not approved for use on that grain. The company said it would take a month to dispose of the 4,000 truckloads of cereal in Illinois, Pennsylvania, and Utah landfills. Use this example to illustrate Type I and Type II error in quality control. What is the public interest in cereal inspection? (Data are from *Detroit Free Press,* August 20, 1994, p. 9A.)

DO IT YOURSELF

17.68 Buy a bag of M&Ms. (a) As a measure of quality, take a sample of 100 M&Ms and count the number with incomplete or illegible "M" printed on them. (b) Calculate the sample proportion with defects. (c) What ambiguity (if any) did you encounter in this task? (d) Do you feel that your sample was large enough? Explain.

17.69 Examine a square meter (or another convenient unit) of paint on your car's driver door. Be sure the area is clean. (a) Tally the number of paint defects (scratch, abrasion, embedded dirt, chip, dent, rust, other). You may add your own defect categories. (b) Repeat, using a friend's car that is either older or newer than yours. (c) State your findings succinctly.

17.70 Buy a box of Cheerios (or your favorite breakfast cereal). (a) As a measure of quality, take a sample of 100 Cheerios, and count the number of Cheerios that are broken. (b) Calculate the sample proportion with defects. (c) What ambiguity (if any) did you encounter in this task? (d) Do you feel that your sample was truly random? Explain.

Web Data Sources

Source	Web Site
American Society for Quality (books, training, videos)	www.qualitypress.asq.org
Deming Society (philosophy, references)	www.deming.org
MedStat (health care quality benchmarking)	www.medstat.com
Perry Johnson, Inc. (ISO 9000 training)	www.pji.com
Quality Digest Magazine (current issues)	www.qualitydigest.com
QCI International (training videos)	www.qci-intl.com

Related Reading

Alwan, Layth C. *Statistical Process Analysis.* Irwin/McGraw-Hill, 2000.

Besterfield, Dale H. *Quality Control.* 7th ed. Prentice-Hall, 2004.

Birkenstock, James M. *The ISO 9000 Quality System Checklist.* McGraw-Hill, 1997.

Boardman, Thomas J. "The Statistician Who Changed the World: W. Edwards Deming, 1900–1993." *The American Statistician* 48, no. 3 (August 1994), pp. 179–87.

Bossert, James L. *Supplier Management Handbook.* 5th ed. ASQC: 1994.

Box, George; and Alberto Luceño. *Statistical Control by Monitoring and Feedback Adjustment.* Wiley, 1997.

Brue, Greg. *Six Sigma for Managers.* McGraw-Hill, 2002.

Evans, James R.; and William M. Lindsay. *Management and the Control of Quality.* South-Western, 2001.

George, Michael L. *Lean Six Sigma.* McGraw-Hill, 2002.

Grant, Eugene; and Richard Leavenworth. *Statistical Quality Control.* 7th ed. McGraw-Hill, 1996.

Hawkins, Douglas M.; and David H. Olwell. *Cumulative Sum Charts and Charting for Quality Improvement.* Springer, 1998.

Hogg, Robert V. "Let's Use CQI in Our Statistics Programs." *The American Statistician* 53, no. 1 (February 1999), pp. 7–14.

Jonglekar, Anand M. *Statistical Methods for Six Sigma.* Wiley, 2003.

Juran, Joseph. *Juran's Quality Handbook.* McGraw-Hill, 1998.

Kotz, Samuel; and Norman L. Johnson. *Process Capability Indices.* Chapman & Hall, London, 1992.

Montgomery, Douglas C. *Introduction to Statistical Quality Control.* 4th ed. Wiley, 2000.

Roy, Ranjit. *A Primer on the Taguchi Method.* Society of Manufacturing Engineers, 1990.

Pyzdek, Thomas. *The Six Sigma Handbook.* McGraw-Hill, 2003.

Rao, R.; and R. Khattree, eds. *Handbook of Statistics: Statistics in Industry, 23.* Elsevier Science, 2003.

Ross, Joel E. *Total Quality Management.* 2nd ed. St. Lucie Press, 1994.

Ryan, Thomas P. *Statistical Methods for Quality Improvement.* 2nd ed. Wiley, 2000.

Smith, Gerald M. *Statistical Process Control and Quality Improvement.* 5th ed. Prentice-Hall, 2004.

LearningStats Unit 17   Quality

LearningStats Unit 17 illustrates the tools and applications of statistical process control, capability analysis, and control chart patterns. Your instructor may assign specific modules, or you may pursue those that sound interesting.

Topic	LearningStats Modules
Quality overview	Quality Overview Process Control Overview
Terminology	Terminology of Quality
Control charts	Basic Control Charts Other Control Charts
Capability	Capability Explained Capability Indexes
Control chart patterns and rules	Control Chart Patterns
Student reports	Level Shift and Trend Cycle and Oscillation Mixtures and Instability
Other	What Is Six Sigma?

Key: = PowerPoint = Excel

Visual Statistics

Visual Statistics Modules on Quality

Module	Module Name
21	Visualizing Statistical Process Control
13	Visualizing Goodness-of-Fit Tests

Visual Statistics Modules 21 and 13 are designed to help you

- Understand how control limits are constructed.
- Be able to interpret simple control charts.
- Recognize out-of-control processes and their typical causes.
- Apply pattern recognition rules to control charts.
- Test a sample for normality.

The worktext (included on the CD in .PDF format) contains lists of concepts covered, objectives of the modules, overviews of concepts, illustrations of concepts, orientations to module features, learning exercises (basic, intermediate, advanced), learning projects (individual, team), self-evaluation quizzes, glossaries of terms, and solutions to self-evaluation quizzes.

APPENDIX

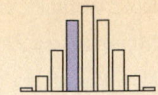

EXACT BINOMIAL PROBABILITIES

									π									
n	X	.01	.02	.05	.10	.15	.20	.30	.40	.50	.60	.70	.80	.85	.90	.95	.98	.99
2	0	.9801	.9604	.9025	.8100	.7225	.6400	.4900	.3600	.2500	.1600	.0900	.0400	.0225	.0100	.0025	.0004	.0001
	1	.0198	.0392	.0950	.1800	.2550	.3200	.4200	.4800	.5000	.4800	.4200	.3200	.2550	.1800	.0950	.0392	.0198
	2	.0001	.0004	.0025	.0100	.0225	.0400	.0900	.1600	.2500	.3600	.4900	.6400	.7225	.8100	.9025	.9604	.9801
3	0	.9703	.9412	.8574	.7290	.6141	.5120	.3430	.2160	.1250	.0640	.0270	.0080	.0034	.0010	.0001	—	—
	1	.0294	.0576	.1354	.2430	.3251	.3840	.4410	.4320	.3750	.2880	.1890	.0960	.0574	.0270	.0071	.0012	.0003
	2	.0003	.0012	.0071	.0270	.0574	.0960	.1890	.2880	.3750	.4320	.4410	.3840	.3251	.2430	.1354	.0576	.0294
	3	—	—	.0001	.0010	.0034	.0080	.0270	.0640	.1250	.2160	.3430	.5120	.6141	.7290	.8574	.9412	.9703
4	0	.9606	.9224	.8145	.6561	.5220	.4096	.2401	.1296	.0625	.0256	.0081	.0016	.0005	.0001	—	—	—
	1	.0388	.0753	.1715	.2916	.3685	.4096	.4116	.3456	.2500	.1536	.0756	.0256	.0115	.0036	.0005	—	—
	2	.0006	.0023	.0135	.0486	.0975	.1536	.2646	.3456	.3750	.3456	.2646	.1536	.0975	.0486	.0135	.0023	.0006
	3	—	—	.0005	.0036	.0115	.0256	.0756	.1536	.2500	.3456	.4116	.4096	.3685	.2916	.1715	.0753	.0388
	4	—	—	—	.0001	.0005	.0016	.0081	.0256	.0625	.1296	.2401	.4096	.5220	.6561	.8145	.9224	.9606
5	0	.9510	.9039	.7738	.5905	.4437	.3277	.1681	.0778	.0313	.0102	.0024	.0003	.0001	—	—	—	—
	1	.0480	.0922	.2036	.3281	.3915	.4096	.3602	.2592	.1563	.0768	.0284	.0064	.0022	.0005	—	—	—
	2	.0010	.0038	.0214	.0729	.1382	.2048	.3087	.3456	.3125	.2304	.1323	.0512	.0244	.0081	.0011	.0001	—
	3	—	.0001	.0011	.0081	.0244	.0512	.1323	.2304	.3125	.3456	.3087	.2048	.1382	.0729	.0214	.0038	.0010
	4	—	—	—	.0005	.0022	.0064	.0284	.0768	.1563	.2592	.3602	.4096	.3915	.3281	.2036	.0922	.0480
	5	—	—	—	—	.0001	.0003	.0024	.0102	.0313	.0778	.1681	.3277	.4437	.5905	.7738	.9039	.9510
6	0	.9415	.8858	.7351	.5314	.3771	.2621	.1176	.0467	.0156	.0041	.0007	.0001	—	—	—	—	—
	1	.0571	.1085	.2321	.3543	.3993	.3932	.3025	.1866	.0938	.0369	.0102	.0015	.0004	.0001	—	—	—
	2	.0014	.0055	.0305	.0984	.1762	.2458	.3241	.3110	.2344	.1382	.0595	.0154	.0055	.0012	.0001	—	—
	3	—	.0002	.0021	.0146	.0415	.0819	.1852	.2765	.3125	.2765	.1852	.0819	.0415	.0146	.0021	.0002	—
	4	—	—	.0001	.0012	.0055	.0154	.0595	.1382	.2344	.3110	.3241	.2458	.1762	.0984	.0305	.0055	.0014
	5	—	—	—	.0001	.0004	.0015	.0102	.0369	.0938	.1866	.3025	.3932	.3993	.3543	.2321	.1085	.0571
	6	—	—	—	—	—	.0001	.0007	.0041	.0156	.0467	.1176	.2621	.3771	.5314	.7351	.8858	.9415
7	0	.9321	.8681	.6983	.4783	.3206	.2097	.0824	.0280	.0078	.0016	.0002	—	—	—	—	—	—
	1	.0659	.1240	.2573	.3720	.3960	.3670	.2471	.1306	.0547	.0172	.0036	.0004	.0001	—	—	—	—
	2	.0020	.0076	.0406	.1240	.2097	.2753	.3177	.2613	.1641	.0774	.0250	.0043	.0012	.0002	—	—	—
	3	—	.0003	.0036	.0230	.0617	.1147	.2269	.2903	.2734	.1935	.0972	.0287	.0109	.0026	.0002	—	—
	4	—	—	.0002	.0026	.0109	.0287	.0972	.1935	.2734	.2903	.2269	.1147	.0617	.0230	.0036	.0003	—
	5	—	—	—	.0002	.0012	.0043	.0250	.0774	.1641	.2613	.3177	.2753	.2097	.1240	.0406	.0076	.0020
	6	—	—	—	—	.0001	.0004	.0036	.0172	.0547	.1306	.2471	.3670	.3960	.3720	.2573	.1240	.0659
	7	—	—	—	—	—	—	.0002	.0016	.0078	.0280	.0824	.2097	.3206	.4783	.6983	.8681	.9321
8	0	.9227	.8508	.6634	.4305	.2725	.1678	.0576	.0168	.0039	.0007	.0001	—	—	—	—	—	—
	1	.0746	.1389	.2793	.3826	.3847	.3355	.1977	.0896	.0313	.0079	.0012	.0001	—	—	—	—	—
	2	.0026	.0099	.0515	.1488	.2376	.2936	.2965	.2090	.1094	.0413	.0100	.0011	.0002	—	—	—	—
	3	.0001	.0004	.0054	.0331	.0839	.1468	.2541	.2787	.2188	.1239	.0467	.0092	.0026	.0004	—	—	—
	4	—	—	.0004	.0046	.0185	.0459	.1361	.2322	.2734	.2322	.1361	.0459	.0185	.0046	.0004	—	—
	5	—	—	—	.0004	.0026	.0092	.0467	.1239	.2188	.2787	.2541	.1468	.0839	.0331	.0054	.0004	.0001
	6	—	—	—	—	.0002	.0011	.0100	.0413	.1094	.2090	.2965	.2936	.2376	.1488	.0515	.0099	.0026
	7	—	—	—	—	—	.0001	.0012	.0079	.0313	.0896	.1977	.3355	.3847	.3826	.2793	.1389	.0746
	8	—	—	—	—	—	—	.0001	.0007	.0039	.0168	.0576	.1678	.2725	.4305	.6634	.8508	.9227
9	0	.9135	.8337	.6302	.3874	.2316	.1342	.0404	.0101	.0020	.0003	—	—	—	—	—	—	—
	1	.0830	.1531	.2985	.3874	.3679	.3020	.1556	.0605	.0176	.0035	.0004	—	—	—	—	—	—
	2	.0034	.0125	.0629	.1722	.2597	.3020	.2668	.1612	.0703	.0212	.0039	.0003	—	—	—	—	—
	3	.0001	.0006	.0077	.0446	.1069	.1762	.2668	.2508	.1641	.0743	.0210	.0028	.0006	.0001	—	—	—
	4	—	—	.0006	.0074	.0283	.0661	.1715	.2508	.2461	.1672	.0735	.0165	.0050	.0008	—	—	—
	5	—	—	—	.0008	.0050	.0165	.0735	.1672	.2461	.2508	.1715	.0661	.0283	.0074	.0006	—	—
	6	—	—	—	.0001	.0006	.0028	.0210	.0743	.1641	.2508	.2668	.1762	.1069	.0446	.0077	.0006	.0001
	7	—	—	—	—	—	.0003	.0039	.0212	.0703	.1612	.2668	.3020	.2597	.1722	.0629	.0125	.0034
	8	—	—	—	—	—	—	.0004	.0035	.0176	.0605	.1556	.3020	.3679	.3874	.2985	.1531	.0830
	9	—	—	—	—	—	—	—	.0003	.0020	.0101	.0404	.1342	.2316	.3874	.6302	.8337	.9135

π

n	X	.01	.02	.05	.10	.15	.20	.30	.40	.50	.60	.70	.80	.85	.90	.95	.98	.99
10	0	.9044	.8171	.5987	.3487	.1969	.1074	.0282	.0060	.0010	.0001	—	—	—	—	—	—	—
	1	.0914	.1667	.3151	.3874	.3474	.2684	.1211	.0403	.0098	.0016	.0001	—	—	—	—	—	—
	2	.0042	.0153	.0746	.1937	.2759	.3020	.2335	.1209	.0439	.0106	.0014	.0001	—	—	—	—	—
	3	.0001	.0008	.0105	.0574	.1298	.2013	.2668	.2150	.1172	.0425	.0090	.0008	.0001	—	—	—	—
	4	—	—	.0010	.0112	.0401	.0881	.2001	.2508	.2051	.1115	.0368	.0055	.0012	.0001	—	—	—
	5	—	—	.0001	.0015	.0085	.0264	.1029	.2007	.2461	.2007	.1029	.0264	.0085	.0015	.0001	—	—
	6	—	—	—	.0001	.0012	.0055	.0368	.1115	.2051	.2508	.2001	.0881	.0401	.0112	.0010	—	—
	7	—	—	—	—	.0001	.0008	.0090	.0425	.1172	.2150	.2668	.2013	.1298	.0574	.0105	.0008	.0001
	8	—	—	—	—	—	.0001	.0014	.0106	.0439	.1209	.2335	.3020	.2759	.1937	.0746	.0153	.0042
	9	—	—	—	—	—	—	.0001	.0016	.0098	.0403	.1211	.2684	.3474	.3874	.3151	.1667	.0914
	10	—	—	—	—	—	—	—	.0001	.0010	.0060	.0282	.1074	.1969	.3487	.5987	.8171	.9044
12	0	.8864	.7847	.5404	.2824	.1422	.0687	.0138	.0022	.0002	—	—	—	—	—	—	—	—
	1	.1074	.1922	.3413	.3766	.3012	.2062	.0712	.0174	.0029	.0003	—	—	—	—	—	—	—
	2	.0060	.0216	.0988	.2301	.2924	.2835	.1678	.0639	.0161	.0025	.0002	—	—	—	—	—	—
	3	.0002	.0015	.0173	.0852	.1720	.2362	.2397	.1419	.0537	.0125	.0015	.0001	—	—	—	—	—
	4	—	.0001	.0021	.0213	.0683	.1329	.2311	.2128	.1208	.0420	.0078	.0005	.0001	—	—	—	—
	5	—	—	.0002	.0038	.0193	.0532	.1585	.2270	.1934	.1009	.0291	.0033	.0006	—	—	—	—
	6	—	—	—	.0005	.0040	.0155	.0792	.1766	.2256	.1766	.0792	.0155	.0040	.0005	—	—	—
	7	—	—	—	—	.0006	.0033	.0291	.1009	.1934	.2270	.1585	.0532	.0193	.0038	.0002	—	—
	8	—	—	—	—	.0001	.0005	.0078	.0420	.1208	.2128	.2311	.1329	.0683	.0213	.0021	.0001	—
	9	—	—	—	—	—	.0001	.0015	.0125	.0537	.1419	.2397	.2362	.1720	.0852	.0173	.0015	.0002
	10	—	—	—	—	—	—	.0002	.0025	.0161	.0639	.1678	.2835	.2924	.2301	.0988	.0216	.0060
	11	—	—	—	—	—	—	.0003	.0029	.0174	.0712	.2062	.3012	.3766	.3413	.1922	.1074	
	12	—	—	—	—	—	—	—	.0002	.0022	.0138	.0687	.1422	.2824	.5404	.7847	.8864	
14	0	.8687	.7536	.4877	.2288	.1028	.0440	.0068	.0008	.0001	—	—	—	—	—	—	—	—
	1	.1229	.2153	.3593	.3559	.2539	.1539	.0407	.0073	.0009	.0001	—	—	—	—	—	—	—
	2	.0081	.0286	.1229	.2570	.2912	.2501	.1134	.0317	.0056	.0005	—	—	—	—	—	—	—
	3	.0003	.0023	.0259	.1142	.2056	.2501	.1943	.0845	.0222	.0033	.0002	—	—	—	—	—	—
	4	—	.0001	.0037	.0349	.0998	.1720	.2290	.1549	.0611	.0136	.0014	—	—	—	—	—	—
	5	—	—	.0004	.0078	.0352	.0860	.1963	.2066	.1222	.0408	.0066	.0003	—	—	—	—	—
	6	—	—	—	.0013	.0093	.0322	.1262	.2066	.1833	.0918	.0232	.0020	.0003	—	—	—	—
	7	—	—	—	.0002	.0019	.0092	.0618	.1574	.2095	.1574	.0618	.0092	.0019	.0002	—	—	—
	8	—	—	—	—	.0003	.0020	.0232	.0918	.1833	.2066	.1262	.0322	.0093	.0013	—	—	—
	9	—	—	—	—	—	.0003	.0066	.0408	.1222	.2066	.1963	.0860	.0352	.0078	.0004	—	—
	10	—	—	—	—	—	—	.0014	.0136	.0611	.1549	.2290	.1720	.0998	.0349	.0037	.0001	—
	11	—	—	—	—	—	—	.0002	.0033	.0222	.0845	.1943	.2501	.2056	.1142	.0259	.0023	.0003
	12	—	—	—	—	—	—	—	.0005	.0056	.0317	.1134	.2501	.2912	.2570	.1229	.0286	.0081
	13	—	—	—	—	—	—	—	.0001	.0009	.0073	.0407	.1539	.2539	.3559	.3593	.2153	.1229
	14	—	—	—	—	—	—	—	—	.0001	.0008	.0068	.0440	.1028	.2288	.4877	.7536	.8687
16	0	.8515	.7238	.4401	.1853	.0743	.0281	.0033	.0003	—	—	—	—	—	—	—	—	—
	1	.1376	.2363	.3706	.3294	.2097	.1126	.0228	.0030	.0002	—	—	—	—	—	—	—	—
	2	.0104	.0362	.1463	.2745	.2775	.2111	.0732	.0150	.0018	.0001	—	—	—	—	—	—	—
	3	.0005	.0034	.0359	.1423	.2285	.2463	.1465	.0468	.0085	.0008	—	—	—	—	—	—	—
	4	—	.0002	.0061	.0514	.1311	.2001	.2040	.1014	.0278	.0040	.0002	—	—	—	—	—	—
	5	—	—	.0008	.0137	.0555	.1201	.2099	.1623	.0667	.0142	.0013	—	—	—	—	—	—
	6	—	—	.0001	.0028	.0180	.0550	.1649	.1983	.1222	.0392	.0056	.0002	—	—	—	—	—
	7	—	—	—	.0004	.0045	.0197	.1010	.1889	.1746	.0840	.0185	.0012	.0001	—	—	—	—
	8	—	—	—	.0001	.0009	.0055	.0487	.1417	.1964	.1417	.0487	.0055	.0009	.0001	—	—	—
	9	—	—	—	—	.0001	.0012	.0185	.0840	.1746	.1889	.1010	.0197	.0045	.0004	—	—	—
	10	—	—	—	—	—	.0002	.0056	.0392	.1222	.1983	.1649	.0550	.0180	.0028	.0001	—	—
	11	—	—	—	—	—	—	.0013	.0142	.0667	.1623	.2099	.1201	.0555	.0137	.0008	—	—
	12	—	—	—	—	—	—	.0002	.0040	.0278	.1014	.2040	.2001	.1311	.0514	.0061	.0002	—
	13	—	—	—	—	—	—	—	.0008	.0085	.0468	.1465	.2463	.2285	.1423	.0359	.0034	.0005
	14	—	—	—	—	—	—	—	.0001	.0018	.0150	.0732	.2111	.2775	.2745	.1463	.0362	.0104
	15	—	—	—	—	—	—	—	—	.0002	.0030	.0228	.1126	.2097	.3294	.3706	.2363	.1376
	16	—	—	—	—	—	—	—	—	—	.0003	.0033	.0281	.0743	.1853	.4401	.7238	.8515

APPENDIX

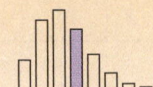

EXACT POISSON PROBABILITIES

							λ								
X	0.1	0.2	0.3	0.4	0.5	0.6	0.7	0.8	0.9	1.0	1.1	1.2	1.3	1.4	1.5
0	.9048	.8187	.7408	.6703	.6065	.5488	.4966	.4493	.4066	.3679	.3329	.3012	.2725	.2466	.2231
1	.0905	.1637	.2222	.2681	.3033	.3293	.3476	.3595	.3659	.3679	.3662	.3614	.3543	.3452	.3347
2	.0045	.0164	.0333	.0536	.0758	.0988	.1217	.1438	.1647	.1839	.2014	.2169	.2303	.2417	.2510
3	.0002	.0011	.0033	.0072	.0126	.0198	.0284	.0383	.0494	.0613	.0738	.0867	.0998	.1128	.1255
4	—	.0001	.0003	.0007	.0016	.0030	.0050	.0077	.0111	.0153	.0203	.0260	.0324	.0395	.0471
5	—	—	—	.0001	.0002	.0004	.0007	.0012	.0020	.0031	.0045	.0062	.0084	.0111	.0141
6	—	—	—	—	—	—	.0001	.0002	.0003	.0005	.0008	.0012	.0018	.0026	.0035
7	—	—	—	—	—	—	—	—	—	.0001	.0001	.0002	.0003	.0005	.0008
8	—	—	—	—	—	—	—	—	—	—	—	—	.0001	.0001	.0001

							λ								
X	1.6	1.7	1.8	1.9	2.0	2.1	2.2	2.3	2.4	2.5	2.6	2.7	2.8	2.9	3.0
0	.2019	.1827	.1653	.1496	.1353	.1225	.1108	.1003	.0907	.0821	.0743	.0672	.0608	.0550	.0498
1	.3230	.3106	.2975	.2842	.2707	.2572	.2438	.2306	.2177	.2052	.1931	.1815	.1703	.1596	.1494
2	.2584	.2640	.2678	.2700	.2707	.2700	.2681	.2652	.2613	.2565	.2510	.2450	.2384	.2314	.2240
3	.1378	.1496	.1607	.1710	.1804	.1890	.1966	.2033	.2090	.2138	.2176	.2205	.2225	.2237	.2240
4	.0551	.0636	.0723	.0812	.0902	.0992	.1082	.1169	.1254	.1336	.1414	.1488	.1557	.1622	.1680
5	.0176	.0216	.0260	.0309	.0361	.0417	.0476	.0538	.0602	.0668	.0735	.0804	.0872	.0940	.1008
6	.0047	.0061	.0078	.0098	.0120	.0146	.0174	.0206	.0241	.0278	.0319	.0362	.0407	.0455	.0504
7	.0011	.0015	.0020	.0027	.0034	.0044	.0055	.0068	.0083	.0099	.0118	.0139	.0163	.0188	.0216
8	.0002	.0003	.0005	.0006	.0009	.0011	.0015	.0019	.0025	.0031	.0038	.0047	.0057	.0068	.0081
9	—	.0001	.0001	.0001	.0002	.0003	.0004	.0005	.0007	.0009	.0011	.0014	.0018	.0022	.0027
10	—	—	—	—	—	.0001	.0001	.0001	.0002	.0002	.0003	.0004	.0005	.0006	.0008
11	—	—	—	—	—	—	—	—	—	—	.0001	.0001	.0001	.0002	.0002
12	—	—	—	—	—	—	—	—	—	—	—	—	—	—	.0001

							λ								
X	3.1	3.2	3.3	3.4	3.5	3.6	3.7	3.8	3.9	4.0	4.1	4.2	4.3	4.4	4.5
0	.0450	.0408	.0369	.0334	.0302	.0273	.0247	.0224	.0202	.0183	.0166	.0150	.0136	.0123	.0111
1	.1397	.1304	.1217	.1135	.1057	.0984	.0915	.0850	.0789	.0733	.0679	.0630	.0583	.0540	.0500
2	.2165	.2087	.2008	.1929	.1850	.1771	.1692	.1615	.1539	.1465	.1393	.1323	.1254	.1188	.1125
3	.2237	.2226	.2209	.2186	.2158	.2125	.2087	.2046	.2001	.1954	.1904	.1852	.1798	.1743	.1687
4	.1733	.1781	.1823	.1858	.1888	.1912	.1931	.1944	.1951	.1954	.1951	.1944	.1933	.1917	.1898
5	.1075	.1140	.1203	.1264	.1322	.1377	.1429	.1477	.1522	.1563	.1600	.1633	.1662	.1687	.1708
6	.0555	.0608	.0662	.0716	.0771	.0826	.0881	.0936	.0989	.1042	.1093	.1143	.1191	.1237	.1281
7	.0246	.0278	.0312	.0348	.0385	.0425	.0466	.0508	.0551	.0595	.0640	.0686	.0732	.0778	.0824
8	.0095	.0111	.0129	.0148	.0169	.0191	.0215	.0241	.0269	.0298	.0328	.0360	.0393	.0428	.0463
9	.0033	.0040	.0047	.0056	.0066	.0076	.0089	.0102	.0116	.0132	.0150	.0168	.0188	.0209	.0232
10	.0010	.0013	.0016	.0019	.0023	.0028	.0033	.0039	.0045	.0053	.0061	.0071	.0081	.0092	.0104
11	.0003	.0004	.0005	.0006	.0007	.0009	.0011	.0013	.0016	.0019	.0023	.0027	.0032	.0037	.0043
12	.0001	.0001	.0001	.0002	.0002	.0003	.0003	.0004	.0005	.0006	.0008	.0009	.0011	.0013	.0016
13	—	—	—	—	.0001	.0001	.0001	.0001	.0002	.0002	.0002	.0003	.0004	.0005	.0006
14	—	—	—	—	—	—	—	—	—	.0001	.0001	.0001	.0001	.0001	.0002
15	—	—	—	—	—	—	—	—	—	—	—	—	—	—	.0001

λ

X	4.6	4.7	4.8	4.9	5.0	5.1	5.2	5.3	5.4	5.5	5.6	5.7	5.8	5.9	6.0
0	.0101	.0091	.0082	.0074	.0067	.0061	.0055	.0050	.0045	.0041	.0037	.0033	.0030	.0027	.0025
1	.0462	.0427	.0395	.0365	.0337	.0311	.0287	.0265	.0244	.0225	.0207	.0191	.0176	.0162	.0149
2	.1063	.1005	.0948	.0894	.0842	.0793	.0746	.0701	.0659	.0618	.0580	.0544	.0509	.0477	.0446
3	.1631	.1574	.1517	.1460	.1404	.1348	.1293	.1239	.1185	.1133	.1082	.1033	.0985	.0938	.0892
4	.1875	.1849	.1820	.1789	.1755	.1719	.1681	.1641	.1600	.1558	.1515	.1472	.1428	.1383	.1339
5	.1725	.1738	.1747	.1753	.1755	.1753	.1748	.1740	.1728	.1714	.1697	.1678	.1656	.1632	.1606
6	.1323	.1362	.1398	.1432	.1462	.1490	.1515	.1537	.1555	.1571	.1584	.1594	.1601	.1605	.1606
7	.0869	.0914	.0959	.1002	.1044	.1086	.1125	.1163	.1200	.1234	.1267	.1298	.1326	.1353	.1377
8	.0500	.0537	.0575	.0614	.0653	.0692	.0731	.0771	.0810	.0849	.0887	.0925	.0962	.0998	.1033
9	.0255	.0281	.0307	.0334	.0363	.0392	.0423	.0454	.0486	.0519	.0552	.0586	.0620	.0654	.0688
10	.0118	.0132	.0147	.0164	.0181	.0200	.0220	.0241	.0262	.0285	.0309	.0334	.0359	.0386	.0413
11	.0049	.0056	.0064	.0073	.0082	.0093	.0104	.0116	.0129	.0143	.0157	.0173	.0190	.0207	.0225
12	.0019	.0022	.0026	.0030	.0034	.0039	.0045	.0051	.0058	.0065	.0073	.0082	.0092	.0102	.0113
13	.0007	.0008	.0009	.0011	.0013	.0015	.0018	.0021	.0024	.0028	.0032	.0036	.0041	.0046	.0052
14	.0002	.0003	.0003	.0004	.0005	.0006	.0007	.0008	.0009	.0011	.0013	.0015	.0017	.0019	.0022
15	.0001	.0001	.0001	.0001	.0002	.0002	.0002	.0003	.0003	.0004	.0005	.0006	.0007	.0008	.0009
16	—	—	—	—	—	.0001	.0001	.0001	.0001	.0001	.0002	.0002	.0002	.0003	.0003
17	—	—	—	—	—	—	—	—	—	—	.0001	.0001	.0001	.0001	.0001

λ

X	6.1	6.2	6.3	6.4	6.5	6.6	6.7	6.8	6.9	7.0	7.1	7.2	7.3	7.4	7.5
0	.0022	.0020	.0018	.0017	.0015	.0014	.0012	.0011	.0010	.0009	.0008	.0007	.0007	.0006	.0006
1	.0137	.0126	.0116	.0106	.0098	.0090	.0082	.0076	.0070	.0064	.0059	.0054	.0049	.0045	.0041
2	.0417	.0390	.0364	.0340	.0318	.0296	.0276	.0258	.0240	.0223	.0208	.0194	.0180	.0167	.0156
3	.0848	.0806	.0765	.0726	.0688	.0652	.0617	.0584	.0552	.0521	.0492	.0464	.0438	.0413	.0389
4	.1294	.1249	.1205	.1162	.1118	.1076	.1034	.0992	.0952	.0912	.0874	.0836	.0799	.0764	.0729
5	.1579	.1549	.1519	.1487	.1454	.1420	.1385	.1349	.1314	.1277	.1241	.1204	.1167	.1130	.1094
6	.1605	.1601	.1595	.1586	.1575	.1562	.1546	.1529	.1511	.1490	.1468	.1445	.1420	.1394	.1367
7	.1399	.1418	.1435	.1450	.1462	.1472	.1480	.1486	.1489	.1490	.1489	.1486	.1481	.1474	.1465
8	.1066	.1099	.1130	.1160	.1188	.1215	.1240	.1263	.1284	.1304	.1321	.1337	.1351	.1363	.1373
9	.0723	.0757	.0791	.0825	.0858	.0891	.0923	.0954	.0985	.1014	.1042	.1070	.1096	.1121	.1144
10	.0441	.0469	.0498	.0528	.0558	.0588	.0618	.0649	.0679	.0710	.0740	.0770	.0800	.0829	.0858
11	.0244	.0265	.0285	.0307	.0330	.0353	.0377	.0401	.0426	.0452	.0478	.0504	.0531	.0558	.0585
12	.0124	.0137	.0150	.0164	.0179	.0194	.0210	.0227	.0245	.0263	.0283	.0303	.0323	.0344	.0366
13	.0058	.0065	.0073	.0081	.0089	.0099	.0108	.0119	.0130	.0142	.0154	.0168	.0181	.0196	.0211
14	.0025	.0029	.0033	.0037	.0041	.0046	.0052	.0058	.0064	.0071	.0078	.0086	.0095	.0104	.0113
15	.0010	.0012	.0014	.0016	.0018	.0020	.0023	.0026	.0029	.0033	.0037	.0041	.0046	.0051	.0057
16	.0004	.0005	.0005	.0006	.0007	.0008	.0010	.0011	.0013	.0014	.0016	.0019	.0021	.0024	.0026
17	.0001	.0002	.0002	.0002	.0003	.0003	.0004	.0004	.0005	.0006	.0007	.0008	.0009	.0010	.0012
18	—	.0001	.0001	.0001	.0001	.0001	.0001	.0002	.0002	.0002	.0003	.0003	.0004	.0004	.0005
19	—	—	—	—	—	—	.0001	.0001	.0001	.0001	.0001	.0001	.0001	.0002	.0002
20	—	—	—	—	—	—	—	—	—	—	—	—	.0001	.0001	.0001

| | | | | | | | λ | | | | | | | | |
X	8.0	8.5	9.0	9.5	10.0	11.0	12.0	13.0	14.0	15.0	16.0	17.0	18.0	19.0	20.0
0	.0003	.0002	.0001	.0001	—	—	—	—	—	—	—	—	—	—	—
1	.0027	.0017	.0011	.0007	.0005	.0002	.0001	—	—	—	—	—	—	—	—
2	.0107	.0074	.0050	.0034	.0023	.0010	.0004	.0002	.0001	—	—	—	—	—	—
3	.0286	.0208	.0150	.0107	.0076	.0037	.0018	.0008	.0004	.0002	.0001	—	—	—	—
4	.0573	.0443	.0337	.0254	.0189	.0102	.0053	.0027	.0013	.0006	.0003	.0001	.0001	—	—
5	.0916	.0752	.0607	.0483	.0378	.0224	.0127	.0070	.0037	.0019	.0010	.0005	.0002	.0001	.0001
6	.1221	.1066	.0911	.0764	.0631	.0411	.0255	.0152	.0087	.0048	.0026	.0014	.0007	.0004	.0002
7	.1396	.1294	.1171	.1037	.0901	.0646	.0437	.0281	.0174	.0104	.0060	.0034	.0019	.0010	.0005
8	.1396	.1375	.1318	.1232	.1126	.0888	.0655	.0457	.0304	.0194	.0120	.0072	.0042	.0024	.0013
9	.1241	.1299	.1318	.1300	.1251	.1085	.0874	.0661	.0473	.0324	.0213	.0135	.0083	.0050	.0029
10	.0993	.1104	.1186	.1235	.1251	.1194	.1048	.0859	.0663	.0486	.0341	.0230	.0150	.0095	.0058
11	.0722	.0853	.0970	.1067	.1137	.1194	.1144	.1015	.0844	.0663	.0496	.0355	.0245	.0164	.0106
12	.0481	.0604	.0728	.0844	.0948	.1094	.1144	.1099	.0984	.0829	.0661	.0504	.0368	.0259	.0176
13	.0296	.0395	.0504	.0617	.0729	.0926	.1056	.1099	.1060	.0956	.0814	.0658	.0509	.0378	.0271
14	.0169	.0240	.0324	.0419	.0521	.0728	.0905	.1021	.1060	.1024	.0930	.0800	.0655	.0514	.0387
15	.0090	.0136	.0194	.0265	.0347	.0534	.0724	.0885	.0989	.1024	.0992	.0906	.0786	.0650	.0516
16	.0045	.0072	.0109	.0157	.0217	.0367	.0543	.0719	.0866	.0960	.0992	.0963	.0884	.0772	.0646
17	.0021	.0036	.0058	.0088	.0128	.0237	.0383	.0550	.0713	.0847	.0934	.0963	.0936	.0863	.0760
18	.0009	.0017	.0029	.0046	.0071	.0145	.0255	.0397	.0554	.0706	.0830	.0909	.0936	.0911	.0844
19	.0004	.0008	.0014	.0023	.0037	.0084	.0161	.0272	.0409	.0557	.0699	.0814	.0887	.0911	.0888
20	.0002	.0003	.0006	.0011	.0019	.0046	.0097	.0177	.0286	.0418	.0559	.0692	.0798	.0866	.0888
21	.0001	.0001	.0003	.0005	.0009	.0024	.0055	.0109	.0191	.0299	.0426	.0560	.0684	.0783	.0846
22	—	.0001	.0001	.0002	.0004	.0012	.0030	.0065	.0121	.0204	.0310	.0433	.0560	.0676	.0769
23	—	—	—	.0001	.0002	.0006	.0016	.0037	.0074	.0133	.0216	.0320	.0438	.0559	.0669
24	—	—	—	—	.0001	.0003	.0008	.0020	.0043	.0083	.0144	.0226	.0328	.0442	.0557
25	—	—	—	—	—	.0001	.0004	.0010	.0024	.0050	.0092	.0154	.0237	.0336	.0446
26	—	—	—	—	—	—	.0002	.0005	.0013	.0029	.0057	.0101	.0164	.0246	.0343
27	—	—	—	—	—	—	.0001	.0002	.0007	.0016	.0034	.0063	.0109	.0173	.0254
28	—	—	—	—	—	—	—	.0001	.0003	.0009	.0019	.0038	.0070	.0117	.0181
29	—	—	—	—	—	—	—	.0001	.0002	.0004	.0011	.0023	.0044	.0077	.0125
30	—	—	—	—	—	—	—	—	.0001	.0002	.0006	.0013	.0026	.0049	.0083
31	—	—	—	—	—	—	—	—	—	.0001	.0003	.0007	.0015	.0030	.0054
32	—	—	—	—	—	—	—	—	—	.0001	.0001	.0004	.0009	.0018	.0034
33	—	—	—	—	—	—	—	—	—	—	.0001	.0002	.0005	.0010	.0020
34	—	—	—	—	—	—	—	—	—	—	—	.0001	.0002	.0006	.0012
35	—	—	—	—	—	—	—	—	—	—	—	—	.0001	.0003	.0007
36	—	—	—	—	—	—	—	—	—	—	—	—	.0001	.0002	.0004
37	—	—	—	—	—	—	—	—	—	—	—	—	—	.0001	.0002
38	—	—	—	—	—	—	—	—	—	—	—	—	—	—	.0001
39	—	—	—	—	—	—	—	—	—	—	—	—	—	—	.0001

APPENDIX

STANDARD NORMAL AREAS

Example: $P(0 < z < 1.96) = .4750$

This table shows the normal area between 0 and z.

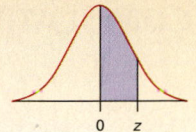

z	.00	.01	.02	.03	.04	.05	.06	.07	.08	.09
0.0	.0000	.0040	.0080	.0120	.0160	.0199	.0239	.0279	.0319	.0359
0.1	.0398	.0438	.0478	.0517	.0557	.0596	.0636	.0675	.0714	.0753
0.2	.0793	.0832	.0871	.0910	.0948	.0987	.1026	.1064	.1103	.1141
0.3	.1179	.1217	.1255	.1293	.1331	.1368	.1406	.1443	.1480	.1517
0.4	.1554	.1591	.1628	.1664	.1700	.1736	.1772	.1808	.1844	.1879
0.5	.1915	.1950	.1985	.2019	.2054	.2088	.2123	.2157	.2190	.2224
0.6	.2257	.2291	.2324	.2357	.2389	.2422	.2454	.2486	.2517	.2549
0.7	.2580	.2611	.2642	.2673	.2704	.2734	.2764	.2794	.2823	.2852
0.8	.2881	.2910	.2939	.2967	.2995	.3023	.3051	.3078	.3106	.3133
0.9	.3159	.3186	.3212	.3238	.3264	.3289	.3315	.3340	.3365	.3389
1.0	.3413	.3438	.3461	.3485	.3508	.3531	.3554	.3577	.3599	.3621
1.1	.3643	.3665	.3686	.3708	.3729	.3749	.3770	.3790	.3810	.3830
1.2	.3849	.3869	.3888	.3907	.3925	.3944	.3962	.3980	.3997	.4015
1.3	.4032	.4049	.4066	.4082	.4099	.4115	.4131	.4147	.4162	.4177
1.4	.4192	.4207	.4222	.4236	.4251	.4265	.4279	.4292	.4306	.4319
1.5	.4332	.4345	.4357	.4370	.4382	.4394	.4406	.4418	.4429	.4441
1.6	.4452	.4463	.4474	.4484	.4495	.4505	.4515	.4525	.4535	.4545
1.7	.4554	.4564	.4573	.4582	.4591	.4599	.4608	.4616	.4625	.4633
1.8	.4641	.4649	.4656	.4664	.4671	.4678	.4686	.4693	.4699	.4706
1.9	.4713	.4719	.4726	.4732	.4738	.4744	.4750	.4756	.4761	.4767
2.0	.4772	.4778	.4783	.4788	.4793	.4798	.4803	.4808	.4812	.4817
2.1	.4821	.4826	.4830	.4834	.4838	.4842	.4846	.4850	.4854	.4857
2.2	.4861	.4864	.4868	.4871	.4875	.4878	.4881	.4884	.4887	.4890
2.3	.4893	.4896	.4898	.4901	.4904	.4906	.4909	.4911	.4913	.4916
2.4	.4918	.4920	.4922	.4925	.4927	.4929	.4931	.4932	.4934	.4936
2.5	.4938	.4940	.4941	.4943	.4945	.4946	.4948	.4949	.4951	.4952
2.6	.4953	.4955	.4956	.4957	.4959	.4960	.4961	.4962	.4963	.4964
2.7	.4965	.4966	.4967	.4968	.4969	.4970	.4971	.4972	.4973	.4974
2.8	.4974	.4975	.4976	.4977	.4977	.4978	.4979	.4979	.4980	.4981
2.9	.4981	.4982	.4982	.4983	.4984	.4984	.4985	.4985	.4986	.4986
3.0	.49865	.49869	.49874	.49878	.49882	.49886	.49889	.49893	.49896	.49900
3.1	.49903	.49906	.49910	.49913	.49916	.49918	.49921	.49924	.49926	.49929
3.2	.49931	.49934	.49936	.49938	.49940	.49942	.49944	.49946	.49948	.49950
3.3	.49952	.49953	.49955	.49957	.49958	.49960	.49961	.49962	.49964	.49965
3.4	.49966	.49968	.49969	.49970	.49971	.49972	.49973	.49974	.49975	.49976
3.5	.49977	.49978	.49978	.49979	.49980	.49981	.49981	.49982	.49983	.49983
3.6	.49984	.49985	.49985	.49986	.49986	.49987	.49987	.49988	.49988	.49989
3.7	.49989	.49990	.49990	.49990	.49991	.49991	.49992	.49992	.49992	.49992

APPENDIX

CUMULATIVE STANDARD NORMAL DISTRIBUTION

Example: $P(z < -1.96) = .0250$

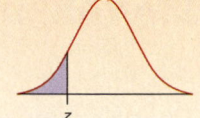

This table shows the normal area less than z.

z	.00	.01	.02	.03	.04	.05	.06	.07	.08	.09
−3.7	.00011	.00010	.00010	.00010	.00009	.00009	.00008	.00008	.00008	.00008
−3.6	.00016	.00015	.00015	.00014	.00014	.00013	.00013	.00012	.00012	.00011
−3.5	.00023	.00022	.00022	.00021	.00020	.00019	.00019	.00018	.00017	.00017
−3.4	.00034	.00032	.00031	.00030	.00029	.00028	.00027	.00026	.00025	.00024
−3.3	.00048	.00047	.00045	.00043	.00042	.00040	.00039	.00038	.00036	.00035
−3.2	.00069	.00066	.00064	.00062	.00060	.00058	.00056	.00054	.00052	.00050
−3.1	.00097	.00094	.00090	.00087	.00084	.00082	.00079	.00076	.00074	.00071
−3.0	.00135	.00131	.00126	.00122	.00118	.00114	.00111	.00107	.00104	.00100
−2.9	.0019	.0018	.0018	.0017	.0016	.0016	.0015	.0015	.0014	.0014
−2.8	.0026	.0025	.0024	.0023	.0023	.0022	.0021	.0021	.0020	.0019
−2.7	.0035	.0034	.0033	.0032	.0031	.0030	.0029	.0028	.0027	.0026
−2.6	.0047	.0045	.0044	.0043	.0041	.0040	.0039	.0038	.0037	.0036
−2.5	.0062	.0060	.0059	.0057	.0055	.0054	.0052	.0051	.0049	.0048
−2.4	.0082	.0080	.0078	.0075	.0073	.0071	.0069	.0068	.0066	.0064
−2.3	.0107	.0104	.0102	.0099	.0096	.0094	.0091	.0089	.0087	.0084
−2.2	.0139	.0136	.0132	.0129	.0125	.0122	.0119	.0116	.0113	.0110
−2.1	.0179	.0174	.0170	.0166	.0162	.0158	.0154	.0150	.0146	.0143
−2.0	.0228	.0222	.0217	.0212	.0207	.0202	.0197	.0192	.0188	.0183
−1.9	.0287	.0281	.0274	.0268	.0262	.0256	.0250	.0244	.0239	.0233
−1.8	.0359	.0351	.0344	.0336	.0329	.0322	.0314	.0307	.0301	.0294
−1.7	.0446	.0436	.0427	.0418	.0409	.0401	.0392	.0384	.0375	.0367
−1.6	.0548	.0537	.0526	.0516	.0505	.0495	.0485	.0475	.0465	.0455
−1.5	.0668	.0655	.0643	.0630	.0618	.0606	.0594	.0582	.0571	.0559
−1.4	.0808	.0793	.0778	.0764	.0749	.0735	.0721	.0708	.0694	.0681
−1.3	.0968	.0951	.0934	.0918	.0901	.0885	.0869	.0853	.0838	.0823
−1.2	.1151	.1131	.1112	.1093	.1075	.1056	.1038	.1020	.1003	.0985
−1.1	.1357	.1335	.1314	.1292	.1271	.1251	.1230	.1210	.1190	.1170
−1.0	.1587	.1562	.1539	.1515	.1492	.1469	.1446	.1423	.1401	.1379
−0.9	.1841	.1814	.1788	.1762	.1736	.1711	.1685	.1660	.1635	.1611
−0.8	.2119	.2090	.2061	.2033	.2005	.1977	.1949	.1922	.1894	.1867
−0.7	.2420	.2389	.2358	.2327	.2296	.2266	.2236	.2206	.2177	.2148
−0.6	.2743	.2709	.2676	.2643	.2611	.2578	.2546	.2514	.2483	.2451
−0.5	.3085	.3050	.3015	.2981	.2946	.2912	.2877	.2843	.2810	.2776
−0.4	.3446	.3409	.3372	.3336	.3300	.3264	.3228	.3192	.3156	.3121
−0.3	.3821	.3783	.3745	.3707	.3669	.3632	.3594	.3557	.3520	.3483
−0.2	.4207	.4168	.4129	.4090	.4052	.4013	.3974	.3936	.3897	.3859
−0.1	.4602	.4562	.4522	.4483	.4443	.4404	.4364	.4325	.4286	.4247
−0.0	.5000	.4960	.4920	.4880	.4841	.4801	.4761	.4721	.4681	.4641

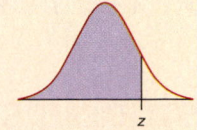

This table shows the normal area less than z.

z	.00	.01	.02	.03	.04	.05	.06	.07	.08	.09
0.0	.5000	.5040	.5080	.5120	.5160	.5199	.5239	.5279	.5319	.5359
0.1	.5398	.5438	.5478	.5517	.5557	.5596	.5636	.5675	.5714	.5753
0.2	.5793	.5832	.5871	.5910	.5948	.5987	.6026	.6064	.6103	.6141
0.3	.6179	.6217	.6255	.6293	.6331	.6368	.6406	.6443	.6480	.6517
0.4	.6554	.6591	.6628	.6664	.6700	.6736	.6772	.6808	.6844	.6879
0.5	.6915	.6950	.6985	.7019	.7054	.7088	.7123	.7157	.7190	.7224
0.6	.7257	.7291	.7324	.7357	.7389	.7422	.7454	.7486	.7517	.7549
0.7	.7580	.7611	.7642	.7673	.7704	.7734	.7764	.7794	.7823	.7852
0.8	.7881	.7910	.7939	.7967	.7995	.8023	.8051	.8078	.8106	.8133
0.9	.8159	.8186	.8212	.8238	.8264	.8289	.8315	.8340	.8365	.8389
1.0	.8413	.8438	.8461	.8485	.8508	.8531	.8554	.8577	.8599	.8621
1.1	.8643	.8665	.8686	.8708	.8729	.8749	.8770	.8790	.8810	.8830
1.2	.8849	.8869	.8888	.8907	.8925	.8944	.8962	.8980	.8997	.9015
1.3	.9032	.9049	.9066	.9082	.9099	.9115	.9131	.9147	.9162	.9177
1.4	.9192	.9207	.9222	.9236	.9251	.9265	.9279	.9292	.9306	.9319
1.5	.9332	.9345	.9357	.9370	.9382	.9394	.9406	.9418	.9429	.9441
1.6	.9452	.9463	.9474	.9484	.9495	.9505	.9515	.9525	.9535	.9545
1.7	.9554	.9564	.9573	.9582	.9591	.9599	.9608	.9616	.9625	.9633
1.8	.9641	.9649	.9656	.9664	.9671	.9678	.9686	.9693	.9699	.9706
1.9	.9713	.9719	.9726	.9732	.9738	.9744	.9750	.9756	.9761	.9767
2.0	.9772	.9778	.9783	.9788	.9793	.9798	.9803	.9808	.9812	.9817
2.1	.9821	.9826	.9830	.9834	.9838	.9842	.9846	.9850	.9854	.9857
2.2	.9861	.9864	.9868	.9871	.9875	.9878	.9881	.9884	.9887	.9890
2.3	.9893	.9896	.9898	.9901	.9904	.9906	.9909	.9911	.9913	.9916
2.4	.9918	.9920	.9922	.9925	.9927	.9929	.9931	.9932	.9934	.9936
2.5	.9938	.9940	.9941	.9943	.9945	.9946	.9948	.9949	.9951	.9952
2.6	.9953	.9955	.9956	.9957	.9959	.9960	.9961	.9962	.9963	.9964
2.7	.9965	.9966	.9967	.9968	.9969	.9970	.9971	.9972	.9973	.9974
2.8	.9974	.9975	.9976	.9977	.9977	.9978	.9979	.9979	.9980	.9981
2.9	.9981	.9982	.9982	.9983	.9984	.9984	.9985	.9985	.9986	.9986
3.0	.99865	.99869	.99874	.99878	.99882	.99886	.99889	.99893	.99896	.99900
3.1	.99903	.99906	.99910	.99913	.99916	.99918	.99921	.99924	.99926	.99929
3.2	.99931	.99934	.99936	.99938	.99940	.99942	.99944	.99946	.99948	.99950
3.3	.99952	.99953	.99955	.99957	.99958	.99960	.99961	.99962	.99964	.99965
3.4	.99966	.99968	.99969	.99970	.99971	.99972	.99973	.99974	.99975	.99976
3.5	.99977	.99978	.99978	.99979	.99980	.99981	.99981	.99982	.99983	.99983
3.6	.99984	.99985	.99985	.99986	.99986	.99987	.99987	.99988	.99988	.99989
3.7	.99989	.99990	.99990	.99990	.99991	.99991	.99992	.99992	.99992	.99992

APPENDIX

STUDENT'S *t* CRITICAL VALUES

This table shows the *t*-value that defines the area for the stated degrees of freedom (v).

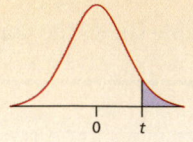

	Confidence Level						Confidence Level			
	.80	.90	.95	.98	.99		.80	.90	.95	.98	.99
	Significance Level for Two-Tailed Test						Significance Level for Two-Tailed Test				
	.20	.10	.05	.02	.01		.20	.10	.05	.02	.01
	Significance Level for One-Tailed Test						Significance Level for One-Tailed Test				
v	.10	.05	.025	.01	.005	v	.10	.05	.025	.01	.005
1	3.078	6.314	12.706	31.821	63.656	36	1.306	1.688	2.028	2.434	2.719
2	1.886	2.920	4.303	6.965	9.925	37	1.305	1.687	2.026	2.431	2.715
3	1.638	2.353	3.182	4.541	5.841	38	1.304	1.686	2.024	2.429	2.712
4	1.533	2.132	2.776	3.747	4.604	39	1.304	1.685	2.023	2.426	2.708
5	1.476	2.015	2.571	3.365	4.032	40	1.303	1.684	2.021	2.423	2.704
6	1.440	1.943	2.447	3.143	3.707	41	1.303	1.683	2.020	2.421	2.701
7	1.415	1.895	2.365	2.998	3.499	42	1.302	1.682	2.018	2.418	2.698
8	1.397	1.860	2.306	2.896	3.355	43	1.302	1.681	2.017	2.416	2.695
9	1.383	1.833	2.262	2.821	3.250	44	1.301	1.680	2.015	2.414	2.692
10	1.372	1.812	2.228	2.764	3.169	45	1.301	1.679	2.014	2.412	2.690
11	1.363	1.796	2.201	2.718	3.106	46	1.300	1.679	2.013	2.410	2.687
12	1.356	1.782	2.179	2.681	3.055	47	1.300	1.678	2.012	2.408	2.685
13	1.350	1.771	2.160	2.650	3.012	48	1.299	1.677	2.011	2.407	2.682
14	1.345	1.761	2.145	2.624	2.977	49	1.299	1.677	2.010	2.405	2.680
15	1.341	1.753	2.131	2.602	2.947	50	1.299	1.676	2.009	2.403	2.678
16	1.337	1.746	2.120	2.583	2.921	55	1.297	1.673	2.004	2.396	2.668
17	1.333	1.740	2.110	2.567	2.898	60	1.296	1.671	2.000	2.390	2.660
18	1.330	1.734	2.101	2.552	2.878	65	1.295	1.669	1.997	2.385	2.654
19	1.328	1.729	2.093	2.539	2.861	70	1.294	1.667	1.994	2.381	2.648
20	1.325	1.725	2.086	2.528	2.845	75	1.293	1.665	1.992	2.377	2.643
21	1.323	1.721	2.080	2.518	2.831	80	1.292	1.664	1.990	2.374	2.639
22	1.321	1.717	2.074	2.508	2.819	85	1.292	1.663	1.988	2.371	2.635
23	1.319	1.714	2.069	2.500	2.807	90	1.291	1.662	1.987	2.368	2.632
24	1.318	1.711	2.064	2.492	2.797	95	1.291	1.661	1.985	2.366	2.629
25	1.316	1.708	2.060	2.485	2.787	100	1.290	1.660	1.984	2.364	2.626
26	1.315	1.706	2.056	2.479	2.779	110	1.289	1.659	1.982	2.361	2.621
27	1.314	1.703	2.052	2.473	2.771	120	1.289	1.658	1.980	2.358	2.617
28	1.313	1.701	2.048	2.467	2.763	130	1.288	1.657	1.978	2.355	2.614
29	1.311	1.699	2.045	2.462	2.756	140	1.288	1.656	1.977	2.353	2.611
30	1.310	1.697	2.042	2.457	2.750	150	1.287	1.655	1.976	2.351	2.609
31	1.309	1.696	2.040	2.453	2.744	∞	1.282	1.645	1.960	2.326	2.576
32	1.309	1.694	2.037	2.449	2.738						
33	1.308	1.692	2.035	2.445	2.733						
34	1.307	1.691	2.032	2.441	2.728						
35	1.306	1.690	2.030	2.438	2.724						

Note: As *n* increases, critical values of Student's *t* approach the *z*-values in the last line of this table. A common rule of thumb is to use *z* when *n* > 30, but that is *not* conservative.

APPENDIX

CHI-SQUARE CRITICAL VALUES

This table shows the critical value for the tail areas for the stated degrees of freedom (ν).

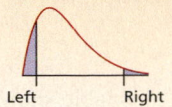

Left   Right

	Left-Tail Area						Right-Tail Area				
ν	.005	.01	.025	.05	.10		.10	.05	.025	.01	.005
1	0.000	0.000	0.001	0.004	0.016		2.706	3.841	5.024	6.635	7.879
2	0.010	0.020	0.051	0.103	0.211		4.605	5.991	7.378	9.210	10.60
3	0.072	0.115	0.216	0.352	0.584		6.251	7.815	9.348	11.34	12.84
4	0.207	0.297	0.484	0.711	1.064		7.779	9.488	11.14	13.28	14.86
5	0.412	0.554	0.831	1.145	1.610		9.236	11.07	12.83	15.09	16.75
6	0.676	0.872	1.237	1.635	2.204		10.64	12.59	14.45	16.81	18.55
7	0.989	1.239	1.690	2.167	2.833		12.02	14.07	16.01	18.48	20.28
8	1.344	1.647	2.180	2.733	3.490		13.36	15.51	17.53	20.09	21.95
9	1.735	2.088	2.700	3.325	4.168		14.68	16.92	19.02	21.67	23.59
10	2.156	2.558	3.247	3.940	4.865		15.99	18.31	20.48	23.21	25.19
11	2.603	3.053	3.816	4.575	5.578		17.28	19.68	21.92	24.73	26.76
12	3.074	3.571	4.404	5.226	6.304		18.55	21.03	23.34	26.22	28.30
13	3.565	4.107	5.009	5.892	7.041		19.81	22.36	24.74	27.69	29.82
14	4.075	4.660	5.629	6.571	7.790		21.06	23.68	26.12	29.14	31.32
15	4.601	5.229	6.262	7.261	8.547		22.31	25.00	27.49	30.58	32.80
16	5.142	5.812	6.908	7.962	9.312		23.54	26.30	28.85	32.00	34.27
17	5.697	6.408	7.564	8.672	10.09		24.77	27.59	30.19	33.41	35.72
18	6.265	7.015	8.231	9.390	10.86		25.99	28.87	31.53	34.81	37.16
19	6.844	7.633	8.907	10.12	11.65		27.20	30.14	32.85	36.19	38.58
20	7.434	8.260	9.591	10.85	12.44		28.41	31.41	34.17	37.57	40.00
21	8.034	8.897	10.28	11.59	13.24		29.62	32.67	35.48	38.93	41.40
22	8.643	9.542	10.98	12.34	14.04		30.81	33.92	36.78	40.29	42.80
23	9.260	10.20	11.69	13.09	14.85		32.01	35.17	38.08	41.64	44.18
24	9.886	10.86	12.40	13.85	15.66		33.20	36.42	39.36	42.98	45.56
25	10.52	11.52	13.12	14.61	16.47		34.38	37.65	40.65	44.31	46.93
26	11.16	12.20	13.84	15.38	17.29		35.56	38.89	41.92	45.64	48.29
27	11.81	12.88	14.57	16.15	18.11		36.74	40.11	43.19	46.96	49.65
28	12.46	13.56	15.31	16.93	18.94		37.92	41.34	44.46	48.28	50.99
29	13.12	14.26	16.05	17.71	19.77		39.09	42.56	45.72	49.59	52.34
30	13.79	14.95	16.79	18.49	20.60		40.26	43.77	46.98	50.89	53.67
31	14.46	15.66	17.54	19.28	21.43		41.42	44.99	48.23	52.19	55.00
32	15.13	16.36	18.29	20.07	22.27		42.58	46.19	49.48	53.49	56.33
33	15.82	17.07	19.05	20.87	23.11		43.75	47.40	50.73	54.78	57.65
34	16.50	17.79	19.81	21.66	23.95		44.90	48.60	51.97	56.06	58.96
35	17.19	18.51	20.57	22.47	24.80		46.06	49.80	53.20	57.34	60.27
36	17.89	19.23	21.34	23.27	25.64		47.21	51.00	54.44	58.62	61.58
37	18.59	19.96	22.11	24.07	26.49		48.36	52.19	55.67	59.89	62.88
38	19.29	20.69	22.88	24.88	27.34		49.51	53.38	56.90	61.16	64.18
39	20.00	21.43	23.65	25.70	28.20		50.66	54.57	58.12	62.43	65.48
40	20.71	22.16	24.43	26.51	29.05		51.81	55.76	59.34	63.69	66.77
50	27.99	29.71	32.36	34.76	37.69		63.17	67.50	71.42	76.15	79.49
60	35.53	37.48	40.48	43.19	46.46		74.40	79.08	83.30	88.38	91.95
70	43.28	45.44	48.76	51.74	55.33		85.53	90.53	95.02	100.4	104.2
80	51.17	53.54	57.15	60.39	64.28		96.58	101.9	106.6	112.3	116.3
90	59.20	61.75	65.65	69.13	73.29		107.6	113.1	118.1	124.1	128.3
100	67.33	70.06	74.22	77.93	82.36		118.5	124.3	129.6	135.8	140.2

APPENDIX

CRITICAL VALUES OF $F_{.10}$

This table shows the 10 percent right-tail critical values of F for the stated degrees of freedom (v).

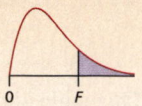

Denominator Degrees of Freedom (v_2)	Numerator Degrees of Freedom (v_1)										
	1	2	3	4	5	6	7	8	9	10	12
1	39.86	49.50	53.59	55.83	57.24	58.20	58.91	59.44	59.86	60.19	60.71
2	8.53	9.00	9.16	9.24	9.29	9.33	9.35	9.37	9.38	9.39	9.41
3	5.54	5.46	5.39	5.34	5.31	5.28	5.27	5.25	5.24	5.23	5.22
4	4.54	4.32	4.19	4.11	4.05	4.01	3.98	3.95	3.94	3.92	3.90
5	4.06	3.78	3.62	3.52	3.45	3.40	3.37	3.34	3.32	3.30	3.27
6	3.78	3.46	3.29	3.18	3.11	3.05	3.01	2.98	2.96	2.94	2.90
7	3.59	3.26	3.07	2.96	2.88	2.83	2.78	2.75	2.72	2.70	2.67
8	3.46	3.11	2.92	2.81	2.73	2.67	2.62	2.59	2.56	2.54	2.50
9	3.36	3.01	2.81	2.69	2.61	2.55	2.51	2.47	2.44	2.42	2.38
10	3.29	2.92	2.73	2.61	2.52	2.46	2.41	2.38	2.35	2.32	2.28
11	3.23	2.86	2.66	2.54	2.45	2.39	2.34	2.30	2.27	2.25	2.21
12	3.18	2.81	2.61	2.48	2.39	2.33	2.28	2.24	2.21	2.19	2.15
13	3.14	2.76	2.56	2.43	2.35	2.28	2.23	2.20	2.16	2.14	2.10
14	3.10	2.73	2.52	2.39	2.31	2.24	2.19	2.15	2.12	2.10	2.05
15	3.07	2.70	2.49	2.36	2.27	2.21	2.16	2.12	2.09	2.06	2.02
16	3.05	2.67	2.46	2.33	2.24	2.18	2.13	2.09	2.06	2.03	1.99
17	3.03	2.64	2.44	2.31	2.22	2.15	2.10	2.06	2.03	2.00	1.96
18	3.01	2.62	2.42	2.29	2.20	2.13	2.08	2.04	2.00	1.98	1.93
19	2.99	2.61	2.40	2.27	2.18	2.11	2.06	2.02	1.98	1.96	1.91
20	2.97	2.59	2.38	2.25	2.16	2.09	2.04	2.00	1.96	1.94	1.89
21	2.96	2.57	2.36	2.23	2.14	2.08	2.02	1.98	1.95	1.92	1.87
22	2.95	2.56	2.35	2.22	2.13	2.06	2.01	1.97	1.93	1.90	1.86
23	2.94	2.55	2.34	2.21	2.11	2.05	1.99	1.95	1.92	1.89	1.84
24	2.93	2.54	2.33	2.19	2.10	2.04	1.98	1.94	1.91	1.88	1.83
25	2.92	2.53	2.32	2.18	2.09	2.02	1.97	1.93	1.89	1.87	1.82
26	2.91	2.52	2.31	2.17	2.08	2.01	1.96	1.92	1.88	1.86	1.81
27	2.90	2.51	2.30	2.17	2.07	2.00	1.95	1.91	1.87	1.85	1.80
28	2.89	2.50	2.29	2.16	2.06	2.00	1.94	1.90	1.87	1.84	1.79
29	2.89	2.50	2.28	2.15	2.06	1.99	1.93	1.89	1.86	1.83	1.78
30	2.88	2.49	2.28	2.14	2.05	1.98	1.93	1.88	1.85	1.82	1.77
40	2.84	2.44	2.23	2.09	2.00	1.93	1.87	1.83	1.79	1.76	1.71
50	2.81	2.41	2.20	2.06	1.97	1.90	1.84	1.80	1.76	1.73	1.68
60	2.79	2.39	2.18	2.04	1.95	1.87	1.82	1.77	1.74	1.71	1.66
120	2.75	2.35	2.13	1.99	1.90	1.82	1.77	1.72	1.68	1.65	1.60
200	2.73	2.33	2.11	1.97	1.88	1.80	1.75	1.70	1.66	1.63	1.58
∞	2.71	2.30	2.08	1.94	1.85	1.77	1.72	1.67	1.63	1.60	1.55

Denominator Degrees of Freedom (ν_2)	Numerator Degrees of Freedom (ν_1)										
	15	20	25	30	35	40	50	60	120	200	∞
1	61.22	61.74	62.05	62.26	62.42	62.53	62.69	62.79	63.06	63.17	63.32
2	9.42	9.44	9.45	9.46	9.46	9.47	9.47	9.47	9.48	9.49	9.49
3	5.20	5.18	5.17	5.17	5.16	5.16	5.15	5.15	5.14	5.14	5.13
4	3.87	3.84	3.83	3.82	3.81	3.80	3.80	3.79	3.78	3.77	3.76
5	3.24	3.21	3.19	3.17	3.16	3.16	3.15	3.14	3.12	3.12	3.11
6	2.87	2.84	2.81	2.80	2.79	2.78	2.77	2.76	2.74	2.73	2.72
7	2.63	2.59	2.57	2.56	2.54	2.54	2.52	2.51	2.49	2.48	2.47
8	2.46	2.42	2.40	2.38	2.37	2.36	2.35	2.34	2.32	2.31	2.29
9	2.34	2.30	2.27	2.25	2.24	2.23	2.22	2.21	2.18	2.17	2.16
10	2.24	2.20	2.17	2.16	2.14	2.13	2.12	2.11	2.08	2.07	2.06
11	2.17	2.12	2.10	2.08	2.06	2.05	2.04	2.03	2.00	1.99	1.97
12	2.10	2.06	2.03	2.01	2.00	1.99	1.97	1.96	1.93	1.92	1.90
13	2.05	2.01	1.98	1.96	1.94	1.93	1.92	1.90	1.88	1.86	1.85
14	2.01	1.96	1.93	1.91	1.90	1.89	1.87	1.86	1.83	1.82	1.80
15	1.97	1.92	1.89	1.87	1.86	1.85	1.83	1.82	1.79	1.77	1.76
16	1.94	1.89	1.86	1.84	1.82	1.81	1.79	1.78	1.75	1.74	1.72
17	1.91	1.86	1.83	1.81	1.79	1.78	1.76	1.75	1.72	1.71	1.69
18	1.89	1.84	1.80	1.78	1.77	1.75	1.74	1.72	1.69	1.68	1.66
19	1.86	1.81	1.78	1.76	1.74	1.73	1.71	1.70	1.67	1.65	1.63
20	1.84	1.79	1.76	1.74	1.72	1.71	1.69	1.68	1.64	1.63	1.61
21	1.83	1.78	1.74	1.72	1.70	1.69	1.67	1.66	1.62	1.61	1.59
22	1.81	1.76	1.73	1.70	1.68	1.67	1.65	1.64	1.60	1.59	1.57
23	1.80	1.74	1.71	1.69	1.67	1.66	1.64	1.62	1.59	1.57	1.55
24	1.78	1.73	1.70	1.67	1.65	1.64	1.62	1.61	1.57	1.56	1.53
25	1.77	1.72	1.68	1.66	1.64	1.63	1.61	1.59	1.56	1.54	1.52
26	1.76	1.71	1.67	1.65	1.63	1.61	1.59	1.58	1.54	1.53	1.50
27	1.75	1.70	1.66	1.64	1.62	1.60	1.58	1.57	1.53	1.52	1.49
28	1.74	1.69	1.65	1.63	1.61	1.59	1.57	1.56	1.52	1.50	1.48
29	1.73	1.68	1.64	1.62	1.60	1.58	1.56	1.55	1.51	1.49	1.47
30	1.72	1.67	1.63	1.61	1.59	1.57	1.55	1.54	1.50	1.48	1.46
40	1.66	1.61	1.57	1.54	1.52	1.51	1.48	1.47	1.42	1.41	1.38
50	1.63	1.57	1.53	1.50	1.48	1.46	1.44	1.42	1.38	1.36	1.33
60	1.60	1.54	1.50	1.48	1.45	1.44	1.41	1.40	1.35	1.33	1.29
120	1.55	1.48	1.44	1.41	1.39	1.37	1.34	1.32	1.26	1.24	1.19
200	1.52	1.46	1.41	1.38	1.36	1.34	1.31	1.29	1.23	1.20	1.15
∞	2.71	1.49	1.42	1.38	1.34	1.32	1.30	1.26	1.24	1.17	1.13

CRITICAL VALUES OF $F_{.05}$

This table shows the 5 percent right-tail critical values of F for the stated degrees of freedom (v).

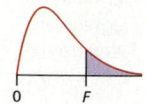

Denominator Degrees of Freedom (v_2)	Numerator Degrees of Freedom (v_1)										
	1	2	3	4	5	6	7	8	9	10	12
1	161.4	199.5	215.7	224.6	230.2	234.0	236.8	238.9	240.5	241.9	243.9
2	18.51	19.00	19.16	19.25	19.30	19.33	19.35	19.37	19.38	19.40	19.41
3	10.13	9.55	9.28	9.12	9.01	8.94	8.89	8.85	8.81	8.79	8.74
4	7.71	6.94	6.59	6.39	6.26	6.16	6.09	6.04	6.00	5.96	5.91
5	6.61	5.79	5.41	5.19	5.05	4.95	4.88	4.82	4.77	4.74	4.68
6	5.99	5.14	4.76	4.53	4.39	4.28	4.21	4.15	4.10	4.06	4.00
7	5.59	4.74	4.35	4.12	3.97	3.87	3.79	3.73	3.68	3.64	3.57
8	5.32	4.46	4.07	3.84	3.69	3.58	3.50	3.44	3.39	3.35	3.28
9	5.12	4.26	3.86	3.63	3.48	3.37	3.29	3.23	3.18	3.14	3.07
10	4.96	4.10	3.71	3.48	3.33	3.22	3.14	3.07	3.02	2.98	2.91
11	4.84	3.98	3.59	3.36	3.20	3.09	3.01	2.95	2.90	2.85	2.79
12	4.75	3.89	3.49	3.26	3.11	3.00	2.91	2.85	2.80	2.75	2.69
13	4.67	3.81	3.41	3.18	3.03	2.92	2.83	2.77	2.71	2.67	2.60
14	4.60	3.74	3.34	3.11	2.96	2.85	2.76	2.70	2.65	2.60	2.53
15	4.54	3.68	3.29	3.06	2.90	2.79	2.71	2.64	2.59	2.54	2.48
16	4.49	3.63	3.24	3.01	2.85	2.74	2.66	2.59	2.54	2.49	2.42
17	4.45	3.59	3.20	2.96	2.81	2.70	2.61	2.55	2.49	2.45	2.38
18	4.41	3.55	3.16	2.93	2.77	2.66	2.58	2.51	2.46	2.41	2.34
19	4.38	3.52	3.13	2.90	2.74	2.63	2.54	2.48	2.42	2.38	2.31
20	4.35	3.49	3.10	2.87	2.71	2.60	2.51	2.45	2.39	2.35	2.28
21	4.32	3.47	3.07	2.84	2.68	2.57	2.49	2.42	2.37	2.32	2.25
22	4.30	3.44	3.05	2.82	2.66	2.55	2.46	2.40	2.34	2.30	2.23
23	4.28	3.42	3.03	2.80	2.64	2.53	2.44	2.37	2.32	2.27	2.20
24	4.26	3.40	3.01	2.78	2.62	2.51	2.42	2.36	2.30	2.25	2.18
25	4.24	3.39	2.99	2.76	2.60	2.49	2.40	2.34	2.28	2.24	2.16
26	4.23	3.37	2.98	2.74	2.59	2.47	2.39	2.32	2.27	2.22	2.15
27	4.21	3.35	2.96	2.73	2.57	2.46	2.37	2.31	2.25	2.20	2.13
28	4.20	3.34	2.95	2.71	2.56	2.45	2.36	2.29	2.24	2.19	2.12
29	4.18	3.33	2.93	2.70	2.55	2.43	2.35	2.28	2.22	2.18	2.10
30	4.17	3.32	2.92	2.69	2.53	2.42	2.33	2.27	2.21	2.16	2.09
40	4.08	3.23	2.84	2.61	2.45	2.34	2.25	2.18	2.12	2.08	2.00
50	4.03	3.18	2.79	2.56	2.40	2.29	2.20	2.13	2.07	2.03	1.95
60	4.00	3.15	2.76	2.53	2.37	2.25	2.17	2.10	2.04	1.99	1.92
120	3.92	3.07	2.68	2.45	2.29	2.18	2.09	2.02	1.96	1.91	1.83
200	3.89	3.04	2.65	2.42	2.26	2.14	2.06	1.98	1.93	1.88	1.80
∞	2.71	3.84	3.00	2.60	2.37	2.21	2.10	2.01	1.94	1.88	1.83

Denominator Degrees of Freedom (v_2)	Numerator Degrees of Freedom (v_1)										
	15	20	25	30	35	40	50	60	120	200	∞
1	245.9	248.0	249.3	250.1	250.7	251.1	251.8	252.2	253.3	253.7	254.3
2	19.43	19.45	19.46	19.46	19.47	19.47	19.48	19.48	19.49	19.49	19.50
3	8.70	8.66	8.63	8.62	8.60	8.59	8.58	8.57	8.55	8.54	8.53
4	5.86	5.80	5.77	5.75	5.73	5.72	5.70	5.69	5.66	5.65	5.63
5	4.62	4.56	4.52	4.50	4.48	4.46	4.44	4.43	4.40	4.39	4.37
6	3.94	3.87	3.83	3.81	3.79	3.77	3.75	3.74	3.70	3.69	3.67
7	3.51	3.44	3.40	3.38	3.36	3.34	3.32	3.30	3.27	3.25	3.23
8	3.22	3.15	3.11	3.08	3.06	3.04	3.02	3.01	2.97	2.95	2.93
9	3.01	2.94	2.89	2.86	2.84	2.83	2.80	2.79	2.75	2.73	2.71
10	2.85	2.77	2.73	2.70	2.68	2.66	2.64	2.62	2.58	2.56	2.54
11	2.72	2.65	2.60	2.57	2.55	2.53	2.51	2.49	2.45	2.43	2.41
12	2.62	2.54	2.50	2.47	2.44	2.43	2.40	2.38	2.34	2.32	2.30
13	2.53	2.46	2.41	2.38	2.36	2.34	2.31	2.30	2.25	2.23	2.21
14	2.46	2.39	2.34	2.31	2.28	2.27	2.24	2.22	2.18	2.16	2.13
15	2.40	2.33	2.28	2.25	2.22	2.20	2.18	2.16	2.11	2.10	2.07
16	2.35	2.28	2.23	2.19	2.17	2.15	2.12	2.11	2.06	2.04	2.01
17	2.31	2.23	2.18	2.15	2.12	2.10	2.08	2.06	2.01	1.99	1.96
18	2.27	2.19	2.14	2.11	2.08	2.06	2.04	2.02	1.97	1.95	1.92
19	2.23	2.16	2.11	2.07	2.05	2.03	2.00	1.98	1.93	1.91	1.88
20	2.20	2.12	2.07	2.04	2.01	1.99	1.97	1.95	1.90	1.88	1.84
21	2.18	2.10	2.05	2.01	1.98	1.96	1.94	1.92	1.87	1.84	1.81
22	2.15	2.07	2.02	1.98	1.96	1.94	1.91	1.89	1.84	1.82	1.78
23	2.13	2.05	2.00	1.96	1.93	1.91	1.88	1.86	1.81	1.79	1.76
24	2.11	2.03	1.97	1.94	1.91	1.89	1.86	1.84	1.79	1.77	1.73
25	2.09	2.01	1.96	1.92	1.89	1.87	1.84	1.82	1.77	1.75	1.71
26	2.07	1.99	1.94	1.90	1.87	1.85	1.82	1.80	1.75	1.73	1.69
27	2.06	1.97	1.92	1.88	1.86	1.84	1.81	1.79	1.73	1.71	1.67
28	2.04	1.96	1.91	1.87	1.84	1.82	1.79	1.77	1.71	1.69	1.66
29	2.03	1.94	1.89	1.85	1.83	1.81	1.77	1.75	1.70	1.67	1.64
30	2.01	1.93	1.88	1.84	1.81	1.79	1.76	1.74	1.68	1.66	1.62
40	1.92	1.84	1.78	1.74	1.72	1.69	1.66	1.64	1.58	1.55	1.51
50	1.87	1.78	1.73	1.69	1.66	1.63	1.60	1.58	1.51	1.48	1.44
60	1.84	1.75	1.69	1.65	1.62	1.59	1.56	1.53	1.47	1.44	1.39
120	1.75	1.66	1.60	1.55	1.52	1.50	1.46	1.43	1.35	1.32	1.26
200	1.72	1.62	1.56	1.52	1.48	1.46	1.41	1.39	1.30	1.26	1.19
∞	2.71	1.67	1.57	1.51	1.46	1.42	1.39	1.35	1.32	1.22	1.17

CRITICAL VALUES OF $F_{.025}$

This table shows the 2.5 percent right-tail critical values of F for the stated degrees of freedom (v).

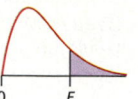

Denominator Degrees of Freedom (v_2)	Numerator Degrees of Freedom (v_1)										
	1	2	3	4	5	6	7	8	9	10	12
1	647.8	799.5	864.2	899.6	921.8	937.1	948.2	956.6	963.3	968.6	976.7
2	38.51	39.00	39.17	39.25	39.30	39.33	39.36	39.37	39.39	39.40	39.41
3	17.44	16.04	15.44	15.10	14.88	14.73	14.62	14.54	14.47	14.42	14.34
4	12.22	10.65	9.98	9.60	9.36	9.20	9.07	8.98	8.90	8.84	8.75
5	10.01	8.43	7.76	7.39	7.15	6.98	6.85	6.76	6.68	6.62	6.52
6	8.81	7.26	6.60	6.23	5.99	5.82	5.70	5.60	5.52	5.46	5.37
7	8.07	6.54	5.89	5.52	5.29	5.12	4.99	4.90	4.82	4.76	4.67
8	7.57	6.06	5.42	5.05	4.82	4.65	4.53	4.43	4.36	4.30	4.20
9	7.21	5.71	5.08	4.72	4.48	4.32	4.20	4.10	4.03	3.96	3.87
10	6.94	5.46	4.83	4.47	4.24	4.07	3.95	3.85	3.78	3.72	3.62
11	6.72	5.26	4.63	4.28	4.04	3.88	3.76	3.66	3.59	3.53	3.43
12	6.55	5.10	4.47	4.12	3.89	3.73	3.61	3.51	3.44	3.37	3.28
13	6.41	4.97	4.35	4.00	3.77	3.60	3.48	3.39	3.31	3.25	3.15
14	6.30	4.86	4.24	3.89	3.66	3.50	3.38	3.29	3.21	3.15	3.05
15	6.20	4.77	4.15	3.80	3.58	3.41	3.29	3.20	3.12	3.06	2.96
16	6.12	4.69	4.08	3.73	3.50	3.34	3.22	3.12	3.05	2.99	2.89
17	6.04	4.62	4.01	3.66	3.44	3.28	3.16	3.06	2.98	2.92	2.82
18	5.98	4.56	3.95	3.61	3.38	3.22	3.10	3.01	2.93	2.87	2.77
19	5.92	4.51	3.90	3.56	3.33	3.17	3.05	2.96	2.88	2.82	2.72
20	5.87	4.46	3.86	3.51	3.29	3.13	3.01	2.91	2.84	2.77	2.68
21	5.83	4.42	3.82	3.48	3.25	3.09	2.97	2.87	2.80	2.73	2.64
22	5.79	4.38	3.78	3.44	3.22	3.05	2.93	2.84	2.76	2.70	2.60
23	5.75	4.35	3.75	3.41	3.18	3.02	2.90	2.81	2.73	2.67	2.57
24	5.72	4.32	3.72	3.38	3.15	2.99	2.87	2.78	2.70	2.64	2.54
25	5.69	4.29	3.69	3.35	3.13	2.97	2.85	2.75	2.68	2.61	2.51
26	5.66	4.27	3.67	3.33	3.10	2.94	2.82	2.73	2.65	2.59	2.49
27	5.63	4.24	3.65	3.31	3.08	2.92	2.80	2.71	2.63	2.57	2.47
28	5.61	4.22	3.63	3.29	3.06	2.90	2.78	2.69	2.61	2.55	2.45
29	5.59	4.20	3.61	3.27	3.04	2.88	2.76	2.67	2.59	2.53	2.43
30	5.57	4.18	3.59	3.25	3.03	2.87	2.75	2.65	2.57	2.51	2.41
40	5.42	4.05	3.46	3.13	2.90	2.74	2.62	2.53	2.45	2.39	2.29
50	5.34	3.97	3.39	3.05	2.83	2.67	2.55	2.46	2.38	2.32	2.22
60	5.29	3.93	3.34	3.01	2.79	2.63	2.51	2.41	2.33	2.27	2.17
120	5.15	3.80	3.23	2.89	2.67	2.52	2.39	2.30	2.22	2.16	2.05
200	5.10	3.76	3.18	2.85	2.63	2.47	2.35	2.26	2.18	2.11	2.01
∞	2.71	5.02	3.69	3.12	2.79	2.57	2.41	2.29	2.19	2.11	2.05

Denominator Degrees of Freedom (ν_2)	Numerator Degrees of Freedom (ν_1)										
	15	20	25	30	35	40	50	60	120	200	∞
1	984.9	993.1	998.1	1001	1004	1006	1008	1010	1014	1016	1018
2	39.43	39.45	39.46	39.46	39.47	39.47	39.48	39.48	39.49	39.49	39.50
3	14.25	14.17	14.12	14.08	14.06	14.04	14.01	13.99	13.95	13.93	13.90
4	8.66	8.56	8.50	8.46	8.43	8.41	8.38	8.36	8.31	8.29	8.26
5	6.43	6.33	6.27	6.23	6.20	6.18	6.14	6.12	6.07	6.05	6.02
6	5.27	5.17	5.11	5.07	5.04	5.01	4.98	4.96	4.90	4.88	4.85
7	4.57	4.47	4.40	4.36	4.33	4.31	4.28	4.25	4.20	4.18	4.14
8	4.10	4.00	3.94	3.89	3.86	3.84	3.81	3.78	3.73	3.70	3.67
9	3.77	3.67	3.60	3.56	3.53	3.51	3.47	3.45	3.39	3.37	3.33
10	3.52	3.42	3.35	3.31	3.28	3.26	3.22	3.20	3.14	3.12	3.08
11	3.33	3.23	3.16	3.12	3.09	3.06	3.03	3.00	2.94	2.92	2.88
12	3.18	3.07	3.01	2.96	2.93	2.91	2.87	2.85	2.79	2.76	2.73
13	3.05	2.95	2.88	2.84	2.80	2.78	2.74	2.72	2.66	2.63	2.60
14	2.95	2.84	2.78	2.73	2.70	2.67	2.64	2.61	2.55	2.53	2.49
15	2.86	2.76	2.69	2.64	2.61	2.59	2.55	2.52	2.46	2.44	2.40
16	2.79	2.68	2.61	2.57	2.53	2.51	2.47	2.45	2.38	2.36	2.32
17	2.72	2.62	2.55	2.50	2.47	2.44	2.41	2.38	2.32	2.29	2.25
18	2.67	2.56	2.49	2.44	2.41	2.38	2.35	2.32	2.26	2.23	2.19
19	2.62	2.51	2.44	2.39	2.36	2.33	2.30	2.27	2.20	2.18	2.13
20	2.57	2.46	2.40	2.35	2.31	2.29	2.25	2.22	2.16	2.13	2.09
21	2.53	2.42	2.36	2.31	2.27	2.25	2.21	2.18	2.11	2.09	2.04
22	2.50	2.39	2.32	2.27	2.24	2.21	2.17	2.14	2.08	2.05	2.01
23	2.47	2.36	2.29	2.24	2.20	2.18	2.14	2.11	2.04	2.01	1.97
24	2.44	2.33	2.26	2.21	2.17	2.15	2.11	2.08	2.01	1.98	1.94
25	2.41	2.30	2.23	2.18	2.15	2.12	2.08	2.05	1.98	1.95	1.91
26	2.39	2.28	2.21	2.16	2.12	2.09	2.05	2.03	1.95	1.92	1.88
27	2.36	2.25	2.18	2.13	2.10	2.07	2.03	2.00	1.93	1.90	1.85
28	2.34	2.23	2.16	2.11	2.08	2.05	2.01	1.98	1.91	1.88	1.83
29	2.32	2.21	2.14	2.09	2.06	2.03	1.99	1.96	1.89	1.86	1.81
30	2.31	2.20	2.12	2.07	2.04	2.01	1.97	1.94	1.87	1.84	1.79
40	2.18	2.07	1.99	1.94	1.90	1.88	1.83	1.80	1.72	1.69	1.64
50	2.11	1.99	1.92	1.87	1.83	1.80	1.75	1.72	1.64	1.60	1.55
60	2.06	1.94	1.87	1.82	1.78	1.74	1.70	1.67	1.58	1.54	1.48
120	1.94	1.82	1.75	1.69	1.65	1.61	1.56	1.53	1.43	1.39	1.31
200	1.90	1.78	1.70	1.64	1.60	1.56	1.51	1.47	1.37	1.32	1.23
∞	2.71	1.83	1.71	1.63	1.57	1.52	1.48	1.43	1.39	1.27	1.21

CRITICAL VALUES OF $F_{.01}$

This table shows the 1 percent right-tail critical values of F for the stated degrees of freedom (v).

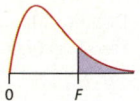

Denominator Degrees of Freedom (v_2)	Numerator Degrees of Freedom (v_1)										
	1	2	3	4	5	6	7	8	9	10	12
1	4052	4999	5404	5624	5764	5859	5928	5981	6022	6056	6107
2	98.50	99.00	99.16	99.25	99.30	99.33	99.36	99.38	99.39	99.40	99.42
3	34.12	30.82	29.46	28.71	28.24	27.91	27.67	27.49	27.34	27.23	27.05
4	21.20	18.00	16.69	15.98	15.52	15.21	14.98	14.80	14.66	14.55	14.37
5	16.26	13.27	12.06	11.39	10.97	10.67	10.46	10.29	10.16	10.05	9.89
6	13.75	10.92	9.78	9.15	8.75	8.47	8.26	8.10	7.98	7.87	7.72
7	12.25	9.55	8.45	7.85	7.46	7.19	6.99	6.84	6.72	6.62	6.47
8	11.26	8.65	7.59	7.01	6.63	6.37	6.18	6.03	5.91	5.81	5.67
9	10.56	8.02	6.99	6.42	6.06	5.80	5.61	5.47	5.35	5.26	5.11
10	10.04	7.56	6.55	5.99	5.64	5.39	5.20	5.06	4.94	4.85	4.71
11	9.65	7.21	6.22	5.67	5.32	5.07	4.89	4.74	4.63	4.54	4.40
12	9.33	6.93	5.95	5.41	5.06	4.82	4.64	4.50	4.39	4.30	4.16
13	9.07	6.70	5.74	5.21	4.86	4.62	4.44	4.30	4.19	4.10	3.96
14	8.86	6.51	5.56	5.04	4.69	4.46	4.28	4.14	4.03	3.94	3.80
15	8.68	6.36	5.42	4.89	4.56	4.32	4.14	4.00	3.89	3.80	3.67
16	8.53	6.23	5.29	4.77	4.44	4.20	4.03	3.89	3.78	3.69	3.55
17	8.40	6.11	5.19	4.67	4.34	4.10	3.93	3.79	3.68	3.59	3.46
18	8.29	6.01	5.09	4.58	4.25	4.01	3.84	3.71	3.60	3.51	3.37
19	8.18	5.93	5.01	4.50	4.17	3.94	3.77	3.63	3.52	3.43	3.30
20	8.10	5.85	4.94	4.43	4.10	3.87	3.70	3.56	3.46	3.37	3.23
21	8.02	5.78	4.87	4.37	4.04	3.81	3.64	3.51	3.40	3.31	3.17
22	7.95	5.72	4.82	4.31	3.99	3.76	3.59	3.45	3.35	3.26	3.12
23	7.88	5.66	4.76	4.26	3.94	3.71	3.54	3.41	3.30	3.21	3.07
24	7.82	5.61	4.72	4.22	3.90	3.67	3.50	3.36	3.26	3.17	3.03
25	7.77	5.57	4.68	4.18	3.85	3.63	3.46	3.32	3.22	3.13	2.99
26	7.72	5.53	4.64	4.14	3.82	3.59	3.42	3.29	3.18	3.09	2.96
27	7.68	5.49	4.60	4.11	3.78	3.56	3.39	3.26	3.15	3.06	2.93
28	7.64	5.45	4.57	4.07	3.75	3.53	3.36	3.23	3.12	3.03	2.90
29	7.60	5.42	4.54	4.04	3.73	3.50	3.33	3.20	3.09	3.00	2.87
30	7.56	5.39	4.51	4.02	3.70	3.47	3.30	3.17	3.07	2.98	2.84
40	7.31	5.18	4.31	3.83	3.51	3.29	3.12	2.99	2.89	2.80	2.66
50	7.17	5.06	4.20	3.72	3.41	3.19	3.02	2.89	2.78	2.70	2.56
60	7.08	4.98	4.13	3.65	3.34	3.12	2.95	2.82	2.72	2.63	2.50
120	6.85	4.79	3.95	3.48	3.17	2.96	2.79	2.66	2.56	2.47	2.34
200	6.76	4.71	3.88	3.41	3.11	2.89	2.73	2.60	2.50	2.41	2.27
∞	2.71	6.63	4.61	3.78	3.32	3.02	2.80	2.64	2.51	2.41	2.32

Denominator Degrees of Freedom (ν_2)	Numerator Degrees of Freedom (ν_1)										
	15	20	25	30	35	40	50	60	120	200	∞
1	6157	6209	6240	6260	6275	6286	6302	6313	6340	6350	6366
2	99.43	99.45	99.46	99.47	99.47	99.48	99.48	99.48	99.49	99.49	99.50
3	26.87	26.69	26.58	26.50	26.45	26.41	26.35	26.32	26.22	26.18	26.13
4	14.20	14.02	13.91	13.84	13.79	13.75	13.69	13.65	13.56	13.52	13.47
5	9.72	9.55	9.45	9.38	9.33	9.29	9.24	9.20	9.11	9.08	9.02
6	7.56	7.40	7.30	7.23	7.18	7.14	7.09	7.06	6.97	6.93	6.88
7	6.31	6.16	6.06	5.99	5.94	5.91	5.86	5.82	5.74	5.70	5.65
8	5.52	5.36	5.26	5.20	5.15	5.12	5.07	5.03	4.95	4.91	4.86
9	4.96	4.81	4.71	4.65	4.60	4.57	4.52	4.48	4.40	4.36	4.31
10	4.56	4.41	4.31	4.25	4.20	4.17	4.12	4.08	4.00	3.96	3.91
11	4.25	4.10	4.01	3.94	3.89	3.86	3.81	3.78	3.69	3.66	3.60
12	4.01	3.86	3.76	3.70	3.65	3.62	3.57	3.54	3.45	3.41	3.36
13	3.82	3.66	3.57	3.51	3.46	3.43	3.38	3.34	3.25	3.22	3.17
14	3.66	3.51	3.41	3.35	3.30	3.27	3.22	3.18	3.09	3.06	3.01
15	3.52	3.37	3.28	3.21	3.17	3.13	3.08	3.05	2.96	2.92	2.87
16	3.41	3.26	3.16	3.10	3.05	3.02	2.97	2.93	2.84	2.81	2.76
17	3.31	3.16	3.07	3.00	2.96	2.92	2.87	2.83	2.75	2.71	2.66
18	3.23	3.08	2.98	2.92	2.87	2.84	2.78	2.75	2.66	2.62	2.57
19	3.15	3.00	2.91	2.84	2.80	2.76	2.71	2.67	2.58	2.55	2.49
20	3.09	2.94	2.84	2.78	2.73	2.69	2.64	2.61	2.52	2.48	2.42
21	3.03	2.88	2.79	2.72	2.67	2.64	2.58	2.55	2.46	2.42	2.36
22	2.98	2.83	2.73	2.67	2.62	2.58	2.53	2.50	2.40	2.36	2.31
23	2.93	2.78	2.69	2.62	2.57	2.54	2.48	2.45	2.35	2.32	2.26
24	2.89	2.74	2.64	2.58	2.53	2.49	2.44	2.40	2.31	2.27	2.21
25	2.85	2.70	2.60	2.54	2.49	2.45	2.40	2.36	2.27	2.23	2.17
26	2.81	2.66	2.57	2.50	2.45	2.42	2.36	2.33	2.23	2.19	2.13
27	2.78	2.63	2.54	2.47	2.42	2.38	2.33	2.29	2.20	2.16	2.10
28	2.75	2.60	2.51	2.44	2.39	2.35	2.30	2.26	2.17	2.13	2.07
29	2.73	2.57	2.48	2.41	2.36	2.33	2.27	2.23	2.14	2.10	2.04
30	2.70	2.55	2.45	2.39	2.34	2.30	2.25	2.21	2.11	2.07	2.01
40	2.52	2.37	2.27	2.20	2.15	2.11	2.06	2.02	1.92	1.87	1.81
50	2.42	2.27	2.17	2.10	2.05	2.01	1.95	1.91	1.80	1.76	1.69
60	2.35	2.20	2.10	2.03	1.98	1.94	1.88	1.84	1.73	1.68	1.60
120	2.19	2.03	1.93	1.86	1.81	1.76	1.70	1.66	1.53	1.48	1.38
200	2.13	1.97	1.87	1.79	1.74	1.69	1.63	1.58	1.45	1.39	1.28
∞	2.71	2.04	1.88	1.77	1.70	1.64	1.59	1.52	1.47	1.32	1.25

APPENDIX

Solutions to Odd-Numbered Exercises

CHAPTER 1

1.5 a. Statistics summarizes data.
   b. Statistics tells us how large a sample to take.
1.7 a. Most would prefer the graph, but both are clear.
   b. A financial planner typically has 16 to 25 years experience.
1.11 a. All combinations have same chance of winning so method did not "work."
   b. No, same as any other six numbers.
1.15 a. Analyze the 80 responses but make no conclusions about nonrespondents.
   b. No, study seems too flawed.
   c. Suggest a new well-designed survey with response incentive.
1.17 a. Attendance, study time, ability level, interest level, instructor's ability, prerequisites.
   b. Reverse causation? Good students make better decisions about their health.
   c. No, causation is not shown.
1.19 A major problem is that we don't know number of students in each major.
   a. Likely fewer philosophy majors to begin with.
   b. Likely more engineers want an MBA, so they take it.
   c. Causation not shown. Physics may differ from marketing majors (e.g., math skills).
   d. The GMAT is just an indicator of academic skills.
1.21 a. "Its R^2 value is quite close to 1, indicating it is a good fit to the actual data. I feel that G.E. is one of the most respected corporations in the world because of its strong management and name recognition. Its valuable assets make it poised for steady growth over the next decade."
   b. "If a country's unemployment rate is too high, it could cause a downturn in their economy's structure."
   c. "This forecast is very unlikely, because you cannot have a negative number of people unemployed."
   d. "This is not a well-designed graph because the title is too long and there are no labels on the axes."
   e. "This graph has no clear border to give a sense of containment. It is dealing with three separate pieces of information. In this graph, the same data is presented, but in a deceptive manner. The sources do not contain enough detail."

CHAPTER 2

2.1 Observation—single data point. Variable—characteristic of an individual that takes on various values.
2.3 a. attribute   b. attribute   c. discrete numerical
   d. continuous numerical   e. continuous numerical
   f. discrete numerical   g. continuous numerical
2.7 a. ratio   b. ordinal   c. nominal   d. interval
   e. ratio   f. ordinal
2.11 a. cross-sectional   b. time series
   c. time series   d. cross-sectional
2.13 a. time series   b. cross-sectional
   c. time series   d. cross-sectional
2.15 a. Census   b. Sample   c. Sample   d. Census
2.17 a. Sample   b. Census   c. Sample   d. Census
2.19 a. Convenience   b. Systematic   c. Judgment or biased
2.25 a. Telephone or Web.   b. Direct observation.
   c. Interview, Web, or mail.   d. Interview or Web.
2.27 Version 1: Most would say yes. Version 2: More varied responses.
2.29 a. Continuous numerical   b. Attribute
   c. Discrete numerical   d. Discrete numerical
   e. Continuous numerical
2.33 Q1 Attribute, nominal   Q2 Continuous, ratio
   Q3 Attribute, nominal   Q4 Continuous, ratio
   Q5 Discrete, ratio   Q6 Discrete, ratio
   Q7 Attribute, nominal   Q8 Attribute, interval
   Q9 Continuous, ratio   Q10 Discrete, ratio
   Q11 Continuous, ratio   Q12 Discrete, ratio
   Q13 Attribute, nominal   Q14 Discrete, ratio
   Q15 Continuous, ratio   Q16 Discrete, ratio
   Q17 Attribute, ordinal   Q18 Attribute, nominal
   Q19 Attribute, ordinal   Q20 Attribute, nominal
2.35 a. statistic   b. parameter
   c. statistic   d. parameter
2.37 a. Number of employees or industry.
   b. Firms may differ in size, etc.
   c. Under representation of chemical companies.
2.39 Use mail or telephone. Census not possible.
2.41 a. Cluster sampling   b. Finite and listable   c. Yes
2.43 a. Cluster sampling.
   b. Yes, if selected stores had the same supplier.
2.45 a. Telephone or mail   b. Finite and listable

2.47 a. Yes.   b. Ordering of the list could influence sample.

2.49 a. Cluster sampling, neighborhoods are natural clusters.
   b. Impractical if potential gain is small.
   c. Picking a day near a holiday with light trash.

2.51 a. systematic.   b. simple random sample.
   c. systematic or simple random sample.
   d. simple random sample or systematic.   e. stratified.

2.53 a. Income, store type   b. Yes
   c. Simple random sample

2.55 a. No   b. Systematic

2.57 Convenience. Cost and Time.

2.59 Education and income could affect who uses the no-call list.
   a. They won't reach those who purchase such services.
   Same response for b and c.

Surveys and Scales

2.61 a. Ordinal.   b. Intervals are equal.

2.63 a. Rate the effectiveness of this professor. 1—Excellent
   to 5—Poor.
   b. Rate your satisfaction with the President's economic
   policy. 1—Very Satisfied to 5—Very dissatisfied.
   c. How long did you wait to see your doctor? Less than
   15 minutes, between 15 and 30 minutes, between 30
   minutes and 1 hour, more than 1 hour.

2.67 a. Likert

CHAPTER 3

3.1 Approximately symmetric with typical values around 25.

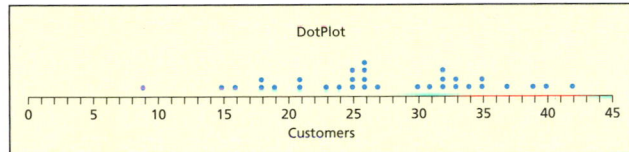

3.3 Sarah's calls are shorter.

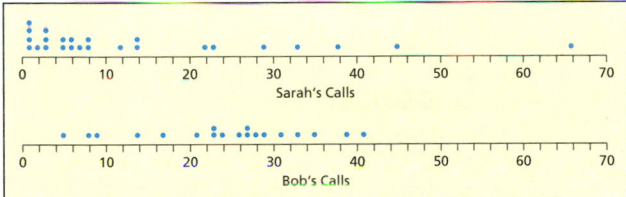

3.5 Sturges' Rule suggests about 6 bins. Slight right skew.

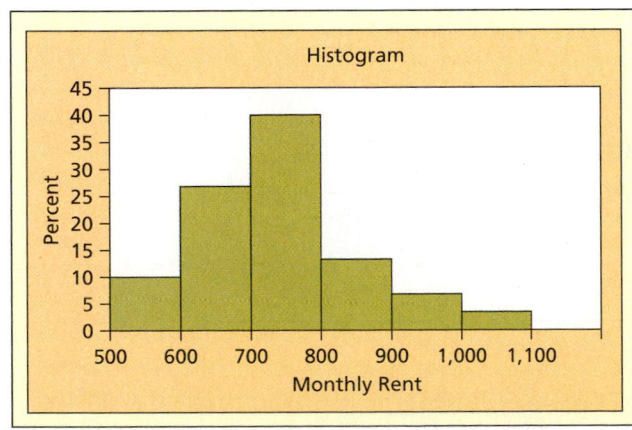

3.7 Declining at a declining rate.

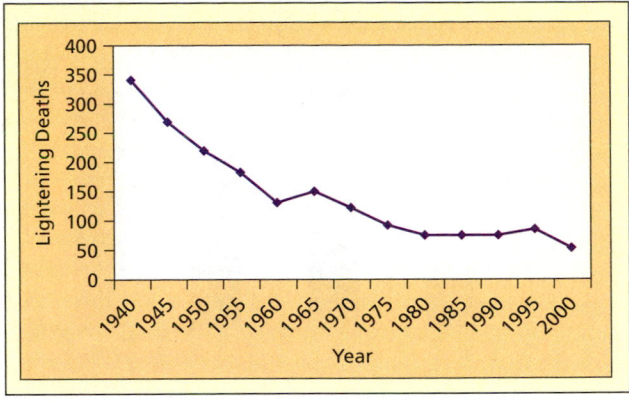

3.9 a. Line chart is clear but not attention-getting. Axis ticks
   not aligned with year or data.

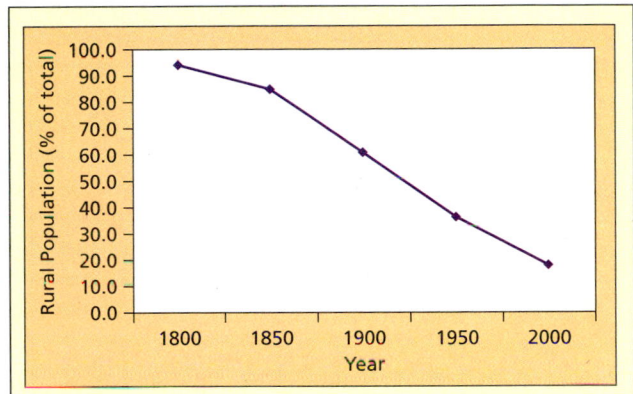

   b. Bar chart has a somewhat more "solid" feel.

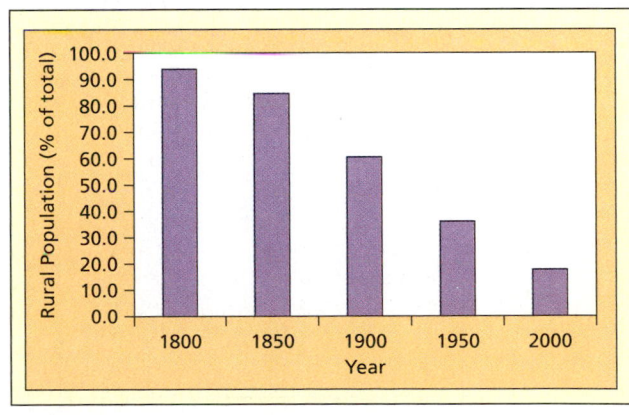

3.11 Chart is fairly easy to interpret as long as the data values are displayed.

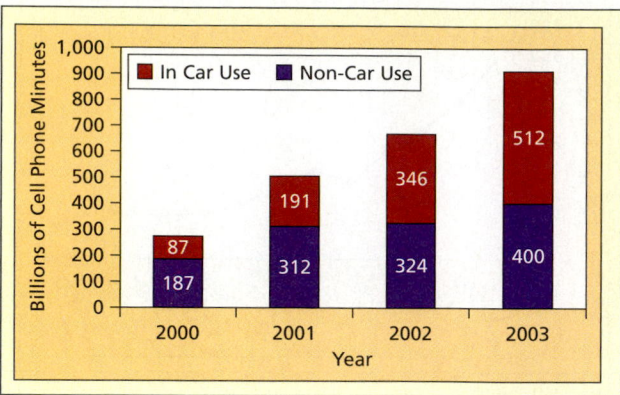

3.13 a. To show more detail, you could start the graph at (20,20).
b. There is a moderate positive linear relationship.

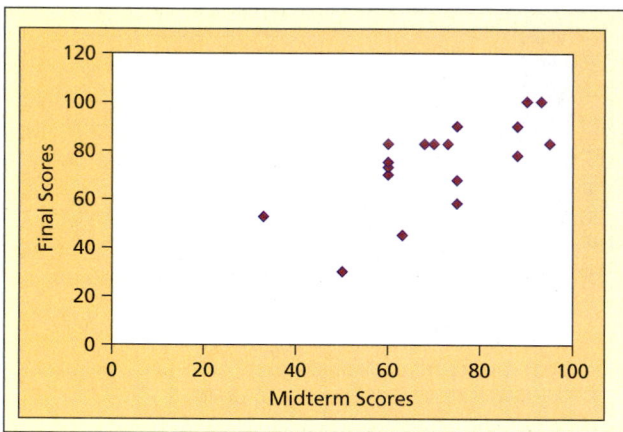

3.15 a. To show more detail, you could start the graph at (.80,100).
b. There is a moderate negative linear relationship.

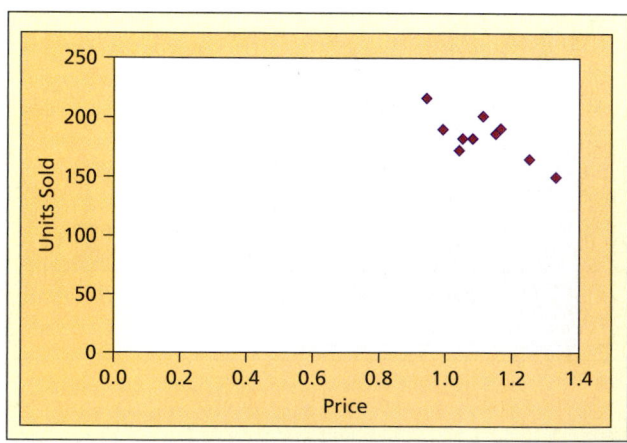

3.17 a. Default pie is clear, but rather small (can be dragged larger).
b. Visually strong, but harder to read due to rotation.
c. Clear, easy to read.

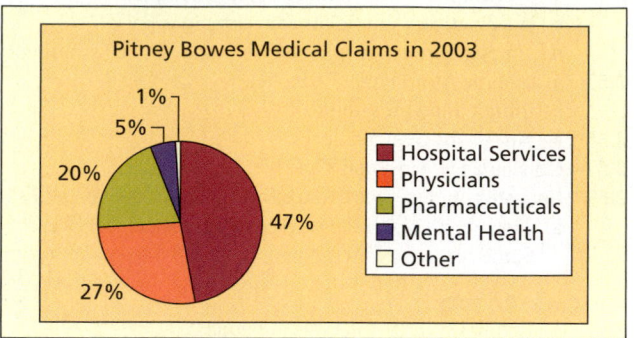

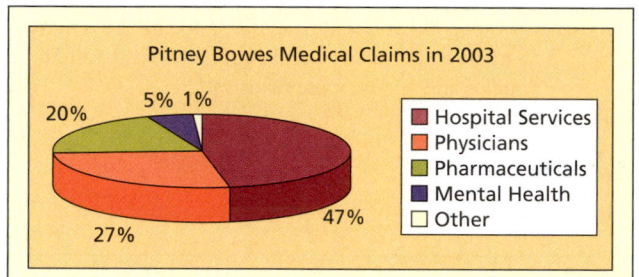

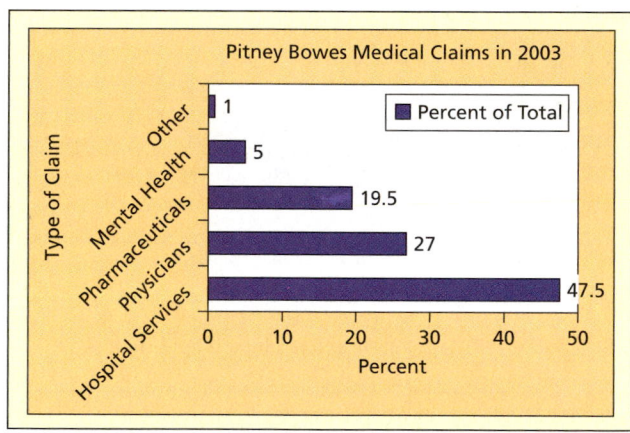

3.19 a.

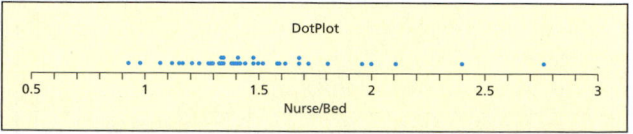

b.

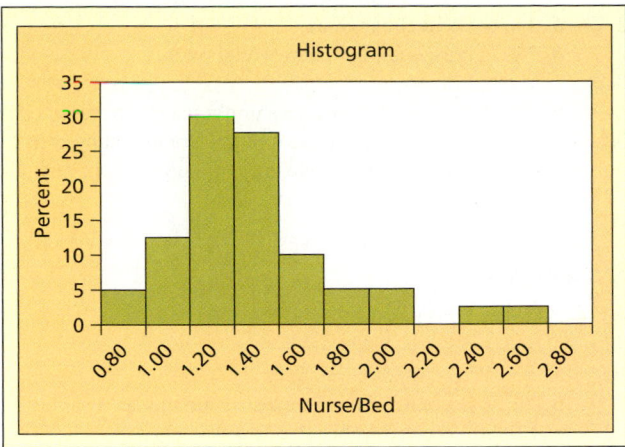

c. Skewed to the right. Half of the data values are between 1.2 and 1.6.

3.21 a. MegaStat's dotplot.

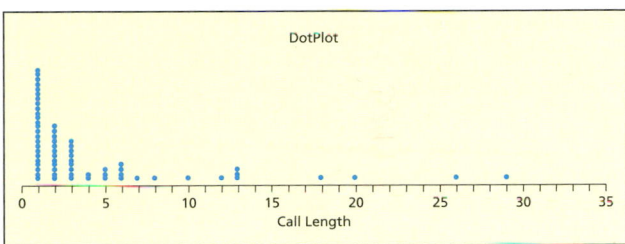

b. MegaStat's histogram.

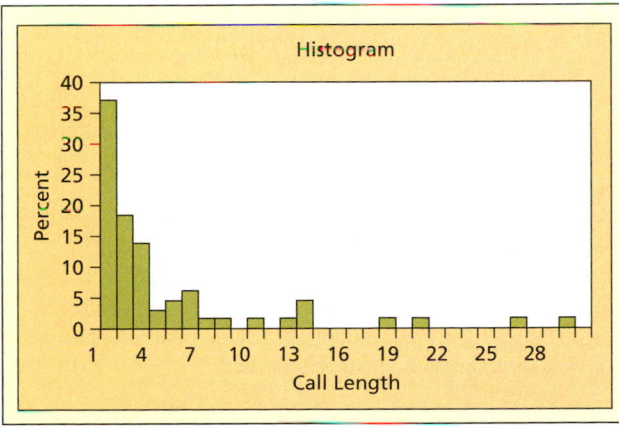

c. Heavily skewed to the right. Central tendency approximately 3 minutes.

3.23 a.

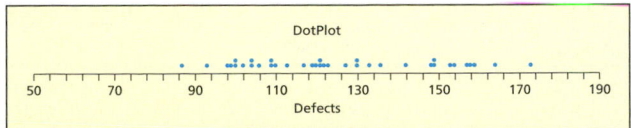

b.

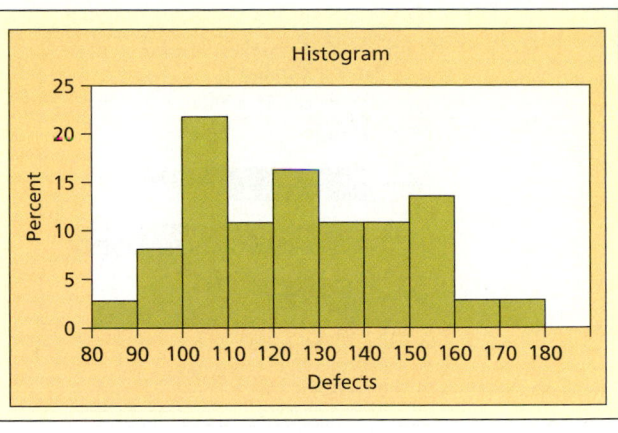

c. Somewhat symmetrical. Central tendency approximately 120–130.

3.25 a. Horizontal bar chart with 3D visual effect.

b. Strengths: Good proportions and no distracting pictures. Weaknesses: No labels on X and Y axes, title unclear, 3D effect does not add to presentation.

c. Vertical bar chart without visual effect and label on X axis.

3.27 a. Map

b. Strengths: Good summary of data, shows geographical differences, just the right amount of information.

c. A histogram of percentages could be informative.

3.29 a. Exploded pie chart.

b. Strengths: Information complete, colorful. Weaknesses: Hard to assess differences in size of pie slices.

c. Sorted column chart with OPEC and non-OPEC countries color coded.

3.31 a. Pictogram.

b. Strengths: Visually appealing; good summary data. Weaknesses: Difficult to assess differences; uses odd-sized pieces to show one category.

c. Column chart with sorted categories: highest to lowest.

3.33 a. Figure (b) gives more detail even though it has a non-zero origin. The fitted line equation overcomes any "exaggeration" in the trend from the use of a non-zero origin.

b. A one hundred mile per hour increase leads to a 7.65 decibel increase.

c. Yes.

d. High noise level, experienced in the cockpit, could cause hearing loss.

3.35 a.

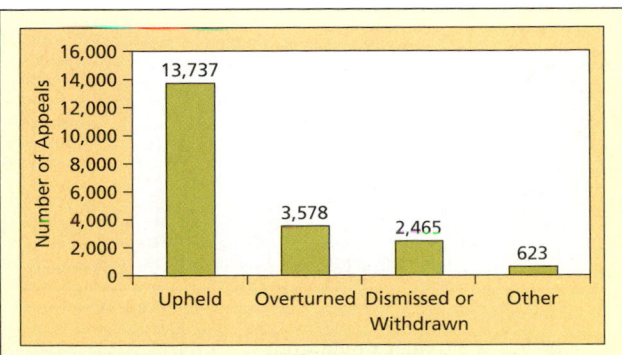

b. Yes, pie chart could be used.

3.37 a.

b. Yes, a vertical column chart would also work.

3.39 a.

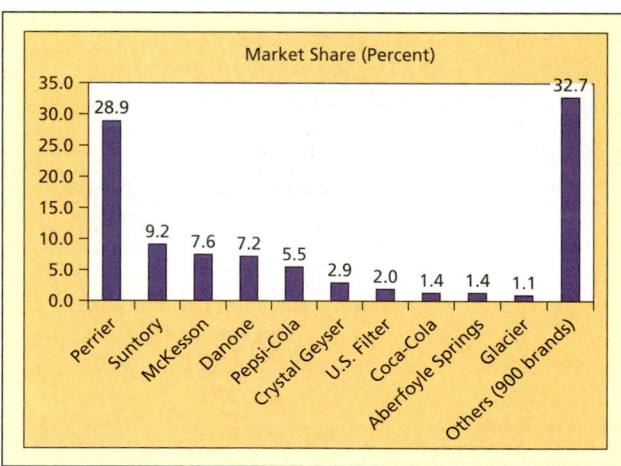

b. Yes, a pie chart could be used.

3.41 a. Graph.

b. Yes, a vertical column chart or line chart could be used. But a table may be clearest, because the large quantity of data tends to clutter the graphs. Also, observers may want to know the actual numbers to compare airlines.

3.43 a.

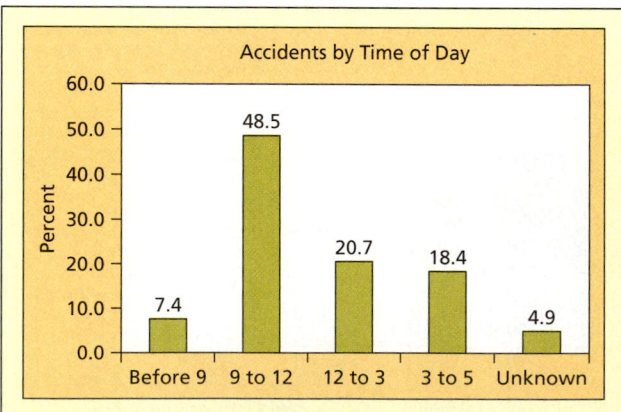

b. Yes, a pie chart would work.

3.45 a. Horizontal bar chart.

b. Yes, a vertical column chart would work.

3.47 a. Pie or vertical bar chart.

b. Yes, a horizontal bar chart would work.

3.49 a. Bar chart.

b. Yes, but so many categories might make it hard to read.

3.51 A chart would not be effective. There are too many categories and nations. The table is clear—no need for any kind of chart.

CHAPTER 4

4.1 b. $\bar{x} = 27.34$, $s = 7.85$.

4.3 b. $\bar{x} = 4.48$, $s = 5.87$.

4.5 a. $\bar{x} = 27.34$, median $= 26$, mode $= 26$.

b. No, $\bar{x}$ is greater than the median and mode.

c. Slightly skewed right.

d. Choose mean or median because data is quantitative.

4.7 b. $\bar{x} = 4.48$, median $= 2$, mode $= 1$.

c. No, $\bar{x} >$ median $>$ mode.

d. Skewed right.

e. Median.

4.9 a. $\bar{x} = 27.34$, midrange $= 25.50$, geometric mean $= 26.08$, 10% trimmed mean $= 27.47$.

b. The measures are all close, especially the mean and trimmed mean.

4.11 a. $\bar{x} = 4.48$, midrange $= 15.0$, geometric mean $= 2.6$, 10% trimmed mean $= 3.61$.

b. No, the midrange is much greater than the other three measures.

c. The data is skewed right.

d. Mean and geometric mean describe the central tendency better than the other two, but also affected by skewness.

4.13 a. Sample A: $\bar{x} = 7$, $s = 1$. Sample B: $\bar{x} = 62$, $s = 1$. Sample C: $\bar{x} = 1001$, $s = 1$.

b. The standard deviation is not a function of the mean.

4.15 a. Stock A: $CV = 21.43\%$. Stock B: $CV = 8.32\%$. Stock C: $CV = 36.17\%$.

b. Directly comparing standard deviation would not be helpful in this case because the means have different magnitudes.

4.17 $s = 5.87$, $MAD = 3.92$.

4.19 b. 18 ($z = 2.30$) and 20 ($z = 2.64$) are unusual observations. 26 ($z = 3.67$) and 29 ($z = 4.18$) are outliers.

c. 87.7% lie within 1 standard deviation and 93.8% lie within 2 standard deviations. 87.7% is much greater than the 68% specified by the empirical rule. The distribution does not appear normal.

d. Yes.

4.21 a. $Q_1 = 1$, $Q_3 = 5$. The middle 50% of the calls last between 1 and 5 minutes.

b. *Midhinge* $= 3$. Calls typically last 3 minutes.

c. The data are heavily skewed to the right.

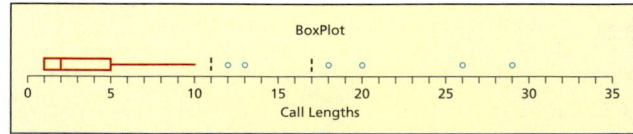

4.23 a. $\bar{x} = 66.15$, median $= 48$, mode $= 48$, and midrange $= 108$.
  b. The median because it is quantitative data, skewed to the right.
  c. A typical catalog has 48 pages.
  d. $s = 36.41$.
  f. 180 ($z = 3.13$) is an outlier, according to the Empirical Rule.

4.25 a.

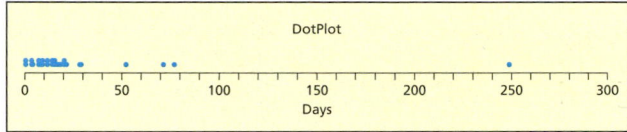

  The distribution is heavily skewed right.
  b. $\bar{x} = 26.71$, median $= 14.5$, mode $= 11$, and midrange $= 124.5$.
  c. $Q_1 = 7.75$, $Q_3 = 20.25$, Midhinge $= 14$, and $CQV = 44.64\%$.
  d. The geometric mean is only valid for data greater than zero.
  e. The median because the data is quantitative and heavily skewed right.

4.27 a. Stock funds: $\bar{x} = 1.329$, median $= 1.22$, mode $= 0.99$. Bond funds: $\bar{x} = 0.875$, median $= 0.85$, mode $= 0.64$.
  b. The central tendency of stock fund expense ratios is higher than bond funds.
  c. Stock funds: $s = 0.5933$, $CV = 44.65\%$. Bond funds: $s = 0.4489$, $CV = 51.32\%$. The stock funds have less variability relative to the mean.
  d. Stock funds: $Q_1 = 1.035$, $Q_3 = 1.565$, Midhinge $= 1.3$. Bond funds: $Q_1 = 0.64$, $Q_3 = 0.99$, Midhinge $= 0.815$. Stock funds have higher expense ratios in general than bond funds.

4.29 a. $\bar{x} = 52.15$, median $= 48.5$, mode $= 47.0$, and midrange $= 60.0$.
  b. Geometric mean $= 50.92$.
  c. All measures of central tendency are fairly close therefore use the mean.

4.31 a.

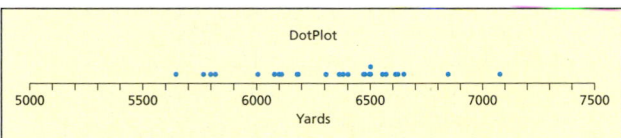

  The dot plot shows that most of the data is centered around 6500 yards. The distribution is skewed to the left.
  b. $\bar{x} = 6,335.52$, median $= 6,400.0$, mode $= 6,500.0$, and midrange $= 6,361.5$.
  c. Best: Median because data is quantitative and skewed left. Worst: Mode worst because the data is quantitative and very few values repeat themselves.
  d. This data is not highly skewed. The geometric mean works well for skewed data.

4.33 a. Male: Midhinge $= 177$, $CQV = 2.82\%$. Female: Midhinge $= 163.5$, $CQV = 2.75\%$. These statistics are appropriate because we have specific percentiles but not the entire data set.

  b. Yes, height percentiles do change. The population is slowly increasing in height.

4.35 a. $\bar{x} = 3012.44$, median $= 2,550.5$. There is no value for the mode.
  b. The typical cricket club's income is approximately £2.5 million.

4.37 a. Lab mouse: $CV = 0.9/18 = 5\%$. Lab rat: $CV = 20/300 = 6.67\%$. The rat has a higher dispersion relative to mean.

4.39 a. Tuition Plans: $CV = 42.86\%$, S&P 500: $CV = 122.48\%$.
  b. The CV shows *relative* risk for each investment.
  c. While the tuition plans have a lower return, there is less risk of losing your investment than if you had invested in stocks.

4.41 a. *Midrange* $= 0.855$.
  b. The methods for estimating the mean and standard deviation are based on a normal distribution.
  c. Normal assumption reasonable.

4.43 a. The distribution is skewed to the right.
  b. This makes sense, most patrons would keep books about 10 days with a few keeping them much longer.

4.45 a. Reasonable to expect the distribution is skewed right.
  b. Mode $<$ median $<$ mean.

4.47 a. Would expect mean to be close in value to the median, or slightly higher.
  b. Life span would have normal distribution. If skewed, more likely skewed right than left. Life span is bounded below by zero, but is unbounded in the positive direction.

4.49 a. It is the midrange, not the median.
  b. The midrange is influenced by outliers. Salaries tend to be skewed to the right. Community should use the median.

4.51 a. and c.

	Week 1	Week 2	Week 3	Week 4
mean	50.00	50.00	50.00	50.00
sample standard deviation	10.61	10.61	10.61	10.61
median	50.00	52.00	56.00	47.00

  b. Based on the mean and standard deviation, it appears that the distributions are the same.

  d.

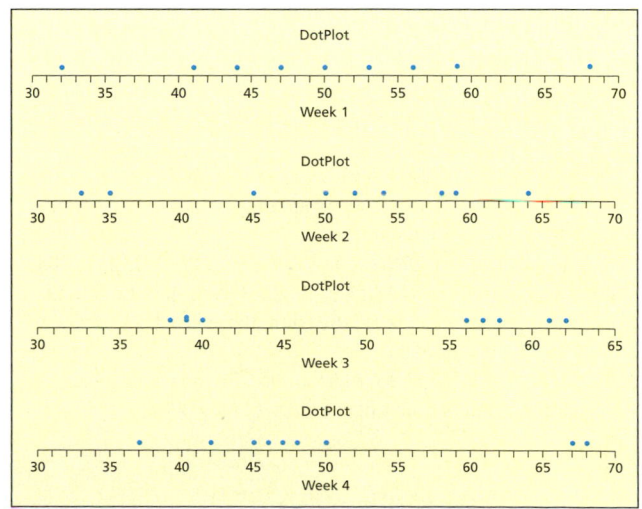

e. Based on the medians and dotplots, distributions are quite different.

4.53 a. 1990: $\bar{x} = 3.98$, $s = 1.93$, $CV = 48.5\%$.
2000: $\bar{x} = 3.47$, $s = 1.83$, $CV = 52.6\%$.

b. The average fertility rate is approximately 4 children per women with standard deviation 1.9. Stayed fairly constant from 1990 to 2000.

c. Frequency table makes it easier to see distribution and create a histogram.

4.55 a. $\bar{x} = 960.7$, $s = 472.2$, $CV = 49.2\%$.

b. Average number of degree days is 960, standard deviation 480.

c. Raw data would have been useful for creating a histogram to see the shape of the distribution.

d. Equal intervals of 250 might have spread data out too far. Yes, it does affect the calculations.

4.57 a. $\bar{x} = 60.2$, $s = 8.54$, $CV = 14.2\%$.

b. No. The class widths increase as the data values get more spread out.

4.59 a. Median falls in class 100–180. We can assign a value of 140 to the median.

b. Unequal class widths were used because the data is quite spread out. This avoids classes with frequency of zero.

CHAPTER 5

5.1 a. S = {(V,B), (V,E), (V,O), (M,B), (M,E), (M,O), (A,B), (A,E), (A,O)}

b. Events are not equally likely. Border's probably carries more books than other merchandise.

5.3 a. S = {(L,B), (L,B′), (R,B), (R,B′)}

b. Events are not equally likely. More right handed people than left handed people.

5.5 a. Expert opinion of stock brokers or empirical.

b. From historical data of IPOs or based on judgments.

5.7 a. Empirical.   b. Historical data of past launches.

5.9 a. $P(A \cup B) = .4 + .5 - .05 = .85$.

b. $P(A \mid B) = .05/.50 = .10$.

c. $P(B \mid A) = .05/.4 = .125$.

5.11 a. $P(S) = .217$.   b. $P(S') = .783$.

c. Odds in favor of S: $.217/.783 = .277$.

d. Odds against S: $.783/.217 = 3.61$

5.13 a. $X = 1$ if the drug is approved, 0 otherwise.

b. $X = 1$ if batter gets a hit, 0 otherwise.

c. $X = 1$ if breast cancer detected, 0 otherwise.

5.15 a. $P(S') = 1 - .246$. There is a 75.4% chance that a female aged 18–24 is a nonsmoker.

b. $P(S \cup C) = .246 + .830 - .232 = .844$. There is an 84.4% chance that a female aged 18–24 is a smoker or is Caucasian.

c. $P(S \mid C) = .232/.830 = .2795$. Given that the female aged 18–24 is a Caucasian, there is a 27.95% chance that they are a smoker.

d. $P(S \cap C') = P(S) - P(S \cap C) = .246 - .232 = .084$. $P(S \mid C') = .014/.17 = .0824$. Given that the female ages 18–24 is *not* Caucasian, there is a 1.4% chance that she smokes.

5.17 $P(A \mid B) = P(A \cap B)/P(B) = .05/.50 = .10$ No, A and B are not independent because $P(A \mid B) \neq P(A)$.

5.19 a. $P(V \cup M) = .70 + .60 - .50 = .80$.

b. $P(V \cap M) \neq P(V)P(M)$ therefore V and M are not independent.

5.21 "Five nines" reliability means $P(not failing) = .99999$. $P(power system failure) = 1 - (.05)^3 = .999875$. The system does not meet the test.

5.23 *Gender* and *Major* are not independent. For example, $P(A \cap F) = .22$. $P(A)P(F) = .245$. Because the values are not equal, the events are not independent.

5.25

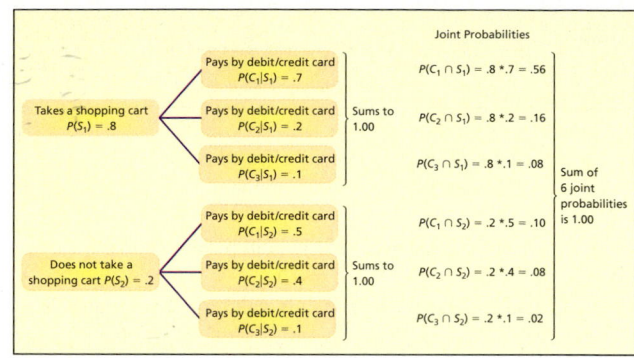

5.27* Let A = using the drug. $P(A) = .04$. $P(A') = .96$. Let T be a positive result. False positive: $P(T \mid A') = .05$. False negative: $P(T' \mid A) = .10$. $P(T \mid A) = 1 - .10 = .90$. $P(T) = (.04)(.90) + (.05)(.96) = .084$. $P(A \mid T) = (.9)(.04)/.084 = .4286$.

5.29* Let W = suitcase contains a weapon. $P(W) = .001$. $P(W') = .999$. Let A be the alarm trigger. False positive: $P(A \mid W') = .02$. False negative: $P(A' \mid W) = .02$. $P(A \mid W) = 1 - .02 = .98$. $P(A) = (.001)(.98) + (.02)(.999) = .02096$. $P(W \mid A) = (.98)(.001)/.02096 = .04676$.

5.31 a. $10^6 = 1,000,000$.

b. $10^5 = 100,000$.   c. $10^6 = 1,000,000$

5.33 a. $7! = 5,040$ ways.   b. No, too many!

5.35 a. $_8C_3 = 56$.   b. $_8C_5 = 56$.

c. $_8C_1 = 8$.   d. $_8C_8 = 1$.

5.41 a. An empirical probability using response frequencies from the survey.

b. Odds for failure: $.44/.56 = .786$ or 11 to 14.

5.43 No, the law of large numbers says that the larger the sample, the closer our sample results will be to the true value. If Tom Brookens increases his times "at bat" he'll get closer and closer to his true batting average, which is probably close to .176.

5.45 a. Empirical or subjective.

b. Most likely estimated by interviewing ER doctors.

c. The sample could have been small, not representative of all doctors.

5.47 a. Subjective.

b. Simulated experiment using a computer model.

c. The estimate is probably not very accurate. Results highly dependent on the simulation and data in the model.

5.49 a. Empirical or subjective.   b. Observation or survey.

c. The estimate is probably not very accurate. Observation is difficult and survey results may be biased.

5.51 H_1 = First child has high cholesterol, N_1 = First child has normal cholesterol, etc. $P(0) = .729$, $P(1) = .243$, $P(2) = .027$, $P(3) = .001$.

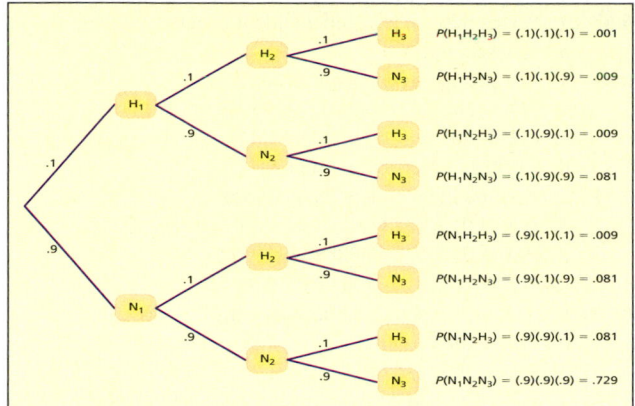

| $P(H_1 H_2 H_3) = (.1)(.1)(.1) = .001$ |
| $P(H_1 H_2 N_3) = (.1)(.1)(.9) = .009$ |
| $P(H_1 N_2 H_3) = (.1)(.9)(.1) = .009$ |
| $P(H_1 N_2 N_3) = (.1)(.9)(.9) = .081$ |
| $P(N_1 H_2 H_3) = (.9)(.1)(.1) = .009$ |
| $P(N_1 H_2 N_3) = (.9)(.1)(.9) = .081$ |
| $P(N_1 N_2 H_3) = (.9)(.9)(.1) = .081$ |
| $P(N_1 N_2 N_3) = (.9)(.9)(.9) = .729$ |

5.53 Odds against an being stolen $= .987/.013 = 76$ to 1.

5.55 P(Detroit Wins) $= 50/51 = .9804$. P(New Jersey Wins) $= 5/6 = .8333$.

5.57 a. $26^3 10^3 = 17{,}576{,}000$.   b. $36^6 = 2{,}176{,}782{,}336$.
c. 0 and 1 might be disallowed since they are similar in appearance to letters like O and I.
d. Yes, 2.2 billion unique plates should be enough.
e. $34^6 = 1{,}544{,}804{,}416$.

5.59 $(7)(6)(5) = 210$.

5.61 a. P(Two aces) $= (4/52)(3/51) = 0.00452$.
b. P(Two red cards) $= (26/52)(25/51) = 0.245098$.
c. P(Two red aces) $= (2/52)(1/51) = 0.000754$.
d. P(Two honor cards) $= (20/52)(19/51) = 0.143288$.

5.63 No, $P(A)P(B) \neq .05$.

5.65 a. Having independent back up power for computers might have eliminated delayed flights.
b. If the cost due to delayed/cancelled flights, weighted by the risk of a power outage, is greater than $100,000, then the airline can justify the expenditure.

5.67 Assuming independence, P(3 cases won out of next 3) $= .7^3 = .343$.

5.69 Assuming independence, P(4 adults say yes) $= .56^4 = 0.0983$.

5.71* See the Excel Spreadsheet in Learning Stats: 05-13 Birthday Problem.xls.
For 2 riders: P(no match) $= .9973$.
For 10 riders: P(no match) $= 0.8831$.
For 20 riders: P(no match) $= 0.5886$.
For 50 riders: P(no match) $= 0.0296$.

5.73 a. i. .4825 ii. .25 iii. .115 iv. .19 v. .64 vi. .3316 vii. .09 viii. .015 ix. .0325.
b. Yes, the vehicle type and mall location are dependent.

5.75 a. i. .5588 ii. .5294 iii. .3684 iv. .4000 v. .1765 vi. .2059.
b. No, P(A−) $= .4705$ and P(A− | F−) $= .3684$. Interest rates moved down 47% of the time and yet the forecasters predictions of a decline showed a 37% accuracy rate.

5.77 a. i. .7403 ii. .1244 iii. .1385 iv. .6205 v. .7098 vi. .9197 vii. .1485 viii. .1274 ix. .0042.
b. Yes, the probability of being a nonsmoker increases with level of education.

5.79*

	Cancer	No Cancer	Totals
Positive Test	4	500	504
Negative Test	0	9496	9496
Totals	4	9996	10000

P(Cancer | Positive Test) $= 4/504 = 0.00794$.

5.81*

	Accident	No Accident	Totals
Right-Handed	3240	5760	9000
Left-Handed	520	480	1000
Totals	3760	6240	10000

P(Left-Handed | Accident) $= 520/3760 = .1383$.

CHAPTER 6

6.1 Only A is a PDF since $P(x)$ sum to 1.

6.3 $E(X) = 2.25$, $V(X) = 1.6875$, $\sigma = 1.299$, right-skewed.

6.5 $E(X) = 1000(.01) + (0)(.999) = \$10$, add $25, charges $35.

6.7 $E(X) = 250(.3) + 950(.3) + 0(.4) = \$360$ million.

6.9 a. $\mu = (20 + 60)/2 = 40$,
$\sigma = \sqrt{[(60 - 20 + 1)^2 - 1]/12} = 11.83$.
b. $P(X \geq 40) = 1/2$, $P(X \geq 30) = 3/4$.

6.11 a. $\mu = (1 + 31)/2 = 16$,
$\sigma = \sqrt{[(31 - 1 + 1)^2 - 1]/12} = 8.944$.
b. Yes, if conception is random.

6.13 Answers may vary.
a. 1 = correct, 0 = incorrect.
b. 1 = insured, 0 = uninsured.
c. 1 = busy, 0 = not busy.
d. 1 = lost weight, 0 no weight loss.

6.15 a. $\mu = 0.8$, $\sigma = 0.8485$ b. $\mu = 4$, $\sigma = 1.5492$
c. $\mu = 6$, $\sigma = 1.7321$ d. $\mu = 27$, $\sigma = 1.6432$
e. $\mu = 56$, $\sigma = 4.0988$ f. $\mu = 16$, $\sigma = 1.7888$

6.17 a. $P(X \leq 3) = .9437$
b. $P(X > 7) = 1 - P(X \leq 6) = .1719$
c. $P(X < 3) = P(X \leq 2) = .0705$
d. $P(X \leq 10) = .00417$

6.19 a. $P(X = 0) = .10737$ b. $P(X \geq 2) = .62419$
c. $P(X < 3) = .67780$ d. $\mu = n\pi = (10)(.2) = 2$
e. $\sigma = \sqrt{(10)(.2)(1 - .2)} = 1.2649$ g. Skewed right.

6.21 a. $P(X = 10) = .00098$ b. $P(X \geq 5) = .62305$
c. $P(X < 3) = .05469$ d. $P(X \leq 6) = .82813$

6.23 a. $\lambda = 1$, $\mu = 1.0$, $\sigma = 1$
b. $\lambda = 2$, $\mu = 2.0$, $\sigma = 1.414$
c. $\lambda = 4$, $\mu = 4.0$, $\sigma = 2.0$ d. $\lambda = 9$, $\mu = 9.0$, $\sigma = 3$
e. $\lambda = 12$, $\mu = 12.0$, $\sigma = 3.464$

6.25 a. $\lambda = 4.3$, $P(X \leq 3) = .37715$
b. $\lambda = 5.2$, $P(X > 7) = .15508$
c. $\lambda = 2.7$, $P(X < 3) = .49362$
d. $\lambda = 11.0$, $P(X \leq 10) = .45989$

6.27 a. $P(X \geq 1) = 1 - .09072 = .90928$
b. $P(X = 0) = .09072$
c. $P(X > 3) = 1 - .77872 = .22128$
d. Skewed right.

6.29 a. If goals arrive independently.
b. $P(X \geq 1) = 1 - .06721 = .93279$
c. $P(X \geq 4) = 1 - .71409 = .28591$
d. Skewed right.

6.31 Let $\lambda = n\pi = (500)(.003) = 1.5$
a. $P(X \geq 2) = 1 - .55783 = .44217$
b. $P(X \leq 4) = .93436$ c. Large n and small π.
d. Yes, $n \geq 20$ and $\pi \leq .05$

6.33 a. Set $\lambda = \mu = (200)(.03) = 6$
b. $\sigma = \sqrt{(200)(.03)(1 - .03)} = 2.413$
c. $P(X \geq 10) = 1 - .91608 = .08392$
d. $P(X \leq 4) = .28506$
e. n is too large without Excel.
f. Yes, $n \geq 20$ and $\pi \leq .05$.

6.35 Distribution is symmetric with small range.

6.37 a. $X =$ number of incorrect vouchers in sample.
b. $P(X = 0) = .06726$ c. $P(X = 1) = .25869$
d. $P(X \geq 3) = 1 - .69003 = .30997$
e. Fairly symmetric

6.39* a. $3/100 < .05$, OK.   b. $10/200 > .05$, not OK.
c. $12/160 > .05$, not OK.   d. $7/500 < .05$, OK.

6.41* a. $P(X = 0) = 0.34868$ (B) or $.34516$ (H).
b. $P(X \geq 2) = .26390$ (B) or $.26350$ (H).
c. $P(X < 4) = .98720$ (B) or $.98814$ (H).
d. $n/N = 10/500 = .02$, so set $\pi = s/N = 50/500 = .1$.

6.43* a. $P(X = 5) = .03125$ when $\pi = .50$
b. $P(X = 3) = .14063$ when $\pi = .25$
c. $P(X = 4) = .03840$ when $\pi = .60$

6.45* a. $\mu = 1/\pi = 1/(.50) = 2$
b. $P(X \leq 10) = 1 - (1 - .50)^{10} = .99902$

6.47* a. $\mu = 9500 + 7400 + 8600 = \$25,500$ (Rule 3), $\sigma^2 = 1250 + 1425 + 1610 = 4285$ (Rule 4), $\sigma = 65.4599$.
b. Rule 4 assumes independent monthly sales (unlikely).

6.49 $E(X) = (100)(1/6) + (-15)(5/6) = 16.67 - 12.50 = \$4.17.$

6.51 a. $\mu = (1 + 44)/2 = 22.5$,
$\sigma = \sqrt{[(44 - 1 + 1)^2 - 1]/12} = 12.698.$
b. What was n? Histogram shape?

6.53 a. $\pi = .80$ (answers will vary).
b. $\pi = .300$ (answers will vary).
c. $\pi = .50$ (answers will vary).
d. $\pi = .80$ (answers will vary).
e. One trial may influence the next.

6.55 a. $P(X = 5) = .59049$ b. $P(X \leq 4) = .32805$
c. Strongly right-skewed

6.57 a. $P(X = 0) = .06250$
b. $P(X \geq 2) = 1 - .31250 = .68750$
c. $P(X \leq 2) = .68750$ d. Symmetric.

6.59 a. $=$BINOMDIST(3,20,0.3,0)
b. $=$BINOMDIST(7,50,0.1,0)
c. $=$BINOMDIST(6,80,0.05,1)
d. $=1-$BINOMDIST(29,120,0.2,1)

6.61 a. $P(X = 0) = .48398$
b. $P(X \geq 3) = 1 - P(X \leq 2) = 1 - .97166 = .02834$
c. $\mu = n\pi = (10)(.07) = 0.7$ defaults

6.63 Binomial with $n = 16$, $\pi = .8$:
a. $P(X \geq 10) = 1 - P(X \leq 9) = 1 - .02666 = .97334.$
b. $P(X < 8) = P(X \leq 7) = .00148.$

6.65 Let $X =$ number of no shows. Then:
a. If $n = 10$ and $\pi = .10$, then $P(X = 0) = .34868.$
b. If $n = 11$ and $\pi = .10$, then $P(X \geq 1) = 1 - P(X = 0) = 1 - .31381 = .68619.$

c. If they sell 11 seats, not more than 1 will be bumped.
d. If $X =$ number who show ($\pi = .90$). Using $= 1 -$ BINOMDIST(9, n, .9, TRUE) we find that $n = 13$ will ensure that $P(X \geq 10) \geq .95$.

6.67 a. Yawns may be non-independent events.
b. Answers will vary.

6.69 a. Are storms independent events?
b. $P(X \geq 5) = 1 - .00181 = .99819$
c. $P(X > 20) = 1 - .95209 = .04791$
d. Fairly symmetric due to large λ.

6.71 a. Assume independent cancellations.
b. $P(X = 0) = .22313$ c. $P(X = 1) = .33470$
d. $P(X > 2) = 1 - .80885 = .19115$
e. $P(X \geq 5) = 1 - .98142 = .01858$

6.73 a. Assume independent defects with $\lambda = 2.4$.
b. $P(X = 0) = .09072$ c. $P(X = 1) = .21772$
d. $P(X \leq 1) = .30844$

6.75 a. $\lambda = 1/30 = 0.033333$, $\sigma = \sqrt{\lambda} = \sqrt{1/30} = .182574$.
b. $P(X \geq 1) = 1 - (.033333)^0 e^{-.033333}/0! = 1 - .9672 = .0328$
c. Appendix B does not have $\lambda = .0333333$.

6.77 a. Assume independent crashes.
b. $P(X \geq 1) = 1 - .13534 = .86466$
c. $P(X < 5) = P(X \leq 4) = .94735$
d. Skewed right.

6.79* a. Set $\lambda = n\pi = (200)(.02) = 4$.
b. $P(X = 0) = .01759$ c. $P(X = 1) = .07326$
d. $P(X = 0) = .01832$ from $=$BINOMDIST(0,200,0.02,0)
$P(X = 1) = .07179$ from $=$BINOMDIST(1,200,0.02,0)
e. Yes, $n \geq 20$ and $\pi \leq .05$.

6.81* a. $\mu = n\pi = (4386)(.00114) = 5$.
b. $\sigma = \sqrt{n\pi(1 - \pi)} = \sqrt{(4386)(.00114)(.99886)} = 2.235$
c. Using $\lambda = 5.0$, $P(X < 5) = P(X \leq 4) = .44049$
d. $P(X > 10) = 1 - .9863 = .0137$
e. Yes, $n \geq 20$ and $\pi \leq .05$.

6.83 a. $N = 52$ cards, $s = 13$ hearts, $n = 5$ dealt.
$P(X = 5 \mid N = 52, s = 13, n = 5) = .0004952$
b. No, since $n/N > .05$.

6.85* a. $\mu = 1/\pi = 1/(.08) = 12.5$ cars
b. $\sigma = \sqrt{(1 - \pi)/\pi^2} = \sqrt{(.92)/(.08)^2} = 11.99$ cars
c. $P(X \leq 5) = 1 - (1 - .08)^5 = .3409$

6.87* a. $\mu = 1/\pi = 1/(.05) = 20$
b. $P(X \leq 29) = 1 - (1 - .05)^{29} = 1 - .2259 = .7741$

6.89 $(b - a + 1)/(b - a + 1) = 1.$

6.91 a. $(233.1)(0.4536) = 105.734$ kg
b. $(34.95)(0.4536) = 15.8533$ kg
c. Rule 1 for the μ, Rule 2 for σ.

6.93* a. By, $\mu_{X+Y} = \mu_X + \mu_Y = 70 + 80 = 150$
b. By Rule 4, $\sigma_{X+Y} = \sqrt{\sigma_X^2 + \sigma_Y^2} = \sqrt{64 + 36} = 10$
c. Rule 4 assumes independent test scores (unlikely).

6.95 Rule 1, $\mu_{vQ+F} = v\mu_Q + F = (2225)(7) + 500 = \$16,075$
Rule 2, $\sigma_{vQ+F} = v\sigma_Q = (2225)(2) = \$4,450$
Rule 1, $E(PQ) = P\mu_Q = (2850)(7) = \$19,950$
$E(TR) - E(TC) = 19,950 - 16,075 = \$3,875$

6.97* a. Binomial $\mu = n\pi = (.25)(250) = 60$
b. Binomial $\sigma^2 = n\pi(1 - \pi) = (240)(.25)(.75) = 45$ so $\sigma = 6.7082$
c. $\mu \pm 1\sigma$ (53.3 to 66.7) and $\mu \pm 2\sigma$ (46.6 to 73.4).

CHAPTER 7

Note: Using Appendix C or Excel will lead to somewhat different answers.

7.1 a. D   b. C   c. C

7.3 a. Area $= bh = (1)(.25) = .25$, so not a PDF (area is not 1).
b. Area $= bh = (4)(.25) = 1$, so could be a PDF (area is 1).
c. Area $= \frac{1}{2}bh = (2)(2) = 2$, so not a PDF (area is not 1).

7.5 a. $\mu = (0 + 10)/2 = 5, \sigma = \sqrt{\dfrac{(10 - 0)^2}{12}} = 2.886751$.

b. $\mu = (200 + 100)/2 = 150, \sigma = \sqrt{\dfrac{(200 - 100)^2}{12}} = 28.86751$.

c. $\mu = (1 + 99)/2 = 50, \sigma = \sqrt{\dfrac{(99 - 1)^2}{12}} = 28.29016$.

7.7 A point has no area in a continuous distribution so $<$ or $\leq$ yields the same result.

7.9 Means and standard deviations differ (X axis scales are different) and so do $f(x)$ heights.

7.11 For samples from a *normal distribution* we expect about 68.26% within $\mu \pm 1\,\sigma$, about 95.44% within $\mu \pm 2\,\sigma$, and about 99.73% within $\mu \pm 3\,\sigma$.

7.13 Using Appendix C-1:
a.. $P(0 < Z < 0.50) = .1915$
b. $P(-0.50 < Z < 0) = P(0 < Z < 0.50) = .1915$.
c. $P(Z > 0) = .5000$.
d. Probability of any point is 0.

7.15 Using Appendix C-1:
a. $P(Z < 2.15) - P(Z < -1.22) = .9842 - .1112 = .8730$
b. $P(Z < 2.00) - P(Z < -3.00) = .9772 - .00135 = .97585$
c. $P(Z < 2.00) = .9772$
d. Probability of any point is 0.

7.17 a. $P(X < 300) = P(Z < 0.71) = .7611$
b. $P(X > 250) = 1 - P(Z < 2.86) = .9979$
c. $P(275 < X < 310) = P(Z < 1.43) - P(Z < -1.07) = .9236 - .1423 = .7813$

7.19 a. $Z = 1.282, X = 13.85$.   b. $Z = 0, X = 10.00$.
c. $Z = 1.645, X = 14.94$.   d. $Z = -0.842, X = 7.47$.
e. $Z = -1.282, X = 6.15$.
f. $Z = \pm 0.675, X = 7.98, 12.03$.
g. $Z = 1.476, X = 14.43$.
h. $Z = \pm 1.960, X = 4.12, 15.88$.
i. $Z = -1.476, X = 5.572$.

7.21 a. $Z = (8.0 - 6.9)/1.2 = 0.92$, so $P(Z < 0.92) = .8212$ (82 percentile).
b. $Z = 1.282, X = 8.44$ lbs
c. $Z = \pm 1.960, X = 4.55$ lbs to 9.25 lbs

7.23 a. $P(X < 110)$ =NORMDIST(110,100,15,TRUE) $= .74751$
b. $P(Z < 2.00)$ =NORMDIST(2,0,1,TRUE) $= .97725$
c. $P(X < 5,000)$ =NORMDIST(5000,6000,1000,TRUE) $= .15866$
d. $P(X < 450)$ =NORMDIST(450,600,100,TRUE) $= .06681$

7.25 a. =NORMINV(0.1,360,9) $= 348.466$
b. =NORMINV(0.32,360,9) $= 355.791$
c. =NORMINV(0.75,360,9) $= 366.070$
d. =NORMINV(0.9,360,9) $= 371.534$
e. =NORMINV(0.999,360,9) $= 387.812$
f. =NORMINV(0.9999,360,9) $= 393.472$

7.27 a. =NORMSINV(RAND())
b. $\mu = 0$ and $\sigma = 1$ (answers will vary)
c. $\mu = 0$ and $\sigma = 1$ (answers will vary)

7.29* Normality OK since $n\pi = (1000)(.07) = 70 \geq 10$, $n(1 - \pi) = (1000)(.93) = 930 \geq 10$. Set $\mu = n\pi = 70$ and $\sigma = \sqrt{n\pi(1 - \pi)} = 8.0684571$.
a. $P(X < 50) = P(Z < -2.54) = .0055$ (using $X = 49.5$)
b. $P(X > 100) = P(Z > 3.78) = 1 - P(Z \leq 3.78) = 1 - .99992 = .00008$ (using $X = 100.5$)

7.31* Normality OK. Set $\mu = 180, \sigma = 4.242641$.
a. $P(X \geq 175) = P(Z \geq -1.30) = 1 - P(Z \leq 1.30) = 1 - .0968 = .9032$ (using $X = 174.5$)
b. $P(X < 190) = P(Z \leq 2.24) = .9875$ (using $X = 189.5$)

7.33* Set $\mu = \lambda = 28$ and $\sigma = \sqrt{28} = 5.2915$.
a. $P(X > 35) = 1 - P(Z \leq 1.42) = 1 - .9222 = .0788$ (using $X = 35.5$)
b. $P(X < 25) = P(Z \leq -0.66) = .2546$ (using $X = 24.5$)
c. $\lambda = 28 \geq 10$, so OK to use normal.
d. .0823 and .2599. Yes, it is good.

7.35 a. $P(X > 7) = e^{-\lambda x} = e^{-(0.3)(7)} = e^{-2.1} = .1225$
b. $P(X < 2) = 1 - e^{-\lambda x} = 1 - e^{-(0.3)(2)} = 1 - e^{-0.6} = 1 - .5488 = .4512$

7.37 $\lambda = 6.0$ alarms/minute or $\lambda = 0.1$ alarms/second.
a. $P(X < 60) = 1 - e^{-\lambda x} = 1 - e^{-(0.1)(60)} = 1 - e^{-6.0} = 1 - .0025 = .9975$
b. $P(X > 30) = e^{-\lambda x} = e^{-(0.1)(30)} = e^{-3.0} = .0498$
c. $P(X \geq 45) = e^{-\lambda x} = e^{-(.0.1)(45)} = e^{-4.5} = .0111$

7.39 $\lambda = 4.2$ orders/hour or $\lambda = .07$ orders/minute.
a. Set $e^{-\lambda x} = .50$, take logs, $x = 0.165035$ hr (9.9 min).
b. Set $e^{-\lambda x} = .25$, take logs, $x = 0.33007$ hr (19.8 min).
c. Set $e^{-\lambda x} = .10$, take logs, $x = 0.548235$ hr (32.89 min).

7.41 MTBE $= 20$ min/order so $\lambda = 1/$MTBE $= 1/20$ orders/min.
a. Set $e^{-\lambda x} = .50$, take logs, $x = 13.86$ min.
b. Distribution is very right-skewed.
c. Set $e^{-\lambda x} = .25$, take logs, $x = 27.7$ min.

7.43* a. $\mu = (0 + 25 + 75)/3 = 33.3333$
b.

$$\sigma = \sqrt{\frac{0^2 + 75^2 + 25^2 - (0)(75) - (0)(25) - (75)(25)}{18}}$$

$= 15.5902$

c. $P(X < 25) = (25 - 0)^2/((75 - 0)*(25 - 0)) = .3333$
d. Shaded area represents the probability.

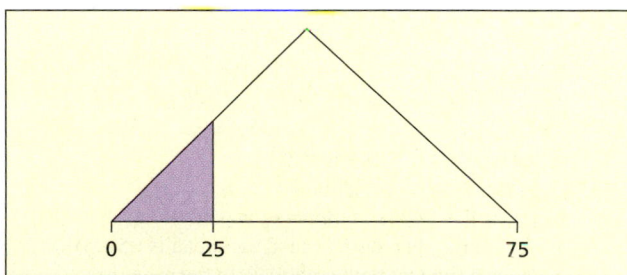

7.45 a. D   b. C   c. C

7.47 a. $\mu = (25 + 65)/2 = 45$ b. $\sigma = 11.54701$
c. $P(X > 45) = (65 - 45)/(65 - 25) = 0.5$
d. $P(X > 55) = (65 - 55)/(65 - 25) = 0.25$
e. $P(30 < X < 65) = (60 - 30)/(65 - 25) = 0.75$

7.49 a. Right-skewed (zero low bound, high outliers likely).
b. Right-skewed (zero low bound, high outliers likely).
c. Normal.   d. Normal.

7.51 a. =NORMINV(0.5,450,80) = 450

b. =NORMINV(0.25,450,80) = 396.04

c. =NORMINV(0.9,450,80) = 552.52

d. =NORMINV(0.2,450,80) = 382.67

e. =NORMINV(0.95,450,80) = 581.59

f. =NORMINV(0.25,450,80) to
=NORMINV(0.75,450,80) or 396.04 to 503.95

g. =NORMINV(0.2,450,80) = 382.67

h. =NORMINV(0.025,450,80) to
=NORMINV(0.975,450,80) or 293.20 to 606.80

i. =NORMINV(0.99,450,80) = 636.11

7.53 a. =1−NORMDIST(130,115,20,TRUE) = .2266

b. =NORMDIST(100,115,20,TRUE) = .2266

c. =NORMDIST(91,115,20,TRUE) = .1151

7.55* a. $P(28 < X < 32) = P(X < 32) - P(X < 28) = .8413 - .1587 = .6826$

b. $P(X < 28) = .1587$

c. 75% of 30 is 22.5, so $P(X < 22.5) = P(Z < -3.75) = .00009$

7.57 $P(1.975 < X < 2.095) = P(-2.00 < Z < +2.00) = .9544$, so 4.56% will not meet specs.

7.59 Using Excel (answers with continuity correction in parentheses):

a. $P(X > 50) = P(Z > .78) = .2177 (.2086)$

b. $P(X < 29) = P(Z < -.54) = .2946 (.3062)$

c. $P(40 < X < 50) = P(X < 50) - P(X < 40) = .2223 (.2439)$

d. Normal distribution assumed.

7.61 a. $P(X > 90) =$1−NORMDIST(90,84,10,TRUE) = .2743

b. Normal distribution assumed.

7.63 a. $P(X > 5200) = $1−NORMDIST(5200,4905,355,TRUE) = 0.2030

7.65 a. 5.3% below John.   b. 69.2% below Mary.

c. 96.3% below Zak.   d. 99.3% below Frieda.

7.67* Probability of making it to the airport in 54 minutes or less is .5000 for A and .0228 for B, so use route A. Probability of making it to the airport in 60 minutes or less is .8413 for A and .5000 for B, so use route A. Probability of making it to the airport in 66 minutes or less is the same for routes A and B.

a. $P(X < 54)$ *Route A*: =NORMDIST(54,54,6,TRUE) = .5000
  Route B: =NORMDIST(54,60,3,TRUE) =.0228

b. $P(X < 60)$ *Route A*: =NORMDIST(60,54,6,TRUE) = .8413
  Route B: =NORMDIST(60,60,3,TRUE) = .5000

c. $P(X < 66)$ *Route A*: =NORMDIST(66,54,6,TRUE) = .9772
  Route B: =NORMDIST(66,60,3,TRUE) = .9772

7.69 =NORMINV(.20) = −0.842, so $x = \mu + z\sigma = 12.5 + (-0.842)(1.2) = 11.49$ inches

7.71* For any normal distribution, $P(X > \mu) = .5$ or $P(X < \mu) = .5$. Assuming independent events:

a. Probability that both exceed the mean is $(.5)(.5) = .25$

b. Probability that both are less than the mean is $(.5)(.5) = .25$

c. Probability that one is above and one is less than the mean is $(.5)(.5) = .25$ but there are two combinations that yield this, so the likelihood is: $.25 + .25 = .50$.

d. $P(X = \mu) = 0$ for any continuous random variable.

7.73* Normality OK since $n\pi \geq 10$ and $n(1 - \pi) \geq 10$. Set $\mu = n\pi = (.25)(100) = 25$ and $\sigma = $ =SQRT(.25*100* $(1 - .25)) = 4.3301$. Then $P(X < 19.5) =$NORMDIST $(19.5,25,4.3301,1) = .1020$.

7.75* Set $\mu = n\pi = (.25)(100) = 25$ and $\sigma = $ =SQRT(.25*100* $(1 - .25)) = 4.3301$.

a. $z = $ NORMSINV(.95) = 1.645 so $x = \mu + z\sigma = 25 + 1.645(4.3301) = 32.12$

b. $z = $ NORMSINV(.99) = 2.326 so $x = \mu + z\sigma = 25 + 2.326(4.3301) = 35.07$

c. Q1 = NORMINV(0.25,25,4.3301) = 22.08
Q2 = NORMINV(0.5, 25,4.3301) = 25.00
Q3 = NORMINV(0.75, 25,4.3301) = 27.92

7.77* Set $\mu = n\pi = (.02)(1500) = 30$ and $\sigma = $ =SQRT(.02* $1500*(1 - .02)) = 5.4222$. Then

a. $P(X > 24.5) = 1 - P(X < 24.5) = $1−NORMDIST(24.5,30,5.4222,1) = .8448

b. $P(X > 40.5) = 1 - P(X < 40.5) = $1−NORMDIST(40.5, 30,5.4222,1) = .0264

7.79 a. $P(X < 10,000) = 1 - e^{-\lambda x} = 1 - e^{-(1/10000)(10000)} = .6321$

b. The distribution is not symmetric as the mean is not equal to the median.

7.81 a. $P(X > 15,000) = e^{-\lambda x} = e^{-(1/25000)(15000)} = 0.5488$

b. Hours in ten years: $(24)(365)(10) = 87,600$, so 25% of 87,600 is 21,900 hours and $P(X < 21900) = 1 - e^{-\lambda x} = 1 - e^{-(1/25000)(21900)} = .5836$. This assumes that failures follow the Poisson model.

7.83* a. $\mu = (300 + 350 + 490)/3 = 380$

b.
$$\sigma = \sqrt{\frac{300^2 + 350^2 + 490^2 - (300)(350) - (300)(490) - (350)(490)}{18}}$$
$$= 40.21$$

c. $P(X > 400) = (490 - 400)^2/((490 - 300)(490 - 350)) = .3045$

7.85* a. $\mu = (500 + 700 + 2100)/3 = 1100$

b.
$$\sigma = \sqrt{\frac{500^2 + 700^2 + 2100^2 - (500)(700) - (500)(2100) - (700)(2100)}{18}}$$
$$= 355.90$$

c. $P(X > 750) = (2100 - 750)^2/((2100 - 500)(2100 - 700)) = .8136$

d. Shaded area represents the probability.

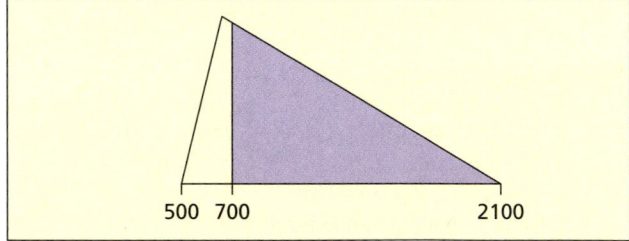

CHAPTER 8

8.1 a. 16   b. 8   c. 4

8.3 a. (4.0252, 4.0448)   b. (4.0330, 4.0370)   c. both are outside expected range

8.5 a. (11.06, 16.94)   b. (33.68, 40.33)

c. (115.12, 126.88)

8.7 (2.4725, 2.4775)

8.9 a. 2.262, 2.2622   b. 2.602, 2.6025

c. 1.678, 1.6779

8.11 a. (33.01, 58.31)   b. Increase n or decrease 95%.

8.13 a. (742.20, 882.80)

8.15 a. (81.87, 88.13) for Exam 1, (82.79, 94.41) for Exam 2, (73.34, 78.66) for Exam 3.
b. Exams 1 and 2 overlap.   c. Unknown σ.

8.17 a. .062   b. .0877   c. .1216

8.19 a. (.2556, .4752)   b. Yes, normal.

8.21 a. (.0152, .0768)   b. Yes, normal.

8.23 a. 0.1507, 0.3199   b. Yes, normal.   c. 136, 769
d. Decrease E and increase confidence.

8.25 25

8.27 97 assuming $\sigma = 25 = R/4$

8.29 47 assuming $\sigma = 86.75 = R/4$

8.31 a. 1692   b. Stratify (e.g., income)

8.33 a. 2401   b. Stratify (e.g., age)

8.35 a. $(-1.16302, 0.803020)$ b. $(-1.15081, 0.79081)$
c. Overlap   d. Same means.

8.37 $(-.1584, .1184)$

8.39 (.0063, .1937)

8.41 (1.01338, 1.94627)

8.43 (5.88, 10.91)

8.45 a. Uneven wear.   b. (0.8332, 0.8355)
c. Normality.   d. 95

8.47 a. (29.443, 39.634)   b. Varying methods
c. Raisin clumps

8.49 a. (19.245, 20.69)   b. Small n.

8.51 a. (33.013, 58.315)   b. Outliers
c. 119   d. (21.26, 40.14)

8.53 a. (29.078, 29.982)   b. Yes   c. 116

8.55 a. (48.515, 56.965)   b. Outliers   c. 75

8.57 a. (.125, .255)   b. Yes   c. 463

8.59 a. (.092, .134)   c. 677

8.61 a. (.595, .733)   b. No

8.63 a. .0127   b. (.121, .171)   c. No
d. (.110, .182)

8.65 a. (.001, .002)   b. No, conclusion is clear.

8.67 (0.0107, 0.0868) with normality, (0.0181, 0.1031) without.

8.69 a. (.914, 1.006)   b. Severity of effect.
c. Use binomial.   d. (.863, .995) from MINITAB

8.71 .04 for 95% CI.

8.73 a. $(-2.51, 0.11)$ b. No

8.75 a. $(-.1063, .0081)$ b. No

CHAPTER 9

9.1 a. Reject in lower tail.   b. Reject in both tails.
c. Reject in upper tail.

9.3 a. Type I error: Admit even though no heart attack. Type II error: Fail to admit when there is a heart attack.
b. Type I error: Allow a landing even though there is enough fuel. Type II error: Fail to let the plane land when there is not enough fuel.
c. Type I error: Go to Staples even though there is enough ink. Type II error: Don't go to Staples and run out of ink.

9.5 a. H_0: Employee not using drugs.
H_1: Employee is using drugs.
b. Type I error: Test positive for drugs when not using. Type II error: Test negative for drugs when using.
c. Employees fear Type I, while employers fear both for legal reasons.

9.7 a. $z = 2.0$, p-value $= .046$.
b. $z = 1.90$, p-value $= .971$.
c. $z = 1.14$, p-value $= .127$.

9.9 a. No.   b. No.   c. Yes.

9.11 a. H_0: $\pi = .997$ versus H_1: $\pi < .997$. Reject H_0 if the p-value is less than 0.05.
b. Yes.
c. Type I error: Throw away a good syringe.
Type II error: Keep a bad syringe.
d. p-value $= .034$
e. Type II increases.

9.13 a. H_0: $\pi = .50$ versus H_1: $\pi > 0.50$. If the p-value is less than .05, reject H_0.
b. p-value $= .0228$.
c. Yes, cost could be high if call volume is large.

9.15 p-value ≈ 0. More than half support the ban.

9.17 a. p-value $= .143$. Standard is being met.
b. Less than five defects observed, cannot assume normality.

9.19 a. $z = 1.50$, p-value $= .1336$.
b. $z = -2.0$, p-value $= .0228$.
c. $z = 3.75$, p-value $= .0001$.

9.21 p-value $= .0062$. The mean weight is heavier than it should be.

9.23 a. Reject H_0 if $z > 1.96$ or $z < -1.96$.
b. $z = 0.78$. Fail to reject H_0.

9.25 a. $t = 1.5$, p-value $= .1544$.
b. $t = -2.0$, p-value $= .0285$.
c. $t = 3.75$, p-value $= .0003$.

9.27 H_0: $\mu \geq 400$ H_1: $\mu < 400$. Reject H_0 if p-value is less than .10. The p-value $= 0.0525$, therefore reject H_0. Decision is close at $\alpha = 0.05$, could be important to a large contractor.

9.29 a. p-value $= .0097$. Reject H_0.

9.31 a. p-value $= .1079$. Fail to reject H_0.
b. (3.226, 3.474) includes 3.25

9.33 a. .3404   b. .7081   c. .9107
Power is lower for each true value of π.

9.35 a. .2595
b. .6388
c. .9123
Power is lower.

9.37 p-value $= .0465$. Reject H_0.

9.39 p-value $= .6202$. Fail to reject H_0.

9.41 a. P(Type I error) $= 0$.
b. You increase the P(Type II error).

9.43 a. H_0: User is authorized.
H_1: User is unauthorized.
b. Type I error: Scanner fails to admit an authorized user.
Type II error: Scanner admits an unauthorized user.
c. Type II is feared by the public.

9.45 P(Type I error) $= 0$.

9.47 a. H_0: Patient does not have appendicitis.
H_1: Patient does have appendicitis.
b. Type I error is high (between .15 and .4) because consequence of a Type II error is fatal.

9.49 About 25% "false alarms."

9.51 a. A two-tailed test.
b. Overfill is unnecessary while underfill is illegal.
c. Normal (known σ).
d. Reject if $z > 2.576$ or if $z < -2.576$.

9.53 a. H_0: $\mu \geq 90$
H_1: $\mu < 90$
b. Student's t.
c. $t = -0.92$. Fail to reject H_0.
d. At least a symmetric population.
e. p-value $= .1936$.

9.55 a. $H_0: \mu \geq 2.268$
$H_1: \mu < 2.268$
If the p-value is less than .05 reject H_0.
p-value $= .0478$. Reject H_0.
b. Usage wears them down.

9.57 p-value $= .0228$. Reject H_0.

9.59 p-value $= .0258$. Fail to reject (close decision) H_0.

9.61 p-value $= .1327$. Fail to reject H_0.

9.63 p-value $= .0193$. Reject H_0. Important to players and universities.

9.65 a. $(.173, .2684)$
b. No, true % could be $>25\%$.

9.67 a. p-value $= .4212$. Fail to reject H_0.
b. Outliers (e.g., Hawkins).

9.69 p-value $= .0794$. Fail to reject H_0.

9.71 $H_0: \pi = .50$ vs. $H_1: \pi > .50$. $P(X \geq 10 \mid n = 16, \pi = .5) = .2272$. Fail to reject H_0.

9.73 a. $(0, .0154)$
b. $np < 10$.
c. Goal is being achieved.

9.77 $\beta = 1 -$ power. The power values are:
$n = 4$: .2085, .5087, .8038, .9543
$n = 16$: .5087, .9543, .9996, 1.0000

9.79 Reject if $X^2 < 9.26$ (d.f. $= 23$). Since $X^2 = 12.77$ do not reject.

CHAPTER 10

Note: Results from Excel except as noted (may not agree with Appendix C, D, or E due to rounding or use of exact d.f.).

10.1 a. $H_0: \pi_1 \geq \pi_2, H_1: \pi_1 < \pi_2, \bar{p} = .4200, z = -2.431$,
$z_{.01} = -2.326$, p-value $= .0075$, so reject at $\alpha = .01$.
b. $H_0: \pi_1 = \pi_2, H_1: \pi_1 \neq \pi_2, \bar{p} = .37500, z = 2.263$,
$z_{.05} = \pm 1.645$, p-value $= .0237$, reject at $\alpha = .10$.
c. $H_0: \pi_1 \geq \pi_2, H_1: \pi_1 < \pi_2, \bar{p} = .25806, z = -1.706$,
$z_{.05} = -1.645$, p-value $= .0440$, reject at $\alpha = .05$.

10.3 a. $H_0: \pi_1 \geq \pi_2, H_1: \pi_1 < \pi_2, \bar{p} = .26000, z = -2.280$.
b. $z_{.01} = -2.326$, can't reject at $\alpha = .01$ (close decision).
c. p-value $= .0113$
d. Normality OK since $n_1 p_1 = 42, n_2 p_2 = 62$, both exceed 10.

10.5 a. $H_0: \pi_1 = \pi_2, H_1: \pi_1 \neq \pi_2, \bar{p} = .11, z = 2.021$,
$z_{.025} = \pm 1.960$ ($p = .0432$) so reject at $\alpha = .05$ (close decision).
b. $(.0013, .0787)$, does not include zero

10.7 a. $p_1 = .28205, p_2 = .05660, H_0: \pi_1 \leq \pi_2, H_1: \pi_1 > \pi_2$,
$\bar{p} = .15217, z = 2.975$, critical value is $z_{.10} = 1.282$,
and p-value $= .0015$, so reject at $\alpha = .10$.
b. Sample is too small since $n_2 p_2 = 3$.
c. Cause-and-effect not demonstrated.

10.9 a. $p_1 = .07778, p_2 = .10448, H_0: \pi_1 = \pi_2, H_1: \pi_1 \neq \pi_2$,
$\bar{p} = .08502, z = -0.669$, critical value is $z_{.025} = 1.960$,
and p-value $= .5036$, so cannot reject at $\alpha = .05$.
b. Normality not OK since $n_1 p_1 = 14$ but $n_2 p_2 = 7$.

10.11 a. $p_1 = .28125, p_2 = .14583, \bar{p} = .22321, H_0: \pi_1 - \pi_2 \leq .10, H_1: \pi_1 - \pi_2 > .10, z = 0.630$, and critical value is $z_{.05} = 1.645$.
b. p-value $= .2644$, cannot reject at $\alpha = .05$

10.13 a. $H_0: \mu_1 \geq \mu_2, H_1: \mu_1 < \mu_2, t = -2.148, df = 28$,
$t_{.025} = -2.048$, p-value $= .0202$, so reject H_0.
b. $H_0: \mu_1 = \mu_2, H_1: \mu_1 \neq \mu_2, t = -1.595, df = 39$,
$t_{.05} = \pm 2.023$, p-value $= .1188$, so can't reject H_0.

c. $H_0: \mu_1 \leq \mu_2, H_1: \mu_1 > \mu_2, t = 1.935, df = 27$,
$t_{.05} = 1.703$, p-value $= .0318$, so reject H_0.

10.15 a. $H_0: \mu_1 = \mu_2, H_1: \mu_1 \neq \mu_2, t = -0.798, df = 48$,
$t_{.05} = \pm 1.677$, can't reject H_0.
b. p-value $= .4288$. Difference is not significant.

10.17 a. $H_0: \mu_1 \leq \mu_2, H_1: \mu_1 > \mu_2, t = 1.902, df = 29$,
$t_{.01} = 2.462$, can't reject H_0.
b. p-value $= .0336$. Would be significant at $\alpha = .05$.

10.19 $H_0: \mu_1 \geq \mu_2, H_1: \mu_1 < \mu_2, df = 14, \bar{x}_1 = 3.38, s_1 = 0.92$,
$\bar{x}_2 = 4.63, s_2 = 1.30, t = -2.22$ ($p = .0217$) so reject H_0
at $\alpha = .025$. Reduction is significant.

10.21 $H_0: \mu_d \leq 0, H_1: \mu_d > 0, t = 1.93, df = 6$, and p-value $= .0509$, so can't quite reject H_0 at $\alpha = .05$.

10.23 $H_0: \mu_d \leq 0, H_1: \mu_d > 0, t = 2.86, df = 9$, and p-value $= .0094$, so reject H_0 at $\alpha = .10$.

10.25 $H_0: \mu_d = 0, H_1: \mu_d \neq 0, t = -1.71, df = 7$, and p-value $= .1307$, so can't reject H_0 at $\alpha = .01$.

10.27 a. $H_0: \mu_1 \geq \mu_2, H_1: \mu_1 < \mu_2, df = 8, \bar{x}_1 = 40.80$,
$s_1 = 2.59, \bar{x}_2 = 48.60, s_2 = 3.13, t = -4.29$,
p-value $= .0013$, so reject at $\alpha = .05$. Significant noise reduction.
b. $H_0: \sigma_1^2 = \sigma_2^2, H_1: \sigma_1^2 \neq \sigma_2^2, df_1 = 4, df_2 = 4$. For two-tailed test $F_R = F_{4,4} = 9.60$, and $F_L = 1/F_{4,4} = 1/9.60 = .104$. Test statistic $F = .6837$ so can't reject equal variances.

10.29 a. $H_0: \mu_1 \leq \mu_2, H_1: \mu_1 > \mu_2, df = 11$ for unequal variances. $\bar{x}_1 = 48.60, s_1^2 = 141.38, \bar{x}_2 = 36.13, s_2^2 = 20.981, t = 3.163$, p-value $= .0045$, so reject H_0 at $\alpha = .05$. International bags are heavier.
b. $H_0: \sigma_1^2 \leq \sigma_2^2, H_1: \sigma_1^2 > \sigma_2^2, df_1 = 11, df_2 = 14$. For two-tailed test, $F_R = F_{9,14} = 2.65$, and $F_L = 1/F_{12,9} = 1/3.07 = .33$. Since $F = 6.74$, international bags have greater variance.

10.31 a. $H_0: \pi_1 \leq \pi_2, H_1: \pi_1 > \pi_2$
b. Reject if $z > z_{.05} = 1.645$.
c. $p_1 = .98000, p_2 = .93514, \bar{p} = .95912, z = 4.507$.
d. Reject at $\alpha = .05$.
e. p-value $= .0000$.
f. Normality is OK since $n_1(1 - \pi_1) = 17$ and $n_2(1 - \pi_2) = 48$ both > 10.

10.33 a. $H_0: \pi_1 = \pi_2, H_1: \pi_1 \neq \pi_2$
b. $p_1 = .17822, p_2 = .14300, \bar{p} = .14895, z = 1.282$,
p-value $= .2000$. Since z is within ± 1.960 for a two-tail test at $\alpha = .05$ and p-value exceeds .05, we fail to reject H_0.

10.35 a. $H_0: \pi_1 = \pi_2, H_1: \pi_1 \neq \pi_2, p_1 = .38492, p_2 = .48830$,
$\bar{p} = .44444, z = -2.506$. Since z does not exceed ± 2.576, we cannot reject H_0.
b. Two-tailed p-value $= .0122$.
c. Normality OK since $n_1 p_1 = 97, n_2 p_2 = 167$ both exceed 10.
d. Gender interests may imply different marketing strategies.

10.37 a. $H_0: \pi_1 \geq \pi_2, H_1: \pi_1 < \pi_2, p_1 = .14914, p_2 = .57143$,
$\bar{p} = .21086, z = -8.003$. Since $z < -2.326$, we conclude that pilots are more likely to approve of night-flying without non-instrument rating.
b. Left-tailed p-value $= .0000$.
c. Normality assumption OK since $n_1 p_1 = 61, n_2(1 - p_2) = 30$ both exceed 10.

10.39 a. $H_0: \pi_1 \leq \pi_2, H_1: \pi_1 > \pi_2, p_1 = .02850, p_2 = .02229$,
$\bar{p} = .02589, z = 2.932$. Reject H_0 since $z > 2.326$.
b. Right-tailed p-value $= .0017$.

c. Normality OK since $n_1 p_1 = 245$, $n_2 p_2 = 185$ both exceed 10.

d. Not a large difference, but life is important.

e. Were smoking, diet, exercise, etc. considered?

10.41 a. $H_0: \pi_1 \leq \pi_2$, $H_1: \pi_1 > \pi_2$, $p_1 = .0042764$, $p_2 = .0016385$, $\bar{p} = .0023388$, $z = 8.254$. Since $z > 2.326$, reject H_0.

b. Left-tailed p-value $= .0000$.

c. Normality OK since $n_1 p_1 = 133$, $n_2 p_2 = 141$ both exceed 10.

d. Yes, risk is almost three times for those with family history.

10.43 a. $H_0: \mu_1 \leq \mu_2$, $H_1: \mu_1 > \mu_2$. Assuming equal variances, $t = 4.089$ with d.f. $= 84$. Since the p-value is $.0000$, reject H_0 at $\alpha = .01$.

10.45 a. $H_0: \pi_1 \geq \pi_2$, $H_1: \pi_1 < \pi_2$, $p_1 = .1402$, $p_2 = .2000$, $\bar{p} = .16396$.

b. $z = -2.777$ and left-tailed p-value $= .0027$. Since $z < -2.326$, reject H_0.

c. Normality OK since $n_1 p_1 = 104$, $n_2 p_2 = 98$ both exceed 10.

d. Many people can't afford them or lack insurance to pay for them.

10.47 a. $H_0: \mu_1 \leq \mu_2$, $H_1: \mu_1 > \mu_2$. Assuming unequal variances, $t = 1.718$ with $\nu = 16$ (using Welch's adjustment). Since the p-value is $.0525$, we fail to reject H_0 at $\alpha = .05$.

b. If we had looked at the same firm in each year, the test would have more power.

10.49 a. Dot plots suggest that the new bumper has less down-time, but variation is similar.

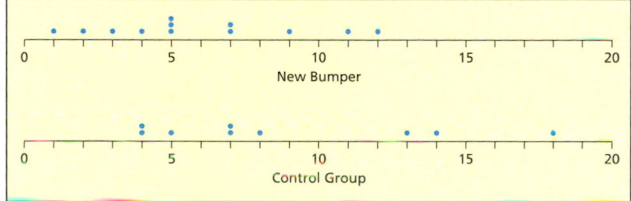

b. $H_0: \mu_1 \leq \mu_2$, $H_1: \mu_1 > \mu_2$.

c. Assuming equal variances, reject H_0 if $t < -1.729$ with df $= 19$.

d. $\bar{x}_1 = 5.917$, $s_1 = 3.423$, $\bar{x}_2 = 8.889$, $s_2 = 4.961$, $s_p^2 = 17.148$, $t = 1.63$, p-value $= .0600$, so fail to reject H_0 at $\alpha = .05$.

10.51 a. Two-tailed test of two means assuming unknown but equal variances.

b. $H_0: \mu_1 = \mu_2$, $H_1: \mu_1 \neq \mu_2$.

c. $t = 2.651$ with df $= 86$. Since the p-value is $.0096$, we easily reject H_0 at $\alpha = .05$. Difference isn't large, but large samples give high power.

d. Students might be more alert in the morning.

e. Yes, the standard deviations are similar.

f. $H_0: \sigma_1^2 = \sigma_2^2$, $H_1: \sigma_1^2 \neq \sigma_2^2$, df$_1 = 41$, df$_2 = 45$. For two-tailed test, $F_R = F_{40,40} = 1.88$, and $F_L = 1/F_{40,40} = 1/1.88 = .53$. Since $F = 7.81^2/6.62^2 = 1.39$, we can't reject H_0.

10.53 a. Dot plots suggest that the means differ and variances differ (outlier in men's salaries).

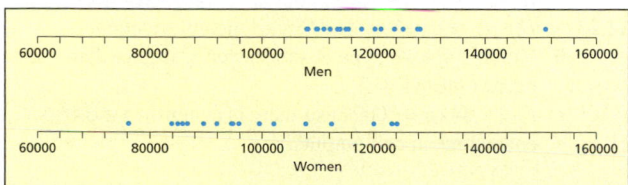

b. $H_0: \mu_1 \leq \mu_2$, $H_1: \mu_1 > \mu_2$.

c. Reject H_0 if $t > 2.438$ with df $= 35$.

d. $\bar{x}_1 = 117{,}853$, $s_1 = 10{,}115$, $\bar{x}_2 = 98{,}554$, $s_2 = 14{,}541$, $s_p^2 = 152{,}192{,}286$, $t = 4.742$.

e. Reject H_0 at $\alpha = .05$. Men are paid significantly more.

f. p-value $= .0000$. Unlikely result if H_0 is true.

g. Yes, the large difference suggests gender discrimination.

10.55 a. Dot plots show strong skewness, but means could be similar.

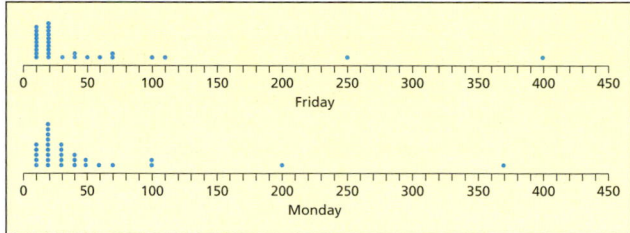

b. $H_0: \mu_1 = \mu_2$, $H_1: \mu_1 \neq \mu_2$. Assume equal variances.

c. Reject H_0 if $t > 2.663$ or if $t < -2.663$ with df $= 58$.

d. $\bar{x}_1 = 50.333$, $s_1 = 81.684$, $\bar{x}_2 = 50.000$, $s_2 = 71.631$, $s_p^2 = 5{,}901.667$. Since $t = .017$ we cannot reject H_0.

e. p-value $= .9866$. Sample result well within chance range.

10.57 a. $H_0: \mu_1 = \mu_2$, $H_1: \mu_1 \neq \mu_2$.

b. For equal variances, df $= 55$, reject H_0 if $t < -1.673$.

c. Since $t = -3.162$ ($p = .0025$) we reject H_0 at $\alpha = .05$. Mean sales are lower on the east side.

10.59 $H_0: \sigma_1^2 = \sigma_2^2$, $H_1: \sigma_1^2 \neq \sigma_2^2$, df$_1 = 30$, df$_2 = 29$. For $\alpha/2 = .025$ $F_R = F_{30,29} = 2.09$, and $F_L = 1/F_{29,30} \cong 1/F_{25,30} = 1/2.12 = .47$. Test statistic is $F = (13.482)^2/(15.427)^2 = 0.76$, so we can't reject H_0.

10.61 Independent samples. $H_0: \mu_1 = \mu_2$, $H_1: \mu_1 \neq \mu_2$. $\bar{x}_1 = 408.25$, $s_1 = 163.72$, $\bar{x}_2 = 412.25$, $s_2 = 168.19$. For equal variances, df $= 14$ and $s_p^2 = 27{,}546$. Since $t = -.05$ ($p = .9622$) do not reject H_0 at $\alpha = .01$.

10.63 Independent samples. $H_0: \mu_1 = \mu_2$, $H_1: \mu_1 \neq \mu_2$. $\bar{x}_1 = 1.8333$, $s_1 = 1.8990$, $\bar{x}_2 = 1.0833$, $s_2 = .9962$. If unequal variances with df $= 16$ (Welch's adjustment) $t = 1.212$ ($p = .2433$) so don't reject H_0 at $\alpha = .10$. Normality is in doubt (Poisson events, small means).

10.65 a. $H_0: \sigma_1^2 \leq \sigma_2^2$, $H_1: \sigma_1^2 > \sigma_2^2$, df$_1 = 11$, df$_2 = 11$. For a right-tail test at $\alpha = .025$, Appendix F gives $F_R = F_{11,11} \cong F_{10,11} = 3.53$. The test statistic is $F = (2.9386)^2/(0.9359)^2 = 9.86$, so conclude that Portfolio A has a greater variance than Portfolio B.

b. These are independent samples. $H_0: \mu_1 = \mu_2$, $H_1: \mu_1 \neq \mu_2$. $\bar{x}_1 = 8.5358$, $s_1 = 2.9386$, $\bar{x}_2 = 8.1000$, $s_2 = .9359$, Assuming unequal variances with df $= 13$ (with Welch's adjustment) we get $t = 0.49$ with p-value $= .6326$, so we cannot reject H_0 at $\alpha = .025$.

CHAPTER 11

11.1 a. $H_0: \mu_A = \mu_B = \mu_C$, H_1: Not all means are equal.

b. One-factor, $F = 5.31$, p-value $= .0223$.

c. Reject H_0 at $\alpha = .05$.

d. Plant B mean likely higher, Plant C lower.

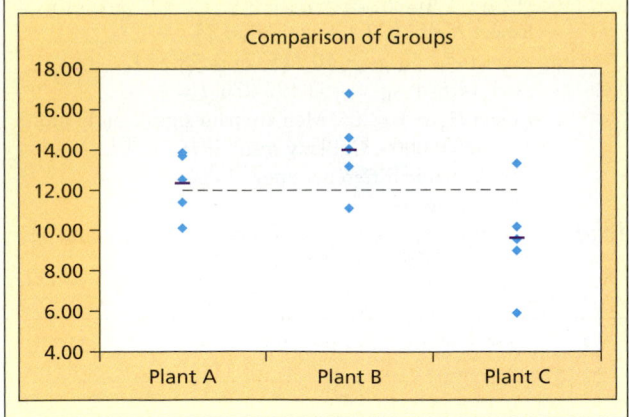

Comparison of Groups — Plant A, Plant B, Plant C

11.3 a. $H_0: \mu_1 = \mu_2 = \mu_3 = \mu_4$, H_1: Not all equal.
  b. One-factor $F = 3.52$, p-value $= .0304$.
  c. Reject H_0 at $\alpha = .05$. GPAs not the same.
  d. Marketing and HR likely higher, accounting and finance lower.

11.5 Only Plant B and Plant C differ at $\alpha = .05$ ($t = 3.23$) using MegaStat Tukey test.

11.7 Only marketing and accounting differ at $\alpha = .05$ (Tukey $t = 3.00$).

11.9 $F_{\max} = 7.027/2.475 = 2.839$. Critical value from Table 11.5 $= 15.5$ (df$_1 = c = 3$, df$_2 = n/c - 1 = 4$). Fail to reject equal variances.

11.11 $F_{\max} = 8.097$. Critical value from Table 11.5 $= 10.4$ (df$_1 = c = 4$, df$_2 = n/c - 1 = 6$). Fail to reject null.

11.13 a. H_0: Mean absenteeism same in all four plants, H_1: Mean absenteeism not the same in all four plants.
  b. ANOVA table: Two factor without replication.
  c. Plant means differ, $F = 41.19$ ($p = .0002$). Blocking factor $F = 8.62$ ($p = .0172$) also significant.
  d. Plant 1, 2 below overall mean, Plant 3, 4 above.

ANOVA table: Two factor without replication

Source	SS	df	MS	F	p-value
Treatments (plant)	216.25	3	72.083	41.19	.0002
Blocks (date)	30.17	2	15.083	8.62	.0172
Error	10.50	6	1.750		
Total	256.92	11			

Mean	n	Std. Dev	Factor Level
20.333	3	1.528	Plant 1
18.000	3	2.000	Plant 2
29.000	3	2.646	Plant 3
25.000	3	2.646	Plant 4
21.500	4	4.041	04-Mar-05
25.250	4	5.377	11-Mar-05
22.50	4	5.508	

11.15 a. H_0: Mean scores same for all five professors, H_1: Mean scores are not the same.
  c. For "professor effect" ambiguous, $F = 3.26$ ($p = .0500$), blocking factor not significant.
  d. Clagmire above overall mean; Ennuyeux slightly below; plots suggest no strong differences.

11.17 a. *Rows*: H_0: Year means the same, H_1: Year means differ.
  Columns: H_0: portfolio type means the same, H_1: portfolio type means differ.
  Interaction(Year × Type): H_0: no interaction, H_1 There is an interaction effect.
  b. ANOVA table: Two factor with replication (5 observations per cell).
  c. Year ($F = 66.82$, $p < .0001$) is highly significant. Portfolio ($F = 5.48$, $p = .0026$) differ significantly, and significant interaction ($F = 4.96$, $p = .0005$).
  d. p-values are very small, indicating significant effects at $\alpha = .05$. Year is strongest result.
  e. Interacton plot lines do cross and support the interaction found and reported above.

ANOVA table: Two factor with replication (5 observations per cell)

Source	SS	df	MS	F	p-value
Factor 1 (portfolio)	1,191.584	2	595.7922	66.82	<.0001
Factor 2 (year)	146.553	3	48.8511	5.48	.0026
Interaction	265.192	6	44.1986	4.96	.0005
Error	427.980	48	8.9162		
Total	2,031.309	59			

11.19 a. *Rows*: H_0: Age group means same, H_1: Age group means differ
  Columns: H_0: Region means same, H_1: Region means differ
  Interaction (Age × Region): H_0: no interaction, H_1: interaction
  b. ANOVA table: Two factor with replication (5 observations per cell).
  c. Age group means ($F = 36.96$, $p < .0001$) differ dramatically. Region means ($F = 0.5$, $p = .6493$) don't differ significantly. Significant interaction ($F = 3.66$, $p = .0010$).
  d. Age group p-value indicates very strong result, interaction is significant at $\alpha = .05$.
  e. Interaction plot lines do cross and support the interaction found and reported above.

11.21 a. $H_0: \mu_1 = \mu_2 = \mu_3 = \mu_4$, H_1: Not all the means are equal.
  b. Graph shows mean Freshmen GPA is lower than overall mean.
  c. $F = 2.36$ ($p = .1000$), fail to reject H_0 at $\alpha = .05$, No significant difference among GPAs.
  d. Reject H_0 if $F > F_{3,21} = 3.07$.
  e. Differences in mean grades large enough (.4 to .7) to matter, but not significant, so cannot be considered important.
  f. Large variances within groups and small samples rob the test of power, suggests larger sample within each group.
  g. Tukey confirms no significant difference in any pairs of means.
  h. $F_{\max} = (0.6265)^2/(0.2826)^2 = 4.91$ which is less than Hartley's critical value 13.7 with df$_1 = c = 4$ and df$_2 = n/c - 1 = 5$, so conclude equal variances.

11.23 a. $H_0: \mu_1 = \mu_2 = \mu_3$, H_1: Not all means are equal.
  b. Graph suggests Type B a bit lower, C higher than the overall mean.
  c. $F = 9.44$ ($p = .0022$) so there is a significant difference in mean cell outputs.

d. Reject H_0 if $F > F_{2,15} = 3.68$.
e. Small differences in means, but could be important in a large solar cell array.
f. Sounds like a controlled experiment and variances are small, so a small sample suffices.
g. Tukey test shows that C differs from B at $\alpha = .01$ and from A at $\alpha = .05$.
h. $F_{max} = (4.57)^2/(4.00)^2 = 1.31$, less than Hartley's 10.8 with $df_1 = c = 3$ and $df_2 = n/c - 1 = 5$, conclude equal variances.

11.25 a. H_0: $\mu_1 = \mu_2 = \mu_3 = \mu_4$, H_1: Not all means equal.
b. Graph shows B higher, D lower.
c. $F = 1.79$ ($p = .1857$) so at $\alpha = .05$ no significant difference in mean waiting times.
d. Reject H_0 if $F > F_{3,18} = 3.16$.
e. Differences in means might matter to patient, but not significant so can't be considered important.
f. Variances large, samples small, so test has low power.
g. Tukey test shows no significant differences in pairs of means.
h. $F_{max} = (11.90)^2/(6.74)^2 = 3.121 = .142$, less than the Hartley's 20.6 with $df_1 = c = 4$ and $df_2 = n/c - 1 = 4$ so conclude equal variances.

11.27 a. *Columns:* H_0: Surface has no effect on mean braking distance, H_1: Surface does effect distance
Rows: H_0: Pumping method has no effect on mean braking distance, H_1: Pumping method does effect distance
b. Graph suggests differences (ice is greater than the other two).
c. Surface: $F = 134.39$ ($p = .0002$), reject H_0. Surface has a significant effect on mean stopping distance. Braking method: $F = 0.72$ ($p = .5387$), cannot reject H_0. Braking method has no significant effect on stopping distance.
d. Reject H_0 if $F > F_{2,4} = 6.94$.
e. For surface, differences large enough to be very importance in preventing accidents.
f. Replication would be desirable, if tests are not too costly.
g. Tukey test shows a difference between ice and the other two surfaces.

11.29 a. H_0: $\mu_1 = \mu_2 = \mu_3 = \mu_4 = \mu_5$, H_1: Not all means equal.
b. Graph shows no differences in means.
c. $F = 0.39$ ($p = .8166$), cannot reject H_0. No significant difference in the mean dropout rates.
d. Reject H_0 if $F > F_{4,45} = 2.61$.
e. Differences not significant, not important.
f. Could look at a different year. But sample is already fairly large.
g. Tukey shows no significant differences in pairs.
h. $F_{max} = (10.585)^2/(3.759)^2 = 7.93$, exceeds Hartley's 7.11 with $df_1 = c = 5$ and $df_2 = n/c - 1 = 9$ so conclude unequal variances.

11.31 *Rows:* H_0: Means same for crash types, H_1: Means differ. *Columns:* H_0: Vehicle means same, H_1: Vehicle means differ.
Interaction (CrashType × Vehicle): H_0: No interaction, H_1: interaction.
Conclusion: both highly significant (crash type and vehicle), but no interaction. Increasing sample size raised F statistics, lowered p-values, which strengthens

conclusions from the smaller sample. Tukey tests show clearer differences in all pairs of crash types, and in all pairs of vehicles. In the smaller sample, not all of these pairs differed significantly.

11.33 Tax audit rate not significantly affected by year ($F = 0.72$, $p = 0.6153$), significantly affected by taxpayer class ($F = 17.08$, $p = 0.0000$).

11.35 a. Two Factor ANOVA
b. Instructor gender p-value ($p = .43$) exceeds $\alpha = .10$, instructor gender means do not differ. Student gender p-value ($p = .24$) exceeds $\alpha = .10$, student gender means do not differ (p-value $> \alpha = .10$). For interaction, the p-value ($p = .03$) suggests significant interaction effect (at $\alpha = .05$).
c. Unlikely that a gender effect was overlooked due to sample size, test should have very good power.

11.37 Call waiting time not affected by day of week ($F = 1.62$, $p = .1760$), is significantly affected by time of day ($F = 3.00$, $p = .0001$).

11.39 a. Two factor, either factor could be of research interest.
b. Pollution affected freeway ($F = 24.90$, $p = .0000$) and by time of day ($F = 21.51$, $p = .0000$).
c. Variances for freeway 2926.7 to 14333.7, for time of day 872.9 to 14333.6. F_{max} ratios are large (4.90 and 16.42), suggesting possibly unequal variances.
d. For freeway, $df_1 = c = 4$ and $df_2 = n/c - 1 = 20/4 - 1 = 4$, Hartley's critical value 20.6, so conclude equal variances. Time of day, $df_1 = c = 5$ and $df_2 = n/c - 1 = 20/5 - 1 = 3$, so Hartley's critical value is 50.7 so conclude equal variances.

11.41 a. One factor.
b. Between Groups $df_1 = 4$ and $df_1 = c - 1$ so $c = 5$ bowlers.
c. p-value 0.000, reject null, conclude there is difference.
d. Sample variances 83.66 to 200.797, $F_{max} = 200.797/83.66 = 2.40$. Hartley's test, $df_1 = c = 5$ and $df_2 = n/c - 1 = 67/5 - 1 = 12$, critical value is 5.30. Not enough variation to reject null hypothesis of homogeneity.

CHAPTER 12

12.1 For each sample: H_0: $\rho = 0$ vs. H_1: $\rho \neq 0$

Sample	df	r	t	t_α	r_α	Decision
a	18	.45	2.138	2.101	.444	Reject
b	28	−.35	−1.977	1.701	.306	Reject
c	5	.6	1.677	2.015	.669	Fail to Reject
d	59	−.3	−2.416	2.39	.297	Reject

12.3 b. −.7328   c. $t_{.025} = 3.183$
d. $t = -1.865$, Fail to reject.   e. p-value = .159

12.5 b. .531   c. 2.131   d. 2.429   e. ±.482
f. Yes, reject.

12.7 a.

	1-Year	3-Year	5-Year	10-Year
1-Year	1.000			
3-Year	−.095	1.000		
5-Year	.014	.771	1.000	
10-Year	.341	.463	.746	1.000

b. $r_{.05} = .576$.

c. Significant positive correlation between years 3 and 5 and 5 and 10.

12.9 a. Each additional sf increases price $150.   b. $425,000.

c. No.

12.11 a. Earning an extra $1,000 raises home price by $2610.

b. No.   c. $181,800, $312,300.

12.13 a. Blazer: Each year reduces price by $1050. Silverado: each year reduces price by $1339.

b. Intercept could indicate price of new car.

c. $10,939.

d. $16,256.

12.15 a. Units Sold = $300 - 150*Price$ (answers will vary).

b. $1 increase in price decreases units sold by 150.

c. No.

12.17 b. *Wait Time* = $458 - 18.5$ *Operators*.

d. $R^2 = .5369$.

12.19 $y = -31.19 + 4.9322x$, $R^2 = .6717$.

12.21 a. $y = 557.45 + 3.00x$

b. (1.2034, 4.806)

c. $H_0: \beta_1 \geq 0$ vs. $H_1: \beta_1 < 0$, p-value $= .0009$, Reject H_0.

12.23 a. $y = 1.8064 + .0039x$

b. intercept: $1.8064/.6116 = 2.954$, slope: $.0039/.0014 = 2.786$ (may be off due to rounding).

c. $df = 10$, $t_{.025} = \pm 2.228$.

12.25 a. $y = 11.1549 + 0.458x$

b. (0.0561, 0.8598). Interval does not contain zero, slope is greater than zero.

c. t test p-value $= .0282$. Conclusion: slope is greater than zero.

d. F statistic p-value $= .0282$. Conclusion: significant relationship between variables.

e. $5.90 = (2.429)^2$

12.27 a. $y = 6.9609 - 0.053x$

b. $(-0.1946, 0.0886)$. Interval does contain zero, slope is not significantly different from zero.

c. t test p-value $= .4133$. Conclusion: slope is not significantly different from zero.

d. F statistic p-value $= .4133$. Conclusion: No significant relationship between variables.

e. $0.74 = (-0.863)^2$

12.45 $t_{critical} = 2.3069$ (from Excel). From sample: $t = 2.3256$. Reject H_0.

12.47 a. 1515.2.

b. No.

c. (1406.03, 1624.37).

12.49 a. $y = 1743.57 - 1.2163x$.

b. $df = 13$. $t_{critical} = 2.160$.

c. Slope is significantly different from zero.

d. $(-2.1671, -0.2656)$. Interval indicates slope is significantly less than zero.

e. $7.64 = (-2.764)^2$

12.51 a. $r = .6771$

b. From sample: $t = 5.8193$. $t_{.01} = 2.423$. Reject H_0.

12.53 b. $r = .749$

c. $df = 13$. $r_{.05} = .514$. Reject H_0.

12.57 b. $y = -4.2896 + 0.171x$, $R^2 = .2474$. Fit is poor.

12.59 a. No significant relationship between variables. (p-value $= .774$).

b. No, study time and class level could be predictors. (Answers will vary.)

12.61 a. The negative slope means that as age increases, price decreases.

b. Intercepts could be asking price of a new car.

c. The fit is good for the Explorer, Pickup, and Taurus.

d. Additional predictors: condition of car, mileage.

CHAPTER 13

13.1 a. *Net Revenue* = $4.31 - 0.082ShipCost + 2.265\ PrintAds + 2.498WebAds + 16.7Rebate\%$

b. Positive coefficients indicate an increase in net revenue; negative coefficients indicate a decrease in net revenue.

c. The intercept is meaningless.

d. 467.16

13.3 a. *df* are 4 (numerator) and 45 (denominator).

b. $F_{.05} = 2.61$.

c. $F = 12.997$. Yes, overall regression is significant.

d. $R^2 = .536$. $R^2_{adj} = .495$.

13.5 a. and c. See Table.

Predictor	Coef	SE	t-value	p-value
Intercept	4.31	70.82	0.0608585	0.9517414
ShipCost	−0.082	4.678	−0.0175289	0.9860922
PrintAds	2.265	1.05	2.1571429	0.0363725
WebAds	2.498	0.8457	2.9537661	0.0049772
Rebate%	16.697	3.57	4.6770308	.0003

b. $t_{critical} = 2.69$. WebAds and Rebate% differ significantly from zero.

13.7 $\hat{y}_i \pm 2.032(3620)$: $\hat{y}_i \pm 7355.84$.

Quick Rule $\hat{y}_i \pm 2SE$: $\hat{y}_i \pm 7240$.

13.27 The sample size is too small relative to number of predictors

13.29 Overall regression not significant (F statistic p-value $= .371$), $R^2 = 0.117$ indicates poor fit. Conclusion: No apparent relationship between cost per load and predictors type of washer and type of detergent used.

13.31 a. Coefficients make sense, except for TrnOvr, which would be expected to be negative.

b. No.

c. With 6 predictors, should have minimum of 30 observations. We have only 23 so sample is small.

d. Rebounds and points highly correlated.

13.33 a. Experience lowers the predicted finish time.

b. No.

c. If the relationship is not strictly linear, it can make sense to include a squared predictor, such as seen here.

CHAPTER 14

14.1 a. Growing at an increasing rate (linear $R^2 = .8338$, quadratic $R^2 = .9219$, exponential $R^2 = .9372$).

b. Diesel fuel may be cheaper, may offer better MPG.

c. Data seems to be growing faster than linear.

d. Exponential model is simple and looks like good fit.

e. Linear seems too conservative (about 40,000 by 2006). Quadratic is reasonable (about 60,000 by 2006) while exponential forecast is rather aggressive (about 80,000 by 2006).

14.3 a. Growing, but may be slowing (linear $R^2 = .9244$, quadratic $R^2 = .9399$, exponential $R^2 = .8785$).

b. Rise of internet, higher speed connections, increased PC use, hacker cult.

c. Trend heavily influenced by 2002 (a slow year) which could be an anomaly.

d. Quadratic has a good fit, but suggests slowing growth. Exponential suggests rapid growth (40 percent anually). Proliferating sales of anti-virus software suggests that firms are betting on the latter.

e. In hindsight, the exponential 2003 prediction (about 240 new viruses) better anticipates the virus explosion of the first decade of the 2000s.

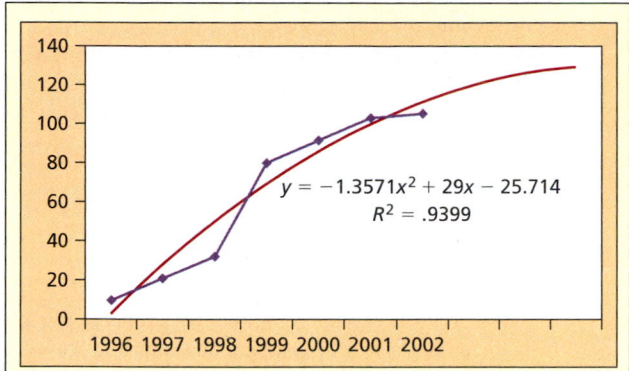

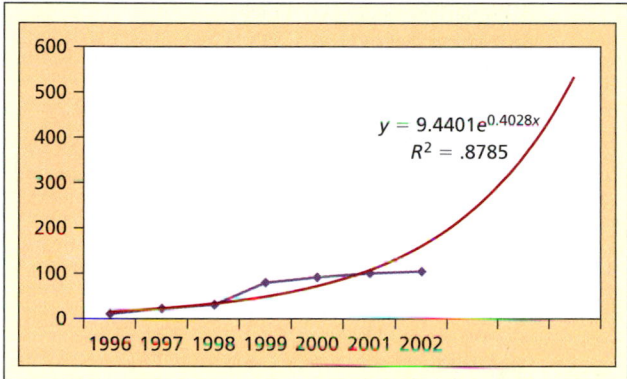

14.5 a. Linear $R^2 = .9898$ (quite a good fit).

b. Rise of health care concerns, change to healthy diet

c. $y_t = 581.73 + 25.55t$.

d. Increased capacity needed for production and distribution.

e. Using $t = 6$, $y_6 = 581.73 + 25.55(6) = 735$.

14.7 Graph shows negative trend and cyclical pattern. Fit improves as α increases (i.e., as we give more weight to recent data). Forecasts are similar for each value of α.

Alpha	.10	.20	0.30
Mean Squared Error	0.039	0.028	0.021
Mean Absolute Percent Error	3.8%	3.1%	2.7%
Percent Positive Errors	42.3%	46.2%	51.9%
Forecast for Period 53	4.30	4.37	4.43

14.9 a. Seasonality exists, but not much trend. Spike in October, 2001 (perhaps a 9-11 reaction).

b. Fit is not very good ($R^2 = .282$, $R^2_{adj} = .036$), and only April ($t = 2.296$, $p = .0278$) shows significant seasonality at $\alpha = .05$. Reasonable, since spring might cause a spike in Corvette sales.

c. Forecasts for 2004:

Period	Forecast	Period	Forecast
January	1,781.46	July	1,916.21
February	2,427.21	August	2,442.21
March	2,532.96	September	2,563.96
April	3,313.96	October	2,866.71
May	2,540.46	November	2,036.21
June	2,284.71	December	1,941.46

14.11 a. Dual scale graph is needed due to differing magnitudes.

b. Electronic sales are large, but have a declining trend ($y_t = 31,578 - 1615.7t$, $R^2 = .9449$). Mechanical sales are small, but with a rising trend ($y_t = 2467 + 40.543t$, $R^2 = .7456$).

c. Electronic sales are falling at 6.27% ($y_t = 32091e^{-0.0627t}$, $R^2 = .9413$) while mechanical are rising at 1.54% ($y_t = 2470.6e^{0.0154t}$, $R^2 = .7465$).

d. Fascination with electronic gadgets may be waning and/or competitors may be moving in on the Swiss watch industry. They may have stronger specialty niche.

e. Linear forecast for electronic is 20,268, mechanical is 2,750.

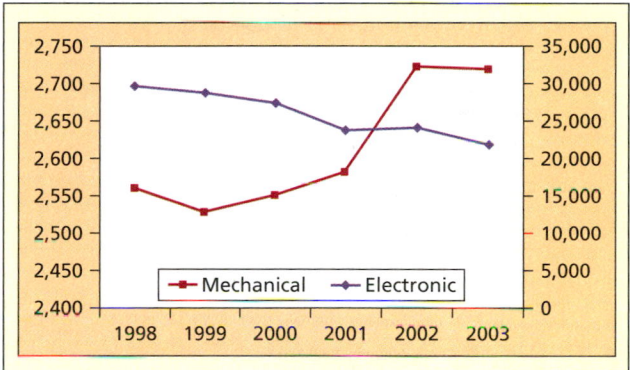

14.13 a. Low in 1948 election, high in 1960 election, fairly steady decline since.

b. Voters may be energized by some elections (e.g., Kennedy-Nixon in 1960).

c. Linear: $y_t = 59.144 - 0.3672t$ ($R^2 = .2007$). Exponential: $y_t = 59.146e^{-0.0067t}$ ($R^2 = .2094$).

d. No one model is very credible for these data, so by Occam's Razor, use linear.

e. About 50 percent (visual judgment forecast).

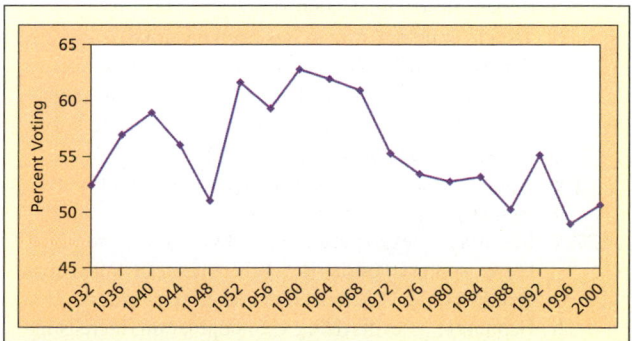

14.15 a. Total credit is growing linearly.
   b. Trend is consistently upward.
   c. Linear is $y_t = 994.86 + 112.45t$ ($R^2 = .9892$), exponential is $y_t = 1061.7e^{0.073t}$ ($R^2 = 0.9920$).
   d. About 2119 (linear model).

14.17 a. Graphs will vary.
   b. Whole milk down, low-fat milk up. Both diet and regular carbonated drinks up. Fruit juices up slightly, beer and wine level or down slightly. Hard liquor is down sharply.
   c–d. Answers will vary, but defend using specific criteria (past fit, recent fit, believability, Occam's Razor).
   e. Answers will vary.

14.19 a. Both have slight downward trends.
   b. Using data from 1980 on and equating women's times to men's times ($148.66 - 0.2186t = 129.96 - .0145t$) and solving for t gives $t = 92$ for year 2137 (recall that 2005 is $t = 26$).
   c. Moving average gives a good fit.
   d. Yes, it is reasonable since trend is slight.

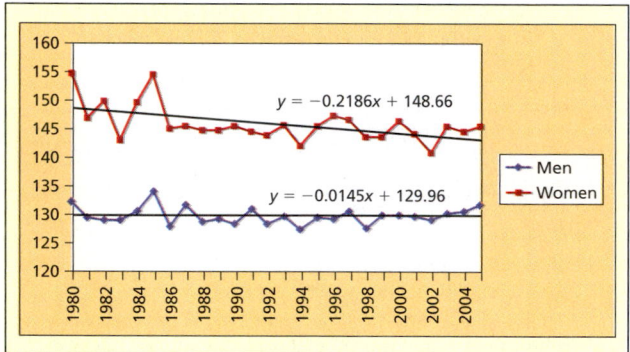

14.21 a. Dramatic increase in shares.
   b. Need to have quick access to travel, unevenness of commercial airplane travel.
   c. $y_t = 3.8256e^{0.4512}$ ($R^2 = 0.9708$). It's a good fit to past data, but can 45.1% annual growth continue?
   d. Answers will vary. 8,000 would be a reasonable judgment, but exponential would be much higher.

14.23 a. Spike in 2001 (due to 2001 terror attacks), otherwise no clear trend.
   b. Positive trend, but poor fit ($R^2 = .1136$)
   c. Fitted trend would not help much.
   d. About 140 (judgment forecast since trend is unclear).

14.25 a. Declines from a little over 10,500 to below 8,500, then rises back toward 10,000.
   b. Trend, while not strong, has been negative. Is 2002 a blip or a turnaround? Linear trend ($y_t = 10,005 - 81.76t$) does not fit the data well ($R^2 = .1834$). Quadratic will give a better fit since it captures the curve, but its forecasts may not be credible.
   c. About 10,000 (judgment forecast since trend is unclear).

14.27 a. Imports and exports are rising, but imports are much larger, so net imports rise. As a percent of world consumption, the U.S. has fallen, leveling at around 25%.
   b. Economic growth, rising U.S. population, increasing vehicle size.

   c. For imports, linear trend is $y_t = 0.5125 + 1.0986t$ ($R^2 = .9016$) and exponential trend is $y_t = 1.7888e^{.2122t}$ ($R^2 = .8885$). The growth rate of 21.22 percent every five years is easy to understand.
   d. For 2005, import may exceed 14 million barrels a day. Believable, given the continued role of oil in the U.S. economy.
   e. Consumers, producers, government, refiners (in other words, all of us) are impacted by use of oil.

14.29 a. Since 1990, SAT scores have upward trends.
   b. Varies with selected series.
   c. Math scores slightly exceed verbal scores, male scores slightly exceed female scores on verbal and math.
   d. Scores may affect high school and college curricula and employers.

14.31 a. Rate declines, then increases.
   b. The following graph shows $\alpha = .20$. Other graphs similar.
   c. For this data $\alpha = .20$ seems to track the recent data well, yet provides enough smoothing to iron out the "blips." It gives enough weight to recent data to bring its forecasts above 1.80 (lagging but reflecting the recent rise in rates). In contrast, $\alpha = .05$ or $\alpha = .10$ provide too much smoothing, so they give a forecast below 1.80. While $\alpha = .50$ gives a good "fit" it does not smooth the data very much.
   d. Smoothing methods are useful since there is no single, consistent trend.

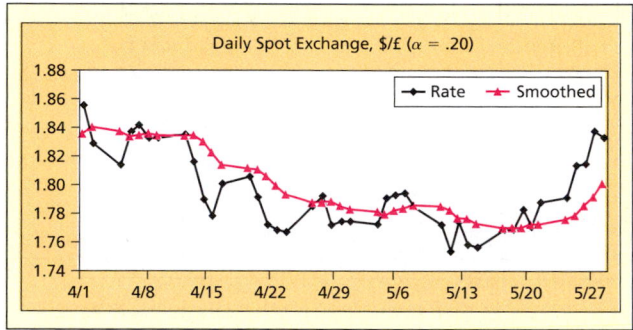

14.33 a. Highly cyclical, but not much trend.
   b. Yes, demand for permits starts to increase before the prime building months of the summer season.
   c. The average month's index is 1.000. Indexes are adjusted so they sum to 12.000.

Month	Index	Month	Index
Jan	0.6494	Jul	1.1219
Feb	0.7225	Aug	1.1252
Mar	1.0554	Sep	1.0294
Apr	1.2505	Oct	1.0911
May	1.1950	Nov	0.8422
Jun	1.1826	Dec	0.7348

   d. April, May, June have the most; January, December, February the least.
   e. No, there is no significant trend ($R^2 = .0179$). Equation is $y = 1.0253x + 1450$

14.35 a. Trend is upward (weakened in 2003 but stronger in 2004) with seasonal fluctuations.

b. The average month's index is 1.000. Indexes are adjusted so they sum to 12.000.

Month	Index	Month	Index
Jan	1.0235	Jul	0.9767
Feb	1.0064	Aug	0.9857
Mar	0.9861	Sep	0.9771
Apr	0.9916	Oct	0.9761
May	0.9977	Nov	1.0320
Jun	0.9852	Dec	1.0617

c. Highest: December, November, January.
Lowest: October, September, July.

d. Yes, this is logical. Credit increases due to the Christmas buying season, drops off during the month of July (vacation) and September and October, kids back to school, waiting for Christmas spending season. Equation is $y = 1.4874x + 210.72$. $R^2 = 0.8344$

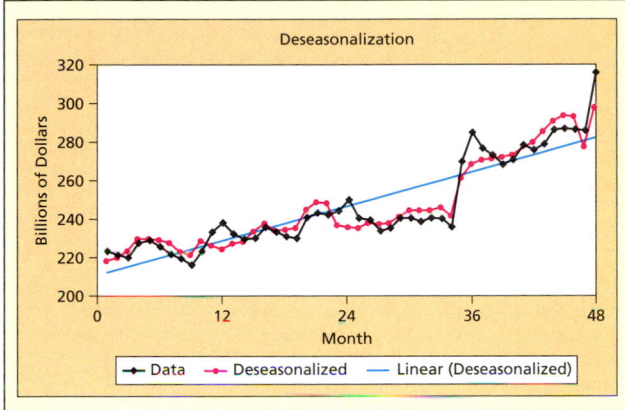

14.37 a. Declines, then rises. No obvious seasonality.

b. Seasonal index are very close to 1.000, though December is a little higher (holiday shopping).

c. To make monthly forecasts, use the trend equation $yt = 1103.8 + 0.0456t$ to predict each month ($t = 85$, $86, \ldots, 96$) and then multiply each month's forecast by its seasonal factor.

Month	Index	Month	Index
Jan	1.0068	Jul	0.9999
Feb	0.9887	Aug	0.9956
Mar	0.9986	Sep	0.9920
Apr	1.0101	Oct	0.9921
May	0.9922	Nov	1.0030
Jun	0.9977	Dec	1.0234

14.39 a. All binaries and time are significant aqt $\alpha = .05$. Each seasonal binary measures the distance from December. Fitted equation is $Permits = 5486 + 576\,Jan + 580\,Feb + 1343\,Mar + 1345\,Apr + 1587\,May + 2526\,Jun + 2665\,Jul + 2933\,Aug + 2387\,Sep + 1910\,Oct + 1215\,Nov - 36.5\,Time$.

Statistic	Coeff	Std Err	t	p
Intercept	5486	231.6	23.69	0.000
Jan	576	283.6	2.03	0.047
Feb	580	283.3	2.05	0.045
Mar	1343	283.0	4.75	0.000
Apr	1345	282.8	4.76	0.000
May	1587	282.6	5.62	0.000
Jun	2526	282.4	8.94	0.000
Jul	2665	282.2	9.44	0.000
Aug	2933	282.1	10.40	0.000
Sep	2387	282.0	8.46	0.000
Oct	1911	281.9	6.78	0.000
Nov	1215	281.9	4.31	0.000
Time	−36.523	2.81	−13.01	0.000

$S = 488.245$ R-Sq = 87.1%   R-Sq(adj) = 84.5%

b. Forecasts for 1997 are obtained from the fitted regression equation using $Time = 73, 74, \ldots, 84$ and the relevant monthly binary coefficients:

Month	Forecast	Month	Forecast
Jan	3,395	Jul	5,266
Feb	3,363	Aug	5,498
Mar	4,090	Sep	4,915
Apr	4,055	Oct	4,402
May	4,261	Nov	3,670
Jun	5,163	Dec	2,418

14.41* To convert a fitted models of the form $y_t = y_0(1 + r)^t$ to Excel's equivalent exponential form $y_t = a\,e^{bt}$, we use the same intercept but set $b = \ln(1 + r)$. This converts the model to a continuously compounded rate of growth (if $b > 0$) or decline (if $b < 0$).

a. $y_t = 123(1.089)^t$ so we set $b = \ln(1.089) = .08525$ and thus $y_t = 123e^{.08525t}$.

b. $y_t = 654(1.217)^t$ so we set $b = \ln(1.217) = .19639$ and thus $y_t = 654e^{.19639t}$.

c. $y_t = 308(0.942)^t$ so we set $b = \ln(.942) = -.05975$ and thus $y_t = 308e^{-.05975t}$.

CHAPTER 15

15.1 a. H_0: *Earnings* are independent of *Approach*

b. Degrees of Freedom = $(r - 1)(c - 1) = (4 - 1)(3 - 1) = 6$

c. CHIINV(.01,6) = 16.81

d. Test statistic is 127.57 ($p = .0000$) so reject null at $\alpha = .01$.

e. *No Clear Effect* and *Business Combinations* contributes the most.

f. All expected frequencies exceed 5.

g. *p*-value is near zero (observed difference not due to chance).

15.3 a. H_0: *Verbal* and *Quantitative* are independent

b. Degrees of Freedom = $(r - 1)(c - 1) = (3 - 1)(3 - 1) = 4$

c. CHIINV(.005,4) = 14.86

d. Test statistic is 55.88 ($p = .0000$), reject null at $\alpha = .005$.

e. *Under 25* and *Under 25* contributes the most.

f. Expected frequency is less than 5 in two cells.

g. *p*-value is nearly zero (observed difference not due to chance).

15.5 a. H_0: *Return Rate* and *Notification* are independent
b. Degrees of Freedom $= (r - 1)(c - 1) =$
   $(2 - 1)(2 - 1) = 1$
c. CHIINV(.025,1) = 5.024
d. Test statistic is 5.42 ($p = .0199$), reject null at $\alpha = .025$.
e. *Returned* and *No* contribute the most.
f. All expected frequencies exceed 5.
g. p-value is less than .025 (observed difference did not arise by chance).
h. $z = 2.33$ (p-value $= .0199$ for two-tailed test).

15.7 a. Bars are similar in length. Vanilla and Mocha are the leading flavors.
b. If uniform, $e_j = 84/4 = 21$ for each flavor.
c. Test statistic is 0.86 with d.f. $= 4 - 1 = 3$ (p-value $= .8358$). Chi-square critical value for $\alpha = .05$ is 7.815, so sample does not contradict the hypothesis that sales are the same for each beverage.

15.9 Expected frequency is $56/7 = 8$ for each age group. Test statistic is 10.000 (p-value $= .1247$). At $\alpha = .05$, critical value for d.f. $= 7 - 1 = 6$ is 12.59. Cannot reject the hypothesis that movie goers are from a uniform population.

Age Class	Obs	Exp	O−E	$(O-E)^2/E$
10 < 20	5	8.000	−3.000	1.125
20 < 30	6	8.000	−2.000	0.500
30 < 40	10	8.000	2.000	0.500
40 < 50	3	8.000	−5.000	3.125
50 < 60	14	8.000	6.000	4.500
60 < 70	9	8.000	1.000	0.125
70 < 80	9	8.000	1.000	0.125
Total	56	56.000	0.000	10.000

15.11 Sample mean $\lambda = 4.948717949$, test statistic 3.483 (p-value $= .4805$) with d.f. $= 6 - 1 - 1 = 4$. The critical value for $\alpha = .05$ is 9.488, cannot reject the hypothesis of a Poisson distribution.

X	P(X)	Obs	Exp	O−E	$(O-E)^2/E$
2 or Less	0.12904	3	5.032	−2.032	0.821
3	0.14326	5	5.587	−0.587	0.062
4	0.17724	9	6.912	2.088	0.631
5	0.17542	10	6.841	3.159	1.458
6	0.14468	5	5.643	−0.643	0.073
7 or More	0.23036	7	8.984	−1.984	0.438
	1.00000	39	39.000	0.000	3.483

15.13 From sample, $\bar{x} = 75.375$, $s = 8.943376$. Set $e_j = 40/8 = 5$. Using Visual Statistics, test statistic is 6.000 (p-value $= .306$) using d.f. $= 8 - 2 - 1 = 5$. Critical value for $\alpha = .05$ is 11.07, cannot reject the hypothesis of a normal distribution.

Score	Obs	Exp	Obs−Exp	Chi-Square
Under 65.09	5	5.000	0.000	0.000
65.09 < 69.34	3	5.000	−2.000	0.800
69.34 < 72.53	5	5.000	0.000	0.000
72.53 < 75.38	3	5.000	−2.000	0.800
75.38 < 78.22	9	5.000	4.000	3.200
78.22 < 81.41	7	5.000	2.000	0.800
81.41 < 85.66	4	5.000	−1.000	0.200
85.66 or more	4	5.000	−1.000	0.200
Total	40	40.000	0.000	6.000

15.15* The probability plot looks linear, but p-value (.033) for the Anderson-Darling test is less than $\alpha = .05$. This tends to contradict the chi-square test used in Exercise 15.13. However, the Kolmogorov-Smirnov test ($D_{Max} = .158$) = does not reject normality ($p > .20$). Data are a borderline case, having some characteristics of a normal distribution. If we have to choose one test, the A-D is the most powerful.

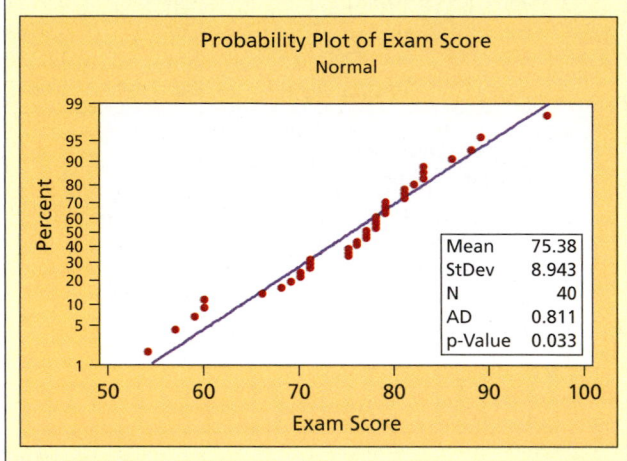

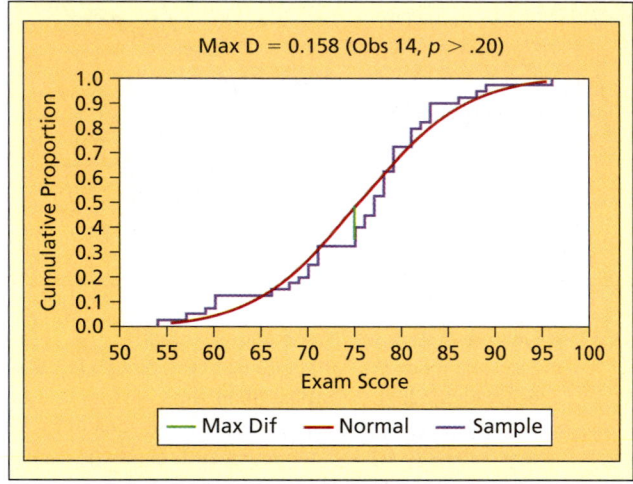

15.17 Is *Satisfaction* independent of *Pay Category?* For d.f. $= (r - 1)(c - 1) = (3 - 1)(2 - 1) = 2$, critical value is CHIINV(.05,2) = 5.991. Test statistic is 4.54 ($p = .1032$), cannot reject the null at $\alpha = .05$. *Salaried* and *Dissatisfied* contributes the most. All expected frequencies exceed 5. The p-value suggests that observed difference would arise by chance 103 times in 1,000 samples if the two variables really were independent, which is not very convincing.

15.19 Is *Grade* independent of *Hand-In Order?* For d.f. $= (r - 1)(c - 1) = (2 - 1)(2 - 1) = 1$, critical value CHIINV(.10,1) = 2.706. Test statistic is 0.23 ($p = .6284$) so cannot reject the null at $\alpha = .10$. *"B" or Better* and *Later Hand-In* contributes the most. All expected frequencies exceed 5. For a two-tailed test of proportions, $p_1 = .4000$, $p_2 = .3333$, $\bar{p} = .3673$, $z = 0.48$ (p-value $= .6284$) which agrees with the chi-square test.

15.21 Is *Graduation* independent of *Sport?* For d.f. $= (r - 1)(c - 1) = (12 - 1)(2 - 1) = 11$, critical value is CHIINV(.01,11) = 24.73. Test statistic is 82.73 ($p = .0000$)

so reject the null at $\alpha = .01$. *Swimming* and *Not Grad in 6 Years* contributes the most. All expected frequencies exceed 5.

15.23 Is *Smoking* independent of *Race?* For d.f. $= (r - 1)(c - 1) = (2 - 1)(2 - 1) = 1$, critical value is CHIINV $(.005,1) = 7.879$. For males, test statistic is 5.84 ($p = .0157$), can't reject the null at $\alpha = .005$. For females, test statistic is 14.79 ($p = .0001$) so reject the null at $\alpha = .005$. *Black* and *Smoker* contributes the most in each test. All expected frequencies exceed 5. The two-tailed test of proportions agrees.

15.25 For d.f. $= (r - 1)(c - 1) = (2 - 1)(2 - 1) = 1$, critical value CHIINV$(.10,1) = 2.706$, test statistic is 1.80 ($p = .1792$) so fail to reject the null at $\alpha = .10$. The lower left cell contributes most. All expected frequencies exceed 5. The two-tailed test of proportions ($z = 1.342$) agrees with the chi-square test. Interestingly, the relationship seems to be inverse (i.e., rates tend to rise when they are predicted to fall).

15.27 For the 2×2 table, d.f. $= 1$, critical value is CHIINV$(.05,1) = 3.841$, test statistic is 7.15 ($p = .0075$) so reject null at $\alpha = .05$. For the 3×3 table, d.f. $= 4$, critical value is CHIINV$(.05,4) = 13.28$, test statistic is 12.30 ($p = .0153$), so reject null at $\alpha = .05$. All expected frequencies exceed 5.

15.29 With d.f. $= (r - 1)(c - 1) = (3 - 1)(3 - 1) = 4$, the critical value is CHIINV$(.01,4) = 2.706$. The test statistic is 54.18 ($p = .0000$) so we reject the null at $\alpha = .01$. All expected frequencies exceed 5.

15.31 If uniform, all expected frequencies would be 9. For d.f. $= 4 - 1 = 3$, critical value is CHIINV$(.10,3) = 6.251$, test statistic is 1.556 ($p = .6695$) so cannot reject the hypothesis of a uniform (it is logical to expect no pattern).

15.33 For d.f. $= 4 - 1 = 3$, critical value is CHIINV$(.05,3) = 7.815$, test statistic is 6.045 ($p = .1095$) so we cannot reject hypothesis that Oxnard follows U.S. distribution.

15.35 For d.f. $= 6 - 1 = 5$, critical value is CHIINV$(.10,5) = 9.236$, test statistic is 4.40 ($p = .4934$) so we can't reject the hypothesis that the die is fair.

15.37* Estimated mean is $\lambda = 1.06666667$. For d.f. $= 4 - 1 - 1 = 2$, critical value is CHIINV$(.025,2) = 7.378$, test statistic is 4.947 ($p = .0843$) so can't reject the hypothesis of a Poisson distribution

X	f_j	$P(X)$	e_j	$f_j - e_j$	$(f_j - e_j)^2/e_j$
0	25	0.344154	20.64923	4.35077	0.917
1	18	0.367097	22.02584	−4.02584	0.736
2	8	0.195785	11.74712	−3.74712	1.195
3 or more	9	0.092964	5.57781	3.42219	2.100
Total	60	1.000000	60.00000	0.00000	4.947

15.39 Mean is $\lambda = 0.702479339$ runs/inning. For d.f. $= 4 - 1 - 1 = 2$, critical value is CHIINV$(.05,2) = 5.991$, test statistic is 95.51 ($p = .0000$) so reject hypothesis that runs per inning are Poisson. In hockey, goals are independent events, while in baseball they are not.

15.41* Answers will vary, but most should confirm the normal distribution and intended μ and σ.

15.43* Answers will vary, but most should confirm the Poisson distribution and intended λ.

CHAPTER 16

16.1 $R = 14$, $z = 0.66$ ($p = .9472$). Fail to reject H_0.

16.3 a. Sample median $= 53.75$. $W = 234.5$, $z = 0.7174$, p-value $= .48$. Median is not significantly different from 50.
   b. Close to a normal distribution. Parametric t test could be justified.

16.5 a. $z = 1.29$, p-value $= .0991$. No difference in medians.
   b. $t = 1.62$, p-value $= .0606$ (assuming equal variances). Same decision but p-value closer to .05.

16.7 a. $H = 6.51$, p-value $= .089$. No difference in medians.
   b. Yes, $F = 2.71$, p-value $= .055$.
   c. Can assume normality for Energy and Retail. Health and Leisure are less obvious.

16.9 $\chi^2 = 3.3$, p-value $= .3476$. No difference in median ratings.

16.11 a.

2004	2005	2004	2005
6	7	17	20
5	5	16	16
10	10	4	4
13	14	14	19
15	15	11	13
19	18	1	1
3	3	20	17
7	6	2	2
8	8	18	12
12	11	9	9

   b. $r_s = .9338$.
   c. Yes, $r_{.01} = .561$.
   e. Pearson: $r = .996$.
   f. Nonnormal data justifies use of Spearman rank correlation.

16.13 $R = 28$, $z = 0.628$ ($p = .5300$). Results are random.

16.15 $R = 15$, $z = 0.49$ ($p = .6245$). Results are random.

16.17 $R = 22$, $z = 1.244$ ($p = .2135$). Results are random.

16.19 $R = 9$, $z = -1.437$ ($p = .1508$). Results are random.

16.21 $H = 0.558$, p-value $= .4549$. No difference in medians.

16.23 From MegaStat Wilcoxon – Mann/Whitney Test: $z = -1.68$, p-value $= .6571$. Medians do not differ.

16.25 $z = -3.06$, p-value $= .0022$. The medians differ.

16.27 $H = 1.46$, p-value $= .4819$. No difference in medians.

16.29 $H = 9.139$, p-value $= .0104$. The medians differ.

16.31 $H = 2.345$, p-value $= .6725$. No difference in median waiting times by day of week.

16.33 $r_s = .812$, $r_{.05} = .514$. Significant rank correlation.

16.35 $r_s = .813$, $r_{.05} = .413$. Significant rank correlation.

CHAPTER 17

17.1 a. See text, p. 732.   b. See text, p. 731.
   c. See text p. 732–733.

17.3 Zero variation is not achievable.

17.5 Answers will vary. Use Likert scales for service attributes.
   a. Cleanliness of vehicle, full gas tank, waiting time for sales help.
   b. Length of queues, friendliness of staff (Likert), interest paid on accounts.
   c. Price, seat comfort, picture quality (Likert scale for all).

17.7 Deming felt most workers want to do a good job, but are often hampered by the work environment, management policies, and fear of reprisal.

17.9 See p. 736.

17.11 See text p. 739.

17.13 a. Sampling frequency depends on cost and physical possibility of sampling.

b. For normal data, small samples may suffice for a mean (Central Limit Theorem).

c. Large samples may be needed for a proportion to get sufficient precision.

17.15 Expect 68.26 percent, 95.44 percent, 99.73 percent respectively.

17.17 $UCL = \bar{\bar{x}} + 3\dfrac{\bar{R}}{d_2\sqrt{n}} = 12.5 + 3\dfrac{.42}{2.326\sqrt{5}} = 12.742$

$LCL = \bar{\bar{x}} - 3\dfrac{\bar{R}}{d_2\sqrt{n}} = 12.5 - 3\dfrac{.42}{2.326\sqrt{5}} = 12.258$

17.19 Estimated σ is $\bar{R}/d_2 = 30/2.059 = 14.572$, UCL = 98.37, LCL = 54.63

$\bar{\bar{x}} = \dfrac{\bar{x}_1 + \bar{x}_2 + \cdots + \bar{x}_9}{9}$

$= \dfrac{72.25 + 74.25 + \cdots + 82.25}{9} = 76.5$

$\bar{R} = \dfrac{R_1 + R_2 + \cdots + R_9}{9}$

$= \dfrac{43 + 31 + \cdots + 41}{9} = 30$

17.21 $\bar{R} = .82$ (centerline)

$UCL = D_4\bar{R} = (2.004)(.82) = 1.64328$

$LCL = D_3\bar{R} = (0)(.82) = 0$

17.23 By either criterion, process is within acceptable standard ($C_p = 1.67$, $C_{pk} = 1.67$).

17.25 Fails both criteria, especially C_{pk} due to bad centering ($C_p = 1.17$, $C_{pk} = 0.67$).

17.27 Yes, safe to assume normality. UCL = .8354, LCL = .1646.

17.29 Services are often assessed using percent conforming or acceptable quality, so we use p charts.

17.31 Answers will vary. Examples:

a. GPA, number of classes retaken, faculty recommendation letters (Likert).

b. Knowledge of material, enthusiasm, organization, fairness (Likert scales for all).

c. Number of bounced checks, size of monthly bank balance errors, unpaid Visa balance.

d. Number of print errors, clarity of graphs, useful case studies (Likert scales for last two).

17.33 Answers will vary. Examples:

a. MPG, repair cost.

b. Frequency of jams, ink cost.

c. Frequency of re-flushes, water consumption.

d. Battery life, ease of use (Likert scale).

e. Cost, useful life, image sharpness (Likert scale).

f. Cost, useful life, watts per lumen.

17.35 $\bar{x}$ is normally distributed from the Central Limit Theorem for sufficiently large values of n (i.e., symmetric distribution) while the range and standard deviation are not.

17.37 a. Variation and chance defects are inevitable in all human endeavors.

b. Some processes have very *few* defects (maybe zero in short run, but not in long run).

c. Quarterbacks cannot complete all their passes, etc.

17.39 Answers will vary (e.g., forgot to set clock, clock set incorrectly, couldn't find backpack, stopped to charge cell phone, had to shovel snow, clock didn't go off, traffic, car won't start, can't find parking).

17.41 Answers will vary (e.g., weather, union slowdown, pilot arrived late, crew change required, deicing planes, traffic congestion at takeoff, no arrival gate available).

17.43 a. $C_p = 1.33$, $C_{pk} = 1.33$ b. $C_p = 1.33$, $C_{pk} = 0.67$

c. Example shows why we need more than just the C_p index. A change in the process mean can reduce the C_{pk} index, even though the C_p index is unaffected.

17.45 a. UCL = 6223, LCL = 5877.

b. Chart violates no rules.   c. Process is in control.

17.47 a. UCL = 1.0939, LCL = 0.9061

b. Chart violates no rules.   c. Process is in control.

17.49 a. $C_p = 1.00$, $C_{pk} = 0.83$.

b. Process well below capability standards (both indices less than 1.33).

c. Technology, cost, door not closed tightly, frequency of door opening.

17.51 Sample mean of 23.025 and standard deviation of 2.006 are very close to the process values ($\mu = 23$, $\sigma = 2$). Histogram is symmetric, but perhaps platykurtic (chi-square or Anderson-Darling test needed).

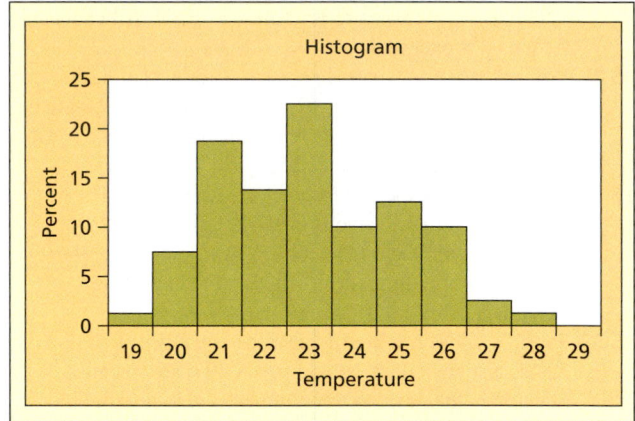

17.53 a. Histogram is arguably normal, but somewhat bimodal (chi-square or Anderson-Darling test needed).

b. $\mu = 8760$, $\sigma = 200$, UCL = 9028, LCL = 8492

c. $\bar{x} = 8785$, $s = 216.14$, UCL = 9075, LCL = 8495

d. Sample is small, may have unreliable estimates of μ and σ.

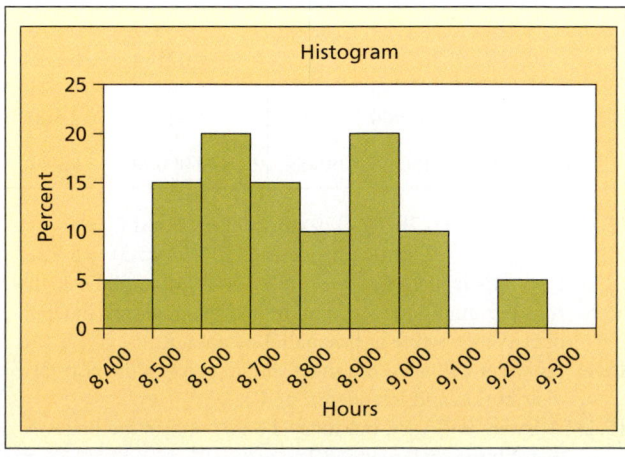

17.55 a. UCL = 470.2, LCL = 459.8.

b. No rules violated. Process in control.

17.57 a. UCL = 12.22095, LCL = 11.75569, centerline = 11.98832.

b. Sample 7 hits the LCL.

c. Histogram approximates normal distribution.

17.59 a. UCL = .1154, LCL = 0.

b. Sample 7 hits the LCL, otherwise in control.

c. Samples are too small to assume normality ($n\pi = 5$). (Better to use MINITAB's binomial option.)

17.61 Chart A: Rule 4.

Chart B: No rules violated.

Chart C: Rule 4.

Chart D: Rules 1, 4.

Chart E: No rules violated.

Chart F: Rules 1, 2.

17.63 Each pattern is clearly evident, except possibly instability in third series.

17.65 a. Type I error: disease not present, but remove meat anyway (sample result shows process out of control when it is not). Type II error: disease is present, but fail to remove the meat (sample result shows process in control when in fact it is not).

b. (27,400,000)/(4,000) = 6,850 two-ton truckloads. But where to put it?

c. NIMBY (not in my backyard).

17.67 Type I error: discard good cereal. Type II error: sell tainted cereal. Public cannot see pesticides, so government is their watch dog agent.

17.67 Type I error: pesticide not present, but remove cereal anyway (sample result shows process out of control when it is not). Type II error: pesticide is at unsafe levels, but fail to remove the cereal (sample result shows process in control when in fact it is not). Consumers cannot see or detect pesticide, so government inspection needed to protect public.

17.69 It may be hard top define a "defective M." Since sampling is easy (and tasty). It should be possible to inspect enough M&Ms to get a reliable confidence interval for π.

17.71 It may be hard to define a "broken Cheerio." Randomness should be attainable.

PHOTO CREDITS

INDEX

CUMULATIVE STANDARD NORMAL DISTRIBUTION

Example: $P(z < -1.96) = .0250$

This table shows the normal area less than z.

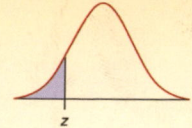

z	.00	.01	.02	.03	.04	.05	.06	.07	.08	.09
−3.7	.00011	.00010	.00010	.00010	.00009	.00009	.00008	.00008	.00008	.00008
−3.6	.00016	.00015	.00015	.00014	.00014	.00013	.00013	.00012	.00012	.00011
−3.5	.00023	.00022	.00022	.00021	.00020	.00019	.00019	.00018	.00017	.00017
−3.4	.00034	.00032	.00031	.00030	.00029	.00028	.00027	.00026	.00025	.00024
−3.3	.00048	.00047	.00045	.00043	.00042	.00040	.00039	.00038	.00036	.00035
−3.2	.00069	.00066	.00064	.00062	.00060	.00058	.00056	.00054	.00052	.00050
−3.1	.00097	.00094	.00090	.00087	.00084	.00082	.00079	.00076	.00074	.00071
−3.0	.00135	.00131	.00126	.00122	.00118	.00114	.00111	.00107	.00104	.00100
−2.9	.0019	.0018	.0018	.0017	.0016	.0016	.0015	.0015	.0014	.0014
−2.8	.0026	.0025	.0024	.0023	.0023	.0022	.0021	.0021	.0020	.0019
−2.7	.0035	.0034	.0033	.0032	.0031	.0030	.0029	.0028	.0027	.0026
−2.6	.0047	.0045	.0044	.0043	.0041	.0040	.0039	.0038	.0037	.0036
−2.5	.0062	.0060	.0059	.0057	.0055	.0054	.0052	.0051	.0049	.0048
−2.4	.0082	.0080	.0078	.0075	.0073	.0071	.0069	.0068	.0066	.0064
−2.3	.0107	.0104	.0102	.0099	.0096	.0094	.0091	.0089	.0087	.0084
−2.2	.0139	.0136	.0132	.0129	.0125	.0122	.0119	.0116	.0113	.0110
−2.1	.0179	.0174	.0170	.0166	.0162	.0158	.0154	.0150	.0146	.0143
−2.0	.0228	.0222	.0217	.0212	.0207	.0202	.0197	.0192	.0188	.0183
−1.9	.0287	.0281	.0274	.0268	.0262	.0256	.0250	.0244	.0239	.0233
−1.8	.0359	.0351	.0344	.0336	.0329	.0322	.0314	.0307	.0301	.0294
−1.7	.0446	.0436	.0427	.0418	.0409	.0401	.0392	.0384	.0375	.0367
−1.6	.0548	.0537	.0526	.0516	.0505	.0495	.0485	.0475	.0465	.0455
−1.5	.0668	.0655	.0643	.0630	.0618	.0606	.0594	.0582	.0571	.0559
−1.4	.0808	.0793	.0778	.0764	.0749	.0735	.0721	.0708	.0694	.0681
−1.3	.0968	.0951	.0934	.0918	.0901	.0885	.0869	.0853	.0838	.0823
−1.2	.1151	.1131	.1112	.1093	.1075	.1056	.1038	.1020	.1003	.0985
−1.1	.1357	.1335	.1314	.1292	.1271	.1251	.1230	.1210	.1190	.1170
−1.0	.1587	.1562	.1539	.1515	.1492	.1469	.1446	.1423	.1401	.1379
−0.9	.1841	.1814	.1788	.1762	.1736	.1711	.1685	.1660	.1635	.1611
−0.8	.2119	.2090	.2061	.2033	.2005	.1977	.1949	.1922	.1894	.1867
−0.7	.2420	.2389	.2358	.2327	.2296	.2266	.2236	.2206	.2177	.2148
−0.6	.2743	.2709	.2676	.2643	.2611	.2578	.2546	.2514	.2483	.2451
−0.5	.3085	.3050	.3015	.2981	.2946	.2912	.2877	.2843	.2810	.2776
−0.4	.3446	.3409	.3372	.3336	.3300	.3264	.3228	.3192	.3156	.3121
−0.3	.3821	.3783	.3745	.3707	.3669	.3632	.3594	.3557	.3520	.3483
−0.2	.4207	.4168	.4129	.4090	.4052	.4013	.3974	.3936	.3897	.3859
−0.1	.4602	.4562	.4522	.4483	.4443	.4404	.4364	.4325	.4286	.4247
−0.0	.5000	.4960	.4920	.4880	.4841	.4801	.4761	.4721	.4681	.4641